The SAGE Handbook of
Child Research

The SAGE Handbook of
Child Research

Edited by

Gary B. Melton, Asher Ben-Arieh,
Judith Cashmore, Gail S. Goodman,
Natalie K. Worley

Los Angeles | London | New Delhi
Singapore | Washington DC

Los Angeles | London | New Delhi
Singapore | Washington DC

SAGE Publications Ltd
1 Oliver's Yard
55 City Road
London EC1Y 1SP

SAGE Publications Inc.
2455 Teller Road
Thousand Oaks, California 91320

SAGE Publications India Pvt Ltd
B 1/I 1 Mohan Cooperative Industrial Area
Mathura Road
New Delhi 110 044

SAGE Publications Asia-Pacific Pte Ltd
3 Church Street
10-04 Samsung Hub
Singapore 049483

Editor: Chris Rojek
Assistant editor: Colette Wilson
Production manager: Cenveo Publisher Services
Marketing manager: Michael Ainsley
Cover design: Wendy Scott
Typeset by: Cenveo Publisher Services
Printed in Great Britain by Henry Ling Limited at the
Dorset Press, Dorchester, DT1 1HD

Library of Congress Control Number: 2013946093

British Library Cataloguing in Publication data
A catalogue record for this book is available from the
British Library

ISBN 978-1-4129-3016-1

Contents

Dedication

The Sage Handbook of Child Research is dedicated to the memory of Stewart Asquith, who conceived of this volume and who was its initial lead editor. He died in April 2009 at age 61 after years of battling multiple myeloma – a personal struggle that characteristically included advocacy and guidance for others through a blog (www.stewartsrevlimid.blogspot.com) under the auspice of Myeloma UK. Also characteristically, Stewart continued as the lead editor of this volume until the day that he was advised to withdraw from an experimental treatment because he was showing no progress in fighting the myeloma.

Even then, after an exhausting array of treatments involving most of his body systems, Stewart found a way to enjoy almost every moment of his life. The following excerpt from his blog, written less than two months before his death, was illustrative:

> Not finished yet! …Just in case you think the myeloma has completely gone for me, [in the two weeks] since the last post (Does sound final, doesn't it!)…, I've finished one bike, nearly finished another; sanded the stairwell; sanded our bathroom door (new bathroom put in) in prep for painting; built a cupboard for Elspeth (screw missing…. I wonder if I have an Ikea gene because various folks have commented on the fact that I also have a screw missing!). So still working away…. Still hanging in there.

I was able to spend time in person with Stewart on only a few occasions. However, he left a strong impression on me, as he did on many others, and I considered him to be not only a distant colleague but also a good friend. My memory of Stewart can be summarized as follows: a doggedly determined Scotsman with a strong love of country, an enthusiasm for folk culture, and a wry sense of humour; above all, a tireless, passionate advocate for children, especially those whose way in life was most unfair (for example, children who had been sexually exploited and trafficked or who had been brutalized in institutions).

Stewart's academic accomplishments were enviable. He was the first holder of the St. Kentigern chair for childhood studies at the University of Glasgow, and in his last years he developed the Centre for Rural Childhood at the University of the Highlands and Islands. However, he was without pretence, and he lost neither his appreciation of the richness of the culture in which he grew up nor his understanding of the hardships that children in poverty and other troubles must overcome. I suspect that he was most comfortable when he was assisting children who were striving to cope with repeated trauma.

Stewart's empathy and determination were rooted in his own experience, as described in his obituary:

> Stewart Asquith was the youngest of six children. His mother was a cinema usherette who took in lodgers to supplement her wages. Stewart never knew his father, nor even clearly established his identity, although he was believed to be a Polish soldier. This combination of childhood deprivation and unresolved questions about his personal origin were to prove driving forces throughout his life and career …
>
> His work was always moulded by strong theoretical principles and moral values, and he was equally appreciated for his personal skills as negotiator, adviser, trusted colleague and friend …

> While he achieved international eminence, he never lost touch with his origins or distanced himself from the ways and lives of the wider community ….[1]

Although *The Sage Handbook of Child Research* was written and edited after Stewart's death, this book was unquestionably his brainchild. Completion of the book was not a task that the ultimate editors had sought, but we were privileged to assume that role. We hope that it communicates the respect that Stewart had for children, especially those who cope each day with challenges that would be forbidding even to most adults. We hope, too, that this book will enable others to illuminate the everyday experiences of children in diverse circumstances around the world and to describe those realities with sensitivity and clarity.

For peace and auld lang syne,
Gary B. Melton

NOTE

1 'Professor Stewart Asquith'. Available at http://www.scotsman.com/news/obituaries/professor-stewart-asquith-1-1034215

Notes on the Editors and Contributors

ABOUT THE EDITORS

The editors of The *SAGE Handbook of Child Research* are diverse in nationality and educational background. However, they share a commitment to advancement of the well-being of children and their parents, a passion for the protection of human rights, a history of distinguished scholarship and public service, and an appreciation of the usefulness of international and interdisciplinary studies in the generation and application of knowledge about children and childhood. Moreover, all of the editors have contributed knowledge relevant to assurance of safety for children in their homes and communities and to creation of conditions conducive to meaningful participation by children in proceedings affecting them.

Asher Ben-Arieh is associate professor of social work at the Hebrew University of Jerusalem, director of its Joseph J. Schwarz MA programs in early childhood and non-profit management, adjunct professor of family and community studies at Clemson University in South Carolina, and director of the Haruv Institute, a non-profit organization for advancement and communication of knowledge useful in child protection practice in Israel and around the world. Prof. Ben-Arieh has been the editor of the annual report on State of the Child in Israel: A Statistical Abstract since 1990. Prof. Ben-Arieh's scholarship has focused on the nature of children's well-being and the factors affecting it, methodology in social indicators research, and the use of child indicators in making and implementing public policy. Prof. Ben-Arieh's work is centred on explication of three constructs: the power of information, the rights of children, and the importance for its own sake of experience in childhood.

Active in both Israeli and international policy debates and scientific discussions in regard to children's well-being, Prof. Ben-Arieh has served on national panels on child health and the situation for children at risk. He also represents Israel on the European Union's working group on child welfare (COST A/19).

Prof. Ben-Arieh was the principal organizer of a global network of scholars involved in monitoring of child well-being. That network developed into the International Society for Child Indicators, which Prof. Ben-Arieh co-chairs. He also founded and now edits the journal Child Indicators Research and a book series on child well-being.

Judith Cashmore, a developmental psychologist, is associate professor of law at the University of Sydney and an adjunct professor at Southern Cross University, where she is the inaugural chair of the advisory board of the Centre for Children and Young People. In 2010,

Prof. Cashmore was honoured as an Officer in the Order of Australia (AO), which recognizes 'distinguished service of a high degree to Australia or to humanity at large.' She received the 2013 Stanley Cohen Distinguished Research Award by the Association of Family and Conciliation Courts for research related to family law.

Prof. Cashmore's research focuses on children's involvement in decisions about their care and protection and their guardianship. Focusing on children's own perceptions, understanding, and experiences of participation in the legal process, Prof. Cashmore takes a child-centred approach to analysis of policy pertaining to these contexts.

Prof. Cashmore has been active in bringing her findings to the attention of legal authorities in Australia. She has frequently led or participated in national or state government committees pertaining to child protection. She is a member of the New South Wales Judicial Commission, which conducts research, provides judicial education, and responds to complaints against judicial officers. She has worked as a consultant to the NSW Bureau of Crime Statistics and Research, the Australian Law Reform Commission, the NSW Department of Community Services, the NSW Community Services Commission, and the NSW Child Protection Council.

Prof. Cashmore is a board member in several non-governmental organizations (e.g., the National Children's and Youth Law Centre). She is an author of Australian non-governmental organizations' shadow report to the U.N. Committee on the Rights of the Child.

Gail S. Goodman is distinguished professor of psychology at the University of California, Davis, and professor of forensic psychology at the University of Oslo. Prof. Goodman also directs UC Davis's Center for Public Policy Research, which applies social science to public policy, especially in regard to child protection, foster care, and assistance to families in poverty.

Prof. Goodman has devoted her career to two related major areas of study: memory development and children's abilities and experiences as victim/witnesses. In the memory development area, she has contributed to understanding of the general relation of emotion to memory and the specific relation of trauma to memory. She also has studied attachment and memory, implicit and explicit memory, and semantic associates and memory. In research on child witnesses, Prof. Goodman has been a leader in study of children's ability to provide testimony about events (especially child abuse) that they have experienced or witnessed. She also has conducted seminal studies on children's experience of the legal process (including testimony itself) and on the psychological effects of the process on child victims. Prof. Goodman's psycholegal research has been cited by US courts at all levels.

Prof. Goodman is also currently studying the effects of child abuse on mental health. That work includes analyses of the relations among child maltreatment, re-victimization, and juvenile delinquency.

Prof. Goodman has served as president of several entities in the American Psychological Association: the Society for Child and Family Policy and Practice, its Section on Child Maltreatment, and the American Psychology-Law Society. She has been a consulting editor of *Child Development*, *Law and Human Behavior,* and *Contemporary Psychology*, among other journals. Among the organizations that have honoured her for research, public service, and/or teaching are APA (twice), its Division of Developmental Psychology, the American Academy of Forensic Psychology, the American Professional Society on Abuse of Children, the National Organization for Victim Assistance, the Society for Child and Family Policy and Practice, and the Society for Psychological Study of Social Issues.

Gary B. Melton is associate director for community development and social policy in the Kempe Center for Prevention and Treatment of Child Abuse and Neglect, professor of paediatrics in the University of Colorado School of Medicine, professor of community and behavioural health in the Colorado School of Public Health, and adjunct professor of family and community studies at Clemson University in South Carolina. Prof. Melton has served as president of the American Orthopsychiatric Association, Childwatch International, the American Psychology-Law Society, and the Society for Child and Family Policy and Practice. He has received awards for distinguished contributions to research and public service from the American Psychological Association (three times), two APA divisions, the American Orthopsychiatric Association, the American Professional Society on Abuse of Children, the American Psychological Foundation, Prevent Child Abuse America, and Psi Chi. He is currently co-editor of the American Journal of Orthopsychiatry and Child Abuse and Neglect.

Prof. Melton has travelled in almost 50 countries. He was a Fulbright professor at the Norwegian Centre for Child Research. He has served as a consultant to the UN Committee on the Rights of the Child, chair of APA's Working Group on the Convention on the Rights of the Child, and a member of an analogous panel for the American Bar Association.

Prof. Melton was vice-chair of the US Advisory Board on Child Abuse and Neglect. He long led a regular congressional briefing series, and he contributed heavily to several amicus briefs in the US Supreme Court and various other appellate courts in the United States.

Natalie K. Worley is a PhD candidate in international family and community studies at Clemson University. Her scholarly interests include community factors in children's well-being, public policy on child maltreatment, and youth participation in community development, particularly in rural areas and developing nations.

Ms Worley is a research assistant in Clemson's Institute on Family and Neighborhood Life. In this position, Ms. Worley participates in the design, implementation, and evaluation of STEM (Science, Technology, Engineering, and Mathematics) curricula for youth in after-school programmes in traditionally underperforming school districts.

For her outstanding performance as a graduate student, Ms. Worley received the Social Work Endowment Award from the University of Tennessee, where she earned her master's degree in social work. As a doctoral student, she received the Graduate Student Award of Excellence from Clemson's College of Health, Education, and Human Development.

Ms. Worley has studied, travelled, and worked in Africa, Australia, the Caribbean, Central America, and Eastern and Western Europe. She completed a master's internship in the South African Education and Environment Project in Cape Town, South Africa. She is currently engaged in program evaluation and strategic planning for Clemson Engineers for Developing Countries in their community development projects in Haiti.

ABOUT THE CONTRIBUTORS

Priscilla Alderson PhD is Professor Emerita of Childhood Studies at the Institute of Education, University of London. With Professor Berry Mayall she designed the Institute's MA course in international children's rights. Recent books include *Young Children's Rights* (Jessica Kingsley/Save the Children, 2008), *The Ethics of Research with Children and Young People: A Practical Handbook* (with V. Morrow, Sage, 2011) and *Childhoods Real and Imagined: An Introduction to Critical Realism and Childhood Studies*, Volume 1 (Routledge, 2013).

Steven R. Asher PhD is a Professor of Psychology and Neuroscience at Duke University. His research focuses on the linkages between social competence and friendship and on the associations between peer relations processes and feelings of loneliness in school. Recent publications examine individual differences in response to challenging situations that arise in friendships. As part of their research, Dr Asher and his doctoral students have created widely used measures for assessing social competence, peer acceptance, friendship quality, and feelings of loneliness. Steven Asher's research is published in major journals in developmental, educational, and clinical psychology and he has co-edited two influential volumes, *The Development of Children's Friendships* and *Peer Rejection in Childhood*, both published by Cambridge University Press. He is a Fellow of the American Psychological Association, the Society for the Psychological Study of Social Issues, the Association for Psychological Science, and the American Educational Research Association.

Else-Marie Augusti PhD is a postdoctoral fellow at the Cognitive Developmental Research Unit, Department of Psychology, University of Oslo, Norway. Dr Augusti's research focuses on maltreated children's cognitive development, and how emotion and executive functions interact in typically developing children compared to maltreated children. Dr Augusti has worked both in the USA and Norway on research concerning children's development. She has published in journals such as the Journal of Traumatic Stress and Child Neuropsychology.

Oscar A Barbarin PhD is the Hertz Endowed Chair in the Department of Psychology at Tulane University in New Orleans. He earned a PhD in clinical psychology at Rutgers University and completed a post-doctoral fellowship in social psychology at Stanford University. His research has focused on the social and familial influences on the development of boys of color. He has developed ABLE, a universal mental health screening tool for young children. His work on children of African descent extends to a 20 year longitudinal study of the effects of poverty and violence on child development in South Africa. He is Co-editor of the *American Journal of Orthopsychiatry*. He chaired the US National Committee for Psychology and served on the Governing Council of the Society for Research in Child Development.

Bryony Beresford is a research director at the Social Policy Research Unit (SPRU) in the University of York, United Kingdom. She has been carrying out applied social research projects concerned with the lives of disabled children and young peoples and their families for over twenty years, publishing widely on this topic. Much of her work is government funded and relates to policy and/or practice issues. Along with other members of her research team, she has been at the forefront of developing methods by which children, including those with autistic spectrum conditions (ASC), who are deaf and/or do not use speech to communicate, can participate directly in research. Recent projects include: specialist mental health services for deaf children; an evaluation of parent training programmes for parents with disabled children; transition experiences for young people with ASC; condition-management transitions for young people with life-limiting conditions.

Stephanie Block PhD is assistant professor at the University of Massachusetts, Lowell. Her research has broadly focused on children in the legal system, the effects of trauma on children's wellbeing and memory for emotional events, and the prevention of child maltreatment. Guided by a social-ecological perspective and interdisciplinary training, she conducts research that generates knowledge and informs public policy relevant to children in the child welfare and legal systems. Dr Block has published in *Applied Developmental Science, Law and Human Behavior, Child Abuse & Neglect,* and *Journal of Applied Social Psychology*.

Marc H. Bornstein is senior investigator and head of child and family research at the Eunice Kennedy Shriver National Institute of Child Health and Human Development. He holds a BA from Columbia College, MS and PhD degrees from Yale University, and an honorary doctorate from the University of Padua. Bornstein has held faculty positions at Princeton University and New York University as well as academic appointments as visiting scientist in Munich, London, Paris, New York, Tokyo, Bamenda, Seoul Trento, and Santiago. Bornstein is a past member of the Governing Council of the SRCD and the Executive Committee of the ISIS. Bornstein has administered both Federal and Foundation grants, sits on the editorial boards of several professional journals, and consults for governments, foundations, universities, publishers, scientific journals, the media, and UNICEF. Bornstein is editor emeritus of *Child Development* and founding editor of *Parenting: Science and Practice*. He is author or editor of numerous scholarly volumes and several children's books, videos, and puzzles and has published widely in experimental, methodological, comparative, developmental, and cultural science as well as neuroscience, pediatrics, and aesthetics. Visit www.cfr.nichd.nih.gov and www.tandfonline.com/HPAR.

Ragnhild Brusdal is a senior researcher at the National Institute for Consumer Research in Norway. Her research fields are all connected to consumption and cover many areas such as household economics, consumption and debt among young grown-ups, and children and consumption in different aspects such as well-being, commercialization and gender equality. Latest publications in this field are; *Children as Consumer* (with Frones, forthcoming), The purchase of moral positions (2012, with Frones) and *Are Parents Gender Neutral when Financing their Children's Consumption*? (2011 with L. Berg).

Lorinda B. Camparo PhD is a professor in the Psychology Department at Whittier College where she has taught and conducted research on enhancing children's narrative reports since 1997. Dr Camparo has published numerous articles and book chapters, and recently co-authored the book, *Evidence-based Child Forensic Interviewing: The Developmental Narrative Elaboration Interview* (with Karen Saywitz, 2014, Oxford University Press). As an active member of The Society for Child and Family Policy and Practice (APA Division 37), Dr Camparo served as Program Chair, Editor of *The Advocate*, and Member-at-Large for Communication & Technology. Dr Camparo has also conducted workshops on interviewing children for lawyers, judges, police officers, and social workers, has served as an expert witness on cases involving children alleging sexual abuse, and as a child development expert, has been interviewed for *World News Tonight* and *Good Morning America*.

Ingrid Cordon is research director and assistant project scientist at the Center for Public Policy Research at the University of California, Davis. She has conducted research and published numerous articles, chapters, and reports on such topics as child maltreatment, children in court, child welfare, juvenile delinquency, memory development, and emotion processing. Dr Cordon received a Bachelor's degree from UCLA (summa cum laude); a Master's degree from California State University, Northridge; and a PhD from UC Davis. She then served as a post-doctoral fellow at the University of Minnesota, Harvard Medical School, and Children's Hospital, Boston. Dr Cordon's educational background includes training in developmental psychology, developmental neuroscience, statistics, and research methods and design. She also served as part-time faculty at California State University, Sacramento.

Lyn Craig is an Australian Research Council Queen Elizabeth II Fellow at the Social Policy Research Centre at the University of New South Wales. Her research interests include parenthood and the time costs of care, work-family balance and the intra-household effects of work-care policy structures.

Tove I. Dahl is a professor of educational psychology in the Department of Psychology at UiT The Arctic University of Norway in Tromsø, Norway. She is also dean of Skogfjorden, the Norwegian language and culture immersion program for youth run by the Concordia Language Villages of Concordia College in Moorhead, Minnesota. Her research endeavors reflect her interest in language, culture and facilitating meaningful and lasting interactions with others. She has studied foreign (and native) language learning and comprehension, peace education and, most recently, the concept of interest and how to use it to build bridges among people who travel and the people and places of their destinations. In all of this research, voice is central – both as something to be expressed and to be heard. Hence her big question for this book's chapter: What happens when we give children voice in the world of research and why should it matter?

Ryan A. Dickson is a Graduate School Dissertation Chair at Northcentral University. He received his MS in psychology from Western Washington University, conducting research on implicit and explicit memory as well as on ethnic identity, and received his PhD from the University of New Hampshire in developmental psychology where he conducted research on autobiographical memory across the lifespan with an emphasis on the reminiscence bump.

Jacinthe Dion PhD is a psychologist and professor at the Université du Québec à Chicoutimi (Quebec, Canada). She is a member of the CRIPCAS (Interdisciplinary Research Centre on Conjugal Problems and Sexual Abuse) and scientific director of the axis 3 of the VISAJ Chair (on youth development). Her research pertains to child sexual abuse among vulnerable populations, such as youth with a disability and Indigenous people, as well as risk factors for body image dissatisfaction.

Amy Dworsky is a senior researcher who has spent much of her career studying vulnerable youth populations including youth aging out of foster care, homeless youth and foster youth who are pregnant and/or parenting. She is currently the PI for several projects: a HUD-funded study of housing programs for youth aging out of foster care; a FSBY-funded impact evaluation of a pregnancy prevention program; and an Illinois Department of Children and Family Services funded study of foster youth who are pregnant and parenting. Previously, Dr Dworsky was the P.I. for the evaluation of an employment program for youth in foster care, a study of runaway and homeless youth who were pregnant and/or parenting; and an investigation of campus support programs for former foster youth. She was also a Co-Investigator for the Midwest Evaluation of the Adult Functioning of Former Foster Youth, a longitudinal study of young people making the transition from foster care to adulthood. Dr Dworsky has a PhD in social welfare from the University of Wisconsin-Madison. Her most recent publications focus on the predictors of homelessness among youth aging out of foster care, the implications of health care reform for young women aging out of foster care and the parenting experiences of runaway and homeless youth.

Ivar Frones is professor of sociology at the University of Oslo, and senior researcher at The Norwegian Center for Child Behavioural Development. His work and international experience covers a variety of areas, with an emphasis on life course analysis, the sociology of childhood and youth, well-being and social exclusion. Frones is a member of the Board of the International Society for Child Indicators, and the founder of the journal Childhood. His numerous publications cover a variety of perspectives on childhood, include *Among Peers* (1995) *Status Zero Youth* (2007), 'On theories of dialogue, self and society' (2007), 'Theorizing indicators: On indicators, signs and trends (2007), and 'The purchase of moral positions' (with Brudsel, 2013). In Scandinavia he has published on digital divides, modern childhood, marginalization and risk, cultural trends and a variety of subjects related to childhood, youth and life course development.

Robert M. Goerge is a senior research fellow at Chapin Hall at the University of Chicago, with more than 25 years of research focused on improving the available data and information on children and families. He is also a Senior Fellow at the UC Computation Institute and at the UC Harris School of Public Policy Studies, where he directs the Master's Degree on Computational Analysis and Public Policy. Dr Goerge developed Chapin Hall's Integrated Database on Child and Family Programs in Illinois, which links the administrative data on child maltreatment, social service receipt, education, criminal and juvenile justice, employment, healthcare, and early childhood programs to provide a comprehensive picture of child and family use of publicly provided or financed service programs. Dr Goerge received his PhD from the School of Social Service Administration of the University of Chicago. He is also co-founder of the International Society for Child Indicators.

Jacqueline Goodnow is a professorial (emeritus) research fellow at the Child and Family Research Centre, Macquarie University, Sydney, Australia. Her main interests have to do with cultural contexts, development, and the relevance of concepts and procedures developed in one context to research in others (cf. Goodnow & Lawrence, in press, Carmichael, *Handbook of Child Psychology*, Vo. 4). Her life has been roughly divided between time in Australia and in the United States, with awards in both countries for distinguished contributions to research. She personally still feels most honored by the citation accompanying inclusion in a list of Distinguished Women in Psychology (American Psychological Association, 1992), ' Significant contributions: Opening up new content areas, indicating not only their significance but also how one might proceed with research; integrating areas of knowledge, bringing together models from several fields ... and consistently underlining the significance ... of the social context'.

Daphna Gross-Manos is a PhD candidate in the Paul Baerwald School of Social Work at the Hebrew University. Her thesis focuses on 'The Relationship of Material Deprivation and Social Exclusion to the Subjective Well-being of Children in Israel'. She serves as the managing editor of *The Journal of Child Indicator Research* and the *Handbook of Child Well-being*. She is also the editor of *The International Society for Child Indicators* newsletter – Indicators. Until 2011 Gross-Manos was a board member of the Israel Social Workers Union for three years. Her awards include the Hebrew University president scholarship and the Luxembourg foundation scholarship. Gross-Manos research interests are: child deprivation; child social exclusion; children subjective well-being; poverty and inequality; social policy.

Whitney Brechwald Guerry PhD is a postdoctoral research scientist in the Department of Pediatrics at Columbia University Medical Center/New York Presbyterian Hospital, where she works with children and families impacted by pediatric cancer and blood diseases. Dr Guerry received her BA from the University of California, Berkeley, and her MA and PhD in clinical psychology from Duke University. Dr Guerry also has received clinical and research training at the University of North Carolina, Chapel Hill and at the Children's Hospital of Philadelphia, where she completed her pre-doctoral clinical internship. Dr Guerry has published research examining the role of peer and other relationships on the physical and socio-emotional well being of children and adolescents. She has a particular interest in how social influence processes may promote positive and negative health-related behaviors in young people.

Harlene Hayne is the vice-chancellor at the University of Otago and she also holds a personal chair in the Psychology Department. Professor Hayne is a Fellow of the Royal Society of New Zealand and of the American Psychological Society. She is also the Co-chair of the Office of the Prime Minister's Science Advisory Committee Working Party on Reducing Social and Psychological Morbidity during Adolescence and the co-director of the Innocence Project, New Zealand. In 2009, Professor Hayne was appointed an Officer of the New Zealand Order of Merit for services to scientific and medical research. She is the Deputy Chair of the Board of Fulbright New Zealand, and a member of the Board of the New Zealand Treasury. Her specialist research interests are memory development, interviews with children in clinical and legal contexts, and adolescent risk-taking.

Scott W. Henggeler PhD is professor at the Medical University of South Carolina and founding director of the Family Services Research Center (FSRC). The FSRC has received numerous awards, including a Points of Light Foundation President's Award in recognition of excellence in service directed at solving community problems. Likewise, Dr Henggeler has received several research and education awards from national organizations including being named one of the twelve people who saved rehabilitation by the American Society of Criminology. He has published 10 books, and his work has been translated into Norwegian, German, Japanese, Dutch, and Spanish. In addition, he has published more than 250 journal articles and book chapters; and has received grants from NIMH, NIDA, NIAAA, OJJDP, CSAT, the Annie E. Casey Foundation, and others. He was Associate Editor of the *Journal of Consulting and Clinical Psychology*, and has been on the editorial boards of more than 10 journals.

Sue D. Hobbs MA is a developmental psychology doctoral student at the University of California, Davis. Her research interests include factors related to child development in the context of child maltreatment and early life stressors. Specifically, she is interested in memory and suggestibility, parent–child attachment, emotion regulation development, and biological stress regulation processes, and how these are associated with child maltreatment and early-life stressors.

Dari Jigjidsuren, a native of Mongolia, earned her PhD from the University of North Carolina at Chapel Hill. Currently Dari is an evaluation specialist at the Frank Porter Graham Child Development Institute in Chapel Hill. Her research interests are on early education, school readiness, and socio-economic factors affecting young children's educational achievement and well-being.

Jan Kampmann is a professor in Childhood research, Dept. for Psychology and Educational studies, Roskilde University, Denmark. For many years Kampmann's research has been on children and young people's everyday life, early childhood education and schooling. His research has been based on institutional ethnography, policy ethnography and participatory action research. He has a special interest in researching implications of gender, class and ethnicity in a children's perspective.

Bong Joo Lee is professor of social welfare at Seoul National University. He earned his PhD from the School of Social Service Administration at University of Chicago. Before joining to the faculty of SNU, he had taught at Boston University School of Social Work and University of Chicago. His research focuses on child indicators, child poverty, child welfare, social development, and social service reform issues. He is a co-editor of *Child Indicators Research*, an international journal on child indicators. He is also on the editorial boards of *Child Abuse & Neglect, Asian Social Work and Policy Review* and *Journal of Asian Pacific Social Work and Development*. He has published many books and papers in domestic and international peer-reviewed journals. Recently, he worked on development of the We Start model, which is a targeted early human capital investment neighborhood program to combat intergenerational transmission of poverty and inequality in Korea. Email: bongjlee@snu.ac.kr; Tel: (82-2) 880-5724; Fax: (82-2) 875-5724

Roger J.R. Levesque is a professor of criminal justice at Indiana University and teaches courses on children's rights at the Maurer School of Law. He is editor-in-chief of the *Journal of Youth and Adolescence* as well as the *New Criminal Law Review*. Professor Levesque's research focuses on the legal regulation of adolescence and the nature of adolescents' rights. In addition to having published numerous journal articles, he is the author of several books dealing mainly with the nature of adolescence, family life, and the laws that shape our intimate lives. He is the author of *Not by Faith Alone: Religion, Law and Adolescence* (New York University Press) and *Adolescence, Media and the Law* (Oxford University Press).

Michael R. McCart PhD is the Associate Director of the Family Services Research Center and an Associate Professor in the Department of Psychiatry and Behavioral Sciences at the Medical University of South Carolina. He holds a secondary appointment in the Department of Pediatrics. Dr McCart's research focuses primarily on the development and evaluation of interventions for adolescents presenting serious clinical problems (e.g., delinquent behavior, substance use, trauma-related psychopathology). He has received grants from the National Institute of Mental Health, the National Institute on Drug Abuse, and the Centers for Disease Control and Prevention to support his research. Dr McCart has published over 50 journal articles and book chapters; and has received awards from the US Department of Justice and the American Professional Society on the Abuse of Children for his research with youth and their families.

Kristina L. McDonald PhD is an assistant professor at the University of Alabama. She received her BA from Illinois Wesleyan University and her MA and PhD from Duke University. She completed postdoctoral training at the University of Maryland and at the Center for the Prevention of Youth Behavioral Problems at the University of Alabama. Her research focuses on the peer relationships of children and adolescents, specifically the social cognitive processes underlying problematic peer interactions as well as how context may affect peer interactions. Her most recent publications address the precursors and consequences for youth who endorse hostile social motivations, like revenge goals; how friendship interactions may influence social cognitions; and how social context may affect peer relationships and social cognitions during peer interactions.

Kelly McWilliams MA is currently a doctoral student at the University of California, Davis in the laboratory of Dr Gail S. Goodman. Her research interests include memory development, emotion understanding, children's eyewitness testimony, children's memory for trauma, and children's experiences in the legal system. Ms. McWilliams has published several articles and book chapters concerning children's memory for abuse and trauma. In addition, she has been awarded grants from NSF and APF to conduct her dissertation work.

Jennifer Mason is professor of sociology and co-director of the Morgan Centre for the Study of Relationships and Personal Life at the University of Manchester, UK. She has conducted research into a wide range of family and relationship matters, including children's kinship. She is an advocate for the creative potential of qualitative mixed methods approaches. She has published widely in the spheres of personal life and relationships, and research methodologies.

Annika Melinder PhD is professor of psychology and director of the Cognitive Developmental Research Unit (EKUP) at the Department of Psychology, University of Oslo, Norway. Dr Melinder holds graduate degrees in experimental and clinical psychology. Her research focuses on neurocognitive development in typical and maltreated children, and legal procedures regarding children as witnesses. She has published extensively including in such journals as *Developmental Psychology, Journal of Experimental Child Psychology*, and *Cognition*.

Terje Ogden PhD is research director at the Norwegian Center for Child Behavioral Development, Unirand and professor at the Institute of Psychology, University of Oslo, Norway. His research interests include clinical trials and implementation of empirically supported interventions (ESI) targeting antisocial children and youth, and the longitudinal development of social competence and externalizing problem behavior in early childhood. Dr Ogden has published several articles on interventions like Multisystemic Therapy, Parent Management Training – the Oregon model, Positive Behavior and Learning Support in schools (N-PALS) and Early Interventions for Children at Risk (the TIBIR project). Publications also include articles on moderators and mediators of interventions, and the large-scale implementation of ESIs.

Charlotte J. Patterson PhD is professor of psychology and director of the interdisciplinary Women, Gender & Sexuality Program at the University of Virginia. Best known for her research on child development in lesbian- and gay-parented families, Patterson is a Fellow of the Association for Psychological Science (APS) and of the American Psychological Association (APA), and a past-President of the Society for Psychological Research on Lesbian, Gay, Bisexual, and Transgender Issues. Patterson has won a number of awards, including the American Psychological Association's 2009 award for Distinguished Contributions to Research in Public Policy, and the Society for the Psychology of Women's 2011 Laura Brown Award for Outstanding Contributions to Lesbian and Bisexual Women's Psychology. Patterson's *Handbook of Psychology and Sexual Orientation*, co-edited with Anthony R. D'Augelli, was published in 2013 by Oxford University Press.

David B. Pillemer is the Dr Samuel E. Paul Professor of Developmental Psychology at the University of New Hampshire and Senior Fellow at the Carsey Institute for Families and Communities. Pillemer's research specialty is autobiographical memory across the life span. He has studied memory development in children, memory and self-esteem, memory and motivation, 'flashbulb' memories of momentous events, memories of educational experiences, and gender and cultural differences in memory performance. He is the author or editor of several books, including *Momentous Events, Vivid Memories and Developmental Psychology and Social Change*.

Juliana Raskauskas is currently associate professor of child development at California State University, Sacramento. Her research interests are in the areas of middle childhood and adolescent development, peer relationships, bullying, and cyber bullying. She has researched bullying both in the United States and New Zealand and published several book chapters and research articles. Notable publications include 'Relations between traditional and internet bullying among adolescent females' in *Developmental Psychology* and "Bullying on the School Bus: A Video Analysis" and "Text-bullying: Associations with Traditional Bullying and Depression among New Zealand Adolescents" in *Journal of School Violence*. Her most recent publication was a chapter called 'Bullying: Students Hurting Students' in the new edition of *Crisis Counseling, Prevention and Intervention in the Schools*.

Kim Rasmussen is associate professor, Mag. Art and PhD at the Department of Psychology and Educational Studies, Roskilde University, Denmark. His research is about childhood and children's life in preschool institutions with focus on children's everyday life, children's culture and children's places. He has done several research projects together with children including children with intellectual disabilities. The approach and empirical methods is often based on children's visual practice and photographs. He is author, co-author or editor of several books including: *Traces of Children's Institutional Life* (2001, co-author), *Childhood in Pictures* (2002, co-author), *Children in the Neighbourhood: The neighbourhood in children* (2004), Children's Places (2005, editor), *The Everyday Life of Children* (with intellectual disabilities) (2008), *Visual Approaches and Methods* (2013, editor).

Eugene C. Roehlkepartain is vice president of research and development at Search Institute, a US-based non-profit organization that provides research, consulting, and other services focused on what young people need to succeed in their families, schools, and communities. He focuses on family strengths and engagement, international youth development, and integrating research and practice for positive community and social change. From 2006–2009 he co-led, with the late Peter L. Benson, Search Institute's Center for Spiritual Development in Childhood and Adolescence. He is author, co-author, or editor of more than 200 publications, including *The Handbook of Spiritual Development in Childhood and Adolescence* (Sage, 2006) and *Nurturing Child and Adolescent Spirituality: Perspectives from the World's Religious Traditions* (Rowman and Littlefield, 2006). He is a PhD candidate in Education, Curriculum, and Instruction with a specialization Family, Youth, and Community at the University of Minnesota, Minneapolis, Minnesota, USA.

Karen J. Saywitz PhD is a professor at the UCLA, School of Medicine, Department of Psychiatry and a developmental and clinical psychologist. For over 20 years, she has directed programs providing mental health services to children and families in the public sector and taught normative child development to students in medicine, law, psychology, and social work. Her research on children in the legal system applies developmental science to legal decision-making. Her work has been cited by the US Supreme Court and numerous appellate courts. She has won national awards for her pioneering research, distinguished teaching, advocacy, and clinical service from organizations such as the American Psychological Association and the American Professional Society on the Abuse of Children. She is a past president of the APA Division of Child, Youth, and Family Services. Her most recent publication is a book titled, Evidence-based Child Forensic Interviewing: The Developmental Narrative Elaboration Interview.

Anna K. Skosireva is a physician educated in Uzbekistan, where she specialized in internal medicine. Subsequently earning an MS degree in international health policy and management from Brandeis University and a PhD degree in international family and community studies from Clemson University, she did her post-graduate studies in social science and health policy. She then completed a post-doctoral research and teaching fellowship in the Institute on Family and Neighborhood Life at Clemson University and a research fellowship in the Canadian Institutes of Health ACHIEVE program at St Michael's Hospital in Toronto. As a physician and sociologist, she integrates perspectives from medicine, health policy, epidemiology, and sociology in her research. Her work is focused on socio-cultural determinants of population health and health disparities, with particular foci on the health of ethnic minorities, children, and people affected by mental illness and drug abuse.

Patricia Sloper was professor of children's healthcare at the Social Policy Research Unit, University of York, UK until her retirement in 2010. Her background is in psychology, and throughout her career her research has focused on the needs and experiences of children with disabilities or chronic illnesses and their families.

Michal Soffer PhD is a senior lecturer at the School of Social Work, Faculty of Social Welfare and Health Sciences, University of Haifa, Israel. Her main research interests are stigma toward disability and illness, as reflected in social policies, structures and processes. She has co-authored a book on women inmates in Israel and published papers on illness-related stigma, mediated images of illness and disabilities, women inmates, and disability-related policies.

Emma Sterrett PhD is a clinical psychologist and an assistant professor in the Kent School of Social Work at the University of Louisville. Her research focuses, in general, on the ways interpersonal relationships affect youth well-being, as well as on dissemination and implementation of evidence-based family and systemic interventions. She has published several papers on family relationships, other contextual influences, and youth psychosocial adjustment among low-income and ethnic minority youth.

Becky Tipper is a sociologist whose research interests include qualitative methods and everyday social life (in particular, family and kin relationships and human-animal interactions). She completed her PhD in Sociology in 2012 at the University of Manchester, UK. Prior to that she worked as an academic researcher. She is currently an Honorary Research Fellow at the Morgan Centre for the Study of Relationships and Personal Life at the University of Manchester.

Anu Toots is a professor of comparative public policy in the Institute of Politics and of Governance, Tallinn University, Estonia. Her research interests include governance of the welfare state, citizenship and education policy. She has been engaged in comparative educational research including large-scale surveys by the International Association for the Evaluation of Educational Achievements (IEA) and education reform analyses by the Council of Europe. Her research articles have appeared in the *Journal of Baltic Studies, International Journal of Educational Research, Studies of Transition States and Societies* and many others.

Karen Tustin PhD recently completed her PhD in psychology from the University of Otago. Karen's research interests include examining age-related changes in childhood amnesia (the inability of adults to recall their infancy and early childhood) across the lifespan and the specific mechanisms responsible for childhood amnesia. In particular, Karen is interested in how the development of episodic memory contributes to our understanding of childhood amnesia. Recent publications include (with Hayne, 2010) 'Defining the boundary: Age-related changes in childhood amnesia' in *Developmental Psychology* and (with Hayne, Gross, McNamee, Fitzgibbon, Tustin, 2011) ' Episodic memory and episodic foresight in 3- and 5-year-old children' in *Cognitive Development*.

Drika Weller PhD is an American Association for the Advancement of Science, Science & Technology Policy Fellow, working at the US Agency for International Development. Dr Weller's work focuses on promoting research-driven solutions to advance the wellbeing of underserved populations, with an emphasis on children and youth. Drika has worked in the US, Asia, Africa, and Eastern Europe. She has published in Child Development, Handbook of Moral Development, and Attachment and Human Development.

Ekaterina Yazykova has addressed questions of legal and psychosocial protections for various vulnerable populations, including children left without parental care, victims of family violence, and communities recovering from armed conflict. She has worked in academic, intergovernmental, and nongovernmental settings on issues that promote recovery and develop confidence in trauma affected individuals and groups. For her doctoral dissertation in international family and community studies at Clemson University, Yazykova conducted field research in communities that were struggling with ethnic strife, poverty, and lack of personal security in post-independence Kosovo. As an intern at the Hague Conference for Private International Law, Yazykova worked on measures to make intercountry adoption a safer practice for children from orphanages in Russia. At Amnesty International, Yazykova reported on violations of rights of disaster victims, victims of domestic abuse, prisoners, and other vulnerable groups in the United States. Yazykova has taught classes on social policy and policy analysis.

INTRODUCTION

The Nature and Scope of Child Research: Learning about Children's Lives

Gary B. Melton, Daphna Gross-Manos, Asher Ben-Arieh and Ekaterina Yazykova

... We must first, all of us, demolish the borders which history has erected ... within our own nations – barriers of race and religion, social class and ignorance. Our answer is the world's hope; it is to rely on youth. The cruelties and the obstacles of this swiftly changing planet will not yield to obsolete dogmas and outworn slogans. It cannot be moved by those who cling to a present which is already dying, who prefer the illusion of security to the excitement and danger which comes with even the most peaceful progress. This world demands the qualities of youth: not a time of life but a state of mind, a temper of the will, a quality of imagination, a predominance of courage over timidity, of the appetite for adventure over the life of ease. ... It is a revolutionary world that we all live in; and thus, as I have said in Latin America and Asia and Europe and in my own country, the United States, it is the young people who must take the lead. Thus you and your young compatriots everywhere have had thrust upon you a greater burden of responsibility than any generation that has ever lived.

These words were uttered in Robert F. Kennedy's Day of Affirmation speech – probably his most famous – at the University of Cape Town on 6 June 1966.[1] Both the historical and rhetorical contexts for these remarks were stirring. Making many allusions to the similar challenges facing South Africa and the United States in the mid 1960s (and before and after), Kennedy called on young people to 'strip the last remnants of that ancient, cruel belief' – 'the dark and poisoning superstition that [the] world is bounded by the nearest hill, [the] universe ends at river's shore', and that the commonality of humanity 'is enclosed in the tight circle of those who share [one's] town or [one's] views and the color of [one's] skin'.

In the most memorable passage of the speech, Kennedy urged his listeners not to be limited by their youthfulness. Reciting a lengthy list of notable young adults – some famous; some little-known – who, as individuals, had 'moved the world', Kennedy proclaimed, 'Each time a man stands up for an ideal, or acts to improve the lot of others, or strikes out against injustice, he sends forth a tiny ripple of hope, and crossing each other from a million different centres of energy and daring, those ripples build a current which can sweep down the mightiest walls of oppression and resistance'.

We have quoted at some length from the Kennedy speech because it starkly presents a common image of the relation of age to political beliefs and actions. Kennedy linked innovation, energy, and 'adventure' to youthfulness, and he tied those attributes to the imagination and courage required to seek greater justice in communities, societies, and the world. In other words, Kennedy associated conventionality – whether grounded in fear, tradition, tired ideas, or complacency – with middle and late adulthood. By contrast, he perceived young people to be drawn to moral principles – to *ideals* – necessary for progress toward 'the enlargement of liberty for individual human beings' – 'the supreme goal and the abiding practice of any *western* society' (emphasis added). Notwithstanding the allusion to Western society, Kennedy clearly believed the traits that he wished to foster to be ones universally associated with youth, 'the only true international community'.

For almost everyone who lived through the past half-century, many images consistent with the concept of youth that Kennedy articulated are indelibly stored in memory. The protests by the 'lost generation' of young people in South Africa – those who were on the barricades (not in schools) while their older leaders were imprisoned (see Cowell, 1990; Hawthorne and MacLeod, 1991) – are but one example. Recall, for example:

- the university and high school students who engaged in sit-ins at racially segregated lunch counters in the American South;
- the students who were in the vanguard of virtually every overthrow of a Latin American dictatorship (see Thomas and Craig, 1973);
- the American university and high school students whose demonstrations, teach-ins, and door-to-door campaigning for anti-war candidates hastened the end of the Vietnam war;
- the French university and lycée students whose protests stimulated weeks of general strikes and permanently changed social norms;
- the Chinese university students who faced tanks and live ammunition in Tiananmen Square;
- the Palestinian boys who challenged Israeli rifles and tanks with stones from the streets of refugee camps during each intifada;
- the German young people who triumphantly disassembled the Berlin wall;
- the Czech university students who filled Wenceslas Square in Prague and peacefully brought down the Communist regime;
- the Iranian youth who risked their lives and liberty to protest apparently corrupt election returns and to bring the resulting government violence to the world's attention;

- the Arab young people who used social media to launch mass demonstrations and to overthrow some long-ruling authoritarian governments.

The extraordinary historical significance of these events is undeniable. Any meaningful account of youth engagement in political life must take them into account. Moreover, the events noted have been so profound in their influence on the course of the second half of the twentieth century and the first decades of the twenty-first century that a reasonable hypothesis would be that achievement of a new political order (at least in the current ethos) is contingent in part on youth participation and maybe even youth leadership in such change.

At the same time, however, the examples suggest that the converse is also true. In other words, although substantial involvement by young people may be necessary for massive political change, such participation is not enough. As illustrated by the variable success of the activists in the Arab Spring in 2011, youthful fervour must be actualized through institutional sponsorship and commitment if it is to be successful (Schwartz, 2011).

BEYOND YOUTHFUL IDEALISM

Youth in political parties

Although the examples given so far are of instances in which youth participation appeared to stimulate democratic change, youth action need not push in such a positive direction. Just as Robert Kennedy presumed young people to be malleable (unfettered by tradition or a solidified ideology), totalitarian regimes have generally regarded childhood to be in the public sphere (Qvortrup, 2008), because it was the context for socialization into the prescribed social and political order. As Toots et al. (Chapter 4, this volume) discuss in more detail, a key element of state power in most such regimes has been the creation of powerful, nearly universal political organizations for children and youth (such as the Hitler Youth, Young Pioneers, and Komsomol; see Wallace and Alt, 2001). Even young children were engaged in celebrations and demonstrations that were linked to parents' workplaces and related adult organizations (Qvortrup, 2008). Hence, youth movements served as forums from which to influence parents, not just children, adolescents, and young adults themselves.

Western political parties have also often established youth organizations to coalesce direct involvement (for example, 'working the polls') in partisan activities (for example, in the United States, Teen Dems, Teen Age Republicans, Young Democrats, and Young Republicans, in the latter two instances, with college branches). Unlike their counterparts in totalitarian regimes, the youth wings of Western political parties are more elitist than mass. They are self-selected, in the same sense that student governments, even if effectively powerless, generally attract and further socialize young people who are and will be active in various aspects of civic life and who already enjoy participation in the battles, drama, and pageantry of political life (Crystal and DeBell, 2002; Glanville, 1999; McFarland and Starmanns, 2009; Sigel and Hoskin, 1981; Youniss, 2011).

For example, the Labour Party camp that was the site of the dreadful terrorist shootings in Norway in 2011 had a tradition of being an entry point into the activities of the long-dominant political party in Norway. Historically, the deliberations of the youth conference had been open only to young people themselves, but most adult leaders of the Norwegian Labour Party had attended the camp when they were adolescents. The camp was thus a peer-governed training ground for politically active young people who already had established a political ideology and party identification and who were apt ultimately to become Labour Party leaders and perhaps office holders.

Except that participants' parents themselves are often politically active, youth branches of

Western political parties are generally semi-autonomous and youth-led, often with weak links to the adult parties with which they are affiliated. Accordingly, these activities are better conceived as democratic political socialization (in this instance, practice in grassroots political organizing) than as orchestrated elements of a state or party apparatus.

It is noteworthy in that regard that the strategies of youth control adopted by fascist and Communist governments were never fully successful (Wallace and Alt, 2001). Despite the authorities' attempts to build and sustain monolithic youth movements, youth subcultures emerged in Nazi Germany and the countries in the Soviet sphere of influence. These informal youth groups did not form an 'opposition' in the ordinary sense. Searching, however, for personal freedom in societies that had little, they tried to differentiate themselves through emulation of Western musical and clothing styles. Official youth organizations tried to co-opt these subcultural expressions by broadening the entertainment available in the established groups.

Children in political life

As in most commentary on 'youth' in politics, so far there has been little discussion of children (distinguished from adolescents and young adults) in this chapter. To some extent, this omission reflects the realities of visible political engagement. University and, to a lesser degree, secondary students were at the centre of most of the examples of youth leadership in political change in the past half-century. At least in part, this centrality was the product of the independence that older youth have as a matter of fact and, at least in regard to those who have passed the age of majority (typically 18; see Convention on the Rights of the Child, 1989, art. 1), as a matter of law.

The focus on adolescents and young adults is also based on the conventional wisdom, crystallized by Erik Erikson (1950, 1968), that the germination of interest in politics occurs during those phases of the life cycle. Throughout the world, this assumption is at the foundation of the placement of formal civic education almost exclusively in secondary schools (see Torney-Purta, Schwille and Amadeo, 1999). Thus, for example, formal school-based political education in Europe occurs primarily in lower secondary education (the equivalent of middle school or junior high in the American system; Eurydice, 2005).

Like other competencies, interests, and values discussed in this volume, however, the assumption that elementary-school-aged children are apolitical ('innocent') is more the product of the social construction of childhood – perhaps coupled with a sense of guilt about the terrible conditions that some children face – than empirical reality. As Robert Coles persuasively demonstrated in his Pulitzer Prize-winning series on *Children in Crisis* (Coles, 1967, 1971a, 1971b, 1977a, 1977b) and his subsequent treatises on the moral (Coles, 1986a), spiritual (Coles, 1990), and political (Coles, 1986b) lives of children (including children in then-conflict-laden societies outside the United States, such as Northern Ireland), children are often profoundly affected by – and cognizant of – the socio-political realities that all too often are troubling or even traumatic.

In his book on *The Political Life of Children*, Coles observed the high frequency with which the word 'really' appears in the conversation of mental health professionals. He confessed that he had for many years failed to attend to children's comments about political matters because he had been trained to believe 'that everything I was hearing was "really" about the patient's *parents*, their beliefs' (1986b: 7). Applying his psychoanalytic education, Coles might have added that he regarded children's political statements as '*really* thinly veiled statements of transference of oedipal strivings onto the authoritative psychiatric interviewer' (Melton, 1987a: 362).

Coles' appreciation of the reality of children's stated concerns about political situations was most powerfully stimulated by Ruby Bridges, the 6-year-old African American child from New Orleans who in 1960 was the first to be integrated into a White elementary school in the American South (see http://www.rubybridges.com/ story.htm). In *The Problem We All Live With* (the centrefold artwork for an issue of *Look* magazine in January 1964), Norman Rockwell famously captured Ruby's dignity on canvas. Accompanied by US marshals, she walked with head held high through a crowd of jeering adults into her classroom of one. (Parents of other children refused to allow them to be in the same classroom as Ruby, and the regular classroom teachers refused to teach her.) First told in a series of articles for the *Atlantic Monthly*, Ruby's story began Coles' series on *Children in Crisis*, which chronicled the situation for children in ethnic minorities, children of migrant workers and sharecroppers, children in impoverished families in Appalachia, and children in wealthy families, all in the United States.[2] Although Ruby did not fully comprehend the situation (for example, she likened the jeering and throwing of objects in her trek into school to the noise and disorder at Mardi Gras), she did understand that her going to the White school had resulted in trouble for her family (such as her father's losing his job). She also understood the hatred in the crowds that lined her way to school. She coped by praying for the people who yelled terrible things or who otherwise tried to frighten her by, for example, displaying a Black doll in a coffin.

Although Ruby Bridges' experience at age 6 was unique, her basic understanding of the situation was not. Even primary-grade children often comprehend the universality of the right to be treated humanely and with dignity. They also have an exquisite awareness of the allocation of authority – who is 'boss' – within the institutions of which children are a part and, in general, show deference to those authorities (Berti and Bombi, 1981;

Furth, 1980; Melton, 1980, 1983a; Melton and Limber, 1992). They also can recognize national political symbols (Dawson, Prewitt and Dawson, 1977). Indeed, by third or fourth grade, most children apply conventional moral judgements (for example, concerns about fairness and social order) to everyday questions pertaining to democratic norms (such as freedom of expression in the school newspaper; see Berti and Bombi, 1981; Furth, 1980; Melton, 1980, 1983a; Melton and Limber, 1992).

Perhaps even more to the point, political ideologies are largely inculcated by that age. Thus, for example, American children in the intermediate grades, regardless of ethnicity, region, or social class, virtually always define and justify children's rights in terms of classically liberal (libertarian) ideals of freedom of expression and autonomy in action. On the other hand, Norwegian children of the same age often offer definitions and justifications based on social and economic rights (such as entitlements to adequate nutrition, education, and health care). In short, although 9-year-olds in the two societies are usually unable to articulate a principled ideology, in fact they have already adopted the libertarian and social democratic values that are dominant in American and Norwegian political cultures, respectively (Melton and Limber, 1992).

Similarly, habits of political activism (such as wearing campaign buttons) are commonly established by early adolescence (Hess and Torney, 1967). So too are commitments to volunteer community service (see, for example, Hashima and Melton, 2008). In general, the period of greatest change in political interest, activity, and identification is middle childhood, not adolescence, even though civic instruction typically occurs in the latter developmental phase (Jennings and Niemi, 1974).

Nonetheless, Furth was correct when he concluded that 'the understanding of what a societal community is and how government functions is only rarely developed in children below age twelve' (1980: 47), *if* he was referring to an ability to articulate facts

and concepts about the political system. Of course, many adolescents and adults also lack sophistication in the mechanisms of political reform (see, for example, McClosky and Brill, 1983; Torney-Purta, Lehmann et al., 2001).

Furth's conclusion has implications for policy and practice to protect children from unwise or ill-informed decisions. For example, there is good reason to be especially careful when considering children's waiver of rights in delinquency proceedings. Such decisions are apt to be made on the bases of erroneous or incomplete beliefs amid the urging of parents, probation officers, and others who demand that juvenile respondents 'talk' (Grisso, 1981) – a problem compounded because young people are inexperienced in seeking and using the advice of lawyers and other professionals.

Nonetheless, it is clearly mistaken to conclude that elementary-school-aged children's limited ability to describe the fine points of the legislative process or to offer abstract reasons for their political attitudes and values implies that elementary-school civic education is a waste of time. To the contrary, insofar as the principal purpose of public education is to prepare children for full participation in community life, a much stronger argument can be made that a civic education curriculum is inadequate if it does not include major components in elementary schools.

More directly to the point of this book and, in particular, to the chapter by Anu Toots et al. (Chapter 4, this volume) on children as political actors, it is also clear that school-age children *are* participants in community life, even when their civic 'participation' is relegated to observation. The belief in elementary-school-age children's 'innocence' and their purported obliviousness to power and politics is a social construction – more like wishful thinking than social fact – designed to maintain consistency with traditional age-based authority relations in the family and, perhaps even more so, the society at large. (Seen from a modern perspective [for example, Zelizer, 1994], the belief that children are outside the marketplace is even more incredible [cf. Brusdal and Frønes, Chapter 7, this volume].) Such reliance on myth historically has served to justify the creation of age-segregated institutional structures to 'socialize' children in groups that are on or outside the boundaries of the community (see, for example, Dahl, 1986; Levine and Levine, 1992; Melton, 1983a, 1987b; Platt, 1980).

Implications for research

There are two important corollaries for research. First, given its moral, social, and political significance, children's participation in the various aspects of civil society should be an important domain of child research. In particular, much more attention should be given to the ways that elementary-school-age and even preschool children are or could be actors (not simply dependent subjects) in community life and to the meaning that such activities (or, conversely, instances of 'protection' from such involvement) have for children themselves.

Second, children's absence (or seeming absence) from some contexts should not necessarily be regarded as indicative of their capacities. As post-Piagetian scholars have demonstrated, 'incompetence' is sometimes a methodological artefact. In other words, the capacity to undertake a task and, by extension, to reason about it may be masked if the means of measurement requires particular verbal skills or vocabulary. Even when such an artefact is not evident, 'incompetence' may reflect a lack of experience or a motivational lacuna that is a product of children's ascribed roles.

In that regard, goals of child 'protection' and 'participation' may sometimes be in conflict. Adults' assumption of responsibilities that may preclude children's own actions is, of course, often morally demanded, even when children have the capacity for greater involvement in community life. Obviously,

children's engagement in paid labour, for example, not only may place them at an unacceptable level of risk to their health and well-being, but it also often precludes their engagement in educational activities that are necessary for optimization of their short- and long-term quality of life. There are also instances in which children are obviously unable to perform (a conventional basketball court is not an asset for a 4-year-old!) and many others in which children's survival and development are necessarily and appropriately in the hands of adults.

Nonetheless, as a general matter, the problem is not zero-sum (adults [usually parents] *or* children). There are two ethical concerns leading to such a conclusion:

> First, ... the fact that the interests of multiple parties are almost always at stake in matters involving children must be taken into account. Such a principle ordinarily implies the need for structures to promote *shared* decision making. Second, taken together, the dual values of autonomy and beneficence imply that children should have opportunities for increasing independence in contexts in which risk is minimized. As a general matter, self-determination is less important than participation in decision making. Nothing is more fundamental to the experience of being taken seriously than simply having a say, being heard politely, and having one's perspective considered – in effect, being part of a conversation about matters of personal significance. In the same vein, children's interests are most likely to be promoted when they are given opportunities for *graduated* decision making – in effect, 'learner's permits' that enable children to gradually assume independence so full autonomy is not exercised until there is some experience with the decision or task.
>
> In short, the human-rights mandate to take children seriously as people usually should not be framed as deference to parents *or* children. Rather, careful efforts to promote the participation of children (as well as parents and other interested adults) – to help them feel they are heard – will usually bring parents *and* children together in shared decision making.
>
> (Melton, 1999: 936 [citations omitted]).

Insights about the nature of children's involvement in everyday life in community settings are at the base of the development of childhood studies, including new directions for empirical child research. The remainder of this chapter provides an overview of such ideas and of their reflection in the contributions by the authors of the chapters in this book. Before addressing the childhood studies movement itself, however, it is useful to take a brief look at the somewhat earlier initial development of ecological psychology, which provided an intellectual foundation for the movement's challenges to traditional concepts and methods in developmental psychology.

THE ECOLOGY OF CHILDHOOD

… One can not go to the scientific literature of child behavior to find what the behavior of children looks like. One must go to the novelists, the diarists, the news reporters. This is true because most data of psychology [and other social sciences] have been assembled in terms of particular problems or theories and this almost always requires the fractionation of behavior to such a degree that its appearance is destroyed. The psychological landscape is strewn with the debris of these dismantling operations.
(Barker and Wright, 1955: 14)

Drawing on the theories of his mentor Kurt Lewin and working more than a half-century ago, Roger Barker and his colleagues at the University of Kansas sought to describe the lives of children in everyday settings. For a quarter-century, Barker and his co-workers copiously recorded observations of children in a multitude of *behaviour settings* (such as the Girl Scouts' cookie sale at the grocery store; the Saturday night social at the American Legion Hall) in 'Midwest', a pseudonym for Oskaloosa, a small town (in 1950, population 707, including 119 children younger than 12 years old) in northeastern Kansas, about 20 miles from the University of Kansas.

As illustrated by the opening quote, Barker believed that the then- (and now-) dominant methods in research on the behaviour of children stripped such activity of practical meaning by isolating children from their ordinary milieu (the 'habitat'):

An essential feature of most methods of psychological diagnosis, testing, and measurement is the creation by the investigator of a special, standard psychological situation within which to observe behavior, thus destroying the natural habitat. Most tests, questionnaires, interviews, and experiments attempt to create for the subject a psychological situation designed for the special purposes of the investigator. To use these methods, except for very limited purposes, would be methodologically parallel to a plant ecologist's importing soil, broadcasting seeds, and coming back later to study the 'natural' vegetation. The task of an ecological field study is to determine the state of affairs that exists independently of the investigator's methods. The questions that exist in a subject's mind are as important as his answers to them. If the investigator asks the questions and poses the problems, he changes the subject's habitat and destroys the very thing he aims to study. Furthermore, free or nondirective interviews can cause profound changes in the subject's perception of himself and his world.
(Barker and Wright, 1955: 12–13)

Thus, in effect, Barker argued for – and undertook – a 'ground-up' science that relied heavily on direct observation of children in the settings of everyday life. This approach consumed most of Barker's adult life. Indeed, Barker and his wife and co-investigator Louise Barker were in many ways participant-observers. They not only worked in Oskaloosa; they also lived there.

Roger Barker's rationale for his approach was primarily scientific. As indicated in the quote opening this section, he believed (like his mentor Lewin) that behaviour was the product of the interaction between person and environment. Omitting or substantially altering either element for the purpose of research diminishes 'ecological validity' (correspondence to real-world phenomena) to an extent that the findings have little meaning. Consequentially, Barker believed, such research also has little usefulness in improving people's well-being.[3]

Barker and his colleagues did contribute important findings of lasting scientific significance. Commonly regarded as the founder of environmental psychology and as a seminal contributor to theory in community psychology, Barker was sensitive to the 'demands' that both physical and social environments exert on human behaviour. (An example of an environmental demand on behaviour would be the design of roadways to minimize or eliminate the possibility that drivers would enter on the wrong side of the road. In the social domain, tasks might be established that, as a side effect, elicit positive interaction or, undesirably, result in pressure to engage in antisocial behaviour or in 'education' in such misbehaviour through modelling.)

In that vein, the Kansas group was particularly influential in its research showing that 'under-populated' (in the original terminology, 'undermanned') settings, such as small schools (Barker and Gump, 1964) and churches (Wicker, 1978) and, more generally, rural communities (see Melton, 1983b), demand frequent, diverse participation, with few people uninvolved, greater personal satisfaction, greater sense of competence, and little segregation by age, ethnicity, or wealth. Consider, for example, this description of the social structure of Midwest:

Midwest children had to tolerate a wide range of individual differences in the inhabitants of most of the behaviour settings they entered, and they had to develop skill in making diverse people fit into the same behavior patterns. The need for participants was so great in relation to the number of inhabitants that selection on the basis of sex, age, social group, intelligence, personality, political beliefs, or wealth was virtually impossible. This tendency was supported by a pervasive democratic ideology. The low degree of segregation meant, further, that most behavior settings had to accommodate a wide range of abilities, motives, and personalities within their standing patterns of behavior. This, in turn, required that children learn early to adjust to a wide range of individual differences. Such adjustment was accomplished partly by special rules and arrangements, but basically it required a great measure of self-control and tolerance.

The lack of segregation in Midwest behavior settings was a factor adding to the richness of life for Midwest children. Not only did they participate in many independent settings with different standing patterns of behaviour but, within most of these settings, a wide range of Midwest citizens was present. The old and the young, the rich and the poor, the bright and the dull rubbed shoulders in most settings.

(Barker and Wright, 1955: 460)

By illustration, one of us (Melton) lived for a long time in Nebraska, one of the most rural states in the United States. In much of the state, not only are the centres of population merely hamlets, but the distances between settlements are great. In tiny school districts in Nebraska, it is common for schools to play eight-man (rather than conventional eleven-man) American football, so that there are enough players to fill all of the positions. Moreover, a boy is likely to play both offence and defence, he may play clarinet in the school band's half-time show, and he may sell advance tickets to the game to people in the community. In a very small community, it is difficult not to be engaged! (The one downside of such an ecology is that it is difficult or even impossible for an individual to specialize and therefore to achieve the highest level of accomplishment in a particular role or skill.)

Barker et al.'s conclusions about the behavioural effects of setting size arose, of course, from their method of simply counting activities (who did what and where they did it). This descriptive research is not only theoretically important. It also has important implications for public policy. Unfortunately, however, in planning school construction, for example, economies of scale and, to some extent, community pride (the false assumption that 'bigger is better') tend to triumph over the long-established fact that youth engagement is greater in small settings. In turn, youth engagement is known to be positively related to students' school attendance, overall achievement, and happiness and inversely related to such negative outcomes as the frequency of delinquent behaviour, dropping out, and depression (Committee on Increasing High School Students' Engagement and Motivation to Learn, 2004; Melton, 2005). Although such findings have not stemmed the growth of ever larger consolidated schools, they have pushed toward innovations to make schools 'feel' smaller (such as 'schools within schools', so that large buildings and the school population itself are divided into largely discrete units).

Barker's team also pioneered in the field of rehabilitation psychology (see, for example, Schoggen, 1978; Wright, 1983 [1960]). They examined the trajectory of changes in the frequency of various behaviours in diverse settings following an injury or illness and treatment. Such data not only provide a picture of the natural history of recovery, but they also suggest ways in which settings might be modified in order to enhance the fit between the individual and the setting.

As in the other contexts mentioned, behaviour ecology is not 'developmental' in the way that the term is ordinarily used. Barker and his colleagues understood that age-related changes in behaviour reflect not only maturational changes in the child but also changes in the nature of the settings in which children of different ages are likely to find themselves. Thus, for example, age might be a variable in behaviour mapping related to a particular disability, but age differences in the types of settings where children are found or the kinds of activities in which they participate would not necessarily mean that the disability is manifested differently among children of different ages or that rehabilitation was differentially effective by age. Changes in the child, whether by maturation or rehabilitation, must be understood as a product of interaction between the child and the setting (including the other people who are a part of a given setting).

That assumption builds the connection between the work of ecological psychologists and that of specialists in childhood studies, which did not develop systematically until about a generation later. In both instances, children's behaviour is understood to be a function of context.

Although Barker and his colleagues did not start from an ideology of childhood in the way that some contemporary scholars

in childhood studies do, Barker et al. made clear that they also valued children's experience for its own sake. They considered the meaning of children's experience in the here and now, not merely as practice for adulthood:

> The children of Midwest occupied positions of power and prestige; they were not a luxury in the community; they performed essential functions. About one-quarter of all performances in Midwest were by children. Even infants penetrated a few settings to the performance level, and younger school children were joint leaders of some settings. The settings children entered to the performance zones were not primarily those which were created especially for children; in fact, more than half of them were 'adult' settings. The meaning of this for the children of Midwest was that their achievements were not relegated to unimportant settings; children had the opportunity to achieve power and status in behavior settings which were generally prestigious.
>
> (Barker and Wright, 1955: 460)

Clearly, however, Barker and his colleagues' perspective was exceptional for the time and indeed for decades to come. We turn now to consideration of the processes by which such attention to children's actual and potential engagement in community life moved to a central point in child research.

HOW CHILDHOOD STUDIES CAME TO BE

Intellectual underpinnings

Child and family studies grew up to a large extent outside universities. Even theoretical scholarship on child development was largely a product of scholarly work undertaken outside academia. For example, Jean Piaget spent most of his career at the International Bureau of Education in Geneva, and much of his 'research' occurred in his own home as he observed the development of his own children. Sigmund Freud developed his theory of child development in his psychiatric office – and then in consultations with *adult* patients! Moreover, as psychoanalysis grew as a field of scholarship and practice, such studies took place in free-standing psychoanalytic institutes.

Analogously, much of the early systematic research on child development took place in free-standing institutes, such as the Merrill-Palmer Institute in Michigan and the Fels Research Institute in Ohio. In the United States, family studies also grew initially outside the principal academic units of universities, as 'domestic science' was typically a feature of Cooperative Extension units in land-grant universities (public universities with an outreach mission and a corps of professional staff with a translational job description and usually without doctorates).

Gradually, however, such work became more 'scientific' and nested within departments of psychology (developmental psychology) and sociology (family sociology) within colleges of arts and sciences in universities. With the new emphasis on application of the scientific method, child and family studies, especially the 'best' such scholarship within programmes in developmental psychology, became heavily laboratory-focused and experimental. As a general rule, internal validity (reduction of sources of 'error') was valued more than external validity (generalizability to real-world settings).

As Adrian James and Alan Prout have pointed out, the developmental theories prominent in child psychology provided a framework of 'rationality', 'naturalness', and 'universality'. Children's behaviour was understood to be largely the product of a natural process, in which the nature of children's reasoning, moral judgements, social behaviour, motor behaviour, psychosexual concerns, and emotional expression all unfolded in predictable, forward-oriented maturational patterns. Such patterns were generally held to be consistent across cultures; in effect, biology was destiny.

Just as development was conceived ordinarily as unidirectional (moving forward through maturation), so too were developmental influences. Adults influenced ('socialized') children, as their capacities expanded.

By implication, therefore, children were 'shaped' by their genes, their level of maturation, and their environment. They were generally not perceived as *actors* in their environment, except perhaps in relation to siblings and peers.

However, dissatisfaction with that organizational and epistemological base began to appear in the 1970s and to be reflected in some new academic structures in the 1980s and (at an increased rate) the 1990s. In arguments consistent with constructivist perspectives (or 'critical studies') arising in multiple disciplines in the humanities and social sciences, historians (for example, Kett, 1977) began to conceive of both 'childhood' and 'adolescence' as 'inventions'. Apart from the epistemologies involved, such arguments were hard to ignore because empirical historical evidence, like cross-cultural research, suggested that the nature and pace of children's development were significantly influenced by their context. Similarly, the societal attributions about children were recognized as social phenomena that have meaning beyond children's objective levels of maturation. Consider, for example, historical and cultural differences in the way that children are depicted in paintings.

Critics like Barker and Bronfenbrenner regarded much of the work about children and families that had emerged in the academy as being intellectually sterile, divorced from the realities of everyday life and unresponsive to the needs of organizations, communities, and societies for expertise in dealing with the complex problems that many children and families face. Such critiques were by-products in part of more general trends toward 'relevance' in the academy, which in turn emanated from the protests of disadvantaged groups that they had been systematically ignored or denigrated in major institutions, including universities.

Developmental research itself began to suggest that biologically grounded 'stage' models, such as Jean Piaget's and those of his intellectual progeny (such as Lawrence Kohlberg), underestimated the importance of both cultural factors and individual differences. Even more to the point here, Piagetians were said to overlook situational factors in children's behaviour that sometimes masked their actual capacities and their potential. (For a succinct review of these criticisms and the counter-arguments in regard to Piagetian theory, see Lourenço and Machado, 1996; see also Narvaez, 2005, on Kohlberg and his critics.)

Other child researchers argued that 'ecological' models are better tools than biological, cognitive-developmental, or social theories alone in understanding child development as a scientific matter and underlying the design of policies and professional practices. Their answer to most questions about the effects of a sometimes potent variable on a malleable outcome was, 'It depends'.

The creation of settings for child research

In order to facilitate holistic responses to the needs of policymakers, educators, clinicians, and others for assistance in serving children and families, many universities and governments again moved outside traditional psychology and sociology departments to form interdisciplinary centres and institutes intended both to generate and transfer knowledge about child ecology or childhood itself. The fact that they are special structures outside conventional university departments and schools (faculties) is an indicator of the fragility of such entities (Melton, 2013). They come and go, and they expand and shrink, with much greater dependence on external sponsors and often on a founder's vision than is typically true for other university units that are more conventionally organized and more predictably funded.

Today the global consortium Childwatch International (based at the University of Oslo) has more than 40 member centres and institutes (some of which are not university-affiliated), and the (American) University Child and Family Policy Consortium has more than 30 member institutions. A look at those lists and the websites of some other child research centres of which the authors were aware showed that some of the largest and best established centres were established in the 1980s (for example, the Norwegian Centre for Child Research, based at the Norwegian University of Science and Technology in Trondheim, 1982; International Centre for Research and Policy on Childhood [CIESPI], Pontifical Catholic University of Rio de Janeiro, 1984; Chapin Hall Center for Children, University of Chicago, 1985; Office of Child Development, University of Pittsburgh, 1986; Center on Children, Families, and the Law, University of Nebraska-Lincoln, 1987), but that most were established in the mid-1990s or later. The only pre-1980 child research centre that we identified was the Children's Rights Centre (established in 1978) at Ghent University in Belgium), which has evolved into the national, multi-university Children's Rights Knowledge Centre (KeKi), founded in 2010.[4]

(This assessment overlooks the small group of much older, once free-standing institutions for child research. For example, the Merrill-Palmer Institute, now the Merrill Palmer Skillman Institute of Wayne State University in Detroit, was established in 1920. The Fels Research Institute for the Study of Human Development [since 1977, absorbed into the lifespan health research programme at the medical school at Wright State University in Dayton, OH], was founded in 1929. However, these institutes were and are conceived as programmes for research on *child development*, not *childhood studies*.)

The growth of centres and institutes was roughly parallel with – or perhaps slightly preceded by – the development of national and international structures for facilitation of scholarship in child studies. In addition to the consortia mentioned earlier, scientific societies and academic journals have been important catalysts for growth of the field. For example, the American Sociological

Association established a Section on Children and Youth in 1992, the European Sociological Association began annual conference programmes on sociology of childhood in 1999 (Research Network 4), and the International Sociological Association created a Research Committee on Sociology of Childhood (RC 53) in 1998. Through the initiative of the Norwegian Centre for Child Research, the journal *Childhood* began publication in 1993, and the *International Journal of Children's Rights* (a spin-off from an international study group convened by the Israeli chapter of Defence for Children International) also published its first issue in 1993.

A loose network of scholars interested in child indicators began meeting in the mid-1990s. That group evolved into the International Society for Child Indicators, which began holding biennial international conferences in 2007 and which initiated the journal *Child Indicators Research* in 2008.

Publication of major treatises in the field followed the initial development of centres and associations supportive of such scholarship. As the list of key texts in Table 1.1

illustrates, scholarship framed in relation to childhood studies became prominent in the early 2000s. The topical development is a still later phenomenon, so that it is only recently that a handbook with the scope of the current volume became possible.

With the development of a full-fledged field of study, graduate programmes specialized at least in part in childhood studies have begun to emerge since 2000, predominantly in Europe but also in Oceania, Latin America, and North America (see, for example, the programmes listed at www.icyrnet.net/index. php?page=links). The degree programmes are predominantly at master's level, as illustrated by the European Network of Masters in Children's Rights, founded in 2009, and a parallel Latin American Network that was initiated by Save the Children Sweden (Rädda Barnen). However, there are a few doctoral programmes in childhood studies, such as those at the Norwegian University of Science and Technology (founded in 2006) and Rutgers University-Camden (founded in 2007). Some other interdisciplinary doctoral programmes have a substantial focus

Table 1.1 Some leading monographs and textbooks on child research

Ben-Arieh, Asher and Frønes, Ivar (eds.) (2009) *Indicators of Children's Well-Being: Theory and Practice in a Multi-Cultural Perspective.* New York: Springer-Verlag.

Ben-Arieh, Asher, Kaufman, Natalie Hevener, Andrews, Arlene B., Goerge, Robert M., Lee, Bong Joo and Aber, Lawrence J. (2001) *Measuring and Monitoring Children's Well-Being.* Dordrecht, Netherlands: Kluwer Academic.

Corsaro, William A. (2005) *The Sociology of Childhood.* 2nd edn. Thousand Oaks, CA: Pine Forge Press. (1st edn, 1997).

James, Allison and James, Adrian L. (2004) *Constructing Childhood: Theory, Policy and Social Practice.* Basingstoke, England: Palgrave Macmillan.

James, Allison and James, Adrian L. (eds.) (2008a) *European Childhoods: Cultures, Politics and Childhoods in Europe.* Basingstoke, England: Palgrave Macmillan.

James, Allison and James, Adrian L. (2008b) *Key Concepts in Childhood Studies.* London: Sage.

James, Allison, Jenks, Chris and Prout, Alan (1998) *Theorizing Childhood.* Cambridge, England: Polity Press.

Kjørholt, Anne Trine (2004) 'Childhood as a social and symbolic space: Discourses on children as social participants in society'. PhD dissertation, Norwegian University of Science and Technology.

Lancy, David F. (2008) *The Anthropology of Childhood: Cherubs, Chattel, Changelings.* Cambridge, England: Cambridge University Press.

Prout, Alan (2004) *The Future of Childhood.* London: Routledge Falmer.

Pufall, Peter B. and Unsworth, Richard P. (eds.) (2004) *Rethinking Childhood.* New Brunswick, NJ: Rutgers University Press.

Qvortrup, Jens, Corsaro, William A., and Honig, Michael-Sebastian (eds.) (2009) *The Palgrave Handbook of Childhood Studies.* Basingstoke, England: Palgrave Macmillan.

on childhood studies (for example, Clemson University's PhD programme in International Family and Community Studies, founded in 2006 and now delivered in both South Carolina and Albania).

The chicken or the egg?

As the discussion thus far shows, the field of childhood studies is young, but it has evolved both organizationally and substantively in logical ways. It is interesting to consider, however, whether the field of childhood studies is stimulating or merely responding to change in the status and well-being of children. Of course, the likelihood is that the process is bidirectional. New ideas generated in the academy gradually make their way into popular consciousness, and scholarly discourse changes in response to popular concerns.

However, in this instance, it is likely that the stronger influences have been from forces outside academia. For example, the upsurge during the 1990s in scholarship on childhood and particularly on children's rights was undoubtedly stimulated in part by the enactment of the Convention on the Rights of the Child (CRC) by the UN General Assembly in 1989 and the nearly unanimous ratification by the global community soon thereafter. The CRC's enactment was enabled in turn by the end of the Cold War and the advances of other disadvantaged groups. Taken together, those developments universalized demands for democracy and challenged the belief that *any* class of people – even the smallest and most vulnerable – could be justifiably denied full recognition as persons entitled to human rights. The implementation of the CRC itself had considerable direct effects on childhood studies by creating a need for monitoring national fulfilment of children's rights and indirect effects by giving new legitimacy to the recognition of children's status as 'persons' in political, legal, and moral life.

However, the enactment of the CRC was not the whole story. For example, it is unlikely that the proliferation of scores of university-based American centres on child and family issues was heavily influenced by the adoption of the CRC, which the United States still has not ratified and which has been given little attention in the American media.[5] Rather, at least in the American case and probably to a substantial degree in other countries, the push for development of centres on children's issues came from foundations, policymakers, and child-serving agencies that demanded – and often indicated a willingness to pay for – expertise and new policy- and practice-specific knowledge that they often could not find in conventional academic departments.

Such demands were grounded in the mismatch between guild- or discipline-based work (in both universities and human services) and the realities of child and family life near the turn of the millennium. As a result, child professionals had been slow to develop and widely apply new modes of family support and human service delivery in response to the sea changes that had occurred since the 1960s in family structure, family attitudes, family law, economic stratification, workplace demands, gender roles, ethnic groups' status, residential mobility, relationship networks, informal support, human-service regulation, and communities' trust of both governmental and voluntary institutions (Melton, 1994, 2010a, 2010b; Melton and Wilcox, 1989). Although the growth of the intellectual framework for childhood studies was a predictable evolution of ideas, the motivation for such change could be found in practical realities.

PREMISES OF CHILDHOOD STUDIES[6]

Descriptive assumptions

So what then are the key ideas that typify the childhood studies movement and correspondingly underlie the new child research? Some core ideas are descriptive tenets about the nature of childhood.

First, *'childhood' is a **social** phenomenon.* Although membership in the class who are called 'children' is defined in part by biological and cognitive maturation, it is by no means the only criterion or even a limiting criterion. Consider, for example, the CRC's definition of 'children' as inclusive of 17-year-olds. That definition leads to the legal fiction of describing – and treating – many teenagers as 'children', when that descriptor would never be used in ordinary conversation.

On the other hand, as the average age for achievement of economic independence continues to increase, the initial assumption of historic 'adult' roles becomes more remote for each cohort of young people. Accordingly, the social status of teenagers and 20-somethings is increasingly ambiguous, as reflected in some scholars' use of a new label ('emerging adults') for many people who would have unequivocally been considered 'young adults' even in the recent past.

Second, *children are **actors**, not merely subjects.* The range of options for children may be limited by objective gaps in skills and knowledge (caused sometimes by inexperience or lack of environmental accommodations more than true incapacity) and, perhaps even more so, in ascribed roles. Almost from the beginning, however, children are active participants in constructing their environment. (See Kampmann, Chapter 8, this volume, for discussion of children's engagement in early childhood programmes.) There is now a consensus that Piaget and other early theorists in child development grossly underestimated young children's abilities and indeed the sophistication of their typical behaviour:

> We now know that infants and young children have a stunning array of biopsychosocial competencies. Even young infants have rudimentary intentions and organized and motivating emotions and are able to react to the meanings of others' intentions and emotions. With these biopsychosocial competencies, infants make meaning about their relation to the world of people and things and about themselves. Of course, their meaning-making is nonsymbolic and radically different from the representational meaning made by older children and adults, but it is meaning nonetheless.
> (Tronick and Beeghly, 2011: 107; citations omitted)

Third, *it is meaningful to conceive of 'children' (or 'adolescents' or 'young children' or 'young people') as a class.* The concept of 'childhood' itself and the descriptions of particular 'childhoods' (circumstances of childhood) often slough over individual and group differences in both the objective reality and the subjective experience of childhood. (In that regard, the title provided for the Convention on the Rights of *the* Child is unfortunate.) However, it is possible for an individual to step from childhood (or adolescence) to adulthood, as provided in law by the age of majority and as may occur in the attributions that both adults and children make about that person, regardless of age or psychological maturity. Therefore, although 'development' is a continuous function, the question of whether an individual is properly classified as a 'child' may have a binary (nominal or ordinal) answer, as illustrated most obviously by rites of passage.

Fourth, as discussed by Toots et al. (Chapter 4, this volume), *childhood may be conceived as a culture in itself with its own institutions, norms, mores, dialect, and styles.* Moreover, it may transcend boundaries both vertically and horizontally. Thus, for example, one may conceive of an American youth subculture, but one may also talk meaningfully about a youth culture that in at least some respects (including music, fashion, games, particular political concerns) may cross national boundaries.

Normative perspective

Giving children a voice

Childhood studies also incorporates a *normative* perspective – values and norms about how children *should* be treated. Perhaps the most basic assumption in that regard has already been noted; namely, children are *people* whose perspective is valuable and sometimes distinctive. In particular, they should have a voice (even if their opinions are not necessarily dispositive) in describing the settings of which they are a part and the effects on their lives of various policies and programmes.

Moreover, effects on children as children, not only as future adults, should be considerations in decision making. Thus, for example, the public good might be advanced by improving children's current quality of life (for example, enhancing recreational opportunities) even if such action cannot be demonstrated to improve children's productivity or happiness as adults.

The emphasis on learning about children's own viewpoint is based on three reasons. First, as already indicated, there is a *moral* dimension. Such research provides a means for children to have a say when their personhood may be in question. Second, there is a *pragmatic* concern. Information about children's own views may better guide the design of policies, practices, and even the physical environment in order to match (in ecological terms, 'fit') children's expectations, so that services are more acceptable and probably more effective. Third, as illustrated by Barker's work, knowledge about children's daily lives and their experiences of the settings in which they are a part is apt to be *scientifically* valuable, so that knowledge better reflects the realities of childhood.

Scholars on childhood typically believe that efforts to obtain more direct information about children's experiences and their behaviour in everyday settings is especially important because of gaps and misconceptions that have long pervaded both popular and professional beliefs about children. In particular, children's capacities as citizens have often been underestimated. To the extent that children's level of performance has been accurately observed, their apparent abilities have often been constrained by their status and the corollary range of their experiences.

In the same vein, children's experience in everyday settings has been given insufficient attention. Partly as a result, topics on which there is basic research suggesting strategies for intervention (for example, educational approaches to improve understanding and exercise of rights; neighbourhood approaches to enhancement of children's safety and well-being) have often not been followed by translations of such knowledge into programmatic trials until decades later, if at all.

Building ethically and empirically sound public policy

In general, public policies affecting children should recognize and accommodate (a) children's capacities, (b) the 'real' developmental differences that shape their experience and their possibilities, and (c) the constraints placed on their performance by their social and legal status (see Melton, 1999, for explication of these points in practical terms). In the first instance, policies and programmes should offer opportunities for children to enhance and apply their skills in relation to matters of concern to them. In the second, efforts should be made to ensure that caring adults are available for consultation and that risks attached to improvident decisions are minimized. In the third, policymakers should recognize the unfairness of holding young people fully responsible for bad behaviour when they have had little opportunity to practise the independent exercise of good judgement. Provision of adequate knowledge for application of these principles will often require innovations in methodology (see the chapters in Part III of this volume, especially Craig, Chapter 25 and Rasmussen, Chapter 24) to enable valid observation of children's everyday behaviour and optimal communication between researchers and child participants at all phases of the process, including diffusion of results (Dahl, Chapter 30; Hayne and Tustin, Chapter 29; Saywitz and Camparo, Chapter 21; Soffer and Ben-Arieh, Chapter 28).

In turn, these new approaches raise complex problems of research ethics. Behavioural research is rarely of direct benefit to the participants, child participants are often unaccustomed to exercise of autonomy, and in many instances they are in populations that are of uncertain competence, low freedom, and high vulnerability (see the examples in Part II of this volume; see also Melton and Stanley, 1996). Moreover, research on children's everyday lives almost inevitably intersects with the complicated legal and social relationships that permeate the settings of which children are a part (see the examples in Part I of this volume, especially Levesque, this volume; see also those chapters that focus on third-party informants (for example, Bornstein, Chapter 26; Goerge and Bong-Lee, Chapter 23)). Given the evolution of children's status, the opportunities for undue intrusions on children's – and third parties' – privacy are rampant (see Melton, 1991), no matter whether the unobtrusive measures are direct observations (as in Barker and colleagues' work), alternative media (such as Rasmussen, Chapter 24, this volume), or analyses of administrative data (including Goerge and Lee, Chapter 23, this volume). Interviews and questionnaires about sensitive matters (including one's associations and use of time), even when intended to be 'innocuous', can be especially intrusive (see Melton, 1991), no matter whether the informants are children themselves (see this in volume, Craig, Chapter 25; Hayne and Tustin, Chapter 29; Saywitz and Camparo, Chapter 21; Soffer and Ben-Arieh, Chapter 28), children as adults (Pillemer and Dickson, Chapter 27), or adults important in the children's lives (Bornstein, Chapter 26, this volume). Increased respect for children with corresponding desire to learn about their experiences ironically raises the risk of violations of their privacy.

THE CONTENTS OF THIS BOOK

The contributors to this volume reflect the topical, disciplinary, and geographic diversity of the field. The following abstracts are intended to guide readers in both selecting chapters of particular interest and identifying themes that develop across chapters. (Abstracts are not included for the introductions to the major sections of the book.)

The book's first topical chapters address childhood in the context of major normative systems: law, politics, and theology. In his discussion of childhood as a legal status, **Roger Levesque** (Chapter 3) revisits some of the controversies surrounding children's rights in law and practice. The on-going debates about the proper allocation of roles, rights, and responsibilities among child, family, and state give shape to the legal status of children and ultimately affect the experiences of childhood, parenthood, and family life. Levesque stresses the significance of the concept of 'evolving capacities' in defining the bounds of children's rights. Unless governments recognize children's capacities in fact, their capacities in law may be empty promises.

In Chapter 4, **Anu Toots, Natalie Worley, and Anna Skosireva** revisit some of the issues raised in the current (introductory) chapter. In particular, they address ways in which young people have been both engaged in and affected by major political changes, and they consider the meaningfulness of 'youth culture' amid such transformations. Toots et al. discuss developmental changes in children's understanding of political life, social factors mediating those changes, and the nature and effectiveness of mechanisms for civic education and political socialization. They also note the growing availability of youth parliaments and other structures for consideration of children's interests in particular settings, especially schools, and sometimes the body politic as a whole. Such structures commonly remain impotent in policymaking, but they nonetheless sometimes facilitate children's political engagement and leadership development.

Eugene Roehlkepartain (Chapter 5) reviews the state of the art in the study of children's religious and spiritual development. Until recently, religion and spirituality in childhood were hardly addressed in scientific literature. In part as a result, however, of the broader concern with childhood, research is growing in regard to children's religious and spiritual beliefs, experiences, and commitments. Although noting methodological challenges, the authors underscore the importance of recognizing that spiritual development, like other aspects of personal development, is a product of interaction between children and systems of influence. Sources of influence in that regard include not only micro-level settings, such as the family, the school, and the religious institution itself, but also the norms and myths in local, ethnic, and societal cultures.

The next three chapters examine children's roles as consumers of, respectively, health care, material goods, and education. The role of health care consumer ('patient') is fraught with vulnerability for both children and adults, at least in the societies that **Priscilla Alderson** (Chapter 6) describes as 'the minority richer world'. Although adults wish to spare children the stress and responsibility of the decision-making process when it comes to treatment choices, children often demonstrate remarkable capacity to weather and navigate through such challenges. Through her discussion of children's experiences in the 'patient' and 'non-patient' zones, Alderson issues an indictment against commercially driven research and service delivery that neglect health needs of children in 'the majority poorer world.' By juxtaposing examples of over-pathologizing generally healthy children and underserving very sick children, Alderson expands the discussion of childhood illness to include consideration of business agendas and other economic influences.

In Chapter 7, **Ragnhild Brusdal and Ivar Frønes** discuss the influences of consumerism as both culture and activity on socialization of children. No longer merely the beneficiaries of their parents' choices in the marketplace, children have become powerful purchasers of goods, services, and experiences, whether directly or through influences on parents and grandparents. For product developers and marketers, children and parents present particularly sought-after consumer groups: children, because their physical size and scope of activities grow rapidly, and their preferences change as they mature and as peer-culture dictates; parents, because they regard purchases for their children as high-priority investments that enable greater choices for their children in the future. Consumption claims greater portions of children's and parents' time, and family schedules involve more paid-for activities with more paid-for things. Childhood itself has becomes commercialized, with market definitions of what a boy or girl of a particular age and status must have and do.

Jan Kampmann (Chapter 8) offers a social commentary on children's activities as learners. Emphasizing the politics of early childhood education and care, Kampmann talks about the increasing bureaucratization of children's learning, as reflected in standardization of goals, methods, and quality assurance. The author criticizes the turn toward 'test culture', which attributes value to competencies that can be planned, controlled, and uniformly measured and which may allocate rewards on the bases of test-score differences that have little practical or scientific meaning. The standards-driven learning environment that functions according to codes and norms places additional requirements on children to de-code the institutional codes and to act appropriately, or 'normally'. International funders may apply these expectations globally, so that schooling becomes defined in practice as 'normal children's normal learning'. In such a context, children's individual experiences, diverse cultural backgrounds, varied systems of belief, and unique social circumstances receive less and less respect.

The buffer against children's domination by professionalized, bureaucratized institutions may be their relationships with family and friends. Increasingly, such relationships are regarded as zones of privacy. In global terms, this shift is in part the result of the welcome downfall of totalitarian regimes, which typically treated child care as an appropriate (and effective) means of socializing children to conform to the norms favoured by the state (Qvortrup, 2008). It also reflects changes in economic organization as technical and structural changes permit or even demand flexibility of places and times for work and, therefore, of communities of residence. The 'retreat' becomes more valuable, and fences are erected both literally and figuratively. This strong trend, which has been in evidence for at least two generations in the West and which shows no signs of abating, has had a substantial cost in social capital, particularly in the number and intensity of sources of social support available to children and their parents (Putnam, 2000), with corollary negative effects on the well-being of children and families (Melton, 2010b, and Melton, in press, and citations therein).

In Chapter 9, **Jennifer Mason and Becky Tipper** engage in a methodological discussion about research on children's experiences of family life. Until recently, few studies directly addressed this topic. Children were implicitly regarded as subjects of parents' influence, and the marital (or cohabitant or non-cohabitant) relationship between parents was treated as a discrete phenomenon. Reciprocity in parent–child (never 'child–parent') relationships and the interaction, identity, and experiences of the family as a whole (including siblings and extended-family or clan members), both among themselves and with unrelated parties, were phenomena largely outside researchers' self-defined field of vision.

The newer research focusing exclusively on children's own perspectives provided insights about family dynamics through children's eyes, but it also presented numerous methodological and ethical problems. A particular challenge lies in uncovering and capturing what Mason and Tipper call 'relationality', so that the various family members' perspectives on their collective interaction, identity, and experience may be captured and interwoven. The socio-cultural

constructions of childhood and family are complex interactive processes that involve 'being, becoming, and developing', and none of these processes can be fully understood in isolation.

Similar considerations apply to friendship networks. Friendship may protect children from bullying, social anxiety, and depression. They offer possibilities for fun, fulfilment, and cooperative learning and service. At the same time, friendship can introduce children to potential losses, group misbehaviour, and victimization by peers. Appreciating these complexities, **Steven Asher, Whitney Brechwald Guerry, and Kristina McDonald** (Chapter 10) describe the nature of children's friendships and their effects on children's socio-emotional and academic adjustment. Although considerable differences in children's friendships can be found within and across cultures, much is universal.

Asher et al. note a large body of research on positive and protective effects of friendship, but they lament that this literature offers little guidance to professionals hoping to help children with friendship problems. The social tasks perspective may provide a useful basis for education of children about specific friendship-related skills, such as helping a friend, resolving conflicts of interest, and coping with a friend's dishonesty or betrayal.

Although the new child research has focused in large part on children in particular settings (especially those settings that are set aside for children), child researchers have also been cognizant of the reality that children's particular situations and expectations affect their adaptation even in those settings. It is noteworthy in that regard that Barker and Wright's (1955) early studies examined the particular activities and experiences of children with disabilities and of African American children in the settings of 'Midwest'. Part II of this book addresses the experiences common in children in particular populations.

In Chapter 12, **Oscar Barbarin, Emma Sterrett, and Dari Jigjidsuren** discuss the well-being of ethnic-minority children in relation to the broader societies of which they are a part. They concentrate their discussion on stress, coping, and resilience among African American children. However, they also address the situation for Kazakh children in Mongolia and ethnic-Russian children in Estonia, and they note the diversity of situations for ethnic minorities in widely diverse societies.

Charlotte Patterson (Chapter 13) discusses a topic of growing interest to researchers and the general public: the intersection of the private matter of sexual orientation and the public domains of legal and policy issues, permitted and accepted institutional practices, and formal and informal systems of support and service provision. She examines these issues from the perspectives of two groups that are in different situations but that have similar interests: youth who are themselves in sexual minorities and children whose parents are in sexual minorities. Family support turns out to be a major factor in the adjustment of young people in both groups. Like Alderson in her discussion of children as patients, Patterson notes children's resilience in hostile situations, such as the social exclusion and public ridicule that youth in sexual minorities and children of parents in sexual minorities often experience.

Patricia Sloper and Bryony Beresford (Chapter 14) consider the situation for children with disabilities, another disparate population that historically has been subjected to stigma. Similar to older research on family life that rarely included children's perspective, studies of the experiences of children with disabilities has relied mostly on data obtained from adults and not from the children themselves. However, recent methodological innovations have enabled researchers to hear directly from children with autistic spectrum disorders, cognitive and perceptual disabilities, and physical, sensory, and communication impairments.

Sloper and Beresford share their experiences in conducting research with children with disabilities. They explore methodological-

challenges that such research presents, including researchers' own prejudices about disability, their need in some instances to rely on non-verbal communication, and their openness to use of non-traditional research tools. For example, Sloper and Beresford describe studies using visual methods with children who do not use speech to communicate, observing or joining in an activity with children with cognitive impairments, and collaborating with researchers who are deaf when conducting research with children who are deaf.

Experienced in research on treatment of juvenile delinquents with serious offence histories, **Michael McCart, Terje Ogden, and Scott Henggeler** (Chapter 15) discuss illegal behaviour among juveniles and the systems of response to such misconduct, with a focus on economically advanced countries of northern Europe and North America – systems that are grounded in diverse assumptions about the nature of childhood and adolescence. McCart et al. review the extensive body of research (including cross-cultural studies) showing multiple determinants of delinquency and indicating the relative effectiveness of complex intervention approaches that integrate responses to the known causes and correlates of delinquency.

In Chapter 16, **Kelly McWilliams and her colleagues** at the University of California, Davis, examine the experiences of children who serve as witnesses in legal proceedings. Child witnesses' involvement varies both within and across countries and may include, for example, participating in multiple forensic interviews, testifying in open court, providing testimony by closed circuit television, or confiding in an assigned professional who will represent a child's voice in court. Although any legal involvement may be stressful, children report greater satisfaction with the legal process when they are treated with respect and allowed to form positive relationships with legal staff.

In Chapter 17, **Kelly McWilliams, Gail Goodman, Juliana Raskauskas, and Ingrid Cordon** discuss contemporary research about child victims of mistreatment, including abuse and neglect by adults and bullying by peers. Taking a comparative approach, McWilliams et al. describe findings from diverse societies, including Egypt, Romania, China, Kenya, Canada, Ireland, South Africa, Philippines, and the United States. Echoing a theme throughout the book, McWilliams et al. stress the importance of hearing children's own voices when studying child victimization, but they caution that children themselves may not realize the seriousness or the wrongfulness of the acts they have experienced. The authors conclude that in order to inform policy and practice adequately, research on child victimization must include the perspectives of both child victims and sympathetic adults.

For a range of reasons (including threats to their safety), many children in both industrialized and developing countries find themselves living away from their families. After being voluntarily placed in alternative care settings by their parents, involuntarily removed because of treatment needs, abuse, or neglect, or separated from their families because of armed conflict or natural disasters, children may spend anywhere from a few weeks to their entire childhoods living somewhere other than their parents' home. In Chapter 18, **Judith Cashmore** discusses the various arrangements for children's out-of-home care, including kinship care, foster care, institutional care, adoption, and independent living, sometimes including homelessness. She gives primary attention to formal foster care settings in industrialized countries (the focus of much of the existing research), but she emphasizes the need for researchers to reach children in informal settings, including those who are homeless.

In other instances, children are in unstable situations because of population-wide problems, not just the difficulties experienced by their families. With or without their families, children who are refugees, asylum seekers, or displaced persons come to the safer parts of the world in search of protection from the dangers of their homeland, including armed conflict, political and religious persecutions, and abhorrent practices, such as bodily mutilations. **Jacqueline Goodnow** (Chapter 19) discusses the challenges of research involving this population of children. Data collection may be particularly difficult, because refugee and displaced children and asylum seekers may avoid interviewers altogether or they may be very cautious in their responses, because they fear being denied their request for protection in the receiving country and then deported. As with other vulnerable groups, researchers need to be open and resourceful, to ensure that participation translates into a positive experience for the children, and to be clear about the intended beneficiaries of the information being generated.

Part III examines the usefulness of various methods for child research. Interviewing is a widely used method in social science research and a standard practice in a variety of applied settings, including health, mental health, and forensic settings. It is the most obvious means of learning about children's expectations and experiences, at least for school-age children and often for preschoolers. **Karen Saywitz and Lorinda Camparo** (Chapter 21) offer practical recommendations for both laboratory and field settings. The science of child interviewing has come a long way since 25 years ago, and today's interviews are informed by considerations of interview structure, rapport development, question composition, interviewer behaviour, cultural factors, language limitations, physical setting, traumatic context, and developmental differences in children. At the centre of a successful interview is respect for the child being interviewed and genuine interest in the child's point of view.

Much of what is known about children's development is the result of longitudinal studies that have relied on reports by family members, independent observers, and, in recent times, children themselves. **Amy Dworsky** (Chapter 22) provides a comprehensive review of national and international longitudinal studies that have involved children as informants. The majority of the studies that followed children from an early age initially relied on parents' and caregivers' reports. Children's own reports were sought when they reached an age (usually 10) when they were perceived to be able to respond to surveys reliably. Dworsky considers the use of developmentally appropriate measures, a particular challenge in longitudinal research because of changes in children's competencies and interests as they mature. She stresses the importance of cross-cultural longitudinal studies that would advance the state of knowledge on universality and specificity of factors that affect children's development.

Rather than gathering new data, investigators of children- and childhood-related phenomena sometimes rely on existing administrative data, collected by various agencies and organizations in public and private sectors. In their review, **Robert Goerge and Bong Joo Lee** (Chapter 23) discuss drawbacks (such as lack of richness) and benefits (including widespread availability; reliability; accuracy; cost efficiency) of administrative data. Research has relied on administrative data about vital statistics (such as births and deaths), education (including test scores; disciplinary actions), health (for example, hospital visits and immunizations), unlawful behaviour (such as arrests and rehabilitation data), economic well-being (including family income and participation in anti-poverty programmes), and child maltreatment (most notably, recorded incidents of child abuse and neglect).

In Chapter 24, **Kim Rasmussen** describes use of children's photography as a relatively unobtrusive, engaging way of tapping children's knowledge and experience and doing so in a way that does not rely heavily on verbal skills. Cameras can be used, for example, on neighbourhood walks to identify the people and places most important to children. Photography is one example of the use of children's artistic expressions as data, whether through archives or work actually produced for research (for example, books analysing and presenting children's letters

to Eleanor Roosevelt (an archive; Cohen, 2002) and posthumously to Martin Luther King (a research effort; Colbert and Harms, 1998)).

Lyn Craig (Chapter 25) discusses time-use studies, which allow scholars of children and childhood a greater understanding of how childhoods are actually lived. (Note that this approach, although in contemporary research no longer relying solely on direct observation, is the one adopted by Barker and his colleagues.) What happens in the minutes, hours, and days of childhood? Although we know about the range of behaviours in which children engage (such as going to school; watching television; doing homework; playing; performing chores), knowledge of the content, sequencing, duration, and intricacies of children's activities is much more limited. Few time-use studies to date have specifically included questions about children's use of time, and fewer still relied on children as primary informants on their use of time. Although these studies present numerous methodological challenges, including recall bias and developmentally appropriate research tasks, such as completing a time diary, studies of children's time use yield invaluable findings relevant to children's health and well-being (for example, an association between children's time use and depression). In general, time-use studies offer an important window on childhood.

Several authors in this volume refer to the newer research that focuses on children's own perspectives and experiences as an element of progress in acquisition of child-related knowledge, most of which has been historically derived from adults' reports. In Chapter 26, **Marc Bornstein** takes a close look at parents' reports as a source of information about children's lives. He discusses strengths and weaknesses of the method that remains widely used in studies of childhood and child development, including studies of very young children, assessments of developmental histories, and studies of aggressive and other behaviours with low base rates.

Bornstein considers questions of parents' knowledge about their children, objectivity in reporting, expectations regarding children, and cultural preferences. Although well suited to answer certain research questions, a parent's report, like any other single source of information, is not sufficient to provide a complete picture of the child's life. A more coherent and valid picture of children's lives emerges when there is an integration of researchers' observations, the child's own accounts, and reports from various others who vary in their relationship to the child, the settings in which they interact with the child, and the values and perspectives that they use for evaluation of the child's behaviour.

Another interesting perspective on childhood is that offered by adults who reminisce about their own early years. Research in this domain has focused in large part on the accessibility and accuracy of early memories, questions that have been of interest because of their potential relevance in some forensic cases and their theoretical significance in regard to the bounds and processes of long-term memory. Starting from this point, **David Pillemer and Ryan Dickson** (Chapter 27) suggest that when adults remember certain childhood experiences, they may reassess the value of those experiences to fit their understanding of the personal significance that the events ultimately had – a perspective children themselves obviously lack. Pillemer and Dickson argue that finding a place in children- and childhood-related research for adults' recollections of childhood next to children's own accounts and direct observations of children would make an important contribution to understanding of 'the true fabric of childhood experience'.

Contemporary researchers who pursue children- and childhood-related inquiries largely agree that studies that involve children as direct sources of information about their own lives and experiences make a valuable contribution to adults' understanding of childhood. In Chapter 28, **Michal Soffer and Asher Ben-Arieh** discuss ways of obtaining reliable information from school-aged children about their own lives. Soffer and Ben-Arieh urge adoption of inclusive and participatory child-centred methodologies. In particular, they suggest use of child-friendly data collection techniques, such as drawing, storytelling, and games.

Continuing the discussion about childhood memories, **Harlene Hayne and Karen Tustin** (Chapter 29) focus on young children's ability to provide information about their lives. Readers will recall that in the chapter on adults' memories of themselves as children (Chapter 27), Pillemer and Dickson review research on earliest memories, commonly dating back to the time when the now-adult child was 3 or 4 years old. Addressing this question, Hayne and Tustin reference a number of studies that reveal that very young children remember experiences before they can talk about them and they can maintain non-verbal representations of experiences for a long time. Inquiries into the workings of memory of very young children produced fascinating discoveries, including one that 2- to 4-year-old children may not apply their emerging vocabulary to descriptions of events that occurred in the past (at six or twelve months earlier). Instead, they use only words that were part of their vocabulary at the time of the event. Another finding that carries significant implications for research on children's own perspectives is that their ability to talk about their past is affected by their parents' practices of narration.

In the concluding chapter (Chapter 30), **Tove Dahl** provides advice about children in research not only as study participants, but also as collaborators with adult researchers at all stages of the research process. Building on developments in participatory action research, Dahl argues that by involving children in research as scientists, both the academic community and the children benefit. Academicians acquire a better understanding of children's subjective experiences of the world, and children are empowered through participation. The benefits spill over to the world at large. The knowledge produced with the help of children as researchers contributes to improvement of the welfare of youth and ultimately the welfare of all.

NOTES

1 The Day of Affirmation speech is available in both written transcript and audio recording at http://www.jfklibrary.org/Research/Ready-Reference/RFK-Speeches/Day-of-Affirmation-Address-news-release-text-version.aspx

2 Coles (1995) also wrote a children's book about Ruby's story.

3 Important similar critiques were made later by Urie Bronfenbrenner (1981, 2004) and his most famous student, James Garbarino (2009). However, Bronfenbrenner and Garbarino placed greater emphasis on addressing problems of policy and practice. Hence, they did not begin with purely unobtrusive naturalistic observations in the way that Barker and his colleagues did.

4 The Myers-JDC-Brookdale Institute in Jerusalem began in 1974, but its child research centre emerged later.

5 Most relevant American professional organizations have indicated that they favour ratification of the CRC. Although discussion of the treaty rarely occurs in the popular media, it may be the case that many professionals in the field have at least passing knowledge of the CRC. Except, however, for specialists in international children's issues, we doubt that many American scholars' work has been materially influenced by the CRC.

6 This section of the introductory chapter does not include references in the ordinary manner, because the ideas herein are found throughout the seminal treatises of child research. Among them are the books cited in Table 1.1.

REFERENCES

Barker, R.G. and Gump, P.V. (1964) *Big School, Small School: High School Size and Student Behavior.* Stanford, CA: Stanford University Press.

Barker, R.G. and Wright, H.F. (1955) *Midwest and its Children: The Psychological Ecology of an American Town.* Evanston, IL: Row, Peterson.

Berti, A.E. and Bombi, A.S. (Gerard Duveen, trans.) (1981) *The Child's Construction of Economics.* Cambridge, England: Cambridge University Press.

Bronfenbrenner, U. (1981) *The Ecology of Human Development: Experiments by Nature and Design.* Cambridge, MA: Harvard University Press.

Bronfenbrenner, U. (ed.) (2004) *Making Human Beings Human: Bioecological Perspectives on Human Development.* Thousand Oaks, CA: Sage.

Cohen, R. (ed.) (2002) *Dear Mrs. Roosevelt: Letters from Children of the Great Depression.* Chapel Hill: University of North Carolina Press.

Colbert, J. and Harms, A.M. (eds.) (1998) *Dear Dr. King: Letters from Today's Children to Dr. Martin Luther King, Jr.* New York: Hyperion.

Coles, R.H. (1967) *Children in Crisis: Vol. 1. A Study in Courage and Fear.* Boston, MA: Little, Brown.

Coles, R.H. (1971a) *Children in Crisis: Vol. 2. Migrants, Sharecroppers, Mountaineers.* Boston, MA: Little, Brown.

Coles, R.H. (1971b) *Children in Crisis: Vol. 3. The South Goes North.* Boston, MA: Little, Brown.

Coles, R.H. (1977a) *Children in Crisis: Vol. 4. Eskimos, Indians, Chicanos.* Boston, MA: Little, Brown.

Coles, R.H. (1977b) *Children in Crisis: Vol. 5. The Privileged Ones: The Well-off and the Rich in America.* Boston, MA: Little, Brown.

Coles, R.H. (1986a) *The Moral Life of Children.* Boston, MA: Atlantic Monthly Press.

Coles, R.H. (1986b) *The Political Life of Children.* Boston, MA: Atlantic Monthly Press.

Coles, R.H. (1990) *The Spiritual Life of Children.* New York: Houghton Mifflin.

Coles, R.H. (1995) *The Story of Ruby Bridges.* New York: Scholastic.

Committee on Increasing High School Students' Engagement and Motivation to Learn (National Research Council and Institute of Medicine, National Academies of Science) (2004) *Engaging Schools: Fostering JHigh School Students' Motivation to Learn.* Washington, DC: National Academy Press.

Convention on the Rights of the Child, GA Res. 44/25, annex, UN GAOR, 44th Sess., Supp. No. 49, at 167, UN Doc. A/44/49 (1989).

Cowell, A. (1990, 17 September) 'In South Africa, a "lost generation"', *NYTimes.com*. Available at http://www.newyorktimes.com/1990/09/17/world-in-south-africa-a-lost-generation.html?src=pm

Crystal, D.S. and DeBell, M. (2002) 'Sources of civic orientation among American youth: Trust, religious valuation, and attributions of responsibility', *Political Psychology*, 23: 113–32.

Dahl, T.S. (1986) *Child Welfare and Social Defence: Science State and the Professions During the Emergence of Child Welfare in Norway.* New York: Oxford University Press.

Dawson, R.E., Prewitt, K. and Dawson, K.S. (1977) *Political Socialization.* 2nd edn. Boston, MA: Little, Brown.

Erikson, E.H. (1950) *Childhood and Society.* New York: Norton.

Erikson, E.H. (1968) *Identity: Youth and Crisis.* New York: Norton.

Eurydice (2005) *Citizenship Education at School in Europe.* Brussels: European Union Publications Office.

Furth, H.G. (1980) *The World of Grown-ups: Children's Conception of Society.* New York: Elsevier.

Glanville, J.L. (1999) 'Political socialization or selection? Adolescent extracurricular participation and political activity in early adulthood', *Social Science Quarterly,* 80: 279–90.

Garbarino, J. (2009) *Children and Families in the Social Environment.* 2nd edn. Piscataway, NJ: Transaction.

Grisso, T. (1981) *Juveniles' Waiver of Their Rights.* New York: Plenum.

Hashima, P. and Melton, G.B. (2008) '"I can conquer a mountain": Ordinary people who provide extraordinary service in Strong Communities', *Family and Community Health,* 31: 162–72.

Hawthorne, P. and MacLeod, S. (1991, 18 February) 'South Africa: The lost generation', *Time.com.* Available at http://www.time.com/time/magazine/article/0,9171,972361-1,00.html

Hess, R.D. and Torney, J.V. (1967) *The Development of Political Attitudes in Children.* Chicago: Aldine.

Jennings, M.K. and Niemi, R.G. (1974) *The Political Character of Adolescence: The Influence of Families and Schools.* Princeton, NJ: Princeton University Press.

Kett, J.F. (1977) *Rites of Passage: Adolescence in America, 1790 to the Present.* New York: Basic Books.

Levine, M. and Levine, A. (1992) *Helping Children: A Social History.* New York: Oxford University Press.

Lourenço, O. and Machado, A. (1996) 'In defense of Piaget's theory: A reply to ten common criticisms', *Psychological Review,* 103: 143–64.

McClosky, H. and Brill, A. (1983) *Dimensions of Tolerance: What Americans Think About Civil Liberties.* New York: Russell Sage Foundation.

McFarland, D.A. and Starmanns, C. (2009) 'Inside student government: The variable quality of high school student councils', *Teachers College Record,* 111: 27–54.

Melton, G.B. (1980) 'Children's concepts of their rights', *Journal of Clinical Child Psychology,* 9: 186–90.

Melton, G.B. (1983a) *Child Advocacy: Psychological Issues and Interventions.* New York: Plenum.

Melton, G.B. (1983b) 'Ruralness as a psychological construct', in Alan W. Childs and Gary B. Melton (eds), *Rural Psychology.* New York: Plenum. pp. 1–13.

Melton, G.B. (1987a) 'Children, politics, and morality: The ethics of child advocacy', *Journal of Clinical Child Psychology,* 16: 357–67.

Melton, G.B. (1987b) 'The clashing of symbols: Prelude to child and family policy', *American Psychologist,* 42: 345–54.

Melton, G.B. (1991) 'Respecting boundaries: Minors, privacy, and behavioral research', in Barbara H. Stanley and Joan E. Sieber (eds), *Social Research on Children and Adolescents: Ethical Issues.* Newbury Park, CA: Sage, pp. 65–84.

Melton, G.B. (1994) 'Introduction: Personal satisfaction and the welfare of families, communities, and society', in Gary B. Melton (ed.), *Nebraska Symposium on Motivation: Vol. 42. The Individual, the Family, and Social Good: Personal Fulfillment in Times of Change.* Lincoln: University of Nebraska Press, pp. xi–xxvii.

Melton, G.B. (1999) 'Parents *and* children: Legal reform to facilitate children's participation', *American Psychologist,* 54: 935–44.

Melton, G.B. (2005) 'Building a context for success: Communities, families, and schools'. Report to the South Carolina Education Oversight Committee.

Melton, G.B. (2010a) 'Angels (and neighbors) watching over us: Child safety in an age of alienation', *American Journal of Orthopsychiatry,* 80: 89–95.

Melton, G.B. (2010b) 'Putting the "community" back into "mental health": The challenge of a great crisis in the health and well-being of children and families', *Administration and Policy in Mental Health and Mental Health Services Research,* 37: 173–6.

Melton, G.B. (2013) 'A swan song (or a fanfare): Some thoughts of an institute director after thirty years of service', *American Journal of Orthopsychiatry,* 83: 1–10.

Melton, G.B. (in press) 'Strong Communities for Children: A community-wide approach to prevention of child maltreatment', in Jill E. Korbin and Richard D. Krugman (eds), *Handbook of Child Maltreatment.* Dordrecht, Netherlands: Springer.

Melton, G.B. and Limber, S.P. (1992) 'What rights mean to children: Children's own views', in Michael Freeman and Philip Veerman (eds), *Ideologies of Children's Rights.* Dordrecht, Netherlands: Martinus Nijhoff, pp. 167–87.

Melton, G.B. and Stanley, B.H. (1996) 'The psychology of research involving special populations', in Barbara H. Stanley, Joan E. Sieber, and G. B. Melton (eds), *Research Ethics: A Psychological Approach.* Lincoln: University of Nebraska Press, pp. 177–202.

Melton, G.B. and Wilcox, B.L. (1989) 'Changes in family law and family life: Challenges for psychology', *American Psychologist,* 44: 1213–16.

Narvaez, D. (2005) 'The neo-Kohlbergian tradition and beyond: Schemas, expertise, and character', in Gustavo Carlo and Carolyn Pope Edwards (eds), *Nebraska Symposium on Motivation: Vol. 51. Moral Motivation Through the Life Span.* Lincoln: University of Nebraska Press, pp. 119–64.

Platt, A.M. (1980) *The Child Savers: The Invention of Delinquency.* Chicago: University of Chicago Press.

Putnam, R.D. (2000) *Bowling Alone: The Collapse and Revival of American Community.* New York: Simon & Schuster.

Qvortrup, J. (2008) 'Macroanalysis of childhood', in Pia Christensen and Allison James (eds.), *Research with Children: Perspectives and Practices.* 2nd edn. Abingdon, England: Routledge, pp. 66–86.

Schoggen, P. (1978) 'Environmental forces on physically disabled children', in Roger G. Barker (ed.), *Habitats, Environments, and Human Behavior.* San Francisco: Jossey-Bass, pp. 125–45.

Schwartz, S. (2011, 28 April) 'Youth and the Arab spring'. Available at http://www.usip.org/publications/youth-and-the-arab-spring

Sigel, R.S. and Hoskin, M.B. (1981) *The Political Involvement of Adolescents.* New Brunswick, NJ: Rutgers University Press.

Thomas, D.B. and Craig, R.B. (1973) 'Student dissent in Latin America: A comparative analysis', *Latin American Research Review*, 8: 71–96.

Torney-Purta, J., Lehmann, R., Oswald, H. and Schulz, W. (2001) *Citizenship and Education in Twenty-Eight Countries: Civic Knowledge and Engagement at Age Fourteen.* Amsterdam: International Association for the Evaluation of Educational Achievement.

Torney-Purta, J., Schwille, J. and Amadeo, J.A. (eds) (1999) *Civic Education Across Countries: Twenty-Four National Case Studies from the IEA Civic Education Project.* Amsterdam: International Association for the Evaluation of Educational Achievement.

Tronick, E. and Beeghly, M. (2011) 'Infants' meaning-making and the development of mental health problems', *American Psychologist*, 66: 107–19.

Wallace, C. and Alt, R. (2001) 'Youth cultures under authoritarian regimes: The case of the Swings against the Nazis', *Youth and Society*, 32: 275–302.

Wicker, A.W. (1978) 'Importance of church size for new members', in Roger G. Barker (ed.), *Habitats, Environments, and Human Behavior.* San Francisco: Jossey-Bass, pp. 257–64.

Wright, B.A. (1983) *Physical Disability: A Psychosocial Approach.* 2nd edn. New York: Harper & Row (1st edn, 1960).

Youniss, J. (2011) 'Civic education: What schools can do to encourage civic identity and action', *Applied Developmental Science*, 15: 98–103.

Zelizer, V.A. (1994) *Pricing the Priceless Child: The Changing Value of Children.* Princeton, NJ: Princeton University Press.

Setting-Specific Issues in Child Research

The Settings of Childhood

Asher Ben-Arieh

We live in a changing world. Whether discussing information technology and the new era of information (Compaine, 2001; Drori, 2005; Jackson, 2008), changing gender roles (Fagot, Rodgers and Leinbach, 2000; Helwig, 1998; Herold and Milhausen, 1999; Montgomery, 2010), the globalization of markets (Alderson, 1999; Alderson and Nielsen, 2002; Berberoglu, 2005; Berger, 2000; Brady, Beckfield and Zhao, 2007), or the emergence of new global cultures (Featherstone, 1990; Franklin, Lury and Stacey, 2000), it seems one consensus can easily be agreed upon – societies have changed dramatically, and many of the institutions within society have changed as well.

Most of the institutions we refer to as central to children and childhood have undergone extraordinary change in the past generation or two. A partial and short list includes: the family; the law; religion and religious practices; political, health, and educational systems; and the economic market and consumption. These and other institutions have changed to such a degree that anything short of acknowledging the fact that we are dealing with 'new' societies would be hard to justify.

The general notion that society has changed is accompanied by the growing acceptance of a new sociology of childhood (Corsaro, 1997; James and Prout, 1997; Mayall, 2002; Qvortrup, 1994) and the consensus that childhood itself has changed as well (Flekkoy and Kaufman, 1997; Jensen et al., 2004). Ample research has shown that childhood and the well-being of children in the twenty-first century differ from how we used to think of them even in the recent past (see, for example, Adamson and Morrison, 1995; Ben-Arieh, 2010, 2009; Bradshaw, 2009; Bradshaw and Mayhew, 2005; Fattore, Mason and Watson, 2007; Hood, 2004, 2007; Land, Lamb and Mustillo, 2001; Lau and Bradshaw, 2010; Richardson, Hoelscher and Bradshaw, 2008; Stanley, Richardson and Prior, 2005). In the realm of this handbook, the concept of child research now differs as well.

Without attempting to address causality or order issues, it is safe to acknowledge that the new society and its changing institutions interact markedly with children and childhood (Arnott, 2008; Hart, 2008; Prout, 2000; Smith, 2007; Thomas, 2007; Tisdall, 2008). Children are affected by these changes as much as they influence them, especially when seen and understood as active agents (Hart, 1999, 1992; Melton, 2005; Tisdall and Davis, 2007; Willow, 2002). As a consequence, childhood and children's lives are even more affected, to such a degree that we are in fact facing a 'new' childhood and dealing with 'different' children (Jensen et al., 2004; John, 2003; Flekkøy and Kaufman, 1997; Piachaud, 2007).

These changes are apparent in a number of domains and fields, the research implications of which are described in the chapters of this volume. From reading these chapters, a clear picture of the 'new child research' emerges. In the remainder of this chapter, I will discuss a short list of issues that are central to childhood and children today which were not necessarily so in the past.

One of these major changes is the new legal status of children and the revolution in children's rights (Alaimo and Klug, 2002; Alderson, 2010; Archard, 1993; Freeman and Veerman, 1999; Hale, 2006; Hart, 1991; Leena, 2010; Reynaert, Bouverne-de Bie and Vandevelde, 2009; Wilcox and Naimark, 1991). Roger Levesque (Chapter 3, this volume) describes how the 'new' legal status of children testifies to the developments and transformations in societal understanding of children and their place in society, ultimately creating new settings for them. However, this new legal setting in children's lives brings with it new challenges for children's well-being in general and child research in particular. Drawing again on Levesque's observations, one must agree that children continue to occupy a peculiar status in law and society. While all modern societies now champion the importance of recognizing and fostering a wide range of children's rights, children still may not actually control their own rights. Perhaps more significantly, a great disjuncture often appears when we examine claims of children's rights and compare them with the reality of children's lives. Children have gained recognition under the law, but it remains to be determined what that recognition means in practice.

Many would argue that the impact of the children's rights revolution extended far beyond their legal status. In many ways a consequence of the children's rights concept, another new setting for children and childhood

is the child's role in political process and socialization. Anu Toots and her colleagues devote their chapter (Chapter 4, this volume) to this issue and its implications for child research. Political socialization research offers insights into the political knowledge and attitudes of children and youth (Furnham and Stacey, 1991; Torney-Purta et al., 2001). Similarly, large-scale longitudinal surveys of youth, such as the American Freshman Survey (Sax et al., 1999), have studied youths' civic values, their motivation to participate in community activities, and the effects of child and youth participation in school and community activities on academic achievement, youth behaviour, and future civic involvement (Eccles and Barber, 1999; Lamborn et al., 1992; Yates and Youniss, 1998). These studies are only starting to unveil the civic setting of childhood in the twenty-first century, yet they are a good start for a thorough discussion of child research in a new society and setting.

In the new setting of childhood, spirituality is no longer a distant and marginal issue. As Eugene Roehlkepartain (Chapter 5, this volume) clearly articulates, if issues of children's religion and spirituality have been relegated to the margins in the social sciences in the past, they are now enjoying a resurgence of interest in and attention to spiritual and religious development. In the 'new' childhood, he argues, spiritual development is a normative developmental process involving critical developmental tasks such as connectedness, belongingness, purpose, and contribution. All persons in all societies 'do' spiritual development, though culture plays a major role in its process and content. Spiritual development does not require divinity or belief in a supernatural power, although many people include these in their own stories. From this perspective, spiritual development 'happens' among secular humanists, atheists, Muslims, Methodists, Buddhists, animists, artists, scientists, young, and old. Spiritual development is a normative developmental process that, like cognitive or social development, is informed and shaped by family, kinship, peers, school, culture, social norms, and programmes.

In addition to spiritual settings, the 'new' childhood is posing new settings in regard to child research in the health domain. As Priscilla Alderson (Chapter 6, this volume) argues, traditional research about children as patients in traditional settings focused on causes, prevention, and treatment of physical and psychological disorders. Indeed, scientific and clinical medical and nursing research, particularly from the 1960s, has brought more benefit to children than any other research field. Society has seen great gains in child health and survival and for preventing and treating children's illnesses, injuries, and impairments. It is social research about child patients' own views and experiences, however, which has shaped the new setting of child health research within the 'new' childhood.

In this new setting, research does not utilize a clear differentiation between sick and healthy children. The new child health research instead identifies pathology within social and political contexts. Paediatricians observe many problems in the unhealthy behaviours and relationships, diet and housing, families and communities that damage children, but they often feel uncertain how to explain, prevent, or cure children's suffering. Health care and social research collect innumerable visible data but seldom consider underlying 'real' explanations.

Ragnhild Brusdal and Ivar Frønes (Chapter 7, this volume) present yet another new setting of childhood – that of consumption and consumerism. Although the majority of the world's children do not live in conditions of affluence and consumerism, new groups of children are continuously entering this world, to such a degree that consumption is a pivotal part of socialization in modern societies. The setting of consumer childhood differs from earlier settings of childhood in terms of the scale and content of consumption, penetrating everyday life and culture. Children's consumption, as illustrated by the concept of shopping, is a display of the economic and moral economy of the family as well as the values of children's cultures and the dynamics of the market.

Child consumerism often is associated with the market for specific childhood products and their related advertisements, but this is only a minor part of children's consumption. The understanding of children as consumers cannot be restricted to what they buy themselves or indirectly through their 'pester power'. Children's engagement in the marketplace includes parents' purchases of computers, books, and education itself as investment in their children's future. Children's place in the economy extends to household safety equipment, family holidays, as well as the hamburgers that children buy with their pocket money. To a large degree, modern settings of childhood are displayed and developed through children's consumption. (We recognize, of course, that many children in developing societies and agricultural communities serve as family breadwinners, not just earners or possessors of discretionary income.)

School and learning pose an additional setting of childhood which has changed dramatically. Jan Kappmann (Chapter 8, this volume) describes how the idea of viewing children as learners, while neither surprising nor unique, has been used in recent years for setting a new agenda in the politics of early childhood education and care. Similarly, one can see how the interest in children's learning has narrowed down the question of how to make learning more efficient by controlling and creating a setting of tests and academic outcomes while diminishing almost all other goals of schools.

I have discussed (even if briefly) the changing nature of family and home settings for children. Jennifer Mason and Becky Tipper (Chapter 9, this volume) describe in greater detail the 'new' settings of the family and the home for children. In regard to child research they argue that the major problem central to the discussion of children as family members is the faulty assumption that family research automatically includes child research and that, by extension, if we have done research on families then we know about children. Until recently (Brannen and O'Brien, 1996), surprisingly little research on 'the family' actually incorporated, let alone focused on, children's everyday experiences of family life. Children were part of the picture, certainly, but more often as the inert recipients of parenting, childcare, and socialization than as active members or participants in their own right.

Peer groups and friendships have always been considered to be a central setting of childhood. Steven Asher and his colleagues (Chapter 10, this volume) analyse the new setting of friendship as well. A close friendship is, for many children, the first non-familial intimate relationship that is freely chosen. Friendships between children often have been contrasted with parent–child relationships by emphasizing the more egalitarian nature of friendships. It is said that, in friendships, children are likely to have similar levels of power. This is in contrast to the parent–child relationship in which there is often a clear asymmetry in the power of the parties involved. This contrast, however, can be overstated. Many peer relationships, and even close friendships, are characterized by imbalances in power, whereas some parent–child relationships have a fairly equal distribution of power. More importantly, the attention to the balance-of-power dimension of peer versus family relationships may result in our overlooking one of the critical differences between children's friendships and their family relationships, namely that children's friendships are typically voluntary relationships (for a discussion of cultures that are exceptions to this, see Kappmann, 1996). In friendships, the parties generally can withdraw from the relationship if things are not going well, whereas in parent–child relationships the parents and children generally stay in contact for life, even if their relationship is stressful or disappointing. In friendship, one or both participants are likely to leave the relationship if large

problems, or sometimes even minor problems, go unresolved.

Finally, I would argue that one of the best 'new' settings to observe and study the status of children's lives in the 'new' society is in the political process, particularly through child participation (see Toots et al.'s discussion). As Levesque describes, children's participation in decision making became an international standard in 1989 with the enactment of the United Nations' Convention on the Rights of the Child (CRC). One of the general principles of the Convention was (and still is) to respect children's opinions and to enable their expression (see arts. 12–17). This principle effectively expands children's autonomy by giving them an opportunity to participate directly in their community life, while also giving them the skills to do so (Cavet and Sloper, 2004; Glanville, 1999; Hart, 1992, 2008; Hinton, 2008; Hinton et al., 2008; Lansdown, 2001; Melton, 2006; Riepl and Wintersberger, 1999).

I end this commentary with the new activity setting of child participation, because it has the most direct impact on child research. The new norm of child participation and, underlying it, the concept of children as active citizens imply that child research itself must change. We must take children's *participation* seriously, so that they can become partners in the quest for knowledge, not merely *subjects* of researchers' manipulations.

NOTE

In this introduction, the language describing the contributors' core ideas is drawn with minimal exception from the chapters themselves.

REFERENCES

Adamson, P. and Morrison, P. (eds.) (1995) *The Progress of Nations.* New York: UNICEF.

Alaimo, K. and Klug, B. (eds.) (2002) *Children as Equals: Exploring the Rights of the Child*. Lanham, MD: University Press of America.

Alderson, A.S. (1999) 'Explaining deindustrialization: globalization, failure, or success?', *American Sociological Review*, 64(5): 701–21.

Alderson, P. (2010) *Review of Young Children's Rights: Exploring Beliefs, Principles and Practice (2nd Edition)*. London: Jessica Kingsley Publishers.

Alderson, A.S. and Nielsen, F. (2002) 'Globalization and the great U-turn: Income inequality trends in 16 OECD countries', *American Journal of Sociology*, 107(5): 1244–99.

Archard, D. (1993) *Children: Rights and Childhood*. London: Routledge.

Arnott, M.A. (2008) 'Public policy, governance and participation in the UK: A space for children?', *International Journal of Children's Rights*, 16(3): 355–67.

Ben-Arieh, A. (2010) 'Developing indicators for child well-being in a changing context', in C. McAuley and W. Rose (eds.), *Child Well-Being: Understanding Children's Lives*. London, UK: Jessica Kingsley Publishers, pp. 129–42.

Ben-Arieh, A. (2009) 'From child welfare to children well-being: The child indicators perspective', in S.B. Kamerman, S. Phipps and A. Ben-Arieh (eds.), *From Child Welfare to Children Well-being: An International Perspective on Knowledge in the Service of Making Policy*. Dordrecht, Netherlands: Springer, pp. 3–22.

Berberoglu, B. (2005) *Globalization and Change*. Lanham, MD: Lexington Books.

Berger, S. (2000) 'Globalization and politics', *Annual Review of Political Science*, 3(1): 43–62.

Bradshaw, J. (2009) 'Child well-being in comparative perspective', *Children Australia*, 34(1): 5–13.

Bradshaw, J. and Mayhew, E. (eds.) (2005) *The Well-being of Children in the UK*. London: Save the Children Fund.

Brady, D., Beckfield, J. and Zhao, W. (2007) 'The consequences of economic globalization for affluent democracies', *Annual Review of Sociology*, 33(1): 313–34.

Brannen, J. and O'Brien, M. (1996) *Children and Families: Research and Policy*. London: Falmer Press.

Cavet, J. and Sloper, P. (2004) 'The participation of children and young people in decisions about UK service development', *Child Care, Health and Development*, 30(6): 613–21.

Compaine, B. (ed.) (2001) *The Digital Divide*. Cambridge: MIT Press.

Corsaro, W.A. (1997) *The Sociology of Childhood*. San Francisco, CA: Pine Forge.

Drori, G.S. (2005) *Global E-litism: Digital Technology, Social Inequality and Transnationality*. New York: Worth Publishers.

Eccles, J.S. and Barber, B. (1999) 'Student council, volunteering, basketball, or marching band: What kind of extracurricular involvement matters?', *Journal of Adolescent Research*, 14(1): 10–34.

Fagot, B.I., Rodgers, C.S. and Leinbach, M.D. (2000) 'Theories of gender socialization', in T. Eckes and H.M., Trautner (eds.), *The Developmental Social Psychology of Gender*. Mahwah, NJ: Lawrence Erlbaum Associates, Inc, pp. 65–8.

Fattore, T., Mason, J. and Watson, E. (2007) 'Children's conceptualisation(s) of their well-being', *Social Indicators Research*, 80(1): 5–29.

Featherstone, M. (1990) 'Global Culture: An Introduction', *Theory Culture Society*, 7(2): 1–14.

Flekkøy, M.G. and Kaufman, N.H. (1997) *The Participation Rights of the Child: Rights and Responsibilities in Family and Society*. London: Jessica Kingsley Publishers.

Franklin, S., Lury, C. and Stacey, J. (2000) *Global Nature, Global Culture*. London: Sage.

Freeman, M. and Veerman, P. (eds.) (1999) *The Ideologies of Children's Rights*. Dordercht: Martinus Nijhoff Publishers.

Furnham, A. and Stacey, B. (1991) *Young People's Understanding of Society*. London: Routledge.

Glanville, J. (1999) 'Political socialization or selection? Adolescent extracurricular participation and political activity in early adulthood', *Social Science Quarterly*, 80(2): 279–90.

Hale, B. (2006) 'Understanding children's rights: Theory and practice', *Family Court Review*, 44(3): 350–60.

Hart, J. (2008) 'Children's participation and international development: Attending to the political', *International Journal of Children's Rights*, 16(3): 407–18.

Hart, R. (1992) *Children's Participation: From Tokenism to Citizenship*. Florence: UNICEF.

Hart, R.A. (1999) *Children's Participation: The Theory and Practice of Including Young Citizens in Community Development and Environmental Care*. New York: UNICEF.

Hart, S. (1991) 'From property to person status: Historical perspective on children's rights', *American Psychologist*, 46(1): 53–9.

Helwig, A.A. (1998) 'Gender-role stereotyping: Testing theory with a longitudinal sample', *Sex Roles*, 38(5-6): 403–23.

Herold, E.S. and Milhausen, R.R. (1999) 'Does the sexual double standard still exist? Perceptions of university women', *Journal of Sex Research*, 36(4): 361–8.

Hinton, R. (2008) 'Children's participation and good governance: Limitations of the theoretical literature', *International Journal of Children's Rights*, 16: 285–300.

Hinton, R., Tisdall, E.K.M., Gallagher, M. and Elsley, S. (2008) 'Introduction: Children's and young people's participation in public decision-making', *International Journal of Children's Rights*, 16(3): 281–4.

Hood, S. (2004) *The State of London's Children Report*. London: Greater London Authority.

Hood, S. (2007) 'Reporting on children's well-being: The state of London's children reports', *Social Indicators Research*, 80(1): 249–64.

Jackson, L.A. (2008) 'Adolescents and the internet', in D. Romer and P. Jamieson (eds.), *The Changing Portrayal of American Youth in Popular Media*. New York: Oxford University Press, pp. 377–410.

James, A. and Prout, A. (eds.) (1997) *Constructing and Reconstructing Childhood: Contemporary Issues in the Sociological Study of Childhood*. London: Falmer.

Jensen, A.M., Ben-Arieh, A., Conti, C., Kutsar, D., Phadraig, M.N. and Nielsen, H.M. (eds.) (2004) *Children's Welfare in Ageing Europe V. I–II*. Trondhiem: Norwegian Centre for Child Research.

John, M. (2003) *Children's Rights and Power: Charging up a New Century*. London: Jessica Kingsley Publication.

Kappmann, L. (1996) 'Amicitia, drujba, shin-yu, philia, Freundschaft, friendship: On the cultural diversity of a human relationship', in W. M. Bukowski, A. F. Newcomb, and W. W. Hartup (eds.), *The Company They Keep: Friendship in Childhood and Adolescence*. Cambridge: Cambridge University Press.

Lamborn, S.D., Brown, B.B., Mounts, N.S. and Steinberg, L. (1992) 'Putting school in perspective: The influence of family, peers, extracurricular participation, and part-time work on academic engagement', in F.M. Newman (ed.), *Student Engagement and Achievement in American Secondary Schools*. New York: Teachers College Press, pp. 153–91.

Land, K.C., Lamb, V.L. and Mustillo, S.K. (2001) 'Child and youth well-being in the United States, 1975–1998: Some findings from a new index', *Social indicators Research*, 56(3): 241–320.

Lansdown, G. (2001) *Promoting Children's Participation in Democratic Decision-Making*. Florence: Innocenti Research Centre.

Lau, M. and Bradshaw, J. (2010) 'Child well-being in the Pacific Rim', *Child Indicators Research*, 3(3): 367–83.

Leena, A. (2010) 'Editorial: Taking children's rights seriously', *Childhood*, 17(1): 5–8.

Mayall, B. (2002) *Towards Sociology for Childhood: Thinking from Children's Lives*. Buckingham: Open University Press.

Melton, G.B. (2005) 'Treating children like people: A framework for research and advocacy', *Journal of Clinical Child & Adolescent Psychology*, 34(4): 646–57.

Melton, G.B. (2006) Background for a general comment on the right to participate: Article 12 and related provisions of the Convention on the Rights of the Child. Prepared for the UN Committee on the Rights of the Child.

Montgomery, H. (2010) 'Learning gender roles', in D.F. Lancy, J. Bock and S. Gaskins (eds.), *The Anthropology of Learning in Childhood*. Lanham, MD: Alta Mira Press, pp. 287–305.

Piachaud, D. (2007) *Freedom to be a Child: Commercial Pressures on Children*. London: Centre for Analyses of Social Exclusion.

Prout, A. (2000) *The Body, Childhood and Society*. London: Macmillan.

Qvortrup, J. (1994) 'Childhood matters: An introduction', in J. Qvortrup, M. Bardy, G. Sgritta and H. Wintersberger (eds.), *Childhood Matters: Social Theory, Practice and Politics*. Aldershot: Avebury, pp. 1–24.

Reynaert, D., Bouverne-de Bie, M. and Vandevelde, S. (2009) 'A review of children's rights literature since the adoption of the United Nations Convention on the Rights of the Child', *Childhood*, 16(4): 518–34.

Richardson, D., Hoelscher, P. and Bradshaw, J. (2008) 'Child well-being in Central and Eastern European Countries (CEE) and the Commonwealth of Independent States (CIS)', *Child Indicators Research*, 1(3): 211–50.

Riepl, B. and Wintersberger, H. (1999) *Political Participation of Youth below Voting Age: Example of European Practice*. Vienna: European Centre for Social Welfare Policy and Research.

Sax, L.J., Astin, A.W., Korn, W.S. and Mahoney, K. M. (1999) *The American Freshman: National Norms for Fall 1999*. Los Angeles, CA: Higher Education Research Institute, UCLA.

Smith, A.B. (2007) 'Children as social actors: An introduction', *International Journal of Children's Rights*, 15(1): 1–4.

Stanley, F., Richardson, S. and Prior, M. (2005) *Children of the Lucky Country? How Australian Society Has Turned Its Back on Children and Why Children Matter*. Australia: Pan Macmillan.

Thomas, N. (2007) 'Towards a theory of children's participation', *International Journal of Children's Rights*, 15(2): 1–20.

Tisdall, E.K.M. (2008) 'Is the honeymoon over? Children and young people's participation in public decision-making', *International Journal of Children's Rights*, 16(3): 419–29.

Tisdall, E.K.M. and Davis, J. (2007) 'Making a difference? Bringing children's and young people 's view into policy-making', *Children and Society*, 18(2): 131–42.

Torney-Purta, J., Lehmann, R., Oswald, H. and Schultz, W. (2001) *Citizenship and Education in 28 Countries: Civic Knowledge and Engagement at Age Fourteen.* Amsterdam: IEA.

Wilcox, B.L. and Naimark, H. (1991) 'The rights of the child: Progress toward human dignity', *American Psychologist*, 46(1): 1–19.

Willow, C. (2002) *Participation in Practice: Children a Young People as Partner in Change.* London: The Children Society.

Yates, M. and Youniss, J. (1998) 'Community service and political identity development in adolescence', *Journal of Social Issues*, 54(3): 495–512.

3

Childhood as a Legal Status

Roger J.R. Levesque

THE PECULIAR LEGAL STATUS OF CHILDREN

The legal status of children reveals important developments and transformations in societal understandings of children and their place in society. The rights of children, the standard on which we most appropriately can evaluate their legal status, have catapulted from an obscure and essentially nonexistent concept to a globally recognized phenomenon at the forefront of modern human rights movements. Much of this transformation occurred at the very end of the last century, and it rapidly spread at an unprecedented pace. Despite these impressive developments, children continue to occupy a peculiar status in law and society. Most notably, all modern societies now champion a wide range of children's rights as important to recognize and foster. Nevertheless, children still may not actually control their own rights even when societies acknowledge the need to recognize children as individuals worthy of independent rights. Perhaps more peculiarly, a great disjuncture often appears when we examine claims of children's rights and compare them with

the realities of children's lives. Children have gained recognition under law, but it remains to be determined more precisely what that recognition means in practice.

The peculiar failures and disjunctions in recognition stem from a variety of sources. The disparity between laws recognizing children's place in society and the reality of their status is the product in part of the traditional view that rights belong only to fully rational, autonomous people capable of exercising free choice. Because most children lack fully developed rational capabilities necessary to be direct recipients of many rights, the law necessarily deems children dependent 'incompetents'. To complicate matters even more, children are not really 'individuals' who can stand alone from all others; children are, in many ways, dependent, and their dependency implies relationships with others. These complexities render the rights of children important to explore, not just to help us decipher the nature of children's legal status in society. A look at the complexities of children's rights also allows us to understand the place of relationships and rights in modern civil society as well as how societies determine everyone's legal status and the benefits that accrue to the various types of legal status societies find worth conferring. In a real sense, examining children's legal status tells us about societies' views of children, child development, and what it means to no longer be a child.

This chapter briefly overviews developments relating to children's legal status, with a particular emphasis on the nature of their rights. We begin by examining prevailing conceptions of ways societies historically have approached the legal status of children and how that status determined the nature of children's rights. We then examine the place of children's status in family law jurisprudence, the major area of law that regulates children's social and legal environments both within and outside families. We proceed with examining groundbreaking developments in conceptions of children's human rights. That analysis permits us to revisit the nature of children's legal status to highlight different ways legal systems could envision children's rights. We conclude by highlighting key points about recent developments in children's legal status. Throughout, we emphasize a persistent shift in conceptions of children's rights: a shift toward full legal personhood status, a status that involves the development of legal systems that directly protect children's rights and a status that views an increasing number of children's rights as no longer derivative of those of their parents. We end by highlighting the significance of recent efforts to revise, reformulate, innovate, and strengthen the rights with which we wish to endow children that will serve as a catalyst for profound cultural changes concerning the legal status of children in families and society.

PREVAILING CONCEPTIONS OF CHILDREN'S LEGAL STATUS

The most central debate in modern conceptions of children's legal status focuses on the proper balance among parents' rights, children's rights, and a community/state's place in recognizing and fostering those rights. Legally, this debate plays out in numerous and varied contexts, including sexual health, child custody, religious freedom, immigration, schooling, crime, child welfare, poverty, medical care, family violence, and even countries' participation in international treaties. The debate becomes particularly vociferous and the stakes especially high in these contexts for the simple reason that championing one view of rights necessarily implicates and may even determine the manner in which a society more broadly approaches the social issues surrounding these particular issues. Thus, in the context of child welfare law, we often witness particularly charged and polarized debates between advocates of parents' rights and those who champion a turn to children's rights (see Levesque, 2008a); the same is true, for example, for legal responses to education (Levesque, 2002a), sexuality (Levesque, 2000), religion (Levesque, 2002b), and free speech (Levesque, 2007). In these areas, critics of the focus on parental rights argue that a focus on parents creates a system that sacrifices children's open futures. The focus on the rights of parents leads to the creation of a system that permits the state to be deferential to parents' rights and resists protecting children's own independent rights, such as the right to protection from maltreatment in their own homes. On the other hand, critics of legal approaches that focus on children themselves contend that these systems create incentives for states to intervene too readily in families, which runs the risk of unfairly removing children from their homes. The debates certainly are complex and become considerably nuanced when one takes a close look at how legal systems operate. Legal systems often adopt a variety of approaches depending on the involved issues, and the approaches often conflict. These general approaches are worth examining briefly given that the manner in which societies conceptualize the legal status of children inevitably results in important implications for (and often reflects perceptions of) children, parents, families, and broader society.

The rights of parents

Conceptions of children's rights operate in the shadow of a long-standing legal principle that still dominates and influences this entire area of law. That principle is quite basic: the law fervently protects the rights of parents to the care and custody of their children. This core principle has deep historical roots and important contemporary adherents who champion parental rights as the most effective way to protect children's interests. The principle drives many jurisdictions and even shapes legal doctrines that focus on children's own rights. In Western countries, most notably, the notion of parents' rights reaches as far back as Roman law. For example, Blackstone's *Commentaries* highlights how Roman law conferred on fathers' nearly complete control over their children, and the courts had no role in mediating this relationship (Blackstone, 1765, 2001). This principle was embodied in the concept of *patria potestas*, which granted the male head of a family full legal authority over his legitimate and adopted children, as well as further descendants in the male line, unless emancipated. This authority was quite expansive, as it included, for example, power over life and death (Flugge, 1996). Not surprisingly, legal analyses describe this view as conceiving children as parental property.

The once dominant conception that children essentially were parental property certainly has faded, but the impulse continues and shapes efforts to conceptualize and develop notions of children's rights. Arguably, the related principle that parents control their children, with minimal state intervention, remains alive and well. Many countries express and follow this legal principle as they struggle to recognize children's rights, with the United States remaining an exemplary staunch supporter of this approach. The modern

expression of this legal principle is found in many iconic Supreme Court decisions establishing that the Constitution protects parents' fundamental right to the care, custody, and management of their children (see *Wisconsin v. Yoder*, 1972). Solicitude for parents' rights continues to play out in several important ways within systems where children find themselves: families, child welfare, schools, juvenile justice, and even religious organizations. Again, these conceptions influence the role of the state: strong protection of parental rights increases protection from states' efforts to intervene in families and the rights of parents. This approach, importantly, does not mean that children do not have rights; it does mean that the extent to which they do (barring extreme cases that warrant a state's taking over parental responsibilities) largely depends on their parents' decisions to respect them.

The focus on parents continues to have considerable appeal beyond the legal rules that would support them. Given the profound attachment to parental rights, rationales for supporting them appear quite persuasive. For example, parents seem particularly well situated to determine and act in a child's best interest, at least in areas not squarely within the state's expertise and not in circumstances when parents' decisions transgress certain limits. Protections from state interventions also safeguard cultural and moral diversity in matters of childrearing. Limiting a state's intrusion into family life ensures that a state does not impose a uniform view of parenting. In democratic societies, this protection from governmental control in the name of diversity is seen as the foundation of democratic principles. Parents' rights also protect parents from state intervention on impermissible grounds, such as race, or for improper reasons, such as preferring one set of parents over another purely for the material benefits available from an alternative family. The focus on parental responsibility also, of course, means that parents have the primary responsibility to support their children and families. This certainly reduces considerable burdens (such as financial ones) that a state would otherwise need to carry if it took children under its charge. Finally, the weight granted parental rights ensures that states offer procedural protections that will provide parents with the resources to counter a state's allegations when they intervene in their children's lives. This certainly would seem particularly important in light of the potential for the dehumanization of parents and children involved in a variety of legal systems. Overall, then, much can be said for systems that bestow on parents the right and duty to direct and control their children's upbringing.

The rights of children

The concept of parental rights may have a long history and retain considerable appeal, but so does the concept of children's rights. The same laws and principles that granted parents' rights also placed on parents the high duty to foster their children's healthy development and prepare them for appropriate roles in society (*Wisconsin v. Yoder*, 1972). The concept of children's rights, just like the concept of parental rights, also has developed in a variety of ways (see Levesque, 1994). For our purposes, three related yet somewhat different views of what should constitute children's rights illustrate the complexity of children's legal status even when we adopt an orientation espousing 'children's rights'.

One approach to ensuring children's rights centres on permitting children to assert rights against their parents. This approach, arguably the earliest recognized strand of children's rights, fundamentally adopts a protectionist view. Legally, the approach dates to the nineteenth century, when courts challenged the view of divine parental authority to control children. This movement located the authority to control children, in part, to a parent's civic duty and with the understanding that the child was a future citizen. This approach bestowed on the state the power to regulate parental authority by ensuring that such authority was exercised in the interests of children as well as the public. The 'child

saving' movement illustrates this trend. That movement spread during the nineteenth century and contributed to the creation of state supported educational systems as well as systems that permitted the removal of children from their homes in order to save them from their families and protect communities (see Myers, 2006). This movement's influence continues to be felt, but the rationales that supported the movement often become entangled with other approaches conceptualizing children's rights.

Another approach to conceiving children's legal rights focuses on claims against the state, such as claims against unnecessary state intervention, which could involve unnecessary intervention in children's relationships with their parents. This preservationist strain of children's rights reflects the view that unnecessary state intervention in families infringes on a child's right to maintain relationships with their parents. This approach has considerable appeal to the extent that preservation reflects respect for both parents' rights and children's own rights. Although this sharing of interests is often ignored (for a notable exception, see Melton, 1996), legal systems have recognized its appeal and significance. Courts in societies known for embracing strong parental rights models have noted, for example, that children and parents share vital interests in preventing the erroneous termination of their relationships (see *Santosky v. Kramer*, 1982). Surprisingly, commentators have tended to shy away from this approach, although some rightly argue that conceptions of children's rights must include more general protections against the state, a claim supported by research indicating that the state may unnecessarily remove children from their homes and have them spend needless time in alternative care away from their families (Guggenheim, 2005).

Yet another, related approach focuses on children's direct interactions with social systems in ways that the law recognizes their interactions as independent from their parents. Perhaps the clearest example of this view involves the recognition of a child's right to access, even absent their parents' permission, social services. Although this approach also remains buttressed by several important rationales, the approach essentially aims to liberate children from their parents' hold over them and to limit a state's power to control them more than they would adults. The approach certainly recognizes that not all children can act independently, a point highlighted by the approach's general claim that children's autonomy should be dictated by their 'evolving capacities'. The most frequently recognized examples include medical decision making without parental or judicial intervention and children's power to waive their own rights when they interact with law enforcement (see Levesque, 2007). These proposals, however, run counter to deeply held societal perceptions of who should guide children's development.

There has been some recognition that adolescents can have an independent right to certain services (such as medical testing). But the major rationales supporting independent rights even for adolescents often are blurred, with some rationales being bottomed on efforts to protect the public from disease and crime rather than protect children from their parents or the state itself. As a result, it remains to be seen how receptive societies will be to efforts that advocate children's independent rights, for example, to freedom of thought, conscience, speech, and religion (Levesque, 2008b). Although this lack of development need not mean that the approach has no currency, it does mean that the extent to which it will succeed necessarily turns on its ability to address prevailing societal perceptions of children's relative status in society, especially in families.

beings. The diverse views of children's rights have important implications to the extent that they most likely lead to strikingly different outcomes. The clearest example involves arguments that children are capable of knowing and exercising their rights. This may work well in some contexts and lead, for example, to what some view as greater protection. The important example of this would be permitting minors to obtain judicial waivers for the usual requirements of obtaining parental permission for medical procedures that parents may not wish their children to have. A judicial waiver could both protect minors from parental harm and protect society from harms that would ensue from minors' lack of access to services. On the other hand, arguing that certain children can be capable of exercising their own rights may lead some states to permit treating them like adults for the purpose of punishing them (see Levesque, 2006). Neither approach works very well when we move outside families, when we focus on potential relationships with other institutions like religious groups, justice systems, and schools as well as the general public. The approaches to conceptualizing children's legal status do account for these relationships, but the tensions that arise leave much to be desired. It is not surprising that all sides of debates offering different conceptions criticize others for fundamentally undervaluing the welfare of children. The reality, however, is that each espouses different ways of resolving the dominant practical tensions that children's rights must confront. We now turn to those and focus on the context in which they tend to arise in the manner that legal systems approach family life.

Preliminary conclusions

Children's legal status necessarily links to societal perceptions of children. Most notably, children's legal status depends on the extent to which, and if so when, society views children as dependent or independent

THE PLACE OF CHILDREN'S LEGAL STATUS IN FAMILY LAW JURISPRUDENCE

The legal status of children closely ties to developments in family law and conceptions of families. Societies have devised special laws that apply to families. Legal systems justify these unique rules by focusing on the family's relational aspects and its intimate nature. As a result, 'family law' typically involves efforts to define the structure of families, responsibilities of members toward one another, and the claims or rights individuals have as family members. In addition, this area of law also includes a focus on the proper relationship between families and the state. The dominant theme that has characterized much of family law has been its casting relationships in families as constituting 'separate spheres' from public life. Jurisprudence typically conceives of the family (the private sphere) and the state (the public sphere) as largely independent of each other. The image of separation generally seeks to capture a vision of family privacy in which direct state intervention remains the exception. This approach relates to and shapes several important tensions in ways legal systems approach rights, including those of children.

The extent to which legal systems separate families and individuals from states' actions necessarily relates fundamentally to the manner that societies balance 'negative' and 'positive' conceptions of rights. Internationally, we know that societies vary in terms of the extent to which they champion negative or positive rights. Although no pure positive or negative rights may exist in practice, these rights are readily distinguishable in theory. Essentially, negative rights seek to prevent the state from violating individuals' autonomy; positive rights impose a duty on the state to provide certain goods and services. Western societies tend to adopt the classic Western notion of rights as negative, as stressing choice and autonomy. As we will see below, much of the modern human rights system has roots in Western political traditions and philosophy, which has led the human rights movement, at least historically, to assume a greater emphasis on negative rights. Other countries and important human rights documents, however, do focus on cultural, economic, and social rights and adopt a more

'positive' approach. This approach highlights ways that governments should support families. Even these approaches, however, recognize the family as the fundamental unit of society and place a focus on protecting families from governments' actions.

Another related tension deals with conceptions of individuals and families. Societies and legal systems vary in the extent to which they view individuals as independent or dependent beings. This stance, in turn, also tends to relate to the extent to which legal systems focus more on negative than on positive rights. The negative rights approach, for example, presents a conception that rests on an individual's capacity to exercise rational choice as an autonomous human being. Under this model, rights comprise negative freedoms to protect the individual's self-determination from violation by the state. In this way, the rights model traditionally pits the individual against the state and erects barriers to protect the individual's selfhood from arbitrary government incursion. The model reflects a fear of governmental tyranny and seeks restrictions on governmental power through legally recognized rights. The approach asserts the status of the individual and the individual's priority over both the state and society. Importantly, the positive rights model also seeks to protect individuals, but it also tends to place focus on the rights and obligations of communities, including the state, to foster individual development. The negative rights model appears less accepting of the view that people are defined by their relationships with others. As expected, legal systems tend to balance their legal systems between these poles and we would be hard pressed to find a legal system that adopted only one approach.

The tension relating to our connections with others versus expressions of our individuality relates to the extent to which children can be deemed as separate from families. The different ways of approaching legal systems and families bring a different impulse to the different, possible conceptions of children's rights. Legal systems valuing non-interference would protect families from intrusion; those valuing support would encourage engagement with services and support systems. These differences also would influence internal family dynamics. Systems that focus on autonomy must find ways to develop children so that they could become autonomous adults. Protection for autonomy need not translate into protection of children's own autonomy. Children, even teenagers, are not fully autonomous in the eyes of the law or societies in general. The history of the classic right to privacy reveals, for example, that the leading cases contributing to the development of this right have involved the rights of adults to procreate, to refrain from procreation, and to raise their children as they see fit. This body of law may lead to placing at the core of the privacy right the fundamental decisions that shape family life, that is, such decisions when made by adults. Given the background of the privacy right in the notions of individual autonomy and family (parental) autonomy, it is clear that a privacy right for children is almost an oxymoron. If adults express their autonomy in part by creating and raising children, it follows that those children can have little or no autonomy of their own and thus no claim to a legal right of privacy. An effort remains, however, to recognize that children must be provided with opportunities to become autonomous, self-reliant persons; and those efforts also seek to protect their autonomy from unwarranted government regulation of certain life-shaping decisions. This impulse is most noticeable in efforts to recognize children's 'evolving capacities', which in some countries has been approached by recognizing the extent to which children have the requisite maturity to exercise their own rights. As we have seen, this is quite significant in that children can well have rights, but they may not necessarily control them: parents often are deemed the ones who have the requisite maturity, experience, and wisdom to exercise the rights of their children. Family law jurisprudence, then, continues to struggle in its effort to balance the appropriate

place of individuals in families and continues to develop ways to determine and affect that balance.

The relegation of children and families to a separate sphere parallels the relationship between the state and federal government as well as federal governments and international governments. Among other things, these spheres have posed an important barrier to the constitutionalization of children's rights and to their development across international borders. Concerns about federalism in the United States are illustrative. Federal courts are reluctant to interfere with matters historically viewed as within individual states' jurisdiction, deeming children's interests both local and private. Children's rights are perceived as part of family law, the paradigmatic turf of the states. While refusing to constitutionalize children's rights and imposing a more national standard, American constitutional traditions have, nonetheless, long recognized parental rights over their children. Although the Constitution is silent on specific rights for children or any other family members, parental rights gained a constitutional foothold during the heyday of court decisions expanding on substantive due process rights. By exercising constitutionally protected rights to physical custody and control over children's upbringing, parents can define the rights of children. The focus on protecting the rights of parents at local levels eventually translates into reluctance to embrace international human rights standards that are perceived, arguably wrongly, as adding yet another level of control over parental rights and moving power increasingly away from local jurisdictions, including federal systems (see Levesque, 1996a).

Given how societies approach jurisprudence regulating family life inevitably has local, federal, and even international dimensions, it should not be surprising to find that the place of children's rights in modern family law jurisprudence presents important implications for public policy. A close look at children's place in family jurisprudence indicates that relationships among children, families, and state are not fixed; the relationships remain potentially dynamic. The place of children in families also illustrates how the family is not a natural entity with a form that is constant and essential; families are societal creations. Relationships among children, families, and the state can be reconfigured, and have been reconfigured, to reflect different sets of expectations and aspirations for children, families, and the more general society. These reconfigurations and aspirations suggest that society would benefit from periodic self-conscious considerations about the continued viability and desirability of historic assumptions about 'the family' as an institution as well as assumptions of children's status in them and society.

These changes are significant for conceptions of children, families, and the law. Even though legal systems continue to characterize families as distinct and separate from the state, for example, the modern state no longer is as distinct as it once (apparently) was; nor are families. Laws still may designate the family as the quintessential 'private' institution, one that is essentially outside the law. For the modern private family, protection from public interference remains the publicly stated norm. State intervention continues to be cast as exceptional, requiring some justification. Yet, families continue to change. What constitutes a family, responsibilities within families, and relationships within families change. And these changes influence the relationship between the family, its members, and the state. As a result, modern legal systems must adapt and perhaps imagine the relationship between the state and families as symbiotic more so than as separate spheres.

In many ways, families and governments are interactive; they define one another. Alterations in the scope or nature of one institution alter the scope or nature of the other. Although law initially defines the family by controlling entry and determining the consequences of its formation, once formed, the family is a powerful constituency within a state. The expectations for the family relieve a state of some obligations. Family actions (or inactions) can place pressure on a state and require adjustments and accommodation that alter the nature of state governments. This symbiosis is undoubtedly part of what is meant when we view families as the building blocks of civil society.

THE INTERNATIONALIZATION OF CHILDREN'S RIGHTS: MOVING FROM RECOGNITION TO IMPLEMENTATION OF CHILDREN'S INDPENDENT LEGAL STATUS

Although the general public is unlikely to have heard about an international movement involving children's human rights, the modern human rights movement has long included special attention to children. The human rights movement contains international treaties and statements that relate directly to children, some that pertain specifically to families, and others that concern them in a more general way through the enumeration of rights for all. An analysis of these documents is beyond the purview of this chapter, especially since one can approach international children's rights by looking at how human rights law addresses, for example, armed conflict (de Berry, 2001), child maltreatment (Levesque, 1999a), child labour (Myers, 2001), health (MacDonald, 2007), homelessness (Panter-Brick, 2002), immigration (Hernandez-Truyol and Luna, 2006), juvenile justice (Levesque, 1996b), education (Levesque, 1998), family violence (Levesque, 1999b, 2001), poverty (Andrews and Kaufman, 1999), etc. For our purposes, it is instructive to examine briefly the most recent and expansive human rights document detailing children's rights: the United Nations' (1989) Convention on the Rights of the Child. The Convention, which was approved unanimously by the United Nations General Assembly in 1989, quickly entered into force in 1990 and was almost universally ratified by all countries a few years later, presents the first and only comprehensive international articulation of children's rights. The treaty is important to examine to the extent that it highlights the nature of children's rights as well as, equally importantly, how those rights are to be respected.

The Convention fundamentally aims to give priority to children in the adoption of state measures and in the allocation of state resources. To achieve this goal, the Convention adopted the following basic principles: (1) children need special legal protection beyond that provided to adults; (2) the ideal environment for a child's survival and development is generally within a protective and caring family setting; and (3) governments and private citizens, including parents, should respect and act in the best interests of children. The treaty further reflects the priority given to children as it delineated six categories of specific and substantive rights: (a) economic rights (including adequate standards of living, social security, and health care); (b) social and cultural rights (including minority rights and educational rights); (c) political and civil rights (including freedoms of thought, conscience and religion, association, expression, and prohibitions against discrimination); (d) legal process rights (civil and criminal procedural rights, prohibitions against certain punishments, and periodic reviews of placements); (e) humanitarian rights (protections during armed conflict); and (f) family rights (parental responsibilities and the right to know and be cared for by parents, maintain contact with parents, and basic rights to a family environment). Although other important rights still do need to be developed (see Freeman, 2000), the enumeration of rights remains quite impressive. The unprecedented and immense breadth of the rights recognized in the Convention, coupled by its focus on a group that has yet to be fully recognized in law, certainly places the Convention in a category of its own. It clearly is one of the greatest achievements of modern human rights law.

The rights enumerated in the Convention certainly are expansive; but the reality is that the 'simple' enumeration of rights is not the same as ensuring that they are taken seriously. The Convention highlights the challenges of placing ideals into practice. Indeed, the manner by which the Convention enumerated rights and charted mechanisms for its implementation has been the subject of considerable controversy. Most notably, the Convention has been criticized relentlessly for being impossible to implement. On its face, this criticism appears considerably valid. Compared to other human rights treaties, the Convention offers the weakest form of legally binding protection. For example, the implementation mechanisms of the Convention do not establish any concrete means of enforcement at the international level. (An optional protocol, at this writing not yet in force, will enable private parties to petition the UN Committee on the Rights of the Child for consideration, after domestic remedies are exhausted, of alleged violations of children's rights. Even in the process, however, the Committee will have no mechanism other than enlistment of international public opinion to enforce its judgments.) Thus, at present, the Convention depends almost exclusively on the regular submission of fact-finding and other reports for monitoring implementation; rather than relying on international courts, enforcement relies on treaty committees and special reporters who scrutinize and regularly report on countries' adherence to the Convention. In addition, the Convention does not directly offer children legal remedies within countries. The Convention, for example, does not mandate direct access to court systems for children who would have their international human rights violated. Instead, the Convention requires countries that ratify the Convention to take steps to ensure respect for the enumerated rights. Furthermore, the Convention introduces and relies on the idea that, in several instances, private individuals have an affirmative duty to act to ensure children's rights. As we have seen above, this focus on private parties may not necessarily result in increasing respect for children's own rights. As a whole, then, the Convention variously and vaguely places burdens on parents, community members, and participating countries to ensure that children's rights are recognized and accepted. In doing so, the Convention requires countries to take steps to develop laws consistent with the Convention's mandates. It is this more programmatic and soft approach to ensuring the recognition and enforcement of children's rights that leaves the Convention open to the criticism that its enforcement mechanisms lack the bite needed to move children's rights to the forefront of countries' political agendas.

Criticisms of the Convention's approach to enforcement are likely to continue, but they, in many ways, obfuscate important developments in thinking of how to envision children's rights. As we have seen above, the traditional approach to ensuring children's rights has been to grant control of their rights to adults, especially parents and family members. The Convention does mark a departure from that tradition. Although precedence is given to the family in terms of promoting its responsibility to assure the protection of children's rights, the majority of provisions are written so that, instead of being parents or families, countries are supposed to 'recognize', 'ensure', 'undertake', 'promote', 'assure', 'respect', 'encourage', 'pursue', and 'take appropriate measures' to ensure rights. More specifically stated, 38 of the 41 substantive articles in the Convention are devoted to enumerating enforceable rights. Of these, 25 have been drafted to place the duty on the government, with no mention of the child's family or parents. In half of the remaining articles, parents are simply mentioned as receiving assistance to carry out the rights guaranteed to the child. The other articles either support the family relationship with the child for the child's benefit or limit parental rights or responsibilities by (1) protecting the child from abuse or parental kidnapping, (2) recognizing the child's 'evolving capacities', and (3) ensuring the child's 'best interests' (see Levesque, 1996a). Although the

Convention may not be a forcefully binding international treaty, it does set into motion a rights agenda for children and does require governments to move in directions that depart from traditional conceptions of children's legal status.

Given the international approach's movement away from traditional conceptions of children's legal status, it is important to highlight the prominent role families continue to have in envisioning children's rights. Despite its strong child-centred language that protects children's independent rights, the Convention still highlights the important role of families in fostering rights. The Convention remains a pro-family document. The Convention 'recognizes the family as the natural environment for child development and makes clear that parents have the primary right and responsibility to raise their own children, without interference from their government' or the United Nations. The Convention further includes numerous provisions aimed to preserve the integrity of the family. For instance, the Preamble asserts that 'the family, as the fundamental group of society and the natural environment for the growth and well-being of all its members and particularly children, should be afforded the necessary protection and assistance so that it can fully assume its responsibilities within the community'. Furthermore, Article 7 imbues the child with the explicit 'right to know and be cared for by his or her parents'. This is the flip-side of the more established right of parents to control their child's custody and upbringing. In this way, the Convention actively protects the family and the parent–child relationship as integral elements of the rights of children. Although the Convention safeguards the parent–child relationship, it maintains 'the best interests of the child' to be 'a primary consideration'. Children's rights are not defined as antagonistic to parents' rights, but rather as their source. Of course, the question remains what the child's 'best interests' actually are, and who gets to define them. However, the rest of the Convention gives content to this open-ended standard and, at least conceptually, it holds the child's best interests as the guiding principle. In addition to emphasizing governmental guidance and enforcement, the Convention lends formal support to the participation and autonomy or self-determination rights of children. That is, nearly one fourth of the substantive articles are participation and self-determination rights, including the following protections and freedoms: personal and national identity, access to information, movement and association, belief, expression, privacy, and development toward independence. To use the language that we have been using throughout, the children's human rights movement seeks to recognize children's independent legal status. Families certainly continue to figure prominently in children's lives, but unlike traditional conceptions of children's rights that saw those rights as determined and controlled by children's parents, families exist to foster children's rights and self-determination.

Despite important criticisms, then, the children's human rights movement remains relatively consistent. The primary model aims to regulate the relationship between children and the government, with parental and familial involvement which, although respected, essentially assumes secondary importance. This approach is truly revolutionary: it limits reliance on parental assurance of children's rights. Although the children's human rights movement remains far from complete and potential conflicts still remain, and although some rights are purely aspirational, the current documents guiding this movement do make clear that governments assume the role of protectors, benefactors and standard-bearers. In a real sense, international human rights law dealing with children abandons the public/private, negative/positive dichotomies. The children's human rights movement uses language indicative of intent to impose human rights obligations protective of children on both state parties and private actors. It does so by granting children a person status independent of their parents. By placing the burden on governments to take affirmative steps toward fostering children's rights, these modern developments go a long way toward assuring children's independent, full legal personhood status.

THE SIGNIFICANCE OF HUMAN RIGHTS APPROACHES TO RECOGNIZING CHILDREN'S LEGAL STATUS

We already have seen the tensions that guide jurisprudence relating to children's legal status as well as those embedded in family law. International developments in children's human rights potentially provide important ways to revisit these tensions and can help transform the manner in which societies view children's legal status. These transformations can occur for a variety of reasons, but all rest on the way that the human rights approach provides a universal standard on which we can evaluate children's status in law and society.

Human rights developments foster the notion that rights are indivisible, that governments have both affirmative obligations as well as obligations to resist infringing in people's lives. This remains a troublesome position for governments that view basic rights as limitations on governmental actions, rather than viewing rights as requiring affirmative state action. It becomes even more troublesome when a government's basic conception of rights also presumes autonomy and a direct relationship between the individual and the state. The position also, of course, continues to be problematic for countries that focus less on limiting government's role in controlling individual's lives. Accepting the human rights approach would mean adopting a completely different stance. It would require protecting the entire gamut of human rights and would no longer presume a direct relationship with the state as a necessary prerequisite for assuring those rights. Human rights developments permit impinging on parental rights. Although human rights law explicitly states that parental rights will be respected, the assertion that their children have state-guaranteed rights necessarily weakens the parental role as traditionally conceived. As the laws now stand, the tendency has been to have the state remain a minor legal actor in children's lives. In contrast, under the human rights approach, the minimalist intervention approach would be replaced by a need for greater state supervision and the inevitable pressure to intervene in family matters. Moreover, the weakening of parental and traditional familial protections would reach far beyond current state intervention to protect children, something which has itself been controversial. The traditional governmental intrusion into the family domain to provide discipline and education would be supplemented by intrusion to ensure that the family appropriately liberates and respects its children. The modern human rights movement embraces civil, political, and religious rights that are, to the extent practicable, bestowed onto children themselves.

Developments in human rights also essentially entail reimaging the role of parents and the family. The human rights movement regards increased governmental 'intervention' in the family as the best protection for children's rights. Governmental intervention between parents and children raises important psychological, social, moral, and political issues. The moral and political implications of this issue already have emerged in the diverging approaches to children's rights. The move toward increasing children's independent rights has been fraught with controversy over the role of the children's voice, the parents' authority, and a government's responsibilities. Resistance is likely to continue. In the United States, for example, the current trend has swung toward respecting greater parental authority. This trend places emphasis on the sovereignty of the normal parent whose affection and self-interest combine to make the child's

autonomy a principal goal of the family. The same is true for non-Western societies, those which have been characterized as viewing children's legal status as one of responsibility for their parents and families (see Panter-Brick, 2002); and this is especially true in societies that perceive children as a family resource (in the context of sub-Saharan Africa, for example, see Rwezaura, 1998), a perception that runs counter to the idea that children are separate individuals vested with certain independent rights. In many ways, the human rights movement adopts a different and opposing stance. Under the human rights framework, not parents but states would ensure that children's rights were respected and recognized; and, in doing so, states also would ensure that parents respect and recognize children's rights. The human rights movements invoke governments as the insurers of children's legal status.

The human rights framework also involves accepting its clear policy choice, a stance that could revolutionize jurisprudence regulating family life. Its potential import in this regard simply cannot be overstated. Underlying the human rights movement is the belief that children's legal personhood should be respected. The movement dictates that children's views should be heard and that their liberty should not be taken capriciously. Furthermore, it requires that their mental health be protected and promoted and that their familial relationships preserved. To implement the human rights movement, legal systems would have to recognize children's capacities. Legal systems no longer would be able to merely salute children's rights while playing down their personhood by ascribing vulnerability and incapacity to them as to render them dependent and rob them of their rights. In addition, legal systems would have to consider children's best interests when making decisions affecting their lives. Although the best interest standard currently pervades jurisprudence that seeks to recognize children's interests in legal responses to their circumstances, the standard leaves virtually unbridled discretion in the hands of those who would determine what constitutes children's interests. The reason for this indeterminacy is that there currently is no statement of key values that should be honoured in matters pertaining to children and families, and societies continue to fluctuate about which rights should be assured children and when those rights should be assured. However, the human rights approach would transform the 'best interests' standard by providing a forthright statement on competing and merging interests in family settings: children come first.

The moral and political implications of the 'children first' stance promoted by the human rights movement become even more obvious when one begins to consider some of its possible legal consequences. The historical record reveals, for example, that when adolescence was conceived, it was merged into the familiar category of childhood, with its attendant need of protection and nurturing. The result of this conception was that adolescents' rights were limited because of their status. Although there was a burgeoning march away from the child as a dependent person and a move toward the view that they could enjoy independent legal rights, most recent legal developments have continued to curtail the rights of adolescents and to subordinate them to adults. For instance, the constitutional rights of minors in the United States are still limited because of their status, because they are always in some form of custody. Thus, adolescents and children not only are subject to control by their parents, but are also subject to control by educational and similar institutions. Moreover, legal systems consistently have declined to require that full legal standards of protection be applied to those relationships. As a result, numerous regulations and practices could be challenged under the human rights standard. These could range from re-examining positions on juvenile nocturnal curfews, cultural or race-matching adoptions, child custody decision making, school curriculum,

prosecution and incarceration of juveniles, corporal punishment in schools, special education programs, out-of-home care for children, illegitimate children's status, and parental notification requirements in teen abortion decision making. That the human rights movement opens the door to debates on these issues is nothing short of phenomenal and offers important opportunities to examine the nature of children's legal status.

In the end, the need to re-examine these areas of jurisprudence, and the great hesitancy to develop mechanisms that foster children's own rights, essentially results in the need to avoid a myopic view of rights when determining the legal status of children. Recent lessons relating to efforts to recognize children's rights again are instructive. Earlier interventionist efforts have highlighted strong reasons for caution (Levesque, 1995; Sealander, 2003). Rights-based models themselves have been challenged for failing to protect children, parents and families (see Levesque, 2008a). Recent examinations of child welfare law reveal, for example, that official decisions are often driven by racial biases and political expediency. Equally problematically, procedural safeguards and court adjudications that are designed to protect rights often do not lead to careful, reliable decisions. In addition, state intervention to protect a child's right to be free from abuse and neglect may be essential in some cases, but intervention also may come at a high cost to the child in the typical child welfare cases when removals are based on such factors as lack of familial resources and less than adequate available alternatives to care. Myopic views of rights might assume that the rights bearer is an autonomous individual seeking freedom from the state. Yet, vulnerable individuals need more than autonomy; they need concrete assistance.

These realities support the conclusion that simply adding resources to current systems will not necessarily 'fix' them because we would need to resolve the fundamental problems associated with myopic views of rights.

Children's relationships are part of a web of complex systems, much of which are not fully understood. It also is unclear whether legal systems would welcome or operationalize findings from social science; any attempt to interfere in children's lives and relations might very well be made without the benefit of findings from research that has at least attempted to understand the nature of those relations. These realities confirm the need to consider the legal status of children as we seek to understand their place in society.

Admittedly, much still needs to be done to turn aspirations into reality (Freeman, 2000; Rwezaura, 1998). Despite words of caution and nagging pessimism about the potential impact of the children's rights movement, the children's human rights movement actually has led to a significant proliferation of regional and international changes in its wake. On the fifteenth anniversary of the adoption of the Convention, UNICEF (2004) conducted an analysis of 50 countries to determine the extent to which countries had engaged in law reform consistent with the Convention's obligations and principles. The study concluded that the Convention had been incorporated into the national legal framework of most of the countries under analysis, either through its automatic integration through existing constitutional principles, constitutional reform, or by legislation specifically designed for that purpose. The study further found that incorporation of the Convention into national legal systems is nearly universal in Central and Eastern Europe and Latin America. Importantly, it also was found that some countries have enacted 'children's codes' while others have opted for more gradual reform of different legislation concerning children, with a focus on regulations. Others have focused more on the design and implementation of programs rather than on law reform itself. All of these efforts constitute critical components of comprehensive approaches to protecting children's rights and ensuring different ways to recognize that children actually do have a legal status.

CONCLUSION: FOSTERING AN APPROPRIATE LEGAL STATUS FOR CHILDREN

Across the globe, children occupy a peculiar legal status. There are many ways to express that status, but it appears clear that a new standard has emerged on which we can evaluate it. The human rights movement has asserted a number of rights for children worldwide. This has resulted in an ambitious agenda to reconfigure children's legal status. This movement gains considerable significance in that, in addition to formulating basic principles to help implement these rights, the international community has taken upon itself a legal obligation to put the recognized rights and principles into practice. The movement has carefully formulated principles to foster the development of rights while still leaving room for some flexibility and cultural interpretation, especially in terms of children's status in families. The movement has heralded a change in the prevailing approaches to determining children's status, from highlighting the needs of children and their dependency on families to defending their rights as citizens. As a result, the movement has fostered efforts to reconstruct the entire concept of children's status. The global community is on the move to recognize that children have their own, independent status.

Recent developments in conceptualizing children's legal status attempt to address two important tensions: inclusion and separation. The first tension involves an effort to extend to children the already recognized foundational rights adults already enjoy. This effort at inclusion would be true for a panoply of rights regardless of a particular country's focus on rights either as protections from governments or as governmental protections in the form of addressing social needs. Regardless of the orientation, addressing children's peculiar status would mean that we must address children's capacity to participate and exercise civil liberties. The second tension involves the extent to which children's peculiar status engenders specific entitlements to respond to vulnerabilities that may arise because of their status in diverse societies. This effort to separate children's specific needs would be true for numerous rights relating, for example, to the need to recognize children as a group for special interventions, such as rendering them a priority group for education, health, and anti-poverty programs as well as efforts to protect them from harm and exploitation due to their special status as children. Regardless of a country's efforts in these areas, recent conceptual developments tell us that children should be taken on their own terms, as individuals requiring distinctive and particular approaches to rights that recognize their peculiar legal status.

A look at legal history reveals that, upon discovering the biasing and excluding effects of a status and then deciding to address it, legal systems' default responses typically seek to incorporate the group into dominant legal responses. Recent developments in conceptualizing children's legal status clearly could be viewed as embracing this approach, but children's peculiar status may require more. Despite the tendency to have children become beneficiaries of new programs and recognitions, a deeper reflection reveals that children are embedded in relationships, especially families, and that their legal status also is embedded in existing areas of jurisprudence, such as family law. This continues to be true throughout legal systems. This reality presents important opportunities and challenges. The focus on children's independent legal status strongly challenges conventional views. Efforts to reconceptualize children's status still recognize the important role of families, but they also seek to ensure that children benefit from shifting moral, political, and practical orientations that ultimately determine how we treat one another. As citizens, children have rights that entitle them to the resources required to protect and promote their development. These rights mean that we must revisit how legal systems define rights, approach relationships, and envision families

if we are to understand and eventually influence the status of children.

ACKNOWLEDGEMENTS

I would like to express my appreciation to Sara M. Walsh, who has helped collect commentaries relating to the rights of children outside the United States.

REFERENCES

Andrews, A.B. and Kaufman, N.H. (eds.) (1999) *Implementing the U.N. Convention on the Rights of the Child: A Standard of Living Adequate for Development.* Westport, CT: Praeger.

Blackstone, W. (1765, 2001) *Commentaries on the Laws of England.* Vol. 1. London: Cavendish.

de Berry, J. (2001) 'Child soldiers and the Convention on the Rights of the Child', *Annals of the American Academy of Political and Social Science*, 575(1): 92–105.

Flugge, S. (1996) 'On the history of fathers' rights and mothers' duty of care', *Cardozo Women's Law Journal*, 3: 377–97.

Freeman, M. (2000) 'The future of children's rights', *Children and Society*, 14(4): 277–93.

Guggenheim, M. (2005) *What's Wrong With Children's Rights.* Boston, MA: Harvard University Press.

Hernandez-Truyol, B. and Luna, J. (2006) 'Children and immigration: International, local, and social responsibilities', *Boston University Public Interest Law Journal*, 15(2): 297–317.

Levesque, R.J.R. (1994) 'International children's rights grow up: Implications for American jurisprudence and domestic policy', *California Western International Law Journal*, 24(2): 193–240.

Levesque, R.J.R. (1995) 'The failures of foster care reform: Revolutionizing the most radical blueprint', *Maryland Journal of Contemporary Legal Issues*, 6(1): 1–35.

Levesque, R.J.R. (1996a) 'Future visions of juvenile justice: Lessons from international and comparative law', *Creighton Law Review* (Special Issue: Issues in Juvenile Justice), 29(4): 1563–85.

Levesque, R.J.R. (1996b) 'International children's rights: Can they make a difference in American family policy?', *American Psychologist*, 51(12): 1251–6.

Levesque, R.J.R. (1998) 'Educating American youth: Lessons from children's human rights law', *Law & Education*, 27(2): 173–209.

Levesque, R.J.R. (1999a) 'Piercing the family's private veil: Family violence, international human rights, and the cross-cultural record', *Law & Policy*, 21(2): 161–87.

Levesque, R.J.R. (1999b) *Sexual Abuse of Children: A Human Rights Perspective*. Bloomington, IN: Indiana University Press.

Levesque, R.J.R. (2000) *Adolescents, Sex, and the Law: Preparing Adolescents for Responsible Citizenship*. Washington, DC: American Psychological Association.

Levesque, R.J.R. (2001) *Culture and Family Violence: Fostering Change through Human Rights Law*. Washington, DC: American Psychological Association.

Levesque, R.J.R. (2002a) *Dangerous Adolescents, Model Adolescents: Shaping the Role and Promise of Education*. New York: Plenum/Kluwer.

Levesque, R.J.R. (2002b) *Not by Faith Alone: Religion, Adolescence and the Law*. New York: University Press.

Levesque, R.J.R. (2006) *The Psychology and Law of Criminal Justice Processes*. Hauppauge, NY: Nova Science Publishers.

Levesque, R.J.R. (2007) *Adolescence, Media and the Law*. New York: Oxford University Press.

Levesque, R.J.R. (2008a) 'Regardless of frontiers: Adolescents and the human right to information', *Journal of Social Issues*, 64(4): 725–47.

Levesque, R.J.R. (2008b) 'Rethinking Laws Regulating Child Protection', in *Child Maltreatment and the Law: Returning to First Principles*. New York: Springer, pp. 169–92.

MacDonald, T.H. (2007) *The Global Human Right to Health: Dream or Possibility*? Oxford: Radcliffe Publishing.

Melton, G.B. (1996) 'The child's right to a family environment: Why children's rights and family values are compatible', *American Psychologist*, 51(12): 1234–8.

Myers, W.E. (2001) 'The right of rights? Child labor in a globalizing world', *Annals of the American Academy of Political and Social Science*, 575(1): 38–55.

Myers, J.E.B. (2006) *Child Protection in America: Past, Present, and Future*. New York: Oxford.

Panter-Brick, C. (2002) 'Street children, human rights, and public health: A critique and future direction', *Annual Review of Anthropology*, 31(1): 147–71.

Santosky v. Kramer, 455 US 745 (1982).

Sealander, J. (2003) *The Failed Century of the Child: Governing America's Young in the Twentieth Century*. New York: Cambridge University Press.

Rwezaura, B. (1998) 'Competing 'images' of childhood in the social and legal systems of contemporary Sub-Saharan Africa', *International Journal of Law, Policy, and the Family*, 12(3): 253–78.

UNICEF (2004) *Summary Report of the Study on the Impact of the Implementation of the Convention on the Rights of the Child*. Florence, Italy: UNICEF Innocenti Research Center.

United Nations (1989) *Convention on the Rights of the Child*, GA res. 44/25, annex, 44 UN GAOR Supp. (No. 49) at 167, UN Doc. A/44/49 (1989), entered into force 2 September 1990.

Wisconsin v. Yoder, 406 US 205 (1972).

4

Children as Political Actors

Anu Toots, Natalie Worley, and Anna Skosireva

INTRODUCTION

It is often assumed, that, as non-voters, young people are not involved in political processes and instead need protection from the adult world. Although the ratification of the Convention on the Rights of the Child brought formal recognition of youth as deserving of citizenship and a unique set of human rights (Sherrod, 2008), the concept of youth political participation remains controversial in many contemporary Western democracies. Children often are regarded as incomplete and incompetent ('becomings' or 'citizens in the making') who need protection and cannot be granted full rights and traditional participation options. At the same time, young people are accused of political apathy or, conversely, of taking overly-radical political actions. At the heart of this paradox is uncertainty about the nature of childhood and changes in its construction brought about by the processes of late modernity (Such, Walker and Walker, 2005).

Despite a limited understanding of children's participation in politics, the topic has long remained unexplored in the research agenda (Alanen, 1994; Prout, Simmons, and Birchall, 2006). Over the last decade,

however, attempts have been made to move away from an age-bound paradigm and reconceptualize 'citizenship' from a child-centred perspective. Researchers emphasize that youth political participation should not be studied in isolation from the debates about political participation in general, since there is no principal difference between child and adult participation in governance (Prout et al., 2006; Tisdall and Bell, 2006). As Weller (2007: 3) observed, 'children, teenagers, and adults alike are all represented as full citizens who throughout their life learn, develop, and exert different forms of citizenship in different spaces'.

The relatively recent development of interest in youth as political actors and the transition from a 'protection' focus to an actor-centred approach is reflected in the research literature, including a growing interest in how youth beliefs and perceptions, family and school contexts, the Internet and other technologies, and participation in voluntary service and civic organizations may influence youths' current and future participation in the political process. Contemporary social structures and democratic governance offer a wide range of possibilities for youth to be engaged in politics as autonomous actors. Thus, when making judgements about the citizenship and political activism of children and adolescents younger than voting age, one should examine all existing practices, from formal student councils to protest graffiti.

POLITICS AND YOUTH SUBCULTURES

The significance of youth as political actors in the United States and worldwide cannot be fully understood without considering the historical aspects of the formation and development of youth subculture. Youth subculture refers to those processes and symbolic systems that young people share that are, to some degree, distinctive from those of their parents and other adults (Austin, 2008). The focus lies on the group aspect: the distinct lifestyles, meaning systems, and modes of expression. Individuals who were born in the context of a certain set of institutions and relations give meaning to their shared social and material life experiences and organize themselves in a defined subculture. Specific events or changes in a specific time give rise to different subcultures, which can be viewed as a way of giving meaning to evolutions in society (Burke, 2000). Thus, a subculture is specific to a defined time. The environment, policies, artefacts, technological evolutions, and organization of social relations do not remain stable over centuries, so a group needs new solutions to address the changes of their distinct reality (Clarke, n.d.).

Youth subcultures are the products of the environment and system conditions in which young people are brought up. Events have a particular effect on people when they are experienced at a formative age. According to Mannheim's (1952) theory, people are significantly influenced by the socio-historical settings that are predominant in their youth. The experiences in these settings not only influence an individual's subsequent values and attitudes into adulthood, but also make the individual an agent of change who,

in turn, affects the events that shape the next generation (Mannheim, 1952; Pilcher, 1994).

Despite the appearance of stability, youth culture is a dynamic, historical process. Youth subcultures are important engines of cultural change and often have played a critical role in historically realigning culture and politics. Human history has abundant examples of youth politics functioning as a catalyst to progressive activism and young people's collective practices restructuring the societal social order, including such recent examples as the 2008 election of President Barack Obama in the United States and the Arab Spring uprisings in the Middle East.

Youth cultures were evident throughout the twentieth century (Fowler, 2008), but the concept of youth subculture as a distinct category has emerged only in the period following World War II (Clarke et al., 2006; Mintz, 2006). Most scholars agree that the conditions necessary for mass youth subcultures to emerge appeared after the formation of modern nation-states and the routinization of life in the industrializing nations of the nineteenth century (Clarke, n.d.). These conditions were markedly different from those which youth experienced in earlier decades. The mass institutions of nation-states, which separate young people from adults and join young people together in large numbers for education, religious instruction, training, work, or punishment, have been consistent locations in which youth subcultures have developed (Austin, 2008). Furthermore, diminished parental influence over children's marriages, greater job opportunities, increased geographical separation between home and work, increased importance of the market and the associated rise of adolescent consumer culture, and the arrival of mass communication also facilitated the creation of youth culture in the post-war period. These factors combined to provide the starting conditions that gave young people shared meanings to their experiences and pushed them to seek solutions for the challenges they face (Clarke, n.d.).

Society quickly became dominated by the social and cultural influences of youth culture by the late 1950s and early 1960s, as large numbers of 'baby boomers' in Western countries entered their teens. As these teens entered the work force, job growth slowed and the labour market demanded higher skills. An increased need for educational credentials elevated the importance of high schools and colleges, creating a heightened age-consciousness that, in turn, was reflected in a growing youth culture (Remy, 2005). The youth culture spread worldwide though fashion, music, and new lifestyle choices. This new culture transformed itself into a worldwide youth movement, with an image of the youth as rebelling and contesting the established system, often starting in settings of higher education. Initially seen as rebels without a cause, and even as deviant and threatening to society, youth culture came to have a goal – the transformation of the world (Forbrig, 2005).

The prominence of youth subcultures in the late 1960s and 1970s was accounted for by a combination of factors. Young people were a much larger group than before. An increased youth income meant that there was a distinct youth market. Higher education further contributed to developing a group social, political, and cultural identity. The young population was dissatisfied with the inaction of their parents, and youth were reacting to the permissive attitudes of their parents (Roszak, 1968). As a result of these factors, a wave of research emerged in the 1960s that recognized the force of youth-created social change and focused on the role of political issues in the transition from adolescence to adulthood (Flanagan and Sherrod, 1998).

A new cohort of young people now conceived of themselves as a transnational social group or a new international social class, which had its own goals, a role to play, and an undeniable power. Mobility and travel were associated with personal freedom (Jobs, 2009), and the expansion of transportation, travel, and communication made behaviours overflow frontiers and 'form a specific civilization extending to millions of young people' (Ferrand, 1968: 60–61). This youth movement had strong repercussions in France after May 1968 and eventually became a global phenomenon, with the young generation rebelling in the United States, Europe, Latin America, and the Middle East (Forbrig, 2005).

Young people increasingly were viewing the world in international terms, participating in it in transnational ways and building a shared political culture across national boundaries. Iconic examples include Che Guevara, the young Argentinean who fought for victory in Cuba before continuing the revolution in Bolivia; Rudi Dutschke, who was from East Germany but led the West German student movement; Daniel Cohn-Bendit, who was the face of the revolutionary events in Paris but had German citizenship and Tariq Ali, who was from Pakistan but became a prominent organizer in Britain (Jobs, 2009). The experience of travel within the emergent youth culture helped to shape a politicized European identity among the young protesters of 1968 and became a turning point in the history of European integration (Jobs, 2009).

Perhaps the most well-known example of young people's transnational political interests of this time period is the distinct subculture that formed in opposition to the Vietnam War. The 'hippie' social movement among youth originated on the West Coast of the United States in the 1960s and was largely a response to the Vietnam War. Opposition to the war was fuelled by the anger of college students over the drafting of young men for duty in the war. These hippies led the anti-war movement in the 1960s and 1970s and were willing to go so far as to engage in physical aggression towards law enforcement officials. The hippie culture had a broader political agenda than just opposing the war: they supported broader lifestyles and political views concerning issues of freedom and the right to self-expression (Movius, 2004). The first major event of the hippie movement that caught the attention of the media was the Summer of Love in winter 1967. About 20,000 activists gathered for a 'human be-in' at the San Francisco Polo Field; the great majority of those who participated were adolescents (Falk and Falk, 2005).

The political events involving youth in the 1960s sparked considerable interest in the systematic study of generations in the United States, largely because of the significant role young people played in the civil rights, free speech, anti-war, and other protest and counterculture movements (Remy, 2005). Researchers attempted to identify 'political generations', birth cohorts who share similar formative experiences and consequently mobilize themselves for political action. The resulting literature suggested that distinct cultural and political identities are shared by those who come of age at moments very close in historical proximity and that adolescence and early adulthood are times of civic and political identity development with lasting effects (Erikson, 1968; Jennings and Niemi, 1981; Smith, 1999). Generational identity and youth culture began to be seen as an extremely powerful social force and the basis for transformative politics and culture.

Unique generational identity is decisive in the magnitude of generational conflict, as young cohorts may share a collective disappointment in the political and cultural systems of a society (Laufer, 1971). As a result, the mere existence of contradictions in society can spur the formation of youth subcultures with new systems of values and norms (Clarke, n.d.). There is historical evidence, at least in the United States, that a search for new political and cultural models was a youth response to being socialized in a system that proclaimed liberal democratic values but did not live up to them in practice (Remy, 2005). Thus, a formation of youth subcultures can be considered an attempt to reconcile the perceived gulf in rhetoric and reality. It also reflects a confrontation with hypocrisy rather than with parental values per se.

Youth subcultures also can be seen as real and symbolic attempts to challenge and influence the equilibrium of perceived power relations between themselves and larger society (Clarke, n.d.). These attempts involve conscious adoption of behaviours that appear threatening to the Establishment, or the 'old'. Therefore, youth culture often is seen as permeated with oppositional defiance, with youth thought to be defining their identity in contradistinction to mainstream adult culture. When a certain culture expresses opposition to hegemonic culture, as is the case with youth subcultures, it is often expressed in forms of resistance. This resistance generally is seen as deviance by youth workers and school officials despite the political nature of resistance itself (Giroux, 1983). Clarke argues that apart from resistance, youth subcultures may draw on strategies such as coexistence, struggle, mobilization, politicization, and organization in order to challenge the dominant culture and to draw attention to structural contradictions within society. These strategies enable young people to win 'space', be that political, economic, or cultural (Clarke, n.d.). There are also symbolic links between youth subculture values and choices of lifestyle, hair, fashion, music, dance, and language. These lifestyles are centred in subjective experience through which the subculture expresses or reinforces its social concerns (Hebdige, 1979).

Hip-hop culture is a prime example of a youth subculture that emerged as a real and symbolic attempt to challenge and influence the equilibrium of power relations. The first to come of age in post-segregation America, a cohort of black Americans born between 1965 and the mid-1980s largely expressed itself through hip-hop music. Hip-hop culture has since evolved beyond its original core elements to encompass language, dress, attitude, and political and social activism (Remy, 2005). Kitwana (2002) identified several factors that have shaped the ideals and construction of hip-hop culture and its reaction to an oppressive mainstream society. For example, the growth of global capitalism in the 1980s and 1990s accelerated income disparities disproportionately affecting black Americans. Despite the gains of the American civil rights movement, segregation and inequality in housing and electoral politics persist. Racial profiling beliefs among African Americans contribute to widespread mistrust of and cynicism about the criminal justice system. The mainstream media often stereotypes and portrays negative images of young blacks, particularly in reporting on crime. Finally, the prevalence of social ills, such as high unemployment, incarceration, gang activity, gun homicide suicide, and HIV/AIDS has contributed to the worldview of hip-hop subculture. The implications of these factors have created an enormous divide between the hip-hop generation and the preceding generation of African Americans, which was influenced by the black Church and the civil rights and Black Power movements. Young blacks are using hip-hop culture to reach and teach black communities about economic and social justice and taking action. Politically radical rap videos have in turn led white teenagers to become more racially tolerant and less likely to identify with reactionary racial political positions (Christenson and Roberts, 1998).

Although the literature has focused predominantly on popular practices in the United States and the United Kingdom, youth subcultures are prevalent in many contemporary societies but remain relatively unknown outside of their immediate geographic region. Many of these subcultures carry common names (such as hip-hop or skinheads) but display variations based on the historical and political conditions of the societies in which they developed (McKay and Goddard, 2009). For example, the hip-hop subculture in Romania has developed to serve much the same function in relation to national politics as African-American hip-hop did in the United States (Şorcaru and Popescu, 2009), while Estonian youth have embraced the subculture as a means to express their local values and attitudes, particularly in relation to gender roles (Kobin and Allaste, 2009).

In another example, when Russian Neo-Nazi groups first appeared in Moscow in 1992, they were more attracted to imitating the music and style of Western skinheads after the fall of the Iron Curtain rather than expressing racist ideologies. After enduring the collapse of the Soviet economic and educational systems and witnessing state violence and xenophobia introduced by mass migration, disillusioned youth began to adopt the political leanings of their Western skinhead counterparts (Salagaev et al., 2009). Many of these groups justify their ethnocentrism as nationalism and view themselves as defenders of their home country (Omel'chenko and Garifzianova, 2009). Skinhead groups within Russia can vary widely in terms of dress code, fluidity of membership in the group, organizational structure, and ideologies. Skinhead groups have a sizable presence across Eastern Europe, in Slovakia, Lithuania, and the Balkans, with the region emerging as the new European front for Neo-Nazi activity (Blazak, n.d.).

South Africa offers another interesting example of youth subcultures developing in a unique historical context. Following World War II, South Africa experienced the rise of apartheid as well as the emergence of two prominent youth subcultures. Black youth were attracted to the *Tstosi* lifestyle, a gang subculture that evolved in the social deprivation and stunted mobility of Johannesburg and Soweto (Glaser, 2000), while white youth were drawn to the Ducktails, a subculture that transcended lines of class and gender and whose members 'were hedonistic, rebellious, apolitical and had little respect for law, education or work' (Mooney, 2005: 42). Although these groups formed, in part, to distinguish themselves from members of the other, they engaged in remarkably similar 'thug' and 'street corner' activities deemed to be anti-social by mainstream society. This rebellious response to social norms is still evident among popular South African youth subcultures. Many black youth now belong to a subculture dubbed *izikhothane*, the defining characteristic of which is the burning of one's own expensive clothes, shoes, alcohol, and money in elaborate public performances of self-expression. Although *izikhothane* has been described in terms ranging from 'escapist ambitions' to youth responding to 'a style-consuming public' (Matheolane, 2012), there is little doubt that this growing youth subculture has captured the attention of mainstream South African society and prompted discussion about the role of consumerism in the lives of today's young people.

Austin (2008) described three trends which emerged in youth subcultures after the 1970s, evidenced in the above examples. First, there emerged recognition of the pre-adolescent segment of the population as a separate economic, social, and cultural market. Youth culture has become younger. Although the pre-adolescent group has limited mobility and autonomy, it is nevertheless segmented from adult and adolescent cultures within the context of institutions such as school, which was a necessary precondition for many aspects of youth culture to emerge. The shared experience of consumer goods, adult authority in socializing institutions, and common sport activities strengthened the cultural connections at an earlier age, while at the same time further distancing pre-adolescents from the experiences of their parents and older siblings. A second trend identified by Austin is that the youth culture acquired new meanings and got older. Young people continued the youth subculture affiliations into adulthood, and youth cultures became 'lifestyles'. Finally, Austin's third trend shows that new information and communication technologies, particularly the Internet, created spaces for new youth cultures to form. The Internet has brought about a unique set of cyber-cultures, allowing

new cultural and political affiliations to emerge, as discussed in greater detail later in this chapter.

CHILDREN AS POLITICAL ACTORS IN NON-DEMOCRATIC AND TRANSITIONAL REGIMES

As the previous section on the emergence of youth subcultures suggests, youth political involvement and the conceptualization of children as political actors are subject to historical context and the dominant political regime. According to Garbarino (2011: 444), 'there is resonance between the way kids relate to authority and the way in which authority is organized in the lives of adults in their society'. In authoritarian societies, rather than being viewed as independent subjects of social relations, children were instead regarded as 'property' of adults. These societies also exhibited a marked absence of a special youth policy. Totalitarian regimes, however, represented a contrasting approach to children, in that childhood was regarded as very public (Qvortrup, 2001). In these systems, children were deliberately and from an early age drawn into the public sphere. They were present at demonstrations and celebrations, and there was a broad network connecting children's activities to adult organizations and parents' workplaces (Kirchhöfer, 1996; Qvortrup, 2001). This involvement implies that children often stood in a privileged position while conversely they were without power and had very little autonomy. In addition, there were powerful political organizations for children and youth with almost universal mobilization of the relevant age group (Wallace and Alt, 2001).

Despite the attempts of authorities in Nazi Germany and Soviet Communist Eastern Europe to gain absolute control of youth through the construction of monolith youth organizations such as Young Pioneer and Komsomol, youth subcultures nevertheless emerged under these regimes. Youth groups used non-political symbols such as American jazz and pop music, long hair, and free-style clothing to demonstrate their non-conformity with official politicized youth organizations. As Wallace and Alt (2001) noted, these young people were not politically opposed to the regime, but they were searching for some personal freedom that was lacking in totalitarian regimes. Both kinds of totalitarian regimes overreacted to this kind of informal and 'unorganized' youth and portrayed adherents of subcultures as enemies of the state. Recognizing the fact that Communist regimes of the 1970s and 1980s used political repressions to a significantly lesser extent compared with the Nazi or Stalinist eras, activists of subculture groups were not criminally punished or arrested. Instead, official youth organizations tried to incorporate alternative subcultures into youth policy, for example by providing new kinds of entertainment and sports.

The breakdown of the Soviet Communist bloc in the 1990s gave impetus to studies of childhood in a period of societal change. Although most of these studies were country-based case studies or small-scale comparative studies, they confirmed general rules that adult–child relations were altered as a consequence of broader macro political and social forces. Additionally, they provided insight into the ways in which children adjust to the circumstances of political turbulence and insecurity.

An early cohort of studies suggested that the prevailing political attitude in transitional societies was neither absolute trust nor active distrust, but rather scepticism of the new regime and its institutions of civil society (Mishler and Rose, 1997). This climate forced a redefinition of social contracts between polity and citizens, particularly for younger generations who were explicitly identified for political socialization and control under previous regimes. In transitional countries such as Bulgaria, Hungary, and Czech Republic, former youth organizations such as Young Pioneer and Komsomol were replaced by Boy and Girl Scouts, 4-H, and church-related social groups. Although these new organizations lacked the overt political functions of government-led youth groups, they nevertheless introduced young people to the concepts of mutual rights and obligations and fostered affinity to their community and nation (Flanagan et al., 1999). Not all youth, however, embraced this new sense of responsibility. Some transitional societies report a marked decrease in youth volunteerism after a successful change in regime as youth negotiate new social contracts (Schwartz, 2010). Other nations experience a delayed transition from adolescence to adulthood as intergenerational relations, rights, and obligations are redefined by both children and adults (see, for example, the case of Serbia in Tomanović and Ignjatović, 2007).

Kirchhöfer's (1996) study of 10- to 14-year-old children in East Germany after the collapse of the Honecker era offers evidence of how children adjust their perception of social relations in transitional societies. Children interviewed in 1990 (just after the fall of the Berlin Wall) had a much weaker sense of privacy, with more cooperative relations between family, school, and local government. In the later post-transitional period (1994), children recounted more individualized experiences and weaker bonds between home, school, and local community. Children were warned to limit contacts with others and were taught that they should not receive or offer help. As a result, families became more closed and schools became more detached from the family. Quite different from the previous Communist era, children in post-totalitarian societies were not encouraged to participate in any public arrangements; their experiences became alienated from political and administrative institutions. As Kirchhöfer (1996: 226) observed, 'childhood appears presently to have been taken out of political structures or political structures seem no longer to function in childhood', leading to a paradox in which open societies seem to discourage the public behaviour of younger citizens.

Nonetheless, adolescents have a unique ability to cope with social and political upheaval of their known regime (Botcheva, Feldman and Leiderman, 2002; Pinquart, Silbereisen and Juang, 2004). A study of 11- to 12-year-old students in Eastern Germany found that adolescents did not suffer from psychological distress after the German unification which brought about the regime change. Authors suggest that this can be explained by individual and age-specific reasons. First, the ability to adapt to social change is strongly related to self-efficacy. High levels of self-efficacy are associated with a decrease in psychological distress. Second, adolescents do not suffer from adult concerns such as unemployment and high inflation; for adolescents, positive changes such as political freedom and better consumption opportunities outweigh the negative aspects of transformation (Pinquart et al., 2004).

In the second half of the 1990s, large cross-national surveys captured first-time comparative data on youth in former authoritarian/totalitarian and democratic countries. Between 1991 and 1997, a survey to measure the link between education and authoritarian/democratic attitudes collected data from nearly 10,000 students (mainly 18- to 27-year-olds) in 44 countries (Farnen and Meloen, 2000). Soon thereafter, the International Association for the Evaluation of Educational Achievements carried out the first Civic Education Study (IEA CIVED) amongst 14-year-olds in 28 countries (Torney-Purta, Schwille, and Amadeo, 1999).

The Farnen-Meloen study collected data over a long period of time and the sample included a wide age cohort; therefore, its findings of transitional societies must be interpreted with the caveat that a rapidly changing social environment potentially alters students' attitudes towards politics and government. Nevertheless, both the Farnen-Meloen study and the IEA CIVED found that young people in post-Communist societies (more often than their peers in continuous democracies) do not possess left- or right-wing leanings. According to Farnen and Meloen, this may be due to the lesser efficacy of post-totalitarian schooling in promoting democratic values. However, the regime bias is not always evident. In the IEA CIVED study, the high performing group – in which students had good civic competencies and strong support of democratic values – included countries with long-standing traditions of democracy as well as emerging democracies. At the same time, there was remarkable diversity in civic competencies and behavioural attitudes within established Western democracies. Regardless of individual nations' democratic histories, Northern and Southern European countries form two distinct groups in terms of teenagers' attitudes towards citizenship and political participation (Lehmann, 2007; Torney-Porta et al., 2001). Thus, not only the governmental regime but also the broader political context and regional political culture seem to play an important role in political socialization.

SCHOOLS AS AGENTS OF POLITICAL SOCIALIZATION

Schools, and educational systems more broadly, are major agents in the political socialization of children and youth. Although the family often is the first introduction to a child's sense of politics, this influence generally is confined to conveying attitudes towards authority and rules and to communicating preference for a particular political party (Davies, 1965; Goldstein, 2009). In contrast, school settings often provide the primary environment for learning about democratic rights and responsibilities, conveying this information in larger and more public groups and by different adults than the child experiences at home (Flekkøy and Kaufman, 1997).

The earliest signs of political consciousness appear in children as young as five years old, the age at which many children enter formalized schooling (Connell, 1971). According to psychological research, children are capable of recognizing political/national symbols as early as age 5 to 7 (Dawson and Prewitt, 1969). At that age, children explain political institutions by their own psychological reactions, often personalizing images (for example, 'Council, the man, he tells the people where the houses should be. He is in London'; Furth, 1980: 43). Most 7- to 8-year-old children are able to distinguish personal and social roles in familiar situations, but they cannot interpret or integrate social events beyond their personal experiences. At that age, children are able to represent hierarchical relations, for example to distinguish the figure of the 'boss' as someone who owns business or government and is very rich. Young children are not able to understand the mechanisms of power representation or mediation that give ground to discussion about authoritarianism at a young age (Berti and Bombi, 1981). Yet authoritarianism decreases with age (Farnen and Meloen, 2000).

At age 9 to 11, children can understand basic social mechanisms such as exchange, different interests, and roles (Berti and Bombi, 1981; Furth, 1980; Stevens, 1982). 'Nevertheless, their understanding of the political system and governmental institutions is still quite vague and their thinking about the general needs of a societal community … is concrete and therefore unsystematic and principally at affective-emotional level' (Furth, 1980: 50). Furth (1980: 47) concludes that 'the understanding of what a societal community is and how government functions is only rarely developed in children below age twelve'. Therefore extensive political education in school starts later, typically at age 12 and culminates at ages 14 to 16, which in Europe corresponds to lower secondary education (Eurydice, 2012). Over 75 per cent of 14-year-old students are able to handle questions on the nature of laws and political rights. Few students, however, can answer more demanding questions on the nature of elections, political reforms, or the social impact of a market economy (Torney-Purta et al., 2001).

Some countries have long-established traditions of teaching civic and citizenship education, whereas others have only recently introduced the subject. Somewhat surprisingly, these decisions do not necessarily correlate to the 'age' of democracy in the country. In France, Scandinavia, and the United States, for example, school has had an explicit role in citizenship education since the beginning of mass education in the nineteenth century (Osler and Starkey, 2005). In contrast, England did not introduce citizenship education as a separate subject until 2002. Some authors argue that the introduction of the subject has been, for many countries, a response to a perceived crisis in democracy featured inter alia by the growing political apathy and anti-social behaviour amongst youth (Biesta and Lawy, 2006; Faulks, 2000; Qualifications and Curriculum Authoriyu, 1998; Weller, 2007).

Social and political context have impacted not only the introduction of political education but, even more importantly, the content and approaches of this education. Anglo-American tradition typically has stressed individual liberties and the concept of 'citizenship', whereas Continental Europe (such as France, Germany, and the Baltic states) has been prone to nationhood and civic knowledge. The dominant contemporary trend, at least in Europe, strongly favours active and multicultural citizenship, which increases pressure to move education policy from teaching passive nationality (*Staatsangehörigkeit*) to active citizenship (*Staatsbürgershaft*; Terkessidis, 2003; Kerr, 2005). Practical implementation of this change, however, has proven difficult. For instance, the Catholic Church and other major conservative actors in Spain have opposed the inclusion of Education for Citizenship since its introduction into the Spanish school system in 2006. Their opposition is based on the claim that such education impinges on parents' rights to be the exclusive source of moral education for their children (Motos, 2010). Former Communist countries in Eastern Europe face additional challenges, since indoctrination and the passing on of factual (often historical) knowledge have been typical pedagogical practices in these countries (Council of Europe, 2004; Torney-Purta et al., 1999).

Although there is basic consensus amongst researchers and policy makers that teaching citizenship is essential to democracy, many issues still remain under debate, primarily due to the contested nature of the concept of citizenship itself. In traditional liberal democracies, citizenship is bound to the nation-state and its mechanism of representation through voting. In the latest theoretical accounts, however, cosmopolitan and communitarian/local models of citizenship are suggested as better suited to the contemporary realities of nation-states and governance (Beck, 2006; Roudometof, 2005). Feminist writers argue that this turn is especially important for children and teenagers, since the adult-centric nature of liberal democracies exclude most youth from active participation (Weller, 2007). Teenagers are engaged at local and cosmopolitan citizenship levels that are illustrated by multiple fluid identities, green issues, Internet-based participation, and selective consumption (Osler and Starkey, 2005; Weller, 2007).

Effective curricula in civic and citizenship education, however, do not reflect these innovative approaches and continue to suffer from adultism and conventional content of representative democracies. Students are predominantly regarded as citizens-in-the-making rather than as actors capable of engaging in current political and civic activities (Gordon and Taft, 2010; James and James, 2004; Jans, 2004; Osler and Starkey, 2005; Weller, 2007). One of the more recent citizenship education curricula in Europe, introduced in England in 2002 (as referenced above), pays more attention to communitarian levels and gives teaching and learning of children's participation skills a central focus (Kerr, 2005). Opponents, however, still find that this curriculum 'fails to acknowledge globalization or even to recognize an international dimension' (Osler and Starkey, 2005: 91–2).

Despite some improvement in formal citizenship education in school, curricula continue to face accusations of 'status quo biases … [which] encourage children to believe in the substantive merits of particular existing laws and institutions' (MacMullen, 2011: 873). Donnelly (2009) suggested a similar bias in classroom education regarding the US Supreme Court, whereby children are taught to be deferential to the wisdom of the Court and those who have participated in popular resistance to the Court are portrayed as villainous.

A key dimension in which formal curricula seem to lag behind the real developments in democratic societies concerns the concept of multiculturalism. In countries with significant class and race differences, migrant children score lower in civic knowledge. This is apparent in the United States, where African-American and Hispanic students demonstrate knowledge below the national average, whereas students with Asian backgrounds perform close to the white students (Baldi et al., 2001). Findings of the Programme for International Student Assessment (PISA) carried out by the Organisation for Economic Co-operation and Development (OECD) show that schools in Germany and Belgium with a high proportion of immigrant children have significantly lower achievement levels, which seems to confirm the critique on institutional discrimination along the race and class lines in these countries (OECD, 2006). Farnen warned that the lower achievement level of minority students is not solely an educational problem. In the 2000 United States presidential elections in Florida, ten times more minority votes (in comparison to white votes) were thrown out and not counted for technical reasons. In such instances, lower knowledge may bring less voice in democratic government systems (Farnen, 2003). Thus, 'for many children, schooling acts neither as a channel of upward mobility nor as an instrument of social change and personal development but as yet another medium of social control' (Boyden, 1997: 213).

Educational systems in general (Alanen, 1994), and particularly in Germany (Terkessidis, 2003), the United States (Farnen, 2003), and the United Kingdom (Kiwan, 2007; Osler and Starkey, 2005; Wyness, 2006) are criticized for their prevailing 'white and middle-class' standards of citizenship. According to these authors, giving up the monopoly of the nation state–school nexus and paying more attention to the non-formal arenas of citizenship helps to overcome this narrow class-centric approach. However, some evolution in approaches to the political socialization of immigrants already can be found in national practices. During 50 years of mass immigration, Germany has practised various approaches to the political education of immigrant children. Prior to the 1980s there was no special education policy targeted to immigrants. After the concept of pedagogy for foreigners (*Ausländerpädagogik*) was introduced in the 1990s, this became the main approach in multicultural education. Today there is a more central focus on immigrant children, but the concept of intercultural education still divides nationals and *Ausländers* (foreigners) and is not built upon civic autonomy of equal individuals (Terkessidis, 2003). Gomolla and Radtke (2002) argue that many German teachers do not envisage school as an educational institution for all citizens. German 'school' tends to be a particular synonym for German culture, and language deficits during school enrolment are seen as an indication of insufficiency for German cultural stability.

Public schools in the United States also struggle to achieve equality in civic education for their diverse student bodies. Children who fall outside of the dominant white, middle-class paradigm tend to be excluded from the design of many civic education programmes and are therefore marginalized from political participation even from a young age. Savit (2009) reported that social studies education – including components of civics, history, economics, and government – has been reduced or eliminated entirely from the curricula of 36 per cent of US public schools

in order to focus on math and literacy as a consequence of the No Child Left Behind policy. These struggling schools that have received low or failing scores by the policy's standards predominantly serve African-American, Hispanic, and lower-income populations. Savit also noted a resulting achievement gap for these populations: 'African American and Hispanic students consistently perform worse than their white counterparts on civics tests; middle- and upper-income students consistently outperform their lower-income peers. Unsurprisingly, the social studies achievement gap manifests itself among adults as well' (p. 1272). Zubrycki (2011) further supported this conclusion, citing the results of studies by the American Enterprise Institute, which argued that civics is as critical an educational topic as math and literacy but that the discrepancy in scores between advantaged and disadvantaged students remains larger for civics than for math or reading scores.

Dominant white and middle-class norms of schooling disproportionately affect the behaviour of immigrant and minority students. These students more clearly understand that they are different (Terkessidis, 2003), causing many students to mask part of their identity by acting the part of their native classmates to achieve academically (Wyness, 2006). Wyness notes that, in comparison to other social arenas like the shopping mall and the night club, schools are more oriented towards national and white and middle-class standards.

Given the traditional view of politics as a male-dominated sphere, one might expect to find further distinct differences in civil knowledge based on gender. However, overall changes in society and educational curricula during late modernity have had their impact, striking a new gender balance. The first IEA civic education study, conducted in 1971, found that male students performed better than females in civic knowledge, and this variance was even more evident in older students (Torney, Oppenheim and Farnen, 1975). More than twenty years later (1999), gender differences in achievement were almost diminished; in several countries girls performed even slightly better than boys (Torney-Purta et al., 2001). The third IEA study showed that earlier trends have been completely reversed: in all 38 participating countries, girls outperformed boys in civic knowledge (Schulz et al., 2010).

In addition to socio-economic and cultural factors, the level of civic knowledge is related to the learners' interest in the topics. Findings of the IEA CIVED survey and Weller's (2007) small-scale study in England support this argument. According to both sets of research, achievement level is higher when the issues seem relevant to the learner. For example, teenagers' knowledge is higher in human rights and lower in electoral issues; 49 per cent of interviewed British students aged 13 to 16 recalled having learned about human rights and deemed it the most useful topic within citizenship classes (Weller, 2007).

The effect of schooling on adolescents' civic competencies remains a complicated issue with diverse and sometimes even contradictory findings. For example, a previous IEA study found that 'the average annual knowledge increment is comparable in size to annual achievement gains in more curriculum-driven domains, such as mathematics' (Amadeo et al., 2002: 46). Yet, compared with the results of math and science knowledge, between-country differences are less remarkable in the area of civics and citizenship. This may be explained by the stronger effect of out-of-school factors like media consumption or dominant value orientations in society. However, none of the possible predictors of civic knowledge (such as home and cultural capital, media use, participation in youth activities) has a major explanatory power (Amadeo et al., 2002). For upper secondary students, school-related factors, such as a classroom climate that is open to discussion, become less important in comparison to adolescents in lower secondary school (Amadeo et al., 2002; Torney-Purta et al., 2001).

In sum, one can conclude that the status of civic and citizenship education in formal schooling is still controversial. On the one hand, the topic has established itself as a separate subject or a cross-curricular theme throughout Europe, North America, and most countries in Latin America, Australasia, and the Far East. At the same time, there is growing criticism of the current state of affairs. Several authors find that formal curricula are overly oriented to compliance and promote only 'proper' (in other words, convenient to policy makers) activism (Weller, 2007); neglect painful issues like racism and xenophobia (Diemer and Li, 2011; Osler and Starkey, 2005); overlook the civic experiences and forms of participation of youth of colour (Bosco, 2010; Kirshner and Ginwright, 2012); and ignore teaching of threats to democracy such as authoritarianism, nationalism, and religious fundamentalism (Farnen and Meloen, 2000). Even when curricula include notions of multiculturalism, critical thinking, and active citizenship, a gap in implementation often still exists (Council of Europe, 2004). Reliance on old-fashioned passive methods of teaching also is reported as an on-going concern across countries (Homana and Barber, 2007; Ireland et al., 2006; Torney-Purta et al., 2001).

FORMS OF YOUTH POLITICAL PARTICIPATION

Camino and Zeldin (2002: 213) have noted that 'whereas engagement is both a right and responsibility of citizenship, and whereas inclusivity benefits both the individual and the collective, it is ironic that pathways for civic engagement remain extremely limited for youth'. Only conventional forms of political activism such as voting or being a member of a political party or a legislative or policy-making body are typically promoted, whereas sparse attention is given to grassroots-level practices, informal youth initiatives, or other unconventional forms of youth political expression. The Millennial Generation (those born from the late 1980s until the early 2000s) prefers new patterns of political participation and does not regard voting as the primary duty of citizens; indeed, voting numbers among young voters remain relatively low, while youth involvement in voluntary and community service in many societies is disproportionately high. This contradiction is largely attributed to the lack of youth-appropriate activities and agendas for political and civic engagement.

In recent years, however, youth and adults alike have challenged the idea of confining youth to the periphery of their communities, leading to unique contemporary means by which youth may become politically and civically engaged, including volunteering, school-based service learning, public policy/ consultation, community coalition involvement, participation in organizational decision making, and youth organizing and activism (Camino and Zeldin, 2002). As Pizmony-Levy (2007) pointed out, it is not important to young people whether their participation is classified as conventional or nonconventional. In all countries except the United States, adolescents tend to support either all or none of them. Thus, young people are efficiently recombining different elements and creating a new style of political participation (Pizmony-Levy, 2007).

Voting

Despite shifting attitudes and growing recognition of alternative contexts for political involvement, the participation of young people in traditional forms of political activism has retained its significance. Voting is still the most supported form of political participation across nations. In countries that participated in the international civic and citizenship education studies carried out by the International Association for the Evaluation of Educational Achievements, an average of 81 per cent of lower and 85 per cent of upper secondary school students intended to vote in national elections in the future (Amadeo et al., 2002; Schulz et al., 2010).

Although overall support for voting is high, there is also remarkable variance across countries, which is associated with the features of the governmental system and political culture of respective nations. In some emerging democracies around the world (for example, Colombia, Guatemala, Republic of Korea, Indonesia, Lithuania), young people are more enthusiastic to vote compared to their peers in established democracies. However, established democracies do not form a single group, and the intention of younger generations to vote seems to be positively associated with a country's effective turnout for elections. For example, in Switzerland, where voter turnout at parliamentary elections is between 42 per cent and 45 per cent, young people below voting age exhibit a comparable intention (42–48 per cent) to vote in the future. Similarly, in Denmark, the effective voter turnout is relatively high (83–87 per cent) and youth intention to vote even higher (91–97 per cent) (Amadeo et al., 2002; Torney-Porta et al., 2001).

The intention to vote in future elections, however, is not always put into practice. Ballington (2002) refers to the well-documented phenomenon that voter turnout is, across countries, lowest among young voters (aged 18–29 years). According to survey estimates, only around 40 per cent of voters age 18 to 24 in the United Kingdom, and fewer than 50 per cent of first-time voters in South Africa, voted in recent parliamentary elections (Ballington, 2002). Furthermore, various election studies report that the turnout rate among young voters is 10 per cent below that of senior citizens in the majority of established democracies (Wattenberg, 2012).

Low trust towards institutions of representative democracy is commonly offered as an explanation for why young people do not vote despite a previous intention to do so (Dalton, 2009). A survey of 15- to 25-year-olds in eight European countries found that 62 per cent of respondents see elections as the most effective form of political participation. At the same time, however, these young people do not trust political parties, which are the core institution of the electoral process. In the case of non-governmental organizations (NGOs), youth attitudes are reversed – NGOs are highly trusted but regarded as non-efficient structures in influencing politics (EUYOUPART, 2005). This contradiction can be explained, at least in part, by a lack of youth's holistic understanding of policy processes. Furthermore, first-time voters often experience a sense of anti-climax after this initial political participation which, despite a continued interest in political matters and support of the democratic process, results in a more critical attitude towards elected officials (Henn, Weinstein and Wring, 2002). It is noteworthy that, while young people do not trust political parties in general, more than half of this population nevertheless identify with a particular party (EUYOUPART, 2005; Schulz et al., 2010).

Volunteering in civic and service organizations

Volunteerism in youth-oriented organizations can provide a broader range of opportunities for youth who may be lacking in certain resources or skills to contribute to the civic well-being of their communities. These organizations and experiences in turn socialize young people to become engaged in politics, both in their youth and later into adulthood, by providing opportunities to develop skills in organizing and leading activities that are generally unavailable in the day-to-day life of most youth (Hanks, 1981). Research has shown that cultural and community service-oriented organizations are more effective than religious, ethnic, and athletic groups at developing youth political participation (McFarland and Thomas, 2006; Quintelier, 2008). Interestingly, membership in multiple voluntary organizations is correlated with greater political activity, while spending the equivalent amount of time in a single organization does not produce a similar increase in political engagement (Quintelier, 2008).

The Civic Voluntarism Model proposed by Verba, Schlozman, and Brady (1995) contributes to an explanation of the unequal participation of more affluent children in more traditional political activities (such as youth councils) by recognizing the unique contributions of both motivation and capacity to one's civic participation, as well as the means by which one is recruited to participate. Motivation is a key factor to participation: one must *want* to be involved. Even with this motivation, however, one might still be limited in the number of appropriate paths for involvement. For youth specifically, age alone can be a significant barrier to participation in traditional forms of political life. A lack of resources such as time, money, and skills may further limit one's capacity to fully participate. Youth are especially vulnerable to a lack of these resources: the majority of their time is spent in school or in school-based activities, many are still financially dependent on a parent or caregiver, and many have not had the opportunity to develop the concrete skills required for effective citizenship as it is traditionally understood. Finally, even given adequate motivation and capacity, one is more likely to become involved in political and civic activities if asked. For example, simply asking young people if they intend to vote does not have the same impact as a direct, personal appeal to do so. In terms of more traditional activities, more affluent youth are more likely to have the requisite combination of capacity and recruitment to make use of their political and civic motivations.

Several factors influence the motivation for youth volunteer participation and subsequent adult political behaviour, including the opportunity to discuss civic and political issues with adults, living in a civic-minded community (Kahne and Sporte, 2008), close familial relationships and parental involvement in the life of a young person (Matthews, Hempel and Howell, 2010; Smith, 1999), living in a household with someone else who is actively involved in volunteering (Zukin et al., 2006), and the social integration of both oneself and the peers in one's social network during teenage years (Settle, Bond and Levitt, 2011). Therefore, simply creating opportunities for youth volunteer engagement is insufficient to foster a sense of political and civic responsibility. Communities must also work to create an environment that actively values and practices civic involvement and encourages youth to question and process their role in the political system.

In order to encourage civically minded youth, thousands of public schools in the US have established a quota of volunteer hours that each student must fulfil as a requisite to graduation. Such school-based service learning and community service – which has experienced resurgence in the past two decades, prompted in large part by the National and Community Service Trust Act of 1993 and the subsequent formation of the Corporation for National Service – provides a viable alternative to traditional community-based volunteering activities. According to Camino and Zeldin (2002: 217), 'school-based service learning is an instructional method that seeks to maximize individual learning while concurrently addressing community needs. Service learning requires schools to offer educational experiences integrating community service, "classroom" knowledge, and critical reflection to promote understanding and skill among students'. In the context of Verba et al.'s Civic Voluntarism Model, these programs address all three components of motivation, capacity, and recruitment to encourage civic participation from a wide range of students that might otherwise be excluded from such activities.

The trend toward incorporating a civic service component into school curricula continues despite inconsistent and weak evidence of its effectiveness in yielding long-term citizenship effects. School policy makers and administrators indicate that service-learning is most important in helping student become more active community members and encouraging student altruism, in addition to having a more general positive impact on students' civic education and academic achievement (Scales and Roehlkepartain, 2004). Numerous students have demonstrated, however, that students who have and have not participated in school-based service activities do not evidence significant differences in feelings of social responsibility (Fenzel and Leary, 1997; Giles and Eyler, 1994), voting behaviours (Jastrzab et al., 1996; long-term commitment to philanthropic behaviour (Ford, 1994), or citizenship attitudes (Ridgell, 1994; Smith, 1994).

Much of the discrepancy in the reported effectiveness of service learning and community service programs has been attributed to the broad variation with which these programs are implemented. The most successful service learning programs clearly specify and communicate learning goals and objectives related to the service; provide quality orientation to and supervision of the service experience; allow for direct contact with those outside of one's institution; and include frequent, quality, and diverse opportunities for reflection (Hurd, 2008). Current research also suggests that the spirit of service-learning is most meaningful when applied to on-going projects – both big and small – rather than isolated or sporadic activity (Fox, 2010). Furthermore, research has demonstrated that service-learning projects have the most positive impact on self-concept and future political participation when they allow students significant voice in and ownership of the project (Morgan and Streb, 2001).

Policy making

Throughout the 1990s, many societies turned attention to the idea that children should participate in public affairs and have a voice in decisions that affect them (Prout et al., 2006). Attempts have been made at national and international levels to introduce structures for young people to participate in forming policies that affect them. These participatory practices – typically in the form of children community councils, youth forums, or parliaments – are particularly prevalent in Europe. For example, a European Youth

Parliament was established in 1990, followed in 1992 by the Council of Europe's adoption of the European Charter on the Participation of Young People in Municipal and Regional Life. More recently, the UK Youth Parliament was established in 2001 and consists of 400 elected members aged 11–18.

Despite the growth of such youth forums and parliaments across different levels of governance, the majority of these structures afford negligible weight to the voice of child participants. Youth political and civic participation largely remains construed, by both children and adults, as an 'adult' activity carried out in 'adult' institutions, where children are little more than a token presence and the meaningful inclusion of children still presents a problem (Jans, 2004; Prout et al., 2006; Roche, 1999; Weller, 2007). Many contemporary participatory structures remain hierarchical and institutionalized, using only traditional methods of administration and often working within electoral cycles. Even those adult politicians who are supportive of children's participation in policy issues regard it primarily as an educational activity for children and not as a way to implement children's voices in the policy (Prout et al., 2006). As a result, well-intentioned initiatives like youth councils and parliaments often become training grounds for making children active citizens in the future, whereas the impact of this involvement on current policies and practices remains marginal.

Few data are available on the impact of child engagement in policymaking. The available data consist primarily of country reports, written by national adult experts, and some case studies with children as interviewees, whereas authentic 'children-made' resources are rare. According to Hendrik (2001), this situation happens more often in areas where children are not recognized as autonomous actors and their views therefore remain undocumented.

A key aspect often criticized in the available literature is that children's participation remains at the lowest level of public engagement (Hart, 1992; Horelli, 1998; Osler and Starkey, 2005; Wyness, 2006). Members of youth councils often feel that they are listened to but not heard and that their proposals are not given serious consideration. According to Weller (2007), teenagers in particular are quite cynical towards formal policy institutions and local MPs. The main reason, highlighted in participants' interviews and diaries, is that teenagers are 'not heard', 'nothing has changed', and there was no real impact as a result of their participation and input. Young representatives lack feedback from the adult elected representatives and city officials, while at the same time, the youth themselves do not effectively communicate with peers outside the organization. There is also a danger that children who are engaged in youth councils tend to be socio-economically better off and, while contributing to the children–adults dialogue, do not reflect the full spectrum of children's needs and experiences (Lansdown, 2001). In this way, a double alienation from politics may occur within disadvantaged youth populations.

Schools offer the most common institutional setting in which young people first participate in issues of policy. In all European countries, for example, there is legislation recommending or enforcing the establishment of student representative bodies and the involvement of students in school decision making. Election of class representatives is the most common activity, while student participation in school governing boards has been enacted in 31 European countries. In the majority of these countries, student involvement consists of informative and consulting functions. Only 10 of these countries, to varying degrees, extend decision-making power to students (Eurydice, 2012).

Despite a similar legal framework for the implementation of these structures, participation rates vary widely across countries. The IEA ICCS study showed that 40 per cent of 14-year-olds participate in student government, council, or parliament and have been involved in decision making on how the school is run. Several countries with very different democratic experiences and political cultures, such as Colombia, Dominican Republic, Greece, Norway, and Poland, were placed above the international mean. In contrast, Estonia, Finland, Korea and Austria each reported low levels of students' participation in decision making (Schulz et al., 2010).

Student councils and other forms of school democracy are mostly viewed as having a positive effect on civic activism of young people (Eurydice, 2012). Councils have the potential to increase a student's sense of belonging and self-efficacy by demonstrating that the school is responsive to students' interests (Ireland, Kerr, Lopes, Nelson, and Cleaver, 2006; Osler and Starkey, 2005). However, poor examples of citizenship in practice within schools have the potential to disengage younger children and teenagers and may therefore have a negative impact on the education of potentially active citizens (Weller, 2007).

Existing data on the impact of student councils on school decision making, or more widely on education policy, are few and conflicting. Despite the prevalence of school-based youth participatory structures, some authors note the irony that the practice of effectively engaging and consulting youth is even less developed in education policy than in other policy areas, and recent education reforms provide rather discouraging support of this suggestion (Osler and Starkey, 2005; Whitty, 2002; Wyness, 2006). In addition, data show that students only moderately believe in the efficacy of councils. Those students who are members of the representative bodies tend to have higher collective efficacy and are more likely to stay politically active after they have completed school (EUYOUPART, 2005). Other students, however, may have critical or even cynical views of student councils, seeing them as 'silly' and 'not serious' (Weller, 2007: 85).

Such conflicting attitudes and research findings can, at least partly, be attributed to rigid organizational structure and authoritarian management practices, the vague role of participative bodies, and excessive bureaucracy in educational systems. Children's participation in schools and education policy usually remains on the lowest level of Arnstein's (1969) participation ladder. Children have the right to voice their interests but rarely to shape decisions, and those decisions over which they are given power are usually inconsequential (such as selecting the theme colours for a school dance). Even rarer are instances of children's involvement in activities such as curriculum development. 'From this point of view, schools seem to experience similar problems to those that characterise democratic societies as a whole, in balancing governance, representation, and participation' (Losito, 2004: 116).

Political protest and graffiti

Over the last half century, there has been a considerable shift in the popular perception of protest actions as a tool of democratic political participation. In their influential book *Political Action*, Barnes and Kaase (1979) considered the traditional view of political protest as a threat to democracy: participation in protest actions was not regarded as a characteristic of a 'good citizen' or something that young people should practice. Democracies today are witnessing a significant increase in protest movements, resulting in many questioning previous theoretical accounts and assumptions about the political preferences of young people. However, the general public remains reluctant to accept political protest as normal youth political activism. On the one hand, much attention is given to the so-called 'apathy thesis', based primarily on age group data and low election turnout figures of the younger generation (Dalton, 2011; Milner, 2010; Wattenberg, 2012). At the same time, schoolchildren who participated in protest marches in the United Kingdom, Germany, and other European countries against the Iraq War were received by adults with confusion, fear, and negativism. The competence of the protesters was questioned, with concerns about the manipulation of youth and possible harm being done to children arising as dominant reactions in the mass media (Cunningham and Lavalette, 2004; Such et al., 2005).

Shifting social norms have affected adolescents' attitudes to political actions. Wattenberg (2012) asserted that although there was a cross-generational consensus about the 'good citizen' in years between 1950 and 1970, in the twenty-first century generations become more divided. Forms of political actions have diversified, and young people today show greater preference for informal grass-roots activities than to 'adult' forms of conventional political action. In the twenty-first century, one can witness increasing readiness amongst adolescents to be engaged in peaceful forms of political protest such as wearing a badge or T-shirt expressing a political message, taking part in a peaceful march, collecting signatures for a petition or boycotting certain products. A majority (51–57 per cent) of students in lower secondary school across 38 countries anticipated doing all of these activities (Schulz et al., 2010). Interest in more radical illegal protest activities has increased slightly as well. In 1999 less than 18 per cent of 14-year-olds across 28 countries considered painting graffiti, blocking traffic, or occupying buildings to demonstrate their political views (Torney-Purta et al., 2001). Ten years later, the percentages of students predicting their participation in these activities ranged from 19 per cent (occupying public buildings) to 27 per cent (spray-painting slogans) (Schulz et al. 2010).

The act of painting graffiti can be used as a demonstration of the shifting attitudes towards such protest activities. Graffiti appears primarily in local spatial environments that adults often do not deem to be legitimate sites of citizenship. However, for children and adolescents, bus stops, shopping centres, and skate parks have long represented important spaces for social communication. In these areas, young people may paint graffiti for purposes other than social rebellion; they can use this medium to communicate messages to the public or to express themselves visually and artistically. Thus, in many ways graffiti can be a positive phenomenon. For example, a content analysis of youth graffiti in Tel Aviv described how fears for democracy and peace in the region often were expressed alongside emotional words about the assassination of Israeli Prime Minister Rabin in 1995. These displays of graffiti were later recognized as a memorial place embraced by the entire community (Klingman and Shalev, 2001).

In another example, from a community in England, teenagers campaigned for skate park facilities and against the demolition of graffiti-sprayed bus stops. In cooperation with the town council, the teenagers repainted the bus stops ('busies'), their favourite space for gathering. The youth's reclaiming of the 'busies' illustrates the ways in which a cooperative attitude by local decision makers can promote teenagers' participation in their own communities, a lesson that Weller (2007: 114) deemed to be 'particularly valuable in the area where there has been notable conflict between the activities of teenagers and other local residents'.

A final example is seen in Kenya's 'peace train', for which that country's Rift Valley Railway officially authorized youth graffiti artists to spray-paint a 10-car commuter train with political icons and messages in the lead up to Kenya's 2013 presidential elections. The railway's decision was made in response to the widespread violence that occurred following the country's 2007 election, when 'young gangs torched, looted and killed … [and] mobs of youth literally tore up the train tracks and sold them for scrap metal' (Warner, 2013). Many of the same young graffiti artists who had been arrested in the past for spray-painting rail cars are now gaining recognition as important partners in Kenya's efforts for peaceful political processes.

Although popular opinion believes that political radicalism among youth is growing, survey data do not support this perceived trend. At the turn of the millennium, youth supporting violent protest as a means of political voice numbered less than half of those who supported non-violent protest (16 per cent and 44 per cent respectively) (Torney-Purta, Schwille, and Amadeo, 1999). Furthermore, only 2–3 per cent of young people age 15–25 in Austria, Estonia, Finland, France, Germany, and Italy report ever having a violent confrontation with police (EUYOUPART, 2005). While younger students have higher levels of trust for the government and higher support for violent forms of participation, older students trust the government less but are also less inclined to see violence as an acceptable solution to political problems (Amadeo et al., 2002).

TECHNOLOGY, YOUTH, AND POLITICAL ACTIVISM

Technology has played a central role in advancing both traditional and unconventional forms of participation and new social movements, introducing innovative means by which young people can gather and share ideas, lobby, network, raise funds, mobilize, recruit supporters, and communicate messages to the public (Forbrig, 2005). Postmodern youth are the first generation to have lived their entire lives in an electronic culture. Technology *is* youth culture today. It is a part of the culture's ideology, lifestyle, and language. New information and communication technologies (ICTs) are critical within the vision of postmodern youth culture. Earl and Schussman (2008) maintained that the affordances of the Internet and digital technologies facilitated the online production of protest activities, which has dramatically reduced the costs of organizing collective actions and accelerated the growth of movement societies.

Although the most popular medium for political information for young people in most countries is television, followed by newspapers and radio (Schulz et al., 2010), increasing accessibility of new media forms such as the Internet and satellite and cable

television have had an effect on overall patterns of media consumption. Norris (2002) categorized political cultures according to the most preferred channel of news media, distinguishing between 'TV cultures' (typical for Southern/Latin Europe and the United States) and 'newspaper cultures' (typical for Northern Europe). Data from IEA and EUYOUPART studies partly support Norris' theory. More than 75 per cent of students in lower and more than 85 per cent in upper secondary school in Estonia, Finland, Norway, and Sweden 'sometimes' or 'often' read newspapers, which exceeds international averages by 5 per cent and 10 per cent, respectively. Students in Chile, Cyprus, Portugal, Hungary, Greece, and Italy, in contrast, favour television news. For example, only 57 per cent of 14-year-olds in Portugal regularly read newspapers, but 89 per cent watch news broadcasts on television (Amadeo et al., 2002). Although there is some deviation from Norris' ideal types, it has become apparent that young people are part of the diversification of media consumption of their respective countries.

ICTs and the Internet in particular have become the tools forging new political communities of young people and facilitating new forms of active youth citizenship and participatory practice (Delli Carpini, 2000; Farthing, 2010; Norris, 2002; Vromen, 2008). The term 'netizenship' has been coined to describe this emerging form of citizenship that has resulted from new interactive ways for youth to create, distribute, and discuss political content (Milner, 2009). Kann et al., (2007) identified three gateways by which youth online presence leads to increased political participation. The first of these gateways is participatory culture. Kann et al. suggested that activities such as multi-player role-playing games allow youth to experience political sovereignty and collective openness, while developing democratic values and political problem-solving skills. The second gateway is political consumerism, which 'involves purchasing or refusing to purchase goods and services based on political, social, or ethical considerations rather than solely on price and quality' (Kann et al., 2007: para. 14). Such purchasing decisions raise youth awareness of significant issues such as labour practices and human rights concerns of which they might otherwise remain unaware. The third gateway identified by Kann et al. includes direct civic engagement, including formal online town hall meetings, informal public discourse in the form of blogs and user-moderated discussion boards, and candidates' presence on social media outlets such as Facebook and Twitter.

Within this shifting paradigm, young people are creating and reshaping new forms of politics. Today's youth and young adults appear to enact political expression in ways that are different from earlier generations – instead of influencing actions of elected officials and the state, they prefer to engage in politics related to lifestyle (Bennett, 2008; Dalton, 2008). This is largely explained by young people's low perception of the efficacy and attractiveness of formal political life (Delgado and Staples, 2007; Ginwright, 2009). Examples of these new forms of political participation are diverse and include such practices as 'boycott Nike' groups on Facebook, buying fair-trade and locally produced foods and goods, electoral blogs, and email campaigns to lobby about the ethics of rainforest agriculture (Farthing, 2010; Pew Research Center, 2004; Owen, 2008; Stolle, Hooghe and Micheletti, 2005). These new forms of participatory practices and social movements reflect the preferences of younger generations for participation in less hierarchical, less bureaucratic, loose informal networks; various lifestyle-related mobilization efforts; and individual actions, such as political consumerism (Inglehart, 1997; Stolle, Hooghe, and Micheletti, 2003).

Politically driven online participation is an important bridge to broader civic and political participation and action. A recent example is the popular uprisings across the Middle East, which were youth driven and galvanized by young people's desire for freedom and an end to authoritarian regimes and

corruption. Young people used the Internet and communication technology for social networking with other politically like-minded Arab youth, to undermine government efforts at censorship and control over information flow, to receive timely information from and communicate messages to the outside world, to raise civic awareness, to share their stories of injustice, and to mobilize and recruit supporters (Hashem, 2009; Hofheinz, 2005). The Internet also played a prominent role in youth engagement and participation in the 2008 US presidential election. There was a 14 per cent increase from the 2004 election in the percentage of 18- to 29-year-olds who reported going online for information about specific campaigns or general politics, compared to a 5 per cent increase for 50- to 64-year-olds. The Obama campaign successfully harnessed this trend to spread the candidate's message of hope and change that was so appealing to the younger generation in a format that was innovative yet familiar to them. The resulting campaign strategy 'combin[ed] digital-age technology with old-fashioned shoe leather' (Von Drehle, 2008), coupling traditional television advertising with the use of unconventional social media such as blogs and regular news feeds and emails. These means of encouraging young people to attend and organize campaign events, recruit friends, and donate money resulted in 'staggering numbers' of people giving small monetary donations online (Bennett, Wells, and Freelon 2010) and a near doubling of the youth vote when compared with the 2000 national election (Kirby et al., 2008).

Despite the growing presence of ICTs and the Internet in the political lives of youth, these technologies are not without limitation. Although ICTs have become more accessible due to declining costs for high-speed Internet access and basic computer models, many youth lack the requisite skills to take full advantage of these technologies, preventing their voices from being heard in electronic political realms (Milner, 2009). This lack of technological skills is particularly noteworthy because, according to a recent survey by Gerodimos (2012), mass media (television, newspapers, radio) continue to play a dominant role in bringing political issues and potential solutions to the attention of young people. Ostman (2012) noted that involvement with online user-generated content (UGC) predicts both offline and online political participation but cautioned that, in contrast to informational media use, UGC involvement is negatively related to political knowledge. Finally, Gerodimos (2012) found the political attitudes of many youth displayed an individual rather a collective orientation; for example, many youth expect or demand tangible benefits for their participation in online civic organizations. These individualistic tendencies run counter to traditional ideas of democratic citizenship, in which one's political actions are for the collective good.

CONCLUSION

Too often, youth are viewed as a problem to be solved, particularly when they exhibit attitudes of behaviours deemed to be 'antisocial' by adult mainstream society (Daiute, Stern, and Lelutiu-Weinberger, 2003). This chapter offered examples of institutions that, when faced with 'problem' youth, dismissed the usual punitive response and created mutually agreeable avenues by which youth could express their social and political views that were the basis of their actions. Such intergenerational collaboration and the recognition, from both sides, of 'both forward- and backward-looking rights and obligations to other generations' (Bohman, 2011: 137) are fundamental to achieving a fair balance of political power between the generations.

Apart from questions of fairness, however, the sceptical view of youth involvement in political life is empirically indefensible. It would be impractical and irresponsible, of course, to assume that children can participate

in political activities in the same way and assume the full extent of political responsibilities that adults do. But neither is it appropriate to assume that children, solely by the nature of being children, 'lack the minimal bundle of cognitive, emotional, and moral capacity necessary for justifiable participation in a democratic polity' (Rehfeld, 2011: 142–3).

Indeed, multiple forms of participation – particularly developments in technology and the growth of social media – may be expanding the modes of meaningful political expression. Eletronic blogs (for example, CommonAction; www.commonaction.blogspot.com) that discuss issues relevant to youth political involvement, virtual classrooms (such as Civic Voices; www.civicvoices.org) for students from around the world to participate in global conversations of democracy and citizenship, online communities (for example, The Freechild Project; www.freechild.org) that aim to connect young people with social change by presenting concrete actions and youth-centred resources, and the ever-increasing reach of technologies such as Facebook, Twitter, and YouTube allow young people to be politically involved while simultaneously exposing them to ideas and viewpoints that guide the development of their individual civic philosophies.

Young people can no longer be viewed as a passive and uniform category in the context of political participation; they do occupy increasingly diverse social positions and actively shape social arenas. As Wyness (2006: 94) noted, 'children are acting with others, making and taking decisions and demonstrating commitments and responsibilities that at the very least confound a "care and control" model of childhood'. Rather than interpreting increased youth activism as an abandonment of childhood and attempting to 'protect' children from political responsibilities, efforts should be made to encourage opportunities which allow children to embrace their rights as a distinctive category of citizens capable of taking action in matters that concern them.

In sum, the nearly universal (and clearly mistaken) assumption by educators and developmentalists that civic education has no place in elementary schools or the lives of children is illustrative of the overarching perspective of this handbook as a while. Historical constructs of childhood have often unduly lowered children's 'competence' and limited their contributions to political life. In response, a broader perspective will both facilitate young people's growth as 'citizens' over the long term and enable their more meaningful and useful participation in the near term.

REFERENCES

Alanen, L. (1994) 'Gender and generation: Feminism and the "child question"', in J. Qvortrup, M. Bardy, G. Sgritta, and H. Wintersberger (eds.), *Childhood matters: Social theory, practice and politics.* Aldershot: Avebury, pp. 3–28.

Amadeo, J.A., Torney-Purta, J., Lehmann, R., Husfeldt, V., and Nikolova, R. (2002) *Civic knowledge and engagement: An IEA study of upper secondary students in sixteen countries.* Amsterdam: IEA.

Arnstein, S. (1969) 'The ladder of citizen participation', *Journal of the Institute of American Planners,* 35(4): 216–24.

Austin, J. (2008) *Youth culture: Encyclopedia of children and childhood in history and society.* Available at http://www/faqs.org/childhood/Wh-Z-and-other-topics/YouthCulture.html

Baldi, S., Perie, M., Skidmore, D., Greenberg, E., Hahn, C., and Nelson, D. (2001) *What democracy means to ninth-graders: U.S. results from the International IEA Civic Education Study.* Washington, DC: US Department of Education.

Ballington, J. (2002) 'Youth voter turnout', in R. L. Pintor and M. Gratchew (eds.), *Voter turnout since 1945: A global report.* Stockholm: IDEA, pp. 111–14.

Barnes, S.H. and Kaase, M. (1979) *Political action: Mass participation in five western democracies.* London: Sage.

Beck, U. (2006) *The cosmopolitan vision.* Cambridge: Polity Press.

Bennett, W.L. (2008) 'Changing citizenship in the digital age', in W. L. Bennett (ed.), *Civic life online: Learning how digital media can engage youth.* Cambridge, MA: MIT Press, pp. 1–24.

Bennett, W.L., Wells, C., and Freelon, D.G. (2009) *Communicating citizenship online: Models of civic learning in the youth web sphere.* Available at http://www.engagedyouth.org/blog/wp-content/uploads/2009/02/ communicatingcitizeshiponline-cloreport.pdf

Berti, A.E. and Bombi, A.S. (1981) *The child's construction of economics.* Cambridge: Cambridge University Press.

Biesta, G.J.J. and Lawy, R.S. (2006) 'From teaching citizenship to learning democracy. Overcoming individualism in research, policy and practice', *Cambridge Journal of Education* 36(1): 63–79.

Blazak, R. (n.d.) 'The racist skinhead movement'. Southern Poverty Law Center. Available at http://www.splcenter.org/get-informed/intelligence-files/ideology/racist-skinhead/racist-skinheads

Bohman, J. (2011) 'Children and the rights of citizens: Nondomination and intergenerational justice', *The Annals of the American Academy of Political and Social Science,* 633: 128–40.

Bosco, F.J. (2010) 'Play, work or activism? Broadening the connection between political and children's geographies', *Children's Geographies,* 8(4): 381–90.

Botcheva, L., Feldman, S, and Leiderman, H. (2002) 'Can stability in school processes offset the negative effects of sociopolitical upheaval on adolescents' adaptation?', *Youth and Society,* 34(1): 55–88.

Boyden, J. (1997) Childhood and the policy makers: A comparative perspective on the globalization of childhood. In A. James and A. Prout (eds.), *Constructing and reconstructing childhood: Contemporary issues in the sociological study of childhood.* London: Routledge Falmer, pp. 190–229.

Burke, B. (2000) *Post-modernism and post-modernity: The encyclopedia of information education.* Available at http://www.infed.org/biblio/b-postmd.htm

Camino, L. and Zeldin, S. (2002) 'From periphery to center: Pathways for youth civic engagement in the day-to-day life of communities', *Applied Developmental Science,* 6(4): 21–20.

Christenson, P.G. and Roberts, D.F. (1998) *It's not only rock and roll: Popular music in the lives of adolescents.* Creskill, NJ: Hampton Press.

Clarke, J. (n.d.) Youth sub-culture. Available at http://dip/youthstudies.eu/wiki/index.php/Clarke

Clarke, J., Hall, S., Jefferson, T., and Roberts, B. (2006) 'Subcultures, cultures, and class: A theoretical overview', in S. Hall and T. Jefferson (eds.), *Resistance through rituals: Youth subcultures post-war Britain.* New York: Routledge, pp. 3–59.

Connell, R.W. (1971) *The child's construction of politics.* Melbourne: Melbourne University Press.

Council of Europe (2004) *All European study on education for democratic citizenship policies*. Strasbourg: Council of Europe Publishing.

Cunningham, S. and Lavalette, M. (2004) '"Active citizens" or "irresponsible truants": School student strike against the war', *Critical Social Policy*, 24(2): 255–69.

Daiute, C., Stern, R., and Lelutiu-Weinberger, C. (2003) 'Negotiating violence prevention', *Journal of Social Issues*, 59(1): 83–101.

Dalton, R. (2008) *The good citizen: How a younger generation is Reshaping American Politics*. Washington, DC: CQ Press.

Dalton, R. (ed.) (2011) *Engaging youth in politics: Debating democracy's future*. New York: IDEBATE Press.

Davies, J.C. (1965) 'The family's role in political socialization', *The Annals of the American Academy of Political and Social Science*, 361(1): 10–19.

Dawson, R.E. and Prewitt, K. (1969) *Political socialization*. Boston, MA: Little, Brown.

Delgado, M. and Staples, L. (2007) *Youth-led community organizing: Theory and action*. New York: Oxford University Press.

Delli Carpini, M.X. (2000) 'Gen.com: Youth, civic engagement, and the new information environment', *Political Communication*, 17(4): 341–9.

Diemer, M.A. and Li, C.H. (2011) 'Critical consciousness development and political participation among marginalized youth', *Child Development*, 82(6): 1815–33.

Donnelly, T. (2009) 'Popular constitutionalism, civic education, and the stories we tell our children', *The Yale Law Journal*, 118: 948–1001.

Earl, J. and Schussman, A. (2008) 'Contesting cultural control: Youth culture and online petitioning', in W. L. Bennett (ed.), *Civic life online: Learning how digital media can engage youth. The John D. and Catherine T. MacArthur Foundation Series on Digital Media and Learning*. Cambridge, MA: The MIT Press, pp. 71–96.

Erikson, E.H. (1968) *Identity: Youth and crisis*. New York: W. W. Norton and Co.

Eurydice (2012) *Citizenship education in Europe*. Brussels: EU Publications Office.

EUYOUPART (2005) *Political participation of young people in Europe – Development of indicators for comparative research in the European Union*. Vienna: SORA. Available at http://www.sora.at/de/start.asp?b=118

Falk, G. and Falk, U.A. (2005) *Youth culture and the generation gap*. New York: Algora Publishing.

Farnen, F. and Meloen, D. (2000) *Democracy, authoritarianism and education: A cross-national empirical survey*. London: Macmillan Press.

Farnen, R. (2003) 'Political socialization, culture and education in 21st century USA and Canada: State of the art in North America', in H. Sünker, R. Farnen, and G. Szell (eds.), *Political socialization, participation and education*. Frankfurt am Main: L Peter Lang, pp. 133–65.

Farthing, R. (2010) 'The politics of youthful antipolitics: Representing the 'issue' of youth participation in politics', *Journal of Youth Studies*, 13(2): 181–95.

Faulks, K. (2000) *Citizenship*. London: Routledge.

Fenzel, M.L. and Leary, T. (1997, March) *Evaluating outcomes of service-learning courses at parochial schools*. Paper presented at the annual meeting of the American Educational Research Association. Chicago, IL.

Ferrand, J. (1968) 'La Jeunesse, nouveau Tiers e'tat (Paris, 1968)'. As cited in Jobs, R. I. (2009). 'Youth movements: Travel, protest, and Europe in 1968'. *The American Historical Review*, 114(2): 376–404.

Flanagan, C.A., Jonsson, B., Botcheva, L., Csapo, B., Bowes, J., Macek, P., and Sheblanova, E. (1999) 'Adolescents and the "Social Contract": Developmental roots of citizenship in seven countries', in M. Yates and J. Youniss (eds.), *Roots of civic identity: International perspectives on community service and activism in youth*. Cambridge University Press: London, pp. 135–6.

Flanagan, C.A. and Sherrod, L.R. (1998) 'Youth political development: An introduction', *Journal of Social Issues*, 54(3): 447–56.

Flekkøy, M.G. and Kaufman, N.H. (1997) *The participation rights of the child: Rights and responsibilities in family and society*. London: Jessica Kingsley Publishers.

Forbrig, J. (2005) *Revisiting youth political participation: Challenges for research and democratic practice in Europe*. Strasbourg: Council of Europe.

Ford, L.E. (1994) *Youth volunteer corps of America: Final evaluation report*. Charleston, SC: College of Charleston.

Fowler, D. (2008) *Youth culture in modern Britain, c.1920 – c.1970. From ivory tower to global movement. A new history*. Hampshire: Palgrave Macmillan.

Fox, K.R. (2010) 'Children making a difference: Developing awareness of poverty through service learning', *The Social Studies*, 101: 1–9.

Furth, H.G. (1980) *The world of grown-ups: Children's conception of society*. New York: Elsevier.

Garbarino, J. (2011) 'What does living in a democracy mean for kids?', *American Journal of Orthopsychiatry*, 81(4): 443–6.

Gerodimos, R. (in press) New media, new citizens: Youth attitudes towards online civic engagement. *Proceedings of the WebScir'09: Society On-Line*. Available at http://journal.webscience.org/182/

Gerodimos, R. (2012) 'On-line youth civic attitudes and the limits of civic consumerism: The emerging challenge to the Internet's democratic potential', in B. Loader and D. Mercea (eds.), *Social media and democracy: Innovations in participatory politics.* London: Routledge, pp.166–89.

Giles, D.E. and Eyler, J. (1994) 'The impact of college community service laboratory on students' personal, social, and cognitive outcomes', *Journal of Adolescence,* 17: 327–39.

Ginwright, S. (2009) *Black youth rising: Activism and radical healing in urban America.* New York: Teacher's College Press.

Giroux, H.A. (1983) *Theory and resistance in education.* South Hadley, MA: Bergin Garvey.

Glaser, C. (2000) *Bo Tsotsi: The youth gangs of Soweto, 1935–1976.* Portsmouth, NH: Heinemann.

Goldstein, E.S. (2009) *Political socialization.* New York: Aldine Publishing.

Gomolla, M. and Radtke, F. (2002) *Institutionelle dicriminierung. Die herstellung ethnisher differenz in der schule.* Opladen: Laske und Budrich.

Gordon, H.R. and Taft, J.K. (2010) 'Rethinking youth political socialization: Teenage activists talk back', *Youth & Society,* 43: 1499.

Hanks, M. (1981) 'Youth, voluntary associations and political socialization', *Social Forces,* 60(1): 211–23.

Hart, R. (1992) *Children's participation: From tokenism to citizenship.* Florence: UNICEF.

Hashem, M.E. (2009) Impact and implications of new information technology on Middle Eastern Youth. *Global Media Journal,* 8(14). Available at http://numerons.in/files/documents/9IT-Impact-on-Middle-Eastern-Youth.pdf

Hebdige, D. (1979) *Subculture: The meaning of style.* London: Methuen.

Hendrik, H. (2001) 'The child as a social actor in historical sources: Problems of identification and interpretation', in P. Christensen and A. James (eds.), *Research with children: Perspectives and practices.* Routledge Falmer, pp. 36–61.

Henn, M., Weinstein, M., and Wring, D. (2002) 'A generation apart? Youth and political participation in Britain', *The British Journal of Politics and International Relations,* 4(2):167–92.

Hofheinz, A. (2005) 'The Internet in the Arab world: Playground for political liberalization', *International Politics and Society,* 3: 78–96.

Homana, G. and Barber, C. (2007) 'School climate for citizenship education: A comparison of England and the United States', in *The Second IEA International Research Conference: Proceedings of the IRC-2660, Vol. 2. Amsterdam*: IEA, pp. 115–30.

Horelli, L. (1998) 'Creating child-friendly environments: Case studies on children's participation in three European countries', *Childhood,* 5: 225–39.

Hurd, C.A. (2008) 'Is service-learning effective? A look at the current research', in S. Shalini (ed.), *Service learning: Perspectives and applications.* Punjagutta, India: ICFAI University Press. Available at http://servicelearning.org/library/resources/7960

Inglehart, R. (1997) *Modernization and postmodernization: Cultural, economic and political change in 43 societies.* Princeton, NJ: Princeton University Press.

Ireland, E., Kerr, D., Lopes, J., Nelson, J, and Cleaver, E. (2006) *Active citizenship and young people: Opportunities, experiences and challenges in and beyond school.* London: DfES.

James, A. and James, A.L. (2004) *Constructing childhood: Theory, policy and social practice.* Basingstoke: Palgrave Macmillan.

Jans, M. (2004) 'Children as citizens: Towards a contemporary notion of child participation', *Childhood,* 11(1): 27–44.

Jastrzab, J., Masker, J., Blonquist, J., and Orr, L. (1996) *Impacts of service: Final report on the evaluation of American conservation and youth service corps.* Washington, DC: Corporation for National Service.

Jennings, M.K. and Niemi, R. (1981) *Generations and politics.* Princeton, NJ: Princeton University Press.

Jobs, R.I. (2009) 'Youth movements: Travel, protest, and Europe in 1968', *The American Historical Review,* 114(2): 376–404.

Kahne, J.E. and Sporte, S.E. (2008) 'Developing citizens: The impact of civic learning opportunities on students' commitment to civic participation', *American Educational Research Journal,* 45(3): 738–66.

Kann, M.E., Berry, J., Grant, C., and Zager, P. (2007) 'The Internet and youth political participation', *First Monday,* 12(8). University of Salford. Available at http://firstmonday.org/htbin/cgiwrap/bin/ojs/index.php/fm/article/viewArticle/1977/1852

Kerr, D. (2005) 'Citizenship education in England – Listening to young people: New insights from the Citizenship Longitudinal Study', *International Journal of Citizenship and Teacher Education,* 1(1): 74–96.

Kirby, E.H., Marcelo, K.B., Gillerman, J., and Linkins, S. (2008) 'The youth vote in the 2008 primaries and caucuses'. Available at http://www.civicyouth.org/PopUps/FactSheets/FS_08_primary_summary.pdf

Kirchhöffer, D. (1996) 'Veränderungen in der alltäglishen Lebensführung Osterberliner Kinder', *Aus Politik und Zeitgeschichte,* B11(8): 31–45.

Kirshner, B. and Ginwright, S. (2012) 'Youth organizing as a developmental context for African American and

Latino adolescents', *Child Development Perspectives*, 6(3): 288–94.

Kitwana, B. (2002) *The hip hop generation: Young blacks and the crisis in African American culture*. New York: Basic Civitas Books.

Kiwan, D. (2007) 'Uneasy relationships? Conceptions of "citizenship", "democracy" and "diversity" in the English citizenship education policymaking process', *Education, Citizenship and Social Justice*, 2(3): 223–35.

Klingman, A. and Shalev, R. (2001) 'Graffiti: Voices of Israeli youth following the assassination of the Prime Minister', *Youth and Society*, 32(4): 403–20.

Kobin, M. and Allaste, A.A. (2009) 'Hip-hop in Rakvere: The importance of the local in global subculture', in G. McKay, C. Williams, M. Goddard, N. Foxlee, and E. Ramanauskaite (eds.), *Subcultures and New Religious Movements in Russia and East-Central Europe*. Bern, Switzerland: Peter Lang AG, pp. 87–110.

Lansdown, G. (2001) *Promoting children's participation in democratic decision-making*. Florence: UNICEF Innocenti Research Centre.

Laufer, R.S. (1971) 'Sources of generational consciousness and conflict', *The Annals of the American Academy of Political and Social Science*, 395(1): 80–94.

Lehmann, R. (2007) 'Predicting the political involvement of European adolescents', in *The Second IEA International Research Conference: Proceedings of the IRC-2006, Vol. 2*. Amsterdam: IEA, pp. 157–67.

Losito, B. (2004) 'Southern Europe Regional Synthesis', in *All-European Study on Education for Democratic Citizenship Policies*. Strasbourg: Council of Europe. MacMullen, I. (2011) 'On status quo bias in civic education', *The Journal of Politics*, 73(3): 872–86.

McFarland, D.A. and Thomas, R.J. (2006) 'Bowling young: How youth voluntary associations influence adult political participation', *American Sociological Review*, 71(3): 401–25.

McKay, G. and Goddard, M. (2009) '(Post-)subculture theory, and practice in East-Central Europe', in G. McKay, C. Williams, M. Goddard, N. Foxlee, and E. Ramanauskaite (eds.), *Subcultures and New Religious Movements in Russia and East-Central Europe*. Bern, Switzerland: Peter Lang AG, pp. 3–15.

Mannheim, K. (1952) *The problem of generations*. In K. Mannheim, *Essays on the sociology of knowledge*. London: Routledge and Kegan Paul (first published in 1923).

Matheolane, M.M. (2012, June 13) 'Youth culture as a metaphor of hope and tragedy'. Mail & Guardian. Available at http://mg.co.za/article/2012-06-12-youth-culture-as-a-metaphor-of-hope-and-tragedy

Matthews, T.L., Hempel, L.M., and Howell, F.M. (2010) 'Gender and the transmission of civic engagement: Assessing the influences on youth civic activity', *Sociological Inquiry*, 80(3): 448–74.

Milner, H. (2010, September) *The Internet: Friend or foe of youth political participation*? Paper presented at the Fifth Biennial Conference of the ECPR, Potsdam, Germany. Available at http://internet-politics.cies.iscte.pt/IMG/pdf/ECPRPotsdamMilner.pdf

Mintz, S. (2006) *Huck's raft: A history of American childhood, Edition 1*. Boston, MA: Harvard University Press.

Mishler, W. and Rose, R. (1997) 'Trust, distrust and skepticism: Popular evaluation of civil and political institution in post-Communist societies'. *The Journal of Politics*, 59(2): 418–51.

Mooney, K. (2005) 'Identities in the Ducktail youth subculture in post-World-War-Two South Africa', *Journal of Youth Studies*, 8(1): 41–57.

Morgan, W. and Streb, M. (2001) 'Building citizenship: How student voice in service-learning develops civic values', *Social Science Quarterly*, 82(1): 154–69.

Motos, C.R. (2010) 'The controversy over civic education in Spain', *European Consortium for Political Research*, 9: 269–79.

Norris, P. (2002) *Democratic phoenix: Reinventing political activism*. New York: Cambridge University Press.

Omel'chenko, E. and Garifzianova, A. (2009) 'Skinheads and defenders of Russia? Power versus friendship in xenophobic youth subcultures', in G. McKay, C. Williams, M. Goddard, N. Foxlee, and E. Ramanauskaite (eds.), *Subcultures and new religious movements in Russia and East-Central Europe*. Bern, Switzerland: Peter Lang AG, pp. 33–61.

Organisation for Economic Co-operation and Development (2006) 'OECD education systems leave many immigrant children floundering, report shows'. Available at http://www.oecd.org/document/17/0,2340,en_2649_201185_36701777_1_1_1_1,00.html

Osler, A. and Starkey, H. (2005) *Changing citizenship: Democracy and inclusion in education*. Maidenhead: Open University Press.

Ostman, J. (2012) 'Information, expression, participation: How involvement in user-generated content relates to democratic engagement among young people', *New Media Society*, 14(6): 1004–21.

Owen, D. (2008) 'Election media and youth political engagement', *Journal of Social Science Education*, 7(2): 14–24.

Pew Research Center (2004) 'Young people more engaged, more uncertain, debates more important to young voters'. Available at http://www.pewtrusts.org/news_room_detail. aspx?id=22948

Pilcher, J. (1994) 'Mannheim's sociology of generations: An undervalued legacy', *British Journal of Sociology*, 45(3): 481–95.

Pinquart, M., Silbereisen, R., and Juang, L. (2004) 'Changes in psychological distress among East German adolescents facing German unification: The role of commitment to the old system and self-efficacy beliefs', *Youth and Society*, 36(1): 77–101.

Prizmony-Levy, O. (2007) 'Sociological perspectives on youth support for social movements', in *The Second IEA International Research Conference: Proceedings of the IRC-2006*. Vol.2. Amsterdam: IEA, pp. 67–86.

Prout, A., Simmons, R., and Birchall, J. (2006) 'Reconnecting and extending the research agenda on children's participation: Mutual incentives and the participation chain', in E. Kay, M. Tisdall, J. M. Davis, M. Hill, and A. Prout (eds.), *Children, young people and social inclusion: Participation for what?* Bristol: Policy Press, pp. 75–104.

Qualifications and Curriculum Authority (1998) *Education for citizenship and the teaching of democracy in schools* (Crick Report). London: QCA.

Quintelier, E. (2008) 'Who is politically active: The athlete, the scout member or the environmental activist? Young people, voluntary engagement and political participation', *Acta Sociologica*, 51(4): 355–70.

Qvortrup, J. (2001) 'Macroanalysis of Childhood', in P. Christensen and A. James (eds.), *Research with children: Perspectives and practices*. Routledge: Falmer, pp. 77–97.

Rehfeld, A. (2011) 'The child as democratic citizen', *The Annals of the American Academy of Political and Social Science*, 633: 141–66.

Remy, S.P. (2005) Generation. New dictionary of the history of ideas 2005. Available at http://www.encyclopedia.com/doc/1G2-3424300311.html

Ridgell, C.E. (1994) *Students' perceptions: Before and after student service-learning*. University of Maryland at College Park.

Roche, J. (1999) 'Children: Rights, participation and citizenship', *Childhood*, 6: 475–93.

Roszak, T. (1968) *The making of a counter culture*. London: Faber and Faber.

Roudometof, V. (2005) 'Transnationalism, cosmopolitanism and globalization', *Current Sociology*, 53(1): 113–35.

Salagaev, A., Shashkin, A., Makarov, A., and Safin, R. (2009) 'From local to global: The transformation of delinquent and radical communities in the Tatarstan Republic of Russia', in G. McKay, C. Williams, M. Goddard, N. Foxlee, and E. Ramanauskaite (eds.), *Subcultures and new religious movements in Russia and East-Central Europe*. Bern, Switzerland: Peter Lang AG, pp. 15–32.

Savit, E. (2009) 'Can courts repair the crumbling foundation of good citizenship? An examination of potential legal challenges to social studies cutbacks in public schools', *Michigan Law Review*, 1007: 1269–303.

Scales, P.C. and Roehlkepartain, E.C. (2004) *Community service and service-learning in U.S. public schools, 2004: Findings from a national survey*. St. Paul, MN: National Youth Leadership Council.

Schulz, W., Ainley, J., Fraillon, J., Kerr, D. and Losito, B. (2010) ICCS 2009 *International Report: Civic knowledge, attitudes, and engagement among lower secondary school students in 38 countries*. Amsterdam: IEA.

Schwartz, S. (2010) *Youth in post-conflict reconstruction: Agents of change*. Washington, D C: United States Institute of Peace.

Settle, J.E., Bond, R., and Levitt, J. (2011) 'The social origins of adult political behavior', *American Politics Research*, 39(2): 239 63.

Sherrod, L.R. (2008) 'Adolescents' perceptions of rights as reflected in their views of citizenship', *Journal of Social Issues*, 64(4): 771–90.

Smith, E.S. (1999) 'The effects of investments in the social capital of youth on political and civic behavior in young adulthood: A longitudinal analysis', *Political Psychology*, 20(3): 553–80.

Smith, M.W. (1994) 'Community service learning: Striking the chord of citizenship', *Michigan Journal of Community Service Learning*, 1(1): 37–43.

Şorcaru, D. and Popescu, F. (2009) 'On linguistic politics: The stylistic testimonies of Romanian hip-hop', in G. McKay, C. Williams, M. Goddard, N. Foxlee, and E. Ramanauskaite (eds.), *Subcultures and new religious movements in Russia and East-Central Europe*. Bern, Switzerland: Peter Lang AG, pp. 125–40.

Stevens, O. (1982) *Children talking politics: Political learning in childhood*. Oxford: Martin Robinson.

Stolle, D., Hooghe, M., and Micheletti, M. (2003) 'Political consumerism – A new phenomenon of political participation?' Paper presented at the ECPR Joint Session, Edinburgh, Scotland.

Stolle, D., Hooghe, M., and Micheletti, M. (2005) 'Politics in the supermarket: Political consumerism as a form of political participation', *International Political Science Review*, 26(3): 245–69.

Such, E., Walker, O., and Walker, R. (2005) 'Anti-war children: Representation of youth protests against the second Iraq War in the British national press', *Childhood*, 12: 301–25.

Terkessidis, M. (2003) 'Migration and political education in Germany: Regarding the neglected question of citizenship', in H. Sünker, R. Farnen, and G. Sze'll (eds.), *Political socialisation, participation and education: Change of epoch – Process of democratization*. Frankfurt am Main: Peter Lang, pp. 197–208.

Tisdall, E.K.M. and Bell, R. (2006) 'Included in governance? Children's participation in "public" decision making', in E. Kay, M. Tisdall, J. M. Davis, M. Hill, and A. Prout (eds.), *Children, young people and social inclusion: Participation for what?* Bristol: Policy Press, pp. 105–20.

Tomanović, S. and Ignjatović, S. (2007) 'The transition of young people in a transitional society: The case of Serbia', *Journal of Youth Studies*, 9(3): 269–85.

Torney, J., Oppenheim, A.N., and Farnen, R. (1975) *Civic education in ten countries: An empirical study*. New York: John Wiley.

Torney-Purta, J. Lehmann, R., Oswald, H., and Schulz, W. (2001) *Citizenship and education in twenty-eight countries: Civic knowledge and engagement at age fourteen*. Amsterdam: IEA.

Torney-Purta, J., Schwille, J., and Amadeo, J. (1999) *Civic education across countries: Twenty-four national case studies from the IEA Civic Education Project*. Amsterdam and Washington, D C: IEA and National Council for Social Studies.

Verba, S., Schlozman, K.L., and Brady, H.E. (1995) *Voice and equality: Civic voluntarism in American society*. Boston, MA: Harvard College.

Von Drehle, D. (2008, January) The year of the youth vote. *Time Magazine*. Available at http://www.time.com/time/magazine/article/0,9171,1708836,00.html

Vromen, A. (2008) 'Building virtual spaces: Young people, participation and the Internet', *Australian Journal of Political Science*, 43(1): 79–97.

Wallace, C. and Alt, R. (2001) 'Youth cultures under authoritarian regimes: The case of the Swings against the Nazis', *Youth and Society*, 32(3): 275–302.

Warner, G. (2013) 'Kenya's graffiti train seeks to promote a peaceful election'. National Public Radio. Available at http://www.npr.org/2013/02/19/171916072/kenyas-graffiti-train-seeks-to-promote-a-peaceful-election?utm_source=nprandutm_medium=facebookandutm_campaign=20130219

Wattenberg, M.P. (2012) *Is voting for young people?* 3rd edition. New York: Pearson.

Weller, S. (2007) *Teenagers' citizenship: Experiences and education*. London: Routledge.

Whitty, G. (2002) *Making sense of education policy: Studies in the sociology and politics of education*. London: Paul Chapman Publishing.

Wyness, M. (2006) *Childhood and society: An introduction to the sociology of childhood*. New York: Palgrave Macmillan.

Zubrycki, J. (2011, 26 October) 'Scholars put civics in same class as literacy and math instruction', *Education Week*, p. 10.

Zukin, C., Keeter, S., Andolina, M., Jenkins, K., and Delli Carpini, M.X. (2006) *A new engagement? Political participation, civic life, and the changing American citizen*. New York: Oxford University Press.

5

Children, Religion, and Spiritual Development: Reframing a Research Agenda

Eugene C. Roehlkepartain

INTRODUCTION

Children's religious and spiritual life is a rich, complex, and sometimes controversial area of research. On the one hand, there is a broad consensus that all children in all societies have, in the words of the Convention on the Rights of the Child, the right 'to freedom of thought, conscience and religion', and parents and guardians have the rights and duties 'to provide direction to the child in the exercise of his or her right in a manner consistent with the evolving capacities of the child' (United Nations Office of the High Commissioner for Human Rights, 1989).

On the other hand, issues of childhood religion and spirituality have too often been relegated to the margins in the social sciences, often presumed to be the parochial concerns of religious institutions, not a core part of human identity and development. However, a resurgence of interest in and attention to spiritual and religious development in the social sciences that began emerging in the 1990s gained additional momentum in the first decade of the twenty-first century.

This chapter examines some of the emerging theory and research on children's religious and spiritual development, participation, and commitments. Then it highlights several questions and methodological issues in the field. In the process, it invites other researchers to consider how they might attend to this dimension of life as part of their own work, thus both enriching their own understanding and also contributing to this nascent but burgeoning field of inquiry within child and adolescent development.

DEFINITIONAL ISSUES IN HISTORICAL PERSPECTIVE

One of the significant challenges in interpreting the role of religious or spiritual development in child development lies in the divergent assumptions and definitions in the field. Indeed, Rew and Wong's (2006: 438) analysis of literature on the relationship between spirituality and adolescent health attitudes and behaviours concluded that the research in this field is 'neither conceptually clear nor firmly grounded in theory'. Indeed, of the 43 studies analysed, 26 were not based on any explicit theoretical or conceptual model. Thus, it is important to look at religious and spiritual development in the context of a family of interrelated but far from synonymous concepts, including religion, religiosity, spirit, spirituality, religious development, and spiritual development. Like any family, this constellation of concepts includes siblings, cousins, parents, and in-laws who may have a little or a lot in common. Understanding what holds them together as well as each of their unique traits and accents is vital for moving beyond caricatures and overgeneralizations.

A voluminous body of recent scholarly literature grapples with these terms. Much of this debate (and it is an active debate) focuses on the relationship between religion and spirituality. Some scholars argue variations of each of the following options: religion and spirituality are synonymous or fused; religion is a sub-domain of spirituality; spirituality is a sub-domain of religion; they are separate domains; or they are distinct, but overlapping domains. (For discussions of this debate, see Reich, 1996; Zinnbauer et al., 1997; Zinnbauer, Pargament and Scott, 1999). What's healthy about this debate is that after decades of disregard, the social sciences are gearing up again to look at these human phenomena. What's less healthy is the continuing confusion about these concepts.

There is a historical cycle to all of this. The golden era of scientific inquiry into this family of ideas occurred among the pioneers of psychology in the late nineteenth and early twentieth centuries. William James, G. Stanley Hall, J. H. Leuba, and Edwin Starbuck considered religion and spirituality to be integral to the field of psychology and central to the understanding of persons' growth and development. More than 100 years ago, William James (1958/1902: 41–2) sought to disentangle the development of one's spirit from institutional or ecclesiastical religion. Using the language of his time, he chose to call the two phenomena 'personal religion' and 'institutional religion'. He described the former as 'the inner dispositions of man himself ... his conscience, his deserts, his helplessness, his incompleteness'. Call it conscience or morality or something else, he

writes, but 'under any name it will be equally worthy of our study'. He then describes this phenomenon 'the primordial thing', the animating force out of which grows art, philosophy, and theology.

Then, for a variety of reasons, this inquiry was marginalized through much of the twentieth century. (For more on this historical context, see Roehlkepartain et al., 2006; Vitz, 2008.) Amid all the explanations, it is fair to say that much of the neglect grew out of social scientists' discomfort with religion as a force in society and in their own lives. Religion, in the *Zeitgeist* of social science, became, at best, a discretionary activity of some people, and at worst, as famously decreed by Albert Ellis, a form of pathology (Ellis, 1980). And Freud (1961: 43) did little to endear developmental scientists to the religious quest when he referred to 'religion as a universal obsessional neurosis', a mere illusion derived from infantile human wishes.

Evidence of this marginalization is evident in the scientific literature. Benson, Roehlkepartain and Rude (2003) searched two broad databases: EBSCO's Social Science Abstracts and PsychINFO, to determine the extent to which religion and spirituality were being addressed in published, peer-reviewed journals between 1990 and 2002. Of the many thousands of studies about children and adolescents, barely one per cent included religion or spirituality as a topic of study. A parallel analysis of six major journals that specialize in child and adolescent development (*Child Development, Developmental Psychology, International Journal of Behavioural Development, Journal of Adolescent Research, Journal of Early Adolescence,* and the *Journal of Research on Adolescence*) found no articles explicitly addressing spiritual development in childhood and adolescence during this time period of more than a decade.

Other reviews have found similar patterns in academic scholarship (see, for example, Davie, 2003; Paloutzian, 1996; Weaver et al., 2000) and, more specifically, the study of adolescence (see Benson and King, 2006;

Bridges and Moore, 2002; King, Ramos and Clardy, 2013; King and Roeser, 2009; Kerestes and Youniss, 2003; Oser, Scarlett and Bucher, 2006) and childhood (including Bartkowski, Xu and Levin, 2008; Houskamp, Fisher and Stuber, 2004; Nye, 1999; Ratcliff and Nye, 2006; Yust et al., 2006).

Thus, religious and spiritual development came to be understood as something like the following: religion is something some people do. Things like spirituality and spiritual development are simply variations on the theme of religion. All of these involve someone's parochial view of gods or God. It is private and personal stuff, best left to those who choose to engage. Accordingly, it is not central to the study of human development. Indeed, though they were writing about the broader study of religious and spiritual development, Hill et al. (2000: 51) captured the reality when they concluded that 'the state of the discipline today can be characterized as sufficiently developed but still overlooked, if not bypassed, by the whole of psychology'.

A variety of explanations have been given for this marginalization. Wulff (1997) identifies some of the more prominent obstacles. Among them is the pervasive personal rejection of religion by social scientists, a fact supported by several studies of academics' attitudes toward religion (Bergin, 1991; Larson and Witham, 1998). Another is the view that religion, like art or music or politics, is a discretionary human activity and not a core, fundamental dynamic of human life. The area may also be shied away from because it is 'politically sensitive and philosophically difficult' (McCrae, 1999: 1211).

However, a different story is emerging. It is too early to know if this new story will gain momentum and rival or overtake the old story. The new story pushes in these directions: spiritual development is a normative developmental process involving critical developmental tasks such as connectedness, belongingness, purpose, and contribution. All persons in all societies 'do' spiritual development, though culture plays a major role in its process and content. Spiritual development does not require divinity or belief in a supernatural power, though a lot of people include these in their own stories. From this perspective, spiritual development 'happens' among secular humanists, atheists, Muslims, Methodists, Buddhists, animists, artists, scientists, young, and old. Spiritual development is a normative developmental process that, like cognitive or social development, is informed and shaped by family, kinship, peers, school, culture, social norms, and programmes.

This resurgence has been fuelled by several major scholarly initiatives. Though far from unified, their combination signifies an emerging and sustained interest in positing the territory, meaning, and importance of spiritual and religious development (see King and Boyatzis, 2004). The Society for Research on Adolescence Study Group on Adolescence in the 21st Century concluded that spiritual values and experiences are research topics deserving more attention (Brown, Larson and Saraswathi, 2002). Spiritual development has been a focus of recent pre-conferences at both the Society for Research in Child Development and the Society for Research on Adolescence.

In addition, Sage published both the *Handbook of Spiritual Development in Childhood and Adolescence* (Roehlkepartain, King et al., 2006) and the *Encyclopaedia of Spiritual and Religious Development* (Dowling and Scarlett, 2006). The prestigious report in the United States titled *Community Programs to Promote Youth Development* (Eccles and Gootman, 2002) names 'spirituality' (or a sense of a 'larger' purpose in life) as a personal asset that facilitates positive youth development. In Great Britain, the National Youth Agency published *A Journey of Discovery: Spirituality and Spiritual Development in Youth Work* (Green, 2006). The most recent edition of *The Handbook of Child Psychology* (the multi-volume 'bible' of developmental psychology) dedicates a chapter to religious and spiritual development (Oser et al., 2006), as does the latest edition of the *Handbook of*

Adolescent Psychology (King and Roeser, 2009).

Still to be resolved in this emerging body of theory and research is a clearer articulation of the relationship between religious and spiritual development. In general, the meaning of religion has evolved to focus more on 'a fixed system of ideas or ideological commitments' (Wulff, 1997: 46), with spirituality being more commonly regarded as 'an individual phenomenon and identified with such things as personal transcendence, supra consciousness sensitivity, and meaningfulness' (Zinnbauer et al., 1997: 551). Some models subsume religiousness as a category within spirituality (see, for example, Helminiak, 2006; MacDonald, 2000).

There are reasons, however, to be cautious about simplistic distinctions that bifurcate religious and spiritual development. For one, children can rarely differentiate between religious and spiritual aspects of life, particularly before early adolescence (Hay and Nye, 1998; Houskamp et al., 2004). More important, many cultures around the world do not distinguish between religion and spirituality; rather, religiosity and spirituality are perceived as inextricably bound and interwoven (Mattis et al., 2006). Indeed, some languages do not have words that distinguish the two concepts, and some cultures see the debate as primarily a North American argument (see, for example, Gottlieb, 2006; Stifoss-Hanssen, 1999). Even in the West, religious belief and traditions are dynamically intertwined with the experiential or 'spiritual' (Marler and Hadaway, 2002; Wuthnow, 1998). Overplaying the distinction can also fuel a stereotype that one (religion) is 'bad' and the other (spirituality) is good (Hill et al., 2000; Pargament, 1999), which isn't borne out by the extant research.

Recent definitional efforts have shifted to identifying a common denominator, which is often described as the sacred. Pargament (1997) suggests that examples of the sacred include the concepts of God, divinity, transcendence, and ultimate reality. Accordingly, spirituality can be defined as 'a search for the sacred, a process through which people seek to discourse, hold on to and, when necessary, transform whatever they hold sacred in their lives' (Hill and Pargament, 2003). Religion also seeks the sacred, creating the doctrine, beliefs, and rituals that bind believers to it and to each other. Alternatively, as Stark suggests, religion seeks to explain existence based on supernatural assumptions, including beliefs about ultimate meaning and the nature of the supernatural (Stark, 2001).

Each of these approaches adds important nuances. However, building on Coles' (1990) pioneering work, we have approached the definitional conundrum by hypothesizing that spiritual development is a core and universal (and understudied) dynamic in human development that may be a wellspring out of which emerges the pursuit of meaning, connectedness to others and the sacred, purpose, and contribution. This set of dynamic developmental process may be (and often is) informed by religion or other systems of ideas and belief. To understand human development fully, we need to examine how this dimension of development dynamically interacts with the other well-known streams of development: cognitive, social, emotional, and moral. My colleagues and I have previously offered the following operational definition:

> Spiritual development is the process of growing the intrinsic human capacity for self-transcendence, in which the self is embedded in something greater than the self, including the sacred. It is the developmental 'engine' that propels the search for connectedness, meaning, purpose and contribution. It is shaped both within and outside of religious traditions, beliefs, and practices.
>
> (Benson et al., 2003: 205–6)

We have continued to struggle with shaping a definition and framework that brings some clarity, structure, and consensus. We engaged an international 'expert panel' of 120 social scientists, religious scholars, and practitioners working with children and adolescents to move toward a greater consensus around these issues across cultures and traditions. Through an iterative, Web-based survey interface, these advisors guided us in developing a theoretical model that was also informed by (and informing) other qualitative and quantitative research in multiple countries that (a) builds on extant literature; (b) resonates across cultures and traditions; (c) reflects the implicit understanding of spiritual development among children and their parents; (d) recognizes the diversities of spiritualities and how children go about this 'work'; and (e) frames new opportunities for further research that will continue to refine and reshape the model.

We see 'spirit' as an intrinsic, animating force that gives energy and momentum to human life. It propels us to look outward to connect our lives with all of life. It also propels us to look inward to create and recreate a link between 'my life' and 'all of life'. Spiritual development, then, is a constant, active, and ongoing process to create and recreate harmony between the 'discoveries' about the self and the 'discoveries' about the nature of life-writ-large. The two journeys (inner and outer) constantly inform each other and are always brought back into balance. Within this understanding are three major dynamics in spiritual development:

- Becoming aware of or awakened to the essence of the self and the essence of life-writ-large.
- Seeking, accepting, and/or experiencing an interconnection between one's inward and outward journeys in a way that brings harmony or coherence.
- Living life in accord with one's essence and one's understanding of or connection to life-writ-large.

Though all persons and cultures engage in these processes, they do so in many different ways. These processes may be active, intentional, or passive, and each may be emphasized more or less in different stages of development, different cultures, traditions, and worldviews. Thus, these dynamics may or may not be grounded in an understanding or experience of transcendence, including an understanding of God, a higher power, or other transcendent forces. Furthermore, the process of spiritual development may be wholly or partially accomplished within a religious context and worldview in which it is fundamentally understood as an experience of divine mystery, God, or other understandings of unseen forces in the world. However, spiritual development is not dependent on such an understanding or belief system.

Furthermore, consistent with current developmental theories, the use of the term 'development' emphasizes the reality of change across time within the domain. It does not imply a linear, invariant, or orderly progression of universal stages, but a set of interactive and dynamic processes and paths that vary in how they are accomplished. These tasks may be worked on multiple times throughout one's life, in any order and/or simultaneously, in cycles, in response to aging, life events, and/or other stimuli, and with potentially deeper, richer, and/or different results in subsequent cycles.

It is also important to recognize that these dimensions are embedded in and interact with physical, social, cognitive, emotional, moral, and other aspects of development in ways that we are only beginning to understand. Furthermore, they are informed by personal, family, religious community, and national beliefs, values, and practices; culture (language, customs, norms, symbols); socio-political realities; meta-narratives, traditions, myths, and interpretive frameworks (including sacred texts and traditions); and significant life events, experiences, and changes. All of these factors add considerable variability (and complexity) to the processes, dynamics, and outcomes of spiritual development.

PREVALENCE OF RELIGIOUS AND SPIRITUAL COMMITMENTS

Two foundational research issues in spiritual and religious development among children are the prevalence of these experiences, beliefs, and commitments and whether and how they affect development outcomes.

As we will discuss below, these questions are themselves fraught with definitional ambiguity. For example, we hypothesize that all young people engage in spiritual development, just as they engage in cognitive or emotional development. However, they may do this more or less intentionally, and they may do it in many different ways. Focusing on religious beliefs and practices is somewhat simpler, since one can ask whether and how children hold (or do not hold) certain beliefs, do or do not engage in certain rituals and practices, are part of particular religious communities and traditions, and so forth.

Even so, these variables only begin to touch on the underlying dynamics and distinctions. Though focused on adults, a study of 'unchurched religion' in the United States, Sweden, and Japan illustrates the complexity (Stark, Hamberg and Miller, 2005). In the United States, engagement in religious institutions ('churched religion') is significantly higher than the other countries. However, a lack of formal religious participation (which is often the default measure of religious commitment in research) is more than offset in Japan and Sweden by what the researchers describe as 'unchurched religion'. This category involves 'a relatively free-floating culture based on loose networks of like-minded individuals who, if they do gather regularly, do not acknowledge a specific religious creed, although they may tend to share a common religious outlook' (Stark, Hamberg and Miller, 2005: 8).

In Japan, for example, only 24 per cent of adults consider themselves to be 'religious'. Yet 88 per cent of Japanese households maintain Buddhist altars, and most Japanese engage in a wide range of established rituals (which would be called 'religions' in the West) in the home and in daily life – though participation in any kind of formal religious community or congregation is almost nonexistent aside from 'imported' religious practices of Christianity and other world religions (Stark et al., 2005).

Unfortunately, we do not have data that adequately capture some of the complexity implied in the above example. Where we do, the research focuses on older children or adolescents (ages 12 to 18), who can more accurately complete written surveys. Even so, the body of research in this age group is also limited. Most current research on religion and spirituality has occurred in a North American or European, Judeo-Christian context, which does not reflect the realities of most children in the world. Lippman and Keith (2006: 110) note that most surveys 'generally reflect a Western monotheistic frame of reference vis-à-vis spirituality and religion, and use terminology and concepts that are found in Judaism, Christianity, and Islam, such as the concept of one God who influences one's life'.

Despite these and other limitations, current research suggests significant levels of religious and spiritual beliefs and practices (broadly defined) among children in different cultures and contexts, though those expressions vary considerably. And a preponderance of the research (using widely varying measures, methods, and theoretical assumptions) points toward a positive impact on children's outcomes.

Some of the broadest evidence we have of religious and spiritual commitments globally come from the World Values Survey, which has been conducted four times since 1981, interviewing adults age 18 and older in nationally representative samples in 81 countries around the world (Inglehart et al., 2004). Unfortunately, the sample consists of adults, but the lowest age cohort, 18 to 24, gives some hints at the diverse patterns that likely formed in the first two decades of life.

Lippman and Keith (2006) examined a subset of the data from 20,000 18- to 24-year-olds in 41 of the countries representing all the regions of the world, focusing on three questions: the importance of religion in their lives, whether they believed in God, how important God was in their lives. They found a wide range in attitudes on all three questions. For example, belief in God ranged from a low of 40 per cent in Sweden to a high of 100 per cent in Pakistan. Young adults indicating that God is 'very important' ranged from a low of 2 per cent in Sweden to 100 per cent in Pakistan. And the percentage of those who place high importance on religion ranges from a low of 0 in Japan to 93 per cent in Nigeria. Lippman and Keith also noted that, 'In general, young adults in less economically developed countries are more likely to be spiritual, as well as religious, than those in more economically developed countries' (2006: 111).

One of the best sources of more detailed data on religious and spiritual beliefs and practices among children (ages 13 to 17) is the landmark National Study of Youth and Religion, led by sociologist Christian Smith (Smith and Denton, 2005). The study involved a nationally representative telephone survey of households containing at least one teenager age 13–17 between July 2002 to January 2003, followed up with in-person interviews in 2003 of a subsample of 267 respondents. (At the time of this writing, another wave of the longitudinal telephone survey has just been reported; see Pearce and Denton, 2011.) At a macro level, US young people reported that religion was important in shaping their daily lives as well as the major life decisions they face. They also reported feeling close to God and had very few doubts about their religious beliefs. Half said that their faith was extremely important or very important in shaping decisions, and only 19 per cent said that their faith was not very important or not at all important.

Finally, Benson and colleagues (2012) reported on an exploratory study of 6275 youth (ages 12 to 25) in eight countries in different regions of the globe in which they examined multiple dimensions of young people's religious and spiritual development, beliefs, and practices. They found that spiritual development is an active developmental process in the lives of a majority of youth in these countries across religious and cultural backgrounds. Using person-centred analyses, they identified different profiles of how young people engaged in the spiritual dimen-

sions of life. These profiles included youth who are high or low across multiple dimensions of their model, as well as those whose profiles emphasize in different combinations several dimensions of spiritual development, including mindfulness, prosocial action, or religious/spiritual practices.

At the same time, these overarching patterns should not be interpreted as evidence that religious and spiritual commitments are deeply and intentionally embedded in the lives of US children. Smith and Denton (2005) argued (based on the in-depth personal interviews) that these commitments are 'somewhere in the background' (p. 129) and that the most common attitude toward religious and spiritual matters is not a dogmatic, sectarian commitment but 'moral therapeutic deism' or a 'whatever' spirituality (p. 118). 'What appears to be the actual dominant religion among U.S. teenagers is centrally about feeling good, happy, secure, at peace' (p. 164). Hence, one might conclude that the United States is a culture that is imbued with an overall religious milieu that forms overall beliefs and attitudes, but that does not necessarily translate into deep personal commitments among young people. In fact, Smith concludes that only about 8 per cent of US teenagers are 'the devoted' for whom religious participation and commitment are central to life.

The situation is quite different in other parts of the world, as data from youth in Europe suggests. For example, among the 9400 respondents between the ages of 15 and 24 in 'The Young Europeans' study, only 19 per cent indicated that they believed and practised a religion. Another 43 per cent of respondents said that they had religious beliefs but they did not practice a religion, and 6 per cent practiced a religion but did not believe. An average of 12 per cent of youth overall identify as agnostic, and 15 per cent describe themselves as atheists (European Commission, 1997; also see Francis and Robbins, 2005; Hughes, 2007).

These disparate findings only begin to raise provocative questions about religious and spiritual commitments among children in different cultures and contexts. Most measures of religious beliefs and practices that are based in Judeo-Christian cultures show wide variation around the world, but they do not take into account the plurality of ways children engage in these aspects of life. Furthermore, as qualitative and quantitative studies delve more deeply into the more complex dynamics of these dimensions of life, new patterns and relationships will inevitably emerge that give new insight into the critical definitional questions, including the relationship between religious and spiritual development and the ways social and cultural ecologies shape these commitments and practices.

THE SOCIAL CONTEXT

Whereas early approaches to spiritual, religious, or faith development underscore individual change or transformation, the field increasingly recognizes the need to shift from an almost-exclusive focus on individuals to transactions between individuals and the various contexts in which they function, including family, peers, and other social relationships, institutional connections (schools, faith communities) and broader national, cultural, ethnic, economic, political, and social contexts (Regnerus, Smith and Smith, 2004; Roehlkepartain, Benson and Scales, 2011).

As a way of framing a broader context, Benson (2006b) offered a theoretical model that seeks to capture a broader, dynamic ecology for spiritual development in which it is understood that children's development (including their religious and spiritual development) occurs within multiple systems of influence and that children are active agents in their own development – with a dynamic interaction between person and context (Figure 5.1). Multiple levels of organizations engaged in human development – from biology and disposition to relationships, social institutions, culture and history – are fused into an integrated system (Lerner, 1976, 1998, 2002). Development has to do with changes in the relations among and between these multiple levels.

At the top of the figure are four circles, representing meaning, purpose, obligation, and contribution. The hypothesis here is that there are compelling (and universal) human motivations toward which spiritual development is drawn. To extend this idea, meaning, purpose, obligation (in the sense of one's moral duty), and contribution (knowing and affirming why one matters) *pull* persons into spiritual development and the animating forces within the person *push* the person forward. Hence, spiritual development is energized by both pull and push, and these dynamically intertwined processes are embedded in, responsive to, and emboldened or compromised by society, life experience, and culture.

Thus, this diagram is suggestive of the multiple dynamics, influences, and interactions that are at play in the shaping of a child's spiritual development, including socializing systems (family, peers, mentors, school, faith community, etc.), culture (language, customs, norms, symbols), and metanarratives and myths. Furthermore, it suggests that life events and experiences, as well as developmental growth, also inform and interact with this process. Within these domains, religious beliefs, communities, narratives, and norms become, in many instances, the specific content and context through which young people's identity, beliefs, and behaviours are formed – thus offering a more complex framework for understanding the interaction between religious and spiritual development.

Consistent with this general approach, Smith and Denton (2005: 240) identified three clusters of interconnected factors that 'may exert positive outcomes in the lives of teenagers':

- 'Moral order' that provides 'substantive cultural traditions grounded in and promoting particular normative ideas of what is good and bad,

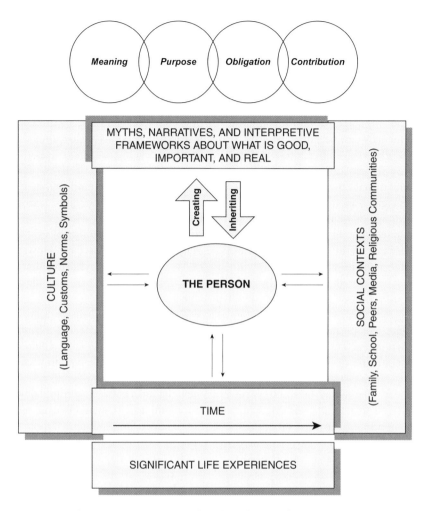

Figure 5.1   Essential Elements in a Comprehensive Theory of Spiritual Development

right and wrong, higher and lower, worthy and unworthy, just and unjust, and so on, which orient human consciousness and motivate human actions' (2005: 241). Moral order includes specific factors such as moral directives, spiritual experiences, and role models.

- 'Learned competencies' involves the ways that religious and spiritual engagement can impart skills and knowledge. These may include community and leadership skills, coping skills, and cultural capital.

- 'Social and organizational ties,' or 'structures of relations that affect the opportunities and constraints that young people face, which significantly affect outcomes in their lives' (2005: 246). Specific factors include social capital, network closure, and extra-community links.

These kinds of factors likely play out in multiple specific contexts within a larger ecological framework. As the research for this field broadens and deepens, scholars are focusing on cultural influences and variations (Mattis et al., 2006), regional, national, and socio-political variations (Verma and Sta. Maria, 2006), family (Boyatzis, Dollahite and Marks, 2006; Dollahite, Marks and Goodman, 2004; Erickson, 1992; King, Furrow and Roth, 2002; Lippman, Michelsen and Roehlkepartain, 2004; Mahoney et al., 2001; Pearce and Haynie, 2004), non-family peer and adult relationships (Oman and Thoresen, 2003; Schwartz et al., 2006), and religious community (Haight, 2002; King and Furrow,

2004; Larson, Hansen and Moneta, 2006; Maton and Sto. Domingo, 2006; Mercer, Matthews and Walz, 2004; Roehlkepartain, 2003a, 2003b; Roehlkepartain and Patel, 2006; Wagener et al., 2003; Yust, 2003).

In each of these cases, it is important to note that the influence of various environmental influences can be either positive or negative. Bartkowski et al. (2008: 16) analyzed family dynamics in early childhood and concluded that 'the family's religious environment can function alternately as a stepping stone or stumbling block for children's development. Frequent parent–child discussions about religion often yield positive effects on child development, while any effects associated with family arguments about religion are deleterious for children.'

Space does not permit delving into the dynamics within each of these relationships and social contexts. In each case, however, we would emphasize the bidirectional nature of the interaction between person and context. Borrowing from McAdams (1993), the myths and narratives that organize and give direction to our lives involve a lifelong creative process in which persons actively create (whether the activity is conscious or not) a story, using source material that can come from many institutions and relationships.

For some, this source material includes the myths inherited from religious traditions. It also includes the myths learned on Grandpa's or Grandma's lap and in the crucible of peer relationships, family, religious institution, school, and community. While the source material creates an abundance of texts, the person may choose to abandon some of the inherited texts, create new narratives, or weave inherited text and created text together in new ways. Thus, we must look for individual differences in the 'rules' persons use to create, accept, reject, or modify texts and narratives – and how those become woven into one's own religious or spiritual identity, commitments, and practices.

IMPACT OF RELIGIOUS AND SPIRITUAL COMMITMENTS

Much of the impetus for addressing religious and spiritual development in research, policy, medicine, child development, and related fields has emerged from the growing body of research that points to the unique power of spiritual development (and related concepts) in impacting children's lives. The current research tends to emphasize spirituality through the lens of religion, and it tends to focus on adolescents who are part of mainstream religious traditions in the United States, especially Christians. However, pending new and emerging research that addresses these limitations, the base provides a reasonable starting point.

The most comprehensive compilation of the extant research is *The Handbook of Spiritual Development in Childhood and Adolescence* (Roehlkepartain, King et al., 2006), which includes chapters that document the links between spiritual development and moral development (Walker and Reimer, 2006); civic development (Donnelly et al., 2006); identify formation (Templeton and Eccles, 2006); coping (Mahoney, Pendleton and Ihrke, 2006); resilience (Crawford, Wright and Masten, 2006); delinquency (Blakeney and Blakeney, 2006); well-being and thriving (King and Benson, 2006); and physical health (Oman and Thoresen, 2006). The handbook also notes the cases in which religious or spiritual practices can lead to harmful outcomes (see, especially, Wagener and Malony, 2006). (Also see Benson et al., 2005; Cotton et al., 2006; Kerestes and Youniss, 2003; Oser et al., 2006; Smith and Denton, 2005; Wong, Rew and Slaikeu, 2006.)

Complementing the handbook is Johnson's (2008: 189) massive review of more than 500 academic articles on the impact of 'organic religion' on people's lives (primarily adults). He describes 'organic religion' as that religion which is 'practiced over time, such as with children who were raised and nurtured in religious homes', thus differentiating it from 'institutional religion'. He examines research that documents various components of 'organic religion' as protecting against health risks such as injury, hypertension, depression, suicide, promiscuous sexual behaviours, alcohol and other drug use, and delinquency. He also reviews studies showing organic religion's association with a variety of prosocial factors, such as longevity, civic engagement, well-being, hope, purpose, and meaning in life, self-esteem, and educational attainment. He concludes:

> The vast majority of studies document the importance of religious influences in protecting youth from harmful outcomes as well as promoting beneficial and prosocial outcomes. The beneficial relationship between religion and health behaviours and outcomes is not simply a result of religion's constraining function or what it discourages – drug use, suicide, or delinquent behaviour – but also of what it encourages, namely, behaviours that can enhance hope, well-being, or educational attainment.
>
> (Johnson, 2008: 198)

By way of illustration of these relationships, Scales (2007b) analyzed data collected by Search Institute among 148,189 middle and high school students in 2003 through a survey that examines a wide range of dynamics in youth development, including religious participation (time spent weekly in a 'church, synagogue, mosque, or other religious or spiritual place') and how important it is to be religious or spiritual. (In this sample, 58 per cent of youth reported weekly religious participation and 50 per cent indicated that being religious or spiritual is 'quite' or 'extremely' important to them.)

Across all racial-ethnic and socio-economic groups, levels of religious participation and importance correlated with other important developmental resources and strengths known as Developmental Assets (Benson, 2006a). For example, religiously active and spiritual youth are at least 60 per cent more likely to experience the assets of 'community values youth', 'youth as resources', 'service to others', 'creative activities', and the value of 'restraint'. And they are 50–59 per cent more

likely to experience the assets of 'positive family communication', 'a caring neighbourhood', 'a caring school climate', 'parent involvement in schooling', and time spent in youth programs.

In addition, young people's religious and spiritual commitments correlate with reduced levels of a wide range of high-risk behaviours and higher levels of thriving. For example, young people who are religiously active are, on average, 39 per cent less likely to engage in 10 high-risk behaviour patterns, especially use of tobacco, illicit drugs, school problems, alcohol abuse, antisocial behaviour, and driving and alcohol. In addition, they are, on average, 26 per cent more likely to have eight indicators of thriving, especially getting good grades in school, resisting danger, maintaining physical health, and leadership (Scales, 2007b).

Of course, we cannot show causality from analysis of cross-sectional data, but only show that there is a statistical relationship. However, the same survey instrument has been used in one community, following 370 students for three years (from 1998 when they were in middle school to 2001 when they were in high school, thus covering a major developmental transition time of early adolescence). Scales (2007a) separately analyzed data from young people who said being spiritual was important or very important to them, versus young people who did not, and from young people who participated at least one hour a week, on average, in a religious community, versus young people who did not.

The study found that young people who were religiously active in middle school were less likely to engage in five high-risk behaviours three years later: alcohol abuse, driving and alcohol, tobacco, illicit drugs, and sexual intercourse. For example, only 13 per cent of youth who were religiously active in middle school had alcohol abuse problems in high school, versus 23 per cent of inactive youth. In addition, a higher percentage of religiously active youth in middle school also exhibited four thriving indicators (resisting danger, informal helping of others, leadership, and overcoming adversity) in high school. The importance placed in middle school on being spiritual or religious had a similar relationship to outcomes three years later.

These longitudinal findings give more confidence in claiming a causal connection between religious and spiritual commitments and child and adolescent outcomes. It is important not to overstate the power of these relationships. Regression analyses showed that when considered alone, apart from any other influences in a young person's world, religious community and spirituality each explain only about 5 per cent of the variation in indexes of risk and thriving created by summing up the individual scores to the various risk patterns and thriving indicators. In other words, single factors rarely explain much of young people's well-being. Rather, life outcomes are shaped by multiple influences operating in multiple parts of young people's worlds, and over multiple points in time.

DIRECTIONS FOR FUTURE RESEARCH

As suggestive as these findings are (like much of the research in the field), our confidence in their broad import must be qualified because of superficial measures (for example, two items), limited methods (mostly cross-sectional surveys or small, non-representative samples), and narrow samples (young people in the United States). Our hope is that the new momentum in this field sets the stage for a wider range of research that will address these limitations. Though the issues are implied above, we summarize key issues for enriching the research base.

Measures

The contrast between the call for deep, multidimensional theoretical frameworks and the 'shallow' measures most often used in

this domain represents one of the major challenges for the future of research in child and adolescent spiritual development. Though the situation is improving (e.g., Benson et al., 2012), the vast majority of studies of spiritual or religious development among children and adolescence have utilized relatively superficial measures, usually religious participation, importance of religion or spirituality, or religious affiliation (Rew and Wong, 2006; Tsang and McCullough, 2003). When multi-item scales are used, they are often denomination or tradition specific (such as assuming a belief in a deity or particular religious tenets), and often they do not provide evidence of scale reliability for use with children or adolescents (Houskamp et al., 2004; Rew and Wong, 2006). Though there are many scales available that address various parts of the terrain of religious or spiritual development (Gorsuch and Walker, 2006; Hill and Hood, 1999), there are relatively few options that address specific dimensions of spiritual development, particularly outside of a North American conceptualization of spirituality. (Those available are helpfully examined and analyzed by Haber, Jacob and Spangler, 2007.) Further complicating the measurement issue is the complexity of language structures within this domain, particularly when seeking to conduct research with children and cross-culturally.

Methods

There is no perfect method for studying religious and spiritual development among children and adolescents. Indeed, given the emergent state of the field, the multidimensionality of the domain, and the inherent limitations of language in these matters, variety in both qualitative and quantitative methods is needed. Qualitative studies (interviews, focus groups, observation, art, journaling, etc.) allow for deeper nuanced examinations of the dynamics, while quantitative approaches lend themselves more readily to examining patterns, relationships, variability, and generalizations. And, of course, combining qualitative and quantitative methods within a particular study framework allows for triangulation and interplay across methods in ways that have potential to enrich the results and strengthen theoretical frameworks.

On the quantitative side, a priority needs to be placed on utilizing more sophisticated measures with more diverse and representative samples while also shifting the balance from cross-sectional studies to longitudinal, intervention designs (Gorsuch and Walker, 2006), and other more complex methods, such as the Experience-Sampling Method (ESM) (Hektner, Schmidt and Csikszentmihalyi, 2006). Quantitative approaches that are appropriate for younger children will also deepen understanding of this domain and the developmental trajectories through childhood (Bartkowski et al., 2008).

A particular challenge in qualitative research is dealing with the tendency of children to simply report the religious beliefs and practices of their parents when asked questions about this dimension of life, particularly when they have not had opportunities to shape their own language for understanding. In-depth interviews (such as Coles, 1990) have significant potential to uncover underlying issues across time, though such methods are time-consuming and costly. However, done well, these qualitative approaches that are analyzed using grounded theory methods (Glaser, 1992; Strauss, 1987) have the potential to inform the underlying theory needed to deepen understanding in this field.

Samples

Virtually every major review article on religious and spiritual development concludes with a lament about the lack of diverse samples (see, for example, Rew and Wong, 2006). As already noted, most research in this domain disproportionately utilizes white, Judeo-Christian samples of young people in the United States. And most of this research is limited to the adolescent years (ages 12 to 18), with very little high-quality research available on younger children. The variability and commonalities we see in those studies that examine religious and spiritual dynamics across cultures, traditions, socio-economic differences, and national boundaries suggests that increasing the diversity and representativeness of quantitative and qualitative samples would yield important understandings for the field – and for overall understanding of the place of religious and spiritual development in child development. In addition, there is a significant need for large enough samples to analyze by individual differences (such as age, gender, race/ethnicity, socio-economic status, family composition, education, and faith tradition).

TOWARD A FIELD OF INQUIRY

In order to contribute to building this field, Search Institute's Center for Spiritual Development in Childhood and Adolescence engaged in a series of exploratory studies with children (primarily ages 12 to 18) in multiple countries (in addition to ongoing secondary analyses of extant datasets) between 2006 and 2009. Each informed our emerging and evolving theory of spiritual development. Three studies merit mention.

First, we have conducted more than 80 focus groups with youth, parents, and youth workers in 13 countries to surface their implicit understanding of spiritual development, its relationship to religious development, and their perceptions of the dynamics that shape young people's developmental trajectories within this domain. Grounded theory analysis allowed for surfacing of themes in this domain from across diverse religious and cultural contexts (Kimball, Mannes and Hackel, 2009), which informed other studies.

Second, we conducted close to 30 interviews with young people who are 'spiritual exemplars' in six countries in different regions of the world (King, Clardy and Ramos, in press). These interviews uncovered the dynamics that occur within the lives of young people whose lives exhibit patterns of optimal development within this domain of life. These structured, in-depth interviews allowed these young people to articulate some of the deeper dynamics that informed our emerging theoretical framework.

Finally, we conducted an exploratory quantitative survey of 6725 young people in eight countries in different parts of the world in which we made empirical tests of both our theoretical assumptions and some of the hypotheses that have emerged from other research (Benson et al., 2012). These early data highlight the challenge of operationalizing a complex, ecological theory and model while also suggesting that it remains a fertile and fruitful approach to investigating this domain of human development.

When combined, these various studies (all of which grow out of shared assumptions and frameworks) set the stage for more systematic and comprehensive data collection by diverse scholars. Our hope is that they will provide frameworks, language, and structure that will facilitate a range of studies that document both the commonalities in spiritual development as a core part of human development as well as the wide diversity of beliefs, practices, and worldviews that shape the particularities of children's spiritual and religious development.

Each of these efforts contributes to expanding and deepening the research tools available for this field. Yet we know that these only begin the process. Our exploratory studies need to be followed with rigorous longitudinal and representative studies. Because we have chosen in this first round to explore broad, cross-cultural issues, additional research efforts are needed that delve deeply into these dynamics within a particular culture, tradition, context, or socializing system, thus reducing some of the variables that need to be considered in analyzing and interpreting the findings. However, studies

must begin to share core theoretical foundations and measures of spiritual development for such an approach to yield results that can be analyzed to advance a shared understanding that is both broad and deep and that reflects the commonalities and particularities in experience, belief, and practices in this domain of life.

REFERENCES

Bartkowski, J.P., Xu, X. and Levin, M.L. (2008) 'Religion and child development: Evidence from the Early Childhood Longitudinal Study', *Social Science Research*, 37(1): 18–36.

Benson, P.L. (2006a) *All Kids Are Our Kids: What Communities Must Do to Raise Caring and Responsible Children and Adolescents (2nd edn)*. San Francisco: Jossey-Bass.

Benson, P.L. (2006b) 'The science of child and adolescent spiritual development: Definitional, theoretical, and field-building challenges', in E.C. Roehlkepartain, P.E. King, L. Wagener and P.L. Benson (eds.), *The Handbook of Spiritual Development in Childhood and Adolescence*. Thousand Oaks, CA: Sage, pp. 484–97.

Benson, P.L. and King, P.E. (2006) 'Adolescence', in H.R. Ebaugh (ed.), *Handbook on Religion and Social Institutions*. New York: Springer, pp. 121–38.

Benson, P.L., Roehlkepartain, E.C. and Rude, S.P. (2003) 'Spiritual development in childhood and adolescence: Toward a field of inquiry', *Applied Developmental Science*, 7(3): 204–12.

Benson, P.L., Scales, P.C., Syvertsen, A.K. and Roehlkepartain, E.C. (2012) 'Is youth spiritual development a universal developmental process? An international exploration', *Journal of Positive Psychology*, 7(6): 453–70.

Benson, P.L., Scales, P.C., Sesma, A., Jr. and Roehlkepartain, E.C. (2005) 'Adolescent spirituality', in K.A. Moore and L.H. Lippman (eds.), *What Do Children Need to Flourish? Conceptualizing and Measuring Indicators of Positive Development*. New York: Springer, pp. 25–40.

Bergin, A.E. (1991) 'Values and religious issues in psychotherapy and mental health', *American Psychologist*, 46(4): 394–403.

Blakeney, R.F. and Blakeney, C.D. (2006) 'Delinquency: A quest for moral and spiritual integrity?', in E.C. Roehlkepartain, P.E. King, L. Wagener and P.L. Benson (eds.), *The Handbook of Spiritual Development in Childhood and Adolescence*. Thousand Oaks, CA: Sage, pp. 371–83.

Boyatzis, C.J., Dollahite, D.C. and Marks, L.D. (2006) 'The family as a context for religious and spiritual development in children and youth', in E.C. Roehlkepartain, P.E. King, L. Wagener and P.L. Benson (eds.), *The Handbook of Spiritual Development in Childhood and Adolescence*. Thousand Oaks, CA: Sage, pp. 297–309.

Bridges, L.J. and Moore, K.A. (2002) *Religion and Spirituality in Childhood and Adolescence*. Washington, DC: Child Trends.

Brown, B.B., Larson, R.W. and Saraswathi, T.S. (2002) *The World's Youth: Adolescence in Eight Regions of the Globe*. Cambridge, UK: Cambridge University Press.

Coles, R. (1990) *The Spiritual Life of Children*. Boston, MA: Houghton Mifflin.

Cotton, S., Zebracki, K., Rosenthal, S.L., Tsevat, J. and Drotar, D. (2006) 'Religion/spirituality and adolescent health outcomes: A review', *Journal of Adolescent Health*, 38(4): 472–80.

Crawford, E., Wright, M.O. and Masten, A.S. (2006) 'Resilience and spirituality in youth', in E.C. Roehlkepartain, P.E. King, L. Wagener and P.L. Benson (eds.), *The Handbook of Spiritual Development in Childhood and Adolescence*. Thousand Oaks, CA: Sage, pp. 355–70.

Davie, G. (2003) 'The evolution of the sociology of religion: Theme and variations', in M. Dillon, *Handbook of the Sociology of Religion*. Cambridge, UK: Cambridge University Press, pp. 61–75.

Dollahite, D.C., Marks, L.D. and Goodman, M. (2004) 'Families and religious beliefs, practices, and communities: Linkages in a diverse and dynamic cultural context', in M.J. Coleman and L.H. Ganong (eds.), *The Handbook of Contemporary Families: Considering the Past, Contemplating the Future*. Thousand Oaks, CA: Sage, pp. 411–31.

Donnelly, T.M., Matsuba, M.K., Hart, D. and Atkins, R. (2006) 'The relationship between spiritual development and civic development', in E.C. Roehlkepartain, P.E. King, L.M. Wagener and P.L. Benson (eds.), *The Handbook of Spiritual Development in Childhood and Adolescence*. Thousand Oaks, CA: Sage, pp. 239–51.

Dowling, E.M. and Scarlett, W.G. (2006) *Encyclopaedia of Religious and Spiritual Development in Childhood and Adolescence*. Thousand Oaks, CA: Sage.

Eccles, J.S. and Gootman, J.A. (eds.) (2002) *Community Programs to Promote Youth Development*. Washington, DC: National Academy Press.

Ellis, A. (1980) 'Psychotherapy and atheistic values: A response to A.E. Bergin's "Psychotherapy and reli-gious values"', *Journal of Consulting and Clinical Psychology*, 48(5): 635–9.

Erickson, J.A. (1992) 'Adolescent religious development and commitment: A structural equation model of the role of family, peer group, and educational influence', *Journal for the Scientific Study of Religion*, 31(2): 131–52.

European Commission (1997) *The Young Europeans: Eurobarometer 47.2*. Available at http://europa.eu.int/comm/public_opinion/archives/eb_special_en.htm

Francis, L.J. and Robbins, M. (2005) *Urban Hope and Spiritual Health: The Adolescent Voice*. Peterborough, UK: Epworth.

Freud, S. (1961) *The Future of an Illusion*. London: Hogarth Press and the Institute of Psycho-Analysis.

Glaser, B. (1992) *Basics of Grounded Theory Analysis*. Mill Valley, CA: Sociology Press.

Gorsuch, R.L. and Walker, D. (2006) 'Measurement and research design in studying spiritual development', in E.C. Roehlkepartain, P.E. King, L. Wagener and P.L. Benson (eds.), *The Handbook of Spiritual Development in Childhood and Adolescence*. Thousand Oaks, CA: Sage, pp. 92–103.

Gottlieb, A. (2006) 'Non-Western approaches to spiritual development among infants and young children: A case study from West Africa', in E.C. Roehlkepartain, P.E. King, L. Wagener and P.L. Benson (eds.), *The Handbook of Spiritual Development in Childhood and Adolescence*. Thousand Oaks, CA: Sage, pp. 150–62.

Green, M. (2006) *A Journey of Discovery: Spirituality and Spiritual Development in Youth Work*. Leicester, UK: National Youth Agency.

Haber, J.R., Jacob, T. and Spangler, D.J.C. (2007) 'Dimensions of religion/spirituality and relevance to health research', *International Journal for the Psychology of Religion*, 17(4): 265–88.

Haight, W. (2002) *African-American Children at Church: A Sociocultural Perspective*. Cambridge, UK: Cambridge University Press.

Hay, D. and Nye, R. (1998) *The Spirit of the Child*. London: Fount/HarperCollins.

Hektner, J.M., Schmidt, J.A. and Csikszentmihalyi, M. (2006) *Experience Sampling Method: Measuring the Quality of Everyday Life*. Thousand Oaks, CA: Sage Publications.

Helminiak, D.A. (2006) 'The role of spirituality in formulating a theory of the psychology of religion', *Zygon*, 41(1): 197–224.

Hill, P.C. and Hood, R.W. (1999) *Measures of Religiosity*. Birmingham, AL: Religious Education Press.

Hill, P.C. and Pargament, K.I. (2003) 'Advances in the conceptualization and measurement of religion and spirituality: Implications for physical and mental health research', *American Psychologist*, 58(1): 64–74.

Hill, P.C., Pargament, K.I., Hood, R.W., McCullough, M.E., Swyers, J.P., Larson, D.B., et al. (2000) 'Conceptualizing religion and spirituality: Points of commonality, points of departure', *Journal for the Theory of Social Behavior*, 30(1): 52–77.

Houskamp, B.M., Fisher, L.A. and Stuber, M.L. (2004) 'Spirituality in children and adolescents: Research findings and implications for clinicians and researchers', *Child and Adolescent Psychiatric Clinics of North America*, 13(1): 221–30.

Hughes, P. (2007) *Putting Life Together: Findings from Australian Youth Spirituality Research*. Fairfield, Australia: Fairfield Press.

Inglehart, R., Basañez, M., Díez-Medrano, J., Halman, L. and Luijkx, R. (2004) *Human Beliefs and Values: A Cross-cultural Sourcebook Based upon the 1999–2002 Values Surveys*. Mexico City: Siglo Veintiuno Editores.

James, W. (1958) *The Varieties of Religious Experience: A Study in Human Nature*. Cambridge, MA: Harvard University Press. (Original work published 1902.)

Johnson, B.R. (2008) 'A tale of two religious effects: Evidence for the protective and prosocial impact of organic religion', in K.K. Kline (ed.), *Authoritative Communities: The Scientific Case for Nurturing the Whole Child*. New York: Springer, pp. 187–226.

Kerestes, M. and Youniss, J.E. (2003) 'Rediscovering the importance of religion in adolescent development', in R.M. Lerner, F. Jacobs and D. Wertlieb (eds.), *Handbook of Applied Developmental Science*: Vol. 1. *Applying Developmental Science for Youth and Families – Historical and Theoretical Foundations*. Thousand Oaks, CA: Sage, pp. 165–84.

Kimball, E.M., Mannes, M. and Hackel, A. (2009) 'Voices of global youth on spirituality and spiritual development: Preliminary findings from a grounded theory study', in M. de Souza, L. Francis, J. O'Higgins-Norman and D. Scott (eds.), *International Handbook of Education for Spirituality, Care and Wellbeing*. Dordrecht: Springer, pp. 329–48.

King, P.E. and Benson, P.L. (2006) 'Spiritual development and adolescent well-being and thriving', in E. C. Roehlkepartain, P.E. King, L. Wagener and P.L. Benson (eds.), *The Handbook of Spiritual Development in Childhood and Adolescence*. Thousand Oaks, CA: Sage, pp. 384–98.

King, P.E. and Boyatzis, C. (Guest editors) (2004) 'Special issue: Exploring adolescent spiritual and religious development: Current and future theoretical and empirical perspectives', *Applied Developmental Science*, 8(1): 2–6.

King, P.E. and Furrow, J.L. (2004) 'Religion as a resource for positive youth development: Religion, social capital, and moral outcomes', *Developmental Psychology*, 40(5): 703–13.

King, P.E., Furrow, J.L. and Roth, N.H. (2002) 'The influence of family and peers on adolescent religiousness', *The Journal for Psychology and Christianity*, 21(2): 109–20.

King, P.E., Clardy, C.E., and Ramos, J.R. (in press) 'Adolescent spiritual exemplars: Exploring adolescent spirituality among diverse youth', *Journal of Adolescent Research*.

King, P.E., Clardy, C.E., and Ramos, J.R. (2013) 'Adolescent spiritual exemplars: Exploring spirituality in the lives of diverse youth', *Journal of Adolescent Research* [published online 12 September 2013]. doi:10.1177/0743558413502534 *Psychology*, 6th ed., Vol. 1: *Theoretical Models of Human Development*. New York: John Wiley, pp. 942–98.

King, P.E., Ramos, J.S., and Clardy, C.E. (2013) 'Searching for the sacred: Religion, spirituality, and adolescent development', in K.I. Pargament, J.J. Exline, and J.W. Jones (eds.), *APA Handbook of Psychology, Religion, and Spirituality (Vol. 1): Context, Theory, and Research*. Washington, DC: American Psychological Association, pp. 513–28.

King, P.E., and Roeser, R.W. (2009) 'Religion and spirituality in adolescent development', in R.M. Lerner and L. Steinberg (eds.), *Handbook of Adolescent Psychology, Volume 1, Individual Bases of Adolescent Development, 3rd Edition*. New York: Wiley, pp. 435–78.

Larson, E.J. and Witham, L. (1998, July) 'Leading scientists still reject God', *Nature*, 394(6691): 313.

Larson, R.W., Hansen, D.M. and Moneta, G. (2006) 'Differing profiles of developmental experiences across types of organized youth activities', *Developmental Psychology*, 42(5): 849–63.

Lerner, R.M. (1976) *Concepts and Theories of Human Development*. Reading, MA: Addison-Wesley.

Lerner, R.M. (1998) 'Theories of human development: Contemporary perspectives', in W. Damon and R. M. Lerner (eds.), *Handbook of Child Psychology: Vol. 1. Theoretical Models of Human Development*. New York: Wiley, pp. 1–24.

Lerner, R.M. (2002) *Concepts and Theories of Human Development* (3rd ed.). Mahwah, NJ: Erlbaum.

Lippman, L.H. and Keith, J.D. (2006) 'The demographics of spirituality among youth: International perspectives', in E.C. Roehlkepartain, P.E. King, L.M. Wagener, and P.L. Benson (eds.), *The Handbook of Spiritual Development in Childhood and Adolescence*. Thousand Oaks, CA: Sage, pp. 109–23.

Lippman, L., Michelsen, E. and Roehlkepartain, E.C. (2004) *Indicators of the Social Context of Families: The Measurement of Family Religiosity and Spirituality.* Unpublished paper prepared for the Office of the Assistant Secretary for Planning and Evaluation, US Department of Health and Human Services.

McAdams, D.P. (1993) *The Stories We Live by: Personal Myths and the Making of the Self.* New York: Guilford.

McCrae, R.R. (1999) 'Mainstream personality psychology and the study of religion', *Journal of Personality*, 67(6): 1209–18.

MacDonald, D.A. (2000) 'Spirituality: Description, measurement, and relation to the five factor model of personality', *Journal of Personality*, 68(1): 157–97.

Mahoney, A., Pargament, K.I., Tarakeshwar, N. and Swank, A.B. (2001) 'Religion in the home in the 1980s and 1990s: A meta-analytic review and conceptual analysis of links between religion, marriage, and parenting', *Journal of Family Psychology*, 15(3): 539–96.

Mahoney, A., Pendleton, S. and Ihrke, H. (2006) 'Religious coping by children and adolescents: Unexplored territory in the realm of spiritual development', in E.C. Roehlkepartain, P.E. King, L.M. Wagener and P.L. Benson (eds.), *The Handbook of Spiritual Development in Childhood and Adolescence.* Thousand Oaks, CA: Sage, pp. 341–54.

Marler, P.L. and Hadaway, C.K. (2002) '"Being religious" or "being spiritual" in America: A zero-sum proposition', *Journal for the Scientific Study of Religion*, 41(2): 288–300.

Maton, K.I. and Sto. Domingo, M.R. (2006) 'Mobilizing adults for positive youth development: Lessons from religious congregations', in E. G. Clary and J. Rhodes (eds.), *Mobilizing Adults for Positive Development.* New York: Kluwer Academic/Plenum, pp. 159–76.

Mattis, J.S., Ahluwalia, M.K., Cowie, S.A.E. and Kirkland-Harris, A.M. (2006) 'Ethnicity, culture, and spiritual development', in E. C. Roehlkepartain, P.E. King, L.M. Wagener and P.L. Benson (eds.), *The Handbook of Spiritual Development in Childhood and Adolescence.* Thousand Oaks, CA: Sage, pp. 283–96.

Mercer, J.A., Matthews, D.L. and Walz, S. (2004) 'Children in congregations; Congregations as contexts for children's spiritual growth', in D. Ratcliff (ed.), *Children's Spirituality: Christian Perspectives, Research, and Applications.* Eugene, OR: Cascade Books, pp. 249–65.

Nye, R.M. (1999) 'Relational consciousness and the spiritual lives of children: Convergence with children's theory of mind', in K.H. Reich, F.K. Oser and W.G. Scarlett (eds.), *Psychological Studies on Spiritual and Religious Development: Vol. 2. Being Human: The Case of Religion.* Lengerich, Germany: Pabst Science, pp. 57–82.

Oman, D. and Thoresen, C.E. (2006) 'Religion, spirituality, and children's physical health', in E.C. Roehlkepartain, P.E. King, L.M. Wagener and P.L. Benson (eds.), *The Handbook of Spiritual Development in Childhood and Adolescence.* Thousand Oaks, CA: Sage, pp. 399–415.

Oman, D. and Thoresen, C.E. (2003) 'Spiritual modelling: A key to spiritual and religious growth?', *International Journal for the Psychology of Religion*, 13(3): 149–65.

Paloutzian, R.F. (1996) Invitation to the psychology of religion (2nd ed.), Needham Heights, MA: Allyn and Bacon.

Pargament, K.I. (1997) *The Psychology of Religion and Coping: Theory, Research, Practice.* New York: Guilford.

Pargament, K.I. (1999) 'The psychology of religion and spirituality? Yes and no', *International Journal for the Psychology of Religion*, 9(1): 3–16.

Pearce, L.C. and Denton, M.L. (2011) *A Faith of their own: Stability and Change in the Religiosity of America's Adolescents.* New York: Oxford University Press.

Pearce, L.D. and Haynie, D.L. (2005) 'Intergenerational religious dynamics and adolescent delinquency', *Social Forces*, 82(4): 1553–72.

Ratcliff, D. and Nye, R. (2006) 'Childhood spirituality: Strengthening the research foundation', in E. C. Roehlkepartain, P. E. King, L. M. Wagener and P. L. Benson (eds.), *The Handbook of Spiritual Development in Childhood and Adolescence.* Thousand Oaks, CA: Sage, pp. 473–83.

Regnerus, M.D., Smith, C. and Smith, B. (2004) 'Social context in the development of adolescent religiosity', *Applied Developmental Science*, 8(1): 27–38.

Reich, K.H. (1996) 'A logic-based typology of science and theology', *Journal of Interdisciplinary Studies*, 8(1–2): 149–67.

Rew, L. and Wong, Y.J. (2006) 'A systematic review of associations among religiosity/spirituality and adolescent health attitudes and behaviors', *Journal of Adolescent Health*, 38(4): 433–42.

Roehlkepartain, E.C. (2003a) 'Building strengths, deepening faith: Understanding and enhancing youth development in Protestant congregations', in R.M. Lerner, F. Jacobs and D. Wertlieb (eds.). *Handbook of Applied Developmental Science, vol. 3: Promoting Positive Youth and Family Development.* Thousand Oaks, CA: Sage Publications, pp. 515–34.

Roehlkepartain, E.C. (2003b) 'Making room at the table for everyone: Interfaith engagement in positive child and adolescent development', in R.M. Lerner, F. Jacobs and D. Wertlieb (eds.). *Handbook of Applied Developmental Science, vol. 3: Promoting Positive Youth and Family Development.* Thousand Oaks, CA; Sage Publications, pp. 535–63.

Roehlkepartain, E.C., Benson, P.L., King, P.E. and Wagener, L.M. (2006) 'Spiritual development in childhood and adolescence: Moving to the scientific mainstream', in E.C. Roehlkepartain, P.E. King, L.M. Wagener and P.L. Benson (eds.). *The Handbook of Spiritual Development in Childhood and Adolescence.* Thousand Oaks, CA: Sage Publications, pp. 1–15.

Roehlkepartain, E.C., Benson, P.L. and Scales, P.C. (2011) 'Spiritual identity: Contextual perspectives', in S.J. Schwartz, K. Luyckx and V.L. Vignoles (eds.), *The Handbook of Identity Theory and Research: Vol. 2 – Domains and Categories.* New York: Springer, pp. 545–62.

Roehlkepartain, E.C., King, P.E., Wagener, L.M. and Benson, P.L. (eds.) (2006) *The Handbook of Spiritual Development in Childhood and Adolescence.* Thousand Oaks, CA: Sage Publications.

Roehlkepartain, E.C. and Patel, E. (2006) 'Congregations: Unexamined crucibles of spiritual development', in E.C. Roehlkepartain, P.E. King, L.M. Wagener and P.L. Benson, *The Handbook of Spiritual Development in Childhood and Adolescence.* Thousand Oaks, CA: Sage Publications, pp. 324–36.

Scales, P.C. (2007a, May) Early spirituality and religious participation linked to later adolescent well-being (Fast Fact). Available at www.spiritualdevelopment-center.org/FastFacts4

Scales, P.C. (2007b, February) Spirituality and adolescent well-being: selected new statistics (Fast Fact). Available at www.spiritualdevelopmentcenter.org/FastFacts2

Schwartz, K.D., Bokowski, W.M. and Aoki, W.T. (2006) 'Mentors, friends, and gurus: Peer and nonparental influences on spiritual development', in E.C. Roehlkepartain, P.E. King, L. Wagener and P.L. Benson (eds.), *The Handbook of Spiritual Development in Childhood and Adolescence.* Thousand Oaks, CA: Sage, pp. 310–23.

Smith, C. and Denton, M.L. (2005) *Soul Searching: The Religious and Spiritual Lives of American Teenagers.* New York: Oxford University Press.

Stark, R. (2001) 'Reconceptualizing religion, magic, and science', *Review of Religious Research,* 43(2): 101–20.

Stark, R., Hamberg, E. and Miller, A.S. (2005) 'Exploring spirituality and unchurched religions in America, Sweden, and Japan', *Journal of Contemporary Religion,* 20(1): 3–23.

Stifoss-Hanssen, H. (1999) 'Religion and spirituality: What a European ear hears', *International Journal for the Psychology of Religion,* 9(1): 25–33.

Strauss, A. (1987) *Qualitative Analysis for Social Scientists.* Cambridge, England: Cambridge University Press.

Templeton, J.L. and Eccles, J.S. (2006) 'The relation between spiritual development and identity processes', in E.C. Roehlkepartain, P.E. King, L. Wagener and P.L. Benson (eds.), *The Handbook of Spiritual Development in Childhood and Adolescence.* Thousand Oaks, CA: Sage, pp. 252–65.

Tsang, J.A. and McCullough, M.E. (2003) 'Measuring religious constructs: A hierarchical approach to construct organization and scale selection', in S.J. Lopez and C.R. Snyder (eds.), *Positive Psychological Assessments: A Handbook of Models and Measures.* Washington, DC: American Psychological Association, pp. 345–60.

Verma, S. and Sta. Maria, M. (2006) 'The changing global context of adolescent spirituality', in E.C. Roehlkepartain, P.E. King, L. Wagener and P.L. Benson (eds.), *The Handbook of Spiritual Development in Childhood and Adolescence.* Thousand Oaks, CA: Sage, pp. 124–36.

Vitz, P. (2008) 'Moral and spiritual dimensions of the healthy person: Notes from the founders of modern psychology and psychiatry', in Kline, K.K. (ed.) *Authoritative Communities: The Scientific Case for Nurturing the whole Child.* New York: Springer, pp. 151–62.

United Nations Office of the High Commissioner for Human Rights (1989) *Convention on the Rights of the Child.* Available at http://www2.ohchr.org/english/law?.htm

Wagener, L.M., Furrow, J.L., King, P.E., Leffert, N. and Benson, P.L. (2003) 'Religious involvement and developmental resources in youth', *Review of Religious Research,* 44(3): 271–84.

Wagener, L.M. and Malony, H.N. (2006) 'Spiritual and religious pathology in childhood and adolescence', in E.C. Roehlkepartain, P.E. King, L. Wagener and P.L. Benson (eds.), *The Handbook of Spiritual Development in Childhood and Adolescence.* Thousand Oaks, CA: Sage, pp. 137–49.

Walker, L.J. and Reimer, K.S. (2006) 'The relationship between moral and spiritual development', in E.C. Roehlkepartain, P.E. King, L. Wagener and P.L. Benson (eds.), *The Handbook of Spiritual*

Development in Childhood and Adolescence. Thousand Oaks, CA: Sage, pp. 224–38.

Weaver, A.J., Samford, J.A., Morgan, V.J., Lichton, A.I., Larson, D.B. and Garbarino, J. (2000) 'Research on religious variables in five major adolescent research journals: 1992–1996', *Journal of Nervous and Mental Disease*, 188(1): 36–44.

Wong, Y.J., Rew, L. and Slaikeu, K.D. (2006) 'A systematic review of recent research on adolescent religiosity/spirituality and mental health', *Issues in Mental Health Nursing*, 27(2): 161–83.

Wulff, D.M. (1997) *Psychology of religion: Classic and contemporary.* New York: John Wiley.

Wuthnow, R. (1998) *After Heaven: Spirituality in America since the 1950s.* Berkeley and Los Angeles: University of California Press.

Yust, K.M. (2003) 'Toddler spiritual formation and the faith community', *International Journal of Children's Spirituality*, 8(2): 133–49.

Yust, K.M., Johnson, A.N., Sasso, S.E. and Roehlkepartain, E.C. (eds.) (2006), *Nurturing Child and Adolescent Spirituality: Perspectives from the World's Religious Traditions.* Portland, OR: Rowman and Littlefield.

Zinnbauer, B.J., Pargament, K.I., Cole, B., Rye, M.S., Butter, E.M., Belavich, T.G., et al. (1997) 'Religion and spirituality: Unfuzzying the fuzzy', *Journal for the Scientific Study of Religion*, 36(4): 549–64.

Zinnbauer, B.J., Pargament, K.I. and Scott, A.B. (1999) 'The emerging meanings of religiousness and spirituality: Problems and prospects', *Journal of Personality*, 67(6): 889–919.

6

Children as Patients

Priscilla Alderson

INTRODUCTION: BROAD AREA OF RESEARCH

Research about health and illness extends very broadly across investigations of health and the spectrum of normality, to determine when illness and the need for treatment begin and to prevent unnecessary treatment. Research about children as patients includes studying the causes, prevention, and treatment of physical and psychological disorders. There have been great gains for child health and survival and in preventing and treating children's illnesses, injuries, and impairments. Social research about child patients' own views and experiences has helped to make medical treatment more humane and ethical, as reviewed later. Childhood is taken in this chapter to begin from birth, except for one example of the foetus as patient.

The more I reflected on the title I was asked to write about, 'children as patients', the more complicated the title appeared to be. This chapter therefore begins by reviewing eight contested meanings of how children are defined as and identify themselves as patients. The borderlines between health and illness tend to be drawn differently in the minority richer world (less than one fifth of

the world's total population of over 7 billion) and the majority poorer world. Later sections will review traditional types of research about children as patients, based on developmental medical and psychological models, illustrated by the example of cognitive behaviour therapy. Traditional methodologies are contrasted with more recent innovative ones, with their expanding concepts of childhood as a social construction, children's rights, their participation, competence, consent, and research ethics. The chapter concludes by reviewing how research with children as patients offers unique insights into children's capacities, their status, and value to their society. The conclusion also discusses enablers and barriers to future research, which is intended to promote the effective, benign, and respectful care of children as patients.

Until around 1990, research mainly concentrated on adults' views about children and was seriously limited in excluding children's own views. Since then, there has been a valuable increase in attention to children's views and experiences. However, research now risks falling into the opposite serious limitation: to attend only to topics and areas that children are assumed to be able to understand and discuss, and to exclude vital 'adult' concerns such as politics and economics. There is a danger of infantilizing child research, and of treating children as if they live in an artificial world of childhood sealed off from the 'real grown-up world'. This inadequate and misleading approach prevents thorough analysis of the social structures and pressures that shape child health and illness and treatments, and also influence how children and adults experience, perceive and describe health and illness. Childhood research is like emancipatory feminist research in challenging patriarchal restrictions. Yet this does not mean simply separating children from adults (or women from men). It involves analysing many ways in which children's lives are restricted and oppressed, as well as nurtured and cherished by adults, and not simply at personal levels but at political levels too. For this reason, the chapter begins by reviewing the politics of child health, which show under-researched areas.

EIGHT CONTESTED MEANINGS OF 'CHILDREN AS PATIENTS'

The sick role

Talcott Parsons (1951) identified disease as biological dysfunction. In contrast, being a patient is a social role. Parsons considered that the patient or sick role is governed by four expectations: exemption from normal role responsibilities; legitimization often by a doctor; wanting to get better; and seeking and cooperating with technically competent help. This section reviews eight examples of how, each year, millions of possibly healthy children are identified as patients and millions of sick and dying children are excluded from that role.

Brief illness

The first group is sick children in the minority-world who are briefly ill, although formerly many of them would have stayed in bed for weeks. Today, the average stay in paediatric wards in the United Kingdom (UK) lasts less than two days. Improved medication to control symptoms and aid rapid recovery has increased uncertainties about the difference between health and minor illness, and about when a child qualifies as a patient. Children who briefly feel unwell, and might hope to become patients, exempted from normal school and housework duties, are now often sent to school or nursery as usual, but with their antibiotics.

Serious chronic conditions

The second group is minority-world children living with serious long-term and potentially fatal conditions, cystic fibrosis or type I diabetes for example. Generally, they maintain high standards of health and well-being. They attend routine healthcare appointments, but few see themselves as patients. They put great efforts into being 'normal', fitting medical routines of diet, physiotherapy, or insulin injections as unobtrusively as possible into their everyday lives and saying 'I want to be like my friends,' 'I just want to get on with life' (Alderson et al., 2006). Hundreds of research papers have been written on these young people's 'non-compliance' with medical regimes, mainly by clinical psychologists who aim to identify the problems and help young people to overcome them (DH and MRC, 2002; and see the Cochrane Collaboration of systematic reviews, which typically begin with thousands of papers and reduce these down to very few examples which meet the criteria of effective convincing research). Young people's resistance could be linked to a reluctance to fit the sick role (although they cannot 'get better' except in terms of managing symptoms more efficiently). Little research attention is paid to the many children who share in effectively managing their condition.

However, I suggest that 'non-compliance' involves differences between ordinary people's broad concepts of social health and healthcare practitioners' narrower concepts of physical health, when they prescribe higher standards of healthy living than the average person would accept. Few adults stick rigidly to advice about diet and exercise, smoking or alcohol. They balance their ideas of 'social health', of 'having fun', being like their friends, and 'living life to the full' with their physical health needs. Children and young people with long-term conditions face similar conflicts when their prescribed very healthy living standards could undermine their social and emotional health by excluding them from friendships, fun, parties, carefree spontaneity, and, most of all, being accepted and included as a normal person. Their physical and social health and survival depend on balancing the demands of being a compliant patient with the vital and very complex challenges of also being 'an ordinary person'. Simply to classify them as patients misses how they have to manage these contradictions at the centre of their daily life and identity.

Sad, bad, mad, or ill?

Until recently, the third group was regarded as within the normal range, or as sad, odd, difficult, or naughty, but not sick. Now they compose the largest and expanding group of minority-world child patients. Their experiences and behaviours are redefined as forms of sickness requiring medical interventions: obesity, shyness, insomnia, hyperactivity (APA, 2013). China Mills (2012: 444–5) reports a marked rise in the UK of NHS prescriptions of the medication Ritalin, for attention deficit hyperactivity disorder (ADHD), from 3500 in 1993 to 250,000 in 2006, while private prescriptions and other treatments for ADHD considerably increased this total, which has continued to rise steeply over the past decade, and in the USA doctors write 2 million prescriptions a month. Neurologists, Baughman and Covey (2006), estimate that each year in the United States (US) between 5 and 8 million children are treated for ADHD. It is claimed that 80 per cent of young children with ADHD also have early-onset bipolar disorder and extensive

medication needs (Papoloses and Papoloses, 2007). These include Zoloft for depression, Ablify for bipolar disorder, Guanfacine for twitchy eyes, and medication for anxiety and depression. A graphic example of children's enforced patient-hood is when they are unwillingly but 'voluntarily' admitted to mental hospital by their parents' agreement, although not their own. Then they are denied the rights held by patients whose admission is enforced by the state.

A survey of child health and well-being in 21 rich countries (UNICEF, 2007b) and in 29 countries (UNICEF, 2013) took six main measures: material well-being; health and safety; educational well-being; family and peer relations (trust, 'just talking with parents', 'kind and helpful peers'); health and risk behaviours (smoking, drinking); violence; and subjective well-being (feeling healthy, liking school, personal satisfaction). Two of the wealthiest countries, the United Kingdom and the United States, had the worst results in 2007. By 2013, the UK had risen to sixteenth out of the 29 richest countries (UNICEF, 2013). The World Health Organization (WHO, 2008) also reported high mortality and morbidity in the United States and the United Kingdom, attributing these results to extreme inequality between groups living in wealth or poverty. The general picture is confirmed by extensive international research (Wilkinson and Pickett, 2009). General paediatricians now treat broadly social rather than medical problems: emotional and behavioural difficulties, obesity, school and other social exclusions, violence and child abuse, dysfunctional families, self-harm and attempted suicide, drug misuse, and teenage pregnancy. These conditions seldom fit the medical model of identifying clinical conditions and their causes, in order to prevent, alleviate, and cure disease. To call all the children in this third group 'patients' can imply and even assume that they are ill and need medical care, but these are questions which will be considered later.

Majority-world children

Fourth and conversely, millions of majority-world children who are severely ill and in urgent need of medical treatment have no hope of becoming patients in terms of receiving diagnoses and formal healthcare. UNICEF (2007a; 2009) estimates that each year over 50 million newborn children are not registered by the state and are therefore not entitled to any state services or protections. An estimated 37 million have no access to professional healthcare. Many families cannot afford to pay for healthcare, and even in the US after the 2010 legal reforms, around 23 million people including children still do not have health insurance. Some progress has been made. UNICEF et al. (2012) reported that although an estimated 12 million children aged under 5 years died in 1990, by 2011 the number had fallen to 6.9 million. Yet that is still almost 19,000 everyday. On violence, 53,000 children are victims of homicide; up to a third of children are severely beaten at home with implements; 150 million girls and 73 million boys are raped or violently sexually abused (UN, 2006). Hazardous child labour, lifelong bonded labour, and trafficking jeopardize child health. Migration of healthcare staff away from poorer countries further reduces the chances of this fourth group of children being treated as patients. 'There are, for example, more nurses from Malawi in Manchester than in Malawi and more doctors from Ethiopia in Chicago than in Ethiopia' (Khor, 2006: para. 6).

Basic services and standards are crucially relevant to 'children as patients' as they prevent them from becoming ill. Yet one in six people in the world does not have clean safe water; one in three has inadequate sanitation. Malnutrition results in the illness, disability, and death of countless children: almost half a billion children suffer severe hunger and 100 million young children have vitamin A deficiency, a major cause of blindness, illness, and death (UNICEF, 2007a). High maternal mortality rates increase infant morbidity and mortality.

Armed conflicts, which tend to occur in urban areas with high child populations and to begin by damaging local sanitation, water, and health services, along with floods, droughts, hurricanes, and enforced migration, increase each year the numbers of children who have serious physical and psychological illness and injury. Numbers of refugees, with numerous health problems, are rising. Over 45.2 million people were displaced in 2012. Of the 15.4 million refugees who fled abroad, an estimated 46 per cent were children aged under 18. Of the almost one million asylum seekers, a record 21,300 applications were by unaccompanied children (UNHCR, 2013). Climate change and pollution from burning fossil fuels are reported to be killing millions of people each year (Levy, 2012), while floods and droughts are forcing up food prices and hunger, especially in the poorest countries with the youngest populations and highest proportion of children (Carty, 2012). Tropical diseases are spreading into the southern US and Europe. The local anxieties of paediatricians about how to prevent and treat social problems for children in group three escalate to a global scale for children in group four, challenging governments and international aid agencies.

Pharmaceutical research relating to children as patients reinforces these inequalities by investing mainly in medication to treat minority-world children, and investing far less in treatments for the diseases that kill and disable most children – tuberculosis, malaria, which infects 500 million people each year, and other tropical infections.

All in the mind?

Fifth is the small but challenging group of children who feel very ill, with nausea, severe pain, exhaustion, and incapacity, but whose doctors refuse to recognize them as ill because they have no identifiable medical sign: for example, no abnormal hormone, blood count, anatomy and x-ray or scan profile, or gene. Conditions such as myalgic encephalopathy (ME) raise debates about whether these are real or imagined illness, and they illustrate further complications of the sick role. To become a patient, it is not enough to suffer extreme and prolonged symptoms. Doctors look for an accepted sign to legitimate illness. Also, the sick role obligation to cooperate with technically competent help (Parsons, 1951) requires effective help with which to cooperate, but so far treatments for ME are mainly ineffective or highly controversial. Children in this fifth group highlight a paradox when doctors refuse to accept them as patients, whereas doctors do accept countless children from group three, who also tend to have no clinical signs and in addition often lack symptoms of pain, nausea, and inertia.

Screening and the worried well

The sixth group is mainly healthy general populations who undergo medical screening. Most screening is an initial broad sweep to find the few who may be potential patients, who will have further tests. Usually, screening is for older age groups, to help practitioners to give them informed advice on healthy lifestyles, or to offer treatment for cancer and other ailments. In contrast, the other routine screening/scanning is prenatal, when the main 'treatment' offered is not lifestyle options but termination of pregnancy if the foetus is impaired or, in some societies, female. Pre-conception screening aims to identify prospective parents who carry genetic conditions; and in vitro fertilization (IVF) may involve checking and selecting embryos before they are implanted into a uterus. Prenatally, 'children as patients' extends to include the foetus and even the IVF embryo because of emphases in prenatal services associated with modern childhood that potentially influence child–parent relationships well before birth: risk, anxiety about imperfection and failure to fulfil potential, costly reliance on medical information and technology (Ehrich et al., 2008).

An unusual example of screening, which brings direct benefit, is when all newborn babies are checked for phenylketonuria, and treatment begins immediately to prevent severe learning difficulties from developing. However, another neonatal screening, for cystic fibrosis when earlier detection and treatment before symptoms develop might improve health and survival rates, raises the usual but so far unresolved controversies associated with almost all screening. Are screening costs recouped by outcomes in terms of healthier lives and disabled lives prevented? Are scarce practitioners better employed in screening or in treatment services? Does earlier detection and treatment, even for serious but rare conditions, produce better outcomes? How does screening itself arouse unnecessary anxiety in the healthy majority, who may become the 'worried well', and when parents may perceive their child as a vulnerable potential patient? Why do so many people ignore advice based on screening results? This is being shown in current screening of school children for obesity.

Genetic screening raises further ethical questions (Clarke and Ticehurst, 2006; Evans et al., 2011). Should children be tested or informed, when no prevention or cure can be offered, and when the condition (Huntington's chorea, breast cancer) might not develop until decades later? If children are found to be carriers of genetic conditions, when they will not have cystic fibrosis, for example, but might pass it on to their children, when should parents and children be informed?

Children who are disabled

Group seven is children who are disabled, when medical services cannot cure or alleviate their physical, sensory, or learning difficulties. While valuing medical services to treat illness, disabled academics have questioned medical 'management' of disability. They contrast the medical with the social model of disability (Oliver, 1990). They criticize the misuse of medical services and time, and the risks of arousing false hopes of a cure. They argue that instead of reducing disability, the medical model can increase its worst aspects, stigma, and exclusion: by identifying and trying to treat the problem within the individual child; by keeping the child and family dependent on healthcare practitioners and on separate services, such as special schools; by constantly comparing the child's failings against 'normal' standards; and by generally expecting disabled children to play the sick role but without hope of recovery.

There are medical debates about whether repeated operations for children who have spina bifida or cerebral palsy increase their infections, pain, and immobility and do more harm than good. One girl in my study of consent to surgery had had over 40 operations (Alderson, 1993). Yet it is hard to research children's private views, because they are so loyal to the adults who care for them (Bluebond-Langner, 1978). Linda aged eight, facing repeated surgery, wanted to know the surgery details and asked, 'What if it goes wrong?' Although, she said: 'My doctor and my mummy decided about my operation. They knew what I wanted. After all she is my mum and I do trust her' (Alderson, 1993: 30). However, although she was cheerful while her mother was present, after her mother and aunt left she said: 'When I get back [from the operation] tomorrow, they'll be in tears for me' (1993: 128). Trying to research private views can be very damaging if researchers raise doubts in children's minds, or try to break through their stoic coping. It is also hard to contact those children and parents who opt out from surgery services.

In contrast, the social model identifies disabling factors not in the child's impairments but in the barriers and negative attitudes of an uncaring society. Special services are replaced in these ways: by inclusive mainstream ones where disabled and non-disabled children live and learn together (Richards and Armstrong, 2010); by assuring access to public buildings and transport; by overcoming negative discriminating attitudes; by respecting and valuing children for themselves, rather than for their performance or 'normality'. Most crucially, the child is regarded as a person, not a patient, and disabilities are not seen as personal medical problems but as political and economic challenges, which disabled and non-disabled children and adults work together to change.

Children in medical research

Finally, group eight is children taking part in medical research, which can draw strange boundaries between supposed 'patients' and 'non-patients'. For example, many children with asthma use inhalers for daily prophylaxis (to prevent rather than treat asthma attacks). If they stop using inhalers, they are likely to react for days or weeks by having more attacks. If the children take part in randomized controlled trials, they may be 'patients' in a treatment arm, or they may be in the arm which has inhalers containing placebo (dummy or non-treatment). In effect they stop being patients when they no longer have treatment, although for all they know they may be reacting to the new drug rather than to having a non-drug. Logic, ethics, and concern for the children's safety would suggest that the best trials compare a new treatment against a known treatment, unless there is not yet an accepted treatment – but there are effective treatments for asthma. It also seems obviously unscientific to compare the effectiveness of a drug against non-treatment of a group of children who are having severe withdrawal reactions after their usual medication is suddenly withheld. Surely that would give an unfair misleading advantage to the new drug. However, the Food and Drug Administration (FDA), the US agency responsible for medical research, prefers placebo trials (Ross, 2006).

British ethical guidance (RCPCH [The Royal College of Paediatrics and Child Health], 1992/2000) insists that children should be involved in medical research only if the research cannot equally well be done on adults, and if the findings are intended to benefit children. US guidance does not have this standard, so that children are recruited simply to increase numbers of subjects in trials, but with no guarantee that they will be studied as a separate group in order to benefit future child patients (Ross, 2006). Despite bioethics safeguards, harmful and fraudulent medical research and practices continue to be reported (Sharav, 2003; Baughman and Covey, 2006; Slesser and Qureshi, 2009; Kolch et al., 2010; Sercombe, 2010; Mills, 2012), such as the use of dangerous experimental drugs on African children (Save the Children, 2007; Boseley, 2010).

Why does dangerous and unscientific medical research continue to be conducted on children despite decades of critical reports and guidelines? And what is the dominant influence in all the above eight examples? The concluding section will address these questions, after the following sections have considered research methodologies. The chapter title, 'children as patients', raises many complications as well as showing how illness and health pervade many aspects of life.

METHODOLOGIES

The broad range

Research about childhood illness covers most research data collection methods: biochemical and genetic laboratory research; clinical experiments, comparisons, and trials; systematic and thematic literature reviews; research on the aetiology, epidemiology, prevention, and treatment of disease; questionnaire surveys for statistical, international, and longitudinal studies; action research; economic evaluations; ethnography and case studies; examining children's essays, diaries, images, and formal records; increasing use of data on the internet; and a range of interactive methods using interviews, focus groups, play, cameras, and drama.

Complex topics, such as childhood cancer, are like a mountain surrounded by many academic or practical disciplines. Each one can see only a limited view of the topic that reveals some aspects and conceals others, ranging from biochemistry to social

experiences of living with cancer. This range of kinds of knowledge also applies to insights about childhood itself. At the intersection between the biological and the social, understanding of child illness is particularly well served by multi-disciplinary and multi-method research.

Traditional developmental research

'Traditional' methods stretch back for over a century. Although they have been complemented and often replaced by newer approaches, which will be described later, they still strongly influence the mainstream research journals and the funders. Indeed, new requirements in many universities to demonstrate the 'impact' of research is leading to new emphases on large, quantitative, positivist health-related projects. Methodologies combine research methods with theories about epistemology (the study of knowing and belief, and how we know and can validate what we know) and ontology (the study of reality, being, and existing things and people, relationships, and structures). Most research on children has been dominated by psycho-medical research models and methods, in which powerful beliefs (epistemology) about the slowly developing child can confuse and distort data about the being/ontology of real children (Alderson, 2013). When adults are perceived positively as fully developed human beings, children are seen partly negatively, in the sense of not yet developed, still deficient, lacking full competencies and therefore dependent and requiring firm adult control as well as protection and care.

The medical model of research is very useful when it searches for pathology, in order to identify and treat it. However, this approach can become a negative over-emphasis on failings and problems in some psychological and social research. The research tends to overlook children's strengths and achievements, and not to value babyhood and childhood as fulfilling times in their own right. Anxiety about problems experienced by children may go to the extremes of perceiving childhood itself as 'toxic' (Palmer, 2007). The medical metaphor that 'the child's remedy is to grow up' (O'Neill, 1988: 463) is another typical example of an ontology that identifies childhood with the sick role and its four expectations (Parsons, 1951) reviewed earlier. Children are exempted or excluded from normal (adult) role responsibilities. Legitimization of the sick role of childhood by paediatricians has a long history from seventeenth-century Dr Locke to twentieth-century Dr Spock (Hardyment, 1984). Wanting to 'get better' can mean wanting to become more adult.

Traditional and mainly quantitative methods

Predominant older child development research approaches include:

1. observations, case studies, tests, and experiments about child behaviour in laboratories, intended to produce generalizations;
2. questionnaire surveys, usually of adults' assessments, which measure children's health and behaviour against prescribed norms;
3. higher scores for childhood problems and morbidity, whereas 'normal' or very good behaviours tend to have negative zero scores;
4. collection of standardized data for statistical and economic analysis;
5. assumptions that all kinds of data on diverse experiences should be quantified, measured, and compared;
6. standardized 'objective' detached relationships between child research subjects and teams of researchers to avoid bias;
7. efforts to produce self-evident data and facts to support evidence-based solutions and policies.

Limitations of traditional methods

These 'hard science' methodologies have brought great gains for child health in clinical research, but are limited in social research about children's views and experiences. The approaches tend to be conservative rather than innovative. Previously used and validated questionnaires are favoured. Britain's longitudinal studies of birth cohorts from 1958, 1970, and 2000 repeat themes and questions from the earlier surveys in order to compare across generations (Dex and Joshi, 2007), despite numerous changes in childhoods and child health across the decades. Systematic reviews examine previously published research sometimes conducted decades ago, often influenced by cautious policy and funding agencies, and with omissions that the reviews can only replicate, for example, the absence of children's own views.

Larger studies, privileged as statistically and epistemologically more convincing, may filter further conservative emphases into reviews because, like oil tankers, they tend to take longer to design and complete or change. When managed by large hierarchical teams, they can be less flexible in their design and processes, and are very costly, which deters risky innovations and prefers tried and tested methods. These can all be ways to silence child patients' voices, although this can limit the relevance, validity, and effectiveness of research evidence and conclusions. Further limitations will be reviewed, numbered to pair with the above numbered research approaches.

1. Observations of child patients based on laboratory animal study models tend to examine children's behaviour, but not their reasoning which can often justify seemingly irrational behaviour. When children feel nervous in strange settings, they may not show their real competence.
2. Normative questionnaires, which concentrate on adults' assessments and include the pre-designed questions and answers, are also liable to miss children's actual experiences and understandings, as well as new and challenging insights.
3. A century of medical and psychological research has emphasized child morbidity and failings over their strengths and contributions.
4. Standardizing data for statistical analysis involves representative samples, hypothetical questions, vignettes, and analysis of separate variables. In contrast, child patients' experiences tend to be diverse, individual, richly personal

narratives, unexpected, and unique interacting combinations of many factors, and these experiences slip elusively through traditional research data collection. Economic research on cost–benefits and what works well is useful, but can be limited and reductionist when benefits vary among different patients, and are hard to define and measure precisely.

5. Assumptions that research equals measuring tend to dismiss valuable data about children's own views and experiences, which may not easily be measured.

6. Attempts at standardized 'objective' detached relationships between child research subjects and researchers to avoid bias can deter and intimidate children. Talk is likely to remain at a superficial 'public' formal level, whereas skilled researchers move beyond this level by encouraging rapport and intimate, frank 'private' talk.

7. Efforts to produce 'self-evident' data to support 'evidence-based' services conceal powerful unexamined theories and assumptions.

Cognitive behaviour therapies (CBTs)

The example of research about CBTs, linked to the high rates of child mental health problems reviewed earlier, illustrates some of the above limitations. An economist has proposed that happiness can be measured and promoted by cost-effective evidence-based CBTs (Layard, 2007). So the UK Government planned to spend £170 million during 2007–2010 on the therapies. However, critics make the following points (Leader and Corfield, 2007) linked to the above seven limitations as indicated by the numbers in brackets.

Happiness and unhappiness are too complex, personal, and diverse to be measured or managed wholly in standardized ways (above limitations 4–5). Proper therapy, Leader and Corfield consider, involves exploring each person's unpredictable problems and deeper reasoning, through the non-judgemental relationship between client and therapist (above limitations 1–4, 6). In contrast, CBT remains at the superficial level of behaviour (limitation 1). Claims that CBT

has been evaluated by trials comparing groups with the same profile and problem and receiving standardized therapy are invalid for these reasons. People's profiles all differ. They each have several and not only one identifiable problem. The problems cannot be wholly predicted or classified in advance. Effective therapy has to be partly spontaneous and responsive. By definition, it cannot be standardized; ironically, therefore, it cannot be evaluated in formal trials (limitations 2, 4–7).

The CBT trial is an example of efforts to research health problems and treatment through formal methods that differ from real clinical practice, so that the findings are of limited practical use. How did the CBTs appear to be effective? The trial was mainly designed by CBT therapists with only short-term follow-up, when CBT can seem to be effective before the symptoms reappear (limitation 7). Research about cost–benefit and what works well can be more thorough when it is independent. For example, independent research by Roberts et al. (2004) found that the UK Government's favoured mentoring of 'anti-social' young people can harm their mental health when mentoring becomes yet another stressful failed relationship for them.

The CBT research and policy emphasize the medical model of individual treatment evaluated with cost-effective economic measures. However, the social model of critical policy, outlined earlier in relation to disabled children, also applies to the whole concept of childhood itself, as the next section considers. Much healthcare research is criticized as being the 'handmaiden' of medical research, collecting social data about health and illness by using conservative research models, which work well in pharmacology but less so in unpredictable social matters. Scambler (2002) criticizes social researchers for spending too much time on collecting and reporting surface appearances and associations (such as poor health indices and behaviours) and too little time on searching for deeper realities and explanations, as considered later. Concepts of childhood and children's rights are among these deeper issues.

The United Nations Convention on the Rights of the Child and children's competence

The UNCRC combines economic welfare rights with liberal civil rights. The UNCRC enshrines children's rights to the best attainable healthcare and an adequate standard of living. Children's civil or participation rights, modified versions of adult autonomy, involve children in expressing their views on all matters that affect them, and adults giving the views 'due weight in accordance with the age and maturity of the child' (UN, 1989: UNCRC Article 12). Potentially, the UNCRC expands the rights of millions of children to higher standards of healthcare and participation. English and Commonwealth law in over 50 countries goes beyond the UNCRC, in respecting the legally valid consent of minors, provided they are competent in having sufficient understanding and discretion to make a wise choice in their best interests (*Gillick v. Wisbech & W Norfolk AHA*).

My research on the age when children are competent to consent to major surgery, in the view of the adults caring for them, studied 120 children aged from 8 to 15 years having elective, mainly orthopaedic, surgery (Alderson, 1993). They were interviewed in hospital the day before their operation and a week later, and I spent months making observations and, with a colleague, interviewing parents and staff. Many of the children had two or more serious long-term illnesses or disabilities and had already had on average four or five operations, so they deeply understood from experience the nature and purpose, risks and hoped-for benefits, attendant pain and immobility, of the planned surgery. Most children showed impressive understanding and maturity (see also Bluebond-Langner, 1978), as if their hard experiences had increased their maturity and coping with complex and distressing events.

> I think they should tell you honestly. You are much less frightened when you know what's going to happen.
> (David, aged 10, in Alderson, 1993: 116)

> Mum kept the information to herself, and she said in the clinic, 'Judy, go out.' I said, 'No.' [The doctor agreed.] Mum changed after that. She realized it's better for me to be informed, and she started explaining things.
> (Judy, aged 12, in Alderson, 1993: 116)

> If I didn't want the operation, my parents wouldn't make me have it. If I was going to die they'd make me. It would be the only sensible thing to do, but I'd agree.
> (Gemma aged 11, in Alderson, 1993: 43)

> I would like to see the age limits [on consent] completely scrapped, and maturity brought in. As you grow up, your age has a stereotype. I'm trying to escape from that stereotype.
> (Robin aged 13, in Alderson, 1993: 43)

The group was unusually experienced, but instead of being exceptional children, might they be ordinary children in exceptional circumstances? Minority-world children are so highly protected from risks that major surgery is a rare time of serious danger. Do most children have latent capacities, which may be demonstrated during serious crises, and which more fortunate children do not have the need or the opportunity to reveal? The evidence from research with disadvantaged majority-world children suggests that very many of them do indeed have great reserves of courage and competence. For example, Invernizzi (Invernizzi and Williams, 2008: 133) observed parents in Peru encouraging their 'children to have small businesses in the street at a very early age as a means of boosting income as well as learning about people, environment and business'. Although it might seem healthier for children to be in school, early independence for very disadvantaged children can help to improve the family's living conditions and diet, and the child's chances of survival, especially if the parents become ill or die.

However, it seems to be hard for adults to recognize these early capacities, which counter dominant developmental theories about childhood deficits unless:

1. they have direct contact with competent children;
2. they then feel forced to reconsider their beliefs and make the paradigm shift of understanding how beliefs about slowly developing childhood/adolescence are social constructs and not simply biological facts; and
3. they work with children to transform their relationships with them, to trust and respect them, and through shared risk-taking to find (sometimes stressfully) how greatly the trust is validated and moves on to new, and arguably increasingly healthy stages of mutual respect.

Each person's own changing experiences and values structure their perceptions of childhood, meaning beliefs about what children and their relations with adults are and should be like. Many adults who research, work with and care for children socially reconstruct the dyads of: the providing adult and helpless needy child; the rescuing protective adult and victim child; the corrective adult and deficient delinquent child; or confident resourceful child–adult partnerships. Childhood research shows how children's views and relationships are worthy of study in their own right and how children actively co-construct their lives, relationships, and contexts, while international comparisons show childhoods vary widely and are not fixed facts. Researchers construct different childhoods through their research design, theories, questions, methods, findings, and conclusions.

SHARING INFORMATION AND DECISION MAKING WITH CHILDREN

When can children begin to be involved in serious complex decisions? When do, or should, adults begin to involve them, for example, in the contentious examples when children are born with ambiguous genitalia? In such cases, surgery is very rarely needed to improve function and is usually cosmetic, primarily in order to reassure parents. Many affected adults now regret that they had surgery as children, and many feel they were assigned to the wrong gender (Preeves, 2003). Parens (2006) and colleagues agreed that, in most cases, surgery should be postponed until the child is old enough to begin to request it, or at least to indicate a clear gender preference that guides surgery decisions.

When can children begin to form and express views that can influence their healthcare? Children who live with a long-term condition can gain profound understanding through social experience, well in advance of their supposed biological developmental stage. For example, they begin to share in managing their diabetes injections and diet early on (Alderson et al., 2006). We interviewed 24 children aged 3 to 12 years about their type I diabetes. From 4 years, some understood that 'insulin is the key that turns sugar into energy', and shared in doing their daily blood tests and injections, although others wanted to wait until they were older. Parents knew that informing, involving, and respecting children were all vital so that they could avoid rows, force, and coercion, and be able to trust their children to be careful about their diet at all times. Ruby (aged 5) could work out from doing her blood test how much cake she could eat at birthday parties. Jessie (6) explained how she did blood tests, and Simba (7) explained why he needed insulin (2006: 30–31).

Some of the children had become very ill before they were diagnosed, and so they had intense experience of the life-threatening nature of their condition. Moogum (7) diagnosed when she was aged 5 years, said, 'My sister was at home in bed and she was crying because she thought I was dead' (2006: 31).

Observations of premature babies have discovered the babies' eloquent body 'language', which adults can 'read' (Als, 2012).

The babies' healthcare needs for quiet, for dim lighting, for resting in individually preferred positions, and also their agency in their own self-healthcare, are ignored in many neonatal units. However, a few 'baby-led' units continually learn from the babies' expressed 'views' and adjust the care accordingly.

How can mental health research interviews with very disturbed young children about parental abuse discover the children's needs and views without distressing them still further? During research interviews, each child aged 4 to 7 years had a small box to decorate with craft materials, creating images of the child on the outside, and of the child's wishes and feelings within (Winter, 2012). Children were able to control the pace, timing, and topics during the interview, such as by saying 'pass the glue' to deflect or pause before answering a hard question. Concentrating on their work also avoided problems of potentially intimidating sustained eye contact. The method created spaces in which children seemed to feel confidence, trust, and some control, so that they were willing to talk rationally in detail in their own time. The family courts usually ignore the views of these children, believing they are too young to form sensible views. Yet the interviews showed that if decisions about residence are made without consulting or explaining to the children, this can undermine their mental health and increase their distress, anxiety, and sense of guilt. Children who are not engaged in the process are at very high risk of needing long-term adolescent and adult mental healthcare. Effective interviews depend on adult interviewers' skill, tact, patience, and psychological stamina to cope with sharing the children's pain.

Repeated nurse research studies about managing children's pain conclude that even young children should be involved in explaining and deciding their needs for pain relief (for example, Kortesluoma et al., 2008). Hospitals give children pain relief pumps after surgery, so that within given limits they can administer their own analgesia and, knowing this, they tend to use less pain relief. More generally, hospitals have changed over the decades from bleak frightening places into attractive colourful family-centred spaces, in response to children's views, from films of distressed lonely young children in the 1950s (Robertson and Robertson, 1989) to today's routine consultations with young people about planning and providing services. For example, they have recommended that reception desks should be low enough for children to see over them.

INNOVATIVE RESEARCH METHODOLOGIES, ETHICS, AND FINDINGS

This section considers closely related aspects of current research: methodologies adapted to respect children's rights and competence and high standards of research ethics. The challenge to the medical model by the social model, described earlier with disabled children, applies equally to childhood. Is childhood a condition of personal disability/deficit? Or are childhood 'deficits' partly or mainly socially and politically ascribed and imposed, much as women used to be seen as inevitably inferior to men? Women's health improved immeasurably when they came to be respected (more or less) as equal to men (Doyal, 1995). We have to research how much of children's physical and mental morbidity stems from their economic and social inequality with adults (far beyond biological differences). The ontology of the child as a real person now, not only a human becoming or future adult, introduces an epistemology of trust in children's own views and experiences as valid sources of knowledge, beyond relying on adult controlled 'facts' about children's observed behaviours.

The UNCRC (1989) has promoted research that consults and respects children's views to form and express their own views in all matters affecting them. All nation states except the USA and Somalia have ratified the UNCRC and thereby agreed to report regularly to the UN review committee, and some involve children in compiling their reports. Governments, service providers including healthcare services, and funding agencies now routinely commission research about children's own views. There are the dangers of token consultation, poor methods of enquiry, and false claims about what children 'want' and 'choose'. Children and their advocates are disappointed that, despite all the funding and effort invested in consulting children, in the UK at least, few of their ideas and requests are implemented (Percy-Smith and Thomas, 2010).

Most consultation is with groups of children. However, consulting with individual child patients before major treatment is an exception that leads the way in several respects. The child is consulted about a practical decision, which will almost definitely be made and implemented, and not referred on to some other agency and probably forgotten. As a patient, the child shares with adult patients the benefits of a long medico-legal history of respect for voluntary consent (Nuremberg Code, 1947) and informed consent (WMA, 1964/2008). The adults concentrate on one child's views and, uniquely, the child patient's views about his or her own body matter most, whereas in other family and group decisions the child's views and interests will be balanced with other people's and may be discounted. So although parents may be the main deciders, within the constraints of available healthcare, they should set the child patient's interests first. If the child disagrees with the decision (in the UK) efforts are usually made to inform and involve the child, sort out fears and misunderstandings, negotiate as much as possible, and avoid imposing a decision on a fearful resisting child. The UK sets high ethical standards (for example, RCPCH, 1992/2000) although these have been undermined by European law on medical research with children (Biggs, 2010).

Participation in topic, aims, and methods

Participative research with children involves newer methods which, to be effective, engage with the topic and aims of participation. In contrast to the numbered conservative methods listed earlier, innovative childhood study methods involve:

1. observing children in the context of their everyday lives where they are the experts; even very young children and those with speech and learning difficulties can communicate beyond words through their body language and everyday activities and relationships;
2. creating with children questionnaires, which are child-friendly in their design and content, instead of relying solely on adults' replies, and also researchers avoiding normative judgements, and instead assuring children that there are no right or wrong answers but that their views matter, while trying to understand children's own standpoints and reasoning (Mayall, 2002);
3. concentrating on competent, positive aspects of child patients' lives, as well as their problems, and considering possible causes of problems beyond children's own failings, besides learning from historical and international examples how different childhoods are reconstructed;
4. attending to children's complex diverse experiences through their narratives and play, by using open questions, semi-structured narrative interviews, and ethnographic observations as well as statistical analysis (questions about economic research are reviewed later);
5. working on qualitative and quantitative data analysis, on theoretical and critical explanations;
6. encouraging rapport and trust between researchers and child participants with high standards of ethical respect for informed consent and confidentiality;
7. having a cautious critical awareness of the differing limitations of every research method, of the tenuous links between data, analysis, findings, recommendations, and possible future policies and practice, while being aware of the risk that research tends to serve the interests of powerful groups over those of children.

Although further developed since 1989 (Christensen and James, 2008), these methodologies have a long history. In the 1950s, several moving films showed young children's lonely anxiety in institutions without their parents (Robertson and Robertson, 1989). The paediatrician who allowed the film *Laura* to be made in his children's ward, which he considered to be very happy, was horrified to see Laura's severe sadness and at first rejected the message of the film. But he became convinced and was a leading advocate of 'mother care in hospital' (MacCarthy, 1979). Maureen Oswin's (1971) powerful ethnographic accounts of her work as a care assistant in children's sub-normality hospitals led to radical policy changes. She graphically explained not only the inadequate mass 'care', but also the children's complex emotions at a time when they were dismissed as 'idiots' and 'vegetables'. After describing a child in tears after her parents' rare visit, Oswin commented 'cabbages don't cry'. Her channelling of children's experiences led to a government inquiry and the fairly rapid transfer of children out of the vast hospitals and into small family units, as well as much more support for parents caring for their children at home as persons and not patients.

Research ethics initially developed within medical research, which incurs the highest risks. The central principles are respect, justice, and avoiding harm when possible, with utilitarian balancing of harms and risks with hoped-for benefits, the basis of medical ethics guidelines, which tended to emerge from publicity about medical scandals involving harm to children. The guidelines help to protect medical research and researchers as well as research subjects. The Nuremberg Code (1947) emerged from the trials about Nazi experiments. Helsinki (WMA, 1964/2008) followed the episode when pregnant women took Thalidomide and their babies were born with deformed limbs. Work by Beecher (1966) and Pappworth (1967) about harmful research on children led to the rise of medico-legal and philosophical bioethics, and to many publications, for example, USNC (1977), Beauchamp and

Childress (1983/2001), Melton et al. (1983), and Nicholson (1986).

During the 1990s, review by research ethics committees (UK) and institution research boards (US) gradually became a routine part of designing healthcare research. During the 2000s this informs and has spread routinely into much social research in the ethics questions that arise at every stage of research from first plans to final dissemination (Alderson and Morrow, 2010).

CONCLUSION

The above review of many aspects of research relating to children as patients raises perplexing contradictions, which are considered in this final section. Are there any general answers or rules, themes, or underlying realities to explain the following puzzles?

Instead of a clear straight line dividing child patients from healthy children, the eight initial examples showed wildly shifting boundaries placing many extremely sick children in the 'non-patient' zones, and many children who are healthy, or who perceive themselves as healthy, in the patient zones. The medical model, intended to promote health, can paradoxically increase the numbers of 'children as patients' who experience disabling stigma, social exclusion, blame, and guilt about their 'abnormalities'. The model tends to overlook children's own views about their distress and needs, and also their strengths and competencies. The pharmaceutical company websites show that research for minority-world children is far more highly funded than research about the vastly greater needs of majority-world children, although many of their illnesses can be prevented and treated, per child, at extremely low cost.

In research and practice, medical models of individual children's illness and failings differ markedly from emancipatory social models. The medical model is appropriate for treatable illness or injury. Yet by searching for problems within individuals, it can reduce social and political problems into 'dysfunctional' children, youth, and families. General paediatricians observe many problems in the unhealthy behaviours and relationships, diet and housing, families, and communities that damage children, but they often feel uncertain how to explain, prevent, or cure children's suffering. The strength of the medical model, to identify/diagnose the main disease or cause of illness, and administer effective treatment instead of simply trying to alleviate its symptoms or effects, is often missing in public child health policies.

In research about children as patients it is necessary to examine the powerful influence of economics. Pharmaceutical companies publicize the problem of 'therapeutic orphans' (illnesses that have no accepted treatment), mainly in the minority world to justify involving more children as research subjects. Yet the companies say less about their very slight changes to marketed drugs and 'orphan drugs' (drugs in search of illnesses), which increase company profits, or about their relative neglect of research for loss-making drugs for majority-world children dying from TB and tropical diseases. Meanwhile, governments promote national and international policies to increase prosperity but which also increase inequalities, thereby damaging child health. Despite governments' aims to 'end poverty', economic inequalities are growing and are the greatest source of physical and mental ill health (Wilkinson and Picket, 2009).

Setting the health of future generations in peril, governments' growth and productivity priorities damage the finite planet. Governments increase their Gross National Product (GNP) not only with 'goods', such as healthcare, housing, and business profits, but also with costly 'bads' linked to illness: dealing with accidents, illness, pollution, and disasters. Above certain poverty levels, paradoxically, a rising GNP involves steady increases in the 'bads' of infant mortality, child abuse and

poverty, teenage suicides, drug use, and mental illness (Douthwaite, 1999). Economic wealth does not necessarily increase child health, social well-being, justice, or equity, once the national average income has passed a certain basic level (not met yet by many sub-Saharan African countries). Instead it tends to increase wealth inequalities, which are clearly linked to worse child health. The first recommended way to promote child health is therefore to reduce inter- and intra-country economic inequalities (Wilkinson and Pickett, 2009; WHO, 2008). Many analysts conclude that the key adverse influence on health is neo-liberal economics (Stiglitz, 2010; Wacquant, 2009) in the growing divisions between wealthy (generally older) and poor (generally younger) generations, resulting in the growth in child poverty, war, and the destruction of natural environments, which all increase child illness. Neo-liberalism involves disorganized deregulated global capitalism, the withdrawal of practical material support for citizens by the welfare state, but also the invasion of state and economic power and control into adults' and children's public and private life. People are then treated less as active determining citizens (agents), than as passive clients (patients) of state services, and as dependent consumers guided by the mass media and drawn into debt.

Economics is the key factor in the initial eight examples. Children become patients when adults are willing and able to pay for their treatment, and when it is profitable for companies to sell treatments. Sick children are denied the status of patient for economic rather than medical reasons and children who are so precious to their family and community may not count, in global policy terms, as worth even the cheapest healthcare. From this perspective, future research to benefit children as patients would promote multi-disciplinary multi-method research, which works: to overcome qualitative/quantitative, factual/constructionist, 'hard/soft', adult-centred/child-centred divisions; to see how contrasting approaches can inform and enrich one another; to combine 'micro' research with individual patients with 'macro' critical political and economic analyses; to attend more critically to connections among data, interpretations, policy recommendations, and practical implementation; to investigate children's many views and experiences seeing how they exercise their rights to be involved in all matters, processes, and decisions that affect their healthcare; to learn about their capacities from child patients' exposure to exceptional risks; and to examine the principled and the cost-effective benefits of humane respect when adults work with child patients as partners.

Barriers to these aims, in Britain at least, include the increasingly commercial nature of research, controlled by funders' agendas, and treated by universities as income generation. However, ways to enable research that is intended to promote the effective, benign, and respectful care of children as patients include the enthusiastic cooperation of many children and parents, of agencies working for children's rights, and of many researchers and practitioners across the world.

REFERENCES

Alderson, P. (1993) *Children's Consent to Surgery*. Buckingham: Open University Press.

Alderson, P. (2008) *Young Children's Rights*. London: Jessica Kingsley/Save the Children.

Alderson, P. and Morrow, V. (2010) *The Ethics of Research with Children and Young People: A Practical Handbook*. London: Sage.

Alderson, P., Sutcliffe, K. and Curtis, K. (2006) 'Children's competence to consent to medical treatment', *Hastings Center Report*, 36(6): 25–34.

Als, H., Duffy, F., McAnulty, G. et al. (2012) 'NIDCAP improves brain function and structure in preterm infants with severe intrauterine growth restriction', *Journal of Perinatology*, 32: 797–803.

APA – American Psychiatric Association. (2013) *Diagnostic and Statistical Manual of Mental Disorders*. Washington, DC: APA.

Baughman, F. and Covey, C. (2006) *The ADHD Fraud: How Psychiatrists Make Patients of Normal Children*. Victoria BC: Trafford.

Beauchamp, T. and Childress, J. (2008) *Principles of Biomedical Ethics*. New York: Oxford University Press.

Beecher, H. (1966) 'Ethics and Clinical Research', *New England Journal of Medicine*, 274(24): 1354–60.

Biggs, H. (2010) *Healthcare Research, Ethics and Law*. London: Routledge.

Bluebond-Langner, M. (1978) *The Private Worlds of Dying Children*. Princeton, NJ: Princeton University Press.

Boseley, S. (2010) 'Nigeria: Drug trial tale of "dirty tricks"', *Guardian Weekly*, 17 December, and see http://www.cbsnews.com/8301-505123_162-42846951/pfizers-nigeria-scandal-doctors-without-borders-stirs-the-pot-to-little-effect/ 5 January 2011 (accessed 7 January 2013).

Carty, T. (2012) *Extreme Weather, Extreme Prices: The Costs of Feeding a Warming World*. Oxford: Oxfam.

Christensen, P. and James, A. (eds.) (2008) *Research with Children*. London: Routledge.

Clarke, A. and Ticehurst, F. (2006) *Living with the Genome: Ethical and Social Aspects of Human Genetics*. Basingstoke: Palgrave Macmillan.

Dex, S. and Joshi, H. (2007) *Parental Care and Employment in Early Childhood*. London: Equal Opportunities Commission.

DH and MRC (Department of Health and Medical Research Council) (2002) *Current and Future Research on Diabetes*. London: Department of Health.

Douthwaite, R. (1999) 'The Need to End Economic Growth', in M. Scott Cato and M. Kennett (eds.), *Green Economics*. Aberystwyth: Green Audit Books, pp. 27–35.

Doyal, L. (1995) *What Makes Women Sick?* Oxford: Blackwell.

Ehrich, K., Williams, C. and Farsides, B. (2008) 'The embryo as moral work object', *Sociology of Health & Illness*, 30(5): 772–87.

Evans, J., Meslin, E. Marteau, T. and Caulfield, T. (2011) 'Deflating the genomic bubble', *Science*, 331(6019): 861–2.

Hardyment, C. (1984) *Dream Babies: Childcare from Locke to Spock*. Oxford: Oxford University Press.

Invernizzi, A. and Williams, J. (eds.) (2008) *Children and Citizenship*. London: Sage.

Khor, M. (2006) 'Medical brain drain hits poor nations', *Third World Network*. Available at http://www.twnside.org.sg/title2/gtrends99.htm.

Kolch, M., Ludolph, A., Plener, P., Fangerau, H., Vitiello, B. and Fegert, J. (2010) 'Safeguarding children's rights in psychopharmacological research: Ethical and legal issues', *Current Pharmacological Design*, 16(22): 2398–406.

Kortesluoma, R., Nikkonen, M. and Serlo, W. (2008) 'You just have to make the pain go away: Children's experiences of pain management', *Pain Management Nursing*, 9(4): 143–9.

Layard, R. (2007) *Happiness: Lessons from a New Science*. London: Penguin.

Leader, D. and Corfield, D. (2007) *Why Do People Get Ill?* London: Penguin.

Levy, P. (2012*) Climate Change Kills Five Million People Every Year*, http://www.policymic.com/articles/21419/climate-change-kills-5-million-people-every-year-here-s-how, accessed 11 July 2013.

MacCarthy, D. (1979) *The Under Fives in Hospital*. London: National Association for the Welfare of Children in Hospital.

Mayall, B. (2002) *Towards a Sociology for Childhood*. Buckingham: Open University Press.

Melton, G., Koocher, G. and Saks, M. (eds.) (1983) *Children's Competence to Consent*. New York: Plenum Press.

Mills, C. (2012) '"Special" treatment, "special" rights', in Freeman, M. (ed.), *Law and Childhood Studies*. Oxford: Oxford University Press, pp. 438–55.

Nicholson, R. (1986) *Medical Research with Children: Ethics, Law and Practice*. Oxford: Oxford University Press.

Nuremberg Code (1947) http://ori.dhhs.gov/education/products/RCRintro/c03/b1c3.html (accessed 26 October 2012).

Oliver, M. (1990) *The Politics of Disablement*. Basingstoke: Macmillan.

O'Neill, O. (1988) 'Children's rights and children's lives', *Ethics*, 98(3): 445–63.

Oswin, M. (1971) *The Empty Hours*. Harmondsworth: Penguin.

Palmer, S. (2007) *Toxic Childhood*. London: Orion.

Papoloses, D. and Papoloses, J. (2007) *The Bipolar Child*. New York: Broadway. Available at www.bipolarchild.com

Pappworth, M. (1967) *Human Guinea Pigs*. London: Routledge and Kegan Paul.

Parens, E. (ed.) (2006) *Surgically Shaping Children*. Baltimore, MD: Johns Hopkins University Press.

Parsons, T. (1951) *The Social System*. Glencoe, IL: Free Press.

Percy-Smith, B. and Thomas, N. (eds.) (2010) *A Handbook of Children and Young People's Participation*. London: Routledge.

Preeves, S. (2003) *Intersex and Identity: The Contested Self*. New Brunswick, NJ: Rutgers University Press.

RCPCH (The Royal College of Paediatrics and Child Health) (1992/2000) 'Guidelines on the ethical conduct of medical research involving children', *Archives of Disease in Childhood*, 82(2): 177–82.

Richards, G. and Armstrong, F. (eds.) (2010) *Teaching and Learning in Diverse and Inclusive Classrooms*. London: Routledge.

Roberts, H., Liabo, K., Lucas, P., DuBois, D. and Sheldon, T. (2004) 'Mentoring to reduce antisocial behaviour', *British Medical Journal*, 328(7438): 512–14.

Robertson, J. and Robertson, J. (1989) *Separation and the Very Young*. London: Free Association Books.

Ross, L.F. (2006) *Children in Medical Research: Access versus Protection*. New York: Oxford University Press.

Save the Children (2007) *Why Social Corporate Responsibility is Failing Children*. London: SCF.

Scambler, G. (ed.) (2001) *Habermas, Critical Theory and Health*. London: Routledge.

Sercombe, H. (2010) 'The "teen brain" research, *Youth & Policy*, 105: 71–80.

Sharav, V. (2003) 'Children in clinical research: A conflict of moral values', *American Journal of Bioethics*, 3(1): 1–99.

Slesser, A. and Qureshi, Y. (2009) 'The implications of fraud in medical and scientific research', *World Journal of Surgery*, 33(11): 2355–9.

Stiglitz, J. (2010) *Freefall: Free Markets and the Sinking of the Global Economy*. London: Allen Lane.

UN (United Nations) (1989) *Convention on the Rights of the Child (UNCRC)*. New York: UNICEF.

UN (United Nations) (2006) *The United Nations Secretary General's Study on Violence against Children*. New York: UN.

UNHCR – UN High Commission for Refugees (2013) 'Global forced displacement at 18 year high'. http://www.unhcr.org.uk/news-and-views/news-list/news-detail/article/un-humanitarian-agencies-announce-major-new-funding-push-for-syria-crisis.html, accessed 11 July 2013.

UNICEF (2007a) *State of the World's Children*. New York: UNICEF.

UNICEF (2007b) *An Overview of Child Well-Being in Rich Countries*. New York: UNICEF.

UNICEF (2009) *Progress for Children*. New York: UNICEF.

UNICEF (2013) *An Overview of Child Well-Being in Rich Countries*. New York: UNICEF.

UNICEF and WHO, The World Bank, UN DESA/Population Division. (2012) *Levels and Trends in Child Mortality*. New York: UNICEF.

USNC (US National Commission for the Protection on Human Subjects of Biomedical and Behavioral

Research). (1977) *Research Involving Children.* Washington, DC: DHEW.

Wacquant, L. (2009) *Punishing the Poor.* London: Duke University Press.

WHO (World Health Organization) (2008) *Closing the gap in a generation.* Commission on Social Determinants of Health, Final Report. Geneva: WHO.

Wilkinson, R. and Pickett, K. (2009) *The Spirit Level.* Harmondsworth: Penguin.

Winter, K. (2012) 'Ascertaining the perspectives of young children in care: Case studies in the use of reality boxes', *Children & Society*, 26(5): 368–80.

WMA (World Medical Association) (1964/2000) *Declaration of Helsinki.* Fernay Voltaire: WMA.

7

Children as Consumers

Ragnhild Brusdal and Ivar Frønes

CHILDREN AS CONSUMERS

Although the majority of children on the planet do not live under conditions of affluence and consumerism, new groups of children are continuously entering this world of 'little emperors'. Discussions of children as consumers illustrate that consumption is a pivotal part of socialization in modern societies. Consumer culture is different from earlier cultures primarily in terms of the scale and content of consumption, penetrating everyday life and culture as illustrated by the concept of shopping. Children's consumption is based on families' economic ability; children's consumption is a display of the economic and moral economy of the family as well as the fads and values of child cultures and the dynamics of the market. The divergent moorings of the child consumer, the peer culture, the family culture, individual style, and social position, produce cultural tension in the realm of consumption, tension that is formulated and displayed through the actual consumption.

The child consumer is often associated with the market for specific childhood products and their related advertisements, but this is only a minor part of children's consumption. The understanding of children as consumers cannot be restricted to what they buy themselves or their 'pester power'. It includes the computer and books purchased by their parents as an investment in children's future, the safety equipment, the family holidays, and the hamburgers that children buy with their pocket money. Modern parenthood is displayed and developed through children's consumption, as is modern childhood.

The deeper structural upheavals of the post-industrial society influence not only patterns of education and upbringing, but also the diversity and intensity of the markets directed towards the child as an individual, as a family member and as a member of social groups. These new changes produce a complex differentiated cultural and economic matrix, where consumption varies with age, gender, class, and cultural factors. The understanding of children as consumers requires an understanding of this matrix, ranging from the market for 'edutainment' for the youngest to the market for autonomy and counter culture for teens. At the heart of this market is a negotiation between parents and children, between social position and individual style, between identity as an expression of individual agency and social structure, and, in the educational society, between the present and the future.

AFFLUENT SOCIETIES AND THE COMMERCIALIZATION OF CHILDHOOD

In the Western world, the child as an individual consumer first emerged in the late nineteenth century. The emergence of the child consumer was part of revitalization and the sanctification of the family with motherhood and childhood at the centre (Cook, 2004). The emergence of this new consumer category is illustrated by ads directed towards the mother that focus on health, hygiene, and medicine. The evolving consumer culture underscored the importance of teaching children good spending habits, gradually integrating consumption into socialization and upbringing, and blurring the boundaries between private and public life (Jacobson, 2004). A child with a toy was a symbol of progress and the pleasures of consumerism (Kline, 1993).

Despite the growth of consumption in everyday culture, particularly in the United States, it was not until the 1950s that the accessibility of consumer goods began to transcend the barriers of social classes. Being a teenager (the term itself coming into wide use in the 1940s (Palladino, 1996)), meant being at the forefront of a new youth market. The teenager encompassed, in principle, boys and girls from all social backgrounds. Their identity as a social group was constituted through the consumption of the new products of leisure and popular culture. When children's purchasing power reached certain levels, they were naturally targeted as specific consumer segments (Pecora, 1998). The market also shaped the consumer. The construction of retail departments as early as 1930 shaped different versions of the child consumer by spatially situated markets separating children by age and gender (Cook, 2003). Although the teenage mark was rooted in both general affluence and the fact that teenagers often were wage earners (or at least working for pocket money), the purchasing power of children was rooted in the growing affluence of the household, that is in the father's income and, increasingly, that of the mother.

An analysis of US advertisements in the early twentieth century reveals that children were even then becoming portals to the new world of consumption (Cross, 2004a). Yet the extensive scale of marketing to children was still a relatively new phenomenon. When Mattel in 1955 bought 52 weeks of advertising on the *Mickey Mouse Club* television show, it was the first time children were addressed as consumers in such a targeted way. This innovation created a strong relationship between the media and the child consumer, and the Disney empire and their Mickey Mouse Clubs were strong actors in the making of the American child (Sammond, 2005).

Commercialization of childhood implies that children's products and activities are offered to them in a distinct market. In the discourse on modern childhood, the phrase 'commercial' is established as both an economic and a cultural category. The normative differentiation of products, where upscale products often escape the label 'commercial', illustrates the interplay of economic and cultural capital within the framework of consumerism. Miles (1998) distinguishes between 'consumption' to purchase something and the term 'consumerism', which conveys that consumption is part of the very fabric of modern life. To become a consumer strongly influences the general process of socialization; the market and its products touch children's lives and culture directly (Kline, 1993).

THE CULTURAL MATRIX OF CHILDHOOD CONSUMPTION

Children's consumption covers a wide range of products and serves many purposes. An object's function is important because objects are integral to specific activities. Newer and better models are important to heighten one's skill; computers need upgrading, and new fashion secures social positions. Activities help develop competence and skills, both related to the activity and to the general social competence needed for social integration. The decline of informal leisure and the rise of organized leisure activities raise the 'entrance fees' as well as the need for equipment and commuting costs. Participation and the development of social capital are increasingly dependent on consumption, children's access to the activities and consumer goods require payment and parental support.

Social identities are staged with the help of consumer goods and practices, and brands have come to function as banners of social identity. The compositions of symbolic products signal whether one 'fits in' with peers and group identity, and how one 'sticks out', expressing individual personality. Consumption is also necessary for 'joining in' in everyday activities (Ridge, 2002).

The modern individual, signalling uniqueness as well as social position and group belonging, is a perfect match for the expanding cultural market. Industries targeting children closely monitor the pulse of cultural trends, contributing to the translation of trends into styles and subgroups. The position of the symbolic matrixes of style is indicated by small children's capacity to recognize brands (Kline, 1993; Hansen et al., 2002; Schor, 2004), a competence acquired through television, advertisements, the shelves they study from the shopping cart, and, not least, from their peers.

Langer (2004) describes the business of brand enchantment and stresses that for children it is not just brands that become intimately associated with culture and identity. Toys and media characters also connect children to products through emotional identification. Disney educates children in the Disney universe, bridging products, brands, and values. Spin-off products marketed through movies

and television are an enormous industry. This entertainment consumption fits well with Campbell's (1987) description of the new hedonistic consumer as a person consuming experiences. The consumption of experiences generates boredom as a theme in everyday life, producing a continual search for new experiences.

Children's consumption and culture have become *global*, producing a combination of increased homogeneity and heterogeneity. Fashion, toys, television, and movies are increasingly travelling around the planet. In all corners of the world you will find McDonald's, Barbie, the latest Disney movie, Bollywood movies, and Japanese Mangas. These homogenizing forces develop parallel to an increasing diversification of style and taste; the once dominant top-ten list of pop music is no longer a meaningful indicator of musical taste. The dynamics of differentiation promote possible hierarchies of styles and rapid change, and one consequence of differentiation is most likely increased consumption. There is an extensive discussion of whether globalization and children's consumer goods are wiping out local cultures (Buckingham, 2000; Kline, 1993; Pecora, 1998; Seiter, 1993).

Technology, another aspect of consumption, permeates childhood. Mobile phones are not only new communication options. They are a new dimension of peer culture with specific styles and accessories. The global sales of ring tones for mobile phones were estimated in 2006 at about $6 billion (US) per year, and the market has continued to grow. Through virtual cities, Internet games, and 'Second Lives,' virtual markets are penetrating the real lives of children, as are socio-virtual spaces such as MySpace and Facebook. Internet games such as 'World of Warcraft' require subscriptions, and the virtual shops with convertible currency are not providing accessories for the avatars for free.

Children are the main consumers in the virtual worlds, and the discussion of banning sex and gambling in these virtual communities have quickly arisen. The virtual worlds represent both a market where products provide the access to various worlds and markets inside the virtual walls of the virtual cities. The virtual and socio-virtual worlds represent both rapidly expanding markets targeting children and new dilemmas for the legal system and parents.

The modern matrixes of consumption are complex, particularly for children, who rapidly change their social and cultural positions as well as their physical size as they progress through childhood. The symbolic power of the commercial forces is illustrated by the clothing industry, designating not only fashion, but also distinctions of age, gender, social class, and cultural subgroups (Cook, 2004). The industry is segmenting age groups as cultural categories and positioning clothes, style, activities, and toys within a matrix of lifestyles and cultural and economic capital.

THE POST-INDUSTRIAL CHILDHOOD AND EDUCATIONAL CONSUMPTION

The post-industrial knowledge society stresses 'human capital' as a key factor in the economy, assigning children the position of the human capital of the future. The expansion of the educational system implies an evolving educational culture which penetrates family life and socialization on all levels, translating individual or social resources into cultural and social capital. Not surprisingly, the educational childhood is catered to by various industries, changing the profile of children's consumption. The piles of superfluous toys in children's rooms in the minority world may easily draw the attention away from the expensive new products designed for the post-industrial childhood, ranging from technology and sports equipment to fashion, safety, design, and educational support. The post-industrial educational society constitutes new patterns of socialization intensively focusing the development of

cultural and social capital, transforming the symbolic matrixes of childhood and family life.

The educational culture of the post-industrial society blurs the lines between educational and leisure activities. Educational activities are often understood as in opposition to commercialization of childhood, while in fact leisure is transformed into educational activities through consumption and edutainment. After-school programmes, participation in organized activities, and school-oriented leisure activities are likely to expand in all post-industrial societies. Public government may support such activities, but they are in general paid for by active parents navigating the educational market for their children (Buckingham, 2007).

'Edutainment' that combines play and educational objectives target the child consumer through their parents seeking to provide their young offspring a head start. 'Baby Einstein' is a line of multimedia products and toys that specializes in interactive activities for children three months to three years old. A division of the Disney Company currently makes these products under the slogan 'Where Discovery Begins.' In 2005, the edutainment market was projected to reach more than $7 billion (US) worldwide by 2011, with the continued increase in affluence and growing educational competition (AllBusiness, 2007). Intensive parenting expands the areas of consumption, making educational and cultural products designed to support children's development and future success, pivotal target areas for commercial products. Intensive parenting also favours a privatization of childhood; the outdoors is no longer teeming with playing children. Children are moved to private areas. The activities substituting traditional play are increasingly based on consumer patterns intending to develop cultural capital and competence, which means that children's play is increasingly framed by the cultural capital and educational orientation of the parents (Kline, 1993).

THE COST OF CHILDREN AND THE STANDARD PACKAGE

For several decades, consumption per capita has increased in most countries, and a substantial proportion of those growing expenditures have been spent on children. The fact that some products such as education and health insurance are public expenditures in some countries (via taxes) while in others they are primarily private expenses, influences the calculation of expenses. The general trend has been growing consumption of communications services, recreation and culture goods, services, and personal effects. Housing has grown more expensive, rooted in the increased size of dwellings and new level of standards (Australian Bureau of Statistics, 2007).

According to the United States department of Agriculture (2013), a middle income family can expect to spend about $241,000 for food, shelter, and necessities related to child rearing expenses over the next 17 years (Lino, 2013), the biggest expense being housing (college expenses not included). In Australia, the costs of raising two children to the age of 21 were calculated to $537,000 (Australian) for a middle-income family, or about 23 per cent of the parents' combined income (Percival et al., 2007). The cost of two children is estimated to about $800000 (Australian) in 2012 (Philips, 2013), an increase that is partly related to the increasing costs of education among middle class families. The increasing costs of education are rooted in series of factors, but do reflect the knowledge economy and the increasing emphasis on high quality education. In China the cost of raising children rose during the 1990s. In 85 per cent of the urban families, children's consumption reached one third or more of family income, illustrating a growing investment in children within an emerging educational society (Ying, 2003).

In the US, consumption inequality among children increased in the period 1981–2001. The increase in the percentage of children living in the bottom quintile is primarily due to the increased number of children living with single mothers (Johnson, Smeeding and Torrey, 2005). In the oil-affluent Norwegian welfare state, children living in relative poverty (as defined by the Organization for Economic Cooperation and Development [OECD]) are primarily children of single mothers and immigrant children in large families. The relativity of the poverty line indicates that poor children in rich countries may consume much more than poor children in poorer environments. The United Nations Children's Fund (UNICEF, 2004) finds that only the Nordic countries (Finland, Norway and Sweden) have a rate of child poverty less than 5 per cent (for example, in Italy the rate was 16.6 per cent and in the United Kingdom 15.4 per cent).

Consumption is culturally defined, and it is more than just a satisfaction of basic needs. Within a common cultural and normative framework a person needs to possess a minimum of goods and participate in a minimum of activities, both related to social integration and activities and as a signal of the support of dominant social norms. This is called the *standard package* (Parsons and Smelser, 2001). If you do not have this minimum, you will likely be excluded from local peer culture as well as from local integration in general. Poverty may entail social exclusion and is part of inclusion and exclusion processes both today as well as in the child's future life. Ridge (2002) focused on the need for 'fitting in' and 'joining in' when looking at children's ability to participate in the social world of their peers. In addition some of these needs have a direct impact on their future lives. The standard package varies with class and time. As consumption has increased dramatically, new items and activities have been gradually added to the standard package. This expansion also tailors standard packages to class and lifestyle. In the educational childhood the educational standard package not only informs people of who you and your family are, but also of where you are heading. As the standard package expands, economically as well as culturally, more parents are becoming inadequate as providers of the consumption modern childhood requires.

An important aspect of children's consumption is about 'joining in', that is, their opportunities to take part in common activities (Ridge, 2002). The fact that children from less affluent families often expressed a greater longing for 'things' than children from more affluent families (Eydal and Jeans, 2006) may be rooted in the profile of cultural as well as economic capital. Chin (2001) shows that consumption among poor black children is constrained by an awareness of limited resources. Deprived children are missing out on a broad range of essential items and activities enjoyed by their peers (Middleton, Ashworth and Braithwaite, 1997; Mayer, 1998), often missing products that generate important social and cultural capital.

PARENTAL PRIORITIES

Children's consumption has to be understood in relation to the cultural, social, and financial capital of the household; the interplay between these factors is also a factor influencing the child's development (Townsend 1979; Middleton et al., 1997; Ridge, 2002;). Parents' economy sets limits to children's spending, and parents' cultural and social capital influences children's lifestyle and values, and their activities and priorities.

From a perspective of consumption and exclusion, poverty is the intersection of low consumption and low income. Pugh (2004) found that income instability was as important as income scarcity for determining priorities concerning children's consumption. In general parents will give their children priority (Kochuyt, 2004), and British single parents receiving government income support spent almost as much as other parents on Christmas presents (Middleton et al., 1997). This indicates that poor families spend disproportionately more on their children than wealthier families (Mayer, 1998), and that

parents make efforts to ensure their children a normal childhood (Edin and Lein, 1997).

Consumption varies nationally and regionally within industrialized countries. North Americans spend almost twice as much on children's toys and video games as Europeans and Asians combined (Langer, 2002). Asian parents invest more in educational activities and products. Privatized, intensive parenting finds its most active representatives among parts of the American middle class. Despite distinctions the general trends remain: the focus on social and cultural capital changes the profile of childhood consumption and establishes the cultural and social capital of the parents as an increasingly salient factor of children's consumption.

In 1996, 21 per cent of children aged 7–12 in Beijing and other big cities in China had their own computer, and 60 per cent had their own video players. In the period between 1990 and 1999 in China children's share of the family's consumption has increased. In 85 per cent of the urban families children's consumption is equal to one third or more of the family income (Ying, 2003). Another study of Chinese children finds that they have increased their buying power considerably and they start spending money at the age of four (Chee, 2000). The gravitation of the centre of high-tech production towards new parts of Asia will most likely contribute to increased consumption of educational products and activities among children. But consumption is not confined to Asia by any means. In 2007 in Norway, 50 per cent of the 8- to 11-year-olds had a television in their rooms, 86 per cent had a Play Station game console, and 26 per cent of the same age group had a personal computer (Borgeraas and Brusdal, 2008).

The interaction between and within families, between the child, the family, and the market varies with historical periods, social class, ethnic background, and local communities. Children in Beijing are involved in about 3000 hours of learning activities per year including school (Ishinger, 2006), a fact which reflects parents' investment in educational activities and products. Toys and outdoor equipment that were once only found in public areas, such as slides and swings, are increasingly found in private gardens, something that illustrates privatization as protection when environments are regarded as unsafe (Jacobson, 2004). Safety products, such as different helmets for different activities, underscore the prevention of risks as a new arena of parental responsibility. The protected childhood, far from the life of Tom Sawyer, produces new areas of parental responsibility and corresponding products.

FITTING IN AND STICKING OUT

The process of individualization is expressed most visibly through consumption. Individualization, as something to be constructed, is a precondition of lifestyles and social identity. Individualization, and the corresponding expressions of individual styles and social identities, has penetrated the life of younger and younger children. What you consume reveals something about you and the group you wish to join. This will differ with age, gender, and social status. What is considered highly valuable in one context may be less valuable in another. Peer relations are often understood through a simple model of peer pressure, and advanced models of consumption have seldom been applied to childhood to date (Martens, Southerton, and Scott, 2007). The cultural and social peer dynamics are better modelled with the concept of fields (Bourdieu, 1984), where positions are negotiated within continuously changing matrixes of symbolic values, where distinctions often are vague and negotiable, especially in the intersections of fields or in zones of transition (Frønes, 1995).

Peer pressure is not primarily rooted in the stability of norms and values. Rather, the intensity of peer pressure is rooted in a search for status, and activity imbued with potential insecurity. Individual identity is negotiated within a set of shared cultural codes. The other is always there even if the participants underline that they do not care about the style or attitudes of others in their development of the self. The structuralized images of strong and stable webs of norms overlook the fact that gender and age are both something children do and negotiate as well as something they are. Consumer goods are used to negotiate and maintain a set of beliefs and ensure social belonging (Douglas and Isherwood, 1979) as well as individual style. The complex matrixes of changing fields and styles, and the simple fact that children are growing up, intensify the importance of symbolic distinctions. Toys or clothes provide cues for sticking out as an individual, for fitting in with peers, as well as cues for social distinction and social class (Elliott and Leonard, 2004; Ridge, 2002).

This dynamics of gender, class, group, ethnicity, and individuality are increasingly permeating the life of the youngest children. Adler and Adler (1998) found that in general popular girls wore designer clothing and had more products in their rooms, and they were also able to participate in more expensive activities such as horse riding. For boys, consumption had little impact on popularity, while athletic ability and coolness were important factors. Ethnicity is also expressed in young people's construction of style (Phenix, 2005). Lamont and Molnar (2001) described how African-Americans use consumption to express and transform their collective identity and individual style.

Muniz and O'Guinn (2001) propose a model of a brand community based on a structured set of social relationships among admirers or users of a brand. This could be local residents, users of special computers, owners of special cars, football supporters, etc. Children's brand communities are partly based on brand identification, but also on the development of 'Toy Universes', where specialized toys referring to different universes make it hard to participate if you don't have the right toy and brand. The idea of brand communities is supported in a British study where children appeared to be part of 'symbolic' brand communities (Elliott and Leonard, 2004).

The meaning of consumption differs between cultures. In the United States diversity is more evident and encouraged, and individual styles emerge, such as urban style, social styles, ethnic styles and the like, while Japanese youth tend towards group conformity. Japanese culture strongly focuses on brands, what is new, and inclusion through specific consumption, and young Japanese are turning towards a stratification system which includes 'brand identity' and consumer hierarchies (White, 1994). Chinese children and parents also take an interest in expensive and new styles and goods (Chadha and Paul, 2006; Ying, 2003). The various markets reflect divergent cultures; different cultural matrixes are transformed into patterns of consumption, and shopping together is also buying and bonding.

THE CONSTRUCTION OF SOCIAL IDENTITIES: AGE, GENDER, CONSUMPTION

Childhood is not static and in childhood there exist a series of oppositional stances defining children. The complexity of the changing matrix of life phase and gender underscores that gender and age are normatively constituted, as well as being something children do (Butler, 2006; Thorne, 2003; West and Zimmerman, 1987). The institutionalization of childhood creates phases and transitions. Peer cultures translate institutionalized age grading into cultural patterns of activities, styles, and toys that signify the various age phases. Age and gender relations, peer group affiliation, and social position are expressed and coordinated by semiotics of consumer goods; in this sense childhood is commodified. The emergence of a nursery – a private room for children – is an example of the confluence of marketing and individualization. Children's rooms have been defined as singular, private areas by commercial markers,

with furniture, toys, and accessories all underscoring style and individuality as well as age.

Active marketing towards children makes commercial forces constitutive of the cultural patterns of childhood as well as of the roles of children and parents and the images of the family. For children, age signifies maturity and status. Heterogeneity of style is increasingly interacting with age and gender producing differentiated spectres of products. The phases and the age differentiations are not stable, as indicated by the changing of the metaphor 'cute' to 'cool', and phases such as tweens (Cross, 2004b). Tweens became a globally significant target group in the 1980s and early 1990s, and tween girls in particular have become a major target of the expanding fashion market (Cook, 2004). The tween category is primarily female and tends to produce a female consumer who is typically white, middle- or upper-class, and heterosexual (Cook and Kaiser, 2004).

For small children, the world appears as pink and blue. Bikes, skis, and knapsacks for school all come in gendered versions. Children's toys and television characters copy themes from the adult culture and present them in exaggerated versions. High-pitched voices, pastel colours, frills, endless quantities of hair, and an innate capacity for sympathy mark female characters. The male characters appear as superheroes with enormous muscles, deep voices, and an earnest and unrelenting capacity for action and bravery (Seiter, 1993).

Children's toys can be seen as a miniature adult world, preparing the child for the roles and hierarchies awaiting them (Barthes, 1973). Traditional toys reflect future tasks and positions, such as engineering kits for boys and household kits for girls, but they occupy just a small corner of the modern toy industry. For the youngest children, edutainment is competing with life in the fairy tales and distanced galaxies, a fantasy that is extremely gendered. As the child ages, consumption is still gendered, but not so obviously in colour and style. But boys and girls treasure different consumer goods and behave differently as consumers (Dittmar, 1992). Toys, clothes, and colours differ, as do play, activities, social patterns, and the way rituals and celebrations are carried out. Gender is construed through visible means, implying that consumption operates at the centre of gender expressions (Drotner, 1991; Nixon, 1996; Wilska, 2005). Traditional concepts such as 'gender roles' lose their dynamics, changing and differentiating fields where children express gender through consumption.

Boys' consumption is often connected to an activity 'doing' while girls' consumption is more related to 'being,' that is, looking good and being concerned with relations. Drotner (1991) describes boys' consumption as more related to what they can do with their body, like sports, while for girls consumption is more connected to using their body as a display for fashion and style. Brands seem to be most important to boys (Phenix, 2005; Wilska, 2005), who seem to prefer brands because they convey status, while girls are more eager to exhibit their personality. A Finnish study found strong traditional gender roles in consumption: boys placed more emphasis on technology and leisure equipment and girls more emphasis on style (Wilska, 2005). The masculine market related to clothes, jewellery, make-up, and so on has been expanding for some decades, as has the focus on brands and distinctions (Edwards, 2000; Nixon, 1992; White, 1994; Wilska, 2005).

As children are directed towards maturity, the toys they loved at a specific age will soon join the heap of waste produced as the child moves along the life course (Gunter and Furnham, 1998). The dominating brands produce life-phase-specific kids' fashion, with an increasingly adult design. An analysis of catalogues published over a 17-year period by H&M (a Swedish clothing and fashion company that operates in 28 countries) showed that girls' clothing had become more like teens in design, even if some styles remained that featured cuteness and cool/cute combinations that satisfy both grandparents and children (Borg, 2006). Fashion has

trickled down, not from upper classes, but from older age groups to younger, especially for girls (Cook and Kaiser, 2004). The fact that children are looking more like teens does not necessarily imply that they are becoming 'teens' at a younger age. The combination of rapidly changing fashion and a complex symbolic matrix of life phases, lifestyles, brands, and gender ensure that clothes and toys cannot be inherited. The Spiderman T-shirt cannot be passed on to the next cohort; they are collecting the next year's superheroes in an ever-changing system of logos. Children can recognize logos at eighteen months, and before reaching their second birthday they may ask for products by brand name (Schor, 2004). Three-year-old girls can be heard in shops insisting on brand-name shoes, and boys of eight discuss the future value of their baseball card collections (Kline, 1993).

As children get older the need for consumer goods increases, both related to the expansion of activities and to the symbolic values of products, as peer influence grows stronger (Middleton et al., 1997; Ridge, 2002). New phases represent challenges both economically and culturally; consumption is the strategic tool for mastering identity transitions (Wærdahl, 2005). This development implies that poverty and exclusion is increasingly experienced with age.

THE CHILD CONSUMER IN THE FAMILY

Modern family life is characterized by negotiation; children have their say in the family when it comes to consumption both as active agents arguing for their own desires and as representatives of the family. Terms like 'nag factor' or 'pester power' illustrate this. The negotiations vary from everyday purchases of food to holiday destinations and are part of the construction of a family as well as of consumption as such. On some areas children are the frontrunners and teach their parents in areas such as new technology and environmentally friendly behaviour (Castells, 2007; Tufte, 2005). Children seem to exert a strong influence on the family's purchases (Atkin, 1978; Ekström, 1995; Jenkins, 1979; Lee and Beatty, 2002; McNeal, 1992). Studies indicate that 70 per cent of the parents were receptive to their children's product requests. For toys and entertainment, the percentage was even higher. A poll by the Center of New American Dream conducted in 2002 found that American children seem to have embraced the pester power; 83 per cent of the children aged 12–13 report that they have asked their parents to buy something that they have seen advertised (Schor, 2004). Children use a variety of different strategies when asking their parents for consumer goods (Palan and Wilkes, 1997).

Chinese children have a strong influence on the family's economy. Almost two-thirds of children between 7 and 12 years old claim to have an influence on the purchase of snacks and children's school supplies, 32 per cent claim to have an influence on the purchase of their clothing and health-related family purchases, while just 4 per cent claim to have an influence on purchase of technology and household goods (Ying, 2003). This does not imply that parents do not buy personal computers (PCs), but that the children do not feel that they are pushing for this educational equipment. (It is also possible that children's say in purchases of electronics has increased since 2003, when iPods, cell phones, etc., were less likely to be features of children's everyday life.)

The merging of education and fashion creates new arenas for negotiations between parents and children. The market provides expensive fashion diaries for the first school day that underline that transitions in school require new clothes of certain brands and lunchboxes of particular styles. Related to sports equipment, both fashion and quality is emphasized, the educational capacities of the computer increase with each new model, and for younger children media characters are available as toys and bed linen. The fashionizing of educational equipment and everyday products are well suited as part of the negotiating processes of the family; fashion clothes, computers, and sports equipment can satisfy both the fitting in and joining in; both parental needs for educational support and protection and children's desire for social positions among peers.

Children are often described as being marginalized in society, but the consumption patterns of modern middle-class families illustrate that children have been moved to the epicentre of the family rituals. The expanding business of amusement parks all over the world shows that the children's wishes have become constitutive events in the life history of the family. However, the centrality of vacations and activities as rituals of the normal childhood and as part of the standard package suggest that children in low-income families may be excluded from these mainstream rituals. Childhood consumption as constitutive of family life and basic childhood rituals and activities illustrates the complex interaction between poverty and social exclusion.

THE DISPLAY OF PARENTHOOD THROUGH CHILDREN'S CONSUMPTION

Advertisements in the first half of the twentieth century offer a glimpse of the conception of child rearing and proper parenthood. The ads show the expanding sphere of children's cultural products – the tools of upbringing – and the moral force of these presentations is that parents who cannot provide them are in some way inadequate (Jacobson, 2004; Kline, 1993). In the postindustrial society the moral obligations of parents are related to educational consumption, particularly among the youngest children. At the symbolic level these products, such as the Baby Einstein toys, display parenting skills and the moral economy of the family (Brusdal, 2007). 'Trophy children' illustrate children's positions in modern conspicuous consumption in the sense of Veblen (1953/1976). In reputable upper-middle-class homes the baby Dior collection functions as approved signs of care and concern about quality, as well as an indication of cultural and economic capital. The need for stimulation of the youngest is underlined by an expansive industry of popular science books targeting parents (Buckingham, 2007).

Ying (2003) emphasizes vicarious consumption among Chinese children, describing how some parents buy things for their children according to their own tastes (like pearl necklaces). Much money is spent on expensive birthday presents, and there is a strong focus on style, which is most prominent in the urban areas. However, there is a worry that the urges for luxury among children will damage the formation of children's healthy character and personality (Ying, 2003), again illustrating the moral dimension of the politics of consumption. The expansion of premium enclaves of expensive designer products to small children may accomplish the paradoxical function often filled by expensive art: to status on the economic level while being above vulgar commercial principles in the cultural dimension.

Family economy is partly a gift economy with the child at the centre. That parents and grandparents take pleasure in children's delight implies that children influence the type of gifts they receive. Money as gifts is not impersonal between adults and children; money implies that the choice of products is left to the child. Some money is earmarked for special types of consumption, like the example of grandparents covering the cost of a computer or a new bicycle. The small things piling up at the children's rooms are often to be understood as marks of greetings. The little gift to the child from a relative may act as a greeting to the family, and the small gifts between peers signal friendship and bonding.

Contemporary parenthood is embedded in consumerism; the boundaries between family values and consumption are blurred and often problematic. Children's desires are often mothers' dilemmas (Seiter, 1993). Schor (2004) underlines that children 'have become conduits from the consumer marketplace into the household, the link between advertisers and the family purse'. Good parents have to protect their children from the perpetual claims from the market, while the children are the antennas into the symbolic codes of the family market they are supposed to be protected from.

SOCIALIZATION AND CONSUMPTION

The post-industrial emphasis on educational products and activities influences socialization both through the use of time and through the increase of highly organized activities, creating debates about the possible stressed and hurried child (Elkind, 1981). However, the market influences socialization in more subtle ways than parents' direct capability to invest in children's development. Children's magazines advance notions of femininity and masculinity, and the glossy images of the lives of celebrities convey the blessing of consumption and wealth. The affluent childhood introduces tensions between ideals of child rearing and the symbolic and normative values of specific products, as well as a broader concern about the deeper hedonistic and shallow values of the consumer society.

Parents seek to establish consumption as part of good upbringing. Allowances are related to tasks and educational efforts with the idea that the process of choosing, saving, and planning will help children to develop into mature consumers as well as into good persons. To spend one's own money also teaches ownership and autonomy. The work related to the allowances is often gendered; boys work outside the home cutting lawns or shovelling snow, while girls clean and baby-sit. Both boys and girls walk dogs and do errands. At a certain age 'real' part-time jobs are available. Jobs are seen as educational projects as well as economic assets; jobs teach the value of money, responsibility, and social experience. Children's motivation is that money provides access to leisure activities and products, making extra work a possible threat to schooling both as a time-consuming activity and as funding for social and cultural distractions.

Becoming a consumer is important for different reasons in different countries. In the United States, the child's allowance is supposed to provide an important lesson, either in spending or saving wisely, but in Japan the relation between money and the building of 'character' is less visible (White, 1994). Japanese parents have high expectations for their children, who in turn are less inclined to disagree with their elders than their American counterparts (White, 1994). Chinese parents pick the brands for their small children, and the later choice of the children seems to correlate with their parents' preferences (Hsieh, Chiu and Lin, 2006). Socialization of consumption is also a socialization of taste, as well as a preparation for social positions and the producing of social and cultural capital (Bourdieu, 1984).

Parents have a strong influence on children's socialization as consumers. A recent study found higher levels of materialism in young consumers with materialistic parents (Goldberg et al., 2003). Middle-class parents tempt their children with heavy subsidies of educational and safe products (such as teenagers' 'language camps' and computers) but not the flashy products of fads and subcultures. Competence and responsibility are buzzwords that are mirrored in modern children's consumer goods, paradoxically also underlining that good things are all on the market.

Worries about the consequences of wealth are salient in affluent societies, but the spoiled child is not a new invention. The early-twentieth-century child-rearing manuals reflected an obsession with order and a fear of children's desires; children were understood as insatiable creatures who needed to be strictly controlled by their parents (Cross, 2004a). The spoiled, self-centred child has been understood as rooted in lenient, permissive parenting, more than in pure materialistic overload. The spoiled child does not get along with peers or adults, while the rich child surrounded by peers understands the world as a market. The parental balance is complex; upbringing and socialization are embedded in the cultural and economic dynamics of the market.

The post-war period has seen the emergence of youthful subcultures identified through consumption, with style and music as the dominating markers. Subcultures are understood as more pointing to ideological and coherent groups than the looser concept lifestyle. Both have permeated childhood in the most recent decades. Lifestyle and subculture strongly link identity and the market, and thereby the market and socialization. The emphasis on personal authentic qualities has paradoxically contributed to the strong impact of the market, through the translation of products into indicators of inner qualities.

THE RISKS OF CONSUMPTION

A characteristic of risk society (Beck, 1992) is that the risks are concealed. This concealment creates a special anxiety and parents feel that a thousand hidden dangers face their children, both physical as well as psychological threats. Today children are precious, and the idea that a child should be harmed is more unacceptable than ever before (Zelizer, 1985). The risk society implies recognition of possible dangers for children, caused by consumer goods as well as consumption in itself, and is part of the modern panorama of risks.

The child as consumer and the child as a learner increasingly overlap. The financial and cultural capitals of the family influence the parental educational investments, creating the possibility that some families will underinvest in modern standard packages. The Poverty and Social Exclusion (PSE) survey of Britain has shown that one third of British children go without at least one item or activity deemed as necessary by the majority of the population, and nearly one fifth (18 per cent) go without two or more items or activities (Gordon et al., 2000). A Finnish study indicated that the social-economic position of the family has little impact on allowances, indicating that this is normatively regulated and that the parents prioritize their children if possible (Lintonen et al., 2007). What seems to differ with social class is the more expensive investment in educational socialization. Lareau (2003) found that middle-class children's lives were scheduled around practices and performances, while working-class and poor children had more free time and spent more time in front of the television. Thus, working-class children were less expensive. This creates the paradox of interacting capital: poor children risk receiving smaller investment in activities and educational products and too much of the cheapest and less healthy investments.

Another worry is that children, driven on by the market, are getting too mature too soon. The last years have brought strong concerns about the sexualization of young girls, ranging from the body image displayed by Barbie and the coming of child beauty pageants and sexualized T-shirts, to the consequences of the total media pressure. The proliferation of sexualized images of girls may not only create a more dangerous environment for tweens and young teens, but it may, as American psychologists have warned, harm their development (American Psychological Association, 2007). Parents' joining organizations that advocate the reduction of the commercial pressure on children and youth illustrates the position of consumption in the modern moral discourses.

Although the cultural and moral aspects of children's consumption – and its risks – have been in focus for some time, the consequences for health have become increasingly prominent in the past decades. On the whole, children are spending less time exercising and more time in front of the TV, computer, or video-game console. Since the 1970s, the percentage of overweight children and adolescents in the United States has more than doubled. Today 10 per cent of

2- to-5-year-olds and more than 15 per cent of children aged 6–19 are overweight, and in most countries obesity is viewed as an epidemic. Combining the percentage of children who are overweight with the percentage who are at risk of becoming overweight, about one in three children is affected in the United States. In the United Kingdom, it is estimated that one in four of 11- to 15-year-old are overweight or obese. In Italy, about 24 per cent of the children are overweight (Mertanen et al., 2005). Obesity has become the most prevalent nutritional problem in most European countries.

Very few children become overweight because of an underlying medical problem. Children are more likely to be obese if their parents are obese, illustrating the correlation between profile of consumption and background related to lifestyles and possibly to genetics. Changing childhood, with less outdoor play, makes physical activities something to be chosen and organized, which often entails a price tag. According to the National Diet and Nutrition Survey (Gregory et al., 2000) in the United Kingdom, 40 per cent of boys and 60 per cent of girls do not get the minimum one hour of daily physical activity as recommended by the health education authority. In China, it is argued that the one-child family has strengthened the child's influence on the family diet as well as on their own; excessive snacking has created health problems and obesity (Ying, 2003).

The latest risks confronting the child consumer can be found on the Internet. Internet games may tempt children to spend most of their time in interactive fairy tales. Virtual sex and gambling raise questions about the risk of losing money, the risk of dangerous liaisons, and the effects on socialization in general.

CHILD DEVELOPMENT, LIFE PHASES, AND CONSUMPTION

Today, children's socialization and development are interwoven with consumption. Models of consumer socialization are in general based on a Piagetian framework of cognitive development, focusing children's capacity to understand the dynamics of marketing at different cognitive stages. In correspondence with Piaget's pre-operational level, children up to the age of 7 years recognize advertisements and brand names, but they do not discriminate between advertisement and other media content. Young children are still not capable of understanding that there is no free meal or free accessories, which is, of course, why small 'free' products appear together with other products (McNeal, 2007). Between 7 and 11 years, children develop capacities to identify the persuasive intent of advertisements and its possible bias. This is also the age phase where children gradually develop the capacity for social decentring – to grasp the perspectives of others. But the process that turns the believing preschooler into a sceptical adolescent does not imply that the young tweens have developed a strong cognitive defence against the forces of the market (John, 1999). Socialization is embedded in the semiotics of consumption, providing the signifiers of maturation and social identities. Tweens and teens are vulnerable actors even if they are capable of the cognitive formal operations in Piaget's sense.

Related to cognitive and social maturation, the strong vulnerability of preschool children is based on their cognitive level as well as their lack of experience. But the development of the cognitive capacities of the first school years does not entail a corresponding cognitive defence, even if children's competences are not to be underestimated. This is partly rooted in the fact that the cognitive level is not the only factor involved in the understanding of children's position as consumers. The stages of social development, shaped by cultural and social factors as well as by biological development, constitute specific vulnerable life phases. The social and cultural changes of the last decade have moved the vulnerability of teenagers to the tween group, and possibly intensified this vulnerability, both because of the modern consumerism and the lower level

of cognitive capacity of the younger group. When psychologists warn against the sexualization of tween girls, it illustrates that the phase is vulnerable for specific commercial pressure. Vulnerability also applies to specific groups; studies that indicate that obese children respond more strongly to advertisements for unhealthy food than other children illustrate the vulnerability of groups at risk.

The knowledge society develops a specific vulnerability related to the economic, cultural, and social capital of the parents; that is, to their capacity to fund or to identify valuable consumption. This may often enhance the vulnerability of specific phases and groups at risk, as illustrated by the stereotyping of brands as indications of success as well as the frequency of early pregnancy among children living under poor conditions. The unavailability of a series of consumer goods may contribute to the shift to risky consumption of products of risky lifestyles.

The line between persuasion and information is more often blurred for children than among older age groups. When sports heroes hailed as role models appear on advertisements for children, it is because they are well suited to exploit these cognitive weaknesses. Modern heroes are increasingly commodified, emerging as figures that merge fame, consumption, and happiness. The fact that their characteristics and lives also function as narratives, reflecting moral values and lifestyles (Wicks, Nairn and Griffin, 2007), illustrates their pivotal and complex position in modern commercialized lives. Many of the narratives of the celebrities permeating children's lives illustrate that not only may consumption be the profit of achievements, but conspicuous consumption may also be understood as the road to fame.

THE CHILD CONSUMER: VULNERABLE OR COMPETENT?

How we view the child and the child consumer has changed throughout history.

Modern childhood studies have stressed the active and competent child (James, Jenks and Prout, 1998; Jenks, 1996; Qvortrup et al., 1994), including their competency as consumers (Willis, 1993; Buckingham, 2000; Zelizer, 2002). In line with this emphasis on children's agency there has been a shift from seeing the child as vulnerable to seeing the child as savvy agent acting on his or her own behalf in the growing children's market. On the one hand, the modern change of the image of the child from 'cute' to 'cool' illustrates that the nineteenth century's sacred and vulnerable child has been more or less replaced by an active child in control of his or her life. On the other hand, the child creating his or her media-inspired 'cool' look appears as a victim as well as an agent. The gradual development of social and cognitive competence and the risk of specific life phases illustrate that the vulnerability of modern children is partly rooted in the expectation of activity and competence.

The parallel existence of vulnerability and competence is salient in all discussions of children as consumers. The perspective of protection often stresses children as 'becoming' and that their competence and vulnerability must be understood in relation to their level of maturity and the possible developmental consequences of lack of protection. Children are vulnerable not only as subjects under socialization, but as children of the present, as illustrated by preschool children being exploited by advertisements tailored to their current comprehension levels (Kunkel, 2004) and the vulnerability of tweens and young teens.

Liberal perspectives claim that needs and wants children express about consumption are actual and not artificially constructed by marketing, or at least not more than among other groups, and that children must learn through their own experiences sooner rather than later. The understanding of children as empowered interpreters and shapers of their world touches clearly on a perspective focusing children as 'being', that is, as socially and culturally competent actors (James et al., 1998; Qvortrup et al., 1994). They see through commercials (Fiske, 1989; Willis, 1993) and construct their own narratives as when Barbies are changed to fit local styles (Chin, 2001). But when the perspective of 'bricolage' (Hebdige, 1979), where the sign systems of youth cultures are understood to transgress conventional distinctions of consumerism, are applied to the semiotics of children's culture, it immediately raises the question of developmental age and life phase. Studies indicate that (older) children are creative consumers, that children are easily influenced by the commercial narratives, and that the commercialization of lifestyles in specific phases, like the tween period, may produce vulnerability and risk.

Some societies seek to meet some of the dilemmas of marketing by banning advertisements to young children, as has been done in Sweden and Norway. The European Union is now considering whether there should be a European-wide ban or regulation. Others seek to regulate special advertisements for products that have identifiable negative consequences. Since April 2007, the United Kingdom has banned junk food advertising during television programmes aimed at small children and extended the ban to all children under age 16 in January 2008. There are also growing concerns about 'hidden messages' in books, school playgrounds, and areas for children's activities.

It has been suggested that childhood is disappearing in the dynamics of media and the market (Elkind, 1981; Postman, 1982). But childhood still evokes the idea of the innocence that the rest of the world has lost, and children's cognitive and socially rooted vulnerability is well documented. The right to autonomy rightfully claimed for children is seldom exemplified on the arena where children daily are invited to exert autonomy: as consumers. Vulnerable or reflective agent, the child consumer is enmeshed in the intersection of the market and the moral economy of the family as well as the society.

REFERENCES

Adler, P. and Adler, P. (1998) *Peer Power*. New Brunswick, NJ: Rutgers University Press.

AllBusiness (2007, 2 May) 'The Worldwide Market for edutainment toys is predicted to reach $7.3 billion by 2011', *AllBusiness*, Available at http://www.allbusiness.com/services/business-services/4330070-1.html

American Psychological Association (2007) *Report of the APA Task Force on the Sexualization of Girls*. Washington, DC: American Psychological Association. Available at www.apa.org/pi/wpo/sexualization.html

Atkin, C. (1978) 'Observation of parent-child interaction in supermarket decision-making', *Journal of Marketing*, 42(4): 41–5.

Australian Bureau of Statistics (2007) *Australian Social Trends 2007: Trends in Household Consumption*, ABS catalogue No. 4102.0. Belconnen, Australia: Australian Bureau of Statistics.

Barthes, R. (1973) *Mythologies*. London: Paladin.

Beck, U. (1992) *Risk Society*. London: Sage.

Borg, E. (2006) *Barndommens små voksne (Childhood grown-ups)*. Report No. 4. Oslo: National Institute for consumer research.

Borgeraas, E. and Brusdal, R. (2008) *Barns forbruk (Children's consumption)*. Oslo: National Institute for Consumer Research.

Bourdieu, P. (1984) *Distinction: A Social Critique of the Judgement of Taste*. London: Routledge and Kegan Paul.

Brusdal, R. (2007) 'If it's good for the child's development then I say yes almost every time: How parents relate to their children's consumption', *International Journal of Consumer Studies*, 31(4): 391–6.

Buckingham, D. (2000) *After the Death of Childhood*. Cambridge: Polity Press.

Buckingham, D. (2007) *Beyond Technology*. Cambridge: Polity.

Butler, J. (2006) *Gender Trouble*. New York: Routledge.

Campbell, C. (1987) *The Romantic Ethic and the Spirit of Modern Consumerism*. Oxford: Blackwell.

Castells, M. (2007) *Mobile Communication and Society*. Cambridge, MA: MIT Press.

Chadha, R. and Paul, H. (2006) *The Cult of the Luxury Brand*. Boston, MA: Nicholas Brealey Publishing.

Chee, B. (2000) 'Eating snacks and biting pressure: Only children in Bejing', in Jun Jing (ed.), *Feeding China's Little Emperors*. Stanford, CA: Stanford University Press, pp. 48–70.

Chin, E. (2001) *Purchasing Power: Black Kids and American Consumer Culture*. Minneapolis: University of Minnesota Press.

Cook, D. (2003) 'Spatial biographies of children's consumption', *Journal of Consumer Culture*, 3(2): 147–69.

Cook, D. (2004) *The Commodification of Childhood*. Durham, North Carolina: Duke University Press.

Cook, D. and Kaiser, S. (2004) 'Betwixt and between', *Journal of Consumer Culture*, 4(2): 203–27.

Cross, G. (2004a) 'Wondrous innocence: Print advertising and the origins of permissive child rearing in the US', *Journal of Consumer Culture*, 4(2): 183–201.

Cross, G. (2004b) *The Cute and the Cool*. Oxford, New York: Oxford University Press.

Dittmar, H. (1992) *The Social Psychology of Material Possessions*. New York: St. Martin's Press.

Douglas, M. and Isherwood, B. (1979) *The World of Goods*. London: Routledge.

Drotner, K. (1991) *To Create One-Self. Youth, Aesthetics, Pedagogy*. Copenhagen: Gyldendal.

Edin, K. and Lein, L. (1997) *Making Ends Meet: How Single Mothers Survive Welfare and Low-wage Work*. New York: Russell Sage Foundation.

Edwards, T. (2000) *Contradictions of Consumption*. Buckingham: Open University Press.

Ekström, K. (1995) 'Children's influence in family decision-making', Doctoral Thesis, Göteborg University.

Elkind, D. (1981) *The Hurried Child*. Cambridge, MA: Addison-Wesley Publisher.

Elliot, R. and Leonard, C. (2004) 'Peer pressure and poverty: Exploring fashion brands and consumption symbolism among children of the "British poor"', *Journal of Consumer Behaviour*, 3(4): 347–59.

Eydal, G.B. and Jeans, C.L. (2006). 'Children, consumption and poverty in Reykjavik', Paper presented at Child and Teen Consumption 2006: 2nd international conference on pluridisciplinary perspectives on child and teen consumption. Copenhagen: Copenhagen Business School.

Fiske, J. (1989) *Reading the Popular*. Boston, MA: Unwin Hyman.

Frønes, I. (1995) *Among Peers: On the Meaning of Peers in the Process of Socialization*. Oslo: Scandinavian University Press.

Goldberg, M., Gorn, G., Peracchio, L. and Bamossy, G. (2003) 'Understanding materialism among youth', *Journal of Consumer Psychology*, 13(3): 278–88.

Gordon, D., Levitas, R., Pantazis, C., Patsios, D., Payne, S., Townsend, P., et al. (2000) *Poverty and Social Exclusion in Britain*. York: Joseph Rowntree Foundation.

Gregory, J. et al. (2000) *National diet and Nutrition Survey: Young People Aged 4 to 18 years,* Volume 1: Report of the Diet and Nutrition Survey. London: TSO.

Gunter, B. and Furnham, A. (1998). *Children as Consumers*. London and New York: Routledge.

Hansen, F., Rasmussen, J., Martensen, A. and Tufte, B. (2002) *Children – Consumption, Advertising and Media Copenhagen*. Copenhagen: Business School Press.

Hebdige, D. (1979) *Subculture: The Meaning of Style*. London: Routlegde.

Hsieh, Y.C., Chiu, H.C., and Lin, C.C. (2006) 'Family communication and parental influence on children's brand attitudes', *Journal of Business Research*, 59(10–11): 1079–86.

Ishinger, B. (2006) 'Education: Raising ambitions', *OECD Observer* No. 257. Available at http://www.oecdobserver.org/news/fullstory.php/aid/2064/Education:_Raising_ambitions.html

Jacobson, L. (2004) *Raising Consumer: Children and the American Market in the Early Twentieth Century*. New York: Columbia University Press.

James, A., Jenks, C. and Prout, A. (1998) *Theorizing Childhood*. Cambridge: Polity Press.

Jenkins, R.L. (1979): 'The influence of children in the family decision-making', *Advances in Consumer Research*, 6(1): 413–18.

Jenks, C. (ed.) (1996) *Sociology of Childhood*. Brookfield: Gregg Revival.

John, D.R. (1999) 'Consumer socialization of children', *Journal of Consumer Research*, 26(3): 183–213.

Johnson, D.S., Smeeding, T. and Torrey, B.B. (2005) 'Economic inequality through the prisms of income and consumption', *Monthly Labor Review*, 128(4): 11–24.

Kline, S. (1993) *Out of the Garden*. New York: Verso.

Kochuyt, T. (2004) 'Giving away one's poverty: On the consumption of scarce resources within the family', *The Sociological Review*, 52(2): 139–61.

Kunkel, D. (2004) 'Task force on advertising and children', in Wilcox, B.L., Cantor, J. Palmer, E., Linn, S. and Dowrick, P. (eds.), *Handbook on Children and Media*. Washington, DC: American Psychological Association.

Lamont, M. and Molnar, V. (2001) 'How Blacks use consumption to shape their collective identity', *Journal of Consumer Culture*, 31(1): 31–45.

Langer, B. (2002) 'Commodification enchantment: Children and consumer capitalism', *Thesis Eleven*, 69(1): 67–81.

Langer, B. (2004) 'The business of branded enchantment', *Journal of Consumer Culture*, 4(2): 251–77.

Lareau, A. (2003) *Unequal Childhoods: Class, Race and Family Life*. Berkely: University of California Press.

Lee, C.K.C. and Beatty, S.E. (2002) 'Family structure and influence in family decision-making', *Journal of Consumer Marketing*, 19(1): 24–41.

Lino, M. (2013) *Expenditures on Children by Families 2012. U.S.* Department of Agriculture. Miscellaneous Publication No. 1528–2012.

Lintonen, T., Wilska, T.A., Koivusilta, L. and Konu, A. (2007) 'Trends in disposable income among teenage boys and girls in Finland from 1977 to 2003', *International Journal of Consumer Studies*, 31(4): 340–8.

McNeal, J. (1992) 'Children as market of influencers', in J. McNeal, *Kids as Customers: A Handbook of Marketing to Children*, Chapter 4. New York: Lexington books, pp. 63–87.

McNeal, J. (2007) *On Becoming a Consumer: Development of Consumer Behavior Patterns in Childhood*. Amsterdam: Academic Press.

Martens, L., Southerton, D. and Scott, S. (2007) 'Bringing children (and parents) into the sociology of consumption: Towards a theoretical and empirical agenda', *Journal of Consumer Culture*, 4(2): 155–82.

Mayer, S. (1998) *What Money Can't Buy*. London: Harvard University Press.

Mertanen, E., Roos, G., and Sarlio-Lähteenkorva, S. (2005) 'Children's diet – responsibilities, ethics and current issues', in G. Tellnes (ed.), *Urbanisation and Health: New Challenges in Health Promotion and Prevention*. Oslo: Unipubforlag, Oslo Academic Press, pp. 89–93.

Middleton, S., Ashworth, K. and Braithwaite, I. (1997) *Small Fortunes*. York: Joseph Rowntree Foundation.

Miles, S. (1998) *Consumerism as a Way of Life*. London: Sage Publications.

Muniz, A. and O'Guinn, T. (2001) 'Brand community', *Journal of Consumer Research*, 27(1): 31–48.

Nixon, S.J. (1996) *Hard Looks: Masculinities, Spectatorship and Contemporary Consumption*. London: UCL Press.

Palan, K.M. and Wilkes, R.E. (1997) 'Adolescent-parent interaction in family decision making', *Journal of Consumer Research*, 24(2): 159–69.

Palladino, G. (1996) Teenagers. New York: Basic Books.

Parsons, T. and Smelser, N.J. (2001) *Economy and Society. A Study in the Integration of Economic and Social Theory*. London: Routledge. (Original work published 1956).

Pecora, N.O. (1998) *The Business of Children's Entertainment*. New York: The Guilford Press.

Percival, R., Payne, A., Harding, A., and Abello, A. (2007). *Honey I Calculated the Kids...It's $537,000: Australian Child Costs in 2007*, AMP.NATSEM Income and Wealth Report No.18. Sydney, Australia: AMP.NATSEM.

Phenix, A. (2005) 'Young people and consumption: Commonalities and differences in the construction of identities', in B. Tufte, J. Rasmussen and L. B. Christensen (eds.), *Frontrunners or Copycats?*, Edition 1, Copenhagen: Copenhagen Business School Press, pp. 78–98.

Philips, B. (2013) AMP.NATSEM Income and Wealth Report Issue 33 - Cost of Kids: The Cost of Raising Children in Australia. Sydney: AMP.

Postman, N. (1982) *The Disappearance of Childhood*. New York: Delacorte Press.

Pugh, A.J. (2004) 'Windfall child rearing', *Journal of Consumer Culture*, 4(2): 229–49.

Qvortrup, J., Bardy, M., Sgritta, G. and Wintersberger, H. (1994) *Childhood Matters*. Aldershot: Avebury.

Ridge, T. (2002) *Childhood Poverty and Social Exclusion*. Bristol: The Policy Press.

Sammond, N. (2005) *Babes in Tomorrowland*. Durham and London: Duke University Press.

Schor, J.B. (2004) *Born to Buy*. New York: Scribner.

Seiter, E. (1993) *Sold Separately*. New Brunswick: Rutgers University Press.

Thorne, B. (2003) *Gender Play*. New Brunswick: Rutgers University Press.

Townsend, P. (1979) *Poverty in the United Kingdom: A Survey of Household Resources and Standards of Living*. Harmondsworth: Penguin Books.

Tufte, B. (2005) *Frontrunners or Copycats?* Copenhagen: Copenhagen Business School Press.

UNICEF (United Nations International Children's Emergency Fund) (2004) *The State of the World's Children 2005: Childhood Under Threat*. New York, USA: UNICEF.

Veblen, T. (1953/1976) *The Theory of the Leisure Class.* New York: The New American Library.

Wærdahl, R. (2005) 'Small distinctions: Socialization of (in-) difference in seemingly homogeneous peer groups', *Sosiologisk Årbok*, 2(1): 119–34.

West, C. and Zimmerman, D.H. (1987). 'Doing gender', *Gender and Society*, 1(2): 125–51.

White, M. (1994) The *Material Child: Coming of Age in Japan and America*. Berkeley, CA: University of California Press.

Wicks, P.G., Nairn, A. and Griffin, C. (2007) 'The role of commodified celebrities in children's moral development: The case of David Beckham', Consumption, Markets and Culture, 10(4): 401–24.

Willis, P. (1993) *Common Culture*. Buckingham: Open University Press.

Wilska, T.A. (2005) 'Gender differences in the consumption of children and young people in Finland', paper presented at the 7th ESA conference, Torun, Poland.

Ying, G. (2003) 'Consumption patterns of Chinese children', *Journal of Family and Economic Issues,* 24(4): 373–9.

Zelizer, V. (1985) *Pricing the Priceless Child*. Princeton, NJ: Princeton University Press.

Zelizer, V. (2002) 'Kids and commerce', *Childhood*, 9(4): 375–96.

8

Young Children as Learners

Jan Kampmann

INTRODUCTION

Learning can be defined as 'every process among living organisms which leads to a permanent change of capacity and which is not simply due to forgetting, biological maturation or aging' (Illeris, 2007: 15). This broad, comprehensive definition enables us to understand learning as a phenomenon that all people experience, regardless of their age. If, however, we parse this definition, learning can denote the *result* – the information or skill that has been acquired. Learning can be also understood as a *cognitive* process mirroring the process of interaction between individuals and their physical and social environments. What we cannot identify is learning itself, the particular moment when change of capacity takes place. Thus, although a mundane experience, how people learn is a topic that continually attracts the attention of researchers and spawns academic controversies.

Learning can take place in institutional, formal settings (for example, schools; places of worship) or non-institutional, informal contexts (for example, family outings; conversations with peers). Thus, of course, learning occurs not only as planned events (for example, the activities organized as elements of a teacher's lesson plan) but also as incidental outcomes of the processes of everyday life. In either instance, the changes in capacity that may result may be permanent.

Curiously, however, young children have traditionally been considered learners only in limited ways. The dominant view in both professional and everyday contexts has been to interpret changes in children's capacity as examples of maturation or socialization, not active learning. To be clear, these processes are not antithetical to a conceptualization of changes in children as examples of learning. Rather, my point is that the concept of learning has not been central in images of childhood. The concepts of learning and children as learners have only recently become significant foci of attention in policy, research, and pedagogical practice.

CHILDREN AS LEARNERS AT A POLICY LEVEL

In recent years, the concept of learning has attained ever greater importance when studying young children, especially in the area of early childhood services. There has been an increasing public growth of 'the politics of early childhood education'. The learning perspective is increasingly visible in government-initiated discussions of curricula even in day care centres and preschools. This process is especially prominent in Western countries, though at varying speeds with varying impact (UNICEF, 2008), and directed by diverse governmental authorities (Neuman, 2008). Early childhood education can be found under administration of education, social welfare, and health agencies (Neuman, 2008).

Whatever the auspice, many Western countries have worked since the 1990s to access, improve quality, and develop more coherent policies and programmes in early childhood education and care (ECEC; see Neuman, 2008). Commonly, there has been a general intensification of the focus on the learning dimension of early childhood education programmes, often in connection with establishment of the national curriculum or similar common guidelines. Internationally, this emphasis can be seen most explicitly in the 'Starting Strong' reports (OECD, 2001; 2006). These developments are expressions of a broader tendency to structure childhood through creation or strengthening of formal international arrangements.

Accordingly, political interest in ECEC goes beyond establishment of the proper number of places for children of preschool age. In the past two decades, national policies have also emphasized qualitative demands and expectations, about the content of activities carried out in the established institutions. Internationally, one can clearly see – again primarily in Western countries – a common tendency to establish requirements for quality, based on the evidence, documentation, evaluation, and common goals for pedagogical work (Bennett, 2008a; 2008b). In this context, it has been clear that even though most countries formulate statements and policies about the caring tasks of early childhood services, focus now is placed on the institution's learning tasks. This can be viewed as an expression of how OECD and the whole preschool sector have become more integrated with primary education – in other words, 'schoolification' (Neuman, 2008).

Even though learning has always had a central place in schools' mission, the formalization of children's learning and the focus on expectations for academic achievements are relatively new for preschool and primary school. Young children's role as students has been accorded a greater attention and given a more central position in both educational policy and professional circles. It is hardly surprising when viewed in relation to modernist understanding of the association between knowledge and social development, expressed in such terms as the 'knowledge society' and 'knowledge economy'. Education, and thereby learning, is attributed an increasingly central role in the continued growth and development of national welfare, competitiveness, and the nation's ability to keep up the 'globalization race', etc. (Apple, Kenway and Singh, 2005).

Lifelong learning has been placed on the international agenda as a high-priority item. Although lifelong learning traditionally has been associated with the extension of education and learning activities into adulthood and working life, there is clearly a parallel increased focus on learning as something that begins early in the lives of human beings (OECD, 2001; 2006). Hence, now more than ever, learning is viewed as something to be integrated into the politics of early childhood education.

INSTITUTIONALIZATION OF CHILDHOOD

The fact that children are now positioned as learners in ECEC reflects a changed understanding of the approach to children. It also represents a changed perception of the importance of public institutions in children's life and development.

Administrative authorities – national, regional and municipal – are inclined to intervene more extensively in ECEC than at any previous time in Western history. This tendency has been concretized in increasing attention to pedagogical content and operation of ECEC programmes. Previously, professionals in the individual institutions generally had the freedom to define the objectives, tools, and methods for their pedagogy. Today this definitional task is increasingly being undertaken by central political and administrative authorities, who have a principal goal of optimizing individual children's learning process and outcomes even in the preschool years. 'Starting Strong' in the OECD context,[1] 'No Child Left Behind' and state-level initiatives in the United States,[2] 'Sure Start' in the UK,[3] the 'PISA' surveys in Europe,[4] and similar initiatives and studies have all contributed to strengthening children's learning and preparation to perform in school on equal terms, through their focus on 'breaking the cycle of poverty' and accompanying 'general underachievement'.

This tendency is most immediately visible in developments within early childhood education, because it is here that we most clearly can identify a break from tradition. In reality, however, it is not only the preschool and early school years that have experienced dramatic changes during the last decade. The same development can be seen in the whole school sector in general. In recent decades, here, too, there has been increased focus on describing the content by applying standards for enhancing children's learning benefit (Apple, 2000; 2006).

LEARNING AND NATIONAL CURRICULUM

The increased focus on learning, in both early childhood education and the primary schools, most clearly emerges in the increased focus of establishing a national curriculum and common standards. In North America, Australia, New Zealand, and large parts of Europe and other OECD countries, one observes parallel tendencies toward increased central administration of common goals for early childhood education and primary school (Bloch et al., 2003; Dahlberg, Moss and Pence, 1999; Duncan, 2008; Hultqvist and Dahlberg, 2001; OECD, 2001, 2006; Sylva and Pugh, 2008).

We can discern a clear tendency for key parts of these common objectives to be formulated as demands for fulfillment of pre-defined and partial objectives, which are expressed in terms of standardized types of skills and knowledge. 'Back to Basics' has been one of the buzz phrases applied in this context. Ironically, new norms for children as learners have been presented nostalgically as reflections of purportedly abandoned traditional expectations for centrally formulated policies for early childhood education. Literacy and numeracy have held priority positions in many such formulations. One can say that an increased focus on children's learning also contributes to new demands for normality. Children are expected, at an increasingly younger age, to act in accordance with the learning expectations specified by the increased formalization of their everyday lives.

TESTS AND ASSESSMENTS

In both the school context and early childhood education, use of tests and assessments has increased as part of the attempt to ensure quality through attention to measurable results. The thrust of these requirements is generally the demonstration of literacy and numeracy.

Tests of children's language competencies are common rituals during the transition from day care to school or from primary school to post-primary education. Here again, the focus is specifically on testing children's literacy skills, occasionally combined with other types of competencies, such as their social skills.

This form of test culture has given rise to several criticisms. First, completed early in children's lives, the assessment of their personal development and competencies is reduced to that which can be uniformly measured and assessed. Thus, reliance on standardized test narrows the educational objectives for young children.

Second, even though the tests are presented as being objective and natural, they inherently have cultural biases, which may result in systematic discrimination against ethnic-minority children and children with working-class backgrounds. Thus, assessment programmes often are implicitly focused on the relation of children's and families' 'cultural capital' to the cultural codes of the school.

Third, the tests contribute to increased tracking. Thus, the culture of testing contributes to the reproduction of social and ethnically-based based inequalities in the educational system.

Fourth, the cart pulls the horse. Tests are often not carefully designed to match the goals and values of a broadly based liberal education. Rather, education is organized to support the tests' requirements. Thus, we have 'teaching to the test'.[5] Because children selected for special education or remedial programmes are often tested frequently, they are especially likely to experience a curriculum that is narrowed to address the key objectives of the tests (Apple, 2006; Gillborn, 2008).

Combined, the move toward national curricula and the growing culture of measurement and evaluation are based on bureaucratic and instrumental logic. To the bureaucrat, only that which can be measured, controlled, and planned is of any value. To the pragmatist, the reduction of alternatives that is implicit in contemporary reform promotes the development of competencies that will secure efficiency and rationality in the children's future.

These conceptual problems cannot be laid solely at the feet of politicians, bureaucrats, and business managers. The current emphasis on narrow academic goals started with educators and child researchers.

Originally, the needs for publicly funded care and sufficient institutional capacity were the most important factors in the engagement of the public sector. The professional staff themselves shifted the public discussion by their foci on content, methods, and quality assurance. Preschool and primary school teachers themselves were driving forces in developing educational and pedagogical theory and practice, often with a degree of cooperation from child researchers.

THE DOMINANCE OF DEVELOPMENTAL PSYCHOLOGY

A psychological understanding of children's development and learning has dominated the field of early childhood education. Most systematically, this approach has been expressed in connection with American contributions that have focused on the importance of Developmentally Appropriate Practice (DAP; Bredekamp and Copple, 1997). Inspired by the Swiss developmental psychologist, philosopher, and natural scientist Jean Piaget (1896–1980) and contributions from other cognitively oriented developmental psychologists, this position has had a dominant influence on thinking and conceptual development.

In keeping with the established understandings of developmental psychology regarding 'the child's' development through sequential developmental steps and stages, Bredekamp and Copple (1997) developed a wide range of appropriate and inappropriate practices of working with children of different ages. Piaget and other developmental psychologists related this approach to the construct of 'the universal child', and assumptions that each child has similar paths of cognitive development.[6] This understanding has its origins in a focus on individual children's active participation in the construction and acquisition of knowledge about their environment through well-organized pedagogical learning activities, which appropriately challenges the child's intellectual, linguistic, conceptual, social, and motor skills.

In this approach, play has an important position and function. It is regarded as especially important, because well-organized play can contribute to an optimization of the child's development and learning. Such planned play – together with other pedagogic initiatives – is described as 'developmentally appropriate practice'. It is based partly on early childhood teacher's general theoretical knowledge about child development and partly on more contextualized knowledge about the individual children and their social and cultural context (Bredekamp and Copple, 1997). In their important publication, Bredekamp and Copple present a list of different types of DAP, divided into relevant activities and initiatives for different age groups. By making lists of appropriate and inappropriate activities, they seek to establish new types of early childhood programmes – with organized play as one crucial type of activity in the curriculum. As such, the legitimacy of play is justified in its special ability to promote children's learning.

SOCIOCULTURAL CORRECTIONS TO THE CONCEPT OF LEARNING

Sociocultural theory (Anning, Cullen and Fleer, 2004), activity theory (Engestrom, 1987; Engestrom, Meittenen and Punamaki, 1999), and cultural-historical approaches (Hedegaard, 2001) constitute a mixture of critical positions toward, and extensions of, the way in which Piagetian developmental psychology has made the child's learning central to early childhood education. Sociocultural theory, activity theory, and cultural-historical approaches all have the Russian psychologist L.S. Vygotsky (1896–1934) as the source of their inspiration.

Because of Vygotsky's early death and his connection to the Soviet regime, international interest in his ideas began to emerge only in recent decades (see, for example, Vygotsky, 1978; 1987). The various Vygotsky-inspired positions have much in common, especially in their attempt to establish an alternative to more 'traditional' Piaget-inspired developmental psychological traditions.

The sociocultural approaches accentuate the social character of learning and its contextual grounding, so that the child and the world never encounter each other in unmediated form. Hence, knowledge does not simply exist a priori, as something that the individual child must acquire, but is instead created in a common and contextually specific context as 'situated learning' (Lave and Wenger, 1991). From this perspective, children and adults are co-constructors of both learning (as a process) and knowledge. In the sociocultural approaches, social scientists also break from the concept of development of 'the child' in 'stages', which they regard as characteristic of Piagetian developmental psychology.

With their focus on the co-construction of learning and knowledge, the sociocultural approaches emphasize the importance of adults' active role in circumscribing the types of challenges that face the children with whom they are working. The operational concept here is 'zone of proximal development', which denotes the types of actions, skills, and knowledge that children are not yet able to execute or utilize on their own, but which can be developed with adults' help (Holzman and Newman, 2008; Wood and Attfield, 2005: 96). Adults' task is not to communicate a specific knowledge or skills to the children but instead to provide a necessary support in order for children to be able to pursue and complete the challenges they are confronting. This special support function, called 'scaffolding', is considered a key pedagogical task within sociocultural approaches to early childhood education (Hedegaard, 2001; Jordan, 2004; Wood and Attfield, 2005).

Further, the characterization of learning as a social process means that there is generally not a focus on an individual child's learning process or interaction with her environment or an individual adult but instead on children's engagement in 'communities of learning' (Fleer, Anning and Cullen, 2004; Hedegaard, 2001; Lave and Wenger, 1991). Within such an understanding, learning is not simply a process that takes place through a social exchange from adult to child. Rather, it is a process that is connected to a community of learning, in which knowledge is co-constructed by the participants.

An important element, both as precondition and as objective for children's learning process, is children's movement in the learning community from a peripheral to a participatory position. In institution-based learning, this inclusionary process is or should be initiated by the professionals in the school or early childhood education service. With such an emphasis on inclusion and participation, active democracy also becomes a key dimension in the sociocultural approach to learning. Significantly, play becomes a key pedagogical tool in building a constructive learning environment (Wood, 2004). A number of initiatives in early childhood education have developed from these ideas, including Reggio Emilia pedagogy in Italy (Edwards, Gandini and Forman, 1993; Soler and Miller, 2003; Wood and Attfield, 2005) and *Te Whāriki* from New Zealand (Cowie and Carr, 2004; Smith, 1998; Soler and Miller, 2003; Wood, 2004; Wood and Attfield, 2005).

Despite their internal differences of opinion, the proponents of DAP and the sociocultural approach are in agreement on several points. First, they join in criticism of education as technology. They are especially sceptical of the application of academic demands to children, even those in early childhood. They also criticize the narrowing of education in the name of accountability (Anning, Cullen and Fleer, 2004; Bredekamp, 1991). Second, they generally agree that children's learning should be based on a 'multi-theoretical

perspective' (Wood and Attfield, 2005: 59). This viewpoint apparently opens the way toward a certain overlap and convergence of the two perspectives (Bredekamp, 1991; Bredekamp and Copple, 1997; Wood and Attfield, 2005). Third, DAP adherents and sociocultural theorists commonly share a view that play is a critical element in children's learning (Wood and Attfield, 2005).

THE NEW SOCIOLOGY OF CHILDHOOD AND THE RECONCEPTUALIST CRITIQUE

Thus, the developmental-psychological and sociocultural approaches establish a common critique of contemporary childhood policies on the basis of their theoretical and practical understanding of learning. They suggest that the problem is not the learning perspective per se but instead the narrow understanding of learning that is generally expressed in contemporary public policy.

Other positions in the field can be identified when it comes to formulating a broader critique of the already mentioned forms of institutionalization of children's lives. Here we can speak of positions which, instead of having a cultural or developmental psychological point of departure, are founded on a sociological-pedagogical critique of the educational domination of children's lives, as illustrated by the increased political interest in controlling and specifying the content of early childhood services. Especially in Europe and Australia, this position has been united under the rubric of the 'new sociology of childhood'.[7] A similar viewpoint based primarily in North America and Australia can be identified under the label 'reconceptualists'.[8]

These two positions differ in their starting point: respectively, in the sociology of childhood and in early childhood education. However, their conceptualization of childhood is similar. Both movements challenge the developmental psychology 'monopoly' within child research. They do so because they believe that developmental psychology has contributed to maintaining and legitimating an ahistorical construct of child development as a uniform process (see Burman, 1994; Walkerdine, 1984). Because developmental psychology has had a tendency to define 'the child' in terms of shortcomings, children have been positioned as ignorant and incompetent. In contrast, adults have been portrayed as experts who know what children need and have the competence to act accordingly.

Thus, 'childhood' can be understood as a socially and historically constructed phenomenon. It is imprinted in changing societal structures, generational dynamics, and power relations, which are also connected to specific social and cultural contexts. Hence, one can speak of childhoods rather than childhood in the singular.

Accordingly, both 'new sociologists' and 'reconceptualists' hold that children should be studied in their own right and not reduced to an 'implicit' part of other units of investigation. Children are not just family members in the present and not just social resources for the future. They are not just units of burden appearing as expenses to be considered in public sector planning.

Thus, research on children in their own right – their actions, their everyday life, their social positions, and the cultural, economic, and material conditions that affect them – are essential elements in understanding the lives of children, both individually and collectively. Scholars in both 'new sociology' and 'reconceptualist' camps agree that children should be regarded as *social actors*, so that attention is given to children's own contributions to social development and to transformation of everyday life. Children's contributions should not be understood merely as reproductions but also as productions (creations) of cultural significance, codes, and meaning. Children thus have their own active position in social processes (James, Jenks and Prout 1998; Kampmann, 2005; Wyness, 2006). Especially in the work

of the reconceptualists, readers can find a broader understanding of learning as an element of multiple settings of everyday life, not just institutionalized and professionalized schooling.

Post-structuralist understandings and variations of social constructionism are central to the reconceptualist position (Genishi and Goodwin, 2008; Grieshaber and Cannella, 2001; Jipson and Johnson, 2001; MacNaughton, 2005; Soto, 2000) and parts of the new sociology of childhood (Dahlberg and Moss, 2005; Dahlberg, Moss and Pence, 1999; James and James, 2004, 2008; Lee, 2001; Wyness, 2006). In much of this work, researchers point to the central role and importance of the daily and continuating negotiations about proper adult–child relationships and the ways in which children position themselves in the community of children-negotiated along lines differentiated by gender, sexuality, ethnicity, class, age, etc. (Davies and Harré, 1990).

INSTITUTIONAL CULTURE AND POWER

It is meaningless to speak about everyday life in the school as an institution and, more specifically, about teacher-organized processes and learning, without addressing *power* as a dimension of institutional life. At increasingly younger ages, children become part of a unique institutional culture which, although ideologically oriented toward concern for children's development and learning, has the task of organizing everyday life for a very large group of children and doing so with relatively few adult resources. With the low ratio of adults to children, teachers face daily dilemmas about the attention that they give to individual children's desires and interests. Professional educators typically have the right to define the situation and thus to determine where, when, and how particular children's interests are considered (Devine, 2003). Accordingly, negotiations can and do take place on a daily basis as to how strict or lenient such an adult administration of the children's everyday life can be. Variously, these negotiations can reflect a common and reciprocal interest, conflicts of interest between the children and the adults, or conflicts among children or adults themselves.

The organization of pedagogical activities and learning-oriented initiatives is also marked by negotiations and power. The pedagogical craft consists of working with the children, so that they develop 'institutional autonomy'. In other words, the teachers implicitly direct as many children as possible to enter on their own initiative into activities that the professionals want, without the adults needing to issue explicit orders. This professional behaviour could be understood as consonant with Gramsci's concept of 'hegemony', which 'describes the *process* of establishing dominance within a culture, not by brute force, but with voluntary consent, and by leadership rather than rule' (Procter, 2004: 26). In other words, the interaction between children and adults is enacted in an institutional culture, which is organized around different types of behavioural and communication codes, linked to daily routines, rituals, and regulations. The formal justification for the practices that form the hegemonic institutional culture is then typically based on professional pedagogical terminology, which is connected to the learning intention.

The discourse of learning thus has central importance for our understanding of the processes that we consider 'self-evident' in relation to children's participation in school life. This discourse legitimates the pedagogical organization of everyday life. It thus contributes to definition of what is regarded as appropriate, desirable, and 'normal' behaviour for the children – and for the adults, too. Inspired by the work of Foucault (1991, 1998) on 'technologies of the self', Popkewitz and colleagues (Popkewitz, 1998; Popkewitz and Brennan, 1998) showed how these new normalization processes can be seen as expression of an increased implementation of the intention of creating the 'educated subject' based on an understanding

of what Fendler (2001) called the child's 'developmentality'. In this analytic extension of Foucault's concept of 'governmentality' (1991) to the pedagogical field, Fendler (1998: 185) used a historical perspective to describe the shift in the construction of the educated subject, going from 'disciplining the body and training the mind' to 'governing the soul'.

INSTITUTIONALIZATION OF INDIVIDUALIZATION

In Scandinavia specifically and probably in the western world in general, we can see a new tendency in the demands children are facing. Moving from demands for children to acquire particular knowledge and skills, we now see another type of expectation. The child is expected to be actively involved in self-initiated learning, about not only 'the world', numeracy, and literacy, but also 'myself' and 'each other'. Although pedagogical rationality in the 1970s and 1980s was perceived as being connected with the 'pedagogical inspection', expectations are now more directed to the children's own ability to promote 'introspection', permanently being open for self-reflexive and self-evaluative confessions, which can be linked with Foucault's term 'the technologies of the self' (Foucault, 1988).

Nicolas Rose described this type of 'governing the soul' as the obligation that 'each individual must render his or her life meaningful as … the outcome of individual choices made in furtherance of a biographical project of self realization' (Rose, 1999: ix). Increased weight is laid on invisible pedagogy (Bernstein, 1996), so that some children struggle in decoding the implicit rules of conduct. The rules may not be explicitly stated by the teachers until violations occur. This shift in early childhood education and schooling is significant in the process of children's individualization. As described by the German sociologists Ulrich

Beck and Elisabeth Beck-Gernsheim (2002), the increased focus on individualization in modern Western society is a double-edged sword. On one side, this trend reflects increased possibilities and free space for the individual. On the other, however, are found new demands and increased expectations. Individualization in part reflects a societal concept of 'proper' personality development and identity formation.

Moreover, society places the primary responsibility for this process on publicly organized schools and preschool settings. Accordingly, experience in these institutions is essential if children are to acquire the cultural, social, and personal competences necessary for individualization. Such an *institutionalization of individualization* reflects its unavoidable entanglement with the norms operating in formal school and early childhood education programmes.

This institutionalization of individualization is accompanied ironically by increased *individualization of institutionalization*. In schools, the individualization of institutionalization is reflected in a belief that the culture of schools and preschools can and should be adapted to individual children's unique personality and learning styles (Kampmann, 2004).

At least in Scandinavia, pedagogical commentary has turned in recent years to individual children's 'responsibility for learning'. Thus, early childhood educators have been emphasizing children's obligation to evaluate their own performance and by so doing to develop self-reflexive competencies. Thus, in the politics of early childhood services and primary schools, children have shifted from care-demanding 'play-children' to 'responsible learning subjects' (Kampmann, 2004).

The increased degree of institutionalization of learning in recent years may have doubled the demands on children in both early childhood education and primary schools. To an increasing degree, children must be able to acquire large amounts of knowledge, skills, and competencies, which are defined on the bases of centrally determined curricula, as discussed in the section

on national learning plans. Children are also being expected to acquire the ability and willingness to present, evaluate, and reflect on their thoughts and actions, and their knowledge and social competences. One can speak of a generally increased demand for productivity, in that children must show that they are actively able to apply their knowledge and skills during assessments and tests. At the same time, and to an equal degree, they are expected to perform as responsible, active, reflexive, and 'normal' individuals (Ball, 2008). Thus, children experience a peculiar combination of neo-conservative demands to acquire traditional values and basic knowledge and neo-liberal expectations for expression of individual responsibility and accountability. Children can then be blamed for failure to fulfil these requirements even though they are conflicting.

THE HIDDEN CURRICULUM AND LEARNING

More informal daily productions of meaning, identity, and responsibility reveal a connection of learning perspective to the 'hidden curriculum', as was articulated in the 1970s and 1980s (Giroux and Purpel, 1973; Overly, 1970). The concept itself is often connected to Philip W. Jackson, whose classic book *Life in Classrooms* (1968) introduced the concept and showed how ethnographically inspired classroom research can be helpful in elucidating the phenomenon. Also described as 'unstudied, informal, unexpected, subsidiary, or concomitant learnings' (Overly, 1970: vii), the hidden curriculum takes its point of departure from the relatively simple observation that much more is going on in the daily life of a school than what is planned and described in the curriculum.

Jackson's (1968) empirical data and analyses pointed to three essentially unformulated learning dimensions in the hidden curriculum: the needs (a) to adapt to work within a group, (b) to absorb and adapt to ongoing, daily evaluation, and (c) to comply with institutional authorities. In response to the hidden curriculum, children in schools, even preschools, must acquire competence in comprehension of the institutional cultural code. Children who fail to act in accordance with such norms are classified as the 'under-achieving', 'immature', 'learning disabled', or 'disturbed'. According to McDermott (1993), these and other categories are ready to 'acquire' children and even to make them vulnerable to exclusion.

THE HIDDEN CURRICULUM AND GENDER, ETHNICITY, AND AGE

In line with Jackson's original study, several studies have showed how the hidden curriculum is linked to age, gender, sexuality, ethnicity, ability/disability, etc. For example, gender-based expectations for girls' and boys' behaviour create certain gender normalities, which children learn and acquire in the institution's daily life routine (Grieshaber, 1998; Thorne, 1993). Boys' success as learners is commonly attributed to their intrinsic, natural abilities, but their potential failures are often ascribed to something external: the pedagogy, the methods, the choice of text, or the teachers. For girls, conversely, there is a tendency to attribute their failures to something internal in the form of their natural intellectual capacities, but their success is explained in the context of external factors, such as methods, teachers, or other special circumstances (Cohen, 1998). The focus has shifted, however, to 'failing boys' because boys often score lower than girls when educational outcomes are measured with standardized tests (Arnot et al., 1998, 1999).

Studies also show the existence of a hidden curriculum in which various competences and learning capacities are dependent on their ethnicity or 'race'. Several studies in Europe and North America revealed ways that professionals rank and assess children on the basis of their ethnic origins. Such attribution may not be the product of conscious acts, but they nevertheless form part of the hidden curriculum through which children learn the language of race (Connolly and Troyna, 1998; Devine, 2007; Gillborn and Gipps, 1996; Gitz-Johansen, 2004; Sleeter, 1993; Troyna and Hatcher, 1992; Van Ausdale and Feagin, 2001).

On the global level, a hidden curriculum of Western norms about children and learning is being imposed, for instance, through transnational organizations such as the OECD, which promote universal and imperial approaches to 'normal children's normal learning' as a preconception for 'normal' global development, without really respecting children's diverse experiences or the local culture and priorities (Apple, Kenway and Singh, 2005; Kaufman and Rizzini, 2002).

Within an early childhood education framework, the hidden curriculum constitutes an essential part of children's socialization in the modern society. Just, however, as the original theory of socialization (Parsons, 1951) was criticized for emphasis on the process as a transmission of culture, morality, knowledge, and skills from one generation to the next (the child being reduced to a passive recipient), it is important to recognize that unintended learning processes cannot be described solely in relation to the hidden curriculum. Children's acquisition of cultural codes and requirements for normalization also occurs as part of their own mutual interactions and negotiations.

CHILDREN'S LEARNING THROUGH INTERACTIONS WITH PEERS

With his concept of 'interpretive reproduction', Corsaro (1997) showed how children actively process and interpret their impressions. Their reciprocal interactions, negotiations, play sequences, etc., create raw material for their social interventions and their conceptualization of the world. However, it would be more accurate to term this process as 'interpretive (re-)production' to indicate that children also establish new forms of cultural order and orientation in their everyday social learning. They are not just re-producers but also producers of attitudes, meanings, and cultural codes.

In recent decades, the meaning of the peer culture in connection with young children's everyday lives and learning processes has been accorded substantial attention (see, for example Adler and Adler, 1998; Frønes, 1995). Children's social interaction within the group of friends is important for the development of their ability to orient themselves socially. Children must be able to develop an understanding of how social landscape is composed, and they must also learn to read and orient themselves in accordance to the social map in daily life. Finally, children must develop behavioural competencies and agency so that they can act in and move about in appropriate ways, all of which centres in as elements in the child's ongoing negotiations by which the child takes certain position in the social landscape (Andersen and Kampmann, 1996).

As with adult–child relations, children's relations among themselves are characterized by power, inclusion, and exclusion. Views of gender and ethnicity do not operate only in the interaction among adults and children, or as expressions of social and ideological forces that children simply passively reproduce. Instead, they are also negotiated actively in the children's experimentation with identity (Adler and Adler, 1998; Van Ausdale and Feagin, 2001).

Play constitutes an essential framework for preschool and primary school children, in which the daily social exchange takes place among children. Play centres a well-suited social framework for children to be able to develop, acquire, and test several of their social competencies (Sutton-Smith, 2001).

LEARNING AND RESISTANCE

Another important element in children's learning process in the institutional context is the development of different forms of resistance. As a phenomenon in pedagogical contexts, resistance has generally been framed in relation to elder pupils' more or less conscious resistance to an alienating, often irrelevant educational system (Giroux and Purpel, 1983; Shore and Freire, 1987; Willis, 1978). However, resistance has not been a particularly developed theme within early childhood education settings. Nonetheless, in an exemplary way, Angela Spaulding (1997) showed that children as young as 6 or 7 years old sometimes undertake very advanced forms of resistance against the teacher's attempts to define the classroom and the activities within it. Inspired by Ball (1987), Spaulding investigated what she calls the micropolitical perspectives of the children, whose strategies ranged from active and sustained resistance to different forms of withdrawal. Often they succeeded in evading participation in the formal curriculum and the activities linked to it and in establishing and pursuing their own while avoiding detection by the teacher in doing so. In some instances, such active resistance entailed a conscious cooperation among the children in their attempt to change the relations of power and the right to define the pedagogical situation and the space. Even at this early age, children develop conscious strategies to sabotage the teacher's agenda.

LEARNING AS EVERYDAY PRACTICE AND LIVED EXPERIENCE

Learning among children is, of course, not limited to formal educational institutions. Instead, learning takes place in every context in which the children enter (Illeris, 2007). Learning that contributes to understanding and managing everyday life as children experience it is of central importance to children in early childhood services and primary schools, as it is to older children (Frønes, 1995).

Viewed from the children's perspective, learning is closely linked to their specific everyday experiences in the settings of which they are a part. In this emphatic sense, learning can be understood as connected to the concept of experience. Hegel explicated this human experience as being created through the subject's interaction with and intervention into the material and social environment, whereby the material and social environment is changed. Such action simultaneously affects the subject, who not only obtains experience with the nature of the social and material world, but who also obtains an appreciation of one's own place in the social and material environment, an experience that is self-transforming (cf. Hegel, 1931). In educational jargon, this phenomenon is 'experience-based learning', a concept attributed to John Dewey (1973), who was inspired by Hegel.

Pedagogical scholars must be concerned not only with the question of *how* children develop in their thinking but also the problem of *what* children think about. The emphasis on child participation that is found in the Convention on the Rights of the Child implies the need for new and ongoing interest in children's statements about their experiences, wishes and feelings.

In the research context, there is now an emerging interest in presenting children's views of their own everyday life, often formulated as an intention to establish a children's perspective and to develop research methods which are sensitive to 'children's voice' (Christensen and James, 2000; Clark, Kjørholt and Moss, 2005; Deegan, Devine and Lodge, 2004; Grieg and Taylor, 1999; Kampmann, 1998; Lewis and Lindsay, 2000; Milner and Carolin, 1999). Generally speaking, such studies are designed to learn what children are thinking in settings of daily life. Schutz (1982) tied the everyday-life perspective to an interest in participants' – in this case, children's – understanding of their own experience and its meaning and of their own active involvement in the process of creation of meaning (Nielsen and Kampmann, 2007).

Professionals in early childhood education are challenged to adapt their institution to enable greater attention to children's voice and to integrate such messages into pedagogical activities. Such an effort can be one dimension of a critical pedagogical approach to learning (Darder, Baltodano and Torres, 2009).

LEARNING AND CRITICAL PEDAGOGY

In recent decades, research studies have linked the concepts of critical pedagogy and learning which takes its point of departure in the participants' subjective and lived experiences, This trend was inspired by representatives of critical pedagogy, such as Paolo Freire in South America, Henri Giroux in North America, and Oskar Negt in Europe, all with more or less explicit references to Dewey (and Hegel). All of them pointed toward the necessity for teaching to take on the task of putting these immediate subjective experiences into perspective by relating them to what Oskar Negt called the 'objective meaning'. Objective meaning refers to the ambition to decipher and interpret subjective experiences in relation to the social, cultural, and social contexts of which they are part and from which they derive.

As with Hegel's understanding of experience as an exchange between individuals and their social reality, it is also important for critical pedagogues to maintain that learning is not solely based on the individual's experience, but in the confrontation of the immediate experience with relevant social knowledge. This enables subjective experiences to be placed into a context that increases the participants' understanding of their individual and collective situations.

Shirley Kessler (1991) criticized the tradition of *developmentally appropriate practice* for only or overly determining the learning content on the basis of 'developmental appropriateness' at the cost of genuine considerations about the content of the curriculum. Arguing from a critical pedagogical perspective, Kessler emphasized that it is important to organize the ideas into particular content for presentation to children. Teachers should not uncritically accept centrally determined and pre-defined learning outcomes. With inclusion of critical curriculum considerations, a path is opened for consideration of the content of instruction. This perspective thus points to the importance of the daily negotiations concerning perceptions of legitimate knowledge in the institutional setting.

Kessler's recommendation was that the curriculum for the youngest children should begin with the goal of promotion of democratic norms. Curricular discussions should include examination of the requisites for participation in a democratic community. The view of democracy being advocated in this context is democracy in the 'strong' sense of the word – 'participatory democracy'.

Within the critical pedagogical framework, four key principles should guide the approach to children's learning. First, learning must take children's experiences, social world, interests, speculations, and curiosities as points of departure. Teachers must develop approaches that make it possible for this diversified group of children to see how their own life situation and experiences are echoed and taken seriously in the classroom. Second, these experiences must be linked to society through consideration of the similarities and differences among children. Such diversity becomes a daily resource in producing a wide range of knowledge, developing relevant social skills, and demonstrating the meaning of life in a democracy. Third, integrating these experiences, instruction must consistently include children's active contribution to a participatory democracy. Fourth, in so doing, educators must address some crucial questions at every point where we position children as learners: in whose interest are the learning requirements defined? Whose curriculum is it? Who will ultimately gain the most from the way that the curriculum and pedagogical practices are organized?

These and other similar critical questions will be asked if we insist on the importance

of teachers having the courage to confront the ambiguities of children's learning. On one hand, children's exemplary learning through their individual and common experiences is crucial for elaboration of social knowledge. Constructive agency is necessary for creative transformation of children's everyday life in the long run. On the other hand, the pedagogical and educational ambition to organize children's learning is never innocent or neutral. Power is always a part of children's learning, and the teacher has a crucial position. Accordingly, power mechanisms are part of the daily processes that must be taken seriously as we facilitate children's learning.

NOTES

1 See Bennett (2008a, 2008b) and OECD (2001, 2006) for presentations of Starting Strong.

2 See No Child Left Behind (2001) Public Law 107-110, No Child Left Behind Act of 2001, retrieved from http://www2.ed.gov/policy/eslsec/leg/elsec/leg/esea02/107-110.pdf and Sadovnik et al. (2008) for presentations and critical discussions of this initiative.

3 See the Childcare Act (2006) available at http://www.surestart.gov.uk/.

4 See the OECD Programme for International Student Assessment (PISA) available at www.pisa.oecd.org

5 Numerous critiques of test culture and its destructive effects on early childhood education specifically and education generally are available. See, for example, Apple (2006), Gillborn (2008), Kohn (1999, 2000), and Meier (2000).

6 Although Bredekamp and Copple (1997: 9–15) discuss the importance of including considerations regarding cultural specificities and differentiation in understanding and interpreting children's behaviour and needs, they still apply an understanding of children that is grounded in traditional developmental psychology.

7 For further details, see the key publications of the new sociology of childhood, such as *Constructing and Reconstructing Childhood* (James and Prout, 1990), *Childhood as a Social Phenomenon* (Qvortrup, 1991, 1993) and *Childhood Matters* (Qvortrup et al., 1994). In this connection, an important contribution from the United States has been the work of Corsaro (1997).

8 Swadener and Kessler (Early Education and Development, 1991) and their edited collection entitled *Reconceptualizing the Early Childhood*

Curriculum (Swadener and Kessler, 1992) are seminal texts articulating this perspective. See also Jipson and Johnson (2001).

REFERENCES

Adler, P.A. and Adler, P. (1998) *Peer Power: Preadolescent Culture and Identity*. London: Rutgers University Press.

Andersen, P.Ø. and Kampmann, J. (1996*) Børns legekultur [Children's Play-Culture]*. København: Munksgaard.

Anning, A., Cullen, J. and Fleer, M. (ed.) (2004) *Early Childhood Education: Society and Culture*. London: Sage.

Apple, M. (2000) *Official Knowledge. Democratic Education in a Conservative Age*. 2nd ed. New York: Routledge.

Apple, M. (2006) *Educating the 'Right' way: Markets, Standards, God, and Inequality*. 2nd ed. New York: Routledge.

Apple, M.W., Kenway, J. and Singh, M. (eds.) (2005) *Globalizing Education: Policies, Pedagogies, and Politics*. New York: Peter Lang.

Arnot, M., Gray, J., James, M. and Rudduck, J. (1998) *A Review of Recent Research on Gender and Educational Performance*. OFSTED Research Series, London, The Stationery Office.

Arnot, M., David, M. and Weiner, G. (1999) *Closing the Gender Gap. Postwar Education and Social Change*. Cambridge: Polity Press.

Ball, S.J. (1987) *The Micro-politics of the School: Towards a Theory of School Organization*. London: Methuen.

Ball, S.J. (2008) *The Education Debate*. Bristol, England: Policy Press.

Beck, U. and Beck-Gernsheim, E. (2002) *Individualization*. London: Sage Publications.

Bennett, J. (2008a) *Early Childhood Services in the OECD Countries: Review of the Literature and Current Policy in the Early Childhood Field*. Innocenti, Working Paper 2008-01. UNICEF, Innocenti Research Centre.

Bennett, J. (2008b) *Benchmarks for Early Childhood Services in OECD Countries*. Innocenti Working Paper 2008-02. UNICEF, Innocenti Research Centre.

Bernstein, B. (1996) *Pedagogy, Symbolic Control and Identity: Theory, Research, Critique*. London: Taylor & Francis.

Bloch, M.N., Holmlund, K., Moqvist, I. and Popkewitz, T.S. (eds.) (2003) *Governing Children, Families and Education: Restructuring the Welfare State*. New York: Palgrave Macmillan.

Bredekamp, S. (1991) 'Redeveloping early childhood education: A response to Kessler', *Early Childhood Research Quarterly*, 6(2): 199–209.

Bredekamp, S. and Copple, C. (eds.) (1997) *Developmentally Appropriate Practice in Early Childhood Programs*. Washington, DC: NAEYC.

Burman, E. (1994) *Deconstructing Early Childhood Education. Social Justice, and Revolution*. New York: Peter Lang.

Christensen, P. and James, A. (eds.) (2000) *Research with Children: Perspectives and Practices*. London: Falmer Press.

Clark, A., Kjørholt, A.T. and Moss, P. (eds.) (2005) *Beyond Listening: Children's Perspectives on Early Childhood Services*. Bristol, England: Policy Press.

Cohen, M. (1998) 'A habit of healthy idleness: Boy's underachievement in historic perspective', in Epstein, D., Elwood, J, Hey, V. and Maw, J. (eds.): *Failing Boys? Issues in Gender and Achievement*. Buckingham: Open University Press, pp. 19–34.

Connolly, P. and Troyna, B. (eds.) (1998) *Researching Racism in Education: Politics, Theory and Practice*. Buckingham: Open University Press.

Corsaro, W.A. (1997) *The Sociology of Childhood*. Thousand Oaks, CA: Pine Forge Press.

Cowie, B. and Carr, M. (2004) 'The consequences of socio-cultural assessment', in A. Anning, J. Cullen and M. Fleer (eds.), *Early Childhood Education: Society and Culture*. London: Sage Publication, pp. 95–106.

Dahlberg, G. and Moss, P. (2005) *Ethics and Politics in Early Childhood Education*. London: Routledge Falmer.

Dahlberg, G., Moss, P. and Pence, A. (1999) *Beyond Quality in Early Childhood Education and Care: Postmodern Perspectives*. London: Falmer Press.

Darder, A. Baltodano, M.P. and Torres, R.D. (eds.) (2009) *The Critical Pedagogy Reader*. 2nd. ed. London: Routledge.

Davies, B. and Harré, R. (1990) 'Positioning: The discursive production of selves', *Journal for the Theory of Social Behavior*, 20(1): 43–63.

Deegan, J., Devine, D. and Lodge, A. (eds.) (2004) *Primary Voices: Equality, Diversity, and Childhood in Irish Primary Schools*. Dublin: Institute of Public Administration.

Devine, D. (2003) *Children, Power, and Schooling: How Childhood is Structured in the Primary School*. Stoke on Trent: Trentham Books.

Devine, D. (2007) 'Immigration and the enlargement of children's social space in school', in H. Ziher, D. Devine, A.T. Kjørholt and H. Strandell (eds.), *Flexible*

Childhood? Exploring Children's Welfare in Time and Space. Obdence: University Press of Southern Denmark, pp. 143–165.

Dewey, J. (1973) *Experience and Education*. New York: Collier Books.

Duncan, J. (2008) 'Misplacing the teacher? New Zealand early childhood teachers and early childhood education policy reforms, 198–96', in E. Wood (ed.), *The Routledge Reader in Early Childhood Education*. London and New York: Routledge, pp. 253–270.

Edwards, C., Gandini, L. and Forman, G. (eds.) (1993) *The Hundred Languages of children: The Reggio Emilia Approach to Early Childhood Education*. Norwood, NJ: Ablex.

Engestrom, Y. (1987) *Learning by Expanding: An Activity-Theoretical Approach to Developmental Research*. Helsinki: Orienta-Konsultit.

Engestrom, Y., Meittenen, R. and Punamako, R.L. (eds.) (1999) *Perspectives on Activity Theory*. Cambridge: Cambridge University Press.

Fendler, L. (1998) 'What is it impossible to think? A genealogy of the educated subject' in T.S Popkewitz and M. Brennan (eds.), *Foucault's Challenge. Discourse, Knowledge, and Power in Education*. New York: Teachers College Press, pp. 39–63.

Fendler, L. (2001) 'Educating flexible souls: The construction of subjectivity through developmentality and interaction' in K. Hulqvist and G. Dahlberg (eds.), *Governing the Child in the New Millennium*. London: Routledge Falmer, pp. 119–42.

Fleer, M., Anning, A. and Cullen, J. (2004) 'A framework for conceptualizing early childhood education', in A. Anning, J. Cullen and M. Fleer (eds.), *Early Childhood Education: Society and Culture*. London: Sage Publication, pp. 175–89.

Foucault, M. (1988) 'Technologies of the self', in L.H. Martin, H. Gutman and P.H. Hutton (eds.), *Technologies of the Self: A Seminar with Michele Foucault*. Amherst: University of Massachusetts Press, pp. 16–49.

Foucault, M. (1991) 'Governmentality', in G. Burchell, C. Gordon, and P. Miller (eds.), *The Foucault Effect: Studies in Governmentality*. Chicago: University of Chicago Press, pp. 87–104.

Frønes, I. (1995) *Among Peers: On the Meaning of Peers in the Process of Socialization*. Oslo: Scandinavian University Press.

Genishi, C. and Goodwin, A.L. (eds.) (2008) *Diversities in Early Childhood Education: Rethinking and Doing*. New York: Routledge.

Gillborn, D. (2008) *Racism and Education: Coincidence or Conspiracy*? London: Routledge.

Gillborn, D. and Gipps, C. (1996) *Recent Research on the Achievements of Ethic Minority Pupils: Ofsted Reviews of Research*. London: Institute of Education, London University.

Giroux, H. and Purpel, D. (eds.) (1983) *The Hidden Curriculum and Moral Education*. Berkeley, CA: McCutchan Publishing Corp.

Gitz-Johansen, T. (2004) 'The incompetent child: Representations of ethnic minority children', in H. Brembeck, B. Johansson and J. Kampmann (eds.), *Beyond the Competent Child: Exploring Contemporary Childhoods in the Nordic Welfare Societies*. Frederiksberg: Roskilde University Press, pp. 199–225.

Grieg, A. and Taylor, J. (1999) *Doing Research with Children*. London: Sage.

Grieshaber, S. (1998) 'Constructing the gendered infant', in N. Yelland (ed.), *Gender in Early Childhood*. London: Routledge, pp. 15–35.

Grieshaber, S. and Cannella, G.S. (eds.) (2001) *Embracing Identities in Early Childhood Education: Diversity and Possibilities*. New York: Teachers College Press.

Hedegaard, M. (ed.) (2001) *Learning in Classrooms: A Cultural-Historical Approach*. Aarhus: Aarhus University Press.

Hegel, W.F. (1931) *The Phenomenology of Mind*. New York: Macmillan.

Holzman, L. and Newman, F. (2008) 'Playing in/with the ZPD', in E. Wood (ed.), *The Routledge Reader in Early Childhood Education*. London and New York: Routledge, pp. 85–108.

Hultqvist, K. and Dahlberg, G. (eds.) (2001) *Governing the Child in the New Millennium*. New York and London: Routledge Falmer.

Illeris, K. (2007) *How We Learn: Learning and Non-Learning in School and Beyond*. London: Routledge.

Jackson, P.W. (1968) *Life in Classrooms*. New York: Holt, Rinehart and Winston.

James, A. and James, A.L. (2004) *Constructing Childhood: Theory, Policy and Social Practice*. Basingstoke: Palgrave Macmillan.

James, A. and James, A.L. (eds.) (2008) *European Childhoods: Cultures, Politics, and Childhoods in Europe*. Basingstoke: Palgrave Macmillan.

James, A., Jenks, C. and Prout, A. (1998) *Theorizing Childhood*. Oxford: Polity Press.

James, A. and Prout, A. (eds.) (1990) *Constructing and Reconstructing Childhood: Contemporary Issues in the Sociological Study of Childhood*. London: Falmer Press.

Jipson, J.A. and Johnson, R.T. (eds.) (2001) *Resistance and Representation: Rethinking Childhood Education*. New York: Peter Lang.

Jordan, B. (2004) 'Scaffolding learning and co-constructing understandings', in A. Anning, J. Cullen and M. Fleer (eds.), *Early Childhood Education: Society and Culture*. London: Sage, pp. 31–42.

Kampmann, J. (1998) Børneperspektiv og børn som informanter *[Children's Perspective and Children as Informants]*. København: Børneradet [Children's Council].

Kampmann, J. (2004) 'Socialization of childhood: New opportunities? New Demands?', in H. Brembeck, B. Johansson and J. Kampmann (eds.), *Beyond the Competent Child: Exploring Contemporary Childhoods in the Nordic Welfare Societies*. Fredriksberg: Roskilde University Press, pp. 127–52.

Kampmann, J. (2005). 'Understanding and theorizing modern childhood in Denmark: Tendencies and challenges', in B. Tufte, J. Rasmussen and L.B. Christensen (eds.), *Frontrunners or Copycat*? Holbaek: Copenhagen Business School Press, pp. 20–37.

Kaufman, N.H. and Rizzini, I. (eds.) (2002) *Globalization and Children: Exploring Potentials for Enhancing Opportunities in the Lives of Children and Youth*. New York: Kluwer Academic/Plenum Publishers.

Kessler, S.A. (1991) 'Alternative perspectives on early childhood education', *Early Childhood Research Quarterly*, 6(2): 183–97.

Kohn, A. (1999) *The Schools Our Children Deserve*. Boston, MA: Houghton Mifflin Company.

Kohn, A. (2000) *The Case Against Standardized Testing: Raising the Scores, Ruining the Schools*. Portsmouth, NH: Heinemann.

Lave, J. and Wenger, E. (1991) *Situated Learning: Legitimate Peripheral Participation*. Cambridge: Cambridge University Press.

Lee, N. (2001) *Childhood and Society: Growing up in an Age of Uncertainty*. Buckingham: Open University Press.

Lewis, A. and Lindsay, G. (eds.) (2000) *Researching children's Perspectives*. Buckingham: Open University Press.

MacNaughton, G. (2005) *Doing Foucault in Early Childhood Studies*. London: Routledge.

McDermott, R.P. (1993) 'The acquisition of a child by a learning disability', in Charklin, S. and Lave, J. (eds.), *Understanding Practice: Perspectives on Activity and Context*. Cambridge: Cambridge University Press, pp. 269–305.

Meier, D. (2000) *Will Standards Save Public Education*? Boston, MA: Beacon Press.

Milner, P. and Carolin, B. (eds.) (1999) *Time to Listen to Children: Personal and Professional Communication*. London: Routledge.

Neuman, M.J. (2008) 'Governance of early childhood education and care: Recent developments in OECD countries', in E. Wood (ed.), *The Routledge Reader in Early Childhood Education*. London and New York: Routledge, pp. 163–76.

Nielsen, H.W. and Kampmann, J. (2007) 'Children in command of time and space?', in H. Ziher, D. Devine, A.T. Kjorhølt, and H. Srandell (eds.) (2007), *Flexible Childhood? Exploring Children's Welfare in Time and Space*. Odense: University Press of Southern Denmark, pp. 191–214.

OECD (2001) *Starting Strong: Early Childhood Education and Care*. Paris: OECD Publishing.

OECD (2006) *Starting Strong II: Early Childhood Education and Care*. Paris: OECD Publishing.

Overly, N.V. (ed.) (1970) *The Unstudied Curriculum: Its Impact on Children*. Washington, DC: Association for Supervision and Curriculum Development, NEA.

Parsons, T. (1951) *The Social System*. New York: Free Press of Glencoe.

Popkewitz, T.S. (1998) *Struggling for the Soul: The Politics of Schooling and the Construction of the Teacher*. New York: Teachers College Press.

Popkewitz, T.S. and Brennan, M. (1998) 'Restructuring of social and political theory in education: Foucault and a social epistemology of school practices', in T.S. Popkewitz and M. Brennan (eds.), *Foucault's Challenge: Discourse, Knowledge and Power in Education*. New York: Teachers College Press, pp. 3–35.

Procter, J. (2004) *Stuart Hall*. London: Routledge.

Qvortrup, J. (1991) *Childhood as a Social Phenomenon: An Introduction to a Series of National Reports*. Vienna: European Centre.

Qvortrup, J. (ed.) (1993) *Childhood as a Social Phenomenon: Lessons from an International Project*. Vienna: European Centre.

Qvortrup, J., Brady, M., Sgritta, G. and Wintersberger, H. (eds.) (1994) *Childhood Matters: Social Theory, Practice and Politics*. Aldershot: Avebury.

Rose, N. (1999) *Governing the Soul: The Shaping of the Private Self*. 2nd ed. London: Free Association Books.

Sadovnik, A.R., O'Day, J.A., Bohrnstedt, G.W. and Borman, K.M. (eds.) (2008) *No Child Left Behind and the Reduction of the Achievement Gap*. New York: Routledge.

Schutz, A. (1982) *Life Forms and Meaning Structure*. London: Routledge & Kegan Paul.

Shor, I. and Freire, P. (1987) *A Pedagogy for Liberation: Dialogues on Transforming Education*. New York: Bergin and Garvey.

Sleeter, C. (1993) 'How white teachers construct race', in C. McCarthy and W. Crichlow (eds.), *Race, Identity and Representation in Education*. New York: Routledge, pp. 243–56.

Smith, A.B. (1998) *Understanding Children's Development: A New Zealand Perspective*, 4th ed. Wellington: Bridget Williams Books.

Soler, J. and Miller, L. (2003) The struggle for early childhood curricula. A comparison of the English Foundation Stage Curriculum, Te Whāriki and Reggio Emilia', *International Journal of Early Years Education*, 11(1): 57–67.

Soto, L.D. (ed.) (2000) *The Politics of Early Childhood Education*. New York: Peter Lang.

Spaulding, A. (1997) 'The politics of primaries: The micropolitical perspectives of 7-year-olds', in A. Pollard, D. Thiessen and A. Filer (eds.), *Children and their Curriculum: The Perspectives of Primary and Elementary School Children*. London: Falmer Press, pp. 101–21.

Sutton-Smith, B. (2001) *The Ambiguity of Play*. Cambridge, MA: Harvard University Press.

Sylva, K. and Pugh, G. (2008) 'Transforming the early years in England', in R. Wood (ed.), *The Routledge Reader in Early Childhood Education*. London and New York: Routledge, pp.177–94.

Swadener, B.B. and Kessler, S. (1991) 'Introduction to the special issue', *Early Education and Development*, 2(2): 85–94.

Swadener, B.B. and Kessler, S. (1992) *Reconceptualizing the Early Childhood Curriculum: Beginning the Dialogue*. New York: Teachers College Press.

Sylva, K. and Pugh, G. (2008) 'Transforming the early years in England', in R. Wood (ed.), *The Routledge Reader in Early Childhood Education*. London and New York: Routledge, pp. 177–94.

Thorne, B. (1993) *Gender Play: Girls and Boys in School*. Buckingham: Open University Press.

Troyna, B. and Hatcher, R. (1992) *Racism in Children's Lives: A Study of Mainly White Primary Schools*. London: Routledge.

UNICEF (2008) *The Child Care Transition, Innoccenti Report Card 8*. Florence: UNICEF Innocenti Research Centre.

Van Ausdale, D. and Feagin, J.R. (2001) *The First R: How Children Learn Race and Racism*. Oxford: Rowman and Littlefield Publishers.

Vygotsky, L.S. (1978) *Mind in Society: The Development of Higher Psychological Processes*. Cambridge, MA: Harvard University Press.

Vygotsky, L.S. (1987) *Thinking and Speech*. New York: Plenum Press.

Walkerdine, V. (1984) 'Developmental psychology and the child-centered pedagogy: The insertion of Piaget into early education', in J. Henriques, W. Hollway, C. Urwin, C. Venn and Walkerdine (eds.), *Changing the Subject: Psychology, Social Regulation and Subjectivity*. London: Routledge, pp. 153–202.

Willis, P. (1978) *Learning to Labour: How Working Class Kids Get Working Class Jobs*. Farnborough: Saxon House.

Wood, E. (2004) 'Developing a pedagogy of play' in A. Anning, J. Cullen and M. Fleer (eds.), *Early Childhood Education: Society and Culture*. London: Sage, pp. 19–30.

Wood, E. and Attfield, J. (2005) *Play, Learning and the Early Childhood Curriculum*. 2nd ed. London: Paul Chapman Publishing.

Wyness, M. (2006) *Childhood and Society: An Introduction to the Sociology of Childhood*. Basingstoke: Palgrave Macmillan.

9

Children as Family Members

Jennifer Mason and Becky Tipper

INTRODUCTION

In this chapter, we explore what we see as some of the key issues that have arisen in recent research into children's experiences of family life. The chapter has a methodological focus and develops an argument for a methodological approach, which is sensitive and open, and which is anchored in children's everyday experiences and perspectives. We do not suggest, however, that this is simple or straightforward, and we consider some of the complexities and challenges. We conclude by suggesting that, ironically perhaps, the better that qualitative researchers become in listening to the intimate and real-life detail of children's experiences, the more problematic are the ethical issues raised.

Untangling 'home', 'family', and 'children'

In social science research, the family and the home have traditionally been regarded as the 'natural' setting for children's lives. Indeed, the very term 'family' is taken by some to be synonymous with the presence of children, and this reflects the popular use of 'family' as an adjective, as in 'family-friendly' or

'family car' for example. This apparently natural affinity between children and family is problematic in a number of ways. Families do not always include children, and children do not always have families (Masson and Oakley, 1998). Even where they do, children's lives are lived and experienced in many contexts and settings, not all of which have anything much to do with family, and these may not always be best understood or interpreted through the primary lens of family relationships. But there is a further problem with the assumption that family equates to children, which is central to the discussion of children as family members in this chapter. This is where it is wrongly assumed that family research always or automatically includes child research and that, by extension, if we have done research on families, then we know about children. In fact until relatively recently (Brannen and O'Brien, 1996), surprisingly little research on 'the family' actually incorporated, let alone focused on children's everyday experiences of family life. Children were part of the picture, certainly, but more often as the inert recipients of parenting, childcare and socialization, than as active members or participants in their own right.

The two most important challenges to that position were, first, the 'new' approaches to child research that began in earnest especially in sociology in the late 1980s and early 1990s, and second, the almost simultaneous shift in studies of everyday family life towards an emphasis on 'family practices' (Morgan, 1996) and 'doing family' (rather than family roles, structures, or units). The new approaches to child research emphasized the importance of listening to and valuing children's own perspectives on and experiences of family life in the here and now. In part this was a reaction against particular versions of developmental psychology that used quantitative measures linking socio-economic and family background variables to various 'outcome measures' in adults (thereby circumventing the need to listen to children at all!). This was a sea change from a study of childhood that had only been interested in children because of the adults they were in the process of becoming, as Leena Alanen famously put it (Alanen, 2001). Now there was a move towards treating children as experts on their own lives (for example, Alanen and Mayall, 2001; Christensen and James, 2000; James and Prout, 1996; Mayall, 1994; Thorne, 1997).

Meanwhile, family studies, in a reaction against the long-standing dominance of sociological structural-functionalist approaches, were exploring how family life was done, practised, and negotiated interactively (Finch and Mason, 1993; Morgan, 1996). This opened up the idea that families – and what 'the family is' – were not so much units and structures as sets of relationships. Thus even one's own family of origin was not entirely *given* but was also *made* through interaction and experience (Carsten, 2004; Weeks, Heaphy and Donovan, 2001).

At first, these two bodies of work remained relatively separate. As Smart, Neale and Wade (2001) have pointed out, from the point of view of childhood studies this was in part a conscious effort to explore 'children's own social worlds', outside the domineering presence of the family (see also Mannion,

2007). Gradually, however, they began to influence each other, as it became clear that neither childhood nor family could be fully understood without the other. The consequence was the production of some significant studies that combine an emphasis on how family life is done, practised, and made, to paraphrase David Morgan's concept of 'family practices' (Morgan, 1996), with a focus on children as actors, 'doers', and people with the capacity to reflect upon and provide accounts of their experiences (Brannen and O'Brien, 1996; Mason and Tipper, 2008a, 2008b; Morrow, 1998a; O'Brien, Alldred and Jones, 1996; Punch, 2005; Smart and Neale, 1998; Smart et al., 2001; Solberg, 1997; Thomson et al., 2002). As this work has grown and evolved over the last 20 years or so, certain key issues for researching children as family members have emerged, been debated, and recurred, and these form the focus for the remainder of this chapter. The chapter is organized thematically around these key issues and draws on a range of research studies with children as family members, including our own project exploring children's kinship.[1]

Using 'creative' interviews to explore children's home and family lives

A key challenge for researching children as family members has always been that family life tends to be both private and personal, and it is difficult for researchers to gain direct access to the settings in which it is lived and done. The home is usually seen as the primary site or setting for family relationships, but home (and especially certain regions within it) is often considered a private place (Allan and Crow, 1989) and in any case only a restricted range of relationships may be conducted within any one home. Furthermore, for some children and young people, the home can be an oppressing and alienating place (Valentine, Butler and Skelton, 2001), and this has implications both for the ease with which researchers can gain access to the home and understanding about family life via that route, as well as the ethics of attempting to do so. Family life and relationships for any child are also lived in other settings, including in 'public' places such as schools, shopping centres, restaurants and of course in other people's homes (Finch, 2007; James and Prout, 1996; Mayall, 1994; Morgan, 1996). However, catching and observing the moments when family relationships are 'naturally' done in these settings may pose practical and ethical challenges for researchers. We shall expand upon these later.

Furthermore, connections and relationships between family and kin members are not only conducted face to face in physical places at particular moments in time, but also in virtual or less tangible ways, including through memory, stories, and imaginations, across time (sometimes several generations' worth of time) and space (Bryceson and Vuorela, 2002; Mason, 2004; Smart, 2007; Urry, 2002), and of course via digital media. This means that there is not always a physical place, or a temporal moment, where researchers can go to observe or engage with children's family lives as they are going on.

It is for this reason perhaps that the qualitative interview method has come to be relied upon so heavily in family research in general and in recent years has gained ground in relation to researching children in families in particular. Interviews can enable research participants to 'report on' aspects of family life that take place outside the interview setting, as well as enabling interviewer and interviewee to 'co-construct' or evoke the contexts and practice of family life through an interactive exchange (Mason, 2002).

However, traditionally, children have not been seen as legitimate interview subjects in the social sciences, partly because it was assumed that they did not have the verbal, recall, or reasoning capacities. Also though, in family research at least, it had previously been assumed either that adults could unproblematically report on children's behalf, or that children's perspectives would provide no

new knowledge. The 'new approaches to child research' lobby challenged this status quo, however, by arguing that children, even very young children, are quite capable of participating in interviews, and that data generated through interview-based interactions with children are very rich and revealing of their own experiences of family life in ways that proxy interviews with adults could never be (Neale and Smart, 1998). It was thus acknowledged that children were experts on their own lives, and some researchers have argued that children are capable of incisive articulation, sophisticated observation, and moral reasoning about family life (Ackers, 1999; Alderson, 1995; Smart et al., 2001).

However, researchers have not straightforwardly assumed that children will respond well to the kinds of interview techniques often used with adults, particularly those that rely on context-free question-answer formats, concentrated primarily on abstract reasoning through talk or text, in a one-to-one interaction. Instead, many researchers have looked for more creative approaches, where interviews include the use of drawing, collage, pictures, photography, video, making models and play. The aim here is usually to engage children in ways that they will feel comfortable with, and which chime with their everyday lives, thus helping them to articulate their experience. The idea is to be able to 'listen on all channels' (Clark and Moss, 2001) in ways flexible enough to 'tune in' to children's family and kinship (Mason and Tipper, 2008a).

This kind of interview-based research with children has produced detailed and nuanced knowledge of what children say is important about family, what family relationships are like and what they involve, what really matters in family life (Edwards et al., 2006; Morrow, 1998a, 1998b, 2003; Punch, 2005; Smart et al., 2001), and who counts as family.

Knowledge generated in this way can fill gaps in our understandings of family life, which previously focused only on adult experience. For example, some studies start by asking children who is important to them or who counts as family, and then explore how children 'do' and live their family lives. These have been much more illuminating of children's experiences and perspectives than research that 'places children in a particular family setting' – such as a nuclear family household – 'and extrapolates from there' (Morrow, 2003: 116). Through studies of this kind we have discovered that 'extended' kin, including grandparents, aunts, uncles and cousins, step- and half-kin, are often highly significant for children, as are networks of friends and peers, and relationships with animals (Mason and Tipper, 2008a, 2008b; Morrow, 1998a, 1998b, 2003; Pryor, 2003). This kind of work adds considerably to our understanding of how relationships with kin vary across cultures, because it starts by asking who is important and who counts, rather than assuming a specific model applies to all. We also know from this kind of work that 'like-family' relationships with unrelated adults and children are a central part of children's kinship (Mason and Tipper, 2008a).

This kind of experiential knowledge can also provide an important corrective to existing assumptions, for example, in relation to children's experience of parental separation and re-partnering, where knowledge derived from children's experience challenges assumptions previously made in law, social care, policy, and academic scholarship about what is and is not good for children under such circumstances. Specifically, for example, we now know that 'children may experience their parents' behaviour after divorce as more of a problem than the divorce itself' (Smart et al., 2001: 155), and that quality of relationship is more important than household or family structure (Morrow, 2003). And we know that children may struggle to be perceived and treated as full-fledged family members rather than personal chattels for parents to bicker over in conflictual divorces (Neale, Flowerdew and Smart, 2003). And importantly, we know that for teenagers whose parents have separated sometime in the past, parental separation is

not necessarily now what defines their lives or challenges them, despite popular assumptions that parental divorce unequivocally damages and defines children for life (Flowerdew and Neale, 2003).

Evoking the contexts and settings of children's family lives

Some researchers have built into their research an ethnographic emphasis on 'real settings' where family life is lived out and 'done' (Morgan, 1996), by using methods that help researcher and child get as close to the situations and contexts as possible, with the aim of *evoking* the kinds of family experiences and interactions that take place in and through them. The idea is therefore a little different to the 'true' ethnographic aim of actually 'being there' in real time to observe or participate in interactions as they take place, although such real-time participant observation is often an additional benefit of such methods, as we shall argue below. Using real settings in this more 'evocative' way can include, for example, conducting interviews in children's homes (sometimes in children's bedrooms, and often including 'house tours'), or outdoor/walking interviews in neighbourhoods, 'the street', playgrounds, clubs, schools or in gardens and yards. In all of these instances, children can 'show' as well as 'tell' what life is like, and the co-constructed interview is thus not only based firmly in their everyday worlds, but it is also a multi-sensory experience. Children can act as researchers themselves with these kinds of methods too. Other ways of evoking settings can include picture elicitation using children's own photos or drawings of places, events, people, or animals, to hear children's perspectives or to start conversations about family life (Cook and Hess, 2007; Darbyshire, MacDougall and Schiller, 2005).

Researchers do not usually assume that they can personally visit or even virtually access every relevant setting with children, of course. But doing the research as close as possible to where children's lives are lived helps to produce a more closely observed and textured picture. Significantly, it draws the dimensions of place, space, environment, physicality, materiality, the sensory and so on into the frame of reference (Darbyshire et al., 2005), and these have been argued to be highly relevant for children's family and kin relationships, as we shall show below.

Some of these issues are not necessarily specific to child research. Indeed, there has been a good deal of debate over how 'different' child research participants are from adult participants. So, for example, Mauthner (1997) suggests that children have quite different competencies, whereas Punch (2002) argues that research with both children and adults requires a similar kind of creative engagement on the part of the researcher. Certainly, the methodological logic that informs the emphasis on real settings and contextual ways of evoking real life applies equally to adults' everyday family lives too, and it should not be interpreted simply as a reaction to the purported incapacity of children to articulate and reason in the abstract. Recent family research is beginning to see the importance of using methods that are either embedded in or evoke the everyday contexts of family life for adults and children, recognizing that abstract articulations about family may bear little relation to experience and lived realities (Mason, 2002, 2008).

There is another sense in which using 'real settings' in this way is important for understanding children as family members, and that helps to bring into focus the relational nature of family and kinship, which can sometimes be obscured if researchers use more abstracted interview methods with individual children. Relationships are not the property of individuals, and they do not exist solely within individual experience. They exist and are enacted between individuals in interactions, and research needs to be able to uncover this 'relationality'. Methods that evoke the real settings and contexts of relationships are likely to be able to observe and bring their interactivity into focus, and this

raises some enduring questions about children, agency, and relationality to which we now turn.

Children's voices, relationality, and the question of multiple perspectives on family life

If family and kinship are relational and interactive, then surely the accounts and voices of others, not only children, are part of that nexus? This is a controversial issue, especially in the context of child research where battles to centre the experience of children have been hard won in the face of the otherwise domineering presence of adults, parents and family in research findings. There has been much focus on 'listening to children's voices' because they have so long been sidelined in mainstream academic research. But how far is there then a contradiction between listening to children and acknowledging their agency on the one hand, and yet incorporating other perspectives and voices in our analyses on the other? There are two linked concerns here. One is that we need a range of perspectives on family life and relationships, but there is a genuine concern that children's perspectives should not be crowded out. The other is that if the very nature of the 'thing' that we are seeking to understand is *relationality* in this interactive sense, then we may simply not be able to understand it if we only talk to individual children.

Mannion (2007) argues that listening to children's voices is not enough, and that to understand children's lives at all, we need to contextualize them especially within social and adult–child relations. 'Childhood' only really makes sense in the context of interactions, including those between adults and children. Mannion is explicitly criticizing the tendency of recent childhood research to focus *solely* on 'children's perspectives'. Of course, many childhood theorists do write about the importance of relationality and the idea of 'generationing' as the active and interactive practices that help to define and constitute generations in relation to each other, so these ideas are not absent in child research by any means (see especially Alanen, 2001; Alanen and Mayall 2001; James and Prout, 1996). However, those concepts often refer to the mutual and interactive construction of childhood and adulthood at a societal level, rather than the full set of everyday interactions and relationalities that might constitute personal family relations (although see Punch, 2005). Sometimes there is perhaps a difference between philosophies and theories of childhood on the one hand, and the practice and pragmatics of research with children on the other. In the latter, practical decisions have to be made about when and how to centre children's voices (Alderson, 1995), and whether to seek, allow, or exclude those of others, and more generally, how exactly one might research this thing called 'relationality'.

There are different possible approaches to these rather vexed questions. First is the approach that seeks children's individual accounts, notwithstanding the recognition by theorists that relationality and context are important. The logic here is that it is nevertheless children's experience and their accounts of relationality and family that are of primary interest, not least because these have been silenced in the past. Here, there is often a particular concern to allow children to speak privately and independently in one-to-one interviews with researchers, so that they can give their perspectives unfettered by the interruptions or dominance of others. However, to secure such conditions may mean removing the interaction from the 'real settings' of family life mentioned above. The logic is partly connected to ideas about ideal interview conditions (quiet, private, and so on), and this is an assumption commonly made in family law, for example. But sometimes there may also be an implicit assumption that children are particularly *susceptible* to outside influence and that their accounts are more likely to be diluted by others, especially adults. The concern to give children a 'voice' which is *isolated from adult voices*

may reflect deep-seated assumptions about how *competent* children are to resist or reframe other people's perspectives. Are they seen as in need of protection from outside influences? Are special conditions required in order for them to articulate their points of view? How far is this a reasonable response to structures of adult power in an adult-centric society, and how far does it reflect ideas that are anathema to the perspectives of child researchers, for example that children are unfinished, inarticulate and more malleable than adults? It is also worth pointing out that privacy and independence – and indeed agency – for children in research are all compromised to some extent by the requirement under most research ethics regimes to have the consent of a parent/guardian for their child's participation.

A second approach, which can be complementary to the first, favours gaining multiple separate accounts, for example, from children and their parents, or multiple family members within and across generations (for example, Punch, 2005; Smart and Neale, 2001). This approach is informed by the idea that there are different parties and different perspectives on relationships, each of which has validity, and that no one individual has total knowledge of a nexus of relationships and relationalities. From this perspective, the best way to understand the experience of children as family members is to gather separate accounts from children and key others, and then analyse these in relation to each other.

The key question here for the child researcher though is how to put the accounts together to create a meaningful picture of children's lives as family members. There is some very insightful work on how to manage multiple accounts, including those that appear to diverge from each other, and to make sense of what they say about the complexities and relationalities of family life (McCarthy, Edwards and Gillies, 2003). We should not expect different perspectives on family life to be the same, of course, not least because relationalities are not 'flat' uniform things that we can simply find the one truth of, but instead they are intersections of relationships, perspectives, interactions, and so on. But the use of terms like 'convergent' or 'dissonant data' when analysing multiple accounts (for example, Perlesz and Lindsay, 2003) can push us in that direction and may be problematic. In child research we need to be cautious, because it is tempting for researchers to presume the adult view is more reliable or more 'true' and to occlude those of children, especially if accounts are seen to be in competition (or in triangulation for that matter). The value, for understanding relationality, of holding differential accounts simultaneously in focus can thus be overlooked.

However, although different accounts can provide multiple perspectives on sets of relationships, they arguably only take us so far in exploring the relationalities of family and kinship, precisely because they are based on individually generated accounts and reflections. Some researchers have therefore sought to interview children jointly with others, especially siblings, sometimes in addition to conducting individual interviews (Punch, 2005; Edwards et al., 2006; Flowerdew and Neale, 2003). The value of this approach is that the interview works as a kind of 'staged interaction', thus allowing the researcher to see some aspects of relationality in action so to speak.

There is also considerable value in 'unstaged interactions'. For example, in our own study of children's kinship, our initial idea was to gain children's accounts, unmediated by adults, through one-to-one or paired interviews. But we started to achieve further multiple perspectives without asking for them, as parents, siblings, and cousins who happened to be around at the time commented, interrupted, interjected, or simply interacted with the interviewees. We quickly discovered that doing interviews in homes, gardens, neighbourhoods (shared spaces) about kinship (shared relationships) invites interest and comment from others in the household or setting who also partake in those relationships. What we found interesting and valuable about this was precisely that

the interactions and other perspectives were incidental, 'off camera' and interstitial, and they gave significant insights into the lived realities of children's family and kinship. Debates and interactions happened in 'real-time' rather than only in a subsequent analysis where separately generated accounts are later compared and contrasted. Of course, the risk here is that children's accounts are eclipsed or silenced by others present – the very concern that leads some research to seek private and individual interviews with children.

To illustrate some of the issues here, consider the case of Tamsin, an eight-year-old girl in our study, who was interviewed at one end of an open-plan living room, with her mother in earshot. At one point, it became clear that she would have liked to discuss a slightly ambivalent relationship that she had with her grandmother. She hinted at some issues, but then whispered (referring to her mother) 'I can't say very much 'cause she's there'. On the one hand, we might argue that this kind of implicit censorship limits what children may include in their accounts, and certainly we did not get to hear the full story about Tamsin's grandmother. On the other hand, the dynamic of the whispered explanation itself was quite revealing of the subtleties in how Tamsin's relationships with her mother and grandmother are lived. Her relationship with her grandmother should be seen as being constructed partly in this context, in relation to her mother's perceptions, and in turn affecting the relationship she has with her mother. Interaction and input from parents and siblings forms a crucial part of children's everyday experience of family. When parents, explicitly or implicitly, define what is relevant or accessible, this goes some way to reflecting the relational realities of children's everyday lives: their kinship relations take place in these contexts of interaction, debate, and constraint. As such, these interactions form part of the data and can inform our understanding of children's lives and kinship. Tamsin's voice was not completely eclipsed, but neither was it unfettered and she, along with other children we interviewed, was able to assert her perspective as the most legitimate at key points in her interview, as the following quotation illustrates:

> Becky: and how long ago did you move?
> Mum: two years
> Tamsin: will you stop answering! It's supposed to be me that she's talking to
> Mum: sorry (laughter)

Tamsin and her mother both knew that we were seeking children's perspectives and that we were interviewing *Tamsin*, and we can see the value of framing the research in that way. The kinds of data that we were able to generate about interactions and interruptions are ethnographic but are different from what might be achieved solely through observation or even through a joint interview. They illustrate, contextualize, and add depth to what is still essentially the *child's* account. Instead of multiple accounts that have to be collated or harmonized, we were able to gain some insight into relationships in action and in motion. Because the interview is explained as being about children's perspectives, children maintain the right to assert their point of view (often quite forcefully, as did Tamsin) in ways they might not if we had said we were interested in *everyone's* perspective.

Sensory, physical, and tactile elements in children's experience of family life

As researchers increasingly explore the experience of children as family members, they are (slowly!) beginning to incorporate understandings of the sensory, physical, tactile, and embodied elements of that experience (Darbyshire et al., 2005; Davies, 2012; Mason and Tipper, 2008b; Pole, 2007; Wilson et al., 2012). Once researchers start to take seriously the idea of listening to children's voices and entering or evoking the real contexts of their family lives, they find that children are highly fluent in visual, non-verbal, embodied, physical, and tactile modes of communication, and they frequently choose to express aspects

of their lives in these ways. Of course, adults can express their worlds in these ways too, but perhaps these forms of communication have a particular salience for children's lives and relationships (Clark and Moss, 2001; Mason, 2008; Mason and Tipper, 2008b).

However, these are not only forms of communication. Recent studies have shown that children's kinship, for example, is 'a highly embodied set of experiences rather than an abstract set of associations' (Mason and Tipper, 2008b). We found in our study that for children, relationships with family and relatives are often about voices, smells, interphysicality, appearance and ways of being. Hugging, tickling, smacking, shouting, looking nice or 'weird', using 'funny voices' or 'catchphrases', laughing, and so on were core elements in interpersonal relationships, and these were often communicated to us through gestures, animation, facial expressions, pictures, noises, and sound effects (Mason and Tipper, 2008b).

These aspects of children's family lives and relationships pose challenges for child research. First, it is difficult to access them using conventional research methods that focus on talk and text, so researchers need to find ways of facilitating children in expressing these dimensions. Using evocative or contextual methods that encourage non-verbal expression can be helpful here, and these are often used in research with children anyway, as we have suggested. However, often the reason for that is to make children feel comfortable and at home rather than explicitly to gain an understanding of sensory dimensions of experience. In our own study, the children's own photographs clearly offered a representation of aspects of being in the physical world, as well as the physical experience of places and localities, and they often also triggered talk about non-verbal aspects including the visual, facial expressions, looks, smells, and non-verbal sound effects. Children can express such dimensions of experience through interview interactions too, provided that researchers are listening and observing on 'all channels' so that these aspects are picked up as 'data' rather than overlooked.

A further challenge though is how then to treat, for example, drawings, pictures, noises, gestures, facial expressions, mimicry, and so on as *data*. There is some interesting work that analyses children's photographs, drawings, and representations of family (for example, Darbyshire et al., 2005; Edwards et al., 2006; O'Brien et al., 1996), and also that attempts to incorporate more 'sensory' material into the text of written transcripts. Here is an example from our own study of how that can be done:

> Jasmine: (talking about her brother Conrad) We fight a lot but he is nice, you know … He is very funny, like entertaining. He is not like funny as in what he says just in how he acts. He is just silly you know. I mean he is just like doing really funny faces not like (sticks her tongue out in a silly face) he will be like you now saying 'helloooo' (in a deep voice with one eyebrow raised).

It is possible, of course, with some forms of analysis and representation to use audio and video clips, and certainly drawings and other visual representations, and there are some fascinating examples of this (see, for example, Bagnoli, 2004; O'Brien et al., 1996; Smart et al., 2001: chapter 3). But we suspect that in general social researchers are, as yet, ill-equipped actually to analyse such materials and extract valid meanings from them in any systematic way. As Komulainen has pointed out, interpreting what is being communicated through pictures and other non-verbal means can be highly ambiguous and we need to be careful that what is read from such methods does not say more about adult judgements than children's experience (Komulainen, 2007). Often, perhaps because of the difficulties involved, such materials are used more for illustration, or to evoke conversation as described above, rather than as analytical objects in their own right.

Here are some examples of visual materials from our study of children's kinship. Figure 9.1 is a 'circles map' where children were asked to map 'who is important to me' by emotional closeness, with themselves at the centre. Figure 9.2 is a neighbourhood map, using model buildings and drawings. Figures 9.3 and 9.4 are examples of photographs taken by children depicting who was important to them, along with associated places and things.

There are further complications in researching children's embodiment and physicality, concerning how we think about and practice ethics and interpersonal sensitivity. For example, the use of photographs or video clips in representations about children's family lives may breach existing conventions in relation to confidentiality and anonymity. In many countries there is also a context of concern or anxiety about the public portrayal of children in images of any kind. Even to ask research questions about how children might be embodied, sensory and physical beings in this context can be fraught with difficulty, and researchers who want to observe or engage with children in these ways face some tricky ethical dilemmas (Pole, 2007). The aim of centring children's experiences and perspectives, which may be part of a mission to further children's rights (to self-determination, self-expression, and so on), can sit uneasily with other aspects of ethical codes such as children's rights to privacy and protection.

Time and development in children's family lives

'Time' has always been central in the 'new' child research, as is manifest in its political, ethical and moral commitment to a 'presentist' orientation, which challenges the prior dominance of developmental approaches to understanding childhood. Yet this concern with valuing children in the present may actually have led, inadvertently perhaps, to a failure fully to appreciate the complex ways in which time, history, and development play in their family lives and relationships. It is interesting to note, for example, that despite an increasing trend towards biographical approaches in understanding adult family

Figure 9.1   A child's 'circles map' depicting who is important to her

Figure 9.2   Pictures of cousins on the refrigerator

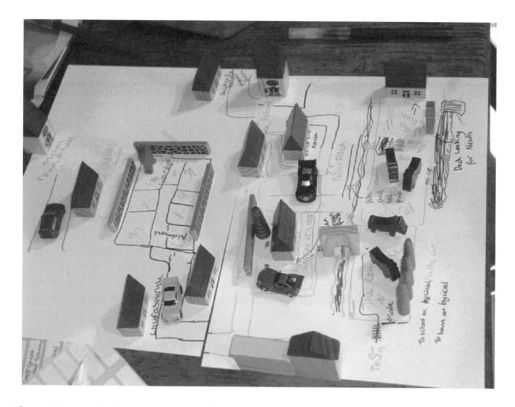

Figure 9.3 A neighbourhood map with models and drawings

Figure 9.4 A child's photograph of her guinea pig's grave

and kinship relations and some fascinating work using sensory memory work with adults to analyse childhood experiences (Widerberg, 2010), there has been little research that systematically applies biographical methods in research with children. This gap may reflect in part the ethics of a presentist orientation which seeks to ensure that children's perspectives are valued in the here and now, rather than being seen as lesser in some way until they reach adulthood. Yet it might also betray an underlying assumption amongst social researchers that children are not fully able to narrate their pasts, and may be unreliable predictors of their futures. Indeed, it may even be felt that children have too little past to bother with.

Whichever way, a lot may be missed if we fail to view children's family lives through a biographical lens. Research which has taken a biographical approach has shown that children and young people are indeed willing and able to narrate the pasts of themselves and others, and that they have a strong sense of the historicity and narrative qualities of their personal and family lives (Mason and Tipper, 2008b; Thomson et al., 2002). It is also clear from this research that children's biographical narratives, and the stories they help to shape and tell about family life, are not simply 'descriptive' or 'factual' accounts but are part of the way in which experiences, memories, identities, and ethical dispositions are shaped. As Smart puts it:

> The young person whose story is one of coping (with parental divorce), and who recalls events and moments when he or she successfully managed adversity, is building a past which helps to shape the kind of person they believe themselves to be. This may, in turn, help to shape how they deal with future adversity and problems.
>
> (2006: 167)

Thus, if we do not use biographical methods, we not only miss out on some of the 'facts' of the story, but also the ways in which stories, narratives and memories are part of identities

and selves and, of course, of family and kinship (Smart, 2007).

Although these kinds of ideas are familiar in research on adult relationships and identities (for example, Lawler, 2002), they have been little applied in child family research. Qualitative longitudinal studies of children and young people's life experiences have started to show the significance of asking them at different points in their lives to look backwards and forwards in family, personal, and historical time, as well as recounting their life experiences in the moment in ways more familiar in 'new' approaches to childhood (Flowerdew and Neale, 2003; Neale and Flowerdew, 2003; Thomson et al., 2002). Yet it is also the case that some more conventional longitudinal studies probably are guilty of assuming that children cannot narrate or reflect on their pasts in reliable ways – hence, the concern is to catch them in and at the (present) moment, in real time so to speak, in sequential waves of a study over many years.

However, there is more at stake in relation to time and children's family lives than just to recognize that children have biographies too and that they can reflect, narrate, remember and anticipate in ways just as legitimate as adults. What we are thinking of here is the very notion of 'development', which has been de-centred if not rejected in many of the 'new' child research agendas. We want to suggest that we do need to recognize that children are both in the process of being and becoming, and so are families and kinship for that matter.

Kinship, for example, is constituted in sets of relationships lived across time (Finch and Mason, 1993; Morgan, 1996). Events, practices, experiences, interactions, and of course stories and narratives are *formative* in how kinship develops and changes in specific circumstances, and kinship is by necessity and definition a historically saturated state of affairs. There is a clear awareness in people's lived experience of kinship that relationships have a history and a future; that they are developing and becoming (Mason and Tipper, 2008b).

Although kinship is always unfolding and in some senses has no finishing or starting point (because of the infinite nature of ancestry and decendancy), relationships can 'turn out' or end in particular ways, at particular times, just as there are births and beginnings. In other words, shifting and complex conceptualizations and understandings of being, becoming, and *developing* are central in how kinship is understood and practised, and if we are researching children's kinship, we need to find ways of being open to exploring them.

Children, as well as kinship itself, are in the process of being *and becoming*. Developmental discourses are dominant ones with which they and their relatives do engage. Children do *grow up* and *get brought up,* and research on children as family members needs to be able to grasp how that plays out in real lives.

CONCLUSION

In this chapter we have explored some of the key issues that we think have arisen in recent years in the development of research concerned with children as family members. We have focused on methodological concerns in researching children's family experiences, more than on the substance of those experiences per se. We have argued for the importance of methodologies that are sensitive to the contexts and settings of children's lives, the relationality of family, the sensory and physical aspects of children's experience, and the subtleties of time in processes of kinship. We think that such methodologies offer great potential for understanding children as family members.

We shall conclude by teasing out two underlying issues which are highly salient for our methodological discussion. The first concerns the cultural variation in what might constitute families in general, and children's families and family experiences in particular. We shall suggest that the kind of methodological approach

we have argued for can and should be sensitive to cultural variation in experience and context. The second concerns the interaction of ethical and methodological issues, which themselves, of course, vary considerably across different cultural contexts. We shall suggest that, ironically perhaps, the kind of 'experience near' (Geertz, 1983) approach that we have advocated brings with it some considerable ethical challenges.

We argued earlier that starting with children's own perspectives on their experiences allows researchers to build a sense of what family is and means for children from the bottom up, rather than using the lens of one ideal model with which to view children's lives or to measure them against. It is important also to recognize the salience of cultural constructions of childhood, and of adult–child relationships and responsibilities, and of family and kinship, because these help to frame children's experiences.

It is significant, for example, that in some places (for example, in many of the Scandinavian countries), there is a long tradition of children's participation, and the idea that family life should be democratic in some way is fairly well established. The idea of children as active participants both in family life and in research fits well with this ethos, and it is not surprising that some of the most important scholarship in the 'new approaches' to children and family research has come from these contexts. In Norway, for example, Gullestad's research on 9–15-year-old girls who regularly look after young children after school, and Solberg's work on the domestic and work roles of children at home both were illustrative of a context in which children can have family roles that might appear to be at odds with the (less responsible, less 'agentic') way in which childhood is conceptualized and experienced elsewhere (Gullestad, 1993; Solberg, 1997). Their work also pointed to significant gender differences in the kinds of care work that children do in families in Norway, with girls developing and claiming more expertise in family care than boys.

Cultural contexts themselves, as well as differences for different groups of children within them (based on ethnicity, gender, access to resources, and so on), vary enormously, and it is not possible to address all the variations here. Instead, we want to emphasize the importance of methods and approaches that are open enough to register the distinctive nature of children's family lives in different settings and that are culturally sensitive. Gullestad and Solberg's approaches, for example, are both in the interpretivist phenomenological tradition, which is valued in the Scandinavian academic context and which is attuned to the routines and intricacies of daily lives. Interpretivist, anthropologically inspired approaches can be applied in very different contexts, for example to understanding the lives of street children in the majority world, for whom kinship, family and the whole idea of democracy and rights, have very different meanings from those for Western children (Mizen and Ofosu-Kusi, 2007), or children in rural South American communities (Punch, 2002). Oral history and narrative approaches have revealed distinctive elements of Caribbean and African American kinship and have enabled understandings to emerge of the importance of 'lateral' kinship structures or chains. For example, Chamberlain's work on Caribbean kinship showed how adult siblings and lateral kin are very often involved in childcare and support (Chamberlain, 1999). Carol Stack's classic work showed the importance of genealogically unrelated others in children's family lives, as 'other mothers' (Stack, 1997; see also Olwig, 2003), as well as the significance of understanding how everyday family life interacts with political, economic and cultural contexts.

Cultural and socio-political differences in the contexts of children's family lives may also be associated, more or less directly, with different approaches to understanding the ethical issues involved in the aims and practice of researching children as family members. We have hinted at some ethical dilemmas – including in how to reconcile ideas about children's participation and agency with the importance for understanding relationality of gaining more than the child's perspective. Also, we suggested that the aim of advancing close and detailed understanding of the contexts of children's lives, especially if these require researcher access to 'private' or 'backstage' places like children's bedrooms, may be problematic. And if those understandings are to extend to the sensory and embodied experience of children's family lives, then there is a potential conflict between encouraging children's self-expression about these domains on the one hand, and getting too close and too intimate, or even putting them at risk, on the other. How these risks and concerns are perceived and debated translate differently in different political and socio-cultural contexts, depending upon the different interest groups who are party to the debate, the forms of regulation that have developed, and the relative values put upon questions of rights for children (or adults for that matter) – to privacy, to self-determination, to protection from harm and so on. But we think it is important to recognize that the better qualitative researchers become at tapping into children's 'real-life' experiences, the more fraught some of these ethical tensions and contradictions are likely to be.

NOTE

1 The 'Children Creating Kinship' study was funded by the UK Economic and Social Research Council in 2004–2007. The research team was Jennifer Mason, Becky Tipper and Jennifer Flowerdew, at the Morgan Centre for the Study of Relationships and Personal Life, University of Manchester, UK. The research involved 49 'creative' interviews with children aged 7–12 living in the North of England, and some of their parents. http://www.socialsciences.manchester.ac.uk/morgancentre/research/childrens-kinship/

REFERENCES

Ackers, L. (1999) 'Context, culture and values in migration research on children within the European Union',

International Journal of Social Research Methodology, 2(2): 171–81.

Alanen, L. (2001) 'Childhood as a generational condition: Children's daily lives in a central Finland town', in L. Alanen and B. Mayall, *Conceptualising Child-Adult Relationships*. London and New York: Falmer, pp. 149–53.

Alanen, L. and Mayall, B. (2001) *Conceptualizing Child-Adult Relationships*. London and New York: Falmer.

Alderson, P. (1995) *Listening to Children: Children, Ethics and Social Research*. Barkinside: Barnardos.

Allan, G. and Crow, G. (1989) *Home and Family: Creating the Domestic Sphere*. London: Macmillan.

Bagnoli, A. (2004) 'Researching identities with multi-method autobiographies', *Sociological Research Online*, 9(2), Available at http://www.socresonline.org.uk/9/2/bagnoli.html

Brannen, J. and O'Brien, M. (1996) *Children in Families, Policy and Research*. London: Falmer Press.

Bryceson, D. and Vuorela, U. (2002) *The Transnational Family: New European Frontiers and Global Networks*. Oxford and New York: Berg.

Carsten, J. (2004) *After Kinship*. Cambridge: Cambridge University Press.

Chamberlain, M. (1999) 'The family as model and metaphor in Caribbean migration', *Journal of Ethnic and Migration Studies*, 25(5): 251–66.

Christensen, P. and James, A. (eds.) (2000) *Research with Children: Perspectives and Practices*. London and New York: Falmer Press.

Clark, A. and Moss, P. (2001) *Listening to Young Children: The Mosaic Approach*. London: National Children's Bureau/Joseph Rowntree Foundation.

Cook, T. and Hess, E. (2007) 'What the camera sees and from whose perspective: Fun methodologies for engaging children in enlightening adults', *Childhood*, 14(1): 29–45.

Darbyshire, P., MacDougall, C. and Schiller, W. (2005) 'Multiple methods in qualitative research with children: More insight or just more?', *Qualitative Research*, 5(4): 417–36.

Davies, H. (2012) 'Affinities, seeing and hearing like family: exploring why children value face-to-face contact', *Childhood: A Journal of Global Child Research*, 19(1): 8–23.

Edwards, R., Hadfield, L., Lucey, H. and Mauthner, M. (2006) *Sibling Identity and Relationships: Sisters and Brothers*. Abingdon: Routledge.

Finch, J. (2007) 'Displaying families', *Sociology*, 41(1): 65–81.

Finch, J. and Mason, J. (1993) *Negotiating Family Responsibilities*. London: Routledge.

Flowerdew, J. and Neale, B. (2003) 'Trying to stay apace: Children with multiple challenges in their post-divorce family lives', *Childhood*, 10(2): 147–61.

Geertz, C. (1983) 'From a native's point of view: on the nature of anthropological understanding', in C. Geertz, *Local Knowledge: Further Essays in Interpretive Anthropology*. New York: Basic Books, pp. 55–70.

Gullestad, M. (1993) *The Art of Social Relations: Essays on Culture, Social Action and Everyday Life in Modern Norway*. Oslo, Norway: Scandinavian University Press.

James, A. and Prout, A. (1996) *Constructing and Reconstructing Childhood: Contemporary Issues in the Sociological Study of Childhood*. Brighton: Falmer.

Komulainen, S. (2007) 'The ambiguity of the child's "voice" in social research', *Childhood*, 14(1): 11–28.

Lawler, S. (2002) 'Narrative in social research', in T. May (ed.), *Qualitative Research in Action*. London: Sage, pp. 242–58.

Mannion, G. (2007) 'Going spatial, going relational: Why "listening to children" and children's participation needs reframing', *Discourse: Studies in the Cultural Politics of Education*, 28(3): 405–20.

Mason, J. (2008) 'Tangible affinities and the real life fascination of kinship', *Sociology*, 42(1): 29–45.

Mason, J. (2004) 'Managing kinship over long distances: the significance of "the visit"', *Social Policy and Society*, 3(4): 421–9.

Mason, J. (2002) 'Qualitative interviewing: Asking, listening and interpreting', in T. May (ed.), *Qualitative Research in Action*. London: Sage, pp. 225–41.

Mason, J. and Tipper, B. (2008a) 'Being related: How children define and create kinship', *Childhood*, 15(4): 687–706.

Mason, J. and Tipper, B. (2008b) 'Children and the Making of Kinship Configurations', in E. Widmer and R. Jallinoja (eds.), *Beyond the Nuclear Family? Families in a Configurational Perspective, Population, Family and Society, Vol. 9*. Bern, Switzerland: Peter Lang Publishing Group, pp. 137–56.

Masson, J. and Oakley, M.W. (1998) *Out of Hearing: Representing Children in Care Proceedings*. London: Wiley.

Mauthner, M. (1997) 'Methodological aspects of collecting data from children: Lessons from three research projects', *Children and Society*, 11(1): 16–28.

Mayall, B. (1994) *Children's Childhoods Observed and Experienced*. Brighton: The Falmer Press.

McCarthy, J.R., Edwards, R. and Gillies, V. (2003) *Making Families: Moral Tales of Parenting and Step-Parenting*. Durham: Sociology Press.

Mizen, P. and Ofosu-Kusi, Y. (2007) 'Street children visualise their working lives: Public views of the private, private views of the public', paper presented at International Visual Sociology Association, Annual Conference, NewYork University, York, August. Available at http://www2.warwick.ac.uk/fac/soc/sociology/staff/academic/mizenp/mizenp_index/phils_research/ghana/publications

Morgan, D.H.J. (1996) *Family Connections: An Introduction to Family Studies.* Cambridge: Polity Press.

Morrow, V. (1998a) *Understanding Families: Children's Perspectives.* National Children's Bureau: London.

Morrow, V. (1998b) 'My animals and other family: Children's perspectives on their relationships with companion animals', *Antrhozoos*, 11(4): 218–26.

Morrow, V. (2003) 'Perspectives on children's agency within families', in L. Kuczynski (ed.), *Handbook of Dynamics in Parent-Child Relations.* Thousand Oaks, CA: Sage, pp. 109–29.

Neale, B. and Smart, C. (1998) 'Agents or dependants? Struggling to listen to children in family law and family research', *Centre for Research on Family, Kinship and Childhood Working Paper.* Leeds: University of Leeds.

Neale, B., Flowerdew, J. and Smart, C. (2003) 'Drifting towards shared residence?', *Family Law*, 12(1): 904–8.

Neale, B. and Flowerdew, J. (2003) 'Time, texture and childhood: The contours of longitudinal qualitative research', *International Journal of Social Research Methodology*, 6(3): 189–99.

O'Brien, M., Alldred, P. and Jones, D. (1996) 'Children's constructions of family and kinship', in J. Brannen and M. O'Brien (eds.), *Children in Families: Research and Policy.* London: Falmer, pp. 84–100.

Olwig, K.F. (2002) 'Displaced children?: Risks and opportunities in a Caribbean urban environment', in P. Christensen and M. O'Brien (eds.), *Children in the City: Home, Neighbourhood and Community.* London: Routledge Falmer, pp. 46–65.

Perlesz, A. and Lindsay, J. (2003) 'Methodological triangulation in researching families: Making sense of dissonant data', *International Journal of Social Research Methodology*, 6(1); 25–40.

Pole, C. (2007) 'Researching children and fashion: An embodied ethnography', *Childhood*, 14(1): 67–84.

Pryor, J. (2003) 'Children's contact with relatives', in A. Bainham, B. Lindley, M. Richards and L. Trinder (eds.), *Children and their Families: Contact, Rights, Welfare.* Oxford and Portland: Hart Publishing, pp. 47–58.

Punch, S. (2002) 'Youth transitions and interdependent adult-child relations in rural Bolivia', *Journal of Rural Studies*, 18(2): 123–33.

Punch, S. (2005) 'The generationing of power: A comparison of child-parent and sibling relations in Scotland', *Sociological Studies of Children and Youth*, 10(10): 169–88.

Smart, C. (2007) *Personal Life: New Directions in Sociological Thinking.* Cambridge: Polity.

Smart, C. (2006) 'Children's narratives of post-divorce family life: From individual experience to an ethical disposition', *Sociological Review*, 54(1): 155–70.

Smart, C., Neale, B. and Wade, A. (2001) *The Changing Experience of Childhood.* Cambridge: Polity.

Smart, C. and Neale, B. (1998) *Family Fragments?* Cambridge: Polity.

Solberg, A. (1997) 'Negotiating childhood: changing constructions of age for Norwegian children', in A. James and A. Prout (eds.), *Constructing and Reconstructing Childhood: Contemporary Issues in the Sociological Study of Childhood.* Brighton: Falmer, pp. 118–37.

Stack, C.B. (1997) *All our Kin: Strategies for Survival in a Black Community.* New York: Basic Books.

Thomson, R., Bell, R., Holland, J., Henderson, S., McGrellis, S. and Sharpe, S. (2002) 'Critical moments: Choice, chance and opportunity in young people's narratives of transition', *Sociology*, 36(2): 335–54.

Thorne, B. (2007) 'Crafting the interdisciplinary field of childhood studies', *Childhood*, 14(2): 147–52.

Urry, J. (2002) 'Mobility and proximity', *Sociology*, 36(2): 255–74.

Valentine, G., Butler, R. and Skelton, T. (2001) 'The ethical and methodological complexities of doing research with "vulnerable" young people', *Ethics, Place and Environment*, 4(2): 119–25.

Weeks, J., Heaphy, B. and Donovan, C. (2001) *Same Sex Intimacies: Families of Choice and Other Life Experiments.* London: Routledge.

Widerberg, K. (2010) 'In the homes of others: Exploring new sites and methods when investigating the doings of gender, class and ethnicity', *Sociology*, 44(6): 1181–96.

Wilson, S., Houmoller, K. and Bernays, S., (2012) '"Home, and not some house": Young people's sensory construction of family relationships in domestic spaces', *Children's Geographies*, 10(1): 95–107.

10

Children as Friends

Steven R. Asher, Whitney Brechwald Guerry and
Kristina L. McDonald

INTRODUCTION

When two children are friends, they are involved in a close dyadic relationship characterized by a shared history, reciprocal affection, and a recognition by both the child and the friend that the relationship has a special status that sets it apart from mere acquaintanceship or 'colleagueship' (Bukowski, Newcomb and Hartup, 1996; Hartup and Stevens, 1997; Newcomb and Bagwell, 1995; Parker and Asher, 1993b). A close friendship is, for many children, the first non-familial intimate relationship that is freely chosen.

Friendships between children have often been contrasted with parent–child relationships by emphasizing the more egalitarian nature of friendships. It is said that, in friendships, children are likely to have similar levels of power. This is in contrast to the parent–child relationship in which there is often a clearer asymmetry in the power of the parties involved. This contrast, however, can be overstated. Many peer relationships, and even close friendships, are characterized by imbalances in power, whereas some parent–child relationships have a fairly equal distribution of power. More importantly, the attention to the balance-of-power dimension

of peer versus family relationships may result in our overlooking one of the critical differences between children's friendships and their family relationships, which is that children's friendships are typically voluntary relationships (for a discussion of cultures that are exceptions to this, see Krappmann, 1996). In friendships, the parties generally can withdraw from the relationship if things are not going well, whereas in parent–child relationships the parents and children generally stay in contact throughout life even if their relationship is stressful or disappointing. In friendship, one or both participants are likely to leave the relationship if large problems, or sometimes even more minor problems, go unresolved.

The more voluntary aspect of friendship can make friendships hard to achieve and somewhat fragile. When children are asked to name all of their best friends in class on a sociometric friendship nomination measure, about 10 per cent of children have no reciprocated friendship nominations. When a more restrictive 'limited nominations' measure is used in which children are asked to name just their best three friends in a class, close to 25 per cent of children have been found to have no reciprocated friendship nominations (Parker and Asher, 1993b; Rose, 2002). Importantly, some children can even be well liked by peers in general and yet have no best friends in their class. Data from several samples indicate that approximately 6–10 per cent of children who are well liked by their classmates (as assessed by a sociometric rating-scale measure of peer acceptance) actually receive no reciprocal friendship nominations when a limited nomination sociometric measure is also administered (see Parker et al., 1999). Some of the children who lack friends do not succeed in forming friendships, whereas other children may make friends but do not succeed in keeping them (Parker and Seal, 1996). Although most children experience what Bowker (2011) refers to as 'downgrades' in their friendships (very close friends becoming less close over time), it is more concerning when a child is unable to sustain friendships.

Parents typically want their children to have friends and they often worry when their children lack friends. Parents also are concerned when their children have friends, but the friend or the friendship has problematic characteristics that could have potentially negative influences on their children. Yet despite the concerns that parents, as well as educators, have about the health of children's friendship adjustment, there is surprisingly little guidance from the multidisciplinary child development research literature on how to help children with friendship problems (for a discussion, see Bagwell and Schmidt, 2011). This is in contrast to the more extensive research on how social skills interventions affect children's acceptance or general liking by peers (see Asher, Parker and Walker, 1996; Bierman, 2004, for reviews). Studies suggest that directly instructing children in key concepts of social interaction, and then providing children with play or activity (practice) opportunities with peers, as well as opportunities for post-play reflection, can lead to significant improvements in how well accepted children are by their classmates (here, too, see Asher et al., 1996; Bierman,

2004, for reviews). The success of these efforts to promote peer acceptance should not be exaggerated because not all studies have found positive changes, but even their partial successes stand in sharp contrast to the relative lack of data on whether comparable direct instruction efforts would help children to make friends and have friendships of high quality.

In this chapter, we will discuss the power of friendship in children's lives and the ways in which having friends and having high-quality friendships promote social-emotional and academic adjustment. We will also discuss the richness of children's friendships and some of the fascinating complexities and dualities of friendship. We will then consider the influence friends can have for good and for ill. Following this, we will discuss emerging research that examines friendship from a cross-cultural perspective. Finally, as part of a focus on friendship skills intervention, we will discuss the 'friendship tasks' that arise in everyday life with friends and consider how a social tasks perspective may provide a useful basis for teaching social relationship skills for friendship making. Our hope is that this will provide a useful foundation for future intervention efforts because decisions about intervention are not just about how to intervene, but also about the content of what should be promoted or taught. To set the stage for these various sections, we will begin with an orientation to some of the most widely used research strategies and measures used to study friendship.

MEASURING AND UNDERSTANDING FRIENDSHIP IN DIVERSE SETTINGS

Research in schools and other settings

Most research on friendship has taken place in school settings. Since the majority of children's closest friends are likely to be in the same school (Parker and Asher, 1993b), schools offer representative samples of friends, thereby facilitating the generalization of findings. Furthermore, because both participants in the friendship are often in the same grade level or classroom, doing research in the schools also facilitates collecting information about the nature of the relationship from both individuals. So, for example, researchers can learn whether two children view each other as friends, and the interpersonal dynamics of the friendship can be studied by either observing the dyad or by asking each party to the friendship to describe what the other person is like as a friend. This eliminates the problem of shared method variance that would occur if all of the data about a friendship were obtained just from one of the parties. Finally, the concentration of pairs of friends in one context with a large number of fellow students also means that valid observations can be made of how the friendship pair functions in a broader context of friendship cliques and 'crowds'.

Another advantage of the school setting is that obtaining parental permission for children's participation in research studies is facilitated by asking for this permission through the school, a familiar and legitimate organizational structure. Principals, teachers, and central school district administrators, who are known and respected by the community of parents, help to legitimize the research process and to communicate that the research project is carried out with school district approval. As a result, either through signed parental consent forms (see, for example, Rose, 2002) or through a consent process that involves the waiver of written parental consent (see, for example, Demir and Urberg, 2004; Rose and Asher, 1999, 2004), it becomes possible for researchers to have participation rates of 90 per cent or higher. This level of research participation is especially important given the need to include both friendship partners in the study.

One consequence of the attractiveness of studying friendship in school settings is that friendship is generally understudied in homes and other non-school settings. Fortunately, though, there have been some notable exceptions that have offered insight into friendship as it occurs in a wide range of settings. Gottman's (1983) study of how young children come to be friends ('hit it off' with another child) was conducted by having the parent place a tape recorder in the vicinity of two children who were playing at one of their homes. Children who hit it off, compared to those who did not, were better at exchanging information, establishing common enjoyable activities, and managing conflicts that arose during interaction. Youth team sports are another promising but understudied context. In a noteworthy example, Fine (1981, 1987) did an ethnographic study in which he spent summers observing the friendship interactions of boys who were playing Little League baseball. Fine's attention to how children (boys in this case) sometimes provide their peers with instruction in various forms of deviant behaviour (such as forging a parent note when skipping out on school) is an early example of a theme that appears in more recent research on the negative influences friends can have on each other (see later in the chapter for a discussion of 'deviancy training' and other negative influences).

Camp settings also provide excellent natural contexts for the study of friendships (Blachman and Hinshaw, 2002; Hanna, 1998; Parker and Seal, 1996). For example, Parker and Seal (1996) carried out repeated sociometric and loneliness assessments over several weeks and found that chronically friendless children were the most lonely at camp. Camp settings can even be designed to study (or intervene with) populations of students with particular characteristics or special needs. For example, Blachman and Hinshaw (2002) observed the friendship patterns of girls at a five-week summer camp for children with and without attention deficit hyperactivity disorder (ADHD). Compared to girls without a diagnosis, girls with ADHD developed fewer friendships over the course of camp and demonstrated more conflict and relational aggression within the friendships that they did form. The opportunity to detect naturalistic friendship patterns associated with certain characteristics (for example, ADHD symptoms) can be particularly helpful in the development of social intervention strategies for children struggling to make and keep friends.

The laboratory setting is also an advantageous location to study friendship processes, although, like home, sports, and camp settings, the laboratory has been used less frequently. In laboratory settings researchers can arrange the environment to amplify certain friendship processes, carefully record conversations and behaviour, and more easily manipulate variables of interest. Micro-level processes of friendship also can be studied by observing how friends discuss moral issues and personal problems, play a game, carry out a task, or even respond to a difficult play partner (McDonald et al., in press; Newcomb, Brady and Hartup, 1979; Parker and Gottman, 1985; Poulin, Dishion and Haas, 1999; Rose, Schwartz and Carlson, 2005; Underwood et al., 2004). The laboratory thereby becomes an excellent place to do fine-grained analyses of friendship interactions.

Consider, for example, a study by McDonald et al. (2007) who examined the conversations of fourth-grade girls with their close friends. Girls were brought into the lab and asked to talk with their friends as they normally would. Gossip about peers made up a significant portion of friends' conversations (27 per cent) and well-liked girls and their friends gossiped more about peers than did rejected girls and their friends. Further, negative gossip was positively associated with observer ratings of friendship quality, suggesting that gossip may be an important process for children's friendships. Additional observational studies about gossip have found dualities in how gossip amongst friends is related to friendship quality; gossip seems to foster intimacy but may also increase friendship conflict (Banny et al., 2011; Menzer et al., 2012).

We address more dualities in friendship later in the chapter.

To date, there is very little research on the conversations of friends in neighbourhood contexts, such as parks, playgrounds, or the front steps and sidewalks in front of children's homes. However, this kind of research could be facilitated by the use of wireless transmission recording devices (see Asher, Rose, and Gabriel, 2001; Pepler and Craig, 1995). For example, Asher et al. (2001) combined wireless audio transmission methodology with video recording to study children's social interactions in the less formal school contexts of the playground, lunchroom, and physical education. Verbatim transcripts of conversations were possible despite sometimes recording from as far as several hundred feet away. This relatively inexpensive and surprisingly unobtrusive technology (the recorded conversations have an unmistakable naturalness) could be used to study pairs of friends as they interact at great distances from an observer who carries the audio receiving equipment and a synchronized video camera.

One of the methodological challenges of studying friendship is that not only do interactions between friends take place in a variety of settings, but settings may also vary depending on the age of the friends (Rubin, Bukowski and Parker, 2006). During the preschool years, interactions with peers are most likely to occur in the home or organized childcare environments. As children move into the middle childhood years, social encounters among friends occur not only in home and school but in the neighbourhood, in after-school programmes, organized youth sports settings, and increasingly in cyberspace. Whereas many activities of younger children take place in adult-structured and monitored settings, later childhood and adolescence are marked by a significant increase in the amount of time spent in settings that are less monitored by parents and other adults (Larson et al., 1996).

The types of activities children do with each other, and the time spent engaged in these activities, also shifts across development. Young friends tend to engage in fantasy play (such as doll play, sociodramatic play with superheroes) or physical activities (such as going down a slide or building something out of blocks). Older children are more likely to get together to participate in organized group activities, such as dance, scouting organizations, gymnastics, religion-related youth groups, and various team sports. However, they also spend more relaxed time 'hanging out' together playing games, listening to music, talking, or watching television, in a manner that facilitates sociability and enhances the relationship (Zarbatany, Hartmann and Rankin, 1990). Compared to younger children, adolescents spend more of their free time with their friends (Larson and Richards, 1991), averaging several hours a day (Csikszentmihalyi and Larson, 1984).

The introduction and increasing prevalence of internet communication has afforded children and adolescents a new and very engaging realm of social interaction. Most adolescents use the internet to maintain relationships with friends they know from school or from other offline contexts where they have face-to-face contact (Gross, 2004; Gross, Juvonen and Gable, 2002; Reich, Subrahmanyan and Espinoza, 2012; Valkenburg and Peter, 2007). A study of the effects of internet involvement among Dutch pre-adolescents and adolescents found that for youth who use the internet to communicate with existing friends, more online communication was associated with increased feelings of closeness in these relationships (Valkenburg and Peter, 2007). Enhanced intimacy with friends has also been reported in a recent survey study of U.S. high school students' perceptions of their social networking site use (Reich et al., 2012) and among late-adolescent users of online instant messaging programs (Hu et al., 2004). An interesting study from Mikami et al. (2010) found evidence for friendship quality continuity in offline friendship interactions and online social networking websites. In this longitudinal study, higher observed positivity during a face-to-face interaction with a best friend at age 13–14 was associated with a greater number of online friends and a greater number of friends posting positive comments on social networking sites during early adulthood (age 20–22). From the research conducted thus far, it appears that online interaction, while very different from time spent face-to-face with a friend, may be correlated with positive friendship experiences offline. Given the rapid and continuing rise of online communication around the world, future research will no doubt further explore the effects of this medium on the friendships of children and adolescents.

As noted earlier, pairs of friends do not operate in a social vacuum. Friendships often develop between individuals who share similar characteristics, like race or ethnicity (see Graham, Taylor and Ho, 2009 for a review). Even today, cross-ethnicity friendships are less likely to occur than friendships among children of the same ethnicity; however, there is some evidence that the cross-ethnicity friendships that form in highly diverse schools are of similar quality to the friendships of same-ethnicity peers (McDonald et al., 2013). Additionally, as children move into adolescence, their friendships are embedded in cliques and larger, reputation-based groups called 'crowds' (for example, jocks [athletes], academic nerds, populars, and druggies). Children within friendship cliques often have shared interests in particular activities, may share values about school achievement, and may have other shared personal characteristics and traits. Accordingly, children may be affected not only by their immediate friends but also by the nature of the larger groups they are in (Brown, 1990; Brown and Dietz, 2009; Coleman, 1961; Kinney, 1993; Rubin et al., 2006).

Measuring friendship participation and interactive processes between friends

Sociometric assessment

There is a long tradition of using sociometric measures to measure friendship within classrooms (see, for example, Asher and Hymel, 1981; Berndt and McCandless, 2009; Bierman, 2004; Gronlund, 1959; Hallinan, 1976; Moreno, 1934). As mentioned earlier, children can be asked for a limited number of friendship nominations (such as their three best friends) or can respond to an unlimited nomination measure in which they name all their friends in their class, grade, camp, etc. Over the years, several procedural changes have been made in sociometric assessments. First, children are often given a roster with schoolmates' names to circle rather than relying on children's ability to recall and write down their classmates' first and last names. Second, for young children, photographs of schoolmates are used instead of a class roster, again to overcome literacy or memory constraints. Third, researchers increasingly distinguish between unilateral and reciprocal nominations, and investigators often define a friendship as existing when two children mutually nominate one another as opposed to one child nominating the other but the other failing to reciprocate the nomination. With this methodology, children can be assigned a score based on the number of reciprocated friendship nominations they have (for examples, see Parker and Asher, 1993b; Rose, 2002).

Researchers, teachers, and parents sometimes raise concerns about whether there are negative effects on children that result from sociometric assessments. One realistic concern is that some children might talk later with classmates about which children they nominated. This concern can be at least partially addressed by emphasizing to children the importance of confidentiality and by administering sociometric measures just before an academic subject (such as reading or mathematics) is about to begin rather than

just before children are dismissed by the teacher into more interactive contexts such as recess on the playground, or physical education, or the lunchroom. Timing sociometric assessments in this manner is likely to reduce children's conversations about their friendship choices.

The other concerns expressed by researchers, teachers, and parents are that some children might feel badly after completing a sociometric measure (if they think that they aren't liked or that they lack friends) or that the simple act of measuring interpersonal attraction could alter the way children interact with each other. Fortunately, from a series of studies it does not appear that asking children sociometric questions has negative effects on children's interactions with peers or their feelings of well-being. For example, children do not feel more lonely, hurt, or upset after sociometric measures are administered (Bell-Dolan, Foster and Sikora, 1989; Iverson, Barton and Iverson, 1997; Mayeux, Underwood and Risser, 2007), and sociometric assessment does not appear to change their pattern of interactions with others (Bell-Dolan et al., 1989; Hayvren and Hymel, 1984).

It should be emphasized that the studies investigating ethical issues in sociometric assessment have generally examined the effects of asking children who they like most and who they like least rather than studying the effects of asking children to name their best friends. However, the fact that asking children to provide positive and negative nominations does not affect their behavioural interactions with peers or their feelings of loneliness is a good sign, because using negative nomination measures is typically more concerning to researchers, teachers, and parents than is using friendship nominations.

When considering the ethical issues involved in sociometric assessment, it is also important to compare the effects of sociometric measurement to the social experiences (risks) of everyday social life. The potential level of everyday risk for children who are disliked or lack friends is clear. As will be discussed later, children who lack friends are much more likely to be victimized by peers and to experience higher levels of loneliness, social anxiety, and depression. The variety of victimization experiences children face was poignantly illustrated one day when researchers were visiting a classroom to administer a sociometric measure (Asher and Hymel, 1986). The fourth-grade teacher intercepted a note as the children were passing it up and down the rows of the classroom. The note was in the form of a petition that read: 'If you hate Graham, sign here.' All of the children had signed. Fortunately, the teacher intercepting the note before it landed on Graham's desk so that this time Graham was spared. Consistent with this episode is research indicating the wide variety of aversive peer experiences that can be observed in school. Asher et al. (2001) used wireless transmission technology to repeatedly observe 35 children over the course of the school year. Thirty-two different types of rejection could be identified in the recordings of children's social interactions, constituting what is probably an incomplete taxonomy of rejection. Many of these rival the episode involving Graham in their potential hurtfulness and, sadly, even in their creativity. Most concerning is that some of the children in this study experienced a large number of very negative relational events in a single 50-minute lunch and recess period (Paquette and Asher, 2005).

These various strands of evidence pointing to the everyday risks of social life, combined with the lack of evidence that sociometric measures cause harm, lead members of human subjects review committees to feel comfortable approving studies that include sociometric measures, including friendship nomination measures. Research using these measures documents the need to find ways to help children who are having friendship problems and who are at elevated risk.

The stability and qualities of friendship

Measuring how many friends children have does not speak to the stability of children's friendships or to the more qualitative features

of their friendships. To measure the stability of a friendship, children in a class, camp, or other setting ideally would be repeatedly sociometrically surveyed to learn whether friendships are maintained (see, for example, Bowker, 2004; Hallinan, 1976; Parker and Seal, 1996; Proulx and Poulin, 2013). Furthermore, to learn about the qualitative features of friendships such as companionship, help, cooperation, loyalty, confiding, emotional support, conflict, and conflict resolution, children have been observed interacting with their friends (Lansford et al., 2006; Simpkins and Parke, 2001) or have been asked to respond to psychometrically strong measures of friendship quality that use large sets of items to measure specific dimensions of friendship quality (see, for example, Bukowski, Hoza and Boivin, 1994; Parker and Asher, 1993b). Research on stability and other more qualitative features of friendship indicates that these are extremely important dimensions in that children who are able to make and keep friends (Parker and Seal, 1996) and children with higher-quality friendships (Ladd, Kochenderfer and Coleman, 1996; Parker and Asher, 1993b) are less lonely. To illustrate the contribution of friendship quality to well-being, higher levels of companionship and recreation, self-disclosure, validation and support, instrumental help, and ease of conflict resolution each predict to lower levels of loneliness, whereas higher levels of conflict predict to greater loneliness (Parker and Asher, 1993b).

Distinguishing friendship participation from peer acceptance

It is also important to distinguish children's participation in friendships from their overall acceptance by the peer group. Peer acceptance refers to how well a child is liked by the group as a whole (Bukowski and Hoza, 1989; Parker and Asher, 1993a). Research using (a) the average rating children receive on a classroom 'roster-and-rating-scale' sociometric measure (Hymel, 1986; Oden and Asher, 1977) to index acceptance, and (b) mutual friendship nominations to index friendship, indicates that children can be well liked by their peers but not have friends in their class (Parker and Asher, 1993b). Likewise, children can be generally disliked by classmates but still have one or more friends (highly aggressive children are more likely than highly withdrawn children to be in this situation). In a study with older elementary-school students, the correlation between the number of mutual friends a child has in class and how well accepted the child is by the class was .38 (Rose and Asher, 1999).

Evidence pointing to the validity and utility of the friendship-acceptance distinction comes from several lines of inquiry. First, having friends and being liked by peers make distinct contributions to children's early school adjustment (Ladd, 1990; Ladd et al., 1996). Second, having friends and being accepted by peers independently predict to feelings of loneliness at school (Parker and Asher, 1993b) and to whether or not children are victimized by peers (Hodges et al., 1999). These associations hold even when the content of the loneliness measure carefully avoids asking children about aspects of their social lives that are better thought of as assessing the causes of loneliness rather than feelings of loneliness per se (Asher et al., 2013; Parker and Asher, 1993b; see Weeks and Asher, 2012, for a review and analysis). Third, social skills intervention studies have found that children can make gains in peer acceptance yet not make gains in their number of best friends (see Asher et al., 1996, for a review).

THE RICH AND COMPLEX WORLD OF CHILDREN'S FRIENDSHIPS

The power of friendship in children's lives is evident even in early childhood. Anna Freud and Sophie Dann (1951) made a special early contribution to the literature on friendship by documenting the powerful attachments that children exhibited toward their friends. Three-year-old orphaned children were brought from a German concentration camp to reside at a country home in England. The children had known each other since they were a year old and 'had no other wish than to be together and became upset when they were separated from each other, even for short moments' (Freud and Dann, 1951: 131). Freud and Dann's report is a moving and compelling story made even more remarkable by the fact that the first author had grown up (in a literal sense!) in a psychoanalytic tradition, yet was documenting the power of early *peer* relations. The power of early attachments has also been demonstrated in laboratory-based research. Ispa (1981), for example, found that 2-year-old Russian children in the presence of a friend exhibited a level of comfort that was similar to the level of comfort they displayed when they were in the presence of a familiar loving adult caretaker. Later research examining preschool-aged children's reactions to a best friend moving away provides additional insight into the depth of the bond even very young children may form with one another (Park, 1992). In this study of the emotional and behavioural responses of children, ages three to five, to the loss of a friend, mothers of over two-thirds of the sample reported that their children exhibited sadness or loneliness following the departure of their friend.

The psychiatrist Harry Stack Sullivan (1953) also was among the first to call special attention to children's friendships ('chumships' was Sullivan's term). Sullivan focused on the middle childhood period as a time when he believed that friendships become centre stage in children's lives. Sullivan felt passionately about the role of friendship in children's lives:

Just as the juvenile era was marked by a significant change – the development of the need for compeers, for playmates rather like oneself – the beginning of preadolescence is equally spectacularly marked ... by the appearance of a new type of interest in another person ... a specific new type of interest in a *particular* member of the same sex who becomes a chum or a close friend. This change represents the beginning of something very like full-blown, psychiatrically defined *love* ... if you will look very closely at one of your children when he finally finds a chum – somewhere between 8-and-a-half and 10 – you will discover something very different in the relationship – namely, that your child begins to develop a real sensitivity to what matters to another person. And this is not in the sense of 'what should I do to get what I want,' but instead 'what should I do to contribute to the happiness or to support the prestige and feeling of worth-whileness of my chum'.

(Sullivan, 1953: 245)

The dualities of friendship

Children's friendships are marked by certain dualities that make them interesting and complex. First, friendships are both effortful and effortless. Because friendships are typically voluntary, a friend must work to maintain the relationship or risk the friend withdrawing from the relationship (Hartup and Stevens, 1997). Friends expect a lot from each other including companionship, instrumental help, emotional support, and being a reliable ally. Accordingly, some degree of 'relationship work' is expected from both partners to fulfil these obligations. Research on children's friendship expectations suggests how expectations may change over age (see, for example, Bigelow, 1977; Bigelow and LaGaipa, 1975; Hunter and Youniss, 1982). When interviewed or surveyed, young children report friendship expectations that centre on play and companionship. In middle childhood, there is an increased emphasis on sharing, cooperation, and helpfulness. This growth of cognitive sophistication in middle childhood is manifest in older children's increasingly abstract conceptualizations of friends. In addition to an expectation of reciprocity, 9- and 10-year-old friends value loyalty and commitment in one another. Adolescents, in turn, report greater expectations for intimacy, shared confidences (self-disclosure), and emotional support. Meeting the expectations of friendship, then, does take relationship work, and it appears that the friendship expectation bar gets raised over the course of childhood and adolescence.

However, even though the maintenance of friendships takes effort, friendships, at their best, also seem effortless to participants. When a child is with a special friend, the child feels truly known by the other person (Ladd and Emerson, 1984; Swenson and Rose, 2009) and is at ease; words and activities come easily and the child is likely to feel less self-conscious and to behave more spontaneously. In a close friendship, there is a sense that one can be oneself (more authentic) and not be particularly concerned about managing the presentation of self.

Very young children are less likely to have the verbal ability or the ability to reflect about relationships to describe for researchers the more sophisticated friendship expectations that older children and adolescents describe. However, their interactions with friends reveal levels of self-disclosure, authenticity, and emotional support that suggest that more sophisticated friendship processes are indeed present even when children do not have the words to describe them in a friendship expectations interview. In this conversation from Gottman and Parkhurst (1980: 245), four-year-old Naomi reassures her best friend Eric (also four) that he is liked by other children and that he is not a 'dumb-dumb'. The episode gains its charm because it occurs in a fantasy context in which the children are simultaneously working on overcoming Naomi's fear of skeletons, but the themes of self-disclosure and emotional support come through loud and clear:

Naomi: No, it's time for our birthday. We better clean up quickly.
Eric: Well, I'd rather play with my skeleton. Hold on there everyone. Snappers I am the skeleton.
Eric: I'm the skeleton. Ooh, hee… Hugh, ha, ha. You're hiding.
Naomi: Hey, in the top drawer, there's the …
Eric: I am, the skeleton, whoa.
Naomi: There's the feet (clattering).
Eric: (Screams) A skeleton, everyone, a skeleton.
Naomi: I'm your friend. The dinosaur.
Eric: Oh, hi dinosaur. You know, no one likes me.
Naomi: But I like you. I'm your friend.
Eric: But none of my other friends like me. They don't like my new suit. They don't like my skeleton suit. It's really just me. They think I'm a dumb-dumb.
Naomi: I know what. He's a good skeleton.
Eric: I am not a dumb-dumb, and that's so.

Naomi: I'm not calling you a dumb-dumb. I'm calling you a friendly skeleton.

This transcript also illustrates another point about friendship – even among young children close friendships can exhibit a remarkable emotional depth. When older children are asked to describe their friendship they spontaneously mention the degree to which they talk about deeply personal feelings and profound concerns. Consider the comments of two girls (approximately 10 years old) who participated in research on the quality of children's best friendships (Parker and Asher, 1993a: 270):

'Me and Diana can count on trusting one another. Yesterday, me and Diana talked about how our parents got a divorce and how the world is going to end;'
'Jessica has problems at home and with her religion, and when something happens, she always comes to me and talks about it. We've been through a lot together.'

Such descriptions are not hard to find in children's descriptions of their friendships.

To return to the idea of dualities, strong emotional connections between friends are not without risks. The great trust shared by friends is accompanied by considerable vulnerability (see MacEvoy and Asher, 2012). Reliability and loyalty, often the foundation of close relationships, mean that friends risk feelings of hurt and betrayal if this trust ruptures. In thinking about friendship, we tend to think of the many pleasures associated with friendship, but friendship can also be an emotionally challenging relationship context. In fact, participating in friendship exposes children to new types of vulnerabilities. A plan to get together with a friend might be cancelled, a friend could decide to spend time with another child on a given day, a friend could fail to take an interest in the other child's problems, or a friend could want to make all of the activity choices and thereby leave little room for the other child's preferences.

Boys and girls appear to experience this vulnerability within friendships differently.

The friendships of pre-adolescent girls may be particularly susceptible to relationship difficulty and termination. An interview study of 10- to 15-year-olds revealed that compared to boys, girls had experienced a greater number of friendship dissolutions, and girls were more upset by the possibility that their current relationships may end (Benenson and Christakos, 2003). Additionally, studies have shown that girls in late childhood report more sadness in response to hypothetical conflicts with friends (Whitesell and Harter, 1996) and to vignettes depicting transgressions of friendship expectations (MacEvoy and Asher, 2012), compared to their male peers. It is possible that the relatively greater friendship intimacy shared by females (for example Underwood and Buhrmester, 2007) fosters particularly harmful reactions to relationship difficulty. Emotional connection thus may amplify vulnerability to certain negative outcomes.

Still another kind of duality is that friendships are relationships touched by both equality and hierarchy. The tendency for friends to share fairly equal status does not prevent the formation of dominant and subordinate roles within the partnership, nor does it even preclude within-friendship victimization (both verbal and physical, subtle and overt). For example, Grotpeter and Crick (1996) found that for relationally aggressive children, even their friendships were characterized by high levels of relational aggression within the relationship. Furthermore, Murray-Close, Ostrov, and Crick (2007) found that greater intimacy within middle childhood female friendships was associated over time with more relational aggression, suggesting that intimate exchange between friends may actually 'provide ammunition' (p. 198) for damage to close relationships.

Finally, a close friendship fosters multiple opportunities for influence and social support, but these processes are not always beneficial to a child's emotional and behavioural health. As research on friendship has matured, scholars have come to give increasing attention to this particular duality – the many positive functions served by friendships need to be understood in the context of emerging evidence that the influence of friends also can be problematic. Both the positive benefits of friendship as well as the potential negative influences of friends are explored in the following section. We will focus on emotional adjustment outcomes, academic adjustment outcomes, prosocial versus antisocial behaviour outcomes, and risky behaviour outcomes.

THE POSITIVE AND NEGATIVE INFLUENCE OF FRIENDS

The effects of friendship on emotional well-being

Given the potential provisions friendships can provide in children's lives (such as companionship and recreation, help and guidance, validation and emotional support, etc.), it could be predicted that children who do not have friends or have lower-quality friendships would be at risk for various emotional adjustment problems. Having friends provides a child with various benefits like increased self-esteem, decreased likelihood of depression, decreased feelings of loneliness, and protection from victimization (Bagwell, Newcomb and Bukowski, 1998; Hodges, Malone and Perry, 1997; Keefe and Berndt, 1996; McDonald et al., 2010; Parker and Asher, 1993b; Renshaw and Brown, 1993). In a large-scale longitudinal study, involvement in one close friendship in adolescence was the most robust protective factor against negative psychological and social outcomes (Resnick et al., 1997). It is also important to note that the negative effect of lacking friends on children's emotional well-being does not seem to be the result of the correlated factor of being poorly accepted by peers. Indeed, lacking friends and low peer acceptance have been found to make independent contributions to children's feelings of loneliness at school

(Parker and Asher, 1993b; Renshaw and Brown, 1993).

One reason that children lacking friends may feel worse than children with friends is that having friends, and especially friends who are physically strong, can protect children from being victimized by peers (for example Hodges et al., 1997, 1999). Furthermore, having friends who are helpful, or being in a friendship that is more secure, may buffer the association between victimization and the negative effects of this victimization in children and adolescents (Schmidt and Bagwell, 2007; Woods, Done and Kalsi, 2009). This is important because there is also evidence that victimization per se is strongly associated with loneliness (Boivin, Hymel and Bukowski, 1995; Hodges et al., 1997; Kochenderfer and Ladd, 1997).

Although friendships can provide many benefits to children including increases in self-esteem and decreases in loneliness and depression, the benefits of friendship may be moderated by friendship quality and stability. For example, having friendships that are high in positive qualities and that are relatively stable increases self-esteem over time for children, but if children's friendships are high in negative qualities this may not be the case (Keefe and Berndt, 1996). Furthermore, children who are treated badly by their friends (subjected to physical or relational aggression) are more likely to experience adjustment difficulties (including anxiety, social avoidance, loneliness; Crick and Nelson, 2002). By contrast, when children have friendships that are high in qualities such as companionship, emotional support, self-disclosure, and help and guidance, children are less lonely (Parker and Asher, 1993b).

Part of the complexity of peer relationships is that friendship dynamics can also foster emotional difficulties. Although positive friendship qualities are associated with lower levels of social anxiety (La Greca and Lopez, 1998), and social support is related to lower levels of depression symptoms (Gaylord-Harden et al., 2007), it also appears to be that intimate, supportive friendships may, under some circumstances, also stimulate processes that amplify internalizing symptoms. A specific feature of some close relationships is co-rumination (Rose, 2002; Rose, Carlson and Waller, 2007), which includes the tendency for friends to frequently discuss problems, rehash problems in detail, focus on negative emotions, and speculate about various aspects of the problem. Co-rumination represents the confluence of a maladaptive cognitive process – rumination, or dwelling on negative aspects of a problem – and self-disclosure, the process of sharing emotions and thoughts with a partner that is typically characteristic of healthy friendships. Co-rumination can be a harmful type of mutual self-disclosure that may produce negative affective outcomes in friends.

In a cross-sectional study of children and early adolescents, Rose (2002) found that girls reported engaging in more co-rumination with friends than did boys. Furthermore, Rose found that, for girls, co-rumination with close same-sex friends was associated with positive friendship quality with a reciprocated best friend, yet was also correlated with maladaptive emotional adjustment, specifically a composite of self-reported anxiety and depression symptoms.

In a follow-up *longitudinal* study of co-rumination, Rose et al. (2007) found an interesting cyclical pattern. Co-rumination with friends was associated with increased friendship quality six months later, as well as increases in depression and anxiety symptoms. Furthermore, both increased internalizing problems and improved friendship quality predicted more co-rumination between friends six months later. Interestingly, this prospective association between co-rumination and friendship quality and symptoms of anxiety and depression was found for girls only (Rose et al., 2007).

Certain friendship features and processes, then, appear to have particular effects on girls' emotional well-being. Aside from co-rumination, girls' general relational orientation, which includes the propensity to invest in and derive self-relevant information from

relationships, may make girls more vulnerable to internalizing problems (Crick and Nelson, 2002; Rudolph and Conley, 2005), even (or perhaps especially) when involved in a high-quality friendship. Further, while co-rumination may foster emotional difficulties through verbal engagement, depressive symptoms and attributions may also be transmitted over time via a contagion process between friends. Evidence suggests that close adolescent friends can reinforce or maintain both depressive symptoms and depressogenic attributional styles, and these contagion effects may be particularly pronounced among girls and among adolescents who are involved in close, reciprocated friendships (Stevens and Prinstein, 2005).

The effects of friendship on school adjustment

It has long been recognized that having friends makes a contribution to children's overall school adjustment. Importantly, the positive effects of friendship on school adjustment are evident from the first years of school. For example, kindergarten children who enter school with friends from their preschool years or who make friends during the school year are better adjusted to school (such as having better attitudes toward school, lower school anxiety, less absenteeism) at the end of the year than children who do not (Ladd, 1990). Among middle school students, Wentzel, Barry and Caldwell (2004) found that students with a reciprocated friend at the beginning of sixth grade fared better on measures of social and academic adjustment at the end of the school year than did students without a friend. One possible mechanism that may explain this effect is that friends contribute to a sense of emotional security and a sense of belonging, both of which may facilitate motivation and achievement at school. School belonging is enhanced by feeling liked, respected, and valued by other members of the school community (Hamm and Faircloth, 2005). Friends may also directly encourage involvement in extracurricular activities, such as membership in school clubs, which further strengthens school belonging. School belonging in turn is positively related to academic engagement (Connell and Wellborn, 1991), and it may also protect against pregnancy and participation in violence (Resnick et al., 1997), both of which can have adverse effects on academic participation and achievement.

It also seems likely that friends play an important role by aiding one another with homework and by preparing together for upcoming tests. They also can come to the rescue by helping each other when one has missed school and needs notes or information about upcoming assignments. In addition, Zajac and Hartup (1997) reviewed evidence suggesting that children have more creative and productive interactions when engaged in a cognitive task with a friend versus a non-friend.

Again, however, the nature of the friendship relationship may play an important role. Evidence exists that the association between friendship and school adjustment is moderated by the quality of a child's friendship. For example, kindergarteners who report receiving more help from a friend increased more over time in their liking for school than children who did not receive help from a friend (Ladd et al., 1996). Berndt and Keefe (1995) also found that children who report more positive qualities in their friendships, including high levels of prosocial behaviour, support, encouragement, disclosure, and loyalty, report being more involved in class. Conversely, having friendships that are high in negative relationship features, like conflict is predictive of being more disruptive in class over time (Berndt and Keefe, 1995), and, for boys, perceptions of conflict within friendships is associated with less engagement in and liking of school (Ladd et al., 1996).

The academic orientation of a child's friends may also affect a child's academic success and achievement motivation. Longitudinal research indicates that how a child's friends perform academically is associated with the later academic performance of the child (Altermatt and Pomerantz, 2005; Wentzel and Caldwell, 1997). If a child's close friends get higher grades then the child is more likely to improve, but if a child's close friends perform poorly, then the child's performance is likely to suffer (Altermatt and Pomerantz, 2005). This influence may occur through a variety of processes, such as tangible help (or lack thereof) that friends provide each other, discussions they have about schoolwork, or through increasingly similar beliefs and attributions about academic achievement and the causes of academic success and failure (Altermatt and Pomerantz, 2003). It is also important to note that although being friends with children who are high achievers may increase a child's academic performance, this friendship may also increase the child's negative self-evaluation because of the social comparison between the self and the friend (Altermatt and Pomerantz, 2005).

The effects of friendship on prosocial and antisocial behaviour

Just as friends influence the achievement orientation of one another, they also influence children's tendencies to be prosocial in and out of school (Barry and Wentzel, 2006; Hartup and Stevens, 1997; Nelson and Aboud, 1985). The institution of friendship itself is understood by children to be prosocial in nature, characterized by behaviours like sharing and listening (Berndt, 1981), and interactions between friends are more likely to involve prosocial acts than are interactions with non-friend peers (Berndt, 1985). Further, Cillessen et al. (2005) found that adolescent friendships characterized by companionship, closeness, helping, security, and low levels of conflict are associated with later self-reported prosocial behaviour. In Barry and Wentzel's (2006) longitudinal study of prosocial behaviour in 9th- and 10th-grade students, friends' perceived levels of prosocial behaviour were associated with adolescents' own engagement in prosocial behaviour one year later, via the adolescents' pursuit of prosocial goals. Positive affective quality and frequency of contact between friends amplified the degree of influence within these friendships.

Recent research has also focused on the negative effects of antisocial friends. Children who affiliate with antisocial peers (antisocial behaviour includes physical aggression, stealing, and lying) are more likely to become antisocial themselves (see, for example, Keenan et al., 1995; Vitaro et al., 1997). Influence from friends to engage in maladaptive behaviours appears to have both immediately negative consequences (such as punishment for harmful or inappropriate activity) and indirect negative effects, including heightened risk for psychopathology later in development (for example, Kupersmidt et al., 1995). Because high levels of antisocial behaviour are predictive of school dropout (Parker and Asher, 1987), friends who reinforce antisocial behaviour in each other are, in effect, contributing to one another's eventual withdrawal or suspension from school. As noted earlier, this influence can be exacerbated in the context of a high-quality and stable relationship: support, intimacy, companionship, and mutuality can interact with antisocial characteristics in a friend to result in more maladaptive outcomes (for example, Berndt, Hawkins and Jiao, 1999; Piehler and Dishion, 2007).

Research has investigated the specific socialization processes that may occur in interactions between two close friends who socialize one another in a negative direction. The findings indicate that aggressive and antisocial adolescent dyads engage in a process called 'deviancy training' (Capaldi et al., 2001; Dishion et al., 1995; Dishion et al., 1996; Granic and Dishion, 2003), in which positive attitudes toward aggression are encouraged by the way children positively reinforce each other for bringing up references to previous antisocial actions or by talking about antisocial intentions. Indeed,

mutual reinforcement of deviant talk seems to be a primary source of positive affect within these antisocial friendships (Dishion et al., 1996). Relatedly, Piehler and Dishion (2007) found that dyadic mutuality (an interactive process characterized by listening to one another, exhibiting understanding and concern, and responding to utterances contingently), in conjunction with deviant talk content, is associated with higher levels of antisocial behaviour in male and female adolescent friendship pairs. There is also evidence from Bagwell and Coie (2004) that when male friendship dyads are observed interacting in a laboratory setting (playing a game or doing a puzzle together) and are given opportunities for rule-breaking behaviour, aggressive boys are more likely than non-aggressive boys to entice one another to violate the rules (such as peeking at the answer key, playing with items on a supply shelf, making obscene gestures).

The effects of friendship on risky behaviours

Health-risk behaviours in adolescence can also be 'entrenched within close friendships' (Prinstein, Boergers and Spirito, 2001: 295). Through processes like deviancy training, including explicit instruction and encouragement, friends may influence engagement in risky behaviours, including substance use (see Borsari and Carey, 2001, for a review), dysfunctional eating and weight loss attitudes and behaviour (Jones, 2004; Paxton et al., 1999), suicidality (Prinstein et al., 2001), and non-suicidal self-injury (Prinstein et al., 2010). Empirical evidence for the negative influence of friends on health-related behaviour is abundant (see Brechwald and Prinstein, 2011, for a review). For example, affiliation with a friend who drinks alcohol is a significant predictor of alcohol use in adolescence (Dishion and Owen, 2002). Research on cigarette smoking and drug use in adolescence has yielded similar findings (Lynskey, Fergusson and Horwood, 1998).

Adolescents' perceptions of their friends' engagement in behaviours such as drinking, smoking, and unhealthy sexual behaviour may also influence their own engagement in these activities. This is problematic because adolescents tend to overestimate the degree to which their friends participate in risky behaviours (Ross, Greene and House, 1977), and these perceptions of friends' behaviour are more proximal predictors of adolescents' own behaviour than actual rates of friends' behaviour (Fromme and Ruela, 1994). Adolescents who are already experiencing challenging circumstances (for example, family dysfunction or peer rejection) or exhibiting psychological distress (such as symptoms of depression or social anxiety) may be especially vulnerable to deleterious influence from friends (Jaccard, Blanton and Dodge, 2005; Prinstein and Wang, 2005; Vitaro, Brendgen and Tremblay, 2000).

CULTURAL VARIATION IN THE FRIENDSHIPS OF CHILDREN AND ADOLESCENTS

Much of what we know about children's and adolescents' friendships is from research within Western cultures and within schools in which most of the children are middle-class. Very little attention has been paid to how cultural contexts may affect the features of friendship and friendship processes (Bell and Coleman, 1999; Way, 2006). The exploration of cultural variation in children's friendships is just beginning to grow, as more researchers attend to how context may affect peer relationships (see Chen, French and Schneider, 2006). This section reviews cross-cultural research on friendship and suggests ways in which this field may be advanced.

A considerable proportion of the cross-cultural research on friendship is aimed at comparing collectivistic and individualistic cultures. Collectivistic cultures have been defined as stressing harmony in social interactions, obedience, and conformity. They have also been described as having members who are more likely to interact in small groups and form lasting, intimate relationships. In contrast, individualistic cultures are defined as stressing personal achievement, competition, and independence. Individualistic societies are described as having members who form social relationships with many people, in many settings, and these relationships are more fluid and non-intimate (Reis, Collins and Berscheid, 2000; Triandis, 1995; Triandis et al., 1988). Researchers typically assume that the individualistic pattern is more characteristic of Western industrialized societies and that collectivism is more prevalent in Asian cultures (Oyserman, Coon and Kemmelmeier, 2002). Support for this distinction has been found; for example, the friendships of adolescents from South Korea, a collectivistic nation, are highly intimate bonds characterized by more trust, disclosure, unconditional acceptance, and exclusivity, compared to the friendships of adolescents from the United States, a nation typically characterized as individualistic (French et al., 2006).

However, recent evidence suggests that cultures which are typically labelled as collectivistic can vary considerably in the features of their friendships. Indonesian college students, coming from a culture thought to have more collectivistic ideals, reported social networks that were larger than those of college students in the United States. They also reported having friendships that were less close than United States students' friendships. In contrast, South Korean students reported levels of disclosure with friends that were similar to the levels reported by US students, but reported more exclusivity in their friendships than both United States and Indonesian students (French et al., 2006; French, Pidada and Victor, 2005). It seems, then, that two collectivistic cultures, South Korea and Indonesia, were more dissimilar to each other in friendship patterns than they were to the United States, a society thought to be individualistic.

In some collectivistic societies, such as Indonesia, involvement with groups of peers is encouraged while the development of significant, intimate best friendships is de-emphasized. These cultures contrast with other collectivistic societies, like South Korea, in which the development of a few highly close, intimate friendships is encouraged (French et al., 2006; Schneider, 1993; Sharabany, 2006). In Indonesia, family members are comparable to friends as sources of companionship and intimacy (French et al., 2001), which may explain why intimacy with friends is lower than that of South Korean (and American) adolescents (French et al., 2005). Additionally, even within a given society there can be considerable cultural differences regarding friendship. For example, Sharabany (1982) studied Israeli preadolescents raised in a kibbutz, which emphasized communal living and de-emphasized close dyadic relationships. Although Sharabany found that preadolescents raised on the kibbutz spent more time with peers and had larger peer groups than did preadolescents raised in the city, they also reported having fewer friends with whom they could share secrets and who would consider them to be close friends.

Researchers have also begun to explore the friendships of ethnic minority adolescents in understudied American communities, such as low-income, urban contexts (Way, 1998; Way and Chen, 2000). Although there is no direct comparison with European American middle-class samples in these studies, qualitative interviews with adolescents from these communities suggest that they may conceptualize and express closeness and trust in somewhat different ways. These differences may be expressed, for example, through a greater emphasis on instrumental aid, such as sharing money and other resources with friends. Way and colleagues (Way, 1998; Way and Chen, 2000) suggest that instrumental aid may be a less dominant feature in the friendships of middle-class children. Future work should directly compare the friendship conceptualizations and behaviours of low-income white children with low-income students of colour from the same and different neighbourhoods in order to piece apart whether possible differences are attributable to race, socioeconomic status, or other community features.

Additionally, research with minority adolescents suggests that some of the gender differences in friendships found with European American, middle-class children are not universal. DuBois and Hirsch (1990) compared African-American and European-American children from the same town and found that whereas European-American girls reported talking more with friends about personal problems and relying on them more for help than did European-American boys, there were not significant gender differences among African-American boys and girls. Similarly, Way and colleagues (Way et al., 2005) also suggest from their interviews that low-income African-American and Asian-American boys have friendships that are characterized by considerable emotional depth, indeed a level of depth that is similar to that of their female counterparts.

There is a great deal left to learn about cultural differences in friendships. First, the field would greatly benefit from the examination of cultural similarities and differences in how friendship characteristics relate to one another and how these features predict friendship success. For example, Schneider et al. (1997) compared Canadian and Italian children on how friendship quality was associated with friendship stability versus termination. For children from both countries, positive friendship qualities were linked with friendship stability. In a study comparing Canadian and Taiwanese children, however, higher levels of companionship in friendship significantly predicted friendship stability for Taiwanese children but not for Canadian children (Benjamin et al., 2001). Further, for Taiwanese children, negative associations between friendship conflict with friendship closeness, help, and security were stronger than the associations between these features for Canadian children. Benjamin et al. (2001) suggest that in Taiwan norms about harmony in social interactions are stressed, making conflict in friendships more detrimental to overall friendship quality than in Canada. More attention should be given to how friendship features and processes might vary across cultures, because these questions will add much to our understanding of the universalities (or lack thereof) in social relationships.

Additionally, understanding culture and friendship will also be aided through the increased use of observational techniques, rather than relying primarily on self-report methodologies. The use of self-report measures for cross-cultural comparisons makes it difficult to know if differences result from the way that different people define or use certain terms (for example, helpful, confiding, reliable) or instead from cross-cultural differences in how friends interact with and treat one another. In vivo observations of how friends behave with one another could validate or qualify some of the self-reported differences between children of different cultures. For example, it would be important to learn whether observations of Indonesian, Korean, and US adolescents' interactions with friends validate the differences in self-reported disclosure discussed above (French et al., 2005, 2006). Until more observational work is done, it will be difficult to know whether self-report data reflect the cultural salience of certain constructs rather than their actual occurrence (Weisz et al., 1995).

Finally, although there appear to be cultural differences in the salient features of children's friendships, there is likely a greater portion of the friendship experience that is universal. For example, even if there are differences in the relative prominence of certain friendship features, children from many countries, including Germany, Iceland, China, and Russia, mention features like trust, affection, shared activities, a shared history, confiding, and helping in their descriptions of why friendship is important and how it develops (e.g., Gummerum and Keller, 2008). Likewise, across cultures, children with friends are more socially skilled, less aggressive, and less withdrawn than children

without friends (French et al., 2003; Newcomb and Bagwell, 1996). Furthermore, across cultures, including the US, the Netherlands, and Indonesia, homophily is characteristic of friendships; that is, friends resemble each other on behavioural, attitudinal, and ability dimensions (French et al., 2003; Kupersmidt, DeRosier and Patterson, 1995). As research on cultural variation in friendship patterns proceeds, attention needs to be given to the ways that friendships are similar as well as dissimilar across cultures.

INTERVENTIONS FOR FRIENDSHIP: A SOCIAL TASKS PERSPECTIVE

Despite evidence of the powerful and pervasive role of friendship in children's lives, there is very little research on whether direct instruction in social relationship skills can promote improvement in children's success in friendship. By contrast, there is a body of intervention research designed to learn whether teaching children certain social relationship skills would help children to become better accepted by their peers (for reviews see Asher et al., 1996; Bierman, 2004). In these intervention studies, children were coached in various social skills, such as participating in activities, being a responsive, cooperative and helpful partner, and avoiding domineering, aggressive, or disruptive behaviour. Remarkably, despite the relatively brief character of these interventions, many of the studies yielded evidence of increased peer acceptance. Furthermore, there was evidence that when significant gains in acceptance occurred they were maintained at one month (Ladd, 1981) and one year (Oden and Asher, 1977) following intervention.

The need for social skills training focused on friendship is highlighted by two kinds of evidence. First, simply pairing a child who lacks friends with another child from the same classroom for a shared activity can promote a short-term friendship gain but does not appear to have enduring effects, even one month after the activity ends (Lilly, 1971; Rucker and Vincenzo, 1970). Second, the few social skills intervention studies that included a friendship nomination measure as well as a rating-scale measure of peer acceptance found that children who received training made gains in their level of peer acceptance, but not in the number of best friendship nominations that they received from peers (Gresham and Nagle, 1980; Oden and Asher, 1977; Siperstein and Gale, 1983).

This latter finding could be interpreted in at least two different ways. First, it is possible that it simply takes time for poorly-accepted children to change from being among the least well-liked children in their classroom to a position of both being better accepted and having new, close friends. Unfortunately, this possibility cannot be tested from the existing studies since none of them conducted any follow-up measure of friendship beyond one month post-intervention. Oden and Asher (1977) assessed peer acceptance at one year follow-up, but did not include a measure of children's participation in friendships. Second, it is possible that for children to form and maintain high-quality friendships, children need to become more competent in handling the kinds of circumstances and issues that are especially likely to arise in friendship. These circumstances and issues may be qualitatively different from those that children face in gaining acceptance in the broader peer group context. The hypothesis that there are distinct competencies associated with making and keeping friends is discussed in detail in Asher et al.'s (1996) review of social skills training studies. They hypothesized that although children can become better accepted if they learn, for example, to participate, and be cooperative, responsive, and supportive with peers, there may well be challenges that children face in the domain of friendship that require particular understandings, emotional capabilities, and behavioural skills.

One way to conceptualize these friendship-specific challenges is to think of them as consisting of specific 'friendship tasks'. This

social tasks perspective on friendship is in the tradition of several scholars who have examined social competence from a social situational or social tasks perspective (see Argyle, Furnham and Graham, 1981; Dirks, Treat and Weersing, 2007; Dodge, McClaskey and Feldman, 1985; Farrell, Ampy and Meyer, 1998; Goldfried and D'Zurilla, 1969; McFall, 1982). The social tasks of friendship are diverse and likely include initiating a friendship (Gottman, 1983; Gottman, Gonso and Rasmussen, 1975), helping a friend (Ladd and Oden, 1979; Rose and Asher, 2004), seeking help from a friend (Rose and Asher, 2004), resolving conflicts of interest (McDonald and Asher, 2013; Rose and Asher, 1999; Selman and Schultz, 1990), coping when a friend has other friends (Parker et al., 2005), and, perhaps most challenging, coping when a friend violates a core expectation of friendship (MacEvoy and Asher, 2012). Each of these tasks, and many others, calls upon children's emotional, cognitive, and behavioural resources.

It follows from the idea that if friendship involves distinct social tasks, then how children respond to certain friendship tasks should be predictive of children's success in friendship. To put this to a rigorous test, it would be necessary to demonstrate that children's responses to a particular friendship task predict success at friendship even when statistically controlling for level of peer acceptance. This is a somewhat demanding test because peer acceptance and friendship correlate about 0.5 (Parker and Asher, 1993b).

Two studies by Rose and Asher (1999, 2004) adopted this research strategy. In the first of these (Rose and Asher, 1999), children were presented with vignettes depicting fairly benign conflicts of interest with a friend, and indicated the extent to which they would pursue various goals and behavioural strategies in each situation. Results indicated that children's number of friends (indexed by reciprocal limited friendship nominations) and friendship quality with a best friend (indexed by children completing Parker and Asher's, 1993b,

Friendship Quality Questionnaire) were predicted from the goals and strategies that children endorsed in response to the conflict vignettes, even after controlling for peer acceptance. For example, children who endorsed revenge goals in response to conflict had fewer friends, and when they had a friend, their friend was more likely to characterize the friendship as high in conflict. In their second study, Rose and Asher (2004) focused on the task of giving help to a friend in need and the task of seeking help from a friend. Here, too, specific goals and strategies were predictive of success at friendship, controlling for level of acceptance (Rose and Asher, 2004). For example, when a friend was portrayed in a vignette as having tripped and fallen and being laughed at by classmates, the goal of assigning responsibility to the friend and the strategy of blaming the friend for what happened each predicted to having fewer friends. In the potential support-seeking context, having goals and strategies focused on maintaining privacy and keeping the friend 'out of one's business' were negatively associated with the number of friends children had.

Still another task that children face involves responding to a friend when the friend has violated a core expectation of friendship, such as the expectation of maintaining a confidence or helping a friend in need. Recall our earlier discussion of the potential fragility of friendship and the ways in which friendships can be placed at risk. MacEvoy and Asher (2012) examined the interplay between children's interpretations, emotions, and goals in responding to this difficult friendship task. Results from this study suggested that the more children interpreted their friends' behaviour as indicating that their friend did not value them, the more they felt angry and the more they felt sad. Importantly, greater anger was associated with higher levels of endorsement of revenge goals and aggressive strategies, whereas sadness was associated with relationship maintenance goals and with problem-solving strategies. This study highlights the point that

competence in friendship involves a system of interconnected processes, including interpretations of the friend's actions, emotional responses that may follow from the interpretation a child makes, interpersonal goals, and behavioural strategy choices.

We conclude this section and our chapter with a call for intervention research focused on helping children with specific friendship tasks. Intervention research aimed at helping children with friendship should be founded on the idea that friendship competence is complex and goes beyond behavioural skills alone. It is also important that such studies include randomized assignment to experimental conditions and include appropriate control conditions, including an attention-only control condition. Given that intervention effects on friendship may dissipate after a relatively short period of time, a long-term follow-up assessment is essential. Equally important, any examination of the effects of a friendship-specific intervention must include a meaningful assessment of the full range of friendship adjustment indices, including how many friends children have and the quality of those friendships as observed or reported by both the target child and the target child's friends. Because we know that the academic orientation, prosocial behaviour, and antisocial behaviour of friends influence children's adjustment, the characteristics of children's newly made friends also need to be assessed. Additionally, to demonstrate that intervention effects extend beyond any influence on peer acceptance, rigorous outcome studies should measure and control for children's peer acceptance. Together, carefully crafted interventions and outcome studies should yield insights into how children can be helped in their friendships.

REFERENCES

Altermatt, E.R. and Pomerantz, E.M. (2003) 'The development of competence-related and motivational beliefs: An investigation of similarity and influence among friends', *Journal of Educational Psychology*, 95(1): 111–23.

Altermatt, E.R. and Pomerantz, E.M. (2005) 'The implications of having high-achieving versus low-achieving friends: A longitudinal analysis', *Social Development*, 14(1): 61–81.

Argyle, M., Furnham, A. and Graham, J.A. (1981) *Social Situations*. New York: Cambridge University Press.

Asher, S.R., Gorman, A.H., Guerra, V.S., Gabriel, S.W., and Weeks, M.S. (2013) *Children's loneliness in different school contexts*. Manuscript submitted for publication.

Asher, S.R., and Hymel, S. (1981) 'Children's social competence and peer relations: Sociometric and behavioral assessment', in J.D. Wine and M.D. Smye (eds.), *Social Competence*. New York: Guilford Press, pp. 125–57.

Asher, S.R. and Hymel, S. (1986) 'Coaching in social skills for children who lack friends in school', *Social Work in Education*, 8(4): 205–18.

Asher, S.R., Parker, J.G. and Walker, D.L. (1996) 'Distinguishing friendship from acceptance: Implications for intervention and assessment', in W.M. Bukowski, A.F. Newcomb and W.W. Hartup (eds.), *The Company They Keep: Friendship in Childhood and Adolescence*. New York: Cambridge University Press, pp. 366–405.

Asher, S.R., Rose, A.J. and Gabriel, S.W. (2001) 'Peer rejection in everyday life', in M.R. Leary (ed.), *Interpersonal Rejection*. New York: Oxford University Press, pp. 105–42.

Bagwell, K.L. and Coie, J.D. (2004) 'The best friendships of aggressive boys: Relationship quality, conflict management, and rule-breaking behavior', *Journal of Experimental Child Psychology*, 88(1): 5–24.

Bagwell, C.L., Newcomb, A.F. and Bukowski, W.M. (1998) 'Preadolescent friendship and peer rejection as predictors of adult adjustment', *Child Development*, 69(1): 140–53.

Bagwell, C.L. and Schmidt, M.E. (2011) *Friendships in Childhood and Adolescence*. New York: Guilford Press.

Banny, A.M., Heilbron, N., Ames, A., and Prinstein, M.J. (2011) 'Relational benefits of relational aggression: Adaptive and maladaptive associations with adolescent friendship quality', *Developmental Psychology*, 47(4): 1153–66.

Barry, C.M. and Wentzel, K.R. (2006) 'Friend influence on prosocial behavior: The role of motivational factors and friendship characteristics', *Developmental Psychology*, 42(1): 153–63.

Bell, S. and Coleman, S. (Eds.). (1999) *The Anthropology of Friendship*. Oxford, UK: Berg.

Bell-Dolan, D.J., Foster, S.L. and Sikora, D.M. (1989) 'Effects of sociometric testing on children's behavior and loneliness in school', *Developmental Psychology*, 25(2): 306–11.

Benenson, J.F. and Christakos, A. (2003) 'The greater fragility of females' versus males' closest same-sex friendships', *Child Development*, 74(4): 1123–9.

Benjamin, W.J., Schneider, B.H., Greenman, P.S. and Hum, M. (2001) 'Conflict and childhood friendship in Taiwan and Canada', *Canadian Journal of Behavioral Science*, 33(3): 203–11.

Berndt, T.J. (1981) 'Relations between social cognition, nonsocial cognition, and social behavior: The case of friendship', in J.H. Flavell and L.D. Ross (eds.), *Social Cognitive Development: Frontiers and Possible Futures*. Cambridge: Cambridge University Press, pp. 176–99.

Berndt, T.J. (1985) 'Prosocial behavior between friends in middle childhood and early adolescence', *The Journal of Early Adolescence*, 5(3): 307–17.

Berndt, T.J., Hawkins, J.A. and Jiao, Z. (1999) 'Influences of friends and friendships on adjustment to junior high school', *Merrill-Palmer Quarterly*, 45(1): 13–41.

Berndt, T.J. and Keefe, K. (1995) 'Friends' influence on adolescents' adjustment to school', *Child Development*, 66(5): 1312–29.

Berndt, T.J. and McCandless, M.A. (2009) 'Methods for investigating children's relationships with friends', in K.H. Rubin, W.M. Bukowski and B. Laursen (eds.), *Handbook of Peer Interactions, Relationships, and Groups*. New York: Guilford, pp. 63–81.

Bierman, K.L. (2004) *Peer Rejection: Developmental Processes and Intervention Strategies*. New York: Guilford.

Bigelow, B.J. (1977) 'Children's friendship expectations: A cognitive-developmental study', *Child Development*, 48(1): 246–53.

Bigelow, B.J. and LaGaipa, J.J. (1975) 'Children's written descriptions of friendship: A multidimensional analysis', *Developmental Psychology*, 11(6): 857–58.

Blachman, D.R. and Hinshaw, S.P. (2002) 'Patterns of friendship among girls with and without attention-deficit/hyperactivity disorder', *Journal of Abnormal Child Psychology*, 30(6): 625–40.

Boivin, M., Hymel, S. and Bukowski, W.M. (1995) 'The roles of social withdrawal, peer rejection, and victimization by peers in predicting loneliness and depressed mood in childhood', *Development and Psychopathology*, 7(4): 765–85.

Borsari, B. and Carey, K.B. (2001) 'Peer influences on college drinking: A review of the research', *Journal of Substance Abuse*, 13(4): 391–424.

Bowker, A. (2004) 'Predicting friendship stability during early adolescence', *Journal of Early Adolescence*, 24(2): 85–112.

Bowker, J.C. (2011) 'Examining two types of best friendship dissolution during early adolescence', *Journal of Early Adolescence*, 31(5): 656–70.

Brechwald, W.A. and Prinstein, M.J. (2011) 'Beyond homophily: A decade of advances in understanding peer influence processes', *Journal of Research on Adolescence*, 21(1): 166–79.

Brown, B.B. (1990) 'Peer groups and peer cultures', in S.S. Feldman and G.R. Elliott (eds.), *At the Threshold: The Developing Adolescent*. Cambridge, MA: Harvard University Press, pp. 171–96.

Brown, B.B. and Dietz, E.L. (2009) 'Informal peer groups in middle childhood and adolescence', in K.H. Rubin, W.M. Bukowski and B. Laursen (eds.), *Handbook of Peer Interactions, Relationships, and Groups*. New York: Guilford, pp. 361–76.

Bukowski, W.M. and Hoza, B. (1989) 'Popularity and friendship: Issues in theory, measurement and outcome', in T.J. Berndt and G.W. Ladd (eds.), *Peer Relationships in Child Development*. New York: Wiley, pp. 15–45.

Bukowski, W.M., Hoza, B. and Boivin, M. (1994) 'Measuring friendship quality during pre- and early adolescence: The development and psychometric properties of the friendship qualities scale', *Journal of Social and Personal Relationships*, 11(3): 471–84.

Bukowski, W.M., Newcomb, A.F. and Hartup, W.W. (1996) *The Company They Keep: Friendship in Childhood and Adolescence*. New York: Cambridge University Press.

Capaldi, D.M., Dishion, T.J., Stoolmiller, M. and Yoerger, K. (2001) 'Aggression toward female partners by at-risk young men: The contribution of male adolescent friendships', *Developmental Psychology*, 37(1): 61–73.

Chen, X., French, D. and Schneider, B.H. (2006) *Peer Relationships in Cultural Context*. New York: Cambridge University Press.

Cillessen, A.H.N., Jiang, X.L., West, T.V. and Laszkowski, D.K. (2005) 'Predictors of dyadic friendship quality in adolescence', *International Journal of Behavioral Development*, 29(2): 165–72.

Coleman, J.S. (1961) *The Adolescent Society: The Social Life of the Teenager and Its Impact on Education*. New York: Free Press.

Connell, J.P. and Wellborn, J.G. (1991) 'Competence, autonomy, and relatedness: A motivational analysis of self-system processes', in M.R. Gunnar and L.A. Sroufe (eds.), *Self Processes and Development: The Minnesota Symposia on Child Development, Vol. 23*. Hillsdale, NJ: Erlbaum, pp. 43–78.

Crick, N.R. and Nelson, D.A. (2002) 'Relational and physical victimization within friendships: Nobody told me there'd be friends like these', *Journal of Abnormal Child Psychology*, 30(6): 599–607.

Csikszentmihalyi, M. and Larson. R. (1984) *Being Adolescent: Conflict and Growth in the Teenage Years*. New York: Basic Books.

Demir, M. and Urberg, K.A. (2004) 'Friendship and adjustment among adolescents', *Journal of Experimental Child Psychology*, 88(1): 68–82.

Dirks, M.A., Treat, T.A. and Weersing, V.R. (2007) 'The situation specificity of youth responses to provocation by peers', *Journal of Clinical Child and Adolescent Psychology*, 36(4); 621–28.

Dishion, T.J., Capaldi, D., Spracklen, K.M. and Li, F. (1995) 'Peer ecology of male adolescent drug use', *Development and Psychopathology*, 7(4): 803–24.

Dishion, T.J. and Owen, L.D. (2002) 'A longitudinal analysis of friendships and substance use: Bidirectional influence from adolescence to adulthood', *Developmental Psychology*, 38(4): 480–91.

Dishion, T.J., Spracklen, K.M., Andrews, D.W. and Patterson, G.R. (1996) 'Deviancy training in male adolescents' friendships', *Behavior Therapy*, 27(3): 373–90.

Dodge, K.A., McClaskey, C.L. and Feldman, E. (1985) 'Situational approach to the assessment of social competence in children', *Journal of Consulting and Clinical Psychology*, 53(3): 344–53.

DuBois, D.L. and Hirsch, B.J. (1990) 'School and neighborhood friendship patterns of blacks and whites in early adolescence', *Child Development*, 61(2): 524–36.

Farrell, A.D., Ampy, L.A. and Meyer, A.L. (1998) 'Identification and assessment of problematic interpersonal situations for urban adolescents', *Journal of Clinical Child & Adolescent Psychology*, 27(3): 293–305.

Fine, G.A. (1981) 'Friends, impression management, and preadolescent behavior', in S.R. Asher and J.M. Gottman (eds.), *The Development of Children's Friendships*. New York: Cambridge University Press, pp. 29–52.

Fine, G.A. (1987) *With the Boys: Little League Baseball and Preadolescent Culture*. Chicago: University of Chicago Press.

French, D.C., Bae, A., Pidada, S. and Lee, O. (2006) 'Friendships of Indonesian, South Korean, and U.S. college students', *Personal Relationships*, 13(1): 69–81.

French, D.C., Jansen, E.A., Riansari, M. and Setiono, K. (2003) 'Friendships of Indonesian children: Adjustment of children who differ in friendship presence and similarity between mutual friends', *Social Development*, 12(4): 605–21.

French, D.C., Pidada, S. and Victor, A. (2005) 'Friendships of Indonesian and United States youth', *International Journal of Behavioral Development*, 29(4): 304–13.

French, D.C., Riansari, M., Pidada, S., Nelwan, P. and Buhrmester, D. (2001) 'Social support of Indonesian and U.S. children and adolescents by family members and friends', *Merrill-Palmer Quarterly*, 47(3): 377–94.

Freud, A. and Dann, S. (1951) 'An experiment in group upbringing', in A. Freud, H. Hartmann and E. Kris (eds.), *The Psychoanalytic Study of the Child, Vol. 6.* New York: International Universities Press, pp. 127–68.

Fromme, K. and Ruela, A. (1994) 'Mediators and moderators of young adults' drinking', *Addiction*, 89(1): 63–71.

Gaylord-Harden, N.K., Ragsdale, B.L., Mandara, J., Richards, M.H. and Petersen, A.C. (2007) 'Perceived support and internalizing symptoms in African American adolescents: Self-esteem and ethnic identity as mediators', *Journal of Youth and Adolescence*, 36(1): 77–88.

Goldfried, M.R. and D'Zurilla, T.J. (1969) 'A behavioral-analytic model for assessing competence', in C.D. Speilberger (ed.), *Current Topics in Clinical and Community Psychology, Vol. 1.* New York: Academic Press, pp. 151–96.

Gottman, J.M. (1983) 'How children become friends', *Monographs of the Society for Research in Child Development*, 48 (3, Serial No. 201): 1–86.

Gottman, J., Gonso, J. and Rasmussen, B. (1975) 'Social interaction, social competence, and friendship in children', *Child Development*, 46(3): 709–18.

Gottman, J.M. and Parkhurst, J.T. (1980) 'A developmental theory of friendship and acquaintanceship processes', in W.A. Collins (ed.), *Minnesota Symposia on Child Development: Vol. 13: Development of cognition, affect, and social relations.* Hillsdale, NJ: Erlbaum, pp. 197–253.

Graham, S., Taylor, A.Z. and Ho, A.Y. (2009) 'Race and ethnicity in peer relations research', in K.H. Rubin, W.M. Bukowski and B. Laursen (eds.), *Handbook of Peer Interactions, Relationships, and Groups.* New York: Guilford, pp. 232–48.

Granic, I. and Dishion, T.J. (2003) 'Deviant talk in adolescent friendships: A step towards measuring a pathogenic attractor process', *Social Development*, 12(3): 314–34.

Gresham, F.M. and Nagle, R.J. (1980) 'Social skills training with children: Responsiveness to modeling and coaching as a function of peer orientation', *Journal of Consulting and Clinical Psychology*, 48(6): 718–29.

Gronlund, N.E. (1959) *Sociometry in the Classroom.* New York: Harper Brothers.

Gross, E.F. (2004) 'Adolescent internet use: What we expect, what teens report', *Journal of Applied Developmental Psychology*, 25(6): 633–49.

Gross, E.F., Juvonen, J. and Gable, S. (2002) 'Internet use and well-being in adolescence', *Journal of Social Issues*, 58(1): 75–90.

Grotpeter, J.K. and Crick, N.R. (1996) 'Relational aggression, overt aggression, and friendship', *Child Development*, 67(5): 2328–38.

Gummerum, M. and Keller, M. (2008) 'Affection, virtue, pleasure, and profit: Developing an understanding of friendship closeness and intimacy in western and Asian societies', *International Journal of Behavioral Development*, 32(3): 218–31.

Hallinan, M.T. (1976) 'Friendship patterns in open and traditional classrooms', *Sociology of Education*, 49(4): 254–65.

Hamm, J.V. and Faircloth, B.S. (2005) 'The role of friendship in adolescents' sense of school belonging', *New Directions for Child and Adolescent Development*, 107: 61–78.

Hanna, N.A. (1998) 'Predictors of friendship quality and peer group acceptance at summer camp', *The Journal of Early Adolescence*, 18(3), 291–318.

Hartup, W.W. and Stevens, N. (1997) 'Friendships and adaptation in the life course', *Psychological Bulletin*, 121(3): 355–70.

Hayvren, M. and Hymel, S. (1984) 'Ethical issues in sociometric testing: Impact of sociometric measures on interaction behavior', *Developmental Psychology*, 20(5): 844–9.

Hawkins, J.D., Catalano, R.F. and Miller, J.Y. (1992) 'Risk and protective factors for alcohol and other drug problems in adolescence and early adulthood: Implications for substance abuse prevention', *Psychological Bulletin*, 112(1): 64–105.

Hodges, E.V.E, Boivin, M., Vitaro, F. and Bukowski, W.M. (1999) 'The power of friendship: Protection against an escalating cycle of peer victimization', *Developmental Psychology*, 35(1): 94–101.

Hodges, E.V.E., Malone, M.J. and Perry, D.G. (1997) 'Individual and social risk as interacting determinants of victimization in the peer group', *Developmental Psychology*, 33(6): 1032–9.

Hu, Y., Wood, J.F., Smith, V. and Westbrook, N. (2004) 'Friendships through IM: Examining the relationship between instant messaging and intimacy', *Journal of Computer-Mediated Communication*, 10(1): Article 6.

Hunter, F.T. and Youniss, J. (1982) 'Changes in functions of three relations during adolescence', *Developmental Psychology*, 18(6): 806–11.

Hymel, S. (1986) 'Interpretations of peer behavior: Affective bias in childhood and adolescence', *Child Development*, 57(2): 431–45.

Iverson, A.M., Barton, B.A. and Iverson, G.L. (1997) 'Analysis of risk to children participating in a sociometric task', *Developmental Psychology*, 33(1): 104–12.

Ispa, J. (1981) 'Peer support among Soviet day care toddlers', *International Journal of Behavioral Development*, 4(2): 255–69.

Jaccard, J., Blanton, H. and Dodge, T. (2005) 'Peer influences on risk behavior: An analysis of the effects of a close friend', *Developmental Psychology*, 41(1): 135–47.

Jones, D.C. (2004) 'Body image among adolescent boys and girls: A longitudinal study', *Developmental Psychology*, 40(5): 823–35.

Keefe, K. and Berndt, T.J. (1996) 'Relations of friendship quality to self-esteem in early adolescence', *Journal of Early Adolescence*, 16(1): 110–29.

Keenan, K., Loeber, R., Zhang, Q., Stouthamer-Loeber, M. and Van Kammen, W.B. (1995) 'The influence of deviant peers on the development of boys' disruptive and delinquent behavior: A temporal analysis', *Development and Psychopathology*, 7(4): 715–26.

Kinney, D.A. (1993) 'From nerds to normals: the recovery of identity among adolescents from middle school to high school', *Sociology of Education*, 66(1): 21–40.

Kochenderfer, B.J. and Ladd, G.W. (1997) 'Victimized children's responses to peers' aggression: Behaviors associated with reduced versus continued victimization', *Development and Psychopathology*, 9(1): 59–73.

Krappmann, L. (1996) 'Amicitia, drujba, shin-yu, philia, Freundschaft, friendship: On the cultural diversity of human relationships', in W.W. Bukowski, A.F. Newcomb and W.W. Hartup (eds.), *The Company They Keep: Friendship in Childhood and Adolescence*. New York: Cambridge University Press, pp. 19–40.

Kupersmidt, J.B., DeRosier, M.E. and Patterson, C.P. (1995) 'Similarity as the basis for children's friendships: The roles of sociometric status, aggressive and withdrawn behavior, academic achievement and demographic characteristics', *Journal of Social and Personal Relationships*, 12(3): 439–52.

Kupersmidt, J.B., Griesler, P.C., DeRosier, M.E., Patterson, C.J. and Davis, P.W. (1995) 'Childhood aggression and peer relations in the context of family and neighborhood factors', *Child Development*, 66(2): 360–75.

Ladd, G.W. (1981) 'Effectiveness of a social learning method for enhancing children's social interaction and peer acceptance', *Child Development*, 52(1): 171–8.

Ladd, G.W. (1990) 'Having friends, keeping friends, making friends, and being liked by peers in the classroom: Predictors of children's early school adjustment?', *Child Development*, 61(4): 1081–100.

Ladd, G.W. and Emerson, E.S. (1984) 'Shared knowledge in children's friendships', *Developmental Psychology*, 20(5): 932–40.

Ladd, G.W., Kochenderfer, B.J. and Coleman, C.C. (1996) 'Friendship quality as a predictor of young children's early school adjustment', *Child Development*, 67(3): 1103–18.

Ladd, G.W. and Oden, S. (1979) 'The relationship between peer acceptance and children's ideas about helpfulness', *Child Development*, 50(2): 402–8.

La Greca, A.M. and Lopez, N. (1998) 'Social anxiety among adolescents: Linkages with peer relations and friendships', *Journal of Abnormal Child Psychology*, 26(2): 83–94.

Lansford, J. E., Putallaz, M., Grimes, C.L., Schiro-Osman, K.A., Kupersmidt, J.B. and Coie, J.D. (2006) 'Perceptions of friendship quality and observed behaviors with friends: How do sociometrically rejected, average, and popular girls differ?', *Merrill-Palmer Quarterly*, 52(4): 694–720.

Larson, R.W. and Richards, M.H. (1991) 'Boredom in the middle school years: Blaming schools versus blaming students', *American Journal of Education*, 99(4): 418–43.

Larson, R.W., Richards, M.H., Moneta, G., Holmbeck, G. and Duckett, E. (1996) 'Changes in adolescents' daily interactions with their families from ages 10 to 18: Disengagement and transformation', *Developmental Psychology*, 32(4): 744–54.

Lilly, M.S. (1971) 'Improving social acceptance of low sociometric status, low achieving students', *Exceptional Children*, 37(5): 341–7.

Lynskey, M.T., Fergusson, D.M. and Horwood, L.J. (1998) 'The origins of the correlations between tobacco, alcohol, and cannabis use during adolescence', *Journal of Child Psychology and Psychiatry and Allied Disciplines*, 39(7): 995–1005.

MacEvoy, J.P. and Asher, S.R. (2012) 'When friends disappoint: Boys' and girls' responses to transgressions of friendship expectations', *Child Development*, 83(1): 104–19.

Mayeux, L., Underwood, M.K. and Risser, S.D. (2007). 'Perspectives on the ethics of sociometric research with children: How children, peers, and teachers help to inform the debate', *Merrill-Palmer Quarterly*, 53(1): 53–78.

McDonald, K.L. and Asher, S.R. (2013) 'College students' revenge goals across friend, romantic partner, and roommate contexts: The role of interpretations and emotions', *Social Development*, 22(3): 499–521.

McDonald, K.L., Bowker, J.C., Rubin, K.H., Laursen, B., and Duchene, M.S. (2010) 'Interactions between rejection sensitivity and supportive relationships in the prediction of adolescents' internalizing difficulties', *Journal of Youth and Adolescence*, 39(5): 563–574.

McDonald, K.L., Dashiell-Aje, E.N., Menzer, M.M., Rubin, K.H., Oh, W., and Bowker, J.C. (2013) 'Contributions of racial and socio-behavioral homophily to friendship stability and quality among same-race and cross-race friends', *Journal of Early Adolescence,* 33(7): 897–919.

McDonald, K. L., Malti, T., Killen, M., and Rubin, K. H. (in press). 'Best friends' discussions of social dilemmas', *Journal of Youth and Adolescence*.

McDonald, K.L, Putallaz, M., Grimes, C.L., Kupersmidt, J.B. and Coie, J.D. (2007) 'Girl talk: Gossip, friendship, and sociometric status', *Merrill-Palmer Quarterly*, 53(3): 381–411.

McFall, R. (1982) 'A review and reformulation of the concept of social skills', *Behavioral Assessment*, 4(1): 1–33.

Menzer, M.M., McDonald, K.L., Rubin, K.H., Rose-Krasnor, L., Booth-LaForce, C. and Schulz, A. (2012) 'Observed gossip moderates the link between anxious withdrawal and friendship quality in early adolescence', *International Journal of Developmental Science*, 6(3–4): 191–202.

Mikami, A.Y., Szwedo, D.E., Allen, J.P., Evans, M.A. and Hare, A.L. (2010) 'Adolescent peer relationships and behavior problems predict young adults' communication on social networking websites', *Developmental Psychology*, 46(1): 46–56.

Moreno, J.L. (1934) *Who Shall Survive?: A New Approach to the Problem of Human Interrelations*. Washington, DC: Nervous and Mental Disease Publishing.

Murray-Close, D., Ostrov, J.M. and Crick, N.R. (2007) 'A short-term longitudinal study of growth of relational aggression during middle childhood: Associations with gender, friendship intimacy, and internalizing problems', *Development and Psychopathology*, 19(1): 187–203.

Nelson, J. and Aboud, F.E. (1985) 'The resolution of social conflict between friends', *Child Development*, 56(4): 1009–17.

Newcomb, A.F. and Bagwell, C.L. (1995) 'Children's friendship relations: A meta-analytic review', *Psychological Bulletin*, 117(2): 306–47.

Newcomb, A.F. and Bagwell, C.L. (1996) 'The developmental significance of children's friendship relations',

in W.M. Bukowski, A.F. Newcomb, and W.W. Hartup (eds.), *The Company They Keep: Friendship in Childhood and Adolescence*. Cambridge: Cambridge University Press, pp. 289–321.

Newcomb, A.F., Brady, J.E. and Hartup, W.W. (1979) 'Friendship and incentive condition as determinants of children's task-oriented social behavior', *Child Development*, 50(3): 878–81.

Oden, S. and Asher, S.R. (1977) 'Coaching children in social skills for friendship making', *Child Development*, 48(2): 495–506.

Oyserman, D., Coon, H.M. and Kemmelmeier, M. (2002) 'Rethinking individualism and collectivism: Evaluation of theoretical assumptions and meta-analyses', *Psychological Bulletin*, 128(1): 3–72.

Paquette, J.A. and Asher, S.R. (2005, April) 'Children's everyday experiences with social aggression: A wireless observation study', in J. Cassidy and S.R. Asher (Chairs), *The Emotional Consequences of Adverse Peer Experiences in Childhood and Adolescence*. Symposium conducted at the biennial meeting of the Society for Research in Child Development, Atlanta.

Park, K. (1992) 'Preschoolers' reactions to loss of a best friend: Developmental trends and individual differences', *Child Study Journal*, 22(4): 233–53.

Parker, J.G. and Asher, S.R. (1987) 'Peer relations and later personal adjustment: Are low accepted children "at risk"?', *Psychological Bulletin*, 102(3): 357–89.

Parker, J.G. and Asher, S.R. (1993a) 'Beyond group acceptance: Friendship and friendship quality as distinct dimensions of peer adjustment', in W.H. Jones and D. Perlman (eds.), *Advances in Personal Relationships, Vol. 4*. London: Kingsley, pp. 261–94.

Parker, J.G. and Asher, S.R. (1993b) 'Friendship and friendship quality in middle childhood: Links with peer group acceptance and feelings of loneliness and social dissatisfaction', *Developmental Psychology*, 29(4): 611–21.

Parker, J.G. and Gottman, J.M. (1985) 'Making friends with an "extra-terrestrial": Conversational skills for friendship formation in young children'. Paper presented at the biennial meeting of the Society for Research in Child Development, Toronto, Canada.

Parker, J.G., Low, C.M., Walker, A.R. and Gamm, B.K. (2005) 'Friendship jealousy in young adolescents: Individual differences and links to sex, self-esteem, aggression, and social adjustment', *Developmental Psychology*, 41(1): 235–50.

Parker, J.G., Saxon, J.L., Asher, S.R. and Kovacs, D.M. (1999) 'Dimensions of children's friendship adjustment: Implications for understanding loneliness', in K.J. Rotenberg and S. Hymel (eds.), *Loneliness in Childhood and Adolescence.* New York: Cambridge University Press, pp. 201–21.

Parker, J.G. and Seal, J. (1996) 'Forming, losing, renewing, and replacing friendships: Applying temporal parameters to the assessment of children's friendship experiences', *Child Development*, 67(5): 2248–68.

Paxton, S.J., Schutz, H.K., Wertheim, E.H. and Muir, S.L. (1999) 'Friendship clique and peer influences on body image concerns, dietary restraint, extreme weight-loss behaviors, and binge eating in adolescent girls', *Journal of Abnormal Psychology*, 108(2): 255–66.

Pepler, D.J. and Craig, W.M. (1995) 'A peek behind the fence: Naturalistic observations of aggressive children with remote audiovisual recording', *Developmental Psychology*, 31(4): 548–53.

Piehler, T.F. and Dishion, T.J. (2007) 'Interpersonal dynamics within adolescent friendships: Dyadic mutuality, deviant talk, and patterns of antisocial behavior', *Child Development*, 78(5): 1611–24.

Poulin, F., Dishion, T.J. and Haas, E. (1999) 'The peer influence paradox: Friendship quality and deviancy training within male adolescent friendships', *Merrill-Palmer Quarterly*, 45(1), 42–61.

Prinstein, M. J., Boergers, J. and Spirito, A. (2001) 'Adolescents' and their friends' health-risk behavior: Factors that alter or add to peer influence', *Journal of Pediatric Psychology*, 26(5): 287–98.

Prinstein, M.J., Heilbron, N., Guerry, J.D., Franklin, J.C., Rancourt, D., Simon, V. and Spirito, A. (2010) 'Peer influence and nonsuicidal self injury: Longitudinal results in community and clinically-referred adolescent samples', *Journal of Abnormal Child Psychology*, 38(5): 669–82.

Prinstein, M.J. and Wang, S.S. (2005) 'False consensus and adolescent peer contagion: Examining discrepancies between perceptions and actual reported levels of friends' deviant and health risk behaviors', *Journal of Abnormal Child Psychology*, 33(3): 293–306.

Proulx, M.-F. and Poulin, F. (2013) 'Stability and change in kindergartners' friendships: Examination of links with social functioning', *Social Development*, 22(1): 111–25.

Reich, S. M., Subrahmanyam, K., and Espinoza, G. (2012). 'Friending, IMing, and hanging out face-to-face: Overlap in adolescents' online and offline social networks', *Developmental Psychology*, 48(2): 356–68.

Reis, H.T., Collins, W.A. and Berscheid, E. (2000) 'The relationship context of human behavior and development', *Psychological Bulletin*, 126(6): 844–72.

Renshaw, P.D. and Brown, P.J. (1993) 'Loneliness in middle childhood. Concurrent and longitudinal predictors', *Child Development*, 64(4): 1271–84.

Resnick, M.D., Bearman, P.S., Blum, R.W., Bauman, K.E., Harris, K.M., Jones, J., Tabor, J., Beuhring, T.,

Sieving, R.E., Shew, M., Ireland, M., Bearinger, L.H. and Udry, J.R. (1997) 'Protecting adolescents from harm: Findings from the national longitudinal study on adolescent health', *Journal of the American Medical Association*, 278(10): 823–32.

Rose, A.J. (2002) 'Co-rumination in the friendships of girls and boys', *Child Development*, 73(6): 1830–43.

Rose, A.J. and Asher, S.R. (1999) 'Children's goals and strategies in response to conflicts within a friendship', *Developmental Psychology*, 35(1): 69–79.

Rose, A.J. and Asher, S.R. (2004) 'Children's strategies and goals in response to help-giving and help-seeking tasks within a friendship', *Child Development*, 75(3): 749–63.

Rose, A.J., Carlson, W. and Waller, E.M. (2007) 'Prospective associations of co-rumination with friendship and emotional adjustment: Considering the socioemotional trade-offs of co-rumination', *Developmental Psychology*, 43(4): 1019–31.

Rose, A.J., Schwartz, R.A. and Carlson, W. (2005) 'An observational assessment of co-rumination in the friendships of girls and boys', in J.D. Coie and M. Putallaz (Chairs), *The Costs and Benefits of Interpersonal Processes Underlying Girls' Friendships.* Paper presented at the Society for Research in Child Development, Atlanta, Georgia, USA.

Ross, L., Greene, D. and House, P. (1977) 'The false consensus effect: An egocentric bias in social perception and attribution processes', *Journal of Experimental Social Psychology*, 13(3): 279–301.

Rubin, K.H., Bukowski, W.M. and Parker, J.G. (2006) 'Peer interactions, relationships, and groups', in W. Damon (Series Ed.) and N. Eisenberg (Vol. Ed.), *Handbook of Child Psychology: Vol. 3. Social, Emotional, and Personality Development*, 6th edition. New York: Wiley, pp. 571–645.

Rucker, C.N. and Vincenzo, F.M. (1970) 'Maintaining social acceptance gains made by mentally retarded children', *Exceptional Children*, 36(9): 679–80.

Rudolph, K.D. and Conley, C.S. (2005) 'Socioemotional costs and benefits of social-evaluative concerns: Do girls care too much?', *Journal of Personality*, 73(1): 115–37.

Schmidt, M.E. and Bagwell, C.L. (2007) 'The protective role of friendships in overtly and relationally victimized boys and girls', *Merrill-Palmer Quarterly,* 53(3): 439–60.

Schneider, B.H. (1993) *Children's Social Competence in Context.* Oxford, UK: Pergamon.

Schneider, B.H., Fonzi, A., Tani, F. and Tomada, G. (1997) 'A cross-cultural exploration of the stability of children's friendships and the predictors of their continuation', *Social Development,* 6(3): 322–39.

Selman, R.L. and Schultz, L.H. (1990) *Making a Friend in Youth.* Chicago: The University of Chicago Press.

Sharabany, R. (2006) 'The cultural context of children and adolescents: Peer relationships and intimate friendships among Arab and Jewish children in Israel', in X. Chen, D.C. French and B. Schneider (eds.), *Peer Relationships in Cultural Context.* New York: Cambridge University Press, pp. 452-478.

Sharabany, R. (1982). 'Comradeship: Peer group relations among preadolescents in Kibbutz versus City', *Personality and Social Psychology Bulletin,* 8(2): 302–9.

Simpkins, S.D. and Parke, R.D. (2001) 'The relations between parental friendships and children's friendships: Self-report and observational analysis', *Child Development,* 72(2): 569–82.

Siperstein, G.N. and Gale, M.E. (1983, April) 'Improving peer relationships of rejected children'. Paper presented at the biennial meeting of the Society for Research in Child Development, Detroit.

Stevens, E.A. and Prinstein, M.J. (2005) 'Peer contagion of depressogenic attributional styles among adolescents: A longitudinal study', *Journal of Abnormal Child Psychology,* 33(1): 25–37.

Sullivan, H.S. (1953) *The Interpersonal Theory of Psychiatry.* New York, NY: W.W. Norton.

Swenson, L.P. and Rose, A.J. (2009) 'Friends' knowledge of externalizing and externalizing adjustment: Accuracy, bias and the influences of gender, grade, positive friendship quality, and self-disclosure', *Journal of Abnormal Child Psychology,* 37(6): 887–901.

Triandis, H.C. (1995) *Individualism and Collectivism.* Boulder, CO: Westview Press.

Triandis, H.C., Bontempo, R., Villareal, M.J., Asai, M. and Lucca, N. (1988) 'Individualism and collectivism: Cross-cultural perspectives on self-ingroup relationships', *Journal of Personality and Social Psychology,* 54(2): 323–38.

Underwood, M.K. and Buhrmester, D. (2007) 'Friendship features and social exclusion: An observational study examining gender and social context', *Merrill-Palmer Quarterly,* 53(3): 412–38.

Underwood, M.K., Scott, B.L., Galperin, M.B., Bjornstad, G.J. and Sexton, A.M. (2004) 'An observational study of social exclusion under varied conditions: Gender and developmental differences', *Child Development,* 75(5): 1538–55.

Valkenburg, P. and Peter, J. (2007) 'Preadolescents' and adolescents' online communication and their closeness to friends', *Developmental Psychology,* 43(2): 267–77.

Vitaro, F., Brendgen, M. and Tremblay, R.E. (2000) 'Influence of deviant friends on delinquency: Searching for moderator variables', *Journal of Abnormal Child Psychology,* 28(4): 313–25.

Vitaro, F., Tremblay, R.E., Kerr, M., Pagani, L. and Bukowski, W.B. (1997) 'Disruptiveness, friends' characteristics, and delinquency in early adolescence: A test of two competing models of development', *Child Development,* 68(4): 676–89.

Way, N. (1998) *Everyday Courage: The Lives and Stories of Urban Teenagers.* New York, NY: University Press.

Way, N. (2006) 'The cultural practice of friendships among urban youth', in D. French, B. Schneider and X. Chen (eds.), *Friendships in Cultural Context.* New York: Cambridge University Press.

Way, N. and Chen, L. (2000) 'Close and general friendship patterns among African American, Latino, and Asian American adolescents from low-income families', *The Journal of Adolescent Research,* 15(2): 274–301.

Way, N., Gingold, R., Rotenberg, M. and Kuriakose, G. (2005) 'Close friendships among urban, ethnic-minority adolescents', in N. Way and J.V. Hamm (eds.), *Close friendships among adolescents. New Directions for Child and Adolescent Development (No. 107).* San Francisco: Jossey-Bass, pp. 41–59.

Weeks, M.S. and Asher, S.R. (2012) 'Loneliness in childhood: Toward the next generation of assessment and research', in J.B. Benson (ed.) *Advances in child development and behavior* (Vol. 42). San Diego: Academic Press, pp. 1–39.

Weisz, J.R., Chaiyasit, W., Weiss, B., Eastman, K.L. and Jackson, E.W. (1995) 'A multimethod study of problem behavior among Thai and American children in school: Teacher reports versus direct observations', *Child Development,* 66(2): 402–15.

Wentzel, K.R., Barry, C.M. and Caldwell, K. (2004) 'Friendships in middle school: Influences on motivation and school adjustment', *Journal of Educational Psychology,* 96(2): 195–203.

Wentzel, K.R. and Caldwell, K. (1997) 'Friendships, peer acceptance, and group membership: Relations to academic achievement in middle school', *Child Development,* 68(6): 1198–209.

Whitesell, N.R. and Harter, S. (1996) 'The interpersonal context of emotion: Anger with close friends and classmates', *Child Development,* 67(4): 1345–59.

Woods, S., Done, J. and Kalsi, H. (2009) 'Peer victimisation and internalising difficulties: The moderating role of friendship quality', *Journal of Adolescence,* 32(2): 293–308.

Zajac, R.J. and Hartup, W.W. (1997) 'Friends as coworkers: Research review and classroom implications', *The Elementary School Journal,* 98(1): 3–13.

Zarbatany, L., Hartmann, D.P. and Rankin, D. B. (1990) 'The psychological functions of preadolescent peer activities', *Child Development,* 61(4): 1067–80.

PART II

Population-Specific Issues in Child Research

11

Children in Exceptional Circumstances

Judith Cashmore

Children live in a vast range of different circumstances that are distinguished by their racial and cultural identity, their physical and social settings, and their own characteristics and experiences. As Frønes (1993: 1) pointed out, 'There is not one childhood, but many, formed at the intersection of different cultural, social and economic systems, natural and man-made physical environments'. The particular historical, cultural, and social context in which children live their lives means that they experience an enormous diversity of circumstances with a range of opportunities, risks, and resources. The chapters in this section of the handbook deal with some particular circumstances defined, but not limited by, children's ethnicity, sexuality, disabilities, and by particular experiences that include changes in their living circumstances (living away from their families or leaving their country or place of birth with or without their families as refugees or asylum-seekers), their behaviours (breaking the law), and their responses to being abused or bullied, and appearing as witnesses to crimes against them.

As the chapters in this handbook and this section indicate, much of the research on special populations of children and those in

exceptional circumstances is outcome-focused and concerned with measuring how those circumstances affect children's development and longer-term outcomes. The focus for much of this work has been on adverse outcomes and risk and resilience. There has been relatively little attention to children's and young people's perceptions of their circumstances and their experiences, though interest has been growing with the development of Childhood Studies. This has been marked by a respect for children as active constructors of their world and by interest in the diversity as well as the positive aspects of children's experiences and participation rather than just a focus on children's vulnerability.

The aim of this section is to understand the experiences of children and young people in a range of exceptional circumstances. This is important for several reasons. This understanding is first an end in itself – to understand how children experience and construct their world. Particular aspects of children's identities, such as their racial and ethnic background, their sexual identity and their disabilities, influence children's lived experiences, their day-to-day interactions, and the way children and young people see themselves and make meaning of their lives.

While children often have little control over the circumstances in which they find themselves, they are not powerless and they construct their own meanings and 'sub-contexts which most often remain invisible to adults but are most visible and salient to children' (Graue and Walsh, 1998: 12). As Goodnow states in Chapter 19 (this volume), children 'make active efforts at shaping the way events proceed, at constructing or reconstructing their own and others' perceptions of who they are, what they are like, what their past has been or what their possible futures might be'.

Secondly, it is useful in expanding our understanding of children's and young people's development. As Goodnow points out, the development of children in exceptional circumstances can tell us more about children's developmental pathways and the ways in which development is influenced 'by particular experiences and by social and cultural contexts'. Similarly, Masten, Best and Garmezy (1990: 440) pointed to the benefits of studying children's development in non-normative and challenging situations. These include gaining insight into 'the necessary and sufficient qualities of caregiving environments, the significant functions of parenting and other normative protective processes, the range and variation of human responses to challenge, the self-righting properties of development and constraints on those properties, and the linkages or independence among different aspects of cognitive, emotional, and social development'. While the focus here, and in much of the research, is on developmental outcomes and concerned with measuring the impact of children's circumstances on their development, children's experiences and their understanding of those experiences are powerful factors that drive their development (Lerner et al., 2006). Children's views about their experiences are also important indicators of how well they are faring. We know relatively little as yet about the level of congruence between so-called objective adult-instituted measures of children's outcomes and children's own views of how they are faring. To date, there has not been a systematic approach to including children's views about their experiences, and much of this research has been descriptive and not well integrated with outcomes-focused analyses. Until recently there has also been little attention to interdisciplinary approaches, which bring with them a variety of methodological and analytical approaches; this push has, however, been one of the driving forces in the growth of Childhood Studies. There are both theoretical and practical pay-offs from a more integrated approach.

Thirdly, understanding the experiences of children in various exceptional circumstances provides information that is useful in improving their circumstances, especially in relation to the way children are treated and involved in processes that can have a profound effect on their lives. Decision-making processes and interventions to assist children can benefit from an understanding and respect for children's experiences and constructions of their world. Indeed, the effectiveness of interventions intended to assist children may well depend upon it. As indicated earlier, children may have little control over the circumstances in which they find themselves, but their reactions to their circumstances and the way they are treated can influence the outcomes (Graue and Walsh, 1998). Children are not passive recipients of treatments and interventions. They can resist, influence and subvert adult decisions, as Alderson (Chapter 6, this volume) points out in relation to health-related decisions. Child witnesses can refuse to give evidence, children with physical and mental health problems can refuse to comply with treatment, and children in out-of-home care or living with one parent post parental separation may run away or 'act out' if they are unhappy with where they are living. Much of children's bad behaviour at school and elsewhere may also indicate a mismatch with what they are being offered in that setting and its acceptability to children.

Furthermore, Article 12 of the Convention on the Rights of the Child affords children the right to express their views freely and have those views taken into account in all matters affecting them, with their views 'being given due weight in accordance with their age and maturity'. This extends beyond the particular case of procedural rights in judicial and administrative and should include their right to participate – or not – in research that affects them. It is increasingly clear too that adults, even those quite close to children, cannot speak on children's behalf about their experiences, concerns, or wishes – and what they find acceptable or not. Protecting children from their involvement in decisions and processes that affect them (for example, in relation to their adoption or their living arrangements after their parents separate) risks leaving children vulnerable to the subjective interpretation of others (Mendenhall et al., 2004; Parkinson and Cashmore, 2008).

COMMON OBSTACLES IN THE EXPERIENCES OF CHILDREN IN EXCEPTIONAL CIRCUMSTANCES

Children in these exceptional circumstances face a range of social, emotional, and physical challenges in life. In some cases, these circumstances increase the likelihood of adverse outcomes in various areas of their lives or are assumed to do so. Some of these challenges children have in common; others are specific to their particular circumstances and to the particular transitions these children make in their lives. The common challenges involve developing and maintaining a sense of identity and belonging, and dealing with uncertainty, lack of information and control especially in relation to decision-making, as well as limited opportunities in relation to education and other social interactions. The more specific challenges include having to cope with trauma and the loss of loved ones and other personal relationships (abused and neglected children and those who have had to leave their countries as refugees and asylum-seekers), and having to adjust to unfamiliar

and possibly unfriendly environments (refugees, children in racial and ethnic minorities at school and in new neighbourhoods, and children who are detained in juvenile justice facilities). The following discussion outlines several of these challenges as well as perhaps the most important factor contributing to positive experiences and outcomes, the presence of caring and supportive relationships. These relationships are the key to children's developing sense of identity, competence and sense of belonging.

'Assigned' identity and stigma

All children and young people face the task of coming to grips with who they are, developing their identity and sense of self, and working out their own place in the world. This involves learning who they are like and not like, who is important to them, how they understand their background, and what they believe about a host of issues. As Grotevant (1997: 5) stated, the 'construct of identity stands at the interface of individual personality, social relationships, subjective awareness, and external context'. The 'construction' of identity therefore takes place against a complex back-drop which comprises children's cultural and historical context as well as their own genetic make-up and personality, gender, socio-economic status, family composition, and ethnic and racial background. All of these affect children's experiences of the world.

For some groups of children who differ from the mainstream cultural and social groupings in society, however, there are particular challenges in relation to their 'assigned' identity. While Grotevant (1997) pointed out that some aspects of identity such as gender, race, ethnicity, disability, and also adoptive status are assigned, children differ in the extent to which they accept or challenge this assignment. Accepting at a personal level one's disability does not, for example, preclude a child's fight against constructs of disability which overlook their competence. Some aspects, however, may require 'adjustment' to a 'dominant culture' that can be hostile, with particular difficulties such as lack of peer acceptance and reduced access to resources and opportunities. As Sloper and Beresford (Chapter 14, this volume) point out, children with disabilities 'across the globe ... are identified as, and also report, being more likely than their non-disabled peers to experience limited lives, poverty, marginalisation and exclusion'. Immigrant and refugee children face the task of learning the culture of their new community and finding their place within their peer group at school and in their neighbourhood while developing and maintaining their own identity. This assumes particular importance for children who are unaccompanied minors without the support of their family and a sense of belonging.

Perhaps the most difficult aspect for children and youth who are marked out from their peers is their experience of 'feeling different' and being treated differently, both by their peers and by adults. Children are generally finely attuned to differential treatment, and well aware once they are conscious of racial, ethnic, and socioeconomic status of the differences between themselves and others, including, for example, who they can play with and visit (Weinger, 2000). Children can, however, assert and redefine their cultural identity as they grow older and as the context changes. Rumbaut (2005: 158–9) provided various examples of children and young people whose asserted identities evolved over time with changing experiences and information; in one case, 'Joseph' identified as Chinese when he was young because his family spoke Cantonese at home, but then identified as Vietnamese 'when he found out that he was born in Vietnam' and then later as Chinese Vietnamese, and then as Asian American.

When assigned 'status' is less easy to change or redefine and it marks them out in negative ways, children and young people commonly report discomfort and unhappiness about being stereotyped and stigmatized and treated differently. Indeed, some children in out-of-home care report not telling their peers and not wanting anyone at school to know they are in care so that they can avoid being labelled as such and subjected to differential treatment (Unrau, Seita, and Putney, 2008). Similarly, as Patterson (see Chapter 13, this volume) points out, 'many sexual minority youth hesitate to disclose non-heterosexual identities' because of their concerns about rejection by family members and friends. Where their 'identity' becomes known, sexual minority youths, children in out-of-home care and adolescents with mental health problems commonly report harassment, bullying and social exclusion at school and in their community (Moses, 2010). In the absence of positive support and intervention, such difficulties are often the precursors of children and young people becoming aggressive or withdrawn, disengaging from school and failing academically.

Dealing with uncertainty, lack of information, and lack of control

Children and young people making the transition to a new environment such as a new school, neighborhood, or country face a number of challenges that include learning the rules at play there, the language, what is acceptable behaviour, and who 'belongs' there. Where the new environment is potentially unfriendly and even hostile, as it can be for those in ethnic, racial, or sexual minorities, and in residential or juvenile detention centers, the demands are acute. These demands are often exacted as much or more by children's peers as by the adults involved.

For some children – child witnesses, juvenile defendants, and unaccompanied asylum-seeking children – the demands are more formal and involve meeting the expectations of legal and bureaucratic systems. Most children, like some adults, have quite limited understanding of these decision-making processes, so they feel vulnerable to the associated uncertainties. The language may be intimidating and almost incomprehensible with specific and unfamiliar terminology that is delivered in stressful circumstances in relation to traumatic or difficult events. As Goodman et al. (Chapter 16, this volume) and others have pointed out, child witnesses report that the most stressful aspects of giving evidence in court in common law countries include being cross-examined in court and asked complex questions about embarrassing and distressing events (Goodman et al., 1992; Plotnikoff and Woolfson, 2004; Saywitz and Nathanson, 1993; Spencer and Flin, 1993). For child witnesses, juvenile defendants, and refugees, there is also the added concern about whether the 'story' they tell will be believed and how it will be responded to. The consequences of disbelief respectively include an unfavorable verdict and continuing uncertainty or rejection of their claims for protection and refugee status.

Coping with the uncertainty is not made any easier by delays, especially as perceived by anxious children. Matters generally take some time to come before a court and for decisions to be made, and as Goodnow points out, decisions about refugee status are hard to predict and may take considerable time. There is little, if anything, children can do to affect the time scales and indeed they have little control and little knowledge about how to affect the decision-making processes. Anxiety about these processes is also likely to be exacerbated by previous exposure to fearful situations, personal loss, and distrust of adults and those in authority, to be expected among children who have been maltreated or have had to leave their country of origin because of safety concerns. In one study that asked those who had been in out-of-home care as children about their experiences of placement changes, one of the key themes concerned 'not knowing' and the 'loss of power over personal destiny', with little or no forewarning of the changes ahead (Unrau et al., 2008).

Importance of relationships and support

Children's relationships with others, and particularly with caring adults, comprise the most important aspect of children's environments and their lived experiences. As more is being learnt about brain development, the significant role that human relationships play as the 'building blocks of healthy development' is becoming clearer (Collins and Laursen, 1999; Shonkoff and Phillips, 2000). As the National Scientific Council on the Developing Child (2004: 2) stated:

> [R]elationships are the 'active ingredients' of the environment's influence on healthy human development. They incorporate the qualities that best promote competence and well-being – individualized responsiveness, mutual action-and-interaction, and an emotional connection to another human being ... Relationships engage children in the human community in ways that help them define who they are, what they can become, and how and why they are important to other people.
>
> (Working paper 1: 1)

In helping to define children's social reality and their constructions of the world around them, parents and other trusted adults and friends (including peers) provide information, opportunities to learn how to behave, and connections to other resources as well as opportunities to 'participate' in the broad sense of the word (Percy-Smith and Thomas, 2010). Relationships are also the primary place in which children's sense of identity is recognized and respected. Similarly, Garbarino (1993: 4) referred to 'opportunities for development' as 'relationships in which children find material, emotional, and social encouragement compatible with their needs and capacities as they exist at a specific point in their developing lives. For each child, the best fit must be worked out through experience, within some very broad guidelines of basic human needs, and then renegotiated as development proceeds and situations change'. In relation to the way children learn to deal with racial discrimination, Johnson

(2005: 89), for example, outlined the 'mix of intentional and unintentional messages, parental practices, child-rearing behaviors and other interactions at school and in the community' that communicate to African-American children 'how they are to perceive, process and respond to discrimination'. But as Johnson pointed out, children bring their own interpretations to bear on their circumstances, and their perceptions of the safety and quality of their neighborhood and community influence their choices and the way they respond to risky situations and perceived discrimination.

For some children, however, and particularly those who have been abused and neglected or have had to leave their country of origin for reasons of safety, particularly as unaccompanied child refugees, trusted and supportive relationships may be absent or in short supply, at least for some periods in their lives. These children may be very reluctant to disclose what has happened to them, particularly if they distrust adults and those in positions of authority. This of course makes adult-directed external efforts to assist these children very difficult and street children in Western and non-Western countries, for example, often actively resist adult intervention, relying instead on peer relationships (Cashmore, Chapter 18, this volume). This is also an indication that these children and young people are keen to define their own identity and not accept representations of themselves as traumatized or vulnerable. As others have pointed out, such representations can undermine their coping strategies and are often a disservice to children and young people (Dawes, 2000; Ennew, 1994).

ETHICAL AND METHODOLOGICAL ISSUES

One of the key issues in relation to special populations of children concerns their accessibility – both in terms of researchers being able to gain direct access to these children, and having the appropriate methodologies or techniques to engage them. The first concerns ethical issues and the second concerns methodology.

Ethical issues

One of the primary difficulties for researchers wanting to conduct research concerned with children's experiences is gaining access to children to seek their consent to participate in the research. The first step, after obtaining the approval of an appropriate ethical body, is to gain the interest and consent of those who care for and have legal responsibility for the children involved, and control access to them. For children in special circumstances, this is often complicated because of the number of adults involved, their overlapping responsibilities, and because of their concerns about the impact of the research on the children and its perceived value.[1] Access to some special populations of children such as sexual minority children and those who may have been abused or neglected or exposed to family violence may be mediated via educational and other settings. Children with disabilities, with mental health problems, and those in out-of-home care and in juvenile detention centers are generally 'protected' from contact by researchers and others by their carers, legal guardians and parents, and medical or other staff members. Those in authority in these settings can provide or deny access to researchers who wish to conduct research with the children and young people there.

There is, of course, a range of reasons that adults, both within and outside the family, may not allow access to children in their care. Apart from the potential inconvenience and extra work for the adults involved, there tend to be three main concerns. The first is that involving children in research, especially about sensitive issues, may upset or 'destabilize' already 'vulnerable' children. This is a relatively common response in relation to children in out-of-home care or residential care, especially if they have already been subjected to various interventions and changes in their lives (Gilbertson and Barber, 2002; Murray, 2005). It is also understandably a concern for child witnesses in sexual assault and other matters who have often undergone a number of investigative and other preparatory interviews with unknown adults about sensitive material.

While concern for the best interests of the child is quite proper and justifiable, the problem is that the decisions of these gate-keepers may, on the one hand 'silence and exclude' children who would wish to partici-pate in such research and, on the other, coerce children to participate when institu-tional approval is given (Alderson, 2004; Cashmore, 2006; Heath et al., 2007).[2] Several studies have indicated that children may be more willing to participate and less disturbed by their involvement in research than might be expected (Murray, 2005; Priebe, Bäckström, and Ainsaarc, 2010). In a recent Swedish study, for example, Priebe et al. (2010: 438) reported that adolescents and even 'vulnerable subgroups such as sexually abused or sexually inexperienced adolescents' showed little discomfort in answering questions about their sexuality and sexual abuse. Veale (2005) also provided the example of children in rural Rwanda engaged in a social mapping exercise who took a different view from the facilitators about the value of the exercise and whether they should stop when some children became upset. For them, the value was the revelation of their shared experience, with therapeutic aspects beyond the research. On the other hand, it is clear that some children may be quite reluctant to talk about traumatic events and not wish to engage, as Goodnow outlines in relation to refugee children. The issue is respect for the diversity of individual experience and for the agency and dignity of children to determine whether and how they wish to be involved (Fitzgerald et al., 2010; Melton, 1991). This means coming to a new understanding of children's vulnerability as able to sit along-side, rather than preclude children's agency (Graham and Fitzgerald, 2010). Protection and participation are not mutually exclusive.

The second reason that adults involved with children deny consent for them to be approached concerning their research participation is that the children are presumed to be not competent on the basis of their age or 'capacity', either to provide informed consent or to engage with the research (Baker, 2005; Gilbertson and Barber, 2002; Graham and Fitzgerald, 2010; Melton and Stanley, 1996; Thomas and O'Kane, 1998). Heath et al. (2007) outline examples of children, including one child with a severe disability, being 'deemed unable to express a view on their participation' but subsequently or in other ways indicating their wish to do so. In relation to children with disabilities, Sloper and Beresford state in Chapter 14 (this volume) that 'Researchers commonly report being told that children cannot partici-pate, can't communicate, that they won't get anything out of a child (for example, Morris, 2003)'. They go on to advise that they have found it 'useful to explain in detail to gate-keepers about methods that will be used to facilitate communication, showing them any pictures or symbols that will be used, and also reassuring them that the researcher can be flexible in adapting to the child's own means of communication, and will be sensi-tive to any indication that the child is not happy about taking part'.

The third though rarely articulated reason that parents, carers, and legal guardians may refuse consent for children to participate in research is to protect the privacy of the family or to prevent children from revealing problems within the family or institution – in effect, to censor or control the expression of children's views. This is a significant issue in research concerning family violence and child abuse, or other unsafe or illegal behaviours. Children's 'self-reports' about their experience of abuse, family violence, and their involvement in substance use and criminal activity, for example, are important, however, because they provide different and possibly more accurate estimates of the prevalence of these behaviours, which are intended to be 'private' and below the radar of the authorities.[3] Hearing and understanding the perceptions and experiences of children and young people is therefore important in shaping policy and practice in these areas (Cashmore, 2006).

A primary concern therefore about the role that gatekeepers play in allowing or denying access to children for research purposes is that such 'selection practices' can compromise the representativeness of the sample and the validity of the findings (Cashmore, 2006: 970). A related and key concern is that making decisions without consulting children denies them a voice (Christiansen and Prout, 2002). It makes assumptions about children's vulnerability and it excludes their perspectives – perspectives which cannot be assumed to align with those of the adults who might otherwise be making decisions about their lives (Boyden, 2003; Percy-Smith and Thomas, 2010). It excludes children, particularly the most vulnerable and those already marginalized, and is arguably in contravention of their right under Article 12 of the Convention on the Rights of the Child to express their views on matters that affect them. Furthermore, the risks of failing to hear the perspectives of children and young people outside their 'institutional base' have been demonstrated repeatedly by the failures to act in relation to institutional and systems abuse (Utting, 1997) and the treatment of refugee and traveller children in various countries.

Methodological issues

Once children are permitted to be involved in research and agree to do so, researchers need to be able to engage children in the research process and to use appropriate and reliable means of gaining insight into their views and lived experience. This applies to all research with children, as Weller, Hobbs and Goodman have outlined (Chapter 20, this volume), but the need is more acute for children in special populations or whose circumstances are exceptional. The particular considerations for these children concern their willingness to disclose information about their experiences, their need for privacy, and for techniques that engage their interest and demonstrate their capacities.

One of the benefits of the development of Childhood Studies, and its focus on children's competence and participation, is the expansion of the range of techniques for engaging with children that may have particular benefits for children in exceptional circumstances. These include qualitative techniques such as story-games, narratives, ethnographic and other observational tools, and more participatory approaches that allow some insight into children's behaviours, activities, and contexts (Evans, 2012; Greene and Hogan, 2005). Other techniques include the use of photostories, models, drawings, and computer-assisted or interactive 'games' which allow children to communicate their experience and view of the world both verbally and non-verbally (Eldén, 2013). As Sloper and Beresford (Chapter 14, this volume) point out, visual techniques such as the use of photographs, drawing, puppets, and symbol forms of communication can also be appropriate and effective for disabled children.[4] Drawing and computer-assisted games can also break down the barriers and assist younger children and those who are reluctant to talk or prefer to avoid face-to-face interactions. Some computer-assisted techniques can also be helpful in this regard and can provide a stronger sense of privacy by allowing children and young people to respond without having to verbalize their comments and risk others overhearing them (Dodds et al., 2010). On-line surveys on appropriate child-friendly and youth-appropriate websites can also provide for anonymity and privacy on sensitive issues and help overcome some of the accessibility issues for hard-to-reach youth (Cashmore et al., 2010; Curtis et al., 2004). Veale (2005) and others have used a range of such techniques successfully with rural children and street-children in non-Western cultures, including children who have experienced the devastating effects of political violence, genocide, and HIV.

DESIGN AND PARTICIPATORY APPROACHES

Beyond deciding what tools are useful and meaningful in research with children and young people, the emerging and increasingly important issue is how to engage children and young people in active participation in determining both the focus of the research and the research process. Researchers in the Childhood Studies field and elsewhere are increasingly challenging the representation of children as passive participants and 'objects' to be studied rather than citizens and active participants who have some control over the way they are 'researched' and represented. As Veale (2005) pointed out, 'participatory approaches' are more concerned with 'knowledge production than knowledge gathering' and aim to be respectful of children's involvement in the process. Although there is some development of participatory approaches and creative methods that assist in this process, we still have some way to go in designing research that provides for active participation by the children and young people involved – 'participation that may strengthen their capacity to shape or to cope with the situations they encounter' (Goodnow, Chapter 19, this volume, citing Cairns and Dawes, 1996). We also have some way to go in designing studies and developing the analyses to allow us to examine the linkages between the various family, neighbourhood, and community contexts of children's lives and the way in which they interact in the life experiences of children.

NOTES

1 The possible exception here is children who are homeless or living on the streets and for whom there are no obvious or contactable adults who can make such a decision. This independence from adults therefore increases the ethical responsibility of the researcher and any ethical overseeing body to ensure that these children's best interests are foremost in the research process. This includes consideration of the cost–benefits of the research for those involved.

As Garbarino (1993: 3) pointed out, the agenda and ethical responsibility for such research 'must derive not just from the personal interests of researchers but from the needs of children, parents, and teachers for information and from questions asked by and of social policy'.

2 Heath et al. (2007) have sounded a note of caution to researchers concerning the risk that 'blanket' institutional approval for access to children and young people may effectively deny them any real choice because their participation is assumed.

3 Where children disclose maltreatment or risks to their safety and health in research studies, researchers generally have a legal or ethical obligation to report this to the relevant statutory authority (Fisher et al., 2005).

4 Sloper and Beresford in Chapter 14, this volume, have outlined the various techniques and issues concerned with research with children with disabilities especially those with communication impairments and they are not repeated here.

REFERENCES

Alderson, P. (2004) 'Ethics', in S. Fraser, V. Lewis, S. Ding, M. Kellett, and C. Robinson (eds.), *Doing Research with Children and Young People*. London: Sage, pp. 97–112.

Baker, H. (2005) 'Involving children and young people in research on domestic violence and housing', *Journal of Social Welfare and Family Law*, 27(3): 281–97.

Boyden, J. (2003) 'Children under fire: Challenging assumptions about children's resilience', *Children, Youth and Environments* 13(1). Available at http://colorado.edu/journals/cye

Bronfenbrenner, U. (1979) *The Ecology of Human Development*. Cambridge, MA: Harvard University Press.

Cashmore, J. (2006) 'Ethical issues concerning consent in obtaining children's reports on their experience of violence', *Child Abuse & Neglect*, 30(9): 969–77.

Cashmore, J., Parkinson, P., Weston, R., Patulny, R., Redmond, G., Qu, L., Baxter, J., Rajkovic, M., Sitek, T. and Katz, I. (2010) *Shared Care Parenting Arrangements since the 2006 Family Law Reforms: Report to the Australian Government Attorney-General's Department*. Sydney; Social Policy Research Centre, University of New South Wales.

Christiansen, P. and Prout, A. (2002) 'Working with ethical symmetry in social research with children', *Childhood*, 9(4): 477–97.

Collins, W.A. and Laursen, B. (1999) 'Relationships as developmental contexts', *The Minnesota Symposia on Child Psychology, Vol. 30*. Mahwah, NJ: Erlbaum.

Curtis, K., Roberts, H., Copperman, J., Downie, A. and Liabo, K. (2004) '"How come I don't get asked no questions?" Researching "hard to reach" children and teenagers', *Child and Family Social Work*, 9(2): 167–75.

Dawes, A. 2000. *Cultural Diversity and Childhood Adversity: Implications for Community Level Interventions with Children in Difficult Circumstances.* Plenary address to the Children in Adversity Consultation, Refugee Studies Centre, University of Oxford, UK. http://www.childreninadversity.org/ Document Centre.html

Dodds, A.E., Lawrence, J.A., Karantzas, K., Brooker, A., Lin Y.H., Champness, V. and Albert, N. (2010) 'Children of Somali refugees in Australian schools: Self-descriptions of school-related skills and needs', *International Journal of Behavioral Development.* DOI: 10.1177/0165025409365801.

Eldén, S. (2013) 'Inviting the messy: Drawing methods and '"children's voices"', *Childhood*, 20(1): 66–81.

Ennew, J. (1994) 'Parentless friends: A cross-cultural examination of networks among street children and youth', in F. Nestmann and K. Husselmann (eds.), *Social Networks and Social Supports in Childhood and Adolescence.* Berlin: De Gruyter, pp. 409–26.

Evans, R. (2012) 'Towards a creative synthesis of participant observation and participatory research: Reflections on doing research *with* and *on* young Bhutanese refugees in Nepal', *Childhood*, 20(2): 169–84.

Fisher, C.B., Higgins-D'Alessandro, A., Rau, J.M.B., Kuther, T.L. and Belanger, S. (1996) 'Referring and reporting research participants at risk: Views from urban adolescents', *Child Development*, 67(5): 2086–100.

Fitzgerald, R., Graham, A., Smith, A.B. and Taylor, N. (2010) 'Children's participation as a struggle over recognition', in B. Percy-Smith and N. Thomas (eds.), *A Handbook of Children's Participation: Perspectives from Theory and Practice.* New York: Routledge, pp. 293–305.

Frønes, I. (1993) 'Changing childhood', *Childhood*, 1(1): 1–2.

Garbarino, J. (1993) 'Childhood: What do we need to know?', *Childhood*, 1(1): 3–10.

Gilbertson, R. and Barber, J.G. (2002) 'Obstacles to involving children and young people in foster care research', *Child and Family Social Work*, 7(4): 253–58.

Goodman, G.S., Taub, E.P., Jones, P.P., England, P., Port, L.K. and Prado, L. (1992) 'Testifying in criminal court: Emotional effects on child sexual assault victims', *Monographs of the Society for Research in Child Development*, vol. 57, no. 5, Serial No. 229.

Graham, A. and Fitzgerald, R. (2010) 'Children's participation in research: Some possibilities and constraints in the current Australian research environment', *Journal of Sociology*, 46(2): 133–47.

Graue, M.E. and Walsh, D.J. (1998) *Studying Children in Context: Theories, Methods & Ethics.* Thousand Oaks, CA: Sage.

Greene, S. and Hogan, D. (2005) *Researching Children's Experiences.* London: Sage.

Grotevant, H.D. (1997) 'Coming to terms with adoption: The construction of identity from adolescence into adulthood', *Adoption Quarterly*, 1(1): 3–27.

Heath, S., Charles, V., Crow, G. and Wiles, R. (2007) 'Informed consent, gatekeepers and go-betweens: Negotiating consent in child and youth-orientated institutions', *British Educational Research Journal*, 33(3): 403–17.

Johnson, D. (2005) 'The ecology of children's racial coping: Family, school, and community influences', in T.S. Weisner (ed.), *Discovering Successful Pathways in Children's Development: Mixed Methods in the Study of Childhood and Family Life.* Chicago: University of Chicago Press, pp. 87–109.

Lerner, R.M., Lerner, J.V., Almerigi, J. and Theokas, C. (2006) 'Dynamics of individual ←→ context relations in human development: A developmental systems perspective', in M. Hersen and J.C. Thomas (eds.), *Comprehensive Handbook of Personality and Psychopathology: Volume 1. Personality and everyday functioning.* Hoboken, NJ: Wiley, pp. 23–43.

Masten, A.S., Best, K.M. and Garmezy, N. (1990) 'Resilience and development: Contributions from the study of children who overcome adversity', *Development and Psychopathology*, 2(4): 425–44.

Melton, G.B. (1991) 'Preserving the dignity of children around the world: The U.N. Convention on the Rights of the Child', *Child Abuse & Neglect*, 15(4): 343–50.

Melton, G.B. and Stanley, B.H. (1996) 'Research involving special populations', in B.H. Stanley, J.E. Sieber and G.B. Melton (eds.), *Research Ethics: A Psychological Approach.* Lincoln: University of Nebraska Press, pp. 177–202.

Mendenhall, T.J., Berge, J.M., Wrobel, G.M., Grotevant, H.D. and McRoy, R.G. (2004) 'Adolescents' satisfaction with contact in adoption', *Child and Adolescent Social Work Journal*, 21(2): 175–90.

Morris, J. (2003) 'Including all children: finding out about the experiences of children with communication and/ or cognitive impairments', *Children and Society*, 17(5): 337–48.

Moses, T. (2010) 'Being treated differently: Stigma experiences with family, peers, and school staff among adolescents with mental health disorders', *Social Science & Medicine*, 70(7): 985–93.

Murray, C. (2005) 'Children and young people's participation and non-participation in research', *Adoption & Fostering*, 29(1): 57–66.

National Scientific Council on the Developing Child (2004) *Young children develop in an environment of relationships,* Working Paper #1. Available at http://www.developingchild.net

Parkinson, P. and Cashmore, J. (2008) *The Voice of a Child in Family Law Dispute.* Oxford: Oxford University Press.

Percy-Smith, B. and Thomas, N. (eds.), (2010) *A Handbook of Children's Participation: Perspectives from Theory and Practice.* New York: Routledge.

Plotnikoff, J. and Woolfson, R. (2004) *In Their Own Words: The Experiences of 50 Young Witnesses in Criminal Proceedings.* London: National Society for the Prevention of Cruelty to Children.

Priebe, G., Bäckström, M. and Ainsaarc, M. (2010) 'Vulnerable adolescent participants' experience in surveys on sexuality and sexual abuse: Ethical aspects', *Child Abuse & Neglect*, 34(6): 438–47.

Rumbaut, R.G. (2005) 'Sites of belonging: Acculturation, discrimination, and ethnic identity among children of immigrants', in T.S. Weisner (ed.), *Discovering Successful Pathways in Children's Development: Mixed Methods in the Study of Childhood and Family Life.* Chicago: University of Chicago Press, pp. 111–64.

Saywitz, K. and Nathanson, R. (1993) 'Children's testimony and their perceptions of stress in and out of the courtroom', *Child Abuse and Neglect*, 17(5): 613–22.

Shonkoff, J.P. and Phillips, D.A. (2000) (eds.) *From Neurons to Neighborhoods: The Science of Early Childhood Development.* Committee on Integrating the Science of Early Childhood Development. Washington, DC: National Academy Press.

Spencer, J.R. and Flin, R.H. (1993) *The Evidence of Children: The Law and the Psychology* (2nd edn). London: Blackstone.

Thomas, N. and O'Kane, C. (1998) 'The ethics of participatory research with children', *Children & Society*, 12(5): 336–48.

Unrau, Y.A., Seita, J.R. and Putney, K.S. (2008) 'Former foster youth remember multiple placement moves: A journey of loss and hope', *Children and Youth Services Review*, 30(11): 1256–66.

Utting, W. (1997) *People Like Us: The Report of the Review for Safeguards for Children Living Away from Home.* Department of Health/Welsh Office. London: The Stationery Office.

Veale, A. (2005) 'Creative methodologies in participatory research with children', in S. Greene and D. Hogan (eds.), *Researching Children's Experiences.* London: Sage, pp. 253–72.

Weinger, S. (2000) 'Economic status: Middle class and poor children's views', *Children & Society*, 14(2): 135–46.

Williamson, E., Goodenough, T., Kent, J. and Ashcroft, A. (2005) 'Conducting research with children: The limits of confidentiality and child protection protocols', *Children & Society*, 19: 397–409.

12

Research on Ethnic Minority Children: A Tale of Risk and Resilience

Oscar Barbarin, Emma Sterrett and Dari Jigjidsuren

INTRODUCTION

Two striking conclusions emerge from surveying research on minority children. First, many minority children encounter a range of social and material challenges in life that adversely affect development in multiple domains of their lives. Consequently, minority children are at risk for a wide range of developmental difficulties that augur poorly for their future. Second, although children around the world classified as minority are diverse in language, culture, national origin, and material circumstances, they are strikingly similar in the obstacles they encounter and the developmental outcomes they experience relative to the majority populations in their countries. This chapter describes the developmental outcomes often observed among minority children, with a focus on a specific group: children of African descent in the United States. Although the research literature on African-American children encompasses such interesting and important topics as health, acculturation, ethnic identity, self-concept, risky behaviors, and peer relations, this review will concentrate on two specific domains where the effect of minority status is most significant: education and mental health.

We begin by looking at the well-being of minority children outside the United States. We draw broader inferences about how possessing minority group status often puts children at risk for a range of adverse psycho-social outcomes. We then describe social processes at home, at school, and in communities that have been advanced to account for these academic and socio-emotional outcomes. We conclude by exploring the ways in which some children deal and cope with adversity associated with minority status to avoid its negative consequences. In this way, we explore the role of protective factors and resilience in an attempt to account for unexpectedly positive outcomes that accrue to many of the children growing up under conditions of great hardship and risk.

SOME EXAMPLES OUTSIDE THE UNITED STATES

Overview

A defining feature of any society is how well and how generously it responds to the needs of its most vulnerable members, most notably, children. In many cases, it is the children of the minority groups who represent the neediest of the needy. Ethnic-minority status is defined in terms that go beyond race and physical characteristics. Transcendent indicators of minority status are social exclusion and social denigration, in which negative stereotypes and stigma are associated with religion, language, caste, national background, etc. In this way, we would include under the rubric of minorities groups who consider themselves excluded from the mainstream even though they share in – or even have a disproportionately large share of – a society's wealth, such as French Canadians, Indian Sikhs, or Israeli Christians. Consequently, the term *minority* has been applied to a very diverse group of people. Included among them are, for example, the indigenous peoples in North, Central, and South America and Australia, the Hui and Miao people of China, Catholics in Northern Ireland and Iraq, immigrants from former colonies living in Western Europe, the Romani (otherwise referred to as 'travellers' or Gypsies) in Eastern Europe and the Balkans, Turks in Germany, the Tamil in Sri Lanka, and African-Americans, Muslims and Latinos in the United States.

Mongolia

Although these ethnic minority groups are diverse in so many ways, they do share some common features when they are compared with their respective majority populations. Take, for example, the Kazakh people in Mongolia. Kazakhs constitute the largest ethnic minority group (N = 102,000) in Mongolia where the population is under 3 million (National Statistical Office of Mongolia, 2010). The vast majority of Kazakhs reside in the far western Bayan-Olgii province; others are concentrated around mining villages and towns. Kazakh religion, language and culture are very distinct from the Mongolian majority. Kazakhs are the only Muslims in the nation where 90 per cent are Buddhists. They speak Kazakh, a Turkic language primarily used by ethnic minorities in Kazakhstan, Russia and China. Their traditional script, Arabic, has extremely limited use in Mongolia where Cyrillic has been the official script since the late 1940s.

As a group, Kazakhs perform poorly on many socio-economic indicators, including health; but the scarce information collected by Mongolian agencies frequently does not specify ethnicity. It is known, however, that the incidence of poverty is significantly higher, about 49 per cent by national standards (National Statistical Office of Mongolia, 2010) for the majority living in the western region. Also, the percentage of illiterate people among Kazakhs is 1.5 times higher than that of the Mongolian majority. Kazakh women are less literate than their male counterparts, which sharply contrasts the situation for the majority. Educational attainment is highly valued by Mongolian women; indeed, there is an unusual reverse gender gap in education, with Mongolian men less educated than women.

Kazakhs account for 5 per cent of all children under the age of 14, but many Kazakh children are disadvantaged from early years. Fewer Kazakh children attend formal preschool – less than two-thirds of the national average, which is the lowest preschool participation rate in the country (Huang, 2005). As a result, many children in Bayan-Olgii start school ill-prepared or start school much later than others (Mongolian Ministry of Education, 2013); Kazakh children for years have known to be the most likely candidates for dropping out of school compared to their peers in other regions (Huang, 2005). For instance, in the academic year 2012–2013, over 35 per cent of all school drop outs in the nation resided in Bayan-Olgii aimag (Mongolian Ministry of Education, 2013). Poverty and no apparent reason are cited as major causes for leaving school early .

Research shows, however, that there may be other factors contributing to the ethnic disparity in dropout rate (Huang, 2005). The Mongolian Constitution and Education Law recognize the right to learn in native languages, and a number of schools provide instructions in Kazakh. Therefore, Kazakh children starting formal education may choose between Mongolian and Kazakh schools, and having educational instruction in their native language, at least during primary education (Barcus & Werner, 2007). However, low quality of teaching, lack of adequate educational materials in the Kazakh language and the inability of the few existing materials to meet the requirements of the national curriculum make this choice less favorable (UNESCO, 2008). Besides, because of low quality of language instruction, by the sixth or ninth grade when the students transition into full Mongolian instruction, many Kazakh students have not mastered proficiency in either language. In fact, many students continue needing extra support until they graduate. Therefore, they have limited chances for continuing into higher education (available only in Mongolian) or pursuing other career options. For those who choose to attend a Mongolian school, the situation presents different, no less complicated challenges (Huang, 2005). First, these children forgo their right to learn their native language as Kazakh is not offered as a subject, and most of the teaching in Mongolian schools has little or no relevance to Kazakh culture. Besides, Kazakh children experience bullying from peers and Mongolian teachers who may even refuse to accept them into school because of purported lack of language and slow learning. Although many Mongolian teachers recognize the hardworking nature of Kazakh children, they neither want to be burdened by teaching children a second language, nor are they trained or equipped to do so. Therefore, education in a monolingual Mongolian society remains a major challenge for minority Kazakh children and their families.

Estonia

The situation is slightly different for the Russian minority in Estonia. Their minority status has been acquired unexpectedly as a result of socio-political changes and dissolution of the Soviet Union. In fact, prior to that event, 25 million Russians who lived outside the borders of the Russian Federation were frequently viewed as elites in the republics where they resided, with privileges afforded by power, knowledge, and access to resources. In Estonia, one of the Baltic states that is considered highly developed and a 'westernized' part of the Soviet Union, the overall living standards were higher, living space per capita larger, life expectancy longer, and infant mortality lower than the average in the Soviet Union. Attracted by better life and opportunities, or as a result of political, industrial, and military appointments, many Russians moved to Estonia during Communist rule. (Estonia had a permanent presence of Soviet Army, with the largest of the posts concentrated in the border cities of Narva and Sillamae). According to Joeste et al., as cited in A. Park (1994), Russians were the second largest ethnic group after Estonians; Russians comprised 20 per cent of Estonia's population in 1959, 30 per cent in 1989, and 31.4 per cent in 2006.

During the Soviet occupation, Russians played an active role in the social, political, and industrial life of the country, and they were well represented in the bureaucracy and management. Though a minority in numbers, Russians accrued all the privileges of majority status thanks to the hegemony of Moscow. In the Communist era, Estonians prevailed in all organs of power, and 'decision-making positions in the party were always taken by Russians or completely Russianized Estonians, often born and raised in Russia' (Park, 1994: 75). The comprehensive cultural infrastructure of the USSR allowed the Russians to live comfortably anywhere in the country without having to learn the local language; Russian was recognized for official and unofficial business. Instead, Estonian natives were expected to speak Russian (Leino et al., 2006), and Estonian public schools taught Russian as another native language (Kemppainen et al., 2004).

The situation changed radically with the declaration of Estonian independence following the collapse of the Soviet Union in 1991. The abrupt transformation of the political context brought unwelcome changes for the Russian-speaking community and a diminution of their status. Shortly after proclaiming its independence, the Estonian government reversed the privileged position of Russians when they adopted a law granting citizenship only to those who had been citizens of the Republic of Estonia on 16 June 1940, and their descendants. The rest were reduced to the status of 'aliens' ('stateless persons and citizens of a foreign state regardless of the residence period in Estonia') (Park, 1994: 17). The immediate effect of the citizenship law was ineligibility of most ethnic Russian residents of Estonia to participate in the 1992 parliamentary elections, which resulted in the exclusively ethnic Estonian parliament. The government established a naturalization process that required passing a test on Estonian language and history. The language requirement became the major obstacle for obtaining citizenship for hundreds of thousands of ethnic Russians. A study cited by Park (1994: 74) found in 1992 that while 40 per cent of Russians were born in Estonia, fewer than 10 per cent of them could read, speak, and write fluently in Estonian, and 32 per cent did not understand Estonian at all. Most Russians were not ready to leave Estonia, although they were not ready to 'integrate into Estonian culture'. Those Russians who chose to return to Russia often found themselves in the situation of immigrants displaced from their homes and facing the hardships of re-settlement. Returning to their historic homeland was not smooth; others often perceived them as unwelcome strangers (Flynn, 2007).

Russians who remained in Estonia have become disadvantaged and socially marginalized in many aspects: political, economic, and cultural. Without citizenship, ethnic Russians could not own land or vote in national elections; the language requirement further inhibited their life, limiting opportunities for obtaining and sustaining employment. As part of the requirement of joining the EU, the Estonian government has developed a plan for the so-called 'cultural integration' of the Russian-speaking population both for adults and children. To become full Estonian citizens, Russian children are required to speak Estonian, and play and interact with Estonian children. Along with the 'soft integration' of Russian students into the Estonian society, the number of Russian schools decreased from 117 to 104 between 1994 and 2000 (Jubulis, 2003), and the number of bilingual schools has dropped by half. Children in Russian-speaking communities are offered immersion programs. The city of Narva offers a compelling view of the problem. There, 83 per cent of the residents are Russian, and only 3 per cent are Estonian. However, children in Narva attend the country's only immersion school where all subjects are required to be taught in the Estonian language. Russian parents accede to the situation and enroll their children in Estonian-language schools. However, many of those children do not become literate in either Russian or Estonian. The children in these immersion programs drop out of school at much higher rates than Estonian children. Moreover, as their knowledge of Russian culture and history remains modest, questions arise about the identity development of those children.

As dire as their situation may be, these Russian children have considerable advantages over their Kazakh peers in Mongolia who lack access to education, a rich pool of bilingual educational material, and qualified teachers with expertise of teaching bilingual children. Perhaps as a consequence of the difficulties they face, the Russian children who remain in school show signs of resilience and demonstrate strengths over their Estonian peers (Leino et al., 2006). For example, to overcome the obstacles in their way, the persistent Russian children have a better attitude about learning and spend more time on educational activities than do Estonian children. Also, Russian parents demonstrated four times more concern over unfinished school work of the child compared with Estonian parents. Leino et al. (2006) cited the Estonian Statistical Office report that in the analysis of academic success of school graduates, girls with Russian language instruction come at the top followed by girls who study in Estonian, followed by boys with Russian instruction and finally boys with Estonian instruction. Moreover, the trend has been the same for several decades. Researchers believe that Russian students' academic success and their high motivation are related to their need to cope with life in post-Communist society, which demands greater efforts from them than from Estonian children (Kreitzberg, 2002).

Preliminary conclusions

Both Kazakh children in Mongolia and Russian children in Estonia face discrimination and negative attitudes from others. In Estonia, more than two decades after independence and after many Russians have obtained citizenship, negative attitudes toward Russians remain strong. There is fear that Russians may threaten the Estonian independence (Barrington, Herron and Silver, 2003; Kruusvall, 2000) or dilute Estonian culture (Hallik, 2000). Many Estonians consider themselves as more civilized 'westerners' and they see Russians as part of the East, a nation with a cultural history that is significantly different from their own (Aalto, 2003).

Children are affected by the attitudes of adults. As an example, prejudice against minority children exists in both Mongolia and Estonia, but it takes different forms. Although Kazakh children, a minority group in Mongolia, are often rejected by teachers as slow learners and hard to teach, the popular notions among Estonians is that Russian children, a minority group in Estonia, even when young, are more obstreperous and boisterous than Estonian children. Russian children are seen as rougher than Estonian children. As a result of this belief, the ethnic ratio of Russian to Estonian children in kindergartens is limited to 1:5 (Chunn, 2002).

Ethnic minority status can take the form of a social category that has features of *sent* and *received* roles. The *sent* role involves a set of characteristics and expected behaviors attributed by others to an individual or group. Often these attributions are linked to observable features such as facial characteristics, skin color, language, or practices which play an important role in assigning individuals to a social group. They become the basis on which persons outside the group form their reactions and their social response to minority group members. Subtle and not so subtle messages are sent to minority group members by others defining who they are and the place to which they are relegated in the social order. Often these prejudicial messages are reinforced by discriminatory behavior by individuals, groups, and society institutions. These messages, policies, and institutional behaviors sanction minority group members and define who they are in society. These sanctions figure prominently in producing the adverse effects observed in education and mental health. The negative beliefs constitute a sent role that Russians can either adopt or reject. The *sent* role, or the reactions, beliefs, and behaviors of non-minority groups targeted to minority groups, are not the only sources defining minority group status. These messages from these external sources can be embraced or rejected. In this way, minority status is also experienced in terms of a *received* role consisting of the ways individuals or groups define themselves. Unobservable social psychological features such as a shared history, religion, culture, affiliations, a common experience of oppression, and shared world views play a role in what the group defines as part of its identity and how strongly individuals claim membership in a minority group.

ETHNIC MINORITY CHILDREN IN THE UNITED STATES

The last several decades have witnessed increasing diversity in the racial and ethnic composition of the American population. This trend marked by increases in the proportion of racial and ethnic minorities and a decline in the proportion of the White population was noted more than a decade ago by some as 'more dramatic than at any time in the 20th century' (McLoyd, 1998: 3). According to the Population Census records, between the years 2000 and 2010, the population of the United States increased by 27.3 million, but this growth is somewhat disproportionate across different racial and ethnic minority groups. By using race only estimates, non-Hispanic Whites, the largest racial group, had the lowest population growth rate of the all the racial groups – only 1.9 per cent compared with 12.3, 45.6, and 55.6 per cent of growth in the numbers of non-Hispanic black or African-American, Asian, and Hispanic/Latino populations respectively. As a result, the racial composition of the US population is rapidly changing.[1] The Census Bureau projects that Hispanic and Asian populations may triple in less than 40 years, while non-Hispanic Whites will drop to half in total population. It is projected that by 2050, the Hispanic-American population will reach 21.0 per cent; Asian-American, 7.8 per cent; and Black 13.0 per cent. The non-Hispanic White population is projected to drop to 46.3 per cent of the total population. Because minority groups have higher fertility rates, there is a higher proportion of children than adults in the minority population (McLoyd, 1998). In some states, minorities already form the majority of the child population (US Bureau of the Census, 2011). This growth may be explained by a number of factors, including the increased rates of immigration among minorities compared with non-Hispanic Whites and the higher rates of fertility among minority women (McLoyd, 1998).

AFRICAN-AMERICAN CHILDREN

In 2010, there were 10.6 million African-American children making up about 14 per cent of the American population under the age of 18 years. About 39 per cent of African-American children are living in poverty, compared with 13 per cent of European-American children (US Federal Interagency Forum on Child and Family Statistics, 2013). About 57 per cent of African-American children under the age of 18 were growing up in households with a single mother compared with 17 per cent of White children.

For many, ethnic-minority status has its costs. Indeed, cause for alarm about the status of ethnic-minority children can be found in almost every indicator of health and well-being. Minority children are at higher risk for emotional distress, have lower academic achievement, are less likely to complete school, but more likely to present behavioral problems, drop out of school, and engage in antisocial behaviors that may lead to delinquency, poverty, welfare dependence, drug abuse, and incarceration. For example, across the life span, African-American children are more susceptible to a host of life-threatening illnesses which severely diminish their life quality, if not life itself (Blake and Darling, 1994). Infant mortality rates for African-Americans are more than twice that of Whites and Latinos (Hogue and Vasquez, 2002). Over the life span, health problems abound. It is not surprising then that African Americans have a lower life expectancy. Between the ages of 15 and 30 years, mortality rates for young Black males are three times higher than among White males (Minino, Heron and Smith, 2004). Whereas the primary causes of death for White male youths are accidents and cardiovascular disease, homicide, and suicide are the primary and third leading causes of death, respectively, among African-American youths (Blum and Qureshi, 2011). High rates of unemployment and under-employment make life a struggle. Although academic achievement offers a gateway to economic mobility, many of the problems African Americans face related to employment and financial distress have their roots in the educational disadvantages and difficulties minority groups often experience.

Academic indicators

Low academic attainment

The education-related problems of African Americans are legion and have been well documented. African-American children lag behind their White counterparts in reading, writing, mathematics, and science as early as the third grade (Jencks and Phillips, 1998b; Vanneman, Hamilton, Baldwin Anderson and Rahman, 2009). This gap widens as children get older and progress through school but there is also evidence that the gap has narrowed since 1978 (Vanneman et al., 2009). African Americans generally have much lower grades and achievement test scores than Whites from the time they enter school through to high school and college graduation. African Americans are significantly underrepresented among children who are the highest achievers in reading, mathematics, science, and writing and are overrepresented among the lowest achievers in those areas. African- American students are also less likely to enter colleges and universities, complete their degrees, and gain access to graduate and professional training programs than their White counterparts (National Center for Education Statistics, 2012). As a consequence, African-Americans are heavily underrepresented among young adults who earn advanced degrees (Kewalrami et al., 2007).

It is becoming increasingly clear that difficulties related to academic achievement do not begin in high school or college but have their origins much earlier in life. All the available evidence points to the fact that academic difficulties originate in the early years of school. Even at the start of school, African-American children have fewer of the basic school-readiness competencies and knowledge than their peers (Brooks-Gunn, Klebanov and Duncan, 1996; Brooks-Gunn and Markman, 2005; Lee and Burkam, 2002; Magnuson and Waldfogel, 2005). Data on a national sample of beginning kindergarteners in 1998–99 and in 2011 show conclusively that African-American children start school already behind other groups of children with respect to emergent reading and mathematics skills (Mulligan, Hastedt and McCarroll, 2012; Xue and Meisels, 2004). These difficulties are reflected in early and persistent deficits in language and literacy. For example, many come to school with limited vocabularies, limited exposure to print, less ability to recognize letters or numbers, and poorer school readiness (Duncan et al., 2007; Snow, Burns and Griffin, 1998). These differences may arise from differential emphasis in African-American and White American homes on the development of specific skills and in their understanding of the skills children are expected to display by the time that they begin formal schooling. Thus African-American children may lag in the development of reading skills because they enter preschool with more limited vocabularies than European-American children (Farkas and Hibel, 2007). Moreover, the kindergarten and school experience as currently structured is not sufficient to make up the difference (Downey, von Hippel and Broh, 2004; Magnuson and Waldfogel, 2005).

These early differences are important because the gaps they create are never closed by education in elementary school. In fact, it is estimated that about half of the achievement gap observed in middle and high school can be accounted for by differences detected when African-American children are in kindergarten (Ferguson, 1998; Downey, von Hippel and Broh, 2004). These are based on mean differences; there are many exceptions to this pattern in which individual children grow academically and flourish during the later school years.

Findings regarding early deficits and differences in their predominance across racial and socioeconomic groups are important because evidence suggests that there is stability in children's literacy skills, with strong associations between children's skills at school entry and their skills as they progress through the early grades (Whitehurst and Lonigan, 1998; Duncan et al., 2007). In fact, children who enter school with reading deficits and who do not catch up within the first two years of school are at risk for persistent low achievement and eventual school dropout (Whitehurst and Lonigan, 2001), with these children falling further and further behind their more literate peers in reading and maths, especially in the transition to middle school (Chall, Jacobs and Baldwin, 1990; Duncan et al., 2007; Sohn, 2012). This suggests a mismatch between children's incoming skills and the *average* instruction or typical pedagogy in the classroom, which is often tailored to children with higher incoming abilities. The comparative deficits of African-American and Latino children to Asian and European, American children persist for the most part in the subsequent years of schooling (Ferguson, 1998).

Special education

One of the responses that schools have made to persistent underachievement has been to assess, classify, and assign African-American children to classes set aside for those with learning disabilities. African-American children ages 6–21 have a much higher likelihood of being diagnosed with specific learning disabilities, language impairments, emotional disturbances, disabilities, physical and sensory disabilities, or brain injury and assigned to special education than nonminority children (US Department of Education, 2001). African-American youth, particularly African-American males, are most often reported to be behaviorally disruptive in school and as having attention difficulties (Center for Health Statistics, 1988; Council for Exceptional Children [CEC], 2002). This problem is large in scope and reach. As many as 30 per cent of Black males are siphoned from regular classes and schools and re-assigned to special education programs for learning or developmentally disabled and emotionally impaired. African Americans in this age range made up 20 per cent of the children receiving special education services, although they comprised roughly 12 per cent of the population at the time the data were collected.

It is noteworthy that a very large proportion of the African-American children in special education programs are assigned there because of disruptive behavior and emotional impairment, not due to their learning difficulties. Nationwide, African-American students are almost twice as likely to be designated by schools as having an emotional disability. The problems contributing to special education assignment generally are not observed or acted upon in the early childhood years. For example, there were no differences in the rates of special education classification among toddlers and preschoolers at all, let alone behavioral or emotional difficulties. After the age of eight, however, the differential rates of referral to special education for African-American children emerged, with substantial ethnic differences in special education placement (Artiles, Reschly, and Chinn, 2002; Hibel, Farkas, and Morgan, 2010). By this time, the rate of African Americans formally classified by schools as having an emotional disturbance became higher than for children of any other ethnic background. Eleven per cent of African-American children were classified as being emotionally disturbed and thereby eligible for re-assignment to special education compared with 8 per cent of White, 7.7 per cent for American-Indian, 5 per cent for Asian, and 5 per cent for Hispanic youth (US Department of Education, 2005).

Significant overrepresentation of African-American students in emotionally handicapped programs is a central component of the disproportionate representation in special education. This disproportionate re-assignment has become a matter of great controversy in schools in terms of its educational efficacy and a subject of consternation and protest by many in the African-American community, who fear that such assignments contribute to a downward achievement spiral resulting from removal from academically rigorous curricula and in turn contributing a loss of academic motivation and engagement by the student (Fierros and Conroy, 2002).

Emotional and behavioral indicators

Given the large proportion of African-American children classified within schools as behaviorally disturbed or emotionally impaired and assigned to special education programs, we would expect to find similar evidence of emotional and behavioral dysfunction in mental health systems of care. However, this is not the case. Mental health epidemiological research does not yield as striking a portrait of ethnic differences as one would expect from the data reported on special education programs in the school. Findings from mental health prevalence research actually diverge in a number of areas from educational system data. Although the prevalence of conduct-related problems is higher for African Americans and other minority children than it is for non-minority children, rates of emotional difficulties are quite similar between minority and non-minority groups, with depression and suicide rates being lower among African-American children and adolescents (Federal Interagency Forum on Child and Family Statistics, 2013). Among the very serious mental disorders, there are few differences between African Americans and Whites, except in schizophrenia which is diagnosed more frequently among African-American males. In general, African-American children and adolescents also engage in substance abuse at lower rates than their White counterparts.

Conduct problems

Myers (1989) concluded that African-American children and youth of the urban underclass face a negative social and mental health trajectory which includes poor school performance; school dropout; multiple risks for those who become teen parents; as well as involvement in gangs, violence, and substance abuse. There is considerable evidence regarding the disproportionately high rates of behavioral problems from early childhood through adolescence. Teachers, specifically White and Hispanic teachers, have been found to rate African-American youth as higher on externalizing behavior problems than White and Hispanic children. In addition, White and Hispanic teachers have been found to rate African-American children higher on behavior problems than African-American parents (Zimmerman et al., 1995). Similarly, when focusing just on African-American males, teachers have been found to give African-American males higher scores for externalizing behaviors than African-American boys or their parents give themselves, but not to differ significantly from White caregivers' or adolescents' ratings of White youth's externalizing behaviors (Youngstrom, Loeber and Stouthamer-Loeber, 2000).

There is some evidence that these differences in teacher perceptions lead African American students to be referred for disciplinary action at a higher rate than White students. For example, in one study examining disciplinary reports at a middle school, African-American males did not appear to engage in more disruptive behavior than White males, but African Americans did appear to be referred to the office for infractions that were more subjective in interpretation, such as 'disrespect' or 'excessive noise' (Skiba et al., 2002). Similarly, one study found that teachers observing male adolescents with an African American cultural movement style, defined as a stylized, rhythmic way of walking, perceived those youth to be more aggressive, lower in achievement, and more likely to need special education services (Neal et al., 2003). Finally, in clinical settings, African Americans also tend to be overrepresented among children diagnosed with externalizing problems. Among adolescents hospitalized in a psychiatric facility, African Americans have been found to be more likely than Whites to be diagnosed with conduct disorder (Delbello et al., 2001).

Although African-American youth accounted for 15 per cent of the adolescent population, they accounted for 50 per cent of arrests for murder, 25 per cent of arrests for crimes against property, and 66 per cent of youth arrests for rape. It follows that incarceration is a much more common experience for African- American males than White males: White males are incarcerated at a rate of 8.5 per thousand, compared with 48.3 per thousand for African-American males (Barbarin, 2010). Furthermore, the extent to which they are overrepresented in the juvenile justice system increases with the more severe levels of adjudication. For example, while 33 per cent of youth in juvenile court were African-American, 44 per cent of youth who were then detained were African-American. Similarly, for youth with drug offenses, African Americans made up 39 per cent of the cases petitioned but 63 per cent of cases transferred to adult court (Poe-Yamagata and Jones, 2000).

In summary, African-American youth account for 60 per cent of incarcerated youth under the age of 18 though they constitute less than 10 per cent of youth under the age of 18 (Barbarin, 2010). Among adults they represent only about 13 per cent of the overall American population, but nearly half of the prison population is Black. The median arrest rate for White youth is 7.2 arrests per thousand but 12.6 per thousand for Black youth. Three out of four (75 per cent) of juvenile defendants charged with drug offenses in adult court are Black, and almost all of the juveniles sentenced to adult prison for drug offenses are non-White (Fite, Wynn and Pardini, 2009).

Depression

In general, conflicting evidence exists regarding differences in depression rates between African-American and White youth, with some studies finding that Whites report higher rates of depression (Brooks et al., 2002) and others finding that African Americans report higher rates of depression (Roberts, Roberts, and Chen, 1997). Gender differences may partially explain these inconsistencies. Importantly, African-American boys meet diagnostic criteria for depression at a lower rate than their female and White counterparts. For example, an epidemiological study of urban African-American youth

found the lifetime prevalence of depression to be 6.9 per cent among African-American males compared with nearly double that (11.4 per cent) among African-American females (Ialongo et al., 2004).

Even though African-American males appear to exhibit lower rates of depression, there is an important caveat. Some empirical and theoretical work with African-American adults has introduced questions as to whether current diagnostic criteria and methods are appropriate for detecting depression among African Americans. For example, after interviewing African-American adults, Baker (2001) found three alternative presentations of depression that differ from DSM (Diagnostic and Statistical Manual of Mental Disorders) IV criteria, including those who refuse to admit sadness in favor of relying on faith, those who exhibit extreme irritability or a significant change in personality, and those who prioritize taking on multiple tasks over their health. In addition, both African-American adult men and women who are depressed report poorer physical health and more stressful life events than Whites (Brown, Schulberg and Madonia, 1996; Johnson-Lawrence, Griffith and Watkins, 2013; Lincoln et al., 2011). These studies suggest that presentations of depression including irritability, high levels of activity or multi-tasking, and somatic symptoms need to be included when assessing African Americans for depression.

Suicide

Historically, African Americans have exhibited lower rates of suicidal behavior than Whites. The same pattern exists for adolescents with White males more than twice as likely to die since 2005 as a result of suicide than African-American adolescents (14.2 per 100,000 compared with 6.8 per 100,000 in 2010; Federal Interagency Forum on Child and Family Statistics, 2013: Table PHY8.B, 148–9). The pattern over the last two decades or so has been similar for adolescent females but at a considerably lower rate (for example, 3.5 per 100,000 for White compared with

1.1 per 100,000 for African-American ethnic groups females in 2010).

The link between depressive symptoms and conduct problems

The issues of depressed mood and affect in African-American children and their association with other troubling social outcomes has been explored in the work of Shepard Kellam and his colleagues at the Johns Hopkins University Prevention Research Center. They have demonstrated a strikingly high co-morbidity of affective disturbances with conduct problems, concentration difficulties, and academic underachievement. The concurrence of emotional and behavioral disorders was initially greeted with suspicion and treated as an artefact of measurement error. However, the consistency in these findings suggests that these problems often occur together in children. Data gathered at the Johns Hopkins Prevention Research Center with inner-city children has indicated depressed mood in non-clinical, non-referred African-American children, and adolescents in poor communities that were on average equivalent to levels for children and adolescents hospitalized for clinical depression.

These mood disturbances are particularly prevalent among young African-American males in elementary and middle school and among adolescent females. Cross-sectional data reviewed by Barbarin and Soler (1993) showed that depressive symptoms peak for boys at about ages 9–10 (Grades 4–5), then drop to normal levels. For girls, depression was only moderately elevated through age 10, but rises and peaks around ages 15–16. Given potential increased stigma among African Americans in admitting depression (Cooper-Patrick et al., 1997), it is possible that the high rates of conduct problems described below may in fact be depressive symptoms masquerading as or taking the form of aggression, irritability, and disruptive behavior. Recent national figures based on parents' reports of their children's emotional and behavioral difficulties (using the well-known standardized Strengths and Difficulties

Questionnaire) for children ages 4–17 years found little difference between White and African-American children (Federal Interagency Forum on Child and Family Statistics (2013: 173–4).

Other mental disorders

Although the research on many mental disorders among African-American children is scant, for the most part, African-American children appear to exhibit disorders at rates comparable with those of White children, with important caveats. For example, when more objective measures are used, and specifically assessment items that perform comparably in terms of prediction across races, the rate of Attention Deficit Hyperactivity Disorder (ADHD) is similar among African-American and White children. However, when assessments are made using traditional measures which utilize parent-report, African-American children are often found to exhibit lower rates of ADHD (Hillemeier et al., 2007). Similarly, Bipolar Disorder is often underdiagnosed among African Americans, partly because, current assessment practices, such as use of the Mood Disorder Questionnaire, do not appear to be as sensitive in detecting bipolar disorder among African Americans as White Americans (Graves et al., 2007). On the other hand, African- American adolescent males have been found to be more likely to receive a diagnosis of schizophrenia than African-American females and Whites (Delbello et al., 2001).

Substance abuse

In general, African-American youth tend to exhibit lower levels of alcohol abuse and cigarette use than White youth. For example, the Federal Interagency Forum on Child and Family Statistics (2013) indicates that 8–12th grade African-American youth are reportedly using alcohol and smoking cigarettes at significantly lower rates than their White counterparts (see Tables BEH1–3). For example, since 2000, a quite consistent rate of about 11.3 per 100,000 African-American 8–12th grade youth reported having five or more alcoholic beverages in the previous two weeks compared with between 25.7 and 34.6 per 100,000 for their White peers. Similarly in 2012, 4.7 per 100,000 of African-American youth reported smoking cigarettes daily in the prior 30 days compared with 12.1 per 100,000 for White youth. The illicit drug use rate has been lower for African-American than White youth since 1980 but the rates are converging and since 2010 have been quite similar (Federal Interagency Forum on Child and Family Statistics (2013).

Although, for the most part, African-American youth engage in substance abuse at a lower level than their White counterparts, when they do abuse drugs, the social consequences tend to be more serious. For example, the onset of alcohol use before sixth grade has been found to be more strongly related to eighth grade and adult alcohol use among African-American than White males (Horton, 2007). In addition, African Americans are more than 20 times more likely than Whites to be incarcerated due to a drug-related offense and are more likely to make a drug-related emergency room visit, to die from an overdose, and to contract HIV due to intravenous drug use than Whites (Drucker, 1999).

In summary, in spite of these risks and contrary to widely held views, with the exception of conduct disorders, African-American children do not experience overall higher rates of psychological disorders than other groups. Noteworthy is the finding that African-American children tend to score lower than White children on measures of psychopathology when rated by themselves (Karnik et al., 2006) and their parents (Roberts, Alegria, Roberts and Chen, 2005). However, when rated by teachers, African-American children tend to be rated higher on behavior problems than youth of other ethnic backgrounds, but not higher on other forms of psychological problems (Zimmerman et al., 1995). This suggests the potential role of social process, person perception, and distorted judgement in accounting for

discrepancies in reports of conduct problems of African-American children. Next we turn to discuss social processes that may figure into the high prevalence of conduct problems reported for African-American children.

ADVERSITY EXPLAINS MINORITY CHILD OUTCOMES

Linked to minority-group status are a number of adverse social and economic processes that have been advanced to explain the poor outcomes often observed for minority children. These processes are thought to result in material disadvantage, political disenfranchisement, and social marginalization that in turn undermine children's health and development. The adverse effects of race-related stress, stigma associated with minority status, and the negative messages sent to poor children about self compared with others have also been well documented (Fisher, Wallace and Fenton, 2000; McKown, 2013). For example, prejudiced attitudes and discriminatory behavior in the form of stigmatization of children at school, low expectations of their academic potential, denial of work opportunities to adults, and impediments to their career advancement all work against children in ways that are reflected in the academic and mental health data presented above. These adverse processes are manifested in children's life at home, at school, and in the community.

Adversity in family life

The adverse effects of inequality in employment, housing, and education impact health, emotional well-being, and academic performance, and each of these affects the well-being of minority children (Williams, Neighbors, and Jackson, 2003). Children growing up in households characterized by low socioeconomic status and poverty face multiple risks resulting from inordinately high levels of mundane stressors (food insecurity, insufficient material resources for living, and exposure to violence) of social stigma, and insufficient linguistic and cognitive stimulation. The resulting material disadvantage also means that children are subject to higher rates of neonatal insults and injuries, food insecurity, poor nutrition, exposure to toxins, and early gaps in opportunity to learn. Brain development may be compromised by the intake of too little iron and exposure to lead (Pierpoint and Poertner, 1999). In addition, in the United States many ethnic-minority families experience the emotional distress associated with financial instability, factors that undoubtedly impact the quality of parenting (McLoyd, 1998). For many, the strain of limited financial resources has the potential to turn small daily life hassles and unexpected life events into major crises.

Under these conditions, the threats to well-being extend beyond material sufficiency and physical health to emotional well-being. The differential access to resources and differential threats or life stress may lead diverse families to prioritize sets of skills different from those valued by schools. Thus, the forces of discrimination, inequality, and material hardship shape the day-to-day lives of children and give rise to distinctive coping strategies, world views, aspirations, and beliefs about one's place in the world and how life should be lived (Barbarin, 2002). In addition, some behaviors which qualify as problematic in some quarters may represent children's best efforts to cope with a world with expectations that they find difficult to meet or that they simply do not understand.

Adversity at school

Academic underachievement of minority children often results from a combination of adverse circumstances within the child's family and school. With respect to families, parents often carry the burden of significant educational deficits. As a result of their own limited education, parents may lack the

human capital and material resources their economically advantaged peers have to promote the skilled behaviors that are privileged and often required for success in schools. It has been noted that children from more advantaged backgrounds master the rules, expectations, and the discourse styles of schools long before they enter school (Rogoff, 2003). They learn to speak in 'school talk' and to recognize and use print materials appropriately as young children. In contrast, ethnic-minority children sometimes enter school without ever having held a pencil.

As a consequence, minority children often enter school with the twin burdens of skills that have yet to be developed and doubts on the part of teachers that they have the ability to master them. Teachers who most often come from middle-class backgrounds may unconsciously hold stereotyped views of poor and minority children which color their interactions with the children and undermine expectations that minority children can excel academically. They may hold stigmatizing attitudes about minority children (Reyna, 2000). When children adopt postures or behave in ways that reflect a lack of knowledge of school etiquette and decorum, teachers' low expectations may be reinforced.

Many minority children do make a smooth transition into school and learn to meet the behavioral expectation of schools soon after starting. However, for those whose adaptation to school occurs more slowly, child–teacher conflict may arise to supplant the warmth that is propitious for and facilitative of an effective relationship between the child and the teacher. This conflict may take expression in the form of frequent punishment that conveys unmistakably to the child that they do not fit in and that they are not liked by the teacher (Barbarin and Crawford, 2006).

If interpersonal difficulty between the teacher and child were the only obstacle to the child's academic success, the child might overcome it and do well. However, problems in the teacher–child relationship often co-occur with ineffective instruction. Poor and ethnic-minority children attend schools that have more problems, are less safe, and have less adequate facilities and teaching materials (West and Denton, 2001). Moreover, ethnic-minority schools are taught by the least experienced teachers, in schools with fewer resources and physically unattractive spaces. Their schools are plagued by higher rates of violence and over-crowding and poor physical facilities (such as inadequate lighting, plumbing, and heating); have fewer books, smaller libraries, less adequate science labs, less access to the Internet, and fewer music, art, and drama rooms (Evans, 2004). In a study of 240 randomly selected pre-kindergarten programs in six states, pre-kindergarten teachers were moderately responsive and sensitive but were less successful in engaging children and providing learning in specific skills. Both socio-emotional support and teaching quality aspects of the pre-kindergarten experience predicted the acquisition of language, pre-academic, and social skills through the end of the kindergarten year (National Center for Early Development and Learning (NCEDL), 2000). Unfortunately, the pedagogical rigor for minority children does not improve as children advance through their years at school. For example, instruction in classrooms with more ethnic-minority children of low socioeconomic status tends to be more drill and practice, includes fewer conceptual explanations and greater emphasis on competition, and getting the one right answer, focuses more on 'basic' versus 'advanced' inferential and problem-solving skills, is less varied and extensive in topical range, is more repetitive and fragmented, and emphasizes discipline and control of interactions and learning tasks, as well as worksheet activities (Knapp and Woolverton, 1995; Stipek, 2004).

Adversity in communities

Minority children are often relegated to living in communities with access only to substandard housing and levels of violence that pose additional risk to their development (Overstreet, 2000). For example, African Americans have reported higher exposure to environmental danger, such as witnessing or being victim to crime than Whites. African-American adolescents are more likely than adolescents of other ethnic backgrounds to experience the death of a family member and more likely than White adolescents to experience the death of a friend (Rheingold et al., 2003). African Americans report poorer physical health and more stressful life events than Whites (Brown et al., 1996).

Higher exposure to environmental danger, in turn, has been found to be associated with lower school attendance and a lower tendency to avoid trouble (Bowen and Bowen, 1999). Finally, among African Americans, exposure to community violence has been found to be related to an elevated risk for Post-Traumatic Stress Disorder (PTSD) symptoms and depression (Paxton et al., 2004). Many communities adopt punitive approaches to control undesirable behavior which may be more vigorously applied to minority children. On the other hand, there is increasing evidence that neigborhoods and communities can exert positive influences via adaptive 'racial socialization' and supporting positive racial identity to counteract the discrimination children may experience elsewhere (Neblett et al., 2006; Neblett, Rivas-Drake and Umana-Taylor, 2012; O'Brien Caughy et al., 2004).

STRESS, COPING, AND RESILIENCE

Up to this point we have reviewed research which depicts problems in minority children that may result from growing up in environments which place them at high risk for a variety of academic problems and disabilities, injuries, socio-emotional maladjustment, and death. However, minority children are not destined to have problems. Minority children with problems represent only one aspect of a complex story (Weisner, 2002). The adverse effects of minority status described above often arise in the population level and by comparison with non-minority groups. These effects are not always evident at the individual level. Many, if not most, minority children live in nurturing but poor households, experience emotionally supportive and stable personal relationships even in 'broken' homes; develop a positive ethnic identity in spite of rampant denigration of their group; steadfastly pursue education even when its relationship to gainful employment may be uncertain; abstain from addictive substances even though drugs are ubiquitous and life is unkind; and avoid gangs, illegal activity, and incarceration in spite of pressure to belong and the temptation to acquire much needed financial resources by illegal means.

In light of the adversity they face, how can we account for the fact that many minority children are doing remarkably well even by traditional standards of functioning? How do we explain the African-American children who develop the needed skills to acclimate to the academic and social demands of school, take rigorous courses, graduate from high school and attain advanced training in college and graduate or professional schools? What strengths are likely to support them and sustain their efforts to succeed? Although it is important to remain aware of the significant challenges minority children face, in doing so we cannot overlook the resilience many demonstrate. Many positive outcomes arise from personal characteristics of the children themselves and from the ability of families to socialize coping strategies with which to resist degradation of emotional functioning (Carera, Beeghly and Eisenberg, 2012; Luthar and Brown, 2007; Neblett et al., 2012).

Such adverse outcomes are not inevitable. Some children and families are able to overcome the adversities and sources of distress to function well. In fact, some children in spite of the adverse conditions thrive and are coping well. There are a number of possible explanations: relationship in family and at school, quality of the settings, and luck/chance.

If we are to understand and address the issue of minority children and build on their capacity to overcome these obstacles, it is necessary to look beyond the negative statistics to see the children behind the struggle, to understand their views of the world, their struggles, how they construct their own identities, and make sense of the world around them. How do they see their lives and how do they cope with the demands and failure of their social environment? Unfortunately, there is little research focusing on the perspectives of minority children regarding their status as minorities or their lives, in general. There is, however, an increasing body of research concerned with children's perceptions of racial discrimination and racial identity (Brody et al., 2006; Brown and Bigler, 2005; Neblett et al., 2012). However, a few authors engaging in historical and qualitative work have sought to describe the viewpoints of minority children on various aspects of their lives. For example, four decades ago, Coles (1967) recounted the tales of children in various disadvantaged and traumatic conditions. Two decades ago, Kotlowitz (1992) chronicled the lives of two African-American brothers as they coped with the dangers of living in a dangerous inner-city neighborhood. He discovered the resignation of the boys to the violence and crime they witnessed, but also their hopes for growing up into successful adults.

SIGNIFICANCE OF RESEARCH ON MINORITY CHILDREN

What is the significance of research concerning minority children and what are the challenges of doing research in this area? For the US and Europe, persons classified as ethnic minorities are a rapidly growing part of the population on whom the gross national product and outputs will depend. Considering the comparatively low rates of fertility and longer life expectancy among the White population (US Bureau of Census, 2011), it is clear that an increasing proportion of the labour force will come from minority groups. As a result, their productivity, health, and life style will have great impact on the well-being of millions of Americans as well as on their own.

Ethnic-minority children are important from the standpoint of national planning and policy because they are a leading social indicator of the quality of life in the society. The conditions and status of ethnic-minority children reveal much about how well a society is functioning as a whole and much about the effectiveness of a nation's social safety net. When the majority population suffers minor distress, minority populations suffer a major perturbation. When the majority catches a cold, minority groups tend to get pneumonia. The effects of moderate economic downturns or severe natural disasters are magnified in their impact on minority populations. Take as an example the effects of Hurricane Katrina and the subsequent flooding of the city of New Orleans. Many of the middle-class and more affluent majority population suffered the loss of homes. However, the images of minority populations trapped in flooded areas remind us of their suffering as a result of their even more severe devastation from the disaster itself and the failure of the government to respond quickly and adequately.

Minority children are also of interest from a theoretical and empirical standpoint. They present a 'laboratory' for understanding coping and resilience and the factors that facilitate strategies and ways to overcome adversity and promote normal development under adverse circumstances. In this way, they represent an important means by which to interrogate and understand the relations among adversity, risk factors, and the factors that mitigate risks and promote resilience.

Investigations of minority-group children often involve exploration of issues with implications that go far beyond the welfare of a single group. These studies often involve phenomena that are of broad theoretical interest to social researchers and of practical significance to policy makers. Research on minority children has pointed clearly to the adverse effects of poverty, material deprivation, food insecurity, and mundane stress on family life, school quality, and child development. At the same time the salutary effects of warm supportive relationships, positive identity, and socialization of coping strategies in promoting healthy development are evident (Neblett et al., 2012; O'Brien Caughy et al., 2006).

Finally, although much that is written about minority children, including the resilience literature, focuses on their challenges or 'at-risk' status, minorities possess unique strengths and resources. For example, McAdoo (1982) has highlighted the role of extended families as sources of emotional and instrumental support for African-American children. Similarly, clinicians and researchers have noted the fact that African-American families often have more flexible gender roles than White families (Hines and Boyd-Franklin, 2005). This flexibility can help to empower women and make family problem-solving more efficient. In addition, Coll and colleagues (1996) and others since (McKown, 2012; O'Brien et al., 2004) have developed an integrative model of minority child development which, in addition to the social forces of discrimination and marginalization, includes the 'adaptive culture' endemic to minority cultures composed of such positive factors as traditions and acculturation.

METHODOLOGICAL CHALLENGES

Understanding the status of ethnic-minority children and answering questions about the effects of adversity and resilience requires rigorous research. However, the quality of the research on minority children has been beset by a number of methodological challenges that need to be recognized and addressed in future research.

One of the most serious methodological challenges is defining race and ethnicity.

Researchers note that the terms 'race' and 'ethnicity', although much discussed, are continuously redefined and there no consensus on their definitions (Fisher et al., 2000; Lin and Kelsey, 2000). As a result, current classifications of racial and ethnic groups remain unclear and broadly defined. For instance, the US National Institutes of Health identify minority groups as *American Indian-Alaska Native, Asian-Pacific Islander, Black-African-American not of Hispanic origin, and Hispanic* (Hohmann and Parron, 1996). Assignment to racial groups is more complex than is often acknowledged and many of the indicators used in existing studies may be unreliable especially if they involve an external rater as the principal means of classifying ethnicity.

According to Barbarin (1999), few studies use reliable methods for identifying race; most rely on visible features such as skin color and hair texture. Self-identification by study participants has its own problems but may be an essential component of research based on ethnic classification. Many researchers argue that placing minority research participants in those broad categories causes a serious problem because of the great heterogeneity within ethnic groups. Individuals within the same ethnic group may vary greatly by their immigration history, the length of time they spent in the US, language skills, level of acculturation, ethnic-racial identity, perceived minority status, experiences with discrimination, cultural traditions, dietary preferences, religious beliefs, and socioeconomic status (Alvidrez, Azocar and Miranda, 1996; Lin and Kelsey, 2000). For example, in the United States, the ethnic group *Hispanics* or *Latinos* consists of 63 per cent self-identified as Mexican, 9 per cent as Puerto Rican, 3.5 per cent as Cuban, 13.5 per cent as Central and South American, and 7 per cent as another Hispanic group (US Bureau of the Census, 2011). These groups are very different with respect to history and culture and may even have significant language variations.

According to Fisher et al. (2000: 1026), categorizing ethnic minority participants into broad groups dilutes and obscures the 'moderating effects of national origin, immigration, history, religion, and tradition on normative and maladaptive development'. Moreover, that may also seriously affect the quality of the study by leading to inaccurate conclusions. Trimble and Dickson (2004: 412–13) defined this phenomenon as ethnic gloss which means 'overgeneralization or simplistic categorical label used to refer to ethnocultural groups such as American-Indians, Asian-Americans, Hispanics, and African-Americans and nationalistic or indigenous groups where unique cultural and ethnic differences found among group members are ignored'. They also stated that 'ethnic gloss presents the illusion of homogeneity where none exists, and therefore may be considered a superficial, almost vacuous, categorization, which serves only to separate one group from another' (Trimble and Dickson, 2004: 413). This issue is further complicated by the problems of multiple racial origins (for example, a bi-racial child whose parents are African-American and Hispanic), multi-ethnic or fluid identity (for example, a child born in the recently immigrated Chinese family may identify herself/himself with both the Chinese and American cultures or may gradually grow more 'Americanized'; Lin and Kelsey, 2000).

Another concern is selection and recruitment bias. Although a disproportionate percentage of ethnic-minority persons are in poverty, many ethnic-minority persons are not. Nevertheless, many research studies based on the samples of socioeconomically disadvantaged representatives claim that the research findings are generalizable to the broad population of minorities (Hall, 2001).

A thorny methodological issue is cultural validity and measurement equivalence. Using test items that are not culturally appropriate often leads to compromised research findings and may also have serious harmful consequences for research participants (Fisher et al., 2002). Different ethnic groups may have different ideas and preferences while answering study questions. McLoyd (1998) wrote that children from certain cultures may favor extreme responses, for example, when answering Likert scale questions; this kind of answer may seriously affect the validity of the assessment. Such inaccuracies in the assessment may lead to over-identification of the problem studied, for instance, Down's syndrome among representatives of a certain minority group, and may lead to social labelling and stigmatization of that particular group.

Cultural insensitivity and lack of knowledge of the research team can present fundamental problems that go to the heart of the research enterprise. This includes untested assumptions about ethnic-minority groups, selection of the phenomena to be studied, and how research questions are framed. Often researchers may have biases that they may or may not be aware of but which affect the study through untested assumptions about the population and blind spots in the interpretation of findings. Ethnocentric bias results when researchers use the population of European descent as a normative population using tests normed on Caucasian children to assess development of minority children (McLoyd, 1990b) or solo comparison of ethnic-minority children to White children without taking into consideration the effects of discrimination and socioeconomic inequality experienced by the former (Barbarin, 1999). Lee, Spencer, and Harpalani (2003) stated that research that does not reflect the unique background and culture of persons of minority background misses the purpose of the study in failing to understand the research participants. In other words, some studies of minority children simply treat minority children as a population of interest like any other without acknowledging the unique circumstances in which they are growing and developing. By not delving more fully into what their minority status means to them, such research fails to take advantage of the opportunity to interrogate the effects of social context on the dependent variable or phenomenon under study.

If research on minority children attends to the methodological concerns discussed above, it can make an important contribution to society. Understanding and addressing the status of minority children through research can be valuable from the perspective of social justice and civic stability. There are significant gaps in our knowledge about minority status as a received role. What is it that ethnic-minority children come to believe about themselves in reaction to stigma and social exclusion? Additional scholarship needs to focus on contemporary children's understanding of minority status and their perspectives on their life circumstances. Ethnographies covering the lives of ethnic-minority children which offer a window onto their inner lives would be especially valuable.

History has shown that societies who ignore the plight and legitimate grievances of minority groups do so at their own peril. The frustrated aspirations of minority groups for equality and a better life for their children often find active expression in resistance, disruptions of the status quo or passively in a slow decay of the moral order that erodes the foundation of a society from within. Studying minority children provides insights into the ability of a society to protect its most vulnerable. The functioning and well-being of minority children is a barometer of the health of the nation and the capacity of character of a society in responding to the neediest of its members. The study of minority children can lead to important discoveries about a society, the quality of its current functioning, and clues about its future.

NOTE

1 The proportion of non-Hispanic Whites in the population declined from 75.1 per cent in 2000 to 72.4 per cent in 2010, while the proportions represented by other races increased, in some instances rapidly. Black and African Americans changed from 12.3 to 12.6 per cent, Asians from 3.6 to 4.8 per cent, and Hispanic or Latina origin from 12.5 to 16.3 per cent (US Census Bureau, 2011).

REFERENCES

Aalto, P. (2003) *Constructing Post-Soviet Geopolitics in Estonia*. London: Frank Cass.

Alvidrez, J., Azocar, F. and Miranda, J. (1996) 'Demystifying the concept of ethnicity for psychotherapy researchers', *Journal of Consulting and Clinical Psychology*, 64(5): 903–8.

Artiles, A.J., Reschly, D.J., and Chinn, P.C. (2002) 'Overidentification of students of color in special education: A critical overview', *Multicultural Perspectives*, 4(1): 3–12.

Baker, F.M. (2001) 'Diagnosing depression in African Americans', *Community Mental Health Journal*, 37: 31–8.

Barbarin, O. (1999) 'Social risks and psychological adjustment: A comparison of African American and South African children', *Child Development*, 70(6): 1348–59.

Barbarin, O. (2002) 'African American males in kindergarten', in J.U. Gordon (ed.), *The African-American Male in American Life and Thought*. New York: Nova Science Publishers, pp. 1–12.

Barbarin, O. (2010) 'Halting African American boys' progression from pre-K to prison: What families, school, and communities can do!', *American Journal of Orthopsychiatry*, 80(1): 81–8.

Barbarin, O. and Crawford, G. (2006) 'Acknowledging and reducing stigmatization of African American boys', *Young Children*, 61(6): 79–86.

Barbarin, O. and Soler, R. (1993) 'Behavioral, emotional and academic adjustment in a national probability sample of African American children: Effects of age, gender and family structure', *Journal of Black Psychology*, 19(4): 423–46.

Barcus, H.R., & Werner, C. (2007). 'Trans-National Identities: Mongolian Kazakhs in the 21st century'. *Geographische Rundschau International Edition*, 3(2), 4–10.

Barrington, L., Herron, E. and Silver, B. (2003) 'The motherland is calling: Views of homeland among Russians in the near abroad', *World Politics*, 55(2): 290–313.

Blake, W.M. and Darling, C.A. (1994) 'The dilemmas of the African American male', *Journal of Black Studies*, 24(4): 402–15.

Blum, R.W. and Qureshi, F. (2011) *Morbidity and Mortality among Adolescents and Young Adults in the United States*. Baltimore, MA: Johns Hopkins Bloomberg School of Public Health.

Bowen, N.K. and Bowen, G.L. (1999) 'Effects of crime and violence in neighborhoods and schools on the school behavior and performance of adolescents', *Journal of Adolescent Research*, 14(3): 319–42.

Brooks, T., Harris, S.K., Thrall, J.S. and Woods, E.R. (2002) 'Association of adolescent risk behaviors with mental health symptoms in high school students', *Journal of Adolescent Health*, 31(3): 240–6.

Brooks-Gunn, J., Klebanov, P.K. and Duncan, G.J. (1996) 'Ethnic differences in children's intelligence test scores: Role of economic deprivation, home environment, and maternal characteristics', *Child Development*, 67: 396–408.

Brooks-Gunn, J. and Markman, L.B. (2005) 'The contribution of parenting to ethnic and racial gaps in school readiness', *The Future of Children*, 15: 139–68.

Brown, C.S. and Bigler, R.S. (2005) 'Children's perceptions of discrimination: A developmental model', *Child Development*, 76: 533–53.

Brown, C., Schulberg, H.C. and Madonia, M. (1996) 'Clinical presentations of major depression by African Americans and Whites in primary medical care practice', *Journal of Affective Disorders*, 41(3): 181–91.

Carera, N.J., Beeghly, M. and Eisenberg, N. (2012) 'Positive development of minority children: Introduction to the special issue', *Child Development Perspectives*, 6 (3): 207–209.

Center for Health Statistics (1988) Available at http://www.cdc.gov/nchs/

Chall, J.S., Jacobs, V. and Baldwin, L. (1990) *The Reading Crisis: Why Poor Children Fall Behind*. Cambridge, MA: Harvard University Press.

Chunn, J. (ed.) (2002) *The Health Behavioral Change Imperative: Theory, Education, and Practice in Diverse Populations*. New York: Kluwer Academic/Plenum Publishers.

Coles, R. (1967) *A Study in Courage and Fear: Children in Crisis Vol. 1*. Boston, MA: Atlantic-Little.

Coll, G.C., Crnic, K., Lamberty, G., Wasik, B.H., Jenkins, R., Garcia, H.V. and McAdoo, H.P. (1996) 'An integrative model for the study of developmental competencies in minority children', *Child Development*, 67(5): 1891–914.

College Board (1999) *Reaching the Top: A Report of the National Task Force on Minority High Achievement*. New York: College Board.

Cooper-Patrick, L., Powe, N.R., Jenckes, M.W., Gonzales, J.J., Levine, D.M. and Ford, D.E. (1997) 'Identification of patient attitudes and preferences regarding treatment of depression', *Journal of General Internal Medicine*, 12(7): 431–8.

Delbello, M.P., Lopez-Larson, M.P., Soutullo, C.A. and Strakowski, S.M. (2001) 'Effects of race on psychiatric diagnosis of hospitalized adolescents: A retrospective chart review', *Journal of Child and Adolescent Psychopharmacology*, 11(1): 95–103.

Downey, D.B., von Hippel, P.T. and Broh, B. (2004) 'Are schools the great equalizer? School and non-school sources of inequality in cognitive skills', *American Sociological Review*, 69(5): 613–35.

Drucker, E. (1999) 'Drug prohibition and public health: 25 years of evidence', *Public Health Report*, 114(1): 14–29.

Duncan, G.J., Dowsett, C.J., Claessens, A., Magnuson, K., Huston, A.C., Klebanov, P., Pagani, L.S., Feinstein, L., Engel, M., Brooks-Gunn, J., Sexton, H., Duckworth, K. and Japel, C. (2007) 'School readiness and later achievement', *Developmental Psychology*, 43(6): 1428–46.

Eaton, D.K., Kann, L., Kinchen, S., Shanklin, S., Ross, J., Hawkins, J., et al. (2008) Youth risk behavior surveillance – United States, 2007, *MMWR Surveillance Summaries*, 57(4): 1–131.

ECLS-K (1998) *Early Childhood Longitudinal Study-Kindergarten Cohort. Center for Educational Statistics*. US Department of Education

Evans, G.W. (2004) 'The environment of childhood poverty', *American Psychologist*, 59(2): 77–92.

Farkas, F. (2003) 'Racial disparities and discrimination in education: What do we know, how do we know it, and what do we need to know?', *Teachers College Record*, 6: 1119–46.

Federal Interagency Forum on Child and Family Statistics (2013) *America's Children: Key National Indicators of Well-Being, 2013*. Washington, DC: US Government Printing Office.

Ferguson, R. (1998) 'Can schools narrow the Black-White Test Score gap', in C. Jencks and M. Phillips (eds.), *The Black-White Test Score Gap*. Washington, DC: The Brookings Institution Press, pp. 318–74.

Fierros, E.G. and Conroy, J.W. (2002) 'Double jeopardy: An exploration of restrictiveness and race in special education', in D.J. Losen and G. Orfield (eds.), *Racial Inequity in Special Education*. Cambridge, MA: Harvard Education Press, pp. 39–70.

Fisher, C., Wallace, S. and Fenton, R. (2000) 'Discrimination distress during adolescence', *Journal of Youth and Adolescence*, 29(6): 679–95.

Fite, P., Wynn, P. and Pardini, D.A. (2009) 'Explaining discrepancies in arrest rates between black and white juveniles', *Journal of Consulting and Clinical Psychology*, 77(5): 916–27.

Flynn, M. (2007) 'Reconstructing "home/lands" in the Russian Federation: Migrant-centred perspectives of displacement and resettlement', *Journal of Ethnic and Migration Studies*, 33(3): 461–81.

Fryer, R.G. and Levitt, S.D. (2006) 'The Black–White test score gap through third grade', *American Law and Economics Review*, 8: 249–81.

Graves, R.E., Alim, T.N., Aigbogun, N., Chrishon, K., Mellman, T.A., Charney, D.S. and Lawson, W.B. (2007) 'Diagnosing bipolar disorder in trauma exposed primary care patients', *Bipolar Disorders*, 9(4): 318–23.

Hall, G.C.N. (2001) 'Psychotherapy research with ethnic minorities: Empirical, ethical, and conceptual issues', *Journal of Consulting and Clinical Psychology*, 69(3): 502–10.

Green, T.D., Mcintosh, A.S., Cook-Morales, V.J. and Robinson-Zanartu, C. (2005) 'From old schools to tomorrow's schools: Psychoeducational assessment of African American students', *Remedial and Special Education*, 26: 82–92.

Hallik, K. (2000) 'Nationalizing policies and integration challenges', in M. Lauristin and M. Heidmets (eds.), *The Challenge of the Russian Minority: Emerging Multicultural Democracy in Estonia*. Tartu: Tartu University Press. pp. 65–88.

Hibel, J., Farkas, G. and Morgan, P. (2010) 'Who is placed into special education?', *Sociology of Education*, 83(4): 312–32.

Hillemeier, M.M., Foster, E.M., Heinrichs, B. and Heier, B. (2007) 'Racial differences in parental reports of attention-deficit/hyperactivity disorder behaviors', *Journal of Developmental and Behavioral Pediatrics*, 28(5): 353–61.

Hines, P.M. and Boyd-Franklin, N. (2005) 'African American families', in M. McGoldrick, J. Giordano and N. Garcia-Preto (eds.), *Ethnicity and Family Therapy*. New York, NY: Guilford Press. pp. 87–100.

Hogue, C.J. and Vasquez, C. (2002) 'Toward a strategic approach for reducing disparities in infant mortality', *American Journal of Public Health*, 92(4): 552–6.

Hohmann, A.A. and Parron, D.L. (1996) 'Informed consent and religious values: A neglected area of diversity', *Psychotherapy*, 32(2): 293–300.

Horton, E.G. (2007) 'Racial differences in the effects of age of onset on alcohol consumption and development of alcohol-related problems among males from mid-adolescence to young adulthood', *Journal of Ethnicity in Substance Abuse*, 6(1): 1–13.

Hooper, S., Roberts, J., Sideris, J., Burchinal, M. and Zeisel, S. (2010) 'Longitudinal predictors of reading and math trajectories through middle school for African American versus Caucasian students across two samples', *Developmental Psychology*, 46(5): 1018–29.

Huang, S. (2005) *Education of Kazakh Children: A Situation Analysis*. Save the Children-UK. Mongolia. Retrieved from http://www2.ohchr.org/english/bodies/cerd/docs/ngos/soc-full.pdf

Hughes, D., Rodriguez, J., Smith, E.P., Johnson, D.J., Stevenson, H.C. and Spicer, P. (2006) 'Parents' ethnic-racial socialization practices: A review of research and directions for future study', *Developmental Psychology*, 42: 747–70.

Hughes, D., Witherspoon, D., Rivas-Drake, D. and West-Bey, N. (2009) 'Received ethnic-racial socialization messages and youth's academic and behavioral outcomes: Examining the mediating role of ethnic identity and self-esteem', *Cultural Diversity and Ethnic Minority Psychology*, 15: 112–24.

Ialongo, N., McCreary, B.K., Pearson, J.L., Koenig, A.L., Schmidt, N.B., Poduska, J. and Kellam, S.G. (2004) 'Major depressive disorder in a population of urban, African-American young adults: Prevalence, correlates, comorbidity and unmet mental health service need', *Journal of Affective Disorders*, 79(1–3): 127–36.

Jencks, C. and Phillips, M. (1998a) 'America's next achievement test: Closing the black-White test score gap', *The American Prospect*, 40(44): 45–53.

Jencks, C. and Phillips, M. (1998b) *The Black-White Test Score Gap*. Washington, DC: The Brookings Institution Press.

Joe, S., Baser, R.E., Breeden, G., Neighbors, H.W. and Jackson, J.S. (2006) 'Prevalence of and risk factors for lifetime suicide attempts among Blacks in the United States', *Journal of the American Medical Association*, 296(17): 2112–23.

Johnson-Lawrence, V., Griffith, D.M. and Watkins, D.C. (2013) 'The effects of race, ethnicity, and mood/anxiety disorders on the chronic physical health conditions of men from a national sample', *American Journal of Men's Health*, 7(4 Suppl): 58S–67S.

Jubulis, M. (2003) The challenge of the Russian minority: Emerging multicultural democracy in Estonia. *Democratizatsiya*. FindArticles.com. Available at http://findarticles.com/p/articles/mi_qa3996/is_200310/ai_n9310201/

Karnik, N., Jones, P., Campanaro, A., Haapanen, R. and Steiner, H. (2006) 'Ethnic variation of self-reported psychopathology among incarcerated youth', *Community Mental Health Journal*, 42(5): 477–86.

Kemppainen, R., Ferrin, S., Ward, C. and Hite, J. (2004) 'One should not forget one's mother tongue': Russian-speaking parents' choice of language of instruction in Estonia', *Bilingual Research Journal*, 28(2): 207–29.

Kewalrami, A., Gilbertson, L., Fox, M. and Provasnik, S. (2007) *Status and Trends in the Education of Racial and Ethnic Minorities*. US Department of Education, National Center for Education Statistics.

Knapp, M.S. and Woolverton, S. (1995) 'Social class and schooling', in J.A. Banks and C.A. McGee Banks (eds.), *Handbook of Research on Multicultural Education*. New York: Macmillan, pp. 548–69.

Kotlowitz, A. (1992) *There are No Children Here: The Story of Two Boys Growing up in the Other America*. New York, NY: Random Books.

Kreitzberg, P. (2002) 'Organizational dilemmas in Estonian education in 2001', in L. Lebed, U. Kala and U. Laanemets (eds.), *Competing for the Future: Education in Contemporary Societies*. Tallinn Kirjastus: Vali Press, pp. 28–38.

Kruusvall, J. (2000) 'Social perception and individual resources of the integration process', in M. Lauristin and M. Heidmets (eds.), *The Challenge of the Russian Minority: Emerging Multicultural Democracy in Estonia*. Tartu: Tartu University Press, pp. 117–63.

Lee, C., Spencer, M. and Harpalani, V. (2003) 'Every shut eye ain't sleep: Studying how people live culturally', *Educational Researcher*, 32(5): 6–13.

Leino, M., Veisson, M., Ruus, V., Sarv, E., Ots, L. and Veisson, A. (2006) 'New identity of Russian-speaking children in Estonian society', *Social Work and Society*, 4(10): 160–74.

Lin, S.S. and Kelsey, J.L. (2000) 'Use of race and ethnicity in epidemiologic research: Concepts, methodological issues, and suggestions for research', *Epidemiologic Reviews*, 22: 187–202.

Lincoln, K.D., Taylor, R.J., Watkins, D.C. and Chatters, L.M. (2011) 'Correlates of psychological distress and major depressive disorder among African American men', *Research on Social Work Practice*, 21: 278–88.

Luthar, S.S. and Brown, P.J. (2007) 'Maximizing resilience through diverse levels of inquiry: Prevailing paradigms, possibilities, and priorities for the future', *Developmental Psychology*, 19: 931–55.

McAdoo, H.P. (1982) 'Stress absorbing systems in Black families', *Family Relations*, 31(4): 379–488.

McKown, C. (2013) 'Social equity theory and racial-ethnic achievement gaps', *Child Development*, 84(4): 1120–36.

McLoyd, V. (1990) 'The impact of economic hardship on black families and children: Psychological distress, parenting, and socioemotional development', *Child Development*, 61(2): 311–46.

McLoyd, V.C. (1998) 'Socioeconomic disadvantage and child development', *American Psychologist*, 53(2): 185–204.

Magnuson, K.A. and Waldfogel, J. (2005) 'Early childhood care and education: Effects on ethnic and racial gaps in school readiness', *The Future of Children*, 15(1): 169–96.

Minino, A.M., Heron, M.P. and Smith, B.L. (2004) 'Deaths: Preliminary data for 2004', *National Vital Statistics Report, 54*(19). Available at http://www.cdc.gov/nchs/data/nvsr/nvsr54/nvsr54_19.pdf

Mongolian Ministry of Education (2013) Statistics: General Education Data (2012-2013). Retrieved from http://www.meds.gov.mn/data/pdf/Secondary%20education20122013.pdf

Mulligan, G.M., Hastedt, S. and McCarroll, J.C. (2012) *First-Time Kindergartners in 2010-11: First Findings From the Kindergarten Rounds of the Early Childhood Longitudinal Study, Kindergarten Class of 2010–11 (ECLS-K:2011)* (NCES 2012-049). US Department of Education. Washington, DC: National Center for Education Statistics. Retrieved [date] from http://nces.ed.gov/pubsearch

Myers, H.F. (1989) 'Urban stress and mental health in black youth: An epidemiological and conceptual update', in R.L. Jones (ed.), *Black Adolescents.* Berkeley: Cobb and Henry, pp. 123–52.

National Center for Early Development and Learning (NCEDL) (2000) *Multi-State Study of Public Sponsored Pre-K Programs.* Chapel Hill, NC: Frank Porter Graham Child Development Institute, University of North Carolina.

National Center for Education Statistics (1995) *The National Household Education Survey – October, 1995. Approaching Kindergarten: A look at pre-schoolers in the United States.* Washington, DC: US Department of Education.

National Center for Education Statistics (2012) *The Condition of Education.* Washington, DC: United States Department of Education.

National Institute on Drug Abuse (NIDA) (2003) *Drug Use among Racial/Ethnic Minorities, Revised.* Washington, DC: NIDA.

National Statistical Office of Mongolia (2010) *Mongolian Statistical Yearbook 2009.* Ulaanbaatar, Mongolia: Author.

Neal, L., McCray, A.D., Webb-Johnson, G. and Bridgest, S.T. (2003) 'The effects of African American movement styles on teachers' perceptions and reactions', *The Journal of Special Education*, 37(1): 49–57.

Neblett, E.W., Jr., Philip, C.L., Cogburn, C.D. and Sellers, R.M. (2006) 'African American adolescents' discrimination experiences and academic achievement: Racial socialization as a cultural compensatory and protective factor', *Journal of Black Psychology*, 32: 199–218.

Neblett, Jr, E.W. Rivas-Drake, D. and Umaña-Taylor, A.J. (2012) 'The promise of racial and ethnic protective factors in promoting ethnic minority youth development', *Child Development Perspectives*, 6(3): 295–303.

Neblett, E.W., Jr., Chavous, T.M., Nguyen, H.X. and Sellers, R.M. (2009) 'Say it loud – I'm Black and I'm proud': Parents' messages about race, racial discrimination, and academic achievement in African American boys', *Journal of Negro Education*, 78: 246–59.

O'Brien Caughy, M., Nettles, S.M., O'Campo, P.J. and Lohrfink, K.F., Xue, Y. and Meisels, S.J. (2004) 'Early literacy instruction and children's learning in kindergarten: Evidence from the Early Childhood Longitudinal Study — Kindergarten Class of 1998–99', *American Educational Research Journal*, 41(1): 191–229.

Overstreet, S. (2000) 'Exposure to community violence: Defining the problems and understanding the consequences', *Journal of Child and Family Studies*, 9(1): 7–25.

Park, A. (1994) 'Ethnicity and independence: The case of Estonia in comparative perspective', *Europe-Asia Studies*, 46(1): 69–87.

Paxton, K.C., Robinson, W.L., Shah, S. and Schoeny, M.E. (2004) 'Psychological distress for African-American adolescent males: Exposure to community violence and social support as factors', *Child Psychiatry and Human Development*, 34(4): 281–95.

Peters, R.J., Kelder, S.H., Markham, C.M., Yacoubian, G.S., Peters, L.A. and Ellis, A. (2003) 'Beliefs and social norms about codeine and promethazine hydrochloride cough syrup (CPHCS) onset and perceived addiction among urban Houstonian adolescents: An addiction trend in the city of lean', *Journal of Drug Education*, 33(4): 415–25.

Pierpont, J. and Poertner, J. (1999) 'Prevention of infant deaths', in A.J. Goreczny and M. Hersen (eds.), *Handbook of Pediatric and Adolescent Health Psychology.* Needham Heights, MA: Allyn and Bacon, pp. 11–27.

Poe-Yamagata, E. and Jones, M.A. (2000) *And Justice for Some.* Washington, DC: National Council on Crime and Delinquency. Available at http://www.buildingblocksforyouth.org/justiceforsome/jfs.html

Reyna, C. (2000) 'Lazy, dumb, or industrious: When stereotypes convey attribution information in the classroom', *Educational Psychology Review*, 12(1): 85–110.

Rheingold, A., Smith, D.W., Ruggiero, K.J., Saunders, B.E., Kilpatrick, D.G. and Resnick, H.S. (2003) 'Loss, trauma exposure, and mental health in a representative sample of 12–17-year-old youth: Data from the National Survey of Adolescents', *Journal of Loss and Trauma*, 9(1): 1–19.

Roberts, R., Alegria, M., Roberts, C. and Chen, I. (2005) 'Mental health problems of adolescents as reported by their caregivers: A comparison of European, African, and Latino Americans', *Journal of Behavioral Health Services and Research*, 32(1): 1–13.

Roberts, R., Roberts, C. and Chen, Y. (1997) 'Ethnocultural differences in the prevalence of adolescent depression', *American Journal of Community Psychology*, 25(1): 95–110.

Rogoff, B. (2003) *The Cultural Nature of Human Development.* New York: Oxford University Press.

Skiba, R.J., Michael, R.S., Nardo, A.C. and Peterson, R.L. (2002) 'The color of discipline: sources of racial and gender disproportionality in school punishment', *The Urban Review*, 34(4): 317–42.

Snow, C.E., Burns, S.M. and Griffin, P. (eds.) (1998) *Preventing Reading Difficulties in Young Children.* Washington, DC: National Academy Press.

Sohn, K. (2012) 'The dynamics of the evolution of the Black – White Test score gap', *Education Economics*, 20(2): 175–88.

Stipek, D. (2004) 'Teaching practices in kindergarten and first grade: Different strokes for different folks', *Early Childhood Research Quarterly*, 19(4): 548–68.

Trimble, J.E., and Dickson, R. (2004) 'Ethnic gloss', in C.B. Fisher and R.M. Lerner (eds.), *Applied Developmental Science: An Encyclopedia of Research, Policies, and Programs.* Thousand Oaks: Sage, pp. 412–15.

United Nations Educational, Scientific and Cultural Organization [UNESCO] (2008) *National Report on the Situation of Adult Learning and Education (ALE) in Mongolia.* Ulaanbaatar, Mongolia: National Centre for Non Formal and Distance Education, Ministry of Education, Culture and Science. Retrieved from http://www.unesco.org/fileadmin/MULTIMEDIA/INSTITUTES/UIL/confintea/pdf/National_Reports/Asia%20-%20Pacific/Mongolia.pdf

US Census Bureau (2011) *2010 Census Data.* Available at http://www.census.gov/2010census/data/

USFederal Interagency Forum on Child and Family Statistics Data (2013) *America's Children: Key National Indicators of Well-Being, 2013.* Available at http://www. childstats.gov/americaschildren/demo.asp

US Department of Education (2001) *National Household Education Surveys of 2001.* Washington, DC: National Center for Education Statistics.

US Department of Education (2005) *25th Annual (2003) Report to Congress on the Implementation of the Individuals with Disabilities Act (1),* Washington, DC: US Department of Education.

Vanneman, A., Hamilton, L., Baldwin Anderson, J. and Rahman, T. (2009) *Achievement Gaps: How Black and White Students in Public Schools Perform in Mathematics and Reading on the National Assessment of Educational Progress* (NCES 2009-455). Washington, DC: National Center for Education Statistics, Institute of Education Sciences, US Department of Education.

Weisner, T. (2002) 'Ecocultural understanding of children's developmental pathways', *Human Development*, 45(4): 275–81.

West, J. and Denton, K.L. (2001) *Vulnerable Children and At-Risk Families: What Schools Offer Kindergartners and Their Families.* Presented at the biennial meeting of the Society for Research in Child Development, Minneapolis, MN.

Whitehurst, G.J. and Lonigan, C.J. (1998) 'Child development and emergent literacy', *Child Development*, 69(3): 848–72.

Whitehurst, G.J. and Lonigan, C.J. (2001) 'Emergent literacy: Development from pre-readers to readers', in S.B. Neuman and D.K. Dickinson (eds.), *Handbook of Early Literacy Research.* New York: The Guilford Press, pp. 11–29.

Williams, D., Neighbors, H. and Jackson, J. (2003) 'Racial/ethnic discrimination and health: Findings from community studies', *American Journal of Public Health*, 93: 200–8.

Youngstrom, E., Loeber, R. and Stouthamer-Loeber, M. (2000) 'Patterns and correlates of agreement between parent, teacher, and male adolescent rating of externalizing and internalizing problems', *Journal of Consulting and Clinical Psychology*, 68(6): 1038–50.

Zimmerman, R.S., Khoury, E.L., Vega, W.A., Gil, A.G. and Warheit, G.J. (1995) 'Teacher and parent perceptions of behavior problems among a sample of African American, Hispanic, and Non-Hispanic White students', *American Journal of Community Psychology*, 23(2): 181–97.

13

Sexual Minority Youth and Youth with Sexual Minority Parents

Charlotte J. Patterson

INTRODUCTION

Issues related to sexual orientation are increasingly in the public eye. In the daily news, there are discussions of whether lesbian and gay adolescents should be allowed to discuss their sexual identities at school, bring same-sex dates to school dances, or start gay–straight alliances (MacGillivray, 2007; Woog, 1995). Issues such as whether lesbian and gay adults should be allowed to marry, enter into domestic partnerships or civil unions, or adopt children are also common topics of public debate (see, for example, Eskridge, 1996; Sullivan, 1997; Wolfson, 2004). In the Western world today, many topics related to sexual minority identities are at the centre of public discourse.

In the context of expanding public recognition, issues related to sexual orientation are also at the heart of many significant legal and policy issues (Herek, 2007a; Patterson, 2007, 2009). For instance, questions about the extent to which openly lesbian or gay students must be protected from harassment, or about the permissibility of gay–straight alliances in schools have been litigated in more than one jurisdiction (Russell, 2002). Likewise, questions about the legal recognition of same-sex couples' relationships or about the advisability of allowing lesbian and gay adults to adopt children have occupied courts and legislatures in many different jurisdictions (Wald, 2006). Around the world today, many issues related to sexual minority identities are the subject of legal and policy debates (Badgett, 2009; Joslin and Minter, 2008; Murdoch and Price, 2001).

What is known about the role of sexual orientation in human development? Much of the available information stems from social science research in one of two traditions. The first line of work is focused on youngsters who experience same-sex attractions and/or who identify themselves as non-heterosexual, and explores development among gay, lesbian, and bisexual youth (D'Augelli and Patterson, 2001; Russell, 2002; Savin-Williams, 2005). A second tradition of work is focused on children and youth who grow up with lesbian or gay parents, and asks how they are affected, if at all, by parental sexual orientation (Patterson, 2000, 2007, 2009; Stacey and Biblarz, 2001). Both of these two traditions of research are now more than 20 years old, and at least with respect to some central concerns, each has led to relatively clear conclusions.

Interestingly, studies of non-heterosexual youth (hereafter termed 'sexual minority youth') have yielded results that differ greatly from findings of research on children of non-heterosexual parents (hereafter termed 'youth of sexual minority parents'). On the one hand, research on sexual minority youth has revealed that, relative to other youngsters, they are more likely to suffer with a number of mental health difficulties and other problems (Russell, 2002). On the other hand, studies of children of sexual minority parents suggest that, in many ways, their experiences do not differ very much from those of other children (Patterson, 2006, 2009). Thus, although sexual minority youth have often been found to have elevated risks for mental health problems, children of sexual minority parents appear to be no more likely than others to experience difficulties in development.

What special problems might sexual minority youth suffer? Why might sexual minority youth disproportionately experience difficulties while children of sexual minority parents do not? These are central questions to which this chapter is addressed. In the pages that follow, we first acknowledge and explore some aspects of diversity among such families. Overviews of the main conclusions from research with sexual minority youth, and of the main points from research on the offspring of sexual minority parents are then presented. Following the summaries of research in these two lines of work, we ask why they have yielded such markedly different conclusions, what this means, and what can be done to improve the life circumstances of sexual minority youth.

DIVERSITY AMONG FAMILIES WITH SEXUAL MINORITY MEMBERS

Some observers may be inclined to think of families with sexual minority members as a unitary group, but in reality, they are very diverse. For instance, youngsters who are growing up with lesbian or gay parents may have come into their family situations by any of a number of different pathways (Patterson, 2000). Some were born in the context of heterosexual marriages which broke up when one or the other or both parents came out as lesbian or gay. Others have been born to parents who already identified themselves as lesbian or gay. Some have been conceived by single lesbian women or by lesbian couples through donor insemination with sperm from donors; the donors themselves may be known or anonymous. Still others have been conceived by gay couples or by single gay men through donor insemination and surrogacy. Many other children have been adopted or fostered by lesbian or gay parents (Lavner, Waterman and Peplau, 2012). Thus, families in which children are being reared by lesbian or gay parents are themselves a diverse group (Patterson, 1992, 2000).

In addition to the diversity of families headed by lesbian and gay parents, there is also considerable variability in such children's understanding of their families at different ages. Young children whose parents are a same-sex couple often understand that their family differs from some others, but may not appreciate the stigma that attaches to their parents' sexual minority identities. Older children may begin to understand that some people hold negative attitudes about their lesbian or gay parents. By adolescence, when youngsters become acutely aware of any ways in which their families may differ from prevailing norms, worry or embarrassment about lesbian or gay parents may be common. Among young adults, however, more positive views often come to prevail (Lick, Patterson and Schmidt, 2013). Thus, the self-perceived circumstances of young people with sexual minority parents may differ to some degree, as a function of children's age.

Diversity is also notable among sexual minority youth. Some adopt sexual minority identities early in life, whereas others may not do so until later in adolescence or even in adulthood (D'Augelli, Pilkington and Hershberger, 2002). Some may be open about their sexual minority identities with everyone around them, whereas others may be much more selective about disclosure. Some may find conventional gender roles to be quite comfortable, whereas others may be less conventional in their gender expression. Some sexual minority youth live in tolerant, open environments, but others may face harassment and victimization (Kosciw and Diaz, 2006). Thus, the experiences and circumstances of sexual minority youth are extremely varied (D'Augelli and Patterson, 2001; Russell, 2002).

In addition to the kinds of diversity mentioned above, the families of sexual minority individuals also exhibit all the forms of diversity that characterize other families. For instance, individuals and families may differ from one another on the basis of race, ethnicity, religious background, socioeconomic status, immigration status, and a host of other factors. All of these issues may affect the experiences of family members in powerful ways. For example, Rosario, Schrimshaw, and Hunter (2004) found that, in a racially and ethnically diverse sample of sexual minority adolescents, those who were also members of ethnic and racial minority groups were less likely than their white counterparts to be open about their sexual minority identities in their daily lives. They were also less likely than white youth to report involvement in gay social activities. Thus, the experiences of adolescents may vary considerably as a function of race and ethnicity (Rosario et al., 2004).

In view of such diversity, one must recognize that the experiences of 'sexual minority youth' or of 'youth with sexual minority parents' are likely to show considerable variability (D'Augelli and Patterson, 2001; Patterson, 2000). Recognition of variability is hindered by the fact that the largest amount of research has focused on white, middle-class lesbian or gay youth, or on families headed by white, middle-class lesbian mothers. With some notable exceptions, most studies have also been conducted in the United States or the United Kingdom. Thus, most existing research does not highlight much of the diversity among experiences of families with non-heterosexual members (Tasker and Patterson, 2007). In what follows, we consider the results of research to date, with an eye to highlighting variations that may influence the experience of families with sexual minority members.

RESEARCH ON SEXUAL MINORITY YOUTH

Youth who identify as members of a sexual minority (for example, as lesbian, gay, bisexual, transgender, or queer) often live in environments that marginalize, stigmatize, and discriminate against them (D'Augelli and Patterson, 2001; Herek, 2007b; Rivers and D'Augelli, 2001). As a result, sexual minority youth are, as a group, at higher risk than others for many problems in adjustment (D'Augelli et al., 2002). Despite their elevated risk of difficulties, however, resources to support development among sexual minority youth are increasingly available. As a result, changes over time are likely to be significant in this area.

Because of their concerns about rejection by family members and friends, many sexual minority youth hesitate to disclose non-heterosexual identities (Savin-Williams, 2001). Even though sexual minority youth may report awareness of same-sex attractions as early as 8 or 9 years of age, sizeable numbers do not disclose same-sex attractions to anyone, particularly during the years of early adolescence. Some may disclose non-heterosexual identities while still in high school (Herdt and Boxer, 1996). For many sexual minority youth, however, the first disclosure may not occur until late adolescence (D'Augelli, 1991; Savin-Williams, 1998; Savin-Williams and Diamond, 2000). Thus, many youngsters spend their teen years trying to keep their sexual desires and attractions secret from the people around them (Savin-Williams and Diamond, 2000).

As social climates change over time, some gay and lesbian youth are coming out earlier

(Herdt and Boxer, 1996; Savin-Williams, 2005). For example, Floyd and Bakeman (2006) surveyed 767 adults of all ages about their coming out experiences. These researchers found that most participants recalled being aware of same-sex attractions in early adolescence, but most did not recall disclosing lesbian or gay identities to anyone until they were in their twenties. Interestingly, younger adults recalled having come out to parents and others sooner than did older adults. This result suggests the importance of historical change in making possible greater openness about sexual identities (Floyd and Bakeman, 2006). Despite such recent changes, however, many sexual minority youth remain undisclosed through much of adolescence.

When youth do feel ready to talk about their sexual minority identities, they are likely to worry about parental reactions. Most tell at least one friend of their sexual orientation before they disclose to parents (Rosario, Schrimshaw and Hunter, 2009; Savin-Williams, 1998). When parents first hear the news that a son or daughter identifies as non-heterosexual, many have negative responses. Initial reactions might include shock, denial, distress, or even overt anger. Although parental reactions may grow more positive over time, as parents adjust to the reality that a son is gay or a daughter is lesbian, complete acceptance upon first disclosure is uncommon (Savin-Williams, 2001). Thus, even when they have disclosed non-heterosexual identities at home, the likelihood of sexual minority adolescents having strong parental support is not very great. Some youngsters are victimized, disowned, or told to leave home (Rivers and D'Augelli, 2001).

Sexual minority youth may also encounter hostile environments at school. A national survey of sexual minority adolescents in the United States found that about 75 per cent reported hearing antigay remarks or terms 'often' or 'frequently' at school, and that most reported feeling distressed by this experience (Kosciw and Diaz, 2006). In the same survey, nearly two-thirds of sexual minority adolescents reported that they had been harassed or threatened at school, and more than one third reported that they had suffered physical harassment. It is easy to understand, then, that almost two-thirds of sexual minority adolescents reported feeling unsafe at school due to issues related to sexual orientation. Those who reported experiencing harassment also reported missing more days of school, receiving lower grades, and having lower educational aspirations (Kosciw and Diaz, 2006). Victimization of sexual minority youth clearly occurs in some school environments, and it is often associated with educational difficulties among those who are victimized (Rivers and D'Augelli, 2001; Russell, Franz and Driscoll, 2001).

How do sexual minority adolescents cope with being required to spend time in such stressful environments? Some literally fight back, becoming involved in conflicts at school (Kosciw and Diaz, 2006). Without adequate support, and in the face of hostility and victimization, others feel lonely and experience distress (Russell, 2002). Sexual minority adolescents are more likely than other youth to be involved in aggressive fights and to report depressive symptoms (Russell and Joyner, 2001).

Feelings of exclusion and hopelessness may provide an impetus for excessive use of alcohol and drugs, as well as for unsafe sexual activities (Rotheram-Borus and Langabeer, 2001). Statewide surveys of high school students in Massachusetts and in Vermont have revealed that those with same-sex sexual experience were more likely than their peers to have used alcohol and illegal drugs such as marijuana (DuRant, Krowchuk and Sinal, 1998; Faulkner and Cranston, 1998; Garofalo et al., 1998). In a national sample of adolescents, alcohol and drug use were associated with sexual minority status, especially among girls (Russell, Driscoll and Truong, 2002). Alcohol and drug use may themselves be linked in multiple ways with other problem behaviours, such as delinquency and risky sexual behaviour. Unhappy youth who engage in more alcohol and drug use than do their peers are also likely to be more vulnerable to additional mental health problems (Rotheram-Borus and Langabeer, 2001).

As one might expect based on other problems experienced by lesbian and gay youth, sexual minority status is also a risk factor for adolescent suicidality (Russell, 2003). Information from large-scale, population-based studies has shown that adolescents who identify as members of sexual minorities are distinctly more likely than others to report having attempted suicide (Russell, 2003). In a national sample of American adolescents, youngsters who reported either same-sex attractions or same-sex sexual experiences were at least twice as likely as other youth to report having made a suicide attempt (Russell and Joyner, 2001). Studies of sexual minority adults have also reported heightened vulnerability, and have shown that most suicide attempts recalled by adults actually took place during adolescence (Paul, et al., 2002). Thus, as a group, sexual minority youth are at heightened risk of taking their own lives (Remafedi, 1999).

Despite the undoubted challenges faced by many sexual minority youth, greater support is available to them today than ever before, and many youth develop in positive ways. Adolescents who are attracted to same-sex partners or who identify as members of sexual minorities can find information and can initiate contact with other sexual minority individuals via the internet (Russell, 2002). In many cities, sexual minority youth support groups are available in the community; examples include Horizons Youth in Chicago and the Sexual Minority Youth Assistance League (SMYAL) in Washington, DC. More and more student clubs, such as Gay–Straight Alliances, have been formed, with the twin aims of offering support to lesbian, gay, bisexual, transgender and allied students, and of improving school climates for sexual minority youth (GLSEN [Gay, Lesbian and Straight Education Network], 2007).

Gay–Straight Alliances are important resources for sexual minority youth. In schools with Gay–Straight Alliances, sexual minority students are less likely to report hearing anti-gay remarks, less likely to report being victimized, and less likely to report feeling unsafe at school (Kocsiw and Diaz, 2006; Szalacha, 2003). Both sexual minority and other students are likely to describe the climate for sexual minority students as more favourable in schools with such resources than in schools without them (Goodenow, Szalacha and Westheimer, 2006; Szalacha, 2003).

It is not yet clear how best to interpret effects associated with Gay–Straight Alliances. Is the existence of a Gay–Straight Alliance simply a marker for favourable school climate? In other words, do favourable school climates create conditions in which Gay–Straight Alliances can take root? Or do these clubs have a causal influence? In other words, do Gay–Straight Alliances actually succeed in their efforts to improve the climate for sexual minority youth? Some evidence for the latter view comes from interviews with students who have participated in Gay–Straight Alliances. For example, one student commented, 'going to Gay-Straight Alliance ... you don't feel alone ... there's others out there to support you' (Russell et al., 2009: 899). Another said, 'Being the president of a Gay-Straight Alliance is really empowering to me, it gives me a lot of control ... I've devoted a lot of time to it, and that's empowering, knowing that like I have the power to make this change in my school' (Russell et al., 2009: 903). Whether their influence is causal or not, the existence of a Gay–Straight Alliance at a school is clearly associated with a greater sense of support among sexual minority youth (GLSEN, 2007).

In addition to school environments, the reactions of family members and friends to youth disclosure of non-heterosexual identities are also very significant. For example, Rosario and her colleagues (2009) found that reactions to adolescents' disclosure of sexual minority identities accounted for more variation in health outcomes than did the fact of disclosure itself. In particular, teens whose disclosures were met with negative or rejecting reactions showed higher use of alcohol, cigarettes, and marijuana than did those whose disclosures were met with neutral or positive reactions. Similarly, Ryan et al. (2009) found that sexual minority young adults who experienced family rejection of their sexual minority identities were much more likely than others to experience depressive symptoms, to participate in unsafe sexual practices, to use illegal drugs, and to report having considered suicide (Ryan et al., 2009). Thus, physical and mental health outcomes for sexual minority adolescents and young adults are strongly associated with family support or rejection.

As family and community support becomes available to more and more sexual minority youth, they can be expected to have increasingly positive experiences. Even today, many sexual minority youth seem to fare well at home, at school, and in their peer groups (Savin-Williams, 2005). As attitudes become less hostile and as school climates become more welcoming, many more sexual minority youth can be expected to show positive developmental outcomes (Goodenow et al., 2006; Russell, 2002; Russell et al., 2009; Szalacha, 2003).

Overall, however, research has shown that, both at home and at school, sexual minority youth today, on average, encounter greater hostility than do their heterosexual peers. They also are at elevated risk for psychological distress, substance use, risky sexual behaviour, and suicidality. Not all sexual minority youth show these problems, but many do and the risks are very real (Russell, 2002).

RESEARCH ON CHILDREN OF NON-HETEROSEXUAL PARENTS

A considerable amount of empirical research has been conducted with the offspring of lesbian and gay parents, and the findings have been remarkably consistent. This type of work began by focusing on children who had been conceived in the context of heterosexual relationships that had ended in divorce when one of the parents declared a lesbian or gay identity. It has, however, also come to include research with those whose families were formed in other ways, and to involve adolescents as well as children (Patterson, 2002, 2006; Stacey and Biblarz, 2001). Overall, however, most of this research focuses on children with lesbian mothers.

When children grow up with lesbian or gay parents, do they show healthy development? To address this question, some researchers have compared development among children being reared by a divorced lesbian mother with development among those being reared by a divorced heterosexual mother. The most clear-cut result of these studies has been the tremendous similarity between children in the two groups. Results of these studies revealed no reason to believe that the development and adjustment of children whose parents divorced because the mother declared a lesbian identity was very different than that among those whose parents divorced for some other reason (Patterson, 1992, 2000; Stacey and Biblarz, 2001).

One such study compared the adjustment of children with divorced lesbian mothers to that among children with divorced heterosexual mothers (Golombok, Spencer and Rutter, 1983). Golombok and her colleagues reported that both the qualities of behaviour and of relationships were similar in the two groups. For example, standardized reports on children's conduct by teachers and by parents did not differ between the two groups. Similarly, standardized ratings of each child's psychiatric state, made by a child psychiatrist who was unaware of group membership, did not differ between the two groups (Golombok et al., 1983).

This study was subsequently expanded with individual follow-up interviews of the participants as young adults (Tasker and Golombok, 1997). These interviews revealed that the young adult offspring of lesbian mothers had developed along mostly positive trajectories, and that there were few differences between those reared by divorced lesbian versus divorced heterosexual mothers. For example, no differences between the two groups appeared on measures of general conduct or academic attainment. Moreover, those who had been reared by lesbian mothers were no more likely than were those reared by heterosexual mothers to identify themselves as lesbian or gay (Tasker and Golombok, 1997).

Despite the importance of findings from such studies, however, this type of research was characterized by certain limitations. For example, most studies were based on data from small, homogeneous samples that were made up of predominantly well-educated white respondents. Because no efforts to achieve representative sampling were undertaken in the early studies, the degree to which these findings could be generalized to any population was unknown. Most data were also collected from family members themselves, leaving open the possibility that the results might have been affected by any of a number of systematic biases.

Subsequent waves of research in this area made efforts to address such methodological issues. Some studies attempted to identify potential participants through the use of rational sampling frames. For instance, in one study, every family who had conceived and given birth to a child using the resources of a single sperm bank, during a fixed period of time, was invited to participate in research (Chan, Raboy and Patterson, 1998). Because of the sampling methods used in this study, attrition could be evaluated. Findings revealed that – especially among the lesbian mothers who had been invited to participate – attrition was very low. Most families who were invited to participate did in fact participate, making the sample characteristic representative of the population from which it was drawn.

The resulting sample of 80 families included 55 families headed by lesbian mothers and 25 families headed by heterosexual parents (Chan et al., 1998; Fulcher et al., 2006). In families headed by both lesbian and heterosexual couples, one parent was always biologically related (the biological mother) and the other parent (the nonbiological lesbian mother or the father) was not biologically related to the child. Data on child adjustment were collected from teachers as well as from parents, in an effort to compare the views of parents with those of professionals outside the family circle (Chan et al., 1998).

Much like the findings of earlier studies, results showed that children were developing in healthy directions and that there was no apparent impact of parental sexual orientation. For example, on standardized measures of social competence and behaviour problems, teachers and parents agreed that, on average, both those with lesbian and those with heterosexual parents were developing well. There were no significant differences on social competence or behaviour problems as a function of parental sexual orientation (Chan et al., 1998). What made more difference than parental sexual orientation for children's development was the warmth and closeness of relationships with parents. When parents described their relationships with children as warm and supportive, children were described by teachers and others as developing well (Chan et al., 1998; Fulcher et al., 2006).

Even as they provided new information about children born to lesbian mothers, findings from studies like these, however, also raised additional questions. Families who conceive children using the resources of a sperm bank are generally an affluent group. Was it possible that the children of well-educated professionals in this group were protected from many problems that others would encounter? Another issue was that children who participated in this research were quite young. Was it possible that, even if they were developing well during childhood, problems might emerge during adolescence? Questions like these led to concerns that older youth from a more diverse set of families might encounter as-yet undocumented problems (Baumrind, 1995).

An opportunity to examine such issues was presented by the availability of data from large national surveys such as the National Longitudinal Study of Adolescent Health (known as the Add Health Study). The Add Health Study involved a large, ethnically diverse, essentially representative sample of adolescents and their parents in the United States (Bearman, Jones and Udry, 1997). More than 12,000 adolescents (averaging 15 years of age) completed surveys, questionnaires, and interviews, as did their parents and teachers. Unfortunately, parents were not asked directly about their sexual orientation, but they were asked if they were in a 'marriage or marriage-like relationship'. If parents described themselves as being involved in such a relationship, they were asked to report the gender of their partner. Using these data, Wainright and her colleagues identified a group of adolescents whose mothers were living with same-sex partners and compared them with a matched group of adolescents whose mothers were living with other-sex partners (Wainright and Patterson, 2006, 2008; Wainright, Russell and Patterson, 2004).Consistent with earlier findings, results from the Add Health Study revealed few differences in adjustment between adolescents living with same-sex couples and those living with other-sex couples. There were no significant differences between adolescents living with same-sex couples and those living with other-sex couples on self-reported assessments of psychological well-being, such as self-esteem and anxiety; measures of school outcomes, such as grade point averages and trouble in school; or measures of family relationships, such as parental warmth and care from adults and peers (Wainright, Russell and Patterson, 2004). Adolescents in the two groups were equally likely to say that they had been involved in a romantic relationship in the last year, and they were equally likely to report having been sexually active. There were no significant differences in peer relations, self-reported substance use, delinquency, or peer victimization between those reared by same- or other-sex couples (Wainright and Patterson, 2006, 2008). Thus, in findings from the Add Health Study, the gender of parents' partners was not an important predictor of adolescent well-being or adjustment. Not only is it possible for children and adolescents who are parented by same-sex couples to develop in healthy directions, but as demonstrated in the work of Wainright and her colleagues – which was based on an extremely diverse sample of American adolescents – they generally do.

Although the fact of living with same-sex or other-sex couples was not important as a predictor of adolescent development, other aspects of family relationships were significantly associated with adolescent adjustment. Consistent with other findings in the literature on adolescence, qualities of family relationships were clearly linked with adolescent adjustment. Parents who reported warm, close relationships with their offspring had adolescents who described themselves as showing more favourable adjustment, and whose peers described them as better adjusted. More important than the gender of parents' partners for adolescents' adjustment was the quality of relationships within the families they had (Wainright et al., 2004; Wainright and Patterson, 2006, 2008).

The fact that children and adolescents with lesbian or gay parents generally develop in healthy ways should not be taken to suggest that they encounter no challenges. The same antigay comments that 75 per cent of sexual minority youth report hearing 'often' or 'frequently' in their high schools (Kosciw and Diaz, 2006) are also no doubt overheard by adolescents with sexual minority parents. Indeed, in a large-scale study of lesbian and gay parents and their children, 76 per cent of students with sexual minority parents reported hearing antigay remarks (such as 'that is so gay') 'often' or 'frequently' at school (Kosciw and Diaz, 2008). In the same study, 9 per cent of children with sexual minority parents said that they had heard negative comments about lesbian and gay parents at school, and 23 per cent said they felt unsafe at school because they had a sexual minority parent (Kosciw and Diaz, 2008).

Many authors have commented on the fact that children of lesbian and gay parents may encounter antigay attitudes in the course of their daily lives. For instance, in a study of children born to lesbian mothers, Gartrell et al. (2005) reported that a substantial minority had encountered antigay sentiments among their peers or even among their teachers at school. Not surprisingly, those who had such encounters usually remembered having felt distressed or angry about them. There is no evidence, however, that these kinds of experiences have influenced overall development among the offspring of lesbian or gay parents.

After more than 20 years of research, there can be little doubt but that development among the offspring of sexual minority parents is generally similar to that among the offspring of heterosexual parents. Despite the fears and concerns expressed by some observers, nothing in the way of real evidence has emerged to suggest that children of lesbian mothers or of gay fathers develop, on average, in anything less than positive directions. Indeed, the weight of the research suggests that development and adjustment among children of sexual minority parents is at least as favourable as that among children of heterosexual parents.

DISCUSSION

Overall, then, the evidence from social science research about both sexual minority youth and about youth with sexual minority parents appears to be remarkably clear. Although, on average, sexual minority youth appear to be unusually vulnerable to an array of problems in development, youngsters with sexual minority parents appear to share no such vulnerabilities. These findings raise questions about why issues surrounding

sexual minority status play out so differently in the two cases.

Before taking up substantive questions about the impact of sexual minority identities, however, some limitations of the current research should be acknowledged. First, as noted above, most studies have been conducted in the United States and in the United Kingdom. Research is underway in Australia (Crouch et al., 2012, 2013; Short et al., 2007), Canada (Ross, 2005; Vyncke and Julien, 2007), France (Vyncke and Julien, 2007), Germany (Hermann-Green and Gehring, 2007), and the Netherlands (Bos et al., 2008; Bos, Van Balen and Van den Boom, 2007), but there is still very little information about the lives of sexual minority youth or about youth with sexual minority parents from the developing world. Oppression of sexual minority individuals and their families is still very much in evidence around the world, but our knowledge about its impact is still limited. Future research will hopefully yield a more globalized understanding of these issues.

Another limitation of existing research in this area is its frequent reliance on a small number of methods. For instance, many studies have used sampling methods that are likely to locate well-educated, predominantly white participants, rather than people of colour or those with limited education. Many studies rely on self-report methods, rather than on teacher or peer reports, or observational methods. When research has employed representative sampling techniques, more diverse samples have been assembled; and when research has relied on teacher and peer reports on youngsters' development, clearer understanding has emerged (Wainright et al., 2004). Future research will hopefully employ a broad array of methodologies, so as to yield stronger results.

Why do children of sexual minority parents develop in typical ways when sexual minority youth appear to be markedly more vulnerable? One hypothesis can be drawn from the fact that most offspring of lesbian and gay parents themselves identify as heterosexual (Patterson, 2000). Thus, the stigma associated with sexual orientation may fall directly on sexual minority youth, but not so much (or perhaps almost not at all) on youth with sexual minority parents. Both felt stigma, which involves the perception that one is marginalized, and enacted stigma, which involves the enactment of discriminatory or victimizing behaviour, may be involved here (Herek, 2007b). If based on sexual orientation, the impact of both forms of stigma is likely to be greater for sexual minority youth than for youth with sexual minority parents, who are predominantly heterosexual.

A second hypothesis about different levels of adjustment among sexual minority adolescents versus adolescents with sexual minority parents focuses on the issue of gender typicality. In general, sexual minority individuals are more likely than others to show atypical gender expression, and this appears to be true throughout life. For example, sexual minority men are more likely, as boys, to have behaved in conventionally feminine ways; similarly, sexual minority women are more likely, as girls, to have behaved in conventionally masculine ways (Rieger et al., 2008). It may be that gender nonconformity rather than (or in addition to) sexual orientation per se accounts for heightened vulnerability among sexual minority adolescents. Consistent with this view, gender nonconformity has been identified as a risk factor for suicidality among sexual minority youth (D'Augelli et al., 2002; Remafedi, Farrow and Deisher, 1993). It is possible that atypical gender expression is the critical factor underlying differences in adjustment between sexual minority youth and youth with sexual minority parents.

The role of context

It is also possible that either of these two hypotheses may be correct in some but not other contexts. Depending upon the views of others populating a particular environment, there may be more or less stigma associated with sexual minority status or atypical gender expression in that environment. Growing up as a gender nonconforming gay youth in a liberal urban centre is probably very different than doing so in a conservative farming community. In some environments, whether because of prevailing attitudes toward gender atypicality or toward sexual orientation, or because of other factors, sexual minority youth may have problems that are not experienced by youngsters with sexual minority parents. In other environments, there may be no difference in risk for the two groups.

To evaluate these and other viewpoints, new research will be needed. We need to know more about the characteristics of youngsters themselves, as well as more about the social climates in which they live, and about the interactions of all these variables. What are the characteristics and resources of sexual minority youth who adapt well versus those of youth who experience problems in different environments? What are the aspects of social contexts that foster positive development among sexual minority youth, and how can these encouraged? Future studies will hopefully help to clarify some of the critical questions in this area.

In this regard, the experiences of a relatively small group, the so-called 'second generation' sexual minority youth, may be particularly informative (Goldberg, 2007). Members of the 'second generation' are lesbian, gay, and bisexual adolescents or young adults who have sexual minority parents. Do these individuals share the vulnerabilities of sexual minority youth more generally, like other lesbian or gay adolescents? Or do they adapt well, like the offspring of lesbian and gay parents? On the one hand, such youth would seem to be subject to many of the stressors that affect other sexual minority youth. On the other hand, second generation youth may be more likely than other sexual minority youth to have the benefit of supportive guidance from their parents. Results of research with this group of adolescents and young adults seem likely to help us understand more about the nature of stresses and supports among sexual minority youth.

Additional research focused on potential sources of stress or support for sexual minority youth may also be helpful. For example, how are positive correlates of school-based groups such as Gay–Straight Alliances to be interpreted? Do they represent markers (in other words, indicators that a favourable social climate already exists), or causal factors (the creation of more favourable social climates)? And, if the latter, do they also have effects on youngsters who have sexual minority parents, or on other students? What impact might community-based groups designed for sexual minority youth have on their development? If social support for non-heterosexual identities and/or for gender nonconformity are needs that sexual minority youth feel, then opportunities to participate in Gay–Straight Alliances or community-based support groups should benefit them. Despite some promising work that has already been reported, the research agenda in this area is clearly extensive.

As research examines stresses and supports for sexual minority youth, it most often employs categorical schemes for identifying heterosexual and non-heterosexual youth. It is important to bear in mind, however, that especially among girls, and especially in adolescence and young adulthood, sexual identities may be quite fluid (Diamond, 2008). In a 10-year longitudinal study of sexual identities among non-heterosexual young women, Diamond reported that many participants identified themselves in more than one way over time (Diamond, 2008). Thus, a girl who began the study identifying herself as bisexual might grow into a lesbian identity; another young woman might move from a bisexual to a heterosexual identity over time. Likewise, it is clear that, even after undertaking heterosexual marriage and parenthood, some parents may come out as gay or lesbian (Patterson, 2000). Whether or not a particular person identifies as a member of a sexual minority may change over time, and

some individuals reject labels altogether. Secular changes in this regard may be significant.

Thus, the issues under study here are themselves moving targets. As individual attitudes, public opinion, and legal contexts change over time, it is likely that the experiences of sexual minority individuals and also of youngsters with sexual minority parents will also change (Herek, 2007a). With youngsters coming out earlier and school climates becoming more positive, we are already beginning to see such changes (GLSEN, 2007). When sexual minority individuals are seen as equal citizens and when sexual minority individuals are treated equally under the law, individual attitudes as well as public opinion are likely to shift (Russell, 2002). Although they undoubtedly face some special issues, social science research findings suggest that youngsters growing up with sexual minority parents do not face heightened developmental risks (Patterson, 2006). The day has not yet arrived, but one can begin to imagine a future when growing up lesbian, gay, or bisexual will also pose no special burden.

REFERENCES

Badgett, M.V.L. (2009) *When Gay People Get Married: What Happens when Societies Legalize Same-Sex Marriage*. New York: New York University Press.

Baumrind, D. (1995) 'Commentary on sexual orientation: Research and social policy implications', *Developmental Psychology*, 31(1): 130–6.

Bearman, P.S., Jones, J. and Udry, J.R. (1997) *The National Longitudinal Study of Adolescent Health: Research Design*. Available at http://www.cpc.unc.edu/projects/addhealth/design.html

Bos, H.M.W., Sandfort, T.G.M., de Bruyn, E.H. and Hakvoort, E. (2008) 'Same-sex attraction, social relationships, psychological functioning, and school performance in young adolescents', *Developmental Psychology*, 44(1): 59–68.

Bos, H.M.W., Van Balen, F. and Van Den Boom, D.C. (2007) 'Child adjustment and parenting in planned lesbian-parent families', *American Journal of Orthopsychiatry*, 77(1): 38–48.

Chan, R.W., Raboy, B. and Patterson, C.J. (1998) 'Psychosocial adjustment among children conceived via donor insemination by lesbian and heterosexual mothers', *Child Development*, 69(2): 443–57.

Crouch, S.R., McNair, R., Waters, E. and Power, J. (2013) 'What makes a same-sex parented family', *Medical Journal of Australia*, 198(9): 1–3.

Crouch, S.R., Waters, E., McNair, R., Power, J. and Davis, E. (2012) 'ACHESS – The Australian study of child health in same-sex families: Background research, design and methodology', *BMC Public Health*, 12: 646.

D'Augelli, A.R. (1991) 'Gay men in college: Identity processes and adaptations', *Journal of College Student Development*, 32(2): 140–6.

D'Augelli, A.R. and Patterson, C.J. (eds.) (2001) *Lesbian, Gay and Bisexual Identities and Youth: Psychological Perspectives*. New York: Oxford University Press.

D'Augelli, A.R., Pilkington, N.W. and Hershberger, S.L. (2002) 'Incidence and mental health impact of sexual orientation victimization of lesbian, gay, and bisexual youths in high school', *School Psychology Quarterly*, 17(2): 148–67.

Diamond, L. (2008) *Sexual Fluidity: Understanding Women's Love and Desire*. Cambridge, MA: Harvard University Press.

DuRant, R.H., Krowchuk, D.P. and Sinal, S.H. (1998) 'Victimization, use of violence, and drug use at school among male adolescents who engage in same-sex sexual behavior', *Journal of Pediatrics*, 133(1): 113–18.

Eskridge, W.N. (1996) *The Case for Same-Sex Marriage: From Sexual Liberty to Civilized Commitment*. New York: Free Press.

Faulkner, A.H. and Cranston, K. (1998) 'Correlates of same-sex sexual behavior in a random sample of Massachusetts high school students', *American Journal of Public Health*, 88(2): 262–6.

Floyd, F.J. and Bakeman, R. (2006) 'Coming-out across the life course: Implications of age and historical context', *Archives of Sexual Behavior*, 35(3): 287–96.

Fulcher, M., Sutfin, E.L., Chan, R.W., Scheib, J.E. and Patterson, C.J. (2006) 'Lesbian mothers and their children: Findings from the Contemporary Families Study', in A.M. Omoto and H.S. Kurtzman (eds.), *Sexual Orientation and Mental Health: Examining Identity and Development in Lesbian, Gay, and Bisexual People*. Washington, DC: American Psychological Association, pp. 281–99.

Garofalo, R., Wolf, R.C., Kessel, S., Palfrey, J. and DuRant, R.H. (1998) 'The association between health risk behaviors and sexual orientation among a school-based sample of adolescents', *Pediatrics*, 101(5): 859–902.

Gartrell, N., Deck, A., Rodas, C., Peyser, H. and Banks, A. (2005) 'The National Lesbian Family Study: 4. Interviews with the 10 year old children', *American Journal of Orthopsychiatry*, 75(4): 518–24.

GLSEN (Gay, Lesbian and Straight Education Network) (2007) *Gay-Straight Alliances: Creating Safer Schools for LGBT Students and their Allies* (GLSEN Research Brief). New York: Gay, Lesbian, and Straight Education Network.

Goldberg, A.E. (2007) '(How) does it make a difference? Perspectives of adults with lesbian, gay and bisexual parents', *American Journal of Orthopsychiatry*, 77(4): 550–62.

Golombok, S., Spencer, A. and Rutter, M. (1983) 'Children in lesbian and single-parent households: Psychosexual and psychiatric appraisal', *Journal of Child Psychology and Psychiatry*, 24(4): 551–72.

Goodenow, C., Szalacha, L. and Westheimer, K. (2006) 'School support groups, other school factors, and the safety of sexual minority adolescents', *Psychology in the Schools*, 43(5): 573–89.

Herdt, G. and Boxer, A. (1996) *Children of Horizons: How Gay and Lesbian Teens are Leading a New Way out of the Closet*. Boston, MA: Beacon Press.

Herek, G.M. (2007a) 'Science, public policy, and legal recognition of same-sex relationships', *American Psychologist*, 62(7): 713–15.

Herek, G.M. (2007b) 'Confronting sexual stigma and prejudice: Theory and practice', *Journal of Social Issues*, 63(4): 905–25.

Hermann-Green, L.K. and Gehring, T.M. (2007) 'The German Lesbian Family Study: Planning for parenthood via donor insemination', *Journal of Gay, Lesbian, Bisexual and Transgender Family Studies*, 3(4): 351–96.

Joslin, C.G. and Minter, S.P. (2008) *Lesbian, Gay, Bisexual and Transgender Family Law*. Eagan, MN: Thomson/West.

Kosciw, J.G. and Diaz, E.M. (2006) *The 2005 National School Climate Study*. New York: Gay, Lesbian, and Straight Education Network.

Kosciw, J.G. and Diaz, E.M. (2008) *Involved, Invisible, Ignored: The Experience of Lesbian, Gay, Bisexual, and Transgender Parents and Their Children in Our Nation's K-12 Schools*. New York: GLSEN.

Lavner, J.A., Waterman, J. and Peplau, L.A. (2012) 'Can gay and lesbian parents promote healthy development in high-risk children adopted from foster care?', *American Journal of Orthopsychiatry*, 82(4): 465–72.

Lick, D.J., Patterson, C.J. and Schmidt, K. (2013) 'Recalled social experiences and current psychological adjustment among adults reared by lesbian and gay parents'. *Journal of GLBT Family Studies*, 9, 230–53.

MacGillivray, I.K. (2007) *Gay-Straight Alliances: A Handbook for Students, Educators, and Parents*. New York: Routledge.

Murdoch, J. and Price, D. (2001) *Courting Justice: Gay Men and Lesbians v. the Supreme Court*. New York: Basic Books.

Patterson, C.J. (1992) 'Children of lesbian and gay parents', *Child Development*, 63(5): 1025–42.

Patterson, C.J. (2000) 'Sexual orientation and family life: A decade review', *Journal of Marriage and the Family*, 62: 1052–69.

Patterson, C.J. (2002) 'Lesbian and gay parenthood', in M.H. Bornstein (ed.), *Handbook of Parenting*, 2nd Edition. Hillsdale, NJ: Lawrence Erlbaum, pp. 317–38.

Patterson, C.J. (2006) 'Children of lesbian and gay parents', *Current Directions in Psychological Science*, 15(5): 241–44.

Patterson, C.J. (2007) 'Lesbian and gay family issues in the context of changing legal and social policy environments', in K.J. Bieschke, R.M. Perez and K.A. DeBord (eds.), *Handbook of Counseling and Psychotherapy with Lesbian, Gay, Bisexual and Transgender Clients* (2nd Edition). Washington, DC: American Psychological Association, pp. 359–77.

Patterson, C.J. (2009) 'Children of lesbian and gay parents: Psychology, law, and policy', *American Psychologist*, 64(8): 727–36.

Paul, J.P., Catania, J., Pollack, L., Moskowitz, J., Canchola, J., Mills, T., Binson, D. and Stall, R. (2002) 'Suicide attempts among gay and bisexual men: Lifetime prevalence and antecedents', *American Journal of Public Health*, 92(8): 1338–44.

Remafedi, G. (1999) 'Suicide and sexual orientation: Nearing the end of the controversy?', *Archives of General Psychiatry*, 56(10): 885–6.

Remafedi, G., Farrow, J.and Deisher, R. W. (1993) 'Risk factors for attempted suicide in gay and bisexual youth', in L. Garnets and D.C. Kimmel (eds.), *Psychological Perspectives on Lesbian and Gay Male Experiences*. New York: Columbia University Press, pp. 869–75.

Rieger, G., Linsenmeier, J.A., Gygax, L. and Bailey, J.M. (2008) 'Sexual orientation and childhood gender nonconformity: Evidence from home videos', *Developmental Psychology*, 44(1): 46–58.

Rivers, I. and D'Augelli, A.R. (2001) 'The victimization of lesbian, gay and bisexual youths', in A.R. D'Augelli and C.J. Patterson (eds.), *Lesbian, Gay and Bisexual Identities and Youth: Psychological Perspectives*. New York: Oxford University Press, pp. 199–223.

Rosario, M., Schrimshaw, E.W. and Hunter, J. (2004) 'Ethnic/racial differences in the coming-out process of lesbian, gay, and bisexual youths: A comparison of sexual identity development over time', *Cultural Diversity and Ethnic Minority Psychology*, 10(3): 215–28.

Rosario, M., Schrimshaw, E.W. and Hunter, J. (2009) 'Disclosure of sexual orientation and subsequent substance use and abuse among lesbian, gay, and bisexual youths: Critical role of disclosure reactions', *Psychology of Addictive Behaviors*, 23(1): 175–84.

Ross, L.E. (2005) 'Perinatal mental health in lesbian mothers: A review of potential risk and protective factors', *Women and Health*, 41(3): 113–28.

Rotheram-Borus, M.J. and Langabeer, K.A. (2001) 'Developmental trajectories of gay, lesbian, and bisexual youths', in A.R. D'Augelli and C.J. Patterson (eds.), *Lesbian, Gay and Bisexual Identities and Youth: Psychological Perspectives*. New York: Oxford University Press, pp. 97–128.

Russell, S.T. (2002) 'Queer in America: Citizenship for sexual minority youth', *Applied Developmental Science*, 6(4): 258–63.

Russell, S.T. (2003) 'Sexual minority youth and suicide risk', *American Behavioral Scientist*, 46(9): 1241–57.

Russell, S.T., Driscoll, A.K. and Truong, N. (2002) 'Adolescent same-sex romantic attractions and relationships: Implications for substance use and abuse', *American Journal of Public Health*, 92(2): 198–202.

Russell, S.T., Franz, B.T. and Driscoll, A.K. (2001) 'Same-sex romantic attraction and experiences of violence in adolescence', *American Journal of Public Health*, 91(6): 903–6.

Russell, S.T. and Joyner, K. (2001) 'Adolescent sexual orientation and suicide risk: Evidence from a national study', *American Journal of Public Health*, 91(8): 1276–81.

Russell, S.T., Muraco, A., Subramaniam, A. and Laub, C. (2009) 'Youth empowerment and high school gay-straight alliances', *Journal of Youth and Adolescence*, 38(7): 891–903.

Ryan, C., Huebner, D., Diaz, R.M. and Sanchez, J. (2009) 'Family rejection as a predictor of negative health outcomes in white and Latino lesbian, gay, and bisexual young adults', *Pediatrics*, 123(1): 346–52.

Savin-Williams, R.C. (1998) '*And Then I Became Gay': Young Men's Stories*. New York: Routledge.

Savin-Williams, R.C. (2001) *Mom, Dad, I'm Gay: How Families Negotiate Coming Out*. Washington, DC: American Psychological Association.

Savin-Williams, R.C. (2005) *The New Gay Teenager*. Cambridge MA: Harvard University Press.

Savin-Williams, R.C. and Diamond, L.M. (2000) 'Sexual identity trajectories among sexual-minority youths: Gender comparisons', *Archives of Sexual Behavior*, 29(6): 607–27.

Short, E., Riggs, D.W., Perlesz, A., Brown, R. and Kane, G. (2007) *Lesbian, Gay, Bisexual, and Transgender Parented Families*. Melbourne: Australian Psychological Society.

Stacey, J. and Biblarz, T.J. (2001) '(How) Does sexual orientation of parents matter?', *American Sociological Review*, 66(2): 159–83.

Sullivan, A. (1997) *Same-Sex Marriage: Pro and Con – A Reader*. New York: Vintage Books.

Szalacha, L.A. (2003) 'Safer sexual diversity climates: Lessons learned from an evaluation of Massachusetts Safe Schools Program for gay and lesbian students', *American Journal of Education*, 110(1): 58–88.

Tasker, F. and Golombok, S. (1997) *Growing up in a Lesbian Family*. New York: Guilford Press.

Tasker, F. and Patterson, C.J. (2007) 'Research on gay and lesbian parenting: Retrospect and prospect', *Journal of Gay, Lesbian, Bisexual and Transgender Family Studies*, 3(2–3): 9–34.

Vyncke, J.D. and Julien, D. (2007) 'Social support, coming out, and adjustment of lesbian mothers in Canada and France', *Journal of Gay, Lesbian,* *Bisexual and Transgender Family Studies*, 3(4): 397–424.

Wainright, J.L. and Patterson, C.J. (2006) 'Delinquency, victimization, and substance use among adolescents with female same-sex parents', *Journal of Family Psychology*, 20(3): 526–30.

Wainright, J.L. and Patterson, C.J. (2008) 'Peer relations among adolescents with female same-sex parents', *Developmental Psychology*, 44(1): 117–26.

Wainright, J.L., Russell, S.T. and Patterson, C.J. (2004) 'Psychosocial adjustment and school outcomes of adolescents with same-sex parents', *Child Development*, 75(6): 1886–98.

Wald, M.S. (2006) 'Adults' sexual orientation and state determinations regarding placement of children', *Family Law Quarterly*, 40(3): 381–434.

Wolfson, E. (2004) *Why Marriage Matters: America, Equality, and Gay People's Right to Marry*. New York: Simon and Schuster.

Woog, D. (1995) School's Out: *The Impact of Gay and Lesbian Issues on America's Schools*. Boston, MA: Alyson Publications, Inc.

14

Children Who Have Disabilities

Patricia Sloper and Bryony Beresford

INTRODUCTION

In the past, research often relied on adults as proxies for the views of children, and this was particularly the case for children and young people with disabilities, where research which sought the views of children themselves was rare (Beresford, 1997; Ward, 1997). However, there has been increasing recognition of the fact that children's views differ from those of adults and, along with this, research has shown that children who have disabilities hold and can express views, given the right environment and support, and that they value the opportunity to express their views (Cavet and Sloper, 2004). In recent years, there has been considerable growth in research which consults children with disabilities*. It is argued that the exclusion of children with disabilities from research is largely the result of unsuitability of research methods and lack of expertise of researchers in communication with these children rather than the limitations of children themselves (Rabiee, Sloper and Beresford, 2005a). Booth and Booth (1996: 67) suggested that 'researchers should attend

more to their deficiencies than to the limitations of their informants'.

This is consistent with the social model of disability (Oliver, 1990) which, rather than seeing disability as a problem within individuals, views disability as being socially produced by structural factors and attitudes which fail to adapt to the needs of people with physical or learning disabilities. This model distinguishes between impairment, when a part of the body does not work well, and disablement, when social barriers (such as lack of a communication aid or accessible and appropriate information) exclude people with impairments from valued activities. In addition, adults with disabilities have argued that research should go beyond methods which facilitate the participation of people with disabilities as respondents in research, to their involvement in the whole process of research, from the identification of key issues for research and development of research questions, through design, data collection and interpretation, and ownership and dissemination of research findings (Barnes, 1992; Oliver, 1992). There has been considerable development in the field of children's

---

*In the UK 'disabled children' is preferred to 'children with disabilities'. This terminology is grounded in the social model of disability which argues this phrase better reflects the way external factors (such as the physical environment and social attitudes) disable individuals, rather than the impairment itself.

active participation as partners in the various stages of research (Kirby, 2004). Although examples of involvement of children with disabilities at this level are quite rare, there have been some promising research studies that can inform further development in this field (Lewis et al., 2008).

The literature on the participation of children with disabilities both in research and in decision-making about the services they receive suggests that children who participate are generally those who are older, less severely disabled, and most articulate (Franklin and Sloper, 2006, 2009; Lightfoot and Sloper, 2003). Ensuring that as many children with disabilities as possible can express their views in research poses challenges: in seeking methods that are inclusive of children with different types of disabilities, and in working with these children throughout the whole research process. It requires researchers to challenge themselves and the prejudices about disability that are deeply embedded in many societies, and to seek new understandings of communication as more than verbal skill.

A number of key issues emerge from research which has sought to find out, first hand, the lived experiences and the views of children with disabilities. First, their priorities and aspirations are very similar to those of other children (for example, Beresford, 2002; Beresford, Tozer, Rabiee and Sloper, 2007; Foley et al., 2012; King, Cathers, Polgar, MacKinnon and Havens, 2000; O'Grady and Fisher, 2008; Pollock et al., 1997; Rabiee, Sloper and Beresford, 2005b). Thus, desiring positive experiences in terms of friendships, family life, physical and emotional well-being, safety, and success and achievement are common to children with disabilities and their non-disabled peers. However, it is clear from research with children with disabilities that the meaning of these universal aspirations for childhood needs to be redefined so that they are appropriate and relevant for these children. Thus, physical well-being for some children with disabilities will be about the absence of pain or discomfort, but for others, about maintaining physical abilities or physical health despite having a progressive condition. Similarly, experiences of success may be very different from non-disabled peers and, for some children with autistic spectrum disorders, desires with regard to friendships and social networks may well differ significantly from other groups of children (Sloper, Beresford and Rabiee, 2009).

Second, children with disabilities are at greater risk of poorer or restricted life experiences. Across the globe, children with disabilities are identified as, and also report, being more likely than their non-disabled peers to experience limited lives, poverty, marginalization and exclusion (for example, Beresford, 2002; Brown and Gordon, 1987; Cadman, Boyle, Szatmari and Offord, 1987; McMaugh, 2011; Mulderij, 1996; Philpott and Sait, 2001;).

Third, children's reports of the quality of their life, obtained both through subjective accounts and quality of life (QoL) measures, indicate that factors such as the severity of their impairment, physical well-being, and experiences such as marginalization and exclusion significantly affect their quality of life (Connors and Stalker, 2003; Dickinson et al., 2007).

Finally, and something which highlights the fundamental reason why children need to be directly involved in research, children with disabilities and their parents vary in their reports of the impact of the impairment on the child's life. This includes, for example, the stresses they experience, their concerns and worries, self-image, and emotional well-being (for example, Ennett et al., 1991; Raviv and Stone, 1991; Ronen, Streiner and Rosenbaum, 2003; Varni et al., 2005; White-Konig et al., 2007).

Thus, the existing evidence base points strongly to the need for research which works directly with children with disabilities, and indicates that parents or more general research with children cannot be used as substitutes. It also provides compelling evidence for the need for further research in order to inform policy and service development which will improve the life chances of children with disabilities. At the moment, our understanding of the lives of children with disabilities, although considerably better than it was 15 years ago, is still limited and patchy. The methodological challenges associated with working with some groups of children with disabilities are a reason for this. We use the remainder of this chapter to explore issues and share experiences of doing research with children with disabilities.

METHODS TO SUPPORT THE PARTICIPATION OF CHILDREN WITH DISABILITIES AS RESPONDENTS IN RESEARCH

The first issue that researchers face in designing a study is devising methods that are appropriate to the research questions being addressed. Some questions, usually those that are more tightly specified, require quantitative methods, but others are more appropriately addressed through qualitative research. Both types of research pose challenges for the involvement of children with disabilities. Many quantitative methods, such as surveys, require that respondents have at least moderate levels of literacy, and some use standardized measures which have been validated on non-disabled populations.

Qualitative research has traditionally relied heavily on interviews that require verbal skills. Yet many children with disabilities have communication and/or cognitive difficulties. However, these children can be included in research through the use of more innovative methods. Visual methods (such as the use of photographs, drawing, puppets and symbol forms of communication) are valuable research tools to use with any children and can be particularly appropriate for children with disabilities. For children with limited speech and/or learning difficulties visual stimuli can be used in conjunction with conversation to provide a more concrete stimulus to help children to understand and relate to questions. For example, in a study of children's views of respite care services

(Minkes, Robinson and Weston, 1994), a number of visual prompts were used: photos of the respite care homes, staff members and other children; pictures of everyday objects such as food and games; and small books in which the children and their interviewers could build up a pictorial record. For children who do not use speech, visual methods can allow them to give their views, for instance by pointing or other non-verbal cues. In a project on leisure (Murray, 2004), young people with disabilities, some with significant learning and communication impairments, were given disposable cameras and asked to take photographs of activities that they enjoyed, places that they went to, people whom they liked to be with (or for those unable to use cameras, parents photographed activities that the young person enjoyed).

Murray noted the power of the photographs in enabling young people with disabilities to let researchers know about their leisure experiences and desires. In research with young people with severe and moderate learning difficulties, Adams and Swain (2001) took an activity-based approach, involving interactive computer screens, taking photographs, storyboards, and personal record books. Similarly, Lewis et al. (Lewis, Parsons and Robertson, 2005; Lewis, Robertson and Parsons, 2007) used drawing, photography, puppets, ranking, and cue card prompted interviews with disabled children and young people. Through these methods, young people were facilitated to give their views about aspects of their experiences in education.

When negotiating participation in research for children with disabilities, the attitudes of 'gatekeepers', such as social workers, care workers, and parents, may be barriers to children's participation. Researchers commonly report being told that children cannot participate, can't communicate, that they "won't get anything out of" a child (for example, Morris, 2003). We have found it useful to explain in detail to gatekeepers about methods that will be used to facilitate communication, showing them any pictures or symbols that will be used, and also reassuring them that the researcher can be flexible in adapting to the child's own means of communication, and will be sensitive to any indication that the child is not happy about taking part.

Involving children who do not use speech

Children who do not use speech as their main means of communication have frequently been excluded from opportunities to give their views in research or consultation (Morris, 1998, 2003). However, there is a growing body of work that shows the willingness and ability of children with disabilities to communicate their views and feelings (Morris, 1999a; Rabiee, Priestley and Knowles, 2001; SCOPE, 2002; Stalker and Connors, 2003;). It is important to develop communication methods which can maximize children's potential to express themselves and for researchers to learn how a child expresses her/himself. As a young person with communication impairment described:

> We are used to people saying we cannot communicate, but of course they are wrong. In fact we have powerful and effective ways of communicating and we usually have many ways to let you know what it is we have in mind. Yes, we have communication difficulties, and some of those are linked with our impairments. But by far the greater part of our difficulty is caused by 'speaking' people not having the experience, time or commitment to try to understand us or to include us in everyday life.
>
> (SCOPE, 2002: 1–2)

There is a growing body of literature describing ways to involve children with communication impairments in the process of decision-making (for example, Morris, 1999b). Some of this work aims to improve practice in communicating with this group of children, by offering advice and information to those working with them (Morris, 2002; Triangle/NSPCC, 2001; Warrick, 1998) and practical 'tool kits' (for example, Kirkbride, 1999). In research, a simple example of this is the use of emotion pictures ('smiley faces'

or 'thumbs up') to ascertain children's feelings about particular issues. However, these studies have usually explored children's experiences in terms of likes and dislikes about specific situations. There has been less work on how to obtain the views of children with significant communication impairment on more complex issues. One exception to this is the development of a tool called an 'image vocabulary' by Triangle/NSPCC (2002), which aims to enable children to communicate more complex issues, for example around safety and feelings.

Case study

Another example is work that we carried out, with colleagues in the Social Policy Research Unit (Rabiee et al., 2005a). We aimed to facilitate the communication of children who do not use speech, so that they could tell us about an abstract question: the outcomes that they aspired to achieve through the provision of support services. In this study, the challenge was how to break down this concept to make it easier for the children to grasp it, so that the study could go beyond what they liked and disliked to explore what they aspired to achieve and experience. The study used the ideas of 'talking mats' (Murphy, 1998), a visual framework using symbols to help people with communication difficulties to communicate, as a basis to develop a research tool. To make the task more concrete for children who did not use speech, our first task was to identify the areas of children's lives that were important to them and that should be covered in 'talking mats' as well as the ways in which they talked about them. This was done by first interviewing children with disabilities of the same age range who did use speech and could participate in interviews about their aspirations for their lives, then interviewing parents of the children who did not use speech about what outcomes they desired for their children. Data from both sets of interviews were used to inform the content of the 'interviews' with children who did not use speech. The main themes identified were: communication, friends, school, independent skills, mobility, how they were looked after child when they are away from their parents/ carers, activities, and social presentation (Mitchell and Sloper, 2011). Interview data were then used to generate statements for each theme.

When working with children who do not use speech, it is important to find out what communication systems the children use. In all cases, we interviewed parents before the 'interviews' with children and asked about their children's communication needs. Whenever possible, the researcher also met the child at this point, arranged a time to see the child and then was able to work on tailoring the interview methods to the child's needs before the interview took place.

In this study, children all attended schools in the same area and a symbol system called Boardmaker™ was used in these schools, so these symbols were used in the study. The interviews were facilitated by using A4 laminated cards. The area of the child's life was presented at the top of the card with an accompanying symbol(s). The cards were presented in two forms:

- For some areas, the lower half of the card showed three or four characters (faces and names), each assigned to one of the statements (see Figure 14.1). Children were asked which character's statement was most like them and to choose only one statement.
- For other areas, the lower half of the card showed different aspects of the overall area. For example, based on the area of 'My communication aid' the statements were 'Sam wants his communication aid to be faster', 'Adam wants his communication aid to be able to say more things', 'George wants to be able to use his communication aid wherever he is' and 'John wants to have a communication system he can use without help'. Here children could have multiple choices and take as many statements as they wanted (see Figure 14.2).

Male and female versions of the cards were used as appropriate. Separate labels for the statements were attached to the cards. Children could take off their chosen statements and stick them on a mat, labelled with their name, thus building up a picture of what they wanted in their life. In all cases, the interviewer was sensitive to children's non-verbal behaviour, such as facial expression, eye pointing, and body movement, in order to help interpretation of the child's response.

Figure 14.1   A talking mat using a single response option

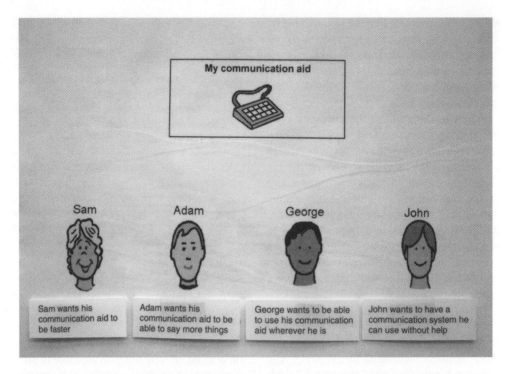

Figure 14.2   Another example of a talking mat utilising a multiple response option

With any method, it is important to try to assess whether a child is able to understand and use the method. In this study, very simple questions to which the interviewer knew the answer, such as the means of transport the child used to get to school and what activities the child most liked doing, were used at the outset to assess whether the child was able to use the tool and to understand the questions.

Children seemed to find this tool fun to use and appreciated the interactive aspect of being able to control what they chose in response to the questions. For many, being able to express their views in this way appeared to be a new experience, and some parents and teachers expressed surprise that children became so involved, maintained their attention, and expressed choices. The children's views showed that they wanted the same outcomes as other children (for instance, to have friends and take part in social activities), but maximizing their opportunities to communicate was fundamental to the achievement of other outcomes. They wanted everyone who looked after them to know their method of communication and to make the effort to understand them. If they used a communication aid, they wanted to be able to take it everywhere they went, but some were not able to do this. They wanted to have more advanced communication aids that were faster and could say more things. They also wanted other people (such as doctors and other professionals) to talk to them in ways they could understand.

Although the 'talking mats' method clearly has potential in facilitating the participation of children who do not use speech, understanding of abstract concepts is still problematic in relation to children with severe cognitive impairment for research which attempts to explore abstract and future ideas such as aspirations, rather than more concrete experiences and immediate likes and dislikes (Ware, 2004). Twelve of the 19 children in the group of children who did not use speech did not participate in 'interviews' because their level of cognitive development was such that they were not able to understand the concepts and questions (Rabiee et al., 2005b).

'Listening''with all the senses

For children with severe cognitive impairment, Morris (2003) highlighted the importance of 'being with' a child as a means of gathering information about their experiences. This may involve observation of a particular situation and/or joining in an activity, and is most valuable if the researcher is able to experience a range of settings with the child. In addition, gathering information from key people who know the child well can help to answer questions that cannot be asked of the child him/herself. Murray (2004) emphasised the importance of understanding 'listening' as more than just hearing messages given in speech, quoting Mason (2000), whose interpretations of listening are clearly relevant to research with children with disabilities:

> Listening is more than pointing your ears in someone's direction and computing the words which come out of their mouths. Listening can mean going for walk with someone and noticing what captures their interest. It can mean learning to recognise situations in which a person becomes upset, or becomes animated; it can mean watching a person's movements, or the activities they choose over others; it can mean creating opportunities for that person to experience new things and observing their response.
> (Mason, 2000: 77–8, quoted in Murray, 2004: 39)

This sort of 'listening' is likely to be more time-consuming and resource-intensive than verbal interviews. However, if research is to be inclusive of all disabled children, then projects need to budget for these increased resources, and research funders need to recognize the value of a more inclusive approach.

Involving children with autistic spectrum disorders

The lack of understanding about the aetiology and nature of autistic spectrum disorders (ASD) means that children with ASD are now a highly researched group in terms of psychological or educational research into the condition itself. However, when it comes to research with children with disabilities which involves working with them directly to explore their views and experiences, children with ASD are often excluded (Preece, 2002) or underrepresented (for example, Morris, 1999b; Rabiee et al., 2001; Watson and Priestley, 1999). The key reason for this discrepancy appears to lie in the nature of the condition. ASD is characterized by impaired communication, difficulties with social interaction, a lack of personal insight, and a restricted range of interests and activities (Wing, 1993). In addition, many children with ASD also have learning difficulties. These impairments present specific challenges to social researchers wishing to work with these children (Preece, 2002). The appearance of an unfamiliar figure (the researcher) may arouse high levels of anxiety and result in the child being unwilling to meet or spend time with the researcher. Difficulties with communication may mean that verbal interaction is very limited or non-existent. In addition, researchers need to be aware that these children may perceive and experience the world in a different way to those without ASD.

Case study

Children with ASD were another of the groups of children we worked with on the project referred to earlier about the outcomes children with disabilities want to achieve in their lives and the role of services to support them in achieving those desired outcomes (Beresford, Tozer, Rabiee and Sloper, 2004, 2007). It soon became apparent in our reading of the literature on ASD and talking with experts in the field that the topic of the research was going to be problematic for most children with ASD. We wanted to find out what children aspired to achieve and what changes they wanted in their lives. However, many children with ASD dislike change and their discomfort in new social situations means that they tend to have quite limited lives and do not have (or want) opportunities to see and/or try new experiences or activities. They may also be quite limited in their abilities to self-reflect or consider their futures. So, a research project which wanted to ask about changes and future aspirations was clearly problematic!

In addition, we needed to consider how we were going to work directly with the children without causing high levels of anxiety. If we did not pay attention to this, it was unlikely that parents would consent to us approaching the children to take part and, ethically, it would be unacceptable to try to work with a child if the researcher's presence was a source of stress and distress.

The research team sought advice from researchers and practitioners who worked with children with ASD in deciding how to modify the research project so that it was meaningful and helped to ensure participation was a positive experience for the children. A number of strategies were incorporated in the research design and fieldwork to address these issues. These included:

- using Social Stories to prepare the child for the research interview;
- using a familiar craft-making activity as the focus of the session;
- using photographs taken by the child;
- restricting the conversation to concrete, 'here and now' experiences.

Social Stories (Gray, 1994) are used to help children with ASD understand and manage specific social situations. They are written for a specific child about a specific situation using a prescribed format which provides detailed, step-by-step information about why a situation is happening and what will happen interspersed, less frequently, with sentences giving gentle advice about how to respond. A Social Story describing the researcher's visit was prepared for each child taking part in the project (see Figure 14.3). The Social Stories were used by the parent a number of times before the researcher's visit. Two of the more able children received the social story directly, written in the form of a letter. Parents subsequently reported these were very helpful, and both the text and photographs had meant they felt their child was prepared for the meeting with the researcher.

A second strategy to alleviate social anxiety was to minimize direct, face-to-face interaction between the child and the researcher. This was achieved by basing the session around a craft activity which involved looking at photographs together and selecting ones to make a poster. Doing this shared activity also meant the researcher sat by, as opposed to opposite, the child. Anecdotal evidence suggested that, like all children, autistic children enjoy looking at photographs, and making a poster was similar to the sorts of projects many of the children did at school.

In terms of actual data collection, we decided to focus on getting a picture of the current aspects of their lives which children viewed positively (with the inference being that this is something they want to keep as part of their lives) and those less positive aspects (possible areas for change). Though limited, this provided data about outcomes the child had achieved and whether they were valued or not. To facilitate the interview, families were sent a disposable camera in advance of the interview and the child was encouraged to take photographs of the people, places, and activities which were important to them. These photographs were used in the poster-making activity and, concurrently, allowed simple questions to be asked. For some, it was also possible to move on to explore in more detail the reasons behind likes and dislikes, and future desires and aspirations. We found the use of photographs and the poster-making activity worked well and was effective in facilitating conversation while keeping social anxiety low. All parents were surprised at how successful the session with the researcher had been. We also believe that, had it been possible, additional visits would have allowed further exploration with their children about their lives, and this is something we would want to incorporate in future projects.

The nature of ASD also raised the issue of consent. As with other researchers (for example, Allmark, 2003), we were not confident that the children would understand the meaning and purposes of the research, or

ROSEMARY VISITS GEORGE AT HOME

This is a photo of Rosemary

Mum and Dad have met Rosemary at home when George was at school.

Rosemary is coming to see George on
Wednesday in the morning. She will come in
her car – a red Polo.

Rosemary will ask George some questions.

She will ask about George's favourite things at school and at home.

Rosemary will ask about the people George knows.

George and Rosemary will make a poster together about George

They will make the poster with photos and drawings.

Rosemary will bring a 'Stop' card with her.

George can hold the Stop card up to stop or have a break.

Rosemary will be at George's house for about an hour.

Then she will go and it will be lunchtime.

It will be OK to meet Rosemary.

Figure 14.3   Example of social story used to prepare children with ASD for research interview

were competent to make a decision based on that information – both requirements for true informed consent (Beauchamp and Childress, 2001). Instead, therefore, an on-going process of assent was adopted. Thus the children's responses to their parents talking to them about taking part in the project (including their reactions as they read through the Social Story) and their engagement in the task of taking the photographs ready for the interview were used as indicators of the child's willingness to meet with and talk to the researcher. Within the interview, any verbal or non-verbal indications that the child did not want the interview to continue were promptly acted upon by the researcher and the interview brought to a close. Written consent was obtained from the parent and this followed provision of written information and a face-to-face meeting with a member of the research team.

Involving deaf children*

Included within the population of children with disabilities are children with sensory impairments including deaf children. In terms of participating in research, the great majority of research involving deaf children has been research into language or other aspects of psychological development. To date, there is little published research on deaf children's views and experiences of their lives and/or how to go about doing research which seeks to directly involve deaf children. More has been written about the doing research with deaf adults and this is useful in terms of alerting researchers to some of the issues which will need to be considered (for example, Baker-Shenk and Kyle, 1990; Jones and Pullen, 1992; Temple and Young, 2004). However, in addition to being deaf-centred, research with

deaf children also needs to be child-centred (Sutherland and Young, 2007).

Language

British Sign Language (BSL) is the sign language used in the UK and, instead of spoken words, uses movements of the hands, body, face, and head. BSL is a complete language in its own right and has a structure and grammar totally different from English (Sutton-Spence and Woll, 1999). It is also an entirely visual language and it has no written form. As with a verbal language, children develop BSL skills over the course of time. In the UK, parents of deaf children are typically encouraged to bring their child up either as a BSL user or to use oral methods of communication (speech, lip-reading, and the use of residual hearing). Thus a research project working with BSL and oral children is essentially being conducted in two languages.

This reality raises two key issues. First, researchers must seek consistency in that procedures are implemented across the two languages (for example, consistency of meaning of questions and tools used to facilitate the interview). Second, researchers are faced with the quandary of how visual data (for example, recordings of an interview conducted in BSL) is to be translated into a printed/written form ready for analysis alongside English transcripts.

In terms of translation, the issue is not simply translation from one spoken/written language into another spoken/written language, but translation from a visual/gestural language into a spoken/written language (Temple and Young, 2004). Different approaches are taken to dealing with this issue. Some researchers have used simultaneous translation from BSL into spoken English during data collection

---

*There are country and cultural differences in the terminology used to identify this population. In the UK, the term 'deaf child' is regarded as the most acceptable. Elsewhere, 'children who are deaf' or 'children with hearing impairments' is the preferred term. The 'people with' language in international parlance (for example, the Convention on the *Rights of Persons with Disabilities* and the *Americans with Disabilities* Act [emphases added]; see also *Publication Manual of the American Psychological Association* (6th ed., § 3.15).) is thought to avoid equating people with their disability."

with the interpretation being recorded and then transcribed. However, the presence of an additional person may be felt to be off-putting for the research participant(s), and this is particularly the case when doing research with children and young people. As with any process of translation, there is the risk of misinterpretation. If translation happens after data collection, researchers need to decide who will do the translation and how that translation will be checked for trueness of meaning.

Enabling children to use their preferred language

Deaf children use a variety of languages and ways of communicating including British Sign Language (BSL), Sign Supported English (SSE is a form of English that additionally uses signs to convey meaning), and/or oral methods of communication. A child may use more than one method of communication and their BSL or SSE may be idiosyncratic and not very fluent. The implication of this is that within a research project, researchers need to be able to meet the range of ways, and abilities, deaf children may choose to communicate. Using methods which reduce reliance on, but do not impede, linguistic ability is therefore important. For example, a card-sorting exercise is essentially a visual technique but also allows or facilitates probing or questioning.

Literacy

Children whose first language is BSL are likely to have lower levels of literacy in English compared with their hearing peers, and among those children who are oral, language development can also be delayed which impacts of levels of literacy (Stern, 2001). Thus researchers need to use research methods which do not rely on reading ability but are instead visual (Sutherland and Young, 2007). They also need to consider the best ways of providing information about their research project to potential participants, including straightforward written and BSL versions.

Deaf culture

Most people who use BSL see themselves as belonging to a distinct linguistic cultural group and are part of the deaf community. Hearing researchers working on a project involving deaf children are also, therefore, doing cross-cultural research. Whilst it is possible to develop an understanding and knowledge of deafness and deaf culture, hearing researchers can never be fully part of deaf culture (Jones and Pullen, 1992). This can only be remedied by the full involvement of deaf people in the entire course of a research project.

Case study

We recently completed a project evaluating specialist mental health services for deaf children (Beresford, Greco and Clarke, 2008). Part of this project involved interviews with children who used the service at the time of referral and then again six to eight months into using the service.

The project posed a range of challenges, not all of which were specific to doing research with deaf children. For instance, there is very little written about how to best gather the views and opinions of children and young people using mental health services, and there are particular matters which need to be taken into account when working with children and young people with mental health difficulties. Those issues aside, there were a number of things we needed to address which were directly concerned with the fact that we were wanting to work directly with deaf children and young people.

Early in the project we recognized that it was vital that the team included deaf researchers. At the beginning, from a position of relative naïveté, we had assumed that we would just use deaf researchers to conduct interviews with children who used BSL. However, it soon became clear to us that without their full and proper involvement the research would be flawed. It also carried an implicit message that the deaf researchers were 'commodities' as opposed to equals within the research team, a criticism rightly levelled at hearing researchers in the past (Baker-Shenk and Kyle, 1990).

Thus three deaf researchers were recruited to the project team. Some of the deaf researchers were fluent in English and BSL; others were fluent in BSL with English as their second language. Although not permanently co-located with the hearing members of the team, they were involved in the development of recruitment materials, interview topic guides and materials, data collection, translation, data analysis, and dissemination (for example, journal articles, presentations at seminars and production of the BSL version of the research summary). They also attended meetings of the research project advisory group. Aside from these concrete tasks or activities, the presence of the deaf researchers on the team and the experience of working with them made a significant contribution to the hearing researchers' understanding and appreciation of deafness.

The interviews with the children taking part in the project were semi-structured and involved a series of predominantly visual activities. The visual activities included drawing a network map of people who the child saw as helping them; a card-sorting exercise of cards carrying a picture and written statement about feelings/emotional difficulties; and the use of rating scales to indicate perceived changes in emotional/mental health difficulties. The map-drawing exercise was used as a warm-up activity. The card-sorting exercise was used to identify the mental health or emotional difficulties which the child was experiencing. The chosen cards were returned to at the second interview when the child used a rating scale to indicate whether or not there had been any change in this area of their life. Questions (or prompts) were used alongside these exercises to elicit further or more depth information about the children's views and/or experiences of the specialist mental health service.

A key task for the team was to ensure the written text on any of visual materials was both accessible and carried the same meaning for those whose first language was BSL and those whose first language was English.

Second, the team had to work together to ensure a shared understanding of the meaning and purpose of the questions included in the written English interview topic guide. The deaf researchers then worked on agreeing how they would pose a question or translate written English text contained on the cards used in the card-sorting exercise.

Children were given the choice of being interviewed in BSL by a deaf researcher or by a hearing researcher using oral means of communication. Interviews conducted in BSL were recorded using a digital camcorder. The deaf researchers wanted to translate the interviews they had conducted rather than use interpreters to translate the recorded interviews. This reduced the risk of misinterpretation. The form of the written data produced varied. Some researchers preferred to write a detailed summary of an interview, others preferred to create a transcript in BSL gloss. Glossing is a method of describing BSL signs whereby the meaning of the sign is written using an English word or words (Sutton-Spence and Woll, 1999).

The hearing researcher who worked with oral children had, at the start of the project, begun taking classes in BSL and had reached 'conversational' level by the time the fieldwork with the children started. This proved extremely useful as she found that some children who chose to have a hearing researcher also used BSL and sometimes used it during the interview. Indeed, some children appeared to be more fluent in BSL than English, which raised questions as to why they had chosen to have a hearing researcher conduct the interview. A number of possible reasons for this were suggested by the deaf researchers. First, it may be that, because of a history of marginalization and oppression of deaf people, the child may view a hearing researcher as more important than a deaf researcher. Second, whilst a child may be using BSL at school, either formally or with peers outside of lessons, it may not be used by the family and the child may, therefore, not feel able to ask for a BSL interviewer. Third, children who use BSL and are also oral may feel confused about their identity. Thus, even if they are skilled signers, if they aspire to be part of the hearing world they will choose a hearing researcher.

Children also chose whether or not their interview was recorded. We had expected that some children would be reluctant for camcorders to be used. This was not the case, and perhaps reflects adults' ambivalence or inexperience of this sort of technology which might not be shared by children and young people. However, we did find that some of children who were using oral methods to communicate did not want their voices recorded. This seemed to be centred on embarrassment about the clarity or sound of their voices. In these situations the researcher took notes during the interview and then made detailed field notes immediately afterwards.

Working in groups

Working in groups is a familiar context for children and young people, and as with research with adults, there is a consensus that focus groups are a very useful and appropriate methodology to use in research with children (Mauthner, 1997). However, it is essential that this methodology will generate the sort of data that 'fits' the research questions and that it is facilitated or moderated by researchers skilled in working with groups. There are some excellent texts on running focus groups with adults and these cover the important general principles of running focus groups (for example, Finch and Lewis, 2003; Krueger, 1994; Litosseliti, 2003).

It is agreed that certain modifications need to be made to accommodate the specific needs, abilities, and developmental stages of children and young people (Hurley, 1998; Mauthner, 1997). Primarily this has to do with size of the group, the ages represented in the group, whether or not to use same- or mixed-sex groups, and the importance of paying attention to social power issues in the group. It is generally agreed that the optimal size of focus groups involving children is smaller, especially when working with young

children, compared to adults. Thus with adults, a group size of 8–12 is seen as ideal; this figure reduces to as low as five when working with young children with a maximum size of around eight for groups of teenagers. In addition, groups work best if they are composed of children of a similar age or with similar cognitive abilities. It is also recommended that researchers consider possible sensitivities (or distractions!) of being in a group with members of the opposite sex and weigh up the disadvantages or advantages of working in single or mixed-sex groups.

Whilst in any group discussion it is important that the researcher pays attention to issues of social power within the group, it is felt that there is greater risk of harm to one or more participants arising from inequities of social power when working with children (for example, intimidation during the group, bullying/teasing after the group). This would seem to especially be the case where the researcher is working with a pre-existing group or with a group of children who already know each other.

Finally, there are also practical issues to address which are not typically encountered when running focus groups for adults. First, unless the research is taking place in school, the participants are likely to be dependent on parents or other carers for transport and associated costs. Thus the timing of the groups has to take account of that. A suitable space for parents to wait (perhaps with other children) needs to be provided. The researchers should also plan how they will deal with the situation of a child wanting to leave during the course of the meeting. Who will look after a child if their parents are not on the premises? How, in such a situation, will the researchers adhere to good practice (in terms of child protection) with regard to not being alone with a single child?

Research with children with disabilities has used focus groups as a methodology, though it appears to be used less frequently with this specific group compared to other groups of children. In our Unit we have used focus groups with children with less severe learning difficulties and physical impairments (for example, Beresford, 2012; Beresford and Sloper, 2003; Franklin and Sloper, 2007; Lightfoot and Sloper, 2003; Mitchell and Sloper, 2001). In the process of conducting these groups we have identified additional issues which need to be considered or addressed. Where children have cognitive impairments, shorter but multiple group discussions are likely to be more fruitful than a single session covering a number of topics. This may also be appropriate for children with conditions which mean they have limited stamina. In addition, when working with groups involving children with physical impairments, it may be necessary to have frequent breaks during the session to allow them to move around to prevent pain and stiffness.

Working with a pre-existing group (for example, at school or members of a social group) seems to be particularly advantageous. Children with disabilities tend to lead more restricted lives than other children and may, therefore, be less familiar and/or more daunted by dealing with a new social situation. For children with learning difficulties, a familiar group means there is not the distraction or sense of inhibition which can happen when a new group is formed. Peers can also help the researcher or other members of the group. For example, they will be familiar with the way a particular child speaks or communicates and can help the researcher understand what a child is trying to say.

Account may also need to be taken of the way an impairment or health condition can impact on participation in a focus group. Researchers therefore need to be well versed with the conditions and impairments of the children, both when considering focus groups as a possible methodology and when planning a focus group. Most children with autistic spectrum disorders are likely to find group situations more stressful than individual interviews and may refuse to participate for this reason.

Children who use augmentative and alternative communication (AAC) to communicate may need to be supported to participate in a group particularly in a group where some children use speech. The group facilitator will need to ensure such children are properly included. It is also likely that, where the group includes children who use AAC, more time will be needed to cover all the topics and thus, again, a number of meetings may be required. The extent to which focus groups can be used if all the members of the group use augmentative and alternative communication assistive technologies has been explored in research with adults (Hemsley, Balandin and Togher, 2008). They point to the importance of the skills of the facilitator and active roles participants play in supporting communication and interaction. Whether or not the children involved have other impairments (for example, hearing, learning difficulties) will also affect the extent to which group members interact with each other and discuss issues as opposed to sequentially answering questions put to them by the facilitator.

We have also encountered situations where health conditions have significantly affected the use of focus group methodology. For a project on the information needs of children with physical disabilities and chronic illnesses (Beresford and Sloper, 2003), individual interviews took place, followed by focus groups attended by children of around the same age and the same condition. It was particularly difficult to arrange the group meetings for the young people with cystic fibrosis. This is because in managing the condition, families and health professionals are keen that contact should not occur between young people who are growing a particular infection (*Pseudomonas cepacia*) and those who are not growing the infection. As a result, the decision was taken to use 'growers' and 'non-growers' groups, rather than splitting by age. The researchers had to liaise with the hospital clinic in the week leading up to a focus group meeting to ascertain the current '*pseudomonas* status' of each participant.

Finally, when running groups with children with disabilities, particular care needs to be taken in the choice of venue in terms of access and self-care facilities. This is likely to require obtaining detailed information about the children's needs *in advance* of the meeting. Our experience is that special schools and hospitals (for example, a physiotherapy department attended by the research participants) can be the best venues in terms of accommodating children's needs. Whilst it could be argued that these places may hold negative connotations, we have found that children like the fact that they are in a familiar place and that we (the researchers) are the visitors and they need to show us around! The familiarity of the venue is also likely to reduce anxiety and promote confidence when working with groups of children with learning difficulties. However, the researcher needs to make sure that group members understand that they are meeting for research purposes and not for the activities they usually participate in at that venue.

Involving children with disabilities in quantitative research

Quantitative research, which for reliability requires all participants to be asked the same questions, can pose particular challenges for the involvement of children who have cognitive impairments or have not developed literacy. However, this should not mean that children with disabilities are never asked for their views in this type of research. Again, the problem is for the researchers to devise ways in which the children can take part. Questionnaires can use pictures and symbols as well as words, and intermediaries, such as researchers, parents, and carers, can read text to children. An extensive stage of development involving children with disabilities themselves is necessary to ensure that important issues for respondents are considered; to find out what words and ideas they use to express these issues; and to ensure that words, pictures, and symbols used are appropriate and likely to be understood. Although these methods will not be accessible to all children with disabilities, particularly

those with severe cognitive impairment, this should not be a reason to exclude all children with disabilities from quantitative research. Whenever possible, alternative ways, such as observation, should be found to include children for whom questionnaires are not accessible, especially to find out if their experiences or views appear to be notably different from those who respond to the questionnaire.

Case study

In our Sharing Value project (Mitchell and Sloper, 2001, 2003), we sought to explore what children with disabilities and their parents particularly valued about the services they received and to create a directory of services commended by parents and children in the UK. First, the project worked with three groups of children and young people with disabilities. We asked them to think of services they used that were really good and what made them good and similarly, any services that they felt were poor and why they were unhelpful or negative. A range of children were included in the groups, including those who used alternative forms of communication. Verbal communication, symbols and electronic voice systems, and activities such as drawing, writing, and posting boxes, were used by the children to communicate their views. Children had clear views on what were the most important criteria for a good service. These were: staff understand my illness or disability; staff know how to help and look after me; staff listen to me; staff ask me for my ideas and take notice of what I say; I can ask staff questions, and they explain things to me; and staff allow me to make choices. It is obvious from these that children prioritized staff attitudes and approach as key aspects within any service. In addition to these core indicators, the children also prioritized certain aspects within different types of services. For example, a key aspect for a leisure service was that it should provide opportunities to meet and make friends.

Using these 'quality criteria' defined by the children, a postal questionnaire was then designed through which a larger number of children with disabilities could nominate a service they thought was very good and could indicate on which criteria they rated the service as good. The questionnaire used both words and drawings and the children were involved in its design, to ensure that both the words and pictures were appropriate for their peers. Clearly, there are limitations when using postal questionnaires, the main one being the heavy reliance on the written word and ability to read. However, the questionnaire could be completed on a number of different levels, and the information accompanying the questionnaires made it clear that children could ask others to read or write information for them.

Participants were asked to nominate a valued service that they used or had used in the past, to indicate service type (by ticking the appropriate pictorial and word depiction), and then to indicate why they valued this service. Participants had a range of methods to choose from. They could tick their service's qualities from options indicated on the questionnaire (these were the quality criteria that had emerged from the discussion groups), and there was space to write their own ideas. If participants did not want to write, they were encouraged to draw a picture of their service and to fill in or ask someone to help them fill in the caption, 'I like my good service because ...'.

Parents were also asked to complete questionnaires, and almost 6000 families returned questionnaires. In half of these, the child with disabilities provided a response, either indicating that they could not think of a really good service to nominate ($n = 2049$) or nominating a service and indicating why they liked it ($n = 780$; Mitchell and Sloper, 2003).

Using standardized measures

The use of standardized self-completion measures (for example, measures of mental health) can be problematic with some groups of children with disabilities. The researcher needs to be sure that the levels of literacy demanded by the measure are suitable for the

children to whom they wish to administer the measure. In addition, it is important to consider whether or not measures standardized on general child populations are appropriate for a particular group of children. For example, standardized measures are typically unsuitable for use with deaf children and young people because of issues with regard to levels of literacy in English and the fact that they have been standardized using populations of hearing children (Bailley and Lauwerier, 2003).

PARTICIPATION OF CHILDREN WITH DISABILITIES IN THE RESEARCH PROCESS

The Sharing Value case study provides an example of children with disabilities being involved in the design of research questionnaires, and the same children were also involved in advising on analysis (see Mitchell and Sloper, 2003). Other studies have also involved children with disabilities in central roles, ranging from advising on to designing and carrying out research.

It is now becoming more common for young people with disabilities to advise research projects, including at proposal, design, and dissemination stages (see for example, Connors and Stalker, 2003; Lewis et al., 2007; Murray, 2002). Lewis et al. (2008) drew together experiences from three research teams that involved 'reference groups' of young people with disabilities who provided input to the research process and influenced research decisions. They highlighted a number of issues that should be considered by researchers and research funders:

- The need to fund such groups properly, and for funding bodies to recognize the importance of this and include provision for it in their budget specifications.
- The value of drawing on existing local disability groups for reference group members, and of creating a standing reference group that can

be drawn on by different projects over time and provide a means to include young people with disabilities from the early stages of planning projects. It is important that the demands on such a group are not too great, and that membership of the group is refreshed over time, so that over-professionalization or politicization is avoided and breadth of views is maintained.

- Clear aims of reference group involvement for everyone, with careful planning for when and how they will be involved, how meetings will be run and by whom (for instance, whether researchers or reference group members will run meetings), and how any facilitators will participate. Flexibility within this general framework is needed to adapt to the needs of participants.
- Consideration of the benefits that participation will provide for group members, for example development of skills and confidence. Monitoring of the group's involvement is important to check that the needs of all partners are being met. Planning for the end of involvement, and if possible identification of other opportunities for participation, is also important as this could mean ending contacts and friendships that have developed.
- Collation of information on good practice on research reference groups, and development by funders of guidance.

Another way of ensuring children and young people with disabilities are involved in all aspects of the research process is to form a consultation group that supports and informs the work of a group of researchers or research unit. This sort of group can be used to help researchers identify topics and methods for future research as well as providing a forum where matters relating to on-going projects can be discussed or checked out (for example, information sheets, interview tools or techniques). The Children and Families team at the Social Policy Research Unit at the University of York has such a group (http://www.york.ac.uk/inst/spru/research/childconsult2.html), which runs in parallel with a similar group for parents. The young people's group is drawn from pupils at the local special school and takes place during school time. This arrangement works well: the young people are familiar with each other

and, because the group meets at the school during the school day, it imposes minimal disruption on the school timetable and does not require alternative transport or post-school care arrangements to be made. The group meets approximately every six weeks for around 45 minutes and is coordinated by two researchers, though the group is used and attended by other researchers in the team.

Ensuring that research participants are informed about the findings and outcomes of a project is good ethical practice. Care needs to be taken to ensure that children with learning difficulties and those with sensory impairments can access research findings. The Norah Fry Research Centre at the University of Bristol is a model of good practice in terms of providing accessible research findings. It produces a magazine and tape for people with learning difficulties which summarizes its research projects (http://www.bristol.ac.uk/Depts/NorahFry/PlainFacts/index.html). The magazine and sound version can be accessed on-line and is also downloadable or can be received as a hard copy. The production of each issue of the magazine is overseen by an advisory group of young people and adults with learning difficulties.

In recent years, there has been considerable growth in the involvement of children and young people as researchers carrying out research and a number of publications describe benefits and costs of such projects and set out guidelines (Broad and Saunders, 1998; France, 2000; Kellett, 2005; Kirby, 1999, 2004; The Routes Project Team, 2001). The recommendations from this literature are relevant to children with disabilities as well as other children. However, involvement of children with disabilities at this level is rare. Whilst research that has involved non-disabled children as researchers points to the benefits and costs of this approach, information on these issues in relation to children with disabilities is lacking.

We do not wish to suggest that there should be a hierarchy of children and young people's participation in research, with young researchers being involved in carrying out the research as the only model to aim for. It is important that young people's involvement is carefully considered in relation to the topic of the research, their own preferences, and the benefits that they and the research will gain from the process. This can be a particular issue with regard to the involvement of young people with cognitive impairment, where the demands on their cognitive and communication skills, particularly of tasks such as interviewing and analysis, are likely to present significant difficulties (Adams and Swain, 2001; Stalker, 1998). The challenge is to aim for appropriate involvement while maintaining the rigour and quality of research. Drawing on the views of young people, respondents, and professional researchers, more evaluations of the process of involvement in research of young people with disabilities are needed.

CONCLUSION

This chapter has described the issues associated with conducting research which is both child-friendly and also meets the specific and sometimes idiosyncratic needs and abilities of the different groups of children who fall within the definition of children with disabilities. Thus, we have reported on the research involving children with physical impairments, sensory impairments, communication impairments, and learning difficulties. We have also explored the very specific issues which need to be addressed when working with children with autistic spectrum disorders. Whilst the primary focus of the research has been in terms of the data collection phase of research, it has also been important to highlight the fact that true participatory research means that children and young people with disabilities should be supported to be involved in setting research agendas, overseeing and advising on the conduct of research and having access to the research findings and sharing in dissemination activities.

During the past decade there has been a significant shift in attitude and practice with regard to the direct involvement of children with disabilities in research about their lives. It is highly unlikely that this chapter would have been commissioned 10 years ago and, if it had, its content would have been very sparse (Beresford, 1997). The volume and diversity of research reported or referred to in this chapter is therefore testament to the progress that has been made over recent years. In order for research with children with disabilities to continue to develop and improve it is imperative that researchers both share their experiences with each other and consult with children about the research agenda and their own experiences in research.

REFERENCES

Adams, J. and Swain, J. (2001) 'Towards participatory research with disabled students', in J. Clark, A. Dyson, N. Meagher, E. Robson and M. Wootten (eds.), *Young People as Researchers: Possibilities, Problems and Politics*. Leicester: National Youth Agency, pp. 29–36.

Allmark, P. (2003) 'The ethics of research with children', *Nurse Researcher*, 10(2): 7–19.

Bailley, D. and Lauwerier, L. (2003) 'Hearing impairment and psychopathological disorders in children and adolescents: Review of the recent literature', *Encephale*, 29(4): 329–37.

Baker-Shenk, C. and Kyle, J.G. (1990) 'Research with deaf people: Issues and conflicts', *Disability, Handicap and Society*, 5(1): 65–75.

Barnes, C. (1992) 'Qualitative research: Valuable or irrelevant?', *Disability, Handicap and Society*, 7(2): 115–23.

Beauchamp, T. and Childress, J. (2001) *Principles of Biomedical Ethics*. Oxford: Oxford University Press.

Beresford, B. (1997) *Personal Accounts: Involving Disabled Children in Research*. London: The Stationery Office.

Beresford, B. (2002) 'Preventing the social exclusion of disabled children', in D. McNeish, T. Newman, and H. Roberts (eds.), *What Works for Children? Effective Services for Children and Families*. Open University Press: Buckingham, pp. 147–64.

Beresford, B. (2012) 'Working on well-being: researchers' experiences of a participative approach to understanding the subjective well-being of disabled young people', *Children & Society*, 26(3): 234–240

Beresford, B. and Sloper, P (2003) 'Chronically ill adolescents' experiences of communicating with doctors: A qualitative study', *Journal of Adolescent Health*, 33(3): 172–9.

Beresford, B., Greco, V. and Clarke, S. (2008) *Evaluating a National Mental Health Service for Deaf Children and Young People.* York: Social Policy Research Unit, University of York.

Beresford, B., Tozer, R., Rabiee, P. and Sloper, P. (2004) 'Developing an approach to involving children with autistic spectrum disorders in a social care research project', *British Journal of Learning Disabilities*, 32(4): 180–5.

Beresford, B., Tozer, R., Rabiee, P. and Sloper, P. (2007) 'Desired outcomes for children and adolescents with autistic spectrum disorders', *Children and Society*, 21(1): 4–16.

Booth, T. and Booth, W. (1996) 'Sounds of silence: Narrative research with inarticulate subjects', *Disability and Society* 11(1): 55–69.

Broad, B. and Saunders, L. (1998) 'Involving young people leaving care as peer researchers in a health research project: A learning experience', *Research, Policy and Planning*, 16(1): 1–9.

Brown, M. and Gordon, W. (1987) 'Impact of impairment on activity patterns of children', *Archives of Physical Medicine and Rehabilitation*, 68(12): 828–32.

Cadman, D., Boyle, M., Szatmari, P. and Offord, D.R. (1987) 'Chronic Illness, disability, and mental and social well-being: Findings of the Ontario Child Health Study', *Pediatrics*, 79(5): 805–13.

Cavet, J. and Sloper, P. (2004) 'Participation of disabled children in individual decisions about their lives and in public decisions about service development', *Children and Society*, 18(4): 278–90.

Connors, C. and Stalker, K. (2003) *The Views and Experiences of Disabled Children and their Siblings: A Positive Outlook.* London: Jessica Kingsley.

Dickinson, H.O., Parkinson, K.N., Ravens-Sieberer, U., Schirripa, G., Thyen, U., Arnaud, C., Beckung, E., Fauconnier, J., McManus, V., Michelsen, S.I., Parkes, J. and Colver, A. (2007) 'Self-reported quality of life of 8-12 year old children with cerebral palsy: A cross-sectional European study', *Lancet*, 369(9580): 2171–8.

Ennett, S.T., DeVellis, B.M., Earp, J.A. Kredich, D., Warren, R.W. and Wilhelm, C.L. (1991) 'Disease experience and psychosocial adjustment in children with juvenile rheumatoid arthritis: Children's versus mothers' reports', *Journal of Pediatric Psychology*, 16(5): 557–68.

Finch, H. and Lewis, J. (2003) 'Focus groups', in J. Ritchie and J. Lewis (eds.), *Qualitative Research Practice.* London: Sage, pp. 170–98.

Foley, K.R., Blackmore, A. M., Girdler, S., O'Donnell, M., Glauert, R., Llewellyn, G. and Leonard H. (2012) 'To feel belonged: The voices of children and youth with disabilities on the meaning of wellbeing', *Child Indicators Research*, 5:375–391.

France, A. (2000) *Youth Research Youth: The Triumph and Success Peer Research Project.* Leicester: Youth Work Press.

Franklin, A. and Sloper, P. (2006) 'Participation of disabled children and young people in decision-making within social services departments: A survey of current and recent activities in England', *British Journal of Social Work*, 36(5): 723–41.

Franklin, A. and Sloper, P. (2007) *Participation of Disabled Children and Young People in Decision-making Relating to Social Care.* York: Social Policy Research Unit, University of York.

Franklin, A. and Sloper, P. (2009) 'Supporting the participation of disabled children and young people in decision-making', *Children and Society*, 23(6): i–iv.

Gray, C. (1994) *The New Social Story Book.* Arlington: Future Horizons.

Hemsley, B., Balandin, S. and Togher, L. (2008) '"I've got something to say": Interaction in a focus group of adults with cerebral palsy and complex communication needs', *Augmentative and Alternative Communication*, 24(2): 110–22.

Hurley, N. (1998) *Straight Talk: Working with Children and Young People in Groups.* York: Joseph Rowntree Foundation.

Jones, L. and Pullen, G. (1992) 'Cultural differences: Deaf and hearing researchers working together', *Disability, Handicap and Society*, 7(2): 189–96.

Kellett, M. (2005) *How to Develop Children as Researchers.* London: Paul Chapman.

King, G., Cathers, T., Polgar, M.J., MacKinnon, E. and Havens, L. (2000) 'Success in life for older adolescents with cerebral palsy', *Qualitative Health Research*, 10(6): 734–49.

Kirby, P. (1999) *Involving Young Researchers: How to Enable Young People to Design and Conduct Research.* York: Joseph Rowntree Foundation/York Publishing Company.

Kirby, P. (2004) *A Guide to Actively Involving Young People in Research: For Researchers, Research Commissioners and Managers.* Eastleigh: Involve.

Kirkbride, L. (1999) *I'll Go First: Planning and Review Toolkit for Use with Disabled Children.* London: The Children's Society.

Krueger, R.A. (1994) *Focus Groups: A Practical Guide for Applied Research*, 2nd Edition. Thousand Oaks: Sage.

Lewis, A., Parsons, S. and Robertson, C. (2007) *My School, My Family, My Life: Telling It Like It Is. A* study drawing on the experiences of disabled children, young people and their families in Great Britain in 2006. London: Disability Rights Commission/ Birmingham, University of Birmingham, School of Education.

Lewis, A., Parsons, S., Robertson, C., Feiler, A., Tarlton, B., Watson, D., Byers, R., Davies, J., Fergusson, A. and Marvin, C. (2008) 'The role and working of reference, or advisory, groups involving disabled people: Reviewing the experiences and implications of three contrasting research projects', *British Journal of Special Education*, 35(2): 78–84.

Lewis, A., Robertson, C. and Parsons, S. (2005) *DRC Research Report – Experiences of Disabled Students and Their Families: Phase 1*. London: Disability Rights Commission/ Birmingham, University of Birmingham, School of Education. Available at http:// www.leeds.ac.uk/disabilitystudies/archiveuk/lewis/ Experiences%201%20full%20report%20word.pdf

Lightfoot, J. and Sloper, P. (2003) 'Having a say in health: Involving young people with a chronic illness or physical disability in local health services development', *Children and Society*, 17(4): 277–90.

Litoseliti, L. (2003) *Using Focus Groups in Research*. London: Continuum.

Mason, M. (2000) *Incurably Human*. London: Working Press.

Mauthner, M. (1997) 'Methodological aspects of collecting data from children: Lessons from three research projects', *Children and Society*, 11(1): 16–28.

McMaugh, A. (2011) 'En/countering disablement in school life in Australia: Children talk about peer relations and living with illness and disability', *Disability & Society*, 26(7): 853–866

Minkes, J., Robinson, C. and Weston, C. (1994) 'Consulting the children: Interviews with children using residential respite care services', *Disability and Society*, 9(1): 47–57.

Mitchell, W. and Sloper, P. (2001) 'Quality in services for disabled children and their families: What can theory, policy and research on children's and parents' views tell us?', *Children and Society*, 15(4): 237–52.

Mitchell, W. and Sloper, P. (2003) 'Quality indicators: disabled children's and parents' prioritizations and experiences of quality criteria when using different types of support services', *British Journal of Social Work*, 33(8): 1063–80.

Mitchell, W. and Sloper, P. (2011) 'Making choices in my life: listening to the ideas and experiences of young people in the UK who communicate non-verbally', *Children and Youth Services Review*, 33 (4): 521–527.

Morris, J. (1998) *Don't Leave Us Out – Involving Disabled Children and Young People with Communication Impairments*. York: Joseph Rowntree Foundation/York Publishing Services.

Morris, J. (1999a) *Hurtling into a Void: Transition to Adulthood for Young Disabled People with 'Complex and Health Support Needs'*. Brighton: Pavilion Publishing.

Morris, J. (1999b) *Space for Us: Finding Out What Disabled Children and Young People Think about their Placements*. London: London Borough of Newham.

Morris, J. (2002) *A Lot to Say! A Guide for Social Workers, Personal Advisors and Others Working with Disabled Children and Young People with Communication Impairments*. London: Scope.

Morris, J. (2003) 'Including all children: finding out about the experiences of children with communication and/or cognitive impairments', *Children and Society*, 17(5): 337–48.

Mulderij, K. (1996) 'Research into the lifeworld of physically disabled children', *Child: Care, Health and Development*, 22(5): 311–22.

Murphy, J. (1998) 'Talking Mats: Speech and language research in practice', *Speech and Language Therapy in Practice*, Autumn issue: 11–14.

Murray, P. (2002) *Hello! Are You Listening? Disabled Teenagers' Experiences of Access to Inclusive Leisure*. York: Joseph Rowntree Foundation/York Publishing Services.

Murray, P. (2004) *Making Connections: Developing Inclusive Leisure in Policy and Practice*. York: Joseph Rowntree Foundation/York Publishing Services.

O'Grady, L. and Fisher, A. (2008) 'Psychological sense of community as a framework to explore adolescence and neighbourhoods', *The Australian Community Psychologist*, 20(2): 44-57.

Oliver, M. (1990) *The Politics of Disablement*. London: Macmillan.

Oliver, M. (1992) 'Changing the social relations of research production', *Disability, Handicap and Society*, 7(2): 101–14.

Philpott, S. and Sait, W. (2001) 'Disabled children: An emergency submerged', in M. Priestley (ed.), *Disability and the Life Course: Global Perspectives*. Cambridge: Cambridge University Press, pp. 151–66.

Pollock, N., Stewart, D., Law, M., Sahagian-Whalen, S., Harvey, S. and Toal, C. (1997) 'The meaning of play for young people with physical disabilities', *Canadian Journal of Occupational Therapy*, 64(1): 25–31.

Preece, D. (2002) 'Consultation with children with autistic spectrum disorders about their experience of short-term residential care', *British Journal of Learning Disabilities*, 30(3): 97–104.

Rabiee, P., Priestley, M. and Knowles, J. (2001) *Whatever Next? Young Disabled People Leaving Care.* York: York Publishing Services.

Rabiee, P., Sloper, P. and Beresford, B. (2005a) 'Doing research with children and young people who do not use speech for communication', *Children and Society*, 19(5): 385–96.

Rabiee, P., Sloper, P. and Beresford, B. (2005b) 'Desired outcomes for children and young people with complex health care needs, and children who do not use speech for communication', *Health and Social Care in the Community*, 13(5): 478–87.

Raviv, D. and Stone, A. (1991) 'Individual differences in the self-image of adolescents with learning disabilities: The roles of severity, time of diagnosis, and parental perceptions', *Journal of Learning Disabilities*, 24(10): 602–11.

Ronen, G.M., Streiner, D.L. and Rosenbaum, P. (2003) 'Health-related quality of life in children with epilepsy: Development and validation of self-report and parent proxy measures', *Epilepsia*, 44(4): 598–612.

SCOPE (2002) *The Good Practice Guide, for Support Workers and Personal Assistants Working with Disabled People with Communication Impairments.* London: Scope.

Sloper, P., Beresford, B. and Rabiee, P. (2009) 'Every Child Matters outcomes: What do they mean for disabled children?', *Children and Society*, 23(4): 256–78.

Stalker, K. (1998) 'Some ethical and methodological issues in research with people with learning difficulties', *Disability and Society*, 13(1): 5–9.

Stalker, K. and Connors, C. (2003) 'Communicating with disabled children', *Fostering and Adoption*, 27(1): 26–35.

Stern, A. (2001, June) 'Deafness and reading', *Literacy Today*, 27. Available at www.literacytrust.org.uk

Sutherland, H. and Young, A. (2007) '"Hate English! Why?..." Signs and English from Deaf children's perspective: Results from a preliminary study of deaf children's experiences of sign bilingual education', *Deafness and Education International*, 9(4): 197–213.

Sutton-Spence, R. and Woll, B. (1999) *The Linguistics of British Sign Language: An introduction.* Cambridge: Cambridge University Press.

Temple, B. and Young, A. (2004) 'Qualitative research and translation dilemmas', *Qualitative Research*, 4(2): 161–78.

The Routes Project Team (2001) *Young People as Researchers: Possibilities, Problems and Politics.* Leicester: National Youth Agency.

Triangle/NSPCC (2001) *Two Way Street – Training Video and Handbook on Communicating with Children Who Do Not Use Speech or Language.* Leicester: NSPCC.

Triangle/NSPCC (2002) *How Is It: An Image Vocabulary for Children About Feelings, Rights and Safety, Personal Care and Sexuality.* Leicester: NSPCC.

Varni, J.W., Burwinkle, T.M., Sherman, S.A., Hanna, K., Berrin, S.J., Malcarne, V.L. and Chambers, H.G. (2005) 'Health-related quality of life of children and adolescents with cerebral palsy: Hearing the voices of the children', *Developmental Medicine and Child Neurology*, 47(9): 592–97.

Ward, L. (1997) *Seen and Heard: Involving Disabled Children and Young People in Research and Development Projects.* York: Joseph Rowntree Foundation.

Ware, J. (2004) 'Ascertaining the views of people with profound and multiple learning disabilities', *British Journal of Learning Disabilities*, 32(4): 175–9.

Warrick, A. (1998) *Communication without Speech: Augmentative and Alternative Communication, Communication Matters.* Oxford: The Ace Centre.

Watson, N. and Priestley, M. (1999) *Life as a Disabled Child: A Qualitative Study of Young People's Experiences and Perspectives*, Final project report to ESRC. Leeds: Disability Research Unit, University of Leeds.

White-Konig, M., Arnaud, C., Dickinson, H., Thyen, U., Beckung, E., Fauconnier, J., McManus, V., Michelsen, S.I., Parkes, J., Parkinson, K., Schirripa, G. and Colver, A. (2007) 'Determinants of child-parent agreement in quality-of-life reports: A European study of children with cerebral palsy', *Pediatrics*, 120(4): 804–14.

Wing, L. (1993) 'The definition and prevalence of autism: A review', *European Child Adolescent Psychiatry*, 2(2): 61–74.

15

Youth Who Have Broken the Law

Michael R. McCart, Terje Ogden and Scott W. Henggeler

INTRODUCTION

Youth who engage in law-breaking behavior are at high risk of presenting significant deleterious outcomes and long-term costs for themselves, their families, and society. In this chapter, the epidemiology and correlates of law-breaking behavior among youth are discussed as bases for understanding the extent and nature of criminal activity among juveniles. In addition, using the juvenile justice system in the United States and the child welfare system in Norway as examples, punitive versus rehabilitative system-wide responses to juvenile offending are discussed. Importantly, research during the past 20 years has led to the development of effective treatments, each of which is family-based, and these are described. Finally, several implications for future research are offered.

EPIDEMIOLOGY OF LAW-BREAKING BEHAVIOR

Law-breaking behaviors among youth are diverse in their seriousness and effects on others. At the less serious end of the continuum

are behaviors that are legally defined in the United States as status offenses. These are behaviors that would not be illegal if performed by an adult (for example, running away from home, truancy, alcohol possession or use, and curfew violations). At the upper end of the continuum are behaviors that have seriously detrimental effects on others, such as rape, robbery, and aggravated assault. In between are criminal activities such as burglary, motor vehicle theft, and vandalism.

Measurement methods

Most youth who break the law never come to the attention of the authorities. Formal (arrest) statistics tend therefore to underestimate the true rates of youths' involvement in illegal acts (Howell et al., 1995). More accurate estimates come from epidemiological studies that gather self-report data from youth regarding their participation in different types of criminal activities (Thornberry and Krohn, 2000). Between 2005 and 2007, the International Self-Report Delinquency Study-2 (Junger-Tas et al., 2010) surveyed random samples of youth in 31 nations regarding their involvement in delinquent behavior. In the United States sample, almost 30 percent of participants reported committing at least one delinquent offense during the past year. The most commonly reported offenses included physical assault (9.7 percent), shoplifting (9.2 percent), and vandalism (8.7 percent). Victim reports comprise a third source of information on criminal behavior. The National Crime Victimization Survey collects data annually on rates of violent victimization (rape/sexual assault, physical assault) among youth in the United States. In 2010, the violent victimization rate among youth aged 12–17 (14.0 per 1000) was more than twice that of adults (6.5 per 1000), and less than half of all violent crimes perpetrated against youth were reported to law enforcement (White and Lauritsen, 2012).

Age and gender trends

Prevalence rates for most types of law-breaking behaviors peak around 17 years of age. Engagement in serious illegal behavior is less common among younger adolescents. When youth do begin participating in criminal acts at a young age (defined as prior to age 14), they are much more likely to continue offending into adulthood (Loeber and Farrington, 2000). In general, boys engage in higher rates of law-breaking behavior compared to girls (Butts et al., 1995; Stahl, Finnegan and Kang, 2007). The only exception to this trend is for the offense of running away from home, which is somewhat more common among female adolescents (US Bureau of Labor Statistics, 2002). However, criminal justice statistics suggest that girls' involvement in law-breaking behavior may be increasing. Since 1983, the female arrest rate in the United States has increased relative to that of males. Although this pattern may reflect a true rise in the rate of law-breaking behavior among girls, it is also possible that law enforcement officials have simply become more likely to arrest girls when they are caught engaging in illegal acts.

Race and cultural differences

Regarding race, African-American and Latino youth in the United States have much higher rates of arrest than do Caucasian youth. Racial effects, however, have failed to consistently emerge in epidemiological studies using self-report methods. Explanations for this discrepancy might include the lower validity of self-report instruments for minorities, as well as racial discrimination in decisions to arrest and incarcerate (Howell et al., 1995; Snyder and Sickmund, 2006).

Research examining cross-cultural differences in rates of law-breaking behavior among youth is limited. To our knowledge, the aforementioned International Self-Reported Delinquency Study-2 (Junger-Tas et al., 2010) is the only investigation that has documented rates of juvenile delinquency in various parts of the world using uniform assessment methodology. Results revealed considerable similarity in the past year prevalence rates of law-breaking behavior across all participating countries. Violent offenses, however, were more common in the United States, Germany, Ireland, and the Netherlands. Moreover, rates of theft were generally higher in countries with more prosperous economies (Junger-Tas et al., 2010).

Psychiatric comorbidity

Studies have identified relatively high rates of psychiatric comorbidity among delinquent youth (Abram et al., 2007). This is perhaps not surprising given that law-breaking behavior and several psychiatric conditions share many of the same biological (for example, prenatal exposure to toxins) and socio-cultural (including poverty and parent–child conflict) risk factors (Fergusson, Lynskey and Horwood, 1996). In a review of the literature, Vermeiren (2003) noted relatively high rates of the co-occurrence of problems such as substance abuse, conduct disorder, posttraumatic stress disorder (PTSD), mood or anxiety disorders, attention deficit/hyperactivity disorder (ADHD), and suicidal behaviors. Across most studies, the risk of psychiatric disturbance among girls was more than twice that of boys. Interestingly, available data also reveal remarkable similarities in rates of psychiatric distress among delinquent youth in different parts of the world (Vermeiren, 2003). When interpreting these data, it is important to note that most research in this area has been conducted with incarcerated or detained youth. Thus, it is unclear whether similarly elevated rates of psychiatric problems are also evident within community samples of delinquent adolescents.

CORRELATES AND DETERMINANTS OF LAW-BREAKING BEHAVIOR

Substantial evidence, including findings from the most rigorous longitudinal studies conducted in this area of research (see, for example, Elliott, 1994; Loeber et al., 1998; Thornberry and Krohn, 2003) supports a multi-determined conceptualization of law-breaking behavior among youth (Henggeler and Sheidow, 2002). The many factors contributing to juvenile offending can be organized using a transactional developmental model (Dodge and Pettit, 2003), which is derived from social ecological theory (Bronfenbrenner, 1979). According to the transactional developmental model, biological predispositions and socio-cultural contexts place youth at heightened risk for engaging in law-breaking behavior, and that risk is mediated by early life experiences with peers and parents.

Biological predispositions

Various biological factors are likely associated with the development of delinquent behavior problems indirectly through youths' temperament. Certain genetic factors and the presence of toxins (such as lead, nicotine, and alcohol) in the prenatal environment predict

dispositions in infancy characterized by emotional reactivity, impulsivity, and resistance to control (Lemola, Stadlmayr and Grob, 2009; Wakschlag and Hans, 2002). Furthermore, these difficult styles of temperament are associated with the development of delinquent behavior problems in later childhood (Caspi et al., 1995). Research overwhelmingly suggests that biological variables tend to exert their strongest influence at an early age, whereas environmental variables become stronger predictors of behavior problems as youth progress through middle childhood and adolescence (Moffitt, 1993).

Cognitive factors

Social information processing

According to the transactional developmental model, relationships among biological, socio-cultural, and life experience factors can lead to patterns of social information processing that are linked with delinquent behavior (Crick and Dodge, 1994). Individuals are hypothesized to process social information in six sequential steps: (1) encoding of information, (2) interpretation of information, (3) specification of an ultimate goal, (4) generation of response options, (5) selection of an optimal response, and (6) enactment of that response. Youths' engagement in law-breaking behavior, particular physical assault, may be associated with faulty processing during any of these steps. For example, delinquent youth tend to search for fewer social cues and generate fewer competent responses in social situations (Dodge and Newman, 1981). Moreover, they display more confidence in their ability to use aggression as a problem solving strategy, and they are more likely to attribute hostile intentions to ambiguous situations (Lochman and Dodge, 1994). Thus, youths with social information processing deficits can be predisposed to behave aggressively, especially when embedded in contexts that support such aggression.

Youths' own explanations for law-breaking behavior

Youth explanations for delinquent offending seem to vary as a function of culture. Tyson and Hubert (2002), for example, examined explanations for delinquency among a multicultural sample of children and adolescents living in Australia. The sample comprised youth who were born in Australia (a traditional individualistic culture) and youth who had recently immigrated to the country from Asia (a traditional collectivist culture). Results indicated that the Australian youth were significantly more likely to emphasize internal explanations for delinquency (for example, emotional maladjustment), while the Asian youth were more likely to emphasize external explanations (such as peer pressure or poor discipline). As noted by the authors, these results are important because a cultural group's beliefs about the causes of juvenile offending may influence their receptivity to specific interventions. For example, youth and families may be reluctant to participate in a particular treatment (or drop out early) if the conceptual and procedural aspects of the intervention are not in line with what they think ought to be done about the problem.

Family factors

Family-level variables play pivotal roles in both the development and attenuation of delinquent behavior. Although several contextual aspects of the family (including single-parenting, maternal depression, marital conflict, and parental involvement in crime) place youth at risk for engaging in delinquent behavior (Alltucker et al., 2006; Deater-Deckard et al., 1998), these generally operate by interfering with important aspects of parenting and family relations. Based on several excellent literature reviews (Biglan et al., 2004; Hoge, Guerra, and Boxer, 2008), antisocial behavior in adolescents is associated most consistently with poor monitoring and supervision, inconsistent and lax discipline,

and poor affective relations with siblings and caregivers. In this regard, coercion theory (Patterson, 1982) offers an excellent example of the link between ineffective parenting and delinquent outcomes. The teenager defies caregiver rules. The caregiver attempts to enforce the rule. The youth escalates his or her defiance verbally or physically. The caregiver acquiesces. Here, the teenager has learned that arguing, threatening, and throwing tantrums can lead to desired outcomes (in other words, negation of rules), and the caregiver has learned that giving in to the adolescent reduced his or her verbal or physical aggression. Similarly, as suggested previously, one can appreciate how caregiver mental health problems, substance abuse, or stress can exacerbate the problem by interfering with caregivers' parenting capabilities.

Peer relations

Decades of correlational and longitudinal research have demonstrated that association with deviant peers (for example, delinquent and/or drug using friends) is a powerful proximal predictor of antisocial behavior in adolescents (Elliott, Huizinga and Ageton, 1985; Keenan et al., 1995). Indeed, leading researchers (see, for example, Dodge, Dishion and Lansford, 2006) have argued cogently that many of the prevailing practices of service systems that aggregate antisocial youths together in group treatment or institutional settings are iatrogenic. Similarly, as discussed subsequently, the most effective treatments of adolescent criminal behavior aim explicitly to minimize youth contact with antisocial peers.

School performance

Delinquent behavior is also consistently associated with poor school performance (for example, low grades, special education placement, reading problems, and frequent suspensions) and with dropping out of school early (Hinshaw, 1992; Stouthamer-Loeber et al., 2002). Furthermore, academic underachievement during adolescence is linked with elevated rates of criminal activity during young adulthood (Loeber et al., 2005). These associations may be explained by the linkages that delinquency and school performance each have with maladaptive parenting, impaired family relations, and association with deviant peers (Leve, Pears, and Fisher, 2002). Researchers have also described various school characteristics that contribute to delinquency, including high student–teacher ratios, poor academic quality, and a lack of perceived fairness and clarity of school rules (Gottfredson et al., 2005; Hellman and Beaton, 1986).

Neighborhood context

Neighborhoods characterized by high levels of poverty, residential mobility, substandard housing, violence, drug use, and social disorganization (defined as a lack of perceived cohesion and social support among neighbors) are associated with elevated rates of juvenile crime and substance use (Sampson, Raudenbush and Earls, 1997; Stewart, Simmons and Conger, 2002). Exposure to interpersonal violence is a particularly salient stressor and has consistently been associated with delinquent behavior. For example, in a cross-sectional sample of youth residing in a low-income urban neighborhood, witnessed violence was positively associated with self-reported aggressive behavior and weapon carrying, even after controlling for the effects of neighborhood disadvantage (Patchin et al., 2006). Similarly, other studies have reported strong associations between childhood physical and sexual abuse and participation in illegal behavior during adolescence and young adulthood (Hubbard and Pratt, 2002; Mersky and Reynolds, 2007; Stewart, Livingston and Dennison, 2008; Widom, 1989).

Developmental pathways

During the past few decades, considerable effort has been expended to understand pathways leading to delinquent outcomes. Initial work in this area was conducted by Moffitt and her colleagues in the context of a 30-year longitudinal study of a birth cohort of 1000 New Zealanders (Moffitt, 1993). Findings from this research revealed two subgroups of youth who could be distinguished from each other based on the age of onset of their lawbreaking behavior. The first group, labeled 'life-course persistent' offenders, began displaying delinquent behavior problems during early childhood. This group tended to possess a number of biologically based risk factors for delinquent behavior, including elevated rates of emotional reactivity, impulsivity, and low verbal intelligence (Moffitt, 1993). They also presented with high rates of peer rejection and tended to come from families characterized by high conflict, parental psychopathology, and low socioeconomic status. The behavior of the life-course persistent youth was highly stable and predictive of later criminality and substance abuse in adulthood (Moffitt, 2003). The second group, labeled 'adolescence-limited' offenders, tended to engage in a time-limited period of rebelliousness and associations with deviant peers during the teenage years. These youth were less likely to have intellectual deficits or impulsive dispositions, came from less disadvantaged family backgrounds, and most desisted from delinquent behavior after transitioning into adult roles. Moffitt's dual taxonomy has since been replicated with other samples of delinquent youth (see, for example, Aguilar et al., 2000; Schaeffer et al., 2006) and serves as a useful framework for specifying two relatively distinct developmental pathways of juvenile offending.

Cross-cultural consistency of findings

Importantly from an international perspective, research conducted in different parts of the world suggests that the characteristics of juvenile offenders and the systems in which they are embedded are similar across diverse cultural populations. For example, descriptive data on juvenile offenders living in the United Kingdom (Hill-Smith et al., 2002), Ireland (Barnes and O'Gorman, 1995), Australia (Cunneen and White, 2007), Turkey (Ozen et al., 2005), and Hong Kong (Wong, 2001) indicate that these youth are characterized by high rates of family dysfunction, deviant peer association, and academic underachievement. Moreover, data from a nationally representative sample of Norwegian adolescents revealed strong associations between poor parental monitoring, parental alcohol use, and adolescent involvement in criminal behavior (Pedersen, 2000).

Next, we discuss intervention models that are being employed in various parts of the world. We begin with a review of the juvenile justice and child welfare systems, which represent government sponsored entities for intervening with youth who are engaging in delinquent activities. Then, several family-based interventions that have proven effective in treating youth law-breaking behavior are discussed.

JUVENILE JUSTICE AND CHILD WELFARE SYSTEMS

Interestingly, the juvenile justice system was initially developed as a model for providing protection and educational remediation for young criminal offenders. Although several countries continue to embrace this type of welfare philosophy, others have adopted a more punishment-oriented approach that places greater emphasis on youth accountability and deterrence. In this section, a general overview on the historical development of the juvenile justice system is provided, and differences in how that system is administered cross-nationally are discussed. A detailed description of the juvenile justice system in the United States is provided as an example of a model that has become almost entirely punishment-based. Comparisons are made between this model and the juvenile justice system in Norway, which has maintained welfare-oriented policies and procedures.

Historical development

As noted by Junger-Tas (2006), global recognition of the need to intervene with delinquent youth emerged around the beginning of the seventeenth century. Strategies that were adopted at that time to address youths' law-breaking behavior included physical punishment (such as flogging, branding) or placement in reformatories, which essentially functioned like youth prisons. Significant changes emerged in the later part of the nineteenth century. During that time, reformers in the United States advocated for increased consideration of the environmental circumstances (for example, parental neglect and neighborhood deprivation) that contributed to juvenile offending. These reformers believed that in order to effectively reduce delinquent behavior among youth, the state needed to assume more of a parental role.

This movement led to the development of the first juvenile court system in Chicago in 1899 (Snyder and Sickmund, 2006). The ultimate aim of that court was to provide protection for children when it was determined that their parents were not providing appropriate supervision. In the years that followed, similar juvenile court systems were created throughout the United States, other common law countries, and Europe. Although juvenile courts in the United States and Europe differed in many ways, they were all based on a similar welfare philosophy. That is, youth who broke the law were viewed as needing early intervention and supervision, as opposed to punishment (Junger-Tas, 2006). Juvenile court hearings were generally informal, extra-legal factors (for example, family functioning, peer influences) were given substantial consideration, and due process protections were considered unnecessary. Disposition options often included verbal warnings, probation, or confinement to a treatment institution.

Juvenile courts continued to function in this way until around the middle of the twentieth century (Junger-Tas, 2006). During that time, public confidence in the effectiveness of institutionalized treatment decreased, and there was a renewed emphasis on the importance of holding youth accountable for their behavior. Several countries, most notably the United States, shifted their focus from the welfare of delinquent youth to an approach that placed greater emphasis on punishment and deterrence (Bishop and Decker, 2006; Bishop and Feld, 2011; Cashmore, 2013; Cunneen and White, 2007; Tonry and Chambers, 2011). Decisions were also made to make juvenile courts more formal, and children accused of a crime were granted increased legal rights (such as right to counsel).

As noted by Junger-Tas (2006), three types of juvenile justice systems appear to be operating in the world today. The first is a punishment- or justice-oriented model that places strong emphasis on youth accountability. This model is practiced in the United States, Canada, Australia, and several European countries, including England, Ireland, and the Netherlands. These countries tend to have lower ages of criminal responsibility (in other words, the age at which youth can be held criminally responsible for their actions). They have also passed laws that make it easier to transfer youth to the adult criminal justice system and to impose adult sentences such as imprisonment. The second type of juvenile justice system is the welfare model, which is still commonly practiced in countries such as Germany, France, and Belgium. The age of criminal responsibility in these countries is higher. Imprisonment is viewed as an intervention of last resort, and most juvenile offenders are diverted to treatment, community service, or mediation programs. The third type of juvenile justice system, as

practiced in the Scandinavian counties (Norway, Denmark, and Sweden) and Scotland, includes a unique mix of justice- and welfare-based principles. These countries are also highly receptive to empirical research and have taken the lead in integrating evidence-based practices into their juvenile justice policies and procedures.

Juvenile justice system in the United States

As described above, when the juvenile justice system was first developed in the United States, its overarching aim was to function as a welfare system by providing support and rehabilitation to young offenders. During the past 20–30 years, the United States' juvenile justice system has undergone a number of changes and currently functions as more of a system of punishment and control as opposed to protection and treatment (Bishop and Decker, 2006). These changes were prompted by what was perceived to be a growing crime problem among the nation's youth in the 1980s and early 1990s. During that time period, the juvenile arrest rate for most types of violent crime increased by more than 100 percent (Synder and Sickmund, 2006). States responded by passing more punitive juvenile justice legislation. The first major change involved the implementation of severe punishments for serious and chronic offenders. This change took the form of increased (and easier) transfers of juveniles to criminal courts for prosecution as adults, greater use of electronic monitoring, and the sentencing of youth to lengthy stays in detention centers.

Youth who break the law in the United States typically enter the juvenile justice system through law enforcement. Once a youth is arrested and charged with a crime, the police can decide to dismiss the charge, refer the youth to juvenile court, or refer the youth to criminal court. According to data from the United States. Department of Justice, the vast majority of arrested adolescents

(67 percent) are referred to the juvenile court for formal case processing (Puzzanchera and Adams, 2011). Charges are dismissed in about 24 percent of cases, and the remaining 9 percent of arrested youth are referred to (adult) criminal court. The primary determining factor for direct referral to criminal court is the age of the youth at the time of the offense. For example, in several states, the upper age of juvenile court jurisdiction is 16 years. Thus, in these states, youth older than 16 years of age are legally defined as adults and are automatically sent to criminal court for prosecution.

Whenever a youth is referred to the juvenile court, an intake worker reviews the circumstances surrounding the arrest and makes a decision about how to proceed with the case. The intake worker may decide to close the case without action or to divert the youth to informal handling by another agency. When a case is handled informally, the youth typically agrees to abide by a specific set of conditions (for example, regular school attendance, no curfew violations) during a set period of time. If the youth complies with these conditions, the charge is dismissed. However, any violation of these conditions can result in an immediate referral back to the court for formal prosecution.

At the time of juvenile court intake, the intake worker may also decide to file a delinquency or waiver petition (Snyder and Sickmund, 2006). A delinquency petition requests that a youth be scheduled for an adjudicatory hearing in juvenile court. A waiver petition requests that the youth be transferred to criminal court. Most states have strict criteria for waivers based on the age of the youth and nature of the offense. The minimum age for judicial waiver to criminal court varies from state to state, with most ranging between 12 and 14 years of age. Offense types that are commonly targeted by waivers include murder, capital crimes punishable by death or life sentences, and other serious violent crimes involving use of a weapon.

A juvenile adjudicatory hearing is analogous in many ways to an adult criminal trial.

Juveniles are represented by counsel (typically a public defender assigned by the court), and the prosecutor and defense attorneys present the facts of the case to a judge. Unlike a criminal court trial, however, adjudicatory proceedings do not involve a jury, and the judge makes the sole determination of guilt. During the hearing process, youth may be held in a detention facility if they are perceived as a threat to the community. Youth may also be ordered to undergo a comprehensive mental health evaluation to determine if a psychiatric or substance abuse problem is contributing to their delinquent behavior. Youth who are adjudicated delinquent (found guilty) of a crime are scheduled for a formal disposition hearing. Dispositions are ordered by the judge and almost always include some form of supervised probation. Dispositions may also include residential placement, participation in psychological or substance abuse counseling, or completion of community service. Recently, several states have expanded their disposition options for youth charged with a serious offense. In these states, offenders may receive what is commonly referred to as a 'blended sentence' involving both juvenile and criminal sanctions. When a blended sentence is ordered by a judge, the criminal sanctions are typically suspended as long as the youth complies with all aspects of the juvenile disposition (such as obeying all conditions of probation; Snyder and Sickmund, 2006).

As noted previously, the juvenile justice system in the United States has become significantly more punitive over the past few decades. This trend is highlighted in a recent report compiled by the National Center for Juvenile Justice (Puzzanchera, Adams and Hockenberry, 2012). According to this report, there was a 30 percent increase in the number of delinquency cases processed by juvenile courts between 1985 and 2009. During that same time period, the number of cases in which a youth was adjudicated delinquent or waived to criminal court increased 45 percent. Dispositions ordered by judges have also become increasingly more punitive.

Over the past 10–20 years, the number of juvenile offenders sent to some form of out-of-home placement has increased 27 percent. Although the juvenile inmate population has declined over time, the United States still incarcerates a larger percentage of youth than any other developed country (Annie E. Casey Foundation, 2013). Interestingly, this movement toward more punitive juvenile justice policies and sanctions in the United States has persisted despite evidence of a substantial decline in the juvenile crime rate since 1994.

Norway's child welfare system

In contrast to the United States, Norway has maintained more of a commitment to the welfare philosophy when intervening with youth who break the law. Although justice-based interventions have become more common in Norway in recent years, they are typically reserved for older and more serious offenders. At present, Norway has no formal juvenile court or juvenile justice system, and the age of criminal responsibility is 15 years. Thus, no child or adolescent may be punished for a delinquent act committed before reaching 15 years of age. Juvenile offenders under age 15 years are typically dealt with by the child welfare system, and those aged 15 to 17 years are the responsibility of the adult criminal justice system.

When youth under age 15 years break the law, they are referred by the police to the child welfare system. The police may investigate the case, but a youth under 15 years of age cannot be arrested or detained. The child welfare system can provide a wide range of interventions that are stepped up gradually according to the seriousness of the youth's situation. Generally, interventions are designed to be in the best interests of the child. In accordance with Norway's Child Welfare Act, voluntary preventive measures in the home must be prioritized. Home-based interventions often take the form of social services to help meet the family's basic needs, family therapy, or assistance in enrolling the youth in prosocial leisure-time activities. Short-term, voluntary care in a foster home may also be implemented, although this is rare.

Youth under the age of 15 years who show serious behavior problems in the form of repeated criminality or persistent substance abuse may, without their consent or the consent of their caregivers, be placed in an institution for observation, examination, and short-term treatment for a period lasting no more than four weeks. If the youth is considered to be in need of more long-term treatment, an order may be made by the county social welfare board to place the child in a treatment or training institution for up to 12 months without the caregiver's consent. According to section 4-25 of the Child Welfare Act, the child welfare service must always consider whether family assistance should be implemented in lieu of placement. If the decision is made to place a youth in an institution, the child welfare system must continue to provide assistance to the family for a set period of time after the youth is released.

Youth aged 15 to 17 years who break the law are typically referred directly to the adult criminal justice system. When a criminal investigation is initiated against a child, the police must immediately inform the child welfare service, although the case is still processed in criminal court. If the prosecuting authorities find that a young person is guilty of a crime, three options are at their disposal. First, prosecution may be waived if an overall evaluation finds that there are weighty reasons for dismissal. This is quite often the case with younger criminal offenders. Second, the prosecuting authority may decide that the case should be remitted to a *mediation board*. The mediation process is designed to give young persons the opportunity to face the victim, apologize for their behavior, and reflect on the consequences of their actions. Third, the youth may receive a more formal sentence that can involve a fine, community service, probation, out-of-home placement in a treatment institution, or imprisonment. It should be noted, however, that there are very few 15 to 17-year-olds in Norwegian prisons today. This is due to the fact that the police, the child welfare service, and the court consistently lean toward other less-restrictive interventions for juvenile offenders. When young persons are imprisoned, special effort is taken to ensure the availability of good health care, education and/or vocational training, and placement close to the family's home. In addition, although Norway does not have special institutions for young offenders, measures are taken to avoid placing young persons together with more experienced criminals.

EVIDENCE-BASED TREATMENTS

As described in the United States Surgeon General's report on youth violence (US Public Health Service, 2001) and the United States National Institutes of Health Consensus Conference (National Institutes of Health, 2006), the general consensus in the field of delinquency treatment in the late 1980s was that 'nothing works'. During the past decade, however, three treatment approaches have emerged as effective in reducing law-breaking behaviors among juvenile offenders: Functional Family Therapy (FFT), Multisystemic Therapy (MST), and Multidimensional Treatment Foster Care (MTFC). Importantly, these treatments share several common features (Henggeler and Sheidow, 2002). They each (a) are comprehensive and address an array of the known risk factors for delinquency discussed previously, (b) view the family as the primary vehicle for achieving favorable clinical outcomes, (c) provide services in community-based settings, (d) use behavioral treatment principles within systemic conceptual frameworks, and (e) rely on strong quality assurance procedures to support therapist fidelity to the respective treatment models and achieve desired outcomes.

Functional family therapy (FFT)

FFT (Alexander et al., 1998) is a family-based treatment for youth with delinquent behavior problems. FFT includes three sequential phases of intervention: (1) engagement and motivation, (2) behavior change, and (3) generalization. During the engagement and motivation phase, therapists work to enhance family members' perceptions of therapist credibility and to create a therapist-family context that is conducive to desired change. To achieve this goal, therapists behave responsively and respectfully toward family members and work to reduce anger and other negative emotions through the use of cognitive reframing techniques. The behavior change phase of FFT involves use of behavioral parent training and family communication training in an attempt to improve family relations in ways that facilitate positive changes in youths' behavior (Alexander and Sexton, 2002). During the generalization phase, therapists aim to sustain clinical improvements by linking families with longer-term support services in the community (such as mental health, social service agencies).

FFT has been evaluated in one randomized controlled trial with male and female status offenders (Alexander and Parsons, 1973), a randomized controlled trial with substance-abusing adolescents (Waldron et al., 2001), and in three quasi-experimental studies that included youth charged with serious delinquent offenses (Barnoski, 2004; Barton et al., 1985; Gordon et al., 1988). Across studies, FFT has been shown to significantly reduce rates of delinquency recidivism and substance use relative to control conditions. Treatment effects have also been maintained as long as five years post-treatment (Gordon, Graves and Arbuthnot, 1995). In addition, a recent large-scale effectiveness trial with juvenile offenders conducted by an independent research group found positive outcomes for FFT on criminal recidivism 12-months post-treatment, but only when therapist adherence to the model was high (Sexton and Turner, 2010).

Multisystemic therapy (MST)

MST is a comprehensive family- and community-based treatment for youth with serious delinquent behavior problems that are at risk for out-of-home placement (Henggeler et al., 2009). Treatment is provided by clinicians using a home-based model of service delivery. Drawing upon evidence-based intervention strategies (such as cognitive-behavioral therapy, pragmatic family therapy), MST clinicians develop and direct interventions toward ameliorating those individual, family, peer, school, and community factors that are linked directly or indirectly with the youth's behavior problems; with caregivers viewed as the keys to achieving sustainable outcomes. For example, behavioral parent training techniques are used to enhance caregivers' capacity to monitor their youth's behavior and whereabouts, and to provide positive consequences for responsible behavior and sanctions for irresponsible behavior. Under the guidance of the therapist, caregivers also develop strategies to promote their youth's school performance, decrease his or her involvement with delinquent peers, and increase his or her participation in prosocial activities (such as sports or church youth groups).

The effectiveness of MST has been demonstrated in 26 published outcome, transportability, and benchmarking studies including 20 randomized trials and 11 independent evaluations (MST Institute, 2012). At least 10 of these studies were conducted with youths presenting serious antisocial behavior. For example, three successful randomized trials with violent and chronic juvenile offenders were published in the 1990s (Borduin et al., 1995; Henggeler et al., 1997; Henggeler, Melton and Smith, 1992), with one producing sustained outcomes at even 22 years post-treatment (Sawyer and Borduin, 2011). Other randomized trials have been conducted with substance-abusing offenders (Henggeler et al., 2006) and juvenile sexual offenders (Letourneau et al., 2009). Importantly, independent replications

have also been published in the United States (see, for example, Timmons-Mitchell et al., 2006) and Europe (Ogden and Hagen, 2006). Findings across these studies have consistently favored MST in comparison with control conditions. A meta-analysis of MST trials (Curtis, Ronan and Borduin, 2004) included seven of these studies (708 total participants, 35 MST therapists), and effect sizes averaged 0.50 for criminal behavior, 1.01 for arrest seriousness, and 0.29 for substance use. Further, these studies typically have been completed in field settings and included few exclusion criteria, features that strengthen support for treatment effectiveness of MST in real-world community practice settings.

Multidimensional treatment foster care (MTFC)

MTFC (Chamberlain and Mihalic, 1998) is the third empirically supported family-based intervention for serious juvenile offenders. Youth receiving MTFC are placed with specially trained foster parents in lieu of residential placement, with the ultimate goal of transitioning the youth back home to his or her biological family. Treatment is provided by a team, consisting of the foster parents, a case manager, individual and family therapists, and other resource staff. Several treatment modalities are integrated to achieve behavior change. For example, behavioral parent training techniques are used to teach foster parents to manage the youth's behavior in a consistent and non-coercive manner. Foster parents also provide intensive supervision of the youth's activities and monitor his or her interactions with peers. Treatment sessions with the biological family are conducted throughout the youth's placement in foster care. These sessions focus on building parents' supervision, discipline, and problem-solving skills. Youth have short-term visits with their family that increase to overnight stays as treatment progresses. In addition to this family-based work, the MTFC team collaborates with school officials to monitor and address youths' behavior in the classroom. Furthermore, individual therapy is offered to assist youth in developing non-violent problem-solving skills.

MTFC has been evaluated in one randomized controlled trial (Chamberlain and Reid, 1998) and in one quasi-experimental study (Chamberlain, 1990) with delinquent boys. More recently, this family-based intervention was also evaluated in randomized controlled trials with both youths (Farmer et al., 2010) and chronically delinquent girls (Leve, Chamberlain and Reid, 2005; Van Ryzin and Leve, 2012). In all three studies, youth receiving MTFC were less likely to run away and more likely to complete treatment compared to youth placed in community residential treatment settings. Youth who received MTFC also engaged in fewer offenses at post-treatment, as measured by official arrest records and self-report of delinquent behavior. Moreover, outcomes have been maintained for up to two years following completion of treatment (Chamberlain, Leve and DeGarmo, 2007; Eddy, Whaley and Chamberlain, 2004). In addition, an independent research group has demonstrated favorable outcomes for MTFC in a randomized effectiveness trial (Westermark, Hansson and Olsson, 2011) and a quasi-experimental study (Westermark, Hansson and Vinnerljung, 2008) involving delinquent youth in Sweden.

IMPLICATIONS FOR FUTURE RESEARCH

In summary, extensive research has documented the characteristics and correlates of law-breaking behavior among youth, and this body of work strongly supports the view that juvenile offending is multi-determined – involving influences at multiple ecological levels. Based largely on this research, several family-based treatments have developed and these have proven effective in reducing the criminal behavior of juvenile offenders. Such treatments, however, must be embedded within services systems. As outlined for the United States and Norway, service systems can vary in the degree of their embrace of rehabilitative approaches versus punishment oriented approaches (Bishop and Feld, 2011; Tonry and Chambers, 2011). In this section, several methodological issues are discussed that may be important to consider when conducting future research on adolescent law-breaking behavior.

Measurement of law-breaking behavior

When conducting studies that examine rates of law-breaking behavior among youth, arrest data should be supplemented with self-report measures of criminal behavior. Sole reliance on arrest data will lead to an underestimation of the rates of delinquent offending because the vast majority of individuals who engage in law-breaking behavior never come to the attention of law enforcement. An example of a self-report measure of juvenile offending that is commonly used in delinquency research is the Self-Report Delinquency Scale from the United States National Youth Survey (SRD; Elliot, Huizinga and Ageton, 1985). The SRD was designed to assess adolescents' participation in criminal acts during the past 90 days and is regarded as one of the best validated self-report measures of delinquency among youth (Thornberry and Krohn, 2000). In addition, researchers should consider supplementing self-report instruments with broad-band measures of behavior problems that allow for the collection of corroborating information from multiple informants (for example, parents and teachers). One well-validated parent-report instrument that assesses behavior problems among youth is the Child Behavior Checklist (CBCL; Achenbach, 2001). This instrument has been translated into multiple languages and includes parallel forms that can be completed by youth, parents, and teachers. Finally, it seems likely that the cultural context (in other words, whether the service system is oriented toward punishment versus rehabilitation) will influence the validity of respondent self-reports. One might expect self-report of offending to be attenuated in systems that are punishment oriented, in much the same way that juvenile sexual offending is under-reported due to stigma and fear of punishment (Letourneau, 2002). Although stringent confidentiality procedures (such as a Federal Certificate of Confidentiality) can be useful in assuring respondents that their responses will be used for research purposes only, the broader issue of system influence on self-reports is largely unknown.

Consideration of developmental trajectories

As noted previously, researchers have identified at least two major developmental pathways along which youth may develop delinquent behavior problems (Moffitt, 1993). The behavior problems of life-course persistent offenders tend to stem from biologically based impairments characterized by impulsivity, high levels of emotional reactivity, and low verbal intelligence. Youth falling on this developmental path tend to show a chronic and persistent pattern of delinquent behavior that extends into adulthood. Adolescence-limited offenders, on the other hand, engage in a time-limited period of rebelliousness and associations with deviant peers during their teenage years. These youth are less likely to present with intellectual deficits or impulsive dispositions, and their behavior problems usually remit once they make the transition into adult roles. Although the ramifications might be important, the differences between these subtypes are seldom examined in the treatment outcome literature. Delinquent adolescents included in treatment studies likely represent a heterogeneous group who may be responding differentially based on the developmental

trajectory of their delinquent behavior. That is, developmental pathway might be an important moderator of treatment effectiveness, with life-course persistent offenders being more difficult to treat because they present less malleable risk factors. On the other hand, the field of rehabilitation would benefit substantially if evidence-based treatments were proven effective with even life-course persistent offenders.

Psychiatric comorbidity

Research has identified elevated rates of anxiety, depression, ADHD, PTSD, and substance abuse problems in samples of delinquent adolescents (Vermeiren, 2003). Of particular interest is whether youth with certain types of comorbid conditions display different patterns of offending behavior over time. For example, some evidence suggests that delinquent youth with a diagnosis of ADHD exhibit more severe, intractable levels of symptomatology and an earlier age of onset compared with those who do not have ADHD (Moffitt, 1993). In contrast, delinquent youth with comorbid anxiety or depressive symptoms tend to show a less persistent course of delinquency (Zahn-Waxler, Klimes-Dougan and Slattery, 2000). The role that these and other psychiatric conditions play in influencing developmental trajectories of offending behavior requires further investigation. Research is also needed to explore whether the presence of comorbid psychiatric problems moderates the effects of commonly used offender-based interventions.

Consideration of cultural differences in explanations of law-breaking behavior

Some data suggest that different cultural groups have different beliefs about the causes of law-breaking behavior among youth. Tyson and Hubert (2002) found that youth from an individualistic culture were more likely to emphasize internal explanations for delinquency (for example, emotional maladjustment), whereas youth from a collectivist culture were more likely to emphasize external explanations (maladaptive parenting, peer influences). These findings might have relevance for individuals conducting clinical research with juvenile offenders. For example, youth and families might be reluctant to participate in a particular treatment if the conceptual and procedural aspects of the intervention are not in line with what they think ought to be done about the problem. On the other hand, the family- and evidence-based treatments noted previously have been embraced by families from a variety of cultures that vary in their individualistic emphases (for example, United States and Australia versus Norway and Sweden). Importantly, however, these treatments place explicit emphasis on building family alliances and considering the role of family culture in the treatment process.

System influences on delinquency research

The nature of the juvenile justice system in different nations can ease or impede the conduct of research on juvenile law breaking. In the United States, for example, adolescent offenders (those aged 12 through 17 years) are clearly identified through arrest and adjudication records, and stakeholders in the juvenile justice system often collaborate with researchers. On the other hand, there is little research on young offenders in Norway, especially those few who are imprisoned. The model, in which most adolescents under 18 years who break the law are transferred to Child Welfare Services, makes it difficult to decide who should be included as a young offender when conducting research. Moreover, the responsibility of the child welfare system is not only those who break the law, but also other children and adolescents who commit non-criminal offenses. Therefore, it is largely left to Child Welfare

Services at the municipal level to define who belongs to the target group (in other words, inclusion criteria for research participants) and who does not. Thus, the definitional power and norms of the various municipal Child Welfare Services are very important for the definition of a young offender. As a result, the prevalence of children and youth with serious behavior problems according to the Child Welfare Act (Section 4-24) may vary substantially among the municipalities. No operational definitions or strict behavioral criteria have been developed to decide who has serious behavior problems. Likewise, the procedure for transferring children and adolescents who break the law to the Child Welfare Services may also lead to an under-reporting of crimes committed by this age group. In order for these children to have a 'clean record', minor criminal offenses might not be formally registered by the police. Consequently it is difficult to study the prevalence of re-offending among young people in Norway, and the actual figures likely underestimate the problem.

Juvenile justice system philosophies and evidence-based treatments

Anecdotal experience in the transport of evidence-based practices to community settings during the past decade (for example, MST has been transported to more than 30 states in the United States and 10 nations worldwide) suggests that the adoption of evidence-based practices is more likely to occur in jurisdictions that emphasize rehabilitation over punishment. For example, several states (such as Connecticut and Florida) and nations (including Norway and Sweden) have implemented large-scale adoption of evidence-based treatments of antisocial behavior in children and adolescents. Less effort, however, has been invested in research-based evaluation of intended and unintended results and consequences of different initiatives. For example, under what circumstances does the initial adoption of an evidence-based practice increase the likelihood of further adoption of evidence-based treatments, and what are the corresponding consequences for existing providers of traditional services? New initiatives are also sometimes introduced without a critical evaluation of their theoretical or empirical underpinnings, which may or may not fit with the local culture. Indeed, as reviewed by Schoenwald and Hoagwood (2001), adoption and implementation of evidence-based practices are likely influenced by a wide variety of provider and system level variables, few of which have been formally examined.

REFERENCES

Abram, K.M., Washburn, J.L., Teplin, L.A., Emanuel, K.M., Romero, E.G. and McClelland, G.M. (2007) 'Posttraumatic stress disorder and psychiatric comorbidity among detained youths', *Psychiatric Services*, 58(10): 1311–16.

Achenbach, T.M. (2001) *Child Behavior Checklist for Ages 6 to 18*. Burlington: University of Vermont, Research Center for Children, Youth, and Families.

Aguilar, B., Sroufe, L.A., Egeland, B. and Carlson, E. (2000) 'Distinguishing the early-onset/persistent and adolescent-onset antisocial behavior types: From birth to 16 years', *Development and Psychopathology*, 12(2): 109–32.

Alexander, J. and Parsons, B. (1973) 'Short-term behavioral intervention with delinquent families: Impact on family process and recidivism', *Journal of Abnormal Psychology*, 81(3): 219–25.

Alexander, J. and Sexton, T. (2002) 'Functional Family Therapy (FFT) as an integrative, mature clinical model for treating high risk, acting out youth', in J. Lebow (ed.), *Comprehensive Handbook of Psychotherapy, Volume IV: Integrative/Eclectic*. New York: John Wiley, pp. 111–32.

Alexander, J., Barton, C., Gordon, D., Grotpeter, J., Hansson, K., Harrison, R., Mears, S., Mihalic, S., Parsons, B., Pugh, C., Schulman, S., Wardron, H. and Sexton, T. (1998) *Blueprints for Violence Prevention, Book Three: Functional Family Therapy*. Boulder, CO: Center for the Study and Prevention of Violence.

Alltucker, K.W., Bullis, M., Close, D. and Yovanoff, P. (2006) 'Different pathways to juvenile delinquency: Characteristics of early and late starters in a sample

of previously incarcerated youth', *Journal of Child and Family Studies*, 15(4): 479–92.

Annie E. Casey Foundation (2013) *Reducing Youth Incarceration in the United States*. Available at: http://www.aecf.org/~/media/Pubs/Initiatives/KIDS%20COUNT/R/ReducingYouthIncarcerationSnapshot/DataSnapshotYouthIncarceration.pdf

Barnes, J. and O'Gorman, N. (1995) 'A descriptive study of juvenile delinquents', *Irish Journal of Psychological Medicine*, 12(2): 53–6.

Barnoski, R. (2004) *Outcome Evaluation of Washington State's Research-Based Programs for Juvenile Offenders*. Olympia, WA: Washington State Institute for Public Policy.

Barton, C., Alexander, J., Waldron, H., Turner, C. and Warburton, J. (1985) 'Generalizing treatment effects of Functional Family Therapy: Three replications', *American Journal of Family Therapy*, 13(3): 16–26.

Biglan, A., Brennan, P.A., Foster, S.L. and Holder, H.D. (2004) *Helping Adolescents at Risk: Prevention of Multiple Problem Behaviors*. New York: Guilford Press.

Bishop, D.M. and Decker, S.H. (2006) 'Trends in international juvenile justice: What conclusions can be drawn?', in J. Junger-Tas and S.H. Decker (eds.), *International Handbook of Juvenile Justice*. Netherlands: Springer, pp. 505–32.

Bishop, D.M. and Feld, B.C. (2011) 'Trends in juvenile justice policy and practice', in B.C. Feld and D.M. Bishop (eds.), *The Oxford Handbook of Juvenile Crime and Juvenile Justice*. New York: Oxford University Press, pp. 898–926.

Borduin, C.M., Mann, B.J., Cone, L.T., Henggeler, S.W., Fucci, B.R., Blaske, D.M. and Williams, R.A. (1995) 'Multisystemic treatment of serious juvenile offenders: Long-term prevention of criminality and violence', *Journal of Consulting and Clinical Psychology*, 63(4): 569–78.

Bronfenbrenner, U. (1979) *The Ecology of Human Development*. Cambridge, MA: Harvard University Press.

Bureau of Labor Statistics (2002) *National Longitudinal Survey of Youth, 1997 Cohort, 1997–2001 (rounds 1–5)*. Chicago, IL: National Opinion Research Center, University of Chicago.

Butts, J.A., Snyder, H.N., Finnegan, T.A., Aughenbaugh, A.L. and Poole, R.S. (1995) *Juvenile Court Statistics 1993*. Washington, DC: Office of Juvenile Justice and Delinquency Prevention.

Cashmore, J. (2013) 'Juvenile justice: Australian court responses situated in the international context', in R. Sheehan, and A. Borowski (eds.), *Australia's Children's Courts Today and Tomorrow*. Dordrecht, Netherlands: Springer, pp. 197–208.

Caspi, A., Henry, B., McGee, R.O. and Moffitt, T.E. (1995) 'Temperamental origins of child and adolescent behavior problems: From age three to fifteen', *Child Development*, 66(1): 55–68.

Chamberlain, P. (1990) 'Comparative evaluation of specialized foster care for seriously delinquent youths: A first step. Community Alternatives', *International Journal of Family Care*, 2(2): 21–36.

Chamberlain, P. and Mihalic, S. (1998) *Blueprints for Violence Prevention, Book Eight: Multidimensional Treatment Foster Care*. Boulder, CO: Center for the study and Prevention of Violence.

Chamberlain, P. and Reid, J.B. (1998) 'Comparison of two community alternatives to incarceration for chronic juvenile offenders', *Journal of Consulting and Clinical Psychology*, 66(4): 624–33.

Chamberlain, P., Leve, L.D. and DeGarmo, D.S. (2007) 'Multidimensional treatment foster care for girls in the juvenile justice system: 2-year follow–up of a randomized clinical trial', *Journal of Consulting and Clinical Psychology*, 75(1): 187–93.

Crick, N.R. and Dodge, K.A. (1994) 'A review and reformulation of social information-processing mechanisms in children's social adjustment', *Psychological Bulletin*, 115(1): 74–101.

Cunneen, C. and White, R. (2007) *Juvenile Justice: Youth and Crime in Australia* (3rd edn), Melbourne: Oxford University Press.

Curtis, N.M., Ronan, K.R. and Borduin, C.M. (2004) 'Multisystemic treatment: A meta-analysis of outcome studies', *Journal of Family Psychology*, 18(3): 411–19.

Deater-Deckard, K., Dodge, K.A., Bates, J.E. and Pettit, G.S. (1998) 'Multiple risk factors in the development of externalizing behavior problems: Group and individual differences', *Development and Psychopathology*, 10(3): 469–93.

Dodge, K.A. and Newman, J.P. (1981) 'Biased decision making processes in aggressive boys', *Journal of Abnormal Psychology*, 90(4): 375–9.

Dodge, K.A. and Pettit, G.S., (2003) 'A biopsychosocial model of the development of chronic conduct problems in adolescence', *Developmental Psychology*, 39(2): 349–71.

Dodge, K.A., Dishion, T.J. and Lansford, J.E. (eds.) (2006) *Deviant Peer Influences in Programs for Youth: Problems and Solutions*. New York: Guilford Press.

Eddy, J.M., Whaley, R.B. and Chamberlain, P. (2004) 'The prevention of violent behaviour by chronic and serious male juvenile offenders: A 2-year follow-up of a randomized clinical trial', *Journal of Emotional and Behavioral Disorders*, 12(1): 2–8.

Elliott, D.S. (1994) 'Serious violent offenders: Onset, developmental course, and termination: The American Society of Criminology 1993 presidential address', *Criminology*, 32(1): 1–21.

Elliott, D.S., Huizinga, D. and Ageton, S.S. (1985) *Explaining Delinquency and Drug Use*. Beverly Hills, CA: Sage.

Farmer, E.M., Burns, B.J., Wagner, H.R., Murray, M. and Southerland, D.G. (2010) 'Enhancing "usual practice" treatment foster care: Findings from a randomized trial on improving youths' outcomes', *Psychiatric Services (Washington, DC)*, 61(6): 555–61.

Fergusson, D.M., Lynskey, M.T. and Horwood, L.J. (1996) 'Factors associated with continuity and change in disruptive behavior patterns between childhood and adolescence', *Journal of Abnormal Child Psychology*, 24(5): 533–53.

Gordon, D., Arbuthnot, J., Gustafson, K.E. and McGreen, P. (1988) 'Home-based behavioral systems family therapy with disadvantaged juvenile delinquents', *The American Journal of Family Therapy*, 16(3): 243–55.

Gordon, D.A., Graves, K. and Arbuthnot, J. (1995) 'The effect of functional family therapy for delinquents on adult criminal behavior', *Criminal Justice and Behavior*, 22(1): 60–73.

Gottfredson, G.D., Gottfredson, D.C., Payne, A. and Gottfredson, N.C. (2005) 'School climate predictors of school disorder: Results from a national study of delinquency prevention in schools', *Journal of Research in Crime and Delinquency*, 42(4): 412–44.

Hellman, D.A. and Beaton, S. (1986) 'The pattern of violence in urban public schools: The influence of school and community', *Journal of Research in Crime and Delinquency*, 23(2): 102–27.

Henggeler, S.W. and Sheidow, A.J. (2002) 'Conduct disorder and delinquency', in D.H. Sprenkle (ed.), *Effectiveness Research in Marriage and Family Therapy*. Alexandria, VA: American Association for Marriage and Family Therapy, pp. 27–51.

Henggeler, S.W., Halliday-Boykins, C.A., Cunningham, P.B., Randall, J., Shapiro, S.B. and Chapman, J. (2006) 'Juvenile drug court: Enhancing outcomes by integrating evidence-based treatments', *Journal of Consulting and Clinical Psychology*, 74(1): 42–54.

Henggeler, S.W., Melton, G.B. and Smith, L.A. (1992) 'Family preservation using multisystemic therapy: An effective alternative to incarcerating serious juvenile offenders', *Journal of Consulting and Clinical Psychology*, 60(6): 953–61.

Henggeler, S.W., Melton, G.B., Brondino, M.J., Scherer, D.G. and Hanley, J.H. (1997) 'Multisystemic therapy with violent and chronic juvenile offenders and their families: The role of treatment fidelity in successful dissemination', *Journal of Consulting and Clinical Psychology,* 65(5): 821–33.

Henggeler, S.W., Schoenwald, S.K., Borduin, C.M., Rowland, M.D. and Cunningham, P.B. (2009) *Multisystemic Treatment of Antisocial Behavior in Children and Adolescents, 2nd Edition.* New York: Guilford Press.

Hill-Smith, A.J., Hugo, P., Hughes, P., Fonagy, P. and Hartman, D. (2002) 'Adolescent murderers: Abuse adversity in childhood', *Journal of Adolescence,* 25(2): 221–230.

Hinshaw, S.P. (1992) 'Externalizing behavior problems and academic underachievement in childhood and adolescence: Causal relationships and underlying mechanisms', *Psychological Bulletin,* 111(1): 127–55.

Hoge, R.D., Guerra, N.G. and Boxer, P. (eds.) (2008) *Treating the Juvenile Offender.* New York: Guilford Press.

Howell, J.C., Krisberg, B., Hawkins, J.D. and Wilson, J.J. (1995) *A Sourcebook: Serious, Violent, and Chronic Juvenile Offenders.* Thousand Oaks, CA: Sage Publications.

Hubbard, D.J. and Pratt, T.C. (2002) 'A meta-analysis of the predictors of delinquency among girls', *Journal of Offender Rehabilitation,* 34(3): 1–13.

Junger-Tas, J. (2006) 'Trends in international juvenile justice: What conclusions can be drawn?', in J. Junger-Tas and S.H. Decker (eds.), *International Handbook of Juvenile Justice.* Netherlands: Springer, pp. 505–32.

Junger-Tas, J., Marshall, I.H., Enzmann, D., Killias, M., Steketee, M. and Gruszczynska, B. (2010) *Juvenile Delinquency in Europe and Beyond: Results of the Second International Self-Report Delinquency Study.* Berlin: Springer.

Keenan, K., Loeber, R., Zhang, Q., Stouthamer-Loeber, M. and Van Kammen, W.B. (1995) 'The influence of deviant peers on the development of boys' disruptive and delinquent behavior: A temporal analysis', *Developmental Psychopathology,* 7(4): 715–26.

Lemola, S., Stadlmayr, W. and Grob, A. (2009) 'Infant irritability: The impact of fetal alcohol exposure, maternal depressive symptoms, and low emotional support from the husband', *Infant Mental Health Journal,* 30(1): 57–81.

Letourneau, E.J. (2002) 'A comparison of objective measures of sexual arousal and interest: Visual reaction time and penile plethysmography', *Sexual Abuse: A Journal of Research and Treatment,* 14(3): 203–19.

Letourneau, E.J., Henggeler, S.W., Borduin, C.M., Schewe, P.A., McCart, M.R., Chapman, J.E. and Saldana, L. (2009) 'Multisystemic therapy for juvenile sexual offenders: 1-year results from a randomized

effectiveness trial', *Journal of Family Psychology,* 23(1): 89–102.

Leve, L.D., Chamberlain, P. and Reid, J.B. (2005) 'Intervention outcomes for girls referred from juvenile justice: Effects on delinquency', *Journal of Consulting and Clinical Psychology,* 73(6): 1181–5.

Leve, L.D., Pears, K.C., and Fisher, P.A. (2002) 'Competence in early development', in J.B. Reid, G.R. Patterson and J. Snyder (eds.), *Antisocial Behavior in Children and Adolescents: A Developmental Analysis and Model for Intervention.* Washington, DC: American Psychological Association, pp. 45–64.

Lochman, J.E. and Dodge, K.A. (1994) 'Social cognitive processes of severely violent, moderately aggressive, and nonaggressive boys', *Journal of Consulting and Clinical Psychology,* 62(2): 366–74.

Loeber, R. and Farrington, D.P. (2000) 'Young children who commit crime: Epidemiology, developmental origins, risk factors, early interventions, and policy implications', *Development and Psychopathology,* 12(4): 737–62.

Loeber, R., Farrington, D.P., Stouthamer-Loeber, M. and Van Kammen, W.B. (1998) *Antisocial Behavior and Mental Health Problems: Explanatory Factors in Childhood and Adolescence.* Mahwah, NJ: Lawrence Erlbaum Associates.

Loeber, R., Pardini, D., Homish, D.L., Wei, E.H., Crawford, A.M., Farrington, D.P., Stouthamer-Loeber, M., Creemers, J., Koehler, S.A. and Rosenfeld, R. (2005) 'The prediction of violence and homicide in youth men', *Journal of Consulting and Clinical Psychology,* 73(6): 1074–88.

Mersky, J.P. and Reynolds, A.F. (2007) 'Child maltreatment and violent delinquency: Disentangling main effects and subgroup effects', *Child Maltreatment,* 12(3): 246–58.

Moffitt, T.E. (1993) 'Adolescence-limited and life-course persistent antisocial behavior: A developmental taxonomy', *Psychological Review,* 100(4): 674–701.

Moffitt, T.E. (2003) 'Life-course persistent and adolescence-limited antisocial behavior: A research review and a research agenda', in B. Lahey, T.E. Moffitt and A. Caspi (eds.), *Causes of Conduct Disorder and Juvenile Delinquency.* New York: Guilford, pp. 49–75.

MST Institute (2012) *Multisystemic Therapy Research at a Glance.* Available at http://mstservices.com/outcomestudies.pdf

National Institutes of Health State-of-the-Science Conference Statement (2006) 'Preventing violence and related health-risking, social behaviors in adolescents, October 13–15, 2004', *Journal of Abnormal Child Psychology,* 34(4): 457–70.

Ogden, T. and Hagen, K.A. (2006) 'Multisystemic therapy of serious behaviour problems in youth: Sustainability of therapy effectiveness two years after intake', *Journal of Child and Adolescent Mental Health*, 11(3): 142–9.

Ozen, S., Ece, A., Oto, R., Tirasci, Y. and Goren, S. (2005) 'Juvenile delinquency in a developing country: A province example in Turkey', *International Journal of Law and Psychiatry*, 28(4): 430–41.

Patchin, J.W., Huebner, B.M., McCluskey, J.D., Varano, S.P. and Bynum, T.S. (2006) 'Exposure to community violence and childhood delinquency', *Crime and Delinquency*, 52(2): 307–32.

Patterson, G.R. (1982) *Coercive Family Process*. Eugene, OR: Castalia.

Pedersen, W. (2000) 'Crime and punishment in Norwegian mid-adolescents: A normal population study', *Journal of Scandinavian Studies in Criminology and Crime Prevention*, 1(1): 87–104.

Puzzanchera, C. and Adams, B. (2011) *Juvenile Arrests 2009*. Washington, DC: US Department of Justice, Office of Justice Programs, Office of Juvenile Justice and Delinquency Prevention.

Sampson, R.J., Raudenbush, S.W. and Earls, F. (1997) 'Neighborhoods and violent crime: A multilevel study of collective efficacy', *Science*, 277(5328): 918–24.

Sawyer, A.M. and Borduin, C.M. (2011) 'Effects of multisystemic therapy through midlife: A 21.9 year follow-up to a randomized clinical trial with serious and violent juvenile offenders', *Journal of Consulting and Clinical Psychology*, 79(5): 643–52.

Schaeffer, C.M., Petras, H., Ialongo, N., Masyn, K.E., Hubbard, S., Poduska, J. and Kellam, S. (2006) 'A comparison of girls' and boys' aggressive-disruptive behavior trajectories across elementary school: Prediction to young adult antisocial outcomes', *Journal of Consulting and Clinical Psychology*, 74(3): 500–10.

Schoenwald, S.K. and Hoagwood, K. (2001) 'Effectiveness, transportability, and dissemination of interventions: What matters when?', *Psychiatric Services*, 52(9): 1190–7.

Sexton, T. and Turner, C.W. (2010) 'The effectiveness of functional family therapy for youth with behavioral problems in a community practice setting', *Journal of Family Psychology*, 24(3): 339–48.

Sheehan, R. and Borowski, A. (eds.) (2013) *Australia's Children's Courts Today and Tomorrow*. New York: Springer.

Snyder, H.N. and Sickmund, M. (2006) *Juvenile Offenders and Victims: 2006 National Report*. Washington, DC: US Department of Justice, Office of Justice Programs, Office of Juvenile Justice and Delinquency Prevention.

Stahl, A., Finnegan, T. and Kang, W. (2007) *Easy Access to Juvenile Court Statistics: 1985–2004*. Available at http://ojjdp.ncjrs.gov/ojstatbb/ezajcs/

Stewart, E.A., Simmons, R.L. and Conger, R.D. (2002) 'Assessing neighborhood and social psychological influences on childhood violence in an African American sample', *Criminology*, 40(4): 801–30.

Stewart, A., Livingston, and Dennison, S. (2008) 'Transitions and turning points: Examining the links between child maltreatment and juvenile offending', *Child Abuse & Neglect*, 32: 51–66.

Stouthamer-Loeber, M., Loeber, R., Wei, E., Farrington, D.P. and Wikstrom, P-O.H. (2002) 'Risk and promotive effects in the explanation of persistent serious delinquency in boys', *Journal of Consulting and Clinical Psychology*, 70(1): 111–23.

Thornberry, T.P. and Krohn, M.D. (eds.) (2003) *Taking Stock of Delinquency: An Overview of Findings from Contemporary Longitudinal Studies*. New York: Kluwer/Plenum.

Thornberry, T.P., and Krohn, M.D. (2000) 'The self-report method for measuring delinquency and crime', *Measurement and Analysis of Crime and Justice*, 4(1): 33–83.

Timmons-Mitchell, J., Bender, M.B., Kishna, M.A. and Mitchell, C.C. (2006) 'An independent effectiveness trial of multisystemic therapy with juvenile justice youth', *Journal of Clinical Child and Adolescent Psychology*, 35(2): 227–36.

Tonry, M. and Chambers, C. (2011), 'Juvenile justice cross-nationally considered' in B.C. Feld and D.M. Bishop (eds), *The Oxford Handbook of Juvenile Crime and Juvenile Justice*. New York: Oxford University Press, pp. 871–897.

Tyson, G.A. and Hubert, C.J. (2002) 'Cultural differences in adolescents' explanations of juvenile delinquency', *Journal of Cross-Cultural Psychology*, 33(5): 459–63.

US Public Health Service (2001) *Youth Violence: A Report of the Surgeon General*. Washington, DC: US Public Health Service.

Vermeiren, R. (2003) 'Psychopathology and delinquency in adolescents: A descriptive and developmental perspective', *Clinical Psychology Review*, 23(2): 277–318.

Van Ryzin, M.J. and Leve, L.D. (2012) 'Affiliation with delinquent peers as a mediator of the effects of multidimensional treatment foster care for delinquent girls', *Journal of Consulting and Clinical Psychology*, 80(4): 588–96.

Wakschlag, L.S. and Hans, S.L. (2002) 'Maternal smoking during pregnancy and conduct problems in high-risk youth: A developmental framework', *Development and Psychopathology*, 14(2): 351–69.

Waldron, H.B., Slesnick, N., Brody, J.L., Turner, C.W. and Peterson, T.R. (2001) 'Treatment outcomes for adolescent substance abuse at 4- and 7-month assessments', *Journal of Consulting and Clinical Psychology*, 69(5): 802–13.

Westermark, P.K., Hansson, K. and Olsson, M. (2011) 'Multidimensional treatment foster care (MTFC): Results from an independent replication', *Journal of Family Therapy*, 33(1): 20–41.

Westermark, P.K., Hansson, K. and Vinnerljung, B. (2008) 'Does Multidimensional Treatment Foster Care (MTFC) reduce placement breakdown in Foster Care?', *International Journal of Child & Family Welfare*, 4: 155–71.

White, N. and Lauritsen, J.L. (2012) *Violent Crimes against Youth, 1994–2010*. Washington, DC: US Department of Justice, Office of Justice Programs, Bureau of Justice Statistics.

Widom, C.S. (1989) 'The cycle of violence', *Science*, 244(4901): 160–6.

Wong, D.S.W. (2001) 'Pathways to delinquency in Hong Kong and Guangzhou', *Violent Youth*, 10(1-2): 91–115.

Zahn-Waxler, C., Klimes-Dougan, B. and Slattery, M.J. (2000) 'Internalizing problems of childhood and adolescence: Prospects, pitfalls, and progress in understanding the development of anxiety and depression', *Development and Psychopathology*, 12(3): 443–66.

16

Children as Witnesses

Kelly McWilliams, Else-Marie Augusti, Jacinthe Dion,
Stephanie D. Block, Annika Melinder, Judith Cashmore,
and Gail S. Goodman

INTRODUCTION

Worldwide, many thousands – if not millions – of children serve as witnesses in legal actions every year. Victims of child maltreatment as well as children who witness or experience other types of illegal activity (for example, domestic violence, murder, kidnapping, robbery, gang violence, war crimes) may be interviewed by authorities and in some countries, they may eventually testify in depositions, in hearings, or at trial. The crimes that lead to legal involvement typically come with their own share of adverse emotional consequences. Then, once a legal case ensues, children may be required to recount these experiences, possibly repeatedly, in formal, complex, and often confusing legal contexts in which the children often fear retribution or feel divided loyalties, which may serve to exacerbate the stress already endured. Even children involved in civil child protection proceedings (often within juvenile courts) may be called, or may seek, to bear witness to the maltreatment they suffered. To provide the most effective help to children who are immersed in the legal system or who are living in its shadows, it is important to compare children's well-being and their own experience in various jurisdictions with diverse policies and procedures in relation to children's testimony.

In this chapter, we briefly review the dependency and criminal court systems of several countries in relation to the treatment and experiences of child witnesses, particularly in regard to child maltreatment. We focus on the United States, Canada, and Norway, but we also describe what we know about the court systems in two Asian countries (more specifically, China and South Korea).

We then turn to children's views of legal involvement. In this way, we can learn from children themselves about their needs within the dependency and criminal court systems. In that regard, the Convention on the Rights of the Child provides children with the right to be heard in legal proceedings that affect their lives. Yet it is unclear how often children actually have this right, even in countries that have ratified the Convention (all members of the United Nations other than the United States, which has ratified the CRC's Optional Protocols, Somalia, which has no working government, and South Sudan, which is a new nation). We close by addressing methodological issues and ideas for future research.

LEGAL SYSTEMS

It is widely believed – and verified in some countries – that most child witnesses enter the legal system because of child maltreatment (Goodman et al., 1999). Moreover, the vast majority of the research on child witnesses in court deals with child abuse cases, particularly child sexual abuse (Quas and Goodman, 2012). Although child maltreatment occurs throughout the world, legal action to protect children or punish offenders is not universal. Some countries have a quite structured and precise process to deal with this offence, but other countries have few guidelines or programmes to deal with victim/witnesses. The involvement of children in the process also differs throughout the world. In some countries with a strong social-welfare orientation (including Israel, Norway, and Sweden), child maltreatment victims rarely testify in criminal court. In the United States, however, child victims often have to testify in a criminal courtroom and submit to direct and cross-examination. As a result, the experiences of child victim/witnesses around the world are vastly different. By examining experiences of child witnesses, we hope to shed light on children's needs in the legal system and discuss legal processes that minimize stress for child witnesses. Next, we examine the legal systems of several different countries: United States, Canada, Norway, South Korea, and China. We provide the most detail about the American courts and then mainly point out important similarities and differences between that system and those of other countries.

United States court system

Children in the United States enter the legal system as witnesses for a variety of reasons. In dependency court, when children testify, they typically do so as a result of allegations of intimate partner violence (which children may witness), child neglect, physical abuse, or child sexual abuse. In most instances in dependency courts, the alleged perpetrator is a parent or other caregiver within the family (US Department of Health and Human Services, 2012). Although parents are not directly punished or imprisoned by the dependency court, they are in jeopardy of loss of custody of their children or of termination of their parental rights altogether, a sanction that the US Supreme Court has recognized as a grave deprivation of rights, tantamount to criminal punishment (*Santosky v. Kramer*, 1982). Moreover, they can be required to accept services (for example, parenting classes) to have their children returned home.

In contrast, most children who testify in criminal court take the stand because they are victims of child sexual abuse (Goodman et al., 1999). In child sexual abuse cases, there may be no other eyewitnesses and no definitive physical evidence (Goodman et al., 1999). Even in criminal court, child witnesses typically testify against a parent or someone else that they know, rather than strangers (Gray, 1993; Whitcomb et al., 1991).

In the United States, when allegations of maltreatment arise, the legal events that follow depend in part on the state where the offense occurred. However, there are many commonalities across states. One of the first major decisions following an allegation is whether or not the child should be removed from the home by police or social services. If the abuse is extrafamilial, the child is likely to remain with the parents. If, however, the maltreatment is intrafamilial and the child appears to be at risk within the home, the child is likely to be taken into 'protective custody' and placed in temporary foster care until a decision can be made about the child's best interests.

The decision to remove a child from the home is a difficult one, as it is often unclear what is in the best interests of the child (Mnookin, 1975). Some children benefit from being removed from the abusive situation, whereas other children may be better off remaining within their family, as long as appropriate services and safeguards are set in place and accepted by the caregiver (Ghetti, Alexander, and Goodman, 2002). A study by Ryan, Warren, and Weincek (1991) examined the type of interventions that were instituted in various child abuse cases. Important factors such as age of victim, relationship to perpetrator, and the nature and frequency of abuse did not predict the course of action taken by the state. Only the role of the victim's mother in protecting the child predicted the type of intervention. More specifically, children with more protective mothers were less likely to be removed from their home following reports of abuse.

Dependency proceedings

Following removal, the dependency court holds a hearing to make a determination about whether the child will return home or remain in the foster care system (to be placed in kinship foster care, nonkinship foster care, or a group home). This decision is usually mandated by law to occur quickly (for example, within 72 hours of the child's removal). At such a hearing in the United States, the parents, the child, and the child protective services agency all have their own attorneys. Relatively few jurisdictions encourage children to attend their dependency hearings and provide direct testimony about their 'wishes' (Khoury, 2008; Krinsky and Rodriguez, 2006; Pitchal, 2008). Instead, the children's attorneys are to consult with the child. However, in court, the children's attorneys tend to represent what they see as the child's best interests, not to advocate the child's own wishes (Myers, 2008), typically to return home (Block et al., 2010). Often the child does not return home at this point. Instead, the caregiver is offered services (such as substance abuse treatment, anger management training, or parenting classes) and the chance to regain custody of the child if sufficient improvement takes place. Otherwise, the child may be adopted but many children remain in foster care for the rest of their childhood, often bounced around from one foster home to another – and not returned home or adopted.

Criminal proceedings

If a criminal investigation into allegations of child maltreatment commences, whether the case is intrafamilial or extrafamilial, the child may undergo several stressful situations, potentially culminating in testifying at trial. In many child abuse cases, children will be given a forensic medical examination to obtain possible physical evidence of the abuse. In child sexual abuse cases, however, physical findings showing abuse are relatively rare. Children may also be subjected to multiple forensic interviews with doctors, social workers, police officers, and attorneys. These interviews can be difficult for children who are asked in detail about personal information, often accusing an important person in their lives (Tedesco and Schnell, 1987).

In the United States legal system, it is now quite common for a trained professional to conduct the main forensic interview of child victims at a Child Advocacy Center (CAC). The first CAC was established more than 25 years ago to address the many issues associated with investigating and prosecuting cases of child maltreatment. Since 1985, over 900 CACs have been created around the United States; many other countries worldwide have instituted CAC systems as well (Santos and Goncalves, 2009). The main focus of a CAC is to coordinate prosecution, child protection, and medical and health services for victims of child maltreatment (Connell, 2009). It has become common practice for a specially trained professional, often a social worker, to conduct the interviews. Interviews at CACs are designed to be child-friendly and to reduce the stress of otherwise being questioned in an intimidating setting, such as a police station or hospital. Although specific CACs are structured differently, all programs within the US National Children's Alliance (NCA) must demonstrate the presence of 10 specific program components, such as child-appropriate/friendly facilities; a multidisciplinary team including law enforcement, child protective services, medical, and mental health professionals; and forensic interviewing and medical evaluations (Connell, 2009; Troxel et al., 2009).

CACs were established in many communities before there was empirical evidence of their value. Recent research has compared the practices of CACs with standard practice within communities without CACs in regard to medical evaluations (Walsh et al., 2007) and forensic interviewing processes (Cross et al., 2007). Victims who were interviewed at a CAC were more likely to receive a medical examination, more likely to have an audio-visual recorded interview performed by a multidisciplinary team, and were given fewer interviews about the abuse. These results suggest that the CAC model is a more thorough process for collecting evidence.[1]

If sufficient evidence is gathered through the investigation, the allegation of child abuse may go to court. In many prosecutions involving child witnesses, children are expected to testify one or more times. If the case goes to trial in a criminal proceeding, it is common in the United States for children to have to testify in open court and face the accused. Children must deal with detailed and challenging questioning, especially during cross-examination, and legal terms and procedures that are often confusing and unfamiliar (Brennan, 1995; Cossins, 2009; Flin, Stevenson and Davis, 1989; Ghetti et al., 2002; Melton et al., 1992; Saywitz and Nathanson, 1993; Spencer and Lamb, 2012; Warren-Leubecker et al., 1989).

When compelling reasons exist in individual cases, however, the majority of states in the United States allow the option for children to testify via alternative methods in criminal proceedings involving physical or sexual abuse. In the legal system, an alternative method is defined as a child's testimony being provided, for example, in closed court, in chambers, by deposition, by audio-visual recording, by closed-circuit television (CCTV), or by another method that allows the parties involved to accurately hear and view the testimony (National Conference of Commissioners on Uniform State Laws, 2002). These methods of testimony are acceptable when, for example, the court finds that testifying in open court would cause a child to suffer such severe emotional trauma that the child could not reasonably be expected to communicate in the physical presence of the accused (Hall and Sales, 2008; *Maryland v. Craig*, 1990).

Although alternative methods of testimony may be less stressful for children, it is not yet clear what their impact is in actual trials. Using samples of 5- to 6-year-olds and 8- to 9-year-olds in a mock trial study, Goodman and colleagues (1998) examined jury-eligible adults' perceptions of CCTV testimony. Although younger children giving their testimony through CCTV had a higher level of accuracy, mock jurors perceived the CCTV testimony as less credible than testimony given live in court. Orcutt, Goodman, Tobey, Batterman-Faunce, and Thomas (2001) also found that mock jurors were equally incapable of determining true versus dishonest testimony when children testified via CCTV as opposed to testifying live in court. On the other hand, the use of CCTV and video-taped interviews, which can serve as children's evidence-in-chief, are now common practice in legal proceedings in Australia, Canada, New Zealand, and the UK. An Australian survey of jurors immediately after the trial finished found that over 90 per cent said that the use of these now normative practices was fair and generally helpful in understanding the child's evidence (Cashmore and Trimboli, 2006). The main predictor of the verdict was the perceived consistency of the children's evidence. Thus, research conducted outside the United States reveals that CCTV may be useful for evaluating children's evidence. It is possible that if CCTV testimony were to become routine in American courtrooms, jurors' perceptions would change.

In the United States and other common-law countries, the legal process that a child witness must endure can be a long and wearing one. This leaves many child witnesses confused and frustrated with the system. However, if children feel that they were 'heard' by the court and treated fairly, they are more likely to feel satisfied with the legal process, even if it is stress-inducing (Cashmore, 1995; Cashmore and Trimboli, 2007; Lind and Tyler, 1988; Tyler and Lind, 2001).

Canadian court system

In Canada, child welfare remains largely under provincial and territorial jurisdictions. As in the United States, the specifics of child protection laws vary among provinces and territories. When the Child and Family Services (the same as Child Protective Services in the United States) respond to concerns about the safety and welfare of children, they first try to obtain the voluntary agreement of the parent to accept either family support services or temporary placement of the child. When parents are believed to be unable to protect their children and voluntary agreement is not obtained, the authorities turn to court action, often described as 'taking a child into care,' similar to a dependency order in the United States (Child and Family Services, 2000).

The prosecution of child physical and sexual abuse is addressed in criminal court through federal laws. Until the 1980s, in Canada, as in other Anglophone jurisdictions, children were perceived to be unreliable witnesses in criminal courts (Spencer and Flin, 1993). Hence, accommodations for children were rare (Bala, 1999; Sas et al., 1996). An attitudinal change toward children's credibility has emerged over the past 30 years in Canada as in other Anglophone jurisdictions, and this led to an increase in the number of children testifying (Sas, 2002). This change was reinforced by the large body of social science research conducted in the United States and elsewhere (Melton and Thompson, 1987; Westcott, Davies and Bull, 2002).

In the 1980s, legislative reforms were undertaken, which resulted in several improvements in forensic practice. These laws, for instance, extended protection to children under 14 years of age by abrogating

the need for corroboration, opening the court to testimony by younger children, and establishing accommodations for children, such as the use of a screen or CCTV. A four-year review of the modifications made by these laws showed more sexual abuse cases were being filed, more young children were being allowed to testify, and several of the techniques for reducing children's stress were being implemented (Sas et al., 1996). Results of a multi-site study in southwestern Ontario involving over 900 cases of prosecuted child abuse revealed that 80 per cent of children testified at the preliminary hearing and 88 per cent at trials (South-Western Ontario Child Witness Network, 1999). In Nova Scotia, more than half of the children involved in the Nova Scotia Department of Justice Victims' Services (2000) testified in court. More recently, legislative reforms led to the passage of a new law for Canadian child witnesses. The findings of recent psychological research influenced this process of legislative reform, which included for instance, new recommendations related to the use of testimonial aids and competency standards for qualifying children under the age of 14 years (Bala et al., 2005).

Many changes in the pertinent law have occurred over the years in Canada. However, there are still obstacles to the implementation of legislative reform. For example, the use of screens, CCTV, videotaped interviews, or a support person is not always implemented, although use of such aids is highly recommended (Bala, Lee and McNamara, 2001; Park and Renner, 1998; South-Western Ontario Child Witness Network, 1999). According to the results of a multi-site survey in 2004, though, the use of aids often occurs, with the screen being the most popular; 60 per cent of crown attorneys request it, 80 per cent of judges grant it, and around 60 per cent of defense attorneys agree to it (Prairie Research Associates Inc., 2004).

Several court preparation programs for children are available across Canada, but few have been evaluated. In 1988, the Child Witness Project was established in Canada to reduce children's stress in court and to empower children in the legal system (Sas et al., 1996). This project included an educational component, stress reduction, and systematic desensitization. A three-year follow-up indicated that the project benefited children in multiple ways, especially in their knowledge of the legal system (Sas et al., 1996). Similar innovations in Canada have included the Victim Assistance Program, which helped children to be more relaxed about the criminal court process (Doueck et al., 1997), and the Calgary Child Witness Court Preparation Program (Barry et al., 2006). These programs demonstrated that it is possible to prepare children for the court process.

Over the past decade or so, several positive changes for child witnesses in the Canadian legal system have resulted from the reforms to the Criminal Code of Canada, the Canada Evidence Act, and the provincial evidence acts (Bala et al., 2005; Welder, 2000). For example, testimonial aids (such as videotapes, hearsay, and CCTV) are progressively used in courts, and support persons are permitted. Moreover, research also indicates that these changes are becoming more accepted by Crown Attorneys, judges, and defence counsel. Overall, the Canadian legal system has developed a more flexible approach with children over the past decade, together with positive progressive changes in legislations.

Norwegian court system

In Norway, the child welfare agency also tries to keep children in their homes and to provide services there. When removal from the home is necessary for the child's safety, however, such action may be initiated in two ways (Melinder, Baugerud, Ovenstad and Goodman, 2013). First, if the child is believed to be in acute danger because of abuse or neglect, child protective services can temporarily remove a child from the home without parental consent. When such emergency action is taken, however, it can be continued for more than six weeks only if a court agrees on the basis of a hearing in which parents may participate. Second, in planned removals, parental consent is required before actual removal. In such cases, the child is not perceived to be in imminent danger, but child welfare authorities do believe that the parents are incapable of providing proper care.

In the dependency courts in Norway, children are not asked to testify or serve as witnesses. Instead, an individual with special knowledge of children (for example, a nurse, a teacher, or a social worker) represents the children. Prior to the court case, the child's representative talks informally with the children about their desires and views. A formal forensic interview does not take place.

According to Norwegian law, however, all children who are at least 7 years old have the right to be heard in cases concerning them. This includes the determination of living arrangements when parents divorce or are believed to be incapable of providing proper care. However, Norwegian authorities strive to elicit children's views in child-friendly environments outside formal legal proceedings. These talks are not video-recorded, but they serve as a basis for a child's representative to present the child's views in court. Thus, children's voices are heard only indirectly; they are instead interpreted to the courts by professionals (Vis and Thomas, 2009).

Even in criminal matters, the justice system in Nordic countries is inquisitorial (Cordon, Goodman and Anderson, 2003; Melinder et al., 2004). Partly as a result, admission of hearsay statements (including videotaped forensic interviews of children) in criminal trials is more accepted in Nordic countries than it is in the United States and other Anglophone countries. Thus, in Norway and other Nordic countries, child witnesses are generally not asked to appear in court to testify. As a practical matter, therefore, children are not allowed to provide direct testimony in criminal courts. Hence, there are few guidelines about courtroom testimony specifically tailored to child witnesses in Norway (Melinder and Korkman, 2010).

Nevertheless, child witnesses are involved in police investigations, and their voices are heard in criminal court indirectly. In Norway, the police department includes specially trained police officers who question children who have either witnessed or been subjected to criminal acts. These police officers conduct each child forensic interview, with the judge, the prosecutor, and defence counsel able to observe the interview through special two-way mirrors. The judge's and attorneys' questions are transmitted to the police officer, who then asks the questions in age-appropriate language. A video-recording of the interview substitutes for live testimony if the case goes to trial.

In a few jurisdictions (as of 2010, five localities), Norwegian judicial authorities have established 'Children's Houses,' which serve as resource centres for children in cases where criminal abuse is alleged. Like many of the CACs in the United States, Children's Houses host the police interviews of children, and they provide medical and psychological assessments. Based on American and Icelandic models, these houses are intended to minimize the stress of legal involvement for vulnerable children.

Chinese and South Korean court systems

In outlining a picture of the treatment of child witnesses around the world, it is important to examine such phenomena in non-Western societies. Although relatively little information has been published about the approach of non-Western countries to child witnesses, some information can be gleaned. Here we discuss legal procedures for children's testimony in Chinese and South Korean courts, especially in child maltreatment cases.

China has ratified the United Nations Convention on the Rights of the Child, but China has no formal child protection system.

Older children can sue their parents, or a case may be brought by relatives on behalf of the child. However, it is unclear how often that occurs. If the child is severely harmed or killed, the parents can be prosecuted. Child rape is a crime in China, although 'rape' lacks a legal definition (Wang, 2009). We have been unable to find evidence of CACs in China or information about how child witnesses are interviewed or treated.

A case example makes the point of how child abuse and child witnesses are handled in China. On 29 October 2009, preschool teachers in Bijie City noticed bruises and injuries on a young female student. When teachers inquired about the injuries, Ting Ting, the injured girl, said that they had been inflicted by her parents. Ting Ting informed her teachers that her parents had burned her bottom with a fire poker to discipline her for talking back to her parents and refusing to do her homework. Ting Ting's teacher reported the abuse to police. When Ting Ting's parents were questioned by police about the abuse, her mother admitted that they had burned her with a fire poker, forced her to kneel on a board of nails, and whipped her with an iron wire. Because China does not have specific laws about child abuse, the parents could be charged only with 'abusing family members'. Ting Ting was too young to sue her parents, and no other family members had come forward to bring legal action on her behalf. The public prosecutor did not pursue the case, because the girl's injuries were perceived not to be severe.

In contrast, South Korea established a child protection system after 1989, with the signing of the Convention on the Rights of Children. Therefore, as a matter of law, children are no longer considered to be possessions of their parents. Amending the child welfare law, South Korea established a child protection system, including provisions for reporting, investigation, and intervention. The focus remains, however, on severe forms of child maltreatment (for example, sexual abuse; severe physical abuse; child abandonment) that are subject to both civil and criminal sanctions. Child victims may be interviewed repeatedly, and there are few special alternative procedures for taking child witnesses' statements (Herskovitz and Kim, 2009). We know of no studies on the emotional effects of legal-system involvement on children in China or South Korea.

CHILDREN'S OWN PERSPECTIVES ON INVOLVEMENT IN THE LEGAL SYSTEM

What can we learn from children themselves about their needs within the dependency court and criminal court systems? In several studies, children have been interviewed about their perspectives on their involvement in the legal process.

Dependency court

Although children's participation in dependency court varies across societies, the overall picture is one of decision making about, but not with, affected children. Research in the United States, and other countries that provide relatively easy access to the legal process, indicates that children whose cases are heard in dependency courts desire a greater voice in decision making (Bessell and Gal, 2009; Chapman, Wall and Barth, 2004). Because dependency courts deal with children's placement in another home, fundamental attachment issues are at stake (Bowlby, 1980; Taylor, 2004).

Block et al. (2010) interviewed 85 children aged 7–10 years as they emerged from their dependency court hearings. These interview findings provide a glimpse of the children's subjective experiences. About half of the children (54 per cent) did not know whether they would return home or remain in their placement. More than one third of the children (37 per cent) did not feel believed or listened to in the courtroom. Children are often discouraged from attending

their dependency court hearings in part because adults fear that the children will be distressed by seeing their parents again and by learning sensitive information about them (Pitchal, 2008). In the Block et al. study (2010), however, most children indicated they felt quite positive about seeing their parent(s) in court and that they did not hear anything about their parents that they did not already know. Most of the children thought that they did well or at least somewhat well in court.

Children were also asked, 'What was the most important thing you wanted the court to do for you?' Nearly three-fourths of the children wanted to return home either immediately or eventually. The following responses were representative:

- 'Go home, and I want my mom to get herself together to get us back, and I don't want to stay in a foster home forever.'
- 'Let me go back home. I will never get to go back home anymore.'

Children who did not want to go back to their homes also expressed poignant wishes:

- 'Be with my foster parents, but have my sisters and my mom come visit me.'
- 'To make my mommy stop beating me and send me to a foster home.'
- 'Put my mom in jail.'

Thus, for many children, attending dependency court had both negative and positive components, with the negatives relating to both the process (for example, not being heard in a meaningful way) and the outcome (such as not being able to return home). Block et al. (2010) concluded that 'although the court cannot always appease a child's wishes, and developmental and socio-emotional factors must be carefully considered, it may be important psychologically, in many cases, to acknowledge children's desires.' In fact, foster youth in a number of countries are now speaking out against their lack of participation: 'Nothing about us without us!' (Bessell and Gal, 2009; Vis and Thomas, 2009).

Forensic interviews

Children who are or might be involved in either civil (dependency) or criminal proceedings may be subjected to forensic interviews. In part because of their emotion-laden and sometimes embarrassing content, such interviews can be a source of stress and discomfort. Children often experience confusion, guilt, embarrassment, fear, sadness, boredom, anger, and doubt during these interviews (Brennan, 1995; Ghetti et al., 2002; Plotnikoff and Woolfson, 2004). Multiple interviews can be emotionally harmful for children, and it has been recommended that the number of interviews should be minimized (Cunningham and Hurley, 2007; Davies, Wilson, Mitchell and Milsom, 1995; Goodman et al., 1992;). The use of CACs and video-taped investigative interviews can potentially decrease the number of interviews because children who are interviewed at a CAC participate in two fewer interviews on average than do their peers in comparison community groups (Cross et al., 2007).

Compared with children interviewed by police or social workers in non-CAC contexts (such as police stations), children interviewed at CACs reported being less frightened by the interview process (Jones et al., 2007). However, the setting for interviews did not significantly affect children's overall satisfaction with the legal process. Regardless of the setting in which interviews took place, the 'average' child reported being moderately satisfied. Whether interviewed at CACs or in more traditional settings, a small percentage of children reported being frustrated with repeated interviews. Nevertheless, the fact that children were less frightened when interviewed at a CAC is important. Research is still needed to determine whether CAC interviewers are able to interview children in a non-leading manner and elicit children's complete and accurate disclosures.

Criminal courts

Many, if not most, legal cases involving child witnesses do not reach the criminal courts. If a case is criminally prosecuted, however, a young witness is thrown into a complex and intimidating legal system designed for legal professionals. As a result, many child witnesses experience feelings of distress and uncertainty. Research reveals that there are short- and long-term effects of involvement in a criminal court trial that go beyond the effects of maltreatment (Goodman et al., 1992; Quas et al., 2005; Quas and Goodman, 2012). Goodman and colleagues (1992) investigated the short-term effects of legal involvement in Colorado courts. This study found that testifying in court was associated with greater behavioural disturbances seven months after testimony. This was exacerbated when children had to testify multiple times, when there was a lack of maternal support, and when no objective evidence of abuse was available. Furthermore, the severity of the abuse and the child's age at the time of testifying predicted the experience and report of adverse effects during court involvement (Goodman et al., 1992). Older children spent more time on the witness stand than did younger children and were treated more harshly (see also Whitcomb et al., 1991). Furthermore, more severe abuse cases resulted in children being on the stand for a longer period of time, regardless of age.

When the children were followed into adolescence and young adulthood, it was found that testifying multiple times in severe cases of abuse was also related to long-term adverse effects. Testifying more frequently in childhood was related to increased levels of internalizing symptoms when the children reached adolescence or young adulthood. In addition, testifying in a case that involved more severe forms of sexual abuse (such as long-lasting abuse, perpetrator being a parental figure, or penetration) predicted higher levels of sexual problems as reported by the victims themselves.

What is it about criminal court that is especially stressful for children? Listening to children provides some helpful answers. When testifying in court, many children report that facing and accusing the defendant is a major source of distress (Brannon, 1994; Goodman et al., 1992; Plotnikoff and Woolfson, 2004; Sas, 1991). For example, in a well-known study conducted in Canada, child sexual abuse victims were interviewed about testifying in criminal court. Regarding the 'worst part of testifying', children indicated that the presence of the accused was the most difficult part. For example: 'Him sitting in front of me and watching me', 'Having him there. And explaining what he did to me', 'Having my dad sit in front of me. I could be responsible for a long jail term' (Sas, 1993: 114).

According to child witnesses, cross-examination by a defence attorney is another particularly difficult part of testifying. A number of studies over the last 20 years or so have provided some understanding of why this is so difficult (Brennan, 1995; Cossins, 2008; Spencer and Lamb, 2012; Zajac, Gross and Hayne, 2003). Brennan (1995) examined specific parts of cross-examination that are especially distressing for children in the Australian courts. The results revealed that children found defence attorneys' complex language, use of confusing and unconnected questions, and a large volume of questions during cross-examination as particularly stressful. Canadian children in Sas's (1993: 118) study, when asked about the defence attorney, stated: 'I hated him because of the way he asked questions – he scared me.' 'She badgered me. I hated her. I don't know how she could defend a guilty man.' 'I met him outside of court and he was okay then, but in court it was a different story. It was like he was trying to prove me guilty.'

Many legal systems have tried to address such issues by developing alternative forms of testifying for child witnesses. Research by Plotnikoff and Woolfson (2004) examined the experiences of 50 child witnesses who testified in criminal court in England, Wales, and Northern Ireland. They found that the majority of child witnesses gave their testimony through a CCTV link. Although they found that many children felt they had no choice about their method of testimony, the majority of children preferred not to give their testimony in open court. In Australia, Cashmore (2002) reported that child witnesses fared best if they were given a choice of testifying live in court or via CCTV. By having a choice, children are given some power in the decision and can determine the mode of testimony that best fits their needs and comfort level.

Goodman et al. (1998) reported that children's anxiety levels were directly related to their lack of legal knowledge (see also Block et al., 2010, for the same findings for dependency court). Specifically, children with more legal knowledge were less stressed about taking the stand in a mock trial. However, children often have relatively little knowledge of the legal system and this lack of knowledge adds to their distress when they are involved in legal proceedings (Ben-Arieh and Windman, 2007; Crawford and Bull, 2006). Children and parents also commonly complain of a lack of information and the slowness of the process (see, for example, Ben-Arieh and Windman, 2007; Goodman et al., 1992). Court preparation for child witnesses has been found to assist in this regard (McAuliff, Nicholson, Amarilio and Ravanshenas, 2012; O'Neill and Zajac, 2013).

Although many child witnesses find the act of testifying face to face with the defendant and being subjected to cross examination in criminal court to be very stressful and emotionally difficult, testifying may still have some benefits to children. Research by Quas et al. (2005) revealed that not testifying was associated with more negative attitudes toward the legal system, and in cases involving less severe abuse, not testifying was associated with higher self-reports on defensive avoidance, a measure of trauma-related psychopathology. If children later believe that as a result of not testifying, the defendant got an overly light sentence or 'walked' (found not guilty or the case dismissed), children often regret not taking the stand.

The act of testifying may be cathartic for some children. When asked about the best part of testifying, Canadian children who reflected on their court experience stated, for example:

- 'Being able to look at [my stepfather] and get it out of my system and let him know I didn't appreciate what he done.'
- 'I finally got it all out of my system and said it in front of a judge.'
- 'When I learned that he wasn't allowed near me.'
- 'I told the truth, that it was over.'

(Child Witness Project, 1993: 114)

Overall, these findings point to potential adverse effects of both testifying and not testifying. When children's testimony is the crucial element in the prosecution case, the key issue is how to facilitate children's testimony so that they are able to provide reliable testimony and their dignity and self-esteem are protected. Listening to children's reports of their experience of the court process, it is clear that they report that children report greater satisfaction with the court process when they are treated with respect, form positive relationships with legal staff, and have access to support persons who are known, supportive, and trusted (Ben-Arieh and Windman, 2007; Goodman et al., 1992).

METHODOLOGICAL CONSIDERATIONS AND FUTURE RESEARCH DIRECTIONS

There are some important methodological considerations and challenges in conducting research with child witnesses. The most common method is to interview children about their experiences and understanding of the processes, but there are ethical and practical challenges in doing so, particularly with young children who may have more difficulty articulating their experience and perceptions of the process. However, interviews and other appropriate methods can provide researchers with rich insights about children's views and needs that affect their participation in legal processes.

The initial methodological challenges arise in the process of recruiting and enrolling child witnesses in research. In most legal cases, social workers, prosecutors, and judges do not readily open courtroom doors to researchers. Legal professionals often want to be convinced that the research will directly benefit their clients. Parents and families are understandably wary of subjecting themselves and their children to more interviews with more strangers. The willingness of a non-offending parent to support research, to discuss their child's well-being, or even to acknowledge the criminal wrongdoing is likely to be affected by their relationship to the alleged offender, with families less likely to participate when the case involved intrafamilial than extrafamilial abuse (Goodman et al., 1992; Malloy et al., 2007). However, it can be empowering for child victims and their families to know that their research participation can help future child victims. With researchers also providing valuable educational services and feedback to legal professionals, collaborations can be mutually beneficial.

Other noteworthy methodological challenges concern missing data and attrition, and the difficulty of replicating the actuality of court processes in quasi-experimental methods. However, experimental analogues of courtroom settings and procedures have enabled tests of legal modifications and testimony conditions. Experimentation with random assignment can then be achieved (Goodman et al., 1998; Nathanson and Saywitz, 2003). Although there are some questions as to the external validity of analogues, this does provide an approximation which allows much to be learned, for instance in terms of the effects of courtroom techniques on children's well-being, jurors' perceptions, and verdicts. Such findings are useful as decisions are made about how best to proceed in cases involving child witnesses.

There are many issues within the study of child witnesses in court that still remain to be explored. There are very few studies, for example, on the emotional effects of testifying in dependency court (but see Runyan et al., 1988). In general, there is little research on child witnesses in dependency court and the extent to which children should be involved in their hearings, although a few courts have been open to such study and legal trends point to greater involvement (see Quas, Cooper and Wandrey, 2009, for review). Regarding criminal court, virtually all studies of child witnesses concern child sexual abuse victims. It is important to know how child witnesses in other types of cases fare and how they feel about their experiences (e.g., child witnesses to domestic homicide; McWilliams, Narr, Goodman, Ruiz and Mendoza, 2013). International research comparing the outcomes and perceptions of children exposed to different court systems and procedures could also be valuable. Overall, research is needed as the courts evolve and change, and as different countries adopt different strategies. To the extent that courts differ, they can provide a natural experiment regarding the best techniques to help child witnesses endure legal involvement. In any such research, it is critical to listen to children about their needs and experiences.

NOTE

1 One of the main criticisms is whether prosecution should be a main goal of CACs or whether their focus should remain solely on victims. There may be an inherent problem with combining a focus on advocacy with a goal of truth seeking (Melton and Kimbrough-Melton, 2006). This mixture could set centres on a dangerous path toward measurement of their success on the number of convictions they obtain. However, there has been no research on whether these conflicts of interest really do affect the accuracy of information obtained or the perceived quality of justice administered. These issues need further investigation.

REFERENCES

Bala, N. (1999) 'Child witnesses in the Canadian criminal courts: Recognizing their capacities and needs', *Psychology, Public Policy, and Law*, 5(2): 323–54.

Bala, N., Duvall-Antonacopoulos, K., Lindsay, R.C.L., Lee, K. and Talwar, V. (2005) 'Bill C- 2: A new law for Canada's child witnesses', *Criminal Report*, 32(6): 48–69.

Bala, N., Lee, J. and McNamara, E. (2001) 'Children as witnesses: Understanding their capacities, needs, and experiences', *Journal of Social Distress and the Homeless*, 10(1): 41–68.

Barry, L., Nixon, K., Tutty, L., M., Wyllie, K. and Mackenzie, J. (2006) *A Review of the Calgary Child Witness Court Preparation Program: Issues and Implication for Child Witnesses and the Criminal Justice System.* Calgary, AB: RESOLVE Alberta.

Ben-Arieh, A. and Windman, V. (2007) 'Secondary victimization of children in Israel and the child's perspective', *Annual Review of Victimology*, 14(3): 321–36.

Block, S., Oran, H., Oran, D., Baumrind, N. and Goodman, G.S. (2010) 'Abused and neglected children in court: Knowledge and attitudes', *Child Abuse & Neglect*, 34(9): 659–70.

Bowlby, J. (1980) *Attachment and Loss: Volume 3.* New York: Basic Books.

Brannon, L.C. (1994) 'The trauma of testifying in court for child victims of sexual assault v. the accused right to confrontation', *Law & Psychology Review*, 18: 439.

Brennan, M. (1995) 'The discourse of denial: Cross-examining child victim witnesses', *Journal of Pragmatics*, 23: 71–91.

Cashmore, J. (1995) 'The perceptions of child witnesses and their parents concerning the court process' in *The Evidence of Children* Monograph Series No 11, Judicial Commission of New South Wales.

Cashmore, J. (2002) 'Innovative procedures for child witnesses', in H. Westcott, G. Davies and R. Bull (eds.), *Children's Testimony: A Handbook of Psychological Research and Forensic Practice.* Chichester: John Wiley & Sons, pp. 203–218.

Cashmore, J. (2007) 'Child witnesses: The judicial role', *The Judicial Review*, 8, 281–294.

Cashmore, J. and Trimboli, L. (2006) Jurors' perceptions of child witnesses in child sexual assault matters. (Research Bulletin and second report in the Evaluation of the Child Sexual Assault Specialist Jurisdiction). Sydney: NSW Bureau of Crime Statistics and Research.

Chapman, M.V., Wall, A., and Barth, R.P. (2004) 'Children's voices: The perception of children in foster care', *American Journal of Orthopsychiatry*, 74(3): 293–304.

Child and Family Services (2000) *Child Welfare in Canada 2000: The Role of Provincial and Territorial Authorities in the Provision of Child Protection Services*. Hull, PQ: Secretariat to the Federal/Provincial/Territorial Working Group on Child and Family Services Information.

Child Witness Project (1993) *Three Years after the Verdict: A Longitudinal Study of the Social and Psychological Adjustment of Child Witnesses Referred to the Child Witness Project*. London, Ontario: London Family Court Clinic Inc.

Connell, M. (2009) 'The child advocacy center model', in K. Kuehnle and M. Connell (eds.), *The Evaluation of Child Sexual Abuse Allegations*. New York: Wiley and Sons, pp. 423–49.

Cordon, I., Goodman, G.S. and Anderson, S. (2003) 'Children in court', in P. Van Koppen and S. Penrod (eds.), *Adversarial Versus Inquisitorial Legal Systems*. NY: Kluwer Academic, pp. 167–89.

Cossins, A. (2009) 'Cross-examination in child sexual assault trials: Evidentiary safeguard or an opportunity to confuse?', *Melbourne University Law Review*, 33: 69–104.

Crawford, E. and Bull, R. (2006) 'Teenagers' difficulties with key words regarding the criminal court process', *Psychology, Crime and Law*, 12(6): 653–67.

Cross, T.P., Jones L.M., Walsh W.A., Simone M. and Kolko D. (2007) 'Child forensic interviewing in Children's Advocacy Centers: Empirical data on a practice model', *Child Abuse and Neglect*, 31(10): 1031–52.

Cunningham, A. and Hurley, P. (2007) *Using Special Accommodations and Testimonial Aids to Facilitate the Testimony of Children*. London, Ontario: Centre for Children and Families in the Justice System, London Family Court Clinic, Inc.

Davies, G., Wilson, C., Mitchell, R. and Milsom, J. (1995) *Videotaping Children's Evidence: An Evaluation*. London UK: The Home Office, Research and Statistics Department.

Doueck, H.J., Weston, E.A., Filbert, L., Beekhuis, R. and Redlich, H. F. (1997) 'A Child Witness Advocacy Program: Caretakers' and Professionals' Views', *Journal of Child Sexual Abuse*, 6(1): 113–32.

Flin, R.H., Stevenson, Y. and Davis, G.M. (1989) 'Children's knowledge of court proceedings', *British Journal of Psychology*, 80(3): 285–97.

Ghetti, S., Alexander, K.W. and Goodman, G.S. (2002) 'Legal involvement in child sexual abuse cases: Consequences and interventions', *International Journal of Law and Psychiatry*, 25(3): 235–51.

Goodman, G.S., Quas, J., Bulkley, J. and Shapiro, C. (1999) 'Innovations for child witnesses: A national survey', *Psychology, Public Policy, and Law*, 5(2): 255–81.

Goodman, G.S., Taub, E.P., Jones, D.P., England, P., Port, L.K., Rudy, L., et al. (1992) 'Testifying in criminal court: Emotional effects on child sexual assault victims', *Monographs of the Society for Research in Child Development*, 57(5): 1–142.

Goodman, G.S., Tobey, A.E., Batterman-Faunce, J.M., Orcutt, H., Thomas, S., Shapiro, C., et al. (1998) 'Face-to-face confrontation: Effects of closed-circuit technology on children's eyewitness testimony and jurors' decisions', *Law and Human Behavior*, 22(2): 165–203.

Gray, E. (1993) *Unequal Justice: The Prosecution of Child Sexual Abuse*. New York: Free Press.

Hall, S.R. and Sales, B.D. (2008) *Courtroom Modifications for Child Witnesses: Law and Science in Forensic Evaluation* (Law and Public Policy: Psychology and the Social Sciences). Washington, DC: American Psychological Association.

Herskovitz, J. and Kim, C. (2009, 9 November) 'South Korea seeks new laws after brutal rape of child', *The Star Online*. Available at http://thestar.com.my/news/story.asp?file=/2009/11/9/worldupdates/2009-11-09T151852Z_01_NOOTR_RTRMDNC_0_-438027-1&sec=Worldupdates

Jones, L., Cross, T.P., Walsh, W.A. and Simone, M. (2007) 'Do child advocacy centers improve families' experiences of child sexual abuse investigations?', *Child Abuse and Neglect*, 31(10): 1069–85.

Khoury, A. (2008) *State-By-State Summary of Youth Involvement in Court*. Washington, DC: American Bar Association Center on Children and Law.

Krinsky, M.A. and Rodriguez, J. (2006) 'Giving voice to the voiceless – Enhancing youth participation in court proceedings', *Nevada Law Journal*, 6: 1302–14.

Lind, E.A. and Tyler, T. (1988) *The Social Psychology of Procedural Justice*. New York: Plenum Press.

Malloy, L.C., Lyon, T.D. and Quas, J.A. (2007) 'Filial dependency and recantation of child sexual abuse allegations', *Journal of the American Academy of Child and Adolescent Psychiatry*, 46(2): 162–70.

Maryland v. Craig, 497 US 836 (1990).

McAuliff, B.D., Nicholson, E., Amarilio, D. and Ravanshenas, D. (2012) 'Supporting children in U.S. legal proceedings: Descriptive and attitudinal data from a national survey of victim/witness assistants', *Psychology, Public Policy, and Law*, 19(1): 98–113.

McWilliams, K., Narr, R., Goodman, G.S., Mendoza, M., and Ruiz, S. (2013) 'Children's memory for their mother's murder: Accuracy, suggestibility, and resistance to suggestion', *Memory*, 21: 591–8.

Melinder, A. and Korkman, J. (2010) 'Children's memory and testimony', in P.A. Granhag (ed.), *Forensic Psychology in Context*. Devon, UK: Willan Publishing, pp. 117–38.

Melinder, A., Baugerud, G.A., Ovenstad, K.S., and Goodman, G.S. (2013). 'Children's memories of removal: A test of attachment theory', *Journal of Traumatic Stress*, 26(1): 125–133.

Melinder, A., Goodman, G.S., Eilertson, D. and Magnussen, S. (2004) 'Beliefs about child witnesses: A national survey', *Psychology, Crime, and Law*, 10(4): 347–65.

Melton, G.B. and Kimbrough-Melton, R.J. (2006) 'Integrating assessment, treatment and justice: Pipe dream or possibility', in S. Sparta and G. Koocher (eds.), *Forensic Mental Health Assessment of Children and Adolescents*. Oxford: Oxford University Press, pp. 30–45.

Melton, G.B. and Thompson, R.A. (1987) 'Getting out of a rut: Detours to less travelled paths in child witness research', in S.J. Ceci, M.P. Toglia, and D.F. Ross (eds.), *Children's Eyewitness Memory*. New York: Springer-Verlag, pp. 209–19.

Melton, G.B., Limber, S.P., Jacobs, J.E. and Oberlander, L.B. (1992) *Preparing Sexually Abused Children for Testimony: Children's Perception of the Legal Process*. Final report to the National Center on Child Abuse and Neglect. Washington, DC: NCCAN.

Mnookin, R. (1975). 'Child custody adjudication: Judicial functions in the face of indeterminacy', *Law and Contemporary Problems*, 39: 226–293.

Myers, J.E.B. (2008) *Myers on Evidence in Child, Domestic, and Elder Abuse Cases*. New York: Kluwer.

Nathanson, R., and Saywitz, K.J. (2003) 'Effects of the courtroom context on children's memory and anxiety', *Journal of Psychiatry and Law*, 31(1): 67–98.

National Conference of Commissioners on Uniform State Laws (2002) *Uniform Child Witness Testimony by Alternative Methods Act*, Chicago, IL: National Conference of Commissioners on uniform state laws.

Nova Scotia Department of Justice Victims' Services Division (2000) *Child Victims and the Criminal Justice System: Study Report*. Halifax, NS: Nova Scotia Department of Justice Victims' Services Division.

O'Neill, S. and Zajac, R. (2013) 'Preparing children for cross-examination: How does intervention timing influence efficacy?', *Psychology, Public Policy, and Law*, 19(3): 307–320.

Orcutt, H.K., Goodman, G.S., Tobey, A.E., Batterman-Faunce, J.M. and Thomas, S. (2001) 'Detecting deception in children's testimony: Factfinders' abilities to reach the truth in open court and closed-circuit trials', *Law and Human Behavior*, 25(4): 339–72.

Park, L. and Renner, K.E. (1998) 'The failure to acknowledge differences in developmental capabilities leads to unjust outcomes for child witnesses in sexual abuse cases', *Canadian Journal of Community Mental Health*, 17(1): 5–19.

Pitchal, E. (2008) 'Where are all the children? Increasing youth participation in dependency proceedings', *UC Davis Journal of Juvenile Law and Policy*, 12: 1–31.

Plotnikoff, J. and Woolfson, R. (2004) *In Their Own Words: The Experiences of 50 Young Witnesses in Criminal Proceedings*. London: National Society for the Prevention of Cruelty to Children.

Prairie Research Associates Inc. (2004) *Multi-Site Survey of Victims of Crime and Criminal Justice Professionals Across Canada*. Ottawa: Policy Centre for Victims Issues, Research and Statistics Division.

Quas, J.A., Cooper, A. and Wandrey, L. (2009) 'Child victims in dependency court', in B.L. Bottoms, C. Nadjowski, and G.S. Goodman (eds.), *Children as Victims, Witnesses, and Offenders*. New York: Guilford Press, pp. 128–49.

Quas, J.A., and Goodman, G.S. (2012). 'Child victims in court: Emotional and attitudinal outcomes', *Psychology, Public Policy, and Law*, 18: 392–414.

Quas, J.A., Goodman, G.S., Ghetti, S., Alexander, K., Edelstein, R., Redlich, A., et al. (2005) 'Childhood sexual assault victims: Long-term outcomes after testifying in criminal court', *Monographs of the Society for Research in Child Development*, 70(2): 1–145.

Runyan, D.K., Everson, M.D., Edelsohn, G.A., Hunter, W.M. and Coulter, M.L. (1988) 'Impact of legal intervention on sexually abused children', *Journal of Pediatrics*, 113(4): 647–53.

Ryan, P., Warren, B.L. and Weincek, P. (1991) 'Removal of the perpetrator versus removal of the victim in cases of intrafamilial child sexual abuse', in D.D. Knudsen and J.A.L. Miller (eds.), *Abuse and Battered: Social and Legal Responses to Family Violence*, pp. 123–35.

Santos, B.R. and Goncalves, I.B. (2009) *Testimony without Fear*. San Paulo, Brazil: Childhood Brazil.

Santosky v. Kramer. 455 U.S. 745. (1982).

Sas, L.D. (1991) *Reducing the System-Induced Trauma for Child Sexual Abuse Victims through Court Preparation, Assessment, and Follow-Up*. Ontario, Canada: London Family Court.

Sas, L.D. (1993) *Three Years after the Verdict*. Ontario, Canada: London Family Court Clinic Inc.

Sas, L.D. (2002) *The Interaction between Children's Developmental Capabilities and the Courtroom Environment: the Impact on Testimonial Competency*, Research Report. Canada: Department of Justice.

Sas, L.D., Wolfe, D.A. and Gowdey, K. (1996) 'Children and the courts in Canada', *Criminal Justice and Behavior*, 23(2): 338–57.

Saywitz, K. and Nathanson, R. (1993) 'Children's testimony and their perception of stress in and out of the courtroom', *Child Abuse & Neglect*, 17(5): 613–22.

South-Western Ontario Child Witness Network (1999) *I'm Doing My Job in Court. Are You? Questions for the Criminal Justice System*. Toronto, ON: Toronto Child Abuse Centre.

Spencer, J.R. and Lamb M.E. (Eds.) (2012) *Children and Cross-Examination: Time to Change the Rules?* Oxford: Hart Publishing.

Tedesco, J.F. and Schnell, S.V. (1987) 'Children's reactions to sex abuse investigation and litigation', *Child Abuse and Neglect*, 11(2): 267–72.

Troxel, N.R., Ogle, C.M., Cordon, I.M., Lawler, M.J. and Goodman, G.S. (2009) 'Child witnesses in criminal court', in B. L. Bottoms, C.J. Najdowski and G.S. Goodman (eds.), *Children as Victims, Witnesses, and Offenders: Psychological Science and the Law*. New York: Guilford Press, pp. 150–67.

Tyler, T.R. and Lind, E.A. (2001) 'Procedural justice', in J. Sanders, and V.L. Hamilton (eds.), *Handbook of Justice Research in Law*. Dordrecht, Netherlands: Kluwer Academic Publishers, pp. 65–92.

US Department of Health and Human Services (2009) *Child Maltreatment, 2007*. Washington, DC: US Department of Health and Human Services.

Vis, S.A. and Thomas, N. (2009). 'Beyond talking — Children's participation in Norwegian care and protection cases', *European Journal of Social Work*, 12: 155–168.

Walsh, W.A., Cross, T.P., Jones, L.M., Simone, M. and Kolko, D.J. (2007) 'Which sexual abuse victims receive a forensic medical examination?: The impact of Child Advocacy Centers', *Child Abuse and Neglect*, 31(10): 1053–68.

Wang, S. (2009, 23 May) 'Underage sex trial tests China's courts', *Asian Times Online*. Available at http://www.atimes.com/atimes/China/KE23Ad03.html.

Warren-Leubecker, A., Tate, C., Hinton, I. and Ozbeck, N. (1989) 'What do children know about the legal system and when do they know it?', in S. Ceci, D. Ross and M. Togllia (eds.), *Perspectives on Children's Testimony*. New York: Springer-Verlag, pp. 158–83.

Welder, A.N. (2000) 'Sexual abuse victimization and the child witness in Canada: Legal, ethical, and professional issues for psychologists', *Canadian Psychology*, 41(3): 160–73.

Westcott, H., Davies, G. and Bull, R. (eds.). *Children's Testimony: A Handbook of Psychological Research and Forensic Practice*. Chichester: John Wiley & Sons.

Whitcomb, D., Runyan, D.K., DeVos, E., Hunter, W.M., Cross, T.P., Everson, M.D., Peeler, N.A., Porter, C.Q., Toth, P.A. and Cropper, C. (1991) *Child Victims as Witnesses: Research and Development Program*. Washington, DC: Office of Juvenile Justice and Delinquency Prevention.

Zajac, R., Gross, J. and Hayne, H. (2003) 'Asked and answered: Questioning children in the courtroom', *Psychiatry, Psychology and Law*, 10(1): 199–209.

17

Child Maltreatment and Bullying

Kelly McWilliams, Gail S. Goodman, Juliana Raskauskas
and Ingrid M. Cordon

INTRODUCTION

The violation of children's rights to personal security is a serious problem throughout the world. All too many children suffer abuse, neglect, and torment at the hands of their parents, caregivers, various authority figures, and even their peers. In this chapter, we explore what is known about child maltreatment not only through research, but also through children's experiences and voices. We examine various forms of maltreatment, focusing on the traditional categories of child abuse and neglect. However, we also include discussion of less traditional forms, specifically bullying and malevolence at the peer-to-peer level. In the process, we review research on the prevalence, seriousness, and discovery of child maltreatment. We also discuss the evolution of public awareness and policy, touching on the various challenges faced when addressing this critical issue. In this regard, we use recent legal cases and various research topics to exemplify how research and policy on child maltreatment and bullying need to be carefully considered.

DEFINITION, CATEGORIES, AND PREVALENCE OF CHILD MALTREATMENT

Definition of child maltreatment

Child maltreatment is a difficult term to define, especially in practice, primarily because of variations in individual and societal standards and expectations for what is appropriate child care. According to the World Health Organization (WHO) Consultation on Child Abuse Prevention (2002), child maltreatment consists of all forms of physical and/or emotional mistreatment, sexual abuse, negligent treatment, or exploitation that result in actual or potential harm to a child's health, development, survival, or dignity in the context of a relationship of trust and/or power. This definition of abuse covers a large spectrum of behaviors. This chapter will focus on physical abuse, sexual abuse, neglect, and emotional/psychological abuse. We will also discuss maltreatment that occurs within peer and sibling relationships, including bullying and other forms of victimization (Finkelhor, Turner and Hamby, 2012; Finklehor, Turner and Ormrod, 2006).

Physical abuse

Although definitions vary, physical abuse is often defined as any acts of commission by a caregiver that result in actual physical harm, or that have the potential for physical harm (WHO, 1999). Injuries that are inflicted through physical abuse take many forms; however, head injuries are particularly concerning because head trauma resulting from physical abuse is the most common cause of death in young children, with children aged 0–2 at highest risk (WHO, 1999).

Sexual abuse

Sexual abuse is typically defined as those acts in which a caregiver or adult in a power and/or trust position uses a child for sexual gratification. Reviews of the empirical literature on child sexual abuse (CSA) reveal that CSA is observed across the world in all societies (Fergusson and Mullen, 1999; Finkelhor, 1994). Young females are at a heightened risk, with female children being victimized two to three times more often than male children although there is increasing evidence that boys and men are more reluctant to disclose sexual abuse than girls and women (Dorahy and Clearwater, 2012; Fergusson and Mullen, 1999).

Neglect

Neglect is the most common form of child maltreatment in the United States and other Western countries (IPSCAN, 2010; US Department of Health and Human Services, 2011). Neglect is defined by the unwillingness or incapacity (because of, for example, parental mental illness, substance abuse, or intellectual disability) of parent, guardian, or custodian of a child to provide the child with food, clothing, shelter, supervision, and/or medical care, where that unwillingness causes substantial risk or harm to the child's welfare. Like physical abuse, neglect can be fatal for very young children (Damashek, McDiarmid Nelson and Bonner, 2013). Neglect has been distinguished from circumstances of poverty, in that people are considered negligent if reasonable resources are available and they fail to use them. In reality, however, neglect and poverty can be difficult

to unravel. Other behaviors are also cause for concern and may be considered neglect, such as exposure of children to drugs, inadequate protection from environmental dangers, abandonment, poor hygiene, and deprivation of a proper education.

Emotional and psychological abuse

In many ways, emotional/psychological abuse is the most difficult form of abuse to define (Trocme et al., 2011), but emotional abuse can be considered to be the failure of a guardian, caregiver, or custodian to provide an appropriately caring and emotionally supportive environment. It includes acts that have the potential for adverse effects on a child's development (WHO, 1999). Examples of emotional/psychological abuse are restricting a child's movement, rejection, and denigration (WHO, 1999).

Peer victimization and bullying

Peer victimization or child-on-child maltreatment, includes bullying and a range of harmful behaviors by a child's peers or siblings (Finkelhor et al., 2006; Finkelhor, Turner and Hamby, 2012). Bullying can be defined as direct or indirect aggressive behaviors by one child (identified as the bully) against another child who is unable to defend himself or herself effectively (the victim; Austin and Joseph, 1996). Bullying may involve direct physical actions, such as hitting or shoving; verbal assaults, such as teasing or name calling; or more indirect actions, such as social isolation or manipulation (Austin and Joseph, 1996; Olweus, 1994, 1997). It also includes cyberbullying using the internet or social media to denigrate and humiliate. Peer victimization and bullying may encompass all of the forms of abuse and violence outlined above, the difference being that the offender is a peer rather than an adult.

Prevalence of child maltreatment worldwide

Violence against children occurs throughout the world (United Nations Study on Violence

Against Children, 2006). However, the actual or 'true' rates of child maltreatment are hard to estimate due to an unknown number of victims not reporting it and many countries lacking the legal and social systems to record or respond to allegations of child maltreatment. Therefore, many of the statistics rely on survey research (for example, interviewing or surveying parents about their treatment of children or interviewing and surveying children themselves). Survey research on child maltreatment has been conducted worldwide and gives us an inkling (albeit likely an underestimation) of the true rate with which violence against children occurs.

The United Nations Study on Violence Against Children (2006) explored child maltreatment internationally and painted a devastating picture. The study revealed that most child maltreatment occurs in everyday settings including the home, school, care and justice systems, work settings, and community. The perpetrators of this violence are most commonly parents, schoolmates, teachers, employers, boyfriends/girlfriends, spouses, and partners. Research conducted worldwide shows that 80 per cent to 98 per cent of children suffer physical punishment in their homes (United Nations Study on Violence Against Children, 2006). WHO stated that the prevalence of forced sexual violence involving touch among boys and girls under 18 is 73 million and 150 million victims, respectively, worldwide. According to a WHO estimate, between 100 and 140 million girls and women in the world have undergone some form of female genital mutilation/cutting (United Nations Children's Fund, 2005). WHO also estimated that 53,000 children worldwide died due to homicide in 2002.

While these numbers are alarming, they do not give us the full picture. As outlined above, child maltreatment can take many different forms and occur in a range of settings. To obtain a better picture of the circumstances under which infringements of children's right to personal security occur, we examine the prevalence of each form of child maltreatment.

Physical abuse

Research on physical abuse reveals that many children worldwide experience physical violence in the course of their childhoods. In the United States in 2010, there were 3.3 million referrals to Child Protective Services involving the alleged maltreatment of approximately 6 million children. About 2 million of the referrals led to investigations or assessments by Child Protective Services (US Department of Health and Human Services, 2011). An estimated 695,000 children were determined to be victims of maltreatment; 17.6 per cent of these children were victims of physical abuse. In Egypt, a cross-sectional study of children found that 37 per cent of children reported being beaten or tied up by their caregivers (Youssef, Attia, and Kamel, 1998). In the Republic of Korea, two-thirds of parents reported whipping their children, and 45 per cent reported they had hit, kicked, or beaten their child (Hahm and Guterman, 2001). In Ethiopia, another study found that 21 per cent of urban school children and 64 per cent of rural school children reported physical injury resulting from physical punishment (Ketsela and Kedebe, 1997).

Sexual abuse

Child sexual abuse, once believed to be uncommon, is all too prevalent throughout the world. In the above sample of CPS cases in the United States in 2010, 9 per cent of children referred to Child Protective Services were confirmed victims of sexual abuse (US Department of Health and Human Services, 2011). An early survey study of 2019 men and women in Great Britain revealed that 10 per cent reported having been sexually abused before the age of 16 (Baker and Duncan, 1985). A more recent study conducted in four provinces of China reported that 16.7 per cent of females and 10.5 per cent of males had an unwanted sexual experience before the age of 16 (Chen, Dunne and Han, 2004). A meta-analysis conducted by Pereda, Guilera, Forns, and Gomes-Benito (2009) included 65 studies, conducted in 22 different countries and examined the prevalence of sexual abuse prior to age 18 as reported retrospectively by men and women from various cultures. They found that 7.9 per cent of men and 19.7 per cent of women world-wide reported some form of sexual abuse prior to the age of 18.

Neglect

International research on child neglect is limited, partly because laws on reporting maltreatment vary and in many countries, reporting neglect is not mandatory. Two studies cited by WHO illustrate different approaches in different countries. One of child neglect in Kenya found that 21.9 per cent of children reported being neglected by their parents (Nairobi, African Network for the Prevention and Protection against Child Abuse and Neglect, 2000). The second, based in Canada, relied on child welfare services data and reported that among the cases of neglect, 19 per cent involved physical neglect, 12 per cent involved abandonment, and 11 per cent involved educational neglect. Neglect is a particularly prevalent form of child maltreatment in developed countries, such as the United States. Approximately 78 per cent of the cases confirmed by CPS in 2010 were classified as involving neglect (US Department of Health and Human Services, 2011), indicating that a large majority of interfamilial child abuse cases confirmed in the United States involve neglect.

Emotional abuse

Emotional abuse is the hardest form of mal-treatment to define internationally, due in large part to the fact that cultures vary greatly in what they view as psychologically harmful to children as a study by WorldSAFE revealed. Sadowski et al. (2004) examined emotional abuse in five countries (Chile, Egypt, India, Philippines, and the United States). They found marked variations in the form emotional mistreatment takes across cultures. For example, threats of abandonment were used frequently in some cultures, such as the Philippines (48 per cent), but rarely in others,

such as in Chile, where only 8 per cent of mothers reported using the threat. Also, cursing at a child is a common practice in Egypt (51 per cent), but rarely carried out in Chile (3 per cent).

Among the 2010 CPS cases in the United States, 8 per cent were characterized as cases of emotional/psychological abuse (US Department of Health and Human Services, 2011). The rates of emotional maltreatment around the world are rarely studied and at this point, mostly unknown. The conse-quences of psychological abuse are also understudied but may vary as a function of cultural context, making it even more diffi-cult to define and measure this practice. It is also likely that emotional abuse is a sequelae of maltreatment generally.

Peer victimization and bullying

Peer victimization and bullying is a problem worldwide. Sampson (2002) argues that bullying takes place in all schools at all grade levels. A study conducted in 35 countries worldwide revealed that approximately 12 per cent of children reported being verbally or physically bullied at least twice in the last 60 days (WHO, 2008). Although bullying takes place around the world, most of the research performed on bullying has been conducted in developed, Western nations. Olweus (1994) studied 140,000 Norwegian children, aged 8 through 16, and discovered that about 15 per cent of them reported being targeted by a bully. A similar study con-ducted in the United Kingdom revealed that of 6758 students ages 8–16, 27 per cent of the children reported being bullied at some point during the duration of the study (Whitney and Smith, 1993). O'Moore and Hillery (1989) examined bullying in Dublin, Ireland, and found that 10 per cent of chil-dren reported being bullied or engaging in bullying behaviors. An examination of inter-mediate school children in South Africa (Greeff and Grobler, 2008) found a very high rate of bullying at 56.4 per cent taking place in grades 4 through 6. Finally, studies con-ducted in Australia, Canada, Italy, Japan,

Spain, and Sweden revealed rates of victimization ranging from 15 per cent to a high of 50 per cent (Baldry and Farrington, 1999; Boulton and Underwood, 1992; Charach, Pepler and Ziegler, 1995; McEachern, Kenny, Blake and Alude, 2005).

Bullying is also a significant problem in the United States. A study conducted by Nansel and colleagues (2001) measured the prevalence of bullying behaviors among US children in grades 6 through 10. They found that 8.5 per cent of children reported being bullied, 10.6 per cent admitted to bullying behavior, and 6.3 per cent revealed they had both been a bully and a victim of a bully. They also found that males are more likely than females to be both perpetrators and targets of bullying. Another US study reported a very high rate of bullying in middle and high schools in the Midwest (Hazler, Hoover and Oliver, 1991), with 77 per cent of participants indicating they had been the target of a bully at some point. A later follow-up study with school-aged children in the same region of the country (Hoover, Oliver and Hazler, 1995) found that 76.8 per cent of the children had been victims of a bully; 14 per cent of these children reported that they had suffered severe reactions due to the abuse. Limber and colleagues (1998) studied bullying in 6500 children in grades 4 through 6 in the southern region of the United States. They found that 1 in 4 children had been bullied regularly, and 1 in 10 children were tormented at least once a week.

Are reports of child maltreatment on the rise or actually decreasing?

Worldwide, reports of child maltreatment are still on the rise. A survey by the International Society for the Prevention of Child Abuse and Neglect (IPSCAN, 2010) of key informants across 75 countries indicated that reports of all forms of child maltreatment are still on the rise internationally. Data released by the federal government in the United States, however, indicate that the prevalence of sexual and physical abuse reports in the US

is declining. Based on a range of data including CPS data, the National Incidence Study, and self-report victimization surveys from 2006, Finkelhor and Jones (2008) reported a decrease in sexual abuse reports ranging from 47 per cent to 69 per cent between 1992 and 2010, and a 29 per cent to 56 per cent decrease in physical abuse reports over the same period (Finkelhor and Jones, 2012). This was not the case, however, for child abuse and neglect fatalities. Their explanation for the decline in sexual and physical abuse was an increase in child protection personnel and law enforcement, aggressive prosecution tactics, and significantly, a growing public awareness of the problem. Substantiated reports of child neglect dropped by 10 per cent. Although the prevalence of some forms of child maltreatment may be declining, at least in the United States, child maltreatment remains a serious problem there and in the world at large.

Methodological issues regarding prevalence estimates

A number of methodological problems plague researchers trying to accurately assess the prevalence of child maltreatment. The prevalence of the various forms of child maltreatment is hard to measure in any one country, and more so for cross-country comparisons. Often, the main data available are only for cases that have been reported and investigated by statutory child protection agencies. Even when survey and other self-report data are available, there are concerns about under-reporting (for example, parents may be loath to disclose mistreatment of their children, and more so in some countries than in others). The serious consequences and stigmas related to child maltreatment in many societies mean that an unknown number of cases go unreported even by the victims. Many victims are too scared, confused, and/or ashamed to disclose the abuse (Pipe et al., 2007). Victims of bullying may be hesitant to come forward about their situation for fear of retaliation.

Another issue that makes assessment difficult is the many different ways that a child abuse case may be handled once an accusation is made. Countries vary in the legal and social structures set up to deal with child maltreatment, making it difficult to find and organize data on all the cases. In many Western countries, abuse by a family member is dealt with by child protective services; however, abuse by a non-caretaker is processed through the criminal justice system and is not generally included in child protective service statistics. Because of these and other limitations, it is not possible to obtain an accurate estimate of the true prevalence of child maltreatment worldwide.

Consequences of maltreatment

A large body of research has documented the adverse outcomes for children growing up in environments of abuse, neglect, and other forms of maltreatment or victimization and bullying. Violence against children has been linked to adverse outcomes across many domains, including children's emotional and social adjustment, cognitive development, and academic functioning (Cicchetti et al., 2003; Eckenrode, Laird and Doris, 1993; Toth, Cicchetti and Kim, 2002; Toth et al., 2011). It is often difficult, however, to differentiate the effects of specific forms of maltreatment frequently co-occur (Cyr et al., in press; Romano, Bell and Billette, 2011). It is also difficult to disentangle the effects of abuse from the other aspects of children's living cirumstances (Fergusson, Boden and Horwood, 2007). It is important to consider how detrimental consequences of maltreatment reach far beyond the individual to touch the community as a whole.

The developmental period during which maltreatment takes place can profoundly influence children's outcomes. When maltreatment occurs in infancy, this is likely to be the most harmful for children's development and may have an impact on the hard-wiring of children's brains (Glaser, 2000). Emotional abuse in infancy and toddlerhood results in

increases in externalizing symptoms, such as aggressive behavior (Manly et al., 2001). Infants and toddlers who experience physical and emotional neglect have been found in a series of studies to have cognitive and language delays, dependency issues, and poor social interactions (Allen and Oliver, 1982; Culp et al., 1991; Egeland and Sroufe, 1981; Gowen, 1993; Hildyard and Wolfe, 2002).

Maltreatment and peer victimization in childhood and adolescence is associated with children's emotional, behavioral, and disciplinary problems and poor performance at school (Boden, Horwood and Fergusson, 2007; Eckenrode et al., 1993; Kim and Cichetti, 2010).

There is also evidence of the longer-term consequences of childhood maltreatment. Adults who experienced maltreatment as children, or were involved in severe bullying, may face cognitive deficiencies and are likely to have more difficulties becoming optimally functioning members of society: Victims of abuse or neglect are at heightened risk for delinquency, adult criminal behavior, and violent criminal behavior (Hildyard and Wolfe, 2002; Kaufman and Widom, 1999; Maxfield and Widom, 1996; Rivera and Widom, 1990; Widom, 2001; Widom and Kuhns, 1996). Peer victimization and bullying is associated with a loss of self-esteem, internalizing problems and the start of suicide ideation that may persist into the adult years (Olweus, 2001; Rigby, 2000; Perren, Ettekal and Ladd, 2013; Reijntjes et al., 2010; Ross, 2003). Individuals who were the aggressor in a bullying relationship are also more likely to engage in delinquent behavior, such as alcohol abuse and smoking (Loeber and Disheon, 1984).

The literature also points to a link between childhood maltreatment and the development of mental health problems and personality disorders, especially in the absence of social support (Sperry and Spatz Widom, 2013). Johnson et al. (1999) found that adults who had been victims of child maltreatment were four times more likely than adults without histories of maltreatment to be diagnosed with a personality disorder. Childhood neglect and physical and sexual abuse have also been linked to other mental health issues such as alcohol problems and dysthymia (Cashmore and Shackel, 2013; Horwitz et al., 2001; Ogawa et al., 1997) and suicidality (Cutajar et al., 2010). Trauma-related psychopathology symptoms (for example, symptoms of Post-Traumatic Stress Disorder, dissociation, and depression) are also often evident (for review, see Alley et al., in press).

It is difficult to pinpoint the effects of maltreatment or bullying in cross-sectional studies because of the correlational nature of the research and the many interrelated factors involved (such as parental dysfunction, substance abuse, poverty). More recent longitudinal studies provide evidence that maltreatment and peer victimization have various adverse effects on children's development, after taking account of a range of other aspects of children's lives and circumstances (Fergusson et al., 2010; Mills et al., 2013; Sperry and Spatz Widom, 2013).

Focusing on peer victimization and bullying, Farrington (1991) argued that society is the ultimate victim of this type of maltreatment because children who are bullied are more likely to mistreat their spouses and children in adulthood, perpetuating the cycle of violence and creating a new generation of aggressive children. Considering the potentially devastating effects of all forms of maltreatment on development, Farrington's argument can be extended beyond bullying to abuse and neglect as well. Society pays the ultimate price when adults carry the damage from earlier maltreatment and cannot reach their full potential and contribute to the success of their communities. For instance, heightened risk of criminal behavior in children with histories of maltreatment goes beyond personal and family consequences, creating pain and destruction within the community as a whole. It is society's responsibility to protect its children and prevent acts that threaten its youngest and most vulnerable members of the population.

Methodological issues regarding determination of maltreatment effects

From a scientific perspective, determining the adverse effects of child maltreatment is a difficult task. To provide a sense of the methodological challenges faced by child maltreatment researchers who attempt to study children's outcomes, we offer a few of the more obvious examples here.

Although many studies examined the outcomes of children with histories of maltreatment, the different definitions of maltreatment and the different sources of data make any cross-study and cross-jurisdictional comparisons very difficult. Studies often rely on vague constructs or definitions from CPS, resulting in considerable variability and low generalizability across studies. In addition, the 'dark figure' associated with unreported maltreatment means that it is not possible for researchers to confidently assess the true consequences of child abuse, neglect, and bullying without knowing whether the studies include representative samples of victims and non-victims in the comparison groups.

As outlined earlier, many children with histories of maltreatment experience other detrimental influences during their development. The environments in which maltreated children are raised make it difficult, if not impossible, to assess unique adverse effects caused by maltreatment per se. Child maltreatment has high rates of co-occurrence, meaning that many children experience more than one form of abuse (such as physical and psychological abuse and rejection; Romano, Bell and Billette, 2011). Children with maltreatment histories may also have resided in households plagued with domestic violence, substance abuse, parental mental illness, and poor nutrition. These interrelated factors can all contribute to poor developmental outcomes for children and are difficult to tease apart.

Despite these challenges (and many more), scientific research on the seriousness of child maltreatment is crucial for an understanding of the adverse effects of abuse, neglect, and bullying on children's development. However, it is also important to hear directly from children about their experiences.

CHILDREN'S PERSPECTIVES OF VIOLENCE

Much of the research conducted on violence against children explores the socio-emotional and cognitive effects of maltreatment and relies on the use of standardized tests, often completed by adults. Some research has asked adults to report retrospectively on their experiences as children. This has some obvious problems methodologically in relation to possible bias and selective or inaccurate memory. Relatively little research examines how children themselves view maltreatment though this area of research is increasing. The United Nations Study on Violence Against Children (2006) is an important departure from that trend, in that children were asked for their own perspectives about experiencing or witnessing violence. Children informed researchers that child maltreatment is not just about the physical 'hurt' but about the 'hurt inside' as well. They revealed that the pain goes beyond the actual experience of violence; it is also caused by adult and community acceptance of the maltreatment. An important issue the children raised was the connection between violence at home, in school, and in the community. Children spoke about how abuse in one setting carries over into other aspects of their daily lives. As one child stated: 'If kids are beaten at home, they are going to beat, that is, if their parents ill-treat them or don't talk to them, kids will beat others because they are beaten. They are going to drag with them what they see at home. This is the basis of violence' (Blanchet-Cohen (2009: 30). Recognizing that child maltreatment is not a compartmentalized issue and affects children in virtually all parts of their lives is vitally important for intervention.

According to the United Nations Study of Violence Against Children (2006), children are most likely to experience violence in the home. Violence in the home takes many forms. As related by the children, it can be in the form of actual physical punishment, witnessing domestic abuse, being yelled at or called names, experiencing sexual abuse, or being neglected. Again as cited by Blanchet-Cohen's study (2009: 31), one child explained that 'parents leave children home [alone] at night to go gamble'. Another child experienced neglect because his parents 'used money to buy drugs'. Yet another child experienced neglect emotionally, 'My stepmother never talks to me or teaches me anything. She ignores me'.

Parents and children often view and define abuse quite differently. A study conducted in South-East Asia revealed that parents considered their violent actions to be appropriate forms of discipline, whereas children viewed them as a direct assault (Baezaley et al., 2006; Blanchet-Cohen, 2009). Another study in Uganda found a similar pattern: parents viewed violence against children as a justifiable means of punishment, used to guide children's future behavior, whereas children described the punishment as assaultive violence (Blanchet-Cohen, 2009; Naker, 2005).

In many countries, violence against children occurs not just in the home, but also in school, at work, and in the community. This abuse is often perpetrated by teachers, students, employers, and significant others. Children who experience abuse outside of the home describe the humiliation of 'public' abuse as equally painful if not more painful than violence at home. One child explained, 'It's not the pain that hurt me, but the feeling of humiliation that I underwent when my classmates laughed at me' (Lansdown, 2006: 19).

Children also express the pain they experience from community acceptance of violent behavior. The children feel that their voices are not heard, and that 'the way our society is set up … kids are not allowed to think for themselves about how they think things should be done ... You are treated as a second-rate citizen' (Ma, 2004: 4). Children believe that child maltreatment often occurs because of adults' abuse of power, a lack of respect for children, and a devaluing of children's perspectives (Blanchet-Cohen, 2009).

Victims of bullying have similar experiences. Bullying usually takes place away from the view of parents, teachers, and other adults, and children are often hesitant to disclose bullying. The majority of children will discuss bullying with their friends; however, most are disinclined to report the maltreatment to adults (Mishna, 2004). One study conducted in Canada found that most children believed telling an adult would only make the abuse worse (Mishna, 2004). McEachern et al. (2005) explained that children are fearful of retaliation or embarrassment that may result from telling an adult. One boy explained, 'They think that if I go to the principal's office and tell him they won't do it anymore, but they'll do it more because you told on them' (Mishna, 2004: 239). McEachern et al. (2005) found that disclosing bullying is not typical behavior for victims, with only half reporting the abuse. Typically, the children who do tell an adult are the children who are regularly victimized. These children will more often tell a parent or 'significant other' at home instead of a teacher or school administrator.

Overall, information concerning children's perspectives of violence provides a valuable tool. Learning first-hand of children's feelings about violence and their insights about the causes of maltreatment is imperative for developing appropriate therapeutic interventions. Without this knowledge, we lack a complete picture of child maltreatment and, arguably, are less able to properly address this serious issue.

The dilemma of listening to children's voices about child maltreatment

It is important to listen to children's voices in understanding their victimization experiences, but there is an important caveat. Children often do not themselves realize the seriousness of the acts they have experienced or how harmful those acts are. It is not uncommon for children to misperceive abusive acts. Instead, they attribute to themselves for being bad. This can promote intergenerational transmission of violence, when abuse victims treat their own children as they themselves were treated. Moreover, community approaches to ending violence against children, which to date appear to hold special promise in preventing child maltreatment and bullying (Melton, 2009), may occur at a level too removed or abstract to be fully realized by individual children. Therefore, research on violence against children and how best to intervene must include not only studies of the effects of child maltreatment, peer victimization and bullying from children's perspectives, but also from the point of view of those adults who, like the present authors, are committed to ending crimes against children.

THE EVOLUTION OF PUBLIC POLICY

Clearly, issues of child maltreatment and bullying are not new and are not unique to any one type of society. Many governments worldwide have accepted children as citizens and have worked towards policies and practices that will protect their youngest and most vulnerable citizens. An important step in child protection was the Convention on the Rights of the Child. Every year, countries that have ratified or acceded to the Convention on the Rights of the Child must go before the UN Committee on the Rights of the Child to report on their progress and answer questions about how well they are fulfilling the treaty.

The Convention stands as a testament to a nearly universal moral and legal recognition of children's rights to protection from 'all forms of violence' (art. 19). Most countries are parties to the Convention. The only exceptions are the United States (a signatory but not a party to the Convention but a party to the Convention's optional protocols against sexual exploitation of children and involvement of children in armed conflicts), Somalia (a signatory but not a party to the Convention, because it has no working government and therefore no capacity to fulfill the treaty), and Kosovo and South Sudan (both new countries with limited capacity to enter into treaties).

Despite these important efforts, it too often takes a drastic event to effect change and create better policies for children. Sensational and disturbing instances of abuse and even murder sometimes finally provide the motivation for society to create policies in an attempt to foster greater protection of children. The dramatic case of Mary Ellen in 1875 led to laws that permit authorities to remove children from home in child maltreatment cases and to the establishment of the New York Society for the Prevention of Cruelty to Children (Jalongo, 2006). Child abuse policy continued to develop, when, in 1962, based on cases of nonaccidental harm to children made evident thanks to advances in radiology, C. Henry Kempe defined the Battered Child Syndrome, and mandated reporting laws followed. The daycare child sexual abuse cases of the 1980s and 1990s also had an effect on research and policy regarding child maltreatment (for example, in the establishment of Child Advocacy Centers for forensic interviewing of children).

In this chapter we have outlined several recent high-profile cases over the last half century, new policies that resulted, and the need for further policy work – ideally of the preventive nature provided by programs like Strong Communities for Children (see below). The examples we discuss next highlight the need for policy to adapt to a changing understanding of children's abilities and needs, and the changing forms of maltreatment, peer victimization and bullying faced by children.

One area of policy change has concerned giving voice to children when child abuse is

alleged. Providing children with a meaningful voice in the legal context has far-reaching implications. Highly sensationalized prosecutions of child sexual abuse at preschools, such as the McMartin and Little Rascals cases in the United States, had the effect of increasing skepticism about children's disclosures of sexual crimes. However, these failed daycare cases of the 1980s and 1990s did not end the prosecution of child sexual abuse. Instead, they led to an increase in scientific research to support optimal interviewing practices for child witnesses in maltreatment cases to bolster children's credibility in court as well as the establishment of specialized Child Advocacy Centers that employ highly trained forensic interviewers. In the end, these changes potentially bring children's voices into court in a way that can support child protection, and they may support due process for those accused.

Even with optimal interviewing, however, children's memory reports are not always as strong and consistent as those of adults. As a result, children's recounting of their experiences can sometimes appear unreliable, even when what they say is true. Take the case of 5-year-old Samantha Runnion. She was kidnapped while playing outside her home, and then raped and murdered. Alejandro Avila was convicted of this horrible crime and is currently on death row, but he was 'on the loose' because jurors had not believed two children in a former child sexual abuse prosecution in which Avila was the defendant. Because he was acquitted in the former case, he was able to murder 5-year-old Samantha. This crime would likely have been avoided if policies and practices were in place to better inform jurors about children's abilities as witnesses and the ways in which children recount their experiences and react to cross-examination in court (Cossins, 2008; Quas, Thompson and Clarke-Stewart, 2005).

Child abuse is not the only form of maltreatment that has gained attention in recent years. Given that bullying is a particularly frequent form of childhood victimization, it is perhaps surprising that until recently it has received less attention from researchers and policy makers than physical and sexual abuse. Much like the sensitization to child sexual abuse in the 1980s and 1990s, the scientific community, funding agencies, and legislators began to give more attention to bullying and other forms of peer violence only after headline-capturing cases mobilized the public.

The problem of bullying was thrust into the national spotlight in the wake of actions carried out by two adolescent boys in Littleton, Colorado. On the morning of 20 April 1999, Eric Harris and Dylan Klebold entered the halls of Columbine High School and shot dead 12 students and 1 teacher, and injured 24 others before turning the guns on themselves. Following this horrific violence, the American public sought some form of understanding of why two teenagers would commit such acts of terror and hatred against their peers. No one knows exactly what drove these two young men to such extremes, but one of the more popular theories is that bullying and torment was the catalyst. Whether or not bullying was the actual cause for the Columbine Shootings, the subject gained national headlines following the tragedy. This attention gave researchers and policy makers a platform to consider the serious consequences of bullying. To date, there are 49 states in the US that have adopted laws concerning bullying and harassment (Sameer and Patchin, 2012).

Bullying took on a new face when cyberbullying became a realm of peer-on-peer maltreatment. Cyberbullying takes place when an individual or group uses technology (such as the Internet or cellular telephone) to engage in hostile or harassing behavior towards another. One famous case of cyberbullying occurred in South Hadley, Massachusetts, in 2009. Phoebe Prince was a 15-year-old girl who was harassed and bullied by older female students following Phoebe's sexual encounters with two older male students at the school. Phoebe received threatening and disturbing messages via social media and text messaging. School officials and faculty were notified of the troubling situation and did little to protect Phoebe from the older bullies. Three months into the torment, Phoebe Prince hanged herself in her family's stairwell (Goldman, 2010).

Another case of cyberbullying that grabbed the headlines was the case of Rutgers University student Tyler Clementi, who had recently come out as a homosexual to his friends and family. One night, while Tyler had a male visitor, his roommate remotely accessed a webcam in the room, briefly viewing Tyler and his companion engaging in sexual activity. Following the encounter Tyler's roommate used the social networking site Twitter to post various homophobic and hateful comments regarding Tyler's sexual activity. Several days later, Tyler Clementi jumped to his death from the George Washington Bridge.

Even before these unfortunate events, researchers suggested the need for school policies as a step in preventing cyberbullying. Agatston, Kowalski, and Limber (2007) recommended implementing bullying prevention programs in which students are educated about the effects of cyberbullying, as well as steps to take to report bullying behavior. They also believe schools should strictly enforce a no-cell-phone-use policy with consistent and strict consequences for students who use their cell phones on school grounds. Finally, these researchers contend that schools should provide parents with literature regarding cyberbullying in an effort to educate them concerning the risks of bullying via technology.

Schools are not the only settings in which cyberbullying has influenced policy. In both the Phoebe Prince and Tyler Clementi cases, the bullies faced legal charges. The justice system is beginning to recognize cyberbullying as a crime. As of April 2012, 14 states have specific laws regarding cyberbullying (Sameer and Patchin, 2012).

Nevertheless, following these notorious cases, as well as a multitude of other incidents, researchers and policy makers decided that the system needed to be updated to deal with the evolution of bullying. In Massachusetts, where Phoebe Prince lived, there is now a law specifically addressing cyberbullying in schools, defining the behavior as 'those behaviors that materially and substantially disrupt the education process or the orderly operation of the school' (Sameer and Patchin, 2012). The behavior includes actions perpetrated 'at a location, activity, function or program that is not school-related, or through the use of technology or an electronic device that is not owned, leased or used by a school district or school, if the bullying creates a hostile environment at school for the victim, infringes on the rights of the victim at school or materially and substantially disrupts the education process or the orderly operation of a school' (Sameer and Patchin, 2012). The state of Massachusetts also now requires bully intervention plans at schools that include annual training for faculty and staff on cyberbullying. New Jersey, where Tyler Clementi was enrolled in college, has the 'Anti-Bullying Bill of Rights Act' which covers harassment via electronic communication (Sameer and Patchin, 2012). These are just two examples of the various new state laws that are directed towards cyberbullying. There is also a federal law pending: The Megan Meier Cyberbullying Prevention Act would result in fines and possible prison sentence of up to two years for individuals convicted of tormenting another through electronic means (Sameer and Patchin, 2012).

However, these policy changes are basically reactive rather than proactive, at least in the sense that the policy reacts to something awful that could have been prevented. In attempts to prevent child maltreatment and bullying in the first place, promising interventions involving entire communities are being implemented and evaluated. For example, Strong Communities for Children is a community-wide program that attempts to make child protection a part of everyday life (Melton, 2009). The ultimate goal to keep children safe from both maltreatment and bullying, according to this intervention strategy, requires that every child and every parent know that when they experience problems, including those involved in raising children, someone in the community will notice and care. In this approach, intervention occurs before parents and children become 'clients' or 'cases' and even without their having to ask for help. Under this community-based intervention, child protection is not just the job of the public child welfare agency, but rather, it involves school staff, civic club members, pediatricians, apartment managers, and everyone else who can volunteer assistance. Opportunities for families to get help are based in ordinary places – schools, churches, parks, libraries, and so forth. This innovative and daring program has achieved promising results, and replications are beginning (Melton, 2009, in press; Melton and Holaday, 2008). Accordingly, there is reason for hope that child maltreatment and bullying can be largely prevented through the evolution of policy on behalf of children.

CONCLUSION

The maltreatment of children is a serious problem throughout the world. Everyday children from all walks of life experience violations of their personal security and bodily integrity. To combat this issue, the community needs to be made aware and finally take responsibility for children's safety and well-being. Law and policy have begun to adapt to the changing forms of maltreatment faced by today's children and youth by creating state and federal laws that prevent torment and cruelty towards others. We have come a long way in recognizing and accepting the seriousness of child maltreatment and bullying, but there is still much more to be done.

Researchers have examined child maltreatment and its devastating effects. This is an important foundation for developing some solutions. Evidence-based interventions need to be brought to schools, homes, and entire communities in an effort to build safe and humane environments for our children. Parents need to be educated about the lasting effects of child maltreatment, as well as trained on ways to identify if their children have become victims. Support systems should be in place throughout the community, creating an environment where parents and children can feel safe and obtain the help they need to prevent acts of violence. There are no short-term solutions, but if communities begin to recognize the problem, they can begin to work towards a solution.

REFERENCES

Agatston, P.W., Kowalski, R., and Limber, S. (2007) 'Students' perspective on cyber bullying', *Journal of Adolescent Health*, 4(6): S59–60.

Allen, R.E. and Oliver, J.M. (1982) 'The effects of child maltreatment on language development', *Child Abuse & Neglect*, 6(3): 299–305.

Alley, D., Narr, R.K., Melinder, A., and Goodman, G.S. (in press) 'Child maltreatment, trauma-related psychopathology, and memory development', in T. Plante (ed.), *Abnormal Psychology Through the Millennium*. Santa Barbara, CA: CIO.

Austin, S. and Joseph, S. (1996) 'Assessment of bully/victim problems in 8 to 11 year-olds', *British Journal of Educational Psychology*, 66(4): 447–56.

Baezaley, H., Bessell, S. Ennew, J., and Waterson, R. (2006) *What children say? Results of comparative research on the physical and emotional punishment of children in South East Asia and the Pacific*. Stockholm: Save the Children Sweden.

Baker, A.W. and Duncan, S.P. (1985) 'Child sexual abuse: A study of prevalence in Great Britain', *Child Abuse & Neglect*, 9(4): 457–67.

Baldry, A.C. and Farrington, D.P. (1999) 'Types of bullying among Italian school children', *Journal of Adolescence*, 22(3): 423–6.

Blanchet-Cohen, N. (2009) *Children, Agency, and Violence: In and Beyond the United Nations Study on the Violence against Children*. UNICEF, Innocenti Research Centre.

Boden, J.M., Horwood, L.J., and Fergusson, D.M. (2007) 'Exposure to childhood sexual and physical abuse and subsequent educational achievement outcomes', *Child Abuse & Neglect*, 31(10): 1101–14.

Boulton, M.J. and Underwood, K. (1992) 'Bully/victim problems among middle school children', *British Journal of Educational Psychology*, 62(1): 73–87.

Cashmore, J. and Shackel, R. (2013) *The Long-term Effects of Child Sexual Abuse*. CFCA paper No. 11. Available at: http://www.aifs.gov.au/cfca/pubs/papers/a143161/index.html

Charach, A., Pepler, D., and Ziegler, S. (1995) 'Bullying at school – a Canadian perspective: A survey of problems and suggestions for intervention', *Education Canada*, 35(1): 12–18.

Chen, J.Q., Dunne, M.P., and Han, P. (2004) 'Child sexual abuse in China: A study of adolescents in four provinces', *Child Abuse & Neglect*, 28(11): 1171–86.

Cicchetti, D., Rogosch, F.A., Maughan, A., Toth, S.L., and Bruce, J. (2003) 'False belief understanding in maltreated children', *Development and Psychopathology*, 15(4): 1067–91.

Cossins, A. (2008) 'Children, sexual abuse and suggestibility: What laypeople think they know and what the literature tells us', *Psychiatry, Psychology and Law*, 15: 153–70.

Culp, R.E., Watkins, R.V., Lawerence, H., Letts, D., Kelly, D.J., and Rice, M.L. (1991) 'Maltreated children's language and speech development: Abused, neglected, and abused and neglected', *First Language*, 11(33): 377–89.

Cutajar, M.C., Mullen, P.E., Ogloff, J.R.P., Thomas, S.D., Wells, D.L., and Spataro, J. (2010) 'Suicide and fatal drug overdose in child sexual abuse victims: A historical cohort study', *Medical Journal of Australia*, 192(4): 184–7.

Damashek, A., McDiarmid Nelson, M., and Bonner, B.L. (in press) 'Fatal child maltreatment: Characteristics of deaths from physical abuse versus neglect', *Child Abuse & Neglect*, available online 11 June 2013.

Dorahy, M.J. and Clearwater, K. (2012) 'Shame and guilt in men exposed to childhood sexual abuse: A qualitative investigation', *Journal of Child Sexual Abuse*, 21(2): 155–75.

Eckenrode, J., Laird, M., and Doris, J. (1993) 'School performance and disciplinary problems among abused and neglected children', *Developmental Psychology*, 29(1): 53–62.

Egeland, B. and Sroufe, L.A. (1981) 'Attachment and early maltreatment', *Child Development*, 52(1): 44–52.

Farrington, D.P. (1991) 'Childhood aggression and adult violence: Early precursors and later life outcomes', in D.J. Pepler and K.H. Rubin (eds.), *The Development and Treatment of Childhood Aggression*. Hillsdale: LEA, pp. 5–30.

Fergusson, D.M. and Mullen, P.E. (1999) *Child Sexual Abuse: An Evidence-Based Perspective*. Thousand Oaks, CA: Sage Publications.

Fergusson, D.M., Boden, J.M., and Horwood, L.J. (2008) 'Exposure to childhood sexual and physical abuse and adjustment in early adulthood', *Child Abuse & Neglect*, 32: 607–19.

Finkelhor, D. (1994) 'The international epidemiology of child sexual abuse', *Child Abuse & Neglect*, 18(5): 409–17.

Finkelhor, D., Turner, H., and Ormrod, R. (2006) 'Kid's stuff: The nature and impact of peer and sibling violence on younger and older children', *Child Abuse & Neglect*, 30(12): 1401–21.

Finkelhor, D. and Jones, L. (2008) *Updated Trends in Child Maltreatment, 2006*. Crimes Against Children Research Center, University of New Hampshire.

Finkelhor, D., Jones, L., and Shattuck, A. (2011) *Updated Trends in Child Maltreatment, 2010*. Crimes Against Children Research Center, University of New Hampshire. Available at http://www.unh.edu/ccrc/pdf/CV203_Updated%20trends%202010%20FINAL_12-19-11.pdf

Finkelhor, D. and Jones, L. (2012) *Have Sexual Abuse and Physical Abuse Declined Since the 1990s?* Crimes against Children Research Center, University of New Hampshire. Available at: http://www.unh.ccrc

Finkelhor, D., Turner, H.A., and Hamby, S. (2012) 'Let's prevent peer victimization, not just bullying', *Child Abuse & Neglect, 36*(4): 271–4.

Glaser, D. (2000) 'Child abuse and neglect and the brain – A review', *Journal of Child Psychology and Psychiatry*, 41: 97–116.

Goldman, R. (29 March 2010) 'Teens indicted after allegedly taunting girl who hanged herself', *abc News*. Available at http://abcnews.go.com/Technology/TheLaw/teens-charged-bullying-mass-girl-kill/story?id=10231357

Gowen, J. (1993) *Effects of Neglect on the Early Development of Children: Final Report*. Washington, DC: National Clearinghouse on Child Abuse and Neglect, Administration for Children & Families.

Greeff, P. and Grobler, A.A. (2008) 'Bullying during the intermediate school phase: A South African study', *Childhood*, 15(1): 127–44.

Hahm, H.C. and Guterman, N.B. (2001) 'The emerging problem of physical child abuse in South Korea', *Child Maltreatment*, 6(2): 169–79.

Hazler, R.J., Hoover, H., and Oliver, R. (1991) 'Student perceptions of victimization by bullies in schools', *Journal of Humanistic Education and Development*, 29(4): 143 50.

Hildyard, K.L. and Wolfe, D.A. (2002) 'Child neglect: Developmental issues and outcomes', *Child Abuse & Neglect*, 26(6-7): 679–95.

Hoover, J.H., Oliver, R., and Hazler, R.J. (1995) 'Bullying: Perceptions of adolescent victims in the Midwestern USA', *School Psychology International*, 13(1): 5–16.

Horwitz, A.V., Widom, C.S., McLaughlin, J., and White, H.R. (2001) 'The impact of childhood abuse and neglect on adult mental health: A prospective study', *Journal of Health and Social Behavior*, 42(2): 184–201.

IPSCAN (2010) *World Perspectives on Child Abuse* (9th ed.).

Jalongo, M.R. (2006) 'The story of Mary Ellen Wilson: Tracing the origins of child protection in America', *Early Childhood Education Journal*, 34(1): 1–4.

Johnson, J.G., Cohen, P., Brown, J., Smailes, E.M. and Bernstein, D.P. (1999) 'Childhood maltreatment increases risk for personality disorders during early adulthood', *Archives of General Psychiatry*, 56(7): 600–6.

Kaufman, J.G. and Widom, C.S. (1999) 'Childhood victimization, running away, and delinquency', *Journal of Research in Crime and Delinquency*, 36(4): 347–455.

Ketsela, T. and Kedebe, D. (1997) 'Physical punishment of elementary school children in urban and rural communities in Ethiopia', *Ethiopian Medical Journal*, 35(1): 23–33.

Kim, J. and Cicchetti, D. (2010) 'Longitudinal pathways linking child maltreatment, emotion regulation, peer relations, and psychopathology' *Journal of Child Psychology and Psychiatry*, 51(6): 706–16.

Lansdown, G. (2006) *Betrayal of Trust: An overview of Save the Children's findings on children's experience of physical and humiliating punishment, child sexual abuse and violence when in conflict with the law*. Stockhom: Save the Children.

Limber, S., Flerx, V., Nation, M. and Melton, G. (1998) 'Bullying among school children in the United States', in M. Watts (ed.), *Contemporary Studies in Sociology (Vol. 18)*. Stamford, CT: Jai Press.

Loeber, R. and Disheon, T.J. (1984) 'Early predictors of male delinquency: A review', *Psychological Bulletin*, 94(1): 68–99.

Ma, S.J. (2004) *Just Listen to Me: Youth Voices on Violence*, Ontario Youth Roundtable Discussions on Violence. Office of Child and Family Advocacy and Voices for Children, Ontario, Canada.

Maxfield, M.G. and Widom, C.S. (1996) 'The cycle of violence: Revisited 6 years later', *Archives of Pediatric and Adolescent Medicine*, 150(4): 390–5.

McEachern, A.G., Kenny, M., Blake, E., and Alude, O. (2005) 'Bullying in schools: International variations', *Journal of Social Sciences*, 8: 51–8.

Melton, G.B. (2009) 'How Strong Communities restored my faith in humanity: Children can live in safety', in K.A. Dodge and D.L. Coleman (eds.), *Community Based Prevention of Child Maltreatment*. New York: Guilford, pp. 82–101.

Melton, G.B. (in press) 'Strong Communities for Children: A community-wide approach to prevention of child maltreatment', in J.E. Korbin and R.D. Krugman (eds.), *Handbook of Child Abuse and Neglect*. New York: Springer.

Melton, G.B. and Holaday, B.J. (eds.) (2008) 'Strong Communities as safe havens for children' (special issue), *Family and Community Health*, 31(2).

Mills, R., Scott, J., Alati, R., O'Callaghan, M., Najman, J.M., and Strathearn, L. (2013) 'Child maltreatment and adolescent mental health problems in a large birth cohort', *Child Abuse & Neglect*, 37(5): 292–302.

Mishna, F. (2004) 'A qualitative study of bullying from multiple perspectives', *Children & Schools*, 26(4): 234–47.

Naker, D. (2005) *Violence against Children: The Voices of Ugandan Children and Adults*. Raising Voices/ Save the Children in Uganda, Kampala: United Nations High Commissioner for Refugees.

Nansel, T.R., Overpeck, M., Pilla, R.S., Ruan, W.J., Simons-Morton, B., and Scheidt, P. (2001) 'Bullying behaviors among US youth: Prevalence and association with psychosocial adjustment', *Journal of the American Medical Association*, 285(16): 2094–100.

Ogawa, J.R., Sroufe, L.A., Weinfield, N.S., Carlson, E.A., and Egeland, B. (1997) 'Development and the fragmented self: Longitudinal study of dissociative symptomatology in a nonclinical sample', *Development and Psychopathology*, 9(4): 855–79.

Olweus, D. (1994) 'Bullying at school: Basic facts and effects of a school based intervention program', *Journal of Child Psychology and Psychiatry and Allied Disciplines*, 35(7): 1171–90.

Olweus, D. (1997) 'Bully/victim problems in school: Knowledge base and an effective intervention program', *Irish Journal of Psychology*, 18(2): 170–90.

Olweus, D. (2001) 'Peer harassment: A critical analysis and some important issues', in J. Juvonen and S. Graham (eds.), *Peer Harassment in School: The Plight of the Vulnerable and Victimized*. New York: Guilford Press, pp. 3–20.

O'Moore, A.M. and Hillery, B. (1989) 'Bullying in Dublin schools', *Irish Journal of Psychology*, 10(3): 426–41.

Pereda, N., Guilera, G., Forns, M. and Gomes-Benito, J. (2009) 'The prevalence of child sexual abuse in community and student samples: A meta-analysis', *Clinical Psychology Review*, 29(4): 328–38.

Perren, S., Ettekal, I., and Ladd, G. (2013) 'The impact of peer victimization on later maladjustment: Mediating and moderating effects of hostile and self-blaming attributions', *Journal of Child Psychology and Psychiatry*, 54(1): 46–55.

Pipe, M.E., Lamb, M.E., Orbach, Y., and Cederborg, A.C. (ds.)(2007) *Sexual Abuse: Disclosure, Delay, and Denial*. New York: Routledge Taylor & Francis Group.

Quas, J.A., Thompson, W.C., and Clarke-Stewart, K.A. (2005) 'Do jurors "know" what isn't so about child witnesses?', *Law and Human Behavior*, 29: 425–56.

Reijntjes, A., Kamphuis, J.H., Prinzie, P., and Telch, M.J. (2010) 'Peer victimization and internalizing problems in children: A meta-analysis of longitudinal studies', *Child Abuse and Neglect*, 34: 244–52.

Rigby, K. (2000) 'Effects of peer victimization in schools and perceived social support on adolescent well-being', *Journal of Adolescence*, 23(1): 57–68.

Rivera, B. and Widom, C.S. (1990) 'Childhood victimization and violent offending', *Violence and Victims*, 5(1): 19–35.

Romano, E., Bell, T., and Billette, J.-M. (2011) 'Prevalence and correlates of multiple victimization in a nationwide adolescent sample', *Child Abuse and Neglect*, 35: 468–79.

Ross, D.M. (2003) *Childhood Bullying, Teasing, and Violence: What School Personnel, other Professionals, and Parents Can Do* (2nd ed.). Alexandria, VA: American Counseling Association.

Sadowski, L.S., Hunter, W.M., Bangdiwala, S.I., and Munoz, S.R. (2004) 'The world studies of abuse in the family environment (WorldSAFE): A model of a multi-national study of family violence', *International Journal of Injury Control and Safety Promotion*, 11(2): 81–90.

Sameer, H. and Patchin, J.W. (2012) 'State cyberbullying laws a brief review of state cyberbullying laws and policies', *Cyberbullying Research Center*. Available at www.cyberbully.us

Sampson, R. (2002) 'Bullying in schools', *Problem-Oriented Guide for Police Series, Guide no. 12*. Available at www.cops.usdoj.gov

Sperry, D.M., & Spatz Widom, C. (2013). 'Child abuse and neglect, social support, and psychopathology in adulthood: A prospective investigation', *Child Abuse & Neglect*, 37, 415–425.

Toth, S., Harris, L., Goodman, G.S., and Cicchetti, D. (2011) 'Influence of violence and aggression on children's psychological development: Trauma, attachment, and memory', in M. Mikulincer and P.R. Shaver (eds.), *Understanding and Reducing Aggression, Violence, and Their Consequences.* Washington, DC: APA Books.

Toth, S.L., Cicchetti, D. and Kim, J. (2002) 'Relations among children's perceptions of maternal behavior, attributional styles, and behavioral symptomatology in maltreated children', *Journal of Abnormal Child Psychology*, 30(5): 487–500.

Trocme, N., Fallon, B., MacLaurin, B., Chamberland, C., Chabot, M. and Esposito, T. (2011) 'Shifting definitions of emotional maltreatment: An analysis child welfare investigation laws and practices in Canada', *Child Abuse and Neglect*, 35: 831–40.

United Nations Children's Fund (2005) *Changing a Harmful Social Convention: Female Genital Mutilation/Cutting.* Innocenti Digest, UNICEF Innocenti Research Center, Florence.

United Nations Study on Violence Against Children (2006) *World Report on Violence against Children.* Geneva: United Nations.

US Department of Health and Human Services, Administration on Children, Youth and Families (2011) *Child Maltreatment 2010.* Washington, DC: US Government Printing Office.

Whitney, I. and Smith, P.K. (1993) 'A survey of the nature and extent of bullying in primary and secondary schools', *Educational Research*, 35(1): 34–9.

Widom, C.S. (2001) 'Child abuse and neglect', in S. O. White (ed.), *Handbook of Youth and Justice.* New York: Plenum. pp. 31–47.

Widom, C.S. and Kuhns, J.B. (1996) 'Childhood victimization and subsequent risk for promiscuity, prostitution, and teenage pregnancy: A prospective study', *American Journal of Public Health*, 86(11): 1607–12.

World Health Organization (WHO) (1999) 'Child abuse and neglect by parents and other caregivers', in *Report of the Consultation on Child Abuse Prevention.* Geneva: World Health Organization.

World Health Organization (WHO) Consultation on Child Abuse Prevention (2002) *World Report on Violence and Health* (eds. E.G. Krug, L.L. Dahlberg, J.A. Mercy, A.B. Zwi, and R. Lozano). Geneva: World Health Organization.

World Health Organization (WHO) (2008) 'Inequalities in young people's health: Health behavior in school-aged children international report from the 2005/2006 survey', *Health Policy for Children and Adolescents*, 5. Available at http://www.hbsc.org/publications/international/

Youssef, R.M., Attia, M.S., and Kamel, M.I. (1998) 'Children experiencing violence I: Parental use of corporal punishment', *Child Abuse and Neglect*, 22: 959–73.

18

Children Living Away from Home

Judith Cashmore

INTRODUCTION

Children live away from their families and without the care of their parents for a range of reasons that vary in prevalence across developed and developing countries.[1] In the developed world, the most common reasons are the forced removal of children from their family by the state because of abuse, neglect, or abandonment, and the relinquishment or voluntary placement of children by parents to an agency. Voluntary placements include respite care and the need for specialized care, especially for children with disabilities or serious medical conditions. Within developed countries, particular sub-populations (for example, First Nation peoples in North America, Aboriginal children in Australia, Maori in New Zealand, and African-American children in the USA) are significantly over-represented for a number of reasons. These include poverty, dispossession, the fragmentation of traditional familial structures, and the high incidence of substance abuse and domestic violence, together with differences in the way they are treated by the child welfare systems and a lack of services in those communities (Thoburn, 2007).

In developing countries, family and environmental calamities are common reasons for children living apart from their parents and away from home. Large numbers of children in African and Asian countries are orphaned as the result of HIV/AIDS, or separated from their parents in the wake of a natural disaster or armed conflict. Internal migration and displacement, and urban and inter-country migration may also involve children's unaccompanied and unauthorized entry to other countries (see Goodnow, Chapter 19, this volume). It is also common for children in a number of countries to be 'shared' with or sent to other family members in kinship arrangements. These arrangements may be voluntary on the part of the birth mothers or imposed upon them by family members or community expectations. The purpose of these arrangements is variously to strengthen kinship bonds, to provide children with a better family environment, greater educational opportunities or instruction in trade, or for children to provide their labour and support in the home of the caregiver (Isiugo-Abanihe, 1985; Verhoef, 2005). There has been a robust debate about the relative benefits for children, their parents, and their caregivers, and in particular some concern about children's feelings about and reactions to these arrangements, especially when children are exploited, abused, or discriminated against in these arrangements (Verhoef, 2005).

Children may also live away from their families for educational purposes in both developed and developing countries. This includes children who move from rural or regional areas to the cities, or overseas, for their schooling. There is also an emerging trend in China and in some Western countries such as Australia, for children who live in the same city as their parents to live in boarding schools for much of the school term because of their parents' work commitments. Until relatively recently, children in Israel also lived in kibbutzim for both social and educational purposes. In developing countries, children also live away from their families as child labourers, often as the result of trafficking.

ARRANGEMENTS FOR CHILDREN LIVING AWAY FROM THEIR FAMILIES

Both within and across the developed and developing world, there is a range of arrangements for children who live away from their parents. These include kinship care, foster care with unrelated people, residential or institutional care, and adoption. There are, however, a number of differences in terminology and in 'historical, political and social contexts' among English-speaking and non-English speaking Western countries as well as developing countries which 'result in different patterns of service delivery for different groups of children' (Thoburn and Courtney, 2011: 211).

Kinship care

It has been quite common, and still is in many countries, for children to live with members of their extended family or kinship group. Kinship care is by far the most prevalent and accepted form of care in developing countries. In many African countries, it includes child-headed families where HIV/AIDS has left many sibling groups without parents or other adult relatives to care for them (Zimmerman, 2005). In Rwanda, for example, it was estimated that about one in eight households consisted of older children caring for their younger siblings (Cantwell, 2005).

In the developed world, kinship care includes care that is arranged within the family without state intervention and support, as well as those arrangements that are organized as a result of and involving state intervention. Formal kinship care with state intervention is a newer placement paradigm and is a result of a clear shift in policy over the last decade or so. There has been a shift from suspicion about the quality of care provided by relatives who are related to the maltreating parent to acknowledgement of the value to children of keeping alive their family and kinship networks, history, and identity. At the same time, kinship carers are helping to meet the shortfall in the supply of suitable carers in many developed countries as the numbers of children coming into and remaining in out-of-home care have been increasing.[2]

Formal foster care

Formal foster care provided by state or non-government agencies has a shorter history than informal foster or kinship care, and is largely confined to developed countries in Western Europe, North America, and Australasia. It can take a variety of forms, determined by the purpose and proposed length of stay. It ranges, for example, from emergency care for abandoned babies and children who need to be removed immediately for their safety and well-being, to short and medium-term care for children who cannot be looked after by their parents on what is expected to be a non-permanent basis. It also includes long-term care for abused and neglected children and for those who cannot be returned home but are unlikely to be adopted.

Much of the literature on children in out-of-home care concerns the provision of formal foster care and the outcomes for the children in these arrangements in developed countries in Europe, North America, and Australasia. Ironically, foster care in the developed world is facing increasing difficulties as a result of more children coming into care and staying longer just as the number of foster carers is falling. At the same time, foster care is being adopted in a number of former socialist countries where there is a move away from state-controlled institutions to foster care and family support (George, van Ouderhoven and Wazir, 2003). In developed countries, there is also a move to specialist or treatment foster care for older children and adolescents whose behaviour and past experiences have made them challenging to care for (Macdonald and Turner, 2008).

Residential or institutional care

Until the last few decades, residential or institutional care was one of the most prevalent forms of care in many countries for children who cannot live with their families.[3] Internationally, the term 'residential care for children and young people' covers an extraordinarily diverse range of provision including the large institutions of the kind often to be found in the former Soviet bloc (Lough and Panos, 2003), the small- to medium-size 'children's homes' or group care facilities run by local government or non-government agencies in many jurisdictions (Sinclair and Gibbs, 1998), and the private sector mental health facilities in the USA, as well as secure units (Courtney and Iwaniec, 2009). They vary in the age and needs of the children they cater for, and their purpose may include care, accommodation, education, and treatment, making cross-national comparisons very complex and difficult (Ainsworth and Thoburn, 2013). There is a great deal of variation in

terms of day-to-day practices, staffing levels, and the nature of staff training, philosophy, the links to the outside world and to the families of residents, resourcing, length of stay, after care provision, and so on. The worst of these were, and in some countries still are, large-scale and impersonal with multiple rotating staff.[4] Concerns about the effects on children, and the risks of physical and sexual abuse and bullying by both carers and residents within residential care institutions, has led to a move away from large-scale institutional care in a number of Western countries, though it continues in various forms and on a smaller scale in group homes for sibling groups and for children with disabilities, and as a base for therapeutic care for troubled older children and adolescents as a last resort for those who cannot be placed in family-based kinship or foster care. In mainland Europe, and particularly the Nordic countries, and Israel, group care is more common than in the UK, US, and other English-speaking countries (Thoburn and Courtney, 2011). It is also still a very common form of care in Eastern Europe, South America, and Asia, though there are now moves in many of these countries toward de-institutionalization in response to the principles and influence of the Convention on the Rights of the Child (Cantwell, 2005; Innocenti Research Centre, 2003; Thoburn, 2007).

Adoption

Adoption involves the termination of the legal relationship between children and their birth parents and the transfer of the parental responsibilities and rights to an adoptive parent.[5] In a number of countries, adoption has been seen as providing the best or only means of meeting children's need for permanency when they cannot remain with their parents. Historically, adoption was used as a means of both satisfying the longing of childless couples for children and providing a 'permanent' family for babies born to 'unmarried' mothers. The nature of adoption in developed countries has, however, changed dramatically over the last 25 years or so, with fewer babies being given up for adoption as a result of demographic and social changes.[6] Adoption in the UK, USA, and Australia is now more often of 'known' children by step-parents or other relatives or of children from other countries. Adoption is, however, not accepted in all cultures. Adoption by 'strangers', for example, is generally not regarded as an acceptable option for children in some cultures and countries (for example, Egypt: Megahead and Cesario, 2008). It is also seen as incompatible with the beliefs and kinship structures of some First Nation's people, including Australian Aboriginal people.

Children are commonly adopted outside the country of their birth via inter-country and international adoption. This was initially an ad hoc humanitarian response after World War II, and then the Korean and Vietnam Wars, and more recently from developing countries, especially in the aftermath of armed conflicts and other disastrous conditions. This practice has, however, provoked increasing criticism and regulation amid growing concern about the rights of children to know and be raised within their own communities. Such concerns have been amplified by reports of gross abuses and trafficking. Although the Convention on the Rights of the Child recognizes 'that inter-country adoption may be considered as an alternative means of [a] child's care, if the child cannot be placed in a foster or an adoptive family or cannot in any suitable manner be cared for in the child's country of origin' (Article 21), it emphasizes the State party's duty to 'ensure that the best interests of the child' are 'the paramount consideration' in any adoption.

More recently, adoption is being used in a number of countries to provide 'permanency' for children who have been through the child protection system. This is based on the view that foster care is inherently temporary and incapable of providing a satisfactory long-term alternative which can give children

a sense of permanence and of 'being wanted'.[7] The rate of adoption of children from the child welfare systems in countries such as Australia, England, Sweden, the USA, and Canada varies markedly. In Australia, for example, very few children are adopted from care.[8] In contrast, in England and the USA, adoption of children in care is actively encouraged by government policy, by using timelines and the dispensation of parental consent, and by incentives to agencies (Quinton and Selwyn, 2009; Thoburn, 2007; Thoburn and Courtney, 2011; Thomas, 2013).

CHILDREN'S EXPERIENCES LIVING AWAY FROM HOME

Although millions of children live away from their families for a range of reasons and in a variety of arrangements, the vast bulk of research concerns children in foster care, residential care, kinship care, and adoption in developed countries, though there is now a quite sizeable literature about homeless children and youth and street-children, especially in developing countries. Most of the research, however, has been concerned with the outcomes for children and young people in these arrangements rather than an understanding of their views and their lived experiences (Dunn, Culhane and Taussig, 2010; Winokur, Holtan and Valentine, 2009). Studies that have sought the views of children and young people have often done so as one aspect of outcome studies in relation to those currently in care; others have relied upon the retrospective accounts of adults looking back and reporting on their time in care, or on the ratings of social workers on the perceived quality of care children were receiving.

More recently, there has been increased interest in and recognition of the value of hearing and understanding what children and young people have to say about their experiences. In research terms, children's own contemporaneous accounts of their experiences can fill out and make more meaningful the measures and interpretation of outcomes-focused research (Gilligan, 2000). For example, as Unrau (2007: 134) pointed out, children's perspectives about what constitutes stability are likely to provide important insights with significant implications for both research and policy:

> Case record data represent placement moves as an artefact of the system instead of an event experienced by children and other people in the context of the system. Ignoring or overlooking the standpoint of foster children in research on placement moves leaves a major gap in understanding this important dimension of the foster care experience, as well as the impressions or scars left by the move experience. Such gaps in research can also lead to incomplete policy. For example, despite the fact that case record data only account for physical living arrangement locations of children, the cut-off value of three or more placements has routinely been interpreted by researchers and policymakers to infer placement stability versus instability.

In relation to practice, children's perspectives can play an important role in contributing to more accurate assessments and to more informed and more workable decisions for children who cannot live with their parents (Gilligan, 2000; Schofield, 2005). As Holland (2009: 232) pointed out, a number of studies using different methodologies have shown that children and adults often have 'different understandings of key concepts or different priorities'. There are also powerful legal, ethical, and therapeutic reasons for listening to and understanding children's perspectives (Cashmore, 2002; Gilligan, 2000). Recognition and respect for children are central to these arguments and in line with the Convention on the Rights of the Child (Archard and Skivenes, 2009; Bessell and Gal, 2011; Melton, 2006).

Types of studies and measures

Most of the research on children's views and experiences of living away from home in the developed countries and some studies in developing countries have been conducted

via large- and small-scale surveys and structured or semi-structured individual interviews with children and young people currently in care or after they have left those arrangements. The survey, interview, and some focus group studies have covered a wide range of topics including (1) children's perceptions of their relationships with their families, carers, case-workers and peers, (2) how they are getting on at school, and health-wise, and the extent to which they understand the reasons for not living at home, (3) whether and how they would like to be involved in the decisions that are made about their lives, and (4) what they think their future holds for them. These areas and the content of the open- and closed-ended questions have, with some notable exceptions (Mason, 2008), generally been determined by the researchers (Alderson and Morrow, 2004; Holland, 2009; Winter, 2006). Most have been conducted by academics, often in collaboration with care agencies; others have been conducted by government and non-government agencies responsible for providing or monitoring children's care (Shaw, 1998; Tarnai and Krebill-Prather, 2008; Wilson and Conroy, 1999) and also by advocacy organizations (McDowall, 2013; Timms and Thoburn, 2003). These include the use of the Looking After Children assessment, a case-planning and review system used in various jurisdictions in the UK, Canada, and Australia to monitor and promote positive care experiences and development for children in care (Kufeldt et al., 2006; Ward, 1998; Wise, 1999).

Although most structured or semi-structured interviews and surveys have comprised a series of open- and closed-ended qualitative and quantitative questions, some have included more innovative approaches and standardized scales. Standardized self-report measures or techniques such as the Kvaebek Family Sculpture Technique (Gardner, 2004a, 2004b) or Family Assessment measure (FAM; Kufeldt, Armstrong and Dorosh, 1995) and a variation on the 'Five Field' map (Heptinstall, Bhopal and Brannen, 2001) have also been used in several studies to obtain children's and adults' perceptions of their relationships with their birth and foster families.

Longitudinal studies

There has been a small number of prospective longitudinal studies of children in the out-of-home care systems in the USA, the UK (Farmer and Lutman, 2010; Schofield, 2003), Australia (Delfabbro, Barber and Cooper, 2002; Fernandez, 2007), Sweden (Andersson, 2005; Vinnerljung and Sallnas, 2008) and Canada (Flynn, Robitaille and Ghazal, 2006). Most have been concerned with the outcomes for children in care but have also sought children's views about their experiences and placements. Most have involved interviews with relatively small samples of about 50–100 children or young people, with the interviews generally supplementing case record analyses and measures from carers, workers, and other professionals. Schofield's study, Growing Up in Foster Care, for example, started with 53 children aged 3–12 in England who had a long-term foster plan in 1997–98, were followed up in 2001–03, and again in 2005–06 but with significant attrition to only 20 children at the third wave; it also involved interviews with foster carers, birth parents, and social workers.

The earliest of these longitudinal studies were three landmark studies – two in the USA by Fanshel and colleagues (Fanshel and Shinn, 1978; Fanshel, Finch and Grundy, 1990) and Festinger (1983) and the other in the UK by Triseliotis (1980). All three were retrospective studies, with young people and young adults interviewed on average about seven or more years after they left foster care. Triseliotis's study in the UK was focused on the experience of foster care through the eyes of 40 children born in 1956–57 who spent between seven and fifteen years in a single foster care home. Children's accounts were matched with the accounts of their foster carers. The largest study, by Fanshel and

Shinn, involved 624 children placed in foster care in New York in 1966 for at least 90 days, but it was concerned more with the impact of moves and other factors on children's outcomes than their experiences per se. Festinger's (1983) study involved 349 young people aged 22 to 25 who had been in foster and residential care in New York for at least five years and was clearly focused on their experiences in care. More recently, there have been a series of studies with young people as they leave care or after they have left out-of-home care, with several small-scale longitudinal studies (Cashmore and Paxman, 2006, in Australia; Stein and Carey, 1986, in England) and some larger longitudinal studies following young people ageing out of care in the USA (Courtney et al., 2007).

There are also several ongoing large-scale prospective longitudinal studies using representative samples of children currently in out-of-home care in the USA. Both the National Survey of Child and Adolescent Wellbeing (NSCAW) and the Longitudinal Studies of Child Abuse and Neglect (LONGSCAN) focus on children who have had contact with child protection services. Both involve sub-samples of children and young people who are or have been in out-of-home care. NSCAW includes a nationally representative sample of 727 children aged 0–14 years, 12 months after they had entered care. LONGSCAN included at one site a sample of 327 maltreated children who entered out-of-home care following their involvement with the child protection system. Both studies, especially NSCAW, have resulted in a number of publications concerning the outcomes for children as well as some on children's perceptions of their time in care (Chapman, Wall and Barth, 2004).[9] More recently, two large-scale longitudinal studies of children entering care and young people leaving care in two states in Australia (New South Wales and Victoria) are underway (NSW: *Pathways of Care, NSW* and Victoria: *Beyond 18*).

Ethnographic or observational studies

Although there have been a number of qualitative studies of children in out-of-home care in Western countries, there have been few ethnographic or observational studies apart from several carried out in residential care (Emond, 2003, 2010; Holland, 2009; Torronen, 2006), foster care (Rees and Pithouse, 2008), and some with homeless young people and those leaving care (Horrocks, 2002; Winter, 2006). Courtney's (2000: 756) call for further research to better understand the outcomes and experiences of children in out-of-home care reflects this:

> Among other things, the field needs rigorously designed ethnographic studies of child welfare agencies, development of grounded theory to help explain the experiences of the system by its various players, and focus group research that can allow service providers, parents, and children to describe what is really happening in the system.

In developing countries, however, there have been quite a few detailed case studies and ethnographic studies, particularly with homeless and street children. A primary aim of such an approach is to build a relationship with children over time that allows the researcher to observe the children's everyday activities and experiences in their natural setting. This was not always the first method of choice but was forced upon the researchers because they failed with their planned survey and interview methods, first in gaining access or trust and secondly in getting reliable information (Turnbull, Hernández and Reyes, 2009). In studies with street children in Kenya, Mexico, Uganda, China, and the USA, researchers have invested months or even years in becoming 'embedded', 'hanging around', and gaining trust by helping out at the soup kitchen, in outreach activities, and by paying for medical treatment. At the same time, they were observing and learning about the experiences and perceptions, inter-relationships and networks of support of these children and young people.

Their time and effort was repaid by much more reliable information and understanding of the diversity and culture and networks among the various sub-groups of children – for example, the 'begging boys', 'market boys', and 'plastic bag boys' in Kaime-Atterhög and Ahlberg's (2008: 1348) study in Kenya. These researchers also came to understand the street-wise competence of street-children in discerning what researchers and other outsiders want and, for example, lying to say their mother is dead to evoke more sympathy (Kaime-Atterhög and Ahlberg, 2008). In one study with street-children in Kampala, Young, and Barrett (2001) used a combination of ethnographic, oral child-led 'radio interviews' and visual methods to obtain information about the children's activities and reflections on their lives. These methods engaged the children's interest and the use of mental map drawings and photo diaries, and also allowed researchers to see spaces and activities that were otherwise inaccessible to them – literally 'through the child's eyes'.

In summary, the most common methods for trying to understand the current or retrospective views and experiences of children living away from their families are semi-structured interviews with older children and young people. In both developed and developing countries, however, more varied and engaging approaches that include ethnographic and visual methods such as photo diaries and mapping are increasingly being used, and there are also attempts to include children who have to date been less accessible, including young children, street-children, and children with disabilities. Apart from some notable exceptions (Schofield et al., 2000), most studies have not included children under 8 or 10, but age-appropriate techniques like those used by Schofield and her colleagues (puppets, eco-maps, pictures, and story-stem completions) are being developed and extended for use with younger children. These include the use of drawings, narratives and life stories, and the 'mosaic approach', which combines a number of tools including child observation, cameras for children to take photos, map-making, and magic carpet 'tours' (Clark and Statham, 2005; Fury, Carlson and Sroufe, 1997).

CHILDREN'S VIEWS AND EXPERIENCES

Children whose adverse circumstances cause them to live away from their families face a number of challenges and transitions that their peers living with their families do not. These include leaving and living apart from their biological parents, changes in their routines and home environment and in their school and neighbourhood settings, the loss of friends, and often multiple moves and insecurity. The challenges facing these children and young people and their poor developmental outcomes are consistently documented in research in Western countries – poor academic attainment, emotional and behavioural problems, poor physical and mental health, and difficulties in maintaining or forming relationships with their carers, their family, and peers. For example, overall young people 'ageing out of care' in Australia and in Canada, England, Ireland, Scotland, and the United States have consistently been shown to have low levels of educational attainment, and high rates of unemployment, mobility, homelessness, financial difficulty, loneliness, and physical and mental health problems (Biehal et al., 1995; Broad, 1999; Courtney et al., 2007; Dixon and Stein, 2005; Kufeldt and McKenzie, 2003; Mendes, 2009; Pecora et al., 2003; Stein, 2004; Stein and Carey, 1986).[10]

There is, however, also considerable variability, with various sub-groups of children entering care for different reasons and for different periods of time. Some children and young people in out-of-home care and after leaving care do well, others less well, and some do very poorly and in so doing, contribute disproportionately to the negative findings (Brand and Brinich, 1999; Brandon and

Thoburn, 2008; Forrester et al., 2009; Jahnukainen, 2007; McCue et al., 2001; Thoburn and Courtney, 2011; Wade et al., 2010; Widom, 1991). The explanations for their poorer outcomes relate both to their pre-care background and experiences, and to particular adverse aspects of their care experience, including the kind of care setting (kinship care, foster care, or residential care), and a range of other factors such as how old they were when they were removed from their family, whether they stayed in care for a short or a long period, and how stable and secure their living arrangements are – as well as likely complex interactions involving gene–environment interdependence (Brandon and Thoburn, 2008; Fernandez and Barth, 2010; Rutter, 2000, 2007).

Not surprisingly, children in care generally fare more poorly than their peers living with their parents. However, the overall conclusion from various longitudinal studies is that children who entered care and stayed there – especially in stable foster or kinship care – were generally 'better off' in terms of their behavioural and emotional adjustment and 'quality of life' than those who returned home or were not removed (Bellamy, 2008; Davidson-Arad, 2005, 2010; Fanshel and Shinn, 1978; Gibbons et al., 1995; Lahti, 1982; Lau et al., 2003; Lawrence, Carlson and Egeland, 2006; Rubin et al., 2007; Sinclair et al., 2005; Taussig, Clyman and Landsverk, 2001; Wald, Carlsmith and Leiderman, 1988).[11] These differences in outcomes occur despite the fact that the children who remained in care have been found to be more likely than those who returned to their families to have behavioural and health problems or disabilities (Landsverk et al., 1996; Littell and Schuerman, 1995). On the other hand, several US studies have reported negative findings for children in care (Doyle, 2007; Lawrence et al., 2006) and a large-scale US study using multiple methods to adjust for selection bias found that out-of-home placement had little effect on children's cognitive skills or behaviour problems (Berger et al., 2009).

Children's own views tend to be more positive though again with some variation. Most children and young people in (foster) care, and after leaving care, in studies in Western countries have consistently reported that they were 'better off' in care than they would have been if they had remained with their parents (Cashmore and Paxman, 1996; Festinger, 1983; Hines, Merdinger and Wyatt, 2005; Johnson, Yoken and Voss, 1995; Kufeldt, Armstrong and Dorosh, 1995; Minty, 1999; Sinclair et al., 2005; Ward, Skuse and Munro, 2005; Wilson and Conroy, 1999).[12] In a number of other studies, at least three-quarters of the children in foster care said they were generally happy and positive about the care they were receiving and how they were treated (Chapman, Wall and Barth, 2004; Delfabbro, Barber and Bentham, 2002; Festinger, 1983; McDowall, 2013; Selwyn, Saunders and Farmer, 2010; Triseliotis, 1984). In a US mixed-method study involving 180 9–11-year-olds, children who had been sexually and emotionally abused and who were satisfied with their current caregivers said they were better off in care whereas those who had been physically abused or were in group care said their lives would have been better at home with their family of origin (Dunn et al., 2010). Although some were ambivalent and others clearly wished that their home circumstances were different so that they could have remained at home, a number of children and young people have said that being in care was better than the alternative – 'being on the streets', 'being dead', or being seriously injured (Cashmore and Paxman, 1996; Hines et al., 2005; Sinclair et al., 2005; Ward et al., 2005). In the words of an American college student who had been in foster care:

> Gosh, anything was better than living with my mother. I never had to worry about any abuse or anything like that in my foster homes. . . . That's when I started being, feeling more comfortable and stuff. ... I mean that's when I really started blooming.
>
> (Hines et al., 2005: 390)

While Flynn et al. (2006) and others have concluded that the views of children and young people in a number of countries have consistently been generally favourable about being in foster care (compared with the alternative), some caution is needed. Most of these studies have involved children in foster care in the United States, England, and Australia and because they are accessible, they are more likely than non-respondents to be in stable care. One small Australian study indicates that Aboriginal children may well be unhappier in out-of-home care than their non-Indigenous counterparts (Higgins et al., 2007) so the possible bias in response needs to be taken into account.

Key aspects of children's experiences in care

Children living in foster care face some common issues – not living with their own families, having to adapt to and learn the rules and expectations in another family, not being sure of their tenure there, and whether or when they can have contact with their own family and possibly return to live with them (Mitchell and Kuczynski, 2010; O'Neill, 2004; Sinclair, 2005).

Several thoughtful reviews of the research literature and the 'messages' from research concerning children in care in the UK and the United States have pointed to a number of key concerns and requirements for children in care (Berridge, 2007; Fox and Berrick, 2007; Gilligan, 2000; Sinclair, 2005). In summary, these include a sense of security and belonging, a feeling of 'normality' including educational opportunities, respect for and contact with their family of origin, and some sense of control and respect for their views.

Sense of security and belonging

Although the outcomes literature in Western countries has understandably focused considerable attention on 'permanency' and 'stability' (particularly the number and pattern of 'placements' children experience during their time in care), children and young people tend to concentrate more on feeling loved and cared for than on 'permanency' per se. For young people in a Californian study, for example, the relational and emotional aspects of permanency were more important than the legal and physical aspects (Sanchez, 2004). In the words of two of these young people:

> The priority should be emotionally stable placements. A place where a youth actually feels comfortable, they feel secure, they feel like they're loved, they feel like they can love. Then think about adoption.
> Legal permanence could be taken off the list and I wouldn't miss it. You can have legal permanency – but without relational or physical permanency, what's the point? By law you have to stay here. Without the last two, the first is not important. They all really feed each other.
> (Sanchez, 2004: 10)

Similarly, Lahti (1982) found that children's sense of permanence came from the inclusiveness of the placement and was associated with the success of the placement; it was not necessarily associated with legal permanence.

Cross-culturally, a small study involving maltreated children living in institutional care in Japan focused on the primacy of emotional well-being and relationships, and in particular the Japanese concept of *Ibasho*. Literally meaning 'whereabouts,' Ibasho 'connotes a place where a person feels a sense of peace, security, satisfaction, acceptance, belonging, and coziness' (Bamba and Haight, 2007: 405). Based on children's views and those of the professional informants, Bamba and Haight (2007: 421) concluded:

> permanency has meaning only to the extent that it facilitates the child's Ibasho creation within the home. If the child is only legally bound to a home, but their psychological needs such as a sense of belonging are not be [sic] met, permanency has little meaning. Legal status is important, but the legal status alone may not meet the 'best interests of the child,' by facilitating children's sense of Ibasho.

When different forms of out-of-home care are compared, children in kinship care generally report feeling more emotionally secure than those in foster care with unrelated people, and children and young people in residential or group care almost always report being less happy, less connected with their carers, and less satisfied with their care experience than those in either kinship or foster care (Chapman, Wall and Barth, 2004; Colton, 1989; Delfabbro, Barber and Bentham, 2002). The evidence in relation to adoption is mixed. On the one hand, some children in long-term permanent placements have said they were keen to be adopted, especially if they had been living with that family since they were quite young (Sinclair et al., 2005). Most who were adopted were happy with their 'new' families (Parker, 1999). Others, and especially older children, however, often do not wish to be adopted particularly if they see it as jeopardizing their relationship with their birth family (Thoburn, 2003).

These findings are consistent with the findings of outcome studies in this and other areas and also with the broader child development literature. As various researchers and commentators back to John Bowlby have pointed out, children's attachments and sense of emotional security and belonging in care are critical aspects of their 'care' experience and important indicators of the 'success' of their placement and of their longer-term outcomes. Stability in children's living arrangements and continuity of place are clearly important and allow children to 'put down roots' and develop a network of relationships, but the critical element of children's lived experience is their perception of the security and quality of the care they receive. This perception or sense of security – of feeling loved and cared for – has been found to be associated with better outcomes for children in out-of-home care and for young people leaving or 'ageing' out of care (Andersson, 2005; Cashmore, 2006; Daniel, Wassell and

Gilligan, 1999; Perry, 2006; Samuels, 2008; Schofield, 2002, 2003; Stein, 2004; Tarren-Sweeney, 2008).

The importance of relationships

Critical to children's sense of security and belonging is the quality of their relationships, both within their living and care arrangements and beyond that. These relationships include those with family members, alternative carers, peers and friends, workers, and mentors.

Family relationships and connections

Living away from their families – and the reasons for doing so – adds a level of complexity, and often considerable ambivalence, to children's relationships with their families and their views about those relationships. Some homeless and street children have chosen to leave, and others have no parents or family members who are available and willing to support them. When children in kinship, foster, and residential care have been removed or sent away from their families, they are often quite ambivalent about their parents, with feelings of loss, anger, and betrayal (Mason, 2008; Messing, 2006; Schofield, 2005). A 15-year-old Australian in Gardner's (2004a: 180) study, for example, commented 'angrily':

> Your Mum, all she did was carry you around for nine months and then she gave birth to you ... My real family are the people around me now, who, you know are there every day for you. ...

The complexity of the ambiguous position for many children in foster care, especially long-term foster care with non-related people, is outlined clearly by one woman who had been in long term care:

> At times I feel ... I'm sort of caught in a no-win situation. She [foster mother] makes me feel like a daughter, but then ... I don't know if it suits her, or she doesn't think about it or what, I'm treated as an outsider. ... And it gets very hard for me. Because I don't know exactly where I'm at.
> (Gardner, 2004b: 195)

Children's views about their families – who they see as 'family', who they call 'mum' and 'dad', and whether and how much they wish to see members of their family of origin – were mixed and diverse. In one Australian study of children in long-term foster care, for example, 65 per cent of children aged 8–15 omitted their biological parents when asked to indicate who they included in their 'family', but 90 per cent included their foster parents; the figures for the adults who were formerly in long-term foster care were similar (59 per cent and 77 per cent, respectively; Gardner, 2004a).

Some children express no wish to see more of their biological parents or be reunited with them. However, most children in kinship and foster care, as well as those in residential care, want to see and have more contact with their family of origin. Most often this is with their siblings, and their mothers more than their fathers (Chapman, Wall and Barth, 2004; Fernandez, 2007; Fox and Berrick, 2007). Children in kinship care report having more contact with their family members than children living with unrelated foster carers, but this generally depends on the relationship between the carers and the parents, in developing and developed countries and in Indigenous communities (Fox and Berrick, 2007; Pecora, Prohn and Nasuti, 1999; Verhoef, 2005).

Peer relationships

For some children without adult carers, their primary relationships are with their peers. For street children and homeless youth, for example, their primary protection and sense of belonging generally come from their peer group (Ayuku et al., 2004; Kaime-Atterhög and Ahlberg, 2008; Kombarakaran, 2004). In a study that involved participant observation, informal interviews and group discussions with 'street boys' in Kenya, three distinct groups of 'market' boys, 'begging' boys, and 'plastic bag' boys were found to have strong bonds of friendship and mutual support in relation to 'food, work, security, shelter, and general welfare' (Kaime-Atterhög and

Ahlberg, 2008: 1353). These street boys, like those reported in other studies and countries, described a strong sense of group solidarity and 'family', variously defined by their own specific form of street economy or work, their music and language, and meeting and sleeping places and lodgings (Beazley, 2003a, 2003b; Oliveira and Burke, 2009).

Peers may also be very important to children's sense of identity and belonging in residential care settings (Bamba and Haight, 2007; Emond, 2003, 2010). Some of these relationships, however, may be unhappy and even harmful, with peers sometimes being the source of sexual harassment and bullying (Freundlich, Avery and Padgett, 2007; Gibbs and Sinclair, 1999). Bryony, quoted in Emond's year long ethnographic study of life in two residential units in Scotland makes the point that life in a children's home is powerfully influenced by fellow residents:

> At the end of the day you only have each other. The staff are lovely but they're paid to be here and there's no getting out of that. They can't be with us every minute so it's up to us to make the place home ... make sure it's the way we want it ... no one is allowed to get too big for their boots here ... it just spoils it for everyone. The staff cannae stop that happening, that's for us to do.
>
> (Bryony, quoted in Emond, 2002)

Children in other forms of care such as kinship and foster care have also indicated in a number of research studies that being placed with their siblings and their friendships with peers at school and elsewhere are very important to them. Indeed, the loss of friends and their connection with school are significant losses for children who enter care and move from one placement to another within out-of-home care. In one American study, a third of the pre-adolescent children in foster care identified friends as the people they missed most when they had to move (Johnson et al., 1995). These are losses that seem often to be underestimated in adult perspectives and understandings of the effects on children of being in care (Mason, 2008; Unrau, Seita and Putney, 2008).

Relationships with workers and mentors

The importance of connectedness and support for children and adolescents in care in Western countries goes beyond their family, carer, and peer relationships. In several studies, children and adolescents as well as young adults formerly in care, who said they had a supportive network or at least one adult other than their parents or carers they could turn to in a crisis, have been found to have more stability in care and better outcomes than those without such support (Andersson, 2005; Cashmore and Paxman, 2006; Farmer, Moyers and Lipscombe, 2004; Lahti, 1982; Perry, 2006). Perry (2006), for example, reported that adolescents in foster care in the US who had strong networks were less likely to have symptoms of depression, and that those in stable placements and in kinship care had stronger networks than those in group care.

Clearly relationships matter both in experiential terms and in terms of their outcomes (Bell, 2002; Fox and Berrick, 2007; Mason, 2008; Schofield, 2002; Winter, 2006). What matters to children and adolescents in these circumstances in relation to people beyond the family is having someone (else) who cares. In a series of recent and not so recent studies, children in care and homeless young people refer to the importance of having workers who are friendly, responsive, trustworthy, reliable, kind, and approachable (Barnes, 2007; Bell, 2002; Davies and Wright, 2008). In a peer research study with homeless young people in the Netherlands, one young person commented on the ideal social worker as being 'someone who doesn't regard you as a client, but treats you as an ordinary human being and trusts you' (de Winter and Noom, 2003: 336).

Normalcy, lack of stigma, or differential treatment

A key issue for children in out of home care is their wish for normalcy – not to be treated differently from other children or stigmatized because they cannot live with their families

(Gilligan, 2001). Adoption may therefore minimize this concern, just as it removes agency workers' intrusions.

In studies in Western countries, a significant minority of children have indicated that they have felt uncomfortable and awkward when asked questions about their 'care status'; they often have not told their peers at school that they were not living with their parents, even when living with relatives (Hines et al., 2005; Kufeldt, Simard and Vachon, 2003; Unrau et al., 2008). Some children in foster care were upset that they were treated differently – and unfairly – compared with the carer's own or biological children. Being included in family holidays, having their own bedroom, and eating the same food were important concerns of children in foster care (Cashmore and Paxman, 1996; Johnson et al., 1995; Sinclair et al., 2005).

Differential treatment is clearly not confined to fostering with non-relatives, however, and although it is generally assumed that there is less stigma attached to children living with relatives than with non-relatives, there is relatively little research evidence to support this (Cuddeback, 2004; Messing, 2006). Certainly none of the adults who were fostered to relatives in a study in Ghana indicated that they would 'give their own children away' to relatives because of their own negative experiences, and some of the children currently fostered indicated that they did not like the way they were treated, particularly when that was different from the other children in the household (Kuyini et al., 2009). In several studies in different communities, some of the children, and adults formerly in kinship care, have reported that they were required to work harder, received poorer quality food and clothing and bedding, and did not receive the same health care when they were ill as the other children in the household (Kuyini et al., 2009; Oni, 1995). In some cases, in both developing and developed countries, children's treatment was clearly abusive (for example, whipping and denigration), though in some countries harsh physical punishment was normative (Kuyini et al., 2009). Children's difficulties were exacerbated by their inability to question what was being done to them and the expectation that they did not report back to their parents on any difficulties they were experiencing (Kuyini et al., 2009; Oni, 1995).

Voice and personal respect

The feeling that they have little control over their lives and what happens to them is a consistent theme in what children and young people in formal and informal care in Western countries say about their experience in care. From children's accounts, this is a result of not being given appropriate information or not understanding why they are in care, feeling that their views are not welcomed or respected, and having few or no choices.

Children's responses to their removal from their families and subsequent changes in their living arrangements indicate that appropriate information is critical at times of transition. The main complaint of children in several US and UK studies concerned the way the transition into care was handled. Most children in several qualitative studies of children aged between 8 and 15 years reported that they were 'removed' without warning and with little explanation about what was happening and why, so that they felt confused, threatened, and abandoned (Folman, 1998; Johnson et al., 1995; Mitchell and Kuczynski, 2010; O'Neill, 2004). A substantial minority of children (40 per cent) in these and other studies did not know why they were in care or were confused about it, and many were uncertain about what was ahead of them when they left their families (Mitchell et al., 2010; Unrau et al., 2008). A 10-year-old Canadian girl, for example, advised case-workers that some information would be helpful:

> Maybe just tell them what's going on and stuff first ... Like you're going to be taking them and just give them a brief example of what's going to be happening and stuff I guess.
>
> (Mitchell et al., 2010: 7)

Children in a range of formal and informal out-of-home care arrangements have commonly reported having few choices and being subject to the decisions made by adults in which their views were often not asked for or not listened to (deWinter and Noom, 2003; Festinger, 1983; Johnson et al., 1995; Unrau et al., 2008). There is, however, considerable evidence that children value having some say in decisions that are made about them and that such participation is associated with the success of their placements (Selwyn et al., 2010; Sinclair et al., 2005; Thomas and O'Kane, 1999). Sinclair (2005), for example, found that children's placements were more likely to disrupt if the children did not want to be fostered or placed into a particular home. Thomas and O'Kane (1999) cited the case of a child being better able to move on and adjust to a change in placement after having some say over the decision even though it did not work out. In some cases, children have exercised some choice in where they wished to live by moving in with former carers or relatives or by forcing a change by 'acting out' or running away (Christiansen, Havik and Anderssen, 2010; Hines et al., 2005; Messing, 2006; Selwyn et al., 2010). In these circumstances, children's behaviour provided the best indication of their views, with one young Norwegian woman saying, 'I didn't want to live there, so I did everything I could to avoid that' (Christiansen et al., 2010: 917).

The focus on children's voices and choices is more apparent as an exception than the rule in the literature from developing countries. Verhoef (2005: 378), for example, referred to children in 'joint venture' foster arrangements, agreed to by both the child's mother and the carer, as being the only group in that study 'where children seemed able to voice their opinions about where they lived'. In other studies about street-children, a number of children in different countries had exercised some choice by leaving their parents to live independently and by resisting any move for them to return home, or to be organized in any institutional way (Lam and Cheng, 2008).

Methodological and ethical issues

Although the value of hearing children's voices, especially vulnerable children, is increasingly recognized in academic research and policy areas, it is not easily achieved. The major barrier is gaining access to children in care and in other living arrangements and then gaining their trust and participation. Children in formal out-of-home care arrangements, those in non-formal or non-existent care arrangements (for example, homeless children and street-children), and younger children are often difficult to access for different reasons.

The logistical and consent processes for children in foster care and residential care in Western countries can be complex and lengthy. The consent of various people and agencies in the child's life is generally required, and there are numerous reasons that carers, birth parents, case-workers, and the statutory and other agencies may not allow access to children in care (Berrick, Frasch and Fox, 2000).[13] Several studies and reviews of the reasons for children's exclusion indicate that, apart from being unwilling or not having the time to cooperate with the research, those involved in making the decision – case-workers and carers – are concerned about the possible distress or upset to the child or the risk of disrupting 'fragile' placements or those that are 'going well' (Gilbertson and Barber, 2002; Heptinstall, 2000; Murray, 2005). Because children are generally the last people to be asked if they would like to participate in telling their story, this omission, even if intended to be protective, raises concerns about children's right to have their say and participate in research, especially more troubled children who may be distressed about their living arrangements. Murray's (2005: 60) review of 38 Quality Protects studies of adoption and fostering in the UK that did involve children found that 'it was not poor response rates from children and young people themselves that accounted for their non-participation in research' but the gatekeeping by those making decisions on their behalf.

There are significant methodological concerns about the exclusion of these children and young people, especially those deemed more 'vulnerable'. It compromises the capacity to generalize from and rely on findings that are based on restricted sampling. As McDonald et al. (1996) noted in their review of outcome studies to assess the long-term effects of foster care, the failure to achieve target sample sizes and retain them was a major problem in all the reviewed studies, and one that was not considered in reporting the findings. Murray (2005) raised another possibility concerning gender bias. In the studies Murray reviewed for which details about gender of the participants were available, there were more girls than boys. This observation led to the tentative hypothesis of 'gendered gatekeeping'. In one study of adoptive children, for example, the bias in favour of girls was 'due to parents passing more invitations to participate in the project to girls rather than boys', rather than to any difference in boys and girls agreeing to participate (Thomas et al., 1999: 13).

For homeless and street-children, gatekeeping and consent processes are less of an issue but accessibility, trust, and the reliability of the information provided may pose significant problems. Therefore, a number of researchers have engaged key informants to gain access and used protracted ethnographic approaches to gain trust. Although homeless and street children may have a degree of autonomy and more fluidity in their lifestyle than children in more traditional living arrangements, they have their own networks and means of protecting their identity and providing group solidarity (Beazley, 2003b). Researchers as 'outsiders' therefore often have a great deal of difficulty breaking through their barriers and need the assistance of key informants to gain access and to provide 'insider information' to let them know when what they are seeing or being told is 'for their benefit' rather than an accurate reflection of their experiences and way of life (Kaime-Atterhög and Ahlberg, 2008; Young and Barrett, 2001). Of course, as Ryen (2008) and Lietz, Langer, and Furman (2006) reminded us, trust, particularly in cross-cultural research, is a critical issue that makes methodological care in the research process vital to research ethics.

CONCLUSION

An increasing body of research is now focusing on children's own perspectives and articulating their experiences of living away from their families, both in developed and developing countries. Much of this research involves qualitative studies based on surveys and structured interviews, and a significant proportion is descriptive, documenting the difficulties that children and young people experience while they are in various forms of out-of-home care and after leaving it. There are, however, signs of some greater breadth in methodology, with more varied and engaging approaches that include ethnographic and visual methods and more appropriate methods for research, including cross-cultural studies, with younger children and with children and young people with disabilities as participants.

Although children's perspectives on their experience in these arrangements are important in their own right, such impressions can be combined with outcomes-focused measures to promote better understanding of what is important for children in both more subjective and objective terms. Better understanding would also result from greater collaboration among scholars in North America, Europe, and the developing countries, and across disciplines. Researchers in these different countries and disciplines, with some notable exceptions, quite often appear to be unaware of their converging areas of interest (Bogolub and Thomas, 2005; Thoburn and

Courtney, 2011). It is important, however, to understand what the effects of the culturally similar and different arrangements are on children, how children experience them, and what makes a difference. Such an understanding has significant implications for better policy and practice for children who for various reasons are unable to or no longer allowed to live with their parents.

ACKNOWLEDGEMENTS

I am very grateful for constructive comments by Robbie Gilligan, Trinity College, Dublin.

NOTES

1 The systems, strategies and challenges involved in 'identifying and enumerating' children outside of family care are outlined by Pullum et al. (2012) for the broad range of children that includes those in foster care and other forms of care, institutionalized children, street children, and those in child-headed households.

2 An increasing number of children in out-of-home care are now in kinship care placements: in New Zealand (75 per cent), Australia (47 per cent), the USA (33 per cent), with lower figures for Western Europe ranging from 15 per cent in Norway, 18 per cent in the UK, and 25 per cent in Sweden and 33 per cent in Belgium (Aldgate and McIntosh, 2006; Australian Institute of Health and Welfare, 2013; Cashmore, 2012; Holtan, 2008).

3 Institutions to cater for abandoned, orphaned or illegitimate children were established from the Middle Ages in Western countries to house abandoned children and orphans, and were later used for children whose parents were unable to care for them, for abused and neglected children, and for children who were 'delinquent'. The Innocenti Institute in Florence, for example, was established in 1419 by the merchants of the powerful Silk Workers Guild who assumed responsibility for all the abandoned children in Florence (Innocenti Research Centre, 2003).

4 There has been increasing concern since the mid-1950s about the effects on infants and children of this style of accommodation, identified in Bowlby's (1951; see also Rutter, 1995) research on the debilitating effects of maternal deprivation on children's development. A conference in 1955 in Italy following the Parliamentary Commission of Inquiry into Poverty of 1951–1952 reported, for example, that: 'children were often housed in large, dark convents or buildings resembling barracks. The children's quarters were vast and their education and development inevitably suffered as a result of this immense anonymity. The interiors were described as being 'shabby, colourless and dull … Nothing to strike a bright note or lift the spirits. Life inside these homes was thoroughly unnatural for children and adolescents, every day being lived to a strict and standardized routine, education imparted in a depersonalized way, with no attention being paid to the individual child. … There was no time and no space for the exercise of personal freedom in these homes of the 1950s' (Ducci, 2003: 3). The Italian commission noted further that staff were often unprepared and that they supervised large numbers of children. As a result, meaningful relationships were impossible (Ducci, 2003). Inquiries in various countries have also revealed serious physical, sexual and emotional abuse and neglect in various institutions, including those run by church-related agencies.

5 Adoption may take various forms – 'open', 'closed', or 'custom' adoption – depending on the extent to which there is information available to, and continuing contact between, the child and the birth parents, and the cultural background of those involved. 'Kafala, for example, is a form of care under Islamic Law, recognized by legal act and considered definitive. Under kafala, the child does not take the name of the host family, nor does he or she acquire inheritance rights, reflecting the precept of Islamic Law whereby blood ties cannot be modified.' (UNICEF International Child Development Centre, 1998: 3).

6 These include the greater availability of contraception, the legalization of abortion, higher workforce participation by women, the disappearance of the stigma of unmarried mothers, and the provision of social welfare support in many countries that has allowed mothers to keep their babies.

7 The push for greater use of adoption for children who can no longer safely live with their families is in response to concern about the psychological harm caused to children by instability, where children 'drift in care' or oscillate in and out of care. There is increased recognition of the deleterious effects of adverse or 'toxic' environments on early brain development (Zeanah, 2009). Where parental substance abuse, violence, and /or mental illness mean that it is unlikely that some young children will ever be able to return to live at home safely, concerns about the inadequacy of the care system and the need for some stability and 'permanence' for these children have led to heightened pressure in England, the USA,

Canada, and Australia to find ways to provide a 'permanent' home for these children.

8 In the year 2011–2012, only 70 children were adopted from care in Australia from a population of 39,621 children in out-of-home care; and only 40 Aboriginal children have been adopted in the last 10 years (Australian Institute of Health and Welfare, 2012).

9 See NSCAW publications at: http://www.acf. hhs.gov/programs/opre/abuse_neglect/nscaw/pres_papers/nscaw_pub/nscaw_pub.pdf

10 Despite the challenges that children in out-of-home care have faced, they are generally required to leave care when they reach the age of majority (generally age 18) with few resources and limited support (Stein and Munro, 2008).

11 With one exception (Davidson-Arad, 2005, 2010: Israel), these studies were conducted in the USA or the UK over the last 30 years or so, varying in relation to the ages of the children involved, the sample size, and the length of follow-up periods. The measures have included personal adjustment, self-esteem, internalizing and externalizing behaviour problems, school achievement, and IQ, based variously on assessments by the child's caregiver, teacher, social worker, or children themselves.

12 Eighty to 90 per cent of children and young people in these studies were satisfied with their experience of being brought up in foster care, but the figures for group homes and residential care were lower.

13 The differences in approach between two researchers in the US and UK are explored in an interesting and insightful dialogue across the Atlantic (Bogolub and Thomas, 2005). While their differences focus on the need to have the consent of birth parents for children to participate in research about their experiences in out-of-home care while the children are still in care, they arise from differences in theoretical background and in approaches to the related methodological and ethical issues.

REFERENCES

Ainsworth, F. and Thoburn, J. (2013) 'An exploration of the differential usage of residential childcare across national boundaries', *International Journal of Social Welfare, online*. DOI: 10.1111/ijsw.12025

Alderson, P. and Morrow, V. (2004) *Ethics, Social Research and Consulting with Children and Young People*. Barkingside: Barnardos.

Aldgate, J. and McIntosh, M. (2006) *Time Well Spent: A Study of Well-Being and Children's Daily Activities*. Edinburgh, UK: Social Work Inspection Agency.

Andersson, G. (2005) 'Family relations, adjustment and well-being in a longitudinal study of children in care', *Child & Family Social Work*, 10(1): 43–56.

Archard, D. and Skivenes, M. (2009) 'Hearing the child', *Child and Family Social Work*, 14(4): 391–9.

Australian Institute of Health and Welfare (2012). *Adoptions Australia 2011–2012*. Child welfare series No. 52. Cat. No. CWS 40. Canberra: AIHW.

Australian Institute of Health and Welfare (2013) *Child Protection Australia 2011–12*. Child welfare series No. 55 Cat. No. CWS 43. Canberra: AIHW.

Ayuku, D.O., Kaplan, C., Baars, H., and de Vries, M. (2004) 'Characteristics and personal social networks of the on-the-street, of-the-street, shelter and school children in Eldoret, Kenya', *International Journal of Social Work*, 47(3): 293–311.

Bamba, S. and Haight, W.L. (2007) 'Helping maltreated children to find their Ibasho: Japanese perspectives on supporting the well-being of children in state care', *Children and Youth Services Review*, 29(4): 405–27.

Barnes, V. (2007) 'Young people's views of children's rights and advocacy services: A case for 'caring' advocacy?', *Child Abuse Review*, 16(3): 140–52.

Beazley, H. (2003a) 'Voices from the margins: Street children's subcultures in Indonesia', *Children's Geographies*, 1(2): 181–200.

Beazley, H. (2003b) 'The construction and protection of individual and collective identities by street children and youth in Indonesia', *Children, Youth and Environments*, 13(1): 1546–2250.

Bell, M. (2002) 'Promoting children's rights through the use of relationship', *Child and Family Social Work*, 7(1): 1–11.

Bellamy, J.L. (2008) 'Behavioral problems following reunification of children in long-term foster care', *Children and Youth Services Review*, 30(2): 216–28.

Berger, L.M., Bruch, S.J., Johnson, E.I., James, S., and Rubin, D. (2009) 'Estimating the "impact" of out-of-home placement on child well-being: Approaching the problem of selection bias', *Child Development*, 80 (6), 1856–76.

Berrick, J., Frasch, K., and Fox, A. (2000) 'Assessing children's experiences of out-of-home care: Methodological challenges and opportunities', *Social Work Research*, 24(2): 119–27.

Berridge, D. (2007) 'Theory and explanation in child welfare: Education and looked-after children', *Child and Family Social Work*, 12: 1–10.

Bessell, S. and Gal, T. (2011) 'Participation in decision-making in out-of-home care in Australia: What do young people say?', *Children and Youth Services Review*, 33: 496–501.

Biehal, N., Clayden, J., Stein, M., and Wade, J. (1995) *Moving on: Young People and Leaving Care Schemes*. London: HMSO.

Bogolub, E.B. and Thomas, N. (2005) 'Parental consent and the ethics of research with foster children: Beginning a cross-cultural dialogue', *Qualitative Social Work*, 4(3): 271–92.

Bowlby, J. (1951) *Maternal Care and Mental Health*. WHO Monograph Series, No. 2. Geneva: World Health Organization.

Brand, A.E. and Brinich, P.M. (1999) 'Behavior problems and mental health contacts in adopted, foster and non-adopted children', *Journal of Child Psychology and Psychiatry*, 40(8): 1221–9.

Brandon, M. and Thoburn, J. (2008) 'Safeguarding children in the UK: A longitudinal study of services to children suffering or likely to suffer significant harm', *Child and Family Social Work*, 13: 365–77.

Broad, B. (1999) 'Young people leaving care: Moving towards "joined up" solutions?', *Children & Society*, 13(2): 81–93.

Cantwell, N. (2005) 'The challenges of out-of-home care. Children without parental care: Qualitative alternatives', *Early Childhood Matters*, 105: 4–14.

Cashmore, J. (2002) 'Facilitating the participation of children and young people in care', *Child Abuse and Neglect*, 26(8): 837–47.

Cashmore, J. (2006) 'Predicting outcomes for young people after leaving care: The importance of 'felt' security', *Child and Family Social Work: Special Issue on Leaving Care*, 11(3): 232–41.

Cashmore, J. (2012) 'Child protection and out-of-home care', in J. Bowes, R. Grace, and K. Hodge (eds.), *Children, Families and Communities: Contexts and Consequences* (4th edn). Melbourne: Oxford University Press, pp. 217–38.

Cashmore, J. and Paxman, M. (1996) *Wards Leaving Care: A Longitudinal Study*. Sydney: NSW Department of Community Services.

Cashmore, J. and Paxman, M. (2006) 'Wards leaving care: Follow up five years on', *Children Australia*, 31(3): 18–25.

Chapman, M.V., Wall, A., and Barth, R.P. (2004) 'Children's voices: The perceptions of children in foster care', *American Journal of Orthopsychiatry*, 74(3): 293–304.

Christiansen, O., Havik, T., and Anderssen, N. (2010) 'Arranging stability for children in long-term out-of-home care', *Children and Youth Services Review*, 32(7): 913–21.

Clark, A. and Statham, J. (2005) 'Listening to young children: Experts in their own lives', *Adoption and Fostering*, 29(1): 45–6.

Colton, M. (1989) 'Foster and residential children's perceptions of their social environments', *British Journal of Social Work*, 19(1): 217–33.

Commission for Children and Young People and Child Guardian (2009) *Views of Young People in Residential Care, Queensland, 2009*. Brisbane: Commission for Children and Young People and Child Guardian.

Courtney, M.E. (2000) 'Research needed to improve the prospects for children in out-of-home placement', *Children and Youth Services Review*, 22(9): 743–61.

Courtney, M.E., Dworsky, A., Cusick, R.G., Havlicek, J., Perez, A., and Keller, T. (2007) *Midwest Evaluation of the Adult Functioning of Former Foster Youth: Outcomes at Age 21*, Chapin Hall Working paper. Chicago, IL: Chapin Hall Center for Children at the University of Chicago.

Courtney, M. and Iwaniec, D. (2009) *Residential Care of Children: Comparative Perspectives*. Oxford: Oxford University Press.

Cuddeback, G.S. (2004) 'Kinship and family foster care: A methodological substantive synthesis of research', *Children and Youth Services Review*, 26(7): 623–39.

Daniel, B., Wassell, S., and Gilligan, R. (1999) 'It's just common sense isn't it? Exploring ways of putting the theory of resilience into action', *Adoption & Fostering*, 23(3): 6–15.

Davidson-Arad, B. (2005) 'Fifteen-month follow-up of children at risk: Comparison of the quality of life of children removed from home and children remaining at home', *Children and Youth Services Review*, 27(1): 1–20.

Davidson-Arad, B. (2010) 'Four perspectives on the quality of life of children at risk kept at home and removed from home in Israel', *British Journal of Social Work*, 40: 1719–35.

Davies, J. and Wright, J. (2008) 'Children's voices: A review of the literature pertinent to looked-after children's views of mental health services', *Child and Adolescent Mental Health*, 13(1): 26–31.

Delfabbro, P.H., Barber, J.G., and Bentham, Y. (2002) 'Children's satisfaction with out-of-home care in South Australia', *Journal of Adolescence*, 25(5): 523–33.

Delfabbro, P.H., Barber, J.G., and Cooper, L.L. (2002) 'Children entering out-of-home care in South Australia: Baseline analyses for a 3-year longitudinal study', *Children and Youth Services Review*, 24(12): 917–32.

deWinter, M. and Noom, M. (2003) 'Someone who treats you as an ordinary human being … homeless youth examine the quality of professional care', *British Journal of Social Work*, 33(3): 325–38.

Dixon, J. and Stein, M. (2005) *Leaving Care: Throughcare and Aftercare in Scotland*. London: Jessica Kingsley.

Doyle, J.J. (2007) 'Child protection and child outcomes: Measuring the effects of foster care', *American Economic Review*, 97, 1583–1610.

Ducci, V. (2003) 'Beyond the orphanage: The process of deinstitutionalizing children in Italy. Post-war developments', in UNICEF *Children in Institutions: The Beginning of the End*, UNICEF Innocenti Research Centre. Florence, Italy: Tipografia Giuntina, pp. 1–24.

Dunn, D.M., Culhane, S.E., and Taussig, H.N. (2010) 'Children's appraisals of their experiences in out-of-home care', *Children and Youth Services Review*, 32: 1324–30.

Emond, R. (2003) 'Putting the care into residential care: The role of young people', *Journal of Social Work*, 3(3): 321–7.

Emond, R. (2010) 'Caring as a moral, practical and powerful endeavour: Peer care in a Cambodian orphanage', *British Journal of Social Work*, 40(1): 63–81.

Fanshel, D. and Shinn, E.B. (1978) *Children in Foster Care: A Longitudinal Study*. New York: Columbia University Press.

Fanshel, D., Finch, S., and Grundy, J. (1990) *Foster Children in a Life Course Perspective*. New York: Columbia University Press.

Farmer, E., Moyers, S., and Lipscombe, J. (2004) *Fostering Adolescents*. London: Jessica Kingsley.

Farmer, E. and Lutman, E. (2010) *Case Management and Outcomes for Neglected Children Returned to Their Parents: A Five Year Follow-up Study*. Report to the Department for Children, Schools and Families: University of Bristol.

Fernandez, E. (2007) 'How children experience fostering outcomes: Participatory research with children', *Child & Family Social Work*, 12(4): 349–59.

Fernandez, E. and Barth, R.P. (eds.) (2010) *How Does Foster Care Work? International Evidence on Outcomes*. London: Jessica Kingsley.

Festinger, T. (1983) *No One Ever Asked Us: A Postscript to Foster Care*. New York: Columbia University.

Flynn, R. J., Robitaille, A., and Ghazal, H. (2006) 'Placement satisfaction of young people living in foster or group homes', in R.F. Flynn, P.M. Dudding and J.G. Barber (eds.), *Promoting Resilience in Child Welfare*. Ottawa: University of Ottawa Press, pp. 191–205.

Folman, R.D. (1998) '"I was tooken": How children experience removal from their parents preliminary to placement in foster care', *Adoption Quarterly*, 2(2): 7–35.

Forrester, D., Goodman, K., Cocker, C., Binnie, C., and Jensch, G. (2009) 'What is the impact of public care on children's welfare? A review of research findings from England and Wales and their policy implications', *Journal of Social Policy*, 38(3): 439–56.

Fox, A. and Berrick, J.D. (2007) 'A response to *No One Ever Asked Us*: A review of children's experiences in out-of-home care', *Child and Adolescent Social Work Journal*, 24(1): 23–51.

Freundlich, M., Avery, R.J., and Padgett, D. (2007) 'Care or scare: The safety of youth in congregate care in New York City', *Child Abuse & Neglect*, 31(2): 173–86.

Fury, G., Carlson, E.A., and Sroufe, A. (1997) 'Children's representations of attachment relationships in family drawings', *Child Development*, 68(6): 1154–64.

Gardner, H. (2004a) 'Perceptions of family: complexities introduced by foster care, part 1: childhood perspectives', *Journal of Family Studies*, 10(2): 170–87.

Gardner, H. (2004b) 'Perceptions of family: Complexities introduced by foster care, part 2: adulthood perspectives', *Journal of Family Studies*, 10(2): 188–203.

George, S., van Oudenhoven, N., and Wazir, R. (2003) 'Foster care beyond the crossroads: Lessons from an international comparative analysis', *Childhood*, 10(3): 343–61.

Gibbons, J., Gallagher, B., Bell, C., and Gordon, D. (1995) *Development after Physical Abuse in Early Childhood. A Follow-Up Study of Children on Protection Registers*. London: HMSO.

Gibbs, I. and Sinclair, I. (1999) 'Treatment and treatment outcomes in children's homes', *Child & Family Social Work*, 4(1): 1–8.

Gilbertson, R. and Barber, J.G. (2002) 'Obstacles to involving children and young people in foster care research', *Child and Family Social Work*, 7(4): 253–8.

Gilligan, R. (2000) 'The importance of listening to children in foster care', in G. Kelly and R. Gilligan (eds.), *Issues in Foster Care: Policy, Practice and Research*. London: Jessica Kingsley, pp. 40–58.

Gilligan, R. (2001) 'The developmental implications for children of life in public care – Irish and international perspectives', *Irish Journal of Psychology*, 21(3-4): 138–53.

Heptinstall, E. (2000) 'Gaining access to looked after children for research purposes: Lessons learned', *British Journal of Social Work*, 30(6): 867–72.

Heptinstall, E., Bhopal, K., and Brannen, J. (2001) 'Adjusting to a foster family: Children's perspectives', *Adoption & Fostering*, 25(4): 6–16.

Higgins, J.R., Higgins, D.J., Bromfield, L.M., and Richardson, N. (2007) *Voices of Aboriginal and Torres Strait Islander Children and Young People in Out-Of-Home Care* (Promising Practices Paper 7). Melbourne: National Child Protection Clearinghouse.

Hines, A.M., Merdinger, J.M., and Wyatt, P. (2005) 'Former foster youth attending college: Resilience and the transition to young adulthood', *American Journal of Orthopsychiatry*, 75(3): 381–94.

Holland, S. (2009) 'Listening to children in care: A review of methodological and theoretical approaches to understanding looked after children's perspectives', *Children & Society*, 23(3): 226–35.

Holtan, A. (2008) 'Family types and social integration in kinship foster care', *Children and Youth Services Review*, 30(9): 1022–36.

Horrocks, C. (2002) 'Using life course theory to explore the social and developmental pathways of young people leaving care', *Journal of Youth Studies*, 5(3): 325–35.

Innocenti Research Centre (2003) *Children in Institutions: The Beginning of the End?* Florence: UNICEF.

Isiugo-Abanihe, U.C. (1985) 'Child fosterage in West Africa', *Population and Development Review*, 11(1): 53–73.

Jahnukainen, M. (2007) 'High-risk youth transitions to adulthood: A longitudinal view of youth leaving the residential education in Finland', *Children and Youth Services Review*, 29(5): 637–54.

Johnson, P.R., Yoken, C., and Voss, R. (1995) 'Family foster care placement: The child's perspective', *Child Welfare*, 74(5): 959–74.

Kaime-Atterhög, W. and Ahlberg, B.M. (2008) 'Are street children beyond rehabilitation? Understanding the life situation of street boys through ethnographic methods in Nakuru, Kenya', *Children & Youth Services Review*, 30(12): 1345–54.

Kombarakaran, F.A. (2004) 'Street children of Bombay: their stresses and strategies of coping', *Children and Youth Services Review*, 26(9): 853–71.

Kufeldt, K. and McKenzie, B. (2003) (eds.) *Child Welfare: Connecting Research, Policy and Practice.* Waterloo, Ontario: Wilfrid Laurier University Press.

Kufeldt, K., Armstrong, J., and Dorosh, M. (1995) 'How children in care view their own and their foster families: A research study', *Child Welfare*, 74(3): 695–715.

Kufeldt, K., Simard, M., and Vachon, J. (2003) 'Improving outcomes for children in care: Giving youth a voice', *Adoption and Fostering*, 27(2): 8–19.

Kufeldt, K., McGilligan, L., Klein, R., and Rideout, S. (2006) 'International perspectives on foster care: The looking after children assessment process: Promoting resilient children and resilient workers', *Families in Society*, 87(4): 565–74.

Kuyini, A.B., Alhassan, A.R., Tollerud, I., Weld, H., and Haruna, I. (2009) 'Traditional kinship foster care in northern Ghana: The experiences and views of children, carers and adults in Tamale', *Child and Family Social Work*, 14(4): 1–10.

Lahti, J. (1982) 'A follow-up study of foster children in permanent placements', *Social Service Review*, 56(4): 556–71.

Lam, D. and Cheng, F. (2008) 'Chinese policy reaction to the problem of street children: An analysis from the perspective of street children', *Children and Youth Services Review*, 30(5): 575–84.

Landsverk, J., Davis, I., Ganger, W., Newton, R., and Johnson, I. (1996) 'Impact of child psychosocial functioning on reunification from out-of-home placement', *Children and Youth Services Review*, 18(4): 447–62.

Lau, A.S., Litrownik, A.J., Newton, R.R., and Landsverk, J. (2003) 'Going home: The complex effects of reunification on internalizing problems among children in foster care', *Journal of Abnormal Child Psychology*, 31(4): 345–59.

Lawrence, C.R., Carlson, E.A., and Egeland, B. (2006) 'The impact of foster care on development', *Development and Psychopathology*, 18(1): 57–76.

Lietz, C.A., Langer, C.L., and Furman, R. (2006) 'Establishing trustworthiness in qualitative research in social work', *Qualitative Social Work*, 5(4): 441–58.

Littell, J.H. and Schuerman, J.R. (1995) *A Synthesis of Research on Family Preservation and Family Reunification Programs.* Washington, DC: Office of the Assistant Secretary for Planning and Evaluation, U.S. Department of Health and Human Services.

Lough, B. and Panos, P. (2003) 'Rise and demise of orphanages in Ukraine', *European Journal of Social Work*, 6(1): 49–63.

Macdonald, G. and Turner, W. (2008) 'Treatment Foster Care for improving outcomes in children and young people', *Cochrane Database of Systematic Reviews*, 1. Art. No.:CD005649.

McCue Horwitz, S., Balestracci, K.M.B., and Simms, M.D. (2001) 'Foster care placement improves children's functioning', *Archives Pediatric and Adolescent Medicine*, 155(11): 1255–60.

McDonald, T.P., Allen, R.I., Westerfelt, A., and Piliavin, I. (1996) *Assessing the Long-Term Effects of Foster Care: A Research Synthesis.* Washington, DC: Child Welfare League of America.

McDowall, J.J. (2013) *Experiencing out-of-home care in Australia: The Views of Children and Young People* (CREATE Report Card 2013). Sydney: CREATE Foundation.

Mason, J. (2008) 'A children's standpoint: Needs in out-of-home care', *Children & Society*, 22(5): 358–69.

Megahead, H.A and Cesario, S. (2008) 'Family foster care, kinship networks, and residential care of abandoned infants in Egypt', *Journal of Family Social Work*, 11(4): 463–77.

Melton, G.B. (2006) Background for a general comment on the right to participate: Article 12 and related provisions of the Convention on the Rights of the Child. Prepared for the UN Committee on the Rights of the Child.

Mendes, P. (2009) 'Young people transitioning from out-of-home care: A critical analysis of Australian and international policy and practice', *Australian Social Work*, 62(3): 388–402.

Messing, J.T. (2006) 'From the child's perspective: A qualitative analysis of kinship care placements', *Children and Youth Services Review*, 28(12): 1415–34.

Minty, B. (1999) 'Annotation: Outcomes in long-term foster family care', *Journal of Child Psychology and Psychiatry*, 40(7): 991–9.

Mitchell, M.B. and Kuczynski, L. (2010) 'Does anyone know what is going on? Examining children's lived experience of the transition into foster care', *Children and Youth Services Review*, 32(3): 437–44.

Mitchell, M.B., Kuczynski, L., Tubbs, C.Y., and Ross, C. (2010) 'We care about care: Advice by children in care for children in care, foster parents and child welfare workers about the transition into foster care', *Child and Family Social Work*, 15(2): 176–85.

Murray, C. (2005) 'Children and young people's participation and non-participation in research', *Adoption & Fostering*, 29(1): 57–66.

O'Neill, C. (2004) '"I remember the first time I went into foster care – it's a long story…" Children, permanent parents, and other supportive adults talk about the experience of moving from one family to another', *Journal of Family Studies*, 10(2): 205–19.

Oni, J.B. (1995) 'Fostered children's perception of their health care and illness treatment in Ekiti Yoruba households, Nigeria', *Health Transition Review*, 5(1): 21–34.

Oliveira, J.O. and Burke, P.J. (2009) 'Lost in the shuffle: Culture of homeless adolescents', *Pediatric Nursing*, 35(3): 154–62.

Parker, R. (1999) *Adoption Now: Messages from Research*. Chichester: John Wiley & Sons.

Pecora, P.J., Le Prohn, N.S., and Nasuti, J.J. (1999) 'Role perceptions of kinship and other foster parents in family foster care', in R. Hegar and M. Scannapieco, *Kinship Foster Care: Policy, Practice, and Research*. New York: Oxford University Press, pp. 155–78.

Pecora, P.J., Williams, J., Kessler, R.C., Downs, A.C., O'Brien, K., Hiripi, E., and Morello, S. (2003) *Assessing the Effects of Foster Care: Early Results from the Casey National Alumni Study*. Connecticut: Casey Family Services. Retrieved on 25 October 2010 from http://www.inpathways.net/casey_alumni_studies_report.pdf

Perry, B.L. (2006) 'Understanding social network disruption: The case of youth in foster care', *Social Problems*, 53(3): 371–91.

Pullum, T., Cappa, C., Orlando, J., Dank, M., Gunn, S., Mendenhall, M., and Riordan, K. (2012) 'Systems and strategies for identifying and enumerating children outside of family care', *Child Abuse & Neglect*, 36 (10): 701–10.

Quinton, D. and Selwyn, J. (2009) 'Adoption as a solution to intractable parenting problems: Evidence from two English studies', *Children and Youth Services Review*, 31(10): 1119–26.

Rees, A. and Pithouse, A. (2008) 'The intimate world of strangers: Embodying the child in foster care', *Child and Family Social Work*, 13(3): 338–47.

Rubin, D.M., O'Reilly, A.L.R., Haffner, L., Luan, X., and Localio, A.R. (2007) 'Placement stability and early behavioral outcomes among children in out-of-home care', in R. Haskins, F. Wulczyn, and M.B. Webb (eds.), *Child Protection: Using Research to Improve Policy and Practice*. Washington, DC: Brookings Institution Press, pp. 171–86.

Rutter, M. (1995) 'Clinical implications of attachment concepts: Retrospect and prospect', *Journal of Clinical Psychology and Psychiatry*, 36(4): 549–71.

Rutter, M. (2000) 'Children in substitute care: Some conceptual considerations and research implications', *Children and Youth Services Review*, 22(9): 685–703.

Rutter, M. (2007) 'Gene–environment interdependence', *Developmental Science*, 10(1): 12–18.

Ryen, A. (2008) 'Trust in cross-cultural research: The puzzle of epistemology, research ethics and context', *Qualitative Social Work*, 7(4): 448–65.

Samuels, G. (2008) *A Reason, a Season, or a Lifetime: Relational Permanence among Young Adults with Foster Care Backgrounds*. Chicago: Chapin Hall Center for Children at the University of Chicago.

Sanchez, R.M. (2004) *Youth Perspectives on Permanency*. San Francisco, CA: California Permanency Project for Youth.

Schofield, G. (2002) 'The significance of a secure base: A psychosocial model of long-term foster care', *Child and Family Social Work*, 7(4): 259–72.

Schofield, G. (2003) *Part of the Family: Pathways through Foster Care*. London: British Agencies for Adoption and Fostering.

Schofield, G. (2005) 'The voice of the child in family placement decision-making', *Adoption & Fostering*, 29(1): 29–44.

Schofield, G., Beek, M., Sargent, K., and Thoburn, J. (2000) *Growing Up in Foster Care*. London: British Agencies for Adoption and Fostering.

Selwyn, J., Saunders, H., and Farmer, E. (2010) 'The views of children and young people being cared for by an independent foster care provider', *British Journal of Social Work*, 40(3): 696–713.

Shaw, C. (1998) *Remember my Messages: The Experiences and Views of 2000 Children in Public Care in the UK*. London: The Who Cares? Trust.

Sinclair, I. (2005) *Fostering Now*. London: Jessica Kingsley.

Sinclair, I. and Gibbs, I. (1998) *Children's Homes: A Study in Diversity*. Chichester: Wiley.

Sinclair, I., Baker, C., Wilson, K., and Gibbs, I. (2005) *Foster Children: Where They Go and How They Get On*. London: Jessica Kingsley Publishers.

Stein, M. (2004) *What Works for Young People Leaving Care?* Ilford: Barnado's.

Stein, M. and Carey, K. (1986) *Leaving Care*. Oxford: Blackwell.

Stein, M. and Munro, E.R. (2008) *Young People's Transitions from Care to Adulthood: International Research and Practice*. London and Philadelphia: Jessica Kingsley Press.

Tarnai, J. and Krebill-Prather, R. (2008) *2008 Survey of Washington State Youth in Foster Care*, Data Report 08-038. Children's Administration, Department of Social and Health Services. Available at http://www. dshs.wa.gov/pdf/ca/YouthSurveyDataRepor.pdf

Tarren-Sweeney, M. (2008) 'Retrospective and concurrent predictors of the mental health of children in care', *Children and Youth Services Review*, 30(1): 1–25.

Taussig, H.N., Clyman, R.B., and Landsverk, J. (2001) 'Children who return home from foster care: A 6-year prospective study of behavioral health outcomes in adolescence', *Pediatrics*, 108(1): 1–7.

Thoburn, J. (2003) 'The risks and rewards of adoption for children in the public care', *Child and Family Law Quarterly*, 15(4): 391–401.

Thoburn, J. (2007) 'Globalisation and child welfare: Some lessons from a cross-national study of children in out-of-home care', *Social Work Monographs*, University of East Anglia, Norwich. Available at http://www.crin.org/bcn/details.asp?id=12962&themeID=1001&topicID=1010

Thoburn, J. and Courtney, M.E. (2011) 'A guide through the knowledge base on children in out-of-home care', *Journal of Children's Services*, 6(4): 210–27.

Thomas, C. (2013) *Adoption for Looked After Children: Messages from Research – An Overview of the Adoption Research Initiative*. London: British Association for Adoption & Fostering.

Thomas, N. and O'Kane, C. (1999) 'Children's participation in reviews and planning meetings when they are looked after in middle childhood', *Child and Family Social Work*, 4(3): 221–30.

Thomas, C., Lowe, N.V., Beckford, V., and Murch, M. (1999) *Adopted Children Speaking*. London: British Agencies for Adoption and Fostering.

Timms, J. and Thoburn, J. (2003) *Your Shout! A Survey of the Views of 706 Children and Young People in Public Care*. London: NSPCC.

Torronen, M. (2006) 'Community in a children's home', *Child and Family Social Work*, 11(2): 129–37.

Triseliotis, J. (1980) *Growing Up Fostered*. Report to the Social Science Research Council. London.

Triseliotis, J. (1984) 'Identity and security in adoption and long term fostering', *Early Child Development and Care*, 15(2-3): 149–70.

Turnbull, B., Hernández, R., and Reyes, M. (2009) 'Street children and their helpers: An actor-oriented approach', *Children and Youth Services Review*, 31(12): 1283–8.

UNICEF International Child Development Centre (1998) 'Intercountry Adoption', *Innocenti Digest* (Dec). Florence: UNICEF.

Unrau, Y.A. (2007) 'Research on placement moves: Seeking the perspective of foster children', *Children and Youth Services Review*, 29(1): 122–37.

Unrau, Y.A., Seita, J.R., and Putney, K.S. (2008) 'Former foster youth remember multiple placement moves: A journey of loss and hope', *Children and Youth Services Review*, 30(11): 1256–66.

Verhoef, H. (2005) ''A child has many mothers': Views of child fostering in north western Cameroon', *Childhood*, 12(3): 369–90.

Vinnerljung, B. and Sallnas, M. (2008) 'Into adulthood: A follow-up study of 718 young people who were placed in out-of-home care during their teens', *Child & Family Social Work*, 13(2): 144–55.

Wade, J., Biehal, N., Farrelly, N., and Sinclair, I. (2010) *Maltreated Children in the Looked After System: A Comparison of Outcomes for Those who Go Home and Those Who Do Not*. Report to Department for Education. York: University of York.

Wald, M.S., Carlsmith, J.M., and Leiderman, P.H. (1988) *Protecting Abused and Neglected Children*. Stanford: Stanford University Press.

Ward, H. (1998) 'Using a child development model to assess the outcomes of social work interventions with families', *Children and Society*, 12(3): 202–11.

Ward, H., Skuse, T., and Munro, E.R. (2005) 'The best of times, the worst of times: Young people's views of care and accommodation', *Adoption & Fostering*, 29(1): 8–17.

Widom, C.S. (1991) 'The role of placement experiences in mediating the criminal consequences of early childhood victimization', *American Journal of Orthopsychiatry*, 61(2): 195–209.

Wilson, L. and Conroy, J. (1999) 'Satisfaction of children in out-of-home care', *Child Welfare*, 78(1): 53–69.

Winokur, M., Holtan, A., and Valentine, D. (2009) 'Kinship care for the safety, permanency, and well-being of children removed from the home for maltreatment', *Cochrane Database of Systematic Reviews 2009*, Issue 1. Art. No.: CD006546.

Winter, K. (2006) 'Widening our knowledge concerning young looked after children: The case for research using sociological models of childhood', *Child & Family Social Work*, 11(1): 55–64.

Wise, S. (1999) *The UK Looking after Children Approach in Australia.* Research Report No.2. Melbourne: Australian Institute of Family Studies.

Young, L. and Barrett, H. (2001) 'Issues of access and identity: Adapting research methods with Kampala street children', *Childhood*, 8(3): 383–95.

Zeanah, C.H. (2009) 'The importance of early experiences: Clinical, research and policy perspectives', *Journal of Loss and Trauma*, 14(4): 266–79.

Zimmerman, B. (2005) 'Orphan living situations in Malawi: A comparison of orphanages and foster homes', *Review of Policy Research*, 22(6): 881–917.

19

Refugees, Asylum Seekers, Displaced Persons: Children in Precarious Positions

Jacqueline J. Goodnow

Refugees, asylum seekers, and displaced persons have a particular status that sets them apart from other migrants, although they face some common tasks (for example, coping with settings that are often geographically and culturally distant from what was once 'home'). Like immigrants in general, they may serve as a base for research on the nature of 'acculturation' (Donà and Ackerman, 2006), on the strategies parents and children use to counter discrimination (Carranza, 2007), and on some particular aspects of development: aspects such as the sense of belonging, perceptions of what the future might hold, and the sense of continuity with the past. Both are also strongly affected by social policies and their implementation. Intake for both, for example, has been described as an act of 'calculated kindness' (Loescher and Scanlan, 1986: 1): a calculation likely to change from one time to another and to require some advance alertness and knowledge.

Refugees, asylum seekers, and displaced persons differ from immigrants, however, in their histories, the challenges that they meet, and their possible futures: in effect, in the mix of their past, present, and future circumstances. Children who are refugees, displaced, or asylum seekers are more likely than child immigrants to have been through periods of upheaval and exposure to violence. When they leave and where they go seldom has been a matter of choice. In the words of a child interviewed by Kidane (2001: 1), 'I did not choose to be here'. They are more likely to have been suddenly uprooted by others, or compelled to leave by hunger or deprivation ('forced migration'). The journey to any next country has often been hazardous, and likely to be marked by time spent in 'refugee camps', 'detention centres', or illegal status in other countries, followed by another expulsion. They are less likely than immigrants to leave or arrive as a standard family unit. One parent may arrive but not others; some siblings may arrive but not others. Some children leave or arrive alone: 'unaccompanied' or 'separated' in official terms.

Different also are the contexts encountered. Refugees, asylum seekers, and displaced persons usually face a maze of bureaucratic categories that determine what they may do: whether, for example, they are allowed to stay or to enter, or whether they are excluded and perhaps face only the option of going back. The assigned 'bureaucratic identity' (Zetter, 1991: 39) may not fit with their own sense of who they are, but it is difficult to change. They face also a host of special tasks: the tasks, for example, of deciphering the criteria for being placed in one category rather than another, and of presenting one's history in ways that meet the set criteria – tasks that are all the more difficult for children who arrive unaccompanied or if there is little help available. Coping with uncertainty is yet another task: decisions about official status are hard to predict and may take a year or more.

That combination of pre-arrival and post-arrival experiences presents a challenge not only to the children who experience them but also to researchers interested in the nature of development and to those who wish to understand their experience and offer effective help. In relation to the nature and the effects of conditions that range from upheaval and exposure to violence to social contexts and social policies, we need to look at what we already know, identify gaps, and ask new questions.

UNDERSTANDING THE CATEGORIES

Refugees, displaced persons, and asylum seekers are terms of international law that have been agreed to by many countries (United Nations, 1951, 1989).

Being categorized as a *refugee* allows entry to a new country or permission to stay (often after unofficial entry), or placement on a list of people who are eligible for entry and may fit a country's quota decisions. For adults, the essential criterion is that they can demonstrate a history of persecution and a 'well-founded' fear of continuing persecution if they stay or return. For children under 18 who arrive without parents or an equivalent adult caregiver ('unaccompanied' or 'separated' minors), the criterion of being 'in need of protection' is often added.[1]

Being categorized as *displaced* means having passed only from one region of a country to another without crossing a clear border between countries: from one end of the Sudan to another, for example. The most likely outcome is to be returned to the region of origin (on a forced or voluntary basis) or a longer stay in 'refugee camps' of some kind.

Being categorized as an *asylum seeker* is equivalent to 'knocking at the door', having clearly crossed a border between countries, but needing to meet the additional criteria for being classed as a 'refugee'. The decision is usually made by immigration authorities and much or most of the waiting time, for those already in a country, may be spent in a detention centre.

SOME CHARACTERISTICS: NUMBER, COMPANY, AGE, GENDER

Research with any group usually starts with some description of the population or the sample. What is known about these three groups? Where are the gaps in knowledge that we would like to fill?

Even when we consider only countries where UN support is provided and those receiving support can be counted, the estimated total number is large. In 2012, the estimated number of people being assisted or supported by UNHCR (United Nations Office of the High Commissioner for Refugees) was 35.8 million (UNHCR, 2013), and 46 per cent were under 18 years of age. Those numbers are expected to increase. Growth is expected to be especially large in the number of people who are denied 'refugee' status because they are regarded as internally displaced or because claims to a 'well-founded fear of persecution' increasingly encounter a 'culture of disbelief' (Marfleet, 2006: 16).[2]

Within this aggregated total are children who arrive unaccompanied by parents and those who arrive without either parent or an equivalent adult caregiver. For the latter group, some estimated numbers are available. Some of these are specific to particular times and places. In the 1980s, for example, Australia's involvement in the war in Vietnam led to refugee status being given to a large number of Vietnamese arriving without the usual papers. Among these were close to 28,000 unaccompanied children (Neumann, 2004). That large and early group has made some longitudinal studies possible (see, for example, Steel et al., 2002).

More recently, a 2012 UN survey across 72 European countries estimated that the number of unaccompanied children was 16,100 (UNHCR, 2013). That number was the highest number on record since UNHCR started collecting such data, perhaps because parents are finding it increasingly difficult to enter as families. One child may then be sent in the hope that he or she will be given particular rights to enter, and perhaps provide the grounds for family reunion (Bhabha and Crock, 2006; Engebrigtsen, 2003). For 2001, however, those reasons were not part of the reasons that children in the UK offered. Their reasons were similar to those offered by adults (persecution, armed conflict, poverty) with the addition of some more child-specific flights from abuse or neglect (Ayotte, 2002).

There is also some information on the extent to which unaccompanied children are successful in their applications for refugee status. Among the 8500 in the UK in 2002, only 9 per cent were granted refugee status. A further 69 per cent were given the less secure status of Exceptional Leave to Remain: a status that carries no guarantee of a permanent future. Not surprisingly, many children facing these decisions feel they are in limbo (Hewett et al., 2005: 14).

Age

Some further breakdown by age is helpful in unpacking the processes that may link particular features of experience to particular outcomes. In other populations, age affects

the kinds of attributions children make for any event. Children who are refugees, asylum seekers, or displaced persons may not show the same variations. They may, for example, have special attributions about the causes of violence or disaster (Hoffman and Bizman, 1996). Age also affects context. Many of the children in refugee camps, for instance, have spent much of their lives in these camps, but we know little about the impact of their age at entry or of the years spent in a camp after that. We would expect those circumstances, however, to affect outcomes such as the images of return or the development of 'a culture of dependency' (Koser, 1997: 11), with children giving more attention to what they think the deciding groups want to hear than to expressions of their own opinions.

Gender

Among children who are applying for refugee status and are 'unaccompanied' or 'separated', the majority are male and aged 15–17 (Bhabha and Crock, 2006; Hewett et al., 2005). Girls then may have fewer opportunities for peer support (Stanley, 2001). In some refugee camps, boys are also more able to take up new opportunities than girls are, with one contributing factor being the time available (girls being given more chores: Brough and Otieno-Hongo, 2010). In other camps, girls may benefit more. Compared with a traditional past, they may experience a greater sense of freedom of movement and reduced control than boys do (Aptekar, Paardekooper and Kuebli, 2000).

Gender may also make a major difference to the kinds of trauma experienced and the likelihood of flight and of being resettled. The 'lost boys from Sudan', for example, were more likely than the girls to be resettled. When their villages were attacked, the boys were often outside the central village area and had more opportunity to flee. After walking long distances, they reached refugee camps concentrated within Kenya (Bixler, 2005). Here they continued to be 'lost boys', in the sense that they tended not to be absorbed into other families. That lack of connectedness and its implication of special need then facilitated their entry into the USA and other countries. In contrast, the seldom-mentioned 'lost girls' in the same camps, fewer in number, were often absorbed into other families, in part because their labour was useful (girls traditionally do domestic chores, fetch water, and mind children) and in part because families can benefit from the receipt of 'bride prices' if the girls are assigned in marriage. Being absorbed may have provided girls some protection from dangers such as rape, but once a child was seen as connected with a family – regardless of its basis – UNHCR decision-makers were less likely to recommend entry into a new country (McKelvey, 2003; Refugees International, 2002).

There is still much to learn about the circumstances in which gender gives rise to differences in children's experiences: a gap that has been remarked on for studies of refugees and of migration in general (see, for example, Mahler and Pessar, 2006). It is, however, clearly a variable to be taken into account when we wish to specify the processes that may underlie various outcomes and experiences.

REASONS FOR RESEARCH AND FOR SOME PARTICULAR DIRECTIONS

Research studies often start from some specific concerns. An interest in school performance, for instance, prompts attention to the level and the regularity of school experience before arrival (Kahin, 1997) and to the kinds of schools attended after arrival (Rutter, 2006). An interest in mental health prompts attention to the fact that some 'become psychological casualties' while 'the large majority do not' (Bracken, Giller and Summerfield, 1995: 1081), possibly related to the availability of parental and other support (Kohli, 2006) and differences in the kinds of trauma experienced.

Overall, however, there are two main reasons for research that involves children who are refugees, displaced, or asylum seekers. Those reasons are often intertwined.

One type of reason lies in adding to developmental theory and research. There is a great deal yet to be learned about the ways in which development is influenced by particular experiences and by social and cultural contexts. The three groups – refugees, displaced persons, asylum seekers – highlight some particular gaps and challenge some current assumptions. They also offer some promising ways forward.

The other kind of reason has to do with various forms of action. This is a long-standing concern in refugee research. (Black, 2001, for example, reviews 50 years of work with this theme.) No one doubts that these children are in need of help. The actions that may be taken range from therapeutic help to individuals to changes in the way decisions are made or in the kinds of social services offered during the asylum-seeking phase or after acceptance. What can research offer? In broad terms, it can (1) document the nature of populations and problems, (2) ask how particular kinds of help come to be given, (3) point to possible lines of action at an individual, local or government level, (4) evaluate the consequences of various actions, and (5) ask how those consequences come about. It can then be both a way of analysing and critiquing various kinds of actions, and a way of building some kind of evidence base for them.

Studies focused on unaccompanied minors provide a particularly interesting example of how those two lines of interest may be intertwined. Since 2001, there has been a surge of research concerning children who arrive without parents or an equivalent caregiver. Some of those studies start from questions about any long-term consequences for children's mental health when they arrive unaccompanied and ways to ameliorate adverse outcomes (see, for example, Steel et al., 2002).

Other studies of unaccompanied children start from concerns with policy. Within the UK, for example, responsibility for unaccompanied children was assigned to social service departments. Many of the articles and reports related to these children then came from social workers, most often with a focus on the quality of the services that could be provided and on steps that could improve that quality (see, for example, Hewett et al., 2005). Others focus on the impact of particular assignments of responsibility (for example, Cemlyn and Brinkman, 2003) and on the strength of the evidence that services can make a difference to outcomes for children (for example, Mitchell, 2003).

A third and last kind of study focused on unaccompanied children starts from an interest in decision-making procedures, often with a focus on children's rights, rather than their need for care and the recognition that detention centres are 'No place for a child' (Crawley and Lester, 2005: 1). A study by Bhabha and Crock (2006) provides an example. It starts from a particular interest in the extent to which interviewing and categorization procedures in several countries respect or violate children's rights (rights that are part of international agreements: United Nations, 1989). The primary concern is with recommendations for change in those procedures. This report highlights also the views people hold about the influence of age. Immigration authorities, for example, usually expect age to bring with it an increased understanding of all kinds of situations but without any consideration of the extent to which a lack of experience could lead to limited understanding in particular situations: a limited understanding, for example, of courts and court procedures. Assumptions about age are also at the core of interest in differences between a 'legal' and a 'psychological perspective' when it comes to assumptions about a young person's capacity to cope and the legitimate end of a state's responsibility (Derlyn and Brokaert, 2008).

What is largely missing, however, is any real focus on children's experiences – of being a refugee, of being new to a country and learning the ways of that community, of being bullied or discriminated against, or of being supported and included (Hopkins and Hill, 2008).

Several research directions could help fill this gap. One proposal (Kohli, 2006: Kohli and Mather, 2003) is that we start from attention to what 'home' means: a first step toward understanding the impact of its loss, a step also emphasized by Papadopoulos (2002). 'Home' is a place that can generate a sense of security, safety, trust, and 'belonging'. It is also a place where events are relatively predictable, where the day-to-day aspects of life usually follow a taken-for-granted routine, and you can anticipate much of how your life's narrative will unfold. It is also a place where others usually understand most of what you do and how you feel. Places of origin do not always contain all those aspects (a feature that may help account for variability in the impact of breaks), but most of them are part of what we think 'home' should be like.

An accompanying proposal is the need to examine the impact of an unchosen and often sudden departure from the area regarded as 'home'. Now what is lost is one or more of some of the previous aspects of 'home'. The shift, Kohli (2006) points out, may contain gains as well as losses. Some of the negative aspects of 'home', for example, may not be repeated in the new context, as is the case for children fleeing violence or political strife.[3] There is a large body of research on children's exposure to domestic and community violence, involving children who do not move from one country to another. There is also a literature on exposure to war and to large-scale conflicts between groups, again without moving away from the same region. These studies contain some of the same observations as those made in studies of refugee children. Common, for example, is the observation that the effects of exposure are heightened when the victim or perpetrator is someone known and previously relied on or trusted (Berman, 1999; Pynoos, 1986; Straker et al., 1996). There is, as well, a common emphasis on effects in the form of a reduced sense of trust and security (Kohli, 2006; Osofsky, 1995). These several areas of research, however, are seldom brought together.

A further direction – an important one – has to do with the development of models that bring together outcomes, circumstances, and processes, together with extensions to effective forms of action. At hand now are descriptions of several effects or outcomes (effects often noted as variable, with some people adversely affected and some not), a variety of circumstances (ranging from exposure to various kinds of violence to the availability of various kinds of support), and a variety of helpful actions (from individual therapeutic care to changes in procedures and services). Closer attention is needed to proposals and research that bring these several pieces together, in ways that avoid one-dimensional models that simply link the number of stressors to the number of psychological problems (Angel, Hjern and Ingleby, 2001).

One example of a move in this direction comes from work by Sack, Clarke and Seeley (1996) with Cambodian refugees in the United States. That work differentiates between effects in the form of depression (these emerge as predominantly linked to recent stress) and effects in the form of post-traumatic stress disorder (these emerge as predominantly linked to pre-arrival trauma and to stresses encountered on arrival or in the early phases of settlement). What is needed for any study of effects, they propose, is a focus on the different pathways that can lead to specific effects.

These several proposals are often directed toward change in the practices of social workers and in their perceptions of their own roles (for example, no longer as 'rescuers' or as simply providers of the state's services). The aim of bringing several parts of the picture together, however, should apply also to people from other professions with an interest in understanding what it means to be a refugee, a displaced person, or an asylum seeker, finding ways to frame their research or their moves toward providing help or support, and seeking to understand the course of development in difficult circumstances.

TAKING ACCOUNT OF BOTH CHILDREN AND FAMILIES

Within developmental theory, there is general agreement that the lives of children and the lives of parents are closely interwoven and that the nature of child–parent relationships is a major influence on the nature of development (Clarke-Stewart and Dunn, 2006). Where do studies involving refugees, displaced persons, or asylum seekers fit into this broader picture? What do they add to it? What might they borrow?

In some approaches to refugees, displaced persons, or asylum seekers, interrelationships receive little direct attention. The categorization given to parents, for example, is regarded as also covering their children. So also are the actions that follow categorization. The whole family, for example, is moved into detention centres, even when these centres are geared predominantly toward holding adult refugees in prison-like conditions. Children as people with specific needs or rights then tend to drop out of the picture. In a reverse kind of exclusion, parents and siblings tend to drop out of the picture when concern focuses only on the traumas a child has experienced.

Both parents and children come into the picture, however, when flow-on effects become the focus. These effects have often been thought of as occurring in only one direction. Events affect parents and these flow on to children. Flow-on effects from children to parents are less often considered: one more gap that invites research and is especially likely to be relevant to refugee children and their families.

Flow-on effects: from parents to children

Although the focus of this chapter is on children's experiences, the experiences of parents matter also. They may in fact cast a long shadow. The children of Holocaust survivors, for example, when compared with the children of parents who have not had those experiences, are more likely to display signs of post-traumatic disorders when they themselves experience occasions of threat and danger: the occurrence, for example, of Scud missiles landing in their areas (Solomon, Kotler and Mulciner, 1988). Up until the threatening experiences occur, these children may show no difference from children whose parents did not have a Holocaust background. The same kind of effect may apply also to refugee families.

One possible basis for effects such as these is that parents provide models for ways of coping with stress. But when they and their children are refugees, displaced persons, or asylum seekers, three further aspects of parenting are likely to be relevant. These have to do with making sense of events, understanding how various systems work, and preparing children for negative encounters.

The making of meaning

We know that adults' responses to negative events are affected by the way they perceive these events: perceive them, for example, as an expectable part of political activity and commitment, or as being outside human agency (the 'hand of God' or the unkindness of fate; Bracken et al., 1995). Some of those perceptions seem likely to flow on to children. Parents' perceptions seem likely, for example, to be one contribution to the finding that some particular ways of viewing conflict (a view, for example, of Israeli/Arab conflict as a necessary part of Israel's fight for survival) helps promote children's adjustment to the tension of continuing conflict (Punamäki, 1996). But parents may not pass on all of their perceptions. The meanings given, for example, may be restricted to what helps young children understand 'why we are here' (Miller, 1996). There is still a great deal to learn about the meanings and the narratives parents give to children of various ages under various circumstances.

Understanding how various systems 'work'

An understanding of how schools 'work' within the USA and the UK, for example, has implications for the experiences and school achievements of children in the general population (Cooper et al., 2002; Furstenberg et al., 1999; Jackson and Marsden, 1990). In more formal terms, it helps if families have cultural capital (Bourdieu and Passeron, 1977). Cultural capital may be in especially short supply among refugee parents who are in new settings – new countries, detention centres, or displacement sites – usually at unexpected times and by unexpected routes.

As research steps, we may then seek to identify the kinds of cultural capital that are most likely to be needed in particular situations and to be in short supply. The capital needed may be an understanding of appeal procedures, school progressions and practices, or how health services may be accessed. In all these circumstances, we can ask what particular knowledge is needed in specific situations, how it may be enhanced, how it may flow from parents to children, and what impact that has on children's perceptions and experiences.

Preparation for negative experiences

We know that African-American parents use a variety of ways to prepare their children for encounters with prejudice (Gonzales and Kim, 1997; Hughes and Chen, 1997). When parents are refugees, asylum seekers, or displaced persons, what difficulties do they anticipate and what strategic steps do they take?

A strong step in that direction is a study by Carranza (2007) focusing on Salvadorian mothers living in Canada after flight from El Salvador. The mothers' particular concern was with preparing their daughters for encounters with racism. To do so, they described themselves as promoting ethnic pride, largely by bringing out a history of oppression and resistance, of adversity and its being overcome: a proud history linking the younger generation to the past. Continued use of Spanish as a 'family affair' united the immediate family and was essential for speaking to older Salvadorians in Canada and to members of the family still in El Salvador. The effectiveness of these methods, Carranza (2007) pointed out, is demonstrated by the daughters' positive comments on the way they feel about being Salvadorian and speaking Spanish, and by their sense of Salvadorian history.

Flow-on effects: from children to parents

One flow-on effect from children to parents takes the form of children providing a reason for parents' struggles. Children's increased likelihood of survival or their achievements in school, for example, seems likely to help make parents feel that their losses were worthwhile. Achievements in school that are lower than expected may have the reverse effect or challenge parents' sense of their effectiveness. Although we have still much to learn about the connections between children's achievement and parents' expectations, experiences, or backgrounds, one study indicates higher expectations and achievements when families come to the United States as refugees rather than as voluntary migrants (Fuligni et al., 2005).

Australia provides an example of a different kind of flow, with the treatment of children in detention centres affecting the way they and their parents were treated. Until 2005, all members of a family (adults and children) – in fact, all people who arrived without official papers or had overstayed their temporary visas – were placed in detention centres. No special provision was made for children (minimal provisions for schooling, little opportunity or place to play, and easy exposure to adults' acts of violent protest). All were held there for whatever time it

took to process adults' claims for refugee status and for residence in Australia, on average over a year but sometimes extending to three, four, or even five years.

These conditions and their extremely damaging effects on children's well-being were made public by psychiatrists who, unlike other professionals, had access to people in detention centres (Human Rights and Equal Opportunity Commission, 2004; Silove, Steel and Mollica, 2001). Public protests led the government of that time to establish in 2005 some less prison-like centres for children and their mothers, treating children now as separable from fathers.[4] The field would benefit from closer attention to assumptions about the needs and interests of children, their separability or inseparability from one or both parents, and flow-on effects both from parents to children and from children to parents.

A special gap: reunions

Refugees, displaced persons, and asylum seekers often do not arrive in the standard units of parents and their children. Children may arrive unaccompanied. So also may fathers. A father, for example, may have been the only one able to leave at an earlier time, the one facing the most risk if he stayed, or the first to be accepted in a new country. Reunion is often hoped for: a hope often not easily met. We need now to ask what sustains that hope, as well as what effects stem from uncertainty about the likelihood of reunion and uncertainty about where other members of the family are and the nature of their lives.

Experiences when families are reunited are also important. How, for example, does reunion with a father proceed when the family has been separated for some years? How do reunions between siblings proceed? Vietnamese parents who fled to Australia and other countries in the 1970s, for example, could often do so with some children but not others. The siblings' reunions with one another did not always go smoothly. When older brothers were the later arrivals, for example, they often expected to pick up again the status that had once gone with being older. Now, however, it was the younger siblings who had the greater expertise, who were more at ease with the new language and knew more about the local scene (Nguyen and Ho, 1995).

Those reunions take place in a new country. Reunions also occur, however, when people return or are returned to their regions of origin (Cornish, Peltzer and McLachlan, 1999; Rousseau, Morales and Foxen, 2001). We need more analyses of how these and other reunions proceed: one more gap in our understanding of family interactions both in general and when one or more members of a family are refugees, asylum seekers, or displaced persons.

APPROACHES TO THE ANALYSIS OF CONTEXTS

From several general analyses of contexts and the way these are specified (see, for example, Cooper and Denner, 1998; Goodnow, 2010), it is useful to select some approaches likely to have particular relevance to children and families who are refugees, asylum seekers, or displaced persons.

The first approach emphasizes *the nature of social categories and category status*. This kind of emphasis appears in the form of UNHCR categories. It appears also in research exploring the social categories people use in the course of everyday life, the usual assumption of out-group homogeneity ('they' are basically all alike; 'we' are diverse individuals), and the extent to which placement in a category is imposed or chosen (Goodnow and Lawrence, 2008; Tajfel and Turner, 1979). People in the position of refugees, asylum seekers, or displaced persons seem especially likely to be in contexts where homogeneity is assumed and where category status is assigned and must be lived with, at least for a while.

In the second approach, contexts are described in terms of *opportunities, resources, and possible paths* (Cooper et al., 2002; Cooper et al., 2005). Particular attention is now given to the paths that are available, known about, and encouraged or discouraged. For refugees, asylum seekers, and displaced persons, the analysis of paths leads to questions about the information available (information, for example, about the extent to which repatriation may be forced or voluntary), and about what people may see as useful preparatory steps for return (Brough and Otieno-Hongo, 2010; Koser, 1997; Miller, 1996). The analysis of paths is also part of research on the way children may be helped to move toward educational paths (Cooper et al., 2002; Dodds et al., 2010). That kind of approach is clearly extendable to children who are refugees, asylum seekers, or displaced persons and, in turn, that extension would add to our general understanding of developmental goals.

In the third approach, contexts are described in terms of the shared views that people hold about others or about events, views often referred to as *'cultural models'* (D'Andrade and Strauss, 1992). This includes the views people hold about children (views, for example, about their needs, their separability from parents, and the special call they may make on our compassion) and variations in the models people hold about the nature and treatment of trauma. There are, for example, differences between Western approaches and traditional perceptions of problems as best treated by silence or ceremonies of purification (Bracken et al., 1995; Silver and Wilson, 1990; Wellenkamp, 1977). The feature of most importance throughout is the extent to which views are shared or are opposed to one another, and the ways in which differences are responded to.

In the fourth approach, contexts are described in terms of shared, taken-for-granted or 'natural' ways of acting, often referred to as *cultural practices* (Goodnow, Miller and Kessel, 1995). Studies of non-refugee groups suggest that it is the disruption of daily practices that helps make unusual events or new contexts disturbing for young children (Love et al., 2005). For people who are Islamic in faith, for example, some ways of acting are seen as a core part of faith: practices related, for instance, to times of prayer and fasting, forms of dress, acceptable food, appropriate interactions between men and women, and appropriate forms of talk between adults and children (Collet, 2007; Kahin, 1997; Rutter, 2006). The contexts that refugees, displaced persons, and asylum seekers encounter seem especially likely to be contexts where one's usual practices are difficult to maintain, with flow-on effects to well-being.

The fifth and last approach focuses on *selective shifts*. What happens when two groups do not totally agree? One possibility is that people use differences to construct new understandings of history, new images of themselves and of each other (Rumbaut, 2005). Out of such interactions, for example, there may emerge new views of what it means to be a Muslim (see, for example, Collet (2007) describing interactions between Somali youth and secular Canadian schools, and Ketner, Buitelaar, and Bosna (2004) describing how Moroccan girls in the Netherlands construct a middle way between their parents' views and the views of the larger society).

Worth extending also are proposals that are not simply about the degree of change but also the areas in which change occurs and the areas where it does not. These partial changes are at the core of what has been called 'segmented assimilation' (Deaux, 2006) or 'selective accommodation' (Giles, Coupland and Coupland, 1991). For refugees, displaced persons, and asylum seekers, what kinds of accommodations occur? What are the 'sticking points' where neither group wishes to give way? To what extent do areas of change or no change reflect relative degrees of power? For people faced with UNHCR categories, for example, power seems to be markedly unequal, leaving little room for selective shifts or negotiation.

At this point, we are still some distance from knowing the forms and bases of accommodations, concessions, or reconstructions that occur in the contexts encountered by refugees, asylum seekers, or displaced persons.

SPECIFYING PERSON–CONTEXT INTERACTIONS

Needed are not only ways to specify the nature of the contexts that people encounter but also the nature of person–context interactions. The significance of these interactions is well recognized in the analysis of other kinds of moves: movements from one neighbourhood to another, for example, or from one school to another. To what extent do those concerns carry over to moves from one country or one large region to another? Where do children who are refugees, displaced persons, or asylum seekers fit into a larger picture? What do they add to it?

To explore those questions, we look at interactions relevant to the availability of knowledge and help, and to the active part that people may play (people are not simply passive recipients of contextual influences).

Person–context interactions: the availability of knowledge and help

To any new setting, people bring meanings and feelings based on experiences in an earlier setting. Past exposure to unexpected violence or betrayal, for example, can give rise to a level of fear, watchfulness, and distrust that may be confirmed or slowly diminished by experiences in a new setting.

Interactions apply also to the knowledge or the information that people bring with them. For parents in a new setting, for example, much depends on how well their understanding fits with what is needed and on whether they find others who know more and are likely to pass on that knowledge. When it comes to services needed by themselves or their children, they may be in particular difficulties when they move into settings where they are without family connections but most people use these connections as the main sources of information (Bloch and Schuster, 2002).

What happens when children arrive alone and are expected to apply for asylum by themselves? What level of understanding do they bring? What kind of information do they need to bring or to have access to? To be given refugee status, they need to know first of all that particular importance is attached to their being under or over 18. They may arrive without papers that prove their age. They may come from countries where there are no such papers. Children who describe themselves as 15, 16, or 17 but have no proof of age often meet with doubt. They become 'age-disputed' cases. For proof, the decision-makers may turn, in ways that must seem strange to children and are not always precise, to advice based on the growth of teeth or on X-rays of wrist bones (Bhabha and Crock, 2006).

Apart from the importance of their age, what else do children need to know? If they are one of a family, they need to know about and to maintain their parents' narratives and silences. If they are unaccompanied minors, they need to understand the meaning of words such as 'persecution', protection', 'asylum', and 'voluntary return'. Ideally, they should have some understanding of the significance attached to the likelihood of return resulting in ill-treatment because of age, gender, or their family's past political activity. They need to describe themselves as being without parents or as separated from them in ways that make return or reunion difficult or impossible. They also need to keep that description unchanged over time, when information is presented to people who may find it doubtful or have an interest in proving that it is not true, with change then regarded as a sign of fabrication.

For children seeking asylum or refugee status, the interesting interactions also include the level of understanding that children bring and the extent to which various contexts provide help in understanding what children are about to encounter. The help available turns out to vary from one country to another (Bhabha and Crock, 2006).[5] Children's understanding and ability to seek and benefit from it will also vary. We need to explore, for example, what children or adults understand by terms such as 'persecution', 'protection', or 'voluntary return' and what they know about sources of help.

Person–context interactions: people take an active part

One example of this kind of interaction is the relationship between the knowledge people bring and the demands of their new settings. Another starts from a principle in developmental theory. This is the principle that children, like their parents, are not simply captives of their contexts. Instead, they make active efforts at shaping the way events proceed, at constructing or reconstructing their own and others' perceptions of who they are, what they are like, what their past has been, or what their possible futures might be.

What evidence is there of these efforts when parents or children are refugees, displaced persons or asylum seekers? Several have been noted. All might be regarded as forms of identity management.

In a familiar kind of move, parents and children put major effort into children doing well in school: a step toward recovering the status they once had, moving up the social/economic scale, or making up for the years lost during a time of upheaval and flight. In a different kind of move, people may themselves choose or decide on a category label. By way of an appeal against a decision, they may challenge an unwanted label. They may ask to be categorized as a refugee or as an immigrant on the basis of their own estimates of success with one or the other self-categorization (Rutter, 2006). They may also seek to have their own labels added to the official names. Many East Timorese granted the right to stay in Portugal and Australia as refugees, for example, defined themselves not as refugees but as people 'in exile' until independence from Indonesia was achieved. That self-description was a signal that return was always their objective (Wise, 2006).

The East Timorese also provide an example of the need to take a questioning look at the extent to which we think of moves into a new country as irrevocable, with a future marked only by degrees and kinds of 'acculturation'. A useful alternative may be a closer look at active moves toward the development of 'transnational' identities. In the course of diaspora, for example, people scatter into several countries. The 'new media' and a greater ease of movement from one country to another, however, now make it easier to stay in contact with one another. Now there are alternatives to simply holding on to the identity you once had or moving toward 'acculturation' (McGown, 1999; Papastergiadis, 1998).

That kind of possibility applies not only to adults but also to children. Children's greater ease in the use of new media may, in fact, make them particularly able to stay in touch with people from their place of origin, establish new connections, and move toward new definitions of what it means to be Assyrian, Cuban, Salvadorian, Somali, or Sudanese.

A last example of active steps comes from people who, after a move to a new country, negotiate their way toward maintaining their own identity. Collet (2007), for example, asked Somali adolescents attending secular Canadian schools about their experiences. For these students, the challenge was often to find ways of fitting their practices into those of the schools. To fit prayers into a school's daily routine, for example, students began by identifying when teachers were less resistant to time being taken out for prayers. Breaks between classes, for example, turned out to be such a time.

METHODOLOGICAL ISSUES

Some particular approaches to the selection of measures and of possible comparison groups can be extended from cross-cultural research and from studies of immigrants to studies concerning refugees, asylum seekers, and displaced children and adults.

Measures

From some earlier studies of exposures to violence comes first the recommendation that we avoid reports of trauma or well-being that come only from mothers rather than from both mothers and children. Parents and adolescents are likely to agree in their reports of pre-migration trauma, but not in their estimates of current well-being or difficulties (parents may often underestimate current difficulties or symptoms: Sack et al., 1996).

Recommended also is care in the use and interpretation of questionnaires or standardized scales for assessing either current well-being or children's experiences. On the latter score, 'we can count exposure to violence items but this does not help us gauge their differential impact' (Cairns and Dawes, 1996: 136). The same type of violence will not affect all communities in the same way.

Some further suggestions have arisen in the course of exploring children's own assessments of their well-being, their experiences, or their images of the future. Among the possibilities that people have turned to are children's drawings (see, for example, Berman, 1999; Miller, 1996), sorting tasks (Hoffman and Bizman, 1996), and computer-interaction tasks (Dodds et al., 2010).

Other methodological challenges include the need to anticipate some particular areas of reluctance or reticence (Gong-Guy, Cravens and Patterson, 1991; Pernice, 1994; Pernice and Brook, 1996; Schweizer, Buckley and Rossi, 2002). These areas cover:

- *Reluctance to engage in one-on-one interviews*, especially with someone outside their own cultural group. Past experiences with one-on-one interviews, and with signing statements, are likely to have been in the course of stressful applications for refugee status. Focus groups may then be a more acceptable procedure. Needed in any case is attention to the frequency of refusals.
- *Reluctance to talk about experience*. This problem has been noted both within families (parents are often reluctant to talk to children about past horrors) and within interviews. One alternative consists of allowing children and young people to construct their own narrative sequences, using their own terms and editing as they proceed. That procedure underlies some informative autobiographies (Bok, 2003; Pung, 2006).
- *A guarded silence from children when it comes to questions about the past or about experiences that might be related to their age*. Needed are ways to ask questions that do not give the appearance of another interrogation (Kohli, 2006). Kohli's (2006) advice to those who work with these children is to accept what children say, and to let any changes from a first statement occur only when the child takes the initiative.
- *Reticence or vagueness about possible futures*. People may be especially reluctant to talk directly about their possible return to a country or region of origin. One alternative comes from a study where 'displaced' children and youth learned to make video productions, to be shown to others in the Kakuma camp (Brough and Otieno-Hongo, 2010). Participants in the programme chose the topics, after being asked what they thought people needed to know before they returned to the Sudan. These topics covered reintegration procedures and current conditions in the Sudan. They also covered topics that adults were often reluctant to talk

about, including HIV/AIDS, provisions for orphaned children, gender biases, conflict resolution, and the contributions that youth could make toward the future of the Sudan. In effect, participants' own concerns were not directly asked about. There was room, however, for these to emerge in the course of discussions about what others needed to know.

Overall, then, there are alternatives or additions to standard ways of assessing experiences, current well-being, or visions of the future, but all are based on respectful interactions (Lawrence, Kaplan and McFarlane, 2013).

Comparisons within and across groups

In most developmental studies, we take for granted the value of comparisons within a group by age or by gender. Some less obvious comparisons are outlined below. Attached to each are some examples and the question: What does this kind of comparison yield?

With the same people, comparisons between one time and another

This is the kind of comparison exemplified by longitudinal studies. It yields some indication of the characteristics likely to be stable or to change and of the conditions that may alter the predictability and course of development. To take an example from Rutter's (2006) study of Somali children in England, these children over time often lose interest in school achievement, especially if they are in schools where many of the 'local' children have little interest in sustained school performance. The same kinds of change may occur also within refugee camps or displacement sites. The variables that go with a sense of well-being or of effort may also change over time. An adult refugee study provides an example. A low level of language proficiency was more closely related to depression after some years in a country than it was shortly after arrival (Beiser and Hou, 2001).

With people from the same cultural group, comparisons between those in one country as against another

This type of comparison becomes more feasible when moves take the form of diaspora, with people from the one region dispersed into different settings. This yields data that add to our understanding of contexts and person–context interactions, and to our understanding of the ways in which people maintain contact across countries (ways that currently range from phone contact or text messages to the sending of remittances: McGown, 1999; Papastergiadis, 1998).

Within a country, comparisons with others who are born in the country but, again for reasons seldom chosen by them, are separated from their home base and 'in care'

For Australian children in out-of-home care, one of the best predictors of successful outcomes is their sense that someone cared what happened to them, that to someone they mattered (Cashmore and Paxman, 2006). The same kind of effect may apply also to separated refugee children, helping us understand some of the processes that underlie effects on well-being and suggesting the kinds of support that are needed.

Within or across countries, comparisons with children who have experienced violent conflicts between social groups but are still on home ground

Cairns and Dawes (1996), for example, have proposed that children in refugee, displaced, or asylum-seeking groups could have a great deal in common with children who have stayed in place but have experienced ethnic or political violence (Cairns and Dawes, 1996; Dawes and Donald, 1994; Punamäki, 1996) or occasions of disaster or terrorism (La Greca et al., 2002). That kind of comparison could allow the violence experienced to be more of a common factor, with the major difference lying in whether or not there has been a major move.

Within a country, comparisons of refugee children with 'local' children in advantaged and disadvantaged positions

All migration studies present the task of separating characteristics such as poverty and disadvantage from refugee or immigrant status. One way forward is suggested by Rutter's (2006) observation that Somali children do as well as other children in the same schools. A study by Dodds et al. (2010) provides an example of closer analysis. It covers three groups: Somali children attending disadvantaged schools, 'local' Australians also in disadvantaged schools, and 'local' children in advantaged schools. All of these fifth- and sixth-graders face a major shift: transition to secondary school. The measures for comparison were children's perceptions of their personal strengths, their skills and, on a four-point scale, how much improvement in each of a set of 14 strengths and skills was needed before going to high school. The overall result was one of similarity across the three groups. Stronger effects from parents' experiences or from current economic disadvantage might well occur with other groups of children or other measures. This type of approach to comparisons, however, can easily be carried over to check on such possibilities.

Comparisons of what happens at one historical time with what happens at another

A study by Straker et al. (1996) provides an example. It focused on groups that stayed in place, but the procedure can also be extended to groups that move. Three groups of township youth with similar mean ages in South Africa were compared: one group in 1987, the others in 1987 and 1992. Exposure to violence was high on all three occasions. On the first two occasions, however, the conflict was between black and white and the lines of division were clearly lines of suppression and resistance. The third was marked by 'black on black' conflict, with many of the victims now not marked by their political alignment. It yielded the largest number of youth taking a negative view of township life and the lowest scores on measures of well-being. The impact of violence then 'seems at least in part to be dependent on the meanings … violence is construed to have and that in turn is dependent on the political context in which it occurs' (Straker et al., 1996: 54).

That study compared three times that were relatively close. What needs to be considered when the periods compared are further apart? Some studies with immigrant groups point to the need to consider both differences in the conditions they leave and the conditions they encounter. Recent immigrants to the United States, for example, come from countries that are different from the earlier waves. They are also arriving in a country that now makes different demands for educational attainment and has different views about the value of diversity. In effect, the models developed at earlier times for acculturation and identity may no longer apply (Portes and Rumbaut, 1996; Rumbaut and Portes, 2001).

Similar comments have been made with reference to asylum seekers (Silove and Ekblad, 2002). In the 1980s and early 1990s, 'boat people' arriving in Australia from Vietnam were welcomed (Vietnamese had been 'allies' and the 'Communist' group they were fleeing from was widely regarded as 'on the other side'). Support was quickly provided and the overall result has been positive. In contrast, recent 'boat people' – together with other arrivals arriving without pre-screening overseas – have usually encountered policies of exclusion and control, a general public suspicion of 'illegals', minimal support and often lengthy periods of mandatory detention. Most of the longitudinal studies now available in Australia and in other countries, Silove and Ekblad (2002) remind us, tend to be based on people who arrived during earlier periods. We should not take it for granted that earlier results will be repeated.

Where then is the value of considering events that have occurred at times more distant from the last 20 to 40 years? History reminds us of several large changes in the way children are regarded, changes that can apply also to current differences across groups or across countries. Changes have occurred, for example, in the values placed on children, the compulsory nature of schools, the ages at which children can enter the paid workforce and become economic contributors to the family, the availability of jobs that require little literacy, the distinctions drawn between males and females, and the perception of children as separable from parents. History dating back several hundred years ago also reminds us, Marfleet (2006, 2008) pointed out, that population flights and exclusions, and terms such as *refuge* or *asylum*, are not new. We may well gain a deeper understanding of current events by becoming more aware of both a recent and a more distant past.

ETHICAL ISSUES

After reviewing studies of children in South Africa who had faced political or ethnically based violence, Cairns and Dawes (1996) recommended that researchers working with vulnerable groups start with two questions. The first: in whose interests is this research being done? Is it the interests of children, of government, or academics? The second: does the research provide any active participation by the people involved, participation that may strengthen their capacity to shape or to cope with the situations they encounter?

Studies of children who are refugees, asylum seekers, or displaced have generally focused on the outcomes for these children compared with those in their new country. Researchers have often started with a concern by governments about their own social and economic interests (Rutter, 2006) and their wish to avoid the emergence of an unskilled underclass within their own boundaries. Research money may flow to studies with immigrants or potential immigrants. Less, however, flows to research with those who are not yet in the country, especially those who face long stays in refugee camps or return to their region or country of origin.

Research with children who are already in the country may still not be directly concerned with the interests or experiences of those children. The driving concern may be researchers' interest in developmental theory: in building concepts that account in general for differences in the course of development, the effects of various contexts or circumstances, and the links between earlier experiences and later outcomes.

Those concepts do matter. Decisions about the needs of children are often based on assumptions about the nature of children or of childhood. Decisions about therapeutic action – for example, the choices made among one-on-one therapy, collective rituals, healing ceremonies – are often based on concepts of trauma or risk and of recovery. Decisions between actions that focus on changes in government policy, the social contexts children encounter, and a recognition of the rights of children are often based on views about the extent to which it is the characteristics of individuals or the characteristics of contexts that matter most and are the proper concern of developmentalists. The flow-on to children's interests may then be indirect. It may also be limited by our working from unquestioned assumptions and, often, from being culture-blind (Bracken et al., 1995; Engebrigtsen, 2003; Summerfield, 1998; Thomas and Byford, 2003).

At the least, Cairns and Dawes (1996) argued, we researchers should ask ourselves how we might meet both goals, especially when we start from an interest in developmental theory. Doing so keeps the interests of children firmly in the picture. It may also alter the theories and the aspects of development we choose as a research focus.

Two studies will serve as examples of how we might proceed. The first is a three-nation study by Bhabha and Crock (2006) comparing the policies of the USA, the UK, and Australia in relation to the rights of children who seek asylum 'alone' (those that arrive without a parent or an equivalent adult and

must themselves then apply for asylum or for refugee status). The main focus in this study was on the extent to which government policies, or the ways in which these are implemented, were in themselves unethical or unlawful and how they could change so that they meet 'the best interests' and 'the rights' of children. The interests of children emerged as often jeopardized by the ways in which the UNHCR criteria are implemented and by children's difficulties in understanding the procedures or the terms used (terms such as 'refugee', 'asylum', or 'voluntary return'). To a smaller extent, however, this study was also concerned with helping children develop a clearer understanding of the terms and procedures they encounter, in effect, an interest also in how children's own skills may be enhanced.

Studies of this kind would not fully meet Cairns and Dawes' (1996) proposal that they should strengthen the position of children by increasing their opportunities for active participation in what happens to them. Opportunities for participation, however, are now part of many action projects, aimed at outcomes such as an increased ability of children and youth to identify their own problems, aims, and possible steps forward, and an increased self-confidence in their ability to do so. The goal of outside helpers is then to help children achieve their own aims – their 'small dreams' (Caouette, 2001: 1) – and to increase their skills and self-confidence, ideally in ways that can be sustained.

The second study, by Brough and Otieno-Hongo (2010), provides a good example of this approach. The starting points for this study were in part questions of law and the need to implement the UNHCR (1996) principle that voluntary return should be based on an informed decision (often not the case with children or youth). The larger base was Freire's (2000) emphasis on dialogue and active participation as bases to empowerment. The population of interest, as we noted earlier, was Sudanese youth within a large long-standing refugee camp in Kenya known as Kakuma.[6] The categorization of most of the people in this camp as 'displaced' meant that return was the most likely future. Many of the children and youth in Kakuma, however, had spent large portions of their lives in this or other camps, so that 'return' was at best a vague concept. They might also be easily regarded, or regard themselves, as having little to say about this topic.

With this kind of difficulty in mind, Brough and Otieno-Hongo (2010) turned to projects that promoted the use, by youth in the camp, of 'participatory video' (part of a surge of interest in the importance of participation and in the way 'new media' open up possibilities for participation). With help from workers associated with UNHCR, the youth in the project learnt the skills needed for video production, chose the topics, and organized their showing to all the people in the camp.[7] The chosen topics, as we mentioned earlier, were oriented toward different facets of return, covering the meaning of voluntary return, the steps that return involves, conditions that currently exist in the Sudan, issues that are often areas of silence (for example, HIV/AIDS, health, gender biases), and the need for particular skills (such as skills in conflict resolution). The result for the community was a general increase in what they knew about return and what it might involve. For the youth themselves, the result was an increased confidence in expressing their opinions and in their sense of agency: their view of themselves as able to make a difference in what happens.

The two studies – by Bhabha and Crock (2006) and by Brough and Otieno-Hongo (2010) – clearly differed in the means adopted to meet the interests of children. They differed also in the extent to which they met both of the criteria that Cairns and Dawes (1996) proposed as ethical frames for any study. Although it may be difficult for any one study to meet both criteria well, giving thought to both priorities – and to the ways in which these shape the studies undertaken – provides an effective starting point for research that aims at ethical goals.

CONCLUSION

This chapter began with the aim of developing research questions and suggesting how they might be approached. Some of these are questions that researchers might ask themselves: questions, for example, about the interests that research serves and the inclusion of an active role for local participants, with benefit both for the research and for the children of interest (Cairns and Dawes, 1996).

A larger set of questions stems from considering the positions and experiences of refugees, asylum seekers, or displaced persons, starting from the official definitions of these category labels and the extent to which these life-changing terms (together with others such as 'voluntary return') are understood and are in any way negotiable. A larger set of questions comes also from taking a developmental perspective on the nature of experiences and their effects. That perspective highlights especially the need to consider the nature of processes, and the mediating or moderating steps that link earlier stresses and later outcomes. Diversity in paths is to be expected, with no inevitably tight connection between earlier trauma and later psychopathology and with attention needed to both those who show clear signs of continuing damage and those who do not. The meanings attached to violence may well provide a significant part of the path.

In short, these population-specific groups present a compelling area for research, not only because we may wish to bring about change in children's lives but also because they offer ways of adding to our understanding of what children encounter and of their development under diverse circumstances.

ACKNOWLEDGEMENTS

For advice on sources and for constructive comment on an earlier draft, I am especially indebted to Judy Cashmore, Katherine

Goodnow, Jeanette Lawrence, and two unnamed reviewers.

NOTES

1 Under special circumstances people may be classed as 'humanitarian refugees'. 'Economic refugees' at any age are excluded.

2 Those estimated numbers do not cover countries where support is minimal and people cannot be counted. There are, for example, sizeable groups of children and young people along the borders of countries such as China, Burma, and Thailand. For that region, a specific action project has brought some details. These young people are most often looking for work. They are often very young (in some places, the age of five is regarded as a 'workable age'). Most are unaccompanied by parents and – not infrequently – they have been sold or trafficked across borders. There is no base, however, for estimating the total number (Caouette, 2001).

3 The next step is the extension of these proposals to the development of helpful actions. Drawing from attachment theory and concepts of 'therapeutic care', Kohli (2006) proposed three 'domains', with actions then designed to meet each of these. The first was the 'domain of cohesion': a domain where assistance is geared toward 'meeting children's practical needs and making sure that the jigsaw of their day-to-day lives fitted together in an orderly way' (Kohli, 2006: 5). An emphasis on meeting children's 'here-and-now' needs was seen as the critical first step, with remembering and dealing with the past to come later.

a. A second was the 'domain of connection'. The connection of most interest is between past and present, between inner and outer worlds. Here assistance needs to start from a respect for silence. A silence that may be interpreted by others only as a state of shock after trauma may be a form of active coping with negative events, a time of thinking one's way through past and present events. Called for also is a careful approach to requests for any stories of the past. Direct requests for accounts of how they came to seek asylum are avoided. Enquiries about losses may be easier to accept. So also may be reminders of daily life in the past (for example, questions about the games you played or the food you usually ate; see Kohli and Mather 2003: 208). In any case, it is seen as best to allow stories about the past to emerge when the children themselves are ready and have come to develop a sense of trust and a feeling of being cared about.

b. The third and last domain was called a 'domain of coherence'. The emphasis falls on 'regenerating the rhythm of ordinary life' (Kohli, 2006: 7), seen as a critical step toward linking the present with a sense of what the past contained. One step toward doing so consists of avoiding the implication that these children are only 'victims of trauma'. That 'image ... is a small part of a broader picture' (Kohli and Mather, 2003: 202). More helpful is a view of these children as 'ordinary children coping with extraordinarily adverse circumstance and trying to make the best use of their own strengths and capabilities' (Kohli, 2006: 7).

4 Changes based on political decisions are inevitable. Since 2007, for example, Australian policy has changed from closing overseas clearance and detention centres to a reversal of this policy. It may easily change again. For the radical change in 2007, however, more complete accounts of events can be found in K. Goodnow (2008) and Marr and Wilkinson (2003). Public protests were part of that change, contributing to recommendations that these detention centres be closed or radically changed. The then-new Labour government elected at the end of 2007 acted on those recommendations. Children were no longer to be placed in detention centres, under any circumstances. That policy, however, was seriously weakened in the course of a large and unanticipated increase in the number of 'illegal' refugees arriving by boat from Indonesia. The detention centre on Christmas Island, established for the processing of refugee status and at one point close to empty, was soon close to full and a new compound came under consideration (Narushima and Saulwick, 2010). No special provision for children – accompanied or unaccompanied – was planned. Nor is it a clear part of the 2012 re-opening of a clearance and detention centre on the island of Nauru. Within the UK, a similar weakening of protection has appeared in the form of children who arrived in Dover being interviewed without any guardian being present and before urgent health needs are met (Silcock, 2010). Between what is supposed to occur and what happens in practice, it seems, gaps can easily occur. What happens in both respects is, unfortunately, a political football in Australia and in other countries.

5 In the UK, under ideal conditions, a guardian advisor is appointed and no interviews are conducted without a non-adversarial adult being present. In the US, children are given a list of phone numbers for legal advisors who may or may not be available or knowledgeable. In effect, the responsibility rests with the children. Australia has provided the least protection, with neither an appointed guardian nor a list of possible advocates. Voluntary child advocates have then been their best sources of help. Again, however, ideal conditions may not always apply. Within

England, for example, children in at least one arrival centre were being interviewed without any guardian present and at a time before their serious health needs have been met. In effect, the conditions that children face in practice often may not meet those specified as part of the rights of the child (United Nations, 1989).

6 A peace settlement in 2005 ended a 20-year civil war within the Sudan. The door was thus opened for return by over four million internally displaced Sudanese persons, including over half a million recognized as refugees (see Browne, 2006; Brough and Otieno-Hongo, 2010, for some descriptions). The people within the camp were far from homogeneous, so that there was some tension when it came to the models and practices that people think should apply. The largest group came from the Sudan: an area in itself made up of several groups with differences in language and a history of distrust or antagonism toward each other. In addition, both traditional and Western views are likely to be encountered and these are likely to have different degrees of power. Kakuma, for example, was a setting where UNHCR representatives increasingly turned over the everyday management of the camp to community leaders. Power in the camp then tended to rest in the hands of senior males who held strongly traditional views of women and girls. Some contrast with those traditions was represented by broad UNHCR policies and by direct encounters with representatives of some NGOs.

7 Brough and Otieno-Hongo's (2010) project, for example, aimed at participation by both boys and girls. To all actual and possible participants, it gave explicit advice on the importance of respecting gender equality. Nonetheless, more boys than girls took up the opportunity to make video productions that took up issues related to the return that both could expect. That result appeared to stem both from differences in available time (girls tended to have more house-based tasks: e.g. cleaning, minding children, fetching water) and in the traditional gender stereotypes held by most of the seniors in the camp.

REFERENCES

Angel, B., Hjern A. and Ingleby, D. (2001) 'Effects of war and organized violence on children: A study of Bosnian refugees in Sweden', *American Journal of Orthopsychiatry*, 71(1): 4–16.

Aptekar, L., Paardekooper, B. and Kuebli, J. (2000) 'Adolescence and youth among displaced Ethiopians: a case study in Kaliti camp', *International Journal of Group Tensions*, 29(1): 101–34.

Ayotte, W. (2000) *Separated Children Coming to Europe – Why They Travel and How They Arrive*. London: Save the Children.

Beiser, N. and Hou, F. (2001) 'Language acquisition, unemployment and depression among Southeast Asian refugees: A 10 year study', *Social Science Medicine*, 53(10): 1321–34.

Berman, H. (1999) 'Stories of growing up amid violence by refugee children of war and children of battered women living in Canada', *Image-Journal of Nursing Scholarship*, 31(1): 57–84.

Bhabha, J. and Crock, M. (2006) *Seeking Asylum Alone: A Comparative Study of Laws, Policy, and Practice in Australia, the UK and the US Regarding Unaccompanied and Separated Children*. Sydney: Themis Press.

Black, R. (2001) 'Fifty years of refugee studies: From research to policy', *International Migration Review*, 35(1): 57–78.

Bixler, M. (2005) *The Lost Boys of Sudan: An American Story of the Refugee Experience*. Atlanta: University of Georgia Press.

Bloch, A. and Schuster, L. (2002) 'Asylum and welfare: Contemporary debates', *Critical Social Policy*, 22(3): 393–414.

Bok, F. (2003) *Escape from Slavery*. New York: St. Martin's Press.

Bourdieu, P. and Passeron, C. (1977) *Reproduction in Education, Society and Culture*. London: Sage.

Bracken, P.J., Giller, J. and Summerfield, D. (1995) 'Psychological responses to war and atrocity: The limitations to current concepts', *Social Science and Medicine*, 40(8): 1073–82.

Brough, M. and Otieno-Hongo, C. (2010) 'Envisioning the return: Participatory video for voluntary repatriation and sustainable reintegration', in H.L. Skartveit and K. Goodnow (eds.), *Changes in Museum Practice: New Media, Refugees, and Participation*. London: Berghahn, pp. 17–34.

Browne, P. (2006) *The Longest Journey: Resettling Refugees from Africa*. Sydney: University of New South Wales Press.

Cairns, E. and Dawes, A. (1996) 'Children: Ethnic and political violence – a commentary', *Child Development*, 67(1): 129–39.

Caouette, Y.M. (2001). *Small Dreams Beyond Reach: The Lives of Migrant Children and Youth Along the Borders of China, Myanmar and Thailand: A Participatory Action Project*. London: Save the Children.

Carranza, M.E. (2007) 'Building resilience and resistance against racism and discrimination among Salvadorian female youth in Canada', *Child and Family Social Work*, 12(4): 390–8.

Cashmore, J. and Paxman, M. (2006) 'Predicting after-care outcomes: The importance of 'felt' security', *Child and Family Social Work*, 11(3): 232–41.

Cemlyn, S. and Brinkman, L. (2003) 'Asylum, children's rights and social work', *Child and Family Social Work*, 8(3): 163–78.

Clarke-Stewart, A. and Dunn, J. (eds.) (2006) *Families Count: Effects on Child and Adolescent Development*. Cambridge: Cambridge University Press.

Collet, N.A. (2007) 'Islam, national identity and public secondary education: Perspectives from the Somali diaspora in Toronto, Canada', *Race, Ethnicity and Education*, 10(2): 131–53.

Cooper, C.R., Cooper, R.G. Jr., Azmitia, M., Chavira, G. and Gullatt, Y. (2002) 'Bridging multiple worlds: How African American and Latino youth in academic outreach programs navigate pathways to college', *Applied Developmental Science*, 6(2): 73–87.

Cooper, C.R. and Denner, J. (1998) 'Theories linking culture and psychology: Universal and community-specific processes', *Annual Review of Psychology*, 49(1): 559–84.

Cooper, C.R., García Coll, C.T., Bartko, W.T., Davis, H. and Chatman, C. (eds.) (2005) *Developmental Pathways through Middle Childhood: Rethinking Contexts and Diversity as Resources*. Mahwah NJ: Erlbaum.

Cornish, F., Peltzer, K. and McLachlan, M. (1999) 'Returning strangers: The children of Malawian refugees come 'home'?', *Journal of Refugee Studies*, 12(3): 113–26.

Crawley, H. and Lester, T. (2005) *No Place for a Child – Children in UK Immigration Detention: Impact, Alternatives and Safeguards*. London: Save the Children.

D'Andrade, R.G. and Strauss, C. (eds.) (1992) *Human Motivation and Cultural Models*. New York: Cambridge University Press.

Dawes, A. and Donald, D. (1994) *Childhood and Adversity: Perspectives from South Africa*. Claremont: David Phillips Publishers.

Deaux, K. (2006) *To be an Immigrant*. New York: Russell Sage Foundation.

Derlyn, I. and Brokaert, E. (2008) 'Unaccompanied children and adolescents: The glaring contrast between a legal and a psychological perspective', *International Journal of Law and Psychiatry*, 31(4): 319–30.

Dodds, A. E., Lawrence, J. A., Karantzas, K., Brooker, A., Lin, Y. H., Champness, V. and Albert, N. (2010) Children of Somali refugees in Australian schools: Self-descriptions of school-related skills and needs. *International Journal of Behavioral Development*. [Published online before print.]

Donà, G. and Ackerman, L. (2006) 'Refugees in camps', in D.L. Sam and J.W. Berry (eds.), *The Cambridge Handbook of Acculturation Psychology*. Cambridge: Cambridge University Press, pp. 218–32.

Engebrigtsen, A. (2003) 'The child's – or the state's – best interests? An examination of the ways immigration officials work with unaccompanied asylum seeking minors in Norway', *Child and Family Social Work*, 8(3): 191–200.

Freire, P. (2000) *Pedagogy of the Oppressed*. New York: Continuum.

Fuligni, A.J., Alvarez, J., Bachman, M. and Ruble, D.N. (2005) 'Family obligation and the academic motivation of young children from immigrant families', in C.R. Cooper, C.T. García Coll, W.T. Bartko, H. Davis and C. Chatman (eds.), *Developmental Pathways Through Middle Childhood: Rethinking Contexts and Diversity as Resources*. Mahwah, NJ: Erlbaum, pp. 261–82.

Furstenberg, F.F., Cook, F.D., Eccles, J., Elder, G.H. and Sameroff, A. (1999) *Managing to Make It: Urban Families and Adolescent Success*. Chicago: University of Chicago Press.

Giles, H., Coupland, N. and Coupland, J. (1991) *Contexts of Accommodation: Developments in Applied Psycholinguistics*. Cambridge: Cambridge University Press.

Gong-Guy, E., Cravens, R.B. and Patterson, T.E. (1991) 'Clinical issues in mental health services delivery to refugees', *American Psychologist*, 46(6): 642–48.

Gonzales, N. and Kim, L. (1997) 'Stress and coping in an ethnic minority context', in A. Wolchik and L.N. Sandler (eds.), *Handbook of Children's Coping: Linking Theory and Intervention*. New York: Plenum Press, pp. 418–511.

Goodnow, J. J. (2010) 'Cultures', in M. Bornstein (ed.), *Cross-Cultural Developmental Science*. Mahwah NJ: Erlbaum, pp. 3–20.

Goodnow, J.J. and Lawrence, J.A. (2008) 'Ethnicity: spotlight on person-context interactions', in J.M. Bowes and R. Grace (eds.) *Children, Families and Communities*, 3rd Ed. Melbourne: Oxford University Press, pp. 61–75.

Goodnow, J.J., Miller, P.J. and Kessel, F. (1995) *Cultural Practices as Contexts for Development*. San Francisco: Jossey-Bass.

Goodnow, K. (2008) *Museums, the Media and Refugees: Stories of Crisis, Control and Compassion*. New York: Berghahn.

Hewett, T., Smalley, N., Dunkerley, D. and Scourfield, J. (2005) *Uncertain Futures: Children Seeking Asylum in Wales*. Cardiff: Save the Children.

Hoffman, M.S. and Bizman, A. (1996) 'Attributions and responses to the Arab-Israeli conflict: A developmental analysis', *Child Development*, 67(1): 117–28.

Hopkins, P.E. and Hill, M. (2008) 'Pre-flight experiences and migration stories: The accounts of unaccompanied asylum-seeking children', *Children's Geographies*, 6(3): 257–268.

Hughes, D. and Chen, L. (1997) 'What and when parents tell their children about race: An examination of race-related socialization in African-American families', *Applied Developmental Science*, 1(4): 200–14.

Human Rights and Equal Opportunity Commission (2004) *A Last Resort: A Summary Guide to the National Inquiry into Children in Immigration Detention*. Sydney: HREOC.

Jackson, B. and Marsden, D. (1990) *Education and the Working Class*. Harmondsworth: Penguin.

Kahin, M. A. (1997) *Educating Somali Children in Britain*. Stoke on Trent: Trentham Books.

Ketner, S.L., Buitelaar, M.W. and Bosna, H.A. (2004) 'Identity strategies among adolescent girls of Moroccan descent in the Netherlands', *Identity: An International Journal of Theory and Research*, 4(2): 145–69.

Kidane, S. (2001) *I Did Not Choose To Be Here: Listening To Refugee Children*. London: British Association for Adoption and Fostering.

Kohli, R.K.S. (2006) 'The comfort of strangers: Social work practice with unaccompanied asylum-seeking children and young people in the UK', *Child and Family Social Work*, 11(1): 1–10.

Kohli, R, and Mather, R. (2003) 'Promoting psychosocial well-being in unaccompanied asylum-seeking young people in the United Kingdom', *Child and Family Social Work*, 8(3): 201–12.

Koser, K. (1997) 'Information and repatriation: the case of Mozambican refugees in Malawi', *Journal of Migration Studies*, 10(1): 1–19.

La Greca, A.M., Silverman, W.K., Vernberg, E.M. and Roberts, M.C. (eds.) (2002) *Helping Children Cope with Disasters and Terrorism*. Washington, DC: American Psychological Association.

Lawrence, J.A., Kaplan, I., and McFarlane,C. (2013) 'The role of respect in research interactions with refugees and asylum seekers', in K. Badcock, E. Riggs, and N. Haslam (eds.), *Values and Vulnerabilities: The Ethics of Research with Refugees and Asylum Seekers*. Bowen Hills, QLD: Australian Academic Press, pp. 103–26.

Loescher, G. and Scanlan, J. (1986) *Calculated Kindness: Refugees and America's Half-Open Door, 1945 to the Present*. New York: Free Press.

Love, E.D., Weisner, T.S., Geis, S. and Huston, A.C. (2005) 'Child care instability and the effort to sustain a working daily routine', in C.R. Cooper, C.T. García Coll, W.T. Bartko, H. Davis and C. Chatman (eds.), *Developmental Pathways Through Middle Childhood: Rethinking Contexts and Diversity as Resources*. Mahwah NJ: Erlbaum, pp. 121–44.

McGown, R. (1999) *Muslims in the Diaspora: The Somali Communities of London and Toronto*. Toronto: University of Toronto Press.

McKelvey, T. (2003, 3 October) 'Where are the "Lost Girls?"', *Slate*. Retrieved 13 August 2007, from http://www.slate.com/id/2089225

Mahler, S.J. and Pessar, P.R. (2006) 'Gender matters: Ethnographers bring gender from the periphery toward the core of migration studies', *International Migration Review*, 40(1): 27–63.

Marfleet, P. (2006) *Refugees in a Global Era*. Basingstoke: Palgrave Macmillan.

Marfleet, P. (2008) ' Forgotten to history: Refugees, historians and museums in Britain', in K. Goodnow (ed.), *Museums, the Media and Refugees: Stories of Crisis, Control and Compassion*. London: Berghahn, pp. 17–25.

Marr, D. and Wilkinson, M. (2003) *Dark Victory*. Sydney: Australia.

Miller, K. (1996) 'The effects of state terrorism and exile on Indigenous Guatemalan refugee children: A mental health assessment and an analysis of children's narratives', *Child Development*, 67(1): 89–106.

Mitchell, F. (2003) 'The social services response to unaccompanied children in England', *Child and Family Social Work*, 8(3): 179–89.

Narushima, Y. and Saulwick, J. (2010, 7 April). Customs puts asylum seekers on separate boats, *Sydney Morning Herald*, p. 7.

Neumann, K. (2004) *Refuge Australia: Australia's Humanitarian Record*. Sydney: University of New South Wales Press.

Nguyen, C. and Ho, M. (1995) Vietnamese-Australian families, in R. Hartley (ed.), *Families and Cultural Diversity in Australia*. Melbourne: Australian Institute of Family Studies, pp. 216–418.

Osofsky, J.D. (1995) 'Children who witness domestic violence: Invisible victims', *Social Policy Report (Society for Research in Child Development)* 9: 1–16.

Papadopoulos, R.K. (ed.) (2002) *Therapeutic Care for Refugees: No Place like Home*. London: Karnac.

Papastergiadis, N. (1998) *Dialogues in the Diaspora: Essays and Conversations on Cultural Identity*. London: Rivers Oram.

Pernice, R. (1994) 'Methodological issues in research with refugees and immigrants', *Professional Psychology: Research and Practice*, 25(3): 207–13.

Pernice, R. and Brook, J. (1996) 'The mental health pattern of migrants: Is there a euphoric period followed by a mental health crisis?' *International Journal of Social Psychiatry*, 42(1): 18–27.

Portes, A. and Rumbaut, R.G. (1996) *Immigrant America: A Portrait.* Berkeley CA: University of California Press.

Punamäki, R.-L. (1996) 'Can ideological commitment protect children's psychosocial well-being in situations of political violence?', *Child Development,* 67: 55–69.

Pung, A. (2006) *Unpolished Gem.* Melbourne: Penguin.

Pynoos, R.S. (1986) 'Traumatic stress and developmental psychopathology in children and adolescents', in J.M. Oldham, M.B. Riba and A. Tasman (eds.), *American Psychiatric Press Review of Psychiatry, Vol. 12.* Washington, DC: American Psychiatric Press, pp. 205–38.

Refugees International (2002) 'Do not forget the lost girls of Sudan,' *Newsletter* 2/11/2002, available at www.refugeesinternational.org

Rousseau, C., Morales, M. and Foxen, P. (2001) 'Going home: Giving voice to memory strategies of young Mayan refugees who returned to Guatemala as a community', *Culture, Medicine and Psychiatry,* 25(2): 135–68.

Rumbaut, R.G. and Portes, A. (2001) *Ethnicities: Children of Immigrants in America.* Berkeley, CA: University of California Press.

Rutter, J. (2006) *Refugee Children in the UK.* Maidenhead: Open University Press.

Sack, W.H., Clarke, G.N. and Seeley, J.M.S. (1996) 'Multiple forms of stress in Cambodian adolescent refugees', *Child Development,* 67(1): 107–16.

Schweizer, R., Buckley, L. and Rossi, D. (2002) 'The psychological treatment of refugees and asylum seekers: What does the psychological literature tell us?', *Mots Pluriel,* 21 [on-line]. Available at http://motspluriels.arts.uwa.edu.au/MP2102sbr.html

Silcock, C. (2010) *United Kingdom: Safe at Last? Children on the Front Line of Border Control.* London: Refugee and Migrant Justice. Available at http://www.crin.org/resources/infodetail.asp?id=22259

Silove, D., and Ekblad, S. (2002) 'How well do refugees adapt after settlement in Western countries?', *Acta Psychiatrica Scandinavia,* 106(6): 401–2.

Silove, D., Steel, Z. and Mollica, R. (2001) 'Detention of asylum seekers: Assault on health, human rights and social development', *The Lancet,* 357(9266): 1436–7.

Silver, S. and Wilson, J. (1990) 'Native American healing and purification rituals for war stress', in J. Wilson, Z. Harel and B. Kahaa (eds.), *Human Adaptation to Stress: From the Holocaust to Vietnam.* New York: Plenum Press, pp. 337–56.

Solomon, Z., Kotler, M. and Mulciner, M. (1988) 'Combat-related traumatic stress disorder among second-generation Holocaust survivors: Preliminary findings', *American Journal of Psychiatry,* 145(7): 865–8.

Stanley, K. (2001) *Cold Comfort: Young Separated Refugees in Britain.* London: Save the Children.

Steel, Z., Silove, D., Phan, T. and Bauman, A. (2002) 'Long-term effect of psychological trauma on the mental health of Vietnamese refugees resettled in Australia: a population-based study', *The Lancet,* 36(9339): 1056–62.

Straker, G., Mendelsohn, M., Moosa, F. and Tudin, P. (1996) 'Violent political contexts and the emotional concerns of township youth', *Child Development,* 67(1): 46–54.

Summerfield, D. (1998) 'A critique of seven assumptions behind psychological trauma programs in war-affected areas', *Social Science & Medicine,* 48(10): 1449–62.

Tajfel, H. and Turner, J. (1979) 'An integrative theory of intergroup conflict', in W.G. Austin and S. Worchel (eds.), *The Social Psychology of Intergroup Relations.* Monterey CA: Brook-Cole, pp. 33–47.

Thomas, S. and Byford, S. (2003) 'Researching unaccompanied asylum seeking children – Ethical issues', *British Medical Journal,* 327(7428): 1400–2.

United Nations (1951) Convention Relating to the Status of Refugees. Geneva: United Nations.

United Nations (1989) *United Nations Convention on the Rights of the Child.* New York: United Nations.

United Nations High Commissioner for Refugees (UNHCR) (1996) *Convention and Protocol Relating to the Status of Refugees.* Geneva: UNHCR.

United Nations High Commission for Refugees (UNHCR) (2013) *Global Trends: Displacement - The New 21st Century Challenge.* Geneva: UNHCR.

Wellenkamp, J. (1977) 'Cultural differences and similarities regarding emotional disclosure: Some examples from Indonesia and the Pacific', in J. Pennebaker (ed.), *Opening up: The Healing Power of Expressing Emotions.* New York: Guilford, pp. 293–311.

Wise, A. (2006) *Exile and Return among the East Timorese.* Philadelphia: University of Pennsylvania Press.

Zetter, R. (1991) 'Labelling refugees: Forming and transforming bureaucratic identity', *Journal of Refugee Studies,* 4(1): 39–63.

PART III

Methods in Research on Children and Childhood

20

Challenges and Innovations in Research on Childhood

Drika Weller, Sue D. Hobbs and Gail S. Goodman

For the past century, developmental psychology has been the pre-eminent discipline to conduct child-related research. In fact, up until the 1970s, relatively few disciplines had a branch of scholarship explicitly devoted to the study of children and childhood, as children's issues were subsumed under other topics (such as education). The last several decades, however, have seen a tremendous increase in child-related scholarship across the disciplines. This movement reached a milestone in 1989 when the United Nations adopted the Convention on the Rights of the Child, setting forth an international decree that children have freedoms and entitlements equal in importance to those of adults.

As academicians were adding child-focused subspecialties within their own disciplines, child-related scholarship across these disciplines remained largely disconnected. Children's (Childhood) Studies developed as its own distinct area of study from the recognition that the viewpoints and methodologies of various disciplines needed to be synthesized in a holistic perspective of children. Children's Studies does not aim simply to accumulate and pull together fragmented pieces of child scholarship. Rather, the goal is to create a whole new, qualitatively different

understanding of children that is more than the sum of its parts (Lenzer, 2001). Each discipline is thus challenged to develop new lines of research that take into account the collective wisdom of interdisciplinary scholarship.

This section of *Children in Childhood* introduces various methodologies to help researchers from different scholarly backgrounds orient themselves to major approaches in child-related research. Backed by a rich history of children's research, developmental psychology offers numerous research methodologies. Many of the authors in this section are developmental psychologists, and many of them reference psychological scholarship in their discussions of child-related research. They note the benefits, challenges, and shortcomings specific to each methodology.

Children's Studies has its own overarching philosophical orientation that guides child-related research. This orientation is based on the principles outlined in the Convention on the Rights of the Child and includes respect for children and their distinctive voices and perspectives. Children's Studies asks that children be considered in their own right and that researchers and scholars interpret the world through children's eyes. Researchers' methodologies should, when possible, involve children as direct participants in research. Children themselves are often their own best informants.

Many methodologies have been developed to achieve these goals. In this section, Saywitz and Camparo discuss interviews of children as one method for generation of knowledge about children's own experience. Interviews allow children to speak for themselves and to reveal thoughts and feelings that parents and other adults may not be aware of. The information gleaned from these interviews has played an important role in creating and changing public policy. For example, children's reports of the distress they experience when testifying in court about painful and embarrassing events have led to changes in the way such testimony is obtained (Quas and Goodman, 2012), with many countries now allowing children to testify in less stressful, noncourt contexts (Applegate, 2006). Children's interviews are useful in a number of situations, such as custody disagreements, criminal investigations, hearings on deportation and relocation status of immigrant parents, and mental health assessments.

Saywitz and Camparo describe several of the most commonly used interview techniques: highly structured diagnostic interviews, semi-structured motivational interviews, largely unstructured ethnographic interviews, and forensic interviews. Each type of interview offers benefits and has limitations. The optimal interview for a given study is determined by the research objective. For example, highly structured interviews allow researchers to compare children's answers easily across different groups, however, interviewers then typically can neither engage in spontaneous probes nor follow up on children's responses. In contrast, unstructured interviews offer considerable flexibility, so that researchers can tap into unexpected information. However, unstructured interviews are not well suited for comparative analyses purposes across samples.

Interviews can pose many challenges that, if the researcher is not careful, can considerably limit the quality of children's reports. It is thus critical that the researcher be attuned to the children's developmental level and culture, and to situational considerations (such as distractions in the interview room or the interviewer's gender). For example, children, particularly young children, are likely to give answers even when they do not understand the questions because they feel pressure to please the interviewer. Such deference to authority figures varies from culture to culture (Quas et al., 1999). However, culture can also influence whether or not children feel comfortable revealing accurate information. If there is a strong cultural stigma around the topic (for example, domestic abuse) or if children's experiences make them feel distrustful about the purpose and potential outcome of the interview, they may be less likely to speak openly and honestly. This reticence may be especially true for marginalized or minority children who have witnessed injustices and feel sceptical about the benefits of the interview. Therefore, it is considered best to use simple open-ended questions and to avoid questions that are complex, leading, or suggestive, or that require simple 'yes' or 'no' responses. The latter types of questions are more likely to result in confusion, misunderstandings, and inaccurate data (Lamb et al., 2009).

It is critical that interviewers make children feel comfortable, put aside any preconceived expectations and remain open to hearing children's own perspectives. Saywitz and Camparo list empirically grounded techniques for putting children at ease and preventing interview mishaps. For example, explaining the purpose of the interview, teaching children to speak up when they need clarification, and emphasizing that children are the 'experts' and the adults are the 'students' can help ensure the quality of interviews.

Asking children to communicate through drawings (Burkitt, Watling and Murray, 2011; Thomas and Silk, 1990), stories

(Bretherton, Prentiss and Ridgeway, 1990), games with blocks or dolls (Woolgar, 1999), or other creative means can also help researchers understand children's worlds. These creative ways may be especially useful with very young children or children who are quiet, non-verbal, or developmentally delayed. In this part, Rasmussen (Chapter 24) discusses how children's photographs can offer distinctive insight into the minds of children. Children enjoy expressing themselves through photographs, especially when they are given freedom to photograph whatever they want and subsequently asked to tell a story about what they have captured. Of interest are the objects, people, and events that catch the children's attention, and the way in which they describe their photographs. Adults need to be open to hearing what children have to say about their photographs and resist the temptation of making assumptions based on their own points of view. Children have their own distinctive way of experiencing the world. Their thoughts and emotions can come to the surface if they are allowed to voice their stories in an accepting environment. Although the use of photographs in research primarily lends itself to qualitative analysis, quantitative analysis can also be conducted if the number of participants is large enough and each photograph is systematically analysed.

Another way to include children in research is to observe them. Whereas other methods that seek to understand children's behaviour sometimes carry greater potential for inaccuracies (for example, self-or adult-reports can be biased; child tests can provoke anxiety in children), behavioural observations offer researchers the advantage of actually observing how children behave.

Observing behaviour, however, is no easy task, and researchers need to follow specific procedures to ensure valid and reliable data. These include using the proper coding system, counterbalancing observations, employing trained observers, and reducing reactivity, as briefly described below. It is critical that researchers use a standardized coding system relevant to the research question and the observed environment. Observations should be conducted at different times of the day to ensure that researchers are capturing a representative sample of behaviour. If more than one child is being repeatedly observed, order of observations should be counterbalanced. Observers must be trained and remain neutral to the children being observed, as inaccuracies will occur if observers are not consistent in their interpretation of the behavioural scales or if they hold preconceptions about the observed children. Researchers must also ensure that children become accustomed to their presence before recording behaviour to avoid reactivity (when individuals behave differently because they are aware they are being observed).

There are different methods to observing behaviour, including ad libitum (unstructured observation that allows the researcher to get a general idea of what is occurring) and focal person sampling (the systematic observation of one child at a time). Each method presents its own limitations and challenges. Ad libitum sampling is unsystematic – the observer may focus on certain individuals or certain behaviours at the expense of ignoring others. During focal person sampling, a child might be difficult to follow and can move out of sight or earshot. Focal person sampling is systematic and allows for easier comparisons across groups, but it can be time consuming and expensive. The research question, as well as the time and cost of the research, will determine the method of sampling.

Conducting time-use studies is another way to document how children spend their time; this approach is particularly useful for understanding children's leisure habits when they are not at school or involved in extra-curricular activities (Olds et al., 2012). In Chapter 25, Craig explains how time-use studies are especially relevant to learning how children spend their private time which often occurs in settings where direct observation feels intrusive (such as the home).

This methodology is frequently used to gather information about maternal employment and its effects on time spent with children; gender differences in parenting, such as the different activities mothers and fathers perform with their children; and time children spend with parents in play and watching television. Time-use studies frequently examine the relation between how time is spent in early childhood and children's outcomes later in life. Time-use studies also tend to focus on a particular group and a distinct set of activities and particular outcomes (for example, obesity and the amount of time spent watching television).

Methods of data collection in time-use studies include stylized questionnaires (for example, participants are asked to reflect back over a period of time and recall their activities), time diaries, direct observation, and experience sampling (using pagers to remind participants to write down what they are doing). All methods offer benefits and drawbacks. For example, both direct observation and experience sampling can be intrusive, expensive, and can miss the recording of important activities. Social desirability and recall bias can pose problems with stylized questionnaires and with time diaries.

Of the time-use data collection methods, time diaries are frequently regarded as the most reliable and valid. Although they can be burdensome for the participant, they are rich with information. Time diaries typically require that research participants record all of their activities that occur within a specified period (often 24–48 hours). They may need to be adapted for use with children; these adaptations may pose some limitations. For example, parents need to fill out time diaries for young children who are not yet able to read or write, or do not have a good grasp of time; thus, not all behaviour will be recorded as parents cannot constantly be with their children. Older children who are able to record information themselves may require a simplified diary, a pre-coded diary with lists of activities that allow children to simply

mark a box next to the behaviour. These diaries do not tap activities that are unlisted; as with all methods, there are advantages and disadvantages to this technique.

Observational measures, interviews, and other means (such as photographs or stories) that require children to act as their own informants can give researchers valuable insight into children's inner states and their behaviour at a given time point. These methods of data collection, however, are limited in that they do not necessarily provide an objective view of children. Collecting child data from the reports of parents, caregivers, teachers, and other knowledgeable adults (in addition to the information researchers obtain from children themselves) can arguably provide a more complete understanding of children.

Parent reports, such as those provided through interviews, surveys, and questionnaires, may be especially useful when children are too young to provide much meaningful information for themselves. In this part (Chapter 26), Bornstein discusses the use of parent and adult reporting in research through written accounts (for example, diaries), interviews, and questionnaires.

Baby diaries, or biographies, are a very early form of parent reporting on child behaviour. One of the most notable is Jean Piaget's diary that documented, in detail, the development of his three children. Piaget's observations played a prominent role in advancing understanding of child development and establishing it as a science. Such diaries can offer more detail than researchers would obtain from other methods. In general, however, biographies documenting parents' observations of their children have significant limitations in research. Reports on one child cannot be easily generalized to other children, observations are usually not systematic, and the findings are likely to be biased by the parents' own perspectives and preferences.

A more systematic and reliable way to obtain information is to conduct questionnaires and interviews with parents and other significant adults in children's lives. Questionnaires in particular are easy to administer to a large, representative sample that can provide results more easily generalizable to the wider population. Adult reports of any kind, however, are subject to similar limitations as those noted above. Even mothers who tend to be most privy to their children's inner worlds have limited insight into the complexities of the children's thoughts and feelings. Adults are not unbiased observers of children, and they may perceive only those dimensions of behaviour that fit with their existing conceptions and that suit their own mental and emotional schemas. For these reasons, obtaining reports from different adults – including grandparents, teachers, and other caretakers – offers a more complete picture of the children. Even areas of disagreement among the adult reporters can be very informative.

Asking *adults* to reflect on their own childhoods offers another way to understand children's experiences. In Chapter 27, Pillemer and Dickson discuss research on adult memory of childhood experiences and highlight three ways in which it can be conducted. Researchers can ask adults to report their earliest memory (Kingo, Bernsten and Krøjgaard, 2013) or to report multiple early childhood memories. Researchers can also use memory prompts to help adults recall specific early childhood events (for example, providing photographs and asking adults to remember the events surrounding the birth of their younger siblings). Each of the three methods yields slightly different results in terms of the age of adults' first reported memory and the richness of their memory descriptions. For example, memory cues tend to enhance adults' ability to remember very early memories. Other factors, including differences in culture and the way questions are asked, also tend to affect results. Open-ended probes identify the average age of the earliest memory recollection at 3 to 4 years, whereas direct questions about targeted events can spark memory recollections for even earlier time periods. Parents' cultures

can influence the extent to which they discuss past events with their children, which in turn affects how children talk about those events in adulthood.

From a research perspective, asking adults to describe their early memories can be challenging for a number of reasons. Memories about early events and the dates they occurred are prone to inaccuracies. Although adults find it difficult to recall early events without prompts, providing prompts can lead to errors in recall. Adults' memories may actually be stories they heard from parents and family members, or reflect a general understanding of a specific type of event.

Adults' memories of early childhood events can become important in practical settings, for example, in criminal investigations where adults are asked to report what they experienced as young children. Adult memories can also provide greater knowledge of what it means to be a child. Adults remember childhood events from a more mature perspective and potentially with greater understanding of an event's context. These memories can complement children's descriptions of events to yield greater understanding of childhood experiences.

Such differences in perspective can also be useful in understanding generational (cohort) phenomena that may result in different 'childhoods' in different historical contexts. In that regard, the limitations of memory, although still relevant, are probably less significant in relation to understanding adolescence or older childhood.

Given the various advantages and limitations of each approach to child research, methodology should ideally vary. In addition, multiple assessments and strategies should be applied when examining the same phenomenon, as each method will provide data and insights that may not be available from other methods. Administrative data, as discussed by Goerge and Lee in this part (Chapter 23), offer researchers information about a number of childhood issues – including medical histories, maltreatment, anti-poverty programmes, education, and juvenile delinquency – and are relatively inexpensive to obtain.

Although administrative data are usually not collected specifically for research purposes, researchers can still draw on such data for their studies. Administrative data can provide answers to questions that cannot be reasonably tackled with other research methods alone. Administrative data are often collected on large populations, which is a prohibitively expensive and time-consuming task to undertake through other means, such as survey methods. Administrative data frequently include historical data that can be used in retrospective longitudinal research. In addition, different datasets can be combined to produce a picture of children and their families that might not be available from other forms of research. Armed with these data, researchers have a better opportunity to create and change policies that affect child well-being.

The challenges of administrative data include the lack of control over how the data are collected or the questions that are asked. Persons collecting the data are not trained researchers so the quality of data collection and data entry can be inconsistent. Use of administrative data can be costly and time-consuming as researchers need to carefully clean, format, and check the meaning of the variables before data analysis. Further, administrative data on children are not as readily available in some countries as in others. Researchers may need to have connections within the government or have a special arrangement with the government research divisions before being granted permission to access the data.

Researchers also need to decide on the type of study that would best answer their questions. In Chapter 22, Dworsky discusses longitudinal studies of children and youth. The major advantage of longitudinal designs is that they allow researchers to make causal predictions with greater confidence as information is gleaned from the chronological sequence of events, and children's development can be examined both before and after

events have taken place. Longitudinal studies can address important developmental questions about environmental influences on children's outcomes, and cross-cultural longitudinal comparisons can increase knowledge of how children's development is affected by factors that are universal versus culture specific. Researchers conducting longitudinal studies with children collect data in a variety of ways, including analysis of existing administrative data, interviews of adults who know the children, and interviews of children themselves.

Two of the methodological challenges of longitudinal studies involving children are attrition and the need for more standardized assessments that can be used for all age groups. Attrition may compromise the quality and the generalizability of the study because children who remain in the study may be different from those who dropped out. Attrition can be reduced by keeping contact with participants between sessions. Assessments can be a problem for longitudinal studies with children because most assessments cannot be used across different age groups given vast developmental differences. At the same time, using different assessments across different age groups can make it more difficult to compare changes over time. Although researchers can modify assessments to make them developmentally appropriate for different age groups, these variants are not necessarily psychometrically sound. Further, children in different cohorts may require different assessments given their values, experiences, and so on. These differences can make it difficult to measure change within groups.

There are a number of methods for conducting research with children, and the chapters represented in this section offer an overview of their many benefits and challenges. All methods have their advantages and limitations. For this reason, it is important to vary and combine different approaches. Methods should also suit the children's capabilities and developmental level, so researchers need to have a solid understanding of child development. Further, children's culture and preferences must be taken into account, as any confusion or discomfort could limit results and research objectives.

In general, Children's Studies tends to place priority on descriptive methodology (in other words, methodology that *describes* rather than *explains* a given phenomenon) and on methodology that asks children to be their own informants. As described in Chapter 28 by Soffer and Ben-Arieh, Chapter 29 by Hayne and Tustin, and Chapter 30 by Dahl, this methodological focus includes observing children and asking what is important to them, what their everyday experiences are, and what they subjectively think and feel. These priorities stem from the philosophy that children's voices and perspectives must be heard and that adults cannot assume they know children's inner worlds and experiences. Other methods, however, are not excluded, as each type of research provides unique insight into children's worlds. Methodologies that aim to make causal connections between children's environments and their outcomes also have a crucial place. Many of the chapters in this section discuss ways that various types of methodology can be used to complement one another in an attempt to make causal connections and with the goal of providing a better environment for children.

One type of research that is not explicitly emphasized in this section of the book but that is often used by developmental psychologists is the experimental method. In experimental studies, researchers manipulate variables in a controlled, laboratory setting to determine causal influences on children's behaviour and thinking (see Cordon et al., 2013; Goodman et al., 2011). The advantage of this type of research is that it allows the researcher to make causal inferences; the limitation is that the setting is often artificial. Overall, researchers must be cautious in generalizing the results.

The 'bottom line' in child-related research is that, regardless of the methodology, researchers strive to *benefit* children. Research can foster insight into the children's world to promote their well-being. Much as the results of a research study in a foreign country ought to be interpreted in light of that culture's mores, codes, and values, children's behaviours should be interpreted in light of their world, their perspectives, and their needs. Adults do not see the world in the same way as children and therefore must remain open to hearing and understanding children's responses and behaviours as if they were still children, too.

This is an exciting time for child research. With the creation of Children's Studies, varied disciplines can come together to create a broader understanding of children than any one discipline can offer on its own. Challenged by new theories and methodologies, the disciplines can generate innovative questions, ideas, and perspectives.

REFERENCES

Applegate, R. (2006) 'Taking child witnesses out of the crown court: A live link initiative', *International Review of Victimology*, 13: 179–200.

Bretherton, I., Prentiss, C. and Ridgeway, D. (1990) 'Family relationships as represented in a story-completion task at 37 and 54 months of age', in I. Bretheron and M. Watson (eds.), *Children's Perspectives on the Family (New Directions for Child Development series vol. 48)*. San Francisco: Jossey-Bass, pp. 85–105.

Burkitt, E., Watling, D., and Murray, L. (2011) 'Children's drawings of significant figures for a peer or an adult audience', *Infant and Child Development*, 20: 466–73. doi: 10.1002/icd

Cordon, I M., Melinder, A.M.D., Goodman, G.S., and Edelstein, R.S. (2013) 'Children's and adults' memory for emotional pictures: Examining age-related patterns using the developmental affective photo system', *Journal of Experimental Child Psychology*, 114: 339–56.

Goodman, G.S., Ogle, C.M., Block, S.D., Harris, L.S., and Larson, R.P. (2011) 'False memory for trauma-related Deese-Roediger-McDermott lists in adolescents and adults with histories of child sexual abuse', *Development and Psychopathology*, 23: 423–8. doi: 10.1017/S0954579411000150

Kingo, O.S., Bernsten, D., and Krøjggard, P. (2013) 'Adults' earliest memories as a function of age, gender, and education in a large stratified sample', *Psychology and Aging*. Advance online publication. doi: 10.1037/a0031356

Lamb, M.E., Orbach, Y., Sternberg, K.J., Aldridge, J., Pearson, S., Stewart, H.L., and Bowler, L. (2009) 'Use of structured investigative e protocol enhances the quality of investigative interviews with alleged victims of child sexual abuse in Britain', *Applied Cognitive Psychology*, 23: 449–67.

Lenzer, G. (2001) 'Children's Studies: Beginnings and purposes', *The Lion and the Unicorn*, 25(2): 181–6.

Olds, T., Ferrar, K., Gomersall, S.R., Maher, C., and Walters, J.L. (2012) 'The elasticity of time: Associations between physical activity and use of time in adolescents', *Health Education & Behavior*, 39: 732–6.

Quas, J.A., and Goodman, G.S. (2012) 'Child victims in court: Emotional and attitudinal outcomes', *Psychology, Public Policy, and Law*, 18: 392–414.

Quas, J.A., Goodman, G.S., Bidrose, S., Pipe, M-E, Craw, S. and Ablin, D.S. (1999) 'Emotion and memory: Children's long-term remembering, forgetting, and suggestibility', *Journal of Experimental Child Psychology*, 72(4): 235–70.

Thomas, G.V. and Silk, A.M.J. (1990) *An Introduction to the Psychology of Children's Drawings*. New York: New York University Press.

Woolgar, M. (1999) 'Projective doll play methodologies for preschool children', *Child Psychology and Psychiatry Review*, 4(3): 126–34.

21

Interviewing Children: A Primer

Karen J. Saywitz and Lorinda B. Camparo

INTERVIEWING CHILDREN: A PRIMER

Research on child interviewing has burgeoned over the past 25 years as expectations about children's agency, competence, and participation in society have changed. Across diverse fields of study, researchers in psychology, medicine, sociology, anthropology, law, social work, nursing, and education have investigated how best to elicit information from children – information about their experiences, perceptions, sensations, attributions, thoughts, and feelings. As informants about their own lives, children have become active participants in building the knowledge base on which public policies about their welfare are predicated. Moreover, their memories, preferences, and perceptions determine everyday decisions that affect individuals of all ages from courtrooms to dinner tables. The goal of this chapter is to provide an overview of the breadth of the field – an introduction to a myriad of issues at play in research on contemporary child interviewing.

Accumulated findings from basic developmental research on children's capabilities and limitations have served as the foundation for expansion to both experimental and applied studies of child interview methods (see, for example, Damon and Lerner, 2006). Changing social trends have propelled the field further. Consider, for example, the nearly universal ratification of the Convention on the Rights of the Child (UN General Assembly, 1989), a document that provides for children to be participants and decision makers in matters that affect their own lives. Managed health care in the United States has expanded demands on medical and mental health professionals to provide more efficient and cost-effective services. The result is less time and fewer resources for in-depth, expensive diagnostic tests and correspondingly greater need to elicit information from children themselves about their presenting symptoms and responses to treatment in both pediatric and psychiatric settings. Increased public concern about child abuse and the consequent legal reforms in reporting and investigating allegations have fuelled research on forensic interviewing techniques to elicit children's memories without tainting their reports (Goodman, 2006).

Widespread liberalization of divorce laws, even in Catholic countries where divorce was not previously allowed, prompts judges, attorneys, psychologists, and parents to consider children's preferences in custody planning based on their descriptions of daily life in both households (Goode, 1993). Recent reforms in adoption and child welfare have increased the need for social workers to monitor children's safety, routines, discipline, and exposure to trauma as efforts are made to strengthen and reunify families who struggle with poverty, drug abuse, or domestic and community violence. Heightened immigration around the world results in more children functioning as informants in decisions concerning deportation and relocation of immigrant parents.

Researchers have made significant strides in understanding the best ways to structure interviews to elicit what children have seen and heard as bystanders, and what they have experienced physically as victims of crime or as patients in health care settings. There has been progress in eliciting children's reliable memories of past events in child eyewitness studies, and their perceptions of their own affective states, behaviours, and coping strategies in the mental health field. Although a full understanding of children as informants about childhood requires integration of multiple sources of information (for example, paper-and-pencil self-report, analyses of videotaped interactions, direct observation, participant-observation, and ratings of peers), this chapter centres on the contribution of the interview method itself. First, we review prominent types of interviews being studied. Then a select set of factors that affect interview outcomes are addressed, including cultural, contextual, and developmental factors. Third, general strategies for interviewing children that are common across purposes and settings are delineated. Finally, a more holistic approach to research is suggested.

TYPES OF INTERVIEWS

Generally, interviews differ from ordinary conversations in that they usually have a definite purpose and a well-defined relationship – the interviewer questions, and the interviewee answers (Sattler, 1998). The interviewer directs the interaction, selects the content and focus, often following a more formal structure. Typically, the purpose is to obtain pertinent and accurate information from the child. In the field, there are often important consequences to the outcome of the interview, including determination of an adult's freedom or incarceration when a child's testimony is at issue, selection of the appropriate medical treatment, or termination of parental rights. Child interviews tend to vary along a continuum. At one end are unstructured interactions that follow the child's lead in order to immerse the researcher in the lives of the children they seek to understand. At the other end of the continuum are highly structured interviews where exact wording of questions are scripted, answers are limited to one-word options, and interviewers have little discretion. In between are semi-structured formats where interviewers follow guidelines and cover predetermined topics but possess a good deal of flexibility in terms of the questions asked. Below we introduce three active areas of research on child interviews: clinical, ethnographic, and forensic.

Clinical interviews

There is a long tradition in child psychiatry and psychology of unstructured clinical interviews guided by various theoretical orientations (for example, psychoanalytic); (see Greenspan and Greenspan, 1991). Given the prevalence and popularity of clinical interviews in the mental health fields (Sattler, 1998), there has been comparatively little scientific research regarding their reliability, validity, or effectiveness over the years. This clinical literature is extensive and beyond the scope of this chapter. In the past 25 years, however, scientific interest has grown. Two sample areas are highlighted below: highly structured diagnostic interviewing to aid assessment and semi-structured motivational interviewing to aid treatment.

Structured diagnostic interviewing

In recent years, researchers, practitioners, and epidemiologists have turned to standardized, structured diagnostic interviews to estimate prevalence of childhood psychopathology in clinical and non-clinical samples or to arrive at psychiatric diagnoses and plan treatment in specific cases. Standardization increases reliability and validity of traditional diagnostic interviews and allows comparisons across studies. Structured interviews reduce interviewer bias and inference; each child is asked a subset of the same set of questions. Some are downward extensions of adult interviews and most have parallel parent and child versions. Structured interviews are thorough, systematic, and do not overlook diagnoses or symptoms. The best researched are the (a) *Diagnostic Interview Schedule for Children* (NIMH DISC-IV; Shaffer et al., 2000), (b) *Diagnostic Interview for Children and Adolescents* (DICA-R; Ezpeleta et al., 1997), (c) *Schizophrenia and Depression Schedule for Children* (K-SADS; Ambrosini, 2000; Birmaher et al., 2009), and (d) *Child Assessment Scale* (CAS; Hodges, Kline, Stern, Cytryn and McKnew, 1982).

To provide a sample of the method, the most highly structured of child interviews, the DISC, is described. The most recent version (NIMH-DISC-IV) is designed for children from 9 to 17 years of age to assess over 30 diagnoses from the American Psychiatric Association's *Diagnostic and Statistical Manual of Mental Disorders* (DSM-IV) and the World Health Organization's *International Statistical Classification of Diseases and Related Health Problems*, 10th version (ICD-10), including Attention Deficit Hyperactivity Disorder, Mood Disorders, and Disruptive Behaviour Disorders.[1] The DISC is cost-effective because it can be administered by trained lay interviewers. The questions are to be read exactly as written and are worded so they can be answered yes or no, sometimes or somewhat. The branching-tree question structure begins with broad 'stem' questions that are asked of everyone followed by 'contingent' questions to determine frequency, duration, and severity of endorsed symptoms. If diagnostic criteria are met, there are additional questions about age of onset, impairment, and treatment. Below are questions from the Separation Anxiety Disorder section (Shaffer et al., 2000):

- Some children worry a great deal about their (parents) being away. Do you worry that something bad might happen to your parents (like they might get sick, or be hurt, or die)?
- What do you worry about? Tell me more about that.
- How long have you been worried about that?
- Do you worry that your parents might go away and not come back?
- How long have you worried about that?
- Do you worry that something bad might happen to you, so you couldn't see your (parents) again (like getting kidnapped or killed)?
- What do you worry about? How long have you worried about that?

Administration time depends on the number of symptoms endorsed and varies from 70 to 120 minutes. Diagnoses are arrived at with a computer algorithm that requires the presence of the requisite number of symptoms for each diagnosis. There are computer-assisted versions of the DISC and versions in English, Spanish, and French. There is a self-administered version using a computer and headphones that is reported to increase the likelihood of youth disclosing sensitive information like suicidality and substance abuse because computers are perceived by youth as less judgemental. The central advantage of structured interviews, such as the DISC, is that their psychometric properties have been tested extensively in clinical and community samples (Shaffer et al., 2000).

According to Sattler's (1998) review of the literature, limitations of structured interviews include the fact that the rigid format may interfere with rapport development, lay interviewers and computers may miss subtle yet important cues and reactions, and one-word answers make meaningful leads difficult to follow up. Such interviews determine whether a diagnosis is present or absent but fail to address a functional analysis of the problem or deeper family, identity, or other intra- and interpersonal issues often used to plan treatment. Interviews are lengthy and there are no guarantees all children will understand questions as intended.

Motivational interviewing

Derived from the substance abuse treatment field, motivational interviewing (MI) techniques have been extended to the treatment of diseases that to some extent are associated with behaviour (such as asthma, diabetes, obesity, teen smoking, alcohol and drug use). Developed by Miller and Rollnick (2002) to help people change, it is defined as a 'client-centered, directive method for enhancing intrinsic motivation to change by exploring and resolving ambivalence' (2002: 25). Typically, interviewer questions are designed to help interviewees articulate the (a) disadvantages of the status quo, (b) advantages of change, (c) optimism for change, and (d) intention to change. Below are a few sample questions.

- How would you like for things to be different?
- What is it you want to change?
- What would be different about your life if you made that change?
- How might you go about making that change?
- What do you think is a good first step?
- What problems do you see that would get in your way?
- How could you deal with them?
- Suppose that one big thing in the way was not there. If it went away magically, how would you make the change?
- If you could make this change right now, by magic, how might things be better for you?

Rubak, Sandbaek, Lauritzen, and Christensen (2005) conducted a meta-analysis of MI effects on variables such as body mass, cholesterol, blood pressure, blood alcohol concentration, and cigarette use. Even though motivational interviews were brief, typically 15 minutes, three out of four studies found significant effects. The authors concluded

that with adults, MI outperforms traditional advice-giving for a broad range of psychological problems and physiological diseases. Although there is reasonable evidence that MI is effective in certain applications, how and why it works is far less clear.

The study of MI with children and adolescents is a relatively recent but rapidly advancing endeavour. MI has been investigated as a prevention and intervention tool with teens to target alcohol and drug use, smoking cessation (Brown et al., 2003), childhood obesity (Smith-Berg et al., 1999), and the management of adolescent diabetes (Channon, Smith and Gregory, 2003). Studies to date have been relatively small, not all have employed control groups, most focus on brief interventions compared to standard care or no treatment control groups. Hence, conclusions are tentative. The originators acknowledge that developmental changes necessitate adaptations that have not yet been tested; however, they believe MI is particularly well suited for preventing and treating high-risk behaviours common in adolescence.

Monti et al. (1999) randomly assigned 13- to 19-year-olds admitted to emergency rooms for alcohol-related events to either a 35–40 minute motivational interview or standard care (5 minutes providing handouts and referrals). At a 6-month follow-up, 18- to 19-year-olds in the MI condition were less likely to report drinking and driving, reported fewer moving violations, and reported fewer alcohol-related injuries and interpersonal conflicts. Among 13- to 17-year-olds, there were no group differences; however, this age group did not report high levels of drinking in the first place.

Researchers have found positive effects of MI with parents to help them implement parenting strategies that assist children in reducing behaviour problems. Dishion, Nelson, and Kavanagh (2003) conducted a randomized field trial targeting the parenting practices of families of young people in a public middle school. They examined the impact of the Family Check Up (FCU) on the course of substance use and deviant peer involvement. The FCU is a brief family-centred intervention that incorporates principles of MI to motivate parents to monitor and manage teens. As in previous research, parents and high-risk adolescents disengaged from each other from grades seven to nine, demonstrating decreased monitoring and communication. However, families who received the FCU intervention maintained monitoring, and at the four-year follow-up in ninth grade, there was a reduction in substance use among youth identified by teachers in sixth grade as high risk.

Also, researchers are testing MI with parents to prevent child abuse. In the United States, when parents referred for physical abuse are mandated to attend parenting programmes by the authorities, attrition rates are as high as 70 per cent (Lundquist and Hansen, 1998). In response, Chaffin et al. (2009) added an MI component to an evidence-based parenting programme, Parent–Child Interaction Therapy (PCIT), as it was transported into a child welfare field setting. In this setting, retention levels were well above what is usually expected or what is typically found in studies of PCIT alone.

Clearly, large-scale studies with children are needed. Researchers have yet to ascertain which motivational interviewing techniques are more or less effective at different stages of development. Some questions require meta-cognitive or perspective-taking skills not yet mastered by young children (for example, 'What is it about your problem that you or other people might see as reasons for concern?'); others are phrased in language too syntactically complex or require advance abstract reasoning skills. However, clinical recommendations to use MI with children and youth are increasing. Authors highlight the similarities between children who are not self-referred but brought to treatment by adults to solve adult-identified problems and addicts who enter treatment under external pressures and remain ambivalent about giving up their addictions. Digiuseppe, Linscott and Jilton (1996) make a good case for studying MI to promote a therapeutic

alliance and cope with the resistance and noncompliance common among children and teens.

Ethnographic interviewing

Ethnography is the study of people as they go about their everyday lives. Originally used by anthropologists to study unfamiliar cultural practices, ethnographic methods engage with children's own views of their lives to understand the cultural underpinnings and developmental pathways that shape children's perceptions of everyday life (Buchbinder, Longhofer, Barrett, Lawon and Floersch, 2006; James, 2001). The literature on the ethnography of childhood is extensive, ballooning over the second half of the twentieth century, in almost all regions of the world, and well beyond the scope of this chapter to review. Readers are referred to Robert LeVine's (2007) historical overview to demonstrate the extent and diversity of ethnographic accounts of childhood. Scholars in sociology and anthropology believe that we are in the midst of a long overdue shift in the paradigm of childhood research away from the exclusive focus on models of physical science (experimentation and manipulation) toward a more naturalist approach to exploring social and psychological phenomena as they exist, unaltered, in the world (James, 2001; Weisner, 2002). James argued that ethnography as a research methodology has enabled children to be recognized as people who can be studied in their own right, shifting from 'seeing children as the raw uninitiated recruits of the social world to seeing them as making a contribution to it, a changed perspective which has steered research toward doing work *with* children rather than *on* them' (James, 2001: 246).

Ethnographic approaches to interviewing are largely unstructured conversations with children engaged in natural activities, supplemented by observation, participant-observation, and full participation in an activity being observed. Bauman and Greenberg (1992) described core characteristics. First, such interviews are unstructured and nondirective, typically without predefined questions which by their nature impose an order upon the flow of information. Interviewees are encouraged to talk about a particular topic. Researchers ask for explanations and elaborations, and they occasionally ask provocative questions. Second, the interviewer collects descriptive data to discover and record children's everyday experiences and how they interpret them through questions like: Could you describe a typical day for me? Could you tell me what happened when you went to the doctor? According to Bauman and Greenberg (1992), interviewers avoid using questions that call for analysis, evaluation, or opinion.

Third, interviewers take on a role of ignorance, encouraging children to take the role of expert or teacher (Christensen, 2004). They strive to take on the 'least adult-like' role possible to minimize power differentials between children and adults that interfere with trust and discourage self-disclosure. Fourth, the interviewer strives to understand the child's experience from his or her point of view, deliberately setting aside, as much as possible, preconceived hypotheses. Lastly, researchers treat the child's language as data, as a window to the ways children structure and categorize experience, communicate culture, and construct reality. Typically, interviewers avoid introducing their own words and instead repeat the child's own expressions when probing.

Ethnographic interviews are common in child care research to help researchers appreciate the lived experience of caregivers, children's play, friendships, and peer conflicts (Buchbinder et al., 2006). Recently they have been used to understand children's experiences living 'on-line' using the Internet, instant messaging, and social networking sites (see Buckingham and Willett, 2006). In the health sector, ethnographic interviews are used extensively to understand what children know about everyday health and well-being, illnesses like leukaemia, and self-care and treatment management; to understand their perceptions of pain and the effects of pain medications; to understand how they consent/assent to therapy or research and how they cope with acute and chronic illness; and finally to understand their decision-making capacity and what they need to know to exercise decision-making abilities to comply with treatment plans (Baylis, Downie and Nuala, 1999; Rebok et al., 2001). Additionally, there is a long tradition of ethnographic methods in educational settings to understand children's experiences of learning and, more recently, bilingual education.

Quantitative researchers sometimes use ethnographic interview data to obtain an initial understanding of the phenomenon under study and to design surveys, questionnaires, or other quantitative instruments. For example, there has been a shift toward patient reported outcomes in clinical trials of medications. As consumers of pediatric health care, children are uniquely positioned to give their perspectives on health care quality (Varni, Limbers and Burwinkle, 2007). Varni and his colleagues used initial interviews of children's perceptions to develop the items for the PEdQL, a measure of health and quality of life tested on over 8500 children, ages 5 to 16, which demonstrates good reliability and construct validity (Varni et al., 2007).

In other sectors, where children are important consumer groups, ethnographic interviews are used to determine children's influence on family food buying practices and consumption to guide marketing and prevention practices. In another mixed-methods study, researchers interviewed Danish children 10–13 years of age and their parents while visiting them at school, buying food in grocery stores, and at home during cooking and eating. In-depth interviews were followed by survey questionnaires to 451 families. Earlier studies had focused on decision dominance and influence (for example, who has the final say in purchases) or family-decision making models that relied exclusively on parental report, viewing children as passive rather than active sources of influence on consumption. These researchers found that everyday routines are an explanatory factor and mediator of children's influence on family food decisions (Mikkelson and Norgaard, 2004). Although the literature on the ethnography of childhood is expanding, there are few ethnographic studies of the interview process itself. However, the literature is peppered with researcher recommendations for facing the challenges of interviewing young children.

Forensic interviews

Forensic interviews are typically employed when legal decisions are pending; hence reliability, accuracy, and trustworthiness of children's reports are paramount. As witnesses to community or domestic violence and as alleged victims of sexual or physical abuse and neglect, children are informants in decisions about adult accountability and punishment. In personal injury cases, the child's responses contribute to a judgement about how an event (such as an accident, exposure to toxic chemical or medical negligence) may have contributed to a medical or psychiatric problem in order to estimate damages. In child protection and law enforcement settings, children's input is utilized to determine risk of physical danger, placement in foster care, termination of parental rights or permanency planning and adoption.

Twenty-five years ago, it was common during pre-trial investigations for child witnesses to be repeatedly interviewed by multiple interviewers from various agencies, each unaware of the other's activities and with no single agency taking responsibility for coordinating the process. Many interviewers lacked training and sensitivity to children's needs, unaware of the dangers of suggestive techniques with young children. Children were interviewed in the presence of siblings and parents — fertile ground for cross-contamination and unseen pressures – and interviews occurred in a wide range of uncontrolled settings, lacking safeguards and objectivity necessary to minimize potential for false accusation.

In contrast, today's forensic interview in the US is more likely to take place in one of the 800 accredited Children's Advocacy Centers (CACs) with a child interview specialist or in the context of a multi-disciplinary team. The hallmark of the child-friendly centres is the fact that they co-locate legal, social service, and medical personnel in one facility where the child has contact with a single highly skilled interviewer often using evidence-based techniques to gather sufficient information for multiple agencies to make a variety of decisions. The effectiveness of these centres or teams has not been tested rigorously yet, but there have been a few quasi-experimental evaluations of the centre model when compared to standard community services (see, for example, Cross, Jones, Walsh, Simone and Kolko, 2007; Miller and Rubin, 2009; Smith, Witte and Ficker-Elhai, 2006; Walsh, Lippert, Cross, Maurice and Davison, 2008).

Field studies have documented the problems that emanate from the use of completely unstructured interviews in the forensic context (Cederborg, Orbach, Sternberg and Lamb, 2000; Westcott and Kynan, 2006). Such interviews are ripe for introduction of bias and suggestion that can distort children's reports. Best-practice guidelines proffered by professional organizations typically describe a semi-structured approach (e.g., American Academy of Child and Adolescent Psychiatry, 2011; American Academy of Pediatrics: Kellog, 2005; American Professional Society on the Abuse of Children, 2012) based on the growing body of relevant scientific research (Ceci, Crossman, Scullin, Gilstrap and Huffman, 2002; Cronch, Viljoen and Hansen, 2006; Goodman and Melinder, 2007; Gudas and Sattler, 2006; Pipe, Lamb, Orbach and Esplin, 2004; Saywitz and Camparo, 2009, 2013; Saywitz, Lyon and Goodman, 2011; Sternberg, Lamb, Davies and Westcott, 2001; Wakefield, 2006). Again, a full review is beyond the scope of this chapter. Here we describe the evidence base, basic guidelines for a semi-structured approach, and three emerging evidence-based protocols.

In the experimental studies that form the evidence base for most forensic guidelines, children participate in a staged or natural event (such as classroom activity, field trip, emergency room visit, or stressful medical procedure) that is recorded or documented by observers, then children are interviewed at various delays about what took place and the accuracy of their reports are compared to the actual event. Studies make comparisons across different interviewing techniques to manipulate variables such as question type (open ended, yes/no, multiple choice, leading) or presence of social support. Comparisons are made across different populations (age group, SES level, or disability). To understand suggestibility and false alarm effects, children are interviewed about fictitious events as well, under various conditions that manipulate variables such as interviewer bias or utilization of memory enhancement strategies. In addition, field studies of actual child witnesses are increasing to complement the highly controlled, laboratory-based analogue studies.

Most guidelines adopt a phased approach, including an initial preparatory phase, a second phase of information gathering, and a third phase of closure.

The initial phase is traditionally a time for introductions and rapport development, but protocols often include (a) practising retelling a narrative that establishes a template for questioning, (b) explicit instructions, (c) a discussion of limitations on confidentiality, and depending on the jurisdiction and purpose (d) informal developmental assessment to ensure children have the linguistic and cognitive capabilities required to answer questions, and/or (e) a competency assessment, promise to tell the truth, or some type of truth–lie discussion (Lyon and Saywitz, 1999).

Preliminary explanations and practice tasks enjoy much empirical support from both field and laboratory studies. Early explanations and ground rules have shown positive effects on amount recalled without increasing errors (McCauley and Fisher, 1995; Mulder and Vrij, 1996; Saywitz, Snyder and Nathanson, 1999; Sternberg, Lamb, Esplin and Baradaran, 1999). Practice recounting everyday narratives (for example, 'Tell me what you did this morning from the time you got up until the time you arrived at the interview.') followed by minimal prompting with open-ended questions shows positive effects in the field on amount of information reported (Roberts, Lamb and Sternberg, 2004) and in the lab on accuracy of recall (see, for example, Brubacher, Roberts and Powell, 2011; Dorado and Saywitz, 2001).

The second interview phase (information-gathering) is an opportunity for children to provide an independent narrative of the event in question with minimal prompting from the interviewer ('Tell me what happened? Tell me more? What happened next? Anything else?'). When children's free recall is exhausted, follow-up questions refer back to information children have mentioned previously, using open-ended questions to help children elaborate, clarify, or justify their perceptions, preferences, and memories prior to more specific and potentially leading question types. Blatantly leading questions are to be avoided, such as, 'He hurt you, didn't he?'

There is overwhelming consensus for the use of open-ended questions that request multi-word responses, encouraging children to tell as much as they can in their own words, in comparison to closed questions that can be answered with a single word or short phrase (option-posing yes/no or multiple choice questions) or can be leading or suggestive (see, for example, Cronch et al., 2006; Lamb et al., 2003; Sternberg et al., 2001; Wood and Garven, 2000). For example, Waterman, Blades, and Spencer (2001) examined 5- and 9-year-olds' tendencies to speculate in response to yes/no and wh- questions (what, who, when, why, how). A majority of children correctly indicated when they did not know the answer to wh-questions but provided responses to yes/no questions even when such questions were unanswerable.

When children's memories are at issue in allegations of abuse, interviewers elicit statements relevant to the participants' identities, locations, physical activities, timing, threats, force, physical sensations, and so forth. Interviewers might explore:

- Specific actions *(You said he touched you, tell me more about how he touched you? What did he do with his hands? What did you see the people do?)*,
- Contexts *(What happened right before? Right after? What made it start? ... stop?)*,
- Emotional states of participants *('What made you think he was mad? What did he do/say to make you think so?)*,
- Other witnesses, or who else knows *(How did your sister learn about that? What did she see? ... hear? What did she do/say when she saw/heard what John did/said?)*, and
- Alternative explanations *(Who else takes care of you? ... on weekends? ... after school? Did John help you the same way as your mom? How was it different/not the same? Tell me more about how the babysitter helps you in the bath?)*.

In contrast, when children's preferences are at issue in custody planning, interviewers gather information on a wide range of topics, times, and places (for example, perceptions of relationships with parents, siblings, friends, relatives, and favourite activities to be preserved in a custody plan, descriptions of bathing, mealtimes, play dates, transportation, and chores). The goal is to gather information that contributes to the decision-making process, rather than condense the task to a question of where the child prefers to live. Interviewers avoid creating a forum that forces children to reject one parent and side with the other. Interviewers strive for neutrality and show an interest in hearing all sides by exploring as many incidents of positive caretaking by both parents as negative. Interviewers might explore:

- What happens when children in the family need help *(What would you do if you were lost? ... fell off your bike? ... felt ill? ... couldn't understand your homework?)*;
- Level of supervision *(When do you stay home alone? When your mom/dad is not there, who takes care of you? What would you do if you needed help and your mom was not there?)*;
- Patterns of conflict resolution *(How do people in your family solve problems when they do not agree?)*;
- Patterns of discipline *(What happens when children in your family do not follow the rules? ... do something they are not supposed to do? What makes your mom/dad happy/sad/upset?)*;
- Knowledge of safety rules *(What are the rules in your dad's/mom's house for keeping children safe?)*; and/or
- Fears and worries *(What could go wrong or make the child not safe?)*.

A third and final interview phase, closure, is routinely recommended although there is little research on this phase. Typically it involves (a) time for re-composure if the child is upset, (b) preparation to help understand the next steps of the legal process, (c) identification of anticipatory coping strategies if children fear negative consequences of revealing disclosures or preferences, and (d) time to address their questions.

Beyond these general guidelines, there are few evidence-based procedures subjected to randomized trials. One is the Cognitive Interview (CI), developed by Geiselman and Fisher, for use with adult witnesses by police officers. CI uses four memory jogging strategies derived from cognitive science to help witnesses recall details. CI has been tested with children in randomized trials in the United States and the United Kingdom. Results show that some of the techniques have been quite helpful (context reinstatement) but others problematic for younger children (change perspective task; McCauley and Fisher, 1995; Milne and Bull, 2003; Saywitz, Geiselman and Bornstein, 1992).

Another evidence-based approach is the Developmental Narrative Elaboration Interview (DNE) developed by Saywitz and her colleagues to help children ages 4 to 12 provide more accurate and detailed narratives of past experiences and perceptions, without tainting children's reports (Saywitz and Camparo, 2013). The DNE is comprised of a core template that lowers task demands to children's developmental level and optional evidence-based memory and communication strategies to improve children's performance. One optional technique, narrative elaboration, guides children to use simple non-leading retrieval cues to elaborate on participants, settings, actions, conversations, and affective states. There is an interim phase of narrative elaboration between free recall and specific questioning using either verbal category cues or visual category cues that involve a pre-interview practice task. Studies using randomized trials in the US, Canada, New Zealand, and Australia show positive effects on the quality and quantity of information children report, without increased errors or false reports of fictitious events (see Saywitz and Camparo, 2013, for review; Brown and Pipe, 2003; Peterson, Warren and Hayes, 2013).

Finally, the US National Institute of Child Health and Human Development (NICHD) Investigative Interview Protocol, developed by Lamb and his colleagues, is a set of structured guidelines for interviewing children about child abuse that has been studied extensively in the field in a wide array of countries and languages (e.g., French, Swedish, Hebrew and English; Lamb, Orbach, Hershkowitz, Esplin and Horowitz, 2007). The guidelines are derived from the extant research on child interviewing. Although we are not aware of any published evaluations with randomized trials of recall for documented events (so that accuracy of children's reports can be assessed), there are ample field-implementation studies to suggest that when field interviewers follow the protocol, they use more of the optimal techniques suggested in the literature (three times more open-ended questions) and avoid more of the suggestive techniques (half the number of suggestive questions) than interviewers who do not follow the protocol, thereby improving the quality of children's reports.

FACTORS AFFECTING INTERVIEWS

Cultural factors

Globalization, immigration, and ethnic diversity are rapidly growing trends worldwide. The need to understand the contributions of cultural factors to interview outcomes is clear. Maguire (2005) argues cogently that although multiculturalism is often framed as a resource in public policy decision-making, the reality is that children living in multicultural contexts are marginalized, excluded from research studies because they (or their parents who need to provide consent) do not speak the dominant language or are deemed too 'hard to reach'. They are interviewed without sensitivity to their preferred language and without appreciation for the fact that interviews are a dialogic process in which language and culture are intertwined (Bakhtin, 1986).

The following are truncated examples from Maguire's research that demonstrate the unique ways bilingual children (a) resisted the interview (CH: 'I can't talk, my lips don't want to move in English today.'), (b) challenged the interviewer (CH: 'You should give kids a choice in what language to use.'), and (c) negotiated rapport (CH: 'I don't want to talk.' I: 'Why?' CH: 'because I don't like to talk in French.' I: 'But you speak it so well.' CH: 'How do you know?'). These examples demonstrate the need for future research and theory to move well beyond the typical ways we have thus far studied and practised cultural differences in interviewing. Dominant theories of language acquisition do not 'explicitly acknowledge the mutually constitutive relationships among children's language development, social interactions, and the socio-culturally embedded nature of their accomplishments and potential, especially from the perspectives of children themselves' (Maguire, 2005: 1).

Most professional guidelines urge interviewers to take racial, cultural, and socioeconomic differences into account, but the empirical research necessary to accomplish this goal is decidedly lacking. Studies of cross-racial, cross-cultural interviews are rare. In one study, researchers compared Caucasian and African-American children's willingness to tell an interviewer they had witnessed an adult steal a purse (Dunkerley and Dalenberg, 2000). The adult 'thief's' race was matched to the race of the child. Caucasian children showed the same level of willingness regardless of interviewer race. However, African-American children were more reluctant to tell a Caucasian interviewer about the transgression.

Additionally, little is known about the effects of culturally defined communication styles on interview behaviour. Not surprisingly, words have different connotations even among same-language speakers from different cultural groups. For example, in Native American communities, kinship terms do not necessarily connote blood-relatives. Uncle can refer to a friendly man, Grandfather, or an old friendly man. Blahauvietz (2005) suggests it may be more useful to ask a Native American child who the important people in her life are or who sleeps in her house rather than make assumptions about a child's use of kinship terms.

Deeper cultural values also shape interview outcomes. Characteristics of Native American communities such as honouring elders with unquestioning allegiance, low levels of community anonymity, and historical mistrust of legal and social institutions may be associated with difficulties establishing rapport or increased rates of false denials of abuse. Willingness to disclose child sexual abuse in Arab and Hispanic families can be influenced by cultural taboos and values of shame, modesty, and an emphasis on virginity in determining marriage prospects (Fontes and Plummer, 2010), while respect and patriarchy can be influential variables among children from South Asian and Indian communities (Giligan and Akhtara, 2006; Gupta and Ailawadi, 2005). Moreover, studies in the United States are beginning to suggest that acculturation can be a more powerful variable than ethnicity itself in children's disclosure of sexual abuse (Katerndahl, Burge, Kellogg and Parra, 2005). To build a knowledge base sufficient to develop culturally competent interview guidelines with children, we need to understand how the suspicion and distrust that stems from children's experiences with migration, displacement, oppression, prejudice, and acculturation affect their interview behaviour. Perhaps an ethnographic approach could supplement existing experimental designs to achieve the deep understanding necessary to accomplish the social objectives that interviews seek to achieve in health care, day care, child protection, justice, education, or law enforcement.

Contextual factors

Contextual factors, such as the physical setting and the psycho-social atmosphere, play a pivotal role in interview outcome. Children perform interview-required skills (such as resisting suggestion, recalling details) better in some contexts (supportive, familiar) than others (intimidating, complex), which accounts for a great deal of their inconsistency across interviews (Price and Goodman, 1990; Revelle, Wellman and Karabenik, 1985). Developmental differences in children's contextual sensitivity suggest that as children mature, they develop a greater ability to resist distraction, to focus attention, and to function independently across settings of varied familiarity and complexity levels. Hence, interviewers who fail to remove intriguing objects that compete for a young child's attention or who answer cell phones during interviews may find it difficult to redirect a young child back to the task at hand.

Context of questioning is thought to influence stress level, motivation, cooperation, attention, retrieval of detail, resistance to suggestion, and communicative competence. In a study of the effects of the courtroom context on children's memory and anxiety during questioning, researchers compared responses of 80 8- to 10-year-olds questioned about a past classroom event. Half were questioned in a mock courtroom environment at a university law school, and half were questioned in a small, private room (Nathanson and Saywitz, 2003). Children questioned in the courtroom showed impaired memory and greater heart rate variability (indicative of a stress response) when compared with children questioned in the private room.

Another essential element of the context is the interviewer. Lamb and Garreston (2003) examined interviewer gender in 672 forensic field interviews in three countries. The amount of information that children provided varied depending on interviewer gender, child gender and age, and question type. Girls of all ages provided more information in response to directive questions posed by female interviewers than by male interviewers. Additionally, in the eyewitness memory literature, interviewer neutrality and bias are the keys to most models of children's suggestibility. Numerous experimental studies demonstrate the power to distort children's reports by manipulating interviewers' a priori knowledge and the interviewer's subsequent use of suggestive questions to introduce misleading information not mentioned by the child previously (see, for example, Bruck, Ceci and Hembrooke, 1998; Ceci et al., 2002; Garven et al., 2000; Malloy, Quas, Melinder, D'Mello and Goodman, 2005).

Studies also find benefits of emotional and social support provided by interviewers (e.g., warmth, eye contact, neutral reinforcement, using the child's name). When interviewers are supportive (as opposed to intimidating or cold/neutral), and social support is not tied to the content of children's responses, it can help children overcome resistance and improve performance, without contaminating their accounts (see Bottoms, Quas and Davis, 2007, for review). In fact, under these conditions, children are more resistant to leading questions when the context is supportive. Moreover, benefits of support are strongest when discussing highly stressful, meaningful life events (Quas, Rush, Klemfuss and Yim, 2013).

Ethnographers also analyse the role of the interviewer, especially issues of inherent and culturally reinforced power differentials as they affect consent/assent to participate in research and medical treatment. They argue that interviewers need to mediate adult–child discrepancies by treating children as cultural experts (Christensen and James 2000; Mandell, 1991; Weisner, 2002). They take steps to counteract children's expectations of adult social roles. For example, Mandell (1991) repeatedly told children, 'I am not a teacher' and 'You will have go to your teacher for that' when conducting interviews on school grounds. Experimental studies confirm that children expect from an early age that adults know more than children (Taylor, Cartwright and Bowden, 1991). In one study, preschoolers were more suggestible when questioned (about the same event with the same questions) by an adult than by an older child (Ceci, Ross and Toglia, 1987). In another study, when asked directly, 8-year-olds said that they believed that the adult asking the questions already knew the answers, even though he had not been present at the event in question (Nathanson and Saywitz, 2003).

Researchers have tried to remedy children's deference to adult knowledge. In several studies, interviewers announced that the interviewer had not been present at the event in question and therefore could not help the child answer the questions. Interviewers emphasized they were most interested in what the *child* remembered and believed. Children who received these instructions made fewer errors when interviewed about past events, although it is not clear whether their perceptions of adult authority status did in fact change as a result of the instructions (see, for example, Mulder and Vrij, 1996; Saywitz and Lyon, 2002; Saywitz and Moan-Hardie, 1994).

Another central element of the context is the rapport between the interviewer and the child. Yet, field studies suggest that interviewers often fail to establish adequate rapport with children before launching into questions about the topic at hand (Westcott and Kynan, 2006). In fact, one study found that when children expressed reluctance, interviewers responded in ways that were counterproductive. Interviewers asked more closed- as opposed to open-ended questions with reluctant than with non-reluctant children (Villalba, Malloy and Lamb, 2013). Not surprisingly, field studies suggest that greater emphasis on rapport building reduces reluctance and aids self-disclosure and cooperation, especially for less talkative children (Hershkowitz, 2009; Lamb, Hershkowitz, Malloy and Katz, 2013). Both field and experimental studies have found that using open-ended prompts during rapport development is associated with more detailed responses to open-ended prompts during the subsequent interview about the topic at hand (Hershkowitz, 2009; Roberts et al., 2004). Thus far, researchers have focused on techniques used by interviewers in preliminary interactions before substantive questioning begins. However, it is important to remember that rapport is a dynamic, transactional process that evolves over the course of the entire interview. Rapport can wax and wane as the interview progresses. With regard to future research, we still know little about how children decide whom to trust and whom not to trust nor the conditions under which techniques designed to overcome resistance, anxiety, or to build trust might have positive, negative, or no effects on memory or self-disclosure.

Developmental factors

Recommendations to use a developmental framework for eliciting and interpreting children's interview behaviour are ubiquitous in the child interview literature (see, for example, Saywitz and Camparo, 1998, 2013; Tang, 2006). The efficacy of a particular questioning technique and the accuracy of a child's self-report depend on maturation in communicative competence (including auditory discrimination and articulation skills, conversational rules, expressive and receptive vocabulary, and syntax), cognition (such as knowledge base, meta-cognitive awareness, reasoning ability, memory, and attention),

and socio-emotional maturity (for example, perspective-taking skills, self-understanding, coping strategies) to name a few relevant domains. A thorough review of the relevant developmental research would be well beyond the scope of this chapter. Instead a few examples in language acquisition, cognition, and self-concept are highlighted.

Often efforts to elicit information from children are frustrated by developmental limitations on children's communicative competence. One study examined how children cope when adults ask incomprehensible questions and whether interview performance can be enhanced by teaching children comprehension monitoring and response strategies. In the study 180 6- and 8-year-old children's memories of a particular event were tested with questions varying in linguistic complexity. When confronted with complex syntax and sophisticated vocabulary that exceeded their level of language comprehension, children in the control group tried to answer questions anyway, but they were as likely to respond incorrectly as correctly. They rarely asked for clarification. This inaccuracy stands in sharp contrast to the high levels of accurate memory for the same events demonstrated when questions were phrased simply, using short utterances and one or two syllable words. In contrast, when a second group was instructed to verbalize their lack of comprehension during the interview, they performed significantly better. And when a third group received the instructions and prepared for the interview with practice detecting and coping with noncomprehension, they showed marked improvement over the other two groups (Cordon, Saetermoe and Goodman, 2005; Saywitz et al., 1999). Studies of field interviews and courtroom testimony have documented how often adults use lengthy, grammatically complex questions with sophisticated vocabulary that exceed a child's level of language comprehension (Korkman, Santilla, Drzewiecki and Sandnabba, 2008).

Developmental trends in cognitive abilities are equally important to children's interview performance and adults' interpretation of children's answers. Interviewers that ask young children questions requiring hypothetical-deductive logic or conventional units of measurement before children have mastered such skills will find fertile ground for misinterpretation (for example, asking *What time was it? How tall was she? How far away was it? How much did he weigh?* before children master the use of hours, minutes, feet, inches, miles, pounds, or dates of the calendar year).

Open-ended interviews about self-concept suggest a child's ability to describe themselves develops gradually as well. Initially self-descriptions focus on observable behaviours ('I run fast'), physical attributes ('I have black hair'), possessions ('I have a cat'), and activities ('I like to play soccer') that are often situation-specific. With growth and experience, they move toward more abstract, psychological, and trait-like descriptions. Over time, children become more accurate in judging their own abilities relative to others, adjusting their self-descriptions to incorporate feedback and past experiences, and self-reflecting, self-monitoring, and self-evaluating. As a result, Cepeda (2010) suggested that interviews with preschoolers about their emotions may be more successful when concrete and action-oriented questions are employed (for example, 'What makes you cry?' rather than 'What makes you sad?'). With age and experience, children develop greater ability to identify feeling states and use a more nuanced vocabulary for describing their feelings. Studies of children's ability to accurately report their own health status, for example symptoms of asthma, suggest that children as young as seven may be dependable and valuable reporters of their health, although data quality improves with age (Olson et al., 2007).

In addition to developmental factors, it is worth noting that researchers are also beginning to find effects of individual differences on interview outcome. For example, children with more self-confidence and higher self-esteem are less likely to acquiesce to adult suggestion. Moreover, individual differences do not operate solely within the child, but affect the child–interviewer dyad. For example, differences in social competence (for example, sociability vs. shyness/withdrawal) are mediated by differential responses of interviewers, which then, in turn, influence children's subsequent behaviour (Gilstrap and Papierno, 2004). Future researchers will need to take into account the dynamic nature of the interview process and study the dyad rather than the child as the unit of analysis.

EMPIRICALLY DERIVED INTERVIEW STRATEGIES

The last two decades of research have resulted in an emerging consensus on some general principles of child interviewing, coalescing around a group of research-based strategies. Although there is still much debate and research to be conducted on the finer points of interviewing, general recommendations include:

1 *Adapt the interview task demands to the child's developmental level.* At a minimum, use language that children comprehend and ask about concepts they can understand (for example, use simple vocabulary, short sentences, concrete terms, proper names and active voice, etc.).
2 *Take time to establish trust and rapport with children through non-suggestive means.*
3 *Provide an age-appropriate, private setting with minimal distractions.*
4 *Promote a supportive, welcoming, non-threatening atmosphere.*
5 *Provide introductions that explain the interviewer's and interviewee's role, the purpose of the interview, what will happen to the information provided. Emphasize that the child is the expert and the adult is genuinely interested in the child's point of view on the subject.*
6. *Provide an opportunity for children to practise answering the questions and providing the kinds of information the interview will demand before moving on to the topic at hand.* Interviews differ from the kind of everyday conversations with adults that children expect: model a template before substantive questioning.

7 *Set ground rules and provide explicit instructions, such as*:

   (a) When memories are at issue, instruct children to be complete – to tell everything they can remember from the beginning to the end, even the little things they might not think are important;

   (b) Instruct children to ask for clarification if they do not understand a question (for example, 'I don't know what you mean'; 'I don't get it'; 'Tell me in new words');

   (c) Give children permission to admit lack of knowledge or recall; give permission to say, 'I don't know' or 'I don't remember', but if they know the answer, to tell the answer;

   (d) Remind children that they are the experts; the interviewer was not present at the incidents under discussion and cannot help children answer the questions;

   (e) Give permission to correct the interviewer if the interviewer says something that is wrong (for example, 'Sometimes I put my guess into a question, tell me if I say something wrong'); or

   (f) When appropriate, instruct children to tell the truth and not to pretend or make up anything.

8 *Remain objective and neutral; Set aside biases and explore alternative hypotheses and explanations.*

9 *To minimize distortion, avoid suggestive techniques that mislead, introduce bias, reinforce interviewer expectations, apply peer pressure, stereotype people, or invite children to pretend and speculate.* Avoid utterances that are coercive ('You cannot play until after you tell me what happened with John'), questions with tags that ask for verification ('He hurt you, didn't he? ... isn't that true?'), negative terms ('Didn't that hurt?'), suppositional questions ('When he hurt you, was he happy or mad?'), and multiple choice questions whenever possible.

10 *To elicit longer, more detailed responses from children, use open-ended questions that require multi-word responses; invite children to elaborate in their own words (for example, 'What happened next? Tell me more. What makes you think so?'); listen attentively and don't interrupt.*

11 *When more focused follow-up questions are needed to elicit details, return to information provided by the child ('You said Tom was there, what did he do?'); use 'Wh' questions that ask for multi-word responses to elicit details (what, where, who, when, how, etc.); rephrase yes/no or multiple-choice questions (for example, 'Did John hit you?' becomes 'What did he do with his* hands?') When yes/no questions are required, follow-up immediately with open-ended prompts to verify that a child's yes or no means what you think it means ('Did you see what happened? Yes. Tell me what you saw.').

12 *When the interview is over, take time for closure, prepare children for next stage of the process, thank children for their effort and invite questions from children.*

NEXT STEP: HOLISTIC APPROACH TO RESEARCH AND PRACTICE

This overview makes clear that children are interviewed daily in the laboratory and in the field in nearly every sector of society. The information they provide helps to discover new knowledge, to set public policy, and to make pivotal decisions in the lives of individuals and families. Despite significant strides in many silos of research on child interviewing, there has been minimal interaction across research sectors, impeding our ability to build cumulative knowledge in this field. In fact, often there has been tension and polarization. Early ethnographic studies were used to criticize formulations in developmental psychology. Developmental psychologists were reluctant to take evidence from field research seriously (LeVine, 2007). In the area of child maltreatment, polarization of researchers and clinicians has been exacerbated by the adversarial nature of the legal system. Greater cross-pollination may well produce new paradigms that individual fields could not develop alone (see Saywitz, Esplin and Romanoff, 2007, for discussion).

Over the last 25 years, distinct domains of research on child interviewing have evolved along separate paths. The cumulative body of knowledge remains fragmented. The aim of this chapter was to illustrate the breadth of the literature and the potential for a cross discipline research agenda. New mixed-methods paradigms may be necessary to create a knowledge base that informs the full range of issues, policies, and decisions on which children's voices are heard.

NOTE

1 Efforts are underway to revise the DISC in order to accommodate changes in the DSM-5 and the ICD-11.

REFERENCES

Ambrosini, P.J. (2000) 'Historical development and present status of the schedule for affective disorders and schizophrenia for school-age children (K-SADS)', *Journal of the American Academy of Child and Adolescent Psychiatry*, 39(1): 49–58.

American Academy of Child and Adolescent Psychiatry (2011) 'Practice parameters for child and adolescent forensic evaluations', *Journal of the American Academy of Child and Adolescent Psychiatry*, 50(12): 1299–312.

American Professional Society on the Abuse of Children (2012) *Practice Guidelines: Forensic Interviewing in Cases of Suspected Abuse*, pp. 1–28. Chicago: APSAC.

Bahkhtin, M. (1986) *The Dialogic Imagination*. Austin: University of Texas Press.

Bauman, L.J. and Greenberg, L. (1992) 'The use of ethnographic interviewing to inform questionnaire construction', *Health Education and Behavior*, 19(1): 9–23.

Baylis, F., Downie, J. and Nuala, K. (1999) 'Children and decision making in health research', *IRB: A Review of Human Subjects Research*, 2(4): 5–10.

Birmaher, B., Ehmann, M., Axelson, D.A., Goldstein, B.I., Monk, K., Kalas, C., Kupfer, D., Gill, M.K., Leibenluft, E., Bridge, J., Guyer, A., Egger, H.L., and Brent, D.A. (2009) 'Schedule for affective disorders and schizophrenia for school-age children (K-SADS-PL) for the assessment of preschool children: A preliminary psychometric study', *Journal of Psychiatric Research*, 43: 680–86.

Blahauvietz, S. (2005) 'Key factors in forensic interviews with Native American children', *National Center for Prosecution of Child Abuse Update*, 18(6), Washington DC: American Prosecutor's Research Institute.

Bottoms, B.L., Quas, J.A. and Davis, S.L. (2007) 'The influence of interviewer-provided social support on children's suggestibility, memory, and disclosures', in M.E. Pipe, M. Lamb, Y. Orbach, and A.C. Cederborg (eds.), *Child Sexual Abuse: Disclosure, Delay, and Denial*. Mahwah, NJ: Lawrence Erlbaum Associates, Publishers. pp. 135–58.

Brown, D. and Pipe, M.-E. (2003) 'Variations on a technique: Enhancing children's recall using Narrative Elaboration training', *Applied Cognitive Psychology*, 17: 377–99.

Brown, R., Ramsey, S., Strong, D., Myers, M., Kahler, C., Lejuez, C., Niaura, R., Palloenen, U., Kazura, A., Goldstein, M. and Abrams, D. (2003) 'Effects of motivational interviewing on smoking cessation in adolescents with psychiatric disorders', *Tobacco Control*, 12(4): 3–10.

Brubacher, S.P., Roberts, K.P. and Powell, M. (2011) 'Effects of practicing episodic versus scripted recall on children's subsequent narratives of a repeated event', *Psychology, Public Policy and Law*, doi:10.1037/a0022793.

Bruck, M., Ceci, S.J. and Hembrooke, H. (1998) 'Reliability and credibility of young children's reports: From research to policy and practice', *American Psychologist*, 53(2): 136–51.

Buchbinder, M. Longhofer, J., Barrett, T., Lawon, T. and Floersch, J. (2006) 'Ethnographic approaches to child care research: A review of the literature', *Journal of Early Childhood Research*, 4(1): 45–63.

Buckingham, D. and Willett, R. (eds.) (2006) *Digital Generations: Children, Young People and New Media*. London: Lawrence Erlbaum.

Ceci, S., Crossman, A., Scullin, M., Gilstrap, L. and Huffman, M. (2002) 'Children's Suggestibility Research: Implications for the Courtroom and the Forensic Interview', in H. Westcott, G. Davies and R. Bull (eds.), *Children's Testimony: A Handbook of Psychological Research and Forensic Practice*. NY: Wiley and Sons, pp. 117–32.

Ceci, S.J., Ross, D.F. and Toglia, M.P. (1987) 'Age differences in suggestibility: Narrowing the uncertainties', in S.J. Ceci, M.P. Toglia and D.F. Ross (eds.), *Children's Eyewitness Memory*. New York: Springer-Verlag, pp. 79–91.

Cederborg, A.C., Orbach, Y., Sternberg, K.J. and Lamb, M.E. (2000) 'Investigative interviews of child witnesses in Sweden', *Child Abuse and Neglect*, 24(10): 1355–61.

Cepeda, C. (2010) *Clinical Manual for the Psychiatric Interview of Children and Adolescents*. Arlington, VA: American Psychiatric Publishing.

Chaffin, M., Valle, L., Funderburk, B., Gurwitch, R., Silovsky, J., McCoy, C. and Kees, M. (2009) 'A motivational intervention can improve retention in PCIT for low-motivation child welfare clients', *Child Maltreatment*, 14(4): 356–68.

Channon, S., Smith, V.J. and Gregory, J.W. (2003) 'A pilot study of motivational interviewing in adolescents with diabetes', *Archives of Disease in Childhood – BMJ*, 88(8): 680–3.

Christensen, P.H. (2004) 'Children's participation in ethnographic research: Issues of power and representation', *Children and Society*, 18(2): 165–76.

Christensen, P.H. and James, A. (eds.) (2000) *Research with Children: Perspectives and Practices*. London: Falmer Press.

Cordon, I.M., Saetermoe, C.L. and Goodman, G.S. (2005) 'Facilitating children's accurate responses: Conversational rules and interview style', *Applied Cognitive Psychology*, 19(3): 249–66.

Cronch, L.E., Viljoen, J.L. and Hansen, D.J. (2006) 'Forensic interviewing in child sexual abuse cases: Current techniques and future directions', *Aggression and Violent Behavior*, 11(3): 195–207.

Cross, T. P., Jones, L. M., Walsh, W. A., Simone, M. and Kolko, D. (2007) 'Child forensic interviewing in Children's Advocacy Centers: Empirical data on a practice model', *Child Abuse and Neglect: The International Journal*, 31(10): 1031–52.

Damon, W. and Lerner, R. (eds.) (2006) *Handbook of Child Psychology*, 6th ed., Vols. 1–4. Hoboken, NJ: John Wiley and Sons.

Digiuseppe, R., Linscott, J. and Jilton, R. (1996) 'Developing therapeutic alliance in child-adolescent psychotherapy', *Applied and Preventive Psychology*, 5(2): 85–100.

Dishion, T.J., Nelson, S.E. and Kavanagh, K. (2003) 'The family check up with high-risk young adolescents: Preventing early onset substance use by parent monitoring', *Behavior Therapy*, 34(4): 553–71.

Dorado, J. and Saywitz, K. (2001) 'Interviewing preschoolers from low and middle income communities: A test of the narrative elaboration recall improvement technique', *Journal of Clinical Child Psychology*, 30(4): 566–78.

Dunkerley, G. and Dalenberg, C. (2000) 'Secret keeping in black and white children as a function of interviewer race, racial identity, and risk for abuse', in K.C. Faller (ed.), *Maltreatment in Early Childhood: Tools for Research-Based Intervention*. New York: Haworth Press, pp. 13–36.

Ezpeleta, L., de la Osa, N., Domenech, J., Navarro, J.B., Losilla, J.N. and Judez, J. (1997) 'Diagnostic agreement between clinicians and the diagnostic interview for children and adolescents (DICA-R) in an outpatient sample', *Journal of Child Psychology and Psychiatry*, 38: 431–40.

Fontes, L. and Plummer, C. (2010) 'Cultural issues in disclosures of child sexual abuse', *Journal of Child Sexual Abuse*, 19: 491–518.

Garven, S., Wood, J.M. and Malpass, R.S. (2000) 'Allegations of wrongdoing: The effects of reinforcement on children's mundane and fantastic claims', *Journal of Applied Psychology*, 85(1): 38–49.

Gilligan, P. and Akhtar, S. (2006) 'Cultural barriers to the disclosure of child abuse in Asian communities: Listening to what women say', *British Journal of Social Work*, 36: 1361–77.

Gilstrap, L.L. and Papierno, P.B. (2004) 'Is the cart pushing the horse: The effects of child characteristics on children's and adults' interview behaviours', *Applied Cognitive Psychology*, 18: 1059–78.

Goode, W.J. (1993) *World Changes in Divorce Patterns*. New Haven: Yale University Press.

Goodman, G.S. (2006) 'Children's eyewitness memory: A modern history and contemporary commentary', *Journal of Social Issues*, 62(4): 811–32.

Goodman, G.S. and Melinder, A. (2007) 'Child witness research and forensic interviews of young children: A review', *Legal and Criminological Psychology*, 12(1): 1–19.

Greenspan, S. and Greenspan, N.T. (1991) *Clinical Interview of the Child*. Washington, DC: American Psychiatric Press.

Gudas, L.S. and Sattler, J.M. (2006) 'Forensic interviewing of children and adolescents', in S. Sparta and G. Koocher (eds.), *Forensic Mental Health Assessment of Children and Adolescents*. New York: Oxford University Press, pp. 115–28.

Gupta, A. and Ailawadi, A. (2005) 'Childhood and adolescent sexual abuse and incest: Experiences of women survivors in India', in S.J. Jejeebhoy, I. Shah, and S. Thapa (eds.), *Sex without Consent: Young People in Developing Countries*, pp. 171–202, New York: Zed Books.

Hershkowitz, I. (2009) 'Socioemotional factors in child abuse investigations', *Child Maltreatment*, 14(2): 172–81.

Hodges, K., Kline, J., Stern, L., Cytryn, L. and McKnew, D. (1982) 'The development of the child assessment interview for research and clinical use', *Journal of Abnormal Child Psychology*, 10(2): 173–89.

James, A. (2001) 'Ethnography in the Study of Childhood', in P.A. Atkinson, A. Coffey, S. Delemont, J. Lofland and L. Lofland (eds.), *Handbook of Ethnography*. London: Sage, pp. 246–57.

Katerndahl, D., Burge, S., Kellogg, N. and Parra, J. (2005) 'Differences in childhood sexual abuse experience between adult Hispanic and Anglo women in a primary care setting', *Journal of Child Sexual Abuse*, 14(2): 85–95.

Kellog, N.D. (2005) 'Clinical report of the American Academy of Pediatrics: The evaluation of sexual abuse in children', *Pediatrics*, 116(2): 506–12.

Korkman, J., Santtila, P., Drzewiecki, T., and Sandnabba, N.K. (2008) 'Failing to keep it simple: Language use in child sexual abuse interviews with 3–8 year old children', *Psychology, Crime & Law*, 14(1): 41–60.

Lamb, M.E. and Garreston, M.E. (2003) 'The effects of interviewer gender and child gender on the informativeness of alleged child sexual abuse victims in forensic interviews', *Law and Human Behavior*, 27(2): 157–71.

Lamb, M.E., Hershkowitz, I., Malloy, L.C. and Katz, C. (March, 2013) *Does Enhanced Focus on Rapport Building Affect Cooperativeness of Reluctant Children in Forensic Interview Contexts?* Paper presented at the annual conference of American Psychology-Law Society, Portland, OR.

Lamb, M.E., Orbach, Y., Hershkowitz, I., Esplin, P.W. and Horowitz, D. (2007) 'A structured interview protocol improves the quality and informativeness of investigative interviews with children: A review of research using the NICHD Investigative Interview Protocol', *Child Abuse and Neglect*, 31(11–12): 1201–31.

Lamb, M.E., Sternberg, K.J., Orbach, Y., Esplin, P.W., Stewart, H. and Mitchell, S. (2003) 'Age differences in young children's responses to open-ended invitations in the course of forensic interviews', *Journal of Consulting and Clinical Psychology*, 71(5): 926–34.

LeVine, R. (2007) 'Ethnographic studies of childhood: A historical overview', *American Anthropologist*, 109(2): 247–60.

Lundquist, L.M. and Hansen, D.J. (1998) 'Enhancing treatment adherence, social validity, and generalization of parent-training interventions with physically abusive and neglectful families', in J.R. Lutzker (ed.), *Handbook of Child Abuse Research and Treatment*. New York: Plenum Press, pp. 449–71.

Lyon, T.D. and Saywitz, K.J. (1999) 'Young maltreated children's competence to take the oath', *Applied Developmental Science*, 3(1): 16–27.

McCauley, M.R. and Fisher, R.P. (1995) 'Facilitating children's eyewitness recall with the revised cognitive interview', *Journal of Applied Psychology*, 80(4): 510–16.

Maguire, M.H. (2005) 'What if you talked to me? I could be interesting! Ethical research considerations in engaging with bilingual/multicultural child participants in human inquiry', *Forum: Qualitative Social Research*, 6(1): 1–17.

Malloy, L., Quas, J., Melinder, A., D'Mello, M. and Goodman, G. (2005) *Effects of Repeated Interviews on the Information Retrieved by Child Witnesses in Forensic Interviews*. Scottsdale, AZ: American-Law Society Convention.

Mandell, N. (1991) 'The least adult role in studying children', in F. Walksler (ed.), *Studying the Social Worlds of Children*. London: Falmer Press, pp. 433–67.

Mikkelsen, M.R. and Norgaard, M.K. (2004) *Children's Influence on Family Decision-Making in Food Buying and Consumption*. Copenhagen: Denmark National Institute of Public Health.

Miller, W.R. and Rollnick, S. (2002) *Motivational Interviewing: Preparing People to Change*. New York: Guilford Press.

Miller, A. and Rubin, D. (2009) 'The contribution of child advocacy centers to felony prosecutions of child sexual abuse', *Child Abuse and Neglect*, 33(1): 12–18.

Milne, R. and Bull, R. (2003) 'Does the cognitive interview help children to resist the effects of suggestive questioning', *Legal and Criminological Psychology*, 8(1): 21–38.

Monti, P.M., Colby, S.M., Barnett, N.P., Spirito, A., Rohsenow, D.J., Myers, M., Woolard, R. and Lewander, W. (1999) 'Brief intervention for harm reduction with alcohol positive older adolescents in a hospital emergency department', *Journal of Consulting and Clinical Psychology*, 67(6): 989–94.

Mulder, M.R. and Vrij, A. (1996) 'Explaining conversations rules to children: An intervention study to facilitate children's accurate responses', *Child Abuse and Neglect*, 10(7): 623–31.

Nathanson, R. and Saywitz, K.J. (2003) 'Effects of the courtroom context on children's memory and anxiety', *Journal of Psychiatry and Law*, 31(1): 67–98.

Olson, L.M., Radecki, L., Frintner, M.P., Weiss, K.B., Korfmacher, J. and Siegel, R.M. (2007) 'At what age can children report dependably on their asthma health status?' *Pediatrics*, 119(1): 93–102.

Peterson, C., Warren, K. L. and Hayes, A.H. (2013) 'Revisiting the Narrative Elaboration training: An ecologically relevant event', *Journal of Cognition & Development*, 14(1): 154–74. doi:10.1080/152483 72.2011.638688

Pipe, M.E., Lamb, M.E., Orbach, Y. and Esplin, P. (2004) 'Recent research on children's testimony about experienced and witnessed events', *Developmental Review*, 24(4): 440–68.

Price, D.W. and Goodman, G.S. (1990) 'Visiting the Wizard: Children's memory for a recurring event', *Child Development*, 61(3): 664–80.

Quas, J. Rush, E., Klemfuss, J.Z. and Yim, I.S., (March, 2013) 'When does interviewer demeanour matter? Effects of Supportive Questioning on children's reports of stressful and nonstressful events', paper reported at the annual conference of the American Psychology-Law Society in Portland, OR.

Rebok, G., Riley, A., Forrest, C., Starfield, B., Green, B., Robertson, J. and Tambor, E. (2001) 'Elementary school-aged reports of their health: A cognitive interviewing study', *Quality of Life Research*, 10(1): 59–70.

Revelle, G., Wellman, H. and Karabenik, J. (1985) 'Comprehension monitoring in preschool children', *Child Development*, 56(3): 654–63.

Roberts, K.P., Lamb, M.E. and Sternberg, K.J. (2004) 'The effects of rapport-building style on children's reports of a staged event', *Applied Cognitive Psychology*, 18: 189–202.

Rubak, S., Sandbaek, A., Lauritzen, T. and Christensen, B. (2005) 'Motivational interviewing: a systematic review and meta-analysis', *The British Journal of General Practice*, 55(513): 305–12.

Sattler, J. (1998) *Clinical and Forensic Interviewing of Children and Families*. San Diego, CA: Jerome M. Sattler, Publisher.

Saywitz, K. and Camparo, L. (1998) 'Interviewing child witnesses: A developmental perspective', *The International Journal of Child Abuse and Neglect*, 22(8): 825–43.

Saywitz, K. and Camparo, L. (2009) 'Contemporary child forensic interviewing: Evolving consensus and innovation over 25 years', in B.L. Bottoms, G.S. Goodman and C.J. Najdowski (eds.), *Child Victims, Child Offenders: Psychology and Law*. Guildford Publications, pp. 102–27.

Saywitz, K.J. and Camparo, L. (2013) *Evidence-based Child Forensic Interviewing: The Developmental Narrative Elaboration Interview*. New York: Oxford University Press.

Saywitz, K.J., Esplin, P. and Romanoff, S.L. (2007) 'A Holistic approach to interviewing and treating children in the legal system', in M.E. Pipe, M.E., Lamb, Y. Orbach and A.C. Cederborg (eds.), *Child Sexual Abuse: Disclosure, Delay, and Denial*. Mahwah, NJ: Lawrence Erlbaum Associates, Publishers, pp. 219–50.

Saywitz, K.J., Geiselman, R.E. and Bornstein, G.K. (1992) 'Effects of cognitive interviewing and practice on children's recall performance', *Journal of Applied Psychology*, 77(5): 744–56.

Saywitz, K. and Lyon, T. (2002) 'Coming to grips with children's suggestibility', in G. Goodman, J. Quas and M. Eisen (eds.), *Memory and Suggestibility in the Forensic Interview*. Mahwah, NJ: Erlbaum Associates, Pub, pp. 85–114.

Saywitz, K.J., Lyon, T.D., and Goodman, G.S. (2011) 'Interviewing Children', in J.E. Myers (ed.), *APSAC Handbook of Child Maltreatment* (3rd ed.). Newberry Park, CA: Sage, pp. 337–360.

Saywitz, K. and Moan-Hardie, S. (1994) 'Reducing the potential for distortion of childhood memories', *Consciousness and Cognition*, 3(3): 257–93.

Saywitz, K.J., Snyder, L. and Nathanson, R. (1999) 'Facilitating the communicative competence of the child witness', *Applied Developmental Science*, 3(1): 58–68.

Shaffer, D., Fisher, P., Lucas, C., Dulcan, M. and Schwab-stone, E. (2000) 'NIMH Diagnostic interview Schedule for Children Version IV (NIMH-DISC-IV): Description, differences from previous versions and reliability of some common diagnoses', *Journal of the American Academy of Child and Adolescent Psychiatry*, 39(1): 28–38.

Smith, D.W., Witte, T.H. and Fricker-Elhai, A.E. (2006) 'Service outcomes in physical and sexual abuse cases: A comparison of child advocacy center-based and standard services', *Child Maltreatment*, 11(4): 354–60.

Smith-Berg, S.M., Stevens, V., Brown, K., Van Horn, L., Gernhofer, N., Peters, E., Greenberg, R., Snetselaar, L., Ahrens, L. and Smith, K. (1999) 'A brief motivational intervention to improve dietary adherence in adolescents', *Health Education Research*, 14(3): 399–410.

Sternberg, K.J., Lamb, M.E., Davies, G.M. and Westcott, H.L. (2001) 'The Memorandum of Good Practice: theory versus application', *Child Abuse and Neglect*, 25(5): 669–81.

Sternberg, K.J., Lamb, M.E., Esplin, P.W. and Baradaran, L.P. (1999) 'Using a scripted protocol in investigative interviews: A pilot study', *Applied Developmental Science*, 3(2): 70–6.

Tang, C.M. (2006) 'Developmentally sensitive forensic interviewing of preschool children: some guidelines drawn from basic psychological research', *Criminal Justice Review*, 31(2): 132–45.

Taylor, M., Cartwright, B.S. and Bowden, T. (1991) 'Perspective-taking and theory of mind: Do children predict interpretive diversity as a function of differentiation in observers' knowledge?', *Child Development*, 62(6): 1334–51.

UN General Assembly (1989) Convention on the Rights of the Child, 20 November 1989, United Nations, Treaty Series, vol. 1577, p. 3, available at: http://www.refworld.org/docid/3ae6b38f0.html [accessed 10 October 2013]

Varni, J.W., Limbers, C.A. and Burwinkle, T.M. (2007) 'How young can children reliably and validly self-report their health-related quality of life?: An analysis of 8,591 children across age subgroups with the PedsQL™ 4.0 Generic Core Scales', *Health and Quality of Life Outcomes*, 5(1): 1–13.

Villalba, D.K., Malloy, L.C. and Lamb, M.E. (2013) *Rapport Building in Investigative Interviews with*

Children. Paper presented at annual convention of the American Psychology-Law Society, Portland, OR.

Wakefield, H. (2006) 'Guidelines on Investigatory Interviewing of Children: What is the consensus in the scientific community?', *American Journal of Forensic Psychology*, 24(3): 57–74.

Walsh, W.A., Lippert, T., Cross, T.P., Maurice, D.M. and Davison, K.S. (2008) 'How long to prosecute child sexual abuse for community using a children's advocacy center and two comparison communities?', *Child Maltreatment*, 13(1): 3–13.

Waterman, A.H., Blades, M. and Spencer, C. (2001) 'Interviewing children and adults: The effect of question format on the tendency to speculate', *Applied Cognitive Psychology*, 15(5): 521–31.

Westcott, H.L. and Kynan, S. (2006) 'Interviewer practice in investigative interviews for suspected child sexual abuse', *Psychology, Crime & Law*, 12(4): 367–82.

Weisner, T.S. (2002) 'Ecocultural understanding of children's developmental pathways', *Human Development*, 45(4): 275–88.

Wood, J.A. and Garven, S. (2000) 'How sexual abuse interviews go astray: Implications for prosecutors, police, and child protection services', *Child Maltreatment*, 5(2): 109–18.

22

Children as Self-Informants in Longitudinal Studies: Substantive Findings and Methodological Issues

Amy Dworsky

INTRODUCTION

One of the first decisions researchers must make when planning a study involving children is whether to use a cross-sectional or longitudinal design. In other words, should a group or groups of children be observed just once or repeatedly over time? The answer largely depends on the purpose of the research. Longitudinal designs are generally preferred when questions about the development of children are of concern. Although developmental changes can be inferred by including children of different ages in a cross-sectional design, any variation observed across age groups may reflect cohort effects (characteristics common to a specific group) rather than individual level change.

Longitudinal studies have two other methodological advantages despite costing more and requiring a longer time. First, they can be used to examine early predictors of later outcomes in a way that a cross-sectional snapshot cannot (Holmbeck, Bruno and Jandasek, 2006; Loeber and Farrington, 1994; Rutter, 1994; Wierson and Forehand, 1994).

Second, although they are not a substitute for randomized experiments, longitudinal studies are more conducive than cross-sectional studies to causal analyses because they provide information about the temporal ordering of events (Menard, 2002; Rutter, 1981, 1994; Wierson and Forehand, 1994).

Even if one is not interested in the methodological advantages of longitudinal designs, there are substantive reasons to care about this type of research. First, longitudinal studies of children have contributed much to our knowledge about both normative and atypical development. Second, they have enhanced our understanding of the role played by individual, family, and environmental factors. And third, longitudinal studies have influenced social, health, and educational policies in both industrialized and developing countries (Shulruf et al., 2007).

This chapter examines the involvement of children in longitudinal research in which data were collected directly from the children being studied. It begins with a review of studies that have followed children over time.

The review provides a brief description of individual studies and, whenever possible, summarizes major findings related to child development or the impact of childhood experiences on young adult outcomes. Longitudinal studies of children in the more highly industrialized parts of the world are distinguished from those of children in countries that are less economically developed. Moreover, because the former group of studies is so much larger than the latter, it is further broken down geographically (United Kingdom, Continental Europe, New Zealand, Australia, Canada, and the United States). The review also includes a handful of studies distinguished by their focus on specific populations: children involved with the child welfare system, children at risk of delinquency, and children who participated in early education or intervention programs. Although this review is not meant to be exhaustive, it is both multidisciplinary and multinational in scope. The review is followed by a discussion of some methodological and ethical issues that arise when children are primary informants in longitudinal research. The chapter concludes with some thoughts about recent trends and future directions.

INVOLVEMENT OF CHILDREN IN LONGITUDINAL RESEARCH

A number of approaches have been used to study children longitudinally. One important distinction is between retrospective studies, which can only look at events that have already happened to the children or youth being studied before the research began, and prospective studies, which can also capture events that happen to children and youth as the study unfolds (Loeber and Farrington, 1994).

Another distinction relates to the source of data (Loeber and Farrington, 1994; Taplin, 2005). Administrative records are often used in longitudinal research, especially when

children are studied retrospectively. Data can also be collected from parents, teachers, or other knowledgeable adults. However, a third option is to collect data directly from the children themselves.

Once viewed as passive objects of study, incapable of providing reliable information about their own lives, children are now recognized as viable informants and included as active participants in research (Goodenough et al., 2003). The inclusion of children's voices is important because, regardless of how much adults know about a given child, or about children in general, they cannot see the world through a child's eyes (Gilligan, 2002; Mahon et al., 1996; Miller, 2000; Oakley, 1994). Nor can adults report on children's internal states (such as feelings, attitudes, motivations). Longitudinal research is no different in this respect.

This is not to say that children are always the best informants. On the contrary, parents, teachers, or other adults may be in a better position to report observable behaviours (Loeber and Farrington, 1994; Taplin, 2005). Children may also be too young to provide meaningful information, particularly during the early years of a longitudinal study. Indeed, it is not uncommon for researchers to collect data from multiple sources over time (Loeber and Farrington, 1994), with children gradually assuming the primary informant role (Holmbeck et al., 2006; Taplin, 2005).

A REVIEW OF LONGITUDINAL STUDIES[1]

Longitudinal studies of children in Great Britain

One of the first large-scale longitudinal studies involving children as informants about themselves was the National Survey of Health and Development (NSHD), a birth cohort study that began in Great Britain more than six decades ago and involved more than

5000 children born in England, Scotland, or Wales during a one-week period in March 1946.[2] It was followed by studies of three later birth cohorts: the National Child Development Study (NCDS) of 1958, the Birth Cohort Study (BCS) of 1970, and the Millennium Cohort Study (MCS) of 2000–2001. Although each birth cohort was defined somewhat differently (Table 22.1), they all included children from throughout Great Britain. At least in the case of the first three studies, data were collected from parents, teachers, school health care professionals, and eventually the children themselves. Data collection has continued through adulthood.

A number of findings have emerged from these studies regarding the importance of experiences during childhood. In analysing data from the 1946 birth cohort, for example, researchers found a positive relationship between parental interest in their children's education and later educational attainment after other factors were taken into account. However, educational attainment was also negatively affected by growing up under socioeconomically disadvantaged circumstances, even among children with high levels of cognitive ability. Behaviour problems were more prevalent among adolescents who had experienced long or multiple hospital admissions by age 5, and among adolescents whose families had been disrupted by parental separation (Wadsworth et al., 2006).

Both the 1958 and 1970 birth cohort studies provided evidence that physical and emotional development during childhood are related to adult health and well-being. For example, data from the National Child Development Study suggest that early social disadvantage can have adverse effects on educational, social, and economic outcomes (Elliot and Vaitlingham, 2008), and that parental separation and divorce may increase the risk of psychological distress and problem drinking in adulthood (Power and Elliot, 2006). Likewise, researchers have used data

from the Birth Cohort Study of 1970 to examine the long-term impact of socioeconomic disadvantage during childhood on later psychological adjustment (Elliot and Shepherd, 2006).

More recently, Growing Up in Scotland (GUS) began following a nationally representative sample of 5000 infants and 3000 toddlers. Data first collected in 2005, then were collected annually until the children were 6 years old and now at key developmental stages through adolescence. Only the primary caregiver, typically the mother, and the caregiver's partner were interviewed while the children were young, but the children themselves begin to be interviewed as they grow older and ultimately become the primary informants.

Other studies in Great Britain have focused on birth cohorts from specific geographic regions. For example, the Newcastle Thousand Families Cohort Study, which was motivated by the city's high infant mortality rate, focused on a sample of more than 1100 children born in Newcastle upon Tyne in May and June of 1947. Known as 'Red Spot Babies' because a red spot had been placed on their medical records, cohort members were followed until 1962 when they were 15 years old, although data were collected from a portion of the cohort at ages 22 and 33, and from the full cohort at age 50.

Data from this study have been used to examine the link between early life experiences and adult health outcomes. They also suggest that childhood disadvantage can increase the risk of criminal offending (Kolvin et al., 1988) and depression (Sadowski et al., 1999).

Another British birth cohort study, Born in Bradford, examined how genes, lifestyle factors and the environment interact to affect development. Researchers will follow approximately 10,000 children whose mothers received prenatal care at the Bradford Royal Infirmary in northern England. Recruitment began in spring 2007 and

Table 22.1 Longitudinal studies of children in Great Britain

Study	Sample	Data collection	Other information
National Survey of Health and Development	All children born in England, Wales, and Scotland during one week in March 1946 (N = 5362)	Data were collected at birth and then at ages 2, 4, 6, 7, 8, 9, 10, 11, 13, 15, 16, 19, 20, 22, 24, 26, 31, 36, 43 and 53 years old.	
National Child Development Study	All native and immigrant children in England, Wales, and Scotland born during a one-week period in 1958 (N ~ 17,500).	Data were collected at birth and then again at ages 7, 11, 16, 23 and 33.	At age 11, children were asked about leisure activities, attitudes towards school, and the life they imagined leading at age 25. At age 16, children were asked about leisure activities, attitudes towards school, school attendance and performance, educational and occupational aspirations, employment and income, sex education, relationships with family, plans for marriage and parenthood, consumption of alcohol and tobacco.
Birth Cohort Study of 1970	All native and immigrant children in England, Wales, Northern Ireland and Scotland born during a one-week period in 1970 (N ~ 17,200). Children born in Northern Ireland were dropped soon after the study began.	Data were collected at birth and then again at ages 5, 10, 16, 26, 30 and 34.	At age 10, children were asked about relationships with parents and peers, school, cigarette smoking, diet, and health. At age 16, they answered questions about a much broader range of topics, kept four-day diaries about nutrition and general activity, and completed a number of educational assessments.
Millennium Cohort Study	All children born in England, Wales, Scotland and Northern Ireland during a 12-month period in 2000–2001 who were living in a random sample of electoral ward at 9 months of age (N = 18,818). Wards were selected to include an adequate representation of low-income, Black and Asian children.	Three waves of data have been collected so far, when the children were 9 months, 3 years and 5 years old. The next wave of data will be collected at age 7.	
Newcastle Thousand Families Cohort Study	> 1100 children born in Newcastle Upon Tyne in May and June 1947.	Data were collected from birth through age 15, and then at ages 22, 33 and 50.	
Born in Bradford	~10,000 children whose mothers received prenatal care at the Bradford Royal Infirmary in Northern England.	Recruitment began in Spring 2007 and then continued for two years.	
Growing Up in Scotland (GUS)	Nationally representative sample of Scottish 5000 infants born between June 2004 and May 2005 and 3000 toddlers born between June 2002 and May 2003.	Data were first collected in 2005 when the mean age of the infants was 10.5 months and the mean age of the toddlers was 34.5 months. Data were collected annually until children were 6 years old and then less frequently through adolescence.	

continued for two years. Because half of the children born in Bradford are of South Asian origin, a parallel study was planned for Mirpur, Pakistan, from which many of Bradford's ethnic minorities immigrated.

Longitudinal studies of children in other European countries

Birth cohort studies have been conducted in a number of other European countries (Table 22.2). Finland has been home to two, both involving children born in the northern provinces of Oulu and Lapland. The first followed children born in 1966; the second followed children born approximately 20 years later (between 1 July 1985 and 30 June 1986). In both cases, data collection took place prenatally, at birth, and then at several points thereafter.

One analysis of data from the 1966 cohort showed that growing up in a single-parent family increased the risk of criminal offending during adulthood, and that the risk was greater the longer children were exposed to single parenthood (Sauvola et al., 2002). Another found that growing up in a single-parent family and being an only child were both associated with a significantly higher risk of various types of personality disorders (Kantojarvi et al., 2008).

A study in Denmark, the Danish Longitudinal Survey of Children (DALSC), is following approximately 6000 Danish children born in 1995 from infancy through to adulthood.

Table 22.2 Longitudinal studies of children in other European countries

Study	Sample	Data collection	Other information
Northern Finland Birth Cohort Studies	12,058 children born in 1966 in the Northern provinces of Oulu and Lapland.	Data were collected at 24 weeks' gestation, at birth, and then at ages 1, 14, and 31.	
	9479 children born between July 1,1985, and June 30,1986 in the Northern provinces of Oulu and Lapland.	Data were collected at 24 weeks' gestation, at birth, at ages 7 or 8, and at ages 15 or 16.	
Danish Longitudinal Survey of Children (DALSC)	6000 Danish children born in 1995.	Data were collected at ages 3 months, 3 years, 5 years and 11 years. A fifth wave of data will be collected at age 14.	
Growing Up in Ireland (National Longitudinal Study of Children in Ireland)	Nationally representative sample of 10,000 9-month-olds randomly selected from the Department of Social & Family Affairs' Child Benefit Register in 2008 and 8000 9-year-olds randomly selected from a nationally representative sample of 750 schools in 2007.	Data were collected at ages 9 months and 3 years for the infant cohort and at ages 9 and 13 for the child cohort. Data were collected from parents, teachers, non-parental caregivers who provide at least 12 hours of childcare each week, and in the case of the older cohort, the children themselves.	Older children were asked about their lives at school and home, activities they enjoy, foods they to eat and perceptions of their community. Their reading and math skills were also assessed.
Growing Up in France (French Longitudinal Study of Children)	~20,000 children born in France during a four-day period in each quarter of 2009.	Data are being collected at birth, six to eight weeks after birth, and at the children's 3rd, 6th and 11th birthdays. Parent interviews will continue into adolescence, and children will be interviewed starting at age 11 or 12.	

Five waves of data have been collected. At the most recent wave of data collection, the children were 15 years old (Hestbæk, 2006). The survey data collected from the children and their parents have been linked to administrative data from the national registry, making it possible to examine the relationship between family background and a wide range of outcomes including health, educational attainment, labour market participation, and receipt of government benefits. One recent analysis of the DALSC data found that parental divorce is negatively related to several dimensions of child well-being (Andersen, Deding and Lausten, 2007). Another found that the negative relationship between child well-being and marital conflict in two-parent families is mediated by parenting style such that the more coercive the parenting, the stronger the relationship becomes (Baviskar, 2008).

Two similarly named, but independent studies are currently underway in Ireland and France. Growing Up in Ireland: The National Longitudinal Study of Children in Ireland will follow a large nationally representative sample of 10,000 nine-month-olds and 8000 9-year-olds. Two waves of data will be collected from the parents or guardians of both cohorts, from teachers and non-parental caregivers, and from the older children. In-depth qualitative interviews will be conducted with the parents of 120 of the older children, and those children will provide information about themselves in the form of essays, drawings, and photo diaries.

Growing Up in France: The French Longitudinal Study of Children will follow the approximately 20,000 children who were born during a four-day period in each quarter of 2009 from birth through adolescence. Data will initially be collected only from the parents, but the children will be interviewed once they are 11 or 12 years old. Information about the content of those interviews or the frequency with which they will occur is not yet available.

Finally, the *European* Longitudinal Study of Pregnancy and Childhood (ELSPAC) is a longitudinal study of European children that is international in scope. Undertaken at the behest of the World Health Organization (WHO), ELSPAC is following a total of more than 40,000 children in Great Britain, the Isle of Man, the Czech Republic, Slovakia, Russia, and the Ukraine to determine whether there are cross-national differences in the way that biological, psychosocial, and environmental factors interact to affect development.[3] Cross-national comparisons are being facilitated by common methodologies and target populations. Data are being collected from parents, teachers, physicians, and the children themselves at key developmental stages beginning prenatally and continuing through adolescence.

Data were first collected directly from the children between 1996 and 1998 when they were, on average, nearly 6 and 1½ years old. The final wave data is currently being collected from the children who are now in their late teens. However, the most recent findings from the study to be published – findings related to the prevalence of conduct disorder among the ELSPAC children – were based on data collected from their mothers, teachers and physicians when the children were age seven (Kukla et al., 2008a, 2008b).

Longitudinal studies of children in New Zealand and Australia

New Zealand and Australia have both been home to a number of longitudinal studies (Table 22.3). The first two longitudinal studies of New Zealand children began in the 1970s. The Christchurch Health and Development Study (CHDS) followed more than 1200 children who were born in the urban Christchurch region during a four-month period in 1977 from birth until age 25. Although data were collected from parents, teachers, medical records, and psychometric

Table 22.3 Birth cohort studies in Australia and New Zealand

Study	Sample	Data collection during childhood/adolescence	Other information
Christchurch Health and Development Study	1265 children born in the urban Christchurch region during a four-month period in 1977.	Data were collected at birth, 4 months, and 12 months, annually until age 16, and then at ages 18, 21 and 25.	
Dunedin Multidisciplinary Health and Development Study	1037 children born at the Queen Mary Maternity Hospital in Dunedin between April 1, 1972 and March 31, 1973.	Data were collected at birth every two years beginning at age 3, every three years beginning at age 15, and less frequently after age 21.	The most recent data were collected at age 32, and future assessments are scheduled for ages 38 and 44.
Competent Children, Competent Learners	307 children living in New Zealand's greater Wellington region. 242 children were added to the study at age 8.	Data were collected in 1993–1994 just before the children's 5th birthday and then every years thereafter, most recently at age 16.	
The Longitudinal Study of New Zealand Children and Families	No information available.	No information available.	
Te Rerenga ā te Pīrere or The Flight Of The Fledgling	Representative sample of 111 Maori children, ages five, eight and eleven, being educated in Māori-language preschools, primary schools, and secondary schools.	Data were collected every year for four years from parents, teachers, principals and the children themselves.	The children were asked about their experiences in the Maori-language schools, their use of the te reo Māori language, their exposure to media and computers, and their engagement in activities.
Australian Temperament Project	Representative sample of 2443 children born in the state of Victoria between September 1982 and January 1983.	Data were collected during each of the first four years (1983–1986) and then every two years thereafter. An additional wave of data was collected in 1995, during study participants' first year of secondary school. The most recent wave of data collection took place in when the study participants were 23–24 years old.	The questionnaires have included measures of temperament, behavioral and school adjustment, substance use, antisocial behavior, depression, health, social competence, civic mindedness and engagement, peer relationships, family functioning, parenting style and family environment.
Growing Up in Australia: The Longitudinal Study of Australian Children	Nationally representative sample of 5107 infants born between March 2003 and February 2004 and 4973 4 to 5 year olds born between March 1999 and February 2000.	Data collection began in 2004 and continued every two years until 2010.	In addition to age-appropriate cognitive assessments, the children are asked about their feelings and their experiences at school.
Aboriginal Birth Cohort	1238 Aboriginal children born in the Top End of the Northern Territory of Australia at the Royal Darwin Hospital between January 1987 and March 1990.	Data were collected shortly after birth, between 1998 and 2001, and again when the children were 16 to 19 years old.	
Longitudinal Study of Indigencus Children or Footprints in Time	Children under age one and children 4 to 5 year olds from Aboriginal and Torres Strait Islander families in remote, rural, and urban areas.	Not yet known.	

tests, the children also played an active role as primary informants.

Researchers involved in the Christchurch study have identified several factors associated with an increased risk of both suicidal thoughts and suicide attempts, including social disadvantage; childhood sexual abuse; adolescent mental health problems, particularly depression (especially relationship breakups); and problems with the law (Fergusson and Lynskey, 1995a, 1995b). They have also found a relationship between exposure to unemployment and increased personal problems during adolescence and young adulthood. However, most of this association was explained by the fact that those with high exposure to unemployment had experienced other difficulties before leaving school, such as lower educational achievement, higher rates of substance use, and criminality (Fergusson, Horwood and Woodward, 2001). Still other analyses of the Christchurch study data suggest that using cannabis at least once a week increases the risk of using other illicit drugs even after controlling for a large number of factors, and that regular cannabis use was related to an increased risk of various problems including depression, suicidal thoughts, unemployment, and criminal behaviour after background factors had been taken into account (Fergusson and Horwood, 2000a, 2000b).

The other longitudinal study of New Zealand children that began in the 1970s, the Dunedin Multidisciplinary Health and Development Study, has been following more than 1000 children since they were born at the Queen Mary Maternity Hospital in Dunedin between 1 April 1972 and 31 March 1973 and will continue to follow them until at least age 44.

Analyses of the Dunedin Study data have revealed a link between antisocial behaviour among boys and poor physical health in adulthood, including injury, sexually transmitted diseases, cardiovascular risk, reduced immune function, and dental disease. However, males who had exhibited high levels of antisocial behaviour as children but reduced their antisocial behaviour by adulthood did not have the same poor health outcomes (Odgers et al., 2007). Other analyses of these data indicate that children who watch much television are more likely to have attention problems in adolescence as reported not only by both their parents and teachers, but also by the teenagers themselves; and this relationship could not be explained by early-life attention difficulties, socioeconomic factors, or intelligence (Landhuis et al., 2007). Finally, there is some evidence that maltreated children may suffer harmful physical and psychological health effects well into adulthood. Specifically, adults who had experienced psychological maltreatment as children were twice as likely to exhibit high levels of inflammation levels as adults who had not been maltreated (Danese et al., 2008).

A somewhat more contemporary study, Competent Children, Competent Learners, is exploring how home and school experiences affect the development of children's cognitive, social, communicative, and problem-solving competencies among more than 500 children from New Zealand's Wellington region (more specifically, Wellington, Hutt, Kapiti and Wairarapa). These children were selected from kindergartens, education and care centres, play centres, family day care, and *aoga amata* (Samoan language nests) in 1993–1994. Data were collected from the children, as well as their parents and teachers, every two years and continued to be collected until they left school.

Analyses of these data have shown that early childhood education continues to contribute to competency levels at age 16, although the associations were weaker than they had been at age 14 (Hodgen, 2007a). They also suggest that quality early childhood education may protect children from getting into trouble at age 16 (Hodgen, 2007b).

In contrast to these regional studies, the Longitudinal Study of New Zealand Children and Families, is examining the development of children throughout New Zealand across a number of domains (including health, educational attainment, and social adjustment). Researchers are particularly interested in how development is affected by factors such as family, school, social networks, community resources, technology, and the mass media.

An early longitudinal study in Australia, the Australian Temperament Project (ATP), has been examining the psychosocial development of a representative sample of 2443 Australian children born in both urban and rural regions of Victoria between September 1982 and January 1983. At least waves of data were collected via mail questionnaires, at least until the study participants were 24 years old. These questionnaires have been completed, at various times, by parents, nurses, teachers, and, beginning at age 11, the children themselves.

Researchers have used the ATP data to explore the relationship between childhood temperament and later outcomes. For example, Blaney et al. (2000) identified high levels of negative emotionality, which includes a propensity to get very angry when frustrated, to respond negatively and intensely, and being moody or cranky, to be major risk factors for the development of eating problems and body dissatisfaction during adolescence. Smart et al. (1999) looked at the pathways to antisocial behaviour and depression at ages 15–16 years old. The best predictors of antisocial behaviour were oppositional behaviour, poor school adjustment, association with 'deviant peers', and low levels of parental monitoring; the best predictors of depression were anxiety problems, low levels of attachment to family, and poor school adjustment at 13–14 years of age. Likewise, Williams et al. (2000) found that the best predictors of teenage substance use were self-reported antisocial behaviour, low levels of emotional control, and having friends who engaged in antisocial behaviour or used substances. Finally, an analysis by Smart et al. (2000) showed that parenting style had a greater impact on the adolescent outcomes of children who were temperamentally at risk for emotional and behavioural difficulties.

In contrast with the Australian Temperament Project, which only involved children born in Victoria, Growing Up in Australia: The Longitudinal Study of Australian Children (LSAC) includes a large, nationally representative sample. LSAC began in 2003–2004 with approximately 10,000 children: 5000 infants who were followed until they were 6 or 7 years old and 5000 4–5-year-olds who were followed until age 10 or 11. Although the parent or guardian who knows the most about the child was the primary respondent, data were also being collected from the children themselves once they were old enough to participate – wave two for the 4- and 5-year-olds and wave three for the infants.

According to the 2006–2007 annual report (Australian Institute of Family Studies, 2008), which was based on data collected during the second wave of interviews, half of the older children, who were age 6 or, 7 felt happy about going to school, 70 per cent enjoyed reading and writing, 70 per cent felt they were doing well at school, and 80 per cent felt their teacher was nice to them. About two-thirds of the children felt happy 'lots of the time' compared with 13 per cent who spent 'lots of the time' feeling scared or worried (Australian Institute of Family Studies, 2008).

Importantly, despite comprising only a small percentage of the total child population, Aboriginal children have been the focus of longitudinal studies in both New Zealand and Australia. For example, one New Zealand study, Te Rerenga ā te Pīrere (or The Flight of the Fledgling), followed a representative sample of 111 Māori children, ages 5, 8, or 11 when the study began, who were being educated in Māori-language schools. Data were collected every year for four years from parents, teachers, principals and the children themselves (Cooper et al., 2004). The researchers found that children who spoke the Māori language more often, and children who had greater exposure to Māori language in school and at home, tended to perform better overall on a variety of assessment tasks than those who did not (Cooper et al., 2004).

In Australia, the Aboriginal Birth Cohort (ABC) study followed more than 1200 Aboriginal children who were born in the Top End of the Northern Territory at the Royal Darwin Hospital between January 1987 and March 1990 (Sayers et al., 2003). This hospital accounts for approximately 90 per cent of the region's Aboriginal births. Their mothers were interviewed within four days of giving birth and follow-up data were collected between 1998 and 2001. A third wave of data was collected when the children were 16 to 19 years old. One of the major findings to emerge from this study is that Aboriginal children from urban areas tend to be healthier than their counterparts in remote areas (Mackerras et al., 2003). This has implications for research on other Indigenous populations because it suggests that what applies to Aboriginal children in remote areas may not generalize to their more urban counterparts.

Motivated by concerns that the number of Indigenous children in the Longitudinal Survey of Australian Children will be too small ($n \approx 350$) for meaningful analysis, another study of Australia's aboriginal children was planned. The Longitudinal Study of Indigenous Children (LSIC), otherwise known as Footprints in Time, was designed to track the long-term development of 2200 children from Aboriginal and Torres Strait Islander families in remote, rural, and urban communities throughout Australia.

Longitudinal studies of children in Canada

Canadian children have been the focus of at least two large-scale longitudinal studies (Table 22.4). The National Longitudinal Survey of Children and Youth (NLSCY) is following a nationally representative sample that excludes children living in institutions or on Indian reserves. Data have been collected

from the mothers (or the person most knowledgeable about the child) and the children every two years since 1994–1995. The sample is augmented at each wave of data collection so that children of all ages continue to be represented, which allows for cross-sectional analyses.

Researchers analysing these data have reported significant differences in school readiness at age 5 related to sex, family characteristics, background, and home environment. They have also found that regardless of household income, daily reading, high positive parent–child interaction, participation in organized sports, lessons in physical activities, and lessons in the arts were associated with higher scores on measures of their readiness to learn. However, children from low-income households were less likely to have those experiences than children in higher-income households, which may explain the overall differences in readiness to learn (Thomas, 2006).

The other large-scale Canadian study has focused exclusively on children born in Québec. Since 1998, the Québec Longitudinal Study of Child Development (QLSCD) has been following a representative sample of more than 2000 children who would have entered school in September 2002 (Jetté, 2002; Plante, Courtemanche and Desgroseilliers, 2002). Data are collected from the mothers (or the person most knowledgeable about the child), and the children participate in age-appropriate activities designed to assess their cognitive abilities. Data collection continued through 2010, when the children are age 12.

Researchers used the data from the QLSCD to assess predictive value of the Early Development Instrument (EDI) – a school readiness measure based on kindergarten teacher ratings of social, emotional, and cognitive development and compared that with the predictive value of more direct school readiness and cognitive tests. They concluded that the EDI is as good a predictor of early school achievement as measures that are more costly and time-consuming to administer (Forget-Dubois et al., 2007).

Table 22.4   Longitudinal studies in Canada

Study	Sample	Data collection during childhood/adolescence	Other information
National Longitudinal Survey of Children and Youth (NLSCY)	Baseline sample of 22,831 children ages birth to 11 from 13,439 households. Sample is augmented at each wave of data collection so that children of all ages continue to be represented. Children are excluded if they are institutionalized or living on Indian reserves.	Data have been collected every two years since 1994–1995.	In-home interviews are conducted with the person most knowledgeable about the child, typically the mother, and the children's cognitive functioning is assessed. Children 10 and older answer questions about a wide range of topics including friends and family, feelings and behaviour, school experiences, puberty, smoking, alcohol, drugs, self-esteem, activities, and health. Youth age 16 and older are interviewed in greater depth.
Québec Longitudinal Study of Child Development	Representative sample of 2223 children born in Québec between October 1997 and July 1998. Excluded children in the Northern Québec administrative region, in Cree or Inuit territory, on Indian reserves, children within an unknown gestational age or born before 24 weeks' gestation.	Data were collected in 1998, when the children were 5 months old, and then annually until 2006.	

Longitudinal studies of children in the United States

Several well-known longitudinal studies of children have taken place in the US (Table 22.5). One study has been following children whose mothers were part of the 1979 National Survey of Youth (NLSY79), a nationally representative sample of 12,686 young people who were 14 to 22 years old in 1979.[4] After sampling weights are applied, the Children of the 1979 National Longitudinal Survey of Youth comprise a nationally representative sample of all children whose mothers were born between 1957 and 1964 and living in the United States in 1978. Data have been collected every other year since the study began in 1986, and sample size has grown significantly over time. Each wave of data collection involves in-person interviews with the children and/or their mothers, interviewer observations of the home

environment, and/or developmental assessments. Although the age of the child determines which data are collected at any given wave, the domains covered include child demographic and family background characteristics; prenatal and child postnatal history; health; home environment; cognitive, motor, social, and emotional development; educational experiences; and adolescent attitudes and behaviours.

Data from the Children of the 1979 NLSY have been used to address a wide range of research questions including questions about how child and adolescent outcomes are affected by family structure, maternal employment, income, and childcare arrangements. Moreover, because the child data can be linked to mother data, the effects of maternal characteristics and experiences on children's development can be examined. The US Department of Labor's Bureau of Labor Statistics maintains an annotated bibliography

Table 22.5 Longitudinal studies of children in the United States

Name of study	Sample	Data collection	Other information
Children of the 1979 National Longitudinal Survey of Youth	Children whose mothers were part of the 1979 National Longitudinal Survey of Youth (NLSY79). Sample size grew from 5255 children belonging to 2922 mothers in 1986 to 8267 children belonging to 3365 mothers in 2004.	Data have been collected every other year since 1986.	Mothers answer questions about the background, home environment, schooling, health, temperament, behavior problems, and/or motor-social development of children younger than age 15. Children ages 10 to 14 answer questions about family, friends, attitudes toward school, school characteristics, grade repetition, school behaviour, parent involvement in education, educational expectations, peer relationships, deviant behaviours, interactions with parents, home responsibilities, time use, jobs, religious attendance, smoking, alcohol and drug use, dating, sexual activity (age 13 and older), gender roles, and family decision making. Children ages 15 and older answer questions about many of these same topics as well as topics more relevant to young adults, including post-secondary education and training, work experience, health, fertility, marital history, parent–child conflict, delinquent or criminal behaviour, use of controlled and uncontrolled substances, access to computers, computer training, volunteer activities, and expectations for the future.
Child Development Supplement (CDS) to the Panel Study of Income Dynamics (PSID)	3563 children, ages birth to 12, from 2394 PSID families in 1997, 2907 children, ages 5 to 18, from 2021 families in 2002–2003 and children who were not yet 18 years old in 2007.	Data were collected in 1997, 2002–2003, and 2007.	
Fragile Families and Child Wellbeing Study	Nearly 5000 children born in a random sample of large US cities between 1998 and 2000. Approximately three-quarters were born to unmarried parents.	Data were collected at birth and then again at ages 1, 3, 5, and 9.	Parent interviews collect information on attitudes, relationships, parenting behaviour, demographic characteristics, health (mental and physical), economic and employment status, neighbourhood characteristics, and program participation. In-home assessments of children's cognitive and emotional development, health, and home environment.
Early Childhood Longitudinal Study – Birth (ECLS-B)	Nationally-representative sample of 10,700 children born in 2001.	Data were collected in 2001–2002 when the children were 9 months old, in 2002–2003 when the children were 2 years old, in 2005–2006 when the children were in preschool, and in 2006–2007 when the children entered kindergarten.	Mothers (or other primary caregivers) were asked about themselves, their families, and their children. Fathers were asked about themselves and their role in their children's lives.

Study	Sample	Data collection	Description
Childhood Longitudinal Study – Kindergarten (ECLS-K)	Nationally representative sample of children who entered kindergarten in the fall of 1998.	Data were collected in the fall and spring of kindergarten (1998–99), in the fall and spring of 1st grade (1999–2000), in the spring of 3rd grade (2002), in the spring of 5th grade (2004), and in the spring of 8th grade (2007).	Fine and gross psychomotor skills were assessed in kindergarten by having children perform a variety of tasks (e.g., building structures with blocks, copying shapes, drawing figures, balancing, hopping, skipping, and walking backwards). Knowledge of academic subjects (e.g., reading, math, science, social studies) was assessed every year but different subject areas were assessed in different grades. Social skills (e.g., cooperation, assertion, responsibility, and self-control) and problem behaviours (e.g., impulsivity and aggression) were also assessed. Children in grades 3, 5 and 8 answered questions about their competence and their popularity with peers. Questions about school and diet were asked when children were in the 5th and 8th grades.
National Institute for Child Health and Development (NIICHD) Study of Early Child Care	1364 children from 10 study sites across the US.	Data were collected at ages 1, 6, 15, 24, 36, and 54 months.	
Early Head Start Research Evaluation Project	~3000 infants and toddlers from low-income families in 17 sites.	Baseline data collected prior to random assignment and when children are 14, 24, and 36 months old.	Data collection included assessments of cognitive, language, and social development; health; resiliency; emotional regulation; and parental attachment.
National Children's Study of the Effects of Environment on Health	National probability sample of ~100,000 children from a nationally representative sample of 105 geographic areas (one or more counties). Neighbourhoods within those areas will be randomly selected.	Recruitment began in 2008. Data will be collected from before birth until age 21.	

of papers based on NLSY79 Child Survey data. The BLS currently contains more than 1200 entries.[5]

Another longitudinal study, the Child Development Supplement (CDS) to the Panel Study of Income Dynamics (PSID), has been following children from a nationally representative sample of American families.[6] These children were 0 to 12 years old in 1997 when the CDS began and remain eligible for the CDS until their 18th birthday.[7] Three waves of CDS data, including diaries for two randomly selected 24-hour periods, cognitive and behavioural assessments, and measures of health and family functioning, have been collected from parents/guardians, teachers, and the children themselves. These data can be linked to family demographic and economic data in the PSID.

The CDS data have been used to study a broad array of developmental outcomes including physical health, emotional well-being, academic achievement, and social relationships. A searchable bibliography of papers based on CDS data is maintained by the University of Michigan's Institute for Social Research.[8]

Other longitudinal studies have followed cohorts of US children. For example, the Fragile Families and Child Well-Being Study sample includes nearly 5000 children born in 20 randomly chosen major US cities between 1998 and 2000. Their parents, approximately three-quarters of whom were unmarried when the children were born, were interviewed shortly after the birth of their child and then when the child was age 1, 3, and 5 years old. Assessments of the children's cognitive and emotional development as well as their home environments took place at ages 3 and 5. Researchers began collecting a fifth wave of data in 2007 when the children were 9 years old. This nine-year follow-up, which continued through 2009, was the first time the children themselves have been interviewed.

Data from the Fragile Families study have been used to address a variety of questions related to child well-being and to unmarried parents' social and economic circumstances, including questions about child support, welfare program participation, father involvement, and parental incarceration. The Center for Research on Child Wellbeing at Princeton University maintains a comprehensive list of all working papers, published articles, books, and book chapters based on Fragile Families data.[9]

Another cohort study, the Early Childhood Longitudinal Study, includes two nationally representative samples of children: a 2001 birth cohort (ECLS-B) that was followed from age 9 months through kindergarten entry in 2006 or 2007 and a 1998 kindergarten entry cohort (ECLS-K) that was followed through the end of 8th grade (Mariner, Romano and Bridges, 1999).[10] Four waves of data were collected from the ECLS-B children and their parents, with additional information provided by childcare providers at waves two and three and by kindergarten teachers at wave four. Although parents were the primary informants, the children participated in activities designed to assess their cognitive, language, social, emotional, and physical development. Data were collected seven times from the ECLS-K children as well as their parents, teachers, and school administrators. The data collection involved assessments of children's fine and gross psychomotor skills, knowledge of academic subjects, and social competence (such as social skills and behaviour problems).

The National Center for Education Statistics has compiled a bibliography of publications based on the ECLS data.[11] One recent report describes how children performed on a number of language, literacy, mathematics, and fine motor skills assessments at age 4 and how their proficiency on those assessments varied by child and family characteristics including socioeconomic status (Chernoff et al., 2007). It also provides information about the children's experiences with non-parental care. Another, which examined the variation in children's gains in reading and math at the end of 5th grade by sex, race/ethnicity, family characteristics, the types of schools attended, and residential as well as school mobility (Princiotta, Flanagan and Hausken, 2006) found that achievement was associated with both poverty status and mother's highest level of education.

At least two longitudinal studies of American children have focused exclusively on early childhood. The National Institute for Child Health and Development (NICHD) Study of Early Child Care followed more than 1300 children from across 10 study sites. Observational data were collected in family, childcare, and laboratory settings six times between ages 1 month and 4.5 years using multiple measures, and telephone interviews provided additional data between waves. Likewise, the Early Head Start Research Evaluation Project is a longitudinal study of low-income children whose families meet Head Start eligibility guidelines. Approximately 3000 children (and their families) in 17 sites were randomly assigned to a comprehensive two-generation program aimed at enhancing child development and supporting families during the first three years of life, or to a comparison group. Data were collected prior to random assignment and then three more times by the children's third birthday. Because neither study was supposed to continue beyond early childhood, the children were not included as primary informants in the original designs.

Finally, one of the largest longitudinal studies of American children, the National Children's Study of the Effects of Environment on Health (NCS) is examining the link between the environment in which children grow up and their development, where environment is broadly defined to include physical surroundings; genetic, biological, and chemical factors; geography; and social, educational, behavioural, family, and cultural influences. Approximately 100,000 children will be followed from before birth to age 21. The sample was selected using a two-stage national probability sampling design, and women who are pregnant or are likely to become pregnant in the near future were recruited beginning in 2008. Women were asked about their pregnancies, and biological and environmental samples will be collected after the children are born.

STUDIES IN THE DEVELOPING WORLD

Longitudinal studies involving children are increasingly being conducted in the developing nations of Asia, Latin America, and sub-Saharan Africa (Harpham et al., 2003). Perhaps the most ambitious of these studies, Young Lives, is examining the causes and consequences of childhood poverty as well as the impact of policy on child well-being in Ethiopia, India (Andhra Pradesh), Peru, and Vietnam over 15 years (Wison, Huttly and Fenn, 2006). Including children from four countries allows development in very different cultural, political, geographic, and social contexts to be compared. The sample includes a younger cohort of approximately 8000 children (2000 in each country) who were born in 2000–2001 and an older cohort of approximately 4000 children (1000 in each country) who were born in 1994.

The first wave of data was collected in 2002 when the younger children were between 6 and 17 months old and the older children were between 7.5 and 8.5 years old. Questionnaires were completed by the children's caregivers but data were also collected directly from the older children who answered questions about a variety of topics and completed tasks designed to measure cognitive abilities. The questionnaires were revised for the second wave of data collection which took place in 2006–2007 when the younger children were five or six years old and the older children were 11 or 12 years old. Several more waves of data were to be collected from the children and their caregivers, including information about the children's sense of self-esteem and self-efficacy as well as the quality of their intra-familial and extra-familial relationships. Each wave of data collection also includes interviews with community leaders (for example, municipal/commune leaders, government officials, village headmen, child health nurses, headmasters, leaders of women's groups, and religious leaders) about the social, economic, and environmental contexts of the communities in which the children live. Community-level data are being obtained from census records and other sources.

Preliminary reports about the children in each of the four countries were published in 2003. Early findings highlighted the many detrimental effects that poverty can have on children's well-being; how household dynamics, especially gender differences and birth order can affect basic child outcomes; the importance of access to quality child-focused services; the increasing marginalization of ethnic minority children in the context of high levels of economic growth; and the limitations of improving child well-being by focusing on the social capital of adults (Department of International Development, 2007).

Other longitudinal studies of children undertaken in developing countries include Birth to Twenty (South Africa), Pelotas Birth Cohort Study (Brazil), Cebu Longitudinal Health and Nutrition Survey (Philippines), the Prospective Cohort Study of Thai Children, and the Jamaican Birth Cohort Study. Each of these studies is briefly described below, and additional information is presented in Table 22.6.

Birth to Twenty is a longitudinal study of more than 3000 children who were born in the Soweto–Johannesburg area of South Africa during a seven-week period in 1990 (Richter et al., 2004, 2007). They are known as Mandela's Children because the study began just weeks after the South African leader was released from prison. At least 16 waves of data were collected, including two each year since age 14, with an overall attrition rate of 28 per cent. Antenatal data are available for the nearly 1600 children whose mothers were recruited during pregnancy. Originally motivated by questions about physical growth and health care receipt, the study shifted its focus to social behaviour

during the preschool years and then to educational progress once the children entered school. In later waves, attention turned towards sexual behaviour, school achievement, substance use, diet, risk of HIV/AIDS, and conflict with the law. The study was replicated with the children of the 1990 birth cohort members.

In 2004, more than 2000 of the Birth to Twenty cohort members responded to a questionnaire about their views on several topics including national identity and future orientation. The youth were very aware of the challenges facing South Africa, yet almost all were proud to be South African and optimistic about the future. As Birth to Twenty moves forward, researchers will examine if and how their views change and what effect those changes might have on their young adult outcomes (University of the Witwatersrand, 2004). However, significant differences were found across racial groups. Black and Coloured youth were more certain about their 'South African-ness' than White or Indian youth. Although Black youth expressed stronger ties to their national identity than White youth, they were less likely to believe that race relationships were more harmonious than they had been in the past (Norris et al., 2008).

Birth cohorts from Pelotas, Brazil have been the focus of two studies. The first involved the nearly 6000 children who were born in maternity hospitals during 1982 (Victora and Barros, 2006).[12] Data were collected from their mothers shortly after birth and then three more times by age four. The children were first interviewed in 1995, when a subsample of the original cohort answered questions about their school performance and HIV/AIDS. Children living in 70 of the city's 265 census tracts were re-interviewed in 1997 and either 2000 or 2001.[13]

A subsample of the 1997 study participants was also involved in an ethnographic study that took place between 1997 and 2001. A series of in-depth interviews was conducted first between ages 15 and 17 and

Table 22.6 Longitudinal studies of children in developing countries

Study	Sample	Data collection	Other information
Young Lives	~ 12,000 children in Ethiopia, India (Andhra Pradesh), Peru and Vietnam including ~8000 born in 2000–2001 and ~ 4000 born in 1994.	Data were collected in 2002 when the younger children were 6 to 17 months old and the older children were 7.5 to 8.5 years old, and then again in 2006–2007 when the younger children were 5 or 6 years old and the older children were 11 or 12 years old. Three further waves of data will be collected.	Older children answered questions about things that make them happy or unhappy, aspects of their immediate environment that they like or dislike, time spent playing with friends, people they turn to when they have problems, school attendance, the things they like and dislike about school, work or other activities they engage in to earn money, and health problems.
Birth to Twenty (BT20)	3275 children born in the Soweto–Johannesburg area of South Africa during a seven-week period in 1990.	Sixteen waves of data have been collected, including two waves each year since age 14. Antenatal data are available for 1594 children whose mothers were recruited during pregnancy.	
Pelotas Birth Cohort Study – 1982 Cohort	5914 children born in Pelotas, Brazil in 1982.	Data were collected shortly after birth and then again in 1983 (sub-sample including only children born from January–April 1982), 1984, 1986, 1995 (sub-sample including 20% of the cohort), 1997 and 2001 (sub-sample including 27% of the cohort).	Several studies of sub-samples, at least two of which included in-depth qualitative interviews.
Pelotas Birth Cohort Study – 1993 Cohort	5249 children born in Pelotas, Brazil in 1993.	Data were collected at ages 1 and 3 months (sub-sample including 13% of the cohort), at ages 6 months, 1 year and 4 years (sub-sample including all low-birth weight children plus 20% of the others), at age 11 (full cohort).	Sub-studies are addressing issues related to oral health, psychological development, mental health, body composition, and ethnography.
Cebu Longitudinal Health and Nutrition Survey	3080 children born to Filipino women from 33 randomly selected Metropolitan Cebu communities between May 1, 1983 and April 30, 1984. 2117 adolescents participated in the 1998–2000 follow-up and 2051 participated in the 2002 follow-up. Attrition was primarily due to out-migration.	Data collected prenatally, immediately after birth, and then bimonthly over the next 24 months. Additional data collected in 1991–2, 1994–5, 1998–2000, 2002 and 2005.	Adolescents were asked about types of emotional relationships (crushes, courting, romantic relationships and dating) and physical behaviours (holding hands, kissing, petting and sexual intercourse) in which they may have engaged as well as diet, education, employment, health, domestic abuse and mental health.
Prospective Cohort Study of Thai Children	4245 children from four regions (i.e., north, northeast, south, central) and the city of Bangkok born during a 1-year period as early as October 15, 2000 and as late as September 14, 2002.	Current plans to follow the cohort until age 24.	
Jamaican Birth Cohort Study	10,527 children born in September and October 1986 (94% of births island-wide).	Data collected shortly after birth, at the end of the pre-school years (ages 5–6), during the primary school years (ages 11–12), during the secondary school years (ages 15–16), and during early adulthood (ages of 18–20). Additional data were collected from children living in Kingston (n = 1720) and St. Andrew (n = 1565) while they were in primary and secondary school.	

then again between ages 18 and 20. Among the topics covered were high-risk sexual behaviours; smoking, drinking and illicit drug use; school failure; violence; family structure and dynamics; peers and key adult figures; and interactions with institutions. Data were also collected from some of the study participants' parents and close friends.

Later findings from the study revealed a strong positive correlation between family income at birth and school achievement at age 18, at least among males. In addition, a case-control analysis comparing females who had given birth by March 2001 with those who had not found that childbearing was associated with family income, parental schooling, being born to a teenage mother, having siblings from different fathers, and school failure before grade four (Victora et al., 2006).

Researchers began following the second cohort in 1993, in part, to evaluate trends in maternal and child health since the original study began. Because of budgetary and logistical constraints, data collection during infancy and childhood was restricted to subsamples of less than 1500 children, or about one quarter of the cohort. Two efforts were made to interview the entire birth cohort. The first took place in 2004 when cohort members were 11 years old; the second in 2008 when cohort members were age 15. More recent publications based on data from the 1993 birth cohort have focused on adolescent risk factors for chronic disease (Victoraet al., 2008).

The Cebu Longitudinal Health and Nutrition Survey (CLHNS), which began as a study of infant feeding patterns, has been examining the long-term effects of prenatal and early childhood nutrition and health on children in the Philippines. Baseline interviews were conducted with more than 3300 pregnant Filipino women, from 33 randomly selected communities in Metropolitan Cebu, who gave birth to more than 3000 children between 1 May

1983, and 30 April 1984. Approximately 2600 of the mothers were surveyed immediately after birth and then 12 times over the next 24 months. Five additional waves of data were collected as of 2005. Only the mothers were interviewed during the first two waves of data collection, but the children, now adolescents, were interviewed, primarily in their homes, during the last three.

Some of the findings from the study have focused on gender differences in adolescents' emotional relationships and physical behaviours. Females started to experience emotional relationships at a younger age than males, but males progressed through types of relationships at a faster pace and tended to engage in physical behaviours, including sexual intercourse, at a younger age than females. For females, moving quickly through types of emotional relationships was associated with a higher risk of sexual intercourse at a younger age. However, this was not the case for males (Upadhyay, Hindin and Gultiano, 2006).

Prospective Cohort Study of Thai Children (PCTC) is an observational, community-based study that is following more than 4000 children from four regions (north, north-east, south, central) and the city of Bangkok beginning at birth and until age 24. Each group of children was born during a one-year period, but because the starting dates were staggered, birthdates ranged from as early as 15 October 2000 to as late as 14 September 2002. The one-year follow-up data were published by Sornsrivichai et al. (2008).

Finally, the Jamaican Birth Cohort Study is following a sample of more than 10,000 children who were born on the island in September and October 1986 (Samms-Vaughan, 2001). Baseline data were collected from medical records, maternal interviews, and physical examinations shortly after birth. Four additional waves of data were collected from parents, teachers, and the children themselves between the end of their preschool years and early adulthood. Children living in Kingston or St. Andrew, who were identified from school records, had their physical measurements taken, were given cognitive assessments, and answered questions about their behaviour while they were in primary and secondary school. The current focus is on how early life experiences affect adult health.

Although an analysis of these data revealed no gender difference in cognitive functioning, researchers did find significant gender differences in academic achievement, with females outperforming their male counterparts, and interpreted this as evidence that boys' academic underachievement has an environmental cause (Samms-Vaughan, McCaw-Binns and Ashley, 2006). Researchers have also used these data to examine urban Jamaican children's exposure to community violence and found extremely high levels at an early age. One-quarter had witnessed severe acts of physical violence and one-fifth had been victims of serious threats or robbery. More than one-third had experienced the murder of a family member of close friend. Children from the lowest socioeconomic group were two to three times more likely to witness violent events than children from the highest socioeconomic group, even after controlling for other factors. However, they were no more likely to be a victim. This may be because children tended to witness violence in their communities but be victimized at school (Samms-Vaughan, Jackson and Ashley, 2005).

LONGITUDINAL STUDIES WITH A SPECIFIC FOCUS

Although most longitudinal studies of children have examined child development broadly defined, some have had a more specific focus. These include studies of pathways to delinquency, child welfare populations, and early childhood education programs.

Longitudinal studies of pathways to delinquency

Longitudinal studies have played a major role is in our understanding of delinquency as well as other antisocial behaviours (Table 22.7). For example, the Longitudinal Cohort Study (LCS), part of the Project on Human Development in Chicago Neighborhoods (PHDCN), followed a sample of 6228 children, representing seven age cohorts (ages 0–1, 3, 6, 9, 12, 15, and 18 at baseline), randomly selected from 80 Chicago neighbourhoods.[14] This accelerated longitudinal design, involving multiple age cohorts, would allow researchers to examine development from infancy to young adulthood in much less time than would be possible if a single cohort were used. Three waves of data were collected over a period of eight years. Children who were at least 6 years old answered questions about a variety of topics including impulse control and sensation-seeking, cognitive and language development, leisure activities, delinquency and substance use, friends, and self-perceptions, attitudes, and values. If they were younger than 18, their primary caregiver was also interviewed.

Researchers have been using data from the LCS to examine how neighbourhood, individual, and family conditions contribute to youth violence, and several major findings have emerged. First, differences in conditions across neighbourhoods, and to a less extent parents' marital status and immigrant generation, seem to account for most of the racial and ethnic differences in rates of youth violence (Sampson, Morenoff and Raudenbush, 2005). Second, neighbourhood safety is the strongest predictor of whether youth will carry firearms (Molnar et al., 2004). Third, youth who have been exposed to violence involving firearms are more likely to engage in serious violence over the next two years than youth who had not been exposed (Bingenheimer, Brennan and Earls, 2005). And finally, early-maturing girls who live in disadvantaged neighbourhoods are at greater

Table 22.7 Longitudinal studies of pathways to delinquency

Study	Sample	Data collection	Other information
Project on Human Development in Chicago Neighborhoods Longitudinal Cohort Study	6228 children and youth from 80 Chicago neighbourhoods randomly selected from seven age cohorts: ages 0–1, 3, 6, 9, 12, 15, and 18.	Three waves of data collected over a period of eight years: 1994–1997, 1997–1999, and 2000–2001.	
Denver Youth Survey	Random sample of 806 boys and 721 girls between the ages of 7 and 15 from Denver's high-crime, disadvantaged neighbourhoods.	Data collected once a year between 1988 and 1992 and then again between 1995 and 2003 from both the children and their primary caregiver.	Topics covered by the interviews included delinquency and violent behaviour, drug use/abuse, gang membership, psychopathology, victimization, sexual behaviour and pregnancy, employment, attachment to family, involvement in conventional activities, attitudes toward delinquent behaviour, impulsiveness, religion, family structure, parental education, occupation, and income, child supervision and monitoring, discipline style and practices, family life events, marital discord/violence, school attendance and achievement, attachment to school, involvement in school activities, involvement with delinquent or drug-using peers, neighbourhood characteristics, and use of mental health services.
Pittsburgh Youth Study	Random sample of 1517 boys from Pittsburgh public schools who were in the first, fourth and seventh grade. A screening tool was used to identify the 30% who exhibited the most disruptive behaviour.	Data collected at 6-month intervals from the boys and their primary caregivers for the first 5 years. 4th grade cohort discontinued after seven assessments, but 1st and 7th grade cohorts continued to be followed into adulthood.	
Rochester Youth Development Study	1000 Children (729 boys and 271 girls) from public schools in Rochester, NY who were 7th and 8th graders in the spring of 1989. Male students and students from high-crime areas were over-sampled because they were thought to be at greater risk of delinquency.	Data collected at 6-month intervals from the youth and one of their parents between 1988 and 1992 and then at 12-month intervals between 1994 and 1997 when the youth were 22 years old.	
Cambridge Study in Delinquent Development	411 boys from a working-class area in South London.	Data were collected at ages 8, 10, 14, 16, 18 and 21, 25, 32 and 48.	Interview topics included living circumstances, employment histories, relationships with females, leisure activities, and self reported offending. Psychological tests measured intelligence, attainment, personality, and psychomotor impulsivity.
High/Scope Perry Preschool Project	Low-income African American children, ages 3 and 4, in Ypsilanti, Michigan from 1962 to 1967. 123 children at high risk for school failure due to low IQ score (i.e., between 70 and 85) randomly assigned to the programme ($n = 58$) or to a control group ($n = 65$).	Data collected every year between ages 3 and 11, and then again at 14–15, 19, 27 and 40.	Outcome measures changed over time, from an initial focus on school performance and behaviour to a broader range of outcomes including delinquency and criminal justice system involvement; marital status and parenthood; high school graduation and pursuit of post-secondary Education; employment and earnings, welfare assistance, and home ownership.

risk for youth violence (Obeidallah et al., 2004).

Three other longitudinal studies were part of the US Office of Juvenile Justice and Delinquency Prevention's Program of Research on the Causes and Correlates of Delinquency: the Denver Youth Survey, which followed a random sample of 1527 children from Denver's high-crime, disadvantaged neighbourhoods; the Pittsburgh Youth Study, which followed a random sample of 1517 boys from Pittsburgh public schools; and the Rochester Youth Development Study, which followed a sample of 1000 students from Rochester, NY who were in seventh or eighth grade in the spring of 1989. Despite differences in sample composition, all three studies involved face-to-face interviews with the children and these interviews covered many of the same topics. Data were also collected from police, court, school, and social service records. Additional information about each of these studies is provided in Table 22.7.

Several important findings have emerged from this research. Childhood maltreatment is associated with an increased risk for later behaviour problems, including serious and violent delinquency, drug use, poor school performance, mental illness, and teenage pregnancy. Second, youth typically progress from engaging in less serious to more serious problem behaviours along one or more developmental pathways including authority conflict, such as defiance and running away; covert actions, such as lying and stealing; or overt actions, such as aggressive and violent behaviour. Third, serious delinquents may have multiple co-occurring problems such as being involved in drug use, precocious sexual activity, school failure, juvenile gangs, and unsupervised gun ownership. Fourth, far too many children are involved in serious violent behaviour before their teenage years. Finally, although boys are still more likely to be involved in serious violence, the rate of serious violence among girls has significantly increased (Kelley et al., 1997; Kelley

et al., 1997; Kelley, Thornberry and Smith, 1997; Office of Juvenile Justice and Delinquency Prevention, 1999; Thornberry and Burch, 1997).

Another longitudinal study of delinquency, the UK Cambridge Study in Delinquent Development, followed more than 400 males from a working-class area of South London into adulthood. They were interviewed a total of nine times between ages 8 and 48 and completed a number of psychological assessments in school. Data were also collected from their parents, teachers, and peers. Some of the most important findings to emerge from the study relate to the early risk factors for delinquency and criminal behaviour. At ages 8 and 10, the best predictors of later offending were disruptive child behaviour; family history of criminality; low intelligence or school achievement; poor parenting; impulsiveness; and economic deprivation (Farrington, 1995, 1999; Farrington et al., 2006).

Longitudinal studies of child welfare populations

A number of longitudinal studies have focused on children involved with the child welfare system (Table 22.8). One of the best examples in the United States, the National Survey of Child and Adolescent Well-Being (NSCAW), is following a nationally representative sample of 5504 children (age 0 to 14 years old) who had been the subject of a Child Protective Services (CPS) investigation between October 1999 and December 2000 and a sample of 727 children who had been placed in out-of-home care between 8 and 18 months before the study began.[15] The children were selected using stratified cluster sampling. Five waves of data were collected for the CPS sample over the first six to eight years after the investigation was closed and four waves of data were collected for the out-of-home care sample over the first four years post-entry. In both cases, data were collected from parents, other caregivers, teachers, caseworkers, administrative records, and the children themselves. In fact, children were considered to be the key respondent if they were at least 11 years old. The interview protocol varied depending on the child's age.

The NSCAW data have been used to address a number of important questions about children who become involved with the child welfare system.[16] However, two analyses are of particular relevance to this discussion. The first examined the perceptions of children in foster care (Chapman, Wall and Barth, 2004) and found that children in out-of-home care are generally satisfied and feel close to their caregivers regardless of placement type. However, these children also wanted more time to visit with their biological parents and believed that when their families are reunified, their relationship with their biological parents will have improved. The second examined the effects of child maltreatment on later outcomes including victimization, delinquency, running away, and school engagement (Tyler et al., 2008). Several significant relationships were found, although some of the relationships varied by gender.

Another US example is the Longitudinal Studies Consortium on Child Abuse and Neglect (LONGSCAN) which has been examining the causes and consequences of child maltreatment, the effects of different interventions, and the factors associated with better or worse outcomes since 1990 across four cities (Baltimore, Chicago, Seattle, and San Diego) and one state (North Carolina). Table 22.8 provides information about the studies that were conducted at each of the five sites. Despite differences in the children's risk of maltreatment and their maltreatment histories, the five sites are using the same measures and methodology. Face-to-face interviews have been conducted with the children and their primary caregivers every other year beginning at age 4 until age 18. Primary caregivers were the principal respondents at ages 4, 6, and 8, but children gradually assumed that role beginning at

age 12. Yearly telephone interviews have been used to help increase retention, and maltreatment data have been collected from case records and other sources.

A wide range of research questions have been addressed using data from the five different LONGSCAN study sites, making it difficult to summarize the findings. Among the topics that have received significant attention are: (1) factors that increase or decrease the likelihood that a child will be maltreated or have mental health, behavioural, or cognitive problems as a consequence of maltreatment; (2) the role of fathers and father figures in the maltreatment of children; (3) the relationship between intimate partner violence and child maltreatment, child development, and behavioural outcomes; (4) the experiences of children during the first 18 months after they had been removed from home and placed in substitute care as well as their adjustment following those first 18 months; and (5) the relationship between classifications, conceptualizations and dimensions of child maltreatment and children's social, emotional and behavioural functioning (Dubowitz et al., 2006; Hunter and Knight, 1998).[17]

Longitudinal studies of child welfare populations have also been conducted in Europe and Australia. For example, Children in Care has been following all Danish children born in 1995 who had ever spent time in an out-of-home placement (Egelund and Hestbæk, 2006). Baseline data were collected in 2003 when the children were 7 or 8 years old. Interviews were conducted with the biological parents (primarily mothers) of the children, and questionnaires were sent to child protective workers and to the children's foster parents or residential care providers. The children were first interviewed and given cognitive assessments at age 11 in 2006 using a Web-based questionnaire. Data will be collected every third year, and children from disadvantaged families in the 1995 Danish birth cohort study are serving as a comparison group. Children born in 1995 who had entered care since the last wave of

Table 22.8 Longitudinal Studies of Child Welfare Populations

Name of study	Sample	Data collection	Other information
National Survey of Child and Adolescent Well-Being (NSCAW)	Nationally representative sample of 5504 children (age 0 to 14 years old) who were the subject of a Child Protective Services (CPS) investigation between October 1999 and December 2000 and a sample of 727 children who were currently in out-of-home care. Each of the eight states with the largest CPS caseloads represented one stratum and all but four of the other states, which were excluded due to laws regarding contact with caregivers, comprised a ninth. Strata were divided into primary sampling units (PSUs), typically one or more counties served by a single CPS agency, and a random sample of 100 PSUs was selected with probability proportionate to size. Children were sampled within PSUs, and children who had been the subject of a CPS investigation were stratified by receipt of child welfare services, type of service received, age and type of abuse/neglect.	Data for the CPS sample were collected 2–6 months after the investigation was closed (11/99 to 4/01), and then 12 months (10/00 to 3/02), 18 months (4/01 to 9/02), 36 months (8/02 to 2/04), and 59–96 months (9/05 to 11/07) post-investigation. For the foster care sample, data were collected approximately 12 months after the child entered care, and then 24 months, 30 months, and 48 months post-entry.	The protocol for children age 4 and younger included assessments of cognitive and language skills that used toys and other objects as well as physical measurements of height, weight, and head circumference. Children age 5 and older were asked about a variety of topics including social competence, relationships with peers and adults, behaviour, mental health, school engagement, academic achievement and exposure to violence. Additional questions about service receipt, substance use, sexual behaviour, maltreatment, injuries and delinquency were only asked of children who were at least 11 years old.
Children in Care (CIC)	576 Danish children born in 1995 who were (or had been) in out-of-home care. Comparison group of children from disadvantaged families.	Data have been collected ever third year since 2003, when the children were 7 or 8 years old.	
Care Pathways and Outcomes	375 children, ages 0 to 5, who were in the care of social services in Northern Ireland on March 31, 2000.	Data from administrative records and case files were analyzed in 2000–2003. Children's current caregivers were interviewed in 2003–2006. Children themselves were interviewed in 2006–2009 and additional data were collected from their caregivers.	
Longitudinal Study of Children Placed in a Swedish Children's Home	All 26 children who were placed for a minimum of four weeks in a Swedish city's one remaining children's home at some time during a two-year period in the early 1980s and who were 0–4 years old at the time of placement.	Seven waves of data have been collected: 3 months after exiting the children's home, 9 months after exiting the children's home, and then at some point between the ages of 5 and 10 years old, between the ages of 10 and 15 years old, between the ages of 15 and 20 years old, between the ages of 20 and 25 years old, and between the ages of 25 and 30 years old.	
Barnardos Find a Family Programme Study	59 Australian children, ages 4 to 15, who had been placed in foster families over a five-year period.	Data collected four months after entry and then at 18- to 24-month intervals thereafter.	

(Continued)

Table 22.8 *(Continued)*

Name of study	Sample	Data collection	Other information
	LONGSCAN		
Chicago Capella Project	300 children (ages 3 to 18 months at the time of recruitment) whose families lived in Chicago's Northern CPS District; had household incomes below the federal poverty threshold; and had (1) received comprehensive services after at least one substantiated maltreatment report within the past 12 months ($n = 100$); (2) received no services despite at least one substantiated maltreatment report within the past 12 months ($n = 100$); or (3) no substantiated maltreatment report within the past 12 months ($n = 100$).		Twelve year olds were asked about a wide range of topics including school and academic achievement, delinquency, behaviour problems, criminal/judicial involvement, abuse or neglect they had experienced, relationships with parents and parental monitoring, relationships with peers, risky behaviours among family and friends, violence, sexual experience, social competence, suicidal thoughts, personal use of tobacco, alcohol and other drugs, drug and alcohol use among family and friends, ethnic identity, future expectations, health and disabilities, puberty, household rules, and father involvement.
Baltimore Longitudinal Study of Child Neglect	333 children recruited from inner-city health care clinics based on risk factors for CPS involvement: 129 children who had been diagnosed with non-organic failure, 83 children who had an HIV-positive or drug-abusing mother, and 121 children whose only known risk factor was poverty.		Fourteen-year-olds were asked about many of the same topics as well as pregnancy and parenthood. Additional topics were covered in the interviews with 16- and/or 18-year-olds,
North Carolina Stress and Social Support (SSS) Study	243 children born in 1986 or 1987 who had been identified as 'high risk' infants. One third had been reported as maltreated.	Data collected every other year beginning in 1990 at age 4 and continuing until age 18.	including employment, family income, household composition, life events, service utilization, social support, coping strategies, independent living skills, self-esteem, personal income, and victimization.
San Diego Longitudinal Study of Maltreated Children Placed in Out-of-Home Care	330 children who had been removed from their homes and placed in foster care before they were 3.5 years old.		
Seattle Long Term Family Study	261 children who had been reported to CPS prior to age 5 and categorized as being at 'moderate risk' of subsequent maltreatment in the absence of intervention.		

data was collected will be added to the study at each new wave. Researchers are examining how risk and protective factors interact with service interventions to affect the developmental outcomes.

Another longitudinal study, Care Pathways and Outcomes, is tracking the outcomes of 375 children, ages 0 to 5, who were in the care of social services in Northern Ireland on 31 March 2000. The first phase of the study (2000–2003) used administrative data and case files to examine the children's placement histories and factors related to the type of care in which they had been placed and whether they remain in care or return home. Phase two (2003–2006) focused on the experiences of a subsample of the children's current caregivers, a group that included foster, adoptive, and birth parents. During the third phase of the study (2006–2009), researchers compared the outcomes of children who have remained in long-term foster care with the outcomes of those who have been adopted and those who have returned home.

A third study examined the experiences of 26 children who were placed in the one remaining residential home for children in a Swedish city during a two-year period in the early 1980s. The children were 0 to 4 years old at the time of their placement and stayed in the home for at least four weeks. Seven waves of data were collected. The first four waves of data collection involved interviews not only with the children but also with their birth and foster parents. During the last three waves of data collection, only the children (by then young adults) were interviewed. Researchers were particularly interested in the relationships between the children and both their birth and foster families, and found that foster family attitudes towards the child's biological family can promote continuity and a sense of security and help foster children deal with their disappointments and come to terms with their family background (Andersson, 2009).

The first study of out-of-home care in Australia to interview children about their experiences in out-of-home care followed 59

children, ages 4 to 15, who had been placed in long-term foster care through the Barnardos Find a Family Programme. Baseline data were collected four months after placement, when the children were, on average, 10.7 years old, and then at 18- to 24-month intervals over a period of five years. Caseworkers, foster parents, birth parents, and children who were at least 8 years old were interviewed. Data from teacher assessments were also collected. Interviews with the children explored their relationships with birth and foster families, the reasons for their placement, and their history in foster care. The children also completed a number of standardized measures.

Data from this study have been used to examine emotional development, familial attachments, and interpersonal skills. Although the children experienced strong feelings of sadness and anxiety at the time of placement, they reported a decrease in emotional problems over time. Self-esteem among these children was generally low and negatively related to younger age of entry and multiple placement changes. Despite strong feelings of attachment to their foster parents, these children wanted more contact with their birth families. Self-perceptions of interpersonal skills at baseline were positively related to the cohesiveness of relationships with foster parents at the first follow-up, and conversely, children who reported more a cohesive relationship with their foster father at baseline perceived themselves as having better interpersonal skills at follow-up (Fernandez, 2007). The data also suggested that children's functioning improved over time as measured by a decline in both internalizing and externalizing behaviours (Fernandez, 2006, 2008).

These examples notwithstanding, the perspective of children has largely been absent from longitudinal studies of child welfare populations (Berrick, Frasch and Fox, 2000; Butler and Williamson, 1994; Fein, Maluccio and Kluger, 1990; Hill and Aldgate, 1996; Triseliotis et al., 1995; Wilson and Conroy, 1999). This omission is prevalent despite increasing recognition that child welfare research should include the perspectives of the children (Curran and Pecora, 1999; Fox and Berrick, 2007; Gilligan, 2000; Hill, 1997). One reason for this absence is that barriers can limit researchers' access to and contact with system-involved children (Gilbertson and Barber, 2002; Heptinstall, 2000). Another is that administrative data can be used to follow children's movement into and out of the child welfare system with minimal attrition and at a much lower cost.

Longitudinal studies of early childhood education interventions

Longitudinal studies of early childhood education programs have been conducted in a number of different countries, including Australia, Canada, Colombia, France, Germany, Great Britain, India, Ireland, Japan, Singapore, South Korea, Sweden, Turkey, and the United States (Table 22.9). Although data have not always been collected directly from the children who participated in the programs, they have frequently been included as informants about themselves.

One example is a study conducted by researchers at the Educational Research Centre of St. Patrick's College that examined the effects of the Rutland Street Project, a two-year, half-day preschool program for 3- to 5-year-old children in one of Dublin's disadvantaged inner-city neighbourhoods. Tests of scholastic ability were administered at program entry and at the end of each of the next five years. Children's perceptual and language development were measured at program entry and age eight. Other data collected at program entry and age 8 included teacher ratings and social worker assessments of home environments. Follow-up interviews were conducted with the children when they were 16 years old.

At the end of the two-year program, children who participated performed significantly better than a comparison group of children from the same geographic area who

had not.[18] However, three years later, those differences had disappeared. By age 16, researchers found no significant differences between the groups with respect to special education placement, absenteeism, truancy, or school behaviour problems. Nor were there differences in work experience or leisure activities. However, children who had participated in the program remained in school longer and were more likely to take the public examinations that qualify students for post-secondary education or vocational training than the non-participants (Kellaghan and Greaney, 1993).

Another example is the Turkish Early Enrichment Project (TEEP), which examined the separate and combined effects of an educational preschool environment and a mother training program on the development of economically disadvantaged children from Istanbul, Turkey. The sample included children attending educational centres, children attending custodial centres (which provided only basic care and supervision), and children not attending any type of day care outside the home. At the beginning of the project's second year, children in each of the three care settings were assigned to a mother training condition or to a no mother training condition. The mothers of children in the training condition participated in a home instruction program focused on developing children's cognitive skills and an enrichment program involving guided group discussions designed to promote child development, maternal well-being, and healthy family relationships. Data were collected from the children and their mothers at the beginning of the intervention in 1982, at the end of the intervention in 1986, and in 1991.

Participation in either the child-focused or parent-focused educational interventions had positive effects on children's cognitive skills, social relationships, and school adjustment at the end of the four-year project. However, follow-up assessments six years later revealed that only the parent-focused intervention was associated with long-term gains as measured by higher primary school

Table 22.9 Longitudinal studies of early childhood education interventions

Name of study	Sample	Data collection	Other information
Rutland Street Project	90 three-year-olds from a disadvantaged inner-city neighbourhood in Dublin, Ireland who attended a two-year preschool programme. Comparison group of 60 eight-year-olds from the same geographic area who had not attended the programme.	Data were collected from the programme children at programme entry, at the end of each of the two programme years at the end of each of the first three primary school grades, and at age 8. Interviews conducted at age 16 with 83 programme participants and 53 non-participants. Outcomes of comparison group were measured five years sooner because they were five years older.	Interviews at age 16 focused on educational careers, first work experience, leisure activities and social deviance.
Turkish Early Enrichment Project (TEEP)	Random sample of 255 low-income children in Istanbul, Turkey. 226 were re-interviewed as adolescents.	Data collected from in 1982, the year before the intervention began in 1986, the year after the intervention ended, and in 1991. In some cases, the participant group included all the children in given age group at a particular centre whereas at other centres children were randomly selected.	Outcome measures included intelligence and cognitive development, academic achievement and primary school grades, and self-concept, school adjustment, aggressiveness and dependency. Follow-up interviews covered attitudes toward school and education, relationships with parents, educational and occupational expectations, self-concept, and social adjustment.
High/Scope Perry Preschool Project	Low-income African American children, ages 3 and 4, in Ypsilanti, Michigan from 1962 to 1967. 123 children at high risk for school failure due to low IQ score (i.e., between 70 and 85) randomly assigned to the programme (n =58) or to a control group (n = 65).	Data collected every year between ages 3 and 11, and then again at 14–15, 19, 27 and 40.	Outcome measures changed over time, from an initial focus on school performance and behaviour to a broader range of outcomes including delinquency and criminal justice system involvement; marital status and parenthood; high school graduation and pursuit of post-secondary education; employment and earnings, welfare assistance, and home ownership.
Abecedarian Early Childhood Intervention Project	111 low income children born between 1972 and 1977 from Chapel Hill and Orange County, North Carolina randomly assigned to the intervention (N = 57) or the control group (N = 54).	Data collected at ages 3, 4, 5, 6.5, 8, 12, 15 and 21.	Early outcome measures included IQ scores, standardized test scores, grade retention, and special education placement. Later outcome measures included educational attainment, employment, and parenthood.
Syracuse Family Development Research Program	216 low-income, single parent African-American families in Syracuse, New York. 108 children were assigned to each the treatment and control groups.	Follow-up data were collected from 119 study participants (65 treatment and 54 controls).	The children were asked what they liked and disliked about themselves (physical attributes, personal attributes), what they saw themselves doing in five years (e.g., school or work); what they perceived to be the worst thing about school; and how they would handle a serious problems such as failing school.
Chicago Longitudinal Study	1150 children who participated in Child-Parent Center Programs as kindergarteners in 1985-1986 and 389 children who participated in an alternative all-day kindergarten program in 5 randomly selected Chicago public schools. All study children were born in 1980 and attended Title I eligible schools.	Data collected in 1989, 1990, 1991, 1995, 1996 and 2002.	

grades and vocabulary scores, more favourable attitudes towards school, and better family and social adjustment. The positive effects of child-focused interventions had largely disappeared (Kagitcibasi, Sunar and Bekman, 2001).

Although the research on early childhood education programs is international in scope, the largest number of studies has taken place in the United States. One of the best known, the Perry Preschool Project, examined the long-term effects of a model program that served low-income African-American children in Ypsilanti, Michigan, from 1962 to 1967. Researchers randomly assigned 123 children at high risk for school failure (those having an IQ between 70 and 85) to a treatment group that received the intervention, which combined classroom instruction and home visiting, or to a control group that did not. Data were collected every year between ages 3 and 11, primarily from mothers and teachers, and then at ages 14, 15, 19, 27, and 40 from the 'children' themselves. Additional information was obtained from school records, police and court records, and standardized tests.

Researchers found significant effects of preschool program participation each time data were collected. At age 10, only 17 per cent of the program participants had been held back a grade or placed in special education compared with 38 per cent of the non-participants. At age 14, program participants were scoring higher on achievement tests, and at age 19, had higher literacy scores and grade-point averages.

Importantly, these differences persisted well into adulthood. Program participants were more likely to have graduated from high school and were less likely to have been arrested than non-participants by age 27. Program participants were more likely to be employed and were earning more each month. They were less likely to be single parents and less likely to be receiving public assistance (Schweinhart, Barnes and Weikart, 1993). Significant differences were still evident at age 40. Participants continued to have higher earnings, fewer arrests, greater home ownership, and less drug use (Schweinhart et al., 2005).

Another widely recognized longitudinal study, the Abecedarian Early Childhood Intervention Project, served low-income children in Chapel Hill and Orange County, North Carolina who were born between 1972 and 1977. A total of 111 children were randomly assigned to a treatment group that participated in a full-day, high-quality centre-based educational intervention with an emphasis on social, emotional, cognitive, and language development from infancy through age 5 or to a control group. Data were collected at ages 3, 4, 5, 6.5, 8, 12, 15, and 21.

Program participation appears to have had a number of long-lasting effects. Program participants consistently scored higher on tests of cognitive ability and academic achievement than non-participants. The former also completed more years of education, were more likely to attend a four-year college, and were older, on average, when their first child was born (Campbell et al., 2002).

A less well-known example of a longitudinal study of an early intervention is the 10-year evaluation of the Syracuse Family Development Research Program (SFDRP) which targeted low-income, single-parent, predominantly African-American families in Syracuse, New York, between 1969 and 1976 (Honig, Lally and Mathieson, 1982). This intervention, which involved home visits, parent training, and individualized day care, began before birth and continued through the preschool years. A total of 216 children were randomly assigned to either a treatment or control group, but follow-up data were only collected from 119. In addition to obtaining information from school, court, and probation department records, interviews were conducted with the children and their parents (who also completed questionnaires).

A 13-year follow-up study by Lally, Mangione and Honig (1988) found significant differences in school performance and juvenile delinquency between the FDRP children and the comparison group, although the differences in academic performance were limited to females. Likewise, Reynolds et al. (2001) found that the FDRP children were less likely to have committed any crimes. However, there was no difference in the number of crimes committed by the youths who committed at least one.

Finally, a somewhat more contemporary example is the Chicago Longitudinal Study, which has been examining the effects of the Chicago Public Schools' Child-Parent Center (CPC) Program, an intervention that provided educational and family support services to children from preschool through third grade. A total of 1539 kindergarteners born in 1980 were enrolled in the CPC program or in an alternative all-day kindergarten program in five randomly selected Title I-eligible schools. Data were collected in 1989, 1990, 1991, 1995, 1996, and 2002. Although the study initially focused on children's feelings about and attitudes towards school, adolescent and early adult outcomes have been assessed across a wide range of domains.

CPC participation was associated with significantly higher achievement test scores at ages 5, 6, 9, and 14, fewer years in special education, and lower rates of grade retention (Reynolds and Temple, 1998). School involvement was much higher among the parents of centre children than among the parents of non-centre children, and centre children were more likely to have graduated from high school and attended college by their early twenties. Delinquency rates were also significantly lower among the CPC participants during early adolescence, and they were less likely to have become involved with the criminal justice system as young adults (Reynolds et al., 2001; Reynolds et al., 2007).

Before concluding this discussion, it is important to point out that because some of the interventions that have been evaluated, particularly in the United States, have been model programs (for example, Perry Preschool School and the Abecedarian Project), the long-term effects that some studies have found may not generalize to the early education programs to which children are more typically exposed (Schweinhart, 2005).

METHODOLOGICAL ISSUES

Involving children in longitudinal research presents several methodological challenges. Assuming children are old enough to participate in an interview, the types of questions they can answer may be limited. As a result, data about children are often collected from their parents or other caregivers at the beginning of a longitudinal study, and then, later from the children once they are able to respond to questions about themselves in a meaningful way. In some cases, the children eventually become primary respondents, either in conjunction with adult informants or exclusively (Taplin, 2005).

Another challenge arises from the need to use developmentally appropriate measures (Runyan et al., 1998). This means not only that children are able to understand the questions, but also that the questions are relevant given the ages of the children to whom they are being asked. In some cases, developmentally appropriate measures already exist. In other cases, pre-existing instruments can be modified or otherwise adapted. However, changing the wording of questions may also change the instrument's psychometric properties as well as reduce the ability to make comparisons across studies (Berrick et al., 2000).

Although this need to use developmentally appropriate measures is not unique to longitudinal research, it is more complicated because what constitutes a developmentally appropriate measure at one age may not at another (West, Hauser and Scanlan, 1998), and using age-inappropriate measures can lead to floor or ceiling effects. Consequently, different measures may need to be used during different waves of data collection. This inconsistency of measurement has implications for assessing change (Holmbeck et al., 2006). In particular, if different measures are used during different waves of data collection, then the data may not be directly comparable across waves. One way to deal with this problem is to use measures for which there are population norms and examine children's standing relative to their peers over time. However, this procedure is not always an option.

The situation is even more complicated when the children or youth being followed belong to different birth cohorts. Hence, what constitutes a developmentally appropriate measure will vary not only between but also within waves. This means that each wave of data collection will require multiple interview protocols, each with different measures (Berrick et al., 2000). Of course, the more domains the interview covers, the more complicated this becomes.

Just as it is important for the instruments that are used to be developmentally appropriate, other aspects of the interview must also take the age of the respondent into account (Berrick et al., 2000). For example, interviewers must be able to develop rapport with children, engage and keep their attention and know how to respond if children appear distressed or disclose that they are being neglected or abused. It is important to provide breaks for children who become distracted, bored, or tired, and to give them the option of rescheduling the interview for another day. Although none of these concerns is unique to longitudinal research, they become even more important if the same children are to be interviewed repeatedly.

Age can also make a difference with respect to the reliability of self-reports. For example, although children are often the best informants about their own feelings and behaviour, the self-reports of children who are at least 10 years old tend to be more reliable than those of younger children (Garbarino and Stott, 1992).

Another major challenge researchers face when they follow children and youth prospectively is sample retention (Taplin, 2005). Retaining children and youth in a study over time is critical for several reasons. First, significant attrition raises questions about sample selection bias. The concern is that the children or youth who continue to participate in the study may be systematically different from those who drop out – a possibility that becomes increasingly likely the more sample size declines over time (Thomas, Frankenberg and Smith, 2001). Second, significant attrition also raises questions about generalizability. In other words, the children or youth from whom data continue to be collected may no longer be representative of the larger population of children or youth. Finally, multivariate techniques for analysing longitudinal data require an adequate sample size. If the sample becomes too small because of attrition, there may not be enough statistical power to detect effects (Guterman, 2004).

A review of longitudinal studies of children and youth by Shulruf et al. (2007) found that an 80 per cent retention rate is achievable. However, attrition rates are generally higher in studies that include large numbers of indigenous peoples and in studies conducted in developing countries where resources are more limited. There is also some evidence that when children or youth are involved in longitudinal research, attrition is most likely to occur during the study's early years (Taplin, 2005). For example, the Canadian Longitudinal Study of Children and Youth had an attrition rate of 11 per cent between the first and second waves of data collection, but the response rate at each of the subsequent waves was 85 per cent to 95 per cent (Soloff, Millward and Sanson, 2003). Similarly, most of the attrition in the South African Birth to Twenty Study occurred during the first two years. Seventy per cent of the 3275 children for whom baseline data were collected were followed for at least 12 years, and the average attrition rate was less than 3 per cent per year (Richter, Norris and de Wet, 2004). Among children in the New Zealand Christchurch Health and Development Study, the attrition rate was

9 per cent between birth and age two, but less than 1 per cent each year after the first two. In fact, cumulative attrition by age 18 was just 19 per cent (Horwood and Fergusson, 1999; Fergusson et al., 1989).

Several strategies have been used to reduce sample attrition (Loeber and Farrington, 1994; Taplin, 2005). One is to collect contact information at the end of each interview for family members, friends, or other people who are likely to know where the children or youth can be found. Another is to obtain permission to search administrative records for information that could be used to locate children and youth. These strategies are particularly important when the children and youth being studied are likely to be highly mobile (for example, children and youth in foster care; homeless children). Still other strategies include maintaining contact with study participants between interviews and providing children or youth (and in some cases their parents or other caretakers) with incentive for continuing participation.

One factor that can affect retention rates is the timing of follow-up interviews. The timing of the follow-up interviews should take into account what is known about the rate of change during different developmental periods. More frequent interviews are needed if change is likely to be rapid (Loeber and Farrington, 1994). Recall errors can also become a problem if the interval between interviews is too long. However, the advantages of collecting data frequently must be weighed against the possibility of sample attrition among respondents for whom frequent data collection has become too much of a burden. Thus, follow-up interviews must be timed to both minimize sample attrition and to maximize the ability to measure change (or stability) during critical developmental periods.

Directly related to this issue of timing is the question of how long children or youth should be followed. Although longer time frames provide more opportunities to observe continuity or change and to identify developmental trends, the knowledge gained from each additional wave of data collection must be balanced against the costs (Farrington, 1991). For this reason, Farrington (1991) has recommended a follow-up period of between seven and eight years.

One final challenge that researchers confront when children are followed over time is how to incorporate comparison or control groups (Taplin, 2005). This is especially important when the children are members of a special population, such as children in foster care or indigenous populations. One option is to use measures that have been used in other longitudinal studies based on nationally representative samples. Of course, any differences between the children being studied and the nationally representative sample must be taken into account. These can include differences in their demographic characteristics as well as differences in geographic region or the time frame during which the data were collected.

ETHICAL ISSUES

Involving children and youth in research *always* raises ethical issues regarding informed consent and confidentiality (Fisher, 1994; Goodenough et al., 2003; Helgesson, 2005; Mishna, Antle and Regehr, 2004). However, a few that pertain specifically to longitudinal research merit special attention.

Questions about children's ability to give informed consent always arise whenever they participate as human subjects in research (Goodenough et al., 2003; Helgesson, 2005; Mishna et al., 2004). Despite some evidence that their capacity to give informed consent has been underestimated (Zwiers and Morrissette, 1999) and may vary even among children of the same age (Miller, 2000), it is generally assumed as a matter of law that children are incapable of giving informed consent, and hence, that decisions about their participation in a study must be made by their parents or legal guardians. (The pertinent federal regulations in the United States require *permission* by parents and *assent* by children in most instances.[19]) However, that approach becomes more problematic when the research in which they are involved is longitudinal. This is the case for two reasons. First, the identity of the primary caregiver can change over time, as might happen if children are moving into and out of foster care. Second, what children can reasonably be expected to understand will increase as they grow older.

Therefore, the information about the study with which children are provided should change over time to reflect their growing cognitive and emotional maturity (Field and Burman, 2004). Moreover, because children's capacity to make voluntary, informed decisions increases as they grow older, study participants who were once too young to give informed consent may eventually become old enough to make decisions for themselves. In fact, it would be possible, as a practical matter, for children to 'nullify' the consent obtained from their parents or legal guardians perhaps years before when the study began (Helgesson, 2005).

Another ethical question that takes on added significance in the case of longitudinal research is whether it is ever ethical for researchers to share information that a child or youth discloses with his or her parents (Macklin, 1992; Mishna et al., 2004). Because parental permission is needed for children to participate in research, parents may expect that they have a right to information that their child reveals, particularly if the information involves risks to their child's well-being. At the same time, researchers must respect children's right to confidentiality, including confidentiality vis-à-vis their parents, because any breach of confidentiality could adversely affect children's continued willingness to participate in the study or, at least, reduce their future candour because of fears that

something else they say might be disclosed. Thus, it is especially important for researchers doing longitudinal studies involving children or youth to anticipate these types of situations, develop a process for dealing with them, and explain that process to both children and their parents in advance.

TRENDS OVER TIME IN LONGITUDINAL STUDIES OF CHILDREN

A recent review of longitudinal studies involving children and youth identified several trends (Shulruf et al., 2007). First, the range of domains covered and the amount of attention they have received have changed over time. Studies that began prior to 1980 were less likely than those that began after 2000 to collect extensive data on the social and physical environments in which children live (such as neighbourhood and schools), whereas studies carried out between 1950 and 1980 were more focused on cognition and antisocial behaviour than those that began in the 1990s, although a reversal of the latter trend may have occurred in recent years (Shulruf et al., 2007).

Directly related to this change in emphasis, longitudinal studies increasingly reflect the growing awareness that children's development is affected by a combination of the internal factors that children bring with them and the larger environmental factors to which children are exposed (Green et al., 1997; West et al., 1998). As a result, more attention is being paid in longitudinal research to context (in other words, the physical, social, family, and school environments in which children live) and the ways in which different factors interact (Nicholson and Rempel, 2004; West et al., 1998). Likewise, there is growing recognition of the importance of what happens during the antenatal period. Concern also has increased about the biological and genetic factors that affect development. Consequently, even before the children are born, longitudinal researchers are increasingly collecting data from the mothers of the children whom they will be studying (Zollinger, 2002).

There has also been a change in sampling methodologies. Studies that began prior to 1990 often relied on sampling frames that included all children born in a specific area and/or on particular dates. More recent studies have tended to use methods that generate more representative samples. These include simple random selection as well as stratified or cluster sampling. The one potential drawback is that more recent studies have tended to have lower initial response rates and higher rates of attrition than studies that sampled all births that occurred within a defined place or time (Shulruf et al., 2007).

Additionally, increasing attention is being paid in longitudinal research to intergenerational factors that affect development (Caspi et al., 2005). This can be seen in the emergence of multi-generational studies. An increasing number of longitudinal studies that began with a cohort of children are now following the children of cohort members. Examples include the Dunedin, New Zealand, study and the Rochester Youth Development Study. Some of these studies actually cover three generations because the original study collected data not only about the children but also about their parents. In fact, the Swiss Etiological Study of Adjustment and Mental Health (SESAM), which is following a sample of 3000 children from before birth until they are 20 years old, their parents, and their grandparents has been a three-generation study from its inception.

Finally, there is an increasing recognition of the need for longitudinal studies that will facilitate comparisons across countries with different social, economic, and institutional environments. Although relatively few longitudinal studies have been international, results from studies conducted in different countries can be compared when similar measures and methodologies are used. These studies are important because they can help us understand which of the factors that affect children's development are culturally specific and which are more universal (Shulruf et al., 2007).

CONCLUSION

As researchers have increasingly come to recognize, children have much to contribute as active participants in longitudinal studies. Parents, teachers, and other adults can provide valuable information about individual children. They may be particularly good informants about observable behaviours and when children are very young. Nevertheless, there are limits to what they can tell us about children's unobservable feelings, attitudes, and thoughts or the motivations that lead children to behave the way they do. Including children's voices in longitudinal research is also essential if our goal is to understand how they perceive not only their own experiences but also the world in which they live, and how those perceptions change over time. Only in this way can we be confident that our policies and practices are truly child-centered.

The number of longitudinal studies involving children from developing countries and indigenous populations is especially encouraging. Such studies are critical if we want to understand how child development and the many factors that affect it vary across place. Regardless, however, where the children whom we are studying live, careful attention must always be given to both the ethical and methodological issues that arise whenever children are involved as active participants in research, issues which can range from informed consent to the scope of child-friendly data collection (Christensen, 2004; Thomas and O'Kane, 1998).

APPENDIX A: WEBSITES WITH INFORMATION ABOUT SPECIFIC STUDIES

1946 National Survey of Health and Development
http://www.nshd.mrc.ac.uk/
1958 National Child Development Study
http://www.cls.ioe.ac.uk/page.aspx?&sitesectionid=724&sitesectiontitle=Welcome+to+the+1958+National+Child+Development+Study
1970 British Cohort Study
http://www.cls.ioe.ac.uk/page.aspx?&sitesectionid=795&sitesectiontitle=Welcome+to+the+1970+British+Cohort+Study
Abecedarian Early Childhood Intervention Project
http://www.fpg.unc.edu/~abc/
Aboriginal Birth Cohort (ABC)
http://www.clancohort.com.au//index.htm
Australian Temperament Project
http://www.aifs.gov.au/atp/pubs/index.html
Barnardos Find a Family Programme
http://www.barnardos.org.au/barnardos/html/rd_projects.cfm
Birth to Twenty
http://web.wits.ac.za/Academic/Health/Research/BirthTo20/
Born in Bradford
http://www.borninbradford.nhs.uk/
Cambridge Study in Delinquent Development
http://sociology-data.sju.edu/8488/8488cb.pdf
Care Pathways and Outcomes
http://www.qub.ac.uk/research-centres/TheCarePathwaysandOutcomesStudy/
Cebu Longitudinal Health and Nutrition Survey (CLHNS)
http://www.cpc.unc.edu/projects/cebu/
Centre for Longitudinal Studies (CLS)
http://www.cls.ioe.ac.uk
Chicago Longitudinal Study of Parent-Child Centers
http://www.waisman.wisc.edu/cls/
Child Development Supplement (CDS) to the Panel Study of Income Dynamics (PSID)
http://psidonline.isr.umich.edu/Studies.aspx
Children in Care (CIC)
http://www.sfi.dk/Default.aspx?ID=4844&Action=1&NewsId=114&PID=10056

Children of the 1979 National Longitudinal Survey of Youth
http://www.bls.gov/nls/handbook/2005/nlshc4.pdf
Christchurch Health and Development Study (CHDS)
http://www.otago.ac.nz/christchurch/research/healthdevelopment/
Competent Children, Competent Learners
http://www.nzcer.org.nz/default.php?products_id=134
Denver Youth Survey
http://ojjdp.ncjrs.org/ccd/denver.html
Dunedin Multidisciplinary Health and Development Study
http://dunedinstudy.otago.ac.nz/
Early Childhood Longitudinal Study (ECLS-B) and (ECLS-K)
http://nces.ed.gov/ecls/index.asp
Early Head Start Research Evaluation Project
http://www.acf.hhs.gov/programs/opre/ehs/ehs_resrch/
European Longitudinal Study of Pregnancy and Childhood (ELSPAC)
http://www.alspac.bristol.ac.uk/
http://www.sci.muni.cz/elspac/www/node/51
Growing Up in Australia: The Longitudinal Study of Australian Children
http://www.aifs.gov.au/growingup/
Growing Up in France: The French Longitudinal Study of Children
http://cls.ioe.ac.uk/page.aspx?&sitesectionid=326&sitesectiontitle=ELFE+(Growing+up+in+France)
Growing Up in Ireland: The National Longitudinal Study of Children in Ireland
http://www.growingup.ie/
Growing Up in Scotland (GUS)
http://www.growingupinscotland.org.uk/
http://www.crfr.ac.uk/gus/publictype.html
High/Scope Perry Preschool Project
http://www.highscope.org/Content.asp?ContentId=219
Jamaican Birth Cohort Study
http://caribbean.scielo.org/scielo.php?script=sci_arttext&pid=S0043-31442005000100004&lng=pt&nrm=iso&tlng=pt

Longitudinal Studies Consortium on Child Abuse and Neglect (LONGSCAN)
http://www.iprc.unc.edu/longscan/

Longitudinal Study of Indigenous Children (LSIC)
http://www.fahcsia.gov.au/about-fahcsia/publications-articles/research-publications/longitudinal-data-initiatives/footprints-in-time-the-longitudinal-study-of-indigenous-children-lsic

Longitudinal Study of New Zealand Children and Families
http://www.msd.govt.nz/about-msd-and-our-work/work-programmes/social-research/longitudinal-study/index.html

Millennium Cohort Study of 2000-2001
http://www.data-archive.ac.uk/deposit/use?id=2167

National Children's Study of the Effects of Environment on Health (NSC)
http://www.nationalchildrensstudy.gov/

National Longitudinal Survey of Children & Youth (NLSCY)
http://www23.statcan.gc.ca/imdb/p2SV.pl?Function=getSurvey&SDDS=4450&lang=en&db=imdb&adm=8&dis=2

National Survey of Child and Adolescent Well-Being (NSCAW)
http://www.acf.hhs.gov/programs/opre/abuse_neglect/nscaw/

Newcastle Thousand Families Cohort Study
http://www.thousandfamilies.com/

NIICHD Study of Early Child Care
http://secc.rti.org/

Northern Finland Birth Cohort Studies
http://kelo.oulu.fi/NFBC/pub/description66.htm
http://kelo.oulu.fi/NFBC/pub/description85.htm

Pittsburgh Youth Study
https://www.ncjrs.gov/html/ojjdp/jjbul9712-2/jjb1297d.html

Program of Research on the Causes and Correlates of Delinquency
http://www.ojjdp.gov/jjbulletin/9810_2/program.html

Project on Human Development in Chicago Neighborhoods
http://www.icpsr.umich.edu/PHDCN/

Prospective Cohort Study of Thai Children
http://elibrary.trf.or.th/project_content.asp?PJID=RDG4310007 (in Thai)

Québec Longitudinal Study of Child Development
http://www.jesuisjeserai.stat.gouv.qc.ca/

Rochester Youth Development Study
http://www.ojjdp.gov/jjbulletin/9810_2/g4.html

Rutland Street Project
http://www.cecde.ie/english/pdf/Policy%20Submissions/Submission%20to%20the%20Curriculum%20Development%20Unit.pdf

Syracuse Family Development Research Program (SFDRP)
http://www.ojjdp.gov/mpg/Syracuse%20Family%20Development%20Research%20Program-MPGProgramDetail-432.aspx

Te Rerenga ā te Pīrere or The Flight Of The Fledgling
http://www.nzcer.org.nz/default.php?products_id=651

The Fragile Families and Child Wellbeing Study
http://www.fragilefamilies.princeton.edu/

Turkish Early Enrichment Project (TEEP)
http://unesdoc.unesco.org/images/0008/000886/088616mb.pdf

Young Lives
http://www.younglives.org.uk/

NOTES

1 Appendix A is a list of websites where information about most of these longitudinal studies can be found.

2 Birth cohort studies focus on a group of people who were born in the same place at about the same time.

3 The British study is known as the Avon Longitudinal Study of Parents and Children or Children of the 90s.

4 African-American, Hispanic, and economically disadvantaged white youth were over-sampled, and data have been collected every year since the *NLSY* began.

5 The annotated bibliography can be found at http://www.nlsbibliography.org/cohort.php3.

6 The PSID itself began in 1968.

7 Youth ages 18 and older are interviewed biennially by phone until they become PSID panel members when they establish households of their own.

8 The searchable bibliography can be found at http://psidonline.isr.umich.edu/Publications/Bibliography/BrowseKeywordsQ.aspx?ID=5

9 The Fragile Families publications collection can be found at http://crcw.princeton.edu/publications/publications.asp

10 Several groups, including children who were low birth weight, twins, and American Indian/Native Alaskan or Asian/Pacific Islander were over-sampled for the ECLS-B.

11 The NCES bibliography can be found at http://nces.ed.gov/ECLS/bibliography.asp

12 Maternity hospitals accounted for 99.2 per cent of the city's births.

13 Most of the males were interviewed as part of the 2000 Army Enlistment Study of draftees. They were given a shorter version of questionnaire in 2001 when the females and the other males were interviewed.

14 The 80 neighbourhoods were selected from among 343 neighbourhoods stratified by SES and racial/ethnic composition.

15 The design originally called for children who had been in out-of-home care for approximately 12 months, but too few children in some primary sampling units fit this criterion.

16 A list of publications based on analyses of NSCAW data can be found at http://www.refworks.com/refshare/?site=010271135929600000/RWWS5A10943/NSCAW

17 Research briefs summarizing the findings from particular studies can be found at http://www.iprc.unc.edu/longscan/pages/researchbriefs/index.htm

18 Children in the comparison group were from the same geographic region but five years older so their outcomes were measured five years sooner.

19 The US National Commission for Protection of Human Subjects of Biomedical and Behavioral Research concluded that 7 years old is a reasonable minimum age for children to be asked for their assent. Consistent with this recommendation, LONGSCAN researchers began asking children to assent once they were 8 years old.

REFERENCES

Andersson, G. (2009) 'Foster children: a longitudinal study of placements and family relationships', *International Journal of Social Welfare*, 18(1): 13–26.

Andersen, A., Deding, M. and Lausten, M. (2007) *How Much Does Parental Divorce Affect Children's Well-Being?* Copenhagen: Danish National Centre for Social Research.

Australian Institute of Family Studies (2008) *The Longitudinal Study of Australian Children: 2006–2007 Annual Report.* Melbourne, Australia: Australian Institute of Family Studies.

Baviskar, S. (2008) *Examining the Relationship between Inter-parental Conflict and Child Outcomes Using Data from the Danish Longitudinal Study of Children.* Copenhagen: The Danish National Centre for Social Research.

Berrick, J., Frasch, K. and Fox, A. (2000) 'Assessing children's experiences of out of home care: Methodological challenges and opportunities', *Social Work Research*, 24(2): 119–27.

Bingenheimer, J., Brennan, R. and Earls, F. (2005) 'Firearm violence exposure and serious violent behavior', *Science*, 308(5726): 1323–6.

Blaney, S.M., Wertheim, E.H., Sanson, A., Prior, M. and Smart, D. (2000) *A Longitudinal and Concurrent Analysis of the Role of Temperament Characteristics in Predicting the Later Development of Disordered Eating in Female Australian Adolescents.* Paper presented at the 35th Australian Psychological Society Conference, October, 2000.

Butler, I. and Williamson, H. (1994) *Children Speak, Children, Trauma and Social Work.* London: Longman.

Campbell, F., Ramey, C., Pungello, E., Sparling, J. and Miller-Johnson, S. (2002) 'Early childhood education: Young adult outcomes from the Abecedarian Project', *Applied Developmental Science*, 6(1): 42–57.

Caspi, A., Moffitt, T., Cannon, M., McClay, J., Murray, R., Harrington, H., Taylor, A., Arseneault, L., Williams, B., Braithwaite, A., Poulton, R. and Craig, I. (2005) 'Moderation of the effect of adolescent-onset cannabis use on adult psychosis by a functional polymorphism in the COMT gene: Longitudinal evidence of a gene X environment interaction', *Biological Psychiatry*, 57(10): 1117–27.

Chapman, M., Wall, A. and Barth, R. (2004) 'Children's voices: The perceptions of children in foster care', *American Journal of Orthopsychiatry*, 74(3): 293–304.

Chernoff, J., Flanagan, K., McPhee, C. and Park, J. (2007) *Preschool: First findings from the Third Follow-Up of the Early Childhood Longitudinal Study, Birth Cohort (ECLS-B).* Washington, DC: National Center for Education Statistics.

Christensen, P. (2004) 'Children's participation in ethnographic research: issues of power and representation', *Children and Society*, 18(2): 165–76.

Cooper, G., Arago-Kemp, V., Wylie, C. and Hodgen, E. (2004) *A Longitudinal Study of Māori Students: Phase 1 Report.* Wellington, New Zealand: New Zealand Council for Educational Research.

Curran, M. and Pecora, P. (1999) 'Incorporating the perspectives of youth placed in family foster care: selected research findings and methodological challenges', in M. Curran and P. Pecora (eds.), *The Foster Care Crisis*. Lincoln, NE: University of Nebraska Press. pp. 99–125.

Danese, A., Moffitt, T., Pariante, C., Ambler, A., Poulton, R. and Caspi, A. (2008) 'Elevated inflammation levels in depressed adults with a history of childhood maltreatment', *Archives of General Psychiatry*, 65(4): 409–15.

Department of International Development (2007) *Young Lives: An International Study of Childhood Poverty*. United Kingdom: Department of International Development, University of Oxford.

Dubowitz, H., English, D., Kotch, J. Litrownik, A., Runyan, D., Thompson, R., Black, M., Calica, R., Hussey, J., Newton, R., Starr, R., Bangdiwala, S., Briggs, E., Everson, M., Graham, J., Knight, E., Landsverk, J. and Lewis, T. (2006) *Research Briefs Volume 2*. Chapel Hill, NC: LONGSCAN Coordinating Center.

Egelund, T. and Hestbæk, A. (2006) *Young Children in Care: A Danish Longitudinal Study on Children from the 1995 Cohort Placed in Care*. Copenhagen: The Danish National Centre for Social Research (SFI).

Elliot, J. and Shepherd, P. (2006) 'Cohort Profile: 1970 British Birth Cohort (BCS70)', *International Journal of Epidemiology*, 35(4): 836–43.

Elliot, J. and Vaitilingham, R. (eds.) (2008) *Now We are 50: Key Findings from the National Child Development Study*. The Centre for Longitudinal Studies, University of London.

Farrington, D. (1991) 'Antisocial personality from childhood to adulthood', *The Psychologist*, 4(9): 389–4.

Farrington, D. (1999) *Cambridge Study in Delinquent Development [Great Britain], 1961–1981*. Ann Arbor, Michigan: Inter-University Consortium for Political and Social Research.

Farrington, D. (1995) 'The development of offending and antisocial behavior from childhood: Key findings from the Cambridge Study in delinquent development', *Journal of Child Psychology and Psychiatry*, 36(6): 929–64.

Farrington, D., Coid, J., Harnett, L., Jolliffe, D., Soteriou, N., Turner, R. and West, D. (2006) *Criminal Careers up to Age 50 and Life Success up to Age 48: New Findings from the Cambridge Study in Delinquent Development*. London: Home Office Research, Development and Statistics Directorate.

Fein, E., Maluccio, A. and Kluger, M. (1990) *No More Partings: An Examination of Long-Term Foster Family Care*. Washington, DC: Child Welfare League of America.

Fergusson, D. and Horwood L. (2000a) 'Cannabis use and dependence in a New Zealand birth cohort', *New Zealand Medical Journal*, 113(1109): 156–58.

Fergusson, D. and Horwood L. (2000b) 'Does cannabis use encourage other forms of illicit drug use?', *Addiction*, 95(4): 505–20.

Fergusson, D. and Horwood, L. (2003) 'Cannabis dependence and psychotic symptoms in young people', *Psychological Medicine*, 33(1): 15–21.

Fergusson, D., Horwood, L., Shannon, F. and Lawton, J. (1989) 'The Christchurch Child Development Study: A review of epidemiological findings', *Paediatric and Perinatal Epidemiology*, 3(3): 278–301.

Fergusson, D., Horwood, L. and Woodward L. (2001) 'Unemployment and psychosocial adjustment in young adults: Causation or selection?', *Social Science and Medicine*, 53(3): 305–20.

Fergusson, D. and Lynskey, M. (1995a) 'Childhood circumstances, adolescent adjustment and suicide attempts in a New Zealand birth cohort', *Journal of the American Academy of Child and Adolescent Psychiatry*, 34(5): 612–22.

Fergusson, D. and Lynskey, M. (1995b) 'Suicide attempts and suicidal ideation in a birth cohort of 16 year old New Zealanders', *Journal of the American Academy of Child and Adolescent Psychiatry*, 34(10): 1308–17.

Fernandez, E. (2006) 'Growing up in care: Resilience and care outcomes', in R. Flynn, P. Dudding and J. Barber (eds.), *Promoting Resilience in Child Welfare*. Ottawa: University of Ottawa Press, pp. 131–56.

Fernandez, E. (2007) 'How children experience fostering outcomes: Participatory research with children', *Child and Family Social Work*, 12(4): 349–59.

Fernandez, E. (2008) 'Psychosocial wellbeing of children in care: A longitudinal study of outcomes', *Child Indicators Research*, 1(3): 303–20.

Field, M. and Berman, R. (2004) *The Ethical Conduct of Clinical Research Involving Children: Executive Summary*. National Academy of Sciences, Committee on Clinical Research Involving Children. Washington, DC: National Academies Press.

Fisher, C. (1994) 'Reporting and referring research participants: Ethical issues for investigators studying children and youth', *Ethics and Behavior*, 4(2): 87–95.

Forget-Dubois, N., Lemelin, J., Boivin, M., Dionne, G., Seguin, J., Vitaro, F. and Tremblay, R. (2007) 'Predicting early school achievement with the EDI: A longitudinal population-based study', *Early Education and Development*, 18(3): 405–26.

Fox, A. and Berrick, J. (2007) 'A response to No One Ever Asked Us: A review of children's experiences in out of home care', *Child and Adolescent Social Work*, 24(1): 23–51.

Garbarino, J. and Stott, F. (1992) *What Children Can Tell Us*. San Francisco, CA: Jossey-Bass.

Gilbertson, R. and Barber, J. (2002) 'Obstacles to involving children and young people in foster care research', *Child and Family Social Work*, 7(4): 253–58.

Gilligan, R. (2002) 'The importance of listening to children in foster care', in G. Kelly and R. Gilligan (eds.), *Issues in Foster Care: Policy, Practice and Research*. London: Jessica Kinsley Publishers, pp. 40–58.

Goodenough, T., Williamson, E., Kent, J. and Ashcroft, R. (2003) 'What did you think about that? Researching children's perceptions of participation in a longitudinal genetic epidemiological study', *Children and Society*, 17(2): 113–25.

Green, P., Hoogstra, L., Ingels, S., Greene, H. and Marnell, P. (1997) *Formulating a Design for the ECLS: A Review of Longitudinal Studies* Working Paper No. 97-24. Washington, DC: U.S. Department of Education, Office of Educational Research and Improvement.

Guterman, N. (2004) 'Advancing prevention research on child abuse, youth violence and domestic violence: Emerging strategies and issues', *Journal of Interpersonal Violence*, 19(3): 299–321.

Harpham, T., Huttly, S., Wilson, I. and de Wet, T. (2003) 'Linking public issues with private troubles: Panel studies in developing countries', *Journal of International Development*, 15(3): 353–63.

Helgesson, G. (2005) 'Children, longitudinal studies and informed consent', *Medicine, Health Care and Philosophy*, 8(3): 307–13.

Heptinstall, E. (2000) 'Gaining access to looked after children for research purposes: Lessons learned', *British Journal of Social Work*, 30(6): 867–72.

Hestbæk, A. (2006) *National Longitudinal Study of Children: A Danish Representative, Longitudinal Study on Children from the 1995 Cohort*. Copenhagen, Denmark: SFI

Hill, M. (1997) 'Participatory research with children', *Child and Family Social Work*, 2(3): 171–83.

Hill, M. and Aldgate, J. (1996) *Child Welfare Services. Developments in Law, Policy, Practice and Research*. London: Jessica Kingsley Publishers.

Hodgen, E. (2007a) *Competent Learners at 16: Competency Levels and Development over Time – Technical Report*. Wellington, New Zealand: Ministry of Education.

Hodgen, E. (2007b) *Early Childhood Education and Young Adult Competencies at Age 16: Technical Report 2 from the Age-16 Phase of the Longitudinal Competent Children, Competent Learners Study*. Wellington, New Zealand: Ministry of Education.

Holmbeck, G., Bruno, E. and Jandasek, B. (2006) 'Longitudinal research in pediatric psychology: An introduction to the special issue', *Journal of Pediatric Psychology*, 31(10): 995–1001.

Honig, A., Lally, J. and Mathieson, D. (1982) 'Personal and social adjustment of school children after five years in the family development research program', *Child Care Quarterly*, 11(2): 136–46.

Horwood, L.J. and Fergusson, D.M. (1999) 'A longitudinal study of maternal labor force participation and child academic achievement', *Journal of Child Psychology and Psychiatry*, 40(7): 1013–24.

Hunter, W. and Knight, E. (1998) *Research Briefs: Volume 1*. Chapel Hill, NC: Consortium for Longitudinal Studies in Child Abuse and Neglect.

Ireland, L. and Holloway, I. (1996) 'Qualitative health research with children', *Children and Society*, 10(2): 155–64.

Jetté, M. (2002) *Survey Description and Methodology – Part I – Statistical Methodology – Longitudinal Aspects of the First Three Rounds 1998 to 2000. Québec Longitudinal Study of Child Development (QLSCD 1998-2002) – From Birth to 29 Months*. Québec: Institut de la statistique du Québec.

Kagitcibasi, C., Sunar, S. and Bekman S. (2001) 'Long-term effects of early intervention: Turkish low-income mothers and children', *Journal of Applied Developmental Psychology*, 22(4): 333–61.

Kantojarvi, L., Joukamaa, M., Miettunen, J., Läksy, K., Herva, A., Karvonen, J., Taanila, A. and Veijola, J. (2008) 'Childhood family structure and personality disorders in adulthood', *European Psychiatry*, 23(3): 205–11.

Kolvin, I., Miller, F., Fleeting, M. and Kolvin, P. (1988) 'Social and parenting factors affecting criminal-offence rates. Findings from the Newcastle Thousand Family Study (1947–1980)', *British Journal of Psychiatry*, 152(1): 80–90.

Kellaghan, T. and Greaney, B. (1993) 'The educational development of students following participation in a pre-school programme in a disadvantaged area in Ireland', Studies and evaluation papers 12. The Hague, Netherlands: Van Leer Foundation.

Kelley, B.T., Huizinga, D., Thornberry, T.P. and Loeber, R. (1997) *Epidemiology of Serious Violence*. Washington, DC: US Department of Justice, Office of Justice Programs, Office of Juvenile Justice and Delinquency Prevention.

Kelley, B.T., Loeber, R., Keenan, K. and DeLamatre, M. (1997) *Developmental Pathways in Boys'*

Disruptive and Delinquent Behavior. Washington, DC: US Department of Justice, Office of Justice Programs, Office of Juvenile Justice and Delinquency Prevention.

Kelley, B.T., Thornberry, T.P. and Smith, C.A. (1997) *In the Wake of Childhood Maltreatment*. Washington, DC: US.Department of Justice, Office of Justice Programs, Office of Juvenile Justice and Delinquency Prevention.

Kukla, L., Hrubá, D., Tyrlík, M. and Matějová, H. (2008a) 'Conduct disorders in seven-year-old children – Results of ELSPAC Study – 1. Co-morbidity', *Journal of Czech Physicians*, 147(5): 269–77.

Kukla, L., Hrubá, D., Tyrlík, M. and Matějová, H. (2008b) 'Conduct disorders in seven-year-old children – Results of ELSPAC Study – 2. Risk Factors', *Journal of Czech Physicians*, 147(6): 311–18.

Lally, J., Mangione, P. and Honig, A. (1988) 'The Syracuse University Family Development Research Program: Long-Range Impact on an Early Intervention with Low-Income Children and Their Families', in D. Powell and I. Sigel (eds.), *Parent Education as Early Childhood Intervention: Emerging Direction in Theory, Research, and Practice. Annual Advances in Applied Developmental Psychology, Volume 3*. Norwood, NJ: Ablex Publishing Corporation, pp. 79–104.

Landhuis, C.E., Poulton, R., Welch, D. and Hancox, R.J. (2007) 'Does childhood television viewing lead to attention problems in adolescence? Results from a prospective longitudinal study', *Pediatrics*, 120(3): 532–7.

Loeber, R. and Farrington, D.P. (1994) 'Problems and solutions in longitudinal and experimental treatment studies of child psychopathology and delinquency', *Journal of Consulting and Clinical Psychology*, 62(5): 887–900.

Mackerras, D., Reid, A., Sayers, S., Singh, G., Bucens, I. and Flynn, K. (2003) 'Growth and morbidity in children in the Aboriginal Birth Cohort Study: The urban–remote differential', *Medical Journal of Australia*, 178(2): 56–60.

Macklin, R. (1992) 'Autonomy, beneficence, and child development: An ethical analysis', in B. Stanley and. Sieber (eds.), *Social Research on Children and Adolescents: Ethical Issues*. London, UK: Sage, pp. 34–46.

Mahon, A., Glendinning, C., Clarke, K. and Craig, G. (1996) 'Researching children: Methods and ethics', *Children and Society*, 10(2): 145–54.

Mariner, C., Romano, Λ. and Bridges, L. (1999) *A Birth Cohort Study: Conceptual and Design Considerations and Rationale*. Working Paper No. 1999-01. Washington, DC: US Department of Education, National Center for Education Statistics.

Menard, S. (2002) *Longitudinal Research*. Thousand Oaks, CA: Sage Publications.

Miller, S. (2000) 'Researching children: Issues arising from a phenomenological study with children who have diabetes mellitus', *Journal of Advanced Nursing*, 31(5): 1228–34.

Mishna, F., Antle, B. and Regehr, C. (2004) 'Tapping the perspectives of children: Emerging ethical issues in qualitative research', *Qualitative Social Work*, 3(4): 449–68.

Molnar, B., Miller, M., Azrael, D. and Buka, S. (2004) 'Neighborhood predictors of concealed firearm carrying among children and adolescents: Results from the project on human development in Chicago neighborhoods', *Archives of Pediatrics and Adolescent Medicine*, 158(7): 657–64.

Nicholson, J. and Rempel, L. (2004) 'Australian and New Zealand birth cohort studies: Breadth, quality and contributions', *Journal of Paediatrics and Child Health*, 40(3): 87–95.

Norris, S., Roeser, R., Richter, L., Lewin, N., Ginsburg, C., Fleetwood, S., Taole, E. And van der Wolf, K. (2008) 'South African-ness among adolescents: The emergence of a collective identity within the Birth to Twenty Cohort Study', *The Journal of Early Adolescence*, 28(1): 51–69.

Oakley, A. (1994) 'Women and children first and last: parallels and differences between children's and women's studies', in B. Mayall (ed.), *Children's Childhoods: Observed and Experienced*. London: The Falmer Press, pp. 13–32.

Obeidallah, D., Brennan, R. Brooks-Gunn, J. and Earls, F. (2004) 'Links between pubertal timing and neighborhood contexts: Implications for girls' violent behavior', *Journal of the American Academy of Child and Adolescent Psychiatry*, 43(12): 1460–8.

Odgers, C., Caspi, A., Broadbent, J., Dickson, N., Hancox, R., Harrington, H., Poulton, R., Sears, M., Thomson, W. and Moffitt, T. (2007) 'Prediction of differential adult health burden by conduct problem subtypes in males', *Archives of General Psychiatry*, 64(4): 476–84.

Office of Juvenile Justice and Delinquency Prevention. (1998) 'Gang membership, delinquent peers and delinquent behavior', *Juvenile Justice Bulletin*. National Criminal Justice number NCJ 171119.

Plante, N., Courtemanche, R. and Desgroseilliers, L. (2002) *Survey Description and Methodology – Part I – Logistics* and Longitudinal Data Collections. *Québec Longitudinal Study of Child Development (QLSCD 1998-2002) – From Birth to 29 Months.* Québec: Institut de la statistique du Québec

Power, C. and Elliot, J. (2006) 'Cohort profile: 1958 British birth cohort (National Child Development Study)', *International Journal of Epidemiology*, 35(1): 34–41.

Princiotta, D., Flanagan, K.D. and Hausken, E.G. (2006) *Fifth grade: Findings from the Fifth-Grade Follow-Up of the Early Childhood Longitudinal Study, Kindergarten Class of 1998–99.* Washington, DC: National Center for Education Statistics.

Reynolds, A. and Temple, J. (1998) 'Extended early childhood intervention and school achievement: Age thirteen findings from the Chicago Longitudinal Study', *Child Development*, 69(1): 231–46.

Reynolds, A., Temple, J., Robertson, D. and Mann, E. (2001) 'Long-term effects of an early childhood intervention on educational achievement and juvenile arrest A 15-year follow-up of low-income children in public schools', *Journal of the American Medical Association*, 285(18): 2339–46.

Reynolds, A., Temple, J., Ou, S., Robertson, D., Mersky, J., Topitzes, J. and Niles, M. (2007) 'Effects of a school-based, early childhood intervention on adult health and well-being: A 19-year follow-up of low-income families', *Archives of Pediatric and Adolescent Medicine*, 161(8): 730–9.

Richter, L., Norris, S. and de Wet, T. (2004) 'Transition from Birth to Ten to Birth to Twenty: the South African cohort reaches 13 years of age', *Paediatric Perinatal Epidemiology*, 18(4): 290–301.

Richter, L., Norris, S., Pettifor, J., Yach, D. and Cameron, N. (2007) 'Cohort Profile: Mandela's children: The 1990 Birth to Twenty study in South Africa', *International Journal of Epidemiology*, 36(3): 504–11.

Runyan, D., Curtis, P., Hunter, W., Black, M., Kotch, J., Bangdiwala, S., Dubowitz, H., English, D., Everson, M., Landsverk, J. (1998) 'Longscan: A consortium for longitudinal studies of maltreatment and the life course of children', *Aggression and Violent Behavior*, 3(3): 275–85.

Rutter, M. (1981) 'Epidemiological/longitudinal strategies and causal research in child psychiatry', *Journal of the American Academy of Child Psychiatry*, 20(3): 513–44.

Rutter, M. (1994) 'Beyond longitudinal data: Causes, consequences, changes, and continuity', *Journal of Consulting and Clinical Psychology*, 62(5): 928–40.

Sadowski, H., Ugarte, B., Kolvin, I., Kaplan, C. and Barnes, A. (1999) 'Early life family disadvantages

and major depression in adulthood', *British Journal of Psychiatry*, 174(2): 112–20.

Samms-Vaughan, M. (2001) Cognition, educational attainment and behaviour in a cohort of Jamaican children. Working Paper No 5. Planning Institute of Jamaica.

Samms-Vaughan, M., Jackson, M. and Ashley, D. (2005) 'Urban Jamaican children's exposure to community violence', *West Indian Medical Journal*, 54(1): 14–21.

Samms-Vaughan, M., McCaw-Binns, A. and Ashley, D. (2006) *The Jamaican Birth Cohort Studies*. Ko'hört: CLS Cohort Studies Newsletter. Centre of Longitudinal Studies, Institute of Education, University of London.

Sampson, R., Morenoff, J. and Raudenbush, S. (2005) 'Social anatomy of racial and ethnic disparities in violence', *American Journal of Public Health*, 95(2): 224–32.

Sauvola, A., Koskinen, O., Jokelainen, J., Hakko, H., Järvelin, M. and Räsänen, P. (2002) 'Family type and criminal behaviour of male offspring: the Northern Finland 1966 Birth Cohort Study', *International Journal of Social Psychiatry*, 48(2): 115–21.

Sayers, S., Mackerras, D., Singh, G., Bucens, I., Flynn, K. and Reid, A. (2003) 'An Australian Aboriginal birth cohort: a unique resource for a life course study of an indigenous population. A study protocol', *BMC International Health and Human Rights*, 3(1): 1.

Schweinhart, L. (2005) *The High/Scope Perry Preschool Study through Age 40: Summary, Conclusions, and Frequently Asked Questions*. Ypsilanti, MI: High/Scope Press.

Schweinhart, L., Montie, J., Xiang, Z., Barnett, W., Belfield, C. and Nores, M. (2005) *Lifetime effects: The High/Scope Perry Preschool Study through Age 40*. Ypsilanti, MI: High/Scope Press.

Schweinhart, L., Barnes, H. and Weikart, D. (1993) *Significant Benefits: The High/Scope Perry Preschool Study through Age 27*. Ypsilanti: High/Scope Press.

Shulruf, B., Morton, S., Goodyear-Smith, R., O'Loughlin, C. and Dixon, R. (2007) 'Designing multidisciplinary longitudinal studies of human development: Analyzing past research to inform methodology', *Evaluation and the Health Care Professions*, 30(3): 207–28.

Smart, D., Sanson, A., Toumbourou, J., Prior, M. and Oberklaid, F. (1999) *Longitudinal Pathways to Adolescent Anti-Social Behavior and Depression*. Paper presented at the Life History Research Society Conference, September, 1999.

Smart, D., Sanson, A., Toumbourou, J., Prior, M. and Oberklaid, F. (2000) *Connections Between Parenting*

Style and Adolescent Problem Behaviors. Paper presented at the International Society for the Study of Behavioral Development, July, 2000.

Soloff, C., Millward, C. and Sanson, A. (2003) *Growing Up in Australia – The Longitudinal Study of Australian Children. Proposed Study Design and Wave 1 Data Collection. Discussion Paper No. 2.* Melbourne: Australian Institute of Family Studies.

Sornsrivichai, V., Chongsuvivatwong, V., Mo-suwan, L. and Intusoma, U. (2008) 'Hospitalized infant morbidity in the prospective Cohort Study of Thai Children project', *Journal of the Medical Association of Thailand*, 91(6): 882–8.

Taplin, S. (2005) *Methodological Design Issues in Longitudinal Studies of Children and Young People in out of Home Care: Literature Review.* Ashfield, New South Wales: NSW Center for Parenting and Research.

Thomas, D., Frankenberg, E. and Smith, J. (2001) 'Lost but not forgotten: Attrition and follow-up in the Indonesia Family Life Survey', *Journal of Human Resources*, 36(3): 556–92.

Thomas, E. (2006) *Readiness to Learn at School Among Five-Year-Old Children in Canada.* Ottawa: Statistics Canada.

Thomas, N. and O'Kane, C. (1998) 'The ethics of participatory research with children', *Child and Society*, 12(5): 336–48.

Thornberry, T.P. and Burch, J. (1997) *Gang Members and Delinquent Behavior.* Washington, DC: US Department of Justice, Office of Justice Programs, Office of Juvenile Justice and Delinquency Prevention.

Triseliotis, J., Borland, M., Hill, M. and Lambert, L. (1995) *Teenagers and the Social Work Services.* London: The Stationery Office.

Tyler, K. A., Johnson, K. A., and Brownridge, D. A. (2008) 'A longitudinal study of the effects of child maltreatment on later outcomes among high-risk adolescents', *Journal of Youth and Adolescence*, 37(5): 506–21.

University of the Witwatersrand (2004) *How the New Generation of Teenagers View South Africa: Editorial Release.* Available at http://web.wits.ac.za/ Academic/Health/Research/BirthTo20/Research/ EditorialReleases/EditorialReleases2004.htm

Upadhyay, U., Hindin, M. and Gultiano, S. (2006) 'Before first sex: Gender differences in emotional relationships and physical behaviors among adolescents in the Philippines', *International Family Planning Perspectives*, 32(3): 110–9.

Victora, C. and Barros, F. (2006) 'Cohort profile: The 1982 Pelotas (Brazil) birth cohort study', *International Journal of Epidemiology*, 35(2): 237–42.

Victora, C., Hallal, P., Araújo, C., Menezes, A., Wells, J. and Barros, F. (2008) 'Cohort profile: The 1993 Pelotas (Brazil) birth cohort study', *International Journal of Epidemiology*, 37(4): 704–9.

Victora, C., Barros, F., Lima, R., Behague, D., Gonçalves, H., Horta, B., Gigante, D. and Vaughan, J. (2006) 'The Pelotas Birth Cohort Study, Rio Grande do Sul, Brazil, 1982–2001', *Cademos Saúde Pública, Rio de Janeiro*, 19(5): 1241–56.

Wadsworth, M., Kuh, D., Richards, M. and Hardy, R. (2006) 'Cohort profile: The 1946 National Birth Cohort (MRC National Survey of Health and Development)', *International Journal of Epidemiology*, 35(1): 49–54.

West, K., Hauser, R. and Scanlan, T. (1998) *Longitudinal Surveys of Children.* Committee on National Statistics, Board on Children, Youth, and Families, Commission on Behavioral and Social Sciences, National Research Council, Institute of Medicine. Washington, DC: National Academy Press.

Wierson, M. and Forehand, R. (1994) 'Introduction to special section: The role of longitudinal data with child psychopathology and treatment: Preliminary comments and issues', *Journal of Consulting and Clinical Psychology*, 62(5): 883–6.

Williams, B., Sanson, A., Toumbourou, J. and Smart, D. (2000) *Patterns and Predictors of Teenagers' Use of Licit and Illicit Substances in the Australian Temperament Project Cohort.* Report commissioned by the Ross Trust. Melbourne: Australian Temperament Project.

Wilson, L. and Conroy, J. (1999) 'Satisfaction of children in out-of-home care', *Child Welfare*, 78(1): 53–69.

Wison, I., Huttly, S. and Fenn, B. (2006) 'A case study of sample design for longitudinal research: Young Lives', *International Journal of Social Research Methodology*, 9(5): 351–65.

Zollinger, G. (2002) 'Longitudinal studies and life-course research: Innovations, investigators, and policy ideas', in E. Phelps, F. Furstenberg and A. Colby (eds.), *Looking at Lives: American Longitudinal Studies of the Twentieth Century.* New York: Russell Sage, pp. 15–36.

Zwiers, M. and Morrissette, P. (1999) *Effective Interviewing of Children: A Comprehensive Guide for Counselors and Human Service Workers.* New York: Taylor & Francis.

23

Use of Administrative Data in Childhood Research

Robert Goerge and Bong Joo Lee

Over the past two decades, there has been a steady increase in the use of administrative data to construct child indicators, to evaluate child and family services and education, and to generally study child well-being and the family and community conditions in which children live. Although the status of the use of administrative data varies from country to country and often within countries, access to this data source by researchers has generally improved, although there are still many bureaucratic, legal, and technical obstacles. These data are typically available in many domains of child well-being, including education, human services, health, juvenile justice, anti-poverty programs, nutrition, and child maltreatment.[1]

Full coverage of all of the issues of the use of administrative data in child research is much more than a single chapter can address. It would be similar to full coverage of survey research with one chapter. There are nuances under every topic that could be addressed in more detail. Simply the number of domains that might affect child well-being is a report in and of itself (see Coulton, 2008). This chapter is intended as an introduction to the topic.

Although it may be an overgeneralization, administrative data are generally more broadly utilized by non-governmental researchers in the United States than in other countries. In part, this has to do with the proliferation of electronic information systems at all levels of government, and particularly at the state level. Although there are exceptions, relatively few national administrative data on child well-being are available in the United States. Researchers must go to state government agencies to access data. Having to go to multiple agencies is often a major deterrent to using administrative data. This is somewhat less the case in Scandinavian countries where more national data are available.

The fact that a national administrative data system exists does not make getting access to the government's administrative data any less challenging. Some European counties, primarily those in Scandinavia, are famous for having excellent administrative data, in part because of the social programs that these countries provide to all citizens (such as national health care). Some Asian countries including South Korea also have administrative data at the national level covering all citizens through programs such as resident registration system and national health insurance system. However, one often has to be 'inside' government or have a special relationship or arrangement with government research divisions in order to obtain access in those cases. Nevertheless, this has been done by more and more researchers. An excellent example is Björklund et al. (2007), who have analyzed the effect of marriage on children using administrative data in Sweden. The researchers used data on youth's grade point average at age 16 as their dependent variable in a number of tests of whether married or cohabiting parents have higher achieving children. They found no difference.

Perhaps the most developed area of the use of administrative data for research is in the area of child indicators. An indicator provides evidence that a certain condition exists or certain results have or have not been achieved (Brizius and Campbell, 1991). Moore and Brown (2006: 91) suggest that 'indicators of child well-being represent an important and complementary strategy for monitoring the success of a society'. Because administrative data provide timely coverage of an entire population, with attention to local indicators, those researchers who are interested in affecting child well-being through policy gravitate towards this source of data.

ADMINISTRATIVE DATA – DEFINING IT, AND ISSUES AROUND USING IT

Administrative data are data regularly and consistently collected in support of an organization's function(s) and stored within an organization's information system (Goerge, 1997). Administrative databases are created primarily to monitor utilization, to determine the consumption of resources, and to ascertain the capacity to supply services. Administrative data are not collected primarily for research purposes, but can become a source for research and statistical compendia. Administrative data are culled from systems that have two basic functions. A particular system may stress one of these functions over the other. The first function is for compliance, accountability, or reimbursement from an external or oversight agency (usually a federal one). The second is internal tracking of individuals or the services that they receive for the purpose of benefit provision, financial functions, decision support, and other activities of the organization. The tracking function is what we think about when we refer to management information systems (MIS) or case management systems. Typically, the tracking system provides richer data, because external reporting in the human services is typically limited to eligibility and benefit receipt.

The characteristics of administrative data point to both the strengths and weakness of it. These characteristics are often contrasted with those of survey data collected through questionnaires where the researcher has control over the items and how the data are going to be collected.

Population coverage

Although it is still the case that management information systems are not universal for child- or family-related programs of interest, they are very common across the domains of interest in developed countries. A particular administrative database typically covers the population receiving a particular service or resource, or those having a particular status. In many cases, data on all individuals who have ever been in the database is kept in the database or archived so that longitudinal information is available. Although data may be purged from the real-time, online systems, historical data are often available in archival formats. The sheer magnitude of the data set typically contrasts with survey research, where small samples are often selected for primary data collection. When it is necessary to represent many geographic areas in a study, primary data collection can be quite costly.

Geographic data

Given the fact that administrative data cover the population of individuals or families with a particular status or receiving a particular service and that their addresses are often available, application of indicators at the state, regional, or local level is quite possible (Banister, 1994; Coulton, 2008). Unlike national social surveys, the population coverage in administrative data allows for state and local indicators to be produced.

Collection of data

Unlike social surveys or census data collection, administrative data collection is done by a professional whose primary responsibility is not data collection. There are both positive and negative aspects of a professional collecting data. These workers are often affected by the data that they enter into the system because of accountability mechanisms or quality assurance, not to mention the results of an analysis of the administrative data, depending on how many operational or policy decisions are based on information from the MIS (Leginski et al., 1989). Also, there are other issues (for example, workers' use of time or confidentiality) that affect the quality of the data entry. Data collection can vary over time because of change in policy, operations, or agency mandates. Finally, workers may take shortcuts or not provide certain data when they understand which data are more or less important in the operation of the agency.

On the positive side, these workers may have an interest in the quality of the data they collect if they actually use the data for their own decision making (Banister, 1992; Hotz et al., 1998; Mugford et al., 1991). For data items that are necessary or mandatory for the successful completion of administration functions, the amount of missing data can be minimal. There may also be considerable access to the subjects or paper records so that incorrect data are more likely to be corrected

than in social surveys or census data. Also, because the data are collected within the normal conduct of business, no interviewer is inserted into the process who may disrupt the lives of those being studied or who may bias responses. This avoidance of interviewer effects may be particularly important around indicators of child maltreatment or mental health problems, when it is difficult for an interviewer to be present during critical events. Finally, administrative data systems often have service payments as a primary purpose. Because those paying and those that are being paid have an interest in being paid the correct amount, there is a built-in system of checks and balances.

Administrative data is also collected very close to the time when the event – birth; service receipt; a change in status – occurs. Also, the date of that event is usually recorded exactly, so that the form of the data is complete in that it contains both the sequence of events and the time at which the event occurred (Coleman, 1981; Tuma and Hannan, 1984). This type of data allows for a full range of cross-sectional, panel, and continuous-time analyses.

Because individual records must be accessed in administrative databases and individuals must usually be contacted in the normal course of providing service or aid, identifying information, such as names, addresses, and Social Security numbers, are usually accurate and maintained over the period in which the individual is in contact with the organization. This information allows for updating of service records, tracking individuals and families over time, and linkage of records to other databases.

Data quality

Before administrative data can be used for research purposes, it is necessary for the researcher to extensively review all data collection procedures and data definitions for all data that will be used for research purposes. This is not a research activity that has a clear step-by-step protocol. Each administrative dataset is documented to a varying extent. Information about quality of the data is often not documented and is only available through interviewing those who maintain the database, use the data, or train those that will collect the data. There are usually multiple interviews and the knowledge about the dataset is often developed in an iterative and interactive manner. A major challenge is finding the individuals in a government agency who actually know about all the fields in a database is also an iterative process. Learning about the reliability, validity, and accuracy of data may only be possible after the data have been analyzed. For example, there may be dramatic variation among counties in a state, which may not be understood until the data are actually analyzed and experts can respond to the results.

Data quality must be assessed on a dataset-by-dataset basis and often on a variable-by-variable basis. Knowing what procedures are undertaken to collect or verify a particular variable is important to know before using the data. Even assumptions about straightforward identifying data must be questioned. Are state or identification numbers verified? How is race or ethnicity determined – by asking the service recipient or by a government official's assessment? Are birth dates verified through actual documents? Are identifiers such as national identification numbers (such as Social Security numbers) verified?

If workers receive sufficient training on the collection of data, we expect the data to be more reliable and valid (Iezzonie, 1992). If clear and complete documentation is available, workers are more likely to provide reliable information. The less training that is available on the more complex data fields, the less these fields should be used, and the more other sources of data should be used for that topic. For example, we have learned that the disability field on foster children's records is extremely poor because workers are given no training on identification and verification of disabilities. Thus, these data

have little reliability. Datasets which have more reliable disability data (educational records, for example) can be used to improve the data on the disabilities of foster children (Goerge et al., 1992). In such instances, links to datasets that are more authoritative on particular variables may be important.

Units of analysis

Administrative data of the kind discussed in this chapter are typically collected at the individual or case level. Very often individuals within a particular case are linked within a database, although much of the activity will be assigned to the grantee or head of household. For example, members of a family will share parts of their same agency identification number and the relationships between members will be tracked. However, the ability to group individuals depends very much on the purpose of the dataset. For example, a birth certificate database should accurately identify the relationship between a child and the child's parents. However, the accuracy of family information may be questionable in school records. From the school's perspective, the important person for a child is the legal guardian, who may be a parent, a relative, or a foster parent.

Cost

The cost of collecting administrative data is often hidden in the operational budgets of organizations (Iezzonie, 1992), while the high costs of collecting national data through surveys are easily determined. The costs of using administrative data for the development of indicators is not much less than that of using survey data after it have been collected. However, the organizations that collect survey data, including the Census, include the cleaning of the data and the formatting of data in the costs of collection. The cleaning and formatting of administrative data is often left up to the analysts that acquire and use the data. In the experience of the authors, the cost of cleaning and formatting is often half to three-quarters of the cost of a particular research project using administrative data. However, the ongoing cost of using these data in subsequent projects may be reduced because of cleaning and formatting done in previous projects.

Access to administrative data

Access to data varies from nation to nation and often with counties and states. In part, this variation depends on privacy and confidentiality statutes regulating particular domains of children's services. However, these statutes are often used by government officials to dissuade potential users of administrative data from pursuing access (Brady et al. 2002). In most cases, research using these data is allowed, especially when the proposed research has potential for improving the program and when data security can be assured. For example, the US Health Insurance Portability and Accountability Act (HIPAA) is quite strong in the protection of identifiable health information. However, with an Institutional Review Board decision and a clear description of how the research will benefit the Medicaid program (the primary public health insurance of low-income children in the USA), it is possible for a researcher to receive these data. There are similar procedures for other programmatic data in the United States. Researchers must be aware of the rules and procedures that govern access if they are to benefit from having administrative data. Many government agencies are appropriately concerned about researchers' protection of the identifying information contained in the administrative data. Security breaches, where identifying information has been divulged, have occurred. Researchers must show that they are able to keep data secure and must be prepared to have their policies and practices audited by the organizations that provide them the data.

Types of research utilizing administrative data

The highest utility of administrative data comes in the potential to link administrative datasets to each other or to survey data (Goerge and Lee, 2002). Although such linkages require access to identifying information of the individuals in the administrative data and survey data, it provides the opportunity to extend individual datasets and combine data from multiple sources. Given that any one administrative dataset is less rich relative to the set of available variables from a researcher's viewpoint, links among individual records across datasets may lead to large numbers of variables that can cover a broad array of topics.

There are three broad categories of linkages using administrative data in studying children, their families, and their contexts: (a) construction of longitudinal data linking individuals' records within a service system over time, (b) composition of variables in interest by linking different information system datasets across service areas, and (c) collection of richer information by linking survey data to administrative data (Goerge and Lee, 2002). The first type of linkage is necessary when 'event' records over time need to be linked to the same individual for a longitudinal study of childhood. For example, a child might receive various health services including newborn screening, immunizations, and other care during his/her childhood. In order to study longitudinal pathways of health status of children, one will need to link those various service records over time for each child in the system. Often a child's official case identification number may change, and the records across cases must be brought together. The second type of linkage is needed to study the relationship among multiple domains of childhood because any single information system does not contain all of the domains of childhood research. The task of linking the data across different systems might be especially challenging when the systems do not share a common ID. Researchers have developed a set of methods know as probabilistic record linkage in order to link records from different sources when there is no common ID (see Jaro, 1985, 1989). In instances, where there is a common identification number, deterministic methods can be used. The third type of linking application is to add data that are not available in one or the other quantitative data source. Typically, researchers use survey data in order to obtain information about 'subjective' well-being that is not available in the administrative data. By the same token, researchers also use administrative data to add 'objective' service event history that can be difficult to obtain through survey method to the survey data. Although survey data are typically richer because they include self-reported data on a range of issues under the control of the researcher for which there might not be administrative data, administrative data are more accurate on issues for which a respondent's memory is otherwise required, such as the program names, the nature and timing of services and education, and income.

Child indicator reports

Ben-Arieh and Goerge (2001) describe the worldwide production of 'State of the Child' reports. In many cases, these child indicators reports rely on administrative data because they can be produced yearly, often at a local level. Surveys other than census data are rarely used to analyze the state of the child at a sub-national level because of their cost. Statistical or service providing agencies can provide data on the population of children and their families because of the ongoing collection of such data. As administrative data become more available, the activity of monitoring child well-being has become more prevalent, as with the Annie E. Casey Foundation's Kids Count initiative.

Evaluations

By definition, administrative data track service receipt status. Thus, administrative data are an excellent resource in evaluation research in human services. Especially when the service is a full-coverage program where experimental evaluation design is not feasible, administrative data provide an opportunity to compare service recipients and service non-recipients by use of quasi-experimental designs. In order to perform these types of research, researchers need an administrative data system that holds both the target program receipt status and the outcome information. The two data elements can come from a single administrative data system or multiple data systems. When data from the multiple systems are needed, the data should be linked across the systems to be used in a program of evaluation research. For example, Lee and Mackey-Bilaver (2007) examined the relationship between the United States Department of Agriculture's Woman, Infant, and Child Supplemental Nutritional Program (WIC) and Food Stamp program participation in the US and young children's health and maltreatment outcomes. (The WIC program is a nutritional program for medically at-risk children under the age of 5, and the Food Stamp program is the primary food support program in the United States for low-income households.) They relied on an individual-level longitudinal database linking administrative datasets on WIC and Food Stamp program participation, Medicaid enrolment and claims, and child abuse and neglect reports in a state in the United States. The study showed that receipt of WIC and/or Food Stamps is associated with a lower risk of abuse and neglect reports, and of diagnosis of several nutrition-related health problems such as anaemia, failure to thrive, and nutritional deficiency. Linking administrative data to survey sample data also provides a unique opportunity to implement advanced evaluation research. Shook-Slack, Lee, and Berger (2007) used linked survey and administrative data to assess relationships between welfare sanction programs and child protective services involvement within a sample of welfare recipients.

An example of a more standard and comprehensive program evaluation using administrative data is the national evaluation of family preservation and reunification programs in the United States. Administrative data provided information on children's placements, re-entries, and subsequent abuse and neglect allegations up to 18 months after entry into the experiment to determine the differences between the experimental and control groups in multiple sites.

Household surveys

Household surveys can be affected by administrative data in two ways. First, as we have noted, administrative data can be linked to survey data in order to extend the type of data, but also in some cases, the longitudinal nature of the data. For example, employment data can be added years after a survey to understand the jobs that individuals have held.

A second use is to provide the sampling frame for a study. Whether the focus is families or providers of services, administrative data provide the list from which a sample can be drawn. This type of data can often be richer than simple directory information so that stratification can be more precise and that survey costs are reduced.

An excellent example of both of these ways of using administrative data is the studies that were aimed at understanding child well-being after welfare reform in the United States (Hotz and Adams, 2001). Many of these studies used administrative data such as child support, wage and earnings, Food Stamps, Medicaid, child abuse and neglect, and child care, in combination with survey data to understand the outcomes of families after welfare reform. In addition, survey researchers relied on lists of current and former welfare program recipients to identify participants for data collection.

Provider studies

While they are growing up, children may interact with many service providers. Just to name a few, they include day care centres, health clinics, hospitals, schools, libraries, museums, and human service agencies. Along with the family, these institutions play a big role in shaping children's daily lives. Administrative data are useful in understanding behaviour of the service providers. Because a typical information management system tracks the operation of an agency by way of storing detailed information on services provided, administrative data can be used to examine the patterns of service provider's behaviour. Lee, Mackey-Bilaver, and Goerge (2003) examined the patterns of program participation in the Food Stamp program and WIC program during the time of welfare reform in an American state using linked administrative data on both programs. The analysis showed that the WIC program was compensated for the falling Food Stamp program participation during welfare reform in the United States.

Administrative data can also be used to describe the supply and demand for services. Such studies combine population data and information about the service capacity of providers. Such work can illuminate how the market for services operates (Goerge et al., 2007).

Geographic analyses

Administrative data are collected on the entire population of individuals and families participating in a given program. Administrative data typically contain extensive geographical identifiers such as full street addresses for the program participants, the location of services provided, and the service providers. These two characteristics of administrative data make it an excellent source for the study of the spread of events of interest over a geographical area (Goerge and Lee, 2002). Coulton's recent report (2008) describes the vast potential of administrative data to produce small geographic area statistics.

ADMINISTRATIVE DATA ACROSS DOMAINS OF CHILD WELL-BEING

The listed domains are intended to be those that are the most primary to child research.

There are many other domains that could be discussed that are critical for families and the care of their children. Adult incarceration, housing, employment, and employment training are among the domains that are critical that we will not address in this chapter.

Vital statistics

Perhaps the best example of the use of administrative data for child indicators is vital statistics – primarily data on births and deaths. While some may claim that these are collected primarily for statistical purposes, each has a clear set of administrative purposes. Many events are triggered or made possible by the fact that a birth or death certificate is issued – essentially anything that requires proof of birth or death. These two sets of data form a cornerstone of the state and federal health statistics. From these two databases, the number of births, teenage births, births to unmarried mothers, and causes of adolescent death, to name just a few, are produced.

These data have been used less for other types of research (Barthet al., 2002) that requires identifiers for linking to other datasets. Simply, the importance of knowing whether or not a child's mother was an adolescent parent makes the birth certificate records an important piece of data for much child research. The use of grouped data may also allow for analyses that may not be possible because of confidentiality. Goerge, Harden, and Lee (2008) conducted an analysis of the effect of adolescent parenthood on the reporting of child maltreatment and entry into foster care using grouped data. Data were grouped by geographic region, race/ethnicity, age of mother, gender of the child, and birth order.

Education

Educational success is a key indicator of a child's well-being and well-becoming.

The child's school achievement and their receipt of school-related services are the indicators of educational success that can be obtained by student information systems (Barth et al., 2002). Student information systems in the United States have become more common over the past decade. Those systems contain information on enrolment, standardized test scores, attendance, grade retention histories, disciplinary actions, and school services. As the nations place a greater emphasis on the accountability of educational systems on children's educational outcomes, we can expect the use of information management systems will be likely to increase in the future. For example, the No Child Left Behind policy in the United States promotes the use of standardized performance measures of the students and schools. This in turn requires the schools collect and store information on key performance measures. Administrative data systems are excellent sources for studying educational domain of childhood and is being increasingly utilized (Data Quality Campaign).

Health

Health is one of the basic developmental domains of the child. There are two kinds of information pertaining to health of children in administrative data. One is the actual health status of children. Birth registration data usually include information on the degree of prenatal care the mother received, birth weight, and APGAR (Appearance Pulse Grimace Activity Respiration) score – a summary measure of the health of a newborn child – which all indicate the health status of a child. The other is the actual health services children received. To name a few, they include data on immunizations, dental care, regular hospital visits, and emergency visits. The medical insurance information management system is usually the good source for service data. For example, Medicaid reimbursement data in the USA contain information on diagnosis provided and medical treatment given for children. South Korea's national health insurance payment data also contain similar information. Researchers have used these kinds of data to construct health status indicators of children (for example, see Lee and Mackey-Bilaver, 2007).

Juvenile justice

Involvement with the juvenile authorities is an indicator of both an adolescent's behaviour and the response of the community to that behaviour. The primary events of interest in juvenile justice domain are arrests, court petition and hearing activity, convictions, and sentence data. Many juvenile courts in the United States do not computerize their records and when they do, they typically only describe court events and very little about the characteristics of the youth and his or her family. As these courts become more focused on youth development, as opposed to punishment, additional data may be required, such as the assets that are available to these youth as they address their juvenile justice system involvement.

Anti-poverty programs

Participation in anti-poverty programs is a powerful indicator of children's economic well-being. In the United States, participation in Temporary Assistance to Needy Families is a major source of information on children who live in below poverty line. Other datasets, such as Medicaid data, Food Stamp program data, and WIC data also provide information on children living in poverty and near-poverty situations. In South Korea, the National Minimum Livelihood Program offer similar information. The anti-poverty program data provide information on three dimensions of poverty that are known to affect children's development. They are timing, duration, and degree of poverty.

The data on service onset date can be used to calculate the timing of poverty in relation to a child's age. It is known that poverty experienced in early ages has a more detrimental effect on a child's development. The data on service duration offer information on poverty duration. The longer the poverty duration, the more negative are their effects on a child's development. The data on income give information on how extreme the child's economic distress is while receiving public assistance. It is known that extreme poverty has a more negative effect on a child's development.

Child maltreatment

Child maltreatment is a basic safety domain of child well-being. Data on child abuse and neglect reports and services provided to children and families are an important source of information to gauge the safety of children in a society. Administrative data typically provide information on reports made to the child protection authorities and the authorities' service responses to the reports. The potential drawback of administrative data on child maltreatment records is that they reflect the combined events of the abuse and/or neglect that actually happened and the reporting behaviours. Depending on the reporting practice of a society, the child maltreatment 'rates' calculated by reports information from child protective agencies would vary.

CONCLUSION

Administrative data can provide a broad array of information on children, their families, and the services and programs in which they participate. Although these data are not as rich as survey data might be, it typically includes data on the population, not a sample, of individuals or families in a program. Across the world, including the USA, coverage of programs by computerized administrative data is incomplete. However, as information systems seemingly become omnipresent and as more accountability is required by governments and other funders, more administrative data will be available. The major question is access, and, at this point in time, there is no analogy to the public-use datasets that are produced for survey data. Researchers must negotiate access on a dataset-by-dataset basis in most situations.

NOTE

1 In this chapter, we refer to this entire range of domains as *children's services*.

REFERENCES

Banister, J. (1994) *FDCH Testimony*. US Congress, August 2.

Barth, R., Locklin-Brown, E., Curraro-Alamin, S. and Needle, B. (2002) 'Administrative data on the well-being of children on and off welfare', in M. Ver Ploeg, A. Moffit, and C. Citro (eds.), *Studies of Welfare Populations: Data Collection and Research Issues*. Washington, DC: National Academy Press, pp. 316–54.

Ben-Arieh, A. and Goerge, R. (2001) 'Beyond the numbers: How do we monitor the state of our children?', *Children and Youth Service Review*, 23(8): 603–31.

Björklund, A., Ginther, D.K. and Sundström, M. (2007) *Does Marriage Matter for Children? Assessing the Causal Impact of Legal Marriage?* (Forschungsinstitut zur Zukunft der Arbeit Institute for the Study of Labor IZA DP No. 3189). Bonn: Germany.

Brady, H., Grand, S.A., Powell, M.A. and Schink, W. (2002) 'Access and confidentiality issues with administrative data', in M. Ver Ploeg, A. Moffit and C. Citro (eds.), *Studies of Welfare Populations: Data Collection and Research Issues*. Washington, DC: National Academy Press, pp. 220–74.

Brizius, J.A. and Campbell, M.D. (1991) *Getting Results: A guide for Government Accountability*. Washington, DC: Council of Governors Policy Advisors.

Coleman, J.S. (1981) *Longitudinal Data Analysis*. New York: Basic Books.

Coulton, C.J. (2008) *Catalogue of Administrative Data Sources for Neighborhood Indicators*. Washington, DC: The Urban Institute.

Goerge, R., Van Voorhis, J., Grant, S., Casey, K., and Robinson, M. (1992) 'Special-Education Experiences of Foster Children: An Empirical Study', *Child Welfare League of America*, 71(5): September/October, 419–38.

Goerge, R. (1997) 'Potential and problems in developing indicators on child well-being from administrative data', in R. Hauser, B. Brown and W. Prosser (eds.), *Indicators of Children's Well-Being*. New York: Russell Sage Foundation, pp. 457–71.

Goerge, R. and Lee, B.J. (2002) 'Matching and Cleaning Administrative Data', in M. Ver Ploeg, A. Moffit and C. Citro (eds.), *Studies of Welfare Populations: Data Collection and Research Issues*. Washington, DC: National Academy Press, pp. 197–219.

Goerge, R., Dilts, J., Yang, D., Wasseman, M. and Clary, A. (2007) *Chicago Children and Youth 1990–2010: Changing Population Trends and Their Implications*. Chicago, IL: Chapin Hall Center for Children at the University of Chicago.

Goerge, R., Harden, A. and Lee, B. (2008) 'Consequences of teen childbearing for child abuse, neglect, and foster care placement', in S.D. Hoffman and R.A. Maynard (eds.), *Kids Having Kids: Economic Costs and Social Consequences of Teen Pregnancy*. Washington, DC: The Urban Institute Press, pp. 257–83.

Hotz, V.J., Goerge, R., Balzekas, J. and Margolin, F. (eds.) (1998) *Administrative Data for Policy-Relevant Research: Assessment of Current Utility and Recommendations for Development*. A Report of the Advisory Panel on Research Uses of Administrative Data of the Northwestern University/University of Chicago Joint Center for Poverty Research. Chicago, IL: The Chapin Hall Center for Children at the University of Chicago.

Hotz, V.J. and Adams, J. (2001) 'The statistical power of national data to evaluate welfare reform', in R. Moffitt and M. Ver Ploeg (eds.), *Evaluating Welfare Reform in an Era of Transition*. Washington, DC: National Academy Press, pp. 209–20.

Iezzonie, L. (1990) 'Using administrative diagnostic data to assess the quality of hospital care', *International Journal of Technology in Health Care*, 6: 272–81.

Jaro, M.A. (1985) *Current Record Linkage Research: Proceedings of the Statistical Computing*. Washington, DC: American Statistical Association.

Jaro, M.A. (1989) 'Advances in record-linkage methodology as applied to matching the 1985 census of

Tampa, Florida', *Journal of the American Statistical Association*, 84(406): 414–20.

Lee, B.J., Mackey-Bilaver, L. and Goerge, R. (2003) 'The patterns of food stamp and WIC participation under welfare reform', *Children and Youth Services Review*, 25(8): 589–610.

Lee, B.J. and Mackey-Bilaver, L. (2007) 'Effects of WIC and food stamp program participation on child outcomes', *Children and Youth Services Review*, 29(4): 501–17.

Leginski, W., Croze, C., Driggers, J., Dumpman, S., Geertsen, D., Kamis-Gould, E., Namerow, M., Patton, R., Wilson, N. and Wurster, C. (1989) Series FN No.10, *Data Standards for Mental Health Decision Support Systems*, National Institute of Mental Health, DHHS Pub No (ADM) 89-1589. Washington, DC: US Govt. Printing Office.

Moore, K. and Brown, B. (2006) 'Preparing indicators for policymakers and advocates', *Social Indicators Research Series*, 27(3): 91–103.

Mugford, M., Banfield, P. and O'Hanlon, M. (1991) 'Effects of feedback of information on clinical practice: A review', *British Medical Journal*, 303(6799): 398.

Shook-Slack, K., Lee, B.J. and Berger, M. (2007) 'Do welfare sanctions increase child protection system involvement? A cautious answer', *Social Service*, 81(2): 207–28.

Tuma, N.B. and Hannan, M.T. (1984) *Social Dynamics: Models and Methods*. Orlando, FL: Academic Press.

24

Children Taking Photos and Photographs: A Route to Children's Involvement and Participation and a 'Bridge' to Exploring Children's Everyday Lives

Kim Rasmussen

INTRODUCTION

It seems both logical and natural to start a chapter about children taking photographs with a photo taken by a child. Therefore you should examine this photo (Figure 24.1) carefully and tell the 'story' you see in the picture. Before you go any further, you could try jotting down a few key words which you can then compare with the narrative that follows.

The photo comes from a pilot project in which children with mental retardation were invited to take photos with a digital camera. The object of the project was, in part, to change typical educational practice so that it was not only the adults in the institution who took photos, but also the children. The other part of the object was to examine what the children would photograph when they had the opportunity to express themselves visually. The project regarded children's

photography/visual expression as a part of children's freedom of expression. (The visual expression aspect seems to be central for children who are mentally retarded and linguistically handicapped.)

The child who took the photo in Figure 24.1 goes to a special kindergarten. The children taking part in the project were allowed to decide for themselves what to photograph from their everyday lives. Each child took a series of photos, and afterwards, the educators spoke with the children about the pictures they had taken. When the educator, with an attempt at an open question, asked the child: 'What's this then?', the child answered in sign language: 'It's a man putting new sand in the sandbox'. This little story that emerges from the photo is a narrative about one of the small (or perhaps 'big' in the eyes of a child) everyday events that took place on one of the days when the child was allowed

Figure 24.1   Photograph taken with a digital camera by a child in the pilot project

to use the camera. The child could have chosen not to photograph it, but nevertheless it has attracted the child's senses, feelings, and attention to such an extent that it was photographed. This may resemble the story you yourself told about the photo. Or the stories may be different from each other.

But the point is that every photo tells a tale. The story can be coaxed out, but the context and the decoding perspective are central to the story that emerges. The story you yourself have attached to the image is based on an imaginary context that you think you can read from some of the information in the photo (man, wheelbarrow, playground, and children). But the story could just as well be something you are reading into the photo on the basis of your pre-understanding/your experience of how children's environments are made manifest in our culture. The child's story is built on the fact that the child, on a daily basis, moves about in the context that has been photographed, and that the child is

the constructor of the photograph. One could ask whether the one tale is truer than the other. Rather than saying that the child's story about the photo is truer or more correct than yours, I would like to point out that the contexts and decoding perspectives are different. Rather than claiming that the one story is truer than the other, one should instead emphasize that photographs and stories that can be teased out of a photo can never be understood independently of the context of which they are part and independent of the decoding perspective lying behind the photo's reception.

Let me underline this point by adding how I myself decoded the photo when I saw it for the first time. What I saw in the photo was namely one of the kindergarten's unofficial celebrations – a highlight of the year. How could this be? Some years ago when I took part in a study about the imprints left by children's everyday lives in day care facilities, assessed on the basis of memories and recollections of 46 young people between 16 and 20 years of age about the time they attended kindergarten, a pattern emerged from the material. Some of them could clearly remember when new sand arrived for the sandbox. This narrative received the same emphasis as the tales they could tell about feast days and holidays like Christmas, Easter, and the summer parties. Here are a few examples of what the young people could remember: 'A big lorry came with the sand and unloaded it in huge piles. For the first couple of weeks the piles of sand were used to jump around in and we played at climbing high mountains ...' (Rasmussen and Smidt, 2001: 129). Another recollection went like this: 'There was an enormous pile of sand lying in the middle of everything, and we had a mountain where we could run around the top and play all sorts of games, for example "King of the Mountain". I remember this as something really good' (Rasmussen and Smidt, 2001: 130). Against this background, the study concluded that new sand in the sandbox must be regarded as an unofficial celebration – in the eyes of the children.

As the study was based on young people's memories, there were no concrete photos or documents about this imprint from institutional life. Therefore I was both surprised and happy when I saw the above photo. I spontaneously decoded the photograph on the basis of the oral accounts about new sand in the sandbox that I had played a part in illustrating in the earlier study. Here, suddenly and unexpectedly, was the concrete picture that matched the stories I knew and the imaginary picture I had.

Against this background, I am also inclined to 'understand/interpret' the child's motive for photographing the man with the wheelbarrow and the new sand. In the child's understanding, the man may be the symbol of an imminent opportunity for playing: namely the games that new sand in the sandbox evokes. One should, naturally, be careful not to ascribe motives to certain children, but the fact that the event which was

photographed is in itself exciting to observe while simultaneously being a symbol of the imminent opportunity for play that primarily takes place once a year is a matter that plays a key role in my reception. One could also say that if the child's photo and statement had stood alone it was probably an example of work performed from a child's perspective, but when the visual and verbal information is placed in a broader frame – whether the frame is theoretical or consists of another study – then a broader and more solid foundation for knowledge is created. These are some of the points as an introduction to the chapter.

In this way, I have simultaneously introduced a number of points to which the article will return in different ways:

- There is a story hidden in every photograph – that is if one can tease it out;
- Photographs can be viewed as a visual expression – therefore they must be regarded as part of children's freedom of expression;
- Photographs are extremely open to interpretation – therefore they can be decoded in several ways;
- The context around a photo is central – just as the decoding perspective is fundamental;
- Children's photography may be regarded as a method with many different potentials that can form part of many contexts.

This introduction with its emphasis on providing *insight* into what can emerge from children's photography will be left here, and I will move on to the broader *overview*.[1]

The objectives and intentions of this chapter

It is the intention of this chapter to present and describe children's photography in different types of projects where children have been invited to participate in a *photographic practice*. These are project types like *development work, evaluation, research,* and *different types of media-educational procedures*. The background for selecting this framework is that children's photography often will enter into and appear in such contexts, just as these contexts will come into play in understanding children's photography. The objective, in addition, is to illustrate what children and adults, respectively, get out of taking part in the different types of projects.

But you must not neglect or underestimate the fact that children taking photos (or making videos, or drawing and painting) could also be used for broader research purposes. The visual approach is an obvious and challenging gateway to gathering facts about children's lives, culture, viewpoints, etc. Children who are quiet or have no voice can be 'heard' with their visual voice. Children who express themselves very well can be understood in new ways when visual materials supply verbal voice, etc. The limitations of what is possible to describe and reflect in this chapter are unfortunately disproportionate to *all* the possibilities of research issues and themes that visual methods invite the innovative and creative researcher to do. But new literature can provide remedy for the limits (see Thomson, 2008).

Next, the intention, a sample of which the introduction has already given, is to contribute critical reflection on the significance and interpretations that adults ascribe to children's photography. Let me add one more thing here. My professional approach to the field of: 'children, involvement, participation and photography' is based on the interdisciplinary universe of cultural sociology and on the ontological views of childhood sociology where children are regarded as social actors who themselves play a part in creating their world and everyday life. I also find it important that children feel they are acknowledged and they experience having a democratic influence on their own lives.

There is no doubt that using photography and adopting a visual approach in producing knowledge about children's lives are embedded in the discourse of qualitative methodology (Emmison and Smith, 2000; Freeman and Mathison, 2009; Knowles and Sweetman, 2004; Leeuwen and Jewitt, 2002). But working

with photos and a visual approach does not exclude the possibility of dealing with quantitative questions and generalizations too. It depends on each single project, how carefully you work out its methodology and how you conduct it in practice. But if the number of participating children and the number of photos are big enough, if the analyzing process comes across in each single photo and/or the generalizations are done carefully and are well reflected in relation to the general knowledge we have about the life of children, then it is possible to exceed purely the qualitative research project. Even though most of this chapter deals with qualitative projects and issues, it will also take account of the question of generalization in a couple of cases.

I hope that the chapter can provide inspiration for social educators, teachers, psychologists, social workers, planners, architects, child and childhood researchers, students, and others who wish to involve children in, and support their participation through, photographic practice.

CHILDREN'S INVOLVEMENT AND PARTICIPATION

Today, in an increasing number of contexts around the world, there is a will to involve children, listen to children, and to allow children to participate actively in different types of projects and processes (Hart, 1997). This applies, for example, to many contemporary pedagogical and educational contexts – contexts where one would perhaps expect to find a long tradition of something like that, but where one is time and again surprised at the low degree to which children genuinely have been involved and have actively participated and decided (when examples in relatively limited reform-pedagogical environments are disregarded). Goodwill toward children and experience with involving others exist in certain contexts in the areas of urban planning, urban development, and modernization of the physical environment (Chawla, 2002). This is also the case in the context of marketing and consumption aimed at children (Seiter, 1993). Likewise, goodwill seems to have put down roots in family and childhood research, which will be exemplified in the chapter. The trend of involving children and respecting children as key informants is not unambiguous and not without exceptions. A random survey among randomly selected children will quickly yield examples of cases where they are kept 'outside'. On the other hand, it cannot be ignored that there is an international trend toward increasingly involving children and taking them into account in localities where children live and move about.

This goodwill is supported by the Convention on the Rights of the Child, and goodwill may in part be a product of this. Article 12 of the Convention states that children who are capable of expressing their own opinions must be ensured the right to freely express these opinions in matters affecting the child (provide direction to a child's right to freedom of thought in a manner consistent with the evolving capacities of the child). Article 13 states that children have the right to freedom of expression, a right that includes the freedom to seek, receive, and communicate information and thoughts of every kind – whether orally, in writing, or in print in the form of art or other means of expression (children's rights to freedom of expression in accordance with age and maturity of the child). But goodwill and rights are not enough. Practical and thoughtful actions are also needed.

In addition, the actions must be regarded as a genuine partnership between children and adults, because that counts. The actions must be carried by mutual respect and recognition. Last but not least, certain media are better than others in terms of involvement, communication, participation, and exchange. It is here that children's photography has something to offer. Projects based on photographing (process) and photography (product) often show that children – in an irresistible, fascinating, and simultaneously delightful way – are involved and actively participate for as long as the project lasts. Experience also shows that projects where children take photographs are usually not insurmountable to undertake – neither financially nor technologically (unlike video, for example, which makes great demands on competence).

ETHICAL CONSIDERATIONS WHEN INVOLVING CHILDREN

Even though experience with projects where children take photographs are largely positive, before starting on a new project and before asking, 'How should I tackle this?', one must critically ask oneself: 'Why invite children to take photographs?'

In other words, one must consider the reasons and arguments behind a project aimed at inviting and involving children in photographic practice. While British child researcher Patricia Alderson does not specifically work with projects that involve children in photographic practice, on a more general level she has pointed out that already at the earliest planning stage one must clarify in whose interests a project with children is being implemented and on what grounds (Alderson, 1995). Environmental psychologist Roger Hart has drawn attention to something similar and taken a critical stance regarding projects that appear to involve children but primarily do so in a way in which children are (mis)used and manipulated (cf. Hart, 1997).

Alderson (1995) points out that not all project ideas require that children are encumbered, their lives intervened in and their time taken up. In other words, there must be good, weighty reasons for involving children. She also urges one to consider in advance what one is going to do with the knowledge one gains almost involuntarily about children's privacy. This seems quite topical in photo projects with children.

When one has achieved clarity with oneself and others concerning a potential project, that the reasons for inviting children to participate in a project are important and good, and has clear grounds for the *why, where* and *what* of the photographic project and *which* children should be invited, then it is important to inform the parties concerned. Here one must consider how much or how little information is needed. Is parental consent necessary or are the children old enough/sufficiently mature to decide for themselves? Finally, some ethical dilemmas arise in connection with dissemination. Who has ownership? Who may make use of the photographs and what may they be used for?

It is difficult to make photos anonymous. What is special about photography, as Susan Sontag, among others, has said, is that it is not merely a picture, but an interpretation of reality, also 'an imprint, a direct impression of reality', which is experienced as not just resembling its motif but as 'a part, an extension of the motif and an effective means of acquiring it, of getting control of it' (Sontag, 1985: 161). Part of the quality of the medium of photography is its 'ability' to freeze details and to concretize. In this context one must carefully consider what consequences the dissemination can have for the children one is thinking of involving. In addition, it is important that there always exists a way out so that children can legitimately leave the project if they lose interest without feeling bad about it.

The ethical problem in connection with projects involving children and photographic practice should not be made light of. But neither should they be regarded as so insuperable that they prevent us from inviting children to photograph where it seems obvious to do so. The ethical reflections will be integrated in the following sections where I present different project types such as development work, evaluation, research, and actual media-educational processes where children have been involved in photographic practice.

EDUCATIONAL DEVELOPMENT WORK WHERE CHILDREN TAKE PHOTOGRAPHS

The following is a description of the educational development project mentioned in the introduction. It has an exemplary element with respect to what often happens when children are invited into and involved in taking photos. At first glance the project may seem 'special', as it is about some 'special children' in a particular special education context. Nevertheless, the project contains exemplary and general elements.

The development project took place in Denmark in 1999 with the participation of teachers and social education workers from three special educational environments. The teachers were working in an ordinary school but in a special class with six children with Down's syndrome. The social education workers came from, respectively, an institution where the six participating children had been diagnosed as having 'severe hearing impairment and autism', and from a special institution where the two participating children had cognitive and speaking problems. The project had, as mentioned, the aim of developing educational practice by allowing the children to take photographs for a period of time. The aim was to study what took place when children with a communication handicap were given the opportunity to take photographs and to communicate through photography. The assumption was that the children would profit from the visual communication.

The children's parents were informed both orally and in writing – and gave their permission. The children were then invited to take part on the understanding that pressure would not be put on anybody to participate and if the children declined that this was absolutely in order.

The project took place over six months and was organized a little differently in the different environments mentioned. This is because it is naturally important that the specific design of a project suits the specific children and adults in context. In one of the institutions, each of the children got a disposable camera with 24 pictures. In the second institution, the children were allowed to use the institution's digital camera. The number of photos here was unlimited, and they could be printed out the same day they were taken together with the children. In the third place, a Polaroid camera was used and here the results could also be seen immediately after the photos were taken.

The children who took part were between 5 and 10 years of age, and all of them were very happy to be invited to take photos. During the preparatory phase the adults had discussed the ethical rules that were to apply to the project. The rule about no children being urged or pressed to take part did not arise as the children were immediately motivated when they had been invited. Some of them, but not all, had taken photographs before. The social education workers and the teachers said that the children were at first very cautious about taking photographs, but also said that the children quickly learned how to look through the viewfinder and manage the technique. The children were not given a task as such but were told that they could photograph as they wished. Part of what was interesting was, after all, to study what the children would photograph and hold on to when they got the opportunity to communicate visually on the basis of self-chosen but unknown criteria.

The adults told us that the children seemed to be especially attentive when they were allowed to go on a photo safari in the institution and the school – or when they took the camera with them on an outing. It seemed that the camera made the children feel more serious than otherwise. The social education workers and the teachers also told about different events and episodes where children and adults had laughed and had more fun than usual. In this way, the project contributed to good spirits and extra fun in daily life. This is not a bad outcome if one also emphasizes the side results of a pilot project and not only its major academic findings.

What, then, did the project result in? Several things deserve mention. In the first place, as already mentioned, the children showed great concentration and attention during the photography project itself. Second, the children were very interested in the development/creation of the photos when they could follow it (cf. Polaroid camera and digital camera). Third, the finished photos gave rise to a great deal of communication when they were being inspected. Among other things, the professionals noticed that some of the children who otherwise were regarded as very quiet and reticent in daily life became quite active and communicative during the project. They looked, pointed, showed, and commented – in either words or sign language. The children were also interested in their photos being put up and looked at. For example, they were interested in showing their photos to other children who visited their class or room. The children thus related to their own photographs.

The most surprising thing about the project however, was that some of the children's photographs proved to be so personal and different from each other that the professionals began changing their view of some of the participating children. They came to regard the children in the light of the visual information they read in the children's photographs.

Figure 24.2 tells something about the children's imagination and ability to stage and cooperate. Simultaneously, it is an example of some children being taken up with angling and framing the world downwards. Four children (one of them is the photographer) have cooperated on this figuration of feet and shoes without the interference of others.

In Figure 24.3, the children had the digital camera with them on their outing. One of the child photographers has 'captured' a section of the carriage – once more with a downward angle. The photo helps us to become aware of the fact that there is a world 'down there' and that the photographer has an eye for this world.

Figure 24.2   Photograph taken cooperatively by four children in the project

Figure 24.3   Photograph taken by a child during an outing as part of the project

One child took close-ups almost exclusively. This observation led to the thought that the child might need glasses. Another child took almost only pictures of 'patterns': the stripes in the curtains, the net in the football goal, the wire fence around the institution, the grid for shoes at the door, the pattern on a friend's blouse, etc. This led to discussions about the child's inner life and experience of the environment. Did the child usually look at the surrounding world by fixing on patterns, stripes, and lines? A third child wanted to take photographs but not hold the camera himself! The social education worker was ordered to hold the camera and take the photos. The child was very insistent on identifying what was to be photographed and was likewise concerned about whether the resulting picture on the display of the digital camera was OK. The members of the project began to speak of this as the child taking photos by proxy, and it was discussed whether the 'result' of this cooperation should be regarded as the child's photograph, the adult's photograph or the photograph of the 'interplay'.

The social education workers also related that some of the children became more courageous and dared to venture further away or to approach areas and things that normally did not interest them. In this way, apart from some quite specific experience of photographing, the children attracted the attention and interest of the professionals in a way that nobody could have imagined in advance.

By means of their pictures, the children could show some of what attracted their attention in daily life. Some of the motifs did not come as any surprise to the adults (photos of the best friend, favourite teacher and the like). But there were also a number of motifs (the child who was interested in stripes and patterns) that made the adults realize that children's visual attention cannot always be communicated and understood through non-visual media (verbal language, sign language,

body language, etc.). In this way, the project illustrated and communicated parts of the aesthetic and visual dimension in children's everyday life and lives.

The project also confirmed the children in being social actors. The children acted and created tracks showing where they had been, what had interested them, and presumably something about what it meant to them. With the mediation of the camera and through the children's photographs, it became possible to *see* what the children momentarily or persistently seemed to find significant.

Theoretically one can discuss whether taking photographs is also creating meaning. But if it is assumed that one does not photograph completely at random, then every photo must express 'some' meaning – whether the meaning is carried by a feeling, an atmosphere, curiosity, or an interest. During the project the children's photos were at least seen as cultural artefacts, an attribution of meaning to the 'moment', the things, the places, the animals, and the persons. This interpretation applies whether or not the children have a developmental disability. Accordingly, photography may assist us to understand the experience of children with language disabilities, who otherwise may not be able to communicate the personal significance of particular events, places, or relationships.

Many of the matters mentioned in connection with the project can be seen again in other project contexts: for example, that the children become physically and creatively active, participatory and engaged, that they help to set an agenda and point to circumstances in such a way that they win the attention of the adults in a different way than they usually do.

Another development project that must be mentioned – because it is drawing attention to the involvement, participation, and empowerment of children with disabilities – is Franziska Meyer's project titled: *Der Weg ensteht im Gehen* (which literally means 'the road occurs while you are walking'). This project, through photography of the city's places and spaces, taught children with Down's syndrome to find their way so they could then move independently in the city on foot, by bus, or by other means (Meyer, 2010). Although the project cannot be described here fully enough to give it justice, it should still be mentioned because it has many qualities to recommend it.

MEDIA EDUCATIONAL PROJECTS WHERE CHILDREN TAKE PHOTOGRAPHS

'Media educational projects' are another type of project involving and inviting children. Many different types of learning processes can take place in such projects (social, cultural, political, etc.), but they always involve learning processes relating to a specific medium, for example, the camera. It is precisely learning processes aimed at using the camera that characterize the projects we are to read about. However, the learning processes in the projects are simultaneously also social, cultural, and political. What is exemplary about the projects is, though, the way in which they involve the children, which is invitingly, respectfully, supportively. In other words, it is the relationship between child and adult that is worth noting.

Some of the projects initiated by photographer and teacher Wendy Ewald are described. This is followed by an account of the project represented by Jim Hubbard and the non-profit organization 'Shooting Back'. In their work both Ewald and Hubbard have striven to involve children in a type of unauthorized grassroots project. At the same time the projects are also examples of the way in which enthusiasts can carry good ideas forward and translate their ideas into practice.

For more than 35 years (her first projects began in 1969), photographer and teacher

Wendy Ewald has run untraditional workshops in, inter alia, Canada, Colombia, Mexico, the USA, India, South Africa, the Netherlands, and Saudi Arabia. For shorter or longer periods of time she has focused her work on children and photography. Her working method is simple and effective, and it has not notably changed throughout the years. She finds some place in the world. Then she looks for a group of children whom she invites to take photos and to participate in a form of workshop. First of all she teaches the children the rudiments of photographic technique. Then they get a camera and she invites them to take pictures of everyday motifs – for example, themselves, family, friends, etc. She points out that in many social contexts photos are only taken on special occasions and for this reason many people have little experience of photographing ordinary events in an ordinary life (Ewald and Lightfoot, 2001). After a while she talks with the children about their dreams and their photos, and in this process she helps them find different photographic and verbal ways of expressing themselves about their world. The imaginary and fantastic universe is manifest in children's lives, and this is therefore a good approach for interaction with the potentials of photography.

The photographic practice that develops in the interaction between the children and Ewald has many features in common with the genre called documentarism, just as it shares likenesses with visual anthropology/visual sociology (Banks, 2001; Banks and Morphy, 1997; Harper, 2012). It gets close to the people who are depicted and gives rise to new insights and realizations. The central, overall goal is, however, for the pupils to acquire skills in interpreting their surroundings and to come to understand themselves through their own expressions. Ewald expresses her intention thus: 'Who we are and where we stand when we watch the world determines how we see and what we record. Children, like professional writers and photographers, must be familiar with the tools of their craft in order to be able to capture what they see: they need to be able to recognize basic concepts in writing and photography' (Ewald and Lightfoot, 2001: 29). However, this educational objective can be achieved in many different ways.

During one of her earliest projects back in 1974, Ewald spent some years at an first nation people reservation in Canada (Ewald, 2000). The children, who were aged between 4 and 16, had never held a camera in their hands before, but they were given a Polaroid camera which they could use to document their lives. The Polaroid technique means that one has an immediate result to relate to. The project gave rise to a manifold portrait of life in the reservation, and some of the photos from the project are reproduced in her book: *Secret Games* (Ewald, 2000). Speaking of the dialectical process between her and the children, she says that while the children were photographing she took photos of the children and their families – if they gave their permission. When the children's photos were compared with her own, it quickly became clear Ewald's photographs were selective and targeted while the children took pictures of everything they saw. One example she gives is when both she and the 14-year-old boy Merton Ward, with whom she became friendly, together photographed a graveyard. She relates:

> My photograph shows what an Indian graveyard looks like. You can read the inscription on the gravestone and see the simple handmade crosses. Merton's picture is grainy, washed out, and the propositions are inaccurate, but his cemetery is a frightening place. No one visits it or places flowers on the graves. Sometimes people see ghosts there. Merton's photograph reflects that fear.
>
> (Ewald and Lightfoot, 2001: 9f)

Through this example and others Ewald discovers and learns that children's photographs tend to be more complicated and disturbed. Ewald interprets the difference as being that children's pictures were far closer to 'what it felt like to be there', and that if the children had not commented on their own pictures,

the pictures would have been difficult to decipher. Thus, the interesting point is that it is not just the children who learn something, but that the teacher, Wendy Ewald, also learns something through a project.

In another project, 'The Best Part of Me', work was explicitly performed on children's self-understanding and how they regarded their bodies. As Ewald says: 'Many times I've heard children describe themselves and their kinships with others in terms of parts of their bodies – "I have Mom's eyes" etc.' (Ewald, 1999: 93). The objective was therefore to take a starting point in this bodily relating, which obviously plays a key role in children's lives but which is seldom thematized. The pupils in third, fourth, and fifth grade at a school in Kentucky were invited along and asked about which parts of their bodies they liked best or that told them most about themselves. Ewald tells further: 'Then, using a view camera so I could focus as closely as I needed to, I took a Polaroid picture of each child. The child and I then looked at the photograph together and discussed changes in composition or background that might reflect the child's vision of him or her. Once we were satisfied with the image, the child took it back into the classroom and wrote about it' (Ewald, 1999: 93). It could, of course, be asked to what extent this kind of project can be regarded as children's photography, and there is no doubt that the project is a borderline case. On the other hand, it could be said that the photographs arose out of interaction between child and adult and where the adult makes herself and the camera into instruments for the child's wishes and ideas. This is something that in many ways is reminiscent of the previously mentioned project where a boy did not want to hold the camera himself but had many ideas and wanted to decide what the social education worker was to photograph. The child–adult relationship seems unusual and interesting in relation to the common child–adult relationship known from mainstream pedagogics and in which there is no doubt of the teacher's power. In the example, Ewald places herself at the disposal of the children's ideas/fantasies and the power that is implicit in this.

At the same time, it must be said that projects that take that slant where the camera not only functions as a visualization instrument but also comes to function as an actual mirror through which the child can view him/herself also contain therapeutical aspects. Where development takes place and work is done on self-portraits and self-thematizations, the therapeutical aspects linked with understanding of self-esteem and self-reflection became extremely tangible. Within media pedagogics one also sees that the boundaries between what is called photo-pedagogics and photo therapy, respectively, are not particularly clear (Schafiyha, 1997). I shall leave Ewald here and turn to another media-educational, photography project that involves children, namely 'Shooting Back'.

Experience from the project entitled 'Shooting Back'

In 1989, the non-profit organization 'Shooting Back' was founded with a view to coordinating workshops on photography, writing, and other media aimed at homeless children and children at risk in an area around Washington. The project started up quite informally and humbly by letting children from homeless families photograph their conditions and everyday lives. The title of the project arose by chance one day when a small 9-year-old boy shouted: 'We're shooting back', when he was standing together with an adult and photographing with a camera that was so big he could hardly hold it. And – the project has certainly shot back, because the margina-lized children and their families have been capturing the attention of the public since the end of the 1980s. The project spread to cities like Minneapolis and Minnesota and to reservations for the indigenous peoples of the USA in Arizona.

This took place when the programme really began to receive media coverage and public interest arose in the children's work.

Jim Hubbard, one of the main figures in 'Shooting Back' from the very beginning, has described how it started. As a professional photographer he worked documenting life among the homeless in Washington, where during the 1980s a growing number of people were forced to live in cars, hotels, and motels as temporary shelters. When he was taking pictures of the families in one of these motels in particular, the children were very interested in holding the camera and looking through the viewfinder. One afternoon, when Hubbard was visiting the Johnson family, the boy Dion showed him a couple of snapshots he himself had taken of the family and some friends. Hubbard relates:

> Both he and his mother were proud of the photos. I offered Dion an opportunity to take pictures and learn more about photography. He accepted and his powerful smile stretched from ear to ear … In large part, this was what moved me to help Dion. This same energy and interest in tapping the creativity of the kids is the common thread running through Shooting Back.
>
> (Hubbard, 1991: 3)

One understands that it all arose without any previous plan and that it was the boy Dion himself who was the driving force because he was so motivated. One also understands that this made the boy proud. He was able to do something that was appreciated by his environment.

When the idea of letting Dion photograph the environment in which he moved had arisen, Hubbard and Dion spent several hours a week together taking photos. Many other children came and asked if they also could take photos with the professional camera when Jim and Dion were moving around the neighbourhood. Hubbard quickly realized that if the children's wishes were to be complied with, it would be necessary to recruit more photographers and freelance photographers as voluntary participants. He managed to find volunteers and the project arose and developed 'from the bottom up' and more or less by chance.

Hubbard describes how life among the homeless is a life 'on the edge'. During the time he spent there, he experienced death, violence, and other tragedies. These terrible events were an everyday occurrence for the children. Hubbard noted, 'As I encountered these children, I realized that they are deprived at many levels ... these children without permanent homes are victims of profound injustice. Myriad factors place them at risk level comparable to that for children in the slums of Calcutta' (Hubbard, 1991: 4). The children were starved of attention and longed for some people who could help them to use and channel their creative energy and skills. Some of the work with the children actually consisted in convincing them that each of them was an important person.

There were only a few rules in the photo project and the idea was simple. The children were to document their world in the neighbourhood. They used a professional camera when a photographer had given them the necessary instructions and they had learned the basic techniques. The key theme was really only letting the children look through the viewfinder and take pictures of the world they sensed.

Another agenda arose when the children's work had been followed for some time. An exhibition was eventually to be made of their works in a space for art. Such an exhibition of the children's work could serve several purposes. The children could make their own case. An exhibition would show the children's creativity and help to teach Americans outside the slums about the injustice and the conditions under which the children lived. These seemed to be a case of both empowerment in relation to the children and of enlightenment in relation to the population.

Hubbard relates further that he and other photographers worked with the children for more than a year. 'Many profound moments occurred during our photographic sessions.

The photographers who came to work with the children in this period were given the opportunity not only to teach but to learn from their young students' (Hubbard, 1991: 5). What is interesting about this statement is that in this project also there is growing acknowledgement of the fact that the learning processes do not only go from the professionals to the children but also move in the opposite direction. This type of recognition was probably partly caused by the openness and receptiveness characteristic of new and untried projects. At the early stage when things are not entirely fixed and where the narratives about what is experienced and what is happening have not grown into rituals and routines either, more untraditional insights will more easily take root. This speaks in favour of the media pedagogue constantly experimenting with his or her practice and not adopting accustomed routines. We all need routines and habits, but if we do not have the courage or energy to experiment we risk not learning anything new ourselves.

In 1989, Hubbard succeeded in establishing the Shooting Back Education and Media Center in Washington. As mentioned before, teaching takes place in this non-profit centre not only in photography and darkroom work but also in painting, drawing, and creative writing. Many talented volunteers lend a helping hand. The exhibition, 'Shooting Back', in Washington, DC, was seen by 10,000 visitors and several millions have seen the story on TV and in the newspapers. 'With our exhibit in Washington, DC, and another in New York City, we have received enormous publicity both nationally and internationally. Our lives have been altered by this experience, and the children are continually having the limits of their world redefined' (Hubbard, 1991: 6).

If one is to briefly summarize some of the key points that seem to be common to Ewald's and Hubbard's work, one could say that their involvement and active participation in photographic practice, the children learn to express themselves in the photographic medium and become more visually conscious of the environment in which they live at the same time as the projects contribute to the children's self-esteem. Both Ewald and Hubbard would seem to have the respect and humility vis-à-vis the children they work with that is decisive for an involvement process resulting in the participating children feeling that both they and their work are recognized and appreciated.[2]

EVALUATION PROJECTS AND CHILDREN'S INVOLVEMENT THROUGH THEIR PHOTOGRAPHY

This section presents yet another type of project that can involve children through photographic practice, namely an evaluation project.

An evaluation wave has washed over children's institutions in recent years. It has become modern to evaluate. But children are not integrated and involved and do not necessarily take an active and serious part in these evaluations. One of the reasons may be that many children find it difficult to be objective and evaluative about their own environments in the way that adults expect. For example, responding to questionnaires or writing small reports does not relate with the way children express themselves and respond. Another reason for children's missing involvement and participation may be the lack of an historical tradition and specific experience of how it is done. People may be perplexed about finding suitable methods.

One may have reservations about fashionable practices that some regard as the product of political correctness (for example, the identification of children as consumers who should evaluate the social service organizations that provide services to them). However, there is no reason for a general dismissal of the relevance of evaluation of children's environments,

especially if the children are genuinely involved and the methods used match the children's skills and desire.

Some years ago, Austrian educational researchers Michael Schrantz and Ulrike Steiner-Löffler pointed out that photography and photos can give children opportunities to explore and assess, for example, the school's 'inner world' without using a mass of verbal argumentation or written objectification. On the basis of practical experience, in an article they told about and demonstrated 'the power of pupils' photographic images when they are asked to take pictures of places they like or dislike (Schrantz and Steiner-Löffler, 1998: 235). Thus, to a high degree they adopt a power perspective on children's involvement and participation in evaluation. The article takes its point of departure in an evaluation project at a school in Vienna, where five boys and nineteen girls in second grade hold to their own views of the school environment through photography. The photos thus provide an opportunity for the children to obtain a means of expression and the teachers acquire valuable insights into the way in which the pupils experience life and their everyday in the school.

When the project began, Schrantz and Löffler had experimented with using photos in school evaluation with different age groups, but not with second-grade children. Therefore, they did not know whether the children could handle the process. The children's teacher, however, was very interested in the idea and willing to try something she had never tried before.

The two evaluation researchers describe how the evaluation was organized. When the children had been introduced to the idea, some self-chosen groups of four to five pupils were set up. These groups or teams were first encouraged to discuss what places in the school they felt it pleasant to be in and what place they did not like. After a while, the children were asked to select about three or four places from each category and to photograph the places in groups. They were then encouraged to discuss whether or not there should be people in the photos. When they had done this, the groups went out and photographed what they had planned. When the pictures had been developed, each team made a poster where the children presented their photos in two categories: the good places and the places where they did not like to be. The children wrote commentaries on their pictures that stated the reasons behind their choices. Subsequently, each group presented their poster to the class. Schrantz and Löffler commented from experience that at this point in the process the pupils usually begin to become involved in heated discussions about their situation at the school in general.

The danger in evaluations consists in the participants experiencing that the evaluations are a ritual action with no practical or concrete consequences. There also is a danger that involving the children is a pseudo-manoeuvre, as we recall Hart warning against at the beginning of the article. Schrantz and Löffler are well aware of this danger and therefore make a general distinction between two different ways of implementing a photo-evaluation project:

(a) Like any other classroom project – which in the final analysis can mean that nobody is interested in changing anything that the children have visually stated they do not like.
(b) But photo evaluation can also be implemented in such a way that what takes place in the individual class is introduced as part of the wider self-evaluation that the school decides on. This will occur when there is an atmosphere at a school that the pupils' 'voice'/photos must be taken seriously, and the school is prepared to take the consequences. This is called giving the pupils 'a photographic voice.' (Schrantz and Steiner-Löffler, 1998: 238)

Some of the things that were discovered through the project were that the positive or negative evaluations made by the children were closely linked to the experiences the pupils had with certain people in certain places. 'We noticed that the connection between places and persons they can relate to was particularly strong in the decision-making process of primary school children …' (Schrantz and Steiner-Löffler, 1998: 239). I interpret this as the children having shown and told through their photos and commentaries that the 'world of the school' in their view is social-physical, that is that the social and the physical are experienced as being closely tied and closer than we adults ordinarily experience and express it, because our world picture is more abstract and it is easier for us to separate things.

A couple of examples can serve to concretize the experience mentioned. Some pupils cannot agree on how to judge the teachers' room. It belongs to the category of hidden and forbidden places (just like the head teacher's office). Some of them think it is attractive because it belongs to a category of taboo places. Others think the opposite because it is associated with boring lessons or punishments that seem to emanate from there.

Another example is the children's afternoon care facility, where the children can spend the afternoon, although monitored by some of the teachers. The girls love this place and enjoy being there together with their friends. But they also like being together with their teacher, who has more time to talk with them personally than here in the school. The boys, on the other hand, regard it as a terrible place because 'everything is forbidden'. Well: same place – but quite different views of the place! One understands that so-called 'reality' can be experienced, seen, and interpreted in many ways. The question is whether there is any meaning in speaking of one reality or if one should rather assume that many realities exist when we speak about 'the world of children'?

Another important finding in the photo-evaluation was that schoolchildren, regardless of age, positively evaluated places where they experience freedom. This observation is not surprising, but it was important to document, because school life is often strictly bound by rules.

Similarly, in another study in which somewhat older children's images of school were examined, children often photographed places in the school that symbolized a 'way out' (for examples, windows or doors): 'We have chosen the exit because freedom lies behind it' (Schrantz and Steiner-Löffer, 1998: 241). The authors added that 'pupils of all ages would choose places where they are allowed to move freely or do manual work' (Schrantz and Steiner-Löffer, 1998: 241). In the photography project, pupils and teachers began to speak with greater clarity about such treasured places in the school.

As this example illustrates, photo-evaluation can give rise to strong feelings. Such affect may emerge because the question of where one feels at ease can involve a 'jungle of feelings'. Also, emotional engagement is an expectable result of children's recognition that their experiences and opinions are appreciated. Moreover, the photographic images themselves often elicit feelings. Researchers must prepare themselves for such affective responses if they use photography as a tool for evaluation.

Evaluation of education and institutional life almost inevitably touches on complex social phenomena. The concrete physical images may thus provide an approachable starting point for discussion of structures and processes that are often hard to describe. At the same time, the themes found in photographs may elicit consideration of quite abstract values, norms, and organizational characteristics.

On the basis of this project it can once more be seen how, through photography and their own photos, children can be involved and become actively creative. As mentioned, it is emphasized that through the camera's visualization children obtain some power that affects the traditional balance of power between teachers and

pupils in the school. The authors also point out that such a project is not just serious. It is also fun, which would seem to correspond to what we heard in the section about the physically and mentally handicapped children. When evaluation researchers say: 'Taking pictures has always been fun ...' (Schrantz and Steiner-Löffler, 1998: 250), in an evaluation context one must add: at any rate as long as this practice remains an alternative to the many more traditional and ritual methods of evaluation.

Evaluating children's urban environment

The reason I have chosen to go further and present American architect Shirl Buss's project from the middle of the 1990s: 'Los Angeles from Young People's Angle of Vision' in the section on evaluation and not in the next on research projects is because it is not possible to clearly categorize the project. (Certain evaluation projects can very well have a research dimension, and certain research projects can similarly have dimensions of evaluation.) At the same time, I find the project exemplary and visionary in relation to involving children in the evaluation not only of their institutions but also of the whole neighbourhood and urban area they move around in on a daily basis.

The objective of the project was to show how children experience the city. Five urban areas in Los Angeles were included and 115 schoolchildren took part with their teachers as assistants. The children took a total of 1740 photos of their homes, neighbourhoods, schools, and communities and arranged them in colourful booklets that were also decorated and painted and claimed texts written by the children. This took place in connection with the participating children analysing and commenting on the pictures and putting words on their experiences.

Figure 24.4 features an extract from a child's booklet. Photo and text interact, while

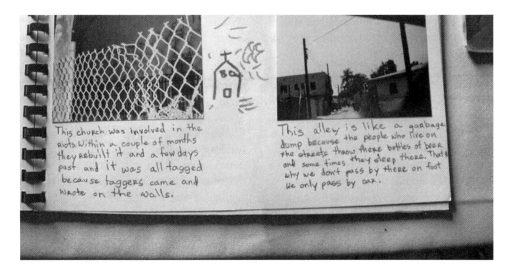

This church was involved in the riots. Within a couple of months they rebuilt it and a few days past and it was all tagged because taggers came and wrote on the walls.

This alley is like a garbage dump because the people who live on the streets throw there bottles of beer and some times they sleep there. That's why we don't pass by there on foot. We only pass by car.

Figure 24.4   Extract from a child's booklet

each on its own would hardly have been comprehensible.

The children were informed of the purpose of the project and the expectations there were of their participation and contributions. The children's photo booklets are rich in information about the environment, and the children's comments add several layers of meaning to the photographic pictures. The children describe their difficult and often hopeless conditions of accommodation and the violence of the inner city. Certain urban landscapes resemble wildernesses and battle zones, but the children also know places with colour, humour, and comfort. Impressions of the city are shown in their photographic pictures and narratives: there are pictures of parks, playgrounds, and public places/spaces. Some schools are experienced as hazardous, although, to a lesser extent than many other places in the immediate environment. On the other hand, shopping streets and malls are among the places where they feel secure, stimulated, and mobile.

Shirl Buss used action-oriented and ethnographic interview methods in the project. Her procedure consisted of children taking disposable cameras home with them at the weekend after which they took photographs of life in the neighbourhood, the

school, and the district. The task was formulated as follows:

- Take photos of places you like and places you don't like (cf. the questions in the school evaluation);
- The pictures may include people.

The children's reaction was unmistakable. They were proud of having been invited and involved in the project and they had a lot of questions: May we take pictures of people living in cardboard boxes? May we take pictures of gang members? etc. When the pictures were developed, they were asked if they wanted to write a short story about each photo in their booklets. They were allowed to say what they liked about each photo, and each of them spent between two and six hours arranging, inserting and writing about their photo collection.

The photographs helped the children with many things:

- Collecting visual information
- Creating an overview of their local environment
- Giving a visual characterization of their life space.

Buss says about her experiences and results that her professional interest actually had to do with children's experience of the spatial syntax of the town, but the children laid the stress somewhere else – namely on the social relations and how they were influenced by the physical world. In this project also, children's photos and narratives contribute to pointing out the way in which the social and the physical are inextricably linked in children's experience.

The project showed that the children regarded their home as the safest place in town. Most of them describe their home as an oasis and a cocoon that was sometimes surrounded by a more violent and unpredictable universe. The project also showed that the neighbourhood was often viewed as a place with many limitations. This negative perception was present even though the neighbourhood might be the starting point for children's demonstration of some measure of independence from their families. Some children described a very restrictive home life with many very tight boundaries for their activities. 'I like my yard but my mother won't allow me to play there because someone could come by on the street and take me' (Buss, 1995: 347). Because of their fear, many children did not make use of the street space in their neighbourhood, but instead moved into narrow playing zones within their yard or home. Statements such as: 'I usually play in the house because they're always shooting' – or 'I don't feel safe in my front yard' – or 'Sometimes there is shooting and I don't want to be the victim' hardly need any elaboration. Buss herself never asks the children about gangs. Nevertheless, four out of five children mention the issue of gangs in the interviews.

Once upon a time the street was an important laboratory for children's physical development, but the children in the study say that streets and roads are the most dangerous places in town. Half of the children interviewed say that they feel frightened, insecure, or nervous being on the street. All the children speak of the uncertainty and danger they associate with the traffic, gangs,

'winos', thieves and 'bad people on the street'. 'I don't feel safe on the street. They can kill innocent people when they shoot'. When children see graffiti, stolen cars, needles, or wine bottles, they associate them with danger – and even with death. 'This alley makes me feel sad and mad because a lot of people have died here and because they like drugs', is a clear statement about the street and an illustrative example of the relation between place and feeling of place.

The photo booklets contain many photos of graffiti, bullet holes, and other signs of local and social conflicts. The children 'read' these traces and attribute meaning to them. Buss says that if we listen to the children and look at their photos, we adults can learn that they feel ill at ease with graffiti and other symbolic representations of social conflict. 'Graffiti is bad. I don't think it's good. It destroys our city'.

As has emerged, the children's photography and the subsequent photo-elicitation method/interviews on the basis of the photographs contributed to creating insight into children's experience of their city. The pictures provided concrete information about the places, and the children's statements provided irrefutable evidence of their experiences and reflections.[3]

RESEARCH PROJECTS BASED ON CHILDREN'S PHOTOGRAPHY

In contrast to the preceding sections, this section is not structured around one or more projects. Much of what has been told and shown about the photography process itself in connection with the previous types of projects would also seem to apply to children's photography in research projects.

But it seems important and appropriate to distinguish between projects which have an educational purpose with those that are intended for research. The main difference between the project types mentioned and research projects appears to be about the methodological work of interpreting children's photographs. In research, it is important to reflect and afterwards inform about the underlying considerations. In media-pedagogical projects, the didactical reflection seems inevitable if you want some sort of guarantee for the processes. Research is directed toward creation of a product (new knowledge), but an educational project could be focussed on the process alone. In research, the aim is also to inform a public which is broader and bigger than the participants (unless we are talking about action research) while educational projects seldom have these ambitions.

However, what one gets to know about the research projects' underlying methodological reflections varies a great deal from one project to the other – that is, what on a more general level is thought about children, children's status as informants, children's photographs, and interviews about them. Researchers may find themselves in a dilemma. Researchers are inclined to emphasize the photos in their reports and to avoid being distracted by methodological concerns. Therefore the methodological reflections are often downgraded to a minimum or completely disappear. It is a shame.

This does not contribute to picture-based research acquiring any special status. But what is even more unfortunate is that the basis on which researchers have arrived at their results tends to remain unclear and difficult to penetrate. Underlying reflections must therefore be recalled and discussed – at least to some degree.

About ten years ago Jon Prosser, writing about picture-based research which he finds contains many potentials, critically but loyally pointed out the following: 'There are no political moves, no general strategies, no overarching methodology, that will alter that status' (of Image-based Research; Prosser, 1998: 108). In my opinion, this critique is also to a certain extent true of the children

and childhood research based on children's photography.

Even though it is not possible within the framework of this chapter to provide more comprehensive methodological reflections about work with children's photography, there are some key aspects that will be focused on here in conclusion. First, projects based on children's photography will be placed in relation to various features of more recent childhood research, which is rich in methodological reflections. This will be followed by a discussion of the issue of 'children's perspective' related to children's photos, and finally, the focus will be on the photo-elicited interview with children.

Some features and characteristics

There are by now quite a few research projects that have gradually included children and children's photography. Several of these studies aim at exploring children's urban and physical environments (see, for example, Buss, 1995; Cele, 2006; Clark, 1999; Jensen, 2008; Kernan, 2005; Orellana, 1999; Wilhjelm, 2002). But children's photography also forms part of projects aimed at other matters. Some examples: Australian researchers Lysaght, Brown, and Westbrook, who have initiated a project involving more than 150 children and young people between the ages of 6 and 18, in which the participants, using disposable cameras, reflect on their everyday life experiences, a project that the researchers describe as 'cross-cultural visual literacy' (Lysaght, Brown and Westbrook, 2007). In other words, the project has an educational aim. Staunæs's study is about young people living and waiting at an asylum centre, and she has provided the young asylum seekers with disposable cameras with a view to telling about this (Staunæs, 1998). Winter's study is about children's perception of home and domesticity, and she asked the children to photograph homes and where they felt at home (Winter, 2004).

The largest photo-based study in which I was involved dealt with children's everyday life and children's perceptions of their institutions (Rasmussen and Smidt, 2002). Eighty-eight children between 5 and 12 years from 13 locations in Denmark were invited to take part in this study. They were given disposable cameras, which they took with them everywhere they went in the course of a week. They were asked to photograph places, persons or situations they found meaningful, and photo-elicited interviews were then conducted. Even this study was based on qualitative methodology. The aim was to get a closer perception of children's childhood and to hear their own views about what they had chosen to picture from everyday life.

The project was made possible because of the number of photographs: nearly 2000 had been taken. With such a quantity the best method was obviously to take a view of the whole range of single pictures and then begin counting them individually according to a category. This led to some interesting interpretations and 'findings' from the material, a few examples of which can be mentioned here.

By examining the range of photos and counting up the actual objects portrayed in the visual material, a significant tendency became clear: most of the photos showed the children's friends – and their pets! It was no surprise to see children's friends, because friendship is a core topic in today's child research. But children's pets were not present in the photos. It may be that some new chapters will have to be written in the near future about children relating to their pets because neither childhood sociology nor family sociology has given this issue enough attention. If we were able to conclude about childhood in general from quantitative tendencies in a qualitative visual study, I would not hesitate to underline this point. When children are informants and when they tell us about everyday life and childhood they also tell us a lot about their pets. However, the topic of children's relationships with pets is nearly absent from the scientific literature. This example gives us some idea of the possibilities available from generalizing connected to visual studies, but the methodology behind working with questions about generalization is not yet well elaborated.

The fact that children's photography has also been employed as a method in different Ph.D projects (see, for example, Cele 2006; Jensen, 2008; Kernan, 2005; Wilhjelm, 2002; and see specifically Cele's study because she focused on some of the methodological issues connected with children's photography) indicates that it is now being accepted among others that are well-known and tested for involving children in the creation of research-based knowledge. This can, moreover, be interpreted as a sign that visualization methods are no longer merely something that interests a small group of well-known professionals who have consciously defined themselves as 'visual anthropologists' or 'visual sociologists'. In other words, the visual approach to studying children's lives and culture seems to have taken root.

CHILDREN'S PHOTOGRAPHY – SEEN IN RELATION TO THE NEW CHILD RESEARCH

When a new form of childhood research emerged in 1990, its characteristics were, inter alia, that:

- Children and childhood should and could be studied 'in their own right';
- Children must be regarded as social actors on an equal footing with adults;
- It was advantageous to include children as informants in empirical childhood studies.

If these points are compared with the projects based on children's photography, it can be seen that the programme statements harmonize with the actual projects.

It has, for example, been said that, 'Children must be *seen as actively involved in the construction of their own lives*, the lives of those around them and of the societies in which they live' (James and Prout, 1997: 4). The projects where children have been invited to take part in research and which photograph parts of their lives would seem to live up to this ontological view. At the same time, research projects in which children take photographs and then are interviewed about their photos must be seen as an approach to research that has not been prevalent for any particularly length of time, namely as British child researcher Berry Mayall has put it, 'research *with* children' – and contrasted with the more traditional: research *on* children (Mayall, 2002).

Researching with children means that the adult researchers enter into a relationship with the participating children in which they interact with the children in ways that have up to now only been relatively vaguely reflected methodologically. One could fundamentally doubt whether the researcher 'can get into' the world of children. But one can get close – there is no reason to doubt this. Experience with children's photography, but also with other more recent methods, has produced empirical material that seems to be inaccessible and unreachable on the basis of more traditional methods (interview, survey, and the like).

In this regard, speaking about children as 'co-researchers' can spontaneously seem sympathetic and right. But as researchers, we must be careful not to name and put children into roles they have not themselves asked for and can hardly assess. In my opinion, doing research with children should not be identical with children being appointed and spoken about as 'co-researchers'. For example, when I have looked at children's photographs and spoken with them I did not regard the children as co-researchers. The children's interest and approach was not 'doing research'. They accepted my invitation to take part because on the basis of my introductory information they felt that it could be fun, and because they had an idea about something they wanted to show me and tell me about. But it is I who

am the researcher. It is I who has researched their lives, and it is I who has defined the framework of the research project. When we look at photos, we cooperate. I could hardly achieve my knowledge without this cooperation. But the knowledge that a project generates is not identical with the children's knowledge. It can come more or less close – but is not identical. It is knowledge that emerges through a form of interpretative interactionism. Interaction and negotiation of significance in and around photographs has taken place in a 'triangular drama' between the children, the visual information that is contained in the photograph, and then myself.

But the process does not end there. I have discussed the knowledge produced further with colleagues when participating in a research network, at seminars, and in other informal contexts such as, working papers, discussion papers, etc. These matters must not be undervalued as they have also have an impact on the knowledge generated which in the final analysis has been published and appears as 'result' or 'findings'.

CHILDREN'S PHOTOGRAPHY AND THE SO-CALLED 'CHILDREN'S PERSPECTIVE'

In research on children and childhood there has been a good deal of talk and discussion about the so-called 'children's perspective' (cf. Gullestad, 1991; Kjørholt, 1991; Tiller, 1991) and the extent to which research can produce knowledge about the world of children as children sense and experience it. This debate seems to be methodologically relevant in relation to the question of the degree to which children's photography is an expression of the much discussed 'children's perspective'.

What, then, has emerged from this debate? Today there would seem to be agreement that the so-called 'children's perspective' is the construction of child researchers and an attempt to get as close as possible to children's experiences and experience while being fully aware that no direct access exists to the world of children. A child researcher and an adult interpretation always come in between.

The research that invites children to take photographs cannot therefore either avoid the fact that children's photographs *cannot* be seen 'unadulterated' and sidestepping the visual perception of adults. The physical perspective that is contained in a photograph taken by a child can, however, be a reminder of how the world 'may' look from the perspective of a small body ('may' in quotation marks because we never only see our environment physically; we see it physically-socially-culturally). Likewise, when children make stories about their photos and tell them to the researcher, then, place is made for the child's voice supported by visual material. But it is an adult ear that is listening and an adult intellect that is interpreting. There is no reason to operate with a naïve concept of 'a children's perspective'. There are many detours on the way to children's innermost sensations, feelings, and experiences. Children's photos can form a 'bridge' between the adult and the world of the child. But one must not mistake the bridge and the 'country' that is difficult to access beyond the bridge/photographs.

On the other hand, neither is there any reason to disallow the fact that many photos are taken in a way that makes the adult aware and thoughtful. (For example, Wendy Ewald and Jim Hubbard stressed that the children had taught them a great deal about the medium in which they otherwise were 'experts' and about the lives of children.)

DECODING CHILDREN'S PHOTOGRAPHS

Simultaneously, the methodological discourse concerning the photograph has pointed out that a photography, after all, only ... shows a segment of time and space, that a photograph is always framed, and that there is always a perspective connected to it (Ewald and Lightfoot, 2001). In addition, encoding and decoding of a medium are not always identical processes (Hall, 1980).

Furthermore, the decoding of a photograph is always determined by several contextual conditions (for example, whether the photographer is present and what the photographer tells about the picture, the context in which the photo is seen – on a PC screen, in a newspaper, in a professional book, in a context with many other people or alone, etc.). As mentioned in the introduction, most photos are very much open to interpretation. This openness to interpretation and the concrete context in which interpretation takes place influences interpretation and understanding.

However, I find it important to allow the child photographers to be the first interpreters of their photos. In the best case, the children's comments and narratives can guide us towards what the children want to show and tell. Then we must hope that we adults can see and hear what the children show and tell, and that we can do this in a way that is not too far away from the children's intentions and creation of meaning.

But it is difficult to imagine that the adults' professionalism will not play a part in their understanding and interpretation of the children's photos and narratives. Architects will probably take a different view of children's photos than will teachers and social workers. Analogously, researchers will apply their theoretical and interpretative baggage. We do not see neutrally and photos do not show anything clearly and objectively (Becker, 1998).

In a certain way one can therefore experience and speak about interviews with children about their own photographs as being 'autodriven' (Clark, 1999), by which is meant that:

- A photo brings a reality into the interview that is based on the participants' perspective;
- The ice between the researcher and the child is quickly broken;
- Photos stimulate the memory – thoughts, feelings, actions and opinions are recalled;

- Photos quickly and easily elicit personal stories and everyday experiences;
- Photos give researchers a collection of non-verbal but valuable information.

Nevertheless one must understand that photo-elicitation is a method that can take many forms. The particular form is partly dependent on the conditions of origin of the photographic material (for example, historical point in time, who the photographer is). The form also partly depends on the research questions under study on which the individual project is based.

CAN PHOTO-DOCUMENTATION BE USEFUL IN DEVELOPING GENERALIZABLE KNOWLEDGE ABOUT CHILDHOOD?

Some kind of generalization could be made at the level at which one might interpret and elaborate about tendencies or patterns internal to the project (a fixed number of children makes it possible to talk about tendencies or patterns in the empirical material). At the same time, we realize 'a general child' or 'a general childhood' exists only as a construction and an abstract picture in our thoughts of children and society.

However, on the one hand, until such reflections are done, I would be cautious about making general conclusions from one project at one location. On the other hand, if you work carefully with the outcome from a photo-based researched project and relate the result to other projects and generally accepted knowledge about childhood, it is not impossible that a local empirical study based on children's photographs can be an important contribution to general narratives about children's lives and the conditions of childhood.

As far as I know, this issue has not been discussed seriously until now among those childhood researchers making visual studies with children. One reason could be that most researchers working with visual studies are primarily influenced by anthropology and micro-sociology rather than by (structural) social science. However, the question mentioned above seems important – today as well in the future, especially if there still will be a growing interest in visual studies based on children's photography.

PHOTO-ELICITED INTERVIEW WITH CHILDREN

Among the first to describe how photographs can be an integrated part of the interview process that has later been called photo-elicitation are the two anthropologists, father and son John and Malcolm Collier (Collier and Collier, 1986) and the sociologist Douglas Harper, who back in 1986 wrote an article entitled: 'Meaning and Work: A Study in Photo Elicitation' (Harper, 1986).[4]

However, both sources deal with the type of photo-elicitation that takes a point of departure in the photographs taken by fieldworkers in a locality or a place, and which are subsequently discussed with local informants. The researchers' phenomenological sensory perception is thus retained in the photograph and the informant provides an interpretation of the objects that can be seen in the picture.

However, the photos taken by children and which they then told about and which have been mentioned in this chapter are different. What is decisive for the interpretation is who has taken the photograph and the context the photo has been taken in, just as the context of the reception is crucial.

It is thus possible to speak of at least four different types of photo-elicitation (see Table 24.1) (all of which, by the way, can involve children in different ways). But only one form corresponds to the photo elicited interviews mentioned in the previous sections.

Table 24.1   Four different types of photo-elicitation

Interviews with a *starting point in already existing* photos but which are *foreign* to the informants Examples: • interviews around historical photos • interviews around documentary photos • interviews around advertising photos • interviews around other photos where the photographer is unknown	Interviews with a *starting point in the sociologist's or anthropologist's photos* (photographic field notes) from the context or locality under study and which the informants themselves come from or relate to
Interviews with a starting point in the informants' *own and already existing and known photos* Examples: • family album • any school photos • holiday photos and the like	Interviews with a *starting point in the informants' photos – taken recently or with a certain research topic* and associated research design Example: • the informants are asked to photograph either a tied and narrowly defined assignment or a relatively free assignment

The scheme shows that there exist several forms of photo-elicited interviews (one can also imagine projects that mix some of the forms mentioned). At the same time it draws attention to the fact that the detachment of the finished photograph from its context of origin has an impact on the interpretation of the photographic picture.

Can all types of photo-elicited interviews be regarded as an invitation to involvement and participation? Even though there cannot be a general answer to this, it is primarily this type of photo-elicited interview building on children's own photographic practice that is identified with children's involvement and participation (Driskell, 2002; Hart, 1997).[5]

Douglas Harper distinguished between photo-elicitation and photo-voice. He has argued that '... photo-elicitation has been more about generating knowledge, and photo-voice has had a subtext of empowerment; that is, a research process that is designed to empower those who traditionally were the focus of academic attention' (Harper, 2012: 155).

With the concepts of photo-elicitation and photo-voice we see that both methods invite cooperation and participation between researcher and informant. At the same time, it becomes clear that photo-elicitation,

while it invites participation, does not necessarily have empowerment as its target. Photo-voice also invites participation and, further, the method has empowerment as a goal.

CONCLUSION

The chapter began with a photo, and it will also conclude with a photo. I have chosen a photo and an accompanying narrative that sum up some of the important points made along the way. Once more I ask you to try and tell the story of this photo. What do you see?

A 9-year-old boy has taken the photo (Figure 24.5), which comes from the photo-project based on a study of children's everyday life and children's experience of their institutions that I mentioned earlier (Rasmussen and Smidt, 2002).

The photo-elicited interview began like this:

– 'Try and tell me something about the picture?'
– 'It's an old hideout that me and Troels built when we were in 1st grade and which has been totally vandalised ...'
– 'By whom?'

Figure 24.5   Concluding example of a child's photography from the project

– 'We think it was some drunken pigs because that's what one of the teachers told us. Some drunken idiots often come at the weekend. They go round the playground and throw bottles and things like that.'
– 'Do you often play in the hideout?'
– 'No, not any more. Because there are a lot of nails sticking out and there are cobwebs all over. So it's not especially nice to be out there.'
– 'Why did you take the picture?'
– 'Because we thought it was a pity that it should just stand there without getting a picture when it was something we spent most time on doing here.'
– 'How much time did you spend making it?'
– 'Oh, I don't know. I think it took a month and then it was completely finished ... and we swept every day and did all sorts of things. And then it was destroyed.'

Photo and narrative show several things. In the first place, they show that *children play a part in creating and staging their own lives.* The boys have created something meaningful, a hideout, which they have worked on for almost a month. The hideout has taken up the boys' physical and mental energies, and one senses that a lot of symbolic creativity has gone into its construction. But it is not only a hideout that can be played in that has been created. A significant place has also been made. The boys are the architects behind its significance, and they can tell about its imprint in words and pictures.

Second, the narrative shows that *children sometimes fight with adults in the arenas in which they both move about.* In this narrative the fight has a sad ending: adults vandalize the boys' hideout. The consequence is that the boys abandon it. This special aspect is extremely interesting because in the public sphere we mostly hear about children and young people vandalizing adults' things and property. But here we hear about the opposite.

Third, the narrative shows that when children get the opportunity to take photographs, *they simultaneously get the power and the means to communicate about key events in their everyday lives.* Even the way the ruined hideout has been photographed does not seem totally accidental: 'Something has gone absolutely wrong here'. The boy himself casually mentioned the symbolic crooked angle: 'I thought I'd take a creative photo'. Such creative expression offers a window to children's experience.

NOTES

1 It is not the intention to provide a complete picture of all projects based on children's photography, but to focus in on examples of different project types and on the experience and key points that I find general and important to pass on.

2 One can easily get an impression of both Ewald's and Hubbard's work through their websites on the internet.

3 In 'Growing Up in an Urbanizing World' (Chawla, 2002) the photo-documentation work on which Buss builds her project is similarly absolutely central. The book is a revival of UNESCO's old project, Growing up in Cities – a pioneer project from the 1970s by the influential urban planner Kevin Lynch, who was trying to understand the reasons why children and young people find their city a good place to grow up or who feel alien and disengaged. The book consists of a collection of article reports made by a team of experts in children's development and urban planning. They describe and analyse the relation between children and their urban environment in eight different countries: Argentina, Australia, India, Norway, Poland, South Africa, the UK and the USA. The focus is on low-income neighbourhoods and they are illustrated through children's involvement and participation with a view to making the cities more responsive to children's needs. The method that is repeated in the eight countries is photo-documentation and interviews. Researchers are asked to give disposable cameras to the children whose neighbourhoods and lives are being studied, to encourage the children to take pictures of the places in the local community that are most important to them – including those they do not like. They are then allowed to discuss and write commentaries on the pictures. The children can later organize and select their photos with a view to making an exhibition and creating public debate about city problems related to children (Chawla, 2002: 244).

4 Other and more recent texts that introduce photo-elicitation are Rose (2007), Lapenta (2011) and Harper (2012).

5 Driskell's book, which is entitled: *Creating Better Cities with Children and Youth – A Manual for Participation*, speaks about 'using a camera' and weights children's active role in connection with documentation.

REFERENCES

Alderson, P. (1995) *Listening to Children. Children, Ethics and Social Research.* Barkingside: Barnardos.

Banks, M. and Morphy, H. (eds.) (1997) *Rethinking Visual Anthropology.* New Haven and London: Yale University Press.

Banks, M. (2001) *Visual Methods in Social Research.* London: Sage.

Becker, H.S. (1998) 'Visual sociology, documentary photography, and photojournalism: It's (almost) all a matter of context', in J. Prosser (ed.), *Image-based Research: A Sourcebook for Qualitative Researchers.* London: Falmer Press.

Buss, S. (1995) 'Los Angeles from young people's angle of vision', *Children's Environment*, 12(3): 340–51.

Cele, S. (2006) *Communicating Place. Methods for Understanding Children's Experience of Place (Stockholm Studies in Human Geography).* ACTA/Stockholm University. Stockholm: Almqvist & Wiksell International.

Chawla, L. (ed.) (2002) *Growing Up in an Urbanising World.* London: Earthscan Publications/UNESCO Publishing.

Clark, C.D. (1999) 'The autodriven interview: A photographic viewfinder into children's experience', *Visual Sociology*, 14(1): 39–50.

Collier, J. and Collier, M. (1986) *Visual Anthropology: Photography as a Research Method.* Albuquerque: University of New Mexico Press.

Driskell, D. (2002) *Creating Better Cities with Children and Youth: A Manual for Participation.* London and Sterling, VA: Earthscan Publications, Ltd. and UNESCO Publishing.

Emmison, M. and Smith, P. (2000) *Researching the Visual: Images, Objects, Contexts and Interactions in Social and Cultural Inquiry.* London: Sage Publications.

Ewald, W. (1999) 'The Best Part of Me', *Double Take*, 5(1): 84–93.

Ewald, W. (2000) *Secret Games: Collaborative Works with Children, 1969–1999*. Zurich: Scalo.

Ewald, W. and Lightfoot, A. (2001) *I Wanna Take Me a Picture. Teaching Photography and Writing to Children*. Boston, MA: Beacon Press.

Freeman, M. and Mathison, S. (2009) *Researching Children's Experiences*. New York and London: The Guilford Press.

Gullestad, M. (1991) 'Hva legger jeg I begrebet barneperspektiv?', *Barn nr*, 1: 63–5.

Hall, S. (1980) 'Encoding/decoding', in S. Hall (ed.), *Culture, Media, Language*. London: Hutchinson, pp. 128–38.

Harper, D. (1986) 'Meaning and work: A study in photo elicitation', *Current Sociology*, 34(3): 24–46.

Harper, D. (2012) *Visual Sociology*. London and New York: Routledge.

Hart, R.A. (1997) *Children's Participation: The Theory and Practice of Involving Young Citizens in Community Development and Environmental Care*. London: UNICEF Earthscan Publications Ltd.

Hubbard, J. (1991) *Shooting Back*. San Francisco: Chronicle Books.

James, A. and Prout, A. (eds.) (1997) *Constructing and Reconstructing Childhood*. London and Washington, DC: Falmer Press.

Jensen, S.M. (2008) *Mellemrum. Om unges hverdagsliv, sociale identiteter og fællesskaber I forstaden, på landet og I byen*. Ph.D. afhandling Inst. f. Psykologi og uddannelsesforskning. RUC.

Kernan, M. (2005) *Using Digital Photography to Listen to Young Children's Perspectives of their Outdoor Play Experiences in Early Childhood Education Settings*. Paper presented at the Childhoods 2005 International Conference, University of Oslo, 29 June–3 July, 2005.

Kjørholt, A.T. (1991) 'Barneperspektivet', *Barn nr*, 1: 66–9.

Knowles, C. and Sweetman, P. (eds.) (2004) *Picturing the Social Landscape. Visual Methods and the Sociological Imagination*. London and New York: Routledge.

Lapenta, F. (2011) 'Some theoretical and methodological views on photo-elicitation', in E. Margolis and L. Pauwels (eds.), *The Sage Handbook of Visual Research Methods*. Los Angeles, London, New Delhi, Singapore, Washington, DC: Sage.

Leeuwen, T.V and Jewitt, C. (eds.) (2002) *Handbook of Visual Analysis*. London: Sage Publications.

Lysaght, P., Brown, I. and Westbrook, R. (2007) 'Voices of children: One lens … many views'. Paper presented at the Conference of the International Visual Sociology Association 2007.

Mayall, B. (2002) *Towards a Sociology for Childhood: Thinking from Children's Lives*. Buckingham, PA: Open University Press.

Meyer, F. (2010) *Der Weg entsteht im Gehen: Eine qualitative Einzelfallstudie zur Raumwahrnehmung und Mobilität von Jugendlichen mit Down Syndrom*. Bern, Berlin, Bruxelles, Frankfurt am Main, New York, Oxford, Wien: Peter Lang Verlagsgruppe.

Orellana, M.F. (1999) 'Space and place in an urban landscape: Learning from children's views of their social worlds', *Visual Sociology* 14: 73–89.

Prosser, J. (1998) 'The status of image-based research', in J. Prosser (ed.), *Image-Based Research: A Sourcebook for Qualitative Researchers*. Bristol, PA: Falmer Press, pp. 97–114.

Rasmussen, K. and Smidt, S. (2001) *Spor af børns institutionsliv*. København: Hans Reitzels Forlag.

Rasmussen, K. and Smidt, S. (2002) *Barndom i billeder*. København: Akademisk Forlag.

Rose, G. (2007) *Visual Methodologies; An Introduction to the Interpretation of Visual Materials*. Los Angeles, London, New Delhi, Singapore, Washington, DC: Sage.

Schafiyha, L. (1997) *Fotopädagogik und Fototerapie. Theorie, Metoden, Praxisbeispiele*. Weinheim und Basel: Beltz Verlag.

Schrantz, M. and Steiner-Löffler, U. (1998) 'Pupils using photographs in school self-evaluation', cited in J. Prosser, 'The status of image-based research', in Prosser (ed.), *Image-Based Research*. London: Falmer Press/ Taylor & Francis Group.

Seiter, E. (1993) *Sold Separately: Parents and Children in Consumer Culture*. New Brunswick, NJ: Rutgers University Press.

Sontag, S. (1985) *Fotografi – Essays Om Billede Og Virkelighed*. København: Fremad.

Sparrman, A. (2002) *Visuell kultur i barns vardagsliv – bilder, medier och praktiker*. Tema Barn: Linköpings universitet.

Staunæs, D. (1998) *Transitliv – Andre Perspektiver På Unge Flygtninge*. København: Politisk Revy.

Thomson, P. (ed.) (2008) *Doing Visual Research with Children and Young People*. London: Routledge.

Tiller, P.O. (1991) '"Barneperspektivet": Om å se og bli sett', *Barn nr*, 1: 72–7.

Wilhjelm, H. (2002) *Barn og omgivelser – virkelighet med flere fortolkninger*. Arkitekthøgskolen i Oslo.

Winter, I.W. (2004) *Hjem Og Hjemlighed – En Kulturfænomenologisk Feltvandring*. DPU.

25

Time-Use Studies

Lyn Craig

INTRODUCTION

Understanding the way individuals spend time is integral to understanding how their lives are lived. How time is used largely determines the progress, achievement, and well-being of individuals, families, communities, and societies (Ironmonger, 2006). There is growing recognition that information on how time is spent is essential for social and health scientists, policy makers, and the community at large. Time-use studies are a window on daily life that, almost uniquely, shows all the things that people actually do.

Time-use data are especially useful in showing activities that occur in the private sphere of the home. A great deal of statistical information is collected on market work, household expenditure, and labour force patterns, but few data sources explore other important aspects of people's lives, such as leisure, domestic, work and socializing with others. Time-use data are therefore also valuable in yielding information about people whose lives are substantially outside the labour market. For example, time use studies have been very useful in exploring the unpaid work of women within the home.

More recently, attention has turned to the potential of time-use research as a tool which can illuminate the lives of children.

Time-use study is increasingly seen to be essential to a full understanding of children's lives (Baxter, 2006; Ben-Arieh and Ofir, 2002; Folbre et al., 2005; Harding, 1997; Ironmonger, 2006). It can offer an objective measure of what children do, where they do it, and who they do it with. The data are useful not only in revealing the lives of children as they are lived, but also have the potential to show associations between early time use and later outcomes. In addition, they can show how parents' time use influences what children do in infancy, and how they use time as they grow. They can highlight children's participation in society and facilitate international and intra-national comparisons. The available information has a wide range of potential applications, both practical and academic. For those interested in child well-being, time-use study is crucial to knowing how children are faring and how their outcomes compare across groups (Harding, 1997).

This chapter begins by tracing contemporary interest in how children use time. The following sections review the existing literature on children's time use derived from both primary and secondary sources. Primary sources comprise time-use studies in which children are the subjects and secondary sources comprise studies of parental time use. In the interests of flow, studies of parental time that provide insight into children's time use will be reviewed first. This is followed by a discussion of time-use research, including the inherent methodological challenges and limitations of conducting time-use studies in which children are the subjects. The chapter concludes with a discussion of why there is a need for more comprehensive, methodologically sound studies into children's time use.

CONTEMPORARY INTERST IN CHILDREN AND TIME

Differing views about children's 'proper' time use have coincided with powerful assumptions about children's roles throughout history and the 'value' of children's time (Aries, 1962; Zelizer, 1985). Concepts of how children should spend their time vary enormously over time and place (Vogler, Morrow and Woodhead, 2009). Childhood has been seen very differently at different times in history and in different cultural contexts. These cultural constructs have profound effects on children's lives. Beliefs about the nature of childhood and corollary expectations about children's 'proper' behaviour can change parents, families and communities' perceptions of what children do and how they spend their time.

Underlying the current interest in what children do is the now ubiquitous agreement that childhood is a distinctive phase of life. Children differ from adults in needs and capabilities, and therefore in the way they can and should spend their time. Beliefs about what constitutes appropriate use of time by children are influenced by normative ideas about child development and the time-dependent maturation process. Childhood is

where the life course starts. There is widespread cultural agreement that the way children spend time in their early years will affect their progress through later transitions (Baxter et al., 2007; Zick, Bryant and Osterbacka, 2001).

Certain activities and pastimes are seen as more developmentally appropriate than others. Children are increasingly segregated from adult activities, especially through formal schooling. The introduction of compulsory schooling throughout the industrialized world has occurred alongside acceptance that the most appropriate goal of childhood is to acquire an education. A key responsibility of contemporary parenthood is to help one's children build human capital (England and Folbre, 1997) – that is, to ensure they develop skills and abilities that will equip and qualify them for gainful employment. Fundamental are literacy and numeracy. For children in the modern West, formal education is their work. A major concern is that if children are not in school, they are not experiencing a proper childhood. At the same time, there is concern that young children are not getting enough parental attention. Because mothers entered the paid work force in large numbers in the middle of the twentieth century, there has been disquiet about the use of substitute care for young children, a worry bolstered by strong reinforcement of cultural prescriptions about mothering (Aries, 1962; Casey, 1989; Ehrenreich and English, 1989).

INSIGHTS FROM STUDIES OF PARENTAL TIME USE

Studies of parental time use provide great insight into how children spend their time. More often than not, this knowledge is derived from studies of maternal time, because mothers spend more time caring for children than do fathers. Among the issues explored in these studies are the effects of maternal employment on time with children, gender differences in parental time use, education as a determinant of parental care time, and parental time investments and later child outcomes.

Maternal employment

A great deal of time-use research has investigated the effects of maternal employment on maternal time with children. Findings indicate that in most Western countries, average parental time spent with children has gone up over time. Even as families are getting smaller, children are spending longer in day care and school, and mothers are more likely to be employed outside the home, parental care time has not fallen (Sayer, Bianchi and Robinson, 2004). Bryant and Zick (1996a) reported similar levels of parental activity time by white parent families in the USA in the 1920s and the 1970s. Bianchi reported similar findings over the period from 1965 to 1998 for time spent with children under the age of 18 (Bianchi, 2000). The impact of structural change in female employment practices on time with children has been outweighed by behavioural change in time mothers spend with children (Craig, 2007a; Sandberg and Hofferth, 2001; Sayer et al., 2004). That is, even as more mothers entered the paid work force, they have changed other aspects of their behaviour so that they are able to allocate more time to children. Some of the changes may involve shifting parent–child time to maximize involvement on weekends or holidays (Craig, 2007a; Yeung, Sandberg, Davis-Kean and Hofferth, 2001). Even within a given time period, however, mothers do not reduce the amount of time they spend with children by the same amount of time as they spend in paid work. Maternal childcare is reduced by far less than an hour for every hour the mother works (Bianchi, 2000; Bittman, Craig and Folbre, 2004; Booth et al., 2002; Bryant and Zick, 1996; Hofferth, 2001; Nock and Kingston, 1988; Sandberg and Hofferth, 2001). Market work and childcare are prioritized, and other activities are curtailed. Mothers make time for employment and childcare by cutting back on sleep, housework, and individual leisure (Bianchi, 2005; Craig, 2007b). Also, employed mothers make compositional changes in their time with children. When they work, 'quality time', in particular, is preserved or protected. Active, engaged childcare time is not reduced as much as non-engaged supervision (Bryant and Zick, 1996; Craig, 2007b; Sandberg and Hofferth, 2001).

Gender differences in parental time use

Gender comparisons have been a large focus of investigations into parental time use. Although mothers still are much more likely to perform the major part of family care, fathers' input is growing too. However, fathers spend a higher proportion of the time they are with children in playing, reading, and talking to children than do mothers. Mothers are still responsible for most of the routine and physical aspects of childcare (Craig, 2006a; Craig and Mullan, 2011a). Also, fathers' increased care seems mainly to take the form of joining in care alongside their wives, rather than taking over and caring for children alone, without their spouse present (Craig, 2006a; Craig and Mullan, 2011a). Studies in the USA found co-resident fathers with wives in paid employment spend slightly more time with their children than men with stay-at-home wives (Fisher, McCulloch and Gershuny, 1999; Gershuny and Robinson, 1988; Sandberg and Hofferth, 2001). However, others have found that fathers' time allocation is not closely linked to maternal employment. Nock and Kingston (1988) found no difference in fathers' time with children according to whether or not their wives worked. Fathers have been found to be somewhat more involved in childcare when non-parental childcare is used (Bittman et al., 2004; Craig, 2007b), but changes to male behaviour are not as marked as the compensatory time adjustments made by mothers (Bianchi, 2000; Bryant and Zick, 1996).

This finding highlights the importance of research which exploits the 'context' information in time diaries, to focus on whom children are with. Although some researchers acknowledge that whom children are with while performing activities may be important (see for example, Fuligni and Brooks-Gunn, 2004; Mullan, 2008), this has rarely been directly addressed in time-use research studies from the child's perspective. The few studies that have paid attention to this issue have explored the relationship between children's gender and the time that they are reading or are doing domestic chores when with their mother or father. This research has shown that time together with both mothers and fathers goes up as children grow (Bryant and Zick, 1996; Mullan, 2008; Stafford and Yeung, 2005; Yeung et al., 2001; Zick et al., 2001). Increasing maternal work hours have been found to have no significant impact on the time that children spend in a range of activities when with their fathers (Yeung et al., 2001). However, *time alone* with fathers does increase with maternal work hours (Mullan, 2008).

Some research has focused on the parental time inputs of single mothers, mostly finding no difference in single and couple mothers' time use, particularly when demographic variables are controlled (Craig, 2005; Craig and Mullan, 2011b; Kalenkoski, Ribar and Stratton, 2006; Kendig and Bianchi, 2008).

Education

Another determinant of parental care time that has been extensively investigated is education. Higher education is associated with more parental time spent with children, by both mothers and fathers, and more time in the activities that develop children's human capital (Craig, 2006b; Sayer, Gauthier and Furstenberg, 2004). Parental education has been found to be positively correlated with children's time reading and doing school work (Bianchi and Robinson, 1997; Hofferth and Sandberg, 2001).

Parental time investments and later child outcomes

An important area of study would be to explore the relationship between the time parents and children spend in activities together, and later child outcomes. For example, Flouri and Buchanan (2004) drew connections between the time spent by fathers and mothers with their children, and children's later attainment at school. They used longitudinal data from the UK National Child Development Study (NCDS), an ongoing study of some 17,000 children who were born in England, Wales, and Scotland in one week in 1958. However, few longitudinal studies of time use are available, as is discussed in more detail below.

STUDYING CHILDREN'S TIME USE

Much of the knowledge we have of how children spend their time is gleaned from studies of parental time use. Although this research has yielded considerable information, awareness has grown in recent years of the importance of engaging directly with children and young people in order to gain greater insight into their subjective understandings of their world. Time-use research is a potentially very useful approach in this regard. Nevertheless, time-use studies in which children directly provide the data are plagued by numerous methodological concerns.

Studies of children's time are few and limited largely because data sources are underdeveloped and partial (Ben-Arieh and Ofir, 2002). Research in this area has been conducted from a range of disciplinary perspectives and addresses disparate aspects of time use. Most research into children's time use has focused on particular activities or populations. Information that captures the whole range of children's activities over a representative sample is much sparser. Agendas, concepts, methods, and interests vary, and as a result, the studies that are available give only a fragmented picture of children's time use. As a result, there is a strong call for children's time use to be studied on a larger scale, on a regular basis and in a way that would allow studies to be collated and harmonized (Baxter, 2006; Ben-Arieh and Ofir, 2002; Fisher and Gershuny, 2008; Ironmonger, 2006). However, there are barriers to furthering this goal. Studies of children's time use are rare partly because of issues that are common to all time-use data collection, and partly because of issues peculiar to children.

TIME-USE RESEARCH

The main methods for collecting time-use data are observation, experience sampling, stylized questionnaires, and time diaries. *Observing people at first hand* is potentially useful, but is very expensive to undertake, can be intrusive, and will miss behaviour that is not actually witnessed by researchers (Ben-Arieh and Ofir, 2002). The *experience-sampling* method involves alerting subjects by a beeper or pager to record their activity at random intervals (Larson, 1989). This method is potentially useful and is relatively non-burdensome. Conversely, it also can be expensive and intrusive and could miss infrequent activities. *Stylized questionnaires* involve asking respondents to estimate how they spent their time during a certain period (for example, the previous day, or in a typical week). This method is relatively simple, inexpensive, and non-intrusive, but can be unreliable. Recall bias is a problem. Some activities may be overestimated or underreported for reasons including social desirability (Kan, 2008; Robinson and Gershuny, 1994). For example, men have been found to overestimate the time that they spend doing housework and parents to overestimate the time that they spend reading to their children (Baxter, 2006; Hofferth, 1999). It can be difficult to estimate time duration from memory, perhaps particularly so for children.

The *time diary*, in which respondents record all the activities they undertake over a certain period (usually 24 or 48 hours), is widely regarded as the most reliable and valid method of time-use data collection (Juster, Ono and Stafford, 2003; Juster and Stafford, 1991; Kan, 2008; Robinson and Gershuny, 1994). Time diaries require respondents to list all their activities in sequential order, and thus provide a comprehensive and exhaustive table of all the things that are done over the time period. These surveys can be conducted at a national level, and some countries have done so over a number of years. For example, the time use of Australians has been investigated by the Australian Bureau of Statistics (ABS) in nationally representative Time-Use Surveys (TUS) conducted in 1992, 1997 and 2006. In these three surveys, all members of sampled households over the age of 15 were required to complete a time diary and to record all they did for two 24-hour periods. Activities were classified into nine broad categories – personal care, employment, education, domestic activities, child care, purchasing, voluntary work and care, social and community interaction, and recreation and leisure – with up to 50 subcategories within each broad category.

Such national time-diary surveys can provide a great deal of information. They collect a range of demographic data and take account of seasonal variation and whether or not the diary-day was a typical one or a holiday. Because weekend activities are often very different from weekday activities, they obtain a cross-section of representative days of the week. They typically ask where respondents are. Because people often do more than one thing at once, many include columns asking 'What else were you doing?' to capture 'secondary' and 'tertiary' activity. In addition, as with the Australian Bureau of Statistics Time-Use Surveys, many national surveys collect data from all household members over a certain age, so researchers can analyse what multiple members of households are doing, how much time they spend in each other's company, which activities are done together and which are done separately. However, such comprehensive surveys impose a heavy burden on the respondent. Others, such as the American Time-Use Survey (ATUS), lessen this burden by requiring only one member per household to respond. Time diaries can be left with the respondent for self-completion, or can be filled out by an interviewer, either face-to-face or over the telephone. The method chosen has implications for respondent burden and for accuracy and social desirability bias (Stewart, 2002). Most time-dairy surveys are conducted at one point in time. More rarely, longitudinal studies collect time diaries at repeat intervals and allow for tracking the time allocation of the same individuals over time (Juster et al., 2003).

The data from national time-use surveys have provided invaluable and rich snapshots of daily life. Moreover, they offer opportunities for cross-national comparisons. To make this possible, the Centre for Time Use Research (CTUR) at Oxford University collates and harmonizes surveys from more than 30 countries as part of the Multinational Time-Use Study (MTUS). Unfortunately, few of the time-use surveys collect data on the time use of children. Some countries do include children in their national samples. For example, the Italian official statistical agency ISTAT in 1989 and 2002–2003 collected information on all members of sampled households down to the age of 3 years. The UK national survey collects data on children as young as 5 years of age. However, most national surveys collect data on respondents from the age of 15 or 18 and over (Fisher and Gershuny, 2008). The Centre for Time-Use Research has laid the groundwork for future comparative work should more data become available, splitting the latest Multinational Time-Use Study versions into adult files (diarists aged 18 and older) and child and youth supplement files (diarists aged less than 18). Currently, the Diaries from Children and Young People (DCYP) supplement only contains diaries

from the UK and Germany, but more will be added progressively. Eventually, the archive will facilitate comparisons of younger people cross-nationally, or with adults in the same country or time period (Fisher and Gershuny, 2008). As more countries add children and young people to their diary data collection, the DCYP supplement will become a more and more valuable resource.

Methodological adaptations in studies of children's time use

Studies of children's time use often require methodological adaptations from those used in studies of adults' time use. These adaptations are usually to the format and content of time diaries and have implications for data quality and comparability. A further methodological issue that arises in children's time-use studies is whether it is children or parents who complete the time diary.

Diaries for young people are presented differently to standard adult diaries, commonly having different format and instructions (Fisher and Gershuny, 2008). In setting up the instrument, survey designers will try to use examples that are relevant to young people. They may use pictures and phrase the instructions in simple, easy-to-follow language. Sometimes supplementary use is made of technology such as portable beepers which remind the children or young people to record their activity (Ben-Arieh and Ofir, 2002; Larson, 1989). Usually, children and young people are asked to fill out 'light' diaries which have fewer details than full adult diaries. Light diaries are often pre-coded and require respondents simply to mark a box indicating their activity, rather than to state what they are doing. Many do not ask young people to record who they were with, where they were and what else they were doing at the same time as the main activity, as most full instruments do.

Although these adaptations make it easier for young people to participate, and therefore may improve response rates, such changes can limit opportunities to compare across age groups. For example, it may appear that children have fewer episodes than adults, when in fact this is an artefact of different diary instruments (Fisher and Gershuny, 2008). Similarly, the light diaries that record only one activity at a time will miss 'secondary' activities. Thus the full duration of some activities will be underestimated, and studies looking for displacement of one activity by another may miss situations in which activities (for example, being online and watching television) are undertaken simultaneously (Vandewater, Bickham and Lee, 2006). The implicit or explicit assumption that daily time has to add up to 24 hours, and that therefore spending time on some activities means less time in others, has some merit, but is not wholly true.

Children as young as 8 and 9 years have contributed to self-report time diaries in some studies (Bianchi and Robinson, 1997; Fisher and Gershuny, 2008). However, the direct participation of children in time-diary surveys is rare, and usually adults fill out the diary on the child's behalf. If the research is conducted outside the home, teachers or care workers can be asked to complete the diary. More typically, diaries are completed by parents. In practice, this is usually mothers. For example, the Growing Up In Australia Longitudinal Study of Australian Children (LSAC) in 2004 started collecting data on two large cohorts of children – infants under 1 year old and other young children aged 4–5 years. The study has a Time-Use Diary (TUD) nested within it. The TUD collects details of the activities of the study children over two 24-hour periods, one a specified weekday and one a specified weekend day. To cut down the respondent burden, the diaries are 'light' and set out 26 pre-coded activities, to a detail level of 15 minutes (Baxter, 2007). The longitudinal nature of the survey means it will eventually yield a great deal of knowledge on children's development and outcomes, including associations between their use of time and other outcomes.

There is a drawback in reliance on parents' reports of children's activities, however. There are gaps in information if parents are not in the constant company of their children. In LSAC there have been problems relating to missing data, especially for the older group, because these children were more likely than the infants to spend a portion of their day in non-parental care (Baxter, 2007). Similarly, in a study of US children, Hofferth and Sandberg (2001) categorized day care as an activity. They found that children who spend more time in day care spend less time in structured and family activities such as church and eating, and in sleep, watching television, play, and reading (Hofferth and Sandberg, 2001). But this conclusion ignores the likelihood that children do many of these things at day care. They may do less of these things together with their parents, but do them in the company of others. Likewise, the pre-coded LSAC does not elicit information on what is done by children while at day care; simply how long children attend (Baxter, 2007).

Capturing the time use of older children or adolescents during periods that they are not under any adult supervision at all is even more problematic. Parents do not necessarily know what children do in their absence (Mullan, 2008; Zuzanek, 2000). Ben-Arieh and Ofir (2002) found that many research papers using time-use data did not even discuss the issue of who provided the information. They caution that this omission is serious, given that some studies relied solely on parents' information even though children spent very little time in their company at all (Gauthier and Furstenberg, 2005; Larson and Richards, 1994).

Ben-Arieh and Ofir (2002) strongly argued that the ideal for researchers would be to elicit information from children themselves. It is now widely recognized that children have valuable insights into their own lives, and there is a developing preference for letting them, as research participants, report on their own experience (Neale and Flowerdew, 2003). Children are not just adults-in-waiting, but are already-present human beings, with their own legitimate perspectives on their own lives (Qvortrup, 1994). Social constructionist research with children emphasizes children's agency and the importance of understanding context in research with children about time (Vogler et al., 2009).

Directly incorporating children's views is not always practicable, however. Collecting time-use data from young people differs from collecting time-use data from adults; and the younger the child is, the more challenging the issues are. Very young children cannot accurately report their own activities. To recall or describe their time use meaningfully, children need to have an understanding of the concept of time (Goldstone and Goldfarb, 1966; Timmer, Eccles and O'Brien, 1985). Children's grasp of time changes as they pass through developmental stages, and only begins when they start to recognize temporal order and gain the ability to describe events in sequence (Nelson and Fivush, 2004). Retrospective recall is often not reliable for children (Orbach and Lamb, 2007). It is necessary to take account of children's developing capability as they grow.

Age of child and time-use research

In an extensive investigation into the current literature on time use from the child's perspective, Ben-Arieh and Ofir (2002) found almost nothing on the time use of infants and young children under age 3. The Longitudinal Study of Australian Children (LSAC) makes an important and ongoing contribution to the reduction of this gap. A few studies of American children have included children as young as age 3 (Bianchi and Robinson, 1997; Mauldin and Meeks, 1990), but there are more studies on 6–11-year-olds, and even more on adolescents (Alsaker, Flammer and Schaffner, 2002; Flammer, Alsaker and Noacke, 1999; Larson, 2001; Zuzanek, 2000).

Because children's capacity to understand time and to report on it increases as they grow, adolescents are unsurprisingly the most researched age group in regard to children's time use and daily activities. As noted, a few national studies include adolescents. In addition, there are some researcher-led studies that cover virtually all aspects of adolescents' time use and activities (Ben-Arieh and Ofir, 2002). However, for children of all ages, most existing time-use studies focus on specific issues, addressing the relationship between time use and particular behaviours, skills, and risk factors.

Non-representative samples

The composition of the research sample has an important influence on the generalizability of the research findings, and few studies of children's time use are drawn from nationally representative samples. Studies that focus on particular groups often emphasize particular activities, such as reading or media use, or particular outcomes, such as depression or obesity. Pointing out that only a comparatively small number of studies explore children's overall activities or their routine daily experiences, Ben-Arieh and Ofir (2002) argue that the focus on separate activities and common use of small non-representative samples means there is currently incomplete knowledge on children's lives, activities, and time use.

Focused studies

The most straightforward thing to measure in time-use studies is duration of time spent in a particular activity. Most small-scale focused studies collect information only on main activities. A justification is that the longer a child is exposed to a particular activity and context, the greater the absorption of knowledge, skills, and competencies that it affords (Larson and Verma, 1999). A drawback is that this type of research offers knowledge about certain activities, but it is incomplete in scope, ungeneralizable in application, and missing a contextual base. Focused studies also often lack some of the demographic variables that could be of interest. They cannot yield information about the other activities that precede, follow, or coincide with the activity of central concern, even if such information is later thought to be important in further illuminating the research question.

Research topic

Furthermore, certain activities have garnered much more research attention than others, particularly in Western countries. Social anxiety about children being in non-parental care when they are small sits alongside concern that they are not in school when older. Concerns that they are too hurried and over-scheduled co-exist with concerns they are not using their time appropriately and therefore are wasting educational opportunities (Daly, 1996; Larson, 2001). Thus the major foci are leisure activities, the use of technology, particularly television and the internet, sport and physical activity, studying, school work, and reading (Alsaker et al., 2002; Bryant and Zick, 1996; Fitzgerald, 2004; Flammer et al., 1999; Harrell et al., 1997; Mullan, 2008; Vandewater et al., 2006; Vandewater, Shim and Caplovitz, 2004; Wake, Hesketh and Waters, 2003).

Investigating the leisure time of a Grade 4 class of American children, for example, one research team found that children's after-school time was spent largely in leisure activities that they chose to do, not in extra school work (Newman et al., 2003). Others have found that an increase in internet use was accompanied by reduced television viewing but that such a change actually stimulated newspaper reading, radio listening, and socializing with friends (Lee and Kuo, 2002). Computer-game and internet use have, however, been found to be negatively associated with good sleep patterns (Van den Bulck, 2004).

Vandewater et al. (2006) assessed whether children's television use interferes with time spent in more developmentally appropriate activities. They found that television viewing was associated with decreased homework

time and decreased time in creative play, but that it did not seem to interfere with time spent reading or in active play. Harrell et al. (1997) looked at the association between school-age children's leisure-time activities and a number of health-related risk factors. Similarly, there is a growing body of research investigating associations among children's activity, media use, and body weight (Vandewater et al., 2004; Wake et al., 2003).

Demographic variables of interest in studies of children's time use

The main demographic variables that have been investigated in studies of children's time allocation are age, gender, maternal employment, and family structure. Children's age has been found to be negatively associated with time spent reading and playing, and positively related to time spent doing domestic and school work (Bianchi and Robinson, 1997; Hofferth and Sandberg, 2001; Mauldin and Meeks, 1990; Mullan, 2008).

There are substantial gender differences in the time that children spend in housework, television watching, reading, and leisure activities (Bianchi and Robinson, 1997; Carvalho, 2002; Douthitt, 2000; Hofferth and Sandberg, 2001; Mauldin and Meeks, 1990; Mullan, 2008). The children of employed mothers in the UK have been found to spend more time alone with their father and to spend more of this time watching television (Mullan, 2008).

Research has also identified differences in children's time use by family structure, some of which compound the effects of gender. For example, a study of children in California found that those living with two parents spent increasingly less time in domestic work as their family income rose, but the domestic work of the children of single parents did not vary with family income. As a consequence of both higher levels of paid and unpaid work, the daughters of single parents were found to have less leisure and less time in school activities than children in two-parent families (Douthitt, 1991, 2000).

The effects of neighbourhood on children's time use

More recently, the effects of neighbourhood and environment on children's time use has become a matter of research interest. Particularly for adolescents, there is concern that particular neighbourhoods engender greater risk-taking or dangerous behaviours (Brooks-Gunn et al., 1997; Kurz, 2002). Neighbourhood issues interact with those of race/ethnicity or socio-economic status. In the USA, black children, those with a single parent, and those who are of lower socio-economic status have been found to have poorer health outcomes, to spend less time in organized sport activities, and to spend more time watching television than other children (Brandes, 2007; Hofferth and Sandberg, 2001; Lareau, 2000). If parents are concerned about children's safety they may not let them play and exercise unsupervised. Sayer and Dwyer (2009) used longitudinal data from the US Panel Study of Income Dynamics' (PSID) Child Development Supplement (CDS) collected in 1997 on a sample of 3563 children aged 12 and younger, and followed up in 2002, to investigate links between neighbourhoods, children's time use, and health outcomes. They found that children in more affluent areas spent more time in active sport, school work, and housework and less time watching television and sleeping than children in poorer areas (Sayer and Dwyer, 2009). Time-use study has also been used to research children's exposure to environmental hazards, finding that 5–12-year-old children spend most of their time indoors at home and concluding that risk assessments should also focus on indoor hazards (Robinson and Thomas, 1991; Silvers et al., 1994).

Children's time use and later child outcomes

A developing research interest is in linking children's own time use to later outcomes, including health and well-being (Harding, 1997; McHale, Crouter and Tucker, 2001). This line of enquiry can complement studies of parental time use and child outcomes. Spending more time in structured leisure activities is associated with fewer depressive symptoms in childhood and adolescence, although the relationship may differ with the age and stage of development (Desha et al., 2005). Time-use studies provide one approach to examining the association between childhood depression and activity participation. However, confidence about causal links between time use and depression, for example, would require more longitudinal data from sources such as the PSID child supplement (CDS) in the USA or the LSAC in Australia.

Comparative studies of children and young people's time use

There is a need for much more comparative research into children and young people's time use. Most cross-national studies have been done in the first world. A comparison of Canadian, Dutch, and Finnish teenagers' time-use data showed that the two most popular free-time activities in all three countries were watching television and socializing with friends, but there were a number of differences among the countries. Canadian teens spent longer in physical leisure than did teens in the Netherlands and in Finland. As well, Finnish teens reported spending two to almost three times more time reading than adolescents in the two other countries (Zuzanek, 2000).

American teens have been found to spend less time on school work than teens in other industrialized countries. American teenagers have more free time, and they spend much of it watching television or socializing with friends compared with teens in Asia (Larson, 2001). Larson found that spending large amounts of time in these activities was related to negative developmental outcomes. However, more of young people's discretionary time is now structured, consisting of voluntary activities like arts, sports, and organizations – activities that may foster initiative, identity, and other positive developmental outcomes (Larson, 2001).

In an important International Labour Organization (ILO) study of children's activities, Rodgers and Standing (1981) investigated the time children spent in domestic work, non-domestic work, non-monetary work, bonded labour, wage labour, schooling, idleness, recreation and leisure, and reproductive activities. They found that participation in productive activities was not all negative for children, but that, as others have also pointed out, enforced labour is a different story (Patrinos and Psacharopoulos, 1995; Rodgers and Standing, 1981; UNICEF, 1992). Industrialization and schooling have been found to be associated with a substantial reduction of children's time spent on household production and market work. As these activities become fewer, school work time increases (Larson and Verma, 1999). Family size, gender, and birth order may also be implicated (Edmonds, 2006; Garcia, 2006). Children in the Philippines have been found to spend more time in market work and household production and less time in school the more siblings they have, with the findings particularly strong for boys with a large number of younger siblings (DeGraff, Bilsborrow and Herrin, 1992).

Interest persists in investigating how children in developing countries spend their time, particularly in the time that they spend in productive activity and labour. However, the area remains significantly under-researched, because data are not available. To a great extent, this gap reflects the difficulty of conducting time-use surveys in developing countries. The difficulties are compounded when the research target is children (Esquivel et al., 2008; World Vision, 2006).

Research on children's time use requires methodological adaptations that limit the depth and breadth of data collected but that are nonetheless essential if data are to be collected at all. Thus, even though research on children's time use is uncoordinated, ad hoc, and largely novel, it has yielded many interesting insights.

FUTURE DIRECTIONS

Recent approaches to research concerning children have moved away from seeing children as in a state of becoming adult to seeing them as interesting research subjects in their own right. It is now widely accepted that children themselves have valuable insights and are experts on their own lives. Use of a combination of methods, particularly observation combined with data gathered directly from children, may be useful as it leads to rich findings (Ben-Arieh and Ofir, 2002).

Time-use studies offer a rich and growing opportunity to explore under-researched aspects of children's lives and under-researched populations of children. This form of research has great potential to provide researchers, policy makers, and society at large with greater insights into how children and young people live their lives, which has implications for their health and well-being. Children's time is regarded as a phenomenon that should be understood and managed. Research their time use gives insight about children's lives as they lead them. It is a window on children's experience and indeed a glimpse at the nature of childhood itself. Moreover, such research has long-term significance because the way that children spend time in the early years will affect their progress through later transitions. Nevertheless, it is evident that such studies are few and limited and that knowledge about children's everyday activities and the way in which different patterns of activity affect children's well-being is insufficient.

Several issues should be considered in order to fully exploit the potential of time-use research in understanding children's lives. Ideally, nationally representative studies of children's time use are required, to give insight into the well-being and outcomes of the nation's children as a whole. Researchers should ensure that their sample includes data from children from birth on and that the protocol covers the full range of daily activities. Where practicable, time diaries should be completed by children and young people themselves. In many instances, however, parents would be required to complete the time diaries. Moreover, it is important that these studies collect data on a range of socio-demographic variables, which also may require parental input. The challenge is to ensure that meeting the goals set out above are weighed against overburdening respondents and those charged with designing, administering, and managing the research.

How children spend their time and the appropriateness of what they do will vary from place to place. Hence, cross-national studies of children's time use are important assets in understanding the significance of culture in children's lives. Although the need is widely noted, most countries have very limited information on the time use of children. Furthermore, the time-use surveys that many countries do conduct are underutilized. As a mode of enquiry, time-use studies are expensive and thorough. There is a need to emphasize the potential of these data sources and a great need to expand upon them to include children.

Time-use research has the potential to yield great insights into the lives of children and young people. However, it also poses unique challenges specific to the method and peculiar to research on children and young people.

REFERENCES

Alsaker, F.D., Flammer, A. and Schaffner, B. (2002) 'Time-use in adolescence: The role of age, gender, and culture', in I. Colozzi and G. Giovannini (eds.), *Unprotected Time of Young People in Europe*. Faenza: Homeless Book, pp. 49–66.

Aries, P. (1962) *Centuries of Childhood*. New York: Vintage Books.

Baxter, J. (2006) 'Patterns of time use over the lifecourse: What we know and what we need to know', Time Use and Gender Seminar. Sydney: University of New South Wales.

Baxter, J. (2007) 'Children's time use in the Longitudinal Study of Australian Children: Data quality and analytical issues in the 4-year cohor', Technical Paper No.4. Melbourne, Australian Institute of Family Studies.

Baxter, J.E., Gray, M., Alexander, M., Strazdins, L. and Bittman, M. (2007) 'Mothers and fathers with young children: Paid employment, caring and wellbeing', Social Policy Research Paper No. 30. Canberra: Department of Families, Community Services and Indigenous Affairs.

Ben-Arieh, A. and Ofir, A. (2002) 'Time for (more) time-use studies: studying the daily activities of children', *Childhood*, 9(2): 225–48.

Bianchi, S.M. (2000) 'Maternal employment and time with children: Dramatic change or surprising continuity?', *Demography*, 37(4): 401–14.

Bianchi, S. (2005) *What Gives When Mothers are Employed?, Time Use and Economic Well-Being*. New York: The Levy Economics Institute of Bard College.

Bianchi, S.M. and Robinson, J.P. (1997) What did you do today? Children's use of time, family composition and the acquisition of social capital, *Journal of Marriage and the Family*, 59(2): 332–4.

Bittman, M., Craig, L. and Folbre, N. (2004) 'Packaging care: What happens when parents utilize non-parental child care', in N. Folbre and M. Bittman (eds.), *Family Time: The Social Organization of Care*. London: Routledge, pp. 171–94.

Booth, C., Clarke-Stewart, A., Vandell, D., McCartney, K. and Owen, M. (2002) 'Child-care Usage and Mother-Infant "Quality Time"', *Journal of Marriage and the Family*, 64(1): 16–26.

Brandes, A.H. (2007) 'Leisure time activities and obesity in school-aged inner city African American and Hispanic children', *Pediatric Nursing*, 33(2): 97–102.

Brooks-Gunn, J., Duncan, G.J., Leventhal, T. and Aber, J.L. (1997) 'Lessons learned and future directions for research on the neighborhoods in which children live', in J. Brooks-Gunn, G.J. Duncan and J.L. Aber (eds.), *Neighborhood Poverty: Vol. 1. Context and Consequences for Children*. New York: Russell Sage Foundation, pp. 279–97.

Bryant, W.K. and Zick, C.D. (1996) 'An examination of parent-child shared time', *Journal of Marriage and the Family*, 58(1): 227–37.

Carvalho, M.J.S. (2002) *Children Time Use and Gender*. Paper presented at the International Sociological

Association Congress, Brisbane, Australia, July.

Casey, J. (1989) *The History of the Family*. Oxford: Basil Blackwell.

Craig, L. (2005) 'The money or the care? A comparison of couple and sole parent households' time allocation to work and children', *Australian Journal of Social Issues*, 40(4): 521–40.

Craig, L. (2006a) 'Does father care mean fathers share? A comparison of how mothers and fathers in intact families spend time with children', *Gender & Society*, 20(2): 259–81.

Craig, L. (2006b) 'Parental education, time in work and time with children: An Australian time-diary analysis', *British Journal of Sociology*, 57: 553–75.

Craig, L. (2007a) *Contemporary Motherhood: The Impact of Children on Adult Time*. Aldershot: Ashgate Publishing.

Craig, L. (2007b) 'How employed mothers in Australia find time for both market work and childcare', *Journal of Family and Economic Issues*, 28(1): 69–87.

Craig, L. and Mullan, K. (2011a) 'How mothers and fathers share childcare: A cross-national time-diary comparison', *American Sociological Review*, 76: 834–61.

Craig, L. and Mullan, K. (2011b) 'Lone and couple mothers' childcare time within context in four countries', *European Sociological Review*, 28: 512–26.

Daly, K.J. (1996) *Families and Time: Keeping Pace in a Hurried Culture*. Newberry Park, CA: Sage Publications.

DeGraff, D.S., Bilsborrow, R.E. and Herrin, A.N. (1992) *The Implications of High Fertility for Children's Time Use in the Philippines*. Population Council Seminar, New York: Population Council.

Desha, L., Ziviani, Nicholson, J. and Martin, G. (2005) *What Underlying Features of Children's Time use are Related to Depressive Symptoms? Study Design*, CDS-II Early Results Workshop: June 24–25, 2005. Ann Arbor, MI: Institute for Social Research, University of Michigan. Available at http://psidonline.isr.umich.edu/Publications/Workshops/CDS2ER/Posters/Desha.pdf

Douthitt, R. (1991) 'Children's time use in single- and two-parent families: Does household organization matter?', *Family and Consumer Sciences Research Journal*, 20(1): 40–51.

Douthitt, R. (2000) 'Time to do the chores? Factoring home-production needs into measures of poverty', *Journal of Family and Economic Issues*, 21(1): 7–22.

Edmonds, E. (2006) 'Understanding sibling differences in child labor', *Journal of Population Economics*, 19(4): 795–821.

Ehrenreich, B. and English, D. (1989) *For Her Own Good: 150 Years of the Experts' Advice to Women*. New York: Anchor Books.

England, P. and Folbre, N. (1997) 'Reconceptualizing human capital', Annual Meeting of the American Sociological Associatio, Toronto, Canada: MacArthur Network on the Family and the Economy.

Esquivel, V., Budlender, D., Folbre, N. and Hirway, I. (2008) 'Time-use Surveys in the South', *Feminist Economics*, 14(3): 107–52.

Fisher, K. and Gershuny, J. (2008) *Diaries from Children and Young People: Supplement of the Multinational Time Use Study*. Oxford: University of Oxford.

Fisher, K., McCulloch, A. and Gershuny, J. (1999) *British Fathers and Children*. Working Paper. University of Essex: Institute for Social and Economic Research.

Fitzgerald, E. (2004) *Counting Our Children: An Analysis of Official Data Sources on Children and Childhood in Ireland*. Dublin: Children's Research Centre.

Flammer, A., Alsaker, F.D. and Noacke, P. (1999) 'Time use in adolescents in an international perspective: The case of leisure activities', in F.D. Alsaker and A. Flammer (eds.), *The Adolescent Experience. European and American Adolescents in the 1990s*. Hillsdale, NJ: Lawrence Erlbaum, pp. 33–60.

Flouri, E. and Buchanan, A. (2004) 'Early father's and mother's involvement and child's later educational outcomes', *British Journal of Educational Psychology*, 74(2): 141–53.

Folbre, N., Yoon, J., Finnoff, K. and Fuligni, A. (2005) 'By what measure? Family time devoted to children in the United States', *Demography*, 42(2): 373–90.

Fuligni, A.S. and Brooks-Gunn, J. (2004) 'Measuring mother and father shared caregiving: An analysis using the panel study of income dynamics – Child development supplement', in R.D. Day (ed.), *Conceptualising and Measuring Father Involvement*. Mahwah, NJ: Lawrence Erlbaum Associates, Inc, pp. 341–57.

Garcia, L. (2006) 'Child labor, home production and the family labor supply', *Revista de Analisis Economico*, 21(1): 59–79.

Gauthier, A. and Furstenberg, F. (2005) 'Historical trends in patterns of time use among young adults', in R.A. Settersten, F. Furstenberg and R.G. Rumbaut (eds.), *On the Frontier of Adulthood: Theory, Research, and Public Policy*. Chicago: University of Chicago Press, pp. 150–76.

Gershuny, J. and Robinson, J.P. (1988) 'Historical changes in the household division of labor', *Demography*, 25(4): 537–52.

Goldstone, S. and Goldfarb, J. (1966) 'The perception of time by children', in A.H. Kidd and J.L. Rivoire (eds.), *Perceptual Development in Children*. New York: International Universities Press, pp. 445–86.

Harding, D. (1997) *Measuring Children's Time Use: A Review of Methodologies and Findings*. Working paper No. 97-01. Center for Research on Child Wellbeing.

Harrell, J.S., Gansky, S.A., Bradley, C.B. and McMurray, R.G. (1997) 'Leisure time activities of elementary school children', *Nursing Research*, 46(5): 246–53.

Hofferth, S. (1999) 'Family reading to young children: Social desirability and cultural biases in reporting', Workshop on measurement of and research on time use. Washington, DC: Committee on National Statistics, National Research Council.

Hofferth, S. (2001) 'Women's employment and care of children in the United States', in T. Van der Lippe and L. Van Dijk (eds.), *Women's Employment in a Comparative Perspective*. New York: Aldine de Gruyter, pp. 151–74.

Hofferth, S. and Sandberg, J. (2001) 'How American children spend their time', *Journal of Marriage and the Family*, 63(2): 295–308.

Ironmonger, D. (2006) *Future Directions of Time Use Research Time Use and Gender Seminar*. Sydney: University of New South Wales.

Juster, F.T. and Stafford, F.P. (1991) 'The allocation of time: Empirical findings, behavioural models, and problems of measurement', *Journal of Economic Literature*, 29(2): 471–522.

Juster, F.T., Ono, H. and Stafford, F.P. (2003) 'An assessment of alternative measures of time use', *Sociological Methodology*, 33(1): 19–54.

Kalenkoski, C.M., Ribar, D.C. and Stratton, L. (2006) *The Effect of Family Structure on Parents' Child Care Time in the United States and the United Kingdom*. IZA DP No. 2441.

Kan, M.Y. (2008) 'Measuring housework participation: The gap between "stylised" questionnaire estimates and diary-based estimates', *Social Indicators Research*, 86(3): 381–400.

Kendig, S. and Bianchi, S. (2008) 'Single, cohabitating, and married mothers' time with children', *Journal of Marriage and Family*, 70(5): 1228–40.

Kurz, D. (2002) 'Caring for teenage children', *Journal of Family Issues*, 23(6): 748–67.

Lareau, A. (2000) 'Social class and the daily lives of children: A study from the united states', *Childhood*, 7(2): 155–71.

Larson, R. (1989) 'Beeping children and adolescents: A method for studying time use and daily experience', *Journal of Youth and Adolescence*, 18(6): 511–30.

Larson, R. (2001) 'How U.S. children and adolescents spend time: What it does (and doesn't) tell us about their development', *Current Directions in Psychological Science*, 10(5): 160–4.

Larson, R. and Richards, M. (1994) *Divergent Realities: The Emotional Lives of Mothers, Fathers, and Adolescents*. New York: Basic Books.

Larson, R.W. and Verma, S. (1999) 'How children and adolescents spend time across the world: Work, play, and developmental opportunities', *Psychological Bulletin*, 125(6): 701–36.

Lee, W. and Kuo, E.C.Y. (2002) 'Internet and displacement effect: Children's media use and activities in Singapore', *Journal of Computer-Mediated Communication*, 7(2). Available at http://jcmc.indiana.edu/vol7/issue2/singapore.html

McHale, S.M., Crouter, A.C. and Tucker, C. (2001) 'Free-time activities in middle childhood: Links with adjustment in early adolescence', *Child Development*, 72(6): 1764–78.

Mauldin, T. and Meeks, C.B. (1990) 'Sex differences in children's time use', *Sex Roles*, 22(9–10): 537–54.

Mullan, K. (2008) *Parental Childcare in the United Kingdom: Concepts, Measurement and Valuation*. PhD Thesis completed at the Institute for Social and Economic Research. Colchester: University of Essex.

Neale, B. and Flowerdew, J. (2003) 'Time, texture and childhood: The contours of longitudinal qualitative research', *International Journal of Social Research Methodology Theory and Practice*, 6(3): 189–99.

Nelson, K. and Fivush, R. (2004) 'The emergence of auto-biographical memory: A social cultural developmental theory', *Psychological Review*, 111(2): 486–511.

Newman, J., Matsopolous, A., Yiping, C. and Kao, C. (2003) 'American children's time use in after-school activities', *Perceptual and Motor Skills*, 97(2): 449–50.

Nock, S.L. and Kingston, P.W. (1988) 'Time with children: The impact of couples' work-time commitments', *Social Forces*, 67(1): 59–85.

Orbach, Y. and Lamb, M. (2007) 'Young children's references to temporal attributes of allegedly experienced events in the course of forensic interviews', *Child Development*, 78(4): 1100–20.

Patrinos, H.A. and Psacharopoulos, G. (1995) 'Educational performance and child labor in Paraguay', *International Journal of Educational Development*, 15(1): 47–60.

Qvortrup, J. (1994) 'Childhood matters: An introduction', in J. Qvortrup, M. Bardy, G. Sgritta and H. Wintersberger (eds.), *Childhood Matters*. Aldershot: Avebury, pp. 4–14.

Robinson, J. and Thomas, J. (1991) *Time Spent in Activities, Locations, and Microenvironments: A California-National Comparison*. Las Vegas: US Environmental Protection Agency.

Robinson, J.P. and Gershuny, J. (1994) 'Measuring hours of paid work: Time-diary vs. estimate questions', *Bulletin of Labor Statistics*, 1: 11–17.

Rodgers, G. and Standing, G. (1981) 'Economic roles of children in low-income countries', *International Labour Review*, 120(1): 31–47.

Sandberg, J. and Hofferth, S. (2001) 'Changes in children's time with parents: United States, 1981-1997', *Demography*, 38(3): 423–36.

Sayer, L., Bianchi, S. and Robinson, J. (2004) 'Are parents investing less in children? Trends in mothers and fathers time with children', *American Journal of Sociology*, 110(1): 1–43.

Sayer, L. and Dwyer, R. (2009) 'Contextual effects of children's time use on health'. Paper presented at Population Association of America Annual Meeting, 20 April – 2 May, Detroit, Michigan.

Sayer, L., Gauthier, A. and Furstenberg, F. (2004) 'Educational differences in parents' time with children: Cross-national variations', *Journal of Marriage and Family*, 66: 1152–69.

Silvers, A., Florence, B.T., Rourke, D.L. and Lorimor, R. (1994) 'How children spend their time: A sample survey for use in exposure and risk assessments', *Risk Analysis*, 14(6): 931–44.

Stafford, F. and Yeung, W.-J. (2005) 'The distribution of children's developmental resources', in D.S. Hamermesh and G.A. Pfann (eds.), *The Economics of Time Use*. New York: Elsevier, pp. 289–313.

Stewart, J. (2002) 'Assessing the bias associated with alternative contact strategies in telephone time use surveys', *Survey Methodology*, 28(2): 157–68.

Timmer, S.G., Eccles, J. and O'Brien, K. (1985) 'How children use time', in F.T. Juster and F.P. Stafford (eds.), *Time, Goods, and Well-Being*. Ann Arbor, MI: The University of Michigan, Institute for Social Research, pp. 353–82.

UNICEF (1992) *Children of the Americas: Child Survival, Protection and Integrated Development in the 1990s*. Santafe de Bogota, Colombia: UNICEF.

Van den Bulck, J. (2004) 'Television viewing, computer game playing, and internet use and self-reported time to bed and time out of bed in secondary-school children', *Sleep*, 27(1): 101–24.

Vandewater, E.A., Bickham, D.S. and Lee, J.H. (2006) 'Time well spent? Relating television use to children's free-time activities', *Pediatrics*, 117(2): 181–91.

Vandewater, E.A., Shim, M. and Caplovitz, A.G. (2004) 'Linking obesity and activity level with children's television and video game use', *Journal of Adolescence*, 27(1): 71–85.

Vogler, P., Morrow, V. and Woodhead, M. (2009) *Conceptualising and Measuring Children's Time Use: A Technical Review*. Oxford: Department of International Development at the University of Oxford.

Wake, M., Hesketh, K. and Waters, E. (2003) 'Television, computer use and body mass index in Australian primary school children', *Journal of Paediatric Child Health*, 39(2): 130–4.

World Vision (2006) *Children's Education, Work and Labour: General Framework and Findings from World Vision Micro-Finance Institutions*. New York: World Vision.

Yeung, J., Sandberg, J.F., Davis-Kean, P. and Hofferth, S. (2001) 'Children's time with fathers in intact families', *Journal of Marriage and the Family*, 63(1): 136–54.

Zelizer, V.A. (1985) *Pricing the Priceless Child*. New York: Basic Books, Inc.

Zick, C.D., Bryant, W.K. and Osterbacka, E. (2001) 'Mothers' employment, parental involvement and the implications for intermediate child outcomes', *Social Science Research*, 30(1): 25–49.

Zuzanek, J. (2000) *The Effects of Time Use and Time Pressure on Parent-Child Relations*. Waterloo: Otium Publications.

26

Parents' Reports About Their Children's Lives

Marc H. Bornstein

INTRODUCTION

> No one can know as well as the attentive parent the subtle and cumulative changes that take place in the world of the child and in his behavior but, on the other hand, no one can distort as convincingly as a loving parent.
> – William Kessen, *The Child* (1965: 117)

There are essentially three main methods for assessing the lives of children – interviewing or testing children themselves, observing and recording them directly, and seeking out people closest to children to report about them. In this chapter, I focus on the third of these methods, describe its advantages and disadvantages, and discuss its validity. In doing so, I draw illustrations principally from parent reports of children's language and temperament as well as children's adaptive and problem behaviors and their health. From a scientific point of view, a historically significant approach to understanding development in children has employed reporters, usually their parents. Since the observations recorded by Charles Darwin, much of the classic information about child development has derived from parental reports. Practically speaking, parent reports

about children are everyday affairs, and they are laden with emotion and meaning, whether they are provoking jealousy as on the playground between parents comparing their child with others, evoking joy when the object of telephone calls to doting grandparents about a child's newest achievement, or invoking concern as the basis of vital anamnesis during paediatric interviews about a child's health.

This chapter focuses on parents' reports about their children's lives, and not on closely allied, active, and well-studied topics of parents' reports about their own parenting cognitions and practices (e.g., Bornstein and Cote, 2004; Bornstein et al., 2010; Pickett et al., 2009; Scrimin et al., 2009; Senese et al., 2012); about their own childhood (e.g., Main, Kaplan and Cassidy, 1985; Putallaz, Costanzo and Smith, 1991); about their parents' parenting (e.g., Nomaguchi and Milkie, 2006); about their family (e.g., Jager et al., 2012); about child reports of their parents' cognitions or practices (e.g., Haines et al., 2008; Sessa et al., 2001; Tein, Roosa and Michaels, 1994); or about others' reports of children (e.g., physicians or caregivers; Pierce et al., 2011).

THE ADVANTAGES AND DISADVANTAGES OF PARENT REPORT

Parental report is one of the most common paths to understanding and evaluating children. Before proceeding to a full discussion of parent report, it may be wise to pause for a critical look at its disadvantages and advantages as a method of child development study and in comparison with its two principal rival contenders, observation and testing.

It has often been argued that the most valid, reliable, and comprehensive information about children must come from observers who know a child best and are with the child most or all of the time – normally, the child's own parents (Thomas et al., 1963). Parent reports (such as child diaries) can be detailed in ways other modes of child study cannot. There are other obvious economic advantages to parent reports, as they are typically rapid, cost-effective, and efficient (Dale et al., 1989).

Normally, parent reports are based on extensive sampling across a wide range of situations and times (Bates, Bretherton and Snyder, 1988; Thal and Bates, 1990), and so provide unique and invaluable information about children and child development, especially when intelligence about context is enlightening or required (Gopnik and Meltzoff, 1986) or when development is otherwise hard to observe or test. For example, the earliest stages of language learning are particularly problematic to observe or to test, in part because the behaviors in question are new, infrequent, and unpredictable (Bates and Carnevale, 1993; Bowerman, 1985). Parent reports are methodologically well suited for assessing the history of developmental phenomena and kinds of behavior whose base rates are low or clinically concerning (such as physical aggression). Several of these considerations underpinned the first child biographies and diaries (discussed immediately below).

Comparatively speaking, diaries, interviews, and questionnaires can provide data not readily available to observation or testing. In some cases, reports may afford the only available source of relevant information, or alternative forms of data may be costly, infeasible, or impossible to obtain for ethical reasons. Children sometimes prove to be poor participants in observations and experiments for numerous reasons, and so parent reports constitute an invaluable substitute (Bornstein et al., 2014). Children may be unwilling to cooperate with strangers in unfamiliar settings (Feldman et al., 2005), and direct observations by unacquainted researchers inevitably involve limited sampling, participant reactivity, context effects (as in the difference between laboratory and home observations), and other potential biases.

All that said, however, the reliability and validity of parent reports can be limited. Aside from methodological shortfalls particular to biographies and diaries (discussed below), parental reports may be compromised for their own reasons. One major drawback is represented by potentially distorting influences that can beset parent-report measures, such as parental bias and uncertainties concerning the objectivity of the reporter (Ash and Guyer, 1991; Miller, 1988). Parents (as Kessen, 1965, observed) are subject to a variety of distortions in their observations. Some reports doubtlessly include objective as well as subjective components (Bates and Bayles, 1984) reflective of extraneous parental characteristics (for example, employment status, achievement orientation, personality, parity, and so forth). In general, parental perceptions are thought to be colored by life circumstances, psychological functioning, and expectations regarding a child or child development. Parent reporters also normally lack professional training, and so their reports may be unsystematic and either overestimate or underestimate the development of the child. Reporting places multiple demands on untrained parents to detect, observe, and interpret various aspects of child development.

Furthermore, most parent reports do not always record observations as they occur, but often employ a retrospective methodology, trying to recall what the child was like from the vantage of some later point in time. Reliance on memory runs many risks dependent on original encoding, faithful retention, amount of time intervening, and surmounting intervening interference (Hefner and Mednick, 1969; McGraw and Molloy, 1941; Mednick and Shaffer, 1963; Pyles, Stolz and MacFarlane, 1935; Robbins, 1963; Wenar, 1963; Wenar and Coulter, 1962). Yarrow, Campbell, and Burton (1970: 68) concluded from an extensive early study of parent reports that their analyses 'brought little honor to retrospective reports as records' of children's development.

Who is reporting makes a difference as well. Children spend time with many adults, including mothers, fathers, grandparents, and childcare providers of various sorts (Clarke-Stewart and Allhusen, 2002; Parke, 2002; Smith and Drew, 2002), and the situations and activities in which children spend time with these different interactants vary. Different conversants and different situations and activities can be expected to give rise to the use of different language forms, for example. As a consequence, any one adult familiar with a particular child may know that child's communicative abilities, but only on the basis of his or her own unique contacts with the child, and when asked to report about that child's communicative ability, different reporters will not necessarily agree (De Houwer, Bornstein, and Leach, 2004). Each of these factors can modify estimations of the child (Achenbach, McConaughy, and Howell, 1987; Bates and Bales, 1984; Bornstein, Gaughran, and Homel, 1986; Kazdin, 1988; Verhulst and Koot, 1992).

Because parental reports can be affected in these various ways, it is often recommended that they be used in combination with objective observations and evaluations by disinterested observers to construct comprehensive

and presumably valid accounts of child development. It may be the case in some circumstances that multiple reporters and multiple methods enhance the scope and validity of child assessment (e.g., Deuchar and Quay, 2000). However, parental perceptions constitute a significant part of the milieu in which the child develops. Parental beliefs therefore merit a status of central interest to child development researchers, as opposed to parents simply being placed in the role of quasi-objective reporters, of a means to validate 'objective' assessments, or of a source of social perceptions about children (St. James Roberts and Wolke, 1984). In short, it is fruitful to look for validity within parental reports per se, without predicating their value on their relations to other measures. In this chapter, I consistently return to consider advantages and disadvantages of parent reports per se and their value in the context of recommendations about multisource multimethod approaches.

HISTORY AND METHODOLOGY OF PARENT REPORTS

Baby biographies and diaries

The eighteenth-century Enlightenment in Europe brought with it a revolutionary concern with understanding individuals, children included. The Swiss philosopher Jean-Jacques Rousseau's (1782) *Confessions* and *Reveries of a Solitary Walker* invented modern autobiography, and his 1762 semi-fictitious *Émile* theorized that education ought not to involve simply imparting knowledge but instead drawing out what is already in the child. Rousseau was among the first philosophers to write about the integrity of childhood as a separate stage of life. Not long after, the German philosopher Dietrich Tiedemann (1787) penned a psychological journal of the growth of his son's sensory, motor, language, and cognitive behavior over the first 30 months, in shorter words a *baby biography*. The first psychological studies of children were descriptions of infants and young in their natural settings usually written by their own parents (Prochner and Doyon, 1997; Wallace, Franklin and Keegan, 1994).

Three types of baby biographies have been distinguished (Wallace et al., 1994). Domestic diaries are the oldest. They were typically recorded by mothers for their personal satisfaction, and they often also provided insights into parental philosophies about the nature of childhood and childrearing. Educational diaries were written to recount the impact of childrearing practices. Finally, scientific diaries usually recount knowledge about child behavior and development.

Both educational and scientific diaries came into their own in the second half of the nineteenth century, which witnessed an intense focus on evolution and development (Lerner et al., 2011). The main stimulus to this development was Darwin, who at that time assembled for publication the observations he made in the early 1840s of his first-born son William Erasmus, nicknamed 'Doddy' (Conrad, 1998). Darwin's publication of 'A Biographical Sketch of an Infant' simultaneously in the German journal *Kosmos* and in the English journal *Mind* in 1877 constituted a turning point in the history of psychology and developmental science. In that paper, Darwin focused specifically on Doddy's sensory, intellectual, and emotional development during the first year.

Darwin's emphasis on development and comparison as general sources of knowledge set the stage for the emergence of developmental science as a formal discipline (Cairns and Cairns, 2006; Lerner et al., 2011). In succeeding years, baby biographies grew in status around the world (Prochner and Doyon, 1997) and have been perennially in style ever since (Dromi, 1987; Greene, 1985; Leopold, 1949; Nelson, 2001; Stern, 1992; Weir, 1962). (In an interesting spinoff of this case-study methodology, K. Nelson, 2006, organized a group of nine scholars in *Narratives from the Crib* to analyze, each from her/his own unique perspective, the same data base of 122 night-time monologues of Emily, a precocious 2-year-old whose solitary speechifying before sleep was surreptitiously audiorecorded by her parents over a yearlong period.) The English-German physiologist William Thierry Preyer's (1881) detailed description of the first three years of his own son's life in *Die Seele des Kindes* established a model for the formal system of developmental examination. Preyer's biography divided child study into categories – sensation, motor activity, expression, and intelligence – that have informed the study of child development ever since. In the early 1890s, the American psychologist James Mark Baldwin (1896) observed that his infant daughter Helen would consistently reach for a yellow cube rather than a blue one. From this, Baldwin deduced that Helen – and by deduction all human infants – must perceive colors because her preferential reaching showed that she discriminated yellow from blue. In the 1960s, Robert Fantz (1964) revived Baldwin to spectacular advantage. Fantz argued that, if babies look preferentially at one of two stimuli, their preference reveals a capacity to discriminate the two. This simple preference technique has yielded revolutionary knowledge about infants and their capacities (see Bornstein, Arterberry and Lamb, 2014). Perhaps the greatest of the twentieth-century baby biographers was the Swiss biologist and philosopher Jean Piaget (see, for example, 1953, 1954, 1962, 1970), most of whose writing and theorizing about perception, cognition, and social development refer to observations and reports of his own three young children: Jacqueline, Lucienne, and Laurent. Thus, developmental science had its formal beginnings in attempts by scientists to do systematically what parents around the world do naturally – simply observe and report about their growing children.

Parental diaries are still in use. To understand sequences of events surrounding disciplinary incidents, Kremer, Smith, and Lawrence (2010) asked parents to keep diaries that could be analyzed subsequently.

Baby biographies and diaries harbor in microcosm many of the advantages and disadvantages of parent reports more generally. Attention paid to their children by important figures (like Darwin and Piaget) excited more general interest not only in children but in the study of children. For these reasons alone, reports by parents (often scientists themselves) have been central to child study. As sources of information, child diaries can be detailed, informative, and thought provoking; talented authors have made exceptional, meticulous, and intuitive observers (see, for example, the child language diary record by Leopold, 1949), and on the basis of close observations, child biographers generated basic descriptive data as well as numerous, novel, and important hypotheses about child development. A very early exemplar was French Count Philippe de Montbeillard's charting of his son's physical growth between 1759 and 1777. His close analysis exemplifies a data base valuable both for the historical record and as a model for child study (see Tanner, 1963). The keen focus on single children also helps to document events that otherwise may be hard to observe, and they are especially valuable theoretically as when they reveal capacities that are supposed to be absent. For example, the earliest stages of language learning are particularly problematic to observe and to test, in part because the behaviors in question are new, infrequent, and unpredictable (Bates and Carnevale, 1993); in this connection, the extensive record by Noji (1973–1977), containing 40,000 child utterances as recorded by a parent and 22,000 child utterances as recorded by other family members, is noteworthy (available through the CHILDES archive; MacWhinney, 2000).

In methodological terms, however, baby biographers frequently observed only a single child, usually their own. Case studies can be telling, but the generalizability of what is observed and reported is always in question. The children who are the typical protagonists of baby biographies could hardly have been representative of the population at large, and,

perhaps like their parents, they may be exceptional. Moreover, baby biographers in history mostly described children growing up in privileged settings that were hardly representative of average childhood experiences of their times (French, 2002). Diarists have never been concerned with comparison groups, and their observations were not always systematic. Also, in reading and evaluating these accounts, it is not possible to determine the extent to which an observed behavior or capacity is limited to either a specific situational circumstance or to a specific child. Frequently, diarists of old were women and men with strong theoretical points of view who tended to see in children and report anecdotes and data that supported their theories.

Interviews, questionnaires, checklists, and focus groups

Parents' biographical recounting of their own spontaneous and sometimes idiosyncratic or haphazard impressions constitutes some prominent types of parental reports. In addition, researchers have used unstructured and structured parent interviews, questionnaires, and checklists to obtain parent reports. Thus, over time parent reports have become much more sophisticated and sound, and today systematic and programmatic reports are a norm. For example, adaptive behavior is conceptualized in psychology as the individual's active modifications to cope more effectively with the demands of her or his natural, social, and designed environments. Adaptation is a major achievement and goal of child development (Herber, 1961; Lazarus, 1999; Scarr, 1996). More generally, adaptation is fundamental to successful growth and development in all organisms and is attained through the organism's interaction with its immediate environment, first, by discerning and selecting those cues in the environment that are critical to successful comprehension of the demands of the environment and, then, by mounting strategies to deal successfully with those demands. Leland (1983) opined that adaptive behaviors include a wide range of developmental achievements involving motor, cognitive, language, socialization, and self-help skills, and Keith, Harrison, and Ehly (1987) likewise contended that adaptive behaviors encompass self-help skills, domestic activities, and interpersonal relationships. Assessment of adaptive behaviors tells how a person copes in everyday life, and psychological measures of adaptive behavior are designed to evaluate what the person actually does vis-à-vis the requirements and challenges of everyday life. For Sparrow, Balla, and Cicchetti (1984: 6), 'adaptive behavior is defined by typical performance, not ability. While ability is necessary for the performance of daily activities, an individual's adaptive behavior is inadequate if the ability is not demonstrated when it is required'.

Adaptive behavior is not measured by testing an individual directly; instead, someone who knows the individual well, and is familiar with the individual's daily habits, is asked (usually in an interview) to rate the individual's typical adaptive behaviors across a variety of contexts. Thus, for Sparrow et al. (1984: 6), 'adaptive behavior is defined by the expectations or standards of other people. The adequacy of an individual's adaptive behavior is judged by those who live, work, and interact with the individual'. The Vineland Adaptive Behavior Scales (VABS; Sparrow et al., 1984) were the first well-normed assessment of adaptive behavior published, and they are acknowledged as the most technically advanced adaptive-behavior scale currently available (diSibio, 1993; Newmark, 1989). The VABS has been evaluated as foremost among 200 adaptive behavior instruments (Doucette and Freedman, 1980; Holman and Bruininks, 1985; Kamphaus, 1987a, 1987b). The Interview Edition, Survey Form asks a parent to assess the child's actual adaptive behavior in four areas: communication, daily living skills, socialization, and motor skills. The VABS Survey Form was normed for 3000 children and youth aged newborn to 18 years, 11 months.

The validity of the VABS is well supported (Sparrow et al., 1984), and Sparrow and Cicchetti (1978) reported high correlations between primary caregivers' estimates of levels of adaptive behavior and independent assessments of those behaviors. For example, Sparrow and Cicchetti (1978) and Tombokan-Runtukahu and Nitko (1992) alike reported high correlations between primary caregivers' estimates of levels of child adaptive behavior and independent teachers' assessments. Both adaptive behavior and, for example, cognitive ability are influenced by general development (Keith et al., 1987): Children with normal intelligence score higher than children with mental retardation on adaptive behavior assessments (Engleman, 1974; Slate, 1983; Sparrow et al., 1984; Tombokan-Runtukahu and Nitko, 1992). The construct of adaptive behavior, generally, and the VABS instrument specifically, which were originally operationalized in the United States, have shown good validity both in other Western settings, such as France and Italy (Bornstein, Giusti, Leach and Venuti, 2005; Frombonne and Achard, 1993; Taverna et al., 2011), and in non-Western contexts, such as Indonesia (Tombokan-Runtukahu and Nitko, 1992).

Another example of a parent interview is the Kiddie Disruptive Behavior Disorders Schedule (K-DBDS; Keenan and Wakschlag, 2002), a semi-structured clinical interview assessing DSM-IV disruptive behavior symptoms (or Oppositional Defiant and Conduct Disorder) in preschool children. Child adaptations include the use of developmentally appropriate examples of behavior and assessing multiple components of core symptoms that are geared to enhance the interview's precision. The K-DBDS also demonstrates good reliability and validity (Keenan et al., 2007).

The acknowledged wellspring of interest and research on the topic of infant temperament is Thomas et al.'s (1963) New York Longitudinal Study (NYLS). The NYLS derived its basic data from extensive parent interviews. On that basis, Thomas and Chess (1977: 21) formulated nine dimensions of infant temperament, including activity level, rhythmicity (regularity), approach or withdrawal, adaptability, intensity of reaction, attention span and persistence, distractibility, quality of mood, and threshold of responsiveness. They further deduced that children could be characterized as difficult, easy, or slow to warm up. Thomas et al.'s (1963) New York Longitudinal Study and the many other investigations which it fostered – notably by Carey (Carey, 1970; Carey and McDevitt, 1978a, 1978b), Bates (Bates, Freeland and Lounsbury, 1979; Lounsbury and Bates, 1982), and Rothbart (Rothbart, 1981; Rothbart and Derryberry, 1981) – are based on parent interviews (and questionnaires, see below) about normal on-going everyday infant and child behavior.

Individual interviews with parents are also a common source of information about parents' goals and values for their children (Gonzalez-Ramos, Zayas and Cohen, 1998; Hurd, Moore and Rogers, 1995; Pachter and Dworkin, 1997). Leyendecker et al. (2002) assessed characteristics mothers would like their child to possess through a structured interview using open-ended questions. Interview techniques have proved especially rewarding in cultural developmental research (Huang et al., 2011). Harwood and colleagues (Harwood, 1992; Harwood et al., 1995; Miller and Harwood, 2002), for example, developed and have utilized a structured interview for Latina mothers, the Socialization Goals Interview. This interview focuses on assessment of five value areas (self-maximization, self-control, lovingness, decency, and proper demeanor) consistent with prevalent Latino cultural values. Tamis-LeMonda et al. (2002) had mothers rank a list of 13 given values from their most important to their least important (based on work by Gonzalez-Ramos, Zayas and Cohen, 1998); this method too required mothers to prioritize their values.

For some topics in child development, interviews have morphed into formal structured questionnaires. Questionnaires can provide rich sources of parent-report data not readily available in observation or amenable to test. Questionnaires about children are also efficient and economical, and replies are presumably based on extensive sampling across a wide range of situations, and so may provide invaluable sources of information about children and child development (Bates, Bretherton and Snyder, 1988; Thal and Bates, 1990).

To evaluate infant temperament, Carey (1970) developed the Infant Temperament Questionnaire (ITQ), later refined by Carey and McDevitt (ITQ-R; 1978a, 1978b). The ITQ is a parent-report instrument on which a parent rates the infant along each of the nine Thomas and Chess dimensions, and it also allows for a summary characterization of infants as easy, slow to warm up, and difficult, as well as intermediate low and intermediate high. Bates (Bates et al., 1979) developed a second parent-report temperament measure, the Infant Characteristics Questionnaire (ICQ). Factor analysis of items in the ICQ yielded four main dimensions of temperament, including fussiness-difficult, unadaptable, dull, and unpredictable. Finally, Rothbart (1981; Gartstein and Rothbart, 2003; Rothbart and Derryberry, 1981; Rothbart and Goldsmith, 1986) developed a third parent-report temperament measure, the Infant Behavior Questionnaire (IBQ and IBQ-R) and the Toddler Behavior Questionnaire (TBQ), also applicable across the early years of life. The six scales of the IBQ are activity level, soothability, fear (distress and latency to approach intense or novel stimuli), distress to limitations (anger/frustration), smiling and laughter, and duration of orienting. These individual scales in turn form factors of Positive and Negative temperament. A successor to the IBQ, the Infant Behavior Questionnaire-Revised (IBQ-R; Gartstein and Rothbart, 2003) consists of 14 scales that yield a three-factor structure of child temperament, including Surgency-Extraversion, Negative Affect, and Attentional Self-regulation/Effortful Control. Infant scales with different names often measure similar constructs. Goldsmith and

Rieser-Danner (1986) had both mothers and childcare teachers of 4- to 8-month-old infants fill out the Revised Infant Temperament Questionnaire (RIT-Q; Carey and McDevitt, 1978a, 1978b), the Infant Characteristics Questionnaire (ICQ; Bates et al., 1979), and the Infant Behavior Questionnaire (IBQ; Rothbart, 1981). Distress to novelty was assessed by all three instruments: IBQ Fear, ICQ Unadaptable, and ITQ Approach-Withdrawal scales. Intercorrelations across the scales were high. For mothers, they ranged from 0.60 to 0.69, with the average $r = 0.64$; for childcare teachers, the intercorrelations ranged from 0.51 to 0.73, with the average $r = 0.63$.

Other studies have used parent-report questionnaires to access like private, sensitive, and infrequent child behaviors, such as the prevalence, stability, and development of physical aggression (Alink et al., 2006; Tremblay et al., 2004) and direct weight-related behaviors (comments to child about weight, encourage child to diet) and indirect weight-related behaviors (dieting, comments about own weight/appearance; Haines et al., 2008).

Checklists constitute a related sort of parent-report instrument. Checklists provide the respondent with a fixed number of items (vocabulary words) and ask the respondent to indicate whether an item applies to the child (knows the word). Checklists use a recognition format, placing fewer demands on the reporter's memory, and offer advantages over other methods in the same way that recognition facilitates memory over recall. Checklists appear to possess increased validity when circumscribed to the child's current status. One widely used contemporary parent-report checklist is the MacArthur Communicative Development Inventories (CDI; Fenson et al., 1993; Fenson et al., 1994). The CDI comprises two different forms: the CDI-Words and Gestures (CDI:WG), appropriate for children between 8 and 16 months of age, assesses receptive and expressive vocabulary, communicative gestures, symbolic behavior, and non-verbal imitation; the CDI-Words and Sentences (CDI:WS), for children between 16 and 30 months, evaluates productive vocabulary, syntax complexity, knowledge of irregular word forms, and overgeneralization of word endings. The CDI for infants asks reporters to indicate whether particular words are understood (comprehension) by the child or understood and said (production). The CDI for toddlers asks about production only. Child language researchers and language and speech diagnosticians and therapists alike have reached positive consensus about this way to measure young children's early communicative and lexical knowledge. CDIs were first developed for American English (http://www.sci.sdsu.edu/cdi/), but have since been adapted to many other languages (http://www.sci.sdsu.edu/cdi/adaptations_ol.htm; see, for example, Thordardottir and Ellis Weismer, 1996, for Icelandic; Maital, Dromi, Sagi and Bornstein, 2000, for Hebrew; and Vollmann, Marschik and Einspieler, 2000, for Austrian German). Other parent-report checklists of child language and communication are the Language Development Survey (LDS; Rescorla, 1989) and the Communication and Early Language (Camaioni et al., 1991).

The parent-report Child Behavior Checklist (CBCL; Achenbach, 1991a) is a widely used index of child psychopathology. (There are also child-report and teacher-report versions.) The CBCL and its associates were developed to be comparable and used as parts of a multiaxial assessment to identify problem behaviors (Achenbach, 1991a). Respondents are asked to report, either now or within the past six months, how often their child had a given problem. Each item is rated as: 0 = *not true or not at all*, 1 = *somewhat or sometimes true*, or 2 = *very true or often true*. The CBCL yields three summary scales; internalizing problems, externalizing problems, and total problem behaviors. For example parent-reported problem behaviors of 1538 inter-country adopted adolescents aged 14 to 18 years were compared with those from general population samples. Parents' reports showed a difference between adopted versus nona-dopted boys (Versluis-den Bieman and Verhulst, 1995). Such measures are also used to gauge the onset of children's symptoma-tology (Todd, Huang and Henderson, 2008).

In the health domain, checklists have seen increasing use as screening devices. For example, diagnoses of autism are waxing in the population, but autism is normally not identified until the third year of life. Likewise, language and other developmental delays are of concern. Parents have access to children continuously from a much earlier period. The Communication and Symbolic Behavior Scales Developmental Profile Infant-Toddler Checklist (SBS-DP-IT-Checklist; Wetherby et al., 2008; Wetherby et al., 2004) is a 24-item multi-purpose parent-report screen. Three autism-specific screening tools that have been used with general population samples include The Checklist for Autism in Toddlers (CHAT: Baird et al., 2000; Baron-Cohen et al., 1992, 1996), The Modified Checklist for Autism in Toddlers (M–CHAT: Kleinman et al., in press; Robins and Dumont-Mathieu, 2006; Robins et al., 2001), and The Early Screening of Autistic Traits Questionnaire (ESAT: Dietz et al., 2006).

Interview protocols, questionnaires, and checklists are helpful in obtaining informa-tion from individuals who are much more familiar with their own children than are professional observers. Interview, question-naire, and checklist techniques may be useful for understanding not only what children do, but why they behave in specific ways. Thus, one can observe infant–parent interactions and then ask parents to explain their infant's history or state (Bornstein et al., 1998).

Focus groups have also been used to gather information from parents about child development and the socialization of children (Gilkerson and Stott, 1997; Gonzalez-Ramos, Zayas, and Cohen, 1998; Guilamo-Ramos et al., 2007). Focus group interviews are gener-ally constructed around a standard set of open-ended questions and assess long-term, abstract socialization values as well as plumb the reasoning behind more specific interactive

practices (Carey and Smith, 1994; Leyendecker et al., 2002). Focus groups are useful to discuss and validate data aggregated from individual interviews (Hurd et al., 1995) and to collect data for use in developing measures or interviews assessing values which may be underrepresented in existing measures (Ruppenthal et al., 2005). Few quantitative measures exist that assess parenting values in different ethnic and cultural groups, and so focus groups in a cross-cultural context can serve as a way of 'minimizing researchers' etic preconceptions and maximizing respondents' emic contribu-tions' (Malgady et al., 1996: 265). In a study of parenting strengths and competencies, Hurd and colleagues (1995) used focus groups and interviews with African-American parents from different socioeconomic statuses and examined data using thematic analysis. Eight themes emerged, including emphases on parental involvement with chil-dren, support from non-parental caregivers, connection with family, achievement and effort, respect for others, fostering self-reliance and self-sufficiency, education, and self-respect and ethnic pride. Other advan-tages of focus groups are that they may be more time efficient relative to conducting individual interviews, and they can elicit communications from people of varying ethnic backgrounds that might not be expressed directly in individual settings. At the same time, however, focus group interac-tions are subject to social processes of conforming and censoring that may limit individual group members' contributions (Carey and Smith, 1994). Individuals who have differing views or thoughts from those of the majority may suppress their opinions or perspectives.

Summary

Different sources of information about a child may contribute valid but different data; however, different data sources can also be used to complement one another and converge to bring into focus a coherent picture of the child. For example, parental report can be comprehensive and often also provides a good representation of emerging skills (Bates et al., 1995; Bornstein and Haynes, 1998). But (as noted) parent reports may reflect parental personality or sociodemographic characteristics instead of or, more probably, in addition to the child or parental perceptions of the child. Interviews obviously also do not equate to questionnaires. Parent report methodologies have much to contribute to the identification and understanding of dimensions of child functioning and development, but they are not without their limitations (Gardner, 2000). All methodologies have their pitfalls; even objective measures through direct observations, often thought to be empirically rigorous, are conducted by researchers unacquainted with the child, are costly, and inevitably suffer from limited sampling, reactivity, and other potential threats to validity. Generally, contemporary research emphasizes the importance of collecting data from multiple informants and applying multiple methodologies to fully describe the nuances and complexities of child development. That said, however, differences in reports between, say, parents and children are not random and the practice of aggregating scores across reporters to integrate data may not be justified.

DESIGN ISSUES IN PARENT REPORTS

A comprehensive discussion of all the niceties and nuances of adult reporting is well beyond the scope of this chapter. For example, Schwarz and Oyserman (2001) identified five steps in responding to a question: understanding the question, recalling relevant behavior, inference and estimation, mapping the answer onto the response format, and 'editing' the answer (for example, for reasons of social desirability). Misinformation and errors are possible at each of these steps (Jobe, 2001). However, a few topics are central to deliberations about parents' reports of their children and so merit brief consideration. Improving our understanding of the nuts and bolts of parents' reports is essential to research on child development and parenting.

Concurrent vs. retrospective parent reports

A basic methodological distinction in this literature partitions concurrent and retrospective parent reports. Because assorted cognitive and motivational factors may undermine respondents' efficient and accurate information about the past (e.g., Bradburn et al., 1987; Henry et al., 1994), biases of various sorts in recalling experiences are widely thought to pervade retrospective reports. However, retrospective reports may not be so poor as usually thought (Bernstein et al., 1994). Relevant data come from fields closely allied to parent reports about their children. Reviewing the literature, Brewin, Andrews, and Gotlib (1993: 91) concluded that 'claims that retrospective reports in general ... are inherently unreliable are exaggerated'. Indeed, there is evidence for the accuracy of retrospective reports of early parental support, for example: using the Parental Bonding Instrument (Parker, Tupling and Brown, 1979), Parker (1984) learned that retrospective ratings of early parental support made by adult children were corroborated by separate reports from their parents. Adults' recalled childhood experiences accord with reports of that time period by their parents. Very likely, retrospective reports are sensitive to a variety of parameters, such as telescoping, the amount of time between the event and the time of reporting, the wording of questions, the informant's emotional state, and so forth (Barsky, 2002). Telescoping can result from compressing the timescale, as when informants systematically move events forward in time when asked to recall when they occurred (Neter and Waksberg, 1964) or when more distant events are recalled with greater error than more recent events. Reports about children by parents are often emotion-laden, and memory accuracy reflects emotional intensity. When participants provide concurrent versus retrospective ratings of positive and negative emotions, retrospective ratings of the intensity of positive and negative affect are higher than concurrent ratings (Thomas and Diener, 1990; see also Parkinson et al., 1995). Generally speaking, past intense events are more likely to come to mind than less intense ones when participants are asked to provide a retrospective reports, resulting in observed discrepancies between concurrent and retrospective reports.

Researchers have devised methods to overcome these issues. The Life History Calendar (LHC; Caspi et al., 1996), for example, is a data-collection method for obtaining reliable retrospective data about one's own life events and activities, but could be adapted for reports about one's children. This retrospective technique gathers time-linked data by asking respondents to recall their pasts. In practice, the LHC is a large grid used to record the events in a respondent's life. Grid rows refer to different activity lines (events or behaviors and life trajectories that are being investigated), and columns divide the grid into time units during which particular events or behaviors may have occurred. The result is continuous information about multiple trajectories and events in the respondent's life. As a research instrument, the LHC is used to collect detailed event-history data; and as a clinical instrument, the LHC is used both as an assessment tool and as a therapeutic guide. A related approach is the Event History Calendar (EHC; Belli, Shay and Stafford, 2001). EHC interviewing methodologies improve recall even for events occurring several years previously (Freedman et al., 1988).

The concurrent versus retrospective issue in parent report is non trivial. Many surveys vital to child development, including notably the Panel Study of Income Dynamics (PSID),

a national probability sample that measures key social and economic variables, rely on retrospective report.

Time frame of parent reports

Parents are often asked to report on their children for a specified reference period. Depending on the study, the length of the reference period may range from short time spans (such as 1 hour or 1 day) to more extended time spans (such as a week, a month, or a year). In specifying a reference period, researchers usually take the assumed frequency of the target phenomenon into account (Sudman and Bradburn, 1983). When the target is likely to be relatively infrequent, researchers usually opt for an extended reference period, otherwise too many parents may report a non-occurrence, which limits possible analyses; when the target is likely to be relatively frequent, researchers usually opt for shorter reference periods, because parents may forget more distant instances of a frequent target. Thus, the reference period may influence which target parents consider to be the referent of the question.

Format of parent reports

Parent reports usually employ recognition formats, in which the caregivers are asked to check the behaviors currently or previously shown by their child: in this way, parent reports are more likely to reflect what the child actually 'knows', more than what parents believe about the child (Camaioni et al., 1991; Dale et al., 1989; Reznick and Goldsmith, 1989). Manipulations of item format can limit the reliance on prospective or retrospective memory. Survey research shows that through careful questionnaire construction it is possible to obtain reliable retrospective reports (e.g., Finney, 1981; Marcus, 1982; Means et al., 1989; Schuman and Presser, 1981).

State-of-the-art of survey interviewing methodology advocates the use of standardized question list (Q-list) instruments (Fowler and Mangione 1990; Kahn and Cannell 1957). Formal characteristics of a question can profoundly affect participants' interpretation (Schwarz, Strack, Muller and Chassein, 1988). When participants report how often they felt 'really annoyed' on one of two different scales (a low-frequency scale that ranged from *less than once a year* to *more than once every three months* or a high-frequency scale that ranged from *less than twice a week* to *several times a day*), those who were exposed to the low-frequency scale subsequently provided more extreme examples of typical annoying situations than those who were exposed to the high-frequency scale. Other aspects of a questionnaire item, such as language, context, and response alternatives, influence self-report (Schwarz, 1999). In situations where clinicians or researchers must rely on retrospective report, use of records (Sudman and Bradburn, 1973) or anchor points (for example, 'was she using words on her first birthday?') may increase reliability of recall (Bonichini, Axia and Bornstein, 2009; Keller et al., 1987; Loftus and Marburger, 1983)

In parent reports about children, social desirability is an issue (Bornstein et al., 2013). Belli et al., (1999) asked citizens if they had voted in the last election and then verified whether or not each individual had voted with county election office records. In their sample, 16.4 percent of the respondents did not accurately report whether or not they had voted, with most individuals claiming they did vote when they actually had not. Behaviors that are embarrassing or socially undesirable tend to be misreported in surveys more often than other types of behaviors (Bradburn, 1983). Presumably, parents wish to report positive things about their children (smiling infants, academically well performing middle-schoolers, athletic adolescents) and resist reporting negative things (cheating,

delinquency, nail-biting). Parental reports may be particularly vulnerable to the influence of social desirability, given the importance placed on having a good child as well as the social and cultural norms that help to define what it means to have a good child. Another factor which could heighten socially desirable responding is parental fear of legal involvement when responding to items associated with possible child misbehavior. Reporting of socially undesirable behaviors can be increased through manipulations of question wording (Catania et al., 1996) and response formats (Belli et al., 1999); however, neither providing information about how rare or commonplace a behavior is (Ong and Weiss, 2000) nor creating a context through attitude statements (Tourangeau and Smith 1996) has reduced socially desirable reporting.

Two (plus 1) metrics of the accuracy of parental reports

How do we know if parent reports are valid? There are two common metrics of agreement over parents' reports of their children's lives. One is relative agreement in terms of order of individual differences. When a parent rates a child high on some characteristic, do other people (or informants) also rate the child high? Do parents and others agree in rating the same children low? The Pearson Product-Moment correlation coefficient is the most commonly used statistic to assess relative agreement between parents' and others' reports of children. It provides information about the order or relative standing of scores from two informants. A correlation of 1.00 indicates that other informants order children in exact accord with parents' ordering of the same children, whereas a correlation of 0.00 indicates random ordering between parents and other informants. For example, Anderson et al. (1985) compared parent diaries of 5-year-old children's time spent in front of television to concurrent automated time-lapse video observations of the children. Parent concurrent diaries correlated highly with video observation ($r = 0.84$).

The second common metric of agreement is in terms of absolute level. Although correlations between parent and other informant reports lend insight into relative correspondence, correlations do not provide information about the magnitude or direction of differences between parents and other reporters. Hence, mean statistics, like the Student t-test, have been used to capture the magnitude of mean level differences. For example, Pillai Riddell, and Craig (2006) examined whether caregiver judgments of infant pain vary systematically with different infant caregiver groups and infant age. Parents, in-patient nurses, and pediatricians viewed videotapes of the behavioral responses of healthy infants (aged 2, 4, 6, 12, and 18 months) to routine immunization injections and provided ratings of both the affective distress and pain intensity they observed. Pediatricians attributed lower levels of pain than parents, and nurses were intermediate and not different from either of the other two groups. Despite an absence of differences in the behavioral reactions of the children, the type of caregiver systematically influenced attributions of pain to infants. Unlike nurses and pediatricians, parents provide care with little to no formal professional training, relying heavily on their personal, familial, and cultural experiences. Although pediatricians also may be parents, their extensive training and specialized medical knowledge would be expected to lead to different approaches to assessing infant pain, and they tend to see a greater number of infants in comparison to in-patient nurses and parents (Huth and More, 1998). Nurses' roles require routine care of ill infants (for example, feeding, play, and medical procedures) akin to parents, but similar to pediatricians they possess a considerable amount of medical knowledge and training (Stevens and Gibbins, 2002).

Logic then suggests that, for a given child characteristic, relative standing and mean level of parent report and other informant might agree, which would lend high credibility to parent report. Or, parent and other informant might agree with respect to relative standing but not mean level, or agree with respect to mean level but not relative standing, or disagree with respect to relative standing and mean level. Each pattern would have its unique implications for how an investigator interprets parent report and child development.

A third and related, although infrequently used, metric asks about parent–other agreement in assigning children to specific categories, say, of type of temperament or diagnostic classification. Here kappa (κ; Cohen, 1960, 1968) would be an appropriate statistical yardstick. For example, Yarrow et al. (1970) included such a categorical comparison in their study of the reliability of maternal retrospective reports of child development. These are the basic and most common indexes of agreement; of course, there are many others (Hartmann, Pelzel and Abbott, 2011) each appropriate to the design of a study.

Every parent-report instrument should have strong psychometric features to support its accuracy, including reliability, validity, sensitivity (true positives), and specificity (true negatives).

ACCURACY AND VALIDITY OF PARENTAL REPORTERS AND REPORTS

Mothers as reporters

For the most part, mothers have been the reporter of choice about children in recognition of the fact that mothers have traditionally and across cultures assumed primary - if not exclusive – responsibility for early childcare, mothers participate in childrearing activities at significantly higher rates than do fathers or others, and beginning prenatally motherhood is unequivocally principal in the health and development of infants and young children (Barnard and Solchany, 2002; Geary, 2000; Hart Research Associates, 1997; Holden and Buck, 2002; Leiderman, Tulkin and Rosenfeld, 1977; Parke, 2002; Weisner and Gallimore, 1977). Given societal dictates that it is mothers who are ultimately responsible for their young children's lives and well-being, women have traditionally become more 'expert' than men in caregiving and knowledge about children, connecting with a largely female network outside the home to gain child-relevant information (Stern, 1995). Not unexpectedly, it is also mothers' parenting that is most consistently associated with developmental and health outcomes in children (Crouter, Helms-Erickson, Updegraff and McHale, 1999; Maccoby and Martin, 1983; Parke, 2002; Rothbaum and Weisz, 1994). Following these lines of thought, many researchers have also assumed that maternal reports of their children's lives are inherently valid, that is accurate reflections of the child.

Generally speaking, then, the large historical and contemporary literatures on child development that derive from 'parent' reports in actuality reflect mothers' assessments of their children. At the outset of their studies of infant temperament, for example, Thomas et al. (1963) proposed that mothers, by virtue of extensive contact with their babies, would serve as the richest source of information about babies and would provide the best assessments of infant temperament. Mothers have the opportunity to observe children across long periods of time and a great diversity of situations, including some that cannot be ethically simulated in the laboratory. So, the mother is often the only informant is developmental research and main analyses often hinge on only mother reports (e.g., Dionne et al., 2003; Tremblay et al., 1999; Vaillancourt et al., 2003). However, mothers' central position in the family can also compromise their perceptions. Feldman, Wentzel, and Gehring (1989) found that mothers' perceptions of family cohesion and power showed the least convergence with the perceptions of other family members and with

observed behavior, whereas fathers and sons provided relatively more objective information about family cohesion. These researchers argued that mothers, by virtue of their traditional responsibility for maintaining family intimacy and stability, may be particularly susceptible to biases in their perceptions of family functioning. Such limitations need to be addressed and may limit the generalizability of findings. (This issue is discussed further under 'perspectives' below.)

Mothers' reports in relation to the developmental literature

The general state of knowledge that parents possess about child development and childrearing constitutes a vital frame of reference from which they interpret their own children, and knowledge about child development affects parents' everyday decisions about their children's care and upbringing, which in turn affects children's development. Parenting knowledge helps parents develop more realistic expectations of their children and more accurate interpretations of their children's behaviors (Bornstein et al., 2008; Bugental and Happaney, 2002). Parents most likely report behavior that they deem as unusual, and knowledge of child development is basic to parents' understanding of what is, and is not, normal for a child of a certain age. In a nutshell, parenting knowledge affects parenting cognitions and practices which in turn affect children.

How do mothers compare with the empirical developmental literature? In one study, mothers of children ranging in age from 6 to 58 months were asked to determine, for separate pairings of language items and play items, which item was more advanced developmentally (Tamis-LeMonda, Chen and Bornstein, 1998). During the assessment, mothers were administered pairs of items from an 11-item language scale and then from an 11-item play scale using a paired-comparisons procedure presented on a computer. The mother's task was to indicate, by pressing a key, which member of the pair she thought to be the more difficult for a child and hence the one to be attained at a later age. In general, mothers' orderings of language and play items alike matched those established in the developmental literature. This procedure was repeated with the same mothers again two weeks later. Mothers' responses were also stable over the short term. However, mothers' knowledge about language development was stronger than, and unrelated to, their knowledge about play, suggesting that maternal knowledge about these two developmental domains is both differentiated and specific. The areas in which parents are more knowledgeable may depend on their goals for their children, what they deem to be important to their children's future, their children's own competencies and interests in specific areas, their parenting experience, and so forth (see Bornstein, 2002; Tamis-LeMonda and Bornstein, 1996).

Mothers' knowledge about child development and childrearing is relevant to parenting, parent–child interactions, and child development as well as to clinical practice. A three-part report investigated parenting knowledge in mothers of young children, where mothers obtained their knowledge, and what factors principally influenced the amount and accuracy of their knowledge (Bornstein et al., 2008). Mothers of 2-year-olds completed a standardized questionnaire of parenting knowledge and provided information about sociodemographic and health status variables as well as sources of support for their parenting. In one study, a large sample of American mothers participated. Mothers' age and education each uniquely contributed to higher scores in parenting knowledge. No differences were found between mothers of girls and boys, mothers' employment status, or birth and adoptive mothers; however, adult mothers scored higher than adolescent mothers, and mothers improved in their knowledge from their first to their second child and they were also stable in relation to parity.

In another study, Japanese and South American immigrant mothers to the United States were compared with Japanese and South American mothers in their countries of origin and to European American mothers in the United States. Immigrant mothers' parenting knowledge was more similar to mothers in their country of origin than to mothers in their country of destination. Nearly all of the questions that Japanese immigrant and South American immigrant mothers experienced difficulty answering concerned normative aspects of children's development and parent–child relationships during infancy. Immigrant mothers' knowledge of parenting increased over time. At the individual level, mothers' cultural cognitions (acculturation, individualism, collectivism) when their infants were 5 months old predicted their parenting knowledge 15 months later. Mothers' acculturation level predicted concurrent parenting knowledge for the Japanese immigrant mothers. Moreover, immigrant mothers' knowledge about child development related to their parenting behavior. For example, immigrant mothers with realistic expectations for infant crying expressed negative affect less frequently when with their baby than mothers who overestimated the amount of time newborns cry or report that they did not know what to expect. Mothers who had greater parenting knowledge overall were more likely to engage in activities that enhanced their children's development (such as talking to their babies more frequently).

In a third study, mothers participated representing six additional countries: Argentina, Belgium, France, Israel, Italy, and Japan. Cross-culturally, Israeli and US mothers scored highest, and Japanese mothers lowest, in parenting knowledge. Parents' knowledge is relevant to the welfare of children as understood by their parents and to clinical evaluations of child health.

Parents' knowledge of child development is important for physician–patient interactions because children's healthcare providers may assume that parents share their knowledge base. However, many report that they lack the skills necessary to interact with parents from different cultures. Because of the large influx of new immigrants to the United States, for example, pediatricians are increasingly likely to see immigrant families in their practice (Bornstein and Cote, 2008). Thus, they do not necessarily understand immigrant families, and immigrant parents may not be able to identify when their children are manifesting developmental problems (which could be mitigated by early intervention).

Increasing healthcare providers' knowledge of parents' cultural beliefs, and increasing healthcare providers' knowledge of child development, are key to creating more meaningful parent–healthcare provider partnerships that ensure, if not enhance, the well-being of children.

Mothers' reports in relation to other informants

Many investigators have sought to establish the convergent validity of maternal reports of, say, child language or temperament by indexing the extent to which maternal reports agree with others' assessments of language or temperament in the same children. Typically father, caregiver, or independent observer ratings have been used for comparison. Attempts to corroborate maternal reports with those of other observers have tended to show varying levels of convergent validity. Parents' reports of childhood behaviors (or even their own childrearing practices) frequently turn out to be less than perfect; Lytton's (1971) early review of studies of the convergence between maternal and objective assessments cited correlations of only 0.30–0.40 (see also, for example, Bates, 1980; Bates et al. 1979; Field and Greenberg, 1982; Hagekull, Bohlin and Lindhagen, 1984; Lounsbury and Bates, 1982; Lytton, 1971; Rothbart and Derryberry, 1981; Sameroff, Seifer and Elias, 1982; Vaughn, Taraldson, Crichton and Egeland, 1981), whereas reliability estimates of inter-observer assessments are typically higher, in the

0.60 to 0.90 range (Riese, 1983; Rothbart, 1986; Wilson and Matheny, 1983). Specifically, Rothbart (1981) reported relatively high IBQ 'household reliability' values in the range of 0.45 to 0.69. Davis, Schoppe-Sullivan, Mangelsdorf, and Brown (2009) reported mothers' and fathers' ratings of difficult temperament were correlated ($r = 0.52$, at 3.5 months and $r = 0.59$, at 13 months).

However, level of agreement between parents may vary with the domain, child age, or other factors. For example, on externalizing problem behaviors of their children, studies have generally found that fathers report fewer problem behaviors than mothers, but that level of disagreement is not influenced by the gender of the child (see the meta-analysis by Duhig et al., 2000). Only a small part of the difference between mother and father reports may be ascribed to rater bias (Hudziak et al., 2003; Ostrov, Crick and Keating, 2005; Van der Valk et al., 2003). Rather, disagreements between mothers and fathers may be attributed to the fact that the two parents have different experiences with their children (Hudziak et al., 2003). Mothers usually spend more time with their children than fathers and, as a result, have more exposure to any problem behaviors of their children (Christensen, Margolin and Sullaway, 1992). Consequently, parental disagreement may reflect actual differences in behaviors of children. On such logic, the use of multiple raters in the study of child development is often recommended (but see below).

Yet another metric against which mothers' reports of children have been assessed is standardized tests of their children. Informatively, high correlations between parent-report scores and child performance on concurrent standardized tests have been reported both for CDI (Dale, 1991; Dale et al., 1989; Feldman et al., 2005; Fenson et al., 1994) and LDS (Rescorla, 1989; Rescorla and Alley, 2001; Rescorla, Hadicke-Wiley and Escarce, 1993). Also a comparison between parental report and professional test scores with follow-up results showed that the two assessment methods yielded similar predictions (Sonnander, 1987).

Overall, a certain amount of skepticism surrounds the validity of maternal reports (Kagan, 1998; Seifer, 2002). For example, some investigators have looked at parents' reports of their children's medical (or even more specifically vaccination) history and found low levels of accuracy when compared with physician's records (McGraw and Molloy, 1941; Pyles et al., 1935; Willis, Brittingham, Lee and Tourangeau, 1999). Not unexpectedly, parents rather consistently over-report the number of vaccinations received by their children. The fact that parents overreport, rather than underreport, vaccinations could indicate a desire to be seen as responsible parents (social desirability). By contrast, however, parents' diaries of their children's spoken words (from 1 year, 2 months to 1 year, 10 months) show good agreement with representative checklists of words (Reznick and Goldfield, 1994). At 1 year, 8 months parent reports of vocabulary correlate with the total number of distinct words in an observed language sample, $r = 0.83$ (Dale, Bates, Reznick and Morisset, 1989). The word production checklist of the CDI correlates with laboratory observations of child vocabulary in the range of 0.60 to 0.80 (Bates and Carnevale, 1993). Maternal ratings of child language competence at 2 years old correlate highly ($r = 0.71$) with observer ratings of child communication and less, but still substantially ($rs = 0.45$ and 0.50), with standardized assessments of children, like the Peabody Picture Vocabulary Test and the Bayley Mental Development Index, respectively (Olson, Bates and Bayles, 1982). Finally, high degrees of agreement ($rs = 0.50–0.52$) obtain between parent report and experimenter assessments of language in clinically referred children (Chaffee et al., 1990).

In a study of infant temperament, Bornstein, Gaughran, and Seguí (1991) compared discrete and observable infant activities (reaching, kicking, smiling, and the like), and they did so with infants when with their mothers and an independent observer on two home visits spaced six days apart. Observers recorded infant behaviors during a structured series of vignettes, and mothers reported on those same behaviors. In addition, mothers completed general questionnaires of infants' activities (corresponding to the assessments) before the first and after the second home visit. Infants were five months old. Items were collected in an Infant Temperament Measure (ITM) designed for the study. Behavioral items in observational forms of the ITM proved psychometrically adequate; they showed individual variation, and mothers and independent observers alike showed significant, if moderate, short-term reliability on ITM items between the two home visits; mothers also showed moderate to high agreement in global ratings before and after the assessment series. No agreement between mothers' ratings made before and after the home visits with observer assessments on the home visits was found, however; but mother–observer agreement for assessments based on the home visits was significant, if moderate. Thus, mothers and observers agreed moderately well in themselves about infant behavior, but provided varying levels of convergence depending on aspects of the measurement situation. When mothers and observers reported about infants over the same time period, they agreed in a significant if moderate way (see, too, Hagekull et al., 1984), but when mothers reported globally about their infants, they did not agree well with what observers reported. Siefer, Sameroff, Barrett and Krafchuck (1994) also reported low correspondence between direct observations and mothers' reports of infant temperament. This pattern of findings suggests that the two kinds of assessors share perceptions of a small but significant proportion of the total variance in infant behavior; that each assessment may be reliable and hold potential validity; that mothers and observers adopt genuinely different 'points of view' of the same behaviors; and that mothers' accounts of their infants may not be 'biased' in the ways some researchers have supposed. When different informants use the same instrument in the same situations in the same circumscribed observation period, it appears to increase agreement (Bornstein, Gaughran and Homel, 1986). Bornstein et al. (1991) found mother–observer agreement for assessments based on shared observations improved substantially.

In short, studies comparing ratings of children's behavior made by mothers and trained observers have identified somewhat overlapping but not identical perceptions across informants (Achenbach et al., 1987; Hinshaw et al., 1992; Phares, Compas and Howell, 1989). Parents demonstrate agreement with observers regarding infant temperament despite the fact the two adults may interact with the infant at different times, elicit different behaviors, and differentially interpret infant behavior (Gartstein and Rothbart, 2003; Parade and Leerkes, 2008). Even if it is true that mothers are the most knowledgeable individuals about their children, it is also true that different individuals, *qua* sources of information about a child, hold different relations to the child, vary in their standards in judging the child, and interact with the child in different conditions with different criteria in mind, and from different perspectives. In many families young children spend considerable time with adults besides their mothers. These individuals include fathers, grandparents, childcare providers, and others (Clarke-Stewart and Allhusen, 2002; Parke, 2002; Smith and Drew, 2002). Also, the situations in which young children spend time with their mothers usually differ from the situations in which they spend time with their other caregivers. Research in temperament and personality, for example, attests that these several factors can result in different estimations of the child (see Achenbach, McConaughy and Howell, 1987; Bornstein et al., 1986; Kazdin, 1988; Verhulst and Koot, 1992). Consider the case of child language. When different adults converse with the same child, they do not necessarily discuss the same topics or use identical words. As a consequence, lexical usage between children and adults typically can be expected to vary across circumstances as well as across conversants. Thus, any one adult familiar with a particular child normally knows that child only on the basis of his or her own interactions with the child. It follows that, if different adults familiar with a child are asked to report about, say, that child's vocabulary, they will not necessarily entirely agree. No single reporter can provide a complete picture of the child. Different speakers and different settings for conversation undoubtedly give rise to the use of different words by both children and adults. This circumstance brings with it the possibility that relying mainly on only one reporter mis- or (more likely) underestimates children. Specifically, mothers may only know about a portion of the words their children know, and hence are limited in what they are able to report. If so, additional data from other reporters are needed for a more complete, accurate, and valid evaluation of the words a particular child knows.

To show what differences can exist across different reporters' assessments of the same child's word knowledge, De Houwer, Bornstein, and Leach (2005) analyzed data from 30 families using (a Dutch version of) the MacArthur Communicative Development Inventory (Zink and Lejaegere, 2002) when the children were 13 months of age. Data were collected from up to three different reporters for the same child (mothers, fathers, and third persons). Each person independently completed a CDI for a given child. The most obvious way of comparing how different reporters assess a particular child is to count the number of words each reporter provides. A simple summing of raw scores for each reporter showed (as expected) large differences in how reporters evaluated the same child. An example makes this finding clear: One young child said seven words according to her mother, eleven words according to her father, and seven words according to her childcare provider. Simply summing these estimates would credit the child with 25 words and averaging across informants would yield 8.33 words. This simple frequency analysis only gives a rough estimate of quantitative differences; however, it does not say anything about the number of different words a child knows or the degrees of agreement between reporters on specific lexical items. Suppose the father claims that his child says 11 words. These words might include the seven words claimed by the mother, or the the two could be completely separate sets, or something in between. When item-by-item comparisons were made, results showed, not unexpectedly, that individual reporters differed from one another substantially in what they reported with regard to child vocabulary knowledge. In no single family did all reporters agree with each other completely for all the words on the CDI. Both within any particular family, and when families are compared with each other, cross-reporter agreement on CDI words was highly variable. There proved to be considerable inter- and intrafamily variation in how different reporters, who were all presumably close to the same child, assessed that particular child's word knowledge. Moreover, when all three reporters were considered together on an item-by-item basis, the child in question was reported to produce 14 different lexical items. Summing overestimates and averaging underestimates the number of different words that the child was able to say. Only an item-by-item comparison across reporters yielded an appropriate cumulative vocabulary score. In comparison with cumulative scores, individual reporter scores typically underestimated children's lexical repertoires (Bornstein et al., 2006).

As stated at the outset of this chapter, there are three main ways to extract information about children: interviewing or testing children themselves, observing and recording them directly, and seeking out people closest to children to report about them. A few studies have compared pairs of procedures in the same children (see, for example, Fenson et al., 1994), but only one study has explored

relations among all three types of methods over the same topic in the same children: experimenter assessments of the child, naturalistic observations of the child, and parent reports about the child. This approach combines the prominent methods for examining the child and emulates the advantages of the multitrait-multimethod perspective (Campbell and Fiske, 1959) in pursuit of comprehensive validity in assessment. Bornstein and Haynes (1998) collected data from 184 20-month-olds and their mothers using two measures of each of the three assessment approaches. They found a high degree of order agreement among the three different sources of information about child language status. Those children who used more words and longer utterances in everyday speech with their mothers were children whom independent experimenters assessed as comprehending and being able to produce more vocabulary, and they were also the children whose mothers independently reported and rated that they knew more words and spoke in more sophisticated ways. This study, perhaps unique for its sample size, multivariate measures, and use of appropriate covariates (maternal verbal intelligence, maternal social desirability, and child sociability), provided stable estimates on the high degrees of order agreement across different perspectives on child language. The results of this study showed convergence among different measures of language in the same children, but the study relied on measures of agreement of children's relative standing on the different approaches, and was not designed to address the issue of absolute levels of vocabulary knowledge (how many words children know) as determined by different methods.

The convergent validity of parent reports cannot be properly evaluated by comparing sets of observations obtained by different methods and with different task demands. In this context, findings regarding poor parent–observer convergence may speak as much to measurement failure as to parent bias. Discrepancies are often contributed to by situational specificity (Achenbach et al., 1987) as when children are seen in different situations, and thus, from different perspectives. Some child behaviors are more obvious in one context than another (such as, attention problems to TV vs. in school). For example, as parents and teachers observe the same children in different settings, it can be expected that their ratings may agree but may not perfectly correlate (Harrison, 1985; Mayfield, Forman and Nagle, 1984; Meanlior and Richman, 1980; Rainwater-Bryant, 1985). Sparrow and Cicchetti (1978), Cicchetti and Sparrow (1981), and Tombokan-Runtukahu and Nitko (1992) all reported high (but not perfect) correlations between primary caregivers' estimates of levels of child adaptive behavior and independent teachers' assessments. To optimize convergence, maternal and observer perspectives need to be investigated simultaneously through a methodology that is time-limited and focused. It is informative in this context to consider the results of an observational paradigm used by Cummings, Zahn-Waxler, and Radke-Yarrow (1981). These investigators trained mothers to observe and report the reactions of their 1- to 2.5-year-olds to emotional expressions of family members. Under these circumstances, mothers' reports closely agreed with those of observers. As in Bornstein et al. (1991), it is telling that mother and observer ratings are comparable when specific behaviors are observed and the observation time frame is coincident for different raters. Understanding sources of discrepancy allows optimizing prediction of later behavior by including systematic sources of bias. In one study, African-American coders rated mothers as less controlling and rated mother–adolescent dyadic interactions as less conflictual, and their ratings were more consistent with the perceptions of the participant African-American mothers and adolescents than were ratings provided by non-African-American coders (Gonzales, Cauce and Mason, 1996).

Mothers' reports in relation to their own children's reports

For children over a certain age, where it is useful and feasible to obtain a report from the child as well as the parent, there seem to be only moderate degrees of agreement between parent and child reports on most target behaviors (Hill, 2002). Investigations of agreement between child reports and parent reports of child emotional and behavior problems, for example, show that children and their parents often do not agree about the number or severity of problems children suffer (see, for example, Seiffge-Krenke and Kollmar, 1998; Waters, Stewart-Brown and Fitzpatrick, 2003). Achenbach et al.'s (1987) meta-analysis of 119 studies showed that the average correlation between parent and child reports of child problems was only 0.25. Correlations were greater for younger children (6 to 11 years) compared with adolescents (12 to 19 years) and were greater for externalizing problems compared to internalizing problems. Others have since reported correlations between parent and child reports of child problems ranging from the 0.20s to the 0.60s (for example, Achenbach, Dumenci and Rescorla, 2002; Theunissen et al., 1998). Overall, the magnitude of correlations between parent and adolescent reports of adolescent problems in community and clinical samples alike are normally low to moderate. Studies of community samples also show that, on average, adolescents report more problems than their parents, whereas studies of clinical samples show that, on average, adolescents report fewer problems than do their parents (Stanger and Lewis, 1993; Thurber and Osborn, 1993; Thurber and Snow, 1990; Waters et al., 2003). Thus, adolescents' Youth Self Report scores differ from parents' Child Behavior Checklist scores. Moreover, discrepancies tend to be larger for externalizing problems, for girls, and for older adolescents.

Similar results appear in other domains of child development. Parent and child report of weight-related behaviors show disagreement (Haines et al., 2008). Disagreements could reflect family member differences in expectations and cognitions regarding the family and familial relationships, which may be more common among families with adolescent children (Paikoff and Brooks-Gunn, 1991; Smetana, 1989).

A question that arises in this connection is whether, in any given community or clinical sample of adolescents and their parents, some adolescents report fewer problems, and others report more problems, than their parents. When some adolescents report fewer problems compared with parent reports, and others in the same sample report more problems than parents, calculating correlations and testing mean differences between adolescents and parents for aggregated samples may mask individual differences and bias agreement indices. Barker, Bornstein, Putnick, Hendricks, and Suwalsky (2007) studied both individual-difference order and group-level mean agreement between adolescent and maternal reports of adolescent internalizing and externalizing problems, taking into account the direction of disagreement. That is, the samples were analyzed and contrasted with agreement indices calculated separately for mother – adolescent dyads where adolescents reported fewer problems than mothers and for dyads where adolescents reported more problems than mothers. When the direction of discrepancies was taken into consideration, parents of adolescents who themselves reported more problems tended also to rate their adolescents as having more problems (in other words, moderate to strong order agreement). Two-thirds to three-quarters of adolescents reported more problems than mothers. Accounting for the direction of discrepancies resulted in improved agreement between adolescents and mothers.

Agreement between African-American mothers and their early adolescent daughters on measures of maternal support, maternal restrictive control, and parent–adolescent conflict were examined in another study (Gonzales et al., 1996). To assess the relative validity of these reports, the study then evaluated dyads against the ratings of independent observers. Additionally, mother and daughter reports were combined to examine validity coefficients based on aggregate scores of each construct. All analyses were based on two sets of objective criterion ratings: ratings provided by coders of similar ethnic background (African-American) and coders who were ethnically dissimilar (non-African-American) to the families they rated. Overall, adolescents provided ratings that accorded more than those of their mothers with both sets of independent ratings. Adolescent ratings of maternal control and parent–adolescent conflict converged at higher levels than ratings provided by mothers. Maternal and adolescent reports of maternal support converged with objective criteria at comparable levels.

Parents consistently perceive families as more loving, more cohesive, and more adaptive to stress and rate family interactions as more open and less conflictual than do their adolescent children (Callan and Noller, 1986; Feldman et al., 1989; Niemi, 1974; Ohannessian, Lerner and Von Eye, 1994). Smetana, Yau, Restrepo, and Braeges (1990) examined adolescents' and parents' views of conflict in relation to independent ratings of their relationship and found mothers' views to be the most discrepant, even more so than fathers' views, whereas adolescents' ratings were found to be congruent with those of trained observers.

Understanding the nature of adolescent–parent discrepancies in reporting has important implications for help-seeking and intervention, and ultimately the well-being of children, because, for example, parents are more likely to seek help for their children than children are for themselves (Berger, Jodl, Allen, McElhaney and Kuperminc, 2005; De Los Reyes and Kazdin, 2005). Understanding informant disagreement (and its sources) likewise has implications for research on childhood disorders because different samples of children will be identified as having problems depending on the reporter (Kazdin, 1994). Depending on their intensity, duration, and whether or not they are resolved, adolescent-parent disagreements can negatively impact adolescent and parent adjustment (Laursen and Collins, 2009; Patterson, Capaldi and Bank, 1991) and parent–child relationships (Belsky et al., 2001) over both the short- and long-term.

Some general observations about parent reports

This discussion of any putative validity of parental report raises ancillary but, nonetheless, important considerations of perspective, domain, accuracy, and reliability. Each has been hinted at to this point, but each merits separate brief deliberation.

Shared vs. unique perspectives

As do any individuals, different family members can experience the same event in different ways (Bartle-Haring, Kenny and Gavazzi, 1999; Deković and Buist, 2005). As just reviewed, research indicates that different family members often answer the same questions about the child differently and they correlate at low to moderate levels (Caster, Inderbitzen and Hope, 1999; Tein, Roosa and Michaels, 1994). Certainly, measurement error contributes to modest correlations among family members' reports about children, but actual differences in perspective doubtlessly contribute as well (Cook and Goldstein, 1993; Eisler, Dare and Szmukler, 1988). Each family member's perspective of the child is to some degree subjective. So, researchers interested in child development often incorporate the perspectives of multiple family members and focus on where those perspectives of the child overlap or converge. Relative to any single family member's perspective of the child, these 'shared perspectives,' which represent the portions of individual perspectives that generalize across, or are shared by, two or more family members, are thought to paint a

more reliable and objective picture of the child (Bartle-Haring et al., 1999; Deković and Buist, 2005). However, this thinking neglects the portion of each family member's perspective of the child that is not shared by any other family member; that is, the portion of each family member's perspective that is idiosyncratic to the individual. Many authorities acknowledge the potential importance of each family member's non-shared or unique perspective on the child (Carlson, Cooper and Spradling, 1991; Cook and Goldstein, 1993; Deal, 1995). In short, each family member has multiple unique perspectives, each specific to a different domain of the child (the specificity principle; Bornstein, 2006). Family members' unique perspectives are subjective and relatively independent of each other. Relative to shared perspectives, researchers have paid far less attention to unique perspectives, the portions of each family member's view of the child that are not shared by any other family member (for an illustration applied to family members' shared and unique perspectives of family dysfunction, see Jager et al., 2012).

One immediate consequence of this unique perspectives view is that 'discrepancies' between reporters about children reflect real differences in the perspectives from which, say, family members or family members and observers view the child (Barnes and Olson, 1985). Children and parents have overlapping but discrete perceptions of each other and of their relationships (Cashmore and Goodnow, 1985; Demo et al., 1987; Jessop, 1982; Noller and Callan, 1988; Phares, Compas and Howell, 1989).

Domains of parent reports

Parent reports cover many domains of child development, parenting, and family life; and the accuracy of parent reports appears to vary by the subject reported. Parent reports first included understanding children – the basic needs, abilities, and accomplishments of children as they grow. Prominent, for example, were expectations about developmental norms and milestones – when a child is expected to attain particular developmental skills. Such expectations are important because they can affect parents' appraisals of their child's development. Do findings of convergence about children extend across multiple domains of development? Parents' attention to, knowledge of, and reports about different specific domains of children's development appear to be specialized and thus vary as a function of the domain being assessed. For example, mothers' knowledge about developments in child language differs from their knowledge about developments in child play, perhaps because of different societal emphases placed on the two domains. In Western cultures, the timely acquisition of key language milestones (for example, first words or combinatorial speech) is considered to be an important child achievement. As a consequence, language skills might be salient to mothers who are vigilant about or actively seek information about their children's normative development in that arena. In contrast, the importance of play as a window on children's abilities is less well recognized. As a consequence of these differential emphases, language achievements may be salient to parents, or parents may be especially motivated to seek out information about early and normative development in this domain. It could be, too, that parents' reports about play might not be as extensive as their reports about language because the two are differentially influenced by individual factors such as parents' education or personal views about the importance of one versus the other domain in children's development.

The idea that parents' reports are specialized derives from new models that suggest that parenting is best conceptualized as multidimensional, modular, and specific, and relates in specific ways to specific developments in children (see, Bornstein, 1989, 1995, 2002, 2006). Parents may be better able to report on some aspects of child development than others, too, because one dimension assesses more nuanced behaviors

that reflect interactional sequences contingent on judgments about the child's moment-to-moment behavior more than another. It may be too that domains that call on the dynamic nature of child development or parenting are more difficult to report about because parents see those domains as shifting contingent on others' behavior.

Parent reports that focus on overt, frequent, concrete, and external behaviors and developmental milestones that are obvious and that parents are likely to notice (for example, 'feeds self with a fork', 'addresses at least two familiar people by name', 'walks as a primary means of getting around') should be more accurate than covert, infrequent, ephemeral, or internal ones. Expectedly, the extent to which parents and children disagree about child problems appears to vary as a function of the problem being assessed (for example, externalizing acting out versus internalizing depression problems). The chances that different evaluators will agree on particular words of the CDI are highest when children understand relatively few words. The larger the child's lexicon, as rated by any one reporter, the more differences tend to emerge between reporters. Maternal reports at four years postpartum for their smoking during pregnancy were more reliable ($r = 0.81$) than for alcohol consumption ($r = 0.53$), presumably because smoking is more habitual and therefore easier to recall (Jacobson and Jacobson, 1990). In a parallel way, recall of the number of sexual partners individuals have over a period of one month, three months, six months, and one year, studied in a group of 285 young, single, heterosexual adults, shows that accuracy rates tend to be lower for individuals who report having more sexual partners (Jaccard et al., 2004). If a parent views temperament or personality to be difficult, then the parent may be more likely to generalize this perception across situations and report more problems in the child. Parents may be more accurate at judging (the relative difficulty of) activities that fall within their child's current age range than they are at judging activities that are above or below their child's current age (Goodnow and Collins, 1990). Mothers' judgments about developmental milestones depend on their children's current developmental level: Mothers are less accurate at estimating the timing of milestones that their children mastered many months earlier, supporting the view that mothers' knowledge is informed by their children's recent rather than past achievements in specific areas. Thus, specific areas of parent reports about children depend on the developmental stage of their child.

Time too is of the essence. Majnemer and Rosenblatt (1994) observed that telescoping varied depending on the milestone the parent was asked to recall. In their study, 91 percent of caregivers recalled the age of their child's first steps within two months of the originally reported age. However, only 59 percent reported word acquisition within two months of the original report; 20 percent of caregivers reported ages that were between six and twenty-five months later than first indicated. Caregivers can report children as having acquired developmental milestones earlier or later than they were actually achieved. This phenomenon, referred to as 'telescoping', can impact retrospective reports provided by caregivers of children. Telescoping of language milestones has been documented in ASD children, resulting in more children meeting language delay criteria as they grew older, in spite of original reports that their language was not delayed (Hus, Taylor and Lord, 2011). There was little evidence of consistent telescoping of caregiver-reported ages of first concern, daytime bladder control, and independent walking (Hus et al., 2011).

Accuracy of parents' reports

Several diverse factors affect the accuracy of parent reports. First, parents' reports generally underestimate true levels of child status. Parents tend to report what they notice, whereas children's competencies typically antecede and exceed their performance. The vehicle of report is a second issue.

Checklists, are normally based on fixed numbers of predetermined items, and so can never provide a complete picture of children. Third, nearly all parental report measures rely on single assessments which are global in that parents are asked to condense a wealth of experience into statements about their children's average or typical behavior. Aggregation improves agreement between mothers and observers (Forman et al., 2003) and is commonly recommended to enhance the reliability and validity of measures derived from multiple reporters (Kenny and Berman, 1980; Schwartz Barton-Henry and Pruzinsky, 1985). However, even when parents are asked to review and report on behaviors occurring within a short time interval (one week in Rothbart's IBQ), the dual tasks of retrospection and summarization can be expected to generate a certain amount of measurement error. For example, the past can be distorted in the service of contemporary needs and constructions (Ross, 1989). (Indeed, children with more favorable characteristics are more likely to be retrospectively reported as wanted by their parents; Rosenzweig and Wolpin, 1993.) Last, it is always uncertain whether mothers (or fathers) and observers define behaviors similarly and employ the same criteria when rating behaviors (Hubert et al., 1982). In this regard, parents' reports are often considered not rigid 'gold standards', but rather 'estimates' of general development. Different informants contribute distinct but overlapping perspectives, as noted earlier, and to report about children it may be essential to include the perspectives of multiple informants, even if they do not correlate well with each other (Achenbach et al., 1987; Feldman et al., 1989; Schwarz et al., 1985).

Short-term reliability of parents' reports

Evidence of test-retest reliability is basic to construct validation. It is psychometrically fundamental, if not requisite, to establish the reliability of parenting reports over brief periods. What are the data on the short-term reliability of parental reports? Individual mothers demonstrate variation in their judgments about children that should be relatively stable over the short term. For example, parental reports about child language and play are stable over one week (Tamis-LeMonda et al., 1998). The six-week test-retest reliability for the MacArthur CDI exceeds 0.90 (Fenson et al., 1993). Sparrow et al. (1984) showed the VABS has high two-week reliability: $r = 0.88$. The reliability of reports of physical aggression are also moderate for 12-month-olds and high for 24- and 36-month-olds (Alink et al., 2006). These findings suggest that mothers have formulated relatively stable schemas about specific areas of their children's accomplishments and that these schemas constitute a relatively consistent part of mothers' knowledge base at least over brief time periods. Similarly, mothers' initial global reports of infant temperament and their follow-on home-based assessments, as well as their final reports, reflect relatively strong reliability (Bornstein et al., 1998). Of course, studies that purport to report reliability of specific measures of children suffer certain noteworthy shortfalls as they draw on the same reporter over a short period, and so shared source and method variance may inflate reliability correlations.

Factors that affect the 'accuracy' of parental reports

Many factors might relate to or determine agreement levels between parents' and others' reports about children. Besides the domain parents are asked to report about, three prominent classes include: factors in the parent, factors in the child, and factors in the relationship between the parent and child.

Factors in the parent

It has been said that 'the aspects of the environment that are most powerful in shaping the course of psychological growth are overwhelmingly those that have meaning to the person in a given situation' (Bronfenbrenner, 1979: 22). In the face of

varying mother–observer convergence estimates about some domains of child development, researchers proposed that parent reports might reflect characteristics of the parent as much or more than those of the child (see, for example, Bates et al., 1979; Sameroff et al., 1982; Vaughn et al., 1981). Important sources of variability are thought to include parents' cognitions, personality and sociodemographic characteristics (Bates and Bayles, 1984; Vaughn, Bradley, Joffe, Seifer and Barglow, 1987). With respect to cognitions, when child behavior is assessed by parent report, both the behavior and the perception of the behavior are assessed. Willis et al. (1999) found that parents had difficulty reporting the number and type of vaccinations immediately following a paediatric appointment while vaccines were administered. This kind of error implicates memory, and in particular encoding (Bornstein et al., 2007; Bornstein, Hahn and Haynes, 2011).

Other individual cognitive factors might include intelligence, attributions, and parents' cognitive structuring of their own childhoods. Discrepancies between parents' and others' reports may reflect parental attributions (De Los Reyes and Kazdin, 2005). That is, parents make assumptions about their child's behavior that others may not make and so the two do not share the same perceptions (Bugental and Happaney, 2002). Biringen (1990) reported that recall of general parental acceptance by mothers (using the Mother–Father–Peer Scale developed by Epstein, 1983) correlated with ratings of observed sensitivity to their infants, observed dyadic physical avoidance (warm and responsive interactions with their infants vs. cool and avoidant ones), level of dyadic harmony existing between themselves and their infants, and their perceptions of their infants' responsiveness to them. The valence of the memory (i.e. negative) may influence the valence parents place on social behavior (having positive or negative childhood peer recollections may alter their child's social interactions). Parental memory leads to parental interpretations. As Schaefer and Keith (1985) observed, people's thoughts and actions are often based on their definition of a situation.

With respect to personality, for example, there is some evidence that mothers' own personality characteristics are associated with their ratings of their infants' temperament (Diener, Goldstein and Mangelsdorf, 1995; Mebert, 1991). A different personality explanation for report inaccuracy is social desirability. Social desirability is the tendency of informants to present information about themselves in a way that enhances their worth (Bornstein et al., 2013). Social desirability often takes the form of emphasizing or exaggerating attributes, attitudes, or behaviors that are socially valued, and minimizing or underreporting ones that are socially disapproved (DeMaio, 1984). The fact that parents over-report rather than under-report vaccinations (Willis et al., 1999) could indicate a desire to be seen as responsible parents. Kagan (1998) argued that parents' answers to questionnaires may be distorted by just such a desire to cast their children in a positive light and to present themselves as consistent. He also suggested that parents interpret survey questions in idiosyncratic ways. Other individual personality factors might include mood state and depressive affect. Pettit and colleagues (Pettit and Laird, 2002; Pettit et al., 2001) found that higher levels of parental warmth and nurturance and a noncoercive parenting style during kindergarten were positively associated with maternal knowledge of adolescent behavior during eighth grade. By contrast, parents who appear indifferent or unattached vis-à-vis their children exhibit low parental knowledge (Dishion and McMahon, 1998). Depressed mothers' reports of infants' negative emotionality are less accurate than those of nondepressed mothers. Maternal depression also predicts discrepancies between adolescent and mother reports of adolescent behavior problems; mothers with increased levels of depression tend to report more problems for their adolescents than adolescents

report for themselves (Berg-Nielsen, Vika and Dahl, 2003).

In another vein, McGillicuddy-DeLisi (1982a; 1982b) asserted that parental beliefs about child development are constructed and modified on the basis of an adult's personal experiences as a parent (see also Bornstein, 1995; Goodnow, 1995; McGillicuddy-DeLisi and Sigel, 1995). Parenting experience (e.g., parity) appears to be associated with greater accuracy of maternal reports. Parents, and young or inexperienced parents in particular, are presumably less able to judge the frequency or intensity of their child's emotional behavior, for example, because they lack knowledge of sufficient comparison children as referents (Forman et al., 2003).

In addition, multiple other parental characteristics, such as age, education and socioeconomic status, have all been identified at one time or another as factors in parents that can affect parent reports (Bugental and Happaney, 2002; De Los Reyes and Kazdin, 2005). Several maternal variables have been identified in this connection, including employment status (Pederson, Zaslow, Cain, Anderson and Thomas, 1976), extraversion, achievement orientation, and parity (Bates et al., 1979), psychological status as measured by mental test batteries (Vaughn et al., 1981), and socioeconomic status, anxiety level, mental health status, and ethnicity (Sameroff et al., 1982). Several researchers have documented a pattern of reduced lexical development in children from low-income families (Hart and Risley, 1995; Whitehurst, 1997). For example, Arriaga, Fenson, Cronan, and Pethick (1998) observed lower CDI scores among low-income children. However, as Fenson et al. (2000: 327) observed, 'it is not yet clear whether the lower scores for low-income children reflect a slower pace of language development or underestimation or incomplete reporting by their parents'. That said, parents from low- and middle-income families complete Age and Stages Questionnaires with comparable accuracy (Squires, Potter, Bricker and Lamorey, 1998).

Some parent characteristics have been found to exhibit stronger relations to reports of child behavior than objective measures of child behavior. In one study, for example, Bates et al. (1979) compared the contribution of infant behaviors with maternal ratings of 'fussy-difficult' temperament against the contribution of maternal personality and sociodemographic characteristics. Maternal variables predicted maternal ratings better than did objectively observed infant behaviors. Similarly, Vaughn et al. (1981) found significant associations between maternal characteristics and maternal temperament ratings, where associations between infant behavior and maternal ratings of temperament failed to reach significance. In a third study, Sameroff et al. (1982) compared maternal ratings of 4-month-olds on Carey's parent-report ITQ first with laboratory and home observations of babies' temperament and then with maternal characteristics such as anxiety level and socioeconomic status. Multiple regression analyses established that maternal variables were better predictors of temperament score variance than were child variables (maternal variables tended to remain significant net child variables, but the reverse was not true). Sameroff et al. (1982: 172) proposed that 'in the face of labile infant behaviors on a changing developmental trajectory, the parents' responses to the questionnaire items must reflect ... their attributions rather than ... [the] infant's behavior.' Finally, beliefs and so reports about children might reflect normative cultural socialization and values (Lightfoot and Valsiner, 1992; Russell and Russell, 1982). As Kessen (1965) observed, parents may be biased informants in various ways: their relationships with offspring, their personality characteristics, their own theories of development, and their efforts to present their children (and themselves) positively can each skew their child reports. For these reasons, there has been continuing vigorous debate concerning the suitability of using parent reports and the extent to which report measures can be made more valid

(cf. Kagan, 1998, with Rothbart and Bates, 1998, 2006).

An enticing extension of this focus on maternal characteristics turns on the possible role of mothers' initial and current reconstructions of their own childhoods for their childrearing intensions as well as their children's development. For example, Main, Kaplan, and Cassidy (1985) developed an Adult Attachment Interview to identify the security status of adults. Parents' recollections of the security of their own attachments relates to their infants' security of attachment (see also Biringen, 1990; Miljkovitch, Pierrehumbert, Bretherton and Halfon, 2004). In addition, mothers' recollections of their own childhood peer relationships relate to their children's social development (Puallatz, Costanzo and Smith, 1991).

Factors in the child

Apart from the specific domain of report, child characteristics, including age, health status, and social competence, can influence parent reports. Children will vary on every given characteristic, and thus for some children reporters might agree, but for other children cross-reporter differences could be substantial.

When parents are involved with a child of a particular age, their reports about the child at that age may be relatively faithful. However, once their child is beyond the age they are asked about, parents appear to rely on generalized stereotypes. That is, parents appear to revert to preconceptions once particular experiences with a child have passed (DeGrada and Ponzo, 1971). When parents of older children are asked to make judgments about younger ones, they typically underestimate children's abilities, a finding that reflects their general bias toward considering young children to be 'babies' (D'Alessio, 1990).

It may be that knowledge about child development is only temporarily informed by current parenting. Parents tend to be more accurate at judging childhood milestones that are close to their own children's current developmental stage. As children advance beyond particular developmental periods, their awareness of the timing of past accomplishments tends to dim. Thus, parents tend to overestimate the ages at which milestones occur when asked to make retrospective judgments. As hypothesized, parents consistently overestimate the ages at which language and play milestones emerge, thereby underestimating the abilities of younger children. The lower accuracy of these parents, as well as the direction of error in their age estimates, accords with the research of DeGrada and Ponzo (1971) and D'Alessio (1977) in which adults were found to systematically underestimate the abilities of young children. Parents are cognitively aware of developments in their children's competencies, but that awareness tends to be circumscribed to the period surrounding children's current or emerging abilities (Tamis-LeMonda et al., 1998). As children develop, parents refocus the spotlight of sensitivity to highlight their children's most recent accomplishments as well as those that are anticipated to occur in the near future.

Children's health status is another individual-difference factor. For example, after a child has received a diagnosis of ASD, caregivers may tend to endorse behaviors, such as language delay, that are consistent with their child's diagnosis (Zwaigenbaum et al., 2007).

Stattin and Kerr (Stattin and Kerr, 2000; Kerr and Stattin, 2000) and others (see, for example, Marshall, Tilton-Weaver and Bosdet, 2005) have suggested that much of the knowledge parents have about their children's behaviors and activities comes from children's open disclosure of information to parents in the first place. Some children are more open than others (Soenens et al., 2006), and so parent reports can be expected to vary accordingly.

Child gender, birth order, and personality, among other factors, may also influence parent report. For example, parents' recall of earlier aggression in children may be biased by current levels of child aggression as it may be by current family situation and the behavior of other children.

Factors in the parent–child relationship and family

Parent reports may be subject to the influence of experience and hence susceptible to feedback from parent–child encounters. That is, insofar as different parents have experienced different developmental histories with their children, their reports might reflect those histories. Thus, parent–child relationship characteristics are influential in parent reports (Holmbeck, Li, Schurman, Friedman and Coakley, 2002; Kazdin, 1994). Parent–adolescent attachment is positively associated with parents' knowledge of their 6th graders' day-to-day experiences (Kerns et al., 2001). By the same token, changes in parent–child relationships, such as increased negative affect associated with parent–child conflict (Collins and Laursen, 2004) or adolescents spending more time with peers (Brown, 2004), tend to disrupt parent–child communication and so attenuate parent-report accuracy. Discrepancies between adolescent and parent reports of problems arise when parent–adolescent relationships are emotionally distant, or if their communication patterns and interactions are negative. If relationships are strained, adolescents may not be willing to share information with parents, undermining parent reports. Parental knowledge is determined by many factors, and the quality of the parent–child relationship is one (Crouter and Head, 2002). Positive parent–child relationships expand knowledge, such as noticing a child's demeanor and enhances a child's motivation to divulge significant information to parents (Crouter et al., 1999; Dishion and McMahon, 1998; Formoso, Gonzales and Aiken, 2000; Jacobson and Crockett, 2000; Kerr and Stattin, 2000). Thus, parent–child relationship quality predicts knowledge: Cohesive parent–adolescent relationships, characterized by emotional connection, positive affect, and positive interaction, are associated with greater parental knowledge (Gondoli et al., 2008).

Finally, factors in the family (family size, structure, SES, ethnicity) apparently matter as well to parent reports (Laursen and Collins, 2009; Paikoff and Brooks-Gunn, 1991). Reciprocally, looking at one kind of child characteristic, temperament, from the point of view of parental reports is telling. Several maternal variables have been identified in this connection, including employment status (Pederson et al., 1976), extraversion, achievement orientation, and parity (Bates et al., 1979), psychological status as measured by mental test batteries (Vaughn et al., 1981), and socioeconomic status, anxiety level, mental health status, and ethnicity (Sameroff et al., 1982).

Summary

Parents seem not to function as perfect reporters of their children's lives; rather, parental (maternal) reports are thought to be colored by life circumstances, psychological functioning, and expectations regarding the child. Perhaps it is fairest to conclude simply that parent reports are simultaneously subjective and objective. Many factors affect the accuracy and validity of parental reporters and reports, including the domain, the reporter, the metric, the child, and the parent–child relationship. Nonetheless, parents' objectivity can be enhanced by asking them to provide specific reports based on observations of their children over specific periods of time, rather than general conclusions about their children's general attributes (Bornstein, Tamis-LeMonda, Suwalsky and Haynes, 1991).

More generally, it is widely acknowledged that no single approach to reporting about child development is best, that no one representation of a developmental phenomenon predominates. For this reason, those who study child development often advocate the wisdom of applying multiple assessments and employing converging operations of different strategies targeted to the same phenomenon. In that way, similarities and differences among all sources of information can be compared, and their implications adequately evaluated. Employing observations, assessments, and reports together overcomes shortfalls of reliance on any single source. Multiple assessments also represent individuals better than do single assessments. It is unlikely that complex developmental phenomena, such as language or temperament or adaptation or problem behaviors or health in children, can be adequately represented from any single perspective. Parents are not trained observers and may be overgenerous, or they may fail to notice subtle aspects of development. Multiple reporters may provide a more accurate picture of a child than any single reporter (Marchman and Martínez-Sussmann, 2002). That said, there is still no 'gold standard' for validating parental report. Each person's experiences with a particular child will differ from that of another person. Hence, each reporter is likely to differ from every other reporter. Furthermore, observation per se distorts and is undeniably intrusive (Heisenberg, 1927). The presence of the observer may represent a kind of novelty that evokes atypical responses from those observed, a phenomenon termed 'reactivity' (Haynes, 1978; Lambert, 1960; Weick, 1968). Thus, observation itself may promote socially desirable or appropriate behaviors and suppress socially undesirable or inappropriate behaviors (for example, adults may display higher rates of positive interactions with children; Baum et al., 1979; Zegiob et al., 1975). In the end, no measure based on a single person's perspective can give a complete picture of the child either. Different reporters evaluating the same child give different, and sometimes divergent, accounts. Having convergent reports about children might in some cases represent a better estimate of children and, consequently, a better understanding and interpretation of childhood. However, when perspectives genuinely diverge, aggregation may equally well mislead.

THE VALUE, MEANING, AND USE OF PARENTAL REPORTS ABOUT CHILDREN AND THEIR PRACTICAL IMPLICATIONS

Given that parental reports represent a child and are the easiest and most economical to obtain, we can ask what they tell us about the child. Predictive validity answers whether a measure provides information that enables expectation of (related) behavior. Predictive validity is important to assess, too, because of concerns that parental perceptions may be biased in some way(s). In the domain of language, for example, parental reports relate concurrently to laboratory measures of child language (Bornstein and Haynes, 1998; Fenson et al., 1994; Marchman and Martinez-Sussmann, 2002) in a generally strong way (median $r = 0.61$; Fenson et al., 1994). A few studies give evidence of associations between items in temperament ratings and concurrently measured target variables, such as aberrant levels of dopamine-beta-hydroxylase (Rapoport et al., 1977) or amount, rated aversiveness, and acoustic properties of infant crying (Lounsbury and Bates, 1982). Predictively, parental report of child language portends subsequent vocabulary and grammar (Fenson et al., 1994) and mean length of longest utterance and semantic diversity in later language (Tamis-LeMonda and Bornstein, 1994). Parental reports of language comprehension in the first year predict Peabody Picture Vocabulary Test scores in the third year (Bates et al., 1988). The correlations in these studies, while statistically significant, are usually relatively small.

Understanding the patterns and processes of child development and childrearing helps parents develop more realistic expectations of their children and more accurate interpretations of their children's behaviors and improves the structure of parent–child interactions and so enhances children's care, upbringing, and development. Mothers who are knowledgeable about general developmental sequences are more likely to organize environments that are appropriate to their children's developing abilities, for example (Hunt and Paraskevopoulos, 1980). Awareness of developmental milestones helps mothers create stimulating and challenging environments for their children and motivates or mediates more meaningful interactions with them (Miller, 1988). More knowledgeable mothers match their children's play levels during free-play interactions (Damast et al., 1996; Tamis-LeMonda and Bornstein, 1991) and adjust the level of their own play over time in close synchrony with changes in their children's play (Tamis-LeMonda and Bornstein, 1991).

Parent reports have consequences for children's well-being, social, and cognitive development (see Goodnow and Collins, 1990; Jacobson et al., 1991; Sigel, 1992). Adolescent mothers who report more positive, more realistic, and more mature expectations about children, parenting, and parent–child relationships have children with better coping skills as rated through observation (Stoiber and Houghton, 1993). Mothers of preterm infants who are more knowledgeable about infant development have babies with higher Bayley Mental Development Index and Psychomotor Development Index scores (Dichtelmiller et al., 1992).

Culture-specific patterns of childrearing are adapted to each specific society's settings and needs; it seems likely, therefore, that cultural variation in parents' childrearing philosophies, values, beliefs, or ideas contributes to differences in their childrearing practices. In anthropology, for example, direct interviews have been used to explore mothers' goals for their children, their sense of caregiving responsibility, and their beliefs about their own roles in helping their children attain those goals as well as their understanding of children's development (Harkness and Super, 2002). In addition, some studies seek mothers' and fathers' interpretations of observed behaviors within their own culture. Other studies have probed mothers' thinking in relation to specific behavioral contexts with their own children.

Pachter and Dworkin (1997) asked mothers from minority (Puerto Rican, African American, West Indian/Caribbean) and majority cultural groups in the United States about normal ages of attainment of typical developmental milestones during the first three years of life: Although all responses fit within a normative developmental range, significant differences emerged across ethnic groups for more than one third of the developmental milestones assessed. What we learn from reports of parents from cultures not our own can be very informative. Gusii and Samoan parents report that it is nonsensical to talk to infants before infants themselves are capable of speech (Ochs, 1988; Richman et al., 1992).

Parents' reports are also manifestly relevant in other realms of children's lives. Parents constitute an 'early warning system' with respect to children's well-being, and as discussed earlier they are vital to healthcare providers' formal evaluations of children. On this account, parent reports have implications for clinical interactions, child diagnosis, and paediatric training. Children and adolescents younger than 15 years of age average more than two visits per year to office-based physicians (Williams, Whitlock, Edgerton, Smith and Bell, 2007). During child health visits, clinicians must ask about and interpret parents' (usually mothers') expectations, concerns, and opinions about their children's health and development (Curran et al., 2007). Accurate and complete developmental anamnesis and surveillance therefore depend on eliciting valid parent reports, properly construing parents' reports, and obtaining relevant developmental histories (among other things). Paediatricians and other practitioners regularly incorporate parental appraisals into their decision making. The early history of study of these reports did not present a pretty picture (see, for example, Brekstad, 1966; Haggard, Brekstad and Skard, 1960; McGraw and Molloy, 1941). For example, a key goal of Functional Family Therapy (FFT; Sexton and Alexander, 2003), which views the family as the unit of intervention, explicitly recognizes the subjective nature of family members' perceptions of the family. Both intra-familial disagreement and family incohesion regarding family dysfunction serve as roadblocks to positive mental health. In addition to the family problems that everyone agrees on (i.e., the family perspective) there are family problems that only a particular family member directly experiences or feels (i.e., unique perspective) and both types of problems contribute independently to the health of family subsystems (Bornstein and Sawyer, 2005; Duvall, 1988; Minuchin, 1985; Olson, 2000).

As clinicians routinely draw on parents' reports during interviews, they need to be aware that parents' reports to the questions clinicians pose are moderated by all of the factors (and more) discussed here. In other words, when interpreting the information parents provide, clinicians must take the sources, biases, and contexts of parents' reports into consideration. One example, especially noteworthy today, is culture (Bornstein and Cote, 2004). Parenting reports differ across cultural groups, and so awareness of such differences is requisite to physicians accurately interpreting parents' reports about child health, development, and behavior during health supervision visits. The work of paediatricians can be enhanced by a better understanding of the state of parents' reports. Practitioners who know more about maternal expectations will be better able to interpret mothers' expressed concerns and opinions about their children's development as well as more accurately appraise their child patients. Parents' reports should be understood as value laden, however, and physicians' interpretations of parents' opinions and concerns about their children will best be construed within the context of parents' cultural belief systems.

Parents have the most experience with their child, are thought to know their child best, and are the clinician's primary source of outside information about their child. As healthcare providers cope in the diminishing time available in office visits, with deciding which health supervision topics to cover from the growing list of potentially useful topics, reports from parents can set priorities and improve practice delivery. For instance, parental concerns about a child's development can be a reliable indicator of developmental delays (Glascoe, 1997, 1999). Healthcare providers often also rely on parents to inform them how well a child responds to treatment, but parents may vary in their accuracy at reporting about their children (Biederman, 2004). One study analyzed data from the 2000 National Survey of Early Childhood Health (NSECH), a telephone survey of 2068 parents of children aged 4 to 35 months. Parents were queried about the frequency of reading with their child, whether their health-care provider discussed reading in the past year, and, if not, whether a discussion of the importance of reading to their child would have been helpful. Approximately one-half of young children were reportedly read to every day by a parent. Significant predictors of daily reading include the child's age, maternal education greater than high school, greater numbers of children's books in the home, and discussion of reading by the healthcare provider. Nearly one-half of parents indicated that they would have found such a discussion helpful (Kuo, Franke, Regalado and Halfon, 2004).

Finally, there is growing interest in subjective and evaluative aspects of parental reports per se. In some domains, effect sizes of environmental influences on children's social development may be larger with direct and structured behavioral observations than parental reports (Collins, Madsen and Susman-Stillman, 2002; Zaslow et al., 2006). However, there is independent value in exploring parents' reports of children in and of themselves. In certain contexts, objective assessments of children may be less useful or predictive than perceptions, attitudes, and beliefs of children in the parental eye. Thus, some developmental phenomena might be best understood by sampling perceptions, attitudes, and beliefs that surround the growing child, and for certain purposes the objective assessment of the child may be less useful or predictive than perception by a parent. So measures from mother (and significant others) might validly index different but equally meaningful kinds of information about children. For example, assessments of infant temperament by non-familial observers may be more predictive than parental perceptions of temperament for some criteria, whereas other aspects of child development might be better understood by sampling the perceptions, attitudes, and beliefs of parents.

CONCLUSIONS

It is generally acknowledged that no single approach to measuring phenomena in child development is best, that no one representation of a developmental phenomenon predominates as a 'gold standard'. Rather, assessment selection is guided by goal, tradition, tractability, or convenience. Moreover, those who study developmental phenomena often advocate the wisdom of applying multiple assessments and employing converging operations of different strategies targeted to the same phenomenon. Agreement emergent among different measures suggests that each may adequately evaluate stable individual variation. Employing observations, assessments, and reports together, however, overcomes the shortfalls of reliance on any single source. Multiple assessments obviously also represent children better than do single assessments, and converging operations are necessary to evaluate whether developmental phenomena adequately reveal inferred capacities, and that apparent performance is not simply an artifact of a given methodology.

It is unlikely that complex developmental phenomena, such as language or temperament, adaptation or behavior problems, or health can be adequately represented from a single perspective, say of parent report. Indeed, conclusions about any research effort depend to a degree on the methods applied to reach them. From a systems perspective, parent reports per se merit a status of central interest. Parent reports have objective as well as subjective sides, but they constitute a significant feature of the milieu in which the child develops. Thus, it may be fruitful to look for evidence of validity within parent reports per se. On this account, parent measures might give evidence of differential predictive validity, parent measures predicting to some developmental criteria, and other measures showing stronger relations to other developmental criteria (Bornstein, 2013). Understanding developmental phenomena can be enhanced by sampling the actions of the child or the attitudes which surround the child. Studies are in order which employ and compare parental reports and other measures, so that method-specific sources of prediction and error can be identified, and patterns of convergence and divergence between parental reports and other methods and measures of children can be better understood.

ACKNOWLEDGEMENTS

This chapter summarizes selected aspects of my research, and portions of the text have appeared in previous scientific publications cited in the references. Research was supported by the Intramural Research Program of the NIH, NICHD. I thank A. De Houwer, A. Dovidio, D.L. Putnick, and K.Woo.

REFERENCES

Achenbach, T.M. (1991a) *Integrative Guide for the 1991 CBCL/4–18, YSR, and TRF Profiles.* Burlington, VT: University of Vermont Department of Psychiatry.

Achenbach, T.M. (1991b) *Manual for the Youth Self-Report and 1991 Profile.* Burlington, VT: University of Vermont Department of Psychiatry.

Achenbach, T.M., Dumenci, L. and Rescorla, L.A. (2002) 'Ten-year comparisons of problems and competencies for national sample youth: Self, parent, and teacher reports', *Journal of Emotional and Behavioral Disorders,* 10(4): 194–203.

Achenbach, T.M., McConaughy, S.H. and Howell, C.T. (1987) 'Child/adolescent behavioral and emotional problems: Implications of cross-informant correlations for situational specificity', *Psychological Bulletin,* 101(2): 213–32.

Alink, L.R., Mesman, J., Van Zeijl, J., Stolk, M.N., Juffer, F., Koot, H.M., Bakermans-Kranenburg, M.J., and Van IJzendoorn, M.H. (2006) 'The early childhood aggression curve: Development of physical aggression in 10-to 50-month-old children', *Child development,* 77(4): 954–66.

Anderson, D.R., Field, D.E., Collins, P.A., Lorch, E.P. and Nathan, J.G. (1985) 'Estimates of young children's time with television: A methodological comparison of parent reports with time-lapse video home observation', *Child Development,* 56(5): 1345–57.

Arriaga, R.I., Fenson, L., Cronan, T. and Pethick, S.J. (1998) 'Scores on the MacArthur Communicative Development Inventory of children from low-and middle-income families', *Applied Psycholinguistics,* 19(2): 209–23.

Ash, P. and Guyer, M.J. (1991) 'Biased reporting by parents undergoing child custody evaluations', *Journal of the American Academy of Child and Adolescent Psychiatry,* 30: 835–8.

Baird, G., Charman, T., Baron-Cohen, S., Cox, A., Swettenham, J., Wheelwright, S., et al. (2000) 'A Screening instrument for autism at 18 months of age: A 6-year follow-up study', *Journal of the American Academy of Child and Adolescent Psychiatry,* 39: 694–702.

Baldwin, J.M. (1896*) Mental Development in the Child and the Race.* New York: Macmillan and Company.

Baldwin, W. (2000) 'Information no one else knows: The value of self-report', in A.A. Stone, J.S. Turkkan, C.A. Bachrach, J.B. Jobe, H.S. Kurtzman, and V.S. Cain (eds.), *The Science of Self-report: Implications for Research and Practice.* Mahwah, NJ: Erlbaum, pp. 3–7

Barker, E.T., Bornstein, M.H., Putnick, D.L., Hendricks, C. and Suwalsky, J.T.D. (2007) 'Adolescent-mother agreement about adolescent problem behaviors: Direction and predictors of disagreement', *Journal of Youth and Adolescence,* 36(7): 950–62.

Barker, E.T., Bornstein, M.H., Putnick, D.L., Hendricks, C., and Suwalsky, J.T.D. (2007) 'Adolescent-mother agreement about adolescent problem behaviors: Direction and predictors of disagreement', *Journal of Youth and Adolescence,* 36: 950–62.

Barnard, K.E. and Solchany, J.E. (2002) 'Mothering', in M.H. Bornstein (ed.), *Handbook of Parenting Vol. 3 Status and Social Conditions of Parenting.* Mahwah, NJ: Lawrence Erlbaum Associates, pp. 3–25.

Barnes, H.L., and Olson, D.H. (1985) 'Parent adolescent communication and the circumplex model', *Child Development*, 56: 438–47.

Baron-Cohen, S., Allen, J. and Gillberg, C. (1992) 'Can autism be detected at 18 months? The needle, the haystack, and the CHAT', *British Journal of Psychiatry, 161*: 839–43.

Baron-Cohen, S., Cox, A., Baird, G., Swettenham, J., Nightingale, N., Morgan, K., et al. (1996) 'Psychological markers in the detection of atism in infancy in a large population', *British Journal of Psychiatry*, 168: 158–63.

Barsky, A.J. (2002) 'Forgetting, fabricating, and telescoping: The instability of the medical history', *Archives of Internal Medicine*, 162: 981–4.

Bartle-Haring, S., Kenny, D., and Gavazzi, S. (1999) 'Multiple perspectives on family differentiation: Analyses by multitrait multimethod matrix and triadic social relations models', *Journal of Marriage and the Family*, 61(2): 491–503.

Bates, E. and Carnevale, G.F. (1993) 'New directions in research on language development', *Developmental Review*, 13(4): 36–70.

Bates, E., Bretherton, I., and Snyder, L. (1988) *From First Words to Grammar: Individual Differences and Dissociable Mechanisms*. Cambridge: Cambridge University Press.

Bates, E., Dale, P. and Thal, D. (1995) 'Individual differences and their implications for theories of language development', in P. Fletcher and B. MacWhinney (eds.), *The Handbook of Child Language*. Oxford: Blackwell, pp. 96–151.

Bates, J.E. (1980) 'The concept of difficult temperament', *Merrill-Palmer Quarterly*, 26(4): 299–319.

Bates, J.E. and Bayles, K. (1984) 'Objective and subjective components in mothers' perceptions of their children from age 6 months to 3 years', *Merrill-Palmer Quarterly*, 30(2): 111–30.

Bates, J.E., Freeland, C.A. and Lounsbury, M.L. (1979) 'Measurement of infant difficultness', *Child Development*, 50(3): 794–803.

Baum, C.G., Forehand, R. and Zegiob, L.E. (1979) 'A review of observer reactivity in adult–child interactions', *Journal of Behavioral Assessment*, 1(2): 167–78.

Belli, R.F., Shay, W.L., and Stafford, F.P. (2001) 'Event history calendars and question list surveys: A direct comparison of interviewing methods', *Public Opinion Quarterly*, 65(1): 45–74.

Belli, R.F., Traugott, M.W., Young, M., and McGonagle, K.A. (1999) 'Reducing vote overreporting in surveys: Social desirability, memory failure, and source monitoring', *Public Opinion Quarterly*, 63: 90–108.

Bernstein, D.P., Fink, L., Handelsman, L., Foote, J., Lovejoy, M., Wenzel, K., Sapareto, E., Ruggiero, and J. (1994) 'Initial reliability and validity of a new retrospective measure of child abuse and neglect', *The American Journal of Psychiatry*, 151: 1132–6.

Berger, L.E., Jodl, K.M., Allen, J.P., McElhaney, K.B. and Kuperminc, G.P. (2005) 'When adolescents disagree with others about their symptoms: Differences in attachment organization as an explanation of discrepancies between adolescent, parent, and peer reports of behavior problems', *Development and Psychopathology*, 17(2): 509–28.

Berg-Nielsen, T.S., Vika, A. and Dahl, A.A. (2003) 'When adolescents disagree with their mothers: CBCL-YSR discrepancies related to maternal depression and adolescent self-esteem', *Child: Care, Health and Development*, 29(3): 207–13.

Biederman, J. (2004) 'Impact of comorbidity in adults with attention deficit/hyperactivity disorder', *Journal of Clinical Psychiatry*, 65(3): 3–7.

Biringen, Z. (1990) 'Direct observation of maternal sensitivity and dyadic interactions in the home: Relations to maternal thinking', *Developmental Psychology*, 26(2): 278–84.

Bögels, S.M., and van Melick, M. (2004) 'The relationship between child-report, parent self-report, and partner report of perceived parental rearing behaviors and anxiety in children and parents', *Personality and Individual Differences*, 37(8): 1583–96.

Bonichini, S., Axia, G., and Bornstein, M.H. (2009) 'Validation of the parent health locus of control scales in an Italian sample', *Italian Journal of Pediatrics*, 35: 1–5.

Bornstein, M.H. (1989) 'Between caretakers and their young: Two modes of interaction and their consequences for cognitive growth', in M.H. Bornstein and J.S. Bruner (eds.), *Interaction in Human Development*. Hillsdale, NJ: Erlbaum, pp. 197–214.

Bornstein, M.H. (1995) 'Parenting infants' in M.H. Bornstein (ed.), *Handbook of Parenting*. Mahwah, NJ: Erlbaum, pp. 3–39.

Bornstein, M.H. (ed.) (2002) *Handbook of Parenting*. Mahwah, NJ: Lawrence Erlbaum Associates.

Bornstein, M.H. (2006) 'Parenting science and practice', in K.A. Renninger, I.E. Sigel, W. Damon and R.M. Lerner (eds.), *Handbook of Child Psychology, 6th Ed.: Vol 4, Child Psychology in Practice*. Hoboken, NJ: John Wiley and Sons Inc., pp. 893–949.

Bornstein, M.H. (2013) '*The specificity principle in parenting and child development: "Everything in Moderation"'*. Unpublished manuscript. Eunice Kennedy Shriver National Institute of Child Health and Human Development.

Bornstein, M.H., Arterberry, M.E., and Lamb, M.E. (2014) *Development in Infancy: An Introduction* (5 edn). New York, NY: Psychology Press.

Bornstein, M.H., and Cote. L. (2004) '*Who is sitting across from me?* Immigrant mothers' knowledge about children's development', *Pediatrics*, 114: 557–64.

Bornstein, M.H., and Cote, L.R. (2004) 'Mothers' parenting cognitions in cultures of origin, acculturating cultures, and cultures of destination', *Child Development*, 75: 221–35.

Bornstein, M.H., and Cote, L.R. (2009) 'Child temperament in three U.S. cultural groups', *Infant Mental Health Journal*, 30: 433–451.

Bornstein, M.H., Cote, L.R., Haynes, O.M., Hahn, C.S. and Park, Y. (2010)') 'Parenting knowledge: Experiential and sociodemographic factors in European American mothers of young children', *Developmental Psychology*, 46: 1677–93.

Bornstein, M.H., Cote, L.R., Haynes, O.M., Hahn, C.-S. and Suizzo, M.-A. (2008) *Mothers' Parenting Knowledge: Experiential, Sociodemographic, and Cultural Factors in U.S., Immigrant, and Cross-national Comparisons.* Unpublished manuscript. Eunice Kennedy Shriver National Institute of Child Health and Human Development.

Bornstein, M.H., Gaughran, J.M., and Homel, P. (1986) 'Infant temperament: Theory, tradition, critique, and new assessments', in C.E. Izard and P.B. Read (eds.), *Measuring Emotions in Infants and Children. Vol. 2: Cambridge Studies in Social and Emotional Development.* New York: Cambridge University Press, pp. 172–99.

Bornstein, M.H., Gaughran, J.M. and Seguí, I. (1991) 'Multimethod assessment of infant temperament: Mother questionnaire and mother and observer reports evaluated and compared at five months suing the Infant Temperament Measure', *International Journal of Behavioral Development*, 14(2): 131–51.

Bornstein, M.H., Giusti, Z., Leach, D.B. and Venuti, P. (2005) 'Maternal reports of adaptive behaviours in young children: Urban-rural and gender comparisons in Italy and United States', *Infant and Child Development*, 14(4): 403–24.

Bornstein, M.H., Hahn, C.-S., and Haynes, O.M. (2010) 'Social competence, externalizing, and internalizing behavioral adjustment from early childhood through early adolescence: Developmental cascades', *Development and Psychopathology*, 22: 717–35.

Bornstein, M.H., Hahn, C.-S., and Haynes, O.M. (2011) 'Maternal personality, parenting cognitions, and parenting practices', *Developmental Psychology*, 47: 658–75.

Bornstein, M.H., Hahn, C.-S., Haynes, O.M., Belsky, J., Azuma, H., Kwak, K., Maital, S., Painter, K.M., Pascual, L., Toda, S., Varron, C., Venuti, P., Vyt, A., and Galperín, C. de G. (2007) 'Maternal personality and parenting cognitions in cross-cultural perspective', *International Journal of Behavioral Development*, 31: 193–209.

Bornstein, M.H. and Haynes, O.M. (1998) 'Vocabulary competence in early childhood: Measurement, latent construct, and predictive validity', *Child Development*, 69(3): 654–71.

Bornstein, M.H., Haynes, O.M., Azuma, H., Galperin, C., Maital, S., Ogino, M., Painter, K., Pascual, L., Pecheux, M., Rahn, C., Toda, S., Venuti, P., Vyt, A. and Wright, B. (1998) 'A cross-national study of self-evaluations and attributions in parenting: Argentina, Belgium, France, Israel, Italy, Japan, and the United States', *Developmental Psychology*, 34(4): 662–76.

Bornstein, M.H., and Hendricks, C. (2012), 'Basic language comprehension and production in >100,000 young children from sixteen developing nations', *Journal of Child Language*, 39: 899–918.

Bornstein, M.H., and Hendricks, C. (2013) 'Screening for developmental disabilities in developing countries', *Social Science and Medicine*,

Bornstein, M.H., Leach, D.B., and De Houwer, A. (2006) 'Child vocabulary across the second year: Stability and continuity for reporter comparisons and a cumulative score', *First Language*, 26: 299–316.

Bornstein, M.H., and Putnick, D.P. (2012) 'Stability of language in childhood: A multiage, multidomain, multimeasure, and multisource study', *Developmental Psychology*, 48: 477–91.

Bornstein, M.H., Putnick, D. L., Lansford, J. E., Pastorelli, C., Skinner, A. T., Sorbring, E., Tapanya, S., Uribe Tirado, L. M., Zelli, Alampay, L.P., Al-Hassan, S.M., Bacchini, D., Bombi, A.S., Chang, L., Deater-Deckard, K., Di Giunta, L., Dodge, K.A., Malone, P.S. and Oburu, P. (2013) *'Agreement in Mother and Father Socially Desirable Responding in Nine Countries'*. Unpublished manuscript. Eunice Kennedy Shriver National Institute of Child Health and Human Development.

Bornstein, M.H., and Sawyer, J. (2005) 'Family systems', in K. McCartney and D. Phillips (eds.), *Blackwell Handbook on Early Childhood Development*. Malden, MA: Blackwell, pp. 381–8.

Bornstein, M.H., Tamis-LeMonda, C.S., Suwalsky, J.T.D. and Haynes, O.M. (1991) *'Family Description Questionnaire'*. Unpublished manuscript. Eunice Kennedy Shriver National Institute of Child Health and Human Development.

Bower, T.G. (1974). *Development in Infancy*. San Francisco, CA: WH Freeman, p. 53.

Bowerman, M. (1985) 'Beyond communicative adequacy: From piecemeal knowledge to an integrated system in the child's acquisition of language', in K. Nelson (ed.), *Children's Language* (Vol. 5). Hillsdale, NJ: Erlbaum, pp. 369–98.

Bradburn, N.M. (1983) 'Response Effects', in P. Rossi, J. Wright, and A. Anderson (eds.), *Handbook of Survey Research*. New York: Academic Press, pp. 289–328.

Bradburn, N.M., Rips, L.J. and Sevel, S.K. (1987) 'Answering autobiographical questions: The impact of memory and inference on surveys', Science, 236: 157–62.

Brekstad, A. (1966) 'Factors influencing the reliability of anamnestic recall', *Child Development*, 37(3): 603–12.

Brewin, C.R., Andrews, B., and Gotlib, I.H. (1993) 'Psychopathology and early experience: A reappraisal of retrospective reports', *Psychological Bulletin*, 113: 82–98.

Bronfenbrenner, U. (1979) *The Ecology of Human Development*, Cambridge, MA: Harvard University Press.

Brown, B.B. (2004) 'Adolescents' relationships with peers', in R.M. Lerner and L. Steinberg (eds.), *Handbook of Adolescent Psychology*. New York: Wiley, pp. 363–94.

Bugental, D.B. and Happaney, K. (2002) 'Parental attributions', in M.H. Bornstein (ed.), *Handbook of Parenting: Vol. 3: Being and Becoming a Parent*. Mahwah, NJ: Erlbaum, pp. 509–35.

Cairns, R.B. and Cairns, B.D. (2006) 'The making of developmental psychology', in R.M. Lerner (ed.), W. Damon (Series Ed.), *Handbook of Child Psychology: Vol. 1. Theoretical Models of Human Development*. Hoboken, NJ: Wiley, pp. 89–165.

Callan, V. and Noller, P. (1986) 'Perceptions of communicative relationships in families with adolescents', *Journal of Marriage and the Family*, 48(4): 813–20.

Camaioni, L., Caselli, M.C., Longobardi, E., and Volterra, V. (1991) 'A parent report instrument for early language assessment', *First Language*, 11: 301–25.

Campbell, D.T. and Fiske, D.W. (1959) 'Convergent and discriminant validation by the multitrait–multimethod matrix', *Psychological Bulletin*, 56(2): 81–105.

Carey, M.A., and Smith, M.W. (1994) 'Capturing the group effect in focus groups: A special concern in analysis', *Quantitative Health Research*, 4(1): 123–7.

Carey, W.B., and McDevitt, S.C. (1978b) 'Revision of the infant temperament questionnaire', *Pediatrics*, 61(5): 735–9.

Carey, W.B. (1970) 'A simplified method for measuring infant temperament', *Journal of Pediatrics*, 77(2): 188–94.

Carey, W.B. and McDevitt, S.C. (1978a) 'Revision of the Infant Temperament Questionnaire', *Pediatrics*, 61(5): 735–39.

Carey, W.B. and McDevitt, S.C. (1978b) 'Stability and change in individual temperamental diagnoses from infancy to early childhood', *Journal of the American Academy of Child Psychiatry*, 17(2): 331–7.

Carlson, C.I., Cooper, C.R., and Spradling, V.Y. (1991) 'Developmental implications of shared versus distinct perceptions of the family in early adolescence', *New Directions for Child and Adolescent Development*, 51: 13–32.

Cashmore, J.A., and Goodnow, J.J. (1985) 'Agreement between generations: A two-process approach', *Child Development*, 56: 493–501.

Caspi, A., Moffitt, T.E., Thornton, A., and Freedman, D. (1996) 'The life history calendar: A research and clinical assessment method for collecting retrospective event-history data', *International Journal of Methods in Psychiatric Research*, 6(2): 101–14.

Caster, J.B., Inderbitzen, H.M., and Hope, D. (1999) 'Relationship between youth and parent perceptions of family environment and social anxiety', *Journal of Anxiety Disorders*, 13(3): 237–51.

Catania, J.A., Binson, D., Canchola, J., Pollack, L.M., and Hauck, W. (1996) 'Effects of interviewer gender, interviewer choice, and item wording on responses to questions concerning sexual behavior', *Public Opinion Quarterly*, 60: 345–75.

Chaffee, C.A., Cunningham, C.E., Secord-Gilbert, M., Elbard, H. and Richards, J. (1990) 'Screening effectiveness of the Minnesota Child Development Inventory Expressive and Receptive Language Scales: Sensitivity, specificity, and predictive value', *Psychological Assessment: A Journal of Consulting and Clinical Psychology*, 2(1): 80–5.

Christensen, A., Margolin, G., and Sullaway, M. (1992) 'Interparental agreement on child behavior problems', *Psychological Assessment*, 4: 419–25.

Chronis-Tuscano, A., Degnan, K., Pine, D., Perez-Edgar, K., Henderson, H., Diaz, Y., Raggi, V., and Fox, N. (2009) 'Stable early maternal report of behavioral inhibition predicts lifetime social anxiety disorder in adolescence', *Journal of American Academy of Child and Adolescent Psychiatry*, 48(9): 1–7.

Cicchetti, D.V., and Sparrow, S.A. (1981) 'Developing criteria for establishing interrater reliability of specific items: Applications to assessment of adaptive behavior', *American Journal of Mental Deficiency*, 86: 127–37.

Clarke-Stewart, K.A. and Allhusen, V.D. (2002) 'Nonparental caregiving', in M.H. Bornstein (ed.), *Handbook of Parenting: Vol. 3. Status and Social Conditions of Parenting*. Mahwah, NJ: Erlbaum, pp. 215–52.

Cohen, J. (1960) 'A coefficient of agreement for nominal scales', *Education and Psychological Measurement*, 20(1): 37–46.

Cohen, J. (1968) 'Weighted kappa: Nominal scale agreement with provision for scaled disagreement or partial credit', *Psychological Bulletin*, 70(4): 213–20.

Collins, W.A. and Laursen, B. (2004) 'Parent-adolescent relationships and influences', in R.M. Lerner and L. Steinberg (eds.), *Handbook of Adolescent Psychology*. New York: Wiley, pp. 331–61.

Collins, W.A., Madsen, S.D. and Susman-Stillman, A. (2002) 'Parenting during middle childhood', in M.H. Bornstein (ed.), *Handbook of Parenting: Vol. 1: Children and Parenting*. Mahwah, NJ: Lawrence Erlbaum Associates Publishers, pp. 73–101.

Conrad, R. (1998) 'Darwin's baby and baby's Darwin: Mutual recognition in observational research', *Human Development*, 41(1): 47–64.

Cook, W.L., and Goldstein, M.J. (1993) 'Multiple perspectives on family relationships: A latent variables model', *Child Development*, 64(5): 1377–88.

Crouter, A.C. and Head, M.R. (2002) 'Parental monitoring and knowledge of children', in M.H. Bornstein (ed.), *Handbook of Parenting: Being and Becoming a Parent*. Mahwah, NJ: Lawrence Erlbaum Associates, pp. 461–83.

Crouter, A.C., Helms-Erickson, H., Updegraff, K. and McHale, S.M. (1999) 'Conditions underlying parents' knowledge about children's daily lives in middle childhood: Between- and within-family comparisons', *Child Development*, 70(1): 246–59.

Cummings, E.M., Zahn-Waxler, C. and Radke-Yarrow, M. (1981) 'Young children's responses to expressions of anger and affection by others in the family', *Child Development*, 52(4): 1274–82.

Curran, L.K., Newschaffer, C.J., Lee, L-C., Crawford, S.O., Johnston, M.V. and Zimmerman, A.W. (2007) 'Behaviors associated with fever in children with autism spectrum disorders', *Pediatrics*, 120(6): 1386–92.

Dale, P.S. (1991) 'The validity of a parent report measure of vocabulary and syntax at 24 months', *Journal of Speech, Language, and Hearing Research*, 34: 565–71.

Dale, P.S., Price, T.S., Bishop, D.V.M., and Plomin, R. (2003) 'Outcomes of early language delay: I. Predicting persistent and transient delay at 3 and 4 years', *Journal of Speech, Language and Hearing Research*, 46: 544–60.

Dale, P.S., Bates, E., Reznick, S., and Morisset, C. (1989) 'The validity of a parent report instrument of child language at 20 months', *Journal of Child Language*, 16(2): 239–50.

D'Alessio, M. (1977) 'Bambino generalizzato e bambino individualizzato nella stereotipa d'eta [Age stereotypes applied to generalized and individualized infants]', in E. Ponzo (ed.), *Il Bambino Seplificato o Inesistente [The simplified or nonexistent infant]*. Rome: Bulzoni, pp. 231–42.

D'Alessio, M. (1990) 'Social representations of childhood: An implicit theory of childhood', in G. Duveen and B. Lloyd (eds.), *Social Representations and the Development of Knowledge*. Cambridge, England: Cambridge University Press, pp. 70–90.

Damast, A.M., Tamis-LeMonda, C.S., and Bornstein, M.H. (1996) 'Mother-child play: Sequential interactions and the relation between maternal beliefs and behaviors,' *Child Development*, 67(4): 1752–66.

Darwin, C. (1877) 'A biographical sketch of an infant', *Mind*, 2: 286–94.

Davis, E.F., Schoppe-Sullivan, S.J., Mangelsdorf, S.C. and Brown, G.L. (2009) 'The role of infant temperament in stability and change in coparenting behavior across the first year of life', *Parenting: Science and Practice*, 9(1): 143–59.

De Houwer, A., Bornstein, M.H. and Leach, D.B. (2005) 'Assessing early communicative ability: A cross-reporter cumulative score for the MacArthur CDI', *Journal of Child Language*, 32(4): 735–58.

De Houwer, A., Bornstein, M.H., and De Coster, S. (2006) 'Early understanding of two words for the same thing: A CDI study of lexical comprehension in infant bilinguals', *International Journal of Bilingualism*, 10: 331–47.

De Los Reyes, A. and Kazdin, A.E. (2005) 'Informant discrepancies in the assessment of childhood psychopathology: A critical review, theoretical framework, and recommendations for further study', *Psychological Bulletin*, 131(4): 483–509.

DeGrada, E. and Ponzo, E. (1971) *La Normalita Del Bambino Come Pregiudizio Dell'adulto [Adult Prejudices About Infant Normality]*. Rome: Bulzoni.

Deković, M., and Buist, K.L. (2005) 'Multiple perspectives within the family: Family relationship patterns', *Journal of Family Issues*, 26(4): 467–90.

DeMaio, T.J. (1984) 'Social desirability and survey measurement: A review', *Surveying Subjective Phenomena*, 2: 257–81.

Demo, D.H., Small, S.A., and Savin-Williams, R.C. (1987) 'Family relations and the self-esteem of adolescents and their parents', *Journal of Marriage and the Family*, 49: 705–15.

Dichtelmiller, M., Meisels, S.J., Plunkett, J.W., Bozynski, M.E.A., Claflin, C. and Mangelsdorf, S.C. (1992) 'The relationship of parental knowledge to the development of extremely low birth weight infants', *Journal of Early Intervention*, 16(3): 210–20.

Diener, M., Goldstein, L. and Mangelsdorf, S. (1995) 'The role of prenatal expectations in parents' report of infant temperament', *Merrill-Palmer Quarterly*, 41(2): 172–90.

Dietz, C., Swinkels, S., Aalen, E.D., Engeland, H., and Buitelaar, J. (2006) 'Screening for autistic spectrum disorders in children aged 14–15 months. II: Population screening with the Early Screening of Autistic Traits Questionnaire (ESAT). Design and general findings', *Journal of Autism and Developmental Disorders*, 36: 713–22.

Dishion, T.J. and McMahon, R.J. (1998) 'Parental monitoring and the prevention of child and adolescent problem behavior: A conceptual and empirical formulation', *Clinical Child and Family Psychology Review*, 1(1): 61–75.

diSibio, M. (1993) 'Conjoint effects of intelligence and adaptive behavior on achievement in a nonreferred sample', *Journal of Psychoeducational Assessment*, 11(4): 304–13.

Donoghue, E.C., and Shakespeare, R.A. (1967) 'The reliability of paediatric case-history milestones', *Developmental Medicine and Child Neurology*, 9: 64–9.

Dorkey, M., and Amen, E.W. (1947) 'A continuation study of anxiety reactions in young children by means of a projective technique', *Genetic Psychology Monographs*, 35: 139–83.

Doucette, J. and Freedman, R. (1980) *Progress Tests for the Developmentally Disabled: An Evaluation*. Cambridge, MA: Abt Books.

Dromi, E. (1987) *Early Lexical Development*. Cambridge: Cambridge University Press.

Duhig, A.M., Renk, K., Epstein, M.K., and Phares, V. (2000) 'Interparental agreement on internalizing, externalizing, and total behavior problems: A meta-analysis Clinical Psychology', *Science and Practice*, 7: 435–53.

Duvall, E.M. (1988) 'Family development's first forty years', *Family Relations*, 57(2): 127–34.

Eisler, I., Dare, C., and Szmukler, G.I. (1988) 'What's happened to family interaction research? An historical account and a family systems viewpoint', *Journal of Marital and Family Therapy*, 14(1): 45–65.

Engleman, D. (1974) 'Quantitative study of adaptive behavior of Ohio educable mentally retarded and normal children', *Dissertation Abstracts International*, 35: 4923 A.

Epstein, N.B., Baldwin, L.M., and Bishop, D.S. (1983) 'The McMaster Family Assessment Device', *Journal of Marital and Family Therapy*, 9(2): 171–80.

Epstein, S. (1983) '*The Mother-Father-Peer Scale*'. Unpublished manuscript. University of Massachusetts, Amherst.

Fantz, R.L. (1964) 'Visual experience in infants: Decreased attention to familiar patterns relative to novel ones', *Science*, 146(3644): 668–70.

Feldman, H.M., Dale, P.S., Campbell, T.F., Colborn, D.K., Kurs-Lasky, M., Rockette, H.E., and Paradise, J.L. (2005) 'Concurrent and predictive validity of parent reports of child language at ages 2 and 3 years', *Child Development*, 76: 856–68.

Feldman, S.S., Wentzel, K.R. and Gehring, T.M. (1989) 'A comparison of the views of mothers, fathers, and pre-adolescents about family cohesion and power', *Journal of Family Psychology*, 3(1): 39–60.

Fenson, L., Dale, P., Reznick, S., Thal, D., Bates, E., Hartung, J. and Reilly, J.S. (1993) *MacArthur Communicative Development Inventories: User's Guide and Technical Manual*. San Diego, CA: Singular Publishing.

Fenson, L., Dale, P.S., Reznick, J.S., Bates, E., Thal, D.J. and Pethick, S.J. (1994) 'Variability in early communicative development', *Monographs of the Society for Research in Child Development*, 59(5), Serial No. 242.

Field, T.M. and Greenberg, R. (1982) 'Temperamental ratings by parents and teachers of infants, toddlers, and preschool children', *Child Development*, 53(1): 160–3.

Finney, H.C. (1981) 'Improving the reliability of retrospective survey measures', *Evaluation Review*, 5: 207–29.

Fogas, B.S., and Wolchik, S.A. (1986, May) 'Multiple reports of stress, parenting and child adjustment following divorce', Paper presented at the Western Psychological Association Convention, Seattle, WA.

Forman, D.R., O'Hara, M.W., Larsen, K., Coy, K.C., Gorman, L.L. and Stuart, S. (2003) 'Infant emotionality: Observational methods and the validity of maternal reports', *Infancy*, 4(4): 541–65.

Formoso, D., Gonzales, N.A. and Aiken, L.S. (2000) 'Family conflict and children's internalizing and externalizing behavior: Protective factors', *American Journal of Community Psychology*, 28(2): 175–99.

Fowler, F.J., and Mangione, T.W. (1990) *Standardized Survey Interviewing*. Newbury Park, CA: Sage.

Freedman, D., Thornton, A., Camburn, D., Alwin, D., and Yong-DeMarco, L. (1988) 'The life history calendar: A technique for collecting retrospective data', *Sociological Methodology*, 18: 37–68.

French, V. (2002) 'History of parenting: The ancient Mediterranean world', in M.H. Bornstein (ed.), *Handbook of Parenting Vol. 2 Biology and Ecology of Parenting*. Mahwah, NJ: Erlbaum, pp. 345–76.

Frombonne, E. and Achard, S. (1993) 'The Vineland Adaptive Behavior Scale in a sample of normal French children: A research note', *Journal for Child Psychology and Psychiatry*, 34(6): 1051–8.

Furstenberg, F.F. Jr., Brooks-Gunn, J. and Morgan, S.P. (1987) *Adolescent Mothers in Later Life*. New York: Cambridge University Press.

Gardner, F. (2000) 'Methodological issues in the direct observation of parent-child interaction: Do observational findings reflect the natural behavior of participants', *Clinical Child and Family Psychology Review*, 3(3): 185–98.

Gartstein, M.A. and Rothbart, M.K. (2003) 'Studying infant temperament via a revision of the infant behavior questionnaire', *Journal of Infant Behavior and Development*, 26(1): 64–86.

Geary, D.C. (2000) 'Evolution and proximate expression of human paternal investment', *Psychological Bulletin*, 126(1): 55–77.

Gilkerson, L. and Stott, F. (1997) 'Listening to the voices of families: Learning through caregiving consensus groups', *Zero to Three*, 17: 9–16.

Glascoe, F.P. (1997) 'Parents' concerns about children's development: Prescreening technique or screening test?', *Pediatrics*, 99(4): 522–8.

Glascoe, F.P. (1999) 'Using parents' concerns to detect and address developmental and behavioral problems', *Journal of the Society of Pediatric Nurses*, 4(1): 24–35.

Goldsmith, H.H. and Rieser-Danner, L.A. (1986) 'Variation among temperament theories and validation studies of temperament assessment', in G.A. Kohnstamm (ed.), *Temperament Discussed: Temperament and Development in Infancy and Childhood*. Lisse: Swets Publishing Service, pp. 1–9.

Gondoli, D.M., Grundy, A.M., Blodgett, S.E.H., and Bonds, D.D. (2008) 'Maternal warmth mediates the relation between mother-preadolescent cohesion and change in maternal knowledge during the transition to adolescence', *Parenting*, 8(4): 271–93.

Gonzales, N.A., Cauce, A.M. and Mason, C.A. (1996) 'Interobserver agreement in the assessment of parental behavior and parent-adolescent conflict: African American mothers, daughters, and independent observers', *Child Development*, 67(4): 1483–98.

Gonzalez-Ramos, G., Zayas, L.H. and Cohen, E.V. (1998) 'Child-rearing values of low-income, urban Puerto Rican mothers of preschool children', *Professional Psychology: Research and Practice*, 29(4): 377–82.

Goodnow, J.J. and Collins, W.A. (1990) *Development According to Parents. The Nature, Sources, and Consequences of Parents' Ideas*. London: Erlbaum.

Gopnik, A., and Meltzoff, A.N. (1986) 'Relations between semantic and cognitive development in the one-word stage: The specificity hypothesis', *Child Development*, 57: 1040–53.

Greene, B. (1985). *Good Morning, Merry Sunshine*. New York: Penguin.

Guilamo-Ramos, V., Dittus, P., and Jaccard, J. (2007) 'Parenting practices among Dominican and Puerto Rican mothers', *Social Work*, 52(1): 17–30.

Güngör, D., and Bornstein, M.H. (2010) 'Culture-general and -specific associations of attachment avoidance and anxiety with perceived parental warmth and psychological control among Turk and Belgian adolescents', *Journal of Adolescence*, 33: 593–602.

Hagekull, B., Bohlin, G. and Lindhagen, K. (1984) 'Validity of parental reports', *Infant Behavior and Development*, 7(1): 77–92.

Haggard, E.A., Brekstad, A. and Skard, A.G. (1960) 'On the reliability of the anamnestic interview', *Journal of Abnormal and Social Psychology*, 61: 311–18.

Haines, J., Neumark-Sztainer, D., Hannan, P., and Robinson-O'Brien, R. (2008) 'Child versus parent report of parental influences on children's weight-related attitudes and behaviors', *Journal of Pediatric Psychology*, 33(7): 783–8.

Harkness, S. and Super, C.M. (2002). 'Culture and parenting', in M.H. Bornstein (ed.), *Handbook of Parenting Vol. 2 Biology and Ecology of Parenting*. Mahwah, NJ: Erlbaum, pp. 253–80.

Hart Research Associates (1997) *Key Findings from a Nationwide Survey among Parents of Zero-To Three-Year-Olds*. Washington, DC: National Center for Infants, Toddlers, and Families.

Hart, B. and Risley, R.T. (1995) *Meaningful Differences in the Everyday Experience of Young American Children*. Baltimore, MD: Paul H. Brookes.

Hartmann, D.P., Pelzel, K.E., and Abbott, C. B. (2011) 'Design, measurement, and analysis in developmental research', in M.H. Bornstein and M.E. Lamb (eds.), *Developmental Science: An Advanced Textbook* (6th ed.). New York: Psychology Press, pp. 109–97.

Harwood, R.L. (1992) 'The influence of culturally derived values on Anglo and Puerto Rican mothers' perceptions of attachment behavior', *Child Development*, 63(4): 822–39.

Harwood, R.L., Miller, J.G., and Lucca Irizarry, N. (1995) *Culture and Attachment: Perceptions of the Child in Context*. New York: Guilford.

Haynes, S. N. (1978) *Principles of Behavioral Assessment*. New York: Gardner.

Hefner, L.T. and Mednick, S.A. (1969) 'Reliability of developmental histories', *Pediatrics Digest*, 8: 28–39.

Heisenberg, W. (1927) 'Uber den anschaulichen Inhalt der Quantentheoretischen Kinematik and Mechanik', *Zeitschrift für Physik*, 43(3): 172–98.

Henry, B., Moffitt, T.E., Caspi, A., Langley, J., and Silva, P.A. (1994) 'On the "remembrance of things past": A longitudinal evaluation of the retrospective method', *Psychological Assessment*, 6: 92–101.

Herber, R.F. (1961). 'A manual on terminology and classification in mental retardation', Monograph Supplement, *American Association of Mental Deficiency*, 65: 499–500.

Hill, J. (2002) 'Biological, psychological, and social processes in the conduct disorders', *Journal of Child Psychology and Psychiatry*, 43(1): 133–64.

Hinshaw, S.P., Han, S.S., Erhardt, D., and Huber, A. (1992) 'Internalizing and externalizing behavior problems in preschool children: Correspondence among parent and teacher ratings and behavior observations', *Journal of Clinical Child Psychology*, 21: 143–50.

Holden, G.W. and Buck, M.J. (2002) 'Parental attitudes toward childrearing', in M.H. Bornstein (ed.), *Handbook of Parenting Vol. 3 Status and Social Conditions of Parenting*. Mahwah, NJ: Lawrence Erlbaum Associates. pp. 537–62.

Holman, J. and Bruininks, R.H. (1985) 'Assessing and training adaptive behaviors', in K.L Lakin and R.H. Bruininks (eds.), *Strategies for Achieving Community Integration and Developmentally Disabled Citizens*. Baltimore, MD: Paul H. Brooks, pp. 73–104.

Holmbeck, G.N., Li, S.T., Schurman, J.V., Friedman, D. and Coakley, R.M. (2002) 'Collecting and managing multisource and multimethod data in studies of pediatric populations', *Journal of Pediatric Psychology*, 27(1): 5–18.

Huang, L., Malone, P.S., Lansford, J.E., Deater-Deckard, K., Di Giunta, L., Bombi, A. S., Bornstein, M.H., Chang, L., Dodge, K.A., Oburu, P., Pastorelli, C., Skinner, A.T., Sorbring, E., Tapanya, S., Uribe Tirado, L.M., Zelli, A., Alampay, L., Al-Hassan, S.M., and Bacchini, D. (2011) 'Measurement invariance of mother reports of discipline in different cultural contexts', *Family Science*, 2: 212–19.

Hubert, N.C., Wachs, T.D., Peters-Martin, P. and Gandour, M.J. (1982) 'The study of early temperament: Measurement and conceptual ideas', *Child Development*, 53(3): 571–600.

Hudziak, J.J., Van Beijsterveldt, C.E.M., Bartels, M., Rietveld, M.J. H., Rettew, D.C., Derks, E.M., et al. (2003) 'Individual differences in aggression: Genetic analyses by age, gender, and informant in 3-, 7-, and 10-year-old Dutch twins', *Behavior Genetics*, 33: 575–89.

Hunt, J., McV. and Paraskevopoulos, J. (1980) 'Children's psychological development as a function of the inaccuracy of their mother's knowledge of their abilities', *Journal of Genetic Psychology*, 136(2): 285–98.

Hurd, E.P., Moore, C., and Rogers, R. (1995) 'Quiet success: Parenting strengths among African Americans', *Families in Society*, 76(7): 434–43.

Hus, V., Taylor, A., and Lord, C. (2011) 'Telescoping of caregiver report on the Autism Diagnostic Interview–Revised', *Journal of Child Psychology and Psychiatry*, 52(7): 753–60.

Huth, H.M. and More, S.M. (1998) 'Prescriptive theory of acute pain management in infants and children', *Journal of the Society of Pediatric Nurses*, 3(1): 23–30.

Jaccard, J., McDonald, R., Wan, C.K., Guilamo-Ramos, V.G., Dittus, P. and Quinlan, S. (2004) 'Recalling sexual partners: The accuracy of self-reports', *Journal of Health Psychology*, 9(6): 699–712.

Jacobson, J.L. and Jacobson, S.W. (1990) 'Methodological issues in human behavioral teratology', *Advances in Infancy Research*, 6: 111–48.

Jacobson, S.W., Jacobson, J.L., Sokol, R.J., Martier, S.S., Ager, J.W. and Kaplan, M.G. (1991) 'Maternal recall of alcohol, cocaine, and marijuana use during pregnancy', *Neurotoxicology and Teratology*, 13(5): 535–40.

Jager, J., Bornstein, M.H., Putnick, D.L., and Hendricks, C. (2012) 'Family members' unique perspectives of the family: Examining their scope, size, and relations to individual adjustment', *Journal of Family Psychology*, 26: 400–10.

Jager, J., Bornstein, M.H., Putnick, D.L., and Hendricks, C. (2012) 'Family members' unique perspectives of the family: Examining their scope, size, and relations to individual adjustment', *Journal of Family Psychology*, 26: 400–10.

Jessop, D.J. (1982) 'Topic variation in levels of agreement between parents and adolescents', *Public Opinion Quarterly*, 46: 538–559.

Jobe, J.B. (2001) 'Cognitive processes in self-report', in A.A. Stone, J.S. Turkkan, C.A. Bachrach, J.B. Jobe, H.S. Kurtzman, and V.S. Cain (eds.), *The Science of Self-report: Implications for Research and Practice* (25-28). Mahwah, NJ: Erlbaum.

Kagan, J. (1998) 'Biology and the child', in N. Eisenberg (ed.) and W. Damon (Series ed.), *Handbook of Child Psychology: Vol. 3. Social, Emotional and Personality Development*. New York: Wiley, pp. 177–235.

Kahn, R.L., and Cannell, C.F. (1957) *The Dynamics of Interviewing.* New York: Wiley.

Kamphaus, R.W. (1987a) 'Conceptual and psychometric issues in the assessment of adaptive behaviour', *The Journal of Special Education*, 21(5): 27–35.

Kamphaus, R.W. (1987b) 'Defining the construct of adaptive behavior by the Vineland Adaptive Behavior Scales', *Journal of School Psychology*, 25(1): 97–100.

Kazdin, A.E. (1988) 'The diagnosis of childhood disorders: Assessment issues and strategies', *Behavioral Assessment*, 10(1): 67–94.

Kazdin, A.E. (1994) 'Informant variability in the assessment of childhood depression', in W.M. Reynolds and H.F. Johnston (eds.), *Handbook of Depression in Children and Adolescents.* New York: Plenum, pp. 249–71.

Keenan, K. and Wakschlag, L. (2002) *The Kiddie Disruptive Behavior Disorders Schedule (K-DBDs), Preschool Version 1.1*, Unpublished manuscript. Chicago, IL: University of Chicago.

Keenan, K. and Wakschlag, L.S. (2002) 'Can a valid diagnosis of disruptive behavior disorder be made in preschool children?', *American Journal of Psychiatry*, 159(3): 351–8.

Keenan, K., Wakschlag, L.S., Danis, B., Hill, C., Humphries, M., Duax, J. and Donald, R. (2007) 'Further evidence of the reliability and validity of DSM-IV ODD and CD in preschool children', *Journal of the American Academy of Child and Adolescent Psychiatry*, 46(4): 457–68.

Keith, T.Z., Harrison, P.L. and Ehly, S.W. (1987) 'Effects of adaptive behavior on achievement: Path analysis of a national sample', *Professional School Psychology*, 2(3): 205–15.

Keller, M.B., Lavori, P.W., Friedman, B., Nielsen, E., Endicott, J., McDonald-Scott, P., and Andreasen, N.C. (1987) 'The Longitudinal Interval Follow-up Evaluation: A comprehensive method for assessing outcome in prospective longitudinal studies', *Archives of General Psychiatry*, 44: 540–8.

Kenny, D.A. and Berman, J.S. (1980) 'Statistical approaches to the correction of correlational bias', *Psychological Bulletin*, 88(2): 288–95.

Kerns, K.A., Aspelmeier, J.E., Gentzler, A.L., and Grabill, C.M. (2001) 'Parent–child attachment and monitoring in middle childhood', *Journal of Family Psychology*, 15(1): 69–81.

Kerns, K.A., McInerney, R.J., and Wilde, N.J. (2001) 'Time reproduction, working memory and behavioural inhibition in children with ADHD', *Child Neuropsychology*, 7(1): 21–31.

Kerr, M. and Stattin, H. (2000) 'What parents know, how they know it, and several forms of adolescent

adjustment: Further support for a reinterpretation of monitoring', *Developmental Psychology*, 36(3): 366–80.

Kessen, W. (1965) *The Child.* London: Wiley.

Klee, T., Pearce, K., and Carson, D.K. (2000) 'Improving the positive predictive value of screening for developmental language disorder', *Journal of Speech, Language, and Hearing Research*, 43: 821–33.

Kleinman, J.M., Robins, D.L., Ventola, P.E., Pandey, J., Boorstein, H.C., Esser, E.L., Wilson, L.B., Rosenthal, M.A., Sutera, S., Verbalis, A.D., Barton, M., Hodgson, S., Green, J., Dumont-Mathieu, T., Volkmar, F., Chawarska, K., Klin, A., and Fein, D., (2008). 'The Modified Checklist for Autism in Toddlers: A follow-up study investigating the early detection of autism spectrum disorders', *Journal of Autism and Developmental Disorders*, 38: 827–39.

Kremer, M., Smith, A.B., and Lawrence, J.A. (2010) 'Family discipline incidents: An analysis of parental diaries', *Journal of Family Studies*, 16(3): 251–63.

Kuo, A.A., Franke, T.M., Regalado, M. and Halfon, N. (2004) 'Parent report of reading to young children', *Pediatrics*, 113(Supplement 5): 1944–51.

Laursen, B., and Collins, W.A. (2009) 'Parent-child relationships during adolescence', in R.M. Lerner and L. Steinberg (eds.), *Handbook of Adolescent Psychology, Vol. 2: Contextual Influences on Adolescent Development* (3rd ed.). Hoboken, NJ: Wiley, pp.3–42.

Lazarus, R.S. (1999) *Stress and Emotion: A New Synthesis.* New York, NY: Springer Publishing Co.

Leland, H. (1983) 'Assessment of adaptive behavior', in K.D. Paget, and B.A. Bracken (eds.), *The Psychological Assessment of Preschool Children.* New York: Grune and Stratton, pp. 191–205.

Leopold, W.F. (1949) *Speech Development of a Bilingual Child.* Evanston, IL: Northwestern University Press.

Lerner, R.M., Lerner, J.V., Almerigi, J., Theokas, C., Phelps, E., Gestsdottir, S., Naudeau, S., Jelicic, H., Alberts, A., Ma, L., Smith, L., Bobek, D., Richman-Raphael, D., Simpson, I., Christiansen, E.D. and von Eye, A. (2005) 'Positive youth development, participation in community youth development programs, and community contributions of fifth-grade adolescents: Findings from the first wave of the 4-H Study of Positive Youth Development', *Journal of Early Adolescence*, 25(1): 17–71.

Lerner, R.M., Lewin-Bizan, S., and Warren, A.E.A. (2011) 'Concepts and theories of human development', in M.H. Bornstein and M.E. Lamb (eds.), *Developmental Science: An Advanced Textbook.* New York: Psychology Press, pp. 3–49.

Leyendecker, B., Lamb, M.E., Harwood, R.L., and Scholmerich, A. (2002) 'Mothers' socialisation goals and evaluations of desirable and undesirable every-day situations in two diverse cultural groups', *International Journal of Behavioral Development*, 26(3): 248–58.

Lightfoot, C. and Valsiner, J. (1992) 'Parental belief systems under influence: Social guidance of the construction of personal cultures', in I.E. Sigel, A.V. McGillicuddy-DeLisi and J.J. Goodnow (eds.), *Parental Belief Systems: The Psychological Consequences for Children*. Hillsdale, NJ: Erlbaum, pp. 433–56.

Loftus, E.F., and Marburger, W. (1983) 'Since the eruption of Mt. St. Helens, has anyone beaten you up? Improving the accuracy of retrospective reports with landmark events', *Memory and Cognition*, 11: 114–20.

Lord, C., Shulman, C., and DiLavore, P. (2004) 'Regression and word loss in autistic spectrum disorders', *Journal of Child Psychology and Psychiatry*, 45: 936–55.

Lounsbury, M.L. and Bates, J.E. (1982) 'The cries of infants and different levels of perceived temperamental difficultness: Acoustic properties and effects on listeners', *Child Development*, 53(3): 677–86.

Lytton, H. (1971) 'Observation studies of parent-child interaction: A methodological review', *Child Development*, 42(3): 651–84.

Maccoby, E.E. and Martin, J.A. (1983) 'Socialization in the context of the family: Parent-child interaction', in M. Hetherington (ed.), *Handbook of Child Psychology*. New York: Wiley, pp. 1–103.

MacWhinney, B. (2000) *The CHILDES Project. Tools for Analyzing Talk* (3rd edition). Mahwah, NJ: Erlbaum.

Main, M., Kaplan, N. and Cassidy, J. (1985) 'Security in infancy, childhood, and adulthood: A move to the level of representation', *Monographs of the Society for Research in Child Development*, 50(1–2): 66–104.

Maital, S., Dromi, E., Sagi, A. and Bornstein, M.H. (2000) 'The Hebrew Communicative Development Inventory: Language specific properties and cross-linguistic generalizations', 27(1): 43–67.

Majnemer, A., and Rosenblatt, B. (1994) 'Reliability of parental recall of developmental milestones', *Pediatric Neurology*, 10: 304–8.

Malgady, R.G., Rogler, L.H., and Cortes, D.E. (1996) 'Cultural expression of psychiatric symptoms: Idioms of anger among Puerto Ricans', *Psychological Assessment*, 8(3): 265–8.

Marchman, V. and Martínez-Sussmann, C. (2002) 'Concurrent validity of caregiver/parent report measures of language for children who are learning both English and Spanish', *Journal of Speech, Language, and Hearing Research*, 45(5): 983–97.

Marcus, A.C. (1982) 'Memory aids in longitudinal health surveys: Results from a field experiment', *American Journal of Public Health*, 72: 567–73.

Marshall, S.K., Tilton-Weaver, L.C. and Bosdet, L. (2005) 'Information management: Considering adolescents' regulation of parental knowledge', *Journal of Adolescence*, 28(5): 633–47.

Martin, J.M., and Cole, D.A. (1993) 'Adaptability and cohesion of didactic relationships in families with developmentally disabled children', *Journal of Family Psychology*, 7(2): 186–96.

Mayfield, K.L., Forman, S.G., and Nagle, R.J. (1984) 'Reliability of the AAMD adaptive behavior scale-public school version', *Journal of School Psychology*, 22(1): 53–61.

McGillicuddy-DeLisi, A.V. (1982a) 'Parental beliefs about developmental processes', *Human Development*, 25(3): 192–200.

McGillicuddy-DeLisi, A.V. (1982b) 'The relationship between parental beliefs and children's cognitive development', in L.M. Laosa and I.E. Sigel (eds.), *Families as Learning Environments for Children*. New York: Plenum, pp. 7–24.

McGillicuddy-DeLisi, A.V. and Sigel, I.E. (1995) 'Parental beliefs', in M.H. Bornstein (ed.), *Handbook of Parenting*. Mahwah, NJ: Erlbaum, pp. 333–58.

McGraw, M. and Molloy, L.B. (1941) 'The pediatric anamnesis: Inaccuracies in eliciting developmental data', *Child Development*, 12(3): 255–65.

Means, B., Nigam, A., Zarrow, M., Loftus, E.F. and Donaldson, M.S. (1989) *Autobiographical Memory for Health-Related Events (Series 6: Cognition and Survey Measurement, No. 2)*. Hyattsville, MD: US Department of Health and Human Services.

Mednick, S.A. and Shaffer, J.B.P. (1963) 'Mothers' retrospective reports in child rearing research', *American Journal of Orthopsychiatry*, 33(3): 457–61.

Meisel, S.J. (1989) 'Can developmental screening tests identify children who are developmentally at risk?', *Pediatrics*, 83: 578–85.

Miljkovitch, R., Pierrehumbert, B., Bretherton, I. and Halfon, O. (2004) 'Associations between parental and child attachment representations', *Attachment and Human Development*, 6(3): 305–25.

Miller, A.M. and Harwood, R.L. (2002) 'The cultural organization of parenting: Change and stability of behaviour patterns during feeding and social play across the first year of life', *Parenting: Science and Practice*, 2(3): 241–72.

Miller, S. (1988). 'Parents' beliefs about children's cognitive development', *Child Development*, 59(2): 259–85.

Neligan, G., and Prudham, D. (1969) 'Norms for four standard developmental milestones by sex, social class and place in family', *Developmental Medicine and Child Neurology*, 11: 413–22.

Nelson, K. (ed.) (2006) *Narratives from the Crib*. Cambridge, MA: Harvard University Press.

Nelson, T.D. (2001) *Cradle the Thought: A Journal for the New Mother's First Year*. Austin, TX: Little Bit Publishing.

Neter, J., and Waksberg, J. (1964) 'A study of response errors in expenditures data from household interviews', *Journal of the American Statistical Association*, 59: 18–55.

Newmark, C.S. (ed.) (1989) *Major Psychological Assessment Instruments, Vol. 2*. Needham Heights, MA: Allyn and Bacon.

Niemi, R.G. (1974) *How Family Members Perceive Each Other: Political and Social Attitudes in Two Generations*. New Haven, CT: Yale University Press.

Noji, J. (1973–1977) Yooji no gengo seikatsu no jittai I -IV. Bunka Hyoron Shuppan. (For a brief description in English, see http://childes.psy.cmu.edu/manuals/, East Asian Languages, p. 23.)

Noller, P., and Callan, V.J. (1988) 'Understanding parent-adolescent interactions: Perceptions of family members and outsiders', *Developmental Psychology*, 24: 707–14.

Nomaguchi, K.M., and Milkie, M.A. (2006) 'Maternal employment in childhood and adults' retrospective reports of parenting practices', *Journal of Marriage and Family*, 68(3): 573–94.

Ochs, E. (1988) *Culture and Language Development: Language Acquisition and Socialization in a Samoan Village*. New York: Cambridge University Press.

Ohannessian, C.M, Lerner, R.M. and Von Eye, A. (1994, February) *Discrepancies in Young Adolescents and Their Perceptions of Family Functioning*. Poster presented at the biennial meeting for the Society for Research on Adolescence, San Diego, CA.

Olson, D.H. (2000) 'Circumplex model of marital and family systems', *Journal of Family Therapy*, 22: 144–67.

Olson, S.L., Bates, J.E. and Bayles, K. (1982) 'Maternal perceptions of infant and toddler behavior: A longitudinal, construct validation study', *Infant Behavior and Development*, 5(2-4): 397–410.

Ong, A.D. and Weiss, D.J. (2000) 'The impact of anonymity on responses to sensitive questions', *Journal of Applied Social Psychology, 30*: 1691–1708.

Ostrov, J.M., Crick, N.R., and Keating, C.E (2005) 'Gender- biased perceptions of preschoolers' behavior: How much is aggression and prosocial behavior in the eye of the beholder?', *Sex Roles, 52*: 393–8.

Pachter, L.M., and Dworkin, P.H. (1997) 'Maternal expectations about normal and child development in 4 cultural groups', *Archives of Pediatrics and Adolescent Medicine*, 151(11): 1144.

Paikoff, R.L., and Brooks-Gunn, J. (1991) 'Do parent-child relationships change during puberty?', *Psychological Bulletin*, 110(1): 47–66.

Parade, S.H., and Leerkes, E.M. (2008) 'The reliability and validity of the Infant Behavior Questionnaire-Revised', *Infant Behavior and Development*, 31: 637–46.

Parke, R.D. (2002) 'Fathers and families', in M.H. Bornstein (ed.), *Handbook of Parenting: Vol. 3. Status and Social Conditions of Parenting*. Mahwah, NJ: Erlbaum, pp. 27–73.

Parker, G., Tupling, H., and Brown, L.B. (1979) 'A parental bonding instrument', *British Journal of Medical Psychology*, 52(1): 1–10.

Parker, W.C. (1984) 'Interviewing children: Problems and promise', *Journal of Negro Education*, 53: 18–28.

Parkinson, B., Briner, R.B., Reynolds, S., and Totterdell, P. (1995) 'Time frames for mood: Relations between momentary and generalized ratings of affect', *Personality and Social Psychology Bulletin*, 21: 331–9.

Patterson, G.R., Capaldi, D., and Bank, L. (1991) 'An early starter model for predicting delinquency', in D.J. Pepler and K.H. Rubin (eds.), *The Development and Treatment of Childhood Aggression*. Hillsdale, NJ: Lawrence Erlbaum Associates, Inc, pp.139–68.

Pettit, G.S., and Laird, R.D. (2002) Psychological control and monitoring in early adolescence: The role of parental involvement and earlier child adjustment', in B. Barber (ed.), *Intrusive Parenting: How Psychological Control Affects Children and Adolescents*. Washington, DC: American Psychological Association, pp. 97–123.

Pettit, G.S., Laird, R.D., Dodge, K.A., Bates, J.E., and Criss, M.M. (2001) 'Antecedents and behavior-problem outcomes of parental monitoring and psychological control in early adolescence', *Child Development*, 72: 583–98.

Phares, V., Compas, B.E., and Howell, D.C. (1989) 'Perspectives on child behavior problems: Comparisons of children's self-reports with parent and teacher reports*', Psychological Assessment*, 1: 68–71.

Piaget, J. (1953) *The Origins of Intelligence in the Child*. London: Routledge and Kegan Paul. (Original work published in 1936.)

Piaget, J. (1954) *The Construction of Reality in the Child*. New York: Basic Books. (Original work published 1937.)

Piaget, J. (1962) *The Moral Judgment of the Child*. New York: Collier, 1962. (Originally published, 1932.)

Piaget, J. (1970) 'Piaget's theory', in P. Mussen (ed.), *Carmichael's Manual of Child Psychology* (Vol. 1). New York: Wiley, pp. 703–32.

Pickett, K., Kasza, K., Biesecker, G., Wright, R., and Wakschlag, L. (2009) 'Women who remember, women who do not: A methodological study of maternal recall of smoking in pregnancy', *Nicotine and Tobacco Research*, 1(10): 1166–74.

Pierce, K., Carter, C., Weinfeld, M., Desmond, J., Hazin, R., Bjork, R., and Gallagher, N. (2011) 'Detecting, studying, and treating autism early: The one-year well-baby check-up approach', *Journal of Pediatrics*, 159(3): 458–65.

Pillai Riddell, R.R. and Craig, K.D. (2006) 'Judgments of infant pain: The impact of caregiver identity and infant age', *Journal of Pediatric Psychology*, 32(5): 501–11.

Preyer, W. (1881) *Die Seele des Kindes [The mind of the child.]* Leipzig, T. Grieber. English translation 1888, New York. D. Appleton and Co.

Prochner, L. and Doyon, P. (1997) 'Researchers and their subjects in the history of child study: William Blatz and the Dionne Quintuplets', *Canadian Psychology*, 38(2): 103–10.

Putallatz, M., Costanzo, P.R., and Smith, R.B. (1991) 'Maternal recollections of childhood peer relationships: Implications for their children's social competence', *Journal of Social and Personal Relationships*, 8(3): 403–22.

Pyles, M.K., Stolz, H.R. and MacFarlane, J.W. (1935) 'The accuracy of mothers' reports on birth and developmental data', *Child Development*, 6(3): 165–76.

Rainwater-Bryant, B.J. (1985) *'Comparisons of parent-obtained and teacher-obtained adaptive behavior scores for handicaped children'.* Doctoral dissertation, Memphis State University.

Rapoport, J.L., Pandoni, C., Renfield, M., Lake, G.R. and Ziegler, M.G. (1977) 'Newborn dopamine-beta-hydroxylase, minor physical anomalies, and infant temperament', *American Journal of Psychiatry*, 134(6): 676–9.

Reese, E., and Read, S. (2000) 'Predictive validity of the New Zealand MacArthur Communicative Development Inventory: Words and sentences', *Journal of Child Language*, 27: 255–66.

Rescorla, L. (1989) 'The Language Development Survey: A screening tool for delayed language in toddlers', *Journal of Speech and Hearing Disorders*, 54: 587–99.

Rescorla, L. Hadicke Wiley, M., and Escarce, E. (1993) 'Epidemiological investigation of expressive language delay at age two', *First Language*, 13: 5–22.

Rescorla, L., and Alley, A. (2001) 'Validation of the Language Development Survey (LDS): A parent report tool for identifying language delay in toddlers', *Journal of Speech, Language, and Hearing Research*, 44: 434–45.

Reznick, J.S. Goldsmith, L. (1989) 'A multiple form word production checklist for assessing early language', *Journal of Child Language*, 16: 91–100.

Reznick, J.S. and Goldfield, B.A. (1994) 'Diary versus representative checklist assessment of productive vocabulary', *Journal of Child Language*, 21(2): 465–72.

Ribas, Jr., R. de C., and Bornstein, M.H. (2005) 'Parenting knowledge: Similarities and differences in Brazilian mothers and fathers', *Interamerican Journal of Psychology*, 39: 5–12.

Richman, A.L., Miller, P.M., and LeVine, R.A. (1992) 'Cultural and educational variations in maternal responsiveness', *Developmental Psychology*, 28(4): 614–21.

Riese, M.L. (1983) 'Behavior patterns in full–term and preterm twins', *Acta Geneticae Medicae et Gemellologiae*, 32(3-4): 209–20.

Robins, D.L., and Dumont-Mathieu, T.M. (2006) 'Early screening for autism spectrum disorders: Update on the Modified Checklist for Autism in Toddlers and other measures', *Developmental and Behavioral Pediatrics*, 27: S111–S119.

Robins, D.L., Fein, D., Barton, M., and Green, J.A. (2001) 'The Modified Checklist for Autism in Toddlers: An initial study investigating the early detection of autism and pervasive developmental disorders', *Journal of Autism and Developmental Disorders*, 31: 131–51.

Robbins, L.C. (1963) 'The accuracy of parental recall of aspects of child development and of child rearing practices', *Journal of Abnormal and Social Psychology*, 66(3): 261–70.

Rosenzweig, M.R. and Wolpin, K.I. (1993) 'Maternal expectations and ex post rationalizations: The usefulness of survey information on the wantedness of children', *Journal of Human Resources*, 28(2): 205–29.

Ross, M. (1989) 'The relation of implicit theories to the construction of personal histories', *Psychological Review*, 96(2): 341–57.

Rothbart, M.K. (1981) 'Measurement of temperament in infancy', *Child Development*, 52(2): 569–78.

Rothbart, M.K. and Bates, J.E. (1998) 'Temperament', in W. Damon and N. Eisenberg (eds.), *Handbook of Child Psychology: Vol. 3 Social, Emotional and Personality Development*. New York: Wiley, pp. 105–76.

Rothbart, M.K. and Bates, J.E. (2006) 'Temperament', in D. Kuhn, and R.S. Siegler (ed.), W. Damon (Series ed.), *Handbook of Child Psychology: Vol. 2. Cognition, Perception, and Language*. Hoboken, NJ: Wiley, pp. 99–166.

Rothbart, M.K. and Derryberry, P. (1981) Development of individual differences in temperament', in M.E. Lamb and A. Brown (eds.), *Advances in Developmental Psychology*. Hillsdale, NJ: Erlbaum, pp. 31–86.

Rothbart, M.K. and Goldsmith, H.H. (1986) 'Three approaches to the study of infant temperament', *Developmental Review*, 5(3): 237-60.

Rothbaum, F. and Weisz, J.R. (1994) 'Parental caregiving and child externalizing behavior in nonclinical samples: A meta-analysis', *Psychological Bulletin*, 116(1): 55–74.

Rousseau, J.J. (1781) *Émile, or on education*, trans. with an introd. by Allan Bloom. New York: Basic Books, 1979. (Originally published, 1762).

Rousseau, J.J. (1782) *Reveries of a Solitary Walker*, trans. Peter France. London: Penguin Books, 1980. (Originally published, 1782).

Ruppenthal, L., Tuck, J., and Gagnon, A.J. (2005) 'Enhancing research with migrant women through focus groups', *Western Journal of Nursing Research*, 27(6): 735–54.

Russell, A. and Russell, A. (1982) 'Mother, father, and child beliefs about child development', *Journal of Psychology*, 110(2): 297–306.

Sameroff, A., Seifer, R. and Elias, P. (1982) 'Sociocultural variability in infant temperament ratings', *Child Development*, 53(1): 164–73.

Scarr, S. (1996) 'How people make their own environments: Implications for parents and policy makers', *Psychology, Public Policy, and Law*, 2(2): 204–28.

Schaefer, R.B., and Keith, P.M. (1985) 'A causal model approach to the symbolic interactionist view of the self-concept', *Journal of Personality and Social Psychology*, 48: 963–9.

Schuman, H. and Presser, S. (1981) *Questions and Answers in Attitude Surveys*. New York: Academic Press.

Schwarz, J.C., Barton-Henry, M.S. and Pruzinsky, T. (1985) 'Assessing child-rearing behaviors: A comparison of ratings made by mother, father, child, and sibling on the CRPBI', *Child Development*, 56(2): 462–79.

Schwarz, N. and Oyserman, D. (2001) 'Asking questions about behavior: Cognition, Communication, and questionnaire construction', *American Journal of Evaluation*, 22: 127–60.

Schwarz, N. (1999) 'Self-reports: How the questions shape the answers', *American Psychologist*, 54: 93–105.

Schwarz, N., Hippler, H.J., Deutsch, B., and Strack, F. (1985) 'Response scales: Effects of category range on reported behavior and comparative judgments', *Public Opinion Quarterly*, 49: 388–95.

Schwarz, N., Strack, E., Muller, G., and Chassein, B. (1988) 'The range of response alternatives may determine the meaning of the question: Further evidence on informative function of response alternatives', *Social Cognition*, 6: 107–17.

Scrimin, S., Haynes, O.M., Altoè, G., Bornstein, M.H., and Axia, G. (2009) 'Anxiety and stress in mothers and fathers in the 24 h after their child's surgery', *Child: Care, Health and Development*, 35: 227–33.

Seifer, R. (2002) 'What do we learn from parent reports of their children's behavior? Commentary on Vaughn et al.'s critique of early temperament assessments', *Infant Behavior and Development*, 25(1): 117–20.

Seiffge-Krenke, I. and Kollmar, F. (1998) 'Discrepancies between mothers' and fathers' perceptions of sons' and daughters' problem behavior: A longitudinal analysis of parent-adolescent agreement on internalizing and externalizing problem behavior', *Journal of Child Psychology and Psychiatry*, 39(5): 687–97.

Senese, P.V., Bornstein, M.H., Haynes, O.M., Rossi, G., and Venuti, P. (2012) 'A cross-cultural comparison of mothers' beliefs about their parenting very young children', *Infant Behavior and Development*, 35: 479–88.

Sessa, F.M., Avenevoli, S., Steinberg, L., and Morris, A.S. (2001) 'Correspondence among informants on parenting: Preschool children, mothers, and observers', *Journal of Family Psychology*, 15(1): 53.

Sexton, T., and Alexander, J. (2003) 'Functional Family Therapy: A mature clinical model for working with at-risk adolescents and their families', in T. Sexton, G. Weeks, and M. Robbins (eds.), *Handbook of Clinical Therapy*. New York, NY: Brunner-Routledge, pp. 323–48.

Siefer, R., Sameroff, A.J., Barrett, L.C. and Krafchuck, E. (1994) 'Infant temperament measured by multiple observations and mother report', *Child Development*, 65(5): 1478–90.

Sigel, I.E. (1992) 'The belief-behavior connection: A resolvable dilemma?', in I.E. Sigel, A. V. McGillicuddy-DeLisi and J.J. Goodnow (eds.), *Parental Belief Systems: The Psychological Consequences for Children*. Hillsdale, NJ: Erlbaum, pp. 433–56.

Smetana, J.G. (1989) 'Adolescents' and parents' reasoning about actual family conflict', *Child Development*, 60(5): 1052–67.

Smetana, J.G., Yau, J., Restrepo, A.M. and Braeges, J.L. (1990) *Coordinations in Adolescents' and Parents' Views of Family Conflict*. Paper presented at the biennial meeting for the Society for Research in Adolescence, Atlanta.

Smith, P.K. and Drew, L.M. (2002) 'Grandparenthood', in M.H. Bornstein (ed.), *Handbook of Parenting: Vol. 3. Status and Social Conditions of Parenting*. Mahwah, NJ: Erlbaum, pp. 141–72.

Soenens, B., Vansteenkiste, M., Luyckx, K. and Goossens, L. (2006) 'Parenting and adolescent problem behavior: An integrated model with adolescent self-disclosure and perceived parental knowledge as intervening variables', *Developmental Psychology*, 42(2): 305–18.

Sonnader, K. (1987) 'Parental developmental assessment of 18-month-old children: Reliability and predictive value', *Developmental Medicine and Chid Neurology*, 29: 351–62.

Sparrow, S. and Cicchetti, D. (1978) 'Behavior rating inventory for moderately, severely and profoundly retarded persons', *American Journal of Mental Deficiency*, 82(4): 365–74.

Sparrow, S.S., Balla, D.A. and Cicchetti, D.V. (1984) *Vineland Adaptive Behavior Scales*. Circle Pines, MN: American Guidance Service.

Squires, J., Potter, L., Bricker, D. and Lamorey, S. (1998) 'Parent-completed developmental questionnaires: effectiveness with low and middle income parents', *Early Childhood Research Quarterly*, 13(2): 345–54.

Stanger, C. and Lewis, M. (1993) 'Agreement among parents, teachers, and children on internalizing and externalizing behavior problems', *Journal of Clinical Child Psychology*, 22(1): 107–15.

Stattin, H. and Kerr, M. (2000) 'Parental monitoring: A reinterpretation', *Child Development*, 71(4): 1072–85.

Stern, D. (1992) *Diary of a Baby: What Your Child Sees, Feels, and Experiences*. New York: Basic Books.

Stern, D. (1995) *The Motherhood Constellation: A Unified View of Parent-Infant Psychotherapy*. New York, NY: Basic Books.

Stevens, B.J. and Gibbons, S. (2002) 'Clinical utility and clinical significance in the assessment and management of pain in vulnerable infants', *Clinics in Perinatology*, 29(3): 1–10.

Stoiber, K.C. and Houghton, T.G. (1993) 'The relationship of adolescent mothers' expectations, knowledge, and beliefs to their young children's coping behavior', *Infant Mental Health Journal*, 14(1): 61–79.

St. James Roberts, I., and Wolke, D. (1984) 'Comparison of mothers' with trained-observers' reports of neonatal behavioral style, *Infant Behavior and Development*, 7: 299–310.

Sudman, S., and Bradburn, N.M. (1973) 'Effects of time and memory factors on response in surveys', *Journal of the American Statistical Association*, 68: 805–15.

Tamis-LeMonda, C.S. and Bornstein, M.H. (1994) 'Specificity in mother-toddler language-play relations across the second year', *Developmental Psychology*, 30(2): 283–92.

Tamis-LeMonda, C.S. and Bornstein, M.H. (1996) 'Variation in children's exploratory, nonsymbolic, and symbolic play: An exploratory multidimensional framework', in C. Rovee-Collier and L.P. Lipsitt (eds.), *Advances in Infancy Research*. Norwood, NJ: Ablex, pp. 37–78.

Tamis-LeMonda, C.S., Chen, L.A. and Bornstein, M.H. (1998) 'Mothers' knowledge about children's play and language development: Short-term stability and interrelations', *Developmental Psychology*, 34(1): 115–24.

Tamis-LeMonda, C.S., Užgiris, I.Č, and Bornstein, M.H. (2002) 'Play in parent-child interactions', in M.H. Bornstein (ed.), *Handbook of Parenting*, *Vol. 5: Practical Parenting* (2nd ed.). Mahwah, NJ: Erlbaum, pp. 221–24.

Tanner, J.M. (1963) 'The regulation of human growth', *Child Development*, 34(4): 817–46.

Taverna, L., Bornstein, M.H., Putnick, D.L., and Axia, G. (2011) 'Adaptive behaviors in young children: A unique cultural comparison in Italy', *Journal of Cross-Cultural Psychology*, 42: 445–65.

Tein, J.-Y., Roosa, M.W., and Michaels, M. (1994) 'Agreement between parent and child reports on parental behaviors', *Journal of Marriage and Family*, 56(2): 341–55.

Thal, D. and Bates, E. (1990) 'Continuity and variation in early language development', in J. Colombo and J. Fagen (eds.), *Individual Differences in Infancy: Reliability, Stability, Prediction*. Hillsdale, NJ: Erlbaum, pp. 359–81.

Theunissen, N.C.M., Vogels, H.M., Koopman, H.M., Verrips, G.H.W., Zwinderman, K.A.H., Verloove-Vanhorick, S.P. and Wit. J.M. (1998) 'The proxy problem: Child report versus parent report in health-related quality of life research', *Quality of Life Research*, 7(5): 387–97.

Thomas, A. and Chess, S. (1977) *Temperament and Development*. New York: Brunner-Mazel.

Thomas, A., Chess, S., Birch, H., Hertzig, M. and Korn, S. (1963) *Behavioral Individuality in Childhood*. New York: New York University Press.

Thordardottir, E.T. and Ellis Weismer, S. (1996) 'Language assessment via parent report: Development of a screening instrument for Icelandic children', *First Language*, 16(48): 265–85.

Thurber, S. and Osborn, R.A. (1993) 'Comparisons of parent and adolescent perspectives on deviance', *Journal of Genetic Psychology*, 154(1): 25–32.

Thurber, S. and Snow, M. (1990) 'Assessment of adolescent psychopathology: Comparison of mother and daughter perspectives', *Journal of Clinical Child Psychology*, 19(3): 249–53.

Tiedemann, D. (1787) 'Beobachtungen über die Entwicklung der Seelenfähigkeiten bei Kindern (Observations on the development of children's mental capacities)', *Hissische Beiträge zur Gelehrsamkeit und Kunst*, 2: 313–33 and 486–502.

Todd, R.D., Huang, H., and Henderson, C.A. (2008) 'Poor utility of the age of onset criterion for DSM-IV attention deficit/hyperactivity disorder: Recommendations for DSM-V and ICD-11', *Journal of Child Psychology and Psychiatry*, 49: 942–9.

Tombokan-Runtukahu, J. and Nitko, A.J. (1992) 'Translation, cultural adjustment, and validation of a measure of adaptive behavior', *Research in Developmental Disabilities*, 13(5): 481–501.

Tourangeau, R. and Smith, T.W. (1996) 'Asking sensitive questions: The impact of data collection mode, question format, and question context', *Public Opinion Quarterly*, 60: 275–304.

Tremblay, R.E. (2004) 'Decade of behavior distinguished lecture: Development of physical aggression during infancy', *Infant Mental Health Journal*, 25: 399–407.

Tremblay, R.E., Japel, C., Perusse, D., McDuff, P., Boivin, M., Zoccolillo, M. (1999) 'The search for the age of "onset" of physical aggression: Rousseau and Bandura revisited', *Criminal Behavior and Mental Health*, 9: 8–23.

Vaillancourt, T., Brendgen, M., Boivin, M., and Tremblay, R.E. (2003) 'A longitudinal confirmatory factor analysis of indirect and physical aggression: Evidence of two factors over time?', *Child Development*, 71: 1628–38.

Van der Valk, J.C., Van den Oord, E.J.C.G., Verhulst, F.C., and Boomsma, D. I. (2003) 'Using shared and unique parental views to study the etiology of 7-year-old twins' internalizing and externalizing problems', *Behavior Genetics*, 33: 409–20.

Vaughn, B., Taraldson, B., Crichton, L. and Egeland, B. (1981) 'The assessment of infant temperament: A critique of the Carey Infant Temperament Questionnaire', *Infant Behavior and Development*, 4: 1–17.

Vaughn, B.E., Bradley, C.F., Joffe, L.S., Seifer, R. and Barglow, P. (1987) 'Maternal characteristics measured prenatally predictive of ratings of temperamental "difficulty" on the Carey Infant Temperament Questionnaire', *Developmental Psychology*, 23(1): 152–61.

Verhulst, F.C. and Koot, H.M. (1992) *Child Psychiatric Epidemiology: Concepts, Methods, Findings*. Newbury Park: Sage.

Versluis-den Bieman, H.J.M. and Verhulst, F.C. (1995) 'Self-reported and parent reported problems in adolescent international adoptees', *Journal of Child Psychology and Psychiatry*, 36(8): 1411–28.

Vollmann, R., Marschik, P. and Einspieler, C. (2000) 'Elternfragebogen fur die Erfassung der frühen Sprachentwicklung für (Österreichisches) Deutsch', *Grazer Linguistische Studien*, 54: 123–44.

Wallace, D.B., Franklin, M.B. and Keegan, R.T. (1994) 'The observing eye: A century of baby diaries', *Human Development*, 37(1): 1–29.

Waters, E., Stewart-Brown, S. and Fitzpatrick, R. (2003) 'Agreement between adolescent self-report and parent reports of health and well-being: Results of an epidemiological study', *Child: Care, Health and Development*, 29(6): 501–09.

Weir, R.H. (1962) *Language in the Crib*. The Hague: Mouton.

Weisner, T.S., and Gallimore, R. (1977) 'My brother's keeper: Child and sibling caretaking', *Current Anthropology*, 18(2): 169–90.

Wenar, C. (1963) 'The reliability of developmental histories', *Psychosomatic Medicine*, 25(6): 505–9.

Wenar, C. and Coulter, J.B. (1962) 'A reliability study of developmental histories', *Child Development*, 33(2): 453–62.

Wetherby, A.M., Brosnan-Maddox, S., Peace, V., and Newton, L. (2008) 'Validation of the Infant–Toddler Checklist as a broadband screener for autism spectrum disorders from 9 to 24 months of age', *Autism*, 12(5): 487–511.

Wetherby, A.M., Woods, J., Allen, L., Cleary, J., Dickinson, H., and Lord, C. (2004) 'Early indicators of autism spectrum disorders in the second year of life', *Journal of Autism Developmental Disorders*, 34: 473–93.

Whitehurst, G.J. (1997) 'Language processes in context: Language learning in children reared in poverty', in L.B. Adamson and M.A. Romski (eds.), *Research on Communication and Language Disorders: Contribution to Theories of Language Development*. Baltimore, MD: Brookes, pp. 110–36.

Williams, S.B., Whitlock, E.P., Edgerton, E.A., Smith, P.R. and Bell, T.L. (2007) 'U.S. Preventive Services Task Force. Counseling about proper use of motor vehicle occupant restraints and avoidance of alcohol use while driving: A systematic evidence review for the U.S. Preventive Services Task Force', *Annals of Internal Medicine*, 147(3): 194–206.

Willis, G., Brittingham, A., Lee, L. and Tourangeau, R. (1999) 'Response errors in surveys of children's immunizations', *Vital Health Statistics*, 6(8): 1–16.

Wilson, R.S. and Matheny, A.P. (1983) 'Assessment of temperament in infant twins', *Developmental Psychology*, 19(2): 172–83.

Yarrow, M.R., Campbell, J.D. and Burton, R.V. (1970) 'Recollections of childhood: A study of the retrospective method', *Monographs of the Society for Research in Child Development,* 35, Serial No. 138.

Zaslow, M.J., Weinfield, N.S., Gallagher, M., Hair, E.C., Ogawa, J.R., Egeland, B., Tabors, P.O. and De Temple, J.M. (2006) 'Longitudinal prediction of child outcomes from differing measures of parenting in a low-income sample', *Developmental Psychology*, 42(1): 27–36.

Zegiob, L.E., Arnold, S., and Forehand, R. (1975) 'An examination of observer effects in parent-child interactions', *Child Development*, 46(2): 509–12.

Zink, I. and Lejaegere, M. (2002) *N-CDIs: Lijsten voor Communicatieve Ontwikkeling. Aanpassing en hernormering van de MacArthur CDIs van Fenson et al.* Leuven: Acco. Sage

Zwaigenbaum, L., Thurm, A., Stone, W., Baranek, G., Bryson, S., Iverson, J., Kau, A., et al. (2007) 'Studying the emergence of autism spectrum disorders in high-risk infants: Methodological and practical issues', *Journal of Autism and Developmental Disorders*, 37: 466–80.

27

Adults' Memories of Their Own Childhoods

David B. Pillemer and Ryan A. Dickson

INTRODUCTION

Research examining adults' recollections of their own childhoods has a long history, dating back to the late 1800s (see, for example, Miles, 1895). Clinical interest burgeoned with Freud's 100-year-old discovery of the phenomenon of infantile amnesia: 'What I have in mind is the peculiar amnesia which, in the case of most people, though by no means all, hides the earliest beginnings of their childhood up to their sixth or eighth year' (1905/1953: 174). Freud attributed the inaccessibility of early memories to the blockading force of repression. Adler (1937) emphasized instead the psychological importance of long-lasting early memories, and researchers continue to explore the special meanings of earliest recollections (Barrett, 1980; Saunders and Norcross, 1988; Sutin and Robins, 2005).

In contrast to Freudian and Adlerian explanations for the absence or persistence of childhood memories, research psychologists have long favoured accounts that focus on developmental changes in memory organization and function (see, for example, Piaget, 1962; Waldfogel, 1948). Previous reviews have identified and contrasted alternative

explanations for infantile amnesia (Fivush and Nelson, 2004; Howe and Courage, 1993; Nelson, 1993; Newcombe, Lloyd and Ratliff, 2007; Pillemer, 1998b; Pillemer and White, 1989; Wang, 2003; White and Pillemer, 1979). Proposed causal factors include developmental changes in language, cognitive abilities, self-concept, the quality of parent–child social interaction, and neurological maturation. A shared premise is that early childhood memories are not encoded in a fashion that facilitates their voluntary narrative recall in adulthood. Accordingly, researchers frequently use the indirect strategy of examining qualities of children's memory processes and extrapolating to adults' long-term autobiographical memory failures (see, for example, Fivush and Nelson, 2004; Pillemer and White, 1989; Richardson and Hayne, 2007).

This chapter presents a synthesis of research and theory on adults' memories of childhood. First, we examine memories of early childhood. We look at reported ages of the earliest childhood memory and also at age distributions of childhood memories provided in response to various types of memory prompts. As part of this analysis, we address the issue of memory accuracy and consistency. We also explore emotional content, focusing on the balance of positive and negative themes. We conclude this section with a methodological analysis and critique. Second, we examine individual and group differences in early childhood memories, with a primary focus on the effects of culture and gender. Third, we examine adults' memories of middle childhood and early adolescence. In contrast to the theoretical importance placed upon memories of early childhood, and the voluminous research literature on this topic, recall of personal events occurring later in childhood has been the focus of study only infrequently. We outline reasons for this relative neglect, and we suggest ways to address it. We conclude by exploring implications for research on childhood.

Our analytical approach differs somewhat from the theoretical and methodological perspectives taken by other contributors to this volume. Like many other memory development researchers, our analysis focuses primarily on the accessibility, persistence, accuracy, and consistency of early childhood memories. We do not focus on what can be learned about the subjective and objective experience of childhood from adults' memory reports. For example, a largely unanswered question is how adults' and children's retrospective reports of comparable childhood events might differ based on cognitive and socio-emotional factors. If adults' memories of childhood are distorted, then our understanding of children's everyday lives based on adults' reports may be similarly biased. On the other hand, some aspects of early experience may be revealed more clearly or persuasively in adults' reports than in those provided by children themselves, given that adults have better verbal skills, greater reflective ability, and a broader and deeper perspective on the meaning of events and their long-term consequences. Future research should explore if and how adults' recollections of childhood can contribute to a fuller understanding of the cognitive, social, and emotional world of the child.

ADULTS' MEMORIES OF EARLY CHILDHOOD

Researchers have elicited early childhood memories in three principal ways (Pillemer, 1998b): (a) by asking participants to report and date their earliest childhood memory; (b) by asking participants to report multiple early childhood memories; and (c) by using memory prompts for specific early childhood events with known dates of occurrence.

The earliest childhood memory

The oldest and most common research strategy for determining the starting point for autobiographical recall involves administering questionnaires to adults and asking them to describe and date their earliest childhood recollection. Although memory probes are for the most part open-ended and non-directive, and participants provide their own subjective estimate of their age at the time of the remembered episode, study results have been consistent over the years. Dudycha and Dudycha (1941) reviewed a number of studies published from the 1890s through the 1930s and concluded that 'the earliest remembered experience for most people dates back to their third or fourth year' (673). Results of recent studies are strikingly consistent with these earlier estimates. We have identified 26 studies that used a questionnaire methodology to elicit the earliest childhood memory from adults (see Table 27.1). These studies produced 49 separate estimates of the age of the earliest memory. The distribution of mean ages from these studies is presented in Figure 27.1. The average age of the earliest memory almost always occurs at 3 or 4 years, with an unweighted mean age across the 49 samples of 3.69 years. As is apparent in Table 27.1, some of the variation in age estimates within and across studies is attributable to the effects of culture, which we discuss later in this chapter.

Does the consistent pattern of mean age estimates allow us to confidently set a lower

Table 27.1　Mean age of earliest memory (in years) by study

Study	Sample characteristics	N	Mean age
Bruce et al. (2005)			
Experiment 1 (Remember earliest)		112	4.22
Experiment 2 (Remember earliest)		129	4.36
Dudycha & Dudycha (1933a)[1]		200	3.71
Dudycha & Dudycha (1933b)[1]		233	3.58
Gur-Yaish & Wang (2006)	Israeli	83	4.15
Hankoff (1987)	Male criminal	32	4.37
	Male control	50	3.75
Harpaz-Rotem & Hirst (2005)	Israeli adult		
Experiment 1	Kibbutz	103	4.15
	Non-kibbutz	104	3.08
Howes, Siegel, & Brown (1993)[2]		~300	
	Male	–	3.40
	Female	–	3.07
Jack & Hayne (2007)			
Uncued earliest condition		40	3.92
Kihlstrom & Harackiewicz (1982)		164	3.24
MacDonald, Uesiliana, & Hayne (2000)			
Experiment 1	New Zealand European	32	3.57
	New Zealand Maori	32	2.72
	New Zealand Asian	32	4.82
Experiment 2	New Zealand Asian		
	Male	16	3.30
	Female	16	4.51
Matsumoto & Stanny (2006)	Japanese bilingual	18	3.20
	US monolingual	15	4.00
Miles (1895)	Female	89	3.04
Mullen (1994)			
Experiment 1	Asian	24	3.94
	Caucasian	117	3.21
Experiment 2	Asian	35	3.71
	Caucasian	133	3.27
Experiment 3	Asian	70	3.63
	Caucasian	235	3.23
Experiment 4[3]	Korean	41	4.63
Potwin (1901)		100	
	Male	–	4.40
	Female	–	3.01

(Continued)

Table 27.1 *(Continued)*

Study	Sample characteristics	N	Mean age
Rabbitt & McInnis (1988)	Older adult		
	Low IQ	70	4.79
	Medium IQ	228	3.88
	High IQ	79	3.14
Rule (1983)	First born	27	3.77
	Later born	37	3.70
Rule & Jarrell (1983)		66	3.70
Saunders & Norcross (1988)		184	3.83
Spirrison & McCarley (2001)		107	4.90
Wang (2001)	Caucasian American	119	3.49
	Chinese	137	3.95
Wang, Leichtman, & White (1998)	Chinese	137	3.95
Wang & Ross (2005)[2]			
Experiment 1 (Control condition)	Chinese	~45	3.34
	Asian	~44	4.17
Weigle & Bauer (2000)[4]	Adult deaf	13	3.08
	Adult hearing	12	2.92
West & Bauer (1999)			
Experiment 1	Female	48	3.33
Experiment 2	Male	15	3.33
Westman & Orellana (1996)			
Experiment 1		53	3.10
Westman, Westman, & Orellana (1996)			
Experiment 1 (No modality cue condition)		66	3.30

Note: All subjects were college or graduate students unless otherwise specified. Partial years reported as months were converted to a proportion of year. For example, 3 years 8½ months was converted to 3.71 years. Dashes indicate unknown values and tildes indicate estimates based on authors' descriptions.

[1] Memories from age 5 and above were excluded from original analyses.

[2] Sample sizes were estimated from authors' descriptions.

[3] Included students and their spouses.

[4] Adult hearing mean calculated excluding subject reporting birth memory.

boundary on personal memory? In practical settings, such as court proceedings, should we doubt the veracity of memories for events that occurred before age 3? Not necessarily. First, the age cut-off of approximately 3.5 years is based on *mean scores*, so that approximately one half of the reported events within any given study will occur at an earlier age. For example, Saunders and Norcross (1988) found that the age of the earliest memory ranged from 1 year to 9 years, and that 90 per cent of memories fell between 1.5 and 7 years. Second, it is unclear if participants are able to identify and accurately date their 'true' earliest memory in response to a single questionnaire item. Mullen (1994, Study 3) asked participants to identify ways that they estimated the age of their earliest memory, and some responses do not generate a great deal of confidence: guessing, just

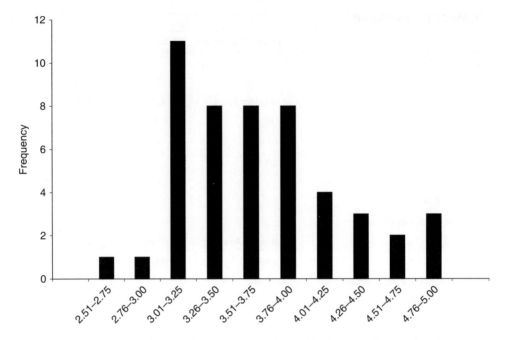

Figure 27.1   Mean age in years of the earliest memory (49 independent samples)

remembering, having an image of how they looked at the time, and linking the memory to a location preceding a family move. Accuracy of memory is addressed in a later section.

Temporal distributions of childhood memories

A second research strategy involves asking research participants to report multiple memories of their childhood or their entire lifetime and then examining the shape of the resulting age distributions. If childhood amnesia exists, very early memories should be scarcer than would be expected as a result of normal forgetting (Wetzler and Sweeney, 1986). Waldfogel (1948) was perhaps the first researcher to adopt this methodological strategy. College students were allotted 85 minutes to record all of their memories up to their eighth birthday. They then dated each memory to the nearest year of occurrence. Very few memories were identified as occurring before age 3, and the rate of increase in

memories accelerated for each year up to age 5, after which the rate of increase diminished. In other words, there is a notable under-representation of memories occurring before age 3 and an especially sharp year-to-year increase up to age 5.

Results of contemporary studies are consistent with Waldfogel's (1948) findings. Rubin (2000) synthesized data from multiple studies, including over 11,000 individual memories. He identified several general strategies for obtaining memories: exhaustive-search methods similar to the one used by Waldfogel (1948), word-cued methods in which memories are given in response to word prompts (Rubin, 1982), and interview methods (Thorne, 1995). The age distribution of memories from the combined studies demonstrates a scarcity of memories before age 3 (only 1.1 per cent of the memory total) and a rapid increase in the number of memories thereafter. The prototypical distribution is well illustrated by Rubin and Schulkind's (1997) analysis of memories provided by college students and older adults in response to word cues. Figure 27.2 displays a paucity of very early memories, a rapid increase

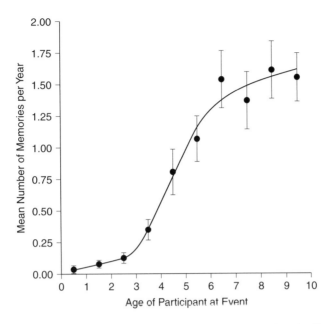

Figure 27.2   Distribution of word-cued autobiographical memories for the first 10 years of life

Source: From 'The Distribution of Important and Word-Cued Autobiographical Memories in 20-, 35-, and 70-Year-Old Adults', by D.C. Rubin and M.D. Schulkind, 1997, *Psychology and Aging, 12*, p. 528. Copyright by the American Psychological Association. Reprinted with permission.

during the preschool years, and a levelling off after age 7.

Memories of targeted childhood events

A different strategy for pinpointing the beginnings of personal memory involves asking participants direct questions about particular past events with known dates of occurrence. Winograd and Killinger (1983) obtained memories of the 1963 assassination of President John Kennedy from adults who were between the ages of 1 and 7 years at the time of the shooting. Memory questions probed personal circumstances such as one's location and ongoing activity when receiving the tragic news. Using a lenient recall criterion, in which respondents had to answer only one memory question, the age drop-off was linear, with very few memories reported by participants who were younger than age 3 in 1963. Using a stricter recall criterion that required

answers to multiple questions, memories were scarce before age 4 and increased rapidly thereafter, with 50 per cent of participants producing detailed recollections by age 6.

One would not expect the shooting of an American president to be easily comprehended by very young preschoolers. Therefore, the onset of personal memories for this episode may be delayed compared to more easily interpretable events. Sheingold and Tenney (1982) examined female college students' recollections of the birth of a sibling. Students answered 20 questions about the birth episode. Participants who were age 3 or younger at the time of the birth rarely were able to answer memory questions, whereas those who were age 4 or older could provide relevant information.

Usher and Neisser (1993) asked college students to answer direct questions about four known childhood events: sibling births, hospitalizations, family moves, and family deaths. For example, questions about a sibling birth included 'Who took care of you while your mother was in the hospital?', 'Where were you the first time you saw the baby?', and 'What was the baby wearing?' A majority of participants who were age 2 at the time of a sibling birth or hospitalization were able to answer some memory questions, whereas many participants answered questions about family deaths and moves only at age 3 or 4.

Eacott and Crawley (1998) examined memories of the birth of a sibling using Usher and Neisser's (1993) procedure but with a much larger sample of participants who had been between ages 2 and 3 at the time of the birth. A majority of participants who were 2 years 4 months or older were able to answer multiple memory questions; remembering before this age was apparent but less extensive. In a follow-up study using the same methodology, Eacott and Crawley (1999) targeted memories of sibling births that occurred between the ages of 1 year 2 months and 1 year 11 months. A majority of participants could answer at least one memory question (60 per cent), and a sizeable minority could answer multiple questions.

Although studies by Usher and Neisser (1993) and Eacott and Crawley (1998, 1999) indicate that personal memories of events occurring even before age 2 or 3 may persist into adulthood, the methodology – asking participants to answer a series of direct questions about particular events – raises serious methodological concerns (see, for example, Loftus, 1993), which will be addressed in a later methodological comparison and critique.

Consistency and accuracy

Age distributions of early memories are orderly and reasonably consistent, but do memories accurately reflect the original events? The possibility exists that memories from the early ages of 2, 3, or 4 years are misremembered or misdated (see also Hayne and Tustin, Chapter 29 this volume). Because it is rarely possible to determine with certainty what happened at the time of the original occurrence, researchers have looked instead for corroboration from other people who were present at the time or who have relevant knowledge. It is important to keep in mind, however, that memories provided by independent observers also are vulnerable to distortion and decay and as such provide a standard for tests of consistency but not factual accuracy (Loftus, 1993).

Howes, Siegel, and Brown (1993) provided some support for the general veracity of earliest memories. College students first reported their earliest childhood memories. They were then asked to contact another person who had been present when the remembered event occurred, to explain the purpose of the study to that person, and to provide them with as little detailed information as possible about the target event. The other person (the 'verifier') then wrote out their independent version of the episode. Participants were excluded if they talked with the verifier prior to obtaining their independent memory or failed to follow other directions and safeguards. Most (80 per cent) memories were either partially or fully verified. Although tests of memory accuracy did not rely on objective factual records, and a minority of memories were judged to be distorted in some way, the high level of consistency between students and verifiers bolsters the credibility of earliest recollections: 'the assumption of a standard or frequent distortion factor in infantile recall was not supported' (Howes et al., 1993: 108).

Bruce, Dolan, and Phillips-Grant (2000) elicited college students' personal memories of events that occurred during the first eight years of life. The researchers obtained permission to write to the participants' parents or other relevant individuals to validate reported memories. Again, memories were frequently validated by these sources: 49/55 memories were judged to be accurate, and two memories differed in only minor ways.

When college students are asked to recall pinpointed early childhood events, such as the birth of a sibling (Eacott and Crawley, 1998, 1999; Usher and Neisser, 1993), their memories also are corroborated frequently by parents. Usher and Neisser (1993) contacted mothers and asked them to answer the same questions that their college student children had answered, and then to rate their children's memories for accuracy. Most of the responses given by college students were judged to be valid, and only 12 per cent were identified as definitely inaccurate. A majority of participants' responses in studies by Eacott and Crawley (1998, 1999) also were verified by their mothers, and only 13 per cent were denied.

Parents usually provide the independent confirmation in studies of memory consistency. Although agreement may be high in part because the remembered events have been rehearsed in family contexts, the evidence supports the general believability and robustness of early memories and is inconsistent with the idea of pervasive memory distortion.

Emotional content

The emotional tone of early memories has long been a topic of research and theory. A historical impetus for both scientific and clinical interest is Freud's repression theory, in which emotion-laden early memories, containing anxiety-provoking remnants of infantile sexuality, are thought to be repressed and replaced by more neutral, surrogate 'screen memories' (Kihlstrom and Harackiewicz, 1982; Pillemer and White, 1989; Waldfogel, 1948). An analysis of emotions expressed in earliest memories provides a test, albeit oversimplified, of the psychoanalytic model. A second reason for scientific and practical interest in emotions accompanying childhood memories involves concerns about the accuracy of early memories of trauma (Alexander, Quas, Goodman, Ghetti, Edelstein, Redlich, Cordon and Jones, 2005; Terr, 1988). A thorough analysis of memories of extreme trauma is beyond the

scope of this chapter, but we return to this issue in our concluding section.

Both positive and negative emotions are well represented in studies of the earliest childhood memory. For example, Kihlstrom and Harackiewicz's (1982) college student participants identified their memories as pleasant (43 per cent), unpleasant (27 per cent), or neutral (30 per cent). Saunders and Norcorss (1988) reported a similar distribution of self-identified emotional tones: pleasant (43 per cent), unpleasant (32 per cent), and neutral (25 per cent). Dudycha and Dudycha's (1933b) participants identified fear (30 per cent), joy (28 per cent), anger (10 per cent), and wonder or curiosity (8 per cent) as the predominant emotions accompanying their memories. Wang (2001) also found a mixture of positive and negative emotions in earliest memories. Waldfogel (1948) had students report multiple early childhood memories. His analysis of emotion terms that students used to describe the remembered experiences revealed a 'wide variety of emotional experiences' (p. 18), with joy (approximately 30 per cent) and fear (approximately 15 per cent) being the most common reactions.

Howes et al. (1993) coded earliest memories for emotional content (a single memory could be coded as containing both positive and negative affect); they identified a preponderance (55 per cent) of negative emotions, with 19 per cent involving positive emotions and 29 per cent falling into no-affect-reported or explicitly non-emotional categories. It is unclear whether differences in method (for example, using researchers' content coding to identify emotions rather than obtaining participants' self-evaluations of emotional tone) contributed to the comparatively high incidence of negative memories in this study.

Emotions expressed in earliest memories appear to be comparable to emotions accompanying memories of events occurring at older ages. West and Bauer (1999) compared earliest and later memories (occurring after age 7) directly, using the same sample of participants and the same methodology, and concluded that 'there do not appear to be systematic differences in the emotional content of early and later memories' (273). Pillemer and White (1989) also noted a similar range of positive and negative emotions in earliest memories and in memories of later life events, such as those occurring during the college years.

The range of feelings accompanying earliest memories is inconsistent with the idea that negative emotional reactions are hidden by banal screen memories: 'memories of troubling experiences from early childhood appear to be no less common than negative memories from adulthood' (Pillemer and White, 1989: 308). But simple distributions of emotions expressed in early episodes do not address the important issue of memory accuracy or consistency across emotional categories. Howes et al. (1993) examined whether certain types of emotional memories are more likely than others to be independently verified: proportions of fully and partially verified memories were quite similar across positive (67 per cent), negative (65 per cent), and no-affect-reported (60 per cent) emotion categories.

Memory complexity

Studies have identified age-related changes not only in memory incidence, but also in memory complexity, elaboration, or completeness. Winograd and Killinger (1983) analyzed the number of questions that participants could answer regarding their personal circumstances when learning of the Kennedy assassination. Informational complexity of memories increased markedly for respondents who had been older than age 4 at the time of the shooting. When college students answered direct questions about sibling births, family moves, family deaths, and hospitalizations, their memories showed age-related increases in elaboration from 2 to 3 years and again from 3 to 4 years (Usher and Neisser, 1993). Davis, Gross, and Hayne

(2008) elicited students' memories of a sibling birth using open-ended probes rather than direct questions; they identified a consistently low level of reported information between the ages of 1 and 3, followed by a strong increase in memory elaboration at age 4 and a levelling off at age 5.

A different way to identify age trends in informational complexity involves comparing fragmentary and intact memories. Bruce, Wilcox-O'Hearn, Robinson, Phillips-Grant, Francis, and Smith (2005) asked college students to report two distinct types of memories. They elicited event memories by asking for 'the earliest personal event in your life that you can remember ... it is a story about an event or incident in your life ... it has a beginning and an end and you will be able to recall some specific details about what happened' (571). The probe for fragment memories requested 'the earliest memory fragment in your life that you can remember. A memory fragment is not a story with a beginning and an end ... it is nothing more than an isolated fragment that sticks in your mind' (571). Results supported the idea that earliest memories become more complete and story-like with increasing age: the mean age of the earliest memory fragment (3.52 years) was younger than the mean age of the earliest memory story (4.36 years).

Analyses of informational complexity support the idea that memories formed later in childhood are richer than memories formed earlier. Memories from the first two years of life are scarce, and 'when memories do begin to appear, they are relatively thin and incomplete' (Usher and Neisser, 1993: 164). These analyses also provide indirect support for the idea that adults' memory reports are trustworthy. If early events are shaped, reinterpreted, and distorted from an adult's perspective as part of the remembering process, why would memories of learning about the Kennedy assassination (Winograd and Killinger, 1983) or a sibling birth (Davis et al., 2008) show marked increases in complexity precisely at ages 4 or 5? It is difficult to attribute sudden age-related increases in memory elaboration to the influence of family stories or to other distorting reconstructive processes operating during recall.

Comparison of methods

Studies published over the past 100 years have produced a reasonably consistent picture of adults' early childhood memories. There is a scarcity of memories before age 2 or 3, and a rapid increase in memory incidence and richness thereafter. But the overall picture is not entirely consistent. For example, between-study variation exists in the reported age of the earliest memory. Although some of the variation is undoubtedly due to sampling error or to differences in participant characteristics, differences in study methodology also are apparent and potentially influential (Davis et al., 2008; Jack and Hayne, 2007; Loftus, 1993; White and Pillemer, 1989).

Studies using open-ended probes consistently identify the average age of the earliest memory as occurring between ages 3 and 4, whereas some studies employing direct questions about targeted events identify age boundaries at or even before 2 years. These findings are not entirely contradictory. Because the mean age of the earliest childhood memory is a statistical abstraction rather than a lower limit, occasional reports of isolated memories from before age 3 should be expected. In addition, identifying a single earliest lifetime memory without cues of any sort is a challenging task (Pillemer and White, 1989); self-generated strategies that people use to identify their earliest memory are not well known. Specific probes help to structure the search process and could lead to greater success in identifying very early memories.

On the other hand, asking direct questions about targeted events may overestimate the degree to which very early memories are available to adults' purposeful recall efforts.

Some of the questions appear to be answerable using simple inference or general knowledge rather than specific episodic memory (Davis et al., 2008; Loftus, 1993). For example, in Usher and Neisser's (1993) influential study, answers to questions such as 'Who took care of you while your mother was in the hospital?' could be based on general knowledge rather than a precise memory of a pinpointed early childhood episode.

Davis and colleagues (2008) showed that study outcomes are in fact strongly influenced by variations in scoring criteria. Participants were asked to recall the circumstances of a sibling birth in response to direct questions used previously by Usher and Neisser (1993) and Eacott and Crawley (1998). Answers were scored using three different criteria: (1) a lenient system used by Usher and Neisser (1993) and Eacott and Crawley (1998) in which any informative response was accepted; (2) a somewhat stricter system used by Sheingold and Tenney (1982) in which answers were required to be specific; and (3) a new system based on suggestions by Loftus (1993) in which responses were required to be so detailed that they could not have been a product of guessing. For example, acceptable answers to the question 'What was the baby wearing?' included 'a blanket' using the most lenient scoring system, 'a slightly pale pink towel' using the intermediate scoring system, and 'a bright pink floral wrap' using the strict scoring system. Not surprisingly, choice of scoring criteria matters. Using the criteria adopted by Usher and Neisser and by Eacott and Crawley, Davis et al. (2008) found that fully 100 per cent of their college student participants were able to answer at least three memory questions about a sibling birth that had occurred when they were 1 year old. This surprising result suggests that participants were relying at least in part on general knowledge rather than on precise memory images or content. Using the strictest scoring criteria, only 40 per cent of respondents who were age 5 when a sibling was born received credit for three valid answers to memory questions.

The authors made a case for using the intermediate scoring criteria, in which responses are required to be specific but not so overly detailed that many apparently reasonable responses are disqualified.

Even among researchers who use the same general methodological approaches, minor variations in how memory questions are asked can be influential. For example, the degree to which instructions stress that participants should decline to answer direct questions when they have no corresponding specific personal memory may be important (Eacott and Crawley, 1998). Bruce et al. (2005) demonstrated a dramatic effect of question type: requests for disconnected fragmentary memories produced a younger mean age of the earliest memory than requests for fully formed, story-like memories.

Given the potential impact of method on reported outcomes, study results cannot be accepted simply at face value. The valuable research strategy used by Hayne and colleagues (Davis et al., 2008; Jack and Hayne, 2007), in which different methodological approaches are implemented and compared within the same study, can inform both critiques of prior research and the design of new studies.

Culture and gender

Culture and gender are the among the most prominent individual difference variables in autobiographical memory research. Other potential influences include intelligence (Rabbit and McInnis, 1988), personality (Kihlstrom and Harickiewicz, 1982; Myers and Brewin, 1994; Spirrison and McCarley, 2001), and handedness or inter-hemispheric interaction (Christman, Propper and Brown, 2006). We limit our analysis to gender and culture because relevant studies are plentiful and because gender and cultural effects have well-articulated theoretical implications for the development of autobiographical memory.

Gender and cultural differences in early memory have attracted intense scientific interest in large part because they bear directly on a major new theory of autobiographical memory development, what has been called the social construction or social interaction model (Hudson, 1990; Nelson, 1993; Pillemer, 1998a, 1998b; Pillemer and White, 1989; Wang, 2003) or the social cultural theory (Fivush, Haden, and Reese, 2006; Fivush and Nelson, 2004; Nelson and Fivush, 2004; Wang, 2008). According to this theoretical perspective, autobiographical memory development is much more than the predetermined evolution of an internal cognitive system. Development occurs as a result of social interactions involving parents and family members. Parents engage their children in memory talk from a very early age, even before the child has the language skills necessary to contribute fully. With increasing age the child slowly assumes more and more conversational responsibility. These parent-guided conversations show the child what personal memory is and how to use it to forge social connections, solve problems, and construct an autobiographical sense of self (Fivush et al., 2006).

One implication of the social interaction model is that memory should vary as a function of the amount and quality of parent–child talk about the past. Fivush and colleagues have extensively examined reminiscing in parent–child dialogues (summarized by Fivush et al., 2006). Highly elaborative mothers eagerly engage their children in memory talk by using open-ended questions and by providing and encouraging detailed event descriptions. Less elaborative mothers use a more sparse and informational questioning style in which they seek out answers to particular questions rather than personal details. Children of highly elaborative parents also adopt an elaborative memory style and produce richer and more detailed personal memories than children of less elaborative parents (Reese, Haden and Fivush, 1993). Memory styles are modifiable: children whose mothers received training in elaborative reminiscing techniques produce memories that are more detailed and under some circumstances more accurate than do children of untrained mothers (Boland, Haden, and Ornstein, 2003; Reese and Newcombe, 2007).

Comparisons between males and females, and among cultural groups, provide a natural laboratory for examining how distinctive styles of social interaction in childhood contribute to memory performance. Do adults representing different cultural and gender groups vary systematically in the ways that childhood is remembered? Do corresponding cultural and gender differences exist in parent–child talk about the personal past? Research has provided affirmative answers to both of these questions.

Culture

Researchers have identified consistent relationships between cultural identity and adults' earliest recollections (for reviews, see Leichtman, Wang and Pillemer, 2003; Pillemer, 1998a; Wang, 2003; Wang, 2008 provides a detailed summary of individual studies). Comparisons frequently involve Caucasian and Asian participants, in part because of the availability of large numbers of Asian students attending American universities and in part because of distinctive cultural patterns of child socialization. When adults are asked to recount their earliest memory, Caucasians often describe events that occurred earlier in childhood than do Asians (see Table 27.1). Mullen's (1994) initial analysis focused on college students, graduate students, and adults affiliated with universities in the Boston area. In three separate studies, the age of the earliest memory for Asians (representing both Asian Americans and foreign Asians from various countries of origin) was later than Caucasians by 8.8 months, 5.3 months, and 4.9 months. When Mullen obtained memories from individuals who had grown up in Korea and who completed questionnaires written in Korean, the average age of the earliest memory was substantially older than in mixed Asian college samples.

Mullen's (1994) discovery of a younger age of the earliest memory for Caucasian students compared to Asian students was confirmed in a series of studies conducted by Wang and colleagues (Wang, 2001; Wang and Ross, 2005). The expected cultural difference also was evident when American and Taiwanese college students were asked to report their earliest memories involving the self, mother, family, friend, and surroundings (Wang, 2006). In each of these five domains, memories recounted by Caucasians were notably earlier than memories recounted by Asians. Fiske and Pillemer (2006) elicited college students' earliest memories of dreams; they identified a higher incidence and earlier occurrence of childhood dream memories among Caucasians than among Asians. Matsumoto and Stanny (2006) provided an exception to the predicted pattern of results: Japanese college students reported a younger age of earliest memory than did Caucasian students. Although the sample sizes were small, this discrepant finding for Japanese students indicates that differences between Asian sub-groups should be examined more carefully in future research.

Cultural differences in early memory content also are apparent (Wang, 2001, 2003, 2008; Wang and Ross, 2005). Wang (2003) summarized the differences as follows: 'Childhood memories reported by American adults tend to be voluminous, specific, self-focused, and emotionally elaborate, whereas memories provided by Chinese are often skeletal, generic, centered on relationships, and emotionally unexpressive'(65). The characteristic qualities of Caucasians' earliest memories – high specificity, high elaboration, richness of personal detail – support the development of a well-articulated independent sense of self, whereas the qualities of Asians' earliest memories – low specificity, brevity, and communal themes – are consistent with a later-developing, other-centred self-concept.

According to the social interaction hypothesis, cultural differences in the age and content of early memories should be linked to corresponding differences in socialization practices. Mullen and Yi (1995) looked directly at patterns of parent–child memory talk among Caucasian families in the United States and Asian families in Korea. Mother–child conversations were recorded and analyzed; talk about specific episodes that the child had experienced was three times higher in the United States than in Korea. Wang and colleagues have reported parallel findings (summarized in Wang, 2003), in which Caucasian mothers reminisce with their children using a more elaborative conversational style and Chinese mothers adopt a less elaborative, factual questioning style. Presumably, the encouragement that Caucasian children receive to remember and talk about specific personal episodes facilitates their long-term recall years later.

Cultural differences in parent–child memory talk appear to reflect different world views about the processes and goals of human development (Fivush et al., 2006; Leichtman et al., 2003; Pillemer, 1998a; Wang, 2003). In general, Western cultures place a premium on the development of an autonomous, independent sense of self, whereas Asian cultures value interdependence and social connectedness. In the United States, 'personal event memories with specific details and elaboration are an important way for people to distinguish themselves as unique individuals ... a coherent, elaborate, well-integrated life history with the individual cast as the central character is indispensable for psychological integrity and well-being' (Wang, 2003: 73). In Asian cultures, detailed personal memories do not contribute as strongly to a coherent sense of self: 'the construction of identity is less dependent on a unique autobiographical history but more on a web of relationships' (Wang, 2003: 73).

Asian–Caucasian differences in dream recall provide additional support for a connection between earliest memories and socialization practices (Fiske and Pillemer, 2006). As mentioned previously, Caucasian college students were more likely to remember childhood dreams and had a younger age of the earliest dream memory. Participants also were questioned about dream-related behaviours and attitudes. Consistent with the social interaction hypothesis, Caucasians were more likely to report talking about their earliest dream with a parent; they received stronger encouragement to talk about their dreams; they were more comfortable sharing their dreams with their parents; they were more likely to talk about their dreams with others in adulthood; and they rated their dreams as more important.

MacDonald, Uesiliana, and Hayne (2000) examined earliest memories of New Zealand college students representing three distinct cultural groups: Europeans (mostly Northern European descent), Asians (mostly Chinese), and Maori (indigenous population). The mean age of the earliest memory for Asians (4.8 years) was predictably older than for Europeans (3.6 years), but Maori participants produced an even younger memory age (2.7 years). The age of the earliest memory for the Maori group is consistent with cultural values: Maori culture places a strong emphasis on both 'personal and tribal history' (MacDonald et al., 2000: 373). A follow-up study (Reese, Hayne and MacDonald, 2008) provided only mixed support for the social interaction hypothesis. Maori mothers were actually less elaborative than European mothers when talking with their children about recent shared past events, although they were somewhat more elaborative when telling the child about a highly significant past event: the child's birth. By adopting an elaborative memory style when recounting truly important family episodes, Maori mothers 'may be helping their children to encode a wide range of early memories in a richer way and later to retain these early memories into adulthood' (Reese et al., 2008: 122). Nevertheless, the authors acknowledge that other explanations are plausible, such as a greater willingness among Maori participants to report earliest memories that are fragmentary rather than story-like.

Harpaz-Rotem and Hirst (2005) conducted a unique test of the social interaction model by comparing memories of Israeli adults raised either in a traditional family setting or a kibbutz. Although these groups of participants do not represent different cultures in a technical sense, the family environments differ greatly. Kibbutz-raised children live in a group facility where a trained nurse is responsible for the care of multiple children. Because parent–child contact is more limited in a kibbutz than in a traditional home, memory talk about personally experienced past events may occur less frequently. As predicted, the mean age of the earliest memory for adults raised at home (3.08 years) was younger than the mean age for children raised in a kibbutz (4.15 years). A second study compared adolescents who had grown up in a traditional kibbutz to adults who had grown up in a reformed kibbutz, where children sleep in their parents' house and go to group care only during the day. The mean age of the earliest memory for adults raised in a traditional kibbutz (4.02 years) was older than the mean age for adults who were raised in a reformed kibbutz (2.93 years). A parent questionnaire confirmed that participants from traditional kibbutzim spent less time with parents than participants from reformed kibbutzim. The authors speculated that the traditional kibbutz 'reduces the opportunity for initiating episodes to co-construct the past' (Harpaz-Rotem and Hirst, 2005: 58).

Associations between the mean age of adults' earliest memories, cultural values, and socialization practices are compatible with social interaction theory. Because the data are correlational in nature, support for the theory is indirect. The case for social interaction is strengthened because other potential explanatory factors do not lead to straightforward predictions about cultural differences (Harpaz-Rotem and Hirst, 2005). Long-term memory differences between Asians and Caucasians, or between traditional and reformed kibbutz members, could be due to different rates of brain maturation, cognitive development, or language development, but there is no obvious empirical or theoretical rationale for such predictions.

Cultural variation in socialization practices provides the most compelling explanation for the highly consistent pattern of findings across diverse studies.

Gender

Gender differences in adults' recall of early childhood events and early socialization experiences also bear upon the social interaction model of autobiographical memory development (Fivush and Nelson, 2004; Pillemer, 1998a). When adults are asked to recount their earliest childhood memory, women sometimes, but not always, recount episodes that occurred at earlier ages than do men. For example, an early study by Potwin (1901) identified a substantially younger mean age of the earliest memory for college women (3.01 years) than for college men (4.40 years). More recently, Mullen (1994) found that female college students reported earlier memories than male students in three separate studies, although some differences were small (Study 1: 0.8 months; Study 2: 5.2 months; Study 3: 1.3 months) and only the largest gender effect was statistically significant. Other researchers, including Harpaz-Rotem and Hirst (2005), Kihlstrom and Harackiewicz (1982), and Wang (2001), failed to find significant sex differences in the age of the earliest memory. Rubin's (2000) synthesis of studies that elicited multiple childhood memories from respondents revealed a similar pattern: 'gender differences are at best very small. Females might have slightly more memories for ages two, three, and four, but it is not clear whether this difference is reliable' (268).

MacDonald et al.'s (2000) cross-cultural analysis provides the only strongly contrary evidence to a possible female advantage in recall of early memories. The researchers found no gender differences in New Zealand European and Maori samples, but a significant difference for New Zealand Asians in which females actually had much older earliest memories than did men (differences of 31 months and 14.5 months in two studies). This surprising finding will be revisited in a later discussion of the social interaction hypothesis as it relates to gender differences. When their analyses focused on memory content rather than memory age, MacDonald et al. discovered that earliest childhood memories reported by women contained more information than memories reported by men across all three cultural groups.

Although support for a younger age of the earliest memory for women than for men is weak and inconsistent, the evidence for gender differences is more convincing when probes specifically target emotional memories. Cowan and Davidson (1984) asked college students to report 'one of your earliest memories in which you had a strong emotional reaction to another human being' (102); the median age at the time of the remembered emotional event was 5.5 years for females and 7.0 years for males. When college students provide childhood memories in response to emotion cues, females recall more memories than males and they retrieve them more rapidly. When recall is open-ended rather than cued, women remember more emotional but not non-emotional early memories than men do (Davis, 1999).

According to the social interaction model, gender differences in early socialization should mirror observed differences in adults' childhood memories. Fivush et al. (2006) provided a review and analysis of how mothers and fathers engage in memory talk with their sons and daughters. One principal finding is that parents engage in more elaborative reminiscing with girls than with boys (Reese and Fivush, 1993; Reese et al., 1996). In addition, mothers appear to adopt a more elaborative memory style when talking about emotional memories with daughters than with sons. Preschoolers' memories also reflect differences in emotional expression: 'girls are providing more elaborated and more emotionally rich narratives of their personal past than are boys' (Fivush et al., 2006: 1576).

Gender differences in parent–child reminiscing are consistent with the finding that women's early memories tend to be more detailed than men's memories, and especially that women have greater access to early memories involving emotions. An important caveat is the indirect and at times post hoc nature of analyses linking early socialization to gender differences in adults' memories of childhood. Consider the contrary findings of MacDonald et al. (2000), in which Asian women in New Zealand reported a substantially older age of the earliest memory than did Asian men. The authors pointed out that Asian boys and girls may be socialized differently with a 'greater family emphasis on the personal experiences and accomplishments of sons relative to daughters' (MacDonald et al., 2000: 374). Yet other research examining the age of Asians' and Caucasians' earliest childhood memories has failed to identify significant culture-by-gender interactions (Wang, 2001, 2006). In sum, cultural comparisons provide more extensive, consistent, and convincing support for the social interaction hypothesis than do gender comparisons.

MEMORIES OF MIDDLE CHILDHOOD AND ADOLESCENCE

The preceding analysis of early childhood memories is based on a large body of theoretically motivated research. Scientific interest in adults' memories of early childhood flows in part from a fascination with the provocative psychoanalytic concept of infantile amnesia and the contrasting theoretical perspectives offered by modern developmental psychology. Although research psychologists have for the most part eschewed repression as a primary explanatory factor, the idea of a dramatic change in autobiographical memory during the preschool years has provided an organizing structure for memory research and a 'dramatic forum for demonstrating the explanatory power and real-world applicability of developmental science' (Pillemer, 1998b: 897; see also Saywitz and Camparo, Chapter 21). The convergence of theory and research has increased our understanding of early memory but at the same time has diverted attention from the potential importance of later developmental transitions.

Research has targeted adults' memories of middle childhood and adolescence far less frequently and systematically than memories of early childhood. Newcombe et al. (2007) observed that empirical studies of childhood memory 'rarely include data on events experienced at later ages, such as 10 or 12 years'(42). Thorne (2000) noted that personality psychologists' interest in autobiographical memories has been 'relegated to internalized representations of early childhood experiences'(45) and she called for a greater focus on memories of adolescence. The occasional study has examined age-related changes in memory content. For example, Thorne (1995) identified a lower incidence of episodes involving parents, and a higher incidence of episodes involving peers, in memories of adolescence than in memories of middle childhood. But the absence of an overarching theoretical structure or organizational framework for individual studies makes it difficult to summarize the findings concisely and meaningfully.

One way to shift scientific attention to middle childhood and early adolescence is to direct the memory search to this specific age range. Collins, Pillemer, Ivcevic, and Gooze (2007) asked college students and middle-aged adults to recount life events that had occurred when they were between ages 8 and 18. Participants described life episodes when they felt especially good or especially bad about themselves. Memories were then plotted as a function of age of occurrence. Figure 27.3 presents separate age distributions of positive and negative memories reported by college students (Collins et al., 2007, Study 2). The incidence of positive memories increases markedly at ages 17 and 18. In contrast, the distribution of negative memories is relatively flat, with only a modest age-related increase. To determine if the sharp rise in positive memories at the end of the requested age interval was tied specifically to late adolescence, college stu-

dents were asked to report a positive and a negative memory occurring between the ages of 10 and 15 (Collins et al., 2007, Study 3). In this case, age distributions of positive and negative memories were quite similar, each showing a modest age-related increase consistent with conventional decay theories of memory.

Collins et al.'s (2007) findings support recent research and theory on what has been termed the reminiscence bump (Berntsen and Rubin, 2002; Rubin and Berntsen, 2003). When older adults are asked to recall life episodes, memories are overrepresented (they form a 'bump') between the ages of 15 and 30. Importantly, the memory peak in late adolescence and early adulthood occurs for positive but not negative life events. Berntsen and Rubin (2002) proposed a life script explanation for the divergent positive and negative age distributions. According to the theory, recall of positive events is guided by temporally constrained cultural expectations that identify positive landmark events during late adolescence and early adulthood. Predictable positive experiences include graduating from high school, gaining college acceptance, getting married, landing a job, and having a baby. A life script points the memory search to the age period where these positive events are expected to occur (but see Dickson, Pillemer, and Bruehl, 2011, for an alternative perspective). In contrast, the age of occurrence of major negative life events is not scripted or highly predictable, such that negative memories are spread more evenly across the life span. The 8- to 18-year age interval used by Collins et al. (2007) captures the beginning of the upward-sloping component of the reminiscence bump. Consistent with the life script theory, only positive memories showed a marked age-related rise during late adolescence. In addition, predictable events marking the major life transition from high school to college – high school graduation and awards, and college acceptance – occurred frequently in positive memories only.

By specifically targeting memories from middle childhood and adolescence, Collins

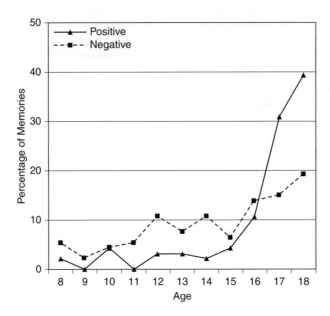

Figure 27.3   Age distributions of positive and negative memories between the ages of 8 and 18 years for Babson College students

Source: From 'Cultural Scripts Guide Recall of Intensely Positive Life Events', by K.A. Collins, D.B. Pillemer, Z. Ivcevic, and R.A. Gooze, 2007, *Memory & Cognition, 35,* p. 654. Copyright by the Psychonomic Society, Inc. Reprinted with kind permission from Springer Science and Business Media.

et al. (2007) revealed an age-dependent, theoretically meaningful pattern of results. When adults reminisce about their childhoods, we should expect not only a scarcity of very early memories, but also an overrepresentation of positive memories in late adolescence. Because highly salient personal memories may inform or direct current attitudes, behaviours, and self-perceptions (Bluck, Alea, Habermas and Rubin, 2005; Pillemer, 2003), vivid recollections of pivotal events from late adolescence could prove to be especially influential over the life course. Beliefs about 'who we are' may be anchored by memories representing the formative transition to adulthood. The clustering of positive memories in adolescence could have important implications for theories of adult self-concept and personal identity (Thorne, 2000).

Research on the reminiscence bump identifies late adolescence as a critical transition point for autobiographical memory, and this age period is likely to draw increasing scientific attention. What about the neglected decade between ages 6 and 16? Like early childhood and adolescence, middle childhood and pre-adolescence also are marked by developmental changes in brain structure and function, cognition, socialization, and sexuality. Discovering whether and how these changes influence, and are reflected in, adults' memories of childhood is a promising direction for new research.

CONCLUSION

Research on adults' recollections of childhood has enhanced our scientific understanding of long-term autobiographical memory. For example, the temporal distribution of earliest memories is well established, with almost all studies reporting a mean age of the earliest memory at 3 years or older. In addition, the contents of adults' early memories are frequently corroborated by other individuals who are knowledgeable about the remembered events, thereby increasing our confidence in the validity of retrospective reports. Memory characteristics vary predictably across studies using different participant groups and methodologies. For example, the mean age of the earliest memory is consistently earlier for Caucasian than for Asian adults. In contrast to research on earliest childhood memories, studies of adults' memories of middle childhood are notably underrepresented in the scientific literature, and this is a fertile topic for new research.

Although research on adults' memories of childhood has provided a fuller scientific understanding of long-term recall processes, it has much less to say about the everyday *experience* of childhood. What, if anything, can be learned from adults' recollections of childhood that is not evident from children's own accounts or, for that matter, from adults' direct observations of children? These different sources of information may provide distinct yet complementary perspectives. Consider, as just one of many possible examples, adults' memories of strict parental discipline in childhood. Early experiences of 'being punished' are remembered and reinterpreted from an adult's longer view in which the past is connected to the present. When evaluated from the distant perspective of adulthood, the vividly remembered indignities and discomforts of childhood punishment could be offset in part by perceived long-term benefits (for example, 'My Dad was very tough on me, but he helped to make me into who I am today'). In contrast, children's contemporary stories of strict parental discipline, like direct observations of affected children, are unlikely to contain a parallel future-oriented perspective.

Other contributors to this volume draw attention to an issue that developmental researchers have for the most part failed to address: What value should be placed on children's own voices in research and policy decisions? Whether or not children are given

voice in such matters could be influenced by discrepancies between children's current accounts and adults' retrospective accounts. If adults assume that their own perspectives on early life experiences are more valid or useful than those of children, the impact of children's voices is diminished. For researchers interested in capturing the true fabric of childhood experience, a triangulated approach that incorporates and balances adults' memories of childhood, children's current accounts, and direct observations of children is likely to prove most useful and insightful.

ACKNOWLEDGEMENTS

Preparation of this chapter was supported by the Dr. Samuel E. Paul Chair in Developmental Psychology, held by David B. Pillemer. Kie Kuwabara and Michelle D. Leichtman provided valuable feedback on the chapter.

REFERENCES

Adler, A. (1937) 'Significance of earliest recollections', *International Journal of Individual Psychology*, 3: 283–7.

Alexander, K.W., Quas, J.A., Goodman, G.S., Ghetti, S., Edelstein, R.S., Redlich, A.D., Cordon, I.M. and Jones, D.P.H. (2005) 'Traumatic impact predicts long-term memory for documented child sexual abuse', *Psychological Science*, 16(1): 33–40.

Barrett, D. (1980) 'The first memory as a predictor of personality traits', *Journal of Individual Psychology*, 36(2): 136–49.

Berntsen, D. and Rubin, D.C. (2002) 'Emotionally charged autobiographical memories across the lifespan: The recall of happy, sad, traumatic and involuntary memories', *Psychology & Aging*, 17(4): 636–52.

Bluck, S., Alea, N., Habermas, T. and Rubin, D.C. (2005) 'A tale of three functions: The self-reported uses of autobiographical memory', *Social Cognition*, 23(1): 91–117.

Boland, A.M., Haden, C.A. and Ornstein, P.A. (2003) 'Boosting children's memory by training mothers in the use of an elaborative conversational style as an event unfolds', *Journal of Cognition and Development*, 4(1): 39–65.

Bruce, D., Dolan, A. and Phillips-Grant, K. (2000) 'On the transition from childhood amnesia to the recall of personal memories', *Psychological Science*, 11(5): 360–4.

Bruce, D., Wilcox-O'Hearn, A., Robinson, J.A., Phillips-Grant, K., Francis, L. and Smith, M.C. (2005) 'Fragment memories mark the end of childhood amnesia', *Memory & Cognition*, 33(4): 567–76.

Christman, S.D., Propper, R.E. and Brown, T.J. (2006) 'Increased interhemispheric interaction is associated with earlier offset of childhood amnesia', *Neuropsychology*, 20(3): 336–45.

Collins, K.A., Pillemer, D.B., Ivcevic, Z. and Gooze, R.A. (2007) 'Cultural scripts guide recall of intensely positive life events', *Memory & Cognition*, 35(4): 651–9.

Cowan, N. and Davidson, G. (1984) 'Salient childhood memories', *Journal of Genetic Psychology*, 145(1): 101–7.

Davis, P.J. (1999) 'Gender differences in autobiographical memory for childhood emotional experiences', *Journal of Personality and Social Psychology*, 76(3): 498–510.

Davis, N., Gross, J. and Hayne, H. (2008) 'Defining the boundary of childhood amnesia', *Memory*, 16(5): 465–74.

Dickson, R.A., Pillemer, D.B. and Bruehl, E.C. (2011) 'The reminiscence bump for salient personal memories: Is a cultural life script required?', *Memory & Cognition*, 39: 977-91.

Dudycha, G.J. and Dudycha, M.M. (1933a). 'Adolescents' memories of preschool experiences', *Journal of Genetic Psychology*, 42(2): 468–80.

Dudycha, G.J. and Dudycha, M.M. (1933b) 'Some factors and characteristics of childhood memories', *Child Development*, 4(3): 265–78.

Dudycha, G.J. and Dudycha, M.M. (1941) 'Childhood memories: A review of the literature', *Psychological Bulletin*, 38(8): 668–82.

Eacott, M.J. and Crawley, R.A. (1998) 'The offset of childhood amnesia: Memory for events that occurred before age three', *Journal of Experimental Psychology: General*, 127(1): 22–33.

Eacott, M.J. and Crawley, R.A. (1999) 'Childhood amnesia: On answering questions about very early life events', *Memory*, 7(3): 279–92.

Fiske, K.E. and Pillemer, D.B. (2006) 'Adult recollections of earliest childhood dreams: A cross-cultural study', *Memory*, 14(1): 57–67.

Fivush, R., Haden, C.A. and Reese, E. (2006) 'Elaborating on elaborations: Role of maternal reminiscing style in cognitive and socioemotional development', *Child Development*, 77(6): 1568–88.

Fivush, R. and Nelson, K. (2004) 'Culture and language in the emergence of autobiographical memory', *Psychological Science*, 15(9): 573–7.

Freud, S. (1953) 'Three essays on the theory of sexuality', in J. Strachey (ed.), *The Standard Edition of the Complete Psychological Works of Sigmund Freud*, *Vol. 7*. London: Hogarth Press. (Original work published 1905), pp. 135–243.

Gur-Yaish, N. and Wang, Q. (2006) 'Self-knowledge in cultural contexts: The case of two western cultures', in A.P. Prescott (ed.), *The Concept of Self in Psychology*. New York: Nova Science, pp. 129–43.

Hankoff, L.D. (1987) 'The earliest memories of criminals', *International Journal of Offender Therapy and Comparative Criminology*, 31(3): 195–201.

Harpaz-Rotem, I. and Hirst, W. (2005) 'The earliest memory in individuals raised in either traditional and reformed kibbutz or outside the kibbutz', *Memory*, 13(1): 51–62.

Howe, M.L. and Courage, M.L. (1993) 'On resolving the enigma of infantile amnesia', *Psychological Bulletin*, 113(2): 305–26.

Howes, M., Siegel, M. and Brown, F. (1993) 'Early childhood memories: Accuracy and affect', *Cognition*, 47(2): 95–119.

Hudson, J.A. (1990) 'The emergence of autobiographical memory in mother-child conversation', in R. Fivush and J.A. Hudson (eds.), *Knowing and Remembering in Young Children*. New York: Cambridge University Press, pp. 166–96.

Jack, F. and Hayne, H. (2007) 'Eliciting adults' earliest memories: Does it matter how we ask the question?', *Memory*, 15(6): 647–63.

Kihlstrom, J.F. and Harackiewicz, J.M. (1982) 'The earliest recollection: A new survey', *Journal of Personality*, 50(2): 134–48.

Leichtman, M.D., Wang, Q. and Pillemer, D.B. (2003) 'Cultural variations in interdependence and autobiographical memory: Lessons from Korea, China, India, and the United States', in R. Fivush and C.A. Haden (eds.), *Autobiographical Memory and the Construction of the Narrative Self*. Mahwah, NJ: Erlbaum, pp. 73–97.

Loftus, E.F. (1993) 'The reality of repressed memories', *American Psychologist*, 48(5): 518–37.

MacDonald, S., Uesiliana, K. and Hayne, H. (2000) 'Cross-cultural and gender differences in childhood amnesia', *Memory*, 8(6): 365–76.

Matsumoto, A. and Stanny, C.J. (2006) 'Language-dependent access to autobiographical memory in Japanese-English bilinguals and US monolinguals', *Memory*, 14(3): 378–90.

Miles, C. (1895) 'Minor studies from the psychological laboratory of Clark University: VIII. A study of individual psychology', *American Journal of Psychology*, 6(2): 534–58.

Mullen, M.K. (1994) 'Earliest recollections of childhood: A demographic analysis', *Cognition*, 52(1): 55–79.

Mullen, M.K. and Yi, S. (1995) 'The cultural context of talk about the past: Implications for the development of autobiographical memory', *Cognitive Development*, 10(3): 407–19.

Myers, L.B. and Brewin, C.R. (1994) 'Recall of early experience and the repressive coping style', *Journal of Abnormal Psychology*, 103(2): 288–92.

Nelson, K. (1993) 'The psychological and social origins of autobiographical memory', *Psychological Science*, 4(1): 7–14.

Nelson, K. and Fivush, R. (2004) 'The emergence of autobiographical memory: A social cultural developmental theory', *Psychological Review*, 111(2): 486–511.

Newcombe, N.S., Lloyd, M.E. and Ratliff, K.R. (2007) 'Development of episodic and autobiographical memory: A cognitive neuroscience perspective', in R.V. Kail (ed.), *Advances in Child Development and Behavior, Vol. 35*. San Diego, CA: Elsevier. pp. 37–85.

Piaget, J. (1962) *Play, Dreams and Imitation in Childhood*. New York: Norton.

Pillemer, D.B. (1998a) *Momentous Events, Vivid Memories: How Unforgettable Moments Help Us Understand the Meaning of Our Lives*. Cambridge, MA: Harvard University Press.

Pillemer, D.B. (1998b) 'What is remembered about early childhood events?', *Clinical Psychology Review*, 18(8): 895–913.

Pillemer, D.B. (2003) 'Directive functions of autobiographical memory: The guiding power of the specific episode', *Memory*, 11(2): 193–202.

Pillemer, D.B. and White, S.H. (1989) 'Childhood events recalled by children and adults', in H.W. Reese (ed.), *Advances in Child Development and Behavior, Vol. 21*. Orlando, FL: Academic Press, pp. 297–340.

Potwin, E.B. (1901) 'Study of early memories', *Psychological Review*, 8(6): 596–601.

Rabbitt, P. and McInnis, L. (1988) 'Do clever old people have earlier and richer first memories?', *Psychology and Aging*, 3(4): 338–41.

Reese, E. and Fivush, R. (1993) 'Parental styles of talking about the past', *Developmental Psychology*, 29(3): 596–606.

Reese, E., Haden, C.A. and Fivush, R. (1993) 'Mother-child conversations about the past: Relationships of

style and memory over time', *Cognitive Development*, 8(4): 403–30.

Reese, E., Haden, C.A. and Fivush, R. (1996) 'Mothers, fathers, daughters, sons: Gender differences in autobiographical reminiscing', *Research on Language and Social Interaction*, 29(1): 27–56.

Reese, E., Hayne, H. and MacDonald, S. (2008) 'Looking back to the future: Maori and Pakeha mother-child birth stories', *Child Development*, 79(1): 114–25.

Reese, E. and Newcombe, R. (2007) 'Training mothers in elaborative reminiscing enhances children's autobiographical memory and narrative', *Child Development*, 78(4): 1153–70.

Richardson, R. and Hayne, H. (2007) 'You can't take it with you: The translation of memory across development', *Current Directions in Psychological Science*, 16(4): 223–7.

Rubin, D.C. (1982) 'On the retention function for autobiographical memory', *Journal of Verbal Learning and Verbal Behavior*, 21(1): 21–38.

Rubin, D.C. (2000) 'The distribution of early childhood memories', *Memory*, 8(4): 265–9.

Rubin, D.C. and Berntsen, D. (2003) 'Life scripts help to maintain autobiographical memories of highly positive, but not highly negative, events', *Memory and Cognition*, 31(1): 1–14.

Rubin, D.C. and Schulkind, M.D. (1997) 'Distribution of important and word-cued autobiographical memories in 20-, 35-, and 70-year-old adults', *Psychology and Aging*, 12(3): 524–35.

Rule, W.R. (1983) 'Birth order and earliest memory', *Perceptual and Motor Skills*, 56(2): 601–2.

Rule, W.R. and Jarrell, G.R. (1983) 'Intelligence and earliest memory', *Perceptual and Motor Skills*, 56(3): 795–8.

Saunders, L.M.I. and Norcross, J.C. (1988) 'Earliest childhood memories: Relationship to ordinal position, family functioning, and psychiatric symptomatology', *Individual Psychology*, 44(1): 95–105.

Sheingold, K. and Tenney, Y.J. (1982) 'Memory for a salient childhood event', in U. Neisser (ed.), *Memory Observed: Remembering in Natural Contexts*. San Francisco: Freeman, pp. 201–12.

Spirrison, C.L. and McCarley, N.G. (2001) 'Age at earliest reported memory: Associations with personality traits, behavioral health, and repression', *Assessment*, 8(3): 315–22.

Sutin, A.R. and Robins, R.W. (2005) 'Continuity and correlates of emotions and motives in self-defining memories', *Journal of Personality*, 73(3): 793–824.

Terr, L. (1988) 'What happens to early memories of trauma? A study of twenty children under age five at the time of documented traumatic events', *Journal of the American Academy of Child and Adolescent Psychiatry*, 27(1): 96–104.

Thorne, A. (1995) 'Developmental truths in memories of childhood and adolescence', *Journal of Personality*, 63(2): 139–63.

Thorne, A. (2000) 'Personal memory telling and personality development', *Personality and Social Psychology Review*, 4(1): 45–56.

Usher, J.A. and Neisser, U. (1993) 'Childhood amnesia and the beginnings of memory for four early life events', *Journal of Experimental Psychology: General*, 122(2): 155–65.

Waldfogel, S. (1948) 'The frequency and affective character of childhood memories', *Psychological Monographs*, 62, Whole No. 291.

Wang, Q. (2001) 'Culture effects on adults' earliest childhood recollection and self-description: Implications for the relation between memory and the self', *Journal of Personality and Social Psychology*, 81(2): 220–33.

Wang, Q. (2003) 'Infantile amnesia reconsidered: A cross-cultural analysis', *Memory*, 11(1): 65–80.

Wang, Q. (2006) 'Earliest recollections of self and others in European American and Taiwanese young adults', *Psychological Science*, 17(8): 708–14.

Wang, Q. (2008) 'Where does our past begin? A socio-cultural perspective on the phenomenon of childhood amnesia', *Psychological Science Agenda*, 22(3): 3–7.

Wang, Q., Leichtman, M.D. and White, S.H. (1998) 'Childhood memory and self-description in young Chinese adults: The impact of growing up an only child', *Cognition*, 69: 73–103.

Wang, Q. and Ross, M. (2005) 'What we remember and what we tell: The effects of culture and self-priming on memory representations and narratives', *Memory*, 13(6): 594–606.

Weigle, T.W. and Bauer, P.J. (2000) 'Deaf and hearing adults' recollections of childhood and beyond', *Memory*, 8(5): 293–309.

West, T.A. and Bauer, P.J. (1999) 'Assumptions of infantile amnesia: Are there differences between early and later memories?', *Memory*, 7(3): 257–78.

Westman, A.S. and Orellana, C. (1996) 'Only visual impressions are almost always present in long-term memories, and reported completeness, accuracy, and verbalizability of recollections increase with age', *Perceptual and Motor Skills*, 83: 531–9.

Westman, A.S., Westman, R.S. and Orellana, C. (1996) 'Earliest memories and recall by modality usually involve recollections of different memories: Memories are not amodal', *Perceptual and Motor Skills*, 82: 1131–5.

Wetzler, S.E. and Sweeney, J.A. (1986) 'Childhood amnesia: An empirical demonstration', in D.C. Rubin (ed.), *Autobiographical Memory*. New York: Cambridge University Press. pp. 191–221.

White, S.H. and Pillemer, D.B. (1979) 'Childhood amnesia and the development of a socially accessible memory system', in J.F. Kihlstrom and F.J. Evans (eds.), *Functional Disorders of Memory*. Hillsdale, NJ: Erlbaum, pp. 29–73.

Winograd, E. and Killinger, W.A., Jr. (1983) 'Relating age at encoding in early childhood to adult recall: Development of flashbulb memories', *Journal of Experimental Psychology: General*, 112(3): 413–22.

28

School-Aged Children as Sources of Information about Their Lives

Michal Soffer and Asher Ben-Arieh

INTRODUCTION

Children's participation in research about their well-being and daily life is crucial for a number of reasons. First, it signifies respect, and it is a meaningful part of treating children as people (Banister and Booth, 2005; Melton, 2005a). Involving children in research is a way of including them, respecting them, and recognizing their dignity as the research process becomes an arena for children to be heard and listened to; that is, it gives children the experience of 'having a voice' (Banister and Booth, 2005; Curtin, 2000).

The second reason for involving children in research is that it is one aspect of the right of children to participate in processes that involve decisions regarding their lives, which is stressed by Article 12 of the Convention of the Rights of the Child (Melton, 2005b, 2006; Munro, Holmes and Ward, 2005). Because research is part of the decision-making process, it is crucial for children to be involved in it.

Third, children are the best possible sources of information about their lives. Therefore, it is methodologically desirable to use them as sources of information. Arguably, if children are participants in a study, then any other sources of information are merely proxies, an identity that creates numerous problems (Ben-Arieh, 2005; Ben-Arieh and Ofir, 2002). Debate about such issues is on-going; the only consensus is that children's participation in research requires consideration of special methodological and ethical concerns.

One of the reasons for this on-going debate is that some studies pose risks to participants' safety and well-being (Bragadottir, 2000; Munro et al., 2005). With school-aged children, the danger of causing harm is amplified, and the research process could potentially become a power relations zone. Hence, 'the power dynamics of age' or 'power relations' (Curtin, 2000; Kirk, 2007; Mauthner, 1997) and the 'issues of power and privilege' (Eder and Corsaro, 1999) are major areas of concern for research with children (Ben-Arieh, 2005).

Further, as Punch (2002) argues, because our society is adult-dominated, children's position as a social group is inferior to that of adults. Children are perceived as vulnerable. Although notions of vulnerability are to some extent real, they also serve as a means to control children. The discourse of 'protection' (see Lowden, 2002) may result in discarding children's views, insights, and opinions. In some cases, forms of parents' protection could deny the child's participation in the research process (Kirk, 2007).

In research, children are considered 'captive subjects' (Pearn, 1984). Thus, it is vital to make sure that they are not abused or exploited (Lind et al., 2003; Munro et al., 2005; Pearn, 1984). The main threat of exploitation concerns issues of consent before the start of the research process and throughout the process itself (Kirk, 2007). Even if a child consents to participating in the research process, however, the risk of exploitation throughout the process still remains.

The power relations that exist between researcher/adult and subject/child pose critical ethical and methodological questions. For example, how can researchers achieve true consent? How can they collect valid and reliable data? Should they use traditional adult research measures such as questionnaires, or are special techniques required? How are they to interpret the data collected? These and other challenges can and should be met while conducting research with children.

THE RATIONALE FOR USING CHILDREN AS SOURCES OF INFORMATION IN STUDIES ABOUT THEIR LIVES

In light of the potential problems that accompany research with children, one may ask whether it is wise to involve school-aged children in research and use them as sources of information. Historically, for example, treatment research has been slow to incorporate children – so much so that regulations in the United States require prospective grantees in health research to justify exclusion of children.

The importance of involving school-aged children in research about their lives is embedded in three different justifications: normative-legislative, theoretical, and practical-methodological. The normative-legislative justification stems from children's rights; the theoretical aspect includes adult perceptions of children and childhood and emphasizes the need for a subjective point of view; and the practical justification simply suggests that because children know most about their lives, they are the best sources of information.

Children's rights

In addressing the normative-legislative justification for involving school-aged children in research about their lives, one must realize that a major shift in the status of children occurred during the twentieth century. Children were seen for many decades mainly as adults' property, but now they are considered persons (Hart, 1991). Discourses of protection and nurturance rights have been replaced by discourses of self-determination rights (Brodin and Stancheva-Popkostadinov, 2009; Hart, 1991; Hesson, Bakal and Dobson, 1993), from mere survival needs to well-being needs (Ben-Arieh, 2006).

In 1989, the United Nations adopted the Convention on the Rights of the Child (CRC). The CRC addresses a full range of rights for children (Ben-Arieh, 2005; Melton, 2011), particularly emphasizing children's rights in relation to decision-making processes regarding their lives (Garth and Aroni, 2003; Kirk, 2007; Melton, 2005a, 2005b; Munro et al., 2005). The right to participate is among the most important children's rights (for a detailed discussion, see Melton, 2006), and it has contributed to a growing interest in children's perspectives in many fields (Kirk, 2007). The right to participate in research may also be seen as a social obligation to contribute to the formation of knowledge (Bragadottir, 2000).

The change in children's rights discourse prompted a change in scholars' and some policymakers' images of children. School-aged children are now seen as having rights that go beyond 'survival needs' per se; they have the right to participate and to be actively involved in decision-making processes that affect their lives. Furthermore, and most important, these new self-determination rights are legal rights, part of many societies' normative systems. The normative-legislative justification for involving school-aged children in research as sources of information about their lives claims that this involvement serves as an extension of the right to participate and is a manifestation of what Garth and Aroni (2003: 562) term 'inclusion as a philosophy'.

From passive beings to active persons: The shifting perspective of children and childhood and the need for a subjective view

In this section we address the theoretical justification for involving school-aged children in research about their lives. The definition of childhood, which once was dominated by socialization theory and developmental psychology, is now shifting. Socialization theory was criticized for viewing children as 'unfinished', 'empty' of societal and cultural views; developmental psychology (especially the Piagetian view) and socialization theory perceive childhood in terms of progress in thought and behaviour and, as a consequence, view children as a unified group that progresses similarly regardless of individual and cultural differences (Eder and Corsaro, 1999; Kirk, 2007; LeVine, 2007). Qvortrup (1994) argues that such perceptions, which consider childhood as a path to adulthood, contributed to the neglect of the study of childhood as a distinct phase. Children are not merely passive objects, and they should be studied from a subjective point of view (Davis, 2007; Qvortrup, 1999). Similarly, interactionism and social construction theories argue that childhood is socially constructed and thus depends on the context in which it occurs. These theories emphasize that children have different experiences and knowledge and actively shape their worlds (Eder and Corsaro, 1999; Kirk, 2007; Qvortrup, 1994). Hence, children are active participants in creating their social world (Qvortrup, 1999).

The theoretical shifts in the perception of children and childhood that result in the acknowledgement that children possess knowledge supply the theoretical justification for children as sources of information about their lives. This view of children as being in possession of knowledge is embedded in the practical-methodological justification for using children as sources of information about their lives.

School-aged children know the most about their lives

In this section, we address the practical-methodological justification for involving school-aged children in research about their lives. The tendency to gather data from parents or other adults in research about children is embedded in concerns about the reliability and validity of data, which this chapter will discuss in detail (Docherty and Sandelowski, 1999). However, a growing amount of researchers argue that because children know the most about their daily life, researchers should ask them about it directly (Ben-Arieh, 2005). Children should be sources of information about their lives because only direct interviews with children will reveal to us their subjective feelings and perspectives (Docherty and Sandelowski, 1999). Children's actual experiences are different from what adults think they know about children's worlds and experiences (Ben-Arieh and Ofir, 2002; Garth and Aroni, 2003). Kirk (2007) frames these differences in perspective and experience between children and adults as 'cultural differences'. In this respect, Davis (2007) quotes Cooper, who calls children 'unrivalled experts in their own fields'.

From a practical-methodological stance, questioning adults about children's lives is not beneficial simply because they cannot serve as proxy measures of children's experiences. Evidence shows that adult proxies do not validate children's social worlds (Ben-Arieh, 2005). This has been recently stressed by Kirk (2007) who conducted a thematic review of qualitative research that was conducted with children and adolescents for over the last few decades. Hence, for example, parents do not really know how children spend their time (see Funk, Hagan and Schimming, 1999, for a study of children in grades 3 to 5) or what they are worried about (see, for example, Gottlieb and Bronstein, 1996, for a study of 6th graders). Likewise, in a study of secondary victimization of children who were victims of abuse and violence, researchers found that 14- to 18-year-old children's perspectives and needs differed from those of their parents (Ben-Arieh and Windman, 2007). The researchers (one of us included) concluded that children's perspectives should be addressed and considered while providing support services throughout the criminal justice process.

In a study that designed separate measures for children with epilepsy between the ages of 6 and 15 and their parents, to assess children's health-related quality of life (HRQL), the researchers concluded that parents cannot truly account for their children's experience and thus serve mainly as a complementary measure (Ronen, Streiner and Rosenbaum, 2003).

METHODS FOR CONDUCTING RESEARCH WITH SCHOOL-AGED CHILDREN

Having established the importance and justifications for using school-aged children as sources of information about their lives, we shall review the various methods used when conducting studies with school-aged children (for a review of significant methods, see also Fargas-Malet et al., 2010). Note that we review the methods that are suitable for research with *school-age* children; some of these methods may not be appropriate for younger children. It is vital to understand

that the researchers' choice of methods is embedded in their vantage point considering childhood and children (Kirk, 2007; Punch, 2002).

The literature on the methods of conducting research with children presents non-standard terminology. The same term or phrase is often used to describe quite different phenomena. Furthermore, the distinction between research methods and means of data collection is unclear. This section is the product of an attempt to make sense of the literature and organize it in a comprehensible way.

Self-report via structured questionnaires

Structured, open-ended questionnaires that are completed by child participants are prevalent in quantitative research with children. For example, Araujo, Medic, Yasnovsky, and Steiner (2006) used the Response Evaluation Measure-71-Youth version (REM-Y-71) to assess defence reactions among school-age children (grades 3–8; age range: 8–15). The German Youth Institute's (Deutsche Jugendinstitut, DJI) longitudinal study project 'How Do Children Grow Up?', started in 2001, retrieved data from school-age children (5–12) by questionnaires 'in a face-to-face' interview (Alt, 2005: 168).

Other studies report the development of self-report measures meant specifically to measure a child-specific phenomenon (for example, school climate) or other phenomena that occur in adults and children (such as depression) but have different expressions or aspects, or that simply need to be adjusted to children's experiences. For example, Walden, Harris, and Catron (2003) developed a self-report measure of emotion (How I Feel, HIF) for 8- to 12-year-olds. Similarly, Marshall et al. (1997) designed a self-report measure for examining internalizing symptoms (Internalizing Symptoms Scale for Children, ISSC) in elementary school children (grades 3–6), and Ronen et al. (2003)

designed a self-report health-related quality of life (HRQL) measure that assesses the impact of epilepsy on children (defined as between 6 and 15 years old) with the disease.

Questionnaires serve also as a means for collecting data in international studies about children. For instance, the IEA (International Association for the Evaluation of Educational Achievement) Civic Education Study was designed to assess 'civic content knowledge and skills in interpreting political communication' (Lehmann, 2004: 9) in 28 countries among 14- to 18-year-olds, via self-report questionnaires as well as other data collection methods (Lehmann, 2004). The Health Behaviour in School-Aged Children (HBSC) surveys, conducted in 35 countries and regions every four years since 1982, rely mainly on self-report questionnaires for 11-, 13-, and 15-year-olds (Currie and Roberts, 2004). The OECD (Organization for Economic Cooperation and Development) Program for International Student Assessment (PISA), designed to examine children's acquired knowledge and skills that promote full participation in society and adult life, consists of surveys with 15-year-olds in 32 countries including 28 OECD countries and Brazil, China, Latvia, and the Russian Federation (OECD, n.d). The Trends in International Mathematics and Science Study (TIMSS), conducted every four years since 1995, uses, among other techniques, self-report questionnaires administered to 4th-grade students to measure and compare mathematics and science achievement between students of 28 countries (National Center for Education Statistics, n.d.). The multinational project for monitoring and measuring children's well-being offers a rich list of indicators and measures of children's well-being, among them self-report questionnaires designed to collect information from children themselves (Israel National Council for the Child, 2007).

Questionnaires can be administered either on paper or online. Mangunkusumo and colleagues (2006) found that 5th-grade children

(10–12 years old) preferred the Internet version of a questionnaire about health and health behaviors among children. Similarly, Borgers et al. (2003, 2004) argue that their use of a computerized questionnaire provided a better response quality – more stability of answers – than typically present in paper-and-pencil surveys.

Stritzke, Dandy, Durkin, and Houghton (2005) tried another means of electronic data collection among school-age children that was reliable. Specifically in a study of attitudes toward alcohol and tobacco use, 9- to 13-year-old children answered open-ended questions over the telephone by pressing the keys of a touch-tone phone.

In 1998–99, Princeton University's Center for Research on Child Wellbeing, in collaboration with the National Evaluation Team for the Urban Health Initiative at the Center for Health and Public Service at New York University's Robert F. Wagner Graduate School, conducted a Survey of Parents and Youth (SPY, later renamed the Survey of Adults and Youth [SAY]). SPY examined trends in 13–17-year-olds' access to parental and community resources via random-digit-dial (RDD) telephone survey with parents and children in the United States (see National Study of Youth and Religion, 2008: 1, note 1). Ybarra and Mitchell (2004) argue that telephone surveys with youths are preferable to school surveys because they are cheaper and can reach a variety of youth populations, not just those who study in school.

A similar method of telephone surveys was adopted by the Swedish Level-of-Living Survey (LNU), a longitudinal survey conducted in Sweden since 1968. In the 2000 survey, data were collected directly from children (10 and 18 years of age) via structured questionnaires that were electronically recorded, and the children gave their answers in writing. The researchers argue that this method ensured confidentiality, saved time, and, similar to telephone surveys, reduced costs (Swedish Institute for Social Research, 2010).

It is also possible to combine written questionnaires with telephone interviews. For example, starting in 2004, the German Youth Institute's (Deutsche Jugendinstitut, DJI) longitudinal study examined the transition from school to the labour market to work among German students via classroom questionnaires during the last four months of compulsory schooling, followed by telephone interviews (German Youth Institute, 2007).

Non-participant observations

Non-participant observations can also serve as a means of collecting data in research with children in both quantitative and qualitative studies. In non-participant observation, the researcher is an external observer who documents and reports the children's behavior. Direct and constant observation of children's activities eliminates the burden on children by freeing them from the need to record their actions. It is considered more objective and has been found to be valuable as a supporting technique. Nevertheless, it may alter the child's behavior, and it is usually time-consuming, costly, and impractical for large samples, thus harming its prospects for wider use (Plewis, Creeser and Mooney, 1990; Verma, Kaur and Saraswathi, 1995).

Spot observation, in which children observe other children's activities in randomly selected times, helps to reduce the observer's intrusive effect and is more feasible for larger samples. The method's limitations lie in its continuous burden of resources and the fact that it fails for observation of children in late or very early hours and in settings other than children's homes or neighborhoods (Larson and Kleiber, 1993; Verma et al., 1995).

Ethnography

Non-participant observation has been criticized as a method to learn *about* children, not *from* them (Docherty and Sandelowski,

1999). One common way to conduct research *with* children and not *about* them is ethnography – in other words, qualitative research. Drawing on the increasingly important children's rights movement, researchers have been developing inclusive and participatory child-centered methodologies that place the voices of children as social actors at the center of the research process (Barker and Weller, 2003). These forms of 'rights-oriented research' could help us to enhance our understanding of children's experiences (Melton, 2005b).

Those who view research with children as different from research with adults use ethnography – qualitative research – as a means of understanding children's worlds (Punch, 2002). Qualitative research methods as a whole are believed to be useful when conducting research with younger children who can experience difficulties in verbalizing their experiences or in direct questioning (Nelson and Quintana, 2005).

In ethnography, the researcher is engaged in learning about a social unit (Nelson and Quintana, 2005). Eder and Corsaro (1999: 521) argue that ethnography is suitable for research with children because it is longitudinal by nature and involves what they refer to as 'intensive observation', thus allowing the researcher to account for various aspects of children's lives in detail and to learn how children interpret their experiences.

Ethnography allows flexibility because the research process is not a linear one but instead is an act of constant alteration of the findings via an on-going process of feedback. Entering children's worlds is difficult because of the power imbalance between children and adults, which we discussed earlier. Some ethnographic researchers claim that although it is difficult, it is a challenge that can be overcome, whereas others argue that the researchers' participation should be kept to a minimum to avoid compromising the findings of the study (Eder and Corsaro, 1999). The literature on ethnography with children reports two means of data collection: 'ethnographic observation', which is also called 'participant observation', and the interview.

Participant observation

Participant observation is frequently used in ethnography and other qualitative studies. In this form of data collection, the researcher is situated within the researched phenomenon – the studied unit, while interacting with the research participants. The researcher commonly documents the participants, behaviors, responses, and other aspects of the researched situation. This means of data collection overcomes communication difficulties (Tetnowski and Franklin, 2003) and thus is suitable in research with children.

Interviews

Interviews are a common method to collect data in qualitative studies with children; for example, Garth and Aroni (2003) used in-depth semi-structured interviews as a means of data collection from 6- to 12-year-old children with cerebral palsy and their mothers in relation to communication in medical consultations. Nelson and Quintana (2005) argue that interviewing children for research purposes may be via direct questions or through storytelling or written vignettes, for example, to elicit negative emotions among 10- and 13-year-olds (Reijntjes, Stegge, Terwogt and Hurkens, 2007). Vignettes involve asking the child to express his or her feelings and thoughts about a situation that involves other people.

The interview allows reactions to general questions as well as space for the child to share his or her experience in detail. Asking more specific questions in the course of the interview helps focus the child on the subjects of interest to the researcher (Nelson and Quintana, 2005). Thus, the interview starts with general issues and narrows down to the researcher's topics of interest (Tetnowski and Franklin, 2003). Note that Curtin (2000) claims that elementary school children should be interviewed for a maximum of 30 minutes. Although interviews can be individual, interviewing a group of children is an efficient way to gather information (Curtin, 2000).

Focus groups

Focus groups are a type of group interview; they consist of a number of participants (Kitzinger, 1995). They are a common method of data collection with adults, but are infrequently used in research with children between the ages of 6 and 12 (Kennedy, Kools and Krueger, 2001). One of the main advantages of using focus groups with children is that they require reliance on only verbal communication (Kitzinger, 1995). In focus groups, participants are considered experts (Heary and Hennessy, 2002; Kitzinger, 1995), so this is a useful method to enter children's worlds, and it signifies respect toward the participants (Heary and Hennessy, 2002).

Focus groups with small children (6–10 years old) should include four to six participants (Kennedy et al., 2001). Although Kennedy et al. (2001) argue that these groups could include both boys and girls, Heary and Hennessy's (2002) review of the literature on focus groups with participants under the age of 18 revealed that most researchers suggest otherwise. Nonetheless, their review revealed scarce and inconclusive evidence to support both views. In the end, the answer may depend on the age of the children.

When conducting focus groups with children, it is advisable not to include children who differ greatly in age (Heary and Hennessy, 2002; Kennedy et al., 2001) or other socio-demographic features (Heary and Hennessy, 2002). The duration of the discussion could vary from 45 minutes to 90 minutes at the most, depending on the age group (Heary and Hennessy, 2002; Kennedy et al., 2001). A similar technique for collecting data from children is what Nelson and Quintana (2005) call 'conversations'. They argue that stimulating conversations about a certain topic among groups of children can be a good source of information.

Self-report questionnaires, participant and non-participant observations, individual interviews, and group interviews by means of focus groups are all documented methods for collecting data in both qualitative and quantitative research. Although, as suggested earlier, these means of data collection should be adjusted to fit the particular research project, research with children is unique because it draws heavily on the use of 'child-friendly' techniques to collect data.

'Child-friendly' techniques

Many researchers employ 'child-friendly' techniques when they are conducting research with children (Kirk, 2007; Punch, 2002), especially in qualitative studies. Child-friendly techniques are 'task-centred' (Punch, 2000) and 'open-ended techniques' (Nelson and Quintana, 2005), which are also influenced by 'participatory rural appraisal' (PRA; Kirk, 2007).

Examples of child-friendly techniques used in research with school age children are sentence completion (Nelson and Quintana, 2005; Punch, 2000); art and play therapy methods (Docherty and Sandelowski, 1999), such as drawing (Bland, 2012; Curtin, 2000; Eldén, 2013; Kennedy et al., 2001; Nelson and Quintana, 2005; Punch, 2000), sculpting (Nelson and Quintana, 2005), and photography (Banister and Booth, 2005; Punch, 2000; Stephenson, 2009); writing a diary (Ben-Arieh and Ofir, 2002; Punch, 2000); responding to a written vignette (Reijntjes et al., 2007); worksheets (Punch, 2000); PRA techniques, which measure mobility inside and outside the community via diagrams and activity tables (Punch, 2000); storytelling (Davis, 2007; Nelson and Quintana, 2005); videotaping a story (Curtin, 2000); reacting to a video recording (Curtin, 2000); talking to a pretend friend (Curtin, 2000); play and games (Kennedy et al., 2001; Nelson and Quintana, 2005); role play (Curtin, 2000;

Kennedy et al., 2001); 'draw and write' techniques (Backett-Milburn and McKie, 1999; Banister and Booth, 2005); 'think-aloud' techniques (Nelson and Quintana, 2005); and body movement (Nelson and Quintana, 2005).

Child-friendly techniques can serve as a means for collecting data for themselves or as an opening to another method of data collection, such as an interview. Thus, these techniques do not rule out the use of adult-oriented methods while studying children (Munro et al., 2005; Punch, 2002). For example, 'draw and write' techniques are used for themselves or as an opening to an interview (Backett-Milburn and McKie, 1999). 'Think-aloud' techniques are commonly used in education and cognitive developmental research, and they usually involve stimulating the child via written or visual material that serves as an opening to a subsequent interview (Nelson and Quintana, 2005).

Backe-Hansen (2005) recommended combining several methods of data collection (such as survey data, qualitative data, and administrative data) while conducting research with children. This approach was adopted in a study of children and young people's (ages 8–14) well-being in the Nordic countries (Backe-Hansen, 2005).

Child-friendly techniques can be used in combination with other data collection methods, including adult methods (Munro et al., 2005; Punch, 2002). For example, in focus groups for children, in addition to conversation, nonverbal methods are also suggested, such as drawing, acting different roles, and playing games (Kennedy et al., 2001). An interview with a child may be conducted while engaging in 'play, drawing and body movement' and listening to the child's storytelling (Nelson and Quintana, 2005: 350). Another child-friendly variation on the common interview, a 'storytelling interview', was designed by Davis (2007) for 7- to 8-year-old children. In a storytelling interview, the child tells a story orally and is asked questions.

The advantages for engaging in child-friendly techniques while conducting research with children all follow from the assumptions that it is difficult to communicate with children, because 'children prefer fun methods', children 'are more competent at these methods', 'children may have a short attention span', and 'children are more used to visual and written techniques' (Kirk, 2007: 1257). Punch (2002) adds to these reasons the fact that children are not accustomed to being treated as equals, so child-friendly techniques are useful because of their perceived familiarity to children.

Furthermore, child-friendly methods are perceived as a means for dealing with the unequal power relations between children and adults (Punch, 2002) and thus serve as a way to 'elicit the children's perspective' (Curtin, 2000). Similarly, Davis (2007: 172) argues that a storytelling interview 'promises a more socially inclusive or democratic approach to data collection'. Aside from dealing with power relations, child-friendly techniques may act as a bridge between adults' communication styles and those of children (Curtin, 2000). It is worth noting that Punch (2000) suggests calling these techniques 'child-sensitive', 'person-friendly', or 'research-friendly' techniques rather than 'child-friendly' techniques.

Although they are prevalent and popular in conducting research with children, child-friendly techniques have also been criticized for various reasons. Some studies have found that the assumption that these methods are always enjoyable for all children is not always correct (Backett-Milburn and McKie, 1999; Kirk, 2007; Punch, 2002). Furthermore, when techniques such as art and play therapy are used alone, they do not provide direct information from children. Instead, such techniques are means of learning about children (Docherty and Sandelowski, 1999). Similarly, Backett-Milburn and McKie (1999) argue that 'projective techniques', as opposed to direct methods of learning about children's worlds (for example, conversations and participant observation), limit children's participation in the research process and preserve the power relations and ethnocentric view of adults by casting them as interpreters of children's works (such as pictures) – what children 'really' think.

ETHICAL DILEMMAS IN STUDIES THAT INVOLVE SCHOOL-AGED CHILDREN

The need for methodological adjustments is not the only problem to take into account when conducting research with school-aged children; the literature also emphasizes the ethical dilemmas that surround such research. Ethical judgment is required when planning and conducting any study (Bragadottir, 2000). Many ethical issues present in social research with children are common to work with participants of any age (Ben-Arieh, 2005). However, the differences between children and adult participants lie in the sharpness of these issues when children are concerned (Fargas-Malet et al., 2010; Kirk, 2007).

Informed consent

The issues most commonly raised by commentators on the ethics of research involving children are informed consent and confidentiality (Punch, 2002). Although informed consent is necessary in any study that involves human participants, research with children is different in two major aspects: (1) a child's competence to make a reasoned decision may be questionable in law if not in fact (see Melton et al., 1983), and (2) both child and adult guardians (usually a parent) must participate in decision making about research (see, for example, Munro et al., 2005).

Informed consent is the manifestation of the principle of autonomy in the research setting (Lowden, 2002). The ethical principle of autonomy means that 'all people have unconditional worth and the right to self-determination' (Lind et al., 2003: 506).

Informed consent is valid only after the maximum amount of information is given (Bragadottir, 2000; Kirk, 2007; Pearn, 1984). Valid consent relies on volunteering, capacity, and comprehension. In younger children, all three elements are questioned (Lind et al., 2003).

Lowden (2002) has argued that competency (the ability to reach a meaningful decision) is acquired mainly by receiving information and proper explanations. When adults decide what information is relevant to the child, or what 'is in the child's best interest', they can inhibit the development of competence. Furthermore, common beliefs about children's rights and prejudices regarding their abilities play a major part in developing competence to consent in children.

Various studies in the literature have discussed the question of the child's age in relation to informed consent. They have yielded mixed results and multiple interpretations (Bragadottir, 2000; Lind et al., 2003; Pearn, 1984). Pearn (1984) claimed that informed consent should be requested from all children over 10 years old. Melton (2006) argued that international law requires that any children who can express their feelings and thoughts should be asked if they wish to participate. Bragadottir (2000) emphasized the need for age-adapted information when consent is sought. The connections among age, cognitive ability, and consent are manifest in legislation. For example, Hesson et al. (1993) studied Canadian law, which was influenced by Piagetian research. Thus they believe that because formal operational thinking is stabilized at age 14, most adolescents have acquired the cognitive skills required for competency.

While criticizing developmental psychology, Lowden (2002) argued that competence depends not on age but on children's experiences, such as illness, disability, and treatment, which could shape their understanding. This claim has received empirical evidence; for example, in a study of children and adolescent patients (ages 7–20) in a paediatric

unit the researchers found that knowledge of research participation was connected to psychological factors rather than to developmental factors such as age and cognitive development (Dorn, Susman and Fletcher, 1995).

Some researchers have suggested that with subjects under the age of majority, one should gain assent (Lind et al., 2003; Unguru et al., 2010). Nonetheless, researchers have revealed that assent can be gained from the majority of elementary school children (Curtin, 2000). Assent is defined as 'the process of concurring with someone to agree to treatment or involvement in research, but it does not entail a demonstration of understanding or reasoning ability' (Lind et al., 2003: 506).

One example of gaining both a guardian's consent and the child's assent is a four-year study designed to investigate the development of the understanding of children's rights and of child participation in a cultural and religious comparative perspective, among children ages 7 to 8 and 12 to 13 (Ben-Arieh et al., 2006). Informed consent from guardians consisted of a signed consent form following a letter of invitation that provided information about the study. Similarly, children's assent consisted of signed assent following a written and oral explanation.

Informed consent is not the only ethical dilemma surrounding research with children. The concept of confidentiality, which, like informed consent, is present in all studies that involve human subjects, is sharpened when school-aged children are considered. This issue is discussed next.

Confidentiality

As we mentioned earlier, confidentiality is essential in all research processes involving human subjects. Pearn (1984) argued that confidentiality in research should be the same for children and adults. Melton (2005, 2006) has emphasized the need to take special care in relation to private and confidential subjects;

researchers should refrain from unnecessary invasion of children's privacy. Similarly, Nelson and Quantina (2005) have stressed the need to protect children's privacy when using qualitative research methods to collect data, as these methods could compromise the child's ability to withhold personal information.

In focus groups, in which a number of participants are interviewed simultaneously, information is revealed not just to the researcher (Heary and Hennessy, 2002) but to other members of the group. 'Draw and write' techniques have also evoked ethical concerns about children's confidentiality because drawings are hard to make anonymous (Backett-Milburn and McKie, 1999).

The principle of confidentiality could be truly at stake if, in the process of research, vital information regarding the child's safety and well-being is exposed. The most extreme form of information is that of abuse: emotional, physical, or sexual. Kirk (2007) found that confidentiality could be compromised in research with children if the researcher learns that the child is at risk. Ben-Arieh (2005) has claimed that it is important to allow children to decide what they want to say about abuse and who they want to say it to. Thus, researchers must assure children that what they tell us will not be passed to other people except in the most extreme circumstances.

QUESTIONS OF VALIDITY, RELIABILITY, AND RESPONSE RATE

Aside from ethical challenges, the literature discusses three related issues that may contribute to the difficulty of conducting research with children: validity, reliability, and response rate. The validity of a study depends on both response rates and reliability. Ben-Arieh (2005) reviewed studies of children's well-being, and reported good response rates. Goodman, Fleitlich-Bilyk, Patel, and Goodman (2007) reported an 83 per cent response rate among Brazilian schoolchildren, ages 7 to 14 years, in a survey that assessed mental health and risk factors. Almqvist et al. (1999) reported a 94.5 per cent response rate among 8- to 9-year-old students who participated in a survey that assessed the prevalence of emotional and behavioral symptoms in children. In a survey examining attitudes toward alcohol and tobacco use among 9- to 13-year-olds, Stritzke et al. (2005: 122) found that '92 per cent of the sample completed the entire study period' of eight weeks. Similarly, Mangunkusumo et al. (2006) reported a 92 per cent response rate among 10- to 12-year-olds who participated in a study comparing Internet to paper administration of questionnaires.

The literature on research with children usually discusses questions of validity and reliability together and is concerned mainly with the following question: can children provide valid and reliable, that is, credible, information? Or is there a need for proxy measures or 'projective' means to collect data about children? In quantitative research, especially in surveys, the question of reliability is primarily interested in the stability of answers over time (see Borgers et al., 2003, 2004).

Some studies have claimed that children lack articulating abilities, have problems recalling data, and cannot understand complex concepts, and thus pose a threat to the authenticity of research findings (Docherty and Sandelowski, 1999). The perception that children are different, are unable to tell reality from fantasy, and have a tendency to not always tell the truth may lead to the conclusion that they are unreliable sources of data (Punch, 2002). These views resemble the once-common medical model perception in educational research that perceives lack of credibility and reliability as defects stemming from the child (Davis, 2007).

Ben-Arieh and Ofir (2002), for example, found concern about the accuracy of children's self-reports throughout the literature in time-use studies with children (see also

Bianchi and Robinson, 1997; Plewis et al., 1990). As was mentioned earlier, these concerns often resulted in using the parents, the guardians, or even other adults such as teachers as sources of information instead of the child (Mederich, Roizen, Rubin and Buckly, 1982).

Arguing against these perceptions, Docherty and Sandelowski (1999) emphasized the fact that even 3-year-olds can recall distressing events. Davis (2007) argued that modern research with children is embedded in an ecological view and thus the responsibility for gaining reliable data lies primarily with the researcher who must know how to connect with children.

The dispute surrounding validity and reliability while conducting research with children, and especially whether children can be credible sources of information, is usually discussed in terms of age. Kirk (2007) found that age and cognition development are widely discussed in relation to reliability and validity of the data. Studies on adults report that response quality is a function of respondent characteristics, mainly cognitive abilities and question phrasing (Borgers et al., 2003, 2004). Borgers et al. (2003: 91), for example, found that 'it appears to be that offering the clearest type of response options produces the best data quality in questionnaire research with children'. Furthermore, Borgers et al. (2004) found that children between the ages of 8 and 16 provided stable answers over time and within a measurement while distinguishing negative from positive questions.

Ben-Arieh and Ofir (2002) have argued that although age is a determining factor in selecting the source of information, we still need to address the question of 'the right age'. We are still facing the practical question of how far down we can go on the age continuum and still get reliable information. The debate is primarily over children younger than 12. Whereas preschool children are considered to be too young to serve as sources of information, the results of studies on elementary school children are mixed (Ben-Arieh, 2005; Ben-Arieh and Ofir, 2002).

A common assumption is that we need the parents or other adults as our source of information when looking, for instance, at time use of children in the age range 6–12 years (Marshall et al., 1997; Sanik and Stattford, 1996). Nevertheless, a number of studies are showing the opposite– young children could be reliable sources of information. For example, Ronen et al. (2003) found that the self-report measure of health-related quality of life (HRQL) was reliable in children who were 8 years old and older. Muris, Meesters, and Fijen (2003) examined the psychometric qualities of the Self-Perception Profile for Children (SPPC), a measure for self-esteem in youths, in a sample of Dutch children and youth (ages 8–14). Similarly, Meesters, Muris, Gjys, Reumerman, and Rooijmans (2003) examined the psychometric qualities of the Children's Somatization Inventory (CSI) among both Dutch school-age children (ages 8–16) and their parents. Both studies concluded that these self-report measures are reliable and valid means of assessing self-esteem and somatization in children. Studies looking at children's understanding of complex concepts such as children and human rights support the notion that children as young as 7 or 8 could be used as reliable sources of information (Melton and Limber, 1992).

Although the issues of reliability and validity may pose some threat to conducting research with children, they are overamplified, but more importantly, they can be dealt with. Some advice on how this can be done is presented next.

CONDUCTING RESEARCH WITH CHILDREN: SOME GENERAL RECOMMENDATIONS

Reflexivity and responsiveness

The literature emphasizes the role of three significant elements in successfully conducting research with school-aged children: reflexivity, responsiveness, and on-going communication. To conduct research with children, researchers should adopt a 'child-centric' approach (Banister and Booth, 2005) and abandon 'ethnocentric views', such as the perception that adult knowledge is superior to that of children (Punch, 2002). Pearn (1984) quotes a sociological view that perceives clinical research as an innovative unit consisting of child and researcher, in which both sides are essential to the process. In addition to questioning their belief system about children and their abilities, maturity, knowledge, and amount of experience, as was mentioned earlier, researchers should also examine their conduct in the research process and whether they were clear in their requests and intentions. A child's difficulty in responding may stem from the researcher rather than from the child's inability (Curtin, 2000).

Reflexivity is most important in research with children; we must constantly question what we know about children's worlds (Kirk, 2007; Mauthner, 1997; Punch, 2002). This 'on-going reflection' means learning from children (Curtin, 2000). It is crucial in research with children to exhibit respect for children who take part in the research process (Melton, 2005; Pearn, 1984). Melton (2005) has stressed the importance of choosing meaningful topics to study that can improve our knowledge about children's worlds.

Punch (2002) has emphasized the need for building rapport with children in a reactive way. Curtin (2000) suggested that to overcome the power relations between the researcher and child, the researcher could develop an 'out of the ordinary' relationship with the child, which is also called 'the least adult role' (see also Banister and Booth, 2005; Kirk, 2007). Similarly, Morrow and Richards (1996: 100) have also suggested that 'using methods which are non-invasive, non-confrontational and participatory, might be one step forward in diminishing ethical problems of imbalanced power relationships between researcher and researched at the point of data collection and interpretation'. Building a trusting partnership could help overcome issues of validity and reliability, although 'the least adult role' may involve ethical and moral complications, especially if the researcher is the only adult around (see Curtin, 2000).

Responsiveness and open-ended research goals and methods are vital when conducting research with children (Kirk, 2007; Mauthner, 1997). Curtin (2000) suggests that when interviewing children, the researcher should be 'flexible and informal', engaging the child in a 'casual conversation' while maintaining some level of structure in the interview (see also Banister and Booth, 2005).

Children and adults have different styles of communication. Thus, being sensitive to nonverbal cues, body language, and tone of voice is vital. Moreover, children make use of fewer words, and so the researcher needs to make sense and meaning from short messages. Researchers are also advised to refrain from general questions, overlong questions, and complicated language and embrace 'kid's language' (for a detailed discussion and further practical suggestions for interviewing children, see Curtin, 2000).

Punch (2002) emphasized the need to conduct the study in children's territory, and Curtin (2000) suggested that interviews should take place in a quiet, private, and neutral place, but one that the child chooses. If the place is unfamiliar to the child, the researcher must give the child some time to adjust. Some researchers suggest using short developmental assessments prior to interviewing a child to adjust the interview to the child's level of comprehension (Docherty and Sandelowski, 1999). Furthermore, it is advisable that while interviewing a child, both researcher and child sit in small-sized chairs. Finally, the presence of a parent or peers, or the use of focus groups may help the child feel more at ease (Curtin, 2000). Using focus groups can also enhance the validity of a study (Heary and Hennessy, 2002).

Encouraging full participation in the research team

A second group of recommendations, suitable for school-age children, but not necessarily for younger children, is about encouraging full participation in the research team. It draws on the principles of responsiveness and on-going communication but goes beyond them.

Kirk (2007) found that researchers tended to choose methods that enabled children's active participation in the research team and the research process. Involving children in the research team could be enjoyable for them (Pearn, 1984). Reviews of studies with children demonstrate that children want to be asked, they want to be asked in an interesting way (to them), they want to be involved in research that matters, and they can contribute to research (Ben-Arieh, 2005); these studies also reported some benefits such as improved self-esteem and the development of altruism (Curtin, 2000; Munro et al., 2005).

An excellent example for full participation of children in research was described by Druin (2002: 13):

> Today, children are most definitely our partners in all that we do at the University of Maryland's Human Computer Interaction Lab. Twice a week, children aged 7–11 join researchers from computer science, education, psychology, art and robotics. Over the summer, the team meets for two intensive weeks eight hours a day to continue our work. Children have remained with our team as long as four years and as short as one year. Together we have become what I now call an 'Intergenerational Design Team' – pursuing projects together, writing papers and creating new technologies. This intergenerational design team has produced research projects…

Children can be involved in the research process in the study design, in defining research problems, in data collection, and in data analysis (Ben-Arieh, 2005; Kirk, 2007; Mason and Danby, 2010). This approximates the role of children as 'design partners' in technology design processes, especially those that support learning. As 'design partners' 'children are considered to be equal stakeholders in the design of new technologies throughout the entire experience (Druin, 2002: 3).

Researchers have shown not only that children know what is important to them, but also that they have clear views on how those issues can and should be measured (Backe-Hensen, 2003). Similarly, Thomas and O'Kane (1998) suggested the selection of research instruments that enable children to choose subjects for discussion and decide what they want to say about them.

Commentators have recommended that researchers talk to children not merely to gain their consent to participate but also after they have finished taking part in the process (Ben-Arieh, 2005; Melton, 2005a). Coming back to meet the child once more after the interview can serve as a means not only of enhancing openness and communication but also of enabling the child to refine and review what he or she told us. Another method is to use group processes, creating a space where children could collectively interpret the research findings (Ben-Arieh, 2005; Kirk 2007; Thomas and O'Kane, 1998). Finally, at the conclusion of the research a smaller group of researchers could be recruited to select and edit their colleagues' comments. The involvement of children in the interpretation and analysis of the data has been found to be very useful (Kefalyew, 1996; Thomas and O'Kane, 1998) because adults and children construct their worlds differently (Kirk, 2007; Punch, 2002). However, analyses of the data should include moral judgment of the findings and choosing the means to apply them; the guideline should be not what is good or best for the child but rather what is morally required (Melton, 2005). When research touches on matters critical to the protection of human dignity, there is a moral obligation to take special care in the application of such information (Melton, 2005). Besides analyzing and providing insight to the meaning of the data, children should also be partners in using the data as part of exercising their right to participation (Ben-Arieh, 2005; see also Casas et al., 2010).

In sum, to overcome methodological barriers regarding the research question of how to measure the questioned phenomenon and how to make sense of the data, the research process should involve children at every step. This is true also in relation to ethical dilemmas such as confidentiality and abuse: there is a greater probability that such vital information would be revealed to a researcher who sees the child as an equal. Even when confidentiality needs to be broken because of the revelation of such facts, it seems that breaching the promise in a trustful, empathetic, supportive environment would benefit the child more than harm him or her. Encouraging full participation in the research team may be beneficial concerning the question of consent. The ethical dilemma of informed consent, as we mentioned earlier, is most important in research with children, so specific recommendations on how to overcome it are addressed next.

Overcoming the ethical dilemmas surrounding the issue of informed consent

When asking children to participate in a research process, it is vital to assure the children that they can withdraw from the process at any time. Children should have as much choice as possible over how to participate in the research (Ben-Arieh, 2005). Kirk (2007) found that qualitative researchers tend to rehearse with children ways of withdrawing and declining to participate in any phase or part of the research. Even after reaching an agreement to participate in the research process, researchers commonly describe the on-going need to check and recheck children's willingness to participate, which could be expressed via nonverbal means of communication (Kirk, 2007; see also Nelson

and Quintana, 2005). Researchers should take special notice of cues of discomfort if peer pressure may be involved, for example in a study that examines a group of children (Nelson and Quintana, 2005).

As we noted earlier, in research involving children, informed consent should be obtained from the child as well as from the guardian. Ben-Arieh (2005) has suggested that studies should be contingent on the child's active agreement, whereas we can settle for passive agreement from the adult involved. We mentioned the distinction between active and passive consent earlier. Informed consent could be gained through opt-in methodology, such as through a formal response to a letter, or an opt-out approach, where consent is considered to be given if subjects do not refuse to participate (Munro et al., 2005). The former approach holds ethical advantages because both the child and adult 'gatekeepers' give consent. However, the need for consent from adult gatekeepers may result in exclusion of children who would have otherwise wanted to take part in the research process.

In sum, although informed consent is a big challenge in research with school-aged children, adopting several simple principles could help. Gaining passive consent from the child's guardian, while relying on the child's active consent, would promote participation. Similar to the need for being reflexive and constantly questioning one's knowledge of children's worlds, consent should be viewed as an on-going process, and repeated affirmation is vital.

CONCLUSION

The change in children's rights discourse, from a discourse of protection and nurturance to a discourse of self-determination, prompted a change in images of children. School-aged children, who were once thought of primarily as vulnerable creatures who thus need to be treasured, protected, and even dominated, are now seen primarily as equals to adults. School-aged children have rights that go beyond 'survival' needs per se: the right to participate and to be actively involved in decision-making processes that affect their lives. Furthermore and most importantly, these new self-determination rights are often legal rights, part of societies' normative systems.

The normative-legislative justification for involving school-aged children in research as sources of information about their lives claims that this involvement serves as an extension of the right to participate. The theoretical shifts in the perception of children and childhood – from views of unfinished adults to persons, from perceptions of a homogenous group to acknowledging personal and cultural differences, and from passive objects to active players who are constantly engaged in creating their worlds – propose the theoretical justification to view children as sources of information about their lives. Put simply, the anachronistic view of adults as being in sole possession of knowledge has fallen to modern views that acknowledge children's knowledge. This attitude toward knowledge possession is embedded in the methodological justification for using children as sources of information about their lives.

The choice of research methods used to conduct research with children depends on the researcher's perception of children and childhood. Traditional research methods are being put aside, clearing the way for new children-centred methods emphasizing full participation of children and their subjective views. Alongside structured questionnaires, non-participant observation, participant observation, and interviews as means of collecting data, there is a tendency to embrace what are known as 'child-friendly' techniques (for example, drawings, diaries, photographs) for collecting data and enhancing participation. The literature calls for a critical view when adopting these methods.

The choice of methods for collecting data is not the only methodological question regarding research with children; validity, reliability, and response rates are also important. These issues are over amplified, relying on only partially realistic fears. Aside from methodological challenges, research with children involves unique ethical dilemmas surrounding informed consent and confidentiality: the need for both child and guardian approval, the need for the on-going consent of the child, and the need to balance protecting children's privacy with promoting participation, especially when using qualitative research methods.

Research with children poses greater methodological and ethical challenges to the researcher, but these can be overcome primarily by engaging in reflexivity, responsiveness, and on-going communication, and via the encouraging of full participation of children in the research team. The first step to designing a successful study is to be aware of the challenges and differences that research with children present. Embracing a 'child-centric' view, that is, 'ownership, active participation and an environment that responds to needs such as shared language and respect' (Banister and Booth, 2005: 172) is essential to truly understand children's worlds.

REFERENCES

Almqvist, F., Kumpulainen, K., Ikaheimo, K., Linna, S.L., Henttonen, I., Huikko, E., Tuompo-Johansson, E., Aronen, E., Puura, K., Piha, J., Tamminen, T., Rasanen, E. and Moilanen, I. (1999) 'Behavioural and emotional symptoms in 8-9-year-old children', *European Child and Adolescent Psychiatry*, 8(4): 7–16.

Alt, C. (2005) 'Data, design and constructs – The first wave of the children's panel', in C. Klockner and U. Paetzel (eds.), *Kindheitsforschung Undkommunale Praxis: Praxisnahe Erkenntnisse aus Der Aktuellen Kindheitsforschung*. Heidelberg: VS Verlag fur Sozialwissenschaften, p. 165–77.

Araujo, K.B., Medic, S., Yasnovsky, J. and Steiner, H. (2006) 'Assessing defense structure in school-age children using the Response Evaluation Measure-71-youth version (REM-Y-71)', *Child Psychiatry and Human Development*, 36(4): 427–36.

Backe-Hensen, E. (2003, April) *Cool, Boring, Difficult or Stupid? What the Children Thought*. Paper presented at the international meeting on methods and techniques in children's research in international comparison at Deutsches Jugendinstitt, Munich.

Backe-Hensen, E. (2005) 'Young people's well-being in the Nordic countries', in C. Klockner and U. Paetzel (eds.), *Kindheitsforschung Undkommunale Praxis: Praxisnahe Erkenntnisse aus Der Aktuellen Kindheitsforschung*. Heidelberg: VS Verlag fur Sozialwissenschaften, p. 77–93.

Backett-Milburn, K. and McKie, L. (1999) 'A critical appraisal of the draw and write technique', *Health Education Research*, 14(3): 387–98.

Banister, E.N. and Booth, G.J. (2005) 'Exploring innovative methodologies for child-centric consumer research', *Qualitative Market Research*, 8(2): 157–75.

Barker, J. and Weller, S. (2003) 'Is it fun? Developing children center research methods', *International Journal of Sociology and Social Policy*, 23(1–2): 33–58.

Ben-Arieh, A. (2005) 'Where are the children? Children's role in measuring and monitoring their well-being', *Social Indicators Research*, 74(3): 573–95.

Ben-Arieh, A. (2006) 'Is the study of the 'state of the children' changing? Re-visiting after 5 years', *Children and Youth Services Review*, 28(7): 799–811.

Ben-Arieh, A. and Ofir, A. (2002) 'Time for (more) time-use studies: Studying the daily activities of children', *Childhood*, 9(2): 225–48.

Ben-Arieh, A. and Windman, V. (2007) 'Secondary victimization of children in Israel and the child's perspective', *International Review of Victimology*, 14(3): 321–36.

Bianchi, S.M. and Robinson, J. (1997) 'What did you do today? Children's use of time, family composition, and the acquisition of social capital', *Journal of Marriage and the Family*, 59(2): 332–44.

Bland, D. (2012) 'Analysing children's drawings: Applied imagination', *International Journal of Research & Method in Education*, 35(3): 235–42.

Borgers, N., Hox, H. and Sikkel, D. (2003) 'Response quality in survey research with children and adolescents: The effect of labeled response options and vague quantifiers', *International Journal of Public Opinion Research*, 15(1): 83–94.

Borgers, N., Hox, H. and Sikkel, D. (2004) 'Response effects in surveys on children and adolescents: The effect of number of response options, negative wording, and neutral mid-point', *Quality and Quantity*, 38(1): 17–33.

Bragadottir, H. (2000) 'Children's rights in clinical research', *Journal of Nursing Scholarship*, 32(2): 179–84.

Brodin, J. and Stancheva-Popkostadinova, V (2009) 'Ethical considerations in child research in light of the convention on the rights of the child', *Journal of Global Change and Governance*, 2(2): 1–16.

Casas, F., González, M., Navarro, D. and Aligué, M. (2012) 'Children as advisers of their researchers: Assuming a different status for children', *Child Indicators Research*, 1–20; DOI 10.1007/s12187–012–9168–0.

Currie, C. and Roberts, C. (2004) 'Introduction', in C. Currie, C. Roberts, A. Morgan, R. Smith, W. Settertobulte, O. Samdal, and V. Barnekow Rasmussen (eds.), *Young People's Health in Context: Health Behaviour in School-aged Children (HBSC) Study: International Report from the 2001/2002 Survey*. Denmark: World Health Organization, pp. 1–6.

Curtin, C. (2000) 'Eliciting children's voices in qualitative research', *The American Journal of Occupational Therapy*, 55(3): 295–302.

Davis, P. (2007) 'Storytelling as a democratic approach to data collection: Interviewing children about reading', *Educational Research*, 40(2): 169–84.

Docherty, S. and Sandelowski, M. (1999) 'Focus on qualitative research methods. Interviewing children', *Research in Nursing and Health*, 22(2): 177–85.

Dorn, L.D., Susman, E.J. and Fletcher, J.C. (1995) 'Informed consent in children and adolescents: Age, maturation and psychological state', *Journal of Health and Adolescent Health*, 16(3): 185–90.

Druin, A. (2002) 'The role of children in the design of new technology', *Behavior and Information Technology*, 21(1): 1–25.

Eder, D. and Corsaro, W. (1999) 'Ethnographic studies of children and youth', *Journal of Contemporary Ethnography*, 28(5): 520–31.

Eldén, S. (2013) 'Inviting the messy: Drawing methods and "children's voices"', *Childhood*, 20(1): 66–81.

Fargas-Malet, M., McSherry, D., Larkin, E. and Robinson, C. (2010) 'Research with children: Methodological issues and innovative techniques', *Journal of Early Childhood Research*, 8(2): 175–92.

Funk, J., Hagan, J. and Schimminq, J. (1999) 'Children and electronic games: A comparison of parents' and children's' perceptions of children's habits and preferences in a United States sample', *Psychological Reports*, 85(3): 883–8.

Garth, B. and Aroni, R. (2003) '"I value what you have to say": Seeking the perspective of children with disability, not just their parents', *Disability and Society*, 18(5): 561–76.

German Youth Institute (2007) 'School-to-Work Transition Longitudinal Study ("DJI Transition Panel")'. Munich, Germany: German Youth Institute. Available at http://www.dji.de/cgi-bin/projekte/output.php?projekt=723

Goodman, A., Fleitlich-Bilyk, B., Patel, V. and Goodman, R. (2007) 'Child, family, school and community risk factors for poor mental health in Brazilian schoolchildren', *Journal of the American Academy of Child and Adolescent Psychiatry*, 46(4): 448–56.

Gottlieb, D. and Bronstein, P. (1996) 'Parent's perceptions of children's worries in a changing world', *Journal of Generic Psychology*, 157(1): 104–18.

Hart, S. N. (1991) 'From property to person status. Historical perspective on children's rights', *American Psychologist*, 46(1): 53–9.

Heary, C.M. and Hennessy, E. (2002) 'The use of focus group interview in pediatric health care research', *Journal of Pediatric Psychology*, 27(1): 47–57.

Hesson, K., Bakal, D. and Dobson, K.S. (1993) 'Legal and ethical issues concerning children's rights of consent', *Canadian Psychology*, 34(3): 317–28.

Israel National Council for the Child (2007) The Multi-National Project for Monitoring and Measuring Children's Well-Being. Chapin Hall at the University of Chicago: Policy Research that benefits Children, Families, and their Communities. Available at http://multinational-indicators.chapinhall.org

Kefalyew, F. (1996) 'The reality of child participation in research', *Childhood*, 3(2): 203–13.

Kennedy, C., Kools, S. and Krueger, R. (2001) 'Methodological considerations in children's focus groups', *Nursing Research*, 50(3): 184–7.

Kirk, S. (2007) 'Methodological and ethical issues in conducting qualitative research with children and young people: A literature review', *International Journal of Nursing Studies*, 44(7): 1250–60.

Kitzinger, J. (1995) 'Qualitative research: Introducing focus groups', *British Medical Journal*, 311(7000): 299–302.

Larson, R. and Kleiber, D. (1993) 'Daily experience of adolescents', in P.H. Tolan and B.J. Cohler (eds.), *Handbook of Clinical Research and Practice with Adolescents*. New York: John Wiley, pp. 125–45.

Lehmann, R. (2004) 'Overview of the IEA civic education study', in W. Schultz and H. Sibberns (eds.), *IEA Civic Education Study Technical Report*. Amsterdam: Multicopy, pp. 7–16.

LeVine, A. R. (2007) 'Ethnographic studies of childhood: A historical view', *American Anthropologist*, 109(2): 247–60.

Lind, C., Anderson, B. and Oberle, K (2003) 'Ethical issues in adolescent consent for research', *Nursing Ethics*, 10(5): 504–11.

Lowden, J. (2002) 'Children's rights: A decade of dispute', *Journal of Advanced Nursing*, 37(1): 100–7.

Mangunkusumo, R.T., Duisterhout, J.S., de Graaff, N., Maarsingh, E.J., de Koning, H. J. and Raat, H. (2006) 'Internet versus paper mode of health and health behavior questionnaires in elementary schools: Asthma and fruit as examples', *Journal of School Health*, 76(2): 80–6.

Marshall, N.L., Coll, C.G., Marx, F., McCartny, K., Keefe, N. and Ruh, J. (1997) 'After-school time and children's behavioral adjustment', *Merrill-Palmer Quarterly*, 43(3): 497–514.

Mason, J., and Danby, S. (2011) 'Children as experts in their lives: Child inclusive research', *Child Indicators Research*, 4(2): 185–9.

Mauthner, M. (1997) 'Methodological aspects of collecting data from children: Lessons from three research projects', *Children and Society*, 11(1): 16–28.

Mederich, E.A., Roizen, J., Rubin V. and Buckly, S. (1982) *The Serious Business of Growing up: A Study of Children's Lives Outside School*. Berkeley: University of California Press.

Meesters, C., Muris, P., Gjys, A., Reumerman, T. and Rooijmans, M. (2003) 'The children's somatization inventory: Further evidence for its reliability and validity in a pediatric and community sample of Dutch children and adolescents', *Journal of Pediatric Psychology*, 28(6): 413–22.

Melton, G.B. (2005a) 'Treating children like people: A framework for research and advocacy', *Journal of Clinical Child and Adolescent Psychology*, 34(4): 646–57.

Melton, G.B. (2005b) 'Building humane communities respectful of children: The significance of the Convention on the Rights of the Child', *American Psychologist*, 60(8): 918–26.

Melton, G.B. (2006) *Background for a General Comment on the Right to Participate; Article 12 and Related Provisions of the Convention on the Rights of the Child*. Report prepared for use by the UN Committee on the Rights of the Child. (September, 2006).

Melton, G.B. (2011) 'Young children's rights', in R.E. Tremblay, M. Boivin, R. deV. Peters (eds.), *Encyclopedia on Early Child Development* Montreal, Quebec: Centre of Excellence for Early Childhood Development and Strategic Knowledge Cluster. Available online at: http://www.child-encyclopedia.com/pages/PDF/MeltonANGxp1.pdf

Melton, G. and Limber, S. (1992) 'What children's rights mean to children: Children's own views', in M. Freeman and P. Veerman (eds.), *The Ideologies of Children's Rights*. Dordrecht, Netherlands: M. Nijhoff Publishers, pp. 167–87.

Melton, G.B., Koocher, G.P. and Saks, M.J. (eds.) (1983) *Children's Competence to Consent*. New York: Plenum.

Morrow, V. and Richards, M. (1996) 'The ethics of social research with children: An overview', *Children and Society*, 10(2): 90–105.

Munro, W.R., Holmes, L. and Harriet, W. (2005) 'Researching vulnerable groups: Ethical issues and the effective conduct of research in local authorities', *British Journal of Social Work*, 35(7): 1023–38.

Muris, P., Meesters, C. and Fijen, P. (2003) 'The self-perception profile for children: Further evidence for its factor structure, reliability, and validity', *Personality and Individual Differences*, 35(8): 1791–1802.

National Center for Education Statistics (n.d.) Trends in International Mathematics and Science Study. National Center for Education Statistics, US Department of Education, Institute of Education Sciences. Available at http://nces.ed.gov/timss/

National Study of Youth and Religion (2008) Methodological Design and Procedures for the National Study of Youth and Religion (NSYR) Longitudinal Telephone Survey (Waves 1, 2, & 3) Chapel Hill, NC: The National Study of Youth and Religion. Retrieved from http://www.youthandreligion.org/sites/default/files/imported/research/docs/master_just_methods_11_12_2008.pdf

Nelson, M.L. and Quintana, S.M. (2005) 'Qualitative clinical research with children and adolescents', *Journal of Clinical Child and Adolescent Psychology*, 34(2): 344–56.

OECD (Organization for Economic Cooperation and Development) (n.d.) The OECD Programme for International Student Assessment. Available at http://www.pisa.oecd.org/pages/0,2987, en_32252351_32235731_1_1_1_1_1,00.html

Pearn, J.H. (1984) 'The child and clinical research', *The Lancet*, 2(8401): 510–12.

Plewis, I., Creeser, A. and Mooney, R. (1990) 'Reliability and validity of time budget data: Children's activities outside school', *Journal of Official Statistics*, 6(4): 411–19.

Punch, S. (2002) 'Research with children the same or different from research with adults?', *Childhood*, 9(3): 321–41.

Qvortrup, J. (1994) 'Childhood matters: An introduction', in J. Qvortrup, M. Brady, G. Sgritta and H. Wintersberger (eds.), *Childhood Matters: Social Theory, Practice and Politics*. Vienna: Avebury, pp. 4–14.

Qvortrup, J. (1999) 'The meaning of child's standard of living', in A.B. Andrews and N. H. Kaufman (eds.), *Implementing the U.N. Convention on the Rights of the Child: A Standard of Living Adequate for Development*. Westport, CT: Prager.

Reijntjes, A., Stegge, H., Terwogt, M.M. and Hurkens, E. (2007) 'Children's depressive symptoms and their regulation of negative affect in response to vignette depicted emotion-eliciting events', *International Journal of Behavioral Development*, 31(1): 49–58.

Ronen, G.M., Streiner, D.L. and Rosenbaum, P. (2003) 'Health-related quality of life in children with epilepsy: Development and validation of self-report and parent proxy measures', *Epilepsia*, 44(4): 598–612.

Sanik, M.M. and Stattford, K. (1996) 'Children's time in household work: Estimation issues', *Journal of Family and Economic Issues*, 17(3–4): 313–25.

Stephenson, A. (2009) 'Horses in the sandpit: Photography, prolonged involvement and "stepping back" as strategies for listening to children's voices', *Early Child Development and Care*, 179(2): 131–41.

Stritzke, W.G., Dandy, J., Durkin, K. and Houghton, S. (2005) 'Use of interactive voice response (IVR) technology in health research with children', *Behavior Research Methods*, 37(1): 119–26.

Swedish Institute for Social Research (2010) Swedish Level-of-Living Survey, LNU2000. Available at http://www.sofi.su.se/pub/jsp/polopoly.jsp?d=9324&a=35617

Tetnowski, J.A. and Franklin, T.C. (2003) 'Qualitative research: Implications for description and assessment', *American Journal of Speech-Language Pathology*, 12(2): 155–64.

Thomas, N. and O'Kane, C. (1998) 'The ethics of participatory research with children', *Children and Society*, 12(5): 336–48.

Unguru, Y., Sill, A. M. and Kamani, N. (2010) 'The experiences of children enrolled in pediatric oncology research: Implications for assent', *Pediatrics*, 125(4): e876–e883.

Verma, S., Kaur, S., and Saraswathi, T.S. (1995) 'Measuring time use by university students', *The Indian Journal of Social Science*, 8(1): 79–89.

Walden, T.A., Harris, V.S. and Catron, T.F. (2003) 'How I feel: A self-report measure of emotional arousal and regulation for children', *Psychological Assessment*, 15(3): 399–412.

Ybarra, M.L. and Mitchell, K.J. (2004) 'Online aggressor/targets, aggressors, and targets: A comparison of associated youth characteristics', *Journal of Child Psychology and Psychiatry*, 45(7): 1308–16.

29

Infants and Young Children as Sources of Information about Their Own Lives: Methodology and Findings

Harlene Hayne and Karen Tustin

INFANTS AND YOUNG CHILDREN AS SOURCES OF INFORMATION ABOUT THEIR OWN LIVES

The ability to share the past with others is a uniquely human ability. To the best of our knowledge, no other species recounts the past. As humans, we share information about things that happened to us days, years, and sometimes decades earlier. We tell stories about our lives in an attempt to educate and entertain and to let the important people in our lives learn something about who we are. We also use the record of our past to gain clues about what might happen in the future or how we should behave in a new situation. As adults, we share literally dozens of stories about ourselves with people we encounter each day – we recount the past to our colleagues, to our family, and to our friends. In the context of the courtroom or the clinic, stories about our past yield information that is sometimes vital to achieving justice or psychological well-being. In the context of the workplace, stories about the past help shape new policies or practices.

What about young children? When do they first begin to record information about their own experiences and when do they begin to share that information with others? How do these abilities change as a function of age and experience? With these questions in mind, the overarching goal of this chapter is two-fold: (1) we will describe some of the experimental techniques that have been used to measure very young children's ability to provide information about their past, and (2) we will summarize some of the key experimental findings in this area, highlighting children's strengths and weaknesses as sources of information about their personal experiences. In this chapter, we will focus primarily on children's ability to remember and recount their *past* experiences, but we recognize that in some instances, children may also be required to describe their potential *future* experiences as well (Hayne, 2007a; Hayne et al., 2011; Hayne and Imuta, 2011).

Nonverbal measures of memory

When we assess the ability of older children and adults to provide information about the past, the primary dependent variable is almost always verbal in nature. That is, we ask participants questions about events from the past (such as 'What happened on your last vacation?' or 'What did you learn in school today?'). In response to these questions, participants provide us with a verbal description of what they remember (for example, 'We spent time with the kids on the beach,' or 'We had a test in English'). In an attempt to gain information about the past, we can also ask older children and adults to complete questionnaires by writing short answers or ticking boxes to tell us something about their past (for example, 'In the last month, how many times have you had a fight with a family member? Smoked a cigarette?'). But even under these test conditions, we are reliant upon the participant's ability to use language as the primary source of information about their own lives. In contrast to this reliance on language, if we want to study the ability of preverbal participants to record or recall the past, we must build nonverbal questions into our experimental procedure and develop behavioural means through which participants can answer us – indicating that they do or do not remember something that they experienced in the past.

Operant conditioning paradigms

Over the past four decades, operant conditioning paradigms have frequently been used as a nonverbal measure of memory during the infancy period. For example, Rovee-Collier and her colleagues (Rovee and Rovee, 1969; for reviews, see Hayne, 2004; Rovee-Collier, 1997; Rovee-Collier and Hayne, 1987) have developed two widely-used operant procedures to study the development of learning and memory in infants and very young children. One procedure, the mobile conjugate reinforcement paradigm, is typically used with 2- to 6-month-old infants. In the mobile

conjugate reinforcement paradigm, infants are placed in a crib beneath an overhead mobile that is suspended from a flexible metal stand. The infant's ankle is attached to the mobile via a piece of ribbon. In this way, the mobile moves each time the infant kicks her leg and the degree of mobile movement is directly proportional to the rate and vigour of kicking.

In the standard mobile conjugate reinforcement paradigm, each infant typically participates in two training sessions. At the start of the first training session, there is a brief period of nonreinforcement during which the ankle ribbon is secured to a second, empty mobile stand that is positioned directly across from the stand supporting the mobile. In this arrangement, the infant can see the mobile and can feel the pressure of the ribbon pulling against the mobile stand each time she kicks, but kicking is ineffective in making the mobile move. This initial period of nonreinforcement provides the opportunity to measure the infant's baseline kick rate prior to the introduction of the contingency. At the completion of this baseline phase, the ribbon is then secured to the stand supporting the mobile and infants quickly learn that kicking produces mobile movement. At the end of the second training session, there is a final period of nonreinforcement, which provides the opportunity to measure what the infant has learned.

Infants' memory of the mobile task is tested after delays ranging from days to weeks. During the test, the infant is once again placed beneath the mobile, but the ribbon is attached to the empty mobile stand (nonreinforcement period). In essence, this test procedure provides the opportunity to 'ask' the infant whether she remembers what to do to make the mobile move. If the infant's kick rate during the test exceeds her baseline kick rate, we infer that she has remembered the contingency; if her kick rate does not exceed baseline, we infer that she has forgotten. Following two standard training sessions, 2-month-old infants typically exhibit excellent memory for up to 24 hours and 6-month-old infants remember for up to two weeks.

A second operant conditioning procedure has also been used to assess memory in older infants (Hartshorn and Rovee-Collier, 1997; Hartshorn et al., 1998a, 1998b). In this task, 6- to 18-month-old infants learn to operate a miniature train by pressing a lever. As in the mobile conjugate reinforcement paradigm, infants typically experience two training sessions; the nonreinforcement phase at the beginning of the first training session constitutes the baseline phase, and the nonreinforcement phase at the end of the second training session constitutes a measure of acquisition. Following a delay ranging from a few days to a few weeks, infants are tested during another period of nonreinforcement. Again, the question is, does the infant remember what to do to make the train move? Consistent with data collected using the mobile conjugate reinforcement paradigm, the duration of retention in the train task increases as a function of age. Six-month-old infants typically remember the task for two weeks and 18-month-old infants remember for up to thirteen weeks.

On the basis of studies conducted using these two paradigms, researchers have learned a considerable amount about age-related differences in infants' ability to record and recall information about their past experiences. For example, the maximum delay after which infants remember the tasks increases dramatically as a function of age. In fact, when the data from the mobile conjugate reinforcement paradigm and the train paradigm are combined, there is a linear increase in retention between 2 and 18 months of age (Hartshorn et al., 1998a). Research with these operant paradigms has also shown that retrieval of the training memory is highly specific to the conditions of original encoding, particularly during early infancy. For example, when 2- to 9-month-olds are trained with a particular mobile or a particular train, they exhibit no retention whatsoever if they are tested with a different mobile or

a different train. As infants mature and gain more experience, however, they are able to retrieve the memory when they are confronted with a similar, but not identical, test stimulus (Hartshorn et al., 1998b). In the train task, for example, 12-month-old infants exhibit the same level of retention irrespective of whether they are tested with the same train or a different one. In short, memory retrieval becomes increasingly more flexible across the infancy period, allowing infants to access their prior experiences in a wider range of situations.

Finally, research conducted with operant conditioning paradigms has also shown that despite substantial forgetting, infants' memory of their prior experience can be restored through the presentation of a reminder treatment. In fact, a very brief exposure to the mobile (Hill, Borovsky and Rovee-Collier, 1988; Rovee-Collier, Sullivan, Enright, Lucas and Fagen, 1987), the train (Hartshorn and Rovee-Collier, 1997), or to the experimental context (Hayne and Findlay, 1995; Rovee-Collier, Griesler and Earley, 1985) is sufficient to alleviate forgetting. In one of the most impressive demonstrations of the reminder phenomenon to date, Hartshorn (2003) trained 6-month-old infants in the operant train paradigm. Infants initially received two eight-minute training sessions and a series of brief reminder treatments 1, 2, 3, 6, and 12 months later. The infants were then tested six months after the final reminder treatment when they were now 2 years old. During this test, infants exhibited excellent retention. Control groups who received only the original training without the interpolated reminder treatments or who received the reminder treatments without original training exhibited no retention whatsoever. Taken together, studies conducted using reminder paradigms clearly indicate that infant memory is robust and long-lasting. On the basis of data like those reported by Hartshorn (2003), we conclude that infants have the capacity to retain information about their early experiences over very long periods of time. Whether they actually do so and how those memories are subsequently expressed is an issue we will return to later in this chapter.

Deferred imitation

The mobile conjugate reinforcement paradigm and train tasks are excellent ways to study the early emergence of long-term memory. The results of these studies clearly show that infants' ability to retain information about simple events in their lives emerges early in development. Furthermore, their ability to retain that information increases dramatically as a function of age and experience. Although the mobile and train tasks are ideally suited for research with 2- to 18-month-old infants, age-related changes in interest and motivation makes them less effective with older infants. For this reason, researchers interested in memory processing by toddlers and young children have turned to briefer, but more complex, experimental tasks. Because the linguistic abilities of toddlers are still extremely limited, the most effective tasks for this age group still require little or no linguistic skill.

Deferred imitation is one nonverbal task that is often used to study memory in infants and very young children. Imitation is a common way in which infants learn new behaviours in the course of their daily lives (Barr and Hayne, 1999; Piaget, 1962), and it has become a popular method to assess learning and memory under more highly-controlled, laboratory conditions (Barr, Dowden and Hayne, 1996; Collie and Hayne, 1999; Hayne, Boniface and Barr, 2000; Meltzoff and Moore, 1994, 1998). Typically, an adult performs a series of actions and the infant is given the opportunity to reproduce those actions after a delay. In a true deferred imitation paradigm, the infant is not given the opportunity to practice the actions and must rely solely on his or her mental representation of the prior demonstration to reproduce the target actions during the test. Furthermore, deferred imitation does not require language comprehension or production on the part of the participant, making it ideally suited for preverbal and early-verbal participants.

Research conducted using the deferred imitation paradigm has confirmed many of the basic findings originally reported for younger participants tested in the mobile conjugate reinforcement and train paradigms. For example, in the deferred imitation task, older participants learn faster, remember longer, and retrieve their prior experiences in a wider range of situations than do younger participants (for review, see Hayne, 2004). Furthermore, despite substantial forgetting, retention in the deferred imitation task can be restored through the presentation of a reminder (Barr, Rovee-Collier and Campanella, 2005). The similarity of the findings obtained with the deferred imitation and operant conditioning paradigms suggest that these age-related changes in memory skill are universal (for review, see Hayne, 2004). Although the absolute duration of retention or the nature of effective retrieval cues may vary as a function of some of the original encoding parameters in a particular task, the overall pattern of findings across tasks is remarkably similar. Given this, the results of research with both kinds of tasks should be considered in concert as we draw conclusions about memory development over the first two years of life.

Verbal measures of memory

Up to this point, we have considered tasks that allow us to assess memory by preverbal participants. But what happens as children begin to talk? When do they first begin to express their memories through language and how does this skill change during the preschool period? Can children report the events of their infancy once they have developed the language skills necessary to do so?

Magic shrinking machine

In an initial attempt to blend the nonverbal procedures commonly used with infants with the verbal procedures commonly used with older children, Simcock and Hayne (2002, 2003) developed the magic shrinking machine to study memory in preschool-age children. In this task, 2- to 4-year-old children learn to perform a series of actions with a machine that is designed to make large objects smaller. After delays ranging from one day to one year, children's verbal and nonverbal recall of the event is assessed. During the verbal portion of the test, children are asked to describe what happened during the event; during the nonverbal portion of the test, they are asked to identify photographs of the objects that had been present and to reproduce the actions that are required to operate the machine. Children's receptive and productive language skills are also measured at the time of the original event and again at the time of the test.

Studies conducted using the magic shrinking machine have yielded four important findings about young children's ability to recall their past experiences. First, the magic shrinking machine event is interesting and entertaining for 2- to 4-year-olds and they are motivated to remember it over long delays. Children in this age range exhibit excellent nonverbal memory for the event when they are tested after delays ranging from one day to one year (Simcock and Hayne, 2002, 2003). Second, there is a dramatic age-related increase in the content of children's verbal reports. Between 2 and 4 years of age, children's verbal recall of the task increases by a factor of eight. Third, children's verbal recall lags behind their general language skill. For example, Simcock and Hayne (2003) compared the amount of verbal information that child reported during the 24-hour interview to the amount of information that he or she could have reported based on his or her productive language skill. Across all ages, children reported 10–30 per cent of what they could have reported about the task based on their concurrent language skills. When the retention interval was increased to six months or one year, this percentage dropped even lower. Taken together, these findings suggest that, although verbal recall increases as language skill increases, children's ability to use their emerging language skills in the service of memory is inferior to

their ability to use that same language to describe events in the here and now.

Finally, studies conducted with the magic shrinking machine have also shown that children find it difficult, if not impossible, to translate their prior, preverbal memories into language after a delay. That is, although children's language skill improved dramatically over long retention intervals that were used in the Simcock and Hayne (2002) study (at 6 or 12 months), their verbal report about the magic shrinking machine after these long retention intervals contained only event-relevant words that were part of their vocabulary at the time of the original event. In no instance did a child use a word or words to describe the event that were not part of his/her productive vocabulary at the time of encoding. Thus, even though children's language skill had improved over the delay, they did not map their new language skills onto their existing memory representation of the event.

Despite a number of anecdotal claims that people can verbally recall events from their infancy and early childhood (for review, see Hayne, 2007b), the Simcock and Hayne study suggests that this feat may be difficult if not impossible (see also Peterson and Rideout, 1998). Subsequent research by Morris and Baker-Ward (2007), however, has shown that, under some highly-constrained conditions, children may be able to map new words on to an existing, preverbal memory representation. In their study, 2-year-olds were shown how to operate a bubble-making machine. For each child, the machine would only operate if a particular colour of bubble mixture was added to it. Some children knew the verbal label for the relevant colour at the time of the original event, and some children did not. During the two-month retention interval between the original event and the test, children were taught the names of the colours during weekly colour training sessions that took place in their preschool. At the time of the test, some of the children who originally did not know the name of the relevant colour had acquired the relevant colour label. The key question was whether any of these children would be able to use this new colour label during the verbal recall phase of the memory test. Morris and Baker-Ward (2007) found that of the children who had learned the name of the relevant colour during the retention interval, approximately 25 per cent of them used that colour label during the verbal phase of the memory interview.

Taken together, what do the findings reported by Morris and Baker-Ward (2007) and Simcock and Hayne (2002) tell us about the fate of preverbal memory? The results of the Simcock and Hayne study clearly show that children can maintain a nonverbal representation of an event over a very long delay, but what about their ability to 'talk' about it? When children are tested after very long delays in the absence of strong contextual support as in Simcock and Hayne, they fail to apply their emerging vocabulary to preverbal aspects of an earlier memory (see also Peterson and Rideout, 1998). When children are tested after shorter delays in the presence of strong contextual support as in Morris and Baker-Ward (2007), on the other hand, they do exhibit some limited ability to map a new word onto an existing memory representation. As acknowledged by Morris and Barker-Ward, however, this ability is extremely 'fragile.' Despite the simplicity of their task and the high level of contextual support that was provided during the test, only a handful of children succeeded in mapping a single word on to their existing preverbal representation of the target event.

It is also important to note that none of the children in the Morris and Baker-Ward or Simcock and Hayne studies could technically be described as preverbal; all of the participants in these two studies had at least some productive language skill at the time of the target event. Whether children (or adults) would ever be able to provide a rich, coherent verbal account of an event that took place prior to any language acquisition has yet to be determined. In our view, the best chance of documenting this kind of phenomenon

might be to examine children's verbal recall of the operant train task following a series of reminder treatments like those used in the Hartshorn (2003) study. Recall that in her procedure, participants took part in the event at the age of six months and were subsequently tested at the age of two years. Given the high level of nonverbal recall that toddlers exhibit of a memory that was originally established during their infancy, it is possible that they may also have some verbal access to this representation. This possibility remains to be tested.

New train task

The magic shrinking machine task described above afforded an excellent opportunity to study verbal and non-verbal memory in very young children, but the 'magical' nature of the task may have made it difficult for the youngest participants to understand the event, which in turn, may have obscured their ability to talk about it, particularly after a delay. Therefore, the next step in the evolution of our research programme was to develop another task that could be used to examine memory development in young children. Our goal in developing this new task was to take a step back, selecting a task that is typically used with infants, and upgrading that task for use with young children. To do this, we modified the operant train procedure originally developed by Rovee-Collier and her colleagues in their work with 6- to 18-month-old infants described above. Recall that in the train task, infants learn to operate a miniature train by pressing a lever (see Figure 29.1, left panel). In our version of the train task, children also learn to operate a miniature train by pressing a lever, but the train apparatus is substantially more complex (see Figure 29.1, right panel). The train occupies an entire room and unexpected events occur as the train passes mountains, bridges, a carousel, etc. Children's verbal and nonverbal recall of the event is assessed after a delay.

Recall that young children tested with the magic shrinking machine provide very lean

Figure 29.1 Rovee-Collier's original train set for use with infants (left) and the modified train set for use with children (right)

verbal reports of their experience of the event. What about the train task? Given that the nature of the task is more simplistic, would children report more about it during a verbal interview? To address these questions, we assessed 3-year-old children's verbal reports about the train task after a 24-hour delay and compared the amount of information they reported with that reported by the 3-year-olds in the Simcock and Hayne (2003) study who were interviewed about the magic shrinking machine after the same delay. As shown in Figure 29.2, we found that the children who took part in the train event reported more than four times the information than did children who took part in the magic shrinking machine event. Thus, the nature of the target experience clearly influences our estimates of children's verbal memory skill. We are currently using the train task to assess children's memory over longer delays.

Personal, real-life experiences
Another way to examine children's memory development is to assess their ability to recount their memories for their own real-life experiences. In these studies, children are asked to describe past events that they nominate or that have been nominated by a parent. This line of research originated with the seminal work of Katherine Nelson and her students, but it has been perpetuated and expanded by a host of other researchers.

Taken together, this large body of work has yielded two consistent findings. First, several studies have shown that parents exhibit different narrative styles when discussing past events with their children. Two distinct styles have been identified; one referred to as elaborative, high elaborative, topic-extending, or reminiscent and the other referred to as low elaborative, repetitive, topic-switching, or practical (for reviews see Farrant and Reese, 2000; Fivush and Reese, 2002; Nelson and Fivush, 2004; Reese, 2002). The narratives of parents who exhibit a high elaborative style are characterized by long and richly detailed descriptions of past events. In contrast, the narratives of parents who exhibit a low elaborative style are often very short; these low-elaborative parents provide few details and often repeat questions over and over in an attempt to elicit the correct response from their child. Although all parents exhibit aspects of both styles, they tend to use one style over the other (Fivush and Reese, 1992).

The second important finding that has emerged from research on adult–child conversations about the past is that a parent's narrative style influences the child's ability to talk about the past (Cleveland and Reese, 2005; Farrant and Reese, 2000; Fivush and Fromhoff, 1988; Hudson, 1990; McCabe and Peterson, 1991; Nelson and Fivush, 2004; Peterson and McCabe, 1994; Reese and Fivush, 1993). Fivush and Fromhoff (1988),

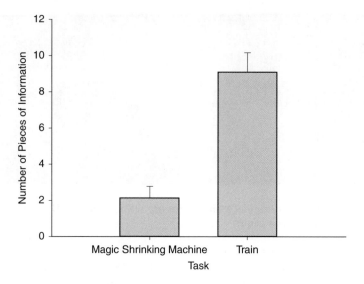

Figure 29.2   The amount of information reported by 3-year-old children about the magic shrinking machine event and the train event after a 24-hour delay

for example, found that 2-year old children of elaborative mothers reported more information when discussing past events than did children of repetitive mothers. Similarly, Hudson (1990) found that the way in which mothers talked to their 2-year-old children about the past affected their children's subsequent memory abilities assessed both with their mother and with an experimenter. In Hudson's study, children of high-elaborative mothers not only recalled more total information, but they also provided more specific information about each event than did children of low-elaborative mothers. Some investigators have also reported long-term effects of parental style on children's past-event narratives. For example, McCabe and Peterson (1991) found that children whose parents used a topic-extending style (similar to the high-elaborative style described above) when the child was 2 years of age provided longer, more well-developed accounts of personally-experienced events when recounting the past one and a half years later. In contrast, a topic-switching maternal style (similar to the low-elaborative style described above) was related to shorter past event narratives at the later age.

Initial research on the relation between adult–child conversations about the past and children's memory development focused primarily on influences from adult to child (especially those from mother to child). That is, individual differences in children's memory-related contributions to conversations about the past were considered within the context of their mother's narrative style (Fivush and Fromhoff, 1988; Hudson, 1990). Additionally, however, some researchers have begun to consider the influence that a child might have on the narrative style adopted by his or her mother (Harley and Reese, 1999; McCabe and Peterson, 1991; Reese and Fivush, 1993; Reese, Haden and Fivush, 1993). One factor that has been shown to influence parental narrative style is a child's gender. Reese and Fivush (1993), for example, found that both mothers and fathers of girls were significantly more elaborative than were mothers and fathers of boys. This stylistic difference in parents' conversations with girls and boys was not due to gender differences in the children's language ability; the MLUs (mean length of utterance in words) of the boys and girls did not differ. Reese and Fivush proposed that parents place more emphasis on the value of reminiscing with their daughters than with their sons. As such, parents alter their own narrative style according to the gender of their child.

It has also been shown that parental narrative style is influenced by the child's ability to participate in memory conversations in the first place. McCabe and Peterson (1991), for example, found evidence for a bidirectional relation between parental narrative style and children's contributions to conversations about the past early in development. In their study, McCabe and Peterson recorded conversations between mothers and their children when the children were 27 and 31 months of age. A number of maternal conversational variables (such as open-ended questions, topic introduction) at 27 months were correlated with children's memory responding (for example, provision of orienting information, clauses per narrative) at 31 months. In addition, certain aspects of children's conversational behaviour (including clauses per narrative, evaluations) at 27 months were correlated with mothers' conversational behaviour (such as open-ended questions, statements introducing new topics, clarifying questions) at 31 months. Furthermore, Reese et al. (1993) found direct long-term child-to-mother relations between parental narrative style and children's contributions to conversations about the past. In their study, there was a significant correlation between children's memory responses at 58 months and maternal elaborations at 70 months. Taken together, the results of McCabe and Peterson (1991) and Reese et al. (1993) suggest that not only are children's memory conversations influenced by their parents' narrative style, but that parents may also adapt their style in response to their child's level of skill or interest.

In all of the studies described above, parents were simply asked to talk about the past with their children, and the experimenters assessed the typical style that each parent adopted. In a move away from this correlational design, some researchers have experimentally manipulated parents' narrative style

and then examined the impact on children's emerging ability to talk about the past. In one of the first experiments of this kind, Peterson, Jesso, and McCabe (1999) gave some low-income mothers specific instruction on how to use a highly elaborative narrative style. The intervention began when the children of these mothers were 3 years old and the children's narrative skills were then assessed two years later. Peterson et al. found that children whose mothers had been taught to use the elaborative style told more complex narratives than did children whose mothers were not taught to use the style (see also Reese and Newcombe, 2007).

In another experimental study of maternal narrative style, McGuigan and Salmon (2004) had mothers and their 3- or 5-year-old children take part in a staged event, a pretend visit to the zoo. The mothers of the children were instructed to use an elaborative narrative style in discussions with their child before, during, or after the staged event. All of the children were then interviewed by an experimenter. McGuigan and Salmon found that elaborative conversations about the event after the event occurred increased the amount of information that children reported more than elaborative talk that occurred prior to or during the event, particularly for the 5-year-old group. This study highlights the importance of past event conversations for children's subsequent recall. Taken together, research of this kind has clearly shown that the way in which parents discuss the past with their preschool-age children has a significant effect on children's ability to recall the past both in the context of their families and in the context of interviews with more unfamiliar conversational partners.

Although the basic mechanisms of memory processing (for example, encoding, retention, and retrieval) are universal, the ways in which they unfold during the course of development are affected by the cultural context in which a child grows up. For example, when discussing the past with their preschool-age children, European American mothers use a more elaborative style than do Chinese mothers

(Wang, 2007). Moreover, the content of these conversations also differs across cultures. For example, European American mothers frequently discuss their child's emotions. They not only encourage the child to articulate his or her own feelings, but they also encourage him or her to describe the events that contributed to that particular emotional state. In contrast, Chinese mothers are more likely to use conversations about the past to teach children appropriate rules of conduct. They focus on rule violation and social norms rather than on the child's emotions (Wang, 2008; Wang and Fivush, 2005).

These cross-cultural differences in parent–child conversations about the past during the preschool period are reflected in children's emerging autobiographical memory skills. For example, European American children refer more to their own feelings and emotions than do Chinese children when they are talking about the past (Wang, 2004). Furthermore, European American adults use more emotion-related information than do Chinese adults when they are describing their memory for events that occurred during early childhood (Wang and Conway, 2004). In fact, cross-cultural differences in the nature of parent-child conversations about the past have been linked to cross-cultural differences in the age of adults' earliest personal memories (MacDonald, Uesiliana and Hayne, 2000; Mullen, 1994; Reese, Hayne and MacDonald, 2008).

Time-line procedure

In addition to talking about the past with their parents, children can also be interviewed about their personal past experiences under more formal interview conditions. In our laboratory, we have recently developed a new procedure that we use to ask children (and adults) about events that have occurred in both the recent and the distant past. In this task, each year of the participant's life is marked on a Time-line that includes photographs of the participant at particular ages (see Figure 29.3). We hypothesized that the Time-line might reinforce the notion of a

linear time sequence, particularly for young children, and that it might provide an external cue for thinking about memories from different epochs of the participant's life.

To date, we have used the time-line task to examine 5- to 20-year-olds' memories for their own real-life experiences. This line of research is still in its infancy, but we have completed a number of studies using the time-line procedure. In our first study, we used the time-line task to ask children, adolescents, and adults about their earliest personal memories. Prior research has shown that when adults are asked to recall their earliest personal memories, most recall an event that took place when they were between 3 and 4 years old, a phenomenon referred to as childhood amnesia. This finding has been obtained in a wide range of different experiments using a wide range of different questioning procedures (for review, see Davis, Gross and Hayne, 2008; Jack and Hayne, 2007, 2010). When interviewed using our time-line procedure, we have shown that the average age of adults' earliest memories also falls between the ages of 3 and 4. In contrast, when children and adolescents are interviewed using this procedure, they recall events that occurred substantially earlier in development (Tustin and Hayne, 2010). This finding suggests that the boundary of childhood amnesia might increase across development. These findings underscore the importance of a developmental perspective when examining a phenomenon like childhood amnesia (see also, Gross, Jack, Davis and Hayne, 2013).

In a replication and extension of our original study, we used the time-line task to interview a group of 12- to 13-year-olds about their earliest personal memories (Jack, MacDonald, Reese and Hayne, 2009). These adolescents had taken part in another study in our laboratory in which we recorded conversations about the past between them and their mothers on a number of different occasions when they were 2 to 4 years old. In our time-line study, we found that, consistent with our earlier findings, these young adolescents reported first memories that were substantially

Figure 29.3 Sample time-lines for (clockwise from top left) 5-year-olds, 8- to 9-year-olds, 18- to 20-year-olds, and 12- to 13-year-olds. These photos have been published with the written permission of the participants and their parents.

earlier than those typically reported by adults. In addition, we also found that the age of their earliest memories was related to their mothers' narrative style during early childhood. That is, those adolescents whose mothers exhibited a more elaborative and evaluative style reported earlier memories than did adolescents whose mothers exhibited a more repetitive narrative style. These findings suggest that the individual differences in parent–child conversations about the past that have been documented in prior studies with preschool-age children have a long-term impact on an individual's memories for their personal past at least through adolescence and perhaps even longer.

The data from our time-line studies have some important implications for our current understanding of memory development. For example, Tulving (2002), Suddendorf (Suddendorf and Corballis, 1997), and others

(Perner and Ruffman, 1995) have argued that children under the age of 4 years old do not store information about their past experiences in an autobiographical format. According to their argument, young children do not encode the 'who,' 'what,' 'where,' and 'when' of their experiences that characterize the autobiographical memories of older children and adults. The findings from our time-line study, however, challenge the notion that young children are not capable of forming and retaining autobiographical memories. For example, the 5-year-old children that we interviewed accurately reported the 'who,' 'what,' 'when,' and 'where' components of events that took place even when they were much younger than 4 (see also, Cleveland and Reese, 2008). Similarly, the older children and adolescents also recalled episodic details of events from this period of development. Thus, although the 18- to 20-year-olds reported more total information about their earliest memories than did any of the younger groups, the basic 'who,' 'what,' 'when,' and 'where' content of the reports did not vary as a function of age. It would seem that, at least during childhood, children are able to store and retain some basic autobiographical aspects of their early experiences.

FIELD TRIPS AND STAGED EVENTS

Once children enter preschool, researchers have the opportunity to assess their memory using field trips and staged events. These procedures have been used to examine young children's memories for complex events that are highly controlled and about which the experimenter is omniscient. In studies of this kind, children experience a novel, entertaining, and often educational event, and, some time later, they are asked to report what they can remember about that event. Past studies conducted in our laboratory have included field trips to the chocolate factory (Gross and Hayne, 1999), pony rides (MacDonald and Hayne, 1996), and trips to the fire station (Butler, Gross, and Hayne, 1995). In other studies, researchers have used staged events such as pretend visits to the doctor to treat a sick teddy bear (Salmon, Bidrose, and Pipe, 1995) or classroom activities during which children and the experimenter make pretend pizza (Kulkofsky, Wang and Ceci, 2007) or participate in a magic show (Principe, Guiliano, and Root, 2008; Principe, Kanaya, Ceci, and Singh, 2006). These kinds of experimenter-controlled events are an ideal way to assess both the content and the accuracy of children's descriptions of past events. Without exception, children find these events enjoyable, and they actively participate in the verbal interviews that follow.

Prior research with these kinds of events has yielded a number of consistent conclusions about children's ability to provide information about events in their lives. First, 3- to 5-year-old children typically report less information about a prior event than do older children or adults (Sutherland and Hayne, 2001). Second, despite the fact that their reports are leaner than those provided by older children, when they are interviewed using open-ended, free recall questions, children as young as 3 to 5 years old provide highly accurate reports of their prior experiences, even when they are interviewed after a delay (Butler et al., 1995; Gross and Hayne, 1999). In the Butler et al. study, for example, 3- and 5-year-olds were interviewed about their field trip to the local fire station. Even when they were interviewed after a delay of three months, 3-year-olds provided highly accurate accounts of what they had done and what they had seen during the trip. In similar kinds of studies with 5- to 6-year-olds, children have continued to report a large amount of accurate information when they are interviewed seven months (Gross, Hayne, and Drury, 2009) to one year later (Gross and Hayne, 1999).

Finally, prior research with young children has shown that some interview techniques are clearly better than others. For example, when they are given the opportunity to draw while recounting the past, young children report substantially more information than they do when they are simply asked to tell. In one study by Gross and Hayne (1998), for example, 3- and 5-year-olds were asked to describe past experiences that had made them feel happy, sad, angry, or scared. Children were either asked to tell the interviewer about the experience or they were asked to draw while telling. In both conditions, only the children's verbal report was analysed. Gross and Hayne found that children who were allowed to draw and tell reported more than twice as much information about their experiences than did children who were only asked to tell (see also, Macleod, Gross and Hayne, 2013; Patterson and Hayne, 2011; Woolford et al., 2013). Importantly, drawing had no effect on the accuracy of children's reports. This same basic finding has now been replicated and extended in a number of subsequent studies (Gross et al., 2009; Salmon, Roncolato, and

Gleitzman, 2003; Wesson and Salmon, 2001). A meta-analysis of this literature has indicated that the effect size associated with the drawing technique is large ($d = 0.95$; Driessnack, 2005).

To date, research on drawing has been motivated primarily by clinical and legal concerns, but there is no reason to believe that drawing would not be effective in other situations in which children's voices should be heard. Recently, Gross et al. (2009) used the drawing technique to assess what children learned about a trip to a museum. In that study, 5- and 6-year-olds were taken on a tour of the Royal Albatross Centre at Taiaroa Head (located near Dunedin, New Zealand, where the children lived). During the tour, they were specifically taught a large number of facts about albatrosses. During the interview 1 to 2 days later, some of the children were given the opportunity to draw and tell about the visit and others were only asked to tell. Consistent with prior research using drawing, children who were given the opportunity to draw reported more total information than did children who were not. In addition, children who drew also reported a larger number of facts about the albatross (for example, details of its life cycle) than did children who did not draw. These findings suggest that drawing may be a particularly powerful tool in educational contexts with young children and raise the possibility that drawing might also help children to talk about a wide range of different experiences.

Although drawing augments the content of children's reports without compromising their accuracy, other interview techniques have been shown to be detrimental. When interviewed using open-ended questions, even preschool-age children can provide highly accurate information about their prior experiences, but when they are asked leading or misleading questions or are exposed to incorrect information, these same children are highly likely to make mistakes. For example, although drawing combined with open-ended questions leads to more complete accounts without decreasing accuracy, when drawing is combined with leading and misleading questions, children make a large number of mistakes (Bruck, Melnyk and Ceci, 2000; Gross, Hayne and Poole, 2006; Strange, Garry and Sutherland, 2003).

Unfortunately, the negative effects of inappropriate questioning and misinformation have been shown using a number of different experimental paradigms. In one study, for example, Leichtman and Ceci (1995) interviewed 3- to 6-year-old children about an event during which they were visited by a male stranger – Sam Stone – 10 weeks earlier. Some of the children were read a series of stories about Sam Stone's 'bad behaviour' before they actually met him. In these stories, Sam Stone was portrayed as particularly clumsy. The rest of the children received no information about Sam prior to the visit. During the target event, Sam entered the classroom, said hello to the children and their teacher, commented on the book the teacher was reading and then left the room. Following the visit, some children received incorrect information about Sam's activities. For these children, the interviewer suggested that Sam had torn a book and soiled a teddy bear. During the final interview, children who received both the stereotype induction that Sam was clumsy and the post-event misinformation that he had torn the book and soiled the bear made the largest number of errors; this finding was particularly prominent in the preschool-age group. The finding that young children are highly susceptible to false suggestions and misleading questioning has been replicated numerous times using a wide range of different events and interview techniques (Goodman and Aman, 1991; Goodman and Reed, 1986; Lyon, Malloy, Quas and Talwar, 2008; Poole and Lindsay, 1995, 2001; Quas et al., 2007).

Recent research has shown that young children are not only influenced by false suggestions provided by adults during a formal interview, but they are also susceptible to information that they overhear during the course of more informal conversations. In a particularly clever series of experiments,

Principe, Ceci, and their colleagues have shown that children incorporate information obtained from their classmates into their own reports of a target event, claiming that they have first-hand knowledge of events that they did not witness (Principe and Ceci, 2002; Principe et al., 2006, 2008). For example, in the first study in this series, 3½- to 5-year-olds participated in a staged event in which they dug for artefacts with an archaeologist (Principe and Ceci, 2002). Some children saw the archaeologist damage two critical 'finds' from the dig whereas other children from the same classrooms did not. When they were interviewed after a delay, children who saw the damage take place reported what happened; more importantly, perhaps, so did children from the same classroom who did not witness these target events. Furthermore, the effect was enhanced when children were interviewed using suggestive questioning techniques. These same findings have been replicated and extended in Principe and Ceci's subsequent research (Principe et al., 2006, 2008, 2010). Taken together, this work highlights the importance of source monitoring in children's ability to provide valid information about their past experiences. Young children are highly likely to confuse events that they have seen with events that they have only heard about, and the probability that they will subsequently report this second-hand information is exacerbated when they are interviewed inappropriately.

The accuracy of children's accounts is paramount when they are interviewed in the course of legal proceedings. In the court, it is vital that children provide accurate reports not only of what they remember, but also what they remember on the basis of their own experience, rather than what they may have learned from others. Despite the importance of accuracy and source monitoring in the court, for the vast majority of situations that children (or adults) encounter, monitoring the source of a piece of knowledge is much less important than the knowledge per se. At the end of the day, children can learn that tigers have stripes by seeing a tiger in a zoo, reading about tigers in a book, or by talking to someone else about tigers. They can also learn that tigers are dangerous without actually being bitten. In both social and educational contexts, learning on the basis of other people's experience can be a fast and efficient way to learn, particularly for young children. In fact, co-opting information from others in the course of social interaction begins in early infancy (Barr and Hayne, 2003; Hanna and Meltzoff, 1993), and the range of sources of information that children will exploit increases dramatically during the preschool period (Simcock and DeLoache, 2006; Simcock and Dooley, 2007). In this way, the same memory mechanisms that have been shown to contaminate children's testimony are actually beneficial to children as they learn about the world around them.

CONCLUSION

In this chapter, we have reviewed some of the research on young children's ability to provide information about events that they have experienced in the past. We have argued that although the basic mechanisms required to record and recall the past are universal and emerge very early during the infancy period, there are age-related changes in these memory skills that continue to take place over a prolonged period of development. As a function of both age and experience, children encode information faster, remember it longer, and are able to retrieve it under a wider range of conditions. Although the experiences of infancy clearly leave their mark on both brain and behaviour, children (and adults) have extremely limited ability to express their memories for these experiences in words. We have also argued that parents (and other adults) play an important role in children's ability to recall the past. Parental narrative style appears to influence what and how much children encode and report about their past experiences, and cross-cultural differences in both the style and content of these early conversations have long-lasting effects on autobiographical memory. Under more formal conditions, interviewers can either enhance or impede the accuracy of children's reports by the nature of the questions that they ask. Although research with young children always raises special ethical concerns, the benefits of this research are substantial. For example, data on young children's susceptibility to misinformation, misleading questions, and rumour mongering have highlighted both their strengths and weaknesses in forensic contexts and have raised public awareness about the importance of proper interview techniques (Goodman, Quas and Redlich, 1998).

In conclusion, young children can be a valuable source of information about their own lives, but they are also highly dependent upon the scaffold that adults provide for them. Although we have focused primarily on children's ability to recall and recount the past in clinical, legal, and educational contexts, the same basic principles undoubtedly apply when children are asked to recall a wide range of different experiences. Furthermore, what children remember about their past undoubtedly influences other aspects of their development and will ultimately shape their views about the important people and events in their lives. In this way, memory provides the springboard for children's cognitive, social, moral, and emotional development.

ACKNOWLEDGEMENTS

Funding for some of the research reported in this chapter was provided by a Marsden grant from the "Royal Society of Zealand" to Harlene Hayne.

REFERENCES

Barr, R., Dowden, A. and Hayne, H. (1996) 'Developmental changes in deferred imitation by 6- to 24-month-old infants', *Infant Behavior and Development*, 19(2): 159–70.

Barr, R. and Hayne, H. (1999) 'Developmental changes in imitation from television during infancy', *Child Development*, 70(5): 1067–81.

Barr, R. and Hayne, H. (2003) 'It's not what you know, it's who you know: Older siblings facilitate imitation during infancy', *International Journal of Early Years Education*, 11(1): 7–21.

Barr, R., Rovee-Collier, C. and Campanella, J. (2005) 'Retrieval protracts deferred imitation by 6-month-olds', *Infancy*, 7(3): 263–83.

Bruck, M., Melnyk, L. and Ceci, S.J. (2000) 'Draw it again Sam: The effect of drawing on children's suggestibility and source monitoring ability', *Journal of Experimental Child Psychology*, 77(3): 169–96.

Butler, S., Gross, J. and Hayne, H. (1995) 'The effect of drawing on memory performance in young children', *Developmental Psychology*, 31(4): 597–608.

Cleveland, E.S. and Reese, E. (2005) 'Maternal structure and autonomy support in conversations about the past: Contributions to children's autobiographical memory', *Developmental Psychology*, 41(2): 376–88.

Cleveland, E.S. and Reese, E. (2008) 'Children remember early childhood: Long-term recall across the offset of childhood amnesia', *Applied Cognitive Psychology*, 22(1): 127–42.

Collie, R. and Hayne, H. (1999) 'Deferred imitation by 6- and 9-month-old infants: More evidence for declarative memory', *Developmental Psychobiology*, 35(2): 83–90.

Davis, N., Gross, J. and Hayne, H. (2008) 'Defining the boundary of childhood amnesia', *Memory*, 16(5): 465–74.

Driessnack, M. (2005) 'Children's drawings as facilitators of communication: A meta-analysis', *Journal of Pediatric Nursing*, 20(6): 415–23.

Farrant, K. and Reese, E. (2000) 'Maternal style and children's participation in reminiscing: Stepping stones in children's autobiographical memory development', *Journal of Cognition and Development*, 1(2): 193–225.

Fivush, R. and Fromhoff, F. (1988) 'Style and structure in mother-child conversations about the past', *Discourse Processes*, 11(3): 337–55.

Fivush, R. and Reese, E. (1992) 'The social construction of autobiographical memory', in M.A. Conway, D.C. Rubin, H. Spinnler and W.A. Wagenaar (eds.), *Theoretical Perspectives on Autobiographical Memory*. The Netherlands: Kluwer, pp. 115–32.

Fivush, R. and Reese, E. (2002) 'Reminiscing and relating: The development of parent-child talk about the past', in J.D. Webster and B.K. Haight (eds.), *Critical Advances in Reminiscence Work: From Theory to Application*. New York: Springer, pp. 109–22.

Goodman, G.S. and Aman, C.J. (1991) 'Children's use of anatomically detailed dolls to recount an event', *Child Development*, 61(6): 1859–71.

Goodman, G.S., Quas, J.A. and Redlich, A.D. (1998) 'The ethics of conducting "false memory" research with children: A reply to Herrmann and Yoder', *Applied Cognitive Psychology*, 12(3): 207–17.

Goodman, G.S. and Reed, R.S. (1986) 'Age differences in eyewitness testimony', *Law and Human Behavior*, 10(4): 317–32.

Gross, J. and Hayne, H. (1998) 'Drawing facilitates children's verbal reports of emotionally laden events', *Journal of Experimental Psychology: Applied*, 4(2): 163–79.

Gross, J. and Hayne, H. (1999) 'Drawing facilitates children's verbal reports after long delays', *Journal of Experimental Psychology: Applied*, 5(3): 265–83.

Gross, J., Hayne, H. and Drury, T. (2009) 'Drawing facilitates children's reports of factual and narrative information: Implications for educational contexts', *Applied Cognitive Psychology*, 23(7): 953–71.

Gross, J., Hayne, H. and Poole, A. (2006) 'The use of drawing in interviews with children: A potential pitfall', in J.R. Marrow (ed.), *Focus on Child Psychology Research*. New York: Nova Publishers, pp. 119–44.

Gross, J., Jack, F., Davis, N. and Hayne, H. (2013) 'Do children remember the birth of a sibling? Implications for the study of childhood amnesia', *Memory*, 21: 336–46.

Hanna, E. and Meltzoff, A.N. (1993) 'Peer imitation by toddlers in laboratory, home, and day-care contexts: Implications for social learning and memory', *Developmental Psychology*, 29(4): 701–10.

Harley, K. and Reese, E. (1999) 'Origins of autobiographical memory', *Developmental Psychology*, 35(5): 1338–48.

Hartshorn, K. (2003) 'Reinstatement maintains a memory in human infants for 1 1/2 years', *Developmental Psychobiology*, 42(3): 269–82.

Hartshorn, K. and Rovee-Collier, C. (1997) 'Infant learning and long-term memory at 6 months: A confirming analysis', *Developmental Psychobiology*, 30(1): 71–85.

Hartshorn, K., Rovee-Collier, C., Gerhardstein, P.C., Bhatt, R.S., Wondoloski, T.L., Klein, P., Gilch, J., Wurtzel, N. and Campos-de-Carvalho, M. (1998a) 'Ontogeny of long-term memory over the first year-and-a-half of life', *Developmental Psychobiology*, 32(2): 69–89.

Hartshorn, K., Rovee-Collier, C., Gerhardstein, P.C., Bhatt, R.S., Klein, P.J., Aaron, F., Wondoloski, T.L. and Wurtzel, N. (1998b) 'Developmental changes in the specificity of memory over the first year of life', *Developmental Psychobiology*, 33(1): 61–78.

Hayne, H. (2004) 'Infant memory development: Implications for childhood amnesia', *Developmental Review*, 24(1): 33–73.

Hayne, H. (2007a) 'Infant memory development: New questions, new answers', in L. Oakes and P. Bauer (eds.), *Short- and Long-term Memory in Infancy and Early Childhood: Taking the First Steps Toward Remembering*. New York: Oxford University Press, pp. 209–39.

Hayne, H. (2007b) 'Verbal recall of preverbal memories: Implications for the clinic and the courtroom', in M. Garry and H. Hayne (eds.), *Do Justice and Let the Sky Fall: Elizabeth Loftus and Her Contributions to Science, Law, and Academic Freedom*. Mahwah, NJ: Erlbaum, pp. 79–103.

Hayne, H., Boniface, J. and Barr, R. (2000) 'The development of declarative memory in human infants: Age-related changes in deferred imitation', *Behavioral Neuroscience*, 114(1): 77–83.

Hayne, H. and Findlay, N. (1995) 'Contextual control of memory retrieval in infancy: Evidence for associative priming', *Infant Behavior and Development*, 18(2): 195–207.

Hayne, H., Gross, J., McNamee, S., Fitzgibbon, O. and Tustin, K. (2011) 'Episodic memory and episodic foresight in 3- and 5-year-old children', *Cognitive Development*, 26: 343–55.

Hayne, H. and Imuta, K. (2011) 'Episodic memory in 3- and 4-year-old children', *Developmental Psychobiology*, 53: 317–22.

Hill, W.L., Borovsky, D. and Rovee-Collier, C. (1988) 'Continuities in infant memory development', *Developmental Psychobiology*, 21(1): 43–62.

Hudson, J.A. (1990) 'The emergence of autobiographical memory in mother-child conversation', in R. Fivush and J.A. Hudson (eds.), *Knowing and Remembering in Young Children*. New York: Cambridge University Press, pp. 166–96.

Jack, F. and Hayne, H. (2007) 'Eliciting adults' earliest memories: Does it matter how we ask the question?', *Memory*, 15(6): 647–63.

Jack, F. and Hayne, H. (2010) 'Childhood amnesia: Empirical evidence for a two-stage phenomenon', *Memory*, 18: 831–44.

Jack, F., MacDonald, S., Reese, E. and Hayne, H. (2009) 'Maternal reminiscing style during early childhood predicts the age of adolescents' earliest memories', *Child Development*, 80(2): 496–50.

Kulkofsky, S., Wang, Q. and Ceci, S.J. (2007) 'Do better stories make better memories? Narrative quality and memory accuracy in preschool children', *Applied Cognitive Psychology*, 22(1): 21–38.

Leichtman, M.D. and Ceci, S.J. (1995) 'The effects of stereotypes and suggestions on preschoolers' reports', *Developmental Psychology*, 31(4): 568–78.

Lyon, T.D., Malloy, L.C., Quas, J.A. and Talwar, V.A. (2008) 'Coaching, truth induction, and young maltreated children's false allegations and false denials', *Child Development*, 79(4): 914–29.

MacDonald, S. and Hayne, H. (1996) 'Child-initiated conversations about the past and memory performance by preschoolers', *Cognitive Development*, 11(3): 421–42.

MacDonald, S., Uesiliana, K. and Hayne, H. (2000) 'Cross-cultural and gender differences in childhood amnesia', *Memory*, 8(6): 365–76.

Macleod, E., Gross, J. and Hayne, H. (in press) 'The clinical and forensic value of information that children report while drawing', *Applied Cognitive Psychology*.

Macleod, E., Gross, J. and Hayne, H. (2013) 'The clinical and forensic value of information that children report while drawing,' *Applied Cognitive Psychology*. Advance online publication. doi: 10.1002/acp.2936

McCabe, A. and Peterson, C. (1991) 'Getting the story: A longitudinal study of parental styles in eliciting narratives and developing narrative skill', in A. McCabe and C. Peterson (eds.), *Developing Narrative Structure*. Hillsdale, NJ: Erlbaum, pp. 217–53.

McGuigan, F. and Salmon, K. (2004) 'The time to talk: The influence of the timing of adult-child talk on children's event memory', *Child Development*, 75(3): 669–86.

Meltzoff, A.N. and Moore, M.K. (1994) 'Imitation, memory, and the representation of persons', *Infant Behavior and Development*, 17(1): 83–99.

Meltzoff, A.N. and Moore, M.K. (1998) 'Object representation, identity, and the paradox of early permanence: Steps toward a new framework', *Infant Behavior and Development*, 21(2): 201–35.

Morris, G. and Baker-Ward, L. (2007) 'Fragile but real: Children's capacity to use newly acquired words to convey preverbal memories', *Child Development*, 78(2): 448–58.

Mullen, M.K. (1994) 'Earliest recollections of childhood: A demographic analysis', *Cognition*, 52(1): 55–79.

Nelson, K. and Fivush, R. (2004) 'The emergence of autobiographical memory: A social cultural developmental theory', *Psychological Review*, 111(2): 486–511.

Patterson, T. and Hayne, H. (2011) 'Does drawing facilitate older children's reports of emotionally laden events', *Applied Cognitive Psychology*, 25: 119–26.

Perner, J. and Ruffman, T. (1995) 'Episodic memory and autonoetic consciousness: Developmental evidence and a theory of childhood amnesia', *Journal of Experimental Child Psychology*, 59(3): 516–48.

Peterson, C., Jesso, B. and McCabe, A. (1999) 'Encouraging narratives in preschoolers: An intervention study', *Journal of Child Language*, 26(1): 49–67.

Peterson, C. and McCabe, A. (1994) 'A social interactionist account of developing decontextualized narrative skill', *Developmental Psychology*, 30(6): 937–48.

Peterson, C. and Rideout, R. (1998) 'Memory for medical emergencies experienced by 1- and 2-year-olds', *Developmental Psychology*, 34(5): 1059–72.

Piaget, J. (1962) *Play, Dreams and Imitation in Childhood*. New York: Norton.

Poole, D.A. and Lindsay, D.S. (1995) 'Interviewing preschoolers: Effects of nonsuggestive techniques, parental coaching, and leading questions on reports of nonexperienced events', *Journal of Experimental Child Psychology*, 60(1): 129–54.

Poole, D.A. and Lindsay, D.S. (2001) 'Children's eyewitness reports after exposure to misinformation from parents', *Journal of Experimental Psychology: Applied*, 7(1): 27–50.

Principe, G.F. and Ceci, S.J. (2002) '"I saw it with my own ears": The effect of peer conversations on preschoolers' reports of non-experienced events', *Journal of Experimental Child Psychology*, 83(1): 1–25.

Principe, G.F., Guiliano, S. and Root, C. (2008) 'Rumor mongering and remembering: How rumors originating in children's inferences can affect memory', *Journal of Experimental Child Psychology*, 99(2): 135–55.

Principe, G. F., Haines, B., Adkins, A. and Guiliano, S. (2010) 'False rumors and true belief: Memory processes underlying children's errant reports of rumored events', *Journal of Experimental Child Psychology*, 107: 407–22.

Principe, G.F., Kanaya, T., Ceci, S.J. and Singh, M. (2006) 'Believing is seeing: How rumors can engender false memories in preschoolers', *Psychological Science*, 17(3): 243–48.

Quas, J.A., Malloy, L.C., Melinder, A., Goodman, G.S., D'Mello, M. and Schaaf, J. (2007) 'Developmental differences in the effects of repeated interviews and interviewer bias on young children's event memory and false reports', *Developmental Psychology*, 43(4): 823–37.

Reese, E. (2002) 'A model of the origins of autobiographical memory', in J. Fagen and H. Hayne (eds.), *Progress in Infancy Research, Vol 2*. Mahwah, NJ: Erlbaum, pp. 215–60.

Reese, E. and Fivush, R. (1993) 'Parental styles of talking about the past', *Developmental Psychology*, 29(3): 596–606.

Reese, E., Haden, C.A. and Fivush, R. (1993) 'Mother-child conversations about the past: Relationships of style and memory over time', *Cognitive Development*, 8(4): 403–30.

Reese, E., Hayne, H. and MacDonald, S. (2008) 'Looking back to the future: Maori and Pakeha mother-child birth stories', *Child Development*, 79(1): 114–25.

Reese, E. and Newcombe, R. (2007) 'Training mothers in elaborative reminiscing enhances children's autobiographical memory and narrative', *Child Development*, 78(4): 1153–70.

Rovee, C.K. and Rovee, D.T. (1969) 'Conjugate reinforcement of infant exploratory behavior', *Journal of Experimental Child Psychology*, 8(1): 33–9.

Rovee-Collier, C., Griesler, P.C. and Earley, L.A. (1985) 'Contextual determinants of retrieval in three-month-old infants', *Learning and Motivation*, 16(2): 139–57.

Rovee-Collier, C. and Hayne, H. (1987) 'Reactivation of infant memory: Implications for cognitive development', in H.W. Reese (ed.), *Advances in Child Development and Behavior*. New York: Academic Press, pp. 185–238.

Rovee-Collier, C. (1997) 'Dissociations in infant memory: Rethinking the development of implicit and explicit memory', *Psychological Review*, 104(3): 467–98.

Rovee-Collier, C., Sullivan, M.W., Enright, M., Lucas, D. and Fagen, J.W. (1987) 'Reactivation of infant memory', in J. Oates and S. Sheldon (eds.), *Cognitive Development in Infancy*. Hillsdale, NJ: Erlbaum, pp. 87–92.

Salmon, K., Bidrose, S. and Pipe, M.-E. (1995) 'Providing props to facilitate children's event reports: A comparison of toys and real items', *Journal of Experimental Child Psychology*, 60(1): 174–94.

Salmon, K., Roncolato, W. and Gleitzman, M. (2003) 'Children's reports of emotionally laden events: Adapting the interview to the child', *Applied Cognitive Psychology*, 17(1): 65–79.

Simcock, G. and DeLoache, J. (2006) 'Get the picture? The effects of iconicity on toddlers' reenactment from picture books', *Developmental Psychology*, 42(6): 1352–7.

Simcock, G. and Dooley, M. (2007) 'Generalization of learning from picture books to novel test conditions by 18- and 24-month-old children', *Developmental Psychology*, 43(6): 1568–78.

Simcock, G. and Hayne, H. (2002) 'Breaking the barrier: Children do not translate their preverbal memories into language', *Psychological Science*, 13(3): 225–31.

Simcock, G. and Hayne, H. (2003) 'Age-related changes in verbal and nonverbal memory during early childhood', *Developmental Psychology*, 39(5): 805–14.

Strange, D., Garry, M. and Sutherland, R. (2003) 'Drawing out children's false memories', *Applied Cognitive Psychology*, 17(5): 607–19.

Suddendorf, T. and Corballis, M. (1997) 'Mental time travel and the evolution of the human mind', *Genetic, Social, and General Psychology Monographs*, 123(2): 133–67.

Sutherland, R. and Hayne, H. (2001) 'Age-related changes in the misinformation effect', *Journal of Experimental Child Psychology*, 79(4): 388–404.

Tulving, E. (2002) 'Episodic memory: From mind to brain', *Annual Review of Psychology*, 53(1): 1–25.

Tustin, K. and Hayne, H. (2010) 'Defining the boundary: Age-related changes in childhood amnesia', *Developmental Psychology*, 46(5): 1049–61.

Wang, Q. (2004) 'The emergence of cultural self-construct: Autobiographical memory and self-description in American and Chinese children', *Developmental Psychology*, 40(1): 3–15.

Wang, Q. (2007) '"Remember when you got the big, big bulldozer?" Mother-child reminiscing over time and across cultures', *Social Cognition*, 25(4): 455–71.

Wang, Q. (2008) 'Emotion knowledge and autobiographical memory across the preschool years: A cross-cultural longitudinal investigation', *Cognition*, 108(1): 117–35.

Wang, Q. and Conway, M. (2004) 'The stories we keep: Autobiographical memory in American and Chinese middle-aged adults', *Journal of Personality*, 72(5): 911–38.

Wang, Q. and Fivush, R. (2005) 'Mother-child conversations of emotionally-salient events: Exploring the functions of emotional reminiscing in European American and Chinese families', *Social Development*, 14(3): 473–95.

Wesson, M. and Salmon, K. (2001) 'Drawing and showing: Helping children to report emotionally laden events', *Applied Cognitive Psychology*, 15(3): 301–20.

Woolford, J., Patterson, T., Macleod, E., Hobbs, L., and Hayne, H. (in press) 'Drawing helps children to talk about their presenting problems during a mental health assessment', *Clinical Child Psychology and Psychiatry*.

Woolford, J., Patterson, T., Macleod, E., Hobbs, L. and Hayne, H. (2013) 'Drawing helps children to talk about their presenting problems during a mental health assessment,' *Clinical Child Psychology and Psychiatry*. Advance online publication. doi: 10.1177/1359104513496261

30

Children as Researchers: We Have a Lot to Learn

Tove I. Dahl

The aftermath of the December 2004 tsunami left tremendous devastation. Thousands of people died, more were left homeless, and entire regions had to be completely rebuilt from the bottom up. This set in motion an unparalleled engagement from outside organizations to help. Basic needs like food, shelter, health care, and sanitation were provided for by the hundreds of organizations that stepped in. Of the 890 agencies involved in the post-tsunami operations in Sri Lanka, however, only 4 per cent had a child focus in their activities, and the majority of those focused primarily on providing for children's physical needs (Plan International, 2005). Aside from a small handful of those 4 per cent, virtually none had prepared their staff to respond to children in other ways.

Meanwhile, substantial reconstruction work was being done by the residents of the afflicted areas themselves (Plan International, 2005). And what did the children do? They helped domestically – advising, encouraging and heartening friends, collecting and sharing food with others, helping with the cooking, caring for and helping siblings and older people, standing in line for goods and services, cheering up their parents, and playing with children whose parents had died. They helped with social services – bringing injured people to hospitals, distributing goods, typing lists of necessary information, helping maintain security at temporary shelters, helping trace scattered families, and constructing coffins. They helped with reconstruction – cleaning, collecting things, dealing with garbage, repairing and building houses, building fences, clearing roadways, and putting down gravel for new roads. They helped disseminate news and information, and they even gave feedback to helping organizations and led prayer groups.

Many were fatefully involved in the lives of others. Imagine the experience of this young Sri Lankan who was left on her own to cope with the aftermath:

> I was going on a trip with my aunt's family. I live with them. When the waves came, my father and I ran to warn another aunt. They did not listen to us. They shouted at us and we rushed back. Everyone was trying to board a bus. A girl cousin gave me her infant baby to hold while she got on the bus. I held the baby and could not enter the bus. Later I gave the baby to another passenger and tried to climb in. Then I saw a small boy cousin of mine struggling to get in. He was alone. I did not want to leave him there. So I got off the bus. We were left behind. I ran with my little cousin. We somehow managed to get into a van. It took

us to a temple far away. We stayed there one day without knowing what happened to our families. I looked after my little cousin and tried to find our families. I told the police and the priest of the temple. They sent us to another camp nearby but my family was not there. On the third day a person from the village said he saw our family in another camp. We stayed in this camp for several weeks before we moved to a temporary house.

(Plan International, 2005: 18)

As significant as her contribution and those of many other children were, it is noteworthy how absent this picture of the young people's tremendous resourcefulness was from the media and from other reports from the aftermath. If all this activity did, indeed, take place, how did some come to know this, and so many others not?

Plan International came to know this through the children themselves. They conducted a large study in India, Indonesia, Sri Lanka, and Thailand that went beyond what the adults saw and experienced in the aftermath (Plan International, 2005). For their study, they consulted directly with children and youth on their own terms about their post-tsunami experiences, gleaning also children's recommendations for what can be done better before, during, and after such disasters that may occur in the future. The findings are, of course, remarkable in terms of revealing what children are capable of. Perhaps even more thought-provoking is how invisible they were until someone thought to ask. On kids' terms.

What else are we missing when we forget to include children and youth in research, forgetting to ask about their experiences, as experts, on their own terms, using their own words or expressions about their lives? As another young Sri Lankan bemoaned, 'When we tried to tell the adults of any gaps in the services, they were angry with us. They told us that children should behave like children and not interfere in adults' work. We do not think it was fair for them to say so' (Plan International, 2005: 5). It is hard to argue with that.

What does it take to involve children directly in the research process? Through

theory, practice, empirical studies, and essays, this chapter is structured to address two different questions that a sceptic might read into the title of this chapter: '*Children* as researchers?' and 'Children as *researchers?*' In trying to understand what the answer to the first question might entail, how children are regarded in different research traditions and what implications those perspectives have for how we involve children in any research process are briefly presented. In exploring what the answer to the second question might entail, methodological and research design considerations for how we can effectively involve children in the research process itself, and the risks and benefits associated with involving children at all are presented. The discussion continues with a series of questions about important ethical considerations that this new and rapidly expanding research approach poses to us as adult researchers – both when responding to research done by children and, surely more and more, when collaborating with children in our own research. It ends with some brief suggestions from the literature for how to effectively conduct one's own research with child collaborators.

CHILDREN AS RESEARCHERS?

Why children as researchers?

Contrary to what we may have looked forward to as children, we must humbly accept that by virtue of being an adult there are things about the human experience that we simply *cannot* know firsthand. This is particularly the case in terms of how children experience the world (Tauer, 2002). The younger the children, the more this is the case. Our memories of our own childhood are influenced by the experiences we have had since, coloured by how we understand the world now. Even if we *could* remember our childhoods as purely as we understood them while children, we cannot escape that they were situated in a particular era - a place and time held together by unique relationships. Though children today may have many experiences like those we had when we were children, our childhood contexts unavoidably render particular aspects of our experiences differently. Likewise, individual differences in how people know and understand the world assures that our own childhoods many not only be different from other children's experiences in important ways across eras, they were likely different in notable ways within our own era. So, relying on our own memories of childhood when trying to understand children from other eras may markedly limit what we could potentially learn from them. To optimize our learning, we have to find ways to listen to children in their own time on their own terms.

What might be the academic benefits?

Acknowledging that children are experts in their own right on the experience of childhood has value. Surely, as groups, children and adults may be similar in many ways and particular subgroups of children and adults may be more similar than they are to peers in their cohort. Nevertheless, there may be some important differences in how children understand and experience the world differently from adults that are worth investigating (O'Kane, 2000). These important differences may manifest themselves in how children understand the world; what kinds of things children remember; the way children communicate (both verbally and non-verbally); children's social and legal status; children's position and strength institutionally, physically, and psychologically; children's dependence upon others; who or what children trust; and children's openness to influence (Hill, 2005). These kinds of things may make the experience of being a child who is impoverished, diabetic, a television watcher, a factory labourer, a person with an ADHD diagnosis, or an armed soldier

different from the experience of an adult in a similar situation.

Equally important to the children's experiences as children are their views on phenomena that involve them. When trying to understand any phenomena fully, those that involve children should also be studied from children's perspectives (McLaughlin, 2005). For example, children can offer valuable insights for people who care about and wish to improve how schools are organized, how back seats in cars are designed, how food is distributed in refugee camps, how the good intentions of health care personnel are actually experienced, or how safe neighborhoods are for all their residents.

What is a child?

The way we think of young people naturally influences how we regard and approach them when it comes to the ethics and methods used in research on the youth experience (Roberts, 2000). The most basic definition of a child, as defined by the Convention on the Rights of the Child (1989) is chronological, including everyone under 18 years of age. However, that definition is much too simplistic in terms of how children have been regarded in research. Some research traditions regard children as objects, others as subjects, and, more recently, as individuals with agency.

When regarded as *objects* of study, children are perceived and treated as people to be acted upon by others, protected as objects in the research process (Christensen and Prout, 2002). In this tradition, children are assumed to be dependent upon adults. In this role, particularly in behavioural research, children are to be observed or involved in systematic experiments where their awareness or interpretation of the investigation's purpose and outcomes are not valued or involved (Woodhead and Faulkner, 2000).

When regarded as *subjects* of study, children take on another role. In this tradition, children are assumed to be thinking, acting, autonomous people, though with a relatively passive role in research (Christensen and Prout, 2002; Woodhead and Faulkner, 2000). Researchers take on a different kind of responsibility for children in this role, initially letting the interests of the investigator fall secondary to the rights of the child by informing children of the nature of their research so that the children can choose themselves whether to participate – even in cases where parental consent has already been secured. However, once they begin participating, in this research tradition children's involvement thereafter is primarily about knowingly participating in research activities on adults' terms.

Most recently, in the spirit of the Convention on the Rights of the Child (1989), children in research have become recognized as *individuals* who are active agents in the world rather than passive participants. In research, then, they are recognized as capable of helping others co-produce new knowledge and understandings (Christensen and Prout, 2002; McLaughlin, 2005). As individuals who act, change, and influence change in others, the social dynamics and interpersonal relationships involved in carrying out research influences how youth (or anyone, for that matter) engage in the research process (Greene and Hill, 2005). Ultimately, this will influence outcomes and how they may be interpreted (McLaughlin, 2005; Woodhead and Faulkner, 2000). As active co-participants in the research process, then, in this tradition it is important to be mindful of how young people are engaged in the research process in order to assure the best quality outcomes.

Regardless of which research tradition we operate within, the question remains whether age should be regarded as a barrier or a variable in the research process. Childhood poses barriers to research if one regards children, because of their age or lack of experience, as vulnerable, incompetent, and/or powerless (Morrow and Richards, 1996). From more traditional research perspectives, those kinds of barriers would limit research. On the other hand, if vulnerability is regarded as a matter

of physical weakness or lack of experience, for example, they can be treated as variables and accounted for in one's research design. If one thinks of competence related to how adult-like one is, then, again, age could be regarded as a barrier that might limit research. On the other hand, if one thinks of children as different from rather than less than adults, then one can also treat the difference as a variable and account for that in one's research design. Finally, if powerlessness is a matter of opportunity, then that, again, could be treated as a variable and accounted for in the opportunities created in one's design.

CHILDREN AS *RESEARCHERS?*

These considerations about what a child is are most relevant when considering whether we should do research with them at all. When reflecting on the possibility of children as researchers, the first question worth raising is what research really is and if it is an endeavour we truly can or ought to engage children in.

Children and science

If we define research as essentially the application of science by scientists, then who are scientists? First, think of science as a way of knowing that entails particular ways of asking questions and seeking out answers in order to critically examine and draw conclusions about the world (Ray, 2000; Spatz and Kardas, 2008). Science has multiple ways of knowing that vary by discipline, and each unique outlook drives the kind of questions we ask and the sorts of tools we employ to reason about empirically derived content (Rosenthal and Rosnow, 2008). Ultimately, we use these methods of science to shape how we draw out those experiences and build reliable bases of knowledge (Bordens and Abbott, 2008; Ray, 2000). Scientists, then, are the thinking, creative individuals who use the scientific method to pursue the knowledge endeavour. Though we may not typically associate children with the role of scientist, its definition is not age-specific and could apply to children provided they, like adult scientist counterparts, participate in applying some version of the scientific method for the purpose of increasing our knowledge base and advancing science.

Children and value added

A second important question is if there is any value added to our research by involving children in research as scientists (Hill, 1997; McLaughlin, 2005). Beyond higher education, there actually is a long and well-developed tradition of involving children in research in order to understand and explore the world for school projects and science fairs. That kind of research is typically about using the scientific method for the purpose of understanding how things work or discovering something new, and such work is definitely perceived as beneficial to young people and potentially beneficial to the creation of new knowledge as well (American Psychological Association Teachers of Psychology in Secondary Schools, 2004). However, the question being posed here is not about whether value is added by having children do research for school projects. Though there may be some overlap between research done for school-related projects and other research, the main focus of this chapter is on the involvement of children in programs of research involving people from higher education working explicitly towards the advancement of theory or the purposeful application of research for children's benefit.

If there is value in involving children in academic or applied research, what impact might findings from such collaborations have? Some of their views may very well not be available to adults any other way than through other children (Kellett, Forrest, Dent and Ward, 2004). By allowing children to be involved in the research process, there are

perspectives that may be shared and understood that would otherwise be missed by adults (Nairn and Smith, 2003). In addition to understanding and experiencing the world differently from adults, children also communicate differently from adults (O'Kane, 2000). That being the case, it is natural to think that the research methods and ethical considerations used with adults may not always be appropriate or sufficient when seeking to fully realize our research potential with young people. So the way we involve children in the research process ought to take those differences into account in deciding what research is pursued and how research is designed.

Indeed, involving children in the research process will influence the kinds of choices we make about the role of the researcher, the methodologies we use, and the way we analyze and interpret the data (Christensen and Prout, 2002; Hogan, 2005). It will also influence the ethical principles and practices we attend to in the process. Because our approach influences how research is conducted, it should not be surprising that involving youth in the data collection and interpretive process has been shown to influence the findings that research yields (Woodhead and Faulkner, 2000).

Potential

In her book on how to train children and youth to do research, Mary Kellett, drawing from her own experience training children to be researchers, asserts that it is absolutely possible for trained young people aged 12–14, and for trained, gifted children aged 9–10, to conduct quality research (Kellett, 2005b). Her belief in children's ability to do research with other children has been validated by a healthy production of interesting studies initiated, carried out, and shared by children at the Children's Research Centre at The Open University in the UK. Roberts (2000: 235), like Kellett, summarizes that if children 'are willing to give their views on subjects on which they are in a sense "experts" … we should be willing to listen to what they have to say, and incorporate their views into our understandings of what it is to be a child or a young person'. In other words, if they can do it, let's assist them and learn from their work. What might be important methodological considerations when we choose to involve children as researchers?

METHODOLOGICAL CONSIDERATIONS

Practical issues related to how we give young people voice through research and what methods we use to do that include: (a) the responsibilities and related caveats of speaking *about* others, (b) the responsibilities and related caveats of speaking *for* others, and (c) how seriously young people's voices are taken by those who it is important for young people to be heard *by* (Fielding, 2004). In sharing what we learn from youth, it is therefore important that when we do speak about or for them, we do so supportively. Better yet, it is beneficial to let youth speak for themselves and engage others in dialog with them. When possible, it can be particularly fruitful to let trained youth engage as (co)researchers where they can be a part of setting and carrying out entire research agendas more or less on their own terms.

Methodologies for research *with* or *by* children are far less developed than methodologies for research *about* children conducted on adult terms. However, there is a growing movement to redress that. This new movement involves complementing the traditional approaches of fields like developmental psychology that typically focus more on the study of 'childhood' with new approaches that focus more on the study of 'the child' (Hogan, 2005). In the 'childhood' tradition, the academic motivation for involving children in research has been for the purpose of developing models that enabled us to predict aspects of *childhood* through normative models of development.

The newer approaches focus more on how children subjectively experience the world *as children*. In these newer approaches, children's everyday lives are foregrounded, including matters about their personal experiences with events, relationships, other people, and with culture. Conversely, adults' interpretations of childhood where the adult researchers assume or are assigned the role of expert recedes to the background. With this switch, we get away from the idea that children are unable to describe themselves to others because they are what Hogan (2005) describes as 'unformed persons' who are passive and dependent with ideas just like those of adults – unreliable informants whose own contributions will show signs of inconsistency. These aspects of the newer approaches have huge implications for how we further develop research methodologies and the choices we make both when designing and carrying out research with young scientists.

If we want to involve children as co-researchers with adults, or even independent researchers under adult supervision, the use of more participatory-oriented approaches to research is appropriate. Such approaches include: action research, Participatory Action Research, Participatory Rural Appraisal, Community-Based Participatory Research, and empowerment evaluation.

Action research

Action research is a process that is concerned with developing practical knowledge in democratic ways that have direct human value (Bradbury and Reason, 2003). It emphasizes the goal of increasing community involvement in using research outcomes. As a research approach, it is inclusive in terms of its co-participants, goal-oriented in terms of its purpose, and broad-minded in terms of what it counts as knowledge and the methods for capturing it. Initially, action research was categorized into four types: diagnostic, participant, empirical, and experimental

(Chein, Cook and Harding, 1948). Though different in focus, they all share the intention of enhancing our fields with quality outcomes based on inclusive methods and research tactics that are characterized by conceptual, theoretical, and methodological integrity (Bradbury and Reason, 2003). Of most relevance to this chapter, however, is the participant brand of action research. It evolved from diagnostic action research (research designed to identify problems and solutions that can inform action) when the diagnostic approach was found to fall short in getting community members to buy into effecting research-suggested changes (Bradbury and Reason, 2003). Participant action research therefore evolved emphasizing the involvement of lay participants in the research itself as a means to increase community investment in research outcomes.

The involvement of lay people in research has been found to limit the range of problems action research can address, given the lay people's lack of specialized skills necessary to meet certain research requirements (Bradbury and Reason, 2003). Participant action research, then, evolved with the dual purpose of engaging lay people in the research process *and* simplifying the processes and methods to suit lay collaborator capacities. Meanwhile, the foundational criteria for action research methods are not firmly established, and guidelines for practice are still being developed. Accordingly, in the process of aligning researchers and lay practitioners, then, a wide variety of methods have been tried and used (Avison, Lau, Myers and Nielsen, 1999).

Methodological changes have not only influenced the craft of research, but also the degree and manner in which researchers and their lay collaborators interface (Avison et al., 1999). However, the lay collaborators who have participated in child-related action research have mostly been adults responsible for children rather than children themselves. Indeed, a survey of journal publications in the fields of medicine and psychology reveals that action research is still not a widely used approach compared to other methods. As a result, very little general action research is done with children at this point.

Participatory Action Research (PAR)

With the increased focus on subjectivity in the human and social sciences, participatory action research (PAR) has grown in recent years (Kidd and Kral, 2005). The goal of PAR is to engage in genuine collaborations through which one seeks knowledge that is useful to the participating group of people. A parallel goal is to use that knowledge in a way that empowers the research participants to be a part of positive change. As such, PAR is about using methods to contribute to social transformation.

PAR, more a philosophy than a method, does have clear methodological implications. Since the philosophy is rooted in the fair representation and empowerment of research participants (Kidd and Kral, 2005; Nieuwenhuys, 2004), perhaps the most direct implication of this method involves the character of the participants themselves. By focusing on socially just action, PAR seeks to provide access to often disenfranchised groups of participants, like children (Kidd and Kral, 2005). Indeed, PAR has been fine-tuned for work with children in particular (Nieuwenhuys, 2004).

Because PAR is highly participatory, and PAR is often used with children, scientific methods have to be managed carefully and appropriately, ensuring reliability and validity while at the same time enabling non-experts to take an active hand in the research process (Kidd and Kral, 2005). Though not all scientific methods lend themselves well to this research approach, many do. To ensure that those that do are used properly, recommendations for PAR practitioners have focused on specifying and meeting methodological criteria in terms of replicability, triangulation, face validity from the co-participants' perspectives, and 'catalytic validity' in terms of how the process catalyzes change.

Because the PAR goal is to actively involve co-participants in the construction of new knowledge that they can later use for themselves and others in positive ways, another important implication of PAR is the importance that is attached to the facilitation of learning among research co-participants (Kidd and Kral, 2005; Nieuwenhuys, 2004). At the same time, researchers have a responsibility to be sure that what is learned by a research group is properly shared with targeted others who can use their findings to improve the conditions or circumstances of the co-participants and others like them. In essence, an adult researcher working with children in the PAR framework then, serves as 'a responsible person who is thinking and rethinking constantly what s/he is doing and is sharing this process of knowledge generation with the youngsters with whom PAR is carried out' (Nieuwenhuys, 2004: 215).

Participatory Rural Appraisal (PRA)

Participatory Rural Appraisal is similar to PAR in philosophy, though it is even more specific in is methodological implications. The goal of this approach is to foster the use of research methods that are as transparent as possible to its constituent groups (O'Kane, 2000). Like PAR, in PRA, everyone involved in research – researchers and co-participants alike – are all considered co-constructors of knowledge. Coming in part from the tradition of Paulo Freire, this means that power, control, and authority are all considered factors of the research process that must be explicitly addressed in the research design. Power relationships can be equalized in research with children by foregrounding children's subjective experiences (Mauthner, 1997). Doing so, however, requires adopting a flexible approach that gives youth the power to influence the terms of their involvement.

In PRA, both the process and product of data collection are equally important (O'Kane, 2000). The process typically involves methods that are dialog- and action-based, encouraging

children to share their knowledge through the telling of stories or anecdotes about their daily lives. Because it is not taken for granted that participants are literate, reading and writing skills are less relied upon than other means of knowledge sharing such as the creation of visual impressions and other active presentations of ideas. This makes PRA an explicitly more child-friendly approach than the other participatory approaches to research.

Community-Based Participatory Research (CBPR)

Community-based participatory research is another approach to research rather than a method per se (Minkler and Wallerstein, 2003). It distinguishes itself from more individual-focused approaches through its characteristic foundation in community work where the approach (a) is participatory, (b) is cooperative, (c) entails co-learning processes, (d) involves the development of systems and the building of community capacity, (e) is empowering, and (f) facilitates a balance between research and action (Minkler and Wallerstein, 2003: 5). The approach forces us to question in important ways what we mean by participation (Which community is involved and who from it is invited to participate in the research process?), knowledge (What kind of knowledge is valued and sought out?), power (What is the context of the research, and who has greater privilege in the relationship between researchers and other research participants?), and practice (What are the research goals?; Wallerstein and Duran, 2003). The answers to the questions determine the degree to which the research meets participatory and community-based goals.

As an approach, there are no definitive principles that apply for all group partnerships (Israel, Schulz, Parker, Becker and Guzman, 2003). However, CBPR practitioners hold that for whichever principles a group agrees upon to guide the research process, it is important that they are monitored and adjusted as needed (Israel et al., 2003). Likewise, for any given project, the definition of community and who the right research partners to seek out from it are will vary by situation and the priorities of the participating community. Also, research designs are not prescribed in CBPR, but rather developed in response to each research context and the research goals of the project co-participants. Finally, since change is an important aspect of CBPR, it is important to be clear in the ongoing planning about what should be disseminated from the project, for what purpose, by and to whom, and through which media.

In order to effectively carry out CBPR projects, there are a number of roles that need to be fulfilled in order to lead them to success. Those roles include that of the leader (or animator), a community organizer, a popular educator, and a participatory researcher (Stoecker, 2003). Which of these are fulfilled by community members and which by researchers may vary as a project evolves, and any one person may fulfil one or more roles.

Empowerment evaluation

Another form of community-based work, empowerment evaluation, has emerged in this wave of participatory approaches to critical inquiry as well. Empowerment evaluation seek to enable individuals and communities who are to be evaluated to become a central part of the evaluation process itself, thus fostering improvement through educated self-determination (Fetterman, 2005). Like PRA, the purpose is to bring often disenfranchised groups to the table and, through their inclusion, give them a meaningful role in decision-making on matters about which they have a vested interest. Empowerment evaluators, then, serve as what has been termed as 'critical friends' – people, like those in PAR and PRA, who help their evaluation constituents understand and master the processes through which they can effect

change. By doing so, the evaluators combine evaluation expertise with 'a commitment to (and expertise in) capacity building' among the community stakeholders (Fetterman, 2005: 13).

Empowerment evaluation, then, aims to help evaluated programs succeed by preparing their own stakeholders to be able to actively take part in planning, implementing, and evaluating their own programs (Wandersman et al., 2005). Ten principles guide this process (though not all 10 may be used in all evaluations). These include the principles of (a) improvement, (b) community ownership, (c) inclusion, (d) democratic participation, (e) social justice, (f) community knowledge, (g) evidence-based strategies, (h) capacity building, (i) organizational learning, and (j) accountability. Because one of the prioritized goals is to give ownership of the evaluation process to the community being evaluated, evaluation practitioners are encouraged to build on local expertise, valuing what community members already know. Thereafter, the evaluation practitioners are encouraged to take a developmental approach to the capacity-building process such that community members are appropriately enabled to grow in their evaluation capacity. The particular tools and concepts used in the evaluation process are then selected, as often as possible, based on what it is believed stakeholders will be able to master the use of and effectively manage, long after evaluation practitioners have left.

By including stakeholders in the evaluation process and evaluating explicitly to help programs flourish, participatory evaluation methods differ from conventional methods of evaluation. Empowerment evaluation therefore serves as an interesting model for research with children. First, instead of being led by external experts, the process is led by communities themselves with the help of external experts as appropriate (Springett, 2003). Rather than relying on predetermined indicators of success, stakeholders are encouraged to identify their own indicators of success. Rather than using scientific objectivity as the primary motivation for method selection, methods are chosen in terms of their simplicity and appropriateness for local capacities.

RESEARCH DESIGN

What all of these participatory methods have in common is a focus on enhancing the rights of an increasingly diverse population of informants to speak, analyze, and act on research at a level that lay participants can arguably manage (Minkler and Wallerstein, 2003). That puts researchers more in the educator and 'critical friend' role than other research approaches do. Yes, academic expertise is crucial for assuring that the work done has both scientific and practical integrity. Yet, at the same time, it should be remembered that empowering people with local expertise is crucial for empowering others to be heard and effect change. Nevertheless, it should be remembered that empowering people has ripple effects, and one should be thoughtful about who ultimately has responsibility for change (Veale, 2005). Depending upon who controls relevant resources, for example, full or part ownership of an issue or situation may not be appropriate or possible. As Veale reminds us, 'In work with children, perhaps more so than with adults, there is a complex relationship between issues of power, control, responsibility and ethics in the research approach and methodology', adding that 'questions about "participation" in child research continue to pose challenges' (Veale, 2005: 270). In light of these admonitions, what factors need to be attended to in order to effectively design and carry out research with child collaborators?

Mindfulness

Experience suggests that building confidence in child participants, adult researchers, and children collaborators is important for the success of any methodology (Save the Children, 2004). In particular, Save the Children advises we be mindful of (a) respect for children, (b) children's enjoyment of the research process, (c) flexibility of mind – remaining open and operating with as few assumptions as possible about the participating children, and (d) presence of mind – appreciating the importance of children's experiences in the here and now.

Time

In order to create a positive environment for research, particularly with children, it may also take quite a bit of time to get to know the people and relevant supportive bodies where research may take place (Greene and Hill, 2005; McLaughlin, 2005; Save the Children, 2004). Time *not* spent on this may have profound effects on the data collected. Likewise, when working with younger children, the work may take longer to complete than when working with older collaborators. If young collaborators are viewed as important for what we seek to learn in our research, then time, again, becomes an important factor to weigh in the formulation for the research design.

Effective research tactics

In research with children, research tactics, like methods, can vary. Still, all have their strengths and weaknesses, and some spring more naturally from our theoretical stance than others (Greene and Hill, 2005). As for all good research, methodological decisions and method-appropriate research tactic choices are important. We simply want to match the ability and training of the researchers to adequately serve the research purpose and the questions being investigated (Kellett et al., 2004). One of the most important additional considerations when making these kinds of decisions when working with children is: Is it a child-friendly approach? (Save the Children, 2004).

The range of research tactics used by youth researchers is, broad and includes both qualitative and quantitative methods. Any number of tactics can be child-friendly as long as they are appropriately adapted and children are appropriately trained to use them well. For example, young researchers have been known in their work to use quite conventional methods like questionnaires, focus groups, email correspondence, interviews, discussion groups, postal questionnaire surveys, text analysis, observation, standard scales, on-line think-aloud protocols, journaling, eliciting responses to world-choice or picture prompts, vignettes with responses, and polls. They have also been known to use some less used traditional methods such as activity-based sessions, let's pretend work, the statement of wishes, 24-hour recall tasks, drawing, filming and photographing, playing games, songs, mapping, drama, pots and beans, diamond rankings, and model building (Alderson, 2000; Carnegie Young People Initiative, 2001; Hill, 1997; Mauthner, 1997; Morrow and Richards, 1996; O'Kane, 2000; Singh, 2007). As for scientific integrity, creativity and triangulation have been found to be as important in research with child collaborators as in any other research (Greene and Hill, 2005; Hart and Tyrer, 2006; Hill, 1997).

THE RESEARCH PROCESS

Children can be involved in either primary or secondary research, though they have tended to be involved far less in the latter than the former (Save the Children, 2004). Secondary research – the critical examination and consideration of research that has already been done by others – is usually done prior to embarking on primary research. Secondary research does not involve the direct collection of information from research participants, yet it can be critical to the shaping of agendas for primary research. Though most of the research illustrations provided here come from primary research, important

learning can come from involving youth in stage-setting secondary research as well.

Though any number of methodologies and research tactics may be used by young researchers, the primary research process itself has several steps that adults may choose to involve children in to varying degrees. For example, in primary research, children may be involved in question identification or formulation, the setting up of the study design, data collection, data analysis, data interpretation, and/or the sharing of the results. However children are involved, it will likely influence the final outcome in ways not possible to achieve with purely adult-led research.

As for how much one should involve children in decision-making, there is quite a bit of uncertainty (Sinclair, 2004). Drawing from Hart's (1997) eight-step ladder model, Nieuwenhuys (2004) underscored that children's participation can be engaged at any number of levels – from pure manipulation, to decoration (including children for the purpose of looking good to others), to token participation, to being assigned tasks that adults have told them to do, to being consulted with about doing tasks that responsible adults have informed them about, to doing tasks that are adult-initiated but that children share in making decisions about, to initiating tasks that children carry out themselves under the direction of responsible adults, or to initiating tasks that children carry out while sharing decision-making with responsible adults along the way.

Clearly, the kind of tasks that children are involved in and the level of participation they are allowed will influence what we can learn from them. The kinds of 'research agendas children prioritize, the research questions they frame and the way in which they collect data are substantially different from adults and all of this can offer valuable insights and original contributions to knowledge', counseled Kellett (2005: 8). However we go about involving children in the research process, it remains important for adults to be present for support, problem-solving and debriefing every step of the way since it is every bit as important for children as for adults that the children be engaged in quality work (McLaughlin, 2005).

Question identification or formulation

Even when adults aim to work with research models that are youth-led, adult-led or co-led by adults and youth, it has typically been adults who have done the secondary research groundwork and who have decided upon the kind of primary research that will be done thereafter (McLaughlin, 2005). That is something, power-wise, that is worth remembering, revisiting and reflecting upon when weighing one's motivations for involving children and setting concrete research goals. In community consultation, often done while research is being developed and approved, researchers go to their targeted communities of participants in order to give them a say in how research questions and designs get developed (Dickert and Sugarman, 2005; Melton, Levine, Koocher, Rosenthal and Thompson, 1988). This is in part to show researcher's genuine concern about doing good work, to give the work legitimacy, to solicit stakeholder interest, to give stakeholders a say in how research evolves, to share responsibility for the research process with stakeholders, to politely show concern for the stakeholder's welfare, and to enhance their benefits and rights as a community of research participants. Such consulting has been shown to yield powerful returns in research done in AIDS and drug testing, disaster relief, emergency treatments, and environmental policy making. Moreover, it has been found to be most productive when consulted communities feel more like partners rather than more 'outside' advisers (Morin, Maiorana, Koester, Sheon and Richards, 2003).

In the actual formulation of research questions, children, as partners, offer unique strengths. For example, they can be important for identifying appropriate topics, questions, and parameters for interviews that other children will respond well to (Alderson, 2001; McLaughlin, 2005). Gillian Mann, for example, collected data from 7- to 11-year-old refugee children about the experience of being refugees in Dar es Salaam (Save the Children, 2004). During her preparations, she befriended three teenage boys who had experience as refugees in the Democratic Republic of the Congo and Tanzania. As she got to know them, she told them about her main research questions and then asked the boys what they thought would be important to explore and why. They took on the task eagerly and offered lots of questions – some that overlapped with Mann's initial questions and others not. Some of their questions included 'How is life different for refugee children compared to Tanzanian children?', 'Do their [refugee children] parents allow them to speak of "home"?' and 'What strategies do children use to hide their refugee identity?' (Save the Children, 2004: 69). Eventually, two teenage Congolese girls joined the team in their discussions, and 10 months were used to fine-tune the final research questions and develop an appropriate research design. This process elegantly built on the principle of exploring what children themselves are interested in or concerned about, yielding, as one would predict, notable returns (Hart and Tyrer, 2006).

Some studies have also shown that children succeed in eliciting responses from peers that language, generational differences, power, and other such matters that can distinguish adults from children might otherwise hinder (Alderson, 2001; Kellett et al., 2004; Nairn and Smith, 2003). Alderson (2000) offered an interesting example of this from a study on a housing estate that had a high incidence of accidents and injuries. When adult researchers asked youth about the accidents and injuries in various ways, the respondents were not very forthcoming with information. When the researchers instead asked the young people themselves how to elicit the desired information, they were encouraged to 'Ask us about our scars' – a strategy that resulted in rich data about the estate's accident events (Alderson, 2000: 143).

In another case from California, the Asians and Pacific Islanders for Reproductive Health (APIRH) organization supports two projects sponsored by the Health, Opportunities, Problem-Solving and Empowerment (HOPE) organization (Cheatham and Shen, 2003). As an organization, their goal is to help young women address disparities in their health, economic, social, and political situations by holding relevant institutions accountable to them. The APIRH went directly to the girls in their target group in order to identify the issues that seemed to matter to them most. They then offered research-related education and training that empowered the girls to develop questions that they wanted to find answers to. In the end, the girls, together with the HOPE staff, created and pretested a questionnaire that they used to pursue questions related to the girls' burning issues.

In yet another case from Durham, England, a paediatrician working with diabetics wanted to improve the health care delivery of the clinic he worked at (Cairns and Brannen, 2005). Recognizing the advantage that children bring to understanding and reaching other children, he sought the help of youth. The mandate provided was to evaluate the clinic and provide concrete pointers for developing a better program for the diabetic young people who used the clinic. Through a program called Investing in Children, five youth and a project administrator were recruited to lead the project. They called it The 730+ Project (730 injections being the minimum number of injections any diabetic may make in a year). The young 730+ group began by interviewing young clients from the clinic. Their investigations eventually developed into two lines of pursuit that they felt mattered most to the quality of young people's clinic experiences. The two main issues were the quality of the physical environment of the clinic itself, and the kind of support and information the young people received about diabetes, especially when first diagnosed. The clinic and greater health community regarded this, and the 730+ group's subsequent work, as a significant contribution to the clinic's improved health care delivery.

Data collection

Because children are younger and not as experienced with research as their adult counterparts, there is a concern that children cannot or will not be as conscientious of the practical and ethical parameters related to data collection. With proper training and/or a healthy collaboration with others who are trained, this need not be a barrier to working with children as researchers (Kellett, 2005a, 2005b; Kellett et al., 2004).

In a study designed and conducted by 12-year-old Paul O'Brien at the Children's Research Centre, for example, there is clear evidence that young people can do thoughtful work of integrity. O'Brien's investigation involved asking 9- to 12-year-olds about their experiences with death (O'Brien, n.d.). First, 160 students were surveyed with a questionnaire, and then eight were selected for a more in-depth interview. In the survey, it turned out that the vast majority of the children had experience with death, most having experience with the loss of relatives and pets. The 10 interview questions posed to the smaller subgroup of participants covered topics like how the children learned about the deaths, how they experienced them, how they dealt with them, how they were supported through them, and how they may have been affected by them in the long term afterwards. Because it was such a personal topic, O'Brien was sensitive about how he went about asking the questions. In his words:

> I did all the interviews on the same day during school time. I was able to use the ICT suite to make it private so nobody could listen in. Each interview lasted about 15 minutes. There was a range of questions about different emotions and different stages of the bereavement. I was trying to make the students as comfortable as possible, as I knew it was an upsetting subject for them to talk about, I gave them a choice of taping the interview using a Dictaphone or for them to write the answers down on an interview sheet.
>
> (O'Brien, n.d.: 2)

In his selection of the research space and his commitment to helping the young people feel comfortable, O'Brien showed the same kind of sensitivity for his participants as his adult counterparts ideally would have. That he also opened up for alternate ways for the participants to respond is also worth noting.

Recognizing and valuing the value of youth expertise, in her Dar es Salaam refugee research, Gillian Mann collaborated with a 14-year-old Congolese girl, Isabelle, during data collection (Save the Children, 2004). Though shy, Isabelle showed remarkable ability to connect with other refugee children and to find creative ways to do the originally planned research more effectively and with greater enjoyment for the participants. Isabelle used Congolese songs and make-believe games that engaged the children's imagination, adapting games that the children already knew to help gather higher-quality data. As Mann summarized, 'Each time we worked together, I learned new skills, new ways of doing things, and new things from the participating children' (Save the Children, 2004: 19). Isabelle also helped Mann establish relationships with families and children that otherwise might not have been possible.

The young 14- to 18-year-old girls in the California HOPE project were also extremely useful in the data collection part of their study (Cheatham and Shen, 2003). They wanted good information from a sizable sample of their 4500 high school peers, so they planted themselves strategically around the school in order to optimize recruitment. They worked hard, and in the end they successfully recorded over 400 responses – a sample size that gave them rich data to work with for deriving representative results. However, the data collection ended up being such a labour-intensive activity that they chose to let others do the data analysis before getting involved again in the dissemination of the results.

Interpreting results

From a participatory standpoint, it is important that research conducted in the genuine spirit of collaboration involve children in data interpretation. Even children can be surprised by their own findings. Of the many things O'Brien learned in his study about how children were affected by death, for example, he was most surprised to find that the children turned to their families, and especially their parents, for help processing the loss (O'Brien, n.d.: 4). As he remarked, 'It was strange that the only people the children asked for comfort from was their family … I would have expected children would really get support from their friends, especially as it seems everyone goes through it'. His reflection is compelling and raises the question about to whom other children, like those in the tsunami, might turn when their parents or friends are absent.

One point to clarify is that allowing children to interpret their data does not preclude others from interpreting them, too. The same data can be interpreted by both children and adults. Such analyst triangulation is recommended as one way of verifying and validating one's findings (Hart and Tyrer, 2006). When interpretations differ, however, involving all relevant parties can be of significant importance, particularly when the goal is to use one's findings to influence action (Jones, 2004). As one researcher reported, using others to respond to one's own interpretations of the data can be quite informative. 'I quickly learned that I got more information from people's *reactions* to my written reports than I did from the original interviews' (Stoecker, 2003: 108, emphasis mine). This level of awareness is important for keeping researcher's biases in check as they seek to represent the authentic voice of their original sources (Grover, 2004).

Ignoring children's input on how findings may be interpreted can have severe consequences – for children and others (Jones, 2004). In a case where both children and adults weighed the information on child labour practices around the world, children agreed with the adults that exploitative and abusive child labour situations should be eliminated, though they did not agree that all aspects of child labour are bad. A surely well-intentioned US bill, the 1993 Harkin Bill, was crafted in response to the negative aspects of child labour practices. It called for a boycott of all child-manufactured goods. This ended up being a decision that the International Labour Organization (ILO) in 2002 claimed 'led to thousands of child workers being dismissed, many of whom then faced destitution' (ILO, 2002: 89 as cited in Jones, 2004: 127). The ILO concluded that not involving children in the research interpretation process was extremely costly in this particular case, painfully illustrating how omitting children from this phase of the research process can sometimes lead to unintended harm.

Sharing results

In addition to the power of including children in the data interpretation phase of research, the ways in which children share their research can significantly impact who gets exposed to it and how it is understood and perceived. Children often present their work through the gray literature of newspapers, reports, posters, wall displays, graphs, pictures, tape-recordings, poems, videos, exhibitions, and PowerPoint presentations like those shared on the web site of the Children's Research Centre (Alderson, 2000, 2001; Kellett et al., 2004). Unlike the academic tradition, their targets are very often the people in their most immediate environments who are most directly implicated by the results (Kellett et al., 2004).

Though academic literature theoretically reaches a more widespread audience than the gray literature may, theory is not the same as practice. Suppose the goal of effective dissemination of results is to awaken interest,

make the findings understandable, and present them in a memorable way to relevant target audiences. That being so, children's methods may be at least as effective, or more, than the more conventional journal articles and book chapters of our fields when it comes to creating awareness and prompting change in targeted audiences. Consider the example that Alderson reported in 2001:

> At the launch of the British Library of a report on pupil democracy in Europe ... school students from Denmark and Sweden described the rights they enjoyed which are far less respected in many British schools. Then Emma and James from Article 12 sternly told the audience to stand up. 'Sit down all of you who are chewing gum', ordered Emma. 'And anyone who has not turned off their mobile phone.' An eminent government adviser sat down. 'And anyone wearing jewellery.' After ten commands almost all the audience was seated. 'If you were at school, you would have a detention and might be told not to attend school next day. But this has nothing to do with education, so why do schools keep doing this?' Emma continued. At the end of their presentation, Emma again ordered everyone to stand and then to sit down if they disagreed with any of her ten statements. These were about making schools more democratic and nearly everyone remained standing, except for the government adviser who sat down at the second statement: 'the convention on the rights of the child should be a part of the national curriculum.' Article 12 vividly demonstrated how out of touch government policy on citizenship education was with most people attending the conference.
> (Alderson, 2001: 145)

Effective presentations can also facilitate action. A year into the 730+ project, after having expanded their inquiry to other implicated groups both within England and abroad, the young research group produced an exhaustive report that identified both the existing challenges as youth saw them and suggestions for solutions (Cairns and Brannen, 2005). Two years into the project, the findings resulted in the rebuilding of the clinic with a space designated exclusively for young people, the beginning of a network of youth support workers for fellow diabetics, improved information provided to newly diagnosed diabetics, and a new magazine targeted for young diabetics. In addition, they had learned about new insulin pump treatments in Sweden that had not been widely known or used in England. Through a presentation together with three Swedish youth to local health managers in Durham, the project group also brought about this new and better form of treatment to the community's youth.

The girls in the HOPE project met similar success. Once the APIRH data were analyzed and the girls were able to summarize the findings and distil recommendations to share, the girls got actively involved in the dissemination of the results (Cheatham and Shen, 2003). They spoke to family and friends, officials from the school and school board, local and state government, and representatives from more than 20 community organizations. 'The survey captured the attention of school authorities and the media in ways that individual accounts had not. The research also provided credibility and legitimacy to the organizing work' (Cheatham and Shen, 2003: 330). In the end, every one of the girls' recommendations was adopted – including the creation and use of educational materials and seminars about sexual harassment for students and school teachers alike. These changes were then spread across the entire school district.

The thrill of communicating one's results successfully should not be underestimated in this process. Getting our ideas across can be as meaningful to a child as it is to adults. This came out clearly in 12-year-old Dominic Cole's feelings after having investigated the impact of brand name advertising vs. celebrity endorsements:

> During the last ten weeks I had two pieces of very exciting news. The first piece of news was that I had been invited to speak at the Cabinet Office in London. I was to prepare a PowerPoint slideshow about whatever subject I wanted and present it to a room full of people in the Top Managers Forum. The second piece of news was that I had also been invited to do my presentation in front of hundreds of young people in Ealing Town Hall. I really enjoyed that too. You can see my PowerPoint presentation on the website it's called 'When can we have *our* say'.
>
> (Cole, n.d.: 2)

RISKS AND BENEFITS

Though these illustrations exemplify that research with children is obviously possible and can yield interesting and important findings, there are clearly risks and benefits uniquely associated with doing such research. When working with children as research partners, as when working with any other research partners, some difficult or even insoluble research dilemmas may arise (Christensen and Prout, 2002). Still, it is possible to examine the risks and benefits beforehand and make informed decisions about when and how to go about dealing with them when entering research collaborations with children.

Risks

Children may not fully understand their rights when involved in research – either as researchers or as participants. Save the Children (2004) has recommended explaining these to children either verbally or in writing before getting involved, though parents often serve as gatekeepers for children, necessarily providing their consent before children are asked for their consent or assent (Pletsch and Stevens, 2001). Knowing that, it is important to understand what kinds of considerations parents weigh when determining whether to consent or not. In one study examining how UK families made the decision to participate in studies designed to learn more about children with diabetes, it was found that parents made their decision to consent based on how they were asked to participate, how disruptive they judged the research to be in the daily lives of their child and family, how beneficial the results might be for their children directly, what kind of opportunities seemed to outweigh the risks, and whether their children, themselves, wanted to participate (Pletsch and Stevens, 2001). Staying involved was another matter. For that, it mattered how able the parents, particularly mothers, were at balancing involvement in the study with their other demands, how positive their interactions were with the research personnel, and what kind of structural support was available in order to remain involved.

In those cases where children have secured parental consent and are asked to be a part of research, it is important both for the youth collaborators and research participants to be clear on the research goals, the time commitment involved, how the data will be handled, and how the data will be shared with participants and others (Hill, 2005). Note that children can be highly dutiful and express that in misdirected loyalties. For example, children can feel bound to their parents' or their own original intentions to participate in research even when they later discover that they rather would not. Some therefore recommend establishing clear ways for children to withdraw once they have begun participating (for example, Save the Children, 2004), and others recommend enlisting an independent advocate to help kids make the best decisions for their own interests (Hill, 2005).

Another risk is that children who serve as research collaborators may come to research underprepared to take on the responsibility and demands of research tasks (though training can take care of a lot of this if done in developmentally appropriate ways; Hart and Tyrer, 2006). Accordingly, any research done with children should be sensitive to the children's developmental capacity (Singh, 2007). With sensitivity to what one learns about participating children's backgrounds, entire studies may additionally require design renegotiation in order to better suit the children who get involved.

On top of these general risks, there are risks that are particularly salient for children involved in research situated in places of stress or conflict when it is 'imperative that research does not cause harm or distress to any of the participants at any time' (Kellett, 2005b: 10). For example, research participants may reveal sensitive information that puts them or their fellow researchers at risk (Hart and Tyrer, 2006; Save the Children,

2004). Likewise, child researchers may put their own health and safety at risk just by being involved (Jones, 2004). Children may raise unrealistic expectations for positive change among their fellow participants. They may also uncover information that is uncomfortable for them to process or manage (Puumala, 2007). In many of these difficult cases, multiple rights (such as children's right to be protected from harm and their right to be heard) may be equally worth protecting yet conflict. In those cases, difficult choices may need to be made and reflected in one's research design (Kellett, 2005b).

Though hardly discussed in the literature, one risk that is relevant for adult researchers who work in institutions of higher education and who collaborate with children is the cost related to time and audience. If research with children takes more time to complete than research conducted with other formally trained adult researchers, it can influence the rate of research output. Likewise, if the media most appropriate for children's findings are in the gray rather than academic literature, then the value of such output may be viewed academically in negative (or, at best, neutral) terms (Hogan, 2005). These matter to decisions related to tenure and promotion and are therefore not trivial considerations, particularly for junior faculty.

Benefits

Weighing in the balance with risks, of course, are the benefits that make the risks worth taking and accommodating. Most compellingly, doing research with children can be directly beneficial to the children themselves. Also important, however, is how useful findings elicited by children researchers are to adults interested in learning more about the world as children experience it.

As for the benefits to young research partners, child–adult research collaborations obviously help children develop the kinds of knowledge and skills necessary to successfully conduct research (for example, communication skills, organizational skills, data collection skills such as observing and interviewing, analytical skills; Hart and Tyrer, 2006; Kellett, 2005b; Nairn and Smith, 2003). Other skills that children might develop are metacognitive and critical thinking skills through the appraisal of one's own and other's research, organizational skills through pulling the whole research endeavour off, logical and lateral thinking skills through the selection of an appropriate methodology for one's question, ability to handle large amounts of information through the collection and management of data, higher order thinking through data analysis, and sharpened writing and communication skills through the formulation and dissemination of one's findings (Kellett, 2005b).

It has been found that doing research can also raise young people's self-awareness, self-confidence, and ability to make accurate judgements about things they have studied (Rose and Shevlin, 2004). For children situated in places of stress or conflict, research also offers them an important learning opportunity – one where they can be a part of identifying problems and solutions to those problems (Hart and Tyrer, 2006). This experience can be fun and stimulating for them. It can also provide an opportunity for them to cooperate with adults and other children with the effect of promoting respect and trust. In a 1997 study done by Khan in Bangladesh, for example, 11 street children ranging in age from 10 to 15 interviewed 51 other street children ranging in age from 7 to 15 about what issues they thought were most important regarding children's worth, dignity, and rights (Alderson, 2001). The purpose was to provide useful information to groups that were planning services to help them. The children identified 11 crucial issues, many of them involving torture and poor treatment by adults (even police), and difficulties for girls in terms of the work they are driven to on the street and its implications for later marriage prospects. Not only were these findings important for the children's own self-awareness, but they also reached a larger

audience. The children shared their findings in four research reports that they were instrumental in producing.

Children can sometimes take what they learn through research and act on it even more directly, reinforcing that they can be actively involved in political action that can help improve services, child-relevant decision-making, and the protection of children in general (Nairn and Smith, 2003; Sinclair, 2004). In a 1995 study done by the International Save the Children Alliance with street boys in New Delhi, twelve 7- to 17-year-old boys learned that 76 per cent of their money was spent on food (Alderson, 2000). Having learned this, some of the boys, with help, took an intensive course on how to cook and serve food to others. They then found a location to cook in and opened up a restaurant. In the spirit of learning from their experience and research findings, they even served some of the food to other street children for free.

Clearly, young people often speak a common language and are able to raise issues with other young people that adults might not be able to (Kellett, 2005b; McLaughlin, 2005). This can be beneficial during any of the research tasks associated with the research process, such as piloting materials as done with the refugees in Tanzania and with the young residents in the accident-prone housing estate (Alderson, 2000; Save the Children, 2004). With young collaborators, then, the range and quality of data collected can be enhanced. On the flip side, children who help generate data can also develop a sense of ownership over the findings. They, like the pupil democracy at the British Library, the HOPE girls and the 730+ group can later be used to help present the findings to new audiences for the whole research team with greater impact than adults may achieve on their own.

ETHICS

Given the risks and benefits associated with doing research with children, when we choose to involve children as researchers, what ethical principles are important for us to consider?

Children scientists and research norms

Though ethical principles in research with children are ultimately about safeguards to protect them, the answers about how to do that are not simple. Why? Because research with children entails an elegant balance of the desire to empower children through participation and the need for associated adults to act professionally within agreed ethical norms (Hill, 1997; McLaughlin, 2005).

We therefore need to weaken what we take for granted in more conventional research paradigms and find ways to enter children's experiences and cultures of communication (Christensen, 2004). More discussion is needed about the ethical questions relevant for this process since once youngsters are viewed as social actors rather than objects, the ethics of working with them becomes more complex. This raises new ethical dilemmas and new responsibilities.

Typically, ethical standards are stronger in the areas of how informants are recruited and informed about a study, how informants give consent to participate, and how to deal with anonymity and confidentiality (Christensen and Prout, 2002; Hill, 2005). However, these matters are problematic in research done with child collaborators (Roberts, 2000). In addition to preparing children for informed consent, for example, we should perhaps also be equally explicit about preparing them for informed *dissent* – particularly when doing research in places of conflict.

Where ethical standards are *not* typically as strong (or outright weak) is in the areas of how to involve children in the research process and design, how to include them in the interpretation of data, and how to involve them in the dissemination of results (Christensen and Prout, 2002). Another area typically overlooked by ethical standards is

the potential benefits or consequences research findings might have for other children and what researchers do with that. Also, where are there committees with child members or child consultants who can help evaluate research that involves them? Because of these kinds of issues, Roberts (2000) warned that 'it is dangerous to assume that because a piece of research has been passed by an ethics committee then it is *ipso facto* an ethical piece of research' (Roberts, 2000: 95).

Three ethical issues that therefore deserve special attention for research with children – in addition to the usual ethical considerations when doing research with adults – include recognition that: (1) children have different competencies than adults, (2) children are potentially vulnerable, and (3) adults may interpret data from children any way they please (Morrow and Richards, 1996). Accordingly, it is important to think ethical symmetry when identifying one's overarching ethical principles for research with children – both as collaborators and as study participants.

Ethical symmetry

The principle of ethical symmetry is about being ethically strategic in how one orients one's work in terms of the rights, feelings, and interests of children (Christensen and Prout, 2002). The starting point of ethical symmetry is the view that the ethical relationship between a researcher and informant is the same, whether the informant is a child or an adult, and, through extrapolation, whether the researcher is a child or an adult. Even though the nature of the relationships in the various researcher-informant constellations is different, the commitment to applying the same ethical principles in all, even if through different means, is the same. This may influence the methodology we choose, how we collect, analyze, and interpret our data, and what kinds of other ethical practices we use. With this as a starting point, there are a number of questions that researchers need to think through in order to make good decisions about ethical symmetry. Here are a few from the literature.

Ethical questions

Not all of the following questions are relevant for all research with children. However, many are and ideally require the establishment of some structural parameters. Nonetheless, many of the questions are within the purview of individuals to weigh and accommodate in research program designs even where structural parameters do not yet exist. Key questions are highlighted below with additional questions that they invite. Answers are not provided here, but are left for us to ponder and address as appropriate in our own research.

1. Who should be responsible when it comes to determining and monitoring the ethics for doing research with children? Related to this overarching question, one can ask:
   a. How do we provide for the safety and welfare of both the child and adult research staff (Save the Children, 2004)?
   b. Who is ethically responsible for child-led research, and who should set those standards and monitor their practice (Kellett, 2005a)?
   c. How should we go about securing ethical approval for youth-led research when ethics committees typically want the research agenda, questions and methodologies figured out before the research begins while research with children is about, in part, giving youth more direct involvement in shaping those very things (Nairn and Smith, 2003)?
   d. What special guidelines, if any, should Ethical Review Boards work with when reviewing research with child researchers or participants (Tauer, 2002)?
2. What kinds of parameters are important to consider for the adults who do research with children researchers?
   a. How do we prepare adults working with children researchers to do ethically appropriate work (Save the Children, 2004)?
   b. What background, skills or training ought researchers directly involved with children

to have? For example, how can we prepare ourselves to use new methods and research tactics effectively? Also, should the identities and criminal histories of all researchers working with children be checked (Hill, 1997; Save the Children, 2004)?
3. What kind of training ought both adults and children receive before beginning data collection?
   a. What should we ensure in the training of children researchers (Save the Children, 2004)?
   b. How should we clearly communicate to children what we as researchers can or cannot do (Save the Children, 2004)?
4. What special needs are raised in research with child researchers when it comes to matters of recruitment, consent and confidentiality?
   a. Should co-researchers also participate with informed consent (McLaughlin, 2005)?
   b. How do we reach groups of children who are literally or metaphorically voiceless (for example, street children, children unable to fill out questionnaires or participate in interviews, children with profound disabilities, displaced children, or Muslim girls; Roberts, 2000)?
   c. How will we recruit children, keeping in mind appropriate representation (Save the Children, 2004)?
   d. How should we prepare children to easily make the decision to choose or *not* to choose to participate as collaborators (Save the Children, 2004)?
   e. When ought it to be necessary or desirable to obtain consent from parents or guardians (Hill, 1997)?
   f. What should be the legal age for children consenting to participate as researchers (Hill, 1997; Kellett, 2005a)?
   g. How should we assure children's confidentiality (Mauthner, 1997)? This can be challenging when family members or teachers close to the children involved might seek insider information even when they know about the confidentiality aspect of a project.
5. How should we deal with research incentives?
   a. Should we offer compensation or incentives to children involved in research – either as researchers or as participants (Save the Children, 2004)?
   b. From whom should we gain approval to employ youth and pay them directly for their work (Nairn and Smith, 2003)?

6. What about when things go wrong?
   a. How do we ensure that we do not distress children through research (Hill, 1997)?
   b. What if research among peers doesn't go well? Then what? What are the ramifications and consequences for the individuals, the project, and the methodology?
   c. How do adults and children alike exit research interactions that may cause or awaken potentially painful experiences (Save the Children, 2004)?
   d. How should we care for children who may need support after being involved in our research (Save the Children, 2004)?
   e. What do we do if children report abusive situations to other children (Hill, 1997)?
7. How far should we go in including children in the sharing of the findings?
   a. If participatory research is about dialog, research with children must be about aligning our work with children's own experiences, interests, values, and everyday routines, while enabling them to express and represent their thoughts on their terms (Christensen, 2004). That so, whose language do we use when soliciting or reporting our results? Adults' reinterpretations of what children express, children's own expressions, or both?
   b. How should we address the personal costs for academicians who choose to do research with children (balancing quality output with expanded time frames for project completion and the use of non-traditional publication venues; Hogan, 2005)?

Children and research participation norms

In addition to these ethical considerations for child research collaborators, we must also be diligent in our ethical considerations for child participants. There must be clarity about which children we involve – both in terms of who is and, equally importantly, who is not included in the participant pool (Roberts, 2000; Sinclair, 2004). Whoever the participants are, child researchers, like their adult partners or guides, will have to be equally diligent in working in ethically appropriate ways. Most of the concerns listed above for child researchers are relevant for child research participants as well. However, there are additional concerns that are unique for the participants themselves. This is particularly the case in contexts where children are living in stressed circumstances (for example, in conflict situations or while undergoing medical care). Accordingly, the medical field has devoted quite a bit of attention to how best to engage youth as research participants, delicately balancing the need to protect children from undue harm or improper use while at the same time involving them in potentially disruptive research that can directly benefit the welfare of other children (Tauer, 2002).

As one researcher summarized, 'On the one hand, we are obligated to protect individual child subjects of research from being harmed or improperly used. On the other hand, the welfare of all children' can often directly benefit from research about them (Tauer, 2002: 128).

Likewise, risk is typically calculated by weighing the possibility of personal risk against the prospect of personal benefit, with acceptable risk being defined as the situation where the prospect of benefit outweighs the possibility of risk (Tauer, 2002). Turning to medicine – a field where child participant rights are extremely important for research involving experimental clinical treatments or drug testing on children – the National Bioethics Advisory Commission defined category of minimal risk as the baseline to use for all such calculations. However, defining that baseline proves to be difficult. If minimal risk is to be akin to risks comparable to those children would ordinarily encounter in their daily lives, then, as Tauer (2000: 129) asked, 'whose daily lives constitute the standard?' Since research with child participants can take place in any variety of settings, including settings of conflict or medical interventions, how that standard is defined is extremely important. As Loretta Kopeman stated, 'It is morally unacceptable to locate children in places with increased risks of harm, and then use that increased risk to redefine "minimal risk" or "justify" higher research risks *for them'* (as cited in Tauer, 2002: 130).

In spite of the moving baseline target, the National Commission has opened the door to allow for research that involves a *minor* increase over minimal risk provided that the research procedures involve (a) experiences commensurate with what children in stressed situations are already experiencing in their lives, (b) learning that can be of benefit to similar groups of children, and (c) knowledge that is vital to understanding or addressing children's adverse experiences or conditions (Tauer, 2002). Indeed, in a study of how mothers chose to consent to allowing their children to choose to participate in research as participants, it was found that the mothers' satisfaction with the experience was primarily influenced by the degree of personal benefit they felt their children gained through their research involvement (Pletsch and Stevens, 2001). In the cases where they felt satisfied, then the social benefit of their children's participation was also important. Where they did not feel satisfied, the social benefit was secondary.

All in all, the research question and context of the research conducted will determine which ethical considerations are most relevant to any given study. Nonetheless, careful consideration beyond what is usual in other research is warranted in order to ensure ethical symmetry in our work with children – whether as research collaborators or as participants. One way to facilitate good decision-making is by considering the rights that one wants to assure children involved in research, for example, welfare rights (contributing to children's well-being), protective rights (children's protection from stress, distress or harm), provision of service rights (children's rights to provide and to receive appropriate services), and choice or participatory rights (children's rights to express their opinions for consideration by others and to make choices about how to do that; Hill, 2005). These rights are as relevant for the child research collaborators as they are for child participants.

QUALITY RESEARCH WITH CHILD COLLABORATORS

We are never fully aware of all the information that might be relevant to any given research question (Koslowski and Thompson, 2002). Research is therefore a process of trying to identify the most relevant information for our questions and findings. Still, it will always be an inexact science. Accordingly, in their general tips to researchers who collaborate with children, Save the Children underscored that 'there is no "right" or "perfect" way to involve children in research'. The best decisions are based on good research questions; research designs that are appropriate for the particular people, place, and time involved; sound ethics; and proper training for all. In the end, they advise that 'doing something is always better than doing nothing' (Save the Children, 2004: 72).

Given all that has been covered in this chapter, what are some concrete ways in which we can facilitate children's competent engagement in research for the purpose of advancing our fields and/or improving the welfare of our youth? The literature offers several recommendations.

First, be clear in one's purpose, identifying questions for which children's perspectives are important (Sinclair, 2004). McLaughlin (2005) recommended that we start by identifying interesting topics about children's experiences or phenomena that involve them. He reminded us, also, that we should not limit ourselves to posing questions that only yield studies by children about other children or child-related phenomena. We should be open to considering children's perspectives on adults as well. Also, not all research with children has to begin with the identification of primary research questions. Though it is typical for adult researchers to prepare for primary research by engaging in secondary research first, engaging children in secondary research can aid in the clarification of even better primary research questions.

Second, pursue questions with methods and research tactics that are appropriate for the nature of the target question, the context in which the question will be pursued, and the resources available to the pursuit. Remember to keep the designs child-friendly. Also, no matter which methods and research tactics we employ, we need to be vigilant about the ethical issues relevant to our designs and adapt our plans accordingly. Strive for ethical symmetry.

We are also reminded to be aware of our taken-for-granted academic assumptions that come from other research traditions (Christensen, 2004). By consciously entering into children's 'cultures of communication', for example, we can become more effective collaborators. We can do so by calibrating our engagement with young partners in order to better understand their perspectives – capturing them on their own terms, the ways children typically express and represent their lives. Remembering that our status as adults influences the way children collaborate with us, being sensitive and responsive to that in the way we build relationships with our young collaborators and the role that we play in shaping the research process can benefit the degree to which children's involvement can genuinely bring new perspectives to the table. Rethinking our researcher role as that of a critical friend rather than that of a controlling expert can be an important part of that process. Figuring out how to weigh children's views along with those of other researchers or stakeholders in the field is critical (Sinclair, 2004). Fortunately, the ideas of this dialogic approach are not brand new. There already exist excellent role models out there to learn from with concrete ideas for how to start and proceed (see, for example, Alderson, 2000, 2001; Hill, 1997; Kellett et al., 2004; Mauthner, 1997; Save the Children, 2004).

Third, educate and train both child *and* adult research collaborators. Educating and training children has been a theme throughout the entire chapter, yet adequate preparation of

all research collaborators matters for the quality of the process and outcome. Kellett (2005b) has already developed a program and materials for educating and training children. Through that work and the work of others, it is clearly evident that education and training in participatory methods need to inspire research designs appropriate for the research question being pursued and sensitive to the background and developmental capacity of all involved. As for *when* education and training should take place, it is recommended that it be offered and supported throughout the whole research process, either through regular meetings (Kellett, 2005b) or through workshops (McLaughlin, 2005). Lastly, throughout this process, youth have expressed that they appreciate being listened to, having people follow through on promises made to them, seeing that confidentiality not breeched, and working with people who respect them (McLaughlin, 2005).

Fourth, recognize that children's lives are fluid, and we need to be flexible in our planning (McLaughlin, 2005). Children live in ever-changing circumstances with multiple obligations to school, home, and other activities. These can make it difficult for young people to make long-term commitments to research collaborations (Alderson, 2000; Hill, 1997; McLaughlin, 2005). Since some children may only be able to make short-term contributions, it is recommended that we build into our designs flexible time frames and different possible roles for children to take that match what they are able to commit to. Recognizing that the research process has many steps that involve different kinds of skills, this is possible to do in a number of different and creative ways. Acknowledging the need for such flexibility can influence the evolution of our research designs. It would therefore be wise to systematically debrief how the work is going to ensure that the validity of the design and the ethics of the work are still appropriate for the task.

Finally, make it meaningful for children to get involved as research collaborators

(Sinclair, 2004). If we make it worth their while to be involved, some children may show enhanced stamina and interest, taking on more challenging tasks or choosing to stay with projects for longer periods of time. McLaughlin (2005) recommended that we amply reward children for their time and efforts. Collaborations can be rewarded with freedom to communicate about things children care about, skill development, awareness of and access to caring adults who listen to them, participation in organizations that respond to children, research stipends, scholarships, opportunities that would otherwise not be available such as research-related travel, certificates of participation that can be used when applying for schools or jobs, and, perhaps most importantly, the chance to make a real difference (Grover, 2004; Mauthner, 1997; Nairn and Smith, 2003; Save the Children, 2004).

It is clear that there is value in giving voice to children. As the tsunami children in Sri Lanka, India, Indonesia, and Thailand, the street children in New Delhi and Bangladesh, and the refugees in Dar es Salaam have illustrated, even children in desperate situations would like a say. They, the HOPE project girls, and Paul O'Brien have also shown that many children would even be willing to be trained to solicit their say in scientifically appropriate and robust ways. Many, such as the tsunami children, the Bangladeshi children, Paul O'Brien, and Dominic Cole, have opened adult eyes to things that were previously unknown or overlooked, and the presentations of their findings have been powerful. Furthermore, many of the findings, like those of the HOPE project girls, the 730+ group, and the New Delhi street children, have already made a difference. Likewise, the tsunami children have been instrumental in helping Plan International identify how to make decisions related to future disasters better. Indeed, what we have learned through children has prompted meaningful work and activities that have been of great importance.

This chapter has been framed by scrutinizing the notion of 'children as researchers'. Our interests combined with how we think about children and how we think about research will ultimately determine the extent to which we will ever find ourselves collaborating in our own research with children. There is a growing movement to think anew about children and exciting research prospects that await us though the active tapping of children's expertise and skills. These can be important for enhancing our understanding of the world. Unquestionably, we have a lot to learn from young collaborators about how they experience it. Much has been done already to get us started. It is now up to us to critically develop this trend further. We must guarantee to our collaborators (including our child-collaborators) and our fields that we will engage only in high-quality work of integrity and purpose.

REFERENCES

Alderson, P. (2000) 'Children as researchers: The effects of participation rights on research methodology', in P. Christensen and A. James (eds.), *Research with Children: Perspectives and Practices*. London, UK: Falmer Press, pp. 241–57.

Alderson, P. (2001) 'Research by children', *International Journal of Social Research Methodology*, 4(2): 139–53.

American Psychological Association Teachers of Psychology in Secondary Schools (TOPASS) (2004) *Conducting Psychological Research for Science Fairs*. Washington, DC: American Psychological Association.

Avison, D., Lau, F., Myers, M. and Nielsen, P.A. (1999) 'Action research', *Communications of the ACM*, 42(1): 94–7.

Bordens, K.S. and Abbott, B.B. (2008) *Research Design and Methods: A Process Approach*, 7th Ed. Boston: McGraw-Hill.

Bradbury, H. and Reason, P. (2003) 'Issues and choice points for improving the quality of action research', in M. Minkler and N. Wallerstein (eds.), *Community-Based Participatory Research for Health*. San Francisco: Jossey-Bass, pp. 201–20.

Cairns, L. and Brannen, M. (2005) 'Promoting the human rights of children and young people: The "Investing in

Children" experience', *Adoption and Fostering*, 29(1): 78–7.

Carnegie Young People Initiative (2001) *UK Full Report*. Fife: Carnegie UK Trust.

Cheatham, A. and Shen, E. (2003) 'Community based participatory research with Cambodian girls in Long Beach, California', in M. Minkler and N. Wallerstein (eds.), *Community-Based Participatory Research For Health*. San Francisco: Jossey-Bass, pp. 316–31.

Chein, I., Cook, S.W. and Harding, J. (1948) 'The field of action research', *American Psychologist*, 3(2): 43–50.

Christensen, P. and Prout, A. (2002) 'Working with ethical symmetry in social research with children', *Childhood*, 9(4): 477–97.

Christensen, P.H. (2004) 'Children's participation in ethnographic research: Issues of power and representation', *Children and Society*, 18(2): 165–76.

Cole, D. (n.d.) *CRC Reflections*. Available at http://childrens-research-centre.open.ac.uk/research.cfm

Convention on the Rights of the Child, G.A. Res. 44/25, UN GAOR Supp. 49 at 165, UN Doc. 4/44 736 (1989).

Dickert, N. and Sugarman, J. (2005) 'Ethical goals of community consultation in research', *American Journal of Public Health*, 95(7): 1123–7.

Fetterman, D.M. (2005) 'The heart and soul of empowerment evaluation', in D.M. Fetterman and A. Wandersman (eds.), *Empowerment Evaluation Principles in Practice*. New York: The Guilford Press, pp. 1–26.

Fielding, M. (2004) 'Transformative approaches to student voice: Theoretical underpinnings, recalcitrant realities', *British Educational Research Journal*, 30(2): 295–312.

Greene, S. and Hill, M. (2005) 'Conceptual, methodological and ethical issues in researching children's experience', in S. Greene and D. Hogan (eds.), *Researching Children's Experience: Methods and Approaches*. London: Sage Publications, pp. 1–21.

Grover, S. (2004) 'Why won't they listen to us? On giving power and voice to children participating in social research', *Childhood*, 11(1): 81–93.

Hart, J. and Tyrer, B. (2006) *Research with Children Living in Situations of Armed Conflict: Concepts, Ethics and Methods* (No. RSC 30). Oxford, UK: University of Oxford.

Hart, R.A. (1997) *Children's Participation: the Theory and Practice of Involving Young Citizens in Community Development and Environmental Care*. London: Earthscan.

Hill, M. (1997) 'Participatory research with children', *Child and Family Social Work*, 2(3): 171–83.

Hill, M. (2005) 'Ethical considerations in researching children's experiences', in S. Greene and D. Hogan (eds.), *Researching Children's Experience: Methods and Approaches*. London: Sage Publications, pp. 61–86.

Hogan, D. (2005) 'Researching "the child" in developmental psychology', in S. Greene and D. Hogan (eds.), *Researching Children's Experience: Methods and Approaches*. London: Sage Publications. pp. 22–41.

Israel, B.A., Schulz, A.J., Parker, E.A., Becker, A.J. 3rd. and Guzman, R. (2003) 'Critical issues in developing and following community based participatory research principles', in M. Minkler and N. Wallerstein (eds.), *Community-based Participatory Research for Health*. San Francisco: Jossey-Bass, pp. 53–76.

Jones, A. (2004) 'Involving children and young people as researchers', in S. Fraser, V. Lewis, S. Ding, M. Kellett and C. Robinson (eds.), *Doing Research with Children and Young People*. London, UK: Sage, pp. 113–30.

Kellett, M. (2005a) *Children as Active Researchers: A New Research Paradigm for the 21st Century?* (No. NCRM/003): The Open University.

Kellett, M. (2005b) *How to Develop Children as Researchers*. London, UK: Paul Chapman Publishing.

Kellett, M., Forrest, R., Dent, N. and Ward, S. (2004) '"Just teach us the skills please, we'll do the rest": Empowering ten-year-olds as active researchers', *Children and Society*, 18(5): 329–43.

Kidd, S.A. and Kral, M.J. (2005) 'Practicing Participatory Action Research', *Journal of Counseling Psychology*, 52(2): 187–95.

Koslowski, B. and Thompson, S. (2002) 'Theorizing is important, and collateral information constrains how well it is done', in P. Carruthers, S. Stich and M. Siegal (eds.), *The Cognitive Basis of Science*. Cambridge, UK: Cambridge University Press, pp. 171–92.

Mauthner, M. (1997) 'Methodological aspects of collecting data from children: Lessons from three research projects', *Children and Society*, 11(1): 16–28.

McLaughlin, H. (2005) 'Young service users as co-researchers', *Qualitative Social Work*, 4(2): 211–28.

Melton, G.B., Levine, R.J., Koocher, G.P., Rosenthal, R. and Thompson, W.C. (1988) 'Community consultation in socially sensitive research: Lessons from clinical trials of treatments for AIDS', *American Psychologist*, 43(7): 573–81.

Minkler, M. and Wallerstein, N. (2003) 'Introduction to community based participatory research', in M. Minkler and N. Wallerstein (eds.), *Community-Based Participatory Research for Health*. San Francisco: Jossey-Bass, pp. 3–26.

Morin, S.F., Maiorana, A., Koester, K.A., Sheon, N.M. and Richards, T.A. (2003) 'Community consultation in HIV prevention research: A study of community advisory boards at 6 research sites', *Journal of Acquired Immune Deficiency Syndromes*, 33(4): 513–20.

Morrow, V. and Richards, M. (1996) 'The ethics of social research with children: An overview', *Children and Society*, 10(2): 90–105.

Nairn, K. and Smith, A. (2003) *Young People as Researchers in Schools: the Possibilities of Peer Research*. Paper presented at the annual meeting of the American Educational Research Association, Chicago, USA.

Nieuwenhuys, O. (2004) 'Participatory action research in the majority world', in S. Fraser, V. Lewis, S. Ding, M. Kellett and C. Robinson (eds.), *Doing Research with Children and Young People*. London, UK: Sage, pp. 206–21.

O'Brien, P. (n.d.) 'How does death affect children?', *Research Studies by CRC Children*. Available at http://childrens-research-centre.open.ac.uk/research.cfm

O'Kane, C. (2000) 'The development of participatory techniques: Facilitating children's views about decisions which affect them', in P. Christensen and A. James (eds.), *Research with Children: Perspectives and Practices*. London, UK: Falmer Press, pp. 136–59.

Plan International (2005) *Children and the Tsunami*. Bangkok: Plan Ltd.

Pletsch, P.K. and Stevens, P.E. (2001) 'Inclusion of children in clinical research: Lessons learned from mothers of diabetic children', *Clinical Nursing Research*, 10(2): 140–61.

Puumala, E. (2007) *Developing a Vulnerable Self: Trans-subjective in Composing Research*. Paper presented at the Methodologies in Peace Research conference, Tromsø, Norway.

Ray, W.J. (2000) *Methods: Toward a Science of Behavior and Experience, 6th Ed.* Belmont, CA: Wadsworth.

Roberts, H. (2000) 'Listening to children and hearing them', in P. Christensen and A. James (eds.), *Research with Children: Perspectives and Practices*. London, UK: Falmer Press, pp. 225–40.

Rose, R. and Shevlin, M. (2004) 'Encouraging voices: Listening to young people who have been marginalized', *Support for Learning*, 19(4): 155–61.

Rosenthal, R. and Rosnow, R.L. (2008). *Essentials of Behavioral Research: Methods and Data Analysis, 3rd Ed.* Boston: McGraw-Hill.

Save the Children (2004) *So You Want to Involve Children in Research?* Stockholm: Save the Children Sweden.

Sinclair, R. (2004) 'Participation in practice: Making it meaningful, effective and sustainable', *Children and Society*, 18(2): 106–18.

Singh, I. (2007) 'Clinical implications of ethical concepts: Moral self-understandings in children taking methylphenidate for ADHD', *Clinical Child Psychology and Psychiatry*, 12(2): 167–82.

Spatz, C. and Kardas, E.P. (2008) *Research Methods in Psychology*. New York: McGraw-Hill Higher Education.

Springett, J. (2003) 'Issues in participatory evaluation', in M. Minkler and N. Wallerstein (eds.), *Community-Based Participatory Research for Health*. San Francisco: Jossey-Bass, pp. 263–88.

Stoecker, R. (2003) 'Are academics irrelevant? Approaches and roles for scholars in community based participatory research', in M. Minkler and N. Wallerstein (eds.), *Community-Based Participatory Research for Health*. San Francisco: Jossey-Bass, pp. 98–112.

Tauer, C.A. (2002) 'Central ethical dilemmas in research involving children', *Accountability in Research*, 9(3-4): 127–42.

Veale, A. (2005) 'Creative methodologies in participatory research with children', in S. Greene and D. Hogan (eds.), *Researching Children's Experience: Methods and Approaches*. London: Sage Publications, pp. 253–72.

Wallerstein, N. and Duran, B. (2003) 'The conceptual, historical, and practical roots of community based participatory research and related participatory traditions', in M. Minkler and N. Wallerstein (eds.), *Community-Based Participatory Research for Health*. San Francisco: Jossey-Bass, pp. 27–52.

Wandersman, A., Snell-Johns, J., Lentz, B.E., Fetterman, D. ., Keener, D., Livet, M., et al. (2005) 'The principles of empowerment evaluation', in D. Fetterman and A. Wandersman (eds.), *Empowerment Evaluation Principles in Practice*. New York: The Guilford Press, pp. 27–41.

Woodhead, M. and Faulkner, D. (2000) 'Subjects, objects or participants? Dilemmas of psychological research with children', in P. Christensen and A. James (eds.), *Research with Children: Perspectives and Practices*. London, UK: Falmer Press, pp. 9–35.

Name Index

Subject Index